CHINA and
U.S. FAR EAST POLICY
1945-1966

A Publication of

CONGRESSIONAL QUARTERLY SERVICE

"The Authority on Congress and National Politics"

1735 K STREET, N.W., WASHINGTON, D.C. 20006

Copyright 1967 by Congressional Quarterly Inc.,
1735 K Street N.W., Washington, D.C., 20006

All reproduction rights, including quotation, broadcasting and publication are reserved for current editorial clients. Second rights are reserved, including use of Congressional Quarterly material in campaign supplements, advertisements and handbooks, without special permission. Rates will be furnished on request.

Published April 1967

Library of Congress Catalog Card Number: 67-22905

Congressional Quarterly Service

Editor and President: Henrietta and Nelson Poynter
Executive Editor: Thomas N. Schroth
Writer and Editor: Peter A. Harkness, Buel W. Patch
Contributors: Joseph Foote, Adrian Spivack, Renee Amrine, Jeanne Kuebler, Judith G. Gault, David Berson, Deborah Roberts
Cover: Howard Chapman, Alison Owings. The symbol on the cover means "China."

FOREWORD

IN the period from 1945 through the beginning of 1967, the world witnessed a dramatic change in the character of the Cold War. The period began with the Republic of China as a close ally and client nation of the United States. It ended with the People's Republic of China posing what, for the American people and their leaders, seemed a more dangerous threat than that of the Soviet Union. By the end of 1966, the relations between the two nations -- one the world's most populous and the other its most powerful -- threatened to culminate in open conflict.

The chasm separating the two countries was more than one of conflicting ideologies; it was between East and West, Orient and Occident, two very different cultures possessing little understanding of each other. While the United States had been Peking's principal enemy for 17 years, America's recognition of Communist China as a potential threat, overshadowing the Soviet Union, had only lately emerged.

The People's Republic had isolated itself in a closed Communist society and, to a large extent, was isolated by other nations. Thus, relatively little was known of the political, economic and social development of China during the mid-century decades -- and less of the actual current conditions in a nation that contained one-fourth of the world's population, occupied more territory than any other country on the globe except Russia and Canada, and promised to gain the prestige and power that go with an arsenal of nuclear weapons.

The United States had become acutely aware of its responsibilities as a Pacific power during World War II. The conflicts in Korea and Viet Nam emphasized the continuing nature of those responsibilities, exemplified by President Johnson's July 1966 speech heralding the coming "Pacific era" in world affairs.

The importance to this country of information about China is self-evident. This book presents a factual and objective account of relations between the United States and China from 1945 through the beginning of 1967, the development of United States Far East policy during this period and the participation of Congress in this policy formation.

TABLE OF CONTENTS

Introduction 1

China and the West 4
Early Contacts with the West 4
Opium War of 1839-1842 5
Future Relations with China 8
Problem of Succession in China 9

Congress and U.S. Far East Policy 11
U.S. Wars - Declared and Undeclared 13
McCarthy and Far East Policy 14
UN Votes on Admission of China 21

"China Lobbies" on Both Sides 23

Chart of Chinese History from 2000 B.C. . . . 29

Map of China 30

Chronology of Events on U.S.-Far East Affairs 35

Before 1945. Revolution of 1911 - Kuomintang-Communist Collaboration - Chiang's Break with Communists - Long March 35

1945. Yalta Decisions - Atomic Bomb - End of World War II - Chiang-Mao Accord - Marshall Appointment 37

1946. Soviet Removal of Machinery from Manria - Sale of War Surpluses to China 39

1947. Mediation Effort Ended - Wedemeyer Mission - U.S. Aid Program - New Red Offensive . . 42

1948. Heavy Fighting in Manchuria - U.S. and British Warned to Leave - Aid Agreement - Mme. Chiang Plea 44

1949. U.S. Declines Request to Mediate - Mao Calls for Surrender - Peiping Falls - State Department White Paper - Nationalists to Formosa . . 46

1950. State Department Writes Off Formosa - McCarthy Charges - Soviet Treaty with Chinese Reds 48

1951. Seoul Falls - UN Truce Appeal - UN Labels China an Aggressor - Truman Dismisses MacArthur . . 55

1952. POW Riot in Korea - Air Raids on North Korea - Truce Talks Pledge - Eisenhower Pledge . . 60

1953. U.S. Hydrogen Bomb - Chiang Unleashed - Korean Armistice - Soviet Hydrogen Bomb 63

1954. Massive Retaliation Doctrine - Nixon on Troops for Indo-China - Dienbienphu - McCarthy Censured 66

1955. China Threatens Formosa - Mutual Defense Treaty with Nationalists - Quemoy and Matsu . . 71

1956. Brinkmanship - Khrushchev Denounces Stalin - Washington Turns Down Peking Bid for Talks . . 75

1957. Eisenhower Pledges Aid to South Viet Nam - Mao's "Hundred Flowers" - U.S. Travel to China . . 79

1958. Reds Purged in China - China Atomic Reactor - "Two Chinas" Concept - Offshore Islands . . . 84

1959. Sino-Soviet Aid Pact - Mao Swims - Tibet Revolt - Liu Chairman - Nehru-Chou Impasse . . . 91

1960. U.S. Aid in Viet Nam - Bishop Walsh Imprisoned - Rhee Resigns - Kennedy-Nixon Debates . . 96

1961. Laos Threatened - Rusk Reaffirms Nationalist China Stand - Bay of Pigs 101

1962. China Warns U.S. - Communist Offensive in Laos - U.S. Troops to Thailand - India-China Dispute 109

1963. Sino-Soviet Feud - Laos Fighting - Lodge Ambassador - Buddhist Demonstrations, Mme. Nhu . . 118

1964. Chou Tours Africa - McNamara on Troops in Viet Nam - Gulf of Tonkin - China A-Explosion . . 132

1965. Bombing of North Viet Nam - Marines Land - Johnson's Hopkins Speech - Ho's Four Points . . 150

1966. End of Bombing Pause - Johnson Meets in Hawaii - Criticism Rises - Red Guards 170

1967. Bombing Question - China Violence - Thant View - Chinese-Russian Clash 214

Tables and Summaries
Korea Conflict -- 3 Years, 150,000 Casualties . . . 52
Cost of "Containment" 106
Defense Dept. Expenditures Since 1948 133
Deepening Viet Nam Crisis 144
Peiping v. Peking 147
U.S. Troop Involvement in Viet Nam 170
A.I.D. & Military Estimates for FY 1966 190

Biographies of China's Leaders 223
Mao Tse-tung 223
Lin Piao 227
Chou En-lai 228
Liu Shao-chi 229
Teng Hsiao-ping 231
Chiang Kai-shek 232
Mme. Chiang Kai-shek 236

Leading Figures in U.S.-Far East Developments 238

Text and Documents 249
Truman Policy Statement 251
Wedemeyer Report 251
China Aid Act of 1948 255
State Dept. Statement on Aid 256
Acheson Policy Statement (1950) 257
Dulles Policy Statement (1955) 261
Rusk Policy Statement (1966) 263
Mansfield Report on Viet Nam 268
Fulbright "Myths and Realities" Speech 273
Testimony at Fulbright Hearings, March 1966 . . 278
Conservative Reaction to China Hearings 311
Chinese Reaction to Hearings 314
Schlesinger Speech 315
Roundtable TV Discussion 317
Lin Piao on People's War 324
Mao's Essays 328
Mao's "Red Book" Quotations 330
Johnson 1966 Address on Asian Policy 333
Viet Nam Constitution 335

INDEX 341

Perhaps we should never have disturbed the slumbering civilization of China. Or else let it awake itself and reach for us. Perhaps China is too vast to be governed by mercy. Yet if the Chinese mind craves order, they must be brought to recognize they are the biggest factor in the world's disorder, and we must untangle the madness of their minds. The most difficult task in the world is to reach the minds of men who hate you. We do not flinch from the immediate tasks; to guard our skies, defend our friends. We cannot flinch from tomorrow's task, to reach the mind of China. We race today to reach the moon; to reach that mind is a task of equal difficulty and far greater urgency."

Theodore H. White,
"China: The Roots of Madness," a television
production, Jan. 31, 1967.

Introduction

In the fall of 1949, as Europe was preoccupied with recovering from the war and the United States with containing Soviet expansion, the dreams of 12 men in China became a reality. A great mass movement, conceived in the summer of 1921, reached its climax. On Oct. 1, 1949, Mao Tse-tung, chairman of the Chinese Communist Party, officially proclaimed the founding of the Chinese People's Republic. The largest country in the world, comprising almost a quarter of its population, had become Communist.

The 12 men had met in Shanghai on July 1, 1921, to attend the First National Congress of the Chinese Communist Party. Although their ideology and political party, borrowed from the West, were new to China, their dreams were not. A revolution had been smouldering in China since the mid-19th century, one which defied far more than existing social conditions. It also sought to destroy the Chinese way of life -- Confucianism, the core of Chinese culture. By the early 20th century, the Manchu Dynasty had been replaced by a republic, new revolutionaries had supplanted old reformers and nationalism had triumphed over Confucianism.

This revolution was accompanied by a century of foreign humiliation of the Chinese people and leaders, dating back to the Opium War (1839-1842) and not finally ending until the victory of the Communists in 1949. These new Western "barbarians," as the Chinese called all foreigners, differed from previous intruders since, for the first time, Chinese culture proved incapable of assimilating that of its invaders. "China's tragedy," Harvard's Dr. John K. Fairbank wrote, "has been, not that she has come up against a more powerful civilization from overseas, but that the alien West has been culturally so different from the old China. Whether Western ways are really and truly 'superior' to the Chinese is unimportant; during the past century they have seemed so to the West. Now they seem so even to Chinese, for the influx of communism, whether we like it or not, must be viewed as the latest phase of a process stimulated by Western contact."

The 1911 revolution in China brought to power a government that had been changed in form, but not in essence. The reforms it had promised failed to materialize, resulting in widespread disillusionment among the young militants who would, years later, launch the real revolution. The traditional system, thousands of years old, would not dissolve overnight. Nor would it halt the advent of the new order; China had to change, whether it wanted to or not.

In the 1920s, the older Kuomintang (National People's Party) revolutionaries became the protectors of the old order they had sought to change. Their revolutionary credo turned reactionary, even to the point where a concentrated effort was made to revive traditional Confucianism. Democracy was sacrificed for national unity and centralized power; economic reform was smothered in bureaucratism. The subsequent waning prestige of the government led to the increased use of police control, and a new militarism emerged for the first time in China's history. As for the peasant masses, the revolution had passed them by.

During the 1930s and 1940s, the situation steadily deteriorated. The Nationalist government, reassured by Chiang Kai-shek's successful campaign against northern warlords in 1927, concentrated on defeating Mao Tse-tung's rebels in the south. By late 1935, the Communists had been forced to flee to northwestern China, taking the legendary Long March, which marked a turning point in their fortunes.

An uneasy alliance between the Kuomintang and the Communists, made in 1937, quickly disintegrated. But the war against the Japanese enabled the Communists, by stressing both united resistance and "agrarian reform," to win support over the entire north China plain area. Party membership increased from 40,000 in 1937 to 1,200,000 in 1945. By the end of the war, the rebels were prepared to challenge the Kuomintang in China's vast countryside.

The swiftness of the Nationalist government's collapse surprised even the elder statesman among revolutionaries, Joseph Stalin, who had shown little confidence in the Chi-

1

nese Communists. Disorder, desertions and demoralization plagued the Nationalist armies, while economic chaos, especially rampant inflation, eroded Kuomintang support in the big cities. Arduous American efforts at mediation were destined for failure. The two sides neither trusted one another nor were inclined to make major concessions while the prospect of eventual total victory persisted.

By 1949, the Chinese Communists had brought together a disciplined and well-indoctrinated army and a party apparatus with which they could exercise extensive political control over the Chinese mainland. For the Chinese people, this new monolithic political structure was in harmony with the past rather than a departure from it. The intensity of the supervision and degree of efficiency increased, and there could be little doubt that the Chinese people, especially the youth, readily accepted the new slogans and programs with enthusiasm. For the forgotten multitude, there was at least hope.

What seemed a new hope for the Chinese people, however, was regarded as a catastrophe by Americans. In the words of Dr. Fairbank: "For a decade the American people had idealized Free China; increasingly the combination of the atomic age and the cold war had intensified their fear of communism. To have Free China become Communist seemed a national disaster. Like the Great Depression, it became political ammunition against the party in office. Governor Dewey used it in the 1948 campaign. Soon the Hiss case, the Fuchs case, the fear of spies and conspiracies, capped by a major war against Communist China in Korea, among other complex factors, took the lid off the McCarthy era."

The Sino-Soviet Treaty of February 1950 and the outbreak of the Korean war four months later undoubtedly intensified America's fear and bitter suspicion of the new Communist government. The Chinese seizure of Tibet, concurrent with her intervention in Korea, was an ominous foreboding to India and other Asian nations. While the Korean War confirmed the fact that the United States had replaced Japan as China's cardinal enemy, it also served the purposes of dictatorial social and economic reorganization in China. The Communist party, by launching a war-time campaign to "suppress counter-revolutionaries," guaranteed its total control over the mainland through property confiscations, thought reform, purges and mass executions. By the end of the Korean conflict, the party's campaign of land reform had already been completed.

Unlike the Manchu leaders, the Chinese Communists took active interest in events in Southeast Asia. With the Korean War deadlocked, it appeared as if the battleground might shift to Indo-China, where the Viet Minh forces were receiving aid from Peking and the French effort was largely financed by the United States. But the Chinese, despite their progress in reorganization, found their internal revolution lagging due to the drain from the Korean struggle, and did not wish to become directly involved. The hostilities in Indo-China therefore ended after seven years of bitter fighting.

The wars in Korea and southern Asia forced the United States to abandon its policy of non-involvement in the Far East and to make new commitments that would, a decade later, overshadow its obligations in Western Europe or, for that matter, anywhere else. A Southeast Asian Collective Defense Treaty was signed in 1954; security treaties were concluded with Japan, Australia, New Zealand, the Philippines, South Korea and Nationalist China, while American military forces in the western Pacific were strengthened. After the French concession in Indo-China, large U.S. economic and military aid programs were initiated in Laos, Cambodia, Thailand and South Viet Nam. The Eisenhower Administration made it clear in 1955 and 1958 that American military power would be utilized to protect the offshore islands still under Nationalist control. The United States had become a Pacific as well as Atlantic power, dedicated to containing the expansion of communism in Asia.

In 1958, the Chinese Communist Party's leadership embarked on the disastrous Great Leap Forward, from which the economy did not recover until 1962. Described as a short cut to pure communism, the rapid mass transferral over to a commune system was ridiculed by the Russians, and its subsequent failure touched off the policy rift between the two countries that would later change the character of the Cold War.

For the Chinese leadership, the second effort to recover the offshore islands in 1958 was disappointing. The Soviet Union, despite its alliance with Communist China, refused to supply the Chinese army with the necessary weaponry to match the U.S.-equipped Nationalist forces on Quemoy and Matsu. Instead, Nikita Khrushchev was in the United States conferring with President Eisenhower, touring Iowa cornfields, eating American hotdogs, and openly fraternizing with China's main enemy. China's first deliberately chosen alliance in history was beginning to crumble.

Although unknown in the West at the time, the Soviet Union had already begun its withdrawal of technicians and blueprints from China in 1958, leaving the complicated business of industrialization to the inexperienced Chinese and a handful of East German advisers.

With the campaign to rid Asia of U.S. influence thwarted, the coalition with the Soviet Union rapidly disintegrating, and the economy teetering on the verge of collapse, the Chinese leadership turned to the underdeveloped nations, offering a mixture of militant anti-Americanism and pledges of military and economic aid. The endeavor was a spectacular failure, and Peking's influence in these countries and in the international Communist movement seriously diminished. Mao Tse-tung's foreign policy suffered grave setbacks in Indonesia, Pakistan, North Viet Nam, North Korea, Cuba, Algeria, Ghana, Upper Volta, Kenya, the Central African Republic, Dahomey, and other nations.

For the American public, China had posed a distant threat compared to the militarily sophisticated Russians. But in 1962, the Cuban missile crisis demonstrated the determination of both the United States and the Soviet Union to avoid total war. Concurrently, the Chinese intrusion into India and its subsequent successful tests of nuclear devices and delivery systems, accompanied by the expansion of the war in South Viet Nam, significantly altered the composition of East-West contention.

By late 1966, Soviet diplomats were no longer attempting to conceal from American officials their apprehension of China's pugnacity, while Chinese propaganda incessantly charged that the United States and the Soviet Union were acting in "collusion" to dominate the world.

The Chinese saw themselves surrounded to the east and south by American "imperialists," and to the north and west by Soviet "revisionists." The United States bombed areas only a few miles away from China's border, constructed vast military complexes in South Viet Nam and Thailand, and stationed armadas off the Chinese coast. The Soviet Union had its single largest military concentration spread along the Manchurian border. Peking felt threatened, but Washington countered that the Chinese suffered from paranoia and said there would only be trouble if China misbehaved, which, in this case, meant intervention in the Viet Nam war.

In both the United States and Communist China there was pressure for reappraisal during 1966. In Washington, leading Sinologists warned that the U.S. strategy was isolating as well as containing China, and was therefore increasing the chance of open conflict. In Peking, more moderate Communist party officials, realizing that China had suffered serious setbacks, urged a less militant and dogmatic approach. By the end of 1966, there were indications that the Johnson Administration was considering a more flexible strategy.

In China, the reactions were quite different. Since the summer of 1966, an aging Mao Tse-tung, the undisputed leader of Communist China for 17 years, had been fighting for his political life. The struggle between the less militant faction of the party's hierarchy and the more canonical Maoist camp penetrated to the lowest levels of party, government and military structures both in the capital and in the provinces. Mao's weapon in the political battle was the "Great Proletarian Cultural Revolution," a Chinese euphemism meaning purge. As its chief architect and executor, Mao chose Marshal Lin Piao, the slight, soft-spoken defense minister and respected military tactician. Lin quickly rose to the second position on the order of precedence in the Communist hierarchy, replacing Head of State Liu Shao-chi, who was dropped to number eight.

The fact that Liu was not dismissed altogether was significant. Both he and the party's general secretary, Teng Hsiao-ping, were considered the most important leaders of the group opposing Mao. It seemed as if Mao and Lin did not possess the power to depose Liu and Teng. Nor were they successful in ousting party leaders in the provinces, despite frenzied attempts by the Cultural Revolution's storm troopers -- the young and militant Red Guards.

The purge did succeed, however, in totally disrupting Chinese life. The turbulence emanating from Peking swept across the countryside, bringing violence and chaos to many areas. Journalists, propagandists, military leaders, educators, scholars and intellectuals were deposed. The nation's entire school system was closed down. The Red Guards, fired by the near-delirious rallies in the capital, raged through the provinces, attacking local party functionaries, disrupting factories and communes, sacking, burning and beating anything or anyone they considered bourgeois, traditional or foreign. Many died, more were injured and still more fought back. "Don't hit people!" Lin Piao finally warned; use "reason, not coercion or force," urged Premier Chou En-lai, who was reported to have assumed greater leadership of the government, party and military apparatus as Mao's star faded in early 1967.

Throughout this reign of terror, the gospel of the Cultural Revolution -- the thought of Chairman Mao, "the Great Teacher, Great Leader, Great Supreme Commander, and Great Helmsman of the Chinese people" -- was spread through China by the Red Guards. In many cases, the campaign of Mao-think seemed ludicrous. Stories of how watermelon salesmen, oil drillers, ping-pong players, farmers, soldiers, swimmers and bureaucrats improved themselves through the study of Mao's thoughts were continually printed in the Chinese press. Mao-thought, the propaganda repeatedly claimed, "marks a completely new stage in the development of Marxism-Leninism." The Russians, increasingly alarmed, publicly scoffed at such ideas.

Throughout the world, China's internal disorders were viewed with a mixture of curiosity and apprehension, exemplified by the vote in the General Assembly in 1966 on China's admission into the United Nations, in which the trend of dwindling opposition to Peking's entry was reversed and the negative vote was actually greater than it had been in 1965.

By the beginning of 1967, the dreams of China's Communist leaders had been only partially fulfilled. Mao's revolution was threatened, both internally and externally, and it was not known whether he controlled events in the People's Republic or was controlled by them. It was generally accepted, however, that the Cultural Revolution and all its implications could well influence the course of Sino-American relations for the last third of the 20th Century. For out of China's political crisis could emerge the great disaster the world had been able to avoid since 1945. Or there could arise a new leadership, more attuned to the tenor of world events.

China and the West

Relations between the United States and Communist China, virtually frozen in mutual hostility since the outbreak of war in Korea in 1950, went through a period of reassessment in Washington during the mid-1960s. Prodded by searching inquiries into Asian policy conducted early in 1966 by two Congressional committees, the Johnson Administration indicated that current American policy toward China was not so rigid as it previously seemed to be.

Even as China was in the midst of confusion and turmoil caused by the denunciation of leaders, the information-by-poster ordeal and the Great Proletarian Cultural Revolution, President Johnson, in his Jan. 10, 1967, State of the Union message put out a friendly hand to China:

> We shall continue to hope for a reconciliation between the people of mainland China and the world community -- including working together in all tasks of arms control, security, and progress on which the fate of the Chinese people, like their fellowmen elsewhere, depends.

> We would be the first to welcome a China which decided to respect her neighbors' rights. We would be the first to applaud her were she to apply her great energies and intelligence to improving the welfare of her people. And we have no intention of trying to deny her legitimate needs for security and friendly relations with her neighboring countries.

Two witnesses heard by the Senate Foreign Relations Committee early in March 1966 -- Prof. A. Doak Barnett of Columbia University and Prof. John K. Fairbank of Harvard strongly urged that the United States abandon its policy of "containment and isolation" of Communist China and substitute a policy of military containment without isolation. The two, both leading authorities on Asian affairs, suggested that the United States encourage Communist Chinese participation in international conferences. *(For text of Barnett statement, see p. 278; Fairbank, p. 284.)*

Vice President Hubert H. Humphrey said in a television interview March 13, 1966, that American policy toward Red China should be one of "containment without necessarily isolation." Humphrey indicated that an attempt would be made to approach China in a manner similar to that followed with the Soviet Union in the late 1950s -- a combination of firmness accompanied by active efforts to explore avenues to better relations. An announcement, March 9, that the United States was easing restrictions on travel of American scholars and scientists to mainland China was viewed as a part of the effort to improve relations with the Asian giant. Furthermore, the State Department disclosed, April 14, that several American universities which had made inquiries had been notified that scientists and scholars from Communist China would be permitted to visit the United States if they applied.

Government spokesmen emphasized the administration's view that if China was isolated from the world community, it was self-imposed isolation. Secretary of State Dean Rusk, testifying on March 16 before the House Foreign

Affairs Subcommittee on the Far East and the Pacific, rejected the contention that the United States had isolated China. Rather Rusk said, China's leaders had "isolated themselves -- both in the non-Communist and Communist worlds."

The Secretary of State outlined ten main components of American policy toward Red China. Basically, his testimony amounted to a re-statement of this country's support of the Nationalist government of Chiang Kai-shek and of Asian nations that wished to resist Asian communism. But Rusk called also for renewed efforts to convince Peking that the United States did not intend to attack mainland China, and for efforts to enlarge possibilities of unofficial contacts with that nation.

"We must keep firmly in our minds," he said, "that there is nothing eternal about the policies and attitudes of Communist China." Rusk added that the United States "must avoid assuming the existence of an unending and inevitable state of hostility between ourselves and the rulers of mainland China."

The new policy obviously fell short of steps urged by critics of the American position who favored recognition of Peking and admission of Red China to the United Nations. China's first reactions to the new policy echoed earlier declarations that only major action, including abandonment of American support of the Chiang government on Taiwan, could bring about any substantial improvement of relations. A *New China* news agency statement, April 19, said: "Rusk persisted in the policy of hostility and aggression toward China while talking no end of 'increasing contacts' and 'restoring friendship' with China."

Some experts on foreign affairs believed that the Chinese intransigence was rooted in the past, when the colonizing nations of Europe, also the United States, imposed their will on a declining Chinese empire. The West's first contacts with China began around 700 years ago. Much of the period since then has been marked by misunderstanding between the two cultures, contempt of the one for the other, exploitation, outright hostility, and occasional resort to arms. Harry Schwartz, *New York Times* expert on Communist affairs, wrote in 1965 that the bitterness and hatred toward the Western nations, and especially the United States, revealed so often by Peking stems from "a century of Chinese humiliation by the West."

Early Contacts With West

Marco Polo, the Venetian adventurer who lived in China for 17 years during the 13th century, was not the first westerner to reach the Celestial Kingdom. Under Alexander the Great, the Greeks had penetrated to central Asia; traders from the Roman empire had some commercial contact with the Chinese. During the reign of the Mongol emperor Kublai Khan, before Marco Polo arrived with his merchant uncles, Roman Catholic missionaries had journeyed from Europe to China and established small communities of Christian converts.

The influence on the West of the writings of Marco Polo was nevertheless wider than that of any occidental who preceded him. His book, *Description of the World*, or *Travels*

This section adapted from Editorial Research Reports, Vol. I, 1966, p. 303.

of Marco Polo, became the principal European source of information on the Far East. A historian, Dun J. Li, has observed that the impact of this work on contemporary Europe was tremendous.

> That a more advanced society existed simultaneously with Europe was hard to believe, and most of the Europeans dismissed the book as mere fable. When the book finally won credence, it aroused great interest in China among the literate Europeans. Its readers included such men as Christopher Columbus. To the religiously devoted, there was a huge pagan world to conquer, and to the worldly merchants, there were enormous profits to be realized.[1]

Marco Polo's journal, Li wrote, paved the way "for the arrival of thousands of Europeans in the centuries to come."

Penetration by the Traders and Missionaries

The greatest influx of westerners into China did not come for several hundred years, not until the European peoples had begun the expansion "which culminated in political domination of the world." The Iberians were the first to arrive. A group of Portuguese traders sailed into Canton harbor in 1517. Though they met with no violence, the emperor, annoyed at their lack of respect, expelled the Portuguese. Others continued to come, trading and often looting along the coast. In an effort to restrict the intruders to a given area, Macao was "lent" to Portuguese merchants as a trading base in 1557.

As the Portuguese traders prospered, traders of other nations followed. The Dutch were the next to arrive; they operated from the Pescadores and Taiwan. By the beginning of the 18th century, England and France had joined in the commerce. The Chinese, hoping to put limits to the widening operations of the foreigners, in 1757 confined all foreign trade to the port of Canton. By 1784 when the first American ship, the Empress of China, sailed for the Orient, the British had established a pre-eminent position in the China trade.

The first extensive cultural contact between China and Europe began at the end of the 16th century, when Jesuit missionaries reached China by sea. The missionaries had a dual role:

> They not only diffused Western ideas in China, including elements of mathematics, astronomy, geography, hydraulics, the calendar, and the manufacture of cannon, but they also introduced Chinese...ideas into Europe. The Jesuits found it easier to influence China's science than her religion. Perceiving this, they used their scientific knowledge as a means of approach to Chinese scholars.[2]

One of the leading Jesuit missionaries was Matteo Ricci, who arrived in Macao in 1582 and in Peking in 1601. Father Ricci revealed an understanding of the Chinese and immersed himself in the study of China's language, literature and philosophy. He sought to detach himself and his mission from identification with the power of the European state and concentrated on cultivating scholars and high government officials. In return for the counsel of Father Ricci and his colleagues on matters of science and technology, the Chinese granted them permission to preach and proselytize. But de-

1 Dun J. Li, The Ageless Chinese: A History (1965), p. 376.
2 Ssu-yu Teng and John K. Fairbank, China's Response to the West (1954), p. 12.

spite the efforts of the Jesuits and of other missionaries who followed them to Peking, the number of Christian converts 100 years after Ricci's arrival in China was estimated at only between 100,000 and 250,000.

Cultural Gap

When Father Ricci was first in Peking, he observed the Chinese looked upon all foreigners "as illiterate and barbarous." They would not condescend "to learn anything from the books of outsiders because they believe that all true science and knowledge belongs to them alone." The Jesuits' superiority in technical subjects finally induced the Chinese to follow their lead, but in other aspects of society and intellectual life the Chinese held to their own views.

The emperor and his court officials, believing Peking to be the center of the world and all other nations inferior, had no understanding of the power of European nations. Scorning trade, they considered commercial contacts with foreigners as privileges they could grant or withhold. Accustomed to dealing with the small tributary states on their borders, they viewed pretentions to sovereignty by others as impertinence.

The first British emissary to China, arriving in 1793, sought an audience with the emperor to establish British representation in Peking, the opening of additional ports to trade, and reductions in Chinese tariffs. To the Chinese, the Briton was no more than a tribute bearer, but the emperor Chien-lung granted him a hearing because he had come so far and was for the first time visiting "a superior country." However, the British requests were rejected as inconsistent with Chinese custom. No other state was allowed permanent representation in Peking.

Differences over trading rights and criminal jurisdiction exacerbated relations between the Chinese and westerners. The Chinese considered permission to trade a favor which could be revoked; but trade was the principal interest of the western voyagers, and they objected to limitations placed upon their activities by designation of where and with whom they could deal. In addition, bribes demanded by local officials doubled, even tripled, the official high tariff rates.

The Chinese insisted that the imperial government had jurisdiction over all criminal cases involving a Chinese national. The foreigners considered Chinese law and court procedures barbarous and were reluctant to accept Chinese jurisdiction. The Chinese held to the principle of joint responsibility for a crime: if one of a ship's crew had committed a crime and could not be found, the ship's captain should be brought to account. The Europeans maintained that only those directly involved were subject to trial and punishment.

Opium War of 1839-1842

Given the vast cultural differences between China and the West, a clash was probably inevitable. "The great tragedy," Harry Schwartz observed, "is that the clash occurred over an issue on which the West's position was morally indefensible by today's standards: the British demand that the Chinese government permit western merchants to sell opium freely to to Chinese." The conflict that became known as the Opium War of 1839-42 was "one that has cast a terrible shadow over China's relations with the West ever since."

Opium originally was shipped to China in quantity by the Portuguese, but this trade was still relatively small in 1729, when the Chinese emperor prohibited the sale and use of opium in China. Despite the ban, the opium traffic grew rapidly as merchants, principally British, pressed the trade with the assistance of corrupt Chinese officials. Not only was the drug traffic a source of large profit; it also provided an alternative to silver in paying for Chinese tea, silk and porcelain.

By the late 1830s, opium addiction had spread from members of the nobility to artisans, merchants, women, and even members of the religious organizations. "If the opium traffic is not stopped," wrote a Chinese official, "the country will become poorer and poorer and its people weaker and weaker." But even a direct appeal to the conscience of Queen Victoria proved unsuccessful. In 1838, Lin Tse-hsu was named imperial commissioner at Canton and directed by the Emperor to end the opium trade once and for all. He ordered that all opium held by foreigners be turned over to the government and burned.

When British traders refused to pledge that they would ship no more opium to China, Lin threatened to ban all commercial traffic. Meanwhile, a Chinese citizen had been killed in Kowloon by a group of English sailors. And when the British rejected Chinese demands for surrender of the sailors, Lin sent war junks toward the British naval force in Hong Kong. The junks were fired upon and so the war began. British naval superiority assured ultimate victory. When the British threatened a direct attack on Nanking, the Chinese sued for peace.

The Treaty of Nanking, signed in 1842, resulted in the opening of China to western traders. The treaty provided for (1) opening of five ports -- Amoy, Canton, Foochow, Ningpo and Shanghai -- to British trade; (2) cession to Britain of the island of Hong Kong; (3) Chinese agreement to uniform and moderate tariffs on imports and exports, subject to change only by mutual consent; and (4) indemnity payments of $21 million. Under a supplementary treaty signed a year later, China granted the British extra-territorial jurisdiction in criminal cases and most-favored-nation status.

Other Western powers, through persuasion and threats of force, demanded and received the same or larger privileges. Because a most-favored-nation clause was incorporated in all later Chinese treaties with Western countries, a concession to one nation automatically became a concession to all. The Treaty of Wang-hsia, concluded with the United States in July 1844, extended the principle of extraterritoriality to civil as well as to criminal cases. France was granted the right to build Roman Catholic missions at treaty ports and freedom to proselytize without interference. Such concessions then were extended to all nations with missionaries in China.

Dun J. Li has pointed out that the Treaty of Nanking, "hopefully hailed by many westerners as the beginning of a new era in the relations between China and the Western world, created only a lull before another storm." The Chinese, with more than 4,000 years of an inward-looking culture, were slow to understand the new reality of European power. Instead of adjusting to the future, they dreamed of the past when the Celestial Emperor dealt peremptorily with the barbarians from the outer world. The policy of conciliation, evasion and negotiation followed by the Manchus for two decades after the Opium War amounted to merely a delaying action as the foreigners moved to enhance their power in China.

Century-Long Humiliation

The Opium War opened more than 100 years of foreign humiliation of the Chinese government and people, a humiliation not fully ended until Mao Tse-tung and the Chinese

Communists triumphed in 1949. Some of the Western nations regarded the Treaty of Nanking as too lenient. They wanted additional ports opened to trade and diplomatic representation at Peking. China's vulnerability was revealed during the Opium War, making a second conflict not unattractive to some Western states.

The second conflict was sparked by two incidents in 1856. One concerned the crew of a British-registered ship, the other the execution of a French Catholic missionary and some of his converts. British and French forces easily defeated the poorly trained Chinese. When the Europeans threatened to attack the city of Tientsin, the Manchu government again sued for peace. The treaties of Tientsin granted new concessions to the West and enlarged older privileges. Britain and France were granted the right to maintain resident ministers at Peking and their nationals received unlimited travel privileges. New ports were opened to trade, and foreign ships were granted navigation rights on the Yangtse river. Indemnities were paid, tariff rates lowered, and protection of missionaries guaranteed.

Utilizing the customary delaying tactics, the Chinese refused to ratify the new treaties. Britain and France renewed the war and the British commander ordered the burning of the Summer Palace in Peking, one of the architectural glories of the empire. The war came to a close with another treaty, signed in Peking in 1860, which gave still more privileges to the Europeans, including cession to the British of the Kowloon peninsula adjoining Hong Kong. The new privileges were extended to the other Western nations which had been accorded most-favored-nation status, including the United States and Russia.

Foreign powers later extended their dominion in Asia. Russia took over all of the mainland north of Korea and Manchuria. France colonized southern Indo-China. Russia in 1868 completed a campaign to gain control of a large part of Sinkiang. Nepal, a tributary state, passed under British control in 1881, and five years later Britain completed the conquest of Burma. At the close of the Sino-Japanese War in 1895, Japan exacted Formosa (Taiwan) from China and won paramount status in Korea. The Germans, French and British gained naval bases and ports on the Chinese mainland in 1898. Finally, following the Boxer uprising [4] and a lengthy siege of the European legation quarter in Peking in 1900, the Western powers imposed heavy indemnities and stationed foreign troops in the capital. "For over a decade after 1900, China was in fact a foreign-occupied country." [5]

The century which began with Chinese pride and arrogance," Robert S. Elegant relates, "ended with Chinese humiliation complete."

---

[3] *Traditionally the Chinese did not allow representatives of tributary states and other foreign lands to reside permanently in China; they were met at the border and escorted to Peking but could not move freely about the capital and the countriside. -- Immanuel C.Y. Hsu,* China's Entrance into the Family of Nations, The Diplomatic Phase 1858-1880 *(1960), pp. 10-11.*

[4] *Boxers were members of a secret sect which sprang up in 1898 among restive peasants. At first opposed by the Empress Dowager and later encouraged as a means of ridding China of foreigners, the Boxers killed scores of missionaries and their converts.*

[5] *Kenneth Scott Latourette,* China *(1904), p. 121. Japan became one of the occupiers after her victory in the Russo-Japanese war of 1904-05. Railroad and other rights in South Manchuria granted by China to Russia in 1898 were transferred to Japan, laying the foundation for Japanese occupation of all of Manchuria in the 1930s.*

Foreign envoys, once scorned, dictated terms in the Imperial City itself. Foreign missionaries, once barely tolerated, ranged everywhere to subvert the people from their proper duties to the Emperor. In violation of Peking's express decrees, hundreds of thousands of Chinese emigranted to serve the imperialists abroad -- and to create the overseas Chinese problem which vexes Southeast Asia today.[6]

China was saved from being carved up into colonies by disagreement among her conquerors, who jealously guarded their spheres of influence. The United States, which had no territorial possessions on the mainland, formalized the precarious status quo by proclaiming the Open Door policy in 1899. That policy guaranteed equality of commercial opportunity and enjoined further territorial seizures. Actually, the Open Door policy, which was supported by British power, was rooted in the most-favored-nation clauses of the Sino-Western treaties.

Sino-Western Relations In 20th Century

The Western powers were able to impose their will in China mainly because of the degenerate state of the Confucian dynasties which had ruled that country for 2,000 years. Chinese failure to recognize until too late that the West was a truly formidable adversary resulted from almost total Chinese ignorance of the world beyond the borders of the Celestial Empire. This lack of knowledge led to collapse of the empire itself, as the Chinese began to learn from the West and to use what they had learned to free themselves from foreign bondage.

Formation of Republic

During the 19th century Chinese resentment at the privileged status of foreigners in their midst periodically flared into violence against westerners. The most serious outbreak was the Boxer Rebellion, but as Chinese youth became more westernized, their resentment was directed at the Chinese authorities and the ineffectual Imperial government. Young students, angered by the corruption, brutality and inefficiency which marked the declining years of the Manchu Dynasty, turned against the customs and religion of the older generation.

The youthful opposition joined in a revolutionary movement led by Sun Yat-sen and supported by overseas Chinese. The Empress Dowager and her successor died in 1908, leaving the succession to an infant emperor. A troop revolt which broke out in three cities in October 1911 led to the proclama- of a republic; the rebellion spread rapidly and by the end of the year a national council had been set up. The council elected Sun Yat-sen president of the republic, and in February 1912 the boy emperor, Pu Yi, was forced to abdicate.

The new leaders had been united only by their opposition to the Manchu Dynasty and China soon splintered into contending states headed by warlords and factions. Between 1913 and 1928, when the Kuomintang or Nationalist Party under the leadership of Chiang Kai-shek established a degree of control over the warring factions, the nation was split into the private domains of various warlords and was demoralized, disorganized, and disunited. During this period, Robert S. Elegant has noted, the only orderly government was "that imposed by foreigners in their various treaty ports."

---

6 *Robert S. Elegant*, The Center of the World: Communism and the Mind of China *(1964), p. 69. See "Overseas Chinese," E.R.R., 1958 Vol. II, pp. 801-806.*

In Westernized treaty ports and in inland hamlets, each new day added new weight to oppressive reality. The young Chinese tended to scorn other Chinese -- and himself -- for their degradation. The chief clubs of China's major cities either excluded Chinese or admitted a few as historical curiosities. The Christian missionary enjoyed extraordinary privileges amounting to immunity from the law.... Foreign warships patrolled the coasts and rivers of China, enforcing payment of taxes for the foreigners' benefit.

"The most idealistic and talented youth of China," Elegant concluded, "grew to maturity in a miasma of hatred."

Decline of Foreign Control

China entered World War I in August 1917, but, when the peace conferees at Paris decided to transfer German holdings in China's Shantung Peninsula to Japan, the representatives of China refused to sign the treaty. However, the Treaty of Versailles benefited China by depriving Austria and Germany of extraterritorial status and special concessions in China.

Further gains were made by the Chinese in the years following the war. At the Washington arms limitation conference of 1921-22, the Western powers and Japan agreed to respect the independence and territorial integrity of China, to refrain from seeking special privileges, and to give the Chinese an opportunity to achieve stable government. The powers agreed also to study the question of extraterritoriality with a view to its abolition. During the conference, furthermore, China and Japan negotiated a treaty, ratified June 2, 1922, under which Japan surrendered the rights and concessions she obtained in Shantung.

The Bolshevik Revolution of November 1917 in Russia had opened the way for China to regain some of the ground lost to the Czars. Under an agreement concluded in 1924, for example, Russian extraterritorial privileges in China were relinquished. Soon thereafter, pressure mounted in China for abolition of the concessions still enjoyed by foreigners in treaty ports. By 1930 more than half of the foreigners in China had lost extraterritorial privileges, but the United States, Great Britain, France and Japan would not give ground. A Chinese attempt to resolve the question by simply decreeing that all remaining extraterritorial privileges would be withdrawn on a certain date was not successful, and some foreigners continued to enjoy such privileges up to World War II.

Civil War and Communist Triumph

The Chinese Communist Party was formally organized in 1921 with no more than 50 registered members. It joined with the Kuomintang in support of Sun Yat-sen in 1924. Several Communists, including Mao Tse-tung, were elected alternate members of the Kuomintang's Central Executive Committee. This first period of cooperation ended in 1927, when the Kuomintang, under Chiang Kai-shek's leadership purged the Communists.

The purge was followed by a lengthy struggle between Communists and Nationalists. The latter were ascendant in the larger part of China, but in 1931 a Soviet republic was proclaimed in southern Kiangsi; under Mao's leadership the area became a microcosm of present-day China. Nationalist armies launched a number of campaigns against the republic, but, plagued by Japanese intrusions in Manchuria, these efforts were unsuccessful. Only in 1934, after a truce with Japan had been signed and an economic blockade of Kiangsi established, did Nationalist pressure damage the Communists. Rather than face annihilation, the Communist forces in 1934-35 staged the famed Long March, described by Harry Schwartz as an "epic of military history."

Harried by government troops, by shortages of food and medicine and by the often harsh climate, Mao's wandering army overcame incredible hardships. It climbed major mountain ranges, crossed turbulent rivers on perilous and primitive bridges and inched its way across great swamps. A year after he had started and 6,000 miles from his starting point, Mao called a halt. He had arrived at the other end of his country, in northern Shensi Province in northwestern China. Fewer than one-third of the 100,000 men who had begun the Long March completed it; most had fallen victim to battle, hunger, cold or disease. But in this poverty-stricken region of China, Mao created a new Communist area, set up his capital in Yenan and started all over.

Confronted by further Japanese aggression in 1937, Communists and Nationalists again entered a period of cooperation. Before long, however, the struggle became a three-sided contest, with each Chinese faction attempting to enlarge its area of control at the expense of its rival while at the same time fighting the Japanese. After World War II ended in the Pacific with Japan's surrender, efforts to form a coalition Chinese government broke down and the civil war between Nationalists and Communists resumed.

By 1949, despite American military and economic aid to Chiang's forces, the Communist armies were clearly headed for victory. Early in that year, Chiang began to shift some of his forces as well as China's gold reserve to Taiwan (Formosa), a large island separated from the mainland by the 100-mile-wide Taiwan Strait. The Nationalist withdrawal was accelerated as the Communists rapidly won most of the mainland. By Oct. 1, 1949, when the People's Republic of China was proclaimed in Peking, few areas were left in Nationalist hands.

Korean War and U.S. Formosan Policy

The United States Government, in a white paper issued in the summer of 1949, placed the blame for Chiang's downfall on the "corruption and incompetence" of the Nationalists. A month after the Nationalists fled the mainland, President Truman said the United States did not have "any intention of utilizing its armed forces to interfere in the present situation" and would not provide military aid or advice to the Nationalists. The Communists began massing a force to invade Taiwan.

"From hindsight," Dun J. Li declares, "it seems that what saved Taiwan from Communist conquest was neither Taipei (capital of Taiwan) nor Washington but a miscalculation on the part of Moscow." Communist North Korea's invasion of South Korea in June 1950 caused the United States to reverse its China policy and support Chiang's regime. President Truman stated, June 27, that in view of North Korea's action, "the occupation of Formosa by Communist forces would be a direct threat to the security of the Pacific area and to the United States forces." He ordered the U.S. Seventh Fleet to prevent any Communist attack on Formosa and to see that all Nationalist air and sea operations against the mainland were halted.

Large-scale intervention of Chinese Communist forces in Korea in November 1950 cemented American support of the Nationalist regime. It also brought a resolution from the United Nations General Assembly declaring Peking guilty of aggression. [7] This declaration marked a turning point in the policy of the United States and certain other nations toward admitting Red China to membership in the world organization. In 1967, however, the permanent seat in the Security Council assigned to China by the UN Charter and China's seat in the General Assembly still were filled by representatives of the Nationalist government.

Since the fighting in Korea and the long drawn-out negotiations over a truce, eventually signed on July 27, 1953, American support of the Nationalist regime remained strong. Late in 1954, Washington signed a mutual defense treaty with Chiang, setting up a vast program of economic and military aid. Taiwan was an island well endowed by nature, and with American aid the real income of its people was doubled. The United States provided almost $2.5 billion in grant economic aid in the 16 years prior to termination of the economic aid program on June 30, 1965. The military assistance program continued.

Future Relations With China

Many observers believed that continued strained relations between the United States and Red China bore the seeds of eventual armed conflict. The American policy of peripheral military containment of mainland China clashed with Peking's interests in two central areas: Taiwan, where U.S. support of the Nationalist government ensured the latter's existence, and in Southeast Asia, where the United States and South Viet Nam were engaged in open conflict with a Chinese ally, North Viet Nam.

In the face of these conflicts, tentative American efforts to improve relations with Peking were rebuffed. Senior diplomatic officials in London were said to have reported April 12, 1966, that the United States, during discussions between the American and Chinese ambassadors in Warsaw, had informed China that it was ready to discuss both a normalizing of relations and Peking's possible membership in the United Nations. The Chinese were said to have rejected the offer, insisting that U.S. forces must withdraw from Viet Nam and that the United States must agree to a global disarmament treaty before the question of improving relations could be taken up.

The State Department denied that the United States had made the reported offer. But Red China's reaction to the publication of Secretary Rusk's statement of March 16 was consistent with past performance. The official New China News Agency called it a "sham" and a "scheme to carry out infiltration in China in the vain hope" that a new generation of Chinese leaders would adopt different policies.

Contacts With Peking

Although the United States and Red China still stood at arm's length, other Western powers expanded their diplomatic and commercial contacts with mainland China. The 49 countries which recognized the Peking regime included Denmark, Finland, France, Great Britain, Netherlands, Norway, Sweden, and Switzerland. [8] When France recognized Red China, Jan. 27, 1964, it was the first Western European country to do so since 1950; the others extended

---

7 On Feb. 1, 1951, by a vote of 44 to 7 with 9 abstentions.
8 Nationalist China is recognized by 56 states; the figures do not include nations at present divided between Communist and non-Communist zones, i.e., Germany, Korea, and Viet Nam.

recognition shortly after the Communists ousted the Nationalists late in 1949.

Opposition of the United States to recognition of Communist China and to its admission to the United Nations played a major role in delaying acceptance of the Peking regime by many other states. But commercial contacts between mainland China and the free world increased despite American efforts to restrict such trade. The United States permitted no trade with Communist China by American exporters or importers. Similar total trade embargoes were imposed by Washington on Cuba, North Korea and North Viet Nam, though American trade in nonstrategic goods with the U.S.S.R. and the Communist countries of Eastern Europe was allowed. A report on East-West trade, issued by the State Department on Dec. 30, 1965, pointed out that in 1964 the value of exports from mainland China to free world nations exceeded $1 billion for the first time; imports from the free world rose 22 percent to a record $977 million.

Seven countries, each of which sold $50 million or more of goods to China, provided almost three-fourths of that country's imports: Australia, Japan, Canada, Argentina, Cuba, the United Kingdom and France (in order of trade volume). Japan was the major supplier of products other than wheat and flour. Major purchasers of Chinese products were Hong Kong, Japan, Cuba, Malaya and Singapore. The only West European countries taking more than $50 million worth of goods from Communist China were Great Britain and West Germany.

Canadian Finance Minister Mitchell Sharp announced April 5, 1966, that China had exercised an option to increase its three-year wheat purchases by about 50 percent. The value of the new agreement could amount to $550 million over the three years beginning Aug. 1. West Germany announced March 17 that it had agreed to guarantee an $87.5-million credit for expansion of China's steel producing facilities in cooperation with Belgian, British, French, Italian and Swiss companies. The United States, at first neutral on the project, later indicated that it opposed the transaction and would try to induce members of the consortium to take another look. It was estimated that the project would boost Chinese steel-making capacity by two million tons.

Two-China Proposals

Differences over trade with China and other Communist countries have periodically ruffled relations between the United States and its Western allies. Secretary Rusk said March 20, 1966, during a television interview that "We are concerned about anything that would lead Peiping to believe that their policy is successful, or anything that would add to the strength of Peiping until there is some indication of change in their policy."

Efforts made periodically to improve the United States' relations with Red China foundered on American support of Nationalist China and, more recently, on U.S. assistance to South Viet Nam. Many observers urged that Washington adopt a "two-China" policy, recognizing that the Communist government was in control of the mainland and that Nationalist rule would be limited, short of a major war, to Taiwan and several small islands. The principal stumbling block in the way of a two-China policy was the refusal of both Chinas to accept it.

Rep. Clement J. Zablocki (D Wis.), chairman of the House Foreign Affairs Subcommittee on the Far East and the Pacific, in 1966 suggested a new two-China approach aimed to surmount present objections. Asserting that it was wishful thinking to suppose that either Mao or Chiang would ever agree to two Chinas in the United Nations, Zablocki proposed temporary adoption of a "no China" formula for the Security Council. Both Chinas would be offered General Assembly seats, and the existing system of permanent Security Council members would be abandoned. Under Zablocki's proposal, the Assembly would elect seven members to serve 20-year terms on the Council along with the temporary members elected for two-year terms. Thus the problem of the permanent seat held by Nationalist China would be bypassed.

Zablocki believed that neither China would be elected to Council membership for the first 20-year period, but that the prospect of election to a 20-year term after that time might induce Communist China to join the world organization.

Problem of Succession in China

Proponents of the American policy of containment without isolation were hopeful that Red China's attitude toward the nations on her periphery and toward the United States might change as the old-line Communist leaders relinquished control and a new leadership took over. Most of the top Chinese officials were engaged in revolutionary warfare all of their adult lives. When they were replaced, some people believed, a less belligerent Chinese government, more concerned with domestic problems and less zealous for world-wide revolution, would take charge.

Mao Tse-tung, chairman of the Communist Party's Central Committee and long the major figure among Chinese Communists, was 73 years old in 1966 and reportedly ailing. The 19 members of the Politburo averaged 66 years of age.

The segment of the population that gave most concern to Chinese leaders was the age group in the twenties and thirties, who were viewed by the top ranks as more interested in bourgeois pleasures and material comforts than in world revolution. The day when the younger generation would take command, however, was several decades away. And many experts believed that the immediate successors of the current leaders would be no more amenable to accommodation with the United States than was the existing regime.

But in mid-1966, all speculation on Mao's possible successor became meaningless, for an unexpected power struggle had developed within the party hierarchy. It soon became apparent that Mao was not enjoying full control -- in fact, he found himself in the minority in his own regime. The failure of the Great Leap Forward (1958-1962) and the subsequent loss of revolutionary zeal had disenchanted the prime officials in the Communist Party apparatus.

In order to put the country's youth to a revolutionary test, and at the same time provide an instrument for purging his opponents, Mao and his new heir apparent, Defense Minister Lin Piao, created the Red Guards, a militant youth group dedicated to the dissemination and preservation of "Mao's thought." Lin Piao had impressed Mao with his ability to organize the army, which was playing an increasingly important role in running the country, since Mao could no longer rely on party officials.

Thus the Great Proletarian Cultural Revolution was created, with the Red Guards as its storm troopers. Its first victims were educators, writers, journalists, intellectuals and propagandists. But on June 2, 1966, it was reported that the mayor of Peking, Peng Chen, and the army's chief of staff, Lo Jui-ching, had been removed from their offices. Other major officials soon followed.

A polarization of the different factions ensued, with Mao and Lin coming out in the minority. Their main opposition centered around President Liu Shao-chi and Teng Hsiao-ping, the party's secretary-general. Liu was dropped from second to eighth place in the party hierarchy, but, significantly, he evidently could not be dismissed altogether.

By late August 1966, the Red Guards had become uncontrollable, beating people, destroying art objects and churches, burning and plundering. But for the first time, they encountered resistance, forcing Peking to send orders to the Red Guards to cool off and a warning to party officials and government employees not to interfere with the activities of the youth group. By late September, however, it was clear that Mao's opposition had grown rather than diminished, as Red Guard units in the provinces met with overwhelming opposition.

By early 1967, Mao and Lin were in real trouble. Liu Shao-chi, who had "confessed" his crimes against Mao in late December 1966, retracted the statement in mid-January 1967. Reports of arrests, suicides, attacks and counter-attacks, bloody clashes, strikes and sabotage led to speculation that China was on the verge of civil war or of shattering into a number of fragments, each controlled by a regional "warlord."

Other China watchers thought those theories too extreme and predicted that either the pro- or anti-Mao forces would win out and eventually return the country to normalcy. Another theory, one which gained some credibility in March 1967, was that Premier Chou En-lai would take over command in a compromise. Still another group contended that Mao was a pawn of Lin Piao, but their "expert" adversaries claimed just the opposite.

In any event, the struggle was regarded as much more than a clash of personalities. Policy also was involved. A defeat for Mao Tse-tung would mean a defeat for his ideology and a victory for pragmatism and moderation. Mao had opposed these attitudes in favor of true communism and political indoctrination, but the voice of the Chinese masses was being heard in early 1967, and, despite his popularity, Mao was in danger of being ground under by the demands of his people.

REVIEW OF CONGRESS' INTEREST IN U.S. FAR EAST POLICY

The principal thrust of Congressional interest in Chinese and Far Eastern affairs changed significantly in the two decades following the Communist takeover of the mainland. In the 1940s, the most vocal Congressional critics of United States policies toward China urged greater U.S. support of the Nationalist government in its civil war against the Communists. In 1966, Congressional critics of U.S. policy suggested a softer stance toward China, involving resumption of trade, diplomatic recognition and admittance of Communist China into the United Nations.

Throughout the postwar period, however, a majority prevailed on Capitol Hill which supported President Truman's hands-off policy toward the Chinese civil war, opposed recognition and UN membership for China and, in an intimately related issue, supported the U.S. military efforts in Viet Nam. For the critics who opposed the escalation of the Viet Nam conflict, there were others who called for more intense measures to win.

Congressional support for the "China lobby" point of view in the 1940s came mostly from Republicans; pressure for a "containment without isolation" policy toward China in the 1960s came for the most part from Democrats, with the Senate Foreign Relations Committee as a base.

This Fact Sheet reviews Congressional debate and actions related to the Far East in the past two decades.

Civil War

During the late 1940s, the Truman Administration maintained a hands-off policy toward the Chinese civil war despite pressure from a vocal minority of Senators and Representatives for the increased involvement of the United States on behalf of Generalissimo Chiang Kai-shek and his Nationalist forces. The only significant concession to this minority was the China Aid Act of 1948:

On Feb. 18, 1948, President Truman sent a special message to Congress recommending a $570 million aid program for China (S 2393). The Administration program made no provision for military aid to the Nationalist government in its struggle against the Communists, who were then making rapid progress in Manchuria. The message said, however, that the proposed shipments of food, raw materials and fertilizers from the United States would permit the Nationalist government "to devote its (own) limited dollar resources to the most urgent of its other needs." On April 2, 1948, Congress passed the bill. The economic aid appropriation had been reduced to $338 million, but $125 million had been added for the Chinese government to use as it saw necessary, which presumably meant for military aid. The total amount was $463 million. On April 3, President Truman signed the bill into law.

But Congressional pressure for more aid continued. On Jan. 18, 1949, the Senate, 83-6, confirmed the nomination of former Under Secretary of State Dean Acheson to succeed Gen. George C. Marshall as Secretary of State. Opposed were Republicans Styles Bridges (N.H.), Homer Capehart (Ind.), William F. Knowland (Calif.), William Langer (N.D.), and Kenneth S. Wherry (Neb.). Wherry, the only one to vote against Acheson's appointment as Under Secretary in 1945, said it was "common knowledge" that Acheson "had been an appeaser of Russia." Although China policy was not a direct issue, it soon became so.

On Feb. 25, 1949, Sen. Pat McCarran (D Nev.) introduced a bill to provide a $1.5 billion loan to Nationalist China for military and economic purposes. Asked for comment by the Senate Foreign Relations Committee, Secretary Acheson wrote April 14, 1949, that there was "no evidence" that such aid would "alter the pattern of current developments in China," to which the U.S. had given $2 billion since 1945 without stemming Communist forces. Sen. Styles Bridges (R N.H.) called for an investigation of China policy, accusing Acheson of what "might be called sabotage of the valiant" Nationalists. Sens. McCarran and Knowland supported Bridges. Sens. Tom Connally (D Texas) and William Fulbright (D Ark.) defended Acheson. No action was taken on McCarran's bill.

On April 14, 1949, however, Congress extended the 1948 China Aid Act by authorizing the President to use unobligated funds as he determined necessary for aid to those areas of China that remained free of Chinese Communist control. The funds were made available until Feb. 15, 1950.

On May 3, 1949, Gen. Claire L. Chennault, wartime leader of the Flying Tigers air group in China and organizer of a Chinese Nationalist airline, told the Senate Committees on Foreign Economic Cooperation and Armed Services that unless the U.S. took immediate steps to save the Nationalists, all Asia would fall to the Communists. Sens. McCarran and Knowland echoed his views. The following month, when it was rumored that the State Department was studying the possibility of recognizing a Chinese Communist regime, 21 Senators (16 Republicans and five Democrats) sent a letter to President Truman expressing bitter opposition to any such move and calling for increased aid to the Nationalists. Sen. Arthur H. Vandenburg (R Mich.) declared in a Senate speech that the U.S. policy toward China had been a "tragic failure." Sen. Tom Connally (D Texas) replied: "Would you send your own sons to fight in the Chinese civil war?"

China White Paper. On Aug. 6, 1949, the State Department released a White Paper on China, making the point that the Nationalists were on the verge of collapse because of the military, economic and political shortcomings of the Chiang regime, and that no amount of additional aid would have prevented their defeat at the hands of Communist forces. The document set off a new burst of criticism from Republicans. Rep. Walter H. Judd (R Minn.) accused Secretary Acheson of "writing off" China.

On Aug. 25, 1949, Rep. Mike Mansfield (D Mont.) called for an investigation of lobbying on behalf of the Nationalists. He suggested that money provided earlier "to help China, but siphoned off for private use, is being used to finance attacks on our Secretary of State and other officials charged with conducting our relations with China." Among groups supporting Chiang and denouncing the White Paper were the China Emergency Committee, headed by Frederick C. McKee, and the American China Policy Committee, headed by Alfred Kohlberg. Talk of a pro-Chiang "China Lobby" persisted for many years, but the issue was never fully clarified.

On Sept. 22, 1949, the Senate passed the Mutual Defense Assistance Act, adding to the funds requested by the President $75 million for use in the "general area" of China. The House accepted the item, for which Sen. William Knowland (R Calif.) was chiefly responsible, and it was retained in the final law.

Five days later, the Senate -- after passing over the nomination 14 times -- confirmed the appointment of W. Walton Butterworth as Assistant Secretary of State for Far Eastern Affairs, 49-27 (D 44-0; R 5-27). Sen. Styles Bridges (R N.H.) led an attack on Butterworth, a career man who had headed the Office of Far Eastern Affairs, calling him the "symbol of failure" in the U.S. China policy.

On Oct. 27, 1949, the Chinese Communists arrested U.S. Consul General Angus Ward in Mukden, raising a storm of official and unofficial protest from the United States. Rep. James G. Fulton (R Pa.) offered himself as a hostage for Ward, who was finally released in December and deported with his staff. The incident, which coincided with the final rout of the Nationalists from the mainland of China, helped to shut the door on any attempt to recognize the new Peking regime.

Disunity Over Asia Policy

Early in 1950, bipartisan cooperation on questions of foreign policy was strained by the charges of Sen. Joseph McCarthy (R Wis.) that American policies in the Far East had been influenced by Communist sympathizers in the State Department (see box); by Republican demands that the President "fire Acheson"; by President Truman's statements that Sen. Styles Bridges (R N.H.) and other minority senators were "trying to sabotage the foreign policy of the United States"; and by continuing complaints from GOP leaders that they were "never consulted" on Far Eastern policy.

A warning that Congressional dissatisfaction with American policy in the Far East went deeper than the Administration apparently had supposed was given early in the 1950 session of Congress when the House Jan. 19 defeated, 191 to 192, a bill to appropriate $60 million for additional economic aid to the Republic of Korea during the period Feb. 15 to June 30. The President had requested $150 million. The appropriation of $60 million was later approved, 240 to 134, but only after an authorization for continued assistance to the Chinese Nationalists on Formosa had been added to it. A new section was inserted in which extended until June 30 the period for expenditure of $103 million remaining from the 1948 China Aid Act.

Korea

Less than five years after V-J Day, the United States in mid-1950 found itself locked in a full-scale war in a little-expected quarter -- Korea (see box). Prompt adoption, by substantially unanimous votes, of the measures needed to deal with Communist aggression in South Korea may have prevented extension of the Korean conflict to

other areas and, to many observers, averted the threat of a third world war. Political disunity receded after President Truman's June 27 action in ordering American forces to South Korea and in a sense reversing previous policy by ordering the 7th Fleet to "prevent any attack on Formosa." Subsequent American set-backs in the conflict brought all but unanimous support for the President's Korean policies and the legislation needed to implement them.

After Communist China's entry into the Korean war and her rejections of two UN appeals for a cease-fire in the conflict, the United States called on the General Assembly to label the Peking regime as an aggressor. Underscoring Congressional support for this move, the House and Senate quickly passed resolutions to the same effect. H Res 77, introduced by House Majority Leader John McCormack (D Mass.), called on the UN to "immediately act and declare the Chinese Communist authorities an aggressor in Korea." The House approved the resolution by a voice vote on Jan. 19, 1951. The Senate Jan. 23, 1951, adopted a similar resolution (S Res 35), introduced by Sen. John McClellan (D Ark.), also by voice vote.

Following Senate action on S Res 35, McClellan called up two other resolutions. S Res 36 declared that Communist China should not be admitted to the UN. Sen. Brien McMahon (D Conn.) said that, although he agreed, the matter should be studied because the U.S. might want to change its position if a split developed between Moscow and Peking. Sen. Spessard Holland (D Fla.) said this would leave the Administration in doubt as to the Senate's views. S Res 36 was adopted, 91-0. The third resolution (S Res 37), calling for "the complete interruption of economic relations" between UN members and Communist China, was referred by voice vote to the Senate Foreign Relations Committee on the motion of Majority Leader Ernest W. McFarland (D Ariz.). No further action was taken on S Res 37.

The House May 15, 1951, passed a resolution identical to S Res 36 after Secretary of Defense George C. Marshall had declared that the United States should use its veto in the Security Council, if necessary, to keep Communist China out of the UN. The Secretary had also said that Formosa "must never be allowed to come under control of a Communist government or a government under Soviet domination."

Also on May 15, 1951, both House and Senate unanimously adopted a resolution (S Con Res 31) which urged the UN General Assembly to "take action leading to... an embargo on the shipment to Communist China of arms, ammunition, and all other materials which might add to the war-making potential of Communist China."

MacArthur. The unity that President Truman had been able to acquire and maintain in Congress was eroded with the President's removal of Gen. Douglas MacArthur April 11, 1951, from his Asian commands. Most Republicans and a few Democrats, dissatisfied with a situation that seemed to promise nothing better than a stalemate in Korea, bitterly attacked the President for his action. Some Republicans, such as Sen. William E. Jenner (Ind.), talked openly of impeachment. Sen. Joseph R. McCarthy (R Wis.) said it was the "greatest victory the Communists have ever won."

In the midst of the storm, MacArthur returned to Washington. In an address before a joint session of Congress April 19, and in subsequent testimony before the joint Senate Foreign Relations-Armed Services Committees, MacArthur recommended that Communist China be block-

U.S. Involvement in Military Situations; Wars Declared

Revolutionary War. On July 4, 1776, the Second Continental Congress, meeting in Philadelphia, unanimously adopted a Declaration of Independence from Great Britain.

War of 1812. On June 1, 1812, President James Madison sent a war message to Congress maintaining that Great Britain was already warring against the United States. On June 18, the Senate voted 19 to 13 and the House 79 to 49 to declare war on Great Britain. A motion declaring a maritime war against France as well as Britain was narrowly defeated in the Senate. On June 19, Madison proclaimed a state of war with Great Britain.

Mexican War. On May 11, 1846, President James K. Polk asked Congress for a declaration of war against Mexico, claiming that a state of war "exists by the act of Mexico herself." On May 11, the House voted 174 to 14 to declare war. The Senate did the same the next day by a vote of 40 to 2. On May 13, Polk signed the declaration of war.

Civil War. President Lincoln insisted that the fighting was between individuals and not governments, thus considering the military action as one to quell an internal disturbance. Therefore, Congress was not asked to make a formal declaration.

Spanish-American War. On April 11, 1898, President William McKinley asked Congress for authority to order "forcible intervention" of the United States to end hostilities in Cuba. On April 20, Congress passed a joint resolution declaring Cuba free and authorizing the President to employ force to expel the Spanish from Cuba. The President signed the resolution the same day. On April 24, 1898, Spain declared war on the United States, and on the following day, at the President's request, Congress formally declared war against Spain, retroactive to April 21.

Incidents with Mexico. On April 21, 1914, on President Wilson's orders, American forces bombarded and then occupied Vera Cruz to prevent a German munitions ship from approaching the harbor. On April 22,

Congress granted Wilson's request for permission to use force to uphold U.S. rights. On March 15, 1916, President Wilson, with the reluctant consent of the Mexican government, ordered 15,000 American troops under Gen. John J. Pershing into Mexico to pursue Pancho Villa, a Mexican bandit.

World War I. On April 2, 1917, President Wilson delivered his war message to Congress. On April 4, the Senate adopted a joint resolution declaring war by a vote of 82 to 6. On April 6, the House adopted the resolution 373 to 50.

World War II. On Dec. 8, 1941, President Roosevelt delivered his war message to Congress. A resolution of war against Japan was adopted immediately by both chambers, with the lone dissenting vote in the House. On Dec. 11, Germany and Italy declared war on the United States. The same day, Congress reciprocated.

The Korean War. On June 27, 1950, the Security Council of the United Nations called on UN members to furnish the Republic of Korea with assistance to repel the armed attack from North Korea. President Truman had ordered air and sea forces to aid South Korea the day before. On June 30, the President ordered ground forces to go into Korea and sent the 7th Fleet to act as a buffer between the Chinese mainland and Formosa. U.S. involvement in Korea was qualified as a UN "police action."

Viet Nam. In 1955, President Eisenhower sent the first military "advisers" into South Viet Nam. President Kennedy announced May 16, 1961, that the military aid would be increased. On Aug. 7, 1964, Congress adopted a joint resolution following the Gulf of Tonkin incident affirming the support of "the determination of the President... to take all necessary measures to repel any armed attack against the forces of the United States and to prevent further aggression..." Dissenting votes were cast by Sens. Morse (D Ore.) and Gruening (D Alaska). Congress also supported executive action with Mutual Security and Foreign Aid appropriations.

aded, that restrictions on "air reconnaissance" of China's coastal areas and Manchuria be removed, and that the restrictions on the forces of the Republic of China on Formosa also be removed, with "logistical support" of their operations against Communist China supplied by the United States. MacArthur said that such actions would quickly bring Communist China to its knees.

Hearings. The joint Senate committee hearings on Far Eastern policy, begun on May 3, 1951, and continued until June 25, put on record a large number of secret documents, including the Wedemeyer report on Korea of September 1947 (part of the report on China which had already been released); the President's version of his talks with MacArthur on Wake Island in October 1950; a Defense Department memorandum of Dec. 6, 1950, which alerted all military commanders to "the greatly increased...possibility of a general war"; and a message to MacArthur by the President, Jan. 13, 1951, which stressed the importance of holding support of "the nations whom we would desperately need... as allies in the event the Soviet Union moves against us." On June 1, over the protest of Secretary of State Dean Ache-

son, the committees voted 15-9 to make public a State Department memorandum of Dec. 23, 1949, which said that Formosa had "no special military significance" and that its loss to the Communists was expected.

Although the hearings were closed, transcripts of the testimony were made public after material directly relating to future war plans had been deleted. A Republican move to hold the hearings in the open was blocked in the Senate, 41 to 37, after all 70 Senators not members of the Foreign Relations or Armed Services committees had been invited to attend by the two committees.

A skillful defense of Administration policies during eight days of testimony and cross-examination apparently restored Secretary Acheson's prestige somewhat. In the House, a Republican amendment to the State Department's fiscal 1952 appropriation (HR 4740) which would have had the effect of removing the Secretary from the federal pay roll was defeated on July 26, 1951, by a standing vote of 171 to 81.

On June 27, 1951, a "Declaration of Faith" prepared by Chairman Richard B. Russell (D Ga.) and issued with the

McCarthy and U.S. Far East Policy

A speech by Sen. Joseph R. McCarthy (R Wis.) Feb. 9, 1950, to the Ohio County Women's Republican Club in Wheeling, W. Va., led to one of the most bitterly controversial investigations in the history of Congress. A special subcommittee of the Senate Foreign Relations Committee was set up to investigate McCarthy's charges that Communists were knowingly employed by the State Department and were directing its policies, especially in the Far East.

Advent of the 'McCarthy Era'. Sen. Millard E. Tydings (D Md.) was appointed Chairman of the Subcommittee; the other members were: Brien McMahon (D Conn.), Theodore F. Green (D R.I.), Henry Cabot Lodge Jr. (R Mass.), and Bourke B. Hickenlooper (R Iowa.)

The Subcommittee held 31 days of hearings between March 8 and June 28, 1950. During the course of the hearings, McCarthy charged ten individuals by name with varying degrees of Communist activities. Named were:

Prof. Frederick L. Schuman, Williams College; Prof. Owen J. Lattimore, Johns Hopkins University; Prof. Harlow Shapley, Harvard; Dorothy Kenyon, New York attorney; Gustavo Duran, former State Department employee, and then a United Nations official; Haldore Hanson, State Department officer; Philip C. Jessup, Ambassador-at-Large; Stephen Brunauer, Navy scientist; his wife, Mrs. Esther Brunauer, State Department officer; and John Stewart Service, Foreign Service officer. McCarthy claimed that Lattimore, Service and Jessup were Communist sympathizers who had influenced American policies in the Far East.

Lattimore Case. On the case of Lattimore, McCarthy said he would "stand or fall." In executive hearings, McCarthy March 20 said Lattimore was "the top of the ring of which (Alger) Hiss was a part." Asked if he was sure Lattimore was the biggest Russian spy, McCarthy said: "By far and away. I think he is the top Russian spy."

Called to testify at McCarthy's request, Louis F. Budenz, former managing editor of the *Daily Worker*, testified April 20, 1950, that he had heard Owen Lattimore described by high Communist party leaders as a concealed member of the party. He claimed that Lattimore had been in a Communist cell in the Institute of Pacific Relations and was instructed to spread the Communist line through publications regarding China.

Lattimore's counsel immediately countered with testimony from Brig. Gen. Elliott R. Thorpe, a retired counterintelligence officer in the Far East, who said Lattimore had been completely cleared by three separate military investigations. An affidavit was then issued from a former Communist, Dr. Bella V. Dodd, who said she had never heard Lattimore's name mentioned as a member or friend while she was on the national committee of the party from 1944 to 1948.

Lattimore spent three days on the stand, April 6 and May 2 and 3. He denied charges that he was a Communist, challenged McCarthy to repeat his charges off the Senate floor "so he can be held accountable in a court of law," and described Budenz as a "professional informer," who was "making a profit."

The Subcommittee re-examined the case of *Amerasia* Magazine, which in 1945 had been found in possession of top secret Government documents. McCarthy in 1950 declared that State Department officials had blocked effective prosecution of the case in order to protect the defendants, whom he called members of an important spy ring.

Report. In the final report (S Rept 2108), filed July 20, 1950, the Democratic majority said no evidence was shown that the *Amerasia* principals were part of a State Department spy ring. The report said the Justice Department had done all it legally could to prosecute the case.

The majority report found "no evidence to support the charge that Owen Lattimore is the 'top Russian spy,' or for that matter, any sort of spy." Each of the other nine primary "cases" submitted by McCarthy was also found to be without substantiation or was rejected because the person involved had never been an employee of the Government.

In its "General Observations," the report said: "It is, of course, clearly apparent that the charges of Communist infiltration or influence upon the State Department are false. This knowledge is reassuring to all Americans whose faith had been temporarily shaken in the security of their Government by perhaps the most nefarious campaign of untruth in the history of our Republic....

"We have seen the technique of the 'Big Lie,' elsewhere employed by the totalitarian dictator with devastating success, utilized here for the first time on a sustained basis in our history."

Security Files. McCarthy had insisted repeatedly during the investigation that all his charges would be proved if loyalty and personnel files were opened to the Subcommittee. Reluctantly, President Truman May 4 announced that he would show the Subcommittee the files of 81 persons McCarthy had accused by name or number. Subcommittee members were allowed to examine the files at the White House, but not to take notes or reveal names of individuals.

Smith Statement. On the Senate floor June 1, 1950, Margaret Chase Smith (R Maine) read a statement, also signed by six other Republicans, criticizing Democratic handling of the Government security problem and blasting "certain elements" of the Republican party which the signers said had tried to exploit "fear, bigotry, ignorance, and intolerance" in pursuit of political victory.

Although he soon lost interest in the Far East, McCarthy and his repeated accusations of Communist influence throughout the Government remained a key domestic issue. Taking over the chairmanship of the Senate Government Operations Committee and the Permanent Investigations Committee in 1953, he investigated the State Department, Voice of America, Department of the Army and other agencies. An opinion-stifling "climate of fear" in many Government agencies was said to be one of the results of his probes. The Army-McCarthy hearings, televised in the Spring of 1954, were the climax of McCarthy's career, and led finally to his censure by the Senate Dec. 2, 1954. McCarthy's influence quickly vanished thereafter. He died May 2, 1957.

approval of all members of the two investigating committees warned the Communists not to misread the evidence of "discord and disagreement" brought out in the hearings.

On Aug. 17, the joint committee voted 20-3 to file no formal report on the investigation. Russell said the group wished to avoid "renewal of bitter controversy" at a time when Korean truce negotiations were in progress. The hearings, he said, had contributed to a better understanding with others of the United Nations and had "forced a definite policy in the Far East when we did not have one." He added that the hearings had been partly responsible for a change in attitude toward the Nationalist Chinese island of Formosa and had led to an economic blockade of Communist China.

An Aug. 19 statement issued by the eight Republican members of the Committee condemned the manner of Gen. MacArthur's dismissal, described the Administration's Far Eastern policy as a "catastrophic failure," asserted that the constitutional authority of the Congress to declare war had been bypassed in Korea, and warned against any peace of "appeasement" with the Chinese Communists. Sen. Wayne Morse (then R Ore.) issued his own statement Sept. 5 praising the President for his actions.

Policy on China in UN

In 1953, following a change of Administration, party, and Congressional leadership, and as negotiators neared agreements in Korea that would lead to the signing of an armistice, the 83rd Congress took new action. On May 27, 1953, the Senate Appropriations Committee approved a rider which ordered American contributions to the United Nations to be withheld in the event that Communist China is admitted into the UN. This action followed introduction by Sen. William F. Knowland (R Calif.), chairman of the Senate Republican Policy Committee, of a resolution for withdrawal from the UN if Communist China were admitted.

After some controversy, the Senate reached a compromise with a declaration that "it is the sense of the Congress that the Communist Chinese Government should not be admitted" to the UN. This provision was later accepted by the House. The price of the Administration success in obtaining a compromise was assurance by President Eisenhower at an emergency White House conference on June 2, 1953, that the U.S. would take active leadership in opposing Communist China's admission under existing conditions and so long as she remained subservient to the Soviet Union.

Korean Treaty. To secure the support of Republic of Korea President Syngman Rhee for an armistice in the Korean conflict (signed July 26, 1953), President Eisenhower had promised to negotiate a mutual security treaty with South Korea, similar to those already in effect between the U.S. and Japan, the Philippines, Australia, and New Zealand. The treaty was signed Oct. 1 and submitted to the Senate for approval Jan. 11, 1954. Secretary of State John Foster Dulles assured the Foreign Relations Committee that the treaty would not obligate the United States to aid South Korea in any attack on North Korea. But in approving the treaty Jan. 19, the Committee added an "understanding" that the pact was not to be construed as requiring the United States "to give assistance to Korea except in the event of an armed attack against territory which has been recognized by the United States as lawfully brought under the administrative control of the Republic of Korea."

The Senate Jan. 26, 1954, approved the understanding by voice vote, then agreed to the treaty 81-6. Sen. John

---

Legislation on China

Congressional action regarding Communist China focused mainly on opposition to the seating of the Peking regime in the United Nations. Congress expressed that opposition 24 times in the past 16 years, generally through resolutions in the form of riders attached to appropriation bills in committee. The most recent such action was taken Oct. 6, 1966, when Congress passed the Foreign Aid appropriations bill for fiscal 1967 (HR 17788), which reiterated Congressional opposition to seating China in the UN.

During the second stage of the Chinese civil war (1945-1949), Congress passed a series of bills granting military and economic aid to Chiang Kai-shek's Nationalist Government. The most notable such action was the China Aid Act of 1948 (S 2393), appropriating $338 million for economic aid and $125 million for military aid to the Chinese.

Since 1950, Congress also agreed to underwrite the cost of containing Communist China. The price was immense, including economic and military aid to Southeast Asia; the financing of three conflicts: Korea, the French effort in Indo-China, and Viet Nam; the development and protection of Taiwan, and the United States' own military operations in the Pacific. Some of the largest military installations in the world were constructed by the United States in Thailand and South Viet Nam.

During the mid-1950s, the Senate ratified three important treaties aimed at containing Communist China militarily: two of the mutual security treaties with South Korea (Jan. 26, 1954) and the Republic of China (Feb. 9, 1955) and the third was the Southeast Asia Collective Defense Treaty (Feb. 1, 1955). In addition, Congress passed resolutions supporting Presidential action in the 1955 Formosa Straits crisis and in the Gulf of Tonkin in 1964.

Stennis (D Miss.), who voted "nay," argued that the U.S. was stretching its commitments too thinly and might not be able to "deliver," while Sen. Russell B. Long (D La.) thought the treaty "would increase the danger of an atomic war."

Formosa

As the eight years of fighting in Indo-China between the French and the Viet Minh ended, and as the Southeast Asia Treaty Organization became a reality, Communist China increased military operations against the offshore islands of Quemoy, Matsu and the Tachens. To underscore its support of the Formosa regime, the United States Dec. 2, 1954, signed a mutual security pact with the Republic of China. Meanwhile, Sen. Knowland (R Calif.) was calling for a blockade of the mainland to force the release of 13 Americans captured in Korea and sentenced Nov. 22, 1954, as spies by the Chinese Communists. Tensions were mounting as the Democratic-controlled 84th Congress convened Jan. 5, 1955, and President Eisenhower asked the Senate for prompt approval of the U.S.-Nationalist security pact.

On Jan. 18, 1955, Communist forces seized the offshore island of Ichiang, 210 miles north of Formosa, and seemed prepared to invade the nearby Tachen islands. The situation led the President to ask Congress, in a special message Jan. 24, for explicit authority to use American armed forces to protect Formosa, the adjoining Pescadores islands, and "related positions and territories." Despite some misgivings concerning aspects of the bill which were quite vague (such as the President's or Secretary Dulles' intent regarding Quemoy, Matsu and the offshore islands), the Democratic leaders in Congress hastened to comply with the President's request. H J Res 159, authorizing him to "employ the armed forces of the United States as he deems necessary" in the defense of Formosa, was reported by the House Foreign Affairs Committee the same day, unanimously and without amendment. The House passed it Jan. 25, 410-3, after hearing Speaker Sam Rayburn state his belief that the resolution added nothing to the Constitutional powers of the

President and should not be taken as a precedent that would bind him in the future. Reps. Barden (D N.C.), Sheehan (R Ill.) and Siler (R Ky.) voted "nay" on the grounds that it amounted to a declaration of war.

On Jan. 26, the Senate Foreign Relations and Armed Services Committees, sitting jointly, voted 27-2 to report the resolution without change, after rejecting amendments to restrict the President's authority. In floor debate Jan. 26-28, Sens. Morse (D Ore.) and Flanders (R Vt.) warned of a "preventative war," while Sens. Kefauver (D Tenn.), Humphrey (D Minn.), and Lehman (D N.Y.) attacked the resolution's ambiguity regarding the offshore islands. But the Senate, by lopsided margins, rejected three restrictive amendments and passed H J Res 159 Jan. 28, 85-3. Voting "nay" were Morse, Langer, and Lehman.

The Presidents' Positions and Actions on Viet Nam

Eisenhower. In an Oct. 23, 1954, letter to South Vietnamese President Ngo Dinh Diem, President Eisenhower said he had instructed the American Ambassador to Viet Nam "to examine with you in your capacity as Chief of Government, how an intelligent program of American aid given directly to your Government, can serve to assist Viet Nam in its present hour of trial, provided that your Government is prepared to give assurances as to the standards of performance it would be able to maintain in the event such aid were supplied. The purpose of this offer," the letter said, "is to assist the Government of Viet Nam in developing and maintaining a strong, viable state, capable of resisting attempted subversion or aggression through military means."

The United States began its direct assistance to South Viet Nam on Jan. 1, 1955. The following month, President Eisenhower sent 200 technicians to Viet Nam and the U.S. Military Advisory Corps (M.A.A.G.) began training the South Vietnamese Army.

Following discussions with Diem on May 12, 1957, a joint statement said that Mr. Eisenhower had assured the South Vietnamese President "of the willingness of the United States to continue to offer effective assistance within the constitutional processes of the United States to meet" the objectives of political stability and economic welfare in Viet Nam."

On May 5, 1960, the Administration announced that the Military Assistance and Advisory Group would be increased by the end of the year from 327 to 685.

Kennedy. On May 5, 1961, President Kennedy was asked during a press conference if he would employ U.S. forces in Viet Nam to prevent Communist domination. Mr. Kennedy replied that the matter was "still under consideration." One week later, the President ordered 100 specially trained jungle fighters (Special Forces) to South Viet Nam. In October 1961, Kennedy sent his military adviser, Gen. Maxwell D. Taylor, to investigate the military situation in South Viet Nam. In a Dec. 14, 1961, message to President Diem, Mr. Kennedy said the United States would "promptly increase our assistance to your defense effort.... I have already given orders to get these programs underway."

During 1962, the number of U.S. military personnel in South Viet Nam increased to approximately 10,000, although the force was still acting in an "advisory" capacity.

In a Sept. 2, 1963, television interview, President Kennedy noted: "In the final analysis, it is their (the Vietnamese) war. They are the ones who have to win it or lose it." He said the United States was prepared to continue assistance to South Viet Nam, but added: "I don't think the war can be won unless the people support the effort."

On Sept. 24, Defense Secretary Robert S. McNamara and Gen. Taylor left for South Viet Nam to review military efforts there. On Oct. 31, Kennedy told a press conference:

"When Secretary McNamara and Gen. Taylor came back, they announced we would expect to withdraw a thousand men from Viet Nam before the end of the year.... If we are able to do that, that would be our schedule."

On Nov. 1, 1963, President Diem was assassinated during a coup d'etat. Three weeks later, President Kennedy was assassinated in Dallas.

Johnson. In an address to a joint session of Congress on Nov. 27, 1963, President Johnson vowed that the United States "will keep its commitments from South Viet Nam to West Berlin." At a June 2, 1964, press conference, after reading President Eisenhower's 1954 letter, Mr. Johnson said the United States was "steadfast in a policy which has been followed for ten years in three Administrations.... In the case of Viet Nam, our commitment today is just the same as the commitment made by President Eisenhower to President Diem in 1954...."

During the summer of 1964, the war escalated at a rapid pace. The number of U.S. troops increased to 25,000. Following attacks on U.S. destroyers in the Gulf of Tonkin, the President asked Congress for a resolution of support, claiming that United States "policy in Southeast Asia has been consistent and unchanged since 1954." Congress passed the resolution Aug. 7, 1964.

On Feb. 7, 1965, President Johnson announced that U.S. planes had made retaliatory air strikes against North Viet Nam.

By late 1966, the war was costing over $2 billion a month, with over 300,000 U.S. troops in South Viet Nam and another 50,000 off its shores.

SEATO Treaty

Senate action on the Southeast Asia Collective Defense Treaty, submitted by the President Nov. 10, 1954, was postponed until the Formosa resolution was approved. The Foreign Relations Committee cleared the treaty Jan. 21, 1955, and the Senate took it up Feb. 1.

The pact, said Chairman Walter F. George (D Ga.), "is inspired by the conviction that a potential aggressor may be deterred from reckless conduct by a clear-cut declaration of our intentions." Reference in the pact to dealing with subversion "does not mean that the United States has undertaken to suppress bona fide local revolutions," he said. Only Sen. William Langer (R N.D.) was opposed as the Senate voted 82-1 to approve ratification Feb. 1, 1955.

China Treaty

On Feb. 8, 1955, the Senate Foreign Relations Committee voted 11-2 to approve the mutual security treaty signed with the Republic of China in December 1954. The committee, however, stated its understanding that its terms "apply only in the event of external armed attack, and that military operations by either party from the territories held by the Republic of China shall not be undertaken except by joint agreement." Two other "understandings" were expressed, to the effect that any extension of the treaty area would require the concurrence of a two-thirds majority in the Senate, and that nothing in the treaty "shall be construed as affecting or modifying the legal status or sovereignty" of Formosa and the Pescadores.

Sen. Wayne Morse (D Ore.) nevertheless proposed adding this last point to the text of the treaty. The Senate rejected the move, 11-57, as it did a second Morse amendment to strike out a reference to defense of "such other territories as may be determined by mutual agreement," 10-60. Ratification of the treaty was then approved Feb. 9, 1955, by a vote of 65-6. Opposed were Sens. Morse (D Ore.), Langer (R N.D.), Lehman, (D N.Y.), Chavez (D N.M.), Gore (D Tenn.), and Kefauver (D Tenn.).

Policy Revisions

In 1957, a handful of Senators advocated revising U.S. China policy, with no substantial results. The most important recommendation was made by Sen. Theodore F. Green (D R.I.), chairman of the Senate Foreign Relations Committee. On Feb. 18, 1957, Green said the U.S. "should recognize Red China sooner or later. We don't like their form of government, but the country is a great country and organized, and I do not myself see why we should recognize these other Communist countries and withhold recognition of China unless we are going to apply that to other Communist countries." Green later amended his original statement by adding that he did not advocate immediate recognition, but that the problem should be studied. On Feb. 19, Secretary of State Dulles told a news conference, when questioned about Green's statement, that it would be "premature, to say the least," to discuss recognizing Communist China, but he added that "none of us are talking here in terms of eternity."

On June 16, 1957, Sen. J. William Fulbright (D Ark.), second-ranking majority member of the Senate Foreign Relations Committee, suggested during a television interview that recognition of Communist China by the United States was inevitable in course of time; the only question was "when and how you do it." Fulbright favored negotiations on recognition and on modification of the embargo in return for such concessions as a Peking pledge to stay out of Formosa.

On July 18, 1957, after pressure was exerted by some Members of Congress and the press, a crack in the American policy of trying to hold Communist China virtually in quarantine showed up for the first time when Secretary of State Dulles offered to validate the passports of a limited number of American newsmen for travel in China for a limited period. The Chinese Communists later refused to allow the newsmen into the country.

Off-Shore Islands

But the rising tide of Congressional sentiment for a revision in U.S. policy toward China was quickly quelled in the fall of 1958 as Communist China resumed military operations against the Nationalist-held offshore islands. As President Eisenhower and Secretary Dulles alternated pledges of "no retreat" with pleas for a cease-fire, Senate Democrats voiced their concern. On Sept. 13, 1958, Sen. John F. Kennedy (D Mass.) commented that in Formosa, "the weight of military, diplomatic, political, and historical judgment would dictate a contrary policy." Kennedy was joined by Sen. Ralph Yarborough (D Texas) on the same day when he asserted that President Eisenhower was getting "bayonet-happy." Sen. Green expressed "profound concern" Sept. 12 over the President's policy of employing armed forces "in a way which might risk deeper military involvement." The President, Green said, "has a duty to request policy guidance from Congress."

On Oct. 4, 1958, 10 Democratic House Members sent a telegram to President Eisenhower making a new demand for a special Congressional session on the Far East. They said they had found "the great majority" of their constituents were "deeply disturbed with the Administration's Quemoy policy," and they believed "we should disentangle ourselves from Chiang Kai-shek's aspirations on Quemoy, and should endeavor to bring the mantle of the UN over Formosa..." On Oct. 8, Sen. Hubert H. Humphrey (D Minn.) joined the Congressmen in advocating UN intervention.

In 1959, the question of a "quarantine" about China arose in both houses of Congress. On Aug. 17, by a 368-2 roll-call vote, the House adopted a resolution (H Con Res 369) restating Congressional opposition to the admission of Communist China to the UN as the representative of China. Voting against the resolution were Reps. William H. Meyer (D Vt.) and Thomas L. Ashley (D Ohio). Reps. Charles O. Porter (D Ore.) and Byron L. Johnson (D Colo.) were paired against it. Rep. Meyer said he would not argue the case for or against admission of Communist China but called the resolution "unnecessary, unwise...useless and possibly harmful." He said that "perhaps the present hatred (between the U.S. and the Communist world) may grow less intense if the pot is not constantly stirred."

Policy Studies

On Nov. 1, 1959, the Senate Foreign Relations Committee released a study prepared by a private research firm, Conlon Associates, Ltd., of San Francisco, Calif., on U.S. foreign policy in Asia. The study recommended that the U.S. gradually shift its policy leading to recognition of Communist China, U.S. support for seating China in the UN, recognition of Nationalist Taiwan as a new republic and its seating in the UN General Assembly. Committee Chairman J. William Fulbright (D Ark.) said the study was "very provocative," and that "while I do not believe that the U.S. should recognize Communist China at the present time... I do not believe it is wise to continue to ignore over 600 million people...in the naive belief that they will somehow go away."

On Jan. 3, 1960, Sen. Henry M. Jackson, chairman of a Senate Government Operations subcommittee, issued a report entitled "National Policy Machinery in Communist China," noting that "the Chinese Communist party has attained a degree of unity and stability at its higher levels which is unequalled by other major Communist parties." The report concluded that the Communist leadership in China had uplifted the country "from a prostrate colossus to a giant on the march, in ten short years."

China was not the only area in the Far East to attract Congressional attention. On Feb. 26, 1960, the Senate Foreign Relations Subcommittee on State Department Organization and Public Affairs, headed by Sen. Mike Mansfield (D Mont.), issued a report citing specific serious shortcomings in the administration of U.S. economic aid to South Viet Nam. The report urged the full Foreign Relations Committee to undertake a study of pay and fringe benefits for Americans in Viet Nam and elsewhere overseas. It also asked for a report from the Secretary of State by September on steps taken to implement the subcommittee's recommendations.

One month after the report was issued, John M. Steeves, the Acting Assistant Secretary for Far Eastern Affairs, told the Senate Foreign Relations Committee that a "grave imbalance of power" existed in the Far East and it was "our countervailing presence which redresses this imbalance." He said Communist China could be expected to maintain pressures and tensions in the area as part of its continuing strategy, and any signs of weakness on the part of the United States would have "grievous effects." Steeves added that he hoped the "crash programs" resulting from the "crisis atmosphere" of the 1950s would be replaced by "the long haul of patient economic development."

Kennedy Administration

Despite reports to the contrary, the Kennedy Administration offered no immediate plans for basic changes in the U.S. China policy. On May 3, 1961, Senate Minority Leader Everett M. Dirksen (R Ill.) introduced a concurrent resolution (S Con Res 34) restating Congressional opposition to the seating of Communist China in the UN. An identical measure was introduced the same day in the House by Rep. Clement J. Zablocki (D Wis.) and 55 other Members (H Con Res 233-288).

Dirksen submitted the resolution, which was also endorsed by Senate Majority Leader Mike Mansfield (D Mont.), following conferences initiated after Senate debate April 14 over the President's reaffirmation of long-standing U.S. policy on the question of Chinese representation in the UN. Asked if the resolution had been approved by Secretary of State Dean Rusk, Dirksen said "that is my definite understanding."

The resolution declared it "the sense of Congress that it supports the President in his affirmation that the United States shall continue to meet its commitments to the people

and Government of the Republic of China and shall continue to support the Government as the representative of China in the United Nations (and) further, the United States shall continue to oppose the seating of the Chinese Communist regime in the United Nations so long as that regime persists in defying the principles of the United Nations Charter. Further, it is the sense of the Congress that the United States supports the President in not according diplomatic recognition to the Chinese Communist regime."

On July 28, 1961, the Senate adopted S Con Res 34 by a 76-0 roll-call vote and sent it to the House. The Senate accepted two amendments offered by Sen. Thomas J. Dodd (D Conn.) which, he said, were designed to justify to the world this country's "determination to keep Red China out of the United Nations." The amendments restated that Communist China should not be seated because it had "flagrantly violated basic human rights," had imposed a brutal regime on the Chinese people, had derived its authority from usurpation and tyranny and had become the "major source of the international illicit narcotics traffic."

Sen. Bourke R. Hickenlooper (R Iowa) later revealed that the Foreign Relations Committee had considered and rejected language which might have been construed as supporting recognition of both Communist China and Nationalist China, the so-called "two China" policy.

On Aug. 31, 1961, the House unanimously passed the resolution. During debate, several Members argued that the language of the resolution was too restrained. Only two Members -- Reps. Thomas L. Ashley (D Ohio) and William Fitts Ryan (D N.Y.) -- spoke against it. Both answered "present" on the roll call. A similar "sense of Congress" rider was added to the foreign aid appropriation bill Sept. 26, 1961, and again in 1962.

Laos, Viet Nam

The 1954 Geneva Agreements on Indo-China failed to resolve the political conflicts of the area, and by 1961, the Communist regime of North Viet Nam was aggressively supporting guerrilla operations against the U.S.-backed governments of Premier Boun Oum in Laos and President Ngo Dinh Diem in South Viet Nam. In 1962, the scale of American aid increased rapidly as more than 10,000 U.S. military personnel undertook to train the expanded forces of President Diem and assist them in countering the highly effective guerrilla techniques of the Communist Viet Cong.

On Feb. 24, 1963, a special report was submitted to the Senate Foreign Relations Committee by a four-man panel headed by Senate Majority Leader Mike Mansfield (D Mont.). In an investigation of U.S. aid to Southeast Asia, the report concluded that "there is no interest of the United States in Viet Nam which would justify, in present circumstances, the conversion of the war...primarily into an American war to be fought primarily with American lives." The report recommended that the U.S. conduct a thorough reassessment of its "over-all security requirement on the Southeast Asia mainland" aimed at consideration of a reduction in the U.S. aid programs, although "extreme caution" should be used, "for if the attempt is made to alter the programs via a Congressional meat axe cut...it runs the risk of not merely removing the fat but of leaving a gap which will lay open the region to massive chaos and, hence, jeopardize the present Pacific structure of our national security."

U.S. Korean-Viet Nam Casualties

KOREAN WAR

(Defense Department Figures)

I. Deaths in battle   33,629
   Other deaths   20,617
   Wounded   103,284

II. The financial cost:
    $18 billion (approximate)

VIET NAM WAR

(January 1961 - April 1967

I. Deaths in battle   8,754
   Other deaths   1,851
   Wounded   51,601
   Current Missing   388
   Current Captured   150

II. The Financial Cost: (Current estimates)

Fortune Magazine, April 1966: "...the current cost works out, at an annual rate, to $13.7 billion..." The article added that a buildup to 400,000 troops would mean that "the cost of the war would run to $21 billion a year -- even more if bombing and tactical air support increased in proportion to the buildup on the ground." [1]

Sen. John Stennis (D Miss.), July 9, 1966: "In my opinion the cost is at or near $2 billion a month." [2]

Secretary of Defense Robert S. McNamara, July 11, 1966: "The best figure I can give you is the one I gave to the Congress earlier this year when I said I thought the incremental costs at that time of Southeast Asia operations were about a billion dollars per month." [3]

Sen. Richard B. Russell (D Ga.), July 12, 1966: "The Secretary of Defense made the statement yesterday that the war in Viet Nam was increasing the expenditures of the Department of Defense by $1 billion a month. That would be $12 billion a year. It is my own opinion that the war in Viet Nam is costing us a good deal more than that amount. I think that it will run closer to $2 billion a month, perhaps somewhere between $1.5 billion and $2 billion a month." [4]

President Johnson, Oct. 22, 1966: For the first time the President cited the cost of the Viet Nam war at $2 billion per month. [5]

[1] William Bowen, "The Vietnam War: A Cost Accounting," Fortune (April 1966), p. 254.

[2] Speech at American Legion Annual Convention, Mississippi Department, Heidelberg Hotel, Jackson, Miss.

[3] Press Conference at Pentagon (July 11, 1966).

[4] Congressional Record, p. 14587.

[5] Impromptu remarks in Sydney, Australia. Reported in the Washington Post, Oct. 22, 1966.

Sen. Mansfield, who had visited Viet Nam in 1955, added: "What is most disturbing is what Viet Nam now appears to be as it was then, only at the beginning of coping with its grave inner problems. All of the current difficulties existed in 1955, along with the hope and energy to meet them. But it is seven years later and two billion dollars of U.S. aid later. Yet, substantially the same difficulties remain, if indeed they have not been compounded."

In South Viet Nam, meanwhile, the regime of President Ngo Dinh Diem's campaign of repression against the nation's Buddhists was met with rising public protest and growing U.S. disenchantment, reinforced by the antagonistic behavior of Diem's brother, secret police chief Ngo Dinh Nhu, and his wife, Mme. Nhu. On Sept. 12, 1963, Sen. Frank Church (D Idaho) proposed a resolution calling for U.S. withdrawal from South Viet Nam if "cruel repressions" of the Buddhists by the government continued. Church charged that the situation in Viet Nam had "worsened" while the U.S. effort had increased.

On Sept. 26, 1963, the House Foreign Operations and Government Information Subcommittee released a report criticizing the State Department's handling of news concerning the conflict in South Viet Nam. "The restrictive United States press policy," the report said, "...contributed to the lack of information in Viet Nam which created an international crisis."

Fulbright Criticism. On March 25, 1964, Sen. J. William Fulbright (D Ark.), chairman of the Senate Foreign Relations Committee, began to criticize the Johnson Administration's Far East policies. In a speech entitled "Old Myths and New Realities," a general criticism of American foreign policy, the Senator called for a re-evaluation of U.S. Far Eastern policies and added that "whatever the outcome of a re-thinking of policy might be, we have been unwilling to take it because of the fear of many government officials, undoubtedly well-founded, that even the suggestion of new policies toward China or Viet Nam would provoke a vehement outcry."

Fulbright asserted that the U.S. should "introduce an element of flexibility, or, more precisely, of the capacity to be flexible, into our relations with Communist China." He added that the foremost of the new realities about China "is that there are not really 'two Chinas' but only one, mainland China, and that is ruled by Communists and likely to remain so for the indefinite future." The Johnson Administration's reaction to Fulbright's speech was cool.

Viet Nam Problems

The conflict in Viet Nam went badly for the United States in 1964. The South Vietnamese government seemed unable to rally its people in the war against the Communists, while the U.S. commitment, both in men and money, was significantly increased. As Congressional concern mounted, President Johnson May 18, 1964, requested $125 million in additional economic and military aid for South Viet Nam. The request for $70 million in additional economic aid and $55 million in additional military aid for Viet Nam was quickly approved May 20 by the House Foreign Affairs Committee, which had been considering the entire $3.4 billion foreign aid bill.

On Aug. 2 and 4, U.S. destroyers patrolling the Gulf of Tonkin off the coast of North Viet Nam reported torpedo attacks by Communist PT boats and President Johnson ordered a retaliatory air strike at their bases resulting in the destruction of 25 boats. On Aug. 5, the President asked Congress to enact a resolution to "give convincing evidence to the aggressive Communist nations, and to the world as a whole, that our policy in Southeast Asia will be carried forward, and that the peace and security of the area will be preserved."

Republicans as well as Democrats endorsed the President's actions. Only Sen. Morse (D Ore.) objected that "continuation of the U.S. unilateral military action in Southeast Asia, which has now taken on the aspects of open aggressive fighting, endangers the peace of the world." On Aug. 7, 1964, the Senate voted 88-2 and the House 414-0 to pass a resolution (S J Res 189, H J Res 1145) declaring support for "the determination of the President as Commander-in-Chief, to take all necessary measures to repel any armed attack against the forces of the United States and to prevent further aggression." Sens. Morse (D Ore.) and Gruening (D Alaska) voted against it. The resolution also affirmed U.S. intentions to aid any member or protocol state of the SEATO pact "requesting assistance in the defense of its freedom" (PL 88-408).

The escalating military situation in South Viet Nam also meant a steep rise in costs. During 1965, the House May 5 and the Senate May 6, by nearly unanimous roll-call votes, passed and sent to the President a bill (H J Res 447) making fiscal 1965 supplemental appropriations of $700 million to meet mounting military requirements in Viet Nam. The actions came less than 53 hours after President Johnson appealed to Congress to "provide our forces with the best and most modern supplies and equipment" and to show "prompt support of our basic course: resistance to aggression, moderation in the use of power; and a constant search for peace." The President signed the bill May 7 (PL 89-18).

Opposition and apprehension about the bill were voiced by a number of Senators: Sens. Joseph S. Clark (D Pa.), Frank Church (D Idaho), and Jacob K. Javits (R N.Y.), expressed approval of the bill, but stressed that their votes should not be construed as endorsement of a "command decision" or "blank check" permitting the President to use U.S. troops in ground combat in Viet Nam.

On May 5, 1965, Sen. Wayne Morse (D Ore.) said: "I say sadly and solemnly, but out of deep conviction, that today my Government stands before the world drunk with military power" and is about to lay the foundation for "intense Asiatic hatred." H J Res 447 gives "the President power to make undeclared war," he said. Senators, Morse added, "can violate your constitutional trust if you want to, but I'll not be with you."

On the following day, Sen. Gaylord Nelson (D Wis.) commented: "Obviously you need my vote less than I need my conscience.... In the cloakrooms and on the floor, numerous distinguished Senators from both sides of the aisle have expressed their concern over the precipitous manner in which we are disposing of this matter."

On June 1, 1965, President Johnson told a news conference that he was asking Congress for a special appropriation of $89 million to begin the economic development program for Southeast Asia he had proposed earlier in the year.

On June 15, the Chairman of the Senate Foreign Relations Committee, Sen. J. William Fulbright (D Ark.) said in a Senate speech it was "clear" that "a complete military victory in Viet Nam...can in fact be attained only at a cost far exceeding the requirements of our interest and our honor" although "the unconditional withdrawal of American support...would have disastrous consequences." Fulbright had met with President Johnson the day before to discuss the Viet Nam situation.

Congressional reaction to Fulbright's speech was, for the most part, negative. On Aug. 4, 1965, President Johnson asked Congress to appropriate an additional $1.7 billion to finance the expanding war in Viet Nam. The new funds were to be added to the fiscal 1966 $45.2-billion defense appropriations bill (HR 9221) which passed the House June 23. Secretary of Defense Robert S. McNamara, appearing before the Senate Armed Services Subcommittee on Military Appropriations Aug. 4, said the additional funds would help provide financing of the war "through January," after which time requests for more funds would be made.

Second Viet Nam Report

As Congressional debate over Viet Nam increased, the Senate Foreign Relations Committee, on Jan. 7, 1966, released a second report on Viet Nam by Senate Majority Leader Mike Mansfield (D Mont.). The new report, entitled "The Viet Nam Conflict: The Substance and the Shadow," concluded that "the situation, as it now appears, offers only the very slim prospect of a just settlement by negotiations or the alternative prospect of a continuance of the conflict in the direction of a general war on the Asian mainland." Militarily, the report said that the large-scale introduction of U.S. forces "has blunted but not turned back the drive of the Viet Cong."

Hearings -- Viet Nam

The Mansfield report and President Johnson's decision to end a 38-day pause in the bombing of North Viet Nam touched off an even more heated Congressional debate, especially in the Senate.

On Feb. 4, 1966, the Senate Foreign Relations Committee began hearings on an Administration bill (S 2793) authorizing $415 million in supplemental fiscal 1966 foreign economic aid, of which $275 million was earmarked for emergency aid to South Viet Nam. The hearings were televised nationally and were used by the Committee as a springboard to conduct a public inquiry into the Administration's "general policy" in Viet Nam. Witnesses included David E. Bell, Administrator of the Agency for International Development; Gen. James. M. Gavin (ret.); George F. Kennan, former Ambassador to the Soviet Union; Gen. Maxwell D. Taylor (ret.), special consultant to President Johnson; Secretary of State Dean Rusk; and Vice President Hubert H. Humphrey, who met informally with the Committee after his return from South Viet Nam.

Authorization. On March 1, 1966, Congress moved nearer to action on supplemental appropriations for U.S. activities in Southeast Asia as it passed several authorizing bills. Passage of the measures came in contrasting atmospheres in the two chambers as Senators continued lengthy and at times acrimonious debate of President Johnson's Viet Nam policies while the House acted quickly and with only limited outright criticism of the increased U.S. commitment to the war. However, 78 Democrats signed a statement which said that their vote for a defense supplemental appropriations authorization did not mean they supported an enlargement of the military effort.

UN Votes on Chinese Representation - 1950-1966

The following table indicates the relative strength of the move for Chinese Communist representation in the UN General Assembly during the years 1950-1963. The China question was on the provisional agenda for the 1964 session but did not come to a vote because of the UN stalemate over peacekeeping assessments.

The 18 votes on the issue:

Year		For	Against	Abstentions
1950	(a) Indian resolution to seat Chinese Communists			
	Rejected	16	32	10
	(b) USSR resolution to unseat Chinese Nationalists			
	Rejected	10	38	8
1951	Moratorium (U.S. resolution not to consider any changes in Chinese representation)			
	Adopted	37	11	4
1952	Moratorium Adopted	42	7	11
1953	Moratorium Adopted	44	10	2
1954	Moratorium Adopted	43	11	6
1955	Moratorium Adopted	42	12	6
1956	Moratorium Adopted	47	24	8
1957	Moratorium Adopted	48	27	6
1958	Moratorium Adopted	44	28	9
1959	Moratorium Adopted	44	29	9
1960	Moratorium Adopted	42	34	22
1961	(a) Five-power resolution (United States, Australia, Colombia, Italy and Japan) making any proposal to change the representation of China an "important question" requiring a two-thirds majority for approval			
	Adopted	61	34	7
	(b) USSR resolution to oust Chinese Nationalists and seat the Communists			
	Rejected	37	48	19*
1962	USSR resolution to oust Chinese Nationalists and seat Communists			
	Rejected	42	56	12*
1963	Albanian resolution to oust Chinese Nationalists and seat Communists			
	Rejected	41	57	12

Two-thirds majority required for adoption.

Year		For	Against	Abstentions
1965	(a) 11-power resolution (U.S., Australia, Brazil, Colombia, Madagascar, Nicaragua, Gabon, Italy, Japan, Philippines, Thailand) declaring 1961 vote on "important question" still in force			
	Approved	56	49	11
	(b) 12-power resolution (Albania, Algeria, Cambodia, Congo-Brazzaville, Cuba, Ghana, Guinea, Mali, Pakistan, Rumania, Somalia, Syria) to oust Chinese Nationalists and seat Communists			
	Rejected	47	47	20*
1966	(a) 15-power resolution (U.S., Australia, Belgium, Bolivia, Brazil, Colombia, Gabon, Italy, Japan, Malagasy Republic, New Zealand, Nicaragua, Philippines, Thailand, Togo) declaring China entry motion an "important question"			
	Approved	66	48	7
	(b) 10-power resolution (Albania, Algeria, Cambodia, Congo-Brazzaville, Cuba, Guinea, Mali, Pakistan, Rumania, Syria) to oust Chinese Nationalists and seat Chinese Communists			
	Rejected	46	57	17*
	(c) Italian proposal (with Belgium, Bolivia, Brazil, Chile, Trinidad, Tobago) to appoint special committee to investigate Red China's position vis a vis UN membership and report to Assembly by July 1967			
	Rejected	34	62	25°

On March 8, 1966, the Senate Foreign Relations Committee began hearings on U.S. policy toward Communist China, an outgrowth of the Viet Nam hearings. Describing the hearings as "educational," Committee Chairman J. William Fulbright (D Ark.) said: "At this stage, perhaps the most effective contribution the Committee can make is to provide a forum for recognized experts and scholars in the field of China."

The main theme to emerge from the next three weeks of testimony was that U.S. policy had not only contained China, but had also attempted to isolate her, which had been both unwise and unsuccessful. Dr. John K. Fairbank of Harvard's East Asian Research Center typified the theme when he concluded: "Containment alone is a blind alley unless we add policies of constructive competition and international contact.... Peiping's rulers shout aggressively out of manifold frustrations.... Isolation intensifies their ailment and makes it self-perpetuating, and we need to encourage international contact with China on many fronts."

The majority of witnesses proposed three basic changes in U.S. policy: official diplomatic recognition of Communist China, an expansion of trade relations, and admission of Communist China into the United Nations. These changes were opposed by a minority of witnesses, one of whom was former Rep. Walter H. Judd (R Minn. 1943-63). Judd said that "our choice -- with Red China just as it was with Japan and Hitler -- is not between checking and not checking, it is whether to check early, while we can, and with allies -- or try to check the aggression later, when it is stronger, closer and we have fewer and weaker friends and allies."

In conclusion, Judd said: "This is the time to stand fast for the basic containment policies that have proved sound and more successful during the last 15 years than most people believed possible.... Until someone can suggest policies that offer better prospects of success, based on something more substantial than speculation, wishful thinking or just hope, I can see no...reason to change present policies and every reason to continue them, always being flexible in our tactics as required by developments...."

On May 19, 1966, the House Foreign Affairs Committee on the Far East and Pacific released a report on its open hearings, held between Jan. 25 and March 10, on U.S. policy towards Asia. The report recommended that the U.S., despite rebuffs, should continue to seek peaceful contacts with China while at the same time preventing her from any aggressive expansion. To do this, it continued, would require both increased assistance and cooperation from Western European allies and increased U.S. efforts to build up the strength of "the independent countries of the continent -- from India and Pakistan to Japan and Korea."

On May 25, 1966, the Senate Foreign Relations Committee held hearings on the "psychological aspects of international relations." The hearings appeared to be an outgrowth of the earlier investigation of U.S. China policy and, in relation to the foreign aid bills, of U.S. policy in Viet Nam. On Aug. 17, the Committee opened hearings on news coverage of the war in Viet Nam. Chairman William Fulbright said the hearings were stimulated by an article in the Washington *Post* which said the United States Information Agency (USIA) was sponsoring visits by foreign newsmen to Viet Nam.

As the war and the American commitment intensified in 1966, so did Congressional debate. While a number of liberal Democrats criticized the President for not doing enough to find a peaceful settlement, both Senate and House Republicans claimed he was not doing enough to win the war. But by the fall of 1966, it was apparent to the Administration's friends and foes that the question was no longer whether the U.S. was going to fight in South Viet Nam or not, but whether Communist China would also become involved.

By the fall of 1966, predictions regarding future Chinese strategy were reduced to educated guesses. Since early spring, China was torn by what the Peking regime labeled as a "great proletarian cultural revolution." Western observers called it a purge. In less than six months, the hierarchy of the Chinese Communist Party had been reshuffled, leaving former defense minister Lin Piao as the heir apparent to Party Chairman Mao Tse-tung. While men connected with the Communist Party machinery had fallen, those somehow connected with Lin rose in prestige.

The purge was not limited to the Peking leadership. It also swept the provinces, claiming party functionaries, educators, intellectuals, propagandists and scientists. Bands of youths known as the Red Guards served as storm troopers and "Mao-think" as its gospel. As it claimed victims, it also created its own opposition, the strength of which was one of the many unknowns.

U.S. Shifts UN Stand

The U.S. ambassador to the United Nations, Arthur J. Goldberg, Nov. 21, 1966, announced U.S. support of an Italian draft resolution proposing that a UN committee explore the question of Chinese representation in the United

Nations and recommend "an equitable and practical solution." Goldberg at the same time stipulated two U.S. conditions for supporting the Italian proposal: the United States would refuse to repudiate its commitments to Nationalist China and would reject any solution of the question that involved the expulsion of the Nationalists from the UN.

The study committee, Goldberg said, ought to obtain answers as to whether the Communist Chinese government would refrain from demanding that Nationalist China be expelled from the United Nations and whether it would be willing to assume the obligations of the UN Charter to refrain from threats of force. Italy Nov. 18 proposed that the special committee be appointed to ask Communist China whether it was willing to comply with the Charter and what its attitude was toward UN representation.

Although the support of the study proposal did not constitute a U.S. commitment to accept a two-China solution, the move was widely felt to be the first break in the hitherto intransigent U.S. position on keeping Communist China out of the world organization.

The Italian resolution, however, was rejected by the General Assembly Nov. 29, with 34 nations for, 62 against, and 25 abstentions. A prior motion was accepted which made a two-thirds majority rule applicable in this case. After voting for the resolution, Goldberg said the United States supported the proposal because it did not want to "prejudge" the committee's findings. France and the Soviet Union opposed the resolution; Britain abstained.

The proposal was similar to a plan circulated by Canadian External Affairs Minister Paul Martin to have Communist China replace the Nationalists as a permanent member of the Security Council and to have both countries represented in the Assembly. Martin did not put the proposal in the form of a draft resolution because a rejection by the Assembly would have ended discussion of the plan.

Background. China was represented at the United Nations by the Nationalist Chinese government in Taiwan, Formosa, while the Communist People's Republic of China in Peking was not represented at all. The "Republic of China" was a founding member of the organization and was a permanent member of the UN Security Council. At the time that the Nationalist government was driven from the Chinese mainland in late 1949, the question arose over whether China should be represented in the United Nations by Chiang Kai-shek's government in Formosa or by Mao Tse-tung's Communist regime at Peking -- in other words, which was entitled to issue credentials for the "Republic of China." The issue, which generally was regarded as one of representation rather than membership, came before the Security Council in January 1950 and later that year was raised in the General Assembly.

The 1950 Security Council vote on the Soviet motion to exclude the Nationalist representative -- at the time considered as a procedural matter and thereby not subject to a big-power veto -- failed to receive majority support of the seven-member body.

Assured of defeat in the Security Council, proponents of Communist China's admittance moves limited subsequent to the General Assembly where their chances appeared to be far better. Since the Peking regime's bid was rebuffed on a 32-16 vote in 1950, the question of Chinese representation was raised in every subsequent General Assembly, except that of 1964, when disputes over assessments kept that body paralyzed.

(Continued on p. 28)

'CHINA LOBBIES' OPERATE FOR BOTH SIDES IN UNITED STATES

The "China Lobby," not as prominent as it was in the early 1950s, still showed signs of life in the mid-1960s. There were registered agents for both the Chinese Nationalists and Communist China currently active, apparently more along commercial lines than for political reasons. The most energetic political activity was concerned with opposition to admission of Communist China into the United Nations and to recognition of or trading with Communist China by the United States.

Background

During the final stages of the Chinese civil war -- which featured many reports of corruption among the Nationalists and the abandonment of U.S.-supplied arms to the Communists -- there was considerable sympathy for the "plague-on-both-your-houses" view of Gen. George Marshall and a policy of "let the dust settle." With the Communist defeat of the Nationalists in 1949, U.S. policy in China became the subject of major political controversy that continued through the 1952 campaign, when conservative Republicans charged that the Truman Administration had "substituted on our Pacific flank a murderous enemy for an ally and friend."

During this period an extensive propaganda war was waged between organizations opposing or supporting the Chinese Nationalists. Groups supporting the Chiang regime charged its opponents with being Communist "dupes" and "fronts"; the latter helped to label the former as the "China Lobby," bought and paid for by the Nationalists. Both charges apparently contained some truth; just how much never was established. But there is no doubt about the outcome of the propaganda battle: the anti-Nationalists were routed by the pro-Nationalists, whose victory was symbolized when President Eisenhower, on taking office in 1953, "unleashed" the Nationalists by rescinding President Truman's 1950 order to the U.S. Seventh Fleet to prevent hostilities in the Formosa Strait.

Policy Groups

Prominently identified with the "China Lobby" in the late 40s and early 50s were the **American China Policy Association,** headed by Alfred Kohlberg, an import-export merchant, and William Loeb, publisher of the Manchester (N.H.) *Union-Leader*; and the **China Emergency Committee,** headed by Frederick C. McKee, a Pittsburgh industrialist. Serving as an adviser to both was Rep. Walter H. Judd (R Minn., 1943-63), long the leading Republican spokesman on China policy. By 1966, neither group was active.

The **Committee to Defend America by Aiding Anti-Communist China** became active in the latter half of 1949 and issued a quantity of literature urging China aid. It was no longer active in 1966. Chairman pro tem of the Committee was Frederick C. McKee. On the Committee's board of directors were ex-Ambassador Arthur Bliss Lane; David Dubinsky, president of the International Ladies Garment Workers (AFL) and second vice president of the American Federation of Labor (AFL), who had been active previously on China issues; James A. Farley, chairman of the board of the Coca-Cola Export Corp., formerly chairman of the Democratic National Committee and Postmaster General.

The **Committee on National Affairs** -- another group headed by Frederick C. McKee -- in 1949 sent Congressmen reprints of an article, "An Aid Plan for Asia," by Harold E. Stassen, then president of the University of Pennsylvania and formerly Governor of Minnesota, calling for a billion-dollar-a-year "MacArthur Plan" for Asia to oppose the Chinese Communists. The Stassen article opposed backing any large central governments, and would extend aid on a project basis. The Committee was no longer active in the 1960s.

The pro-Chiang Kai-shek policy groups formed a loose and broad alliance of individuals having little in common except their opposition to the Chinese Communists. A number of the directors listed on the letterheads of the American China Policy Assn. and the Committee to Defend America by Aiding Anti-Communist China were people who had worked in China as religious or medical missionaries, as had Rep. Judd, or in other similar capacities.

Several of the listed directors were former Communist leaders who broke with Stalinism: Jay Lovestone, of the Committee to Defend America, was once secretary general of the Communist Party, U.S.A. and later a top foreign policy adviser for the AFL-CIO; Freda Utley, of the American China Policy Assn., was a British Communist; other listed directors had similar sympathies or affiliations in the past.

On the other side, there were two prominent anti-Chiang groups:

The **Committee for a Democratic Far Eastern Policy,** which the pro-Chiang groups claimed was under Communist influence, urged a hands-off policy in China. In literature sent Congressmen in 1949, the Committee called for a Congressional investigation of the "Chinese lobby" and private wealth which Chinese officials and individuals "have stowed away in American banks and investments"; an immediate end to all American intervention in China and no dealing with any remnant of the Kuomintang.

In 1950, the Committee circulated "Facts on the Korean Crisis" criticizing the "unprecedented haste" of the United States in persuading the United Nations to censure North Korea.

In October 1950, the Committee sent Congressmen copies of a resolution adopted at a New York City mass meeting, held under its auspices. It urged the United States to: recognize the Chinese Communist Government; help seat it in the United Nations; recognize that Formosa belongs to mainland China; cease giving military aid and advice to military regimes and to European powers for use in Asia; withdraw from Korea.

Among those listed on the Committee's board of directors on the October 1950 letterhead were:

Paul Robeson, concert singer, actor, all-American football player, and co-chairman of the Progressive Party during the Henry A. Wallace campaign in 1948; ex-Rep. Hugh De Lacy (D Wash., 1945-47); Eugene Connolly, former New York City Council member, high official in the American Labor Party in New York and unsuccessful candidate for Congress; Arthur Schutzer, state executive officer of the American Labor Party of New York; Prof. E. Franklin Frazier, head of the Howard University sociology department and author of leading books on the role of the Negro in the United States. Also on the letterhead were officials of unions which had been expelled from the Congress of Industrial Organizations (CIO) in 1950, including Ben Gold, president of the International Fur and Leather Workers Union of the U.S. and Canada. Gold had admitted to a Congressional committee that he was a Communist.

Although the Committee still existed in 1966, its activities appeared to be limited to the publication of literature, most of it written by the Committee's chairman, Maud Russell. The literature was released through the Jefferson Book Shop, 100 East 16th St., N.Y.C., according to the Senate Internal Security subcommittee.

Another group was the **Institute of Pacific Relations,** which came under heavy attack in 1950 during the hearings on Sen. Joseph R. McCarthy's (R Wis.) charges of Communist influence in the State Department.

William L. Holland, secretary of the IPR, in 1950 denied as "utterly false" the McCarthy Communist-front charge. He described the Institute as "a reputable nonpartisan international research organization whose studies of Far Eastern and Pacific countries long have been valued and acclaimed by leading scholars and public figures."

McCarthy's charges came in connection with his attacks on Owen Lattimore, who conducted research in Peiping for the Institute in the early 1930s and was editor of its magazine, "Pacific Affairs," from 1934 to 1941. Holland asserted the charges mainly were a repetition of unsubstantiated allegations made earlier against the Institute's American National Council by Alfred Kohlberg.

In the early 1940s, as a member of the Institute of Pacific Relations, Kohlberg attacked IPR for allegedly harboring Communists and permitting its publications to undercut the Chiang Kai-shek government by giving circulation to the Communist line. His charges were rejected in 1947 by a vote of the IPR trustees.

The IPR also protested to Sen. Pat McCarran (D Nev.) against the seizure of its files in February 1951 at a farm in Lee, Mass., by agents of the Senate Judiciary subcommittee. IPR's Holland said the documents were taken illegally from their place of storage at the country home of Edward C. Carter, a former secretary general of the Institute.

The IPR was governed by an executive committee headed by Gerard Swope, honorary president of the General Electric Co. Vice chairmen were Robert B. Sproul, president of the University of California, and Heaton L. Wren, a Honolulu attorney. Clifford B. Marshall of the Standard-Vacuum Oil Co. was treasurer.

Trustees included former Under Secretary of State Sumner Welles, Secretary of Defense George C. Marshall, Paul C. Smith, editor of the San Francisco *Chronicle,*

W.W. Waymack, formerly of the Des Moines *Register Tribune,* Gordon R. Clapp, then chairman of the Tennessee Valley Authority, author John Hersey, J. Wallace Sterling, president of Stanford University, and Owen Lattimore.

The Institute of Pacific Relations disbanded in 1961, although "Pacific Affairs" was taken over by the University of British Columbia in Vancouver, Canada.

Another organization, established on June 9, 1966, was the **National Committee on United States-China Relations,** with offices in New York and San Francisco. Its acting chairman was Robert A. Scalapino, University of California political science professor. The membership was made up of prominent business, labor, professional, academic and religious leaders.

Scalapino said June 9 the committee hoped to raise $250,000 to finance its activities during the first year, which would include sponsoring seminars, conferences, special studies, and disseminating information throughout the country. He also said the committee would probably not advocate specific policies since its members held so many different views.

Members of the new committee included: John K. Fairbank, director of the East Asian Research Center at Harvard University; A. Doak Barnett, professor in the Department of Public Law and Government at Columbia University; Morton H. Halperin, the Center for International Affairs at Harvard; O. Edmund Clubb, the East Asian Institute at Columbia University; Clark Kerr, the president of the University of California; Roger Hilsman, former Assistant Secretary of State; Robert Gilmore, president of the Center for Peace/War Studies; A. Philip Randolph, vice president of the AFL-CIO; Bayard Rustin, director of the A. Philip Randolph Institute; and Jack Gomperts, former chairman of the World Trade Association.

Americans for a Reappraisal of our Far Eastern Policy was another recent group, established on Oct. 24, 1965, when it linked 30 college campuses by telephone for a national seminar on Far Eastern policy. Organizers of the group included Yale Chaplain William Sloane Coffin, Socialist leader Norman Thomas, author John Hersey, John K. Fairbank, and New York attorney Allard K. Lowenstein. The group's activities since the national "teach-in" were minimal.

In late August 1966, the **Clergymen's Emergency Committee on China** was formed. A news release said the purpose of the group was "to provide factual information and material on Red China to American clergymen and whenever necessary to articulate the sentiments of the majority on the questions of concern."

The chairman of the committee was listed as Rev. Daniel A. Poling and the executive secretary as Rev. David C. Head. The committee's offices were at 432 Madison Ave., N.Y.C.

On Sept. 2, the committee published advertisements in leading newspapers showing the results of a poll of Presbyterian ministers throughout the country concerning U.S. China policy. The advertisements said that 150,000 ministers had been sent questionnaires, and that 30,000 had replied. Of those, the advertisement said, 72.9 percent were opposed to the admission of Communist China into the United Nations and 71.4 percent opposed U.S. recognition of Communist China.

Committee of One Million. In 1953, the pro-Nationalists turned their attention to the problem of keeping

Communist China out of the United Nations. Starting with a petition to the President, signed by prominent members of both parties, a Committee of One Million Against the Admission of Communist China into the United Nations was created. By March 16, 1954, the Committee had collected 500,000 signatures and announced "the expansion of its activities to include opposition to trade with Red China." With its goal of one million signatures on file by August 1954, the Committee closed down.

Then, according to the Committee, "there again began a series of oblique declarations from several major internationally minded American groups hinting at the need to recognize Communist China and admit that regime to the UN for the sake of 'peace'." So, on Feb. 2, 1955 (four days after President Eisenhower signed a resolution empowering him to use force to defend Formosa and 'related positions'), an "historic meeting was held at the home of Ambassador Joseph C. Grew in Washington." The upshot was a decision to reorganize as the Committee of One Million, which has since become, in its own words, "the responsible voice of the overwhelming majority of the American people united in opposing any steps which would strengthen the political, economic, or aggressive power of the Peking regime."

In 1961, the Committee claimed that, after its reorganization, it helped to kill proposed Senate hearings in 1957 on trade with Communist China with the help of "a nation-wide postcard campaign"; organized in 1958 "a letter-writing campaign backing United States policy in the Taiwan Straits"; issued in 1959 a rebuttal to the Conlon Report, a private study urging closer U.S.-Chinese relations, that "helped, in large measure, to refute its recommendations"; and "worked closely with all candidates" in the 1960 campaign, when "those few candidates who openly supported the admission of Communist China to the UN were defeated."

Over the years, the Committee published a number of declarations featuring the names of Congressmen opposed to seating Communist China in the UN. The latest such declaration for the 89th Congress was signed by 51 Senators and 283 Representatives. The declaration listed its opposition to the seating of Communist China in the UN, to granting U.S. diplomatic recognition to Peking, to trade relations between the U.S. and Communist China, and to "any policy of accommodation which might be interpreted as U.S. acquiescence in, or approval of, Communist China's aggression, direct or indirect, against her neighbors." The declaration appeared as an advertisement in the N.Y. *Times*, Washington *Post* and other newspapers in October 1966.

Heading the Committee as honorary chairman as of mid-1966 was former Sen. H. Alexander Smith (R N.J. 1944-59). A nine-member steering committee was composed of Rep. John M. Ashbrook (R Ohio), Sen. Thomas J. Dodd (D Conn.), Sen. Peter H. Dominick (R Colo.), Sen. Paul H. Douglas (D Ill.), former Gov. Charles Edison (D N.J.), Sen. Bourke Hickenlooper (R Iowa), former Rep. Walter H. Judd (R Minn.), Rep. Thomas E. Morgan (D Pa.), chairman of the House Foreign Affairs Committee, and Sen. Hugh Scott (R Pa.). The treasurer was Dr. B. A. Garside; secretary was Marvin Liebman.

Despite evidence of extensive activity on Capitol Hill, the Committee never registered under the lobby law, claiming that it was not engaged in influencing legislation. The Committee received no funds from, nor was in any way connected with, the Chinese Nationalist government, according to Liebman.

Morse Charges in 1952

On April 10, 1952, Sen. Wayne Morse (then R Ore.) read to the Senate what he said were messages sent from the Chinese Embassy in Washington to Generalissimo Chiang Kai-shek reporting activities of the "China Lobby" in Washington. Morse had photocopies of 7 letters and written copies of 17 more. On July 6, 1951, Morse had introduced a bill (S Res 170) providing for an investigation of the China lobby. No action was taken.

Morse said most of the messages were signed with the name Chen Chih-Mai, the Chinese Embassy counselor in Washington, and were sent to Formosa through the communications facilities of the Chinese Nationalist Air Force. The Senator did not say how he had come into possession of the documents. Chen Chih-Mai said April 11 the messages had been sent by Gen. P.T. Mow, dismissed head of the Chinese Aeronautical Commission in Washington, but Chen would not confirm their authenticity.

One of the documents supposedly told Chiang that an associate of William M. Boyle, then chairman of the Democratic National Committee, had agreed to serve as legal adviser to the Chinese Nationalists at a salary of $30,000 a year. The person was hired, according to the translation held by Morse, because he was "capable of reaching the highest levels of the proper authorities."

Another message said Rep. Walter H. Judd (R Minn.) had given Chinese officials "secret information" on U.S. Far Eastern policy. Judd denied April 11 he had given any secret information to any person. Still another cable said William J. Goodwin, then registered as a lobbyist for the Republic of China, said he had "converted" 50 Congressmen to the Nationalist point of view on China.

On June 9, Sen. Morse told the Senate that the documents showed that Chinese Nationalist officials in 1945, 1946, and 1948 instructed their Air Force officers in Washington to spy on U.S. atomic secrets and on "military targets" in the United States. Morse said he had asked the State Department to investigate the authenticity of the cables.

The State Department replied that it did not have the facilities to make an investigation and had referred the matter to the Justice Department. On July 14, 1952, the Justice Department announced that it was proceeding with an investigation.

On Aug. 5, 1952, Sen. Morse said the State and Justice Departments were not able to verify the authenticity of the cablegrams on which he had based his demands for an investigation of the "China Lobby."

Registered Foreign Agents

According to Justice Department records, released in October 1965, there were ten organizations and one individual registered as active agents for Nationalist Chinese principals. The Department listed four individuals registered as active agents for Communist China principals. All filed under the Foreign Agents Registration Act of 1938, which requires all persons and firms working for foreign interests to submit registration statements to the Attorney General.

Agents currently registered for the **Republic of China** (Nationalist China) include:

Agent. KUOMINTANG OF CHINA, HEAD-QUARTERS IN AMERICA, 844 Stockton St., San Francisco, Calif.
Foreign Principal. Kuomintang of China, Central Committee, Taipei, Formosa.

Agent. CENTRAL NEWS AGENCY OF CHINA, NEW YORK BUREAU, 220 E. 42nd St., N.Y.C.
Foreign Principal. Central News Agency of China, Taipei, Formosa.

Agent. CHINESE INFORMATION SERVICE, 1270 Ave. of the Americas, N.Y.C.
Foreign Principal. Chinese Government Information Office, Taipei, Formosa.

Agent. CENTRAL NEWS AGENCY OF CHINA, WASHINGTON BUREAU, 549 National Press Building, Washington 4, D.C.
Foreign Principal. Central News Agency of China, Taipei, Formosa.

Agent. CENTRAL NEWS AGENCY OF CHINA, SAN FRANCISCO BUREAU, 681 Market St., Room 348, San Francisco, 5, Calif.
Foreign Principal. Central News Agency of China, Taipei, Formosa.

Agent. NORDLINGER, RIEGELMAN, BENETAR, AND CHARNEY, 420 Lexington Ave., N.Y.C.
Foreign Principal. Republic of China, Taipei, Formosa.

Agent. WORLD WIDE PHILATELIC AGENCY, INC., 116 W. 32nd St., N.Y.C.
Foreign Principal. Directorate General of Posts, Republic of China, Taipei, Formosa.

Agent. CHINESE INVESTMENT AND TRADE OFFICE, 515 Madison Ave., Suite 1909, N.Y.C.
Foreign Principal. Industrial Development and Investment Center, Taipei, Formosa.

Agent. STERLING MOVIES U.S.A., INC., 375 Park Ave., N.Y.C.
Foreign Principal. Chinese News Service, Taipei, Formosa.

Agent. MYRON W. SOLTER, 1108 16th St., N.W., Washington, D.C.
Foreign Principal. Taiwan Mushroom Packers, United Export Corporation, Taipei, Formosa.

Agent. CHINESE INFORMATION SERVICE, PACIFIC COAST BUREAU, 141 Battery St., Suite 455, San Francisco, Calif.
Foreign Principal. Government Information Office, Executive Yuan, Taipei, Formosa.

Agents currently registered for the **People's Republic of China** (Communist China) include:

Agent. LIUBA SOLOV, 25 W. 43rd St., N.Y.C.
Foreign Principal. China Photo Service, Peking, China.

Queried by Congressional Quarterly, Miss Solov explained that she receives news and feature photographs from Communist China and distributes them to the U.S. news media.

Agent. DAVID ROSEN (doing business as CHINA PUBLICATIONS), 95 Fifth Ave., N.Y.C.
Foreign Principal. Guozi Shudian, China Publications Center, Peking, China.

Rosen told CQ in October 1966 that Guozi Shudian, which means "publishing house" in Chinese, is a wholesale exporter of printed matter from Communist China, selling to agents throughout the world. Mr. Rosen is supposed to pay the publishing house a certain fee. However, it is paid to the Treasury Department, which places it into what is called a blocked account -- where it accumulates but cannot be withdrawn by Communist China or the publishing house. If relations between the two countries were to improve, and the account opened, the money is there for withdrawal.

Agent. PHILIP FRANKFELD (doing business as NEW ERA BOOKS), 80 E. 11th St., N.Y.C.
Foreign Principal. Guozi Shudian, Peking, China.

Agent. HENRY H. NOYES (doing business as CHINA BOOKS AND PERIODICALS), 2929 24th St., San Francisco, Calif.
Foreign Principal. Guozi Shudian, Peking, China.

TERMINATIONS

Agents for the **Republic of China** (Nationalists) who have terminated their registrations with the Justice Department, dating back to 1942, include:

Agent. ROBERT L. FARRINGTON, 1155 15th St., N.W., Washington, D.C.
Foreign Principal. Chinese Government Procurement and Services Mission.

Agent. HAMILTON WRIGHT ORGANIZATION, INC., 30 Rockefeller Plaza, N.Y.C.
Foreign Principal. Government Information Office, Republic of China, Taipei, Formosa.

Agent. DEMOCRATIC AND SOCIALIST PARTY OF CHINA, 777 Sacramento St., San Francisco, Calif.
Foreign Principal. Democratic and Socialist Party of China, Taipei, Formosa.

Agent. COMMITTEE ON PLANNING AND ADVISING FOR CHINESE STUDENTS IN THE UNITED STATES, 125 East 65th St., N.Y.C.
Foreign Principal. Executive Yuan of the Government of China, Taipei, Formosa.

Agent. S. N. FERRIS LUBOSHEZ, 6933 Pinetree Terrace, Falls Church, Va.
Foreign Principal. The Central Trust of China, Taipei and New York.

Agent. MIN YUK SUM (JAMES MOY), 117 Mott St., Apt. 2A, N.Y.C.
Foreign Principal. Chinese Overseas Affairs Commission and the Kuomintang, Taipei, Formosa.

Agent. UNIVERSAL TRADING CORPORATION, 630 Fifth Ave., N.Y.C.
Foreign Principal. National Government of the Republic of China, Formosa.

Agent. COMMERCE INTERNATIONAL CHINA, 64 Hamilton St., Paterson, N.J.
Foreign Principal. Board of Supplies, Executive Yuan, Taipei, Formosa.

Agent. CARSON CHANG, 502 3rd St., S.E., Washington, D.C.
Foreign Principal. China's Fighting League for Free Democracy (headquarters "somewhere in Asia"). The address is unknown "due to the underground nature of its activities."

Agent. HARRY C. LAMBERTON, 1822 Jefferson Pl., N.W., Washington, D.C.
Foreign Principal. Board of Trustees for Rehabilitation Affairs, Taipei, Formosa.

Agent. ALLIED SYNDICATES, INC., 1431 Eye St., N.W., Washington, D.C.
Foreign Principal. Bank of China, N.Y.C.

Agent. LESTER KNOX LITTLE, 190 Exchange St., Pawtucket, R.I.
Foreign Principal. Minister of Finance, Nationalist Chinese Government.

Agent. JOHN WILLIAM FLEMING, 1016 Investment Building, Washington, D.C.
Foreign Principal. Chinese Oil Corporation, 11 Broadway, N.Y.C.

Agents. "CHINESE NATIONALIST DAILY" and "THE YOUNG CHINA" (newspapers), 811 Clay St., San Francisco, Calif.
Foreign Principal. Kuomintang.

Agent. TRANSOCEAN COMMERCE INC., 165 Broadway, N.Y.C.
Foreign Principal. Chinese Film Corporation, Shanghai, China.

Agent. PAUL GUILLUMETTE, INC., 475 Fifth Ave., N.Y.C.
Foreign Principal. Chinese News Service.

Agent. NATIONAL LECTURE MANAGEMENT, 9003 Sudbury Rd., Silver Spring, Md.
Foreign Principal. Chinese News Service.

Agent. CHINA INSTITUTE OF AMERICA, INC.
Foreign Principal. Chinese Nationalist Government.

The Institute was an educational foundation aimed at promoting "culture between the United States and China," whose board of directors in 1951 was headed by Henry R. Luce, editorial chairman of Time Inc.

Agent. DR. SHOU CH'UN MONG, an inspector of educational facilities in the United States, 790 California St., San Francisco, Calif.
Foreign Principal. Chinese Nationalist Government.

Agent. WILLIAM GOODWIN.
Foreign Principal. Chinese News Service, San Francisco Bureau; National Resources Commission of China.

Agent. FREE CHINA POLITICAL ORGANIZATIONS, 736 Grant Ave., San Francisco, Calif.
Foreign Principal. None listed.

Agent. THE COMMITTEE FOR FORMOSAN'S FREE FORMOSA, c/o Tsu-yi Loo, Centennial Hall, University of Minnesota, Minneapolis, Minn.
Foreign Principal. None listed.

Agents for the People's Republic of China, (Communists) who have terminated their registrations with the Department of Justice include:

Agent. IMPORTED PUBLICATIONS AND PRODUCTS, One Union Square, N.Y.C.
Foreign Principal. Guozi Shudian, Peking, China; The China Welfare Institute, Shanghai, China.

Agent. EDWIN S. SMITH, 24 West 45th St., N.Y., N.Y.
Foreign Principal. China Photo Service, Peking, China.

Agent. CHARLES WILLIAM ROSELL (doing business as CHARLES W. ROSELL AND CO.), P.O. Box 828, Big Bear Lake, Calif.
Foreign Principal. The China Welfare Institute of the People's Republic of China, Peking, China.

Agent. FOUR CONTINENT BOOK CORPORATION, 822 Broadway, N.Y.C.
Foreign Principal. People's Republic of China, Kowloon, Hong Kong.

Agent. HELEN BLACK, 15 West 44th St., N.Y.C.
Foreign Principal. Chinese Photo Service, Peking, China.

Agent. FREDERICK V. FIELD, 51 Pine St., N.Y.C.
Foreign Principal. Three Communist China firms and one other.

Communist China's principal representative in the United States was Frederick Vanderbilt Field, a New York millionaire, who was cited for contempt of Congress in 1950 for refusing to tell the Senate Foreign Relations Committee whether or not he was a member of the Communist Party. Field, later indicted by a federal grand jury in Washington, was acquitted in March 1951, after he had pleaded his refusal to testify was a defense against self-incrimination.

In his individual registration, which terminated in April 1951, Field said he was the agent for the Bank of China, China National Aviation Corp., and the Directorate General of Postal Remittances and Savings Bank, all of Peking, and the Chinese Postal Remittances and Savings Bank of Hong Kong. He acted as "attorney-in-fact" for the four concerns, with "authority to manage and conduct their affairs" in the United States. (For more on Field, see below.)

Agent. AMERICAN-CHINESE EXPORT CORPORATION, 51 Pine St., N.Y.C.
Foreign Principal. Eight Communist China firms and two others.

The American-Chinese Export Corporation, which Field headed, acted as an agent for China National Native Produce Corp., China National Egg Products Corp., China National Furs and Wools Corp., China National Bristle Corp., China National Import Corp., China National Oil and Fats Corp., and North China Petroleum Corp., all of Tientsin; China National Tea Corp. of Peking; Leighton Trading Co., Shanghai; and Nam Sun Trading Co., Hong Kong.

The Field Agency's registration stated that the trading corporation had no knowledge as to the character of the Leighton and Nam Sun trading companies but that the others were, "according to our information, government corporations acting under the supervision of the Ministry of Trade of the People's Republic of China."

In both registration statements, Field refused to answer several of the questions on the registration form "in the exercise of my privilege against self-incrimination under the Fifth Amendment of the United States Constitution." These questions concerned:

1. If he had ever used another name.
2. If he was subject to the supervision and control of any individual or organization other than those named in his registration paper.
3. Memberships in clubs, organizations, business, occupations and public activities.

He did list himself as director of Trade Union Service, Inc., owner of a building at 23 West 26th St., N.Y.C., vice president of Eight and Ten West 37th St. Corp., as well as owner of substantial stock holdings in 38 large American industrial corporations. He said he was secretary

and director of Soviet Russia Today Publications, Inc. He listed his affiliations with the Harvard Club, the Century Assn., the Foreign Policy Assn., the American Institute of Pacific Relations and several economic and scientific associations.

According to the House Un-American Activities Committee, Field was listed as the publisher of the *New World Review* in the November 1965 issue, which was published in Mexico. The *New World Review* was the successor of *Soviet Russia Today* and both were listed by the HUAC as "subversive" publications.

CONGRESSIONAL ROLE
(Continued from p. 22)

For each of the years from 1951 through 1960, the United States blocked a vote on Red Chinese representation by a tactic known as the "moratorium formula." The formula was a resolution prohibiting consideration of "any proposals to exclude the representatives of the Republic of China or to seat representatives of the...People's Republic of China." By 1960, however, U.S. majorities had been drastically reduced, and strategy was changed to allow a vote under the "important question" rule which called for a two-thirds majority -- well out of Peking's reach. The "important question" resolution was adopted in 1961 by a vote of 61 to 34. This was followed by the 37-48 rejection of the Soviet proposal to oust the Nationalists and invite the Communists to be represented.

Similar resolutions, considered under the terms of the "important question" resolution requiring a two-thirds majority, were rejected again in 1962 and 1963. In 1965, on a vote requiring a simple majority, the Assembly reaffirmed, 56-49, the procedural decision that any proposal to change the representation of China was an important question. It then rejected the substantive resolution to expel the Nationalist government, 47-47, under the two-thirds majority requirement.

On Nov. 29, 1966, the U.S. policy line scored an appreciable gain when the Assembly defeated an Albanian resolution to substitute Communist China for the Nationalist Government, 46-57 with 17 abstentions. The United States also won increased support for its procedural resolution making the issue an "important question," which required a two-thirds majority; the vote on that resolution was 66-48 with 7 abstentions. *(See p. 20 for UN voting on the question.)*

Dual Representation.   Many advocated an alternative to the seating of either one or the other regime: admit both Chinas to the United Nations -- Communist China as representative of the mainland and the Nationalists

as representatives of Formosa. This solution, they argued, would attract more support. Both countries, however, insisted that there cannot be two Chinas, each claiming to represent all of China.

With the question being one of whose credentials to honor rather than admittance of Communist China as a new member, the problem became one of the knottiest ever brought before the United Nations. A decision by the General Assembly to seat the Communist Chinese would not be binding on the Security Council, where a veto would apply in the absence of agreement to consider the question procedural.

Arguments Against Change.   The United States was consistently against the admission of Communist China since the issue came before the United Nations. The major contentions by members who have opposed Peking's bid were the following:

• The Chinese Communists did not meet the "peace loving" standard for membership laid down in the UN Charter. They practiced aggression, called for violence and were openly contemptuous of the United Nations.

• The Chinese still stand condemned, by vote of the General Assembly in 1951, for aggression against UN forces in Korea. They had committed further aggression in the Formosa Strait, against Tibet and on the border of India. To admit them in the face of such misconduct and to oust the Republic of China, which lived up to the terms of the Charter, would be unthinkable.

• Refusal to seat the Chinese Communists could be said to deny representation to the mainland Chinese, since Peking imposed rule by force and never actively represented the people. The Republic of China, by contrast was still the legal government of all China.

• The reckless policies of the Peking regime might impair the useful work of the United Nations. It would follow that the Chinese Communists would consider their being seated in the United Nations as a complete vindication of their belligerent policies.

CHART OF CHINESE, WORLD HISTORY FROM 2000 B.C.

CHRISTIAN CALENDAR	Outside World	Key Facts	Dynasties	Religion and Thought	Art	Culture	
2000 B.C.	Bronze Age First Dynasty, Babylon-	Emergence from Stone Age	HSIA		Black pottery	Domesticated pig and dog Cultivated millet and wheat Potter's wheel Domesticated ox, goat, sheep, horse	2000 B.C.
1500	Dynasty XVIII, Egypt	Bronze Age		Religion animistic and orgiastic	White incised pottery Bronze ritual vessels and weapons Carved ivory and stone	Script Practice of divination Silk culture Wheeled vehicles Cowry shells	1500
	MOSES	Earliest writing Urban development	SHANG	Recognition of spirit world	Jades	Brush and ink Composite bow Books of bamboo slips	
1000	Iron Age *Rigveda*			Ancestor worship	Turquoise inlay	Wet rice Fowl Water buffalo	1000
	ZOROASTER	Raids cause shift of capital Feudalism	CHOU	*The Odes*		Use of rime	
500	BUDDHA DARIUS ALEXANDER CHANDRAGUPTA ASOKA	Iron Age First law code Canal and wall building		CONFUCIUS MO-TZŬ CHUANG-TZŬ LAO-TZŬ LORD SHANG	Bronze vessels Bronze mirrors Lacquer Jades Palace architecture	Advances in astronomy Traction plow Crossbow Round coins Fighting on horseback Trousers, boots Iron sword	500
		SHIH-HUANG-TI	CH'IN				
		Hsiung-nu raids Expansion under WU-TI	FORMER HAN	Civil examinations SSŬ-MA CH'IEN Canonical research Alchemy	Garden retreats Wall painting Sculpture	Mule, ass, camel introduced Soy bean Football	
A.D.	JESUS	WANG MANG					A.D.
	KANISHKA		LATER HAN	PAN KU PAN CHAO		Paper	
	MARCUS AURELIUS MANI		3 KINGDOMS	Buddhist sūtras translated Taoism Pilgrims to India	Glazed pottery Map of China	Map of China Tea Water mill	
		Buddhism firmly established	TSIN		Calligraphy	Sedan chair	
	ATTILA	South China colonized	WEI / CH'I CHOU / SUNG CH'I LIANG CH'EN	T'AO CH'IEN Chinese nuns	KU K'AI-CHIH Greco-Indian influences in rock temples	Use of coal Kite Firecracker	500
500	MOHAMMED	Grand canal	SUI	Examination system Alien faiths HSÜAN-TSANG	Tomb figurines Painting	Law code Elephant chess Polo game	
	HARUN AL-RASHID	Expansion up to 751 Block printing	T'ANG	HAN YÜ Proscription of Buddhism Printing of all canonical works	Porcelain	Block prints	
		Foot binding	LIAO / 5 Dynasties			Chairs	
1000	WANG AN-SHIH		No. SUNG	Classical renaissance Antiquarianism Judaism	Landscapes Private gardens	Paper money Ships for ocean travel Compass	1000
	Magna Carta The Polos	JENGHIS KHAN	CHIN / So. SUNG	Drama CHU HSI Mathematics Islam Christianity Lamaism	Music Cloisonné	Cotton Gunpowder Sorghum Abacus Distillation of liquor- Chaulmoogra oil	
		Mongols expelled CHENG HO voyages Peking rebuilt	YÜAN	Encyclopaedias Gazetteers WANG SHOU-JEN	Old and new styles in painting Colors on porcelain Under glaze blue and enamel	Spectacles Syphilis Maize and sweet potato	
1500	COLUMBUS Magellan	Portuguese traders Spaniards take P.I. Japanese raids The Manchus	MING	Fiction Jesuit influence Critical scholarship Dictionaries		Peanuts Tobacco and snuff Imposition of queue	1500
		K'ANG-HSI era CH'IEN-LUNG era Mohammedan rebellions Tai-p'ing rebellion SUN YAT-SEN	CH'ING	Libraries Literary inquisition Protestant Christianity Western education	European influences	Mexican dollar Opium smoking Factories Steamships Railroads	
1950	Two World Wars	Japanese invasions Communist control	REPUBLIC	Mass education	Archeology	Motor transport Aviation	1950

Source: A Short History of the Chinese People, by L. Carrington Goodrich, Harper & Brothers, 1951.

Capitals of Republic of China

Nanking	Late 1927 - Nov. 1937
Hankow	Nov. 1937 - Oct. 1938
Chungking	Oct. 1938 - May 5, 1946
Nanking	May 5, 1946 - April 23, 1949
Canton	April 23 - Oct. 15, 1949
Chungking	Oct. 15 - Nov. 30, 1949
Chengtu	Nov. 30 - Dec. 8, 1949
Taipei	Dec. 8, 1949 -

Chronology

Chronology of Events

Before 1945

Revolution of 1911 and Overthrow of Monarchy -- Kuomintang-Communist Collaboration, 1923-27 -- Chiang's Break with Communists, 1927 -- Japanese Takeover of Manchuria, 1931-32 -- Long March and Rise of Mao Tse-tung, 1934-35 -- Japan's Attack on China, 1937 -- Kuomintang-Communist Entente, 1937-39 -- Stilwell's Mission to China, 1942-44 -- Cairo Conference and Declaration, 1943 -- Hurley's Mission to China, 1944-45.

China's Revolution. On Oct. 10, 1911, a mutiny of troops at Wuchang in the Yangtze Valley touched off revolution in China. Four months later, on Feb. 12, 1912, the last representative of the ancient Manchu dynasty, the infant Emperor Hsuan T'ung (later known as Henry Pu Yi), abdicated. The act of abdication specified that Yuan Shih-kai, long a servant of the dynasty, was to organize a republican government at Peiping. To unify the country, Sun Yat-sen, father of the revolution and head of a provisional government at Nanking, yielded the presidency to Yuan. Protracted civil strife, fed by rivalries of China's numerous warlords, prevailed over a large part of the country after Yuan Shih-kai died in 1916. In 1917 Sun Yat-sen established at Canton an independent Republic of South China to assume leadership of the struggle for national unification.

Founding of Parties. In 1912, the Kuomintang, a secret organization started before the revolution by Sun Yat-sen and other radical leaders, was turned into a political party, the first in China. On July 1, 1921, about 50 persons attended the first national congress of the Chinese Communist party in Shanghai. The party had been founded earlier that year by eight men, one of whom was Mao Tse-tung.

Kuomintang-Communist Collaboration. From 1923 until 1927, the Kuomintang accepted the aid and counsel of a Soviet mission invited to China to help the country "achieve unification and attain full national independence." The Kuomintang was reorganized, workers and peasants were mobilized in unions to give the party mass support, and a Kuomintang military force was built up under party control. In 1926 military operations were undertaken against northern warlords to extend the area of Kuomintang control.

Chiang-Communist Break. Dissension among Kuomintang leaders, growing since the death of Sun Yat-sen in 1925, came to a head early in 1927. At the end of March, military forces of Gen. Chiang Kai-shek, leader of the right wing, occupied Shanghai, massacred large numbers of workers, and dissolved trade unions. On April 18, 1927, Chiang set up a new government at Nanking. Left-wingers in control of the established government, then at Hankow, gave way to conservative pressures and made their peace with Chiang in June 1927. The Russians were then sent back to Moscow and Chinese Communists moved underground.

Unification of China. In June 1928, Peiping fell to the armies of Feng Yu-hsiang, the "Christian general." On July 25, 1928, the United States became the first country to recognize the Nanking government as the National Government of the Republic of China. China's unification was completed, at least on the surface, when the Manchurian provinces gave their adherence at the end of 1928.

Communists in the South. After the Kuomintang-Communist split, revolting Communist army commanders, including Mao Tse-tung, led thousands of soldiers into southern China. The Communist armies dominated extensive areas there from 1928 until Chiang Kai-shek, after repeated efforts, finally forced them out in October 1934.

Long March and Mao's Rise. In the famous Long March of 368 days, from October 1934 to October 1935, the escaping Communists made their way over 6,000 miles of often difficult terrain to establish a new center of power in the northwestern province of Shensi. Heavy casualties suffered in the first few months of the march, owing to poor leadership, led in January 1935 not only to Mao's assumption of the leadership of the march but also to his election as chairman of the Central Committee of the Chinese Communist Party.

Japan in Manchuria. On Sept. 18, 1931, Japanese troops stationed in South Manchuria to protect a sphere of interest which Japan had held there since 1905, bombarded the city of Mukden and within three days subjected all of South Manchuria to Japanese control. Military occupation of the remainder of Manchuria was completed on Feb. 5, 1932. Meanwhile, on Jan. 7, 1932, Secretary of State Henry L. Stimson had proclaimed at Washington what became known as the Stimson doctrine of nonrecognition of territorial changes brought about by force.

Puppet State of Manchukuo. On Feb. 18, 1932, Manchuria was declared independent, and on March 1 it became the new state of Manchukuo. On March 9, Henry Pu Yi, last of the Manchu emperors, was inaugurated as provisional dictator. On March 1, 1934, Manchukuo became a monarchy with Pu Yi installed as Emperor Kang Teh.

Tangku Truce. On May 31, 1933, Japanese penetration into North China was halted by conclusion of the Tangku truce, which established a demilitarized area stretching from the Great Wall to within 13 miles of Peiping and from the coast 250 miles inland.

Chiang Kidnapped. In December 1936, Chiang Kai-shek was kidnapped by troops of Marshal Chang Hsueh-liang, former Manchurian warlord whose men, instead of fighting, were fraternizing with the Communists. Chiang was held captive at Sian until an understanding was reached to work for a Kuomintang-Communist entente against the Japanese.

Japanese Attack. On July 7, 1937, a clash of Japanese and Chinese troops at the Marco Polo bridge outside of Peiping led to the opening three weeks later of a full-scale Japanese offensive against China.

Kuomintang-Communist Entente. On Sept. 22, 1937, the entente projected in December 1936 began to take form. On that day, the Central Committee of the Chinese Communist Party issued a manifesto proclaiming abandonment of efforts at insurrection and sovietization in favor of cooperation with the government against Japanese aggression. The following day, Chiang announced that the government would give up attempts at military suppression of communism in favor of seeking a political settlement.

Sinking of USS Panay. On Dec. 12, 1937, Japanese aviators bombed and sank the U.S. gunboat *Panay* which was escorting American tankers in the Yangtze River. Two

Americans were killed and others injured. The crisis passed with Japan's tender of abject apologies.

Government Reforms. In March 1938, an Extraordinary National Congress of the Kuomintang, which included Communist Gen. Chou En-lai among the members of its presidium, established a People's Political Council to advise the government. On April 1, 1938, the National Congress adopted a Program of Armed Resistance and National Reconstruction containing a basic outline of principles to be followed by the wartime entente. The program called for governmental, economic and military reforms.

Kuomintang-Communist Friction. Late in 1938, relations between the Kuomintang and the Communists began to cool. In 1939 the government started to enforce a military blockade of Communist-held areas to prevent Communist infiltration of government-held areas. In January 1941, fighting broke out between government and Communist forces in the Yangtze Valley. Similar clashes followed, but efforts to reach a political settlement continued.

Pearl Harbor. On Dec. 7, 1941, the Japanese attacked Pearl Harbor, and on the following day the United States declared war on Japan.

Stilwell's Mission. On Feb 2, 1942, Lt. Gen. Joseph W. Stilwell was ordered to Chungking as Chief of Staff to Generalissimo Chiang Kai-shek. On Feb. 7, 1942, the U.S. authorized a loan of $500 million to China.

Equal Rights for China. On Jan. 11, 1943, the U.S. and China signed a treaty, ratified May 20, 1943, by which the U.S. relinquished extraterritorial and related rights in China. On Dec. 17, 1943, President Roosevelt approved an act repealing discriminatory legislation affecting immigration of Chinese nationals into the U.S. and the naturalization of Chinese.

Recognition of China as Great Power. On Oct. 30, 1943, upon American insistence, a representative of China joined a conference of the Big Three foreign ministers at Moscow to sign a Declaration of Four Nations on General Security. Acceptance of China as a signatory was interpreted as acknowledgement of China's status as a great power and of its right to participate with the other great powers in prosecuting the war, organizing the peace, and establishing machinery for postwar international cooperation.

Cairo Conference. The Cairo Declaration, issued Dec. 1, 1943, following a conference of President Roosevelt and Prime Minister Churchill with Generalissimo Chiang Kai-shek at Cairo, Nov. 22-26, voiced "their purpose that...all the territories Japan has stolen from the Chinese, such as Manchuria, Formosa, and the Pescadores, shall be restored to the Republic of China." The declaration said also that the three powers were "determined that in due course Korea shall become free and independent."

Wallace's Mission. In late June 1944, Vice President Henry A. Wallace held long discussions with Chiang Kai-shek at Chungking. The Generalissimo insisted to Wallace that he desired a political agreement with the Communists.

Hurley's Mission. On Aug. 18, 1944, Major Gen. Patrick J. Hurley was named President Roosevelt's personal representative to China. Hurley arrived at Chungking on Sept. 6 and on Nov. 30, 1944, was appointed U.S. Ambassador to China. His first job was to seek to improve relations between Chiang and Stilwell, but he found the two so near swords' points that he recommended that Stilwell be recalled. On Oct. 24, Lt. Gen. Albert C. Wedemeyer was designated to replace Stilwell. Hurley's second job was to try to bring about a cessation of hostilities between Chinese Nationalists and Communists. In December 1944, he reported that first steps toward that goal had been taken.

1945

Yalta Decisions on Far East -- Hurley's China Activities -- Death of Roosevelt and Succession of Truman -- End of War in Europe -- China's Rank as Great Power in UN -- Atomic Bombs Dropped -- Russia Enters War in Far East -- End of World War II -- Sino-Soviet Alliance -- Chiang-Mao Agreement -- Nationalist-Communist Hostilities -- Hurley's Resignation and Marshall's Appointment.

Yalta Conference. On Feb. 11, President Roosevelt, Prime Minister Winston Churchill, and Soviet Premier Joseph Stalin signed the Yalta Agreement on surrender terms, and postwar treatment of the Axis nations, on policies toward liberated countries, and on plans for the United Nations. The three had met for a week at the Black Sea resort of Yalta.

Roosevelt had been urged by his military planners to seek a definite commitment for intervention of the Soviet Union in the Pacific war. The President also sought Stalin's agreement to giving China an important place in the UN and allowing her to repossess her lost territories.

The U.S. gained guarantees of Soviet entry into the Pacific war. In effect, Outer Mongolia, strategic ports, islands, and railroads were conceded to the Soviet Union following the defeat of Japan "with the concurrence of Generalissimo Chiang Kai-shek," which Roosevelt agreed to obtain. In return, the Soviet Union agreed "to conclude with the Nationalist government of China a pact of friendship and alliance."

It was further agreed that the Far Eastern aspect of the agreement should remain secret because Russia had a neutrality treaty with Japan, and because information usually leaked from the Nationalists to the Japanese and an immediate announcement might sabotage negotiation of differences between Chinese Nationalists and Communists, which the U.S. Ambassador to China, Major Gen. Patrick J. Hurley, felt were close to success. The Yalta terms were not officially disclosed to Chiang Kai-shek until June 15, 1945.

Discussions in China. On Feb. 14, the Nationalist government announced that it had been negotiating with the Chinese Communists for two weeks with the assistance of Patrick J. Hurley, U.S. Ambassador to China.

New Constitution for China. On March 1, Chiang Kai-shek announced that a national assembly would be convened Nov. 11, 1945, to draw up a constitution. Chiang invited the Chinese Communists to attend and to join the Nationalist government. On March 9, the Communists replied that the national assembly would be a "congress of slaves" and demanded that Chiang be removed from office.

U.S. Arms. On April 2, U.S. Ambassador to China Patrick J. Hurley announced that although the U.S. was sending arms and aid to China, none would go to the Communists. On April 28, Hurley noted that the U.S., the U.S.S.R., and Great Britain agreed that China should be unified, but that "the Chinese must furnish their own leadership, make their own decisions and be responsible for their own policies."

Death of Roosevelt. On April 12, President Roosevelt died at Warm Springs, Ga., and Vice President Harry S. Truman took the oath of office as President at the White House.

Hurley and Stalin. On April 15, U.S. Ambassador to China Patrick J. Hurley concluded a conference with Soviet Premier Stalin and Foreign Minister Molotov in Moscow and reported that Stalin "agreed unqualifiedly to America's policy in China as outlined to him during the conversation." On April 19, W. Averell Harriman, U.S. Ambassador to the Soviet Union, who had participated in the conference, stated that he felt the Hurley report, while factually accurate, gave a "too optimistic impression of Marshal Stalin's reactions." Harriman warned that Stalin eventually "would make full use of and would support the Chinese Communists." Harriman said he was certain that Stalin would not cooperate indefinitely with Chiang Kai-shek.

Chiang's Speech. On May 5, Chiang Kai-shek, addressing the Sixth National Congress of the Kuomintang, called for a new constitution and social reforms, including "land equalization and the control of private capital." On May 19, the National Congress adopted a resolution offered by Chiang to legalize all political parties in addition to the already legal Kuomintang. It also voted to end one-party domination of the army and the schools.

V-E Day. On May 8, 1945, the war ended in Europe. Both the U.S. and the U.S.S.R. shifted their attention to the Far East.

China's Place in UN. On June 26, delegates to the organizing conference of the United Nations at San Francisco signed the UN Charter. The Charter made the Republic of China, along with the U.S., the U.S.S.R., the United Kingdom and France, a permanent member of the Security Council and, as such, entitled to exercise the veto power.

Potsdam Conference. On July 17, President Truman, British Prime Minister Churchill and Soviet Premier Stalin met in Potsdam, Germany, to confer on the fate of the defeated Axis nations and the liberated areas. Concerning the Far East, Stalin asserted that the Chinese did not recognize the "preeminent interests of the Soviet Union" in the Manchurian port of Dairen. President Truman indicated that the main interest of the U.S. was internationalization of that port, with the safeguarding of Soviet interests, as agreed at Yalta. Stalin replied that Dairen would be open to all nations and that he did not wish to "add in any respect to the Yalta agreement or to deceive the Chinese." It was reported later that President Truman was satisfied, but that the U.S. Ambassador to the Soviet Union, W. Averell Harriman, was convinced the U.S. should obtain reaffirmation in writing of Stalin's oral assurances.

Russia Enters War. On Aug. 9, the Soviet Union officially declared war on Japan. On the same day, Soviet troops entered Manchuria.

Atomic Bombs. On Aug. 6, a U.S. B-29 bomber, the *Enola Gay*, dropped an atomic bomb on Hiroshima. On Aug. 9, an atomic bomb was dropped on Nagasaki.

Japan Surrenders. On Aug. 14, Japan surrendered to the U.S., the U.S.S.R., Great Britain and China.

Sino-Soviet Alliance. On Aug. 14, Moscow Radio announced that the Soviet Union and the Republic of China had signed a Treaty of Friendship and Alliance, pledging mutual respect for their respective sovereignities and mutual noninterference in their respective internal affairs for a 30-year period. Chinese Premier T.V. Soong, brother of Mme. Chiang Kai-shek, had headed the Chinese delegation to Moscow.

In separate agreements, the Soviet Union was granted ownership and management with China of the main Manchurian railways and joint use with China of Port Arthur as a naval base. Dairen was declared a free port. The Soviet Union agreed to respect Chinese sovereignty in Manchuria. China agreed to recognize the independence of Outer Mongolia if its people so voted in a plebiscite.

Chiang's Appeal. On Aug. 15, Chiang Kai-shek sent a note to Mao Tse-tung in Yenan (considered the Communist "capital") asking him to come to Chungking, the Nationalist government's wartime capital, to confer on "many international and internal problems." On Aug. 26, Mao accepted the invitation and the next day, the U. S. Ambassador to China, Patrick J. Hurley, flew to Yenan to bring Mao to Chungking. On Aug. 28, Mao and Hurley arrived in Chungking.

Victory Message. On Sept. 3, Chiang Kai-shek, in a victory statement to the Chinese people following the defeat of Japan, pledged that, now that the war had ended, "we shall brook no delay in the inauguration of a constitutional policy" and establish China as "a model democratic state in the Far East." Chiang promised economic and social reforms and the convening of a national assembly in which all parties would participate.

Chinese Troops Occupy Hanoi. On Sept. 11, the Chungking government announced that Chinese troops had occupied Hanoi under the Potsdam agreement that Chinese troops would disarm Japanese and liberate prisoners in northern Indo-China. British troops took over from Japanese in southern Indo-China.

Soviet Withdrawal. On Sept. 29, Russian troops began withdrawing from Manchuria.

Chiang-Mao Agreement. On Oct. 11, Mao Tse-tung returned to Yenan from Chungking after six weeks of discussions with Chiang Kai-shek and U.S. Ambassador Hurley. The two sides were reported in general agreement, except on the government of areas liberated from Japanese control by the Chinese Communists. The two leaders agreed that a Political Consultative Conference should be called, but postponed the date from Nov. 12, 1945, to Jan. 10, 1946. On leaving Chungking, Mao said "there are great difficulties, but they can be overcome." On Oct. 21, the Nationalist government disclosed that Communist troops in east-central China had been withdrawing north of the Yangtze River as had been provided in the agreement.

Outer Mongolia. On Oct. 22, the Soviet Union announced that an Outer Mongolian plebiscite showed overwhelming vote for independence from China.

More Fighting. On Oct. 27, the Nationalist government reported that hostilities between Nationalist and Communist forces were continuing in 11 of China's 28 provinces despite the Oct. 11 agreement between Chiang and Mao. On Oct. 29, the government reported that Chinese Communist forces were massing near the area where U.S. ships were scheduled to land Nationalist troops in Manchuria. The report said the Communists had cut the rail lines between Peiping and Hankow. The Communists rejected demands that they withdraw, and on Oct. 31, 100,000 Red troops attacked Tatung. On Nov. 2, as the Communist attacks continued, U.S. transports landed Nationalist troops at Hulutao in Manchuria.

On Nov. 5, the radio in Yenan, the Communist "capital," and the *New China Daily News*, a Communist paper published in Chungking, charged that U.S. troops sent to China to help disarm the Japanese were aiding the Nationalist forces against the Communists. It was reported the following day that U.S. forces might be withdrawn from China to avoid involvement in the civil war. On Nov. 7, the reports were confirmed by Secretary of State James F. Byrnes in Washington.

On Nov. 8, the Nationalist government announced it had 90 divisions off the coast of Manchuria waiting to be landed from U.S. transports. On the same day, Lt. Gen. Albert C. Wedemeyer conceded that U.S. troops in Shanghai had been involved in skirmishes with the Communists. Fighting continued through the month with the Nationalist forces making gains in Manchuria. There were also repeated reports of skirmishing of U.S. troops with Communist forces.

Sino-Soviet Agreement. On Nov. 27, the Nationalist government reported that the Soviet Union, which still had some troops in Manchuria, had agreed to aid the Nationalists in occupying Manchuria and had ordered the Chinese Communist forces to abandon Mukden and Changchun, large cities in eastern Manchuria.

Resignation of Hurley. On Nov. 27, U.S. Ambassador to China Patrick J. Hurley resigned amid growing criticism in U.S. foreign service circles. It was reported that Hurley believed efforts to "prevent the collapse of the Nationalist government..." had been undermined by career men willing to see the Kuomintang's downfall.

Marshall Appointed. On Nov. 27, President Truman appointed Gen. George C. Marshall as the Special Representative of the President in China, with the personal rank of Ambassador.

Hurley at Press Club. On Nov. 28, Major Gen. Patrick J. Hurley told the National Press Club in Washington that "professional foreign service men" were supporting the Chinese Communists and that "we are permitting ourselves to be sucked into a power bloc on the side of colonial imperialism against Communist imperialism." He added that the "colonial imperialists" were Britain, the Netherlands and France and that the Soviet Union was not supporting the Chinese Communists. On the same day, a number of Members of Congress urged that Hurley's charges be investigated.

Troops in Manchuria. On Nov. 29, the Soviet Union announced it had agreed to a request from the Chinese government to defer withdrawing Soviet troops from Manchuria until Nationalist troops could take over.

Fighting in Shantung. On Nov. 30, it was reported that 200,000 Chinese Communist troops had invaded Shantung Province. On Nov. 28, the Chinese Communists in Yenan had charged that the U.S. "recklessly lines up with all the worst elements in China...to attack the Chinese people."

On Dec. 1, Lt. Gen. Albert C. Wedemeyer said the Chinese government was still receiving U.S. military aid through the lend-lease program.

Byrnes on China. On Dec. 4, Secretary of State James F. Byrnes said in a letter to Rep. Jack Z. Anderson (R Calif.) that "we favor the creation of a strong, united and democratic China" and "feel that collaboration" between the Soviet Union, China, the U.S. and Great Britain is "essential" to peace in the Far East.

Hurley's Testimony. On Dec. 5, Major Gen. Patrick J. Hurley told the Senate Foreign Relations Committee that five career diplomats had attempted to undermine U.S. policy in China. He identified them as George A. Atcheson Jr., John S. Service, John Davies, Fulton Freeman and Arthur Ringwalt.

Truman on China Fighting. On Dec. 15, President Truman called on the Chinese to stop fighting. He urged that a national conference of the major political elements in China be convoked to end the internal strife and unify the country. Truman said each political element should be given a fair voice in the Chinese government.

Marshall in China. On Dec. 22, Gen. George C. Marshall arrived in Chungking and met with the Nationalist Premier, T. V. Soong, and with Gen. Chou En-lai of the Communist faction. On Dec. 27, Chou En-lai proposed a "nationwide and immediate unconditional truce."

Moscow Conference. On Dec. 27, U.S. Secretary of State Byrnes, Soviet Foreign Minister Molotov and British Foreign Minister Bevin announced they had reached a series of agreements after 11 days of discussion in Moscow. Concerning China, the three agreed "as to the need for a democratic and unified China under the National government, and for a cessation of civil strife." Molotov said that withdrawal of Soviet forces from Manchuria "had been postponed until Feb. 1 (1946) at the request of the Chinese government." It was reported that Byrnes and Molotov had decided that both Soviet and American troops would be withdrawn from China "at the earliest practicable moment consistent with the discharge of their obligations and responsibilities."

Truce Proposal. On Dec. 31, the Nationalist government in effect accepted Chou En-lai's Dec. 22 truce proposal and suggested that Gen. George C. Marshall act as mediator between the two sides.

1946

Marshall's Efforts to Mediate Between Nationalists and Communists -- Civil War Truce -- Soviet Removal of Machinery from Manchuria -- Nationalist-Communist Clashes in Manchuria -- Government Returns to Nanking -- Truce in Manchuria -- More Fighting -- New U.S. Ambassador -- Sale of War Surpluses to China -- National Assembly Meets -- End of Nationalist-Communist Negotiations -- Adoption of Constitution.

Marshall Mediation. On Jan. 7, Gen. Chang Chun, Nationalist government representative, and Gen. Chou En-lai, Communist representative, met with Gen. George C. Marshall in Chungking.

Truce in Civil War. On Jan. 10, an agreement for cessation of hostilities in China's civil war was reached. Chiang Kai-shek and Mao Tse-tung both ordered their forces to cease hostilities and halt all troop movements. To enforce the truce, it was agreed to establish an executive headquarters in Peiping manned by one representative each of the Nationalist government, the Communists, and the United States. U.S. participation was to be solely for the purpose of assisting the Chinese members in implementation of the cease-fire.

Political Conference. On Jan. 10, the Political Consultative Conference opened in Chungking with a speech by Chiang Kai-shek pledging recognition of fundamental democratic rights. The delegates, representing almost every faction in the country, agreed on immediate organization of a coalition government. Resolutions were offered to convene a National Assembly on May 5 to adopt a constitution, to recognize the legality of all political parties, and to pledge all parties to accept the national leadership of President Chiang Kai-shek. On Jan 31, the P.C.C. adopted the resolutions. It was announced during the conference that both Communists and Nationalists would reduce their military forces.

Charges and Countercharges. On Feb. 15, the Chinese Communist Party in Yenan (the Red "capital") demanded joint control of Manchuria along with the Nationalist government. The statement noted that the Communists controlled an army of 300,000 in Manchuria. On the following day, the Communists charged that Nationalist troops were engaging in "serious fighting" despite the Jan. 10 cease-fire order. Reports grew that Russian troops were shipping Manchurian industrial equipment to the Soviet Union. On Feb. 17, participants in a rally at Chungking accused Russian troops of "raping, slaughtering and looting" in Manchuria. On Feb. 22, 10,000 students in Chungking demonstrated against the Soviet Union and the Chinese Communists.

Military Unification. On Feb. 25, following reports of heavy fighting between Communists and Nationalists in Manchuria, a military accord was signed in Chungking providing for gradual unification of the opposing armies.

Removal of Machinery. On Feb. 26, reports from Manchuria said the Soviet commander in Mukden conceded that "Japanese" machinery was being taken out of Manchuria. On March 1, the U.S. protested the removal as illegal, and anti-Soviet demonstrations broke out all over China.

Chinese Withdrawing from Indo-China. On Feb. 28, China agreed to withdraw its occupation troops from northern Indo-China by March 31, but only in return for concessions on the railway from Haiphong into China, renunciation of French extraterritorial rights in China, and recognition of a special status for Chinese nationals in Indo-China.

Kuomintang Meeting. On March 1-17, the Kuomintang's Central Executive Committee met in Chungking to consider the resolutions adopted by the Political Consultative Conference on Jan. 31. Although the Committee announced its approval of the resolutions, reports circulated that right-wing elements within the Kuomintang were attempting to "sabotage" the P.C.C. program.

Troops in Manchuria. On March 14, the Nationalist government reported 300,000 Soviet troops, 200,000 Chinese Communist troops, and 120,000 Nationalist troops in Manchuria. On March 23, the Chinese Foreign Minister said the Soviet Union had given notice that the deadline for departure of Russian troops from Manchuria, originally Feb. 1, had been moved back to April 30 because of "technical difficulties."

Marshall Returns Home. On March 15, Gen. George C. Marshall, returning from China, reported to the President. On March 16, Marshall said the situation in Manchuria was "extremely critical."

Reports from Manchuria. On March 30, it was reported in Chungking that Soviet troops were evacuating Manchuria and that Nationalist and Communist forces were moving in. Amid repeated reports of fighting between Nationalists and Communists in Manchuria, Gen. Chou En-lai, head of the Communist delegation at Chungking, urged the U.S. to discontinue military aid to the Nationalist government until a new coalition government had been formed. On April 8, the Communist *Emancipation Daily News* in Yenan charged that Chiang Kai-shek wanted to become the dictator of China.

Battle for Changchun. On April 14, Soviet troops evacuated Changchun, capital of Manchuria, and fighting broke out immediately between Nationalists and Communists for control of the city.

Changchun Falls. On April 17, Communist forces occupied Changchun.

Marshall Back in China. On April 18, Gen. George C. Marshall returned to Chungking from Washington and proposed that field teams be sent to Manchuria to implement the Jan. 10 cease-fire agreements.

National Assembly Postponed. On April 24, President Chiang Kai-shek postponed indefinitely the National Assembly scheduled to meet May 5 to draw up a constitution. The Communists had refused to nominate delegates until Nationalist-Communist differences were settled.

Harbin Falls. On April 25, as Russian troops withdrew, Chinese Communist forces occupied the Manchurian city of Harbin. On April 28, the Chinese occupied Tsitsihar, a railroad center in Manchuria.

Government Returns to Nanking. On May 5, the Nationalist government moved from Chungking back to Nanking. Forced out of Nanking by the approach of Japanese forces in November, 1937, the government had fled to Hankow and then, in October 1938, to Chungking.

Changchun Recaptured. On May 23, Nationalist forces recaptured Changchun, capital of Manchuria.

New Truce Sought. On June 2, Gen. George C. Marshall appealed for a new truce.

Truce Announced. On June 7, a 15-day truce went into effect in Manchuria. Both sides announced that, during the truce, agreement would be sought on a permanent truce and on execution of the Feb. 25 agreement for military reunification.

Truce Extended. On June 21, President Chiang Kai-shek announced that the temporary truce in Manchuria had been extended to June 30 at the request of the Communists.

Mao's Demand. On June 24, Chinese Communist party chairman Mao Tse-tung demanded in Yenan that all U.S. military aid to the "Kuomintang dictatorial government" be halted and U.S. troops withdrawn from China. On June 28, Acting Secretary of State Dean Acheson said in Washington that the U.S. would not meddle in China's internal affairs, but would help rebuild the economy if the Chinese wanted such aid.

Truce Ended. On June 30, the temporary truce ended and on July 8, the Nationalist government announced that its troops had renewed the fighting in Manchuria. On July 16, the Communist representative in Nanking, Gen. Chou En-lai, urged Gen. George C. Marshall to use his influence to renew the truce.

New U.S. Ambassador. On July 11, President Truman appointed Dr. J. Leighton Stuart, President of Yenching University in Peiping, as U.S. Ambassador to China. Stuart succeeded Major Gen. Patrick J. Hurley, who had resigned in 1945.

Mme. Sun Urges U.S. Withdrawal. On July 22, Mme. Sun Yat-sen, widow of former Chinese President Sun Yat-sen and sister of Mme. Chiang Kai-shek, said in Shanghai that the U.S. should withdraw its forces from China and halt aid to the Nationalist government until it became "truly representative." Mme. Sun charged that the Nationalists were guilty of "Fascist activities," and that the Americans were "teaming up" with them to prolong the civil war and incite a conflict with the Soviet Union.

Nationalists Refuse Truce. On July 27, the Nationalist government disclosed that it had rejected an appeal from Communist representative Chou En-lai for an unconditional cease-fire in Manchuria, where the Nationalists launched a new offensive. The Yenan radio announced Aug. 2 that the Communist "capital" had been bombed by Nationalist planes.

U.S. Marines Ambushed. On July 29, a U.S. Marine convoy was ambushed by Communist troops near Peiping. Three Americans were killed and 12 wounded. On Aug. 5, Washington announced it had no intention of withdrawing U.S. forces from China.

Marshall-Stuart Statement. On Aug. 10, U.S. Ambassador J. Leighton Stuart and Gen. George C. Marshall issued a joint statement in Nanking asserting that China was in a serious economic condition and that the fighting threatened to "pass beyond the control of those responsible."

Truman's Letter to Chiang. On the same day, President Truman sent a note to President Chiang Kai-shek stating that the United States might have to redefine its position on China unless there was noticeable progress toward a peaceful settlement of differences with the Communists. Chiang issued a statement three days later blaming the Communists for a breakdown in negotiations and stating his demands for peace.

Sale of War Surpluses to China. On Aug. 31, the U.S. signed an agreement for sale to the Nationalists of surplus U.S. war material in China and the Pacific Islands. The announcement caused the Chinese Communists to denounce the U.S. for attempting to mediate between the two Chinese factions while furnishing one of them with war materials.

Marshall-Chou Meeting. On Sept. 11, Gen. Marshall, after visiting Chiang Kai-shek in his summer palace at Kuling, returned to Nanking and met with Gen. Chou En-lai, the Communist representative there. Chou urged Marshall to negotiate another truce for Manchuria. It was reported that Marshall replied that further discussion would be useless because Chiang was now demanding that the Communists not only stop fighting but also withdraw their forces from strategic areas in Manchuria.

Chou's Accusations. On Sept. 19, Gen. Chou En-lai said he would no longer participate in peace negotiations with the Nationalists. Three days later, he asserted that U.S. mediation was "neither fair nor impartial," and that the U.S. wanted China as a base from which to attack the Soviet Union. Chou also accused the U.S. of violating the Dec. 27, 1945, Moscow agreement on withdrawal of troops from China.

Marshall Memorandum. On Oct. 1, Gen. George C. Marshall in a private memorandum informed President Chiang Kai-shek that he would recommend to President Truman that the U.S. discontinue its efforts at mediation unless "a basis for agreement is found . . . without further delays." On the same day, Communist Gen. Chou En-lai informed Marshall that if the Nationalist government did not halt its offensive against Kalgan, a Communist base in Chahar Province, there would be "a total national split." On Oct. 2, the Nationalist government reported to Marshall that its "maximum concessions" would be to issue a cease-fire order if the Communists began to integrate their forces into the Nationalist Army and appointed their delegates to the National Assembly.

Communists Reject Chiang Offer. On Oct. 8, U.S. Ambassador J. Leighton Stuart and Gen. George C. Marshall announced in Nanking that the Communists had rejected Chiang Kai-shek's offer of a conditional cease-fire.

Kalgan Falls. On Oct. 11, the Communist base of Kalgan in Chahar Province was seized by Nationalist forces.

Cease-Fire Offered and Rejected. On Oct. 16, President Chiang Kai-shek announced an eight-point proposal for a cease-fire, integration of the Communist and Nationalist armies, and immediate opening of truce talks with American mediation. Two days later, the Communists · rejected the proposal and suggested instead a military status quo based on troop dispositions before the Nationalists launched their major offensives. On Oct. 21, however, Communists and Nationalists resumed peace talks in Nanking.

Communists Appeal to UN. On Oct. 24, the Chinese Communists radioed an appeal to the United Nations to halt "American infringement of Chinese territorial integrity and security."

Sino-U.S. Treaty. On Nov. 4, a five-year Sino-American Treaty of Friendship, Commerce and Navigation was signed at Nanking.

Elections in U.S. On Nov. 5, the Republican party won a landslide victory in the off-year Congressional elections, gaining a majority in both houses of the 80th Congress.

Nationalist Cease-Fire. On Nov. 8, Chiang Kai-shek ordered Nationalist troops to cease hostilities at noon, Nov. 11, "except as may be necessary to defend their positions." Chiang again invited the Communists to participate in the National Assembly scheduled to meet Nov. 15.

National Assembly Convenes. On Nov. 15, the National Assembly convened in Nanking with the Communists and a majority of third-party representatives boycotting the session. Chiang Kai-shek called the meeting the beginning of constitutional government for China.

Chou's Statement. On Nov. 16, Gen. Chou En-lai, Communist representative in Nanking, charged that the Kuomintang's action in convening the Assembly as contrary to the resolutions adopted Jan. 30 by the Political Consultative Conference. He said the Communist party would not recognize the Assembly and said the Kuomintang had "slammed" the door to negotiations. On the same day, Chou asked Gen. Marshall for transportation back to the Communist capital of Yenan.

Negotiations Cease. On Nov. 19, 1946, Chou En-lai returned to Yenan aboard a U.S. Army plane. With his departure, all negotiations between Communists and Nationalists, carried on intermittently since January, were terminated. A few Communists were left in Nanking to maintain "liaison" with the Nationalist government and representatives of the U.S. By the end of November, fighting had been resumed and the country was braced for full-scale war. On Dec. 4, the Communists notified Gen. Marshall they would not negotiate until the "illegal" Assembly was dissolved and Nationalist troops were withdrawn to positions they held on Jan. 13.

Marshall's Warning. On Dec. 1, Gen. Marshall met with Chiang Kai-shek and warned that the Communist forces were too strong to defeat militarily. He said negotiations offered the only sensible way to avert the complete collapse of China's economy.

Indo-China. On Dec. 18, violent fighting broke out in Viet Nam as Vietnamese guerrillas began their fight for independence from France. On Dec. 20, Ho Chi Minh, president of the Republic of Viet Nam, fled from Hanoi to avoid capture by French troops. On Dec. 23, French Premier Leon Blum pointed out that France recognized Viet Nam's independence, but only within the French Union.

Communist Warning. On Dec. 18, Communist leader Chou En-lai warned in Yenan that "the back of the Kuomintang military offensive" would be broken in six months and that "within a year there will be sweeping changes effective in China's over-all government and economic structure."

Truman Reaffirms U.S. Policy. On Dec. 18, President Truman reaffirmed American belief in a "united and democratic China." He said he would continue the policy of avoiding involvement in Chinese civil strife while "helping the Chinese people to bring about peace and economic recovery in their country."

Constitution of China Adopted. On Dec. 25, 1946, the National Assembly in Nanking adopted a constitution to go into effect on Christmas Day, 1947. The new constitution included a bill of rights and provided for an over-all National Assembly elected by universal suffrage, a President and Vice President elected by the Assembly and a series of five "Yuans" (government councils or departments): executive, legislative, judicial, examination (to control the civil service), and a control Yuan (to supervise public officials.)

1947

Marshall Reports in Washington -- Mediation Effort Ended -- Continuing Hostilities in China -- U.S. Arms Aid -- Wedemeyer's Fact-Finding Mission and Report -- New U.S. Aid Program -- Elections for National Assembly -- Mao Outlines New Red Offensive -- Soviet Mediation Offer Rejected.

Anti-U.S. Demonstrations. On Jan. 1, about 5,000 students in Shanghai demonstrated to protest the alleged rape of a Chinese girl by a U.S. Marine. On Jan. 3, the demonstrations spread to Nanking where U.S. Ambassador J. Leighton Stuart told the crowd that the matter would be investigated. On Jan. 4, Nationalist Premier T.V. Soong ordered the demonstrations to cease.

Marshall Recalled. On Jan. 6, President Truman announced that Gen. George C. Marshall had been recalled to Washington to report in person on the China situation.

Marshall to State Department. On Jan. 7, President Truman announced nomination of Gen. Marshall as Secretary of State, replacing the ailing James F. Byrnes.

Marshall's Report. On Jan. 8, Gen. Marshall's report on China was made public. Marshall blamed the breakdown in Nationalist-Communist negotiations on the air of suspicion and the extremism in both camps. "The salvation of the situation," he said, "would be the assumption of leadership by the liberals in the government and in the minority parties, and successful action on their part under the leadership of the Generalissimo would lead to unity through good government." Marshall added that although some of the Communists' suspicions of the government were justified, they "do not hesitate at the most drastic measures to gain their ends." On Jan. 14, in Yenan, Communist leader Gen. Chou En-lai said that Marshall's assessment of the Kuomintang was correct, but noted that "he did not point out the fact that Chiang Kai-shek is the leader of this reactionary group."

Ho Chi Minh. On Jan. 17, the United Press reported that President Ho Chi Minh of Viet Nam had declared that his country would fight the French until complete independence was granted.

Rejection of Nationalist Offer. On Jan. 27, the Chinese Communists rejected a Nationalist peace offer and reiterated demands that the "false constitution" be nullified and that the military positions held Jan. 13, 1946, in Manchuria be restored.

U.S. Ends Mediation Effort. On Jan. 29, the U.S. announced termination of its efforts to mediate a settlement in China and immediate withdrawal of its troops. U. S. Ambassador J. Leighton Stuart made formal notification to President Chiang Kai-shek and to Wang Ping-nan, the Communist representative in Nanking. On the following day, Wang declared: "The only way out is to fight."

New Nationalist Offensive. On Feb. 2, the Nationalist government launched a new military offensive involving about 500,000 troops in southern Shantung Province. Communist forces either withdrew or deserted.

Communists Asked to Leave. On Feb. 11, the Nationalist government told the Communist delegation in Nanking that its presence was no longer desired. Deadline for departure was set at March 5.

AP Report. On Feb. 15, the Associated Press reported that President Chiang Kai-shek had said in an interview that the United States was responsible for prolonging the civil war because it was withholding arms shipments and credits from the Nationalist government. The AP said Chiang was convinced that the Communists had to be shattered militarily.

China's Economy. On Feb. 16, Chiang Kai-shek pledged his government to a 10-point program of economic rehabilitation. He blamed the nation's steadily increasing economic woes on the Communists and the "cumulative effect of...eight years of war and one year of destructive peace."

Formosa Uprising. On Feb. 28, a major rebellion broke out on the island of Formosa and was immediately suppressed by the Nationalist government. Over 3,000 Formosans were reportedly slain.

Soong Resigns. On March 1, Premier T. V. Soong resigned and President Chiang Kai-shek took his place (while remaining as President).

Hostilities. On March 1, it was reported that Communist forces had launched a new offensive against Changchun, capital of Manchuria, but on March 4, the Nationalist government's commander there stated that the Reds had been driven back. Reports from Yenan, the Communists' "capital," indicated the city was being evacuated as Nationalist forces approached.

Chou's Charge. On March 8, Communist leader Gen. Chou En-lai stated in Yenan that the Nationalist government's "complete collapse" was being averted only by "the support of the U.S."

Yenan Captured. On March 19, Nationalist forces occupied an already abandoned Yenan, the Communist "capital," and claimed to have routed over 100,000 Red troops. U.S. Ambassador J. Leighton Stuart called the claim a "gross exaggeration" and warned that such military actions only over-extended the Nationalist supply lines and drained the national economy. Stuart noted that withdrawal "in the face of enemy pressure" was a Communist military tactic.

Formosa. On March 22, the Central Executive Committee of the Kuomintang demanded the ouster of the Governor General of Formosa, Chen Yi, and blamed him for the conditions that caused the Feb. 28 rebellion there. On March 31, the United Press reported that Chen Yi had resigned.

Soviet Demand. On April 7, the Soviet news agency, *Tass,* reported that Foreign Minister Molotov had demanded that the U.S. withdraw its forces from China. On April 5, five U.S. Marines were killed and 16 wounded during an attack by Communist troops on a Marine ammunition dump near Tangku.

Reorganization at Nanking. On April 16, a government reorganization was announced at Nanking. Gen. Chang Chun was appointed Premier. Dr. Sun Fo, a leftist and son of the founder of the Chinese Republic, Sun Yat-sen, was elected Vice President. Although a number of representatives of third parties (Communists) were installed in office, the Kuomintang's old guard remained in control of the government.

Anti-war Rioting. On May 16, students began rioting at the University of Nanking. Until the end of June, the government was forced to contend with student demonstrations for an end to the civil war and for government action to improve the lagging economy.

New Formosa Governor. On May 16, Dr. Wei Tao-ming assumed office as the new governor of Formosa and on the same day the island officially became a province of China.

U.S. Arms Aid to China. On June 20, as Communist forces in Manchuria closed in on Changchun, the provincial capital, Vice President Dr. Sun Fo appealed in Nanking for more U.S. aid. On June 27, the State Department announced it had sold $6.5 million worth of ammunition to the Nationalist government at one-tenth the procurement cost. On July 2, Secretary of State George C. Marshall said that arms sales to the Nationalist government did not signify U.S. support of the Nanking regime.

Mao's Arrest Ordered. On June 29, the supreme court in Kiangsu Province ordered the arrest of top Communist leader Mao Tse-tung on charges of establishing an "illegal party" and "an all-out revolt intended to overthrow the government."

Open Rebellion Proclaimed. On July 4, the Nationalist government's State Council proclaimed that the Communists were in open rebellion and demanded that the full resources of the country be used to suppress them.

Marshall's Message. On July 6, Secretary of State George C. Marshall told President Chiang Kai-shek that the U.S. was "perturbed over the economic deterioration resulting from the spread of hostilities." Marshall's message warned that the U.S. could "only assist as conditions develop which give some beneficial results."

Wedemeyer Mission. On July 9, President Truman instructed Lt. Gen. Albert C. Wedemeyer, who had been Chiang Kai-shek's chief of staff from late 1945 till mid-1946, to proceed to China on a fact-finding mission "for the purpose of making an appraisal of the political, economic, psychological, and military situations -- current and projected." The President further instructed Wedemeyer to inform Chinese officials and leaders "...that the United States Government can consider assistance in a program of rehabilitation only if the Chinese government presents satisfactory evidence of effective measures looking towards Chinese recovery and provided further that any aid which may be made available shall be subject to the supervision of representatives of the U.S. Government."

India and Pakistan Freed. On Aug. 15, the Indian subcontinent was partitioned into two independent, self-governing members of the British Commonwealth: India and Pakistan.

Wedemeyer Criticism. On Aug. 24, Lt. Gen. Albert C. Wedemeyer, just before leaving China after a month's stay, strongly criticized the Nationalist government for its corruption and inefficiency and the inadequacy of its military effort. Wedemeyer warned that the government could not defeat communism by force, but only with the enthusiastic support of the Chinese people gained through immediate political and economic reforms. The fate of the Nationalist government, he said, depended on the timeliness and effectiveness of reforms. Chinese reaction to the general's criticism was mostly unfavorable, Premier Chang Chun told an American reporter that "Gen. Wedemeyer paid more attention to people outside the government than in it." On Sept. 2, Chang said the government would not change any of its domestic or foreign policies because of the Wedemeyer statements.

Chiang's Admission of Failure. On Sept. 9, the Fourth Plenary Session of the Kuomintang Central Executive Committee opened in Nanking with an address by President Chiang Kai-shek admitting his "failure" to implement the principles of Sun Yat-sen, but blaming the party for China's unsolved problems and absolving himself of all responsibility. Chiang said the Kuomintang was doomed unless there was reform and admitted that the Communists had proven themselves abler and more devoted than the Nationalists.

Nanking Threatened. On Sept. 18, it was reported that Communist forces were threatening Nanking.

Wedemeyer Report. On Sept. 19, 1947, Lt. Gen. Albert C. Wedemeyer submitted his report to President Truman, but it was not made public until the summer of 1949 because of the general's suggestion that Manchuria be placed by the United Nations under the guardianship of a five-power commission that would include the Soviet Union, or under a UN trusteeship. The President and Secretary Marshall both felt this recommendation would be highly offensive to the Chinese, for it would represent the government as incapable of governing its own territory. The report recommended a five-year program of economic and military aid to China. It stipulated that China accept American advisers to assist "in utilizing U.S. aid in the manner for which it is intended." The report further stipulated that China must carry out economic, political and military reforms.

Elections Postponed. On Sept. 26, the Nationalist government's State Council in Nanking postponed elections for the National Assembly from Oct. 21 to Nov. 21, 1947.

Rail Service Interrupted. On Oct. 11, it was reported that the Nationalist government had been unable to keep open any railroad lines between major points in Manchuria.

U.S. Congressmen Visit China. On Oct. 11, members of the House Military Affairs Committee visited President Chiang Kai-shek in Nanking. The Generalissimo told them that the Chinese Communists were agents of the Soviet Union, taking orders and receiving supplies from Moscow. He said "the predicament in Manchuria was an American responsibility" and repeated a plea for more aid.

Anarchy in Shanghai. On Oct. 15, the Nationalist government announced that Shanghai was in a state of anarchy and that the death penalty would be imposed for law violations, especially hoarding of food.

Communist Land Reform. On Oct. 18, the Chinese Communists announced they had embarked on a new land reform program, abolishing the ownership rights of "all landlords."

Aid Agreement Signed. On Oct. 27, a U.S. aid agreement was signed in Nanking to provide the Chinese with food, supplies and other basic essentials of life.

Democratic League Outlawed. On Oct. 28, a Nationalist government decree outlawed the Democratic League, one of the minor parties, on the ground that it was subservient to the Communists.

New Aid Program. On Nov. 10, Secretary of State George C. Marshall, appearing before a joint session of the Senate Foreign Relations and House Foreign Affairs committees, announced the Administration's intention to seek approval of a new China economic aid program. During hearings on the following days, Marshall tentatively estimated that the amount would be in the area of $300 million over a 15-month period beginning April 1, 1948. The Secretary added that the situation in China was "very decidedly one where we have found the greatest difficulty in trying to calculate a course where money could be appropriated with, as I put it, a 70 percent probability of effective use in the situation." On Nov. 15, Nationalist government leaders called the U.S. aid plan a "drop in the bucket" and urged the U.S. to give them $3 billion over a three-year period.

China Elections. On Nov. 21-23, a three-day popular election by secret ballot, the first in China's history, was held to choose representatives for the National Assembly. The government claimed that 20 million voted and that Kuomintang candidates won most of the seats.

New Constitution. On Dec. 25, the new Constitution, adopted by the National Assembly a year earlier, went into effect.

Mao's Report. On Dec. 25, Chairman Mao Tse-tung reported to the Central Committee of the Chinese Communist party. The report, entitled "Turning Point in China," outlined a new Communist offensive. Mao referred to the Kuomintang members as "reactionary forces" and "running dogs of American imperialism." He confidently predicted the "victory of the revolution" but added that, "owing to the backwardness of China's economy, it will be necessary to permit the existence, for a long period, of the capitalist economy represented by the broad petty bourgeoisie and the middle bourgeoisie."

Soviet Mediation Offer. On Dec. 30, President Chiang Kai-shek's private secretary informed the U.S. Embassy that the Soviet Union had offered to mediate between the Chinese factions, but that the Chinese government "neither desired nor believed possible any accomodation with the Chinese Communists at that time."

1948

Heavy Fighting in Manchuria -- U.S. and British Nationals Warned to Leave North China -- Consideration of China Aid by Congress -- Aid Agreement Signed -- State Department Directives to U.S. Embassy at Nanking -- Red Gains in Manchuria -- Americans Urged to Leave Nanking -- Mme. Chiang Pleads for More Aid.

Red Expectations. On Jan. 14, as extremely heavy fighting was taking place around Mukden and Changchun

in Manchuria, the Chinese Communists announced over their radio that they intended to secure all of Manchuria by the end of the year 1948.

Gandhi Dies. On Jan. 30, Mohandas K. Gandhi, the man whose doctrine of nonviolent resistance through civil disobedience made him the leading crusader for India's freedom, was assassinated in New Delhi.

Warning. On Feb. 15, the U.S. and British governments warned their nationals to leave northern China.

China Aid Program. On Feb. 18, President Truman submitted to Congress a $570 million program of economic aid for China. The sum of $510 million was to finance imports of essential civilian commodities and the remaining $60 million to finance selected industrial and transportation reconstruction projects. The President, in an accompanying message, said that while only the Chinese government could stabilize the nation's economy, the aid program should provide "a respite from rapid economic deterioration." Republican reaction to the proposal was summarized by Sen. Styles Bridges (R N.H.), who criticized it for being too late and for not including military aid.

Marshall on Aid Program. On Feb. 20, Secretary of State George C. Marshall, testifying before the House Foreign Affairs Committee on the China program, said it was needed to keep China from falling to the Communists. Marshall recalled that the U.S. had been giving the Nationalists military aid through sales of military equipment used by U.S. forces in China. *(See Aug. 31, 1946)* He criticized the Chinese government for ignoring American military advice which could have aided the Nationalist forces.

Czech Red Coup. On Feb. 20-25, Czech Communists gained control of the government at Prague, assuring Soviet domination of Czechoslovakia.

Bullitt Testimony. On March 2, William C. Bullitt, ex-Ambassador to the Soviet Union, recommended to the House Foreign Affairs Committee that the U.S. give China $100 million in outright military aid and send "the best man that can be found" to coordinate the war against the Communists.

MacArthur's Cable. On March 3, Gen. Douglas MacArthur cabled from Japan to the House Foreign Affairs Committee his recommendation for military aid to China.

Wedemeyer Testimony. On March 4, Lt. Gen. Albert C. Wedemeyer, author of the September 1947 report on China, urged the House Foreign Affairs Committee to provide military aid for China because "I don't think dollars alone will stop Communism."

Chennault's Testimony. On March 10, Maj. Gen. Claire L. Chennault told the House Foreign Affairs Committee that the U.S. ought to send China $1.5 billion worth of military personnel. Chennault said China was strategically important because it flanked the Soviet Union.

Yenan Recaptured. On March 15, it was reported in Peiping that Yenan, former Communist "capital," had been recaptured by Communist forces.

Action in National Assembly. On March 29, the Chinese National Assembly met in Nanking and on April 19 re-elected Chiang Kai-shek as President, but a strong liberal, Li Tsung-jen, was named Vice President over

Chiang's objections. Election of Li led to speculation that the Nationalist government would finally try to solve China's growing economic problems. However, Li said he was powerless to act because Chiang controlled the party machine, government finances, and the army.

On April 9, Chiang reported to the Assembly that seven Nationalist divisions had been "destroyed" while fighting the Communists in Manchuria. He pledged that replacements would be furnished and that Communist forces operating south of the Yellow River (Central China) would be annihilated within six months. Many of the delegates from Manchuria and North China expressed discontent with the government's conduct of the war in their areas.

China Aid Authorized. On April 2, Congress completed action on the foreign aid authorization bill. Economic aid authorized for China was reduced to $338 million, but $125 million was added to the bill for the Chinese government to use as it saw necessary, which presumably meant for military purposes. The total amount authorized thus was $463 million. On April 3, President Truman signed the foreign aid bill.

Yenan's Recapture Confirmed. On April 22, the Nationalist government confirmed that Yenan had been recaptured by the Communists.

Student Riots. On May 5, a student demonstration in Shanghai began an "anti-hunger and anti-civil war" movement that soon spread to other parts of the country.

Demonstrations Banned. On May 18, the Nationalist government prohibited all demonstrations and strikes. Although the order was largely ineffective, a nationwide strike set for June 2 was averted by resort to repressive measures.

New Chinese Premier. On May 24, President Chiang Kai-shek named Dr. Wong Wen-hao the new Premier, succeeding Dr. Chang Chun. Wong, considered a moderate, on May 31 chose an 18-man cabinet that included six non-Kuomintang members. On June 11, he said it would take at least two years to defeat the Communists.

Berlin. On June 18, the Soviet Union instituted its blockade of Berlin.

Inflation in China. On June 30, the Nationalist government reported that living costs had risen 110 percent during the month of June. One U.S. dollar was worth five million Chinese dollars in Shanghai.

Aid Agreement Signed. On July 3, the U.S. and China signed an aid agreement under which the Nationalist government was to receive $275 million for nonmilitary supplies and $125 million for use at its discretion.

Communists in U.S. On July 31, the House Un-American Activities Committee opened hearings on Communist activity in the U.S. before and since World War II. The hearings led to the investigation of disloyalty charges against Alger Hiss.

China Policy Directives. On Aug. 12, Secretary of State George C. Marshall advised the staff of the American Embassy in Nanking (1) that the U.S. "must not directly or indirectly give any implication of support, encouragement or acceptability of coalition government in China with Communist participation," and (2) that the U.S. had "no intention of again offering its good offices as mediator in China." On the following day, a second policy directive advised the embassy that it was "not likely that the situation will make it possible for us at this juncture to formulate any rigid plans for our future policy in China."

Economic Reforms. On Aug. 19, the Nationalist government announced new economic reforms, temporarily lifting morale in many parts of the country. But the reforms failed to halt rapid deterioration of the economic situation.

Tsinan Falls. On Sept. 24, Tsinan, an industrial and railroad center and capital of Shantung Province, fell to the Communists. Chiang Kai-shek on Oct. 10 called the loss "the greatest disaster."

House Report on China. On Oct. 3, the House Foreign Affairs Subcommittee on World Communism, chaired by Rep. Frances P. Bolton (R Ohio), issued a report calling China the "active theatre" in the cold war. The report said the Communists were using China as a testing ground for tactics they might use to take over the world. The Subcommittee recommended that the U.S. give the Nationalist government a "guarantee of territorial and political integrity."

Changchun Falls. On Oct. 20, the capital of Manchuria, Changchun, fell to the Communists after a bloody three-day battle.

Mukden Falls. On Nov. 1, Mukden, regarded as the key to Manchuria, fell to the Communists. Thereafter, the smaller Manchurian cities and towns went down one after another.

Truman Re-elected. On Nov. 2, President Truman surprised almost all political observers by winning re-election. Democrats not only held on to the White House but also regained control of the House and the Senate. Truman's triumph at the polls dealt a serious blow to President Chiang Kai-shek, who felt that a Republican victory would result in more U.S. aid for China. On Nov. 4, President Truman told Congress that "many difficulties" were involved in making aid to China effective and that Americans had to oversee constantly how funds were expended. The U.S., however, had approved Chinese purchases of arms worth $5 million on Nov. 1.

Americans in China Urged to Leave. On Nov. 5, the U.S. advised Americans in Nanking to leave. On Nov. 17, U.S. consular officials warned Americans of the danger of remaining in any part of China except the far South and Formosa. The U.S. Navy began to evacuate Americans from Shanghai.

New Requests for Aid. On Nov. 18, President Chiang Kai-shek asked President Truman for an immediate increase in material aid. Truman's reply was noncommittal. Experts in Washington were said to believe that it would cost $5 billion to "rescue" the Chinese Nationalists, and then only if it were certain the money would be spent wisely. On Nov. 24, President Truman and Secretary of State George C. Marshall conferred on China. Marshall said later that a large U.S. aid program might involve the U.S. directly in the civil war.

New Premier. On Nov. 26, Dr. Sun Fo, son of Sun Yat-sen, succeeded Dr. Wong Wen-hao as Premier.

Mme. Chiang's Visit. On Dec. 1, Mme. Chiang Kai-shek arrived in Washington to plead personally for $3 billion in aid over a three-year period. The Democratic Administration, since the election no longer under severe pressure from Congress, politely ignored her. The Administration was reported to feel that, because China had received $2.5 billion in aid from the U.S. since the end of World War II, because Chiang had never really paid attention to the advice Secretary Marshall had given him in 1946, and, finally, because the Nationalist armies were not fighting with any degree of enthusiasm, only direct American military involvement would stop the Chinese Communists. On Dec.16, Acting Secretary of State Robert A. Lovett said that the U.S. definitely would not get involved in the Chinese civil war, nor, he said, would U.S. aid be increased if a coalition government were formed.

Chiang Called War Criminal. On Dec. 26, the Chinese Communists announced that 45 Kuomintang leaders, including Chiang and his wife, had been condemned as war criminals and would be punished accordingly when captured.

Chiang's Message. On Dec. 31, President Chiang Kai-shek indicated in a New Year's message that he would step aside if the Chinese Communists were willing to negotiate. His offer was immediately rejected.

1949

U.S. Declines Request to Mediate -- Mao Calls on Nationalists to Surrender -- Chiang Retires and Vice President Li Tsung-jen Becomes Acting President -- Peiping Falls -- Government Moves to Canton -- Red Terms for Peace Rejected -- Nanking Falls -- Shanghai Falls -- U.S. China Policy Review -- U.S. Ambassador Leaves China -- State Department's White Paper -- People's Republic Proclaimed -- Acheson Lists Conditions for Recognition -- Canton and Chungking Fall -- Nationalist Government Moves to Formosa.

Foreign Mediation Asked. On Jan. 8, Chinese Foreign Minister requested the American, British, French, and Soviet governments to mediate a restoration of peace with the Chinese Communists. The request was declined by the U.S. on Jan. 12. On Jan. 5, the Communists had announced over their radio that they would "fight to the finish" rather than negotiate with Chiang or any other "war criminal."

Mao's Demands. On Jan. 14, Communist Party Chairman Mao Tse-tung issued an "eight-point program" calling for surrender of the Nationalist government and punishment of the "war criminals" designated on Dec. 26, 1948.

Chiang Retires. On Jan. 21, President Chiang Kai-shek announced his retirement and left Nanking for Feng-hua, his native province. Vice President Li Tsung-jen became Acting President. On Jan. 16, it was announced that the capital would be moved from Nanking, which was threatened by Communist forces, to Canton. On Jan. 19, the Cabinet, still in Nanking, said the Nationalist government should attempt to arrange an immediate cease-fire with the Communists. On Jan. 28, the Communists said they would talk only if the Nationalists heeded Mao's eight-point program and arrested Chiang Kai-shek and other war criminals.

Peiping Falls. On Jan. 31, Peiping fell to the Communists.

Government Moved. On Feb. 5, the Nationalist Government moved from Nanking to Canton, but acting President Li remained in Nanking; although lacking the full support of Premier Sun Fo in Canton, Li continued to work for a peace agreement.

Negotiations for Peace. On Feb. 24, unofficial representatives of Acting President Li met with Communist leaders Mao Tse-tung and Gen. Chou En-lai north of Peiping. On March 3, Premier Sun Fo, joining the peace effort at Li's insistence, announced that the Nationalists would begin formal peace talks with the Communists soon after March 15. On March 5, the Communist radio called Sun a "war criminal."

U.S. Senate Action. On March 10, 50 Senators -- 25 Republicans and 25 Democrats -- requested that the Senate Foreign Relations Committee take immediate action on a $1.5 billion aid-to-China bill introduced by Sen. Pat McCarran (D Nev.).

Sun Fo Replaced. On March 12, following the resignation of Dr. Sun Fo as Nationalist Premier, Gen. Ho Ying-chin was named to the office. A new cabinet was formed, peace delegates chosen, and proposals made for discussions with the Chinese Communists.

Formosa. On March 15, the Chinese Communists announced that they intended to "liberate" Formosa because the U.S. wanted it as "a springboard for future aggression against China proper."

Communists Agree to Talk. On March 26, the Chinese Communists announced that they would participate in peace talks with the Nationalists. The broadcast said the Communists had already chosen their delegates and selected Peiping as the site of the negotiations.

China Aid Extended. On April 14, Congress authorized the President to use unobligated funds, until Feb. 15, 1950, to aid those areas of China that remained free of Chinese Communist control.

Communist Terms. On April 15, the Chinese Communists informed the Nationalist government of their terms for peace. The terms, amounting to unconditional surrender, paralleled the demands listed in Mao's "eight-point program" of Jan. 14. The government was given five days to accept.

Red Terms Rejected. On April 20, the Nationalist government rejected the peace terms but asked for a cease-fire and negotiations.

Yangtze Crossed. On April 20, at midnight, Communist forces crossed the Yangtze River and began a sweep into southern China. The government's cease-fire proposal was ignored.

Officials Flee. On April 23, the Acting President, the Premier, and other officials fled Nanking for Canton.

Nanking Falls. On April 24, Nanking, already abandoned by Nationalist forces, was occupied by the Communists. On the following day, Communist troops invaded the U.S. Embassy and pulled U.S. Ambassador John Leighton Stuart out of bed for questioning.

Chennault's Plea. On May 3, Gen. Claire L. Chennault told the Senate Armed Services Committee that the

U.S. must defend southern China. On May 4, Secretary of State Dean Acheson (who had become Secretary after George C. Marshall resigned in January because of poor health) said that U.S. policy toward China would not change.

Hankow Falls. On May 17, Hankow fell to the Communists.

Shanghai Falls. On May 25, Shanghai fell to the Communists.

New Premier. On June 3, Nationalist Premier Ho Ying-chin was succeeded by Yen Hsi-shan. It was reported that the government was preparing to move the capital from Canton to Chungking.

Reaction in U.S. Senate. On June 24, 21 Senators (16 Republicans, five Democrats) in a letter to President Truman urged him not to recognize the Chinese Communist regime. Sen. Arthur H. Vandenberg (R Mich.) said in the Senate that U.S. policy toward China had been a "tragic failure." Sen. Tom Connally (D Texas), noting that the U.S. had given the Nationalist government over $2 billion in aid since World War II, asked: "Would you send your own sons to fight in the Chinese civil war?" Meanwhile, the Nationalist government continued to seek large-scale aid from the U.S.

Mao on Communist Alliance. On July 1, in a paper called "On People's Democratic Dictatorship," Chinese Communist party Chairman Mao Tse-tung asserted that China must ally itself with "the Soviet Union, with every new democratic country, and with the proletariat and broad masses in all other countries."

Chiang on Anti-Red Alliance. On July 10, Chiang Kai-shek visited President Quirino of the Philippines. The two said they intended to convoke a conference to discuss formation of an anti-Communist alliance.

U.S. Policy Review. On July 27, Secretary of State Dean Acheson announced that U.S. Far Eastern policy was to be subjected to thorough review by a group headed by Ambassador-at-Large Philip C. Jessup and including several nongovernmental members.

Stuart Leaves China. On Aug. 2, U.S. Ambassador John Leighton Stuart, who had remained in Nanking since the Communists took over late in April, left for the U.S.

White Paper on China. On Aug. 5, the State Department issued a White Paper on U.S. policy toward China, with special reference to the period since 1944. Secretary Acheson, in a letter of transmittal to the President, blamed the Nationalist debacle on the inept leadership of the Kuomintang rather than any insufficiency of American aid. Acheson said "the only alternative open to the United States was full-scale intervention in behalf of a government which had lost the confidence of its own troops and its own people." He asserted that intervention on the scale required to overcome the Communists would have been "resented by the mass of the Chinese people, would have diametrically reversed our historic policy, and would have been condemned by the American people."

Criticism of the White Paper came from all sides. Major Gen. Patrick J. Hurley, U.S. Ambassador to China in 1944-45, called it a "smooth alibi for the pro-Communists in the State Department who had engineered the overthrow of

our ally...and aided in the Communist conquest of China." Walter Lippmann wrote that the White Paper "does not even ask, much less does it answer, the crucial questions." Sens. Styles Bridges (R N.H.), William F. Knowland (R Calif.), Pat McCarran (D Nev.), and Kenneth S. Wherry (R Neb.) termed it "a 1,054-page whitewash of a wishful, do-nothing policy which has succeeded only in placing Asia in danger of Soviet conquest." The most stinging comment came from Mao Tse-tung, who called the White Paper "a bucket of cold water, particularly for those who believe that everything American is good and hope that China will model herself on the United States."

Chiang in Korea. On Aug. 8, Generalissimo Chiang and President Syngman Rhee of South Korea in a joint statement urged President Quirino of the Philippines to summon the anti-Communist conference that was proposed on July 10.

People's Republic Proclaimed. On Sept. 21, 1949, the Chinese People's Political Consultative Conference met in Peiping and proclaimed the People's Republic of China. The conference also adopted the Organic Law of the Central People's Government, ratified Mao Tse-tung's "new democratic" program as "the political foundation of the state," and on Sept. 27 renamed the capital Peking (meaning "northern capital") in place of Peiping (meaning "northern peace"). Three days later, Mao was elected chairman of the new government.

Soviet Atomic Explosion. On Sept. 23, 1949, President Truman announced that "We have evidence that within recent weeks an atomic explosion occurred in the U.S.S.R."

New Government Inaugurated. On Oct. 1, the Central People's Government of China was formally inaugurated. Gen. Chou En-lai was named Premier and Foreign Minister.

Soviet Recognition. On Oct. 2, the Soviet Union recognized the Chinese Communist government and terminated relations with the Nationalist government. In the following days, all other Soviet bloc countries did likewise.

U.S. Position. On Oct. 3, a State Department official said the U.S. would not recognize the Chinese Communist government without first consulting Congress.

Conference on Far East Policy. On Oct. 6, Secretary of State Acheson opened at the State Department a three-day conference on U.S. Far Eastern policy. The conference was attended by 24 leading scholars, academicians, and businessmen. A majority agreed that the U.S. ought to recognize the Chinese Communist government, establish trade relations with Red China, and withdraw recognition from the Nationalist government. Of those who did not concur, Harold E. Stassen was the most prominent. He contended that recognition of Communist China "would be a very sad mistake in our world policy," meaning the U.S. would not only have to withdraw recognition of the Nationalist government, but also "join in an affirmative action to throw the Nationalist government out of the United Nations."

Acheson News Conference. On Oct. 12, Secretary Acheson listed three conditions a new government must meet before receiving U.S. recognition: (1) It must exercise effective control in the country it purports to govern; (2) it must recognize its international obligations; and (3) it must govern with the consent of the people. The Secretary doubted whether Communist China adhered to the standards of international behavior required under the second condition.

Canton to the Reds. On Oct. 15, Canton was occupied by the Communists. The Nationalist capital was moved to Chungking.

Li Flees. On Nov. 20, Acting President Li Tsung-jen flew to Hong Kong. Shortly thereafter, he went on to New York for medical treatment.

Chungking Falls. On Nov. 30, Chungking was occupied by Communist forces. The Nationalist government moved on to Chengtu, but opposition to the Communists in mainland China was fading fast.

Nationalists to Formosa. On Dec. 8, officials of the Nationalist government flew to Formosa, where they set up headquarters the next day. On Dec. 10, Chiang Kai-shek arrived in Formosa.

British Recognize Peking. On Dec. 16, British Foreign Minister Ernest Bevin informed Secretary of State Acheson of a cabinet decision to recognize the Chinese Communist government early in January. The decision was believed to be influenced by the vulnerability of Hong Kong.

Indian Recognition. On Dec. 30, the Indian government announced recognition of the Chinese Communist government.

1950

State Department Writes Off Formosa -- Britain Recognizes Chinese Communist Government -- Acheson on Far East Policy -- Acheson-Vishinsky Exchange -- Dispute Over China's Seat in UN -- Soviet Boycott of Security Council -- McCarthy's Charges on Communists in State Department -- Soviet Treaty with Chinese Communists -- Chiang Resumes Presidency -- Start of Korean War -- UN and U.S. Action -- Seoul Captured -- Chiang Leashed -- Russians Return to UN Security Council -- U.S. Army Expansion -- Wage-Price Control Authority -- Seoul Recaptured -- Truman and MacArthur at Wake Island -- Red Chinese "Volunteers" in Korea -- UN Troops Retreat -- UN Asks Cease-fire Negotiations -- Truman Proclaims National Emergency -- Communist Offensive Against Seoul.

State Department Advisory. On Jan. 3, United Press reporter Earnest Hoberecht revealed that the State Department had notified all its posts that fall of Formosa to the Communists was to be expected and the public should be told that the island meant little to U.S. security.

No Aid for Formosa. On Jan. 5, President Truman announced in Washington that the United States would "not provide military aid or advice to Chinese forces on Formosa." Secretary of State Dean Acheson followed the President, explaining that the Nationalists on Formosa were able to obtain all the required military equipment for themselves. All they needed, Acheson said, was the "will to resist." The Secretary added the President's decision was proof to the world that the U.S. would keep her promises not to meddle in the internal affairs of China.

The announcement shocked both the Nationalists and Republicans. Sen. Robert A. Taft (R Ohio) called it "in-

consistent with what we have agreed to do in stopping the advance of communism in Europe," and Sen. William F. Knowland (R Calif.) said the decision "accelerated the spread of communism in Asia."

Britain Recognizes Peking. On Jan. 6, Great Britain recognized the Chinese Communist government at Peking.

Peking Accepts British Recognition. On Jan. 9, the Chinese Communist Government announced acceptance of British recognition and implied it would not take hostile action against Hong Kong.

Soviet Walkout in UN. On Jan. 10, Soviet delegate Jacob A. Malik walked out of a meeting of the U.N. Security Council when it refused to take immediate action to oust the Nationalist Chinese representative. He returned two days later.

Acheson on Formosa Policy. On Jan. 10, Secretary of State Dean Acheson testified at an executive session of the Senate Foreign Relations Committee. In explaining Formosa policy, Acheson said the first line of U.S. defense in the western Pacific would include Japan, Okinawa, and the Philippines, but not Formosa. He gave no indication that the American Government was considering recognition of Communist China.

Acheson's Press Club Speech. On Jan. 12, just after President Truman had reaffirmed his "hands off Formosa" policy at a news conference, Secretary Acheson addressed the National Press Club in Washington. He asserted that Russia had been "detaching the northern areas of China from China," and that the day would come when the Soviets would have to contend with "the righteous anger and the wrath and the hatred of the Chinese people." He said the United States must avoid "the unenviable position which the Russians have carved out for themselves" and must not divert the attention of the people of Asia from Russian "imperialism" by such "ill-conceived adventures" as occupation of Formosa.

Acheson added that the U.S. could not instill in the new nations of south Asia the "will to fight communism," but would be willing to grant them economic aid and advice if there were a "fighting chance" they could emerge without turning to communism.

Second Soviet Walkout in UN. On Jan. 13, Russian delegate Jacob A. Malik walked out of the Security Council meeting only one day after his return from the first walkout. Malik said Russia would boycott the Council until it ousted the Chinese delegate, who had been serving as the Council's January president. The second walkout followed the Council's rejection of a Soviet resolution for exclusion of the Chinese Nationalists as no longer legally entitled to represent China in the UN.

American Personnel Recalled. On Jan. 14, 1950, the State Department recalled all official personnel from Communist China, following seizure of the U.S. consulate in Peking.

Acheson Press Conference. On Jan. 18, Secretary Acheson said that seizure of the Peking consulate made it obvious that Communist China did not want U.S. recognition.

Nationalist Air Attacks. On Jan. 18, the Nationalists announced that their planes had destroyed 2,000 Communist landing craft assembled around the Luichow Peninsula for an attack on Nationalist-occupied Hainan Island, across the Gulf of Tonkin from Viet Nam.

Chou Arrives in Moscow. On Jan. 19, Chinese Communist Premier and Foreign Minister Chou En-lai arrived in Moscow to participate in treaty talks with the Russians.

Vishinsky Answers Acheson. On Jan. 21, Soviet Foreign Minister Andrei Y. Vishinsky denounced Secretary Acheson's charge that Russia had been grabbing northern Chinese territory as "false and crudely slanderous." The Soviet Foreign Minister insisted that the two countries based their relations on a "stable foundation of respect for the independence and the territorial integrity of both states." He said that "normal people cannot doubt the fact that Manchuria, Inner Mongolia, and Sinkiang continue to be a part of China, being of its organic whole." Vishinsky accused Acheson of lying to cover up "the failure of his own policy in China."

State Department Answers Vishinsky. On Jan. 25, the State Department published a detailed statement in support of American charges that the U.S.S.R. was dominating areas of northern China, including Outer Mongolia, Manchuria, Inner Mongolia, and Sinkiang. The statement concluded: "How long this process of penetration and detachment will take will depend on the Soviet timetable -- and of course on any resistance that may arise in China. The strategic points such as communication and industry appear already well under U.S.S.R. control."

Tibet's Appeal. On Jan. 31, the Tibetan radio broadcast an appeal for aid against invasion by the Communist Chinese.

UN China Dispute. On Feb. 3, the Nationalist Chinese delegate in the UN told a Security Council committee that he would veto a resolution to recognize the right of the Communist regime to represent China in the organization. On Feb. 8, the committee decided that the General Assembly would have to solve the problem of Chinese representation.

McCarthy's First Charge. On Feb. 11, Sen. Joseph R. McCarthy (R Wis.) charged in Wheeling, W. Va., that 57 Communists were working in the State Department. The Department denied the charges two days later.

Sino-Soviet Treaty. On Feb. 14, the Soviet Union and Communist China announced signing of a 30-year Treaty of Friendship, Alliance, and Mutual Assistance, and conclusion of two subsidiary agreements -- one promising eventual return to China of Soviet-held properties in Manchuria and the other extending to China a $300 million loan for industrial equipment.

The two governments declared Russia's 1945 treaty with Nationalist China null and void, promised mutual assistance in case of "the resumption of aggression on the part of Japan or any other state that may collaborate in any way with Japan in acts of aggression," pledged both to work for peace under the UN, guaranteed the "independent status" of the Mongolian People's Republic, and made provisions for the restoration of Port Arthur, Darien, and the Chinese Changchun Railway to full Chinese control.

Foreign Ministers Vishinsky of the U.S.S.R. and Chou En-lai of China signed the pacts after nine weeks of ne-gotiation in Moscow. Following the signing, Chou claimed the two countries were welded into a force of 700 million people "which it is impossible to defeat."

Acheson's Comment. On Feb. 15, Secretary Acheson commented that he felt the Sino-Soviet Treaty was detrimental to China since the U.S.S.R. would attempt to use it to convert China into a Soviet satellite. On the same day, the *New York Times* reported that secret sections of the treaty gave Russia the right to supply "advisers" to the Chinese Communist army and Chinese Communist Party organization and bound China to supply several hundred thousand Chinese workers for Russian projects in Siberia.

Chiang's Promise. On Feb. 19, in a New Year's (Chinese) message scattered by leaflet over mainland coastal cities, Chiang Kai-shek promised that the Nationalists would soon launch a mass offensive on the mainland, execute Mao Tse-tung and try Stalin as a war criminal.

McCarthy's Second Charge. On Feb. 20, Sen. Joseph R. McCarthy (R Wis.) renewed his charge that there were 57 Communists in the State Department. He added that the loyalties of 81 employees were "questionable" and that some were being protected by superiors. Two days later the Senate voted unanimously for an investigation by the Foreign Relations Committee.

Chiang Reclaims Presidency. On March 1, Chiang Kai-shek announced he was reclaiming the Presidency of China from Gen. Li Tsung-jen, who had been in New York for medical treatment since December 1949. Li called Chiang a "dictator" and said he would return to Formosa and overthrow him. Li had lunch with President Truman the next day.

UN Representation Debate. On March 8, 1950, UN Secretary-General Trygve Lie implied in a memorandum to all the delegations that the Communists should be permitted to take China's seat at the UN. Lie said UN policy should be to deal with whatever government exercises "effective authority" in a country and was "habitually obeyed by the bulk of its population." Secretary Acheson replied that the U.S. would not vote to seat the Communists while it recognized the Nationalists, but would also refrain from using the veto and accept the majority decision of the UN. Acheson's statement was severely criticized in Congress.

McCarthy Lists Reds. On March 8, Sen. McCarthy (R Wis.) accused Ambassador-at-Large Philip C. Jessup of having "an unusual affinity for Communist causes." He said also that Secretary of State Dean Acheson's wife was a sponsor of the Washington branch of the Women Shoppers, which, he asserted, was a Communist front. McCarthy later added eight more names to his list of alleged security risks, including those of Prof. Owen J. Lattimore of Johns Hopkins University, and John Stewart Service, a veteran U.S. career diplomat, both of whom had advised the State Department in formulation of Far Eastern policies.

Nationalist Raids. On March 10, dispatches from Hong Kong reported widespread damage from Nationalist bombing of Canton and Shanghai.

Acheson Speech. On March 15, Secretary Acheson warned the Chinese they were headed for "grave trouble" if they followed their leaders in "aggressive or subversive adventures beyond their own borders." Speaking in San

Francisco, he said the U.S. led "the real democratic revolution that has been going on all over the world since long before Communism as a world conspiracy had been thought of."

Famine in China. On the same day, the Communists reported by radio that as many as 16 million people faced immediate starvation in China.

Another McCarthy Charge. On March 23, Sen. McCarthy charged that Russia's "top espionage agent in America" was a consultant on Far Eastern affairs in the State Department and had access to secret files. Sen. Millard E. Tydings (D Md.), chairman of the Foreign Relations subcommittee studying McCarthy's charges, said the man in question had performed menial tasks for the Department five years before and only for four months. McCarthy said this was "completely untrue." Three days later, it was disclosed that the man McCarthy had in mind was Prof. Owen Lattimore of Johns Hopkins University, who called the charges "moonshine" and "a hallucination."

Chiang Appeals for Aid to Famine Victims. On March 28, Chiang Kai-shek appealed from Formosa for world aid to famine victims in China. He said the Nationalists would drop the food by plane.

Truman Denounces McCarthy. On March 30, President Truman denounced McCarthy, Sen. Styles Bridges (R N.H.), and Sen. Kenneth S. Wherry (R Neb.) as saboteurs of American foreign policy and said they were the Kremlin's greatest asset in the Cold War. McCarthy answered in a Senate speech that he had "proof" that Lattimore had been a member of the Communist party for years.

Lattimore Defies McCarthy. On April 6, Prof. Owen Lattimore confronted McCarthy before the Senate Foreign Relations subcommittee. To McCarthy's charge that Lattimore was the architect of the country's policy of abandoning China to the Communists, Lattimore replied: "I wish I had more influence. If I had, I think the Communists would not now control China." Lattimore called McCarthy a "base and contemptible liar" said he was "either a fool or an enemy of his country." He dared the Senator to accuse him off the Senate floor of being a Communist or a Soviet spy. McCarthy answered that he would not repeat his charges without Congressional immunity unless the Government gave him Lattimore's loyalty files. Two weeks earlier, the Senator had said he would quit when the day came that he was afraid to repeat outside the Senate any charges he had made in the chamber.

McCarthy Charges Tempered. On April 8, Sen. McCarthy, in New Jersey to accept the 1950 Americanism award of the Marine Corps League, said Lattimore, Jessup, and Service had followed the Communist line in the Far Eastern policies they had advocated, but he avoided calling Lattimore a spy.

Charge Filed in UN. On April 10, the Chinese Nationalist delegate filed a charge with the UN Secretariat that Russia was furnishing men and planes for the Chinese Communist air force and urged action on his request for UN observation of the Chinese civil war.

Famine Reported Again. On April 15, Peking reported that famine had affected 40 million people in China since 1949 and that seven million were in "a most serious plight."

Russia Answers Nationalist Charge. On April 18, the Soviet Union called "slanderous" the Nationalist charge that Russians were serving in the Chinese air force.

Budenz Testifies. On April 20, Louis F. Budenz, former managing editor of the *Daily Worker*, testified before the Senate Foreign Relations subcommittee that he had heard Owen Lattimore described by high Communist Party leaders as a concealed member of the party. Budenz denied Sen. McCarthy's description of Lattimore as the "top Soviet agent in America," but said that Lattimore had been in a Communist cell in the Institute of Pacific Relations and was instructed to spread the Communist line regarding China through publications.

Lattimore's counsel immediately countered with testimony from Brig. Gen. Elliott R. Thorpe, a retired counter-intelligence officer in the Far East, who said that Lattimore had been completely cleared by three separate military investigations. An affidavit was then issued from a former Communist, Dr. Bella V. Dodd, who said she had never heard Lattimore's name mentioned as a member or a friend while she was on the national committee of the party from 1944 until 1948.

McCarthy Attacks Gen. Marshall. On April 20, before the American Society of Newspaper Editors in Washington, Sen. McCarthy said Gen. George C. Marshall was "completely unfitted" to be the Secretary of State during the China crisis, and therefore had to follow advice from people like Lattimore.

Acheson Attacks McCarthy. On April 22, Secretary of State Acheson called the McCarthy attacks "mad" and "vicious."

Hainan Evacuated. On April 23, Chiang Kai-shek ordered evacuation of the 125,000 Nationalist troops on Hainan Island. Hoihow, capital of Hainan, was occupied by Communist troops the same day.

Truman Speech. On April 24, President Truman, addressing the Federal Bar Association, said the internal security of the U.S. was not threatened by Communists. He denounced those who called others Communists without proof and smeared the character of people who disagreed with their views.

Hanson Accused. On April 27, Sen. McCarthy said that Budenz, in a closed session of the Senate Foreign Relations Subcommittee, had named another State Department official, Haldore Hanson, as an active member of the Communist party. This accusation was denied by Sen. Brien McMahon (D Conn.), another member of the Subcommittee investigating McCarthy's charges. McMahon said that the Subcommittee had unanimously authorized him to report that McCarthy's statement was not accurate. Sen. McCarthy replied that he might have misquoted Budenz, who said that Hanson was not "now" a member of the party, but McCarthy insisted that Hanson "was a Communist and was doing the work of the Communists."

Hearings Continue. On May 2, Lattimore returned to the witness stand before the Foreign Relations subcommittee and denounced McCarthy and Budenz. He said McCarthy "debased" Senate procedures, "has lied, distorted and vilified," and "has disgraced his party and the people of his state and nation." Lattimore called Budenz a "paid informer and unscrupulous finger man" whose motive was money.

Truman Opens Files. On May 4, President Truman agreed to allow the Subcommittee to examine the State Department's loyalty files on 81 of the persons Sen. McCarthy had named.

Nationalists Appeal. On May 5, the Chinese Nationalist Parliament voted to appeal for U.S. military aid "before it is too late." Chiang Kai-shek said the U.S. should give the Nationalists as much aid as the Russians were giving the Chinese Communists, in order to prevent Communist invasion of Formosa or Southeast Asia.

McCarthy Denounces Truman. On May 6, Sen. McCarthy, speaking in Chicago, termed the President's decision to release the State Department's files as "a phony offer of phony files." The next day, in Wisconsin, he said one file had been "thoroughly raped" and material from it removed. Sen. Millard E. Tydings (D Md.), chairman of the Foreign Relations subcommittee studying McCarthy's charges, replied that the files were "complete." He said that if McCarthy could prove that anyone tampered with them, "we will put whoever is responsible in jail."

Report of Peking-Ho Chi Minh Agreement. On May 8, the *New York Times* reported that French intelligence had information that Communist China had a secret military aid agreement with Ho Chi Minh, leader of the Indo-Chinese (Viet Minh) rebels.

Truman Discusses Famine. On May 9, in a speech in Wyoming, President Truman accused the Soviets of being "heartlessly indifferent" toward China's worst famine in a century. He said the U.S. would attempt to get relief to stricken areas in China through private American agencies. The President asserted that the Chinese Communists had "sent to the Soviet Union food which is desperately needed by the Chinese people."

McCarthy Speech. On May 15, Sen. McCarthy demanded in Atlantic City that President Truman fire Secretary of State Dean Acheson and Ambassador-at-Large Philip C. Jessup, whom he called "Pied Pipers of the Politburo." The next week, the State Department issued a list of seven "factual inaccuracies" in McCarthy's speech, and contended that he had "utterly failed to prove there is a single Communist" in the Department.

Declaration of Conscience. On June 1, seven Republican Senators, led by Sen. Margaret Chase Smith (R Maine), issued a "Declaration of Conscience" denouncing McCarthy's tactics as "selfish political exploitation of fear, bigotry, ignorance, and intolerance." In a Senate speech, Sen. Smith criticized "character assassinations," "trial by accusation," and "political smears," without mentioning McCarthy by name. The other signers were: Sens. Aiken (Vt.), Hendrickson (N.J.), Ives (N.Y.), Morse (then R Ore.), Thye (Minn.) and Tobey (N.H.).

McCarthy Accuses Three More. On June 6, Sen. McCarthy said the State Department still employed in "high positions" at least three persons listed by the FBI three years ago as Communist agents. The Department answered that the new charges are "absolutely false" and that the FBI list to which McCarthy referred was a preliminary working document prepared by a State Department security officer. The Department insisted that "no persons" on the list were "now employed...except those whose loyalty has been thoroughly checked."

UN Chinese Issue. On June 6, UN Secretary-General Trygve Lie disclosed that he had asked the Big Four Powers (U.S., Russia, Britain, and France) to end their deadlock over Chinese representation in the UN. It was generally understood that Lie wanted the Western powers to admit Communist China and let Peking occupy China's permanent seat in the Security Council.

Acheson Answers. The following day, Secretary Acheson told a news conference that the U.S. would not be "coerced" by Soviet walkouts into admitting Communist China to the UN. He said the U.S. did not favor transfer of Chinese representation to the Communists but would not use the veto to block the transfer if a majority of the Security Council so voted.

Bradley Testimony. On June 9, Gen. Omar N. Bradley, chairman of the Joint Chiefs of Staff, told a Senate Appropriations subcommittee that U.S. armed forces were not in shape to fight a major war and would not be for a year; however, they were being built up to the point where they could repel an enemy attack.

Korean War. Early in the morning of June 25, 1950, North Korea launched a surprise invasion of South Korea. About 75,000 North Korean troops poured across the 38th Parallel, attacking at six main points along the border and making two amphibious landings on South Korea's east coast. The North Korean radio immediately began broadcasting statements that the attack was "defensive" and that the South Koreans had attempted to invade the North.

UN Acts. That afternoon, the UN Security Council adopted a resolution calling for an immediate cease-fire in Korea and withdrawal of the northern invaders. The resolution also called on member nations "to render every assistance to the UN in the execution of this resolution." The latter section provided a basis for extension of American air and sea support to South Korea. The resolution was adopted 9-0 with Yugoslavia abstaining. A probable Soviet veto was avoided because of the continued Russian boycott of the Security Council over the Chinese representation question. Two days later, Russia and North Korea asserted that the cease-fire resolution was invalid because neither the Soviet Union nor Communist China attended the session at which it was adopted.

Truman Orders Military Action. On June 27, President Truman announced that he had ordered U.S. air and naval forces in the Far East to go to the aid of South Korea; had ordered the Seventh Fleet to prevent any attack on Formosa; and had ordered a speedup of military assistance to French forces in Indo-China and a strengthening of U.S. forces in the Philippines.

UN Sanctions. Late that evening, the UN Security Council adopted a resolution urging UN members to give South Korea the assistance "necessary to repel the armed attack," thus in effect endorsing action already taken by President Truman.

Senate Hearings Suspended. On June 28, the Senate Subcommittee investigating Sen. McCarthy's charges against the State Department voted to call off its hearings "for the time being." McCarthy called the inquiry "a disgrace to the Senate and an insult to the intelligence of the country." Subcommittee Chairman Millard E. Tydings said that all of McCarthy's accusations had been disproved.

Korea Conflict Took Three Years and 150,000 U.S. Casualties

"LIBERATED" from Japan in 1945 only to become a hostage to the Cold War, Korea remained divided at the 38th parallel, its two halves occupied by American and Russian troops until 1948 when Communist refusal to accept UN-supervised elections led to establishment of rival regimes -- the Soviet-sponsored People's Republic (North) and the U.S.-backed Republic of (South) Korea. Having withdrawn all troops in 1949 -- in line with a policy of disengagement -- the U.S. was unprepared for involvement in the war that began with a massive attack on South Korea by North Koreans June 24, 1950 (U.S. time) and lasted three years at a cost of more than 150,000 American casualties. The war spanned three distinct phases.

Phase I. Minus the Soviet delegate (on boycott since January 1950) the UN Security Council June 25, 1950 called for a cease fire and withdrawal of North Koreans. Mr. Truman, advised by Gen. MacArthur in Tokyo that "complete collapse" of ROK forces was imminent, ordered him June 26 to furnish air and naval support and to place the 7th Fleet in Formosa Strait to discourage Chinese Communist-Nationalist hostilities. Next day the Security Council effectively endorsed Truman's initiative, calling on UN members to "furnish such assistance as may be necessary to repel the armed attack and to restore international peace." Asked by MacArthur June 30 to authorize use of American ground forces, Truman promptly agreed and the U.S. became fully committed to repelling the aggressor. One week later MacArthur was designated UN Supreme Commander.

Paced by Soviet tanks, North Korean forces led by Premier Kim Il Sung quickly captured Seoul, the capital of President Syngman Rhee's ROK regime, whose demoralized troops scattered before the rapidly advancing enemy. By the end of July, however, two U.S. divisions from Japan had stopped the advance at a perimeter surrounding Pusan, southeastern port city, where buildup of U.S. troops and supplies proceeded. MacArthur then won approval of Joint Chiefs of Staff for amphibious assault on Inchon, port of Seoul, executed successfully Sept. 15, 1950. While the Xth Corps retook Seoul, the 8th Army broke out of the Pusan perimeter and by the end of September North Koreans were in flight across the 38th parallel.

Authorized by JCS to move north of the parallel to attain "destruction" of North Korean forces -- but forbidden to cross into Manchuria or send planes north of the border -- MacArthur sent American and ROK troops into North Korea, moving up to the Yalu River by the end of October. Despite evidence of a buildup of Chinese forces on both sides of the border, MacArthur ordered a final offensive to start Nov. 25, 1950, announcing that if successful "this should for all practical purposes end the war."

Phase II. The 8th Army offensive immediately buckled under the weight of an estimated 200,000 Chinese "volunteers" massed yet undetected in North Korea, and MacArthur proclaimed the onset of an "entirely new war." With U.S. and ROK forces in full retreat and suffering heavy casualties, MacArthur urged Washington to carry the war to the Chinese mainland, through the use of strategic bombing and

Nationalist forces on Formosa. Having from the outset been determined to confine the issue to Korea, and now concerned lest World War III break out in the Far East, President Truman and his advisers rejected MacArthur's proposals and ordered him to regroup his forces and hold as much of Korea as possible. Under the field command of Gen. Matthew B. Ridgway, U.S. and ROK forces pulled back to the Han River south of Seoul early in January, then began a counter-attack that retook Seoul in mid-March and recrossed the 38th parallel April 3, 1951.

Reflecting the see-saw situation in Korea, the UN had swung from a limited objective at the outset to the restoration of a united and democratic Korea (approved by the General Assembly Oct. 7, 1950 as victory loomed) back to the limited objective of a cease fire and the status quo ante (resolved Dec. 14 as UN forces retreated). On Feb. 1, 1951, the General Assembly condemned Communist China as an aggressor but restated its limited objective. As Ridgway's forces again approached the 38th parallel in March, President Truman was readying an offer to negotiate a settlement when MacArthur issued his own call for Chinese surrender. On April 11, 1951, the President fired MacArthur, naming Ridgway to his place. (See p. 269)

Phase III. --After turning back a new offensive begun April 22, UN forces were holding positions along a line just north of the 38th parallel when, on June 23, 1951, Soviet Deputy Foreign Minister Jacob Malik proposed a cease fire and armistice along the parallel. Truce talks began July 10 and continued for two years, during which heavy but limited engagements were fought with neither side mounting the forces needed for a decisive breakthrough.

By the time President Eisenhower took office Jan. 20, 1953 -- having redeemed a campaign promise by flying to Korea after his election -- the only remaining issue concerned repatriation of prisoners, with the U.S. refusing to turn over North Koreans and Chinese unwilling to return. On March 5 Soviet Premier Joseph Stalin died; three weeks later, the Chinese agreed to the screening of prisoners by a neutral commission, and the talks moved ahead rapidly to the signing of an armistice agreement July 26.

Repatriation was completed Sept. 6, the UN turning over 76,000 prisoners and the Communists about 13,000. Many American prisoners had died from mistreatment; others had been "brainwashed" by their captors and used to buttress Communist charges that the U.S. had engaged in "germ warfare." When political talks that began Oct. 26 showed the Communists prepared to stall indefinitely, U.S. envoy Arthur H. Dean walked out Dec. 12, 1953, and no further agreement was reached. Faced with evidence that North Korea was violating the truce terms in numerous respects, the UN Command announced its decision in mid-1957 "to restore the relative balance of military strength" by modernizing South Korean equipment, beginning with the delivery of F-100 jet fighters. At the end of 1964, Korea was still split into two hostile camps.

Seoul Captured. On June 28, Seoul, capital of South Korea, fell to advancing North Korean troops.

Nationalists Stop Fighting. On June 28, the Chinese Nationalist government ordered its forces to cease attacks on the Chinese mainland in compliance with a request by President Truman when he ordered the Seventh Fleet to defend Formosa from attack. Announcing, June 27, that he had asked Formosa to call off raids on the mainland, Truman said that "The Seventh Fleet will see that this (later dubbed the 'leashing' of Chiang Kai-shek) is done."

President Authorizes Use of U.S. Troops. On June 30, President Truman authorized Gen. MacArthur to send supporting ground forces from Japan to Korea. Truman also ordered the Navy to blockade the entire Korean coast and authorized the Air Force to bomb North Korea.

Troops Land. Hours after the President's announcement, 1,000 American troops landed in South Korea from Japan under heavy air cover.

Marines Ordered. On July 3, Marine ground and air units were ordered to Korea.

UN Action. On July 7, the UN Security Council voted to appoint Gen. MacArthur as UN commander in Korea.

Truman Authorizes Draft. On July 7, President Truman authorized the armed forces to use the draft if necessary to build up their strength. Three days later, the Army put in a call for 20,000 draftees.

Stalin Offers Deal on Korea. On July 15, Premier Stalin said in a note to Indian Prime Minister Nehru that if the Communists were given China's seat on the Security Council, Russia would be willing to return to the Council and help negotiate peace in Korea.

Report Denounces McCarthy. On July 17, the three Democratic members of the Senate Foreign Relations subcommittee that investigated McCarthy's charges reported that there were no Communists in the State Department and denounced the Senator as a "liar." Their report called McCarthy's campaign "a fraud and a hoax perpetrated on the Senate of the United States and the American people... perhaps the most nefarious campaign of half-truths and untruth in the history of this republic." McCarthy answered that the report was "a green light to the Red 5th column in the U.S. ...a signal to the traitors, Communists and fellow travelers in our government that they need have no fear of exposure from this Administration." The full Foreign Relations Committee voted to end the inquiry for good the next day.

$10 Billion Request. On July 19, President Truman requested $10 billion from Congress for a huge rearmament program for the Korean War.

Russians Return to UN. On Aug. 1, the Soviet delegate, Jacob A. Malik, returned to the Security Council, ending the six and one-half month Russian boycott without explanation or condition. The same day, the Council voted to override an order by Malik, as president of the Council for August, that Communist China take the Chinese seat in that body.

Aid to Viet Minh. On Aug. 12, the Viet Nam government in Saigon announced that the Chinese Communists had initiated a large-scale program of military aid to Ho Chi Minh's Indo-Chinese rebels.

North Korean Capital Moved. On Aug. 15, the North Korean government was moved from Pyongyang to Seoul, in South Korea. The North Korean army had pushed Gen. MacArthur's UN forces to a small perimeter around the southern seaport city of Pusan, where supplies and men streamed in from Japan, the U.S., Britain, Australia, Canada, the Netherlands, and Turkey.

Republican Charges. On Aug. 16, Sen. Kenneth S. Wherry (R Neb.), GOP floor leader, charged that "the blood of our boys in Korea is on (Secretary of State Dean) Acheson's shoulders and no one else." The following day, the President called Wherry's attack "a contemptible statement and beneath comment." The Republican members of the Senate Foreign Relations Committee had charged, earlier in the week, that "the major troubles of the world today" were caused by the "failure and refusal" of Presidents Roosevelt and Truman to recognize the true aims of the Russians. They accused the Administration of "subtle betrayals of China" and of a Far Eastern policy which "consistently temporized with and capitulated to the ruthless demands" of the Communists, and resulted in giving the Kremlin "a green light to grab whatever it could in China, Formosa, and Korea."

Communist Chinese Demands. On Aug. 24, the Communist Chinese demanded that the UN Security Council order U.S. "armed invading forces" to withdraw from Formosa. The demands referred to the 7th Fleet. Chinese Foreign Minister Chou En-lai said Communist China was "determined to liberate" Formosa and all other Nationalist territories from "the tentacles of the U.S. aggressors."

Chinese Forces. On Aug. 25, U.S. Army spokesmen said that two Chinese Communist armies were massed on the Korean-Manchurian border and that 120 Russian tanks had been shipped from Manchuria to North Korea. Three days later, the Nationalist Chinese government asserted that four Chinese Communist armies had been in North Korea for a month.

U.S. Denies Aggression. On Aug. 25, U.S. Ambassador to the United Nations Warren R. Austin denied that the U.S. was engaging in acts of aggression in Formosa.

MacArthur Statement on Formosa. On Aug. 26, MacArthur urged that Formosa be turned into a U.S. defense stronghold.

Truman Orders Withdrawal of Statement. On Aug. 28, President Truman directed that the General's statement be withdrawn to "avoid confusion as to the U.S. position on Formosa." The President was criticized by Senate Republicans for "gagging" MacArthur.

Acheson News Conference. On Aug. 30, Secretary Acheson said the U.S. was doing everything possible to convince Communist China that there were no American designs on Formosa or any other Chinese territory. Acheson said the Chinese would have no justification for entering the Korean War.

Malik Steps Down. On Aug. 31, Soviet delegate Jacob A. Malik's month as president of the UN Security Council ended. During August he was successful in blocking debate on the Korean War.

Truman Announces Military Expansion. On Sept. 1, President Truman announced over nationwide radio and television that he planned to double the strength of U.S. armed forces "to close to three million" men.

Russia Uses Veto. On Sept. 6, Russia vetoed a UN Security Council resolution to condemn North Korea for "continued defiance of the UN." The Council then voted 8-1 against a Soviet resolution to demand that all "foreign troops" leave Korea.

Defense Production Act Approved. On Sept. 8, President Truman signed the Defense Production Act of 1950. The Act gave the President authority to impose wage, price and rationing controls, to assign priorities on war materials, and to regulate consumer credit. Hoarding of food or other materials was made subject to heavy penalties.

Landing at Inchon. On Sept. 15, a large UN amphibious force landed at Inchon, 18 miles from South Korea's capital of Seoul and 150 miles north of the battlefront. At the same time, MacArthur's forces near Pusan, at the bottom of the peninsula, launched a major offensive. The North Koreans soon found themselves cut off from supplies and communications with the North and their military position disintegrating. The North Korean government already had complained to the UN that U.S. planes had completely wiped out all heavy industry and most medium and light industry, condemning Koreans to "unemployment, destitution, and famine."

MacArthur's Report. On Sept. 18, Gen. MacArthur reported to the UN Security Council that Russia "has provided and is now providing" a large amount of arms aid to the North Koreans. Russia denied the charge.

Red China Barred Again. On Sept. 19, the Chinese Communists were barred from taking China's seat in the UN General Assembly. An Indian motion to seat the Communists lost 33-16 with 10 abstentions. A Russian motion to oust the Nationalist Chinese lost 38-10 with 8 abstentions.

Seoul Recaptured. On Sept. 26, Gen. MacArthur announced that Seoul had been recaptured, three months to the day after the first Communist forces had entered the city.

Chou's Threat. On Oct. 1, Chinese Foreign Minister Chou En-lai warned that his government would not stand aside if "the imperialists wantonly invaded the territory of North Korea."

UN Decision. On Oct. 7, the UN General Assembly adopted a resolution calling for "all appropriate steps" to "ensure conditions of stability throughout Korea." Gen. MacArthur was authorized by implication to do whatever he deemed necessary about invading North Korea. The General immediately ordered invasion.

Truman and MacArthur Meet. On Oct. 15, President Truman and Gen. MacArthur met on Wake Island to discuss the Korean situation and U.S. policy throughout the Far East. Truman said later that he and MacArthur were in "complete unanimity" and that MacArthur was "one of America's great soldier-statesmen."

Pyongyang Falls. On Oct. 19, Pyongyang, capital of North Korea, fell to U.S. and South Korean forces. One week later, South Korean troops reached the Manchurian border.

Chinese Communists Accept Invitation. On Oct. 24, the Chinese Communists accepted an invitation to attend a UN Security Council discussion of alleged U.S. aggression in Formosa. (*See below, Nov. 28.*)

Chinese Troops Enter War. In the last days of October, American and South Korean troops were badly defeated at the center of the battlefront when they encountered Chinese and North Korean forces, tanks, and sophisticated Soviet rocket weaponry.

Tibet Invaded. On Oct. 25, Peking announced that Chinese Communist forces had been ordered to invade Tibet.

Use of "Volunteers" Admitted. On Nov. 1, a North Korean broadcast said China had decided to let "volunteers" fight in defense of Yalu River power plants that served Manchurian industry.

MacArthur's Report. On Nov. 6, Gen. MacArthur reported to the Security Council that "UN forces are meeting a new foe...are presently in contact with Chinese Communist military units deployed for action against the forces of the United (UN) Command." The General said that a "new war" had begun with the Chinese intervention.

Council Invites Communists. On Nov. 8, the UN Security Council voted to invite the Chinese Communist government to be represented at discussions of MacArthur's report. The U.S. suggested that the Council "summon" the Chinese, rather than "invite" them, but the latter word was used. Efforts had been made a day earlier, by a committee of the UN Korean Commission, to convince the Chinese that the UN did not intend to overrun their electrical installations on the Korean border.

GOP Demands New Investigations. On Nov. 9, Sen. Bourke B. Hickenlooper (R Iowa) demanded a new Senate investigation of the McCarthy charges of Communist infiltration of the State Department and another probe of the Administration's enforcement of the Internal Security Act. In the following days, he was supported by other Republican Senators, including Sen. Homer Ferguson (R Mich.), Sen.-elect Everett M. Dirksen (R Ill.), and Sen.-elect John Marshall Butler (R Md.). Butler had defeated Sen. Millard E. Tydings, chairman of the subcommittee that investigated the McCarthy charges. The demands for a new investigation were made in the wake of Republican gains in the off-year elections. Although the GOP was still in a slight minority in both houses of Congress, the Republican-Dixiecrat coalition often controlled legislative decisions.

Peking Answers Invitation. On Nov. 11, Peking refused the UN invitation of Nov. 8 to discuss Gen. MacArthur's report.

Red China Message to UN. On Nov. 15, the Chinese Communists sent a message to the UN through the Soviet delegation asserting that the "sincere desire of the Chinese to assist the Koreans against U.S. aggression is absolutely natural, just, magnanimous, and lawful."

Acheson's Statement. On the same day, Secretary of State Acheson told reporters that the U.S. was ignorant of Chinese motives and that an effort should be made to determine whether a sincere but needless fear caused the Chinese to intervene in Korea. Acheson hinted that he would welcome direct talks with the Chinese Communists, but warned that deliberate precipitation of a war by China would be "a tragedy of the most colossal nature" and would be met by firm UN action.

UN Offensive Launched. On Nov. 24, UN forces launched an offensive on the western front that met little resistance.

Chinese Open Drive. On Nov. 26, the Chinese Communists opened an enormous counter-offensive that shattered the center of the UN line.

Communist China at UN. On Nov. 28, Red China, carrying out its Oct. 24 acceptance of an invitation to attend a UN Security Council debate on alleged U.S. aggression, told the Council that it should penalize the U.S. for "armed aggression" against China, Formosa, and Korea. The spokesman for a 9-man delegation said China would "liberate" Formosa and aid the Communists in Indo-China, the Philippines, and Japan. "The Chinese people have arisen," he concluded.

Acheson Speech. On Nov. 30, Secretary Acheson warned Peking that it faced its "hour of decision." He said no one "can guarantee that war will not come.... Whether reason will prevail is only partly for us to decide. We must hope and strive for the best while we prepare for the worst."

Truman Statement. On Dec. 1, President Truman contended that the Chinese "are being forced into battle against our troops," and that UN forces "are in Korea to put down an aggression that threatens not only the whole fabric of the United Nations, but all human hopes of peace and justice."

Russian Vetoes. The same day, the Soviet Union vetoed a Security Council resolution requesting the Chinese Communists to withdraw their troops from Korea on assurance that China's legitimate interests would be protected.

Reds Regain Pyongyang. On Dec. 4, the Communists reoccupied the North Korean capital of Pyongyang after it had been abandoned by UN forces retreating to the 38th Parallel. Americans trapped in the northeast began fighting their way to the sea.

Truman-Attlee Conference Ends. On Dec. 8, a five-day Washington conference of President Truman and British Prime Minister Clement R. Attlee ended with a joint statement that there would be "no appeasement" of Red China over Korea. Both leaders agreed to abide by UN decisions, although they disagreed on whether China should be admitted to the UN. Following the Truman-Attlee talks, leading Republicans let up on criticism of Administration Far Eastern policy and called for national unity to meet the crisis. Gov. Thomas E. Dewey (R N.Y.), titular head of the GOP, said Dec. 8: "We can survive if we mobilize America's enormous potential strength and achieve a united front at home and with enough other free nations."

UN Asks for Cease-Fire. On Dec. 14, the UN General Assembly adopted a resolution asking Red China to negotiate with the UN for a cease-fire in Korea. A three-man UN committee was created to seek a truce.

Cease-Fire Plea Rejected. On Dec. 16, the head of the Red Chinese delegation which had appeared before the UN Security Council, Nov. 28, said the Communists would not stop fighting in Korea until all their demands were met.

President Proclaims National Emergency. On the same day, President Truman proclaimed "the existence of a national emergency" as a result of Korean setbacks. He warned the American people on a nationwide broadcast that

"our homes, our nation, all the things we believe in, are in great danger." The President also announced creation of a new Office of Defense Mobilization.

Red Chinese Delegation Departs. On Dec. 19, Red China's visiting delegation at the UN departed for Peking.

Offensive Begins. On Dec. 31, the Chinese Communists and North Koreans began an offensive against Seoul with a heavy artillery barrage.

1951

Seoul Falls to Reds Again -- UN Truce Appeal -- UN General Assembly Labels Red China an Aggressor -- Seoul Recaptured -- MacArthur Hints UN Attack on China and Suggests Negotiations -- State Department Reprimand -- MacArthur Letter to Martin -- Truman Dismisses MacArthur -- MacArthur Hearings in Senate -- Soviet Initiative on Korean Truce -- Ridgway's Truce Proposals -- Truce Talks Begin -- Talks Shifted to Panmunjom -- Provisional Agreement and Lull in Fighting -- Provisional Agreement Lapses but Negotiations Continue.

Seoul Falls Again. On Jan. 4, Seoul fell to the Communists for the second time. UN forces abandoned the city in the face of impossible odds.

Taft's Views. On Jan. 5, Sen. Robert A. Taft (R Ohio) said in the Senate that President Truman violated the Constitution by sending troops to Korea without obtaining approval from Congress. Two days later, he suggested that the United States pull out of Korea and establish a new defense line based on Formosa and Japan. On Jan. 9, Taft offered to join President Truman in formulating a coalition foreign policy. He urged that the U.S. let Chiang Kai-shek's Nationalist troops launch an immediate attack on Red China.

New UN Truce Appeal. On Jan. 13, the UN General Assembly's Political Committee appealed for acceptance of a new cease-fire and truce plan to stop the Korean War and establish peace in the Far East. On Jan. 17, Communist China rejected the appeal and said it would not talk peace until UN troops left Korea and U.S. forces gave up protecting Formosa.

House and Senate Resolutions. On Jan. 19, the House adopted, by almost unanimous voice vote, a resolution asking that the UN immediately declare Communist China an aggressor in Korea. Four days later, the Senate adopted a similar resolution by a vote of 91-0.

UN Resolution on Red China. On Jan. 20, U.S. Ambassador to the UN Warren R. Austin, appearing before the UN Political Committee, introduced a resolution to declare Communist China guilty of aggression in Korea and demand withdrawal of its forces from that country. The U.S. could not find a co-sponsor for the resolution even though it had many supporters. India led an opposition Arab-Asian bloc of 12 nations which contended that the UN should attempt to negotiate with China rather than risk spreading the war beyond Korea. The Indian delegate, Sir Benegal N. Rau, told the Committee that the resolution would follow a "disastrous course" and would "isolate China even more than at present." He said that economic sanctions would harm the Chinese people far more than their leaders and added that the Communists might have acted in Korea because of "suspicious Chinese nationalism and not of aggressive communism."

Modified Chinese Position. On Jan. 22, India delivered at the UN a new communication from the Chinese which modified their earlier rejection of a cease-fire in Korea. The Communists offered to agree to a cease-fire as soon as a seven-nation Far Eastern peace conference went into session. The note added that "definite affirmation of the legitimate status of the People's Republic of China in the UN must be insured." In Washington, the State Department said the U.S. would be "stupid" to accept the new Chinese terms since they carried no guarantees on troop withdrawal or truce inspection. On Jan. 24, Indian Prime Minister Nehru said he was "convinced" the Chinese Communists were "eager to have negotiations." The same day, Ambassador Austin said the Chinese must be shown "you can't shoot your way into the UN." He insisted on condemnation of the Communists and "immediate" study of possible ways to punish them for aggression.

Last Warning. On Jan. 29, India told the UN Political Committee that the Communist Chinese had warned they would not talk peace if the UN branded them as aggressors.

Red China Labeled an Aggressor. The next day, the U.S. resolution cleared the Political Committee by a vote of 44-7 with eight abstentions. On Feb. 1, the General Assembly itself adopted the resolution by the same vote. The resolution condemned Communist China as an aggressor against Korea and the UN but left open a door for peace talks through a standing UN good offices committee.

Chinese Reaction. On Feb. 3, the Chinese Communists declared that adoption of the resolution "blocked the path to a peaceful settlement" and was "...an insult to the Chinese people."

Stalin Statement. On Feb. 16, Soviet Premier Stalin warned: "If Britain and the U.S. reject finally the proposals made by the People's Government of China, the war in Korea can only end in a defeat of the interventionists." He called the UN resolution a "shameful decision," said the UN was being turned into an instrument of war, and asserted that it should have condemned the U.S., which "appropriated" Formosa and "invaded" Korea.

Offensive Thwarted. On Feb. 18, the Chinese Communists abandoned an attempt to break through the UN front in central Korea. UN forces launched a counter-offensive, which led eventually to the recapture of Seoul and drove most Communist forces back across the 38th Parallel.

MacArthur Warning. On March 7, Gen. MacArthur warned that the Korean War "cannot fail" to become a "theoretical military stalemate" if the UN does not use more men and allow attacks on the enemy's Manchurian sanctuary. He said the Communists were building a new offensive for the spring and advised UN members to resolve "obscurities which now becloud" UN objectives in Korea.

Seoul Recaptured. On March 14, Seoul was reoccupied by UN troops. It was the fourth time the capital had changed hands since the outbreak of hostilities. One week later, UN forces occupied Chunchon, a highway and rail center eight miles south of the 38th Parallel. Its capture again raised the question of whether UN forces should cross the parallel.

MacArthur Statement. On March 24, Gen. Douglas MacArthur implied that the UN might soon decide to attack Red China proper. He also suggested that the enemy commander-in-chief meet him in the field for truce negotiations.

Reaction in Washington. The same day, the State Department said the political issues "which General MacArthur has stated are beyond his responsibility as a field commander, are being dealt with in the UN and by intergovernmental consultations." On March 26, the State Department received assurances from the Defense Department that MacArthur would be told to clear any future statements having political overtones. The following day, Defense Secretary George C. Marshall vetoed a full-scale invasion of North Korea by UN forces.

MacArthur's Warning. On April 2, Gen. MacArthur warned of an impending Communist offensive by over 500,000 troops. On April 5, in a letter read to the House of Representatives by Minority Leader Joseph W. Martin Jr. (R Mass.), MacArthur urged use of Chinese Nationalists to open a second front against the Communists on the mainland.

Ho Chi Minh's Orders. On April 7, Indo-Chinese rebel leader Ho Chi Minh broadcast orders to his forces to abandon conventional tactics against the French and resume guerrilla raids. "We are to begin a new war of attrition," he said. The French attributed the orders to recent Viet Minh military setbacks. French military officers said Indo-China was safe for the remainder of the year, unless there was Chinese "intervention."

MacArthur Dismissed. On April 11, 1951, General of the Army Douglas MacArthur, 71, was dismissed by President Truman from all his commands in the Far East and replaced by Lt. Gen. Matthew B. Ridgway, 56, who had commanded the U.S. Eighth Army in Korea for three months. The White House charged that MacArthur had repeatedly violated orders not to make public statements demanding expansion of the war against Communist China. It was revealed later that the letter from MacArthur to House Minority Leader Martin had been the deciding factor in the President's decision.

GOP Reaction. On the day of the President's announcement, Republicans in Congress met, phoned MacArthur in Tokyo and got his consent to appear before a joint session of Congress, and then delivered an onslaught of protest against the President. House Minority Leader Martin said some GOP conferees had talked of "impeachments." Sen. Joseph R. McCarthy (R Wis.) said the dismissal was "perhaps the greatest victory the Communists have ever won." Sen. William E. Jenner (R Ind.) said "Our only choice is to impeach President Truman," and Sen. William F. Knowland (R Calif.) warned of a Far Eastern "Munich." A few Republicans, including Sens. Henry Cabot Lodge (Mass.), Leverett Saltonstall (Mass.), and Wayne Morse (then-R Ore.), and most Democrats backed the President.

President's Rebuttal. On the night of April 11, the President addressed the nation by television and radio. He said he had to dismiss MacArthur because the general could not agree with the policy of continuing the "difficult and bitter task" of repelling the Communists in Korea without letting the "limited war" become "a general war." The President predicted the Communist forces would launch a spring offensive, but said he was "confident" it would fail.

MacArthur's Return. On April 19, Gen. MacArthur addressed a joint session of Congress following a hero's welcome back to the U.S. MacArthur asserted that the Joint Chiefs of Staff had shared his military views on Korea. He said the Korean War must not be stalemated, that Manchuria should be bombed and Red China blockaded. He also favored equipping the Nationalists on Formosa for an invasion of the Chinese mainland. His conclusion -- "Old soldiers never die, they just fade away" -- brought thunderous applause from the Congress and galleries. The next day, the General, his wife and son, were given the largest official welcome in New York City's history.

New Red Offensive Launched. On April 22, the Chinese Communists and North Koreans launched their expected spring offensive and pushed UN forces south of the 38th Parallel. UN commanders said their forces would retreat in good order and inflict heavy casualties on the massive Communist forces, while avoiding heavy UN casualties. A Communist air offensive in support of the ground attack never materialized, and U.S. planes continued to bomb supply lines and troop concentrations.

MacArthur Hearings Announced. On April 24, Democratic leaders announced that the Senate Foreign Relations Committee and the Senate Armed Services Committee would open joint hearings May 3 on Gen. MacArthur's dismissal and U.S. Far Eastern policy.

Red Offensive Thwarted. On May 1, the Chinese Communist forces abandoned their attempt to recapture Seoul in the first phase of their spring offensive.

Reports on Korea and Wake Island Made Public. On May 1, the Senate Armed Services Committee released the Korean section of Gen. Albert C. Wedemeyer's report on China, which had been· submitted to the President in September, 1947. (The remainder of the report, on U.S. involvement in the Chinese civil war, was included in the China White Paper published in August, 1949.) The report predicted invasion of South Korea by a Soviet-trained and Soviet-dominated North Korean army, and listed general recommendations on what the U.S. should do in South Korea. On May 2, a summary of the Wake Island conference of President Truman and Gen. MacArthur in mid-October 1950 was made public by the Senate Foreign Relations and Armed Services committees. The report implied that the President had been misled by Gen. MacArthur on the possibility of Chinese intervention in Korea. It said MacArthur had told the President that China could not move more than 60,000 men across the Yalu River from Manchuria and that the UN air force could "slaughter" that number before they reached Pyongyang, the North Korean capital. From New York, MacArthur denied the validity of the report.

MacArthur's Testimony. On May 3, MacArthur told a joint session of the Senate Foreign Relations and Armed Services committees that the U.S. should serve an ultimatum on Red China to participate in truce talks or its "actions in Korea would be regarded as a declaration of war against the nations engaged there and those nations would take such steps as they felt necessary to bring the

thing to a conclusion." MacArthur added that if Peking defied the ultimatum, the U.S. should use air power to block delivery of Russian supplies to China, institute a naval blockade of Chinese ports, and equip Nationalist Chinese forces for an attack on the mainland. The General doubted that the Soviet Union would intervene. MacArthur said the Joint Chiefs of Staff had recommended to the Defense Department Jan. 12, 1951, that air operations over Manchuria be authorized, that the Chinese Nationalists be given "logistical" support, and that a naval blockade be instituted. He said he did not question "in the slightest" the right of President Truman to recall him, but the manner in which it was done "jeopardized" the national interest because it removed him too abruptly from the middle of vital and immediate operations. He said the reasons for the dismissal were "invalid," for "I have carried out every directive I have ever received."

Marshall's Testimony. On May 7, Defense Secretary George C. Marshall, another five-star general, told the two committees that the Chinese Communists could not be as easily defeated as MacArthur had indicated, and that extension of the hostilities to China would risk "all-out war with the Soviet Union...at the expense of losing our allies and wrecking the coalition of free peoples throughout the world." Marshall admitted that MacArthur had never disobeyed straight military orders, but he said the "cumulation" of MacArthur's public statements challenging Washington's policies so disturbed allied relations that he had to be dismissed. The abruptness of the General's recall, Marshall said, was due in part to a "leak" of the impending ouster.

Communist Retreat. By May 10, Chinese and North Korean troops had retreated almost to the 38th Parallel, where they regrouped for another attack.

Bradley Testimony. On May 15, the Chairman of the Joint Chiefs of Staff, Gen. Omar N. Bradley, began six days of testimony before the two Senate committees. He said that to expand the war beyond Korea "would probably delight the Kremlin more than anything else we could do." MacArthur's plans, Bradley said, would put the U.S. "in the wrong war, at the wrong time, and with the wrong enemy." He added that MacArthur should have resigned if he wanted to disagree publicly with the Administration.

Another Red Offensive. On May 16, the Chinese Communist and North Korean troops launched their second spring offensive with more "human sea" attacks, pushing UN forces farther south of the 38th Parallel. But within a week, enormous casualties forced the Reds again to retreat across the 38th Parallel. The U.S. estimate of Communist casualties for one day alone was 10,000.

Joint Chiefs on MacArthur. Following Gen. Bradley, the other Joint Chiefs testified before the committees investigating Gen. MacArthur's dismissal. They generally agreed with Bradley that MacArthur erred in advocating extension of the war to China.

Tibet Occupied. On May 27, Radio Peking announced the "peaceful liberation" of Tibet by Communist China. Tibet was said to have agreed to become a virtual province of China.

Acheson's Testimony. On June 1, Secretary of State Dean Acheson testified before the committees that Mac-

Arthur's program for air and sea attacks on China might break up the world anti-Communist alliance if carried out by the U.S. alone, and probably would not bring victory in the Korean War. Reviewing history, the Secretary said the Soviet Union was in a position to take much more in Manchuria than the rights it was promised at the 1945 Yalta Conference, and that Chiang Kai-shek approved the deal for getting Russia into the Pacific war. He said the Chinese Nationalist regime was responsible for its own defeat, and pointed out that it had been given $2 billion worth of U.S. aid during the civil war. Acheson added that MacArthur in 1945 had recommended bringing Chinese Nationalists and Communists together, which the General later denied in a letter to Sen. Knowland (R Calif.). When Sens. Morse (then-R Ore.) and McMahon (D Conn.) demanded an investigation of the activities of pro-Chinese Nationalists in the U.S. -- the so-called "China lobby" -- Acheson promised the full cooperation of the Administration.

Reaction to Acheson's Testimony. The Secretary's testimony before the committees brought new demands that he resign. Sen. Robert A. Taft (R Ohio) said Acheson's policies would result in "turn(ing) over both Korea and Formosa to the Communists." Sen. Styles Bridges (R N.H.) said the Administration's Korean policy was limited to "the immoral course of kill, kill, kill and hope somebody will be willing to negotiate."

Marshall Visits Front. On June 8, Secretary of Defense George C. Marshall visited the Korean front and reported later that he could not "conceive of the Korean War going on for years," but that the Chinese Communists had "the problem of 'face,' the importance of which is hard for us to understand." Although Marshall said his trip dealt with military problems, the South Koreans were afraid it foreshadowed a truce along the 38th Parallel, which they would consider "humiliating." South Korean President Syngman Rhee said "The Yalu River is our objective."

Staging Area Overrun. On June 13, UN forces completed occupation of the "Iron Triangle," a Communist staging area in central North Korea.

Wedemeyer's Testimony. On June 11-13, Lt. Gen. Albert C. Wedemeyer, U.S. China theatre commander, 1944-46, was the first witness since MacArthur himself to uphold the dismissed general's views before the Senate committees. The Korean War, he said, was a "bottomless pit" for UN forces. The U.S. should either "go it alone" and step up the attack on Communist China, or withdraw from Korea and harass the Communists by sea and air. Wedemeyer said the West should stop letting Russia tie up its forces wherever it saw fit; it should seize the initiative in the world struggle.

The committees heard from five other witnesses, all of whom were critical of some phases of the Administration's Far East policy. They were former Defense Secretary Louis Johnson; Vice Admiral Oscar C. Badger, former U.S. naval commander in the Far East; Maj. Gen. Patrick J. Hurley (Ret.), a former ambassador to Nationalist China; Maj. Gen. Emmett O'Donnell, former commander of U.S. strategic bomber forces in the Far East; and Maj. Gen. David C. Barr, one-time chief of a military mission to China and a division commander in Korea.

Truce Plea. On June 23, Jacob A. Malik, Soviet delegate to the UN, said Russia would like to see negotia-

tion of a cease-fire in Korea based on the 38th Parallel. The State Department immediately answered that "adequate means for discussing an end to the conflict are available." Malik later stated that political and territorial questions should not be taken up in truce negotiations but considered later. Secretary Acheson said the U.S. would be satisfied if the Communists withdrew behind the 38th Parallel and gave satisfactory guarantees against a renewal of aggression. President Truman said he was hopeful but cautious.

Senate Committees' Warning. On June 27, the Senate Armed Services and Foreign Relations committees unanimously warned in a preliminary statement that "those who threaten us" should not "mistake the temper of our people" because of any "discord and disagreement" produced by the hearings. Misunderstanding America's attitude might lead aggressors to "plunge the world into war...(and) they could never win," the committees said.

Bid for Cease-Fire Parley. On June 30, Gen. Matthew B. Ridgway, commander of UN forces in Korea, broadcast the first specific proposal for a military cease-fire conference. He said: "I am informed you may wish a meeting to discuss an armistice providing for the cessation of hostilities and all acts of armed force in Korea, with adequate guarantees for the maintenance of such armistice. Upon receipt of word from you that such a meeting is desired, I shall be prepared to name my representative (and) suggest a date at which he could meet with your representative. I propose that such a meeting could take place aboard a Danish hospital ship in Wonsan harbor."

Communist Answer. On July 1, the Communists answered that the meeting should be held in the area of Kaesong on the 38th Parallel. Two days later, Gen. Ridgway accepted the offer.

Truce Talks Begin. On July 10, military truce negotiations began in Kaesong between five-man delegations of the UN and North Korean-Chinese Communist commands. The chief negotiators were Vice Adm. Charles Turner Joy, 56, U.S. Navy commander in the Far East, and Lt. Gen. Nam Il, 38, chief of staff of the North Korean Army. Negotiations were delayed when the Communists barred UN war correspondents from the Kaesong area. Adm. Joy refused to negotiate without their presence and talks were interrupted for three days. Finally the Kaesong area was neutralized, and newsmen from both sides mingled around the conference house but were not allowed inside. The second delay concerned Communist demands that the UN withdraw from Korea. The U.S. claimed this was a political issue and did not belong on the agenda of military armistice talks.

Agenda Agreement. On July 26, the negotiators agreed on an agenda, with this order of business: (1) a military demarcation line and the establishment of a demilitarized zone; (2) the composition, organization, and functions of an organization to supervise the implementation of the truce; (3) exchange of prisoners; and (4) recommendations to the governments of the countries concerned on both sides. The negotiations then centered on the first point. The Communists wanted the line on the 38th Parallel, while the UN insisted on the existing battle lines, north of the parallel. A subcommittee was formed to work out a proposal.

New McCarthy Charge. On Aug. 9, Sen. Joseph R. McCarthy (R Wis.) named 26 past or present employees of the State Department, including Ambassador-at-Large Philip C. Jessup and Consul General John Carter Vincent, who, he said, were suspected of disloyalty.

Outcome of MacArthur Inquiry. On Aug. 17, the Senate Armed Services and Foreign Relations committees voted 20-3 not to make any formal report on the investigation of Gen. MacArthur's dismissal. Chairman Richard B. Russell (D Ga.) of the Armed Services Committee said a report might renew "bitter discussion of methods for waging war" and "would not help" Korean truce negotiations. Two days later, 8 of the 12 Republicans on the committees released voluminous "conclusions" on the investigation. Highlights of the statement were:

"The removal of Gen. MacArthur was within the constitutional powers of the President, but the circumstances were a shock to the national pride."

"There was no serious disagreement between Gen. MacArthur and the Joint Chiefs of Staff as to military strategy in Korea."

"The testimony revealed only one positive plan for victory in the Korean War, the plan advocated by Gen. MacArthur."

Under Acheson, "American foreign policy has been primarily to conciliate certain of our associates in the United Nations rather than to advance the security of the United States."

"We have not been convinced that Chiang lost China for any other reason than that he did not receive sufficient support, both moral and material, from the United States."

Truce Talks Halted. On Aug. 23, the Communists halted the Korean truce talks, charging that a UN plane had attacked a jeep carrying their chief negotiator, Korean Lt. Gen. Nam Il. The U.S. denied the charge.

McCarthy Broadcast. On Aug. 24, Sen. McCarthy charged in a radio broadcast that President Truman had issued an executive order in 1948 forbidding Government employees to "give Congress the truth about Communists who are in our Government." McCarthy asserted also that Ambassador-at-Large Philip C. Jessup was once the editorial director of the official publication of a Communist-front organization. He did not mention the organization's name. The Senator said that State Department aide John Stewart Service had been giving "top-secret military information" to Philip Jaffe, who "has been named under oath as a Communist spy." He added that the President had been given favorable mention in the Communist *Daily Worker* in 1944 and wrote the paper a complimentary note. The State Department called the charges "a typical McCarthy mixture of quarter-truth, half-truth, and untruth" and said the Senator was repeating charges that had already been answered.

Justice Douglas's Statement. On Aug. 31, Associate Supreme Court Justice William O. Douglas said on his return from the Far East that U.S. recognition of Communist China would help undermine Peking's ties with Moscow and be "a real political victory" for the West. He said it would "require straightforward and courageous thinking by all Americans, but it is the only logical course."

Japanese Peace Treaty Signed. On Sept. 8, 48 non-Communist nations signed a peace treaty with Japan in San Francisco. Russia refused to sign.

UN Admits Strafing. On Sept. 11, the UN command admitted that one of its planes had strafed the site of the stalled truce talks by accident.

Marshall Resigns. On Sept. 12, Gen. George C. Marshall, 70, resigned as Secretary of Defense and was replaced by Deputy Defense Secretary Robert A. Lovett.

South Korean Deaths. On Sept. 15, the South Korean government announced that one million South Korean civilians had been killed in the war with the Communists.

Communist Offer. On Sept. 20, the Communists offered to resume the Korean truce negotiations in Kaesong. One week later, Gen. Ridgway proposed that the conference be moved from Kaesong to Songhyen, eight miles away. Songhyen was in "no-man's land" while Kaesong was behind Communist lines. The Communists rejected the Ridgway proposal on Oct. 4, insisting that the talks be held in Kaesong. Ridgway refused but said he would let the Communists name the site, as long as it was in "no-man's land."

McCarthy Charges. On Oct. 2, Sen. McCarthy told a Foreign Relations Subcommittee investigating Philip C. Jessup's nomination as a U.S. delegate to the UN, that Jessup's alleged association with Red-front organizations made him unfit to represent the U.S. The following day, Jessup answered that McCarthy's testimony consisted of "barefaced falsehoods, distortions, and misrepresentations."

Atom Tests. On Oct. 6, Soviet Premier Stalin was quoted as confirming that the Russians were testing atomic weapons.

Agreement on Panmunjom. On Oct. 8, Communist and UN commands reached a tentative agreement to resume Korean truce talks in Panmunjom, an abandoned village six miles from Kaesong.

Soviet Rejection. On Oct. 18, it was disclosed that the Soviet Union had rejected the U.S. contention that Korean truce talks should deal only with military arrangements for a cease-fire on present battle lines.

Jessup Rejected. On Oct. 18, a Senate Foreign Relations Subcommittee voted 3-2 against confirming Philip C. Jessup as a U.S. delegate to the UN. The next day, the Senate confirmed the nine other appointments, but avoided voting on Jessup. On Oct. 22, two days after Congress adjourned, President Truman gave the Ambassador-at-Large a recess appointment, saying that charges against him were "utterly without foundation." The President added that the Senate had confirmed Jessup five times previously, three times as a UN delegate.

Korean Negotiations Resume. On Oct. 25, truce negotiations resumed in Panmunjom after a 63-day lapse. A new agreement for neutralizing the conference area had been arranged. On Nov. 1, a subcommittee reached agreement on an armistice line for the eastern half of the front. The Communists had abandoned their insistence on the 38th Parallel, but the dispute continued as to where the line should be drawn in the west. UN negotiators rejected a number of Communist proposals for a cease-fire while negotiations were going on, because they feared it would give Communist forces opportunity to prepare a new offensive.

Provisional Agreement. On Nov. 27, the two sides reached a provisional agreement to establish a cease-fire line following the existing battle front, to make the line permanent if a comprehensive armistice agreement was concluded within 30 days, and to let the provisional cease-fire agreement lapse if a general agreement was not reached by Dec. 27. On the following day, Nov. 28, fighting ceased on almost the entire front, although the provisional agreement obligated neither side to stop fighting until other truce questions were settled. Air action increased in the first part of December, but no major air or ground fighting occurred from mid-month to year's end.

Armistice Negotiations Continue. On Dec. 27, no final armistice agreement having been reached, the provisional agreement lapsed. However, truce negotiators continued efforts to resolve differences on arrangements for enforcing an armistice, exchanging prisoners, etc.

1952

French Stand on Indo-China War -- Washington Meeting on Indo-China -- Warning on Aggression in Southeast Asia -- Proposal for Korean Peace Conference -- Testimony on Far East at McCarthy Hearings -- Deadlock on Korean Prisoners of War -- POW Riot in Korea -- New Air Raids on North Korea -- Release of POWs Wanting to Stay in South Korea -- Indefinite Recess of Truce Talks -- Eisenhower's Pledge to Go to Korea.

Indo-China War. On Jan. 6, French Foreign Minister Robert Schuman said France would accept an agreement ending the Indo-China civil war "under conditions which would be honorable for France." He said France was not "concerned with imperialism or conquest" in Indo-China, but did not "want to open the doors to communism."

Truman-Churchill on Aggression. On Jan. 9, President Truman and British Prime Minister Winston Churchill, after conferring in Washington for four days, recorded in a joint statement their full agreement that aggression in Korea and Southeast Asia must be blocked.

GOP Resolution. On Jan. 10, 38 of the 46 Republican members of the Senate, headed by Styles Bridges (R N.H.), sponsored a Senate resolution asserting that Ambassador-at-Large Philip C. Jessup "does not command the confidence of the American people" as a UN delegate. The resolution was not reported from committee.

Washington Conference on Indo-China. On Jan. 11, a secret military conference involving the U.S., Britain, and France was held in Washington to discuss the situation in Indo-China and other threatened areas of Southeast Asia. The French representative said that France would need help if Communist China entered the war in Indo-China. Gen. Omar N. Bradley, chairman of the Joint Chiefs of Staff, represented the U.S. The Associated Press reported four days later that the U.S. had sent 70 shiploads of military equipment to Indo-China since July 1950.

Korean Truce Stalemate. On Jan. 24, Gen. Matthew B. Ridgway, U.N. Supreme Commander in Korea, said the truce talks had reached "a complete state of paralysis."

Warning in the UN. On Jan. 28, the U.S., France, and Britain warned in the UN that if the Soviet Union and Communist China attempted new aggression in Southeast Asia, they would meet the same resistance as in Korea.

Vincent Testimony. On Jan. 30, Foreign Service Officer John Carter Vincent testified before the Senate Internal Security Subcommittee to deny Sen. McCarthy's charges that he was pro-Communist. Vincent said he accompanied former Vice President Wallace to China in 1944 under orders from Secretary of State Cordell Hull to make sure Wallace did not promise too much to Chiang Kai-shek. He added that he had informed the State Department that the Chinese Reds were "definitely Communists and not agrarian democrats."

Truman on McCarthy. On Jan. 31, President Truman assailed Sen. Joseph R. McCarthy (R Wis.) as "untruthful, pathological and a character assassin." McCarthy answered that the President was engaged in "name-calling."

Far East Conference Requested. On Feb. 6, Communist truce negotiators at Panmunjom proposed a full-dress peace conference on Far Eastern questions. Three days later, the UN delegation rejected the proposal, stating that any peace conference should be confined to Korean questions. On Feb. 19, the UN delegation accepted a proposal for a political conference within three months of a cease-fire to settle "the question of the withdrawal of all foreign forces from Korea, the peaceful settlement of the Korean question, et cetera." The term "et cetera" represented a compromise which might open the way to discussion of other Far Eastern questions.

Vincent Cleared. On Feb. 19, the State Department Loyalty and Security Board "completely cleared" John Carter Vincent of charges of pro-communism made against him by Sen. McCarthy.

Lattimore and Fairbank Testimony. On Feb. 26, Prof. Owen Lattimore of Johns Hopkins University testified before the Senate Internal Security Subcommittee. He denied that he was ever a Communist, that the Institute of Pacific Relations, whose magazine he edited from 1934 to 1941, was Communist, or that he influenced the State Department to abandon China to the Communists.

On March 11, Prof. John K. Fairbank of Harvard accused the subcommittee of using tactics similar to those employed by the Communists. Fairbank called charges that he was a Communist "absurd and false" and denied that the Institute of Pacific Relations was infiltrated by Communists. *(For later Fairbank testimony, see 1966.)*

On March 21, Sen. Pat McCarran (D Nev.), chairman of the Senate Internal Security Subcommittee, strongly criticized Lattimore's conduct as a witness before the Subcommittee and charged that he had helped to shape policy toward China that was beneficial to the Communists. Lattimore replied: "I could not expect a fair hearing."

McCarthy Sues Benton. On March 26, Sen. Joseph R. McCarthy sued Sen. William Benton (D Conn.) for libel, slander, and conspiracy. McCarthy demanded $2 million and costs in the U.S. District Court for the District of Columbia. Benton had filed accusations against McCarthy in connection with a resolution he introduced in 1951 for a Senate investigation of the Wisconsin Republican's fitness to hold his seat. McCarthy said Benton attacked him because he was "exposing Communists in the Government."

Communist Truce Offers. On April 6, the Chinese Communists answered a UN demand that prisoners be given the right to refuse repatriation by promising that anti-Communist prisoners would be immune from punishment on political grounds when they were returned to North Korea or Communist China. The Communists said in a Peking broadcast that they were "fully aware" many Communist troops had been forced to change their political views by the UN captors and they "should not be held responsible." On April 9, the Communists offered to drop their nomination of Russia as a truce observer if the UN would agree to allow construction of military airfields in North Korea. The offer was rejected.

Bullitt's Testimony. On April 8, William C. Bullitt, former Ambassador to France and to Russia, appeared before the Senate Internal Security Subcommittee and asserted that some of Prof. Owen Lattimore's actions indicated either that he was "a charlatan" or that he was backing Soviet aims in Asia. Bullitt said the Russians used the Institute of Pacific Relations for propaganda and sought military information from its members.

Deadlock on Korean POWs. On April 24, the Chinese Communists announced they had rejected a new UN prisoner-exchange plan. The Peking Radio said the UN had submitted a list of prisoners to the Communists excluding all those who did not wish to return. The broadcast called the plan "a disgusting American scheme." On April 28, the UN was reported ready to withdraw its opposition to construction of military airbases in North Korea if the Communists would give up their insistence on forced repatriation of prisoners and on nomination of Russia as a "neutral" truce observer. The Communists replied that they could yield on the truce observer question but not on prisoner repatriation. UN officials said they could not agree to forced repatriation of prisoners of war. Peking Radio concluded that the talks had reached a "most crucial deadlock."

Clark to Far East. On April 28, President Truman announced that Gen. Mark W. Clark would succeed Gen. Matthew B. Ridgway as UN Supreme Commander in Korea and Commander of U.S. forces in the Far East. Ridgway was to succeed retiring Gen. Dwight D. Eisenhower as Supreme Allied Commander, Europe.

Truman on Political Gangsters. On May 2, President Truman condemned "political gangsters" who "are motivated by such a lust for power that they are willing to wreck the lives and careers of innocent public servants" by creating "an atmosphere in which a charge is a conviction in the public mind despite the lack of evidence." Truman added, "I think they are worse than Communists, and I think they are partners with them."

Ridgway on Red Negotiators. On May 22, Gen. Matthew B. Ridgway told a joint session of Congress that UN truce negotiators in Korea had to deal with "blind hatred, the vituperative venom, the vicious falsehoods, deliberately employed, which are all inseparable elements of the technique of Communist negotiation." He warned that the Communists' charges of germ and gas warfare against the UN might be an excuse for using germ and gas weapons themselves.

Communist Prisoners Riot. On June 10, Communist prisoners on Koje Island fought with U.S. paratroopers for almost three hours, using spears, knives and clubs for weapons. The prisoners had captured an American general and held him hostage for three days in early May. The new uprising resulted in the deaths of 38 prisoners and one American. Some prisoners had been killed by their comrades because they wanted to surrender. On June 11, President Truman endorsed a proposal that five neutral countries investigate the uprising and UN measures to suppress it.

Power Plants Bombed. On June 23-26, more than 500 U.S. planes bombed five major hydroelectric power plants in the Yalu River area of North Korea in the biggest bombing raid of the war. The plants provided power for industries in Manchuria and large cities in North Korea, including Pyongyang. The Soviet news agency *Tass* reported on June 25 that "the American air pirates have started the massive bombing of peaceful towns which have no military objectives." Secretary of State Dean Acheson apologized to Prime Minister Winston Churchill on June 26 for failing to give Britain advance of the Yalu raids. Some British political leaders feared the raids might lead to world war.

New POW Proposal. On July 1, Maj. Gen. William K. Harrison Jr., who had replaced Vice Adm. Joy as chief UN negotiator in Korea, offered the Communists a new prisoner-exchange proposal: the UN would agree to repatriate "all" prisoners, but only after reclassifying out of POW status those who did not wish to return to North Korea or Red China. The Communists answered two days later that all Chinese and North Koreans would have to be returned.

Senate Committee's Report. On July 2, the Senate Judiciary Subcommittee on Internal Security issued a report charging that Prof. Owen Lattimore of Johns Hopkins University had been a "conscious, articulate instrument of the Soviet conspiracy" and had lied to the Subcommittee five times. The Subcommittee recommended that the Justice Department ask a grand jury to determine whether Lattimore should be indicted for perjury. Lattimore said the charges were "untrue" and "supported by no creditable evidence."

Russian Veto. On July 3, the Soviet Union vetoed a U.S. proposal that the UN Security Council ask the International Red Cross to investigate germ warfare charges against the UN. The Soviet Union then vetoed a U.S. resolution to denounce the Communist charges as "false."

Republican Convention. On July 7, Gen. Douglas MacArthur, in the keynote address at the Republican National Convention in Chicago, asserted that the Administration "gave over to Soviet control the industrial resources of Manchuria" and "condemned" the people of China to "Communist tyranny." MacArthur contended that when the Chinese Communists entered the war, "our leaders lacked the courage to fight to a military decision, even though victory was then readily within our grasp -- a victory which...might well have saved continental Asia from Red domination." He added that the Administration had condemned U.S. forces to a "stalemated struggle" and Korea to "progressive obliteration." The armistice negotiations, in the general's opinion, only served to give the enemy time for military reinforcement.

Talks in Second Year. On July 10, the Korean truce negotiations entered their second year with the delegations engaged in secret talks over the prisoner-exchange deadlock.

Eisenhower and Nixon Slate. On July 11, the Republicans nominated Gen. Dwight D. Eisenhower for President and Sen. Richard M. Nixon (Calif.) for Vice President.

Pyongyang Bombed. On July 11, Pyongyang, the North Korean capital, was heavily bombed in one of the biggest air raids of the war. Gen. J. Lawton Collins, U.S. Army Chief of Staff, warned of still heavier raids if the Communists insisted on "prolonging the war."

U.S. Report on Prisoners. On July 13, the U.S. said in a report to the UN Security Council that more than 100,000 prisoners had said they would do anything rather than return to Communist territory.

Red China Accepts Geneva Accords. On July 16, Chinese Communist Foreign Minister Chou En-lai announced that Communist China had accepted the 1929 and 1949 Geneva conventions on germ warfare, on treatment of the sick, wounded and war prisoners, and on protection of civilians.

Communist Warning. On July 23, the Chinese Communists warned in a radio broadcast that UN forces would "have their heads broken" if full-scale warfare erupted again in Korea. The Communists said they were "determined to fight to the end" to ensure the return of all prisoners.

Stevenson and Sparkman Slate. On July 26, Gov. Adlai E. Stevenson (Ill.) and Sen. John Sparkman (Ala.) were nominated by the Democratic National Convention for President and Vice President.

Plant Bombed. On July 30, 63 B-29s bombed a North Korean aluminum plant 11 miles from the Manchurian border. On Aug. 5, the U.S. announced that the people of 78 North Korean towns and cities had been warned by radio and leaflets that their areas had been marked for destruction and should be evacuated.

Rhee Elected. On Aug. 5, South Korean President Syngman Rhee, 77, won a second four-year term in South Korea's first popular Presidential election.

Stalemate. On Aug. 14, North Korean Premier Kim Il Sung conceded in a speech at Pyongyang that the Korean War had reached a stalemate. He said he would accept an armistice under which the "Americans are not the winners and the Koreans the losers."

Sino-Soviet Talks. On Aug. 19, Chinese Premier and Foreign Minister Chou En-lai arrived in Moscow for the first conference between Chinese and Soviet leaders since the Treaty of Alliance and Friendship was signed in February 1950. The talks were reported to cover the Korean conflict, its toll on the Chinese Communist economy, and Sino-Soviet relations in general.

McCarthy Question. On Aug. 22, GOP nominee Dwight D. Eisenhower said he would support Sen. Joseph R. McCarthy (R Wis.) for re-election to the Senate if the Senator won renomination in the Wisconsin primary. Both Eisenhower and Democratic nominee Adlai E. Stevenson had denounced McCarthy earlier in the week for attacking Gen. George C. Marshall.

Communist Protest. On Aug. 23, the Chinese Communists and North Koreans, protesting air raids in North Korea, accused the U.S. of "blind and wanton bombings" of civilians. On Aug. 29, the U.S. Air Force announced that Pyongyang, the North Korean capital, had undergone the heaviest air raid of the war.

Peking Peace Conference. On Aug. 31, the Chinese Communists announced that an Asian and Pacific Peace Conference, to be held in Peking, would discuss plans to "settle peacefully the Korean question on a fair and reasonable basis" and to "solve reasonably all questions relating to peace in the Asian and Pacific region, including Indo-China, Malaya, and other countries."

Possible UN Action. On Sept. 1, Ernest A. Gross, deputy U.S., representative to the UN, said the U.S. would seek a General Assembly discussion of the Korean problem if an armistice had not been reached by Oct. 14. On Sept. 9, President Miguel Aleman of Mexico submitted several alternative proposals for settling the dispute over exchange of Korean prisoners of war; the Communists rejected all of them.

McCarthy Renominated. On Sept. 9, in the first test of "McCarthyism" at the polls, Sen. Joseph R. McCarthy overwhelmingly won renomination in the Wisconsin Republican primary.

Prisoners Released. On Sept. 20, the UN announced that it had reclassified 11,000 Communist prisoners as South Korean civilians and released them. The Chinese Communists asserted three days later that the action rendered the armistice talks "null and void." On Oct. 1, 52 rioting Chinese Communist prisoners were killed and 113 wounded by U.S. troops at a Cheju Island prison camp. North Korea immediately denounced the "bloody yet cowardly massacre" of the prisoners.

Conference Opens. On Oct. 1, the Asian and Pacific Peace Conference convened in Peking.

McCarthy-Eisenhower Agreement. On Oct. 3, Gen. Eisenhower said in Green Bay, Wis., that he and Sen. McCarthy agreed on the objective of cleansing the Government of "the subversives and the disloyal," but that they differed on methods. McCarthy, who had joined the Eisenhower campaign train for its tour of Wisconsin, added that he and the general agreed "on the important things." The next day, Stevenson called Eisenhower's acceptance of McCarthy "a sorry spectacle."

Eisenhower on Korea. On Oct. 8, Eisenhower criticized the Truman Administration for allowing UN forces to accept the "trap" of negotiations in Korea in June 1951, at a time when they were "driving back" the enemy. Eisenhower said the lull allowed the Communists time to build up their positions. Earlier in the week, the general told an audience in Illinois that "if there must be war" in Asia, "let it be Asians against Asians, with our support on the side of freedom." He added that "the South Korean battle line today should be manned primarily by Koreans" and American troops should be used as reserves.

Recess of Truce Talks. On Oct. 8, the truce teams in Panmunjom agreed to an indefinite recess after the Communists rejected three UN proposals on the voluntary return of prisoners of war.

Peking Conference Adjourns. On Oct. 13, the Asian and Pacific Peace Conference adjourned in Peking after blaming the U.S. for termination of the Korean truce talks and demanding the repatriation of "all prisoners of war... according to the Geneva Convention of 1949."

Truman Attacks Eisenhower. On Oct. 17, President Truman said in Lawrence, Mass., that Russia would have conquered Europe if the U.S. had failed to fight in Korea. The President pointed out that 50 percent more South Koreans than Americans were fighting in Korea. The next day, Truman charged in Providence, R.I., that Eisenhower "held out a false hope to the mothers of America in an effort to pick up a few votes" by calling for U.S. withdrawal of troops from Korea.

UN Rejection. On Oct. 20, UN Supreme Commander Mark W. Clark rejected a Communist offer to resume truce talks. The Communists had refused to accept voluntary repatriation of prisoners.

Korea in First Place. On Oct. 22, the Korean question was given first place on the UN General Assembly's agenda. On the following day, a representative of South Korea was admitted to the Korea debate.

Eisenhower Pledges Korean Trip. On Oct. 24, Gen. Eisenhower pledged to a Detroit audience that "I shall go to Korea" in an effort to end the war. Stevenson denounced the proposed trip as "a slick idea that gets votes by playing upon our hopes for a quick end to the war." President Truman added that Eisenhower was attempting a "superman" approach to the problem and that "anybody who poses and talks like a superman is a fraud."

McCarthy Charge. On Oct. 27, McCarthy charged in a radio and television broadcast that Stevenson had helped the Communist cause and had surrounded himself with leftist advisers, including Wilson W. Wyatt and Arthur Schlesinger Jr. McCarthy said also that the *Daily Worker* had endorsed Stevenson and ordered all Communists to vote for him. Aides of Gen. Eisenhower immediately said their candidate had nothing to do with McCarthy's speech.

Viet Minh Offensive. On Oct. 27, 10,000 Viet Minh troops broke through French defenses at several points in Indo-China.

Soviet Proposal. On Oct. 29, Soviet Foreign Minister Vishinsky sought to transfer the Korean armistice talks from Panmunjom to the UN General Assembly. Vishinsky proposed the creation of a new commission composed of "parties directly concerned" but "not participating" in the Korean conflict to take "immediate measures" to end the war and unify Korea. The proposal won little support, and the Assembly continued to debate Korean prisoner repatriation.

Eisenhower Wins. On Nov. 4, Gen. Eisenhower defeated Gov. Stevenson for the Presidency. The GOP won control of both houses of Congress by narrow margins.

Lie Resigns. On Nov. 10, UN Secretary General Trgyve Lie of Norway resigned on the ground that Soviet hostility toward him prevented his working effectively for a Korean peace.

Vishinsky on POWs. On the same day, Soviet Foreign Minister Andrei Y. Vishinsky told the General Assembly's Political and Security Committee that the Soviet Union would "never budge" from its opposition to voluntary repatriation of Korean prisoners of war. He rejected all pending compromise proposals.

Indian Proposal on POWs. On Nov. 17, India offered a compromise Korean proposal to establish a "neutral" commission on repatriation with an "umpire" named by the General Assembly if the commission was still deadlocked after three weeks of talks. India suggested that the commission should not be employed either "to prevent or effect" the return of prisoners. On Nov. 27, the U.S. announced its support of the Indian proposal, but Soviet Foreign Minister Vishinsky called it a "rotten resolution." On Dec. 3, the General Assembly adopted India's compromise plan by a vote of 54 to 5 with the Soviet bloc in opposition.

Eisenhower Trip to Korea. On Dec. 2, U.S. President-elect Eisenhower departed on a three-day secret visit to Korea. After touring the battlefront and interviewing officials, Eisenhower announced at a press conference in Seoul on Dec. 5 that he had "no panaceas, no tricks" for settling the war. He said it was "difficult...to work out a plan that would bring positive and definite victory without possibly running a grave risk of enlarging the war."

Red Rejection of POW Plan. On Dec. 15, the Peking radio announced rejection of the compromise prisoner-of-war plan adopted by the UN General Assembly on Dec. 3.

Vincent Suspended. On Dec. 15, the State Department suspended John Carter Vincent as U.S. Minister at Tangier and ordered him back to the U.S. The suspension resulted from a report by the Civil Service Commission's Loyalty Review Board that there was "a reasonable doubt as to his loyalty."

Lattimore Indicted. On Dec. 16, Prof. Owen Lattimore was indicted by a federal grand jury in Washington on seven counts of perjury. Johns Hopkins put Lattimore on an indefinite leave of absence with full pay.

Stalin Letter. On Dec. 24, Soviet Premier Joseph Stalin said in answer to a questionnaire from the *New York Times* that he would favor new moves toward ending the Korean War and would welcome a meeting with President-elect Eisenhower.

Chinese Announcement. On Dec. 29, the Chinese Communist government announced that a People's Congress would be assembled in 1953 to begin drafting "an election law and a constitution."

1953

U.S. Hydrogen Bomb -- Chiang Unleashed -- Death of Stalin -- New Korean POW Proposals -- POW Agreement -- Syngman Rhee Frees Anti-Communist POWs -- Signing of Korean War Armistice -- Korean War Casualties -- Soviet Hydrogen Bomb -- U.S. Aid for France in Indo-China War -- Viet Minh Peace Feelers -- Clash Over Plans for Korean Political Conference -- Viet Minh Drive to Borders of Thailand.

McCarthy Criticized. On Jan. 2, the Senate Privileges and Elections Subcommittee released its report on Sen. Joseph R. McCarthy's (R Wis.) fitness to remain in the U.S. Senate. The report criticized the Senator both for his financial transactions and for his efforts to "thwart" the inquiry.

McCarthy had refused six times to appear before the subcommittee, and he denounced the report as a new low in dishonesty and smear." The report made no recommendations for Senate action.

Hydrogen Bomb. On Jan. 7, in his State of the Union Message to Congress, President Truman confirmed the fact that the U.S. had developed a hydrogen bomb. He added that its use would be "unthinkable for rational men."

Eisenhower Assumes Office. On Jan. 20, Dwight David Eisenhower, 62, became the 34th President of the United States. In his inaugural address he promised a continued quest for peace without appeasement.

Taylor Replaces Van Fleet. On Jan. 23, Lt. Gen. Maxwell D. Taylor, 51, was designated to replace retiring Gen. James A. Van Fleet as commander of the U.S. Eighth Army in Korea.

Election in Viet Nam. On Jan. 25, in the first local elections ever held throughout Viet Nam, candidates supporting the pro-French Viet Nam government were successful in all localities except Hanoi. Despite threats of terrorism from the rebels, 80 percent of those registered voted.

Chiang Unleashed. On Feb. 2, President Eisenhower announced in his State of the Union Message that he was "issuing instructions that the Seventh Fleet no longer be employed to shield Communist China" from an attack by Nationalist forces on Formosa. The President said the order did not imply aggressive intent against Red China on the part of the U.S., "but we certainly have no obligation to protect a nation fighting us in Korea."

China and Truce Talks. On Feb. 4, Chinese Communist Premier Chou En-lai requested the U.S. to return to the Korean truce talks. Communist China, he said, was "ready for an immediate cease-fire on the basis of the agreement already reached in Panmunjom." The U.S. answered it would return when the Communists conceded on their demands for forced repatriation of prisoners of war.

Blockade Proposal. On Feb. 6, Rep. Dewey Short (R Mo.), House Armed Services Committee chairman, reported that the President and his advisers were studying proposals for a naval blockade of Communist China. Secretary of State John Foster Dulles and Gen. Omar N. Bradley, chairman of the Joint Chiefs of Staff, told the Senate Foreign Relations Committee on Feb. 10 that the Joint Chiefs still believed that a blockade by the U.S. alone might split the allies and bring on war with the Soviet Union; and that the flow of U.S. arms to the Chinese Nationalists on Formosa was "stepping up."

Chiang's Statement. On Feb. 12, Chiang Kai-shek said the Nationalists could attack Communist China whenever they chose without UN sanction or fear of Soviet intervention. Chiang conceded that his forces were not "adequately equipped" for a full-scale invasion, but he felt they could "not afford to wait until we are fully prepared."

Eisenhower Press Conference. On Feb. 17, President Eisenhower said at his first news conference that he was not then considering blockading or embargoing mainland China. Secretary of State John Foster Dulles told a news conference the following day that the Administration was seeking ways to isolate Communist China from vital trade with non-Communist nations. He said that an embargo and blockade were only two of a "whole series of measures of varying kinds which could be adopted."

Indictment of Russia. On Feb. 25, U.S. Ambassador to the UN Henry Cabot Lodge Jr. delivered a ten-point indictment of the Soviet Union for arming the Communist troops in Korea. Lodge, appearing before the Political and Security Committee of the General Assembly, indicated also that the Eisenhower Administration supported the Korean truce resolution adopted by the Assembly on Dec. 3, 1952, and rejected by the Communists. The Soviet delegate replied on March 2 that the Russians "sold and continue to sell armaments" to Communist China in return for "strategic materials."

Vincent Cleared. On March 4, Secretary of State John Foster Dulles announced that he had cleared career diplomat John Carter Vincent of disloyalty charges. At the same time, Dulles said Vincent's performance of his duties fell short of necessary standards, and he was therefore accepting his application for retirement.

Stalin Dies. On March 4, Moscow Radio announced that Premier Joseph V. Stalin, 73, had suffered a serious brain hemorrhage and was not expected to live. On March 5, Stalin died. On March 6, it was announced that he would be replaced by Georgi M. Malenkov.

New POW Proposals. On March 29, the Communists offered to exchange sick and wounded Korean prisoners while postponing the exchange of those who did not wish to return. Chou En-lai then suggested, March 30, that prisoners who did not desire to return should be handed over "to a neutral state so as to ensure a just solution to the question of their repatriation." UN officials requested clarification as to what countries the Communists would consider "neutral" and as to whether a "neutral" country receiving prisoners would make the decisions as to their repatriation.

Agreement on Sick and Wounded. On April 11, a final agreement was reached on exchange of sick and wounded prisoners in Korea, starting April 20. The Communists asked for a resumption of talks on the entire prisoner issue and assured the UN that it was the only remaining obstacle to a cessation of hostilities.

Laos Mobilizes. On April 14, the Indo-Chinese kingdom of Laos ordered a general mobilization to help the French resist an advance of Viet Minh rebels into the state.

Main Truce Talks Resume. On April 26, the Korean truce talks were resumed at Panmunjom. The Communists immediately rejected UN proposals for prisoners refusing repatriation, but when the UN delegation threatened to recess the talks again, the Communists modified their stand.

Viet Minh Retreat. On May 6, French forces reported that Viet Minh rebels had withdrawn from all of Laos, except the extreme northeastern section.

POW Agreement Signed. On June 8, 1953, after more than a month of proposals and rejections, UN and Communist delegates to the truce talks in Panmunjom signed an agreement on prisoners of war -- an issue that had deadlocked negotiations for a year. The agreement called for establishment of a supervising commission composed of representatives of Czechoslovakia, India, Poland, Sweden, and Switzerland. The UN agreed that all prisoners should be repatriated provided they were willing to go home; each side would be given 90 days to attempt to change the minds of those unwilling to return. The supervising commission would have charge of those who were unwilling, and they would be released after the 90-day "convincer" period ended.

South Koreans Free Prisoners. On June 18, South Korean President Syngman Rhee engineered the release of anti-Communist prisoners in defiance of the UN Command. Rhee announced that he had freed 25,000 North Koreans "on my own responsibility." His action threatened to complicate conclusion of a cease-fire agreement. The Communists were outraged by the deliberate release of the prisoners and the UN expressed formal regret at Rhee's unilateral action.

Rhee Agrees to Armistice. On July 11, the U.S. announced that South Korean President Syngman Rhee had agreed to an armistice on terms acceptable to the UN. On the following day, Rhee and U.S. Assistant Secretary of State for Far Eastern Affairs Walter S. Robertson issued a joint statement implying that Rhee had accepted President Eisenhower's views on a truce and a U.S.-South Korean defense pact. Robertson had been in Seoul for two weeks in an effort to persuade the South Korean president to accept the truce. Truce negotiations had been broken off on June 20 by the Communists after Rhee had released the 25,000 anti-Communist prisoners of war. Secret negotiations were resumed on July 10, but the Communists refused to sign the agreement, asserting that there was only "vague" assurance that the UN could control South Korea.

New Offensive. On July 13, Chinese Communist forces launched their largest offensive since May 1951, in the central-front area of Korea. UN forces retreated about four miles but by July 16 were able to halt the offensive with heavy artillery fire and bombing attacks. UN forces then counter-attacked and regained most of the lost ground.

Armistice Signed. On July 26, an armistice was finally signed. The truce talks had been the longest in history, lasting two years and 17 days and including 575 separate meetings. The agreement provided for a prisoner exchange, freezing of the military fronts as a demarcation line, and establishment of a demilitarized zone four kilometers wide between the opposing forces. The size of forces on both sides also was frozen, but each side was permitted to rotate limited numbers of troops and equipment. A Military Armistice Commission of five UN and five Communist members was to supervise execution of the agreement. A political conference was to be held, after completion of the prisoner exchange, to discuss the future status of Korea and related problems.

Rhee's Pledge. On July 27, South Korean President Syngman Rhee announced that he would observe the truce "for a limited time," pending the political conference. On July 29, Rhee told the *New York Times* it was "inconceiv-

able" that the U.S. would not resume the war if the Communists refused to reunify Korea.

Eisenhower's Warning. On Aug. 4, President Eisenhower told the Governor's Conference in Seattle that Burma, India and Indonesia would be in peril if the Communists overran Indo-China. He said that U.S. economic and military aid to anti-Communist forces there offered the "cheapest way" to avoid a serious threat to American security.

Prisoner Exchange Begins. On Aug. 5, the first UN and Communist prisoners of war in Korea were exchanged at Panmunjom.

Korean War Casualties. On Aug. 7, the UN Command estimated that UN military casualties totaled 455,000, of whom 300,000 were South Koreans. Estimates of Communist casualties ranged from 1,500,000 to 2,000,000. The Defense Department on Aug. 19 announced a total of 142,277 American casualties in Korea: 25,604 dead, 103,492 wounded, 8,529 missing, 2,219 captured, and 2,433 previously listed as captured or missing but later returned to duty.

Hydrogen Bomb. On Aug. 8, Soviet Premier Georgi M. Malenkov commented in a speech that the U.S. had no "monopoly" on the hydrogen bomb. On Aug. 20, Malenkov announced that the Soviet Union had tested a hydrogen bomb. The test was later confirmed by the U.S. Atomic Energy Commission.

Plan for Korean Conference. On Aug. 28, the UN General Assembly approved plans for the political conference called for by the Korean armistice. The plans provided for a meeting of the opposite sides in the Korean War (including the Soviet Union) instead of a "roundtable" discussion attended by neutrals.

Dulles Warns China. On Sept. 2, Secretary of State John Foster Dulles warned Communist China -- "in hope of preventing another aggressor miscalculation" -- that a renewal of the Korean conflict or a transfer of Communist forces into Indo-China might mean war against the mainland itself. The Secretary said the U.S. had learned one lesson from the Korean conflict: "If events are likely which will in fact lead us to fight, let us make clear our intention in advance; then we shall probably not have to fight."

Prisoner Exchange Completed. On Sept. 6, the exchange of Korean prisoners of war was completed. The Communists released 12,760 prisoners (3,597 Americans), and the UN released 75,799 (5,640 Chinese). On Sept. 9, the UN demanded in the Military Armistice Commission that the Communists account for 3,404 other men, including 944 Americans. On Sept. 10, the UN began to move into the neutral truce zone 14,710 Chinese and 7,918 North Koreans who had refused repatriation. A 5,000-man Indian army guard force was being assembled to police the neutral camps.

Aid to French in Indo-China. On Sept. 10, the National Security Council recommended that U.S. aid to France for the war in Indo-China be increased by $385 million. Congress had already provided $400 million. Sen. Mike Mansfield (D Mont.) left, Sept. 15, on a Senate Foreign Relations Committee assignment to study the situation in Indo-China and other parts of Southeast Asia.

Red China and UN. On Sept. 15, the UN General Assembly adopted, 44-10, a U.S. resolution to keep the question of a seat for Communist China off the Assembly's 1953 agenda. Soviet Deputy Foreign Minister Andrei Y. Vishinsky had proposed that the Chinese Communist government replace the Nationalist Chinese in the Assembly. Secretary of State John Foster Dulles, chairman of the U.S. delegation, argued that "the Chinese Communists have not shown...a genuine intention" of ending the aggression in Korea. "Their continued actions elsewhere in Asia are far from reassuring." Vishinsky warned that any final action on the Korean problem would be delayed if the Assembly had to deal with Communist China indirectly.

Preparatory Korean Meeting. On Oct. 10, Communist China and North Korea announced acceptance of American proposals for a meeting to settle details of the Korean political conference. The Communists said the meeting should discuss composition of the conference as well as place and time. The U.S. denied that the Communists had "held all along that neutral nations should participate" in the conference. On the contrary, the Communists had "insisted that participation be limited to the governments concerned on both sides." When the preparatory meeting began, Oct. 26, proceedings were immediately deadlocked by Communist demands that neutral nations be invited to the full-dress conference. Arthur H. Dean, representative of the 16 UN nations that participated in the Korean conflict, said the inclusion of neutrals would turn the conference into "an endless debating society." He said it was "really very funny" to consider the Soviet Union a neutral, since Russia had "played a direct role in the Korean hostilities."

UN Study of Atrocities. On Nov. 11, the UN General Assembly voted 53-5 to examine U.S. complaints of Communist atrocities against UN prisoners.

Indo-China. On Nov. 20, French forces in Indo-China seized Dienbienphu in western North Viet Nam. The fortress had been a stronghold for the Viet Minh rebels.

Viet Minh Peace Feeler. On Nov. 29, Ho Chi Minh, Indo-China's rebel leader, said he would meet French proposals for peace "if having learned the lesson of these (seven) years of war, the French government wishes to have an armistice and settle the question by negotiations." The French government replied that Ho must make his offer through "an official channel." It would then be examined "with a view to re-establishment of a durable peace assuring the independence of these states" and the "liberty and security" of their people.

Dulles on McCarthy. On Dec. 1, Secretary of State John Foster Dulles denounced Sen. Joseph R. McCarthy (R Wis.) for attacking U.S. foreign policy toward allied nations as too soft. The Secretary said the Administration's "clear and firm purpose" was "to treat other free nations as...equals."

UN Atrocity Resolution. On Dec. 3, the UN General Assembly adopted a U.S.-sponsored resolution charging that North Korea, Communist China, and the Soviet Union were guilty of atrocities against prisoners of war. The Assembly expressed "grave concern" over such acts and condemned them as "a violation of rules of international law and basic standards of conduct and morality and as affronting human rights and the dignity and worth of the human person." The resolution was adopted 42-5 with 10

abstentions. Soviet Deputy Foreign Minister Andrei Y. Vishinsky called the charges "lies, fraud, slander and libel."

Korean Meeting Breaks Up. On Dec. 8, UN Representative Arthur H. Dean proposed to the Communists in Panmunjom that Russia attend the Korean political conference, not as a neutral, but as a voting member. The North Korean delegate rejected the proposal, presumably because the requirement to vote would bind the Soviet Union to conference decisions. On Dec. 12, Dean broke off the discussions when the Chinese Communist accused the U.S. of "perfidy." Dean said he would not return until the charge was retracted. He later said it "was perfectly evident that the Communists were trying to build up to becoming so rude and so arrogant that it would be impossible to continue the talks."

Second Viet Minh Peace Bid. On Dec. 10, Ho Chi Minh offered to open negotiations if France would recognize Indo-Chinese independence. On Dec. 19, seventh anniversary of the Indo-Chinese civil war, Ho again broadcast an offer to release "several hundred French war prisoners."

Dean's Prediction. On Dec. 21, Arthur H. Dean predicted on radio and television that there would not be a renewal of fighting in Korea even if the political conference were not held. Dean had returned to Washington after walking out of preliminary discussions in Panmunjom.

Viet Minh Offensive. On Dec. 22, the Viet Minh launched a five-day offensive which severed Indo-China at its narrowest point, driving across both Viet Nam and Laos. The offensive ended when the Communist forces reached the Mekong River, the border of Thailand. On Dec. 25, Thailand declared a state of emergency in all of its eastern provinces and rushed troops to the Mekong area. On Dec. 29, Secretary of State John Foster Dulles said at a news conference that the military significance of the Communist action had been "exaggerated" and there was "no reason...for anybody to get panicky." Dulles added that he "never thought there was much sincerity" in Ho Chi Minh's peace feelers. He warned that Chinese Communist intervention in Indo-China might set off a U.S. reaction "not necessarily confined to the particular area which the Communists chose to make the theater of their new aggression."

1954

Doctrine of Massive Retaliation -- Eisenhower on Indo-China War -- Nixon on Troops for Indo-China -- Geneva Conference (Part I, Korea) -- Fall of Dienbienphu -- Geneva Conference (Part II, Indo-China) -- Ngo Dinh Diem to South Viet Nam -- Indo-China Settlement -- SEATO Treaty -- Senate Censure of McCarthy

Peace Talks. On Jan. 5, the State Department announced that "intermediaries" in Panmunjom were seeking ways to resume planning sessions for the political conference on Korea, but the Communist charge of "perfidy" against the U.S. continued to deadlock the negotiations.

Massive Retaliation. On Jan. 12, Secretary of State John Foster Dulles, addressing the Council on Foreign Relations in New York City, outlined the doctrine of massive retaliation. The threat of "a great capacity to retaliate, instantly, by means and at places of our choosing" was held out as "a maximum deterrent at a bearable cost" against "a potential aggressor...glutted with manpower."

Unrepatriated POWs Returned. On Jan. 21, the Indian forces in Korea, acting for the supervisory commission on prisoners of war, moved back from the neutral truce zone all prisoners who had refused to be repatriated. The UN forces received 14,209 Chinese and 7,582 North Korean prisoners. On Jan. 28, 347 pro-Communists were handed over to the Chinese and North Koreans; the number included 21 Americans.

Viet Minh Invasion. On Jan. 30, the Viet Minh rebels launched an invasion of northern Laos. By Feb. 11, three Viet Minh forces had reached the outer defenses of Luang Prabang, the Laotion royal capital. French forces at Dienbienphu in Viet Nam began attacking Communist troops who had surrounded that stronghold.

Wilson on Indo-China. On Feb. 9, Secretary of Defense Charles E. Wilson said that no U.S. pilots or ground troops would fight in Indo-China. He added that no aid was planned at "any higher level than now." Wilson denied that Indo-China would turn into another Korea for the U.S. "From our view and that of the French," he said, "the war is going along as well as expected at this stage" with "a military victory...both possible and probable."

Eisenhower's Statement. On Feb. 10, President Eisenhower said it would be a "great tragedy" for the U.S. to get involved in the war in Indo-China and that everything he did was calculated to prevent involvement. The French privately protested later that the President's statement had lowered both French and Indo-Chinese morale and might encourage Red China to intervene.

South Korea Offers Troops. On Feb. 12, the South Korean government confirmed that it had offered to send an army division to Indo-China to fight the Viet Minh. France rejected the offer for fear it might lead to intervention by Communist China. On Feb. 16, it was disclosed that the U.S. had offered to train native troops in Indo-China. The French turned down the offer on the ground that their own training methods were superior.

Plans for Geneva. On Feb. 18, the Big Four foreign ministers, conferring in Berlin, agreed on proposals for a Far Eastern peace parley. The plan provided for a meeting in Geneva on April 26 to be attended by South Korea, the U.S., Britain, France, and 13 other nations represented in the UN Korean command and by Communist China, North Korea, and the Soviet Union "for the purpose of reaching a peaceful settlement of the Korean question." The ministers agreed that the problem of Indo-China also would be discussed. They said the conference should not be deemed "to imply diplomatic recognition in any case where it has not already been accorded." When Secretary of State John Foster Dulles returned from Berlin on Feb. 19, he sought to allay the fears of Congressional leaders who felt that if representatives of the United States sat down with representatives of Communist China at a Geneva conference table, it would be tantamount to recognition of the Peking regime.

Indo-China Optimism. On Feb. 18, Walter Bedell Smith, Acting Secretary of State, and Admiral Arthur W. Radford, chairman of the Joint Chiefs of Staff, told a House Foreign Affairs subcommittee that the French would be successful in blocking a Viet Minh victory in Indo-China.

Invitations to Geneva. On Feb. 26, the U.S. announced it had invited all 14 nations that contributed troops to the UN force in Korea to the Korean phase of the Geneva conference.

France to Negotiate. On March 9, the French National Assembly agreed to negotiate an Indo-China peace settlement at the Geneva conference.

Eisenhower on Indo-China Involvement. On March 10, President Eisenhower said he would not involve the U.S. in any conflict, including Indo-China, unless Congress declared war. Sen. John C. Stennis (D Miss.), a member of the Armed Services Committee, had demanded the day before that the U.S. withdraw its Air Force technicians from Indo-China. "We are taking steps that lead our men directly into combat," he said. "Soon we may have to fight or run."

Dienbienphu Offensive. On March 13, the Viet Minh launched an attack on the French stronghold of Dienbienphu. The rebels had completely surrounded the fortress and damaged the airfield, the only means of supply for the French forces.

U.S. Aid in Indo-China. On March 16, it was announced to the French National Assembly that the U.S. was paying 78 percent of the cost of the Indo-Chinese war. U.S. aid in 1954 would amount to $1.4 billion, while the French would provide only $394 million. On March 23, Secretary of State Dulles said in Washington that the U.S. would give France all the supplies and equipment necessary to defeat the Viet Minh rebels. The Secretary predicted the French would win in Indo-China even if the Chinese Communists continued to support the rebels.

Dienbienphu. In the last week of March, the French launched the greatest air attacks of the Indo-Chinese war against Viet Minh supply lines extending from Communist China to rebel forces around Dienbienphu, but Russian-made trucks and an estimated 100,000 coolies continued to pour in military supplies and equipment.

Dulles on Southeast Asia. On March 29, Secretary of State John Foster Dulles said in a New York speech that a Viet Minh victory in Indo-China would lead to Communist domination of all Southeast Asia. He said also that the U.S. would stand firm against recognition of Communist China and against its admission to the UN.

Dienbienphu Attacked. On March 30, Viet Minh forces staged a massive attack on Dienbienphu. After three days of heavy fighting, they had advanced to within a mile of the stronghold's center but then withdrew to regroup.

Dulles on S.E. Asia Defense. On April 5, Secretary Dulles proposed that the U.S. and its allies join in warning Communist China against further aggression in Indo-China or elsewhere in Southeast Asia. Dulles told the House Foreign Affairs Committee that China was "coming awfully close" to the kind of aggression he had said might result in retaliation. On April 10, the Secretary flew to London, and later to Paris to confer on the prospects of establishing "a united front to resist Communist aggression in Southeast Asia." He returned, April 15, with French and British pledges to examine the possibility of "collective defense" for Southeast Asia and the western Pacific.

Nixon on Troops for Indo-China. On April 16, Vice President Richard M. Nixon said at an American Society of Newspaper Editors meeting that the U.S. might have to send troops to Indo-China if the only alternative were Communist domination. Nixon thought the French could win if they had the will, but he feared that a defeat at Dienbienphu would mean France's withdrawal and the fall of Indo-China. The U.S., he said, could not allow a further retreat in Southeast Asia. The Vice President's statement caused dismay in Congress and the press. On April 19, Secretary Dulles said the use of U.S. troops in Indo-China was "unlikely." He termed Nixon's statement "hypothetical."

Dienbienphu Plea. On April 21, the French commander at Dienbienphu appealed for reinforcements of men and supplies "at any cost." At least 45,000 Viet Minh troops had been added to the original four divisions surrounding the French stronghold, which held an estimated 14,000 men. By April 23, rebel forces had pushed to within 700 yards of the center of the fortified town.

Geneva Conference - Part 1. On April 26, at the opening of the first part of the Geneva conference, which was restricted to Korean questions, Communist China's Premier and Foreign Minister, Chou En-lai, demanded that the U.S. and other Western powers be excluded from Far Eastern affairs. Secretary of State John Foster Dulles answered that the "authority of the UN" was "at stake," and if "this conference is disloyal to the UN and its decisions on how to make peace and unify Korea, then each of us will bear a share of responsibility for destroying what protects us all." Chou replied that "the countries of Asia should consult among themselves,...seeking common measures to safeguard peace and security in Asia." He called the U.S. an aggressor "dreaming to impose upon the Chinese people the power of the Kuomintang remnant clique." Chou demanded removal of all foreign military personnel and bases from Asia. The following day, the Soviet Union announced its support of Chou's stand and condemned the U.S. for refusing to recognize Communist China. Soviet Foreign Minister Molotov said that any peace settlement must recognize that "the peoples of Asia have the full right to settle their own affairs."

French Pledge to Viet Nam. On April 28, France pledged "total independence" to Viet Nam, which promised to "maintain and consolidate" its friendship with France.

Indo-Chinese Invited to Geneva. On May 3, Cambodia, Laos and the Viet Minh rebels were invited to the Geneva Conference as preparations began to arrange a truce or peace in Indo-China.

Dulles Goes Home. On May 4, Secretary of State Dulles returned home and said the Geneva Conference was "going just as we expected." The Secretary faced growing criticism in Washington because he had not yet obtained agreement to a Southeast Asian defense alliance. Dulles said the following day that he was at a loss to understand "what has happened (in Geneva) which is alleged to constitute a defeat." President Eisenhower added that "it was never expected that this collective security arrangement would spring into existence overnight."

Dienbienphu Totters. On May 4, Viet Minh forces, by means of "human sea" attacks, pushed to within 500 yards of the French command post in Dienbienphu.

Dienbienphu Falls. On May 7, the French fortress at Dienbienphu was overrun -- the first time in the Indo-Chinese war that a French stronghold had been conquered by direct assault. The final attack climaxed eight weeks of siege. The Communists on May 10 claimed to have taken 10,000 prisoners, including Brig. Gen. Christian de Castries, commander of the fortress. They said an additional 6,000 were killed or wounded.

Dulles Broadcast. On May 7, Secretary of State Dulles said over radio and television that the U.S. might have to make "serious commitments" to defend Southeast Asia, although the President would not order military action in Indo-China without the support of Congress. Dulles added that "Dienbienphu will harden, not weaken, our purpose to stay united."

Geneva Conference -- Part II. On May 8, the Geneva Conference turned its attention to Indo-China. Nine states -- the U.S., France, Britain, Russia, Red China, Cambodia, Laos, North Viet Nam, and South Viet Nam -- participated in the second part of the conference. Discussions were promptly deadlocked by the Communists' refusal to accept independence for Laos and Cambodia.

Britain on Asian Security. On May 18, British Prime Minister Winston Churchill told the House of Commons that "final decisions cannot be taken regarding establishment of a collective defense in Southeast Asia and the Western Pacific" until "the outcome of the Geneva Conference is known." On May 25, Secretary of State Dulles expressed hope that the British would join a Southeast Asia security alliance.

Viet Minh Offer. On May 25, the Viet Minh delegation at Geneva proposed establishment of separate zones in Indo-China during a cease-fire. The Laotian and Cambodian delegations immediately complained that a cease-fire agreement would have to be limited to Viet Nam. The U.S. supported their position. On May 29, the conference ordered direct military talks on a Vietnamese cease-fire agreement, beginning June 1. The U.S., Cambodia, and Laos reiterated their position that Laos and Cambodia had been invaded by foreign troops and that only Viet Nam could be considered in a state of civil war. On June 3, Communist delegates rejected a separate truce for Viet Nam and UN supervision of an Indo-China armistice. They offered as an alternative the creation of a Korean-style cease-fire commission to supervise all three Indo-Chinese states. A U.S.-French compromise to establish a neutral Asian supervisory commission was rejected by the Soviet Union on June 7, and Soviet Foreign Minister Molotov demanded the "withdrawal of all foreign troops from the territory of Indo-China." The following day, Chinese Foreign Minister Chou En-lai endorsed the Soviet demands.

New French Government. On June 13, Pierre Mendes-France replaced French Premier Joseph Laniel, whose government had lost a vote of confidence in the National Assembly on June 12.

Korean Talks Ended. On June 15, the Korean phase of the Geneva talks was terminated by the UN allies, who pointed out that the Communists had rejected "every effort to obtain agreement." The South Korean foreign minister said the failure of the talks left his government "free to take action."

Diem Becomes Premier. On June 15, Ngo Dinh Diem became premier of South Viet Nam. He had lived in France for three years, protesting colonialism in Indo-China.

Chinese Offer at Geneva. On June 1, Chinese Communist Foreign Minister Chou En-lai offered a new compromise proposal on Indo-China at the Geneva Conference, breaking what had seemed an insurmountable deadlock. The Chinese dropped their demand that rebel forces in Laos and Cambodia be recognized as "governments," said those forces would be withdrawn under a cease-fire, and asked that the Viet Minh rebel command represent the Communists in truce talks in Viet Nam.

Talks Continue. On June 19, the French, British, Soviet, and Chinese delegates agreed to go on with the talks. Under Secretary of State Walter Bedell Smith continued to represent the U.S. but played a more or less passive role. Secretary Dulles, who remained in Washington, was not hopeful of favorable results.

French-Chinese Meeting. On June 23, French Premier Mendes-France and Chinese Communist Premier Chou En-lai met in Bern, Switzerland. The two agreed that a unified Vietnamese government should be established but that the military would remain divided; that a general election should be held after a period of truce; and that Laos and Cambodia should remain sovereign but be neutralized.

Eisenhower-Churchill Meeting. On June 28, President Eisenhower and British Prime Minister Churchill issued a joint statement at the conclusion of four days of talks in Washington. The statement urged the formation of a collective defense alliance for Southeast Asia and warned that "if at Geneva the French government is confronted with demands that prevent an acceptable agreement regarding Indo-China, the international situation will be seriously aggravated."

French Withdrawal. On June 29, French forces in Indo-China withdrew from the southern section of the Red River delta to lines around Hanoi and Haiphong.

Communist China-UN Dispute. On July 1, U.S. Senate Majority Leader William F. Knowland (R Calif.) announced that if Communist China were admitted to the UN, he would resign as majority leader to "devote my full efforts" to terminating U.S. membership. Senate Minority Leader Lyndon B. Johnson (D Texas) said on the Senate floor, July 2, that "the American people will refuse to support" the UN if Communist China is admitted. President Eisenhower said he was "completely and unalterably opposed under the present situation to the admission of Red China," but he implied opposition to U.S. withdrawal. On July 3, Vice President Nixon attributed responsibility for the loss of China and for the Southeast Asian crisis to former President Truman and former Secretary of State Dean Acheson. Sen J. William Fulbright (D Ark.) countered that Nixon was attempting to negate "bipartisan responsibility for foreign policy" and

accused the Vice Presisent of "immoral politics." Sen. John J. Sparkman (D Ala.) said Nixon was preparing "an alibi for the loss of Indo-China."

Dismissal of Lattimore Charge. On July 8, a U.S. Court of Appeals in Washington upheld dismissal of an important count in the perjury indictment of Johns Hopkins University Prof. Owen Lattimore. But the court reinstated two charges against Lattimore.

Dulles on Red China in UN. On July 8, Secretary of State John Foster Dulles told a press conference he was "confident" the U.S. could bar Communist China from a seat in the UN. He added that he could see no reason for "American withdrawal from the UN."

Hanoi and Haiphong Attacked. On July 12, Viet Minh forces intensified their attacks on French defenses at Hanoi and Haiphong.

Dulles Confers on Truce. On July 12, Secretary of State Dulles gave some support to Indo-Chinese truce terms advocated by French Premier Mendes-France. Dulles had flown to Paris to meet with the French Premier and British Foreign Secretary Anthony Eden on a collective defense alliance in Southeast Asia.

Indo-China Settlement. On July 21, separate armistice agreements signed in Geneva with Cambodia, Laos and Viet Nam ended the seven and one-half year war in Indo-China. The U.S. refused to sign the agreements but promised that it would use no threat or force to upset them. South Viet Nam also refused to sign. Under the provisions of the agreements, Viet Nam was divided into two parts along the 17th Parallel, the northern section controlled by the Viet Minh and the southern by the pro-French government in Saigon. Rebel forces in southern Viet Nam were to be withdrawn to the north within 10 months and the French were given the same amount of time to evacuate the Hanoi area. Neither foreign troops nor arms and munitions of any kind were to be introduced into Viet Nam. Cambodia and Laos were to be demilitarized (with the exception of two French outposts) and the territorial and political integrity of both was to be recognized by the Communists (rebel forces were permitted to remain in two Laotian provinces on the North Vietnamese border). Civilians were to be allowed to move from North to South Viet Nam or vice versa and war prisoners were to be exchanged within 30 days. An International Control Commission was established, composed of India, Poland, and Canada, to supervise the agreements.

Final Geneva Declaration. On the day the armistice agreements were signed, the Geneva Conference ended with a "final declaration" which obligated the signatories (again not including the U.S. or South Viet Nam) to observe certain additional stipulations:

1. Laos and Cambodia were not to request foreign military aid except for self-defense.

2. The military demarcation line in Viet Nam (the 17th Parallel) was not to be "interpreted as constituting a political or territorial boundary."

3. General elections were to be held in Viet Nam in July 1956 "under the supervision of an international commission composed of representatives of the member states of the International Supervisory (Control) Commission." Consultations on the elections were to be held "from April 20, 1955, onwards."

4. The signatories were to "respect the sovereignty, the independence, the unity, and the territorial integrity"

of Cambodia, Laos and Viet Nam and "refrain from any interference in their internal affairs."

Eisenhower's Reaction.   On July 21, President Eisenhower told a news conference that the Geneva agreement contained "features we do not like, but a great deal depends on how they work in practice." He said he could not offer a better proposal and would therefore not criticize the conference. Eisenhower pointed out that the U.S. "has not itself been party to or bound by the decisions," but has only attempted "to try to be helpful where desired and to aid (in obtaining) a just and honorable settlement." The President added that the U.S. was "actively pursuing discussions (aimed at) rapid organization of a collective defense in Southeast Asia...to prevent further direct or indirect Communist aggression in that general area."

Casualties in Indo-China.   Total pro-French casualties in the Indo-Chinese war were estimated at 253,000 with 92,000 dead or missing. More than 200,000 Viet Minh soldiers died, according to unofficial estimates.

Red Chinese Air Attacks.   On July 23, Chinese Communist fighter planes shot down a British airliner in the South China Sea, 30 miles south of Hainan Island. On July 26, three American planes searching for survivors were fired on by two Chinese Communist aircraft. The American pilots shot down both. Peking expressed regret for the first incident, explaining that the British aircraft was mistaken for a Chinese Nationalist warplane, but it said the U.S. planes had "committed an act of aggression." Secretary of State Dulles called the incident a "belligerent interference with a humanitarian rescue operation being conducted over the high seas."

Rhee Addresses Congress.   On July 28, South Korean President Syngman Rhee appealed to a joint session of the U.S. Congress to support South Korea and Nationalist China in an attack on mainland China. Rhee said only U.S. air and sea power would be necessary; the manpower would be supplied by South Korea and Formosa.

Chou's Statement.   On Aug. 11, Communist China's Foreign Minister, Chou En-lai, urged the "liberation" of Formosa and warned that "foreign aggressors" who intervened would face "grave consequences." On Aug. 17, President Eisenhower commented that the Communists would have to contend with the Seventh Fleet before reaching Formosa. On Aug. 23, about 40 Chinese Communist troops staged a raid on Nationalist-held Quemoy Island, 15 miles from the mainland. The Nationalists countered with heavy sea and air attacks on the mainland during the next two weeks. On Sept. 3, Red artillery began shelling Quemoy and the Nationalists returned the fire.

Creation of SEATO.   On Sept. 8, eight nations signed in Manila a U.S.-sponsored Southeast Asian collective defense treaty. The signatories were Australia, Britain, France, New Zealand, Pakistan, the Philippines, Thailand, and the U.S. The treaty, which established the Southeast Asia Treaty Organization, pledged each of the member states in the event of armed aggression against any one of them to "act to meet the common danger in accordance with its constitutional processes." Member states agreed also to "develop their individual and collective capacity to resist armed attack and to prevent and counter subversive activities directed from without against their territorial

integrity and political stability." A third commitment was to consult on joint measures to meet the threat raised by "any fact or situation (other than armed attack) which might endanger the peace of the area." The area covered by the treaty was defined as the "general area of Southeast Asia, including the "entire territories" of the Asian parties to the treaty, and the "general area of the Southwest Pacific" below a line running to the south of Formosa.

A protocol to the treaty extended its provisions for economic assistance and for protection against aggression to Cambodia, Laos and South Viet Nam. An official "understanding," filed with the treaty, made it clear that the American commitment applied only to "Communist aggression," but that the U.S. would consult with SEATO members in the event of "other aggression or armed attack." The word "Communist" did not appear in the treaty.

Dulles on SEATO.   On Sept. 8, Secretary of State Dulles called the SEATO treaty an "Asiatic Monroe Doctrine." He said in Manila that it "promoted unity rather than disunity" and was "a major step in building security" for Southeast Asia. The Chinese Communists on the same day termed the treaty a U.S. device to incite Asians against Asians.

Dulles Assures Formosa.   On Sept. 12, Secretary Dulles told newsmen in Denver that he believed the Chinese Communists would not invade Formosa. He said that invasion would be impossible against "such opposition as we would interpose" and that, in his opinion, Quemoy also was secure.

China Question in UN.   On Sept. 21, the General Assembly bypassed a Soviet resolution urging admission of Red China to the UN and adopted, by a 43-11 vote, a U.S. resolution putting off debate on the question to September 1955.

Viet Minh in Hanoi.   On Oct. 9, Viet Minh forces occupied Hanoi and were greeted by flag and banner-waving residents.

Eisenhower Note to Diem.   On Oct. 23, President Eisenhower sent a note to South Vietnamese Premier Ngo Dinh Diem urging "needed reforms" in return for U.S. aid. The President said the aid would help South Viet Nam to develop and maintain "a strong viable state capable of resisting attempted subversion or aggression through military means."

Nehru on Red China.   On Oct. 31, Indian Prime Minister Jawaharlal Nehru reported on his return from Communist China that Mao Tse-tung had assured him that China wished to avoid war because it would interfere with the country's economic development. Nehru said that Mao thought the Geneva Conference "had eased the world situation greatly," but he felt that Korea, Formosa, and Indo-China were still major threats to world peace.

U.S. Mid-Term Elections.   On Nov. 2, the Democrats gained slender majorities in both chambers of Congress. President Eisenhower announced his intention to cooperate fully with Democratic leaders.

Debates on China Banned.   On Nov. 15, the Army and Navy confirmed that West Point cadets and Annapolis midshipmen had been ordered not to participate in intercollegiate debates concerning the recognition of Communist China.

Chinese Sentence Americans.   On Nov. 22, a Chinese Communist military tribunal sentenced 11 U.S. airmen and two civilian U.S. Army employees to long prison terms as spies. They had been captured in two groups when their planes were shot down during the Korean War. The State Department sent the "strongest possible protest" to Communist China, and the Defense Department called the charges "utterly false." President Eisenhower said the U.S. would do everything "humanly possible within peaceful means" to obtain release of the prisoners. *(See Aug. 1, 1966)*

Knowland Reaction. On Nov. 27, Senate Majority Leader William F. Knowland (R Calif.) urged that the U.S. establish a naval blockade of mainland China "until these Americans are released."

Dulles on Blockade. On Nov. 29, Secretary of State Dulles told a Chicago audience that a U.S. blockade of Communist China would be an act of war and that imprisonment of the 13 Americans was "a challenge to us...to find ways, consistent with peace, to sustain international rights and justice." Dulles added that the U.S. was obligated to settle disputes within the framework of the UN "in such a manner that international peace is not endangered." On Dec. 1, he said a blockade was "certainly a possibility" if all peaceful efforts to obtain the release of the Americans failed.

Formosa Pact. On Dec. 2, Secretary Dulles signed a treaty for the defense of Formosa in case of Chinese Communist attack. The treaty did not cover Nationalist-held islands along the coast of China.

Senate Censures McCarthy. On Dec. 2, 1954, the Senate by a 67-22 roll-call vote condemned Sen. Joseph R. McCarthy (R Wis.) for failing to cooperate with a Senate subcommittee that had inquired into his financial affairs in 1951-52, and for leveling abusive charges against the bipartisan Select Committee which had recommended that he be censured. The vote culminated a long controversy over what official attitude the Senate should take toward certain of McCarthy's actions. The resolution finally adopted in amended form (S Res 301) had been introduced by Sen. Ralph E. Flanders (R Vt.) on July 30. As introduced, it proposed merely that the conduct of the Senator be condemned as "unbecoming a Member of the United States Senate... contrary to Senatorial traditions," and tending "to bring the Senate into disrepute." When it was objected that the resolution carried no bill of particulars, Flanders and others filed numerous specific charges which were referred to the Select Committee.

The Committee's report, Nov. 8, recommended censure on two principal counts: (1) McCarthy's lack of cooperation in the investigation of his financial affairs; and (2) McCarthy's treatment of Gen. Ralph W. Zwicker when he testified before him as chairman of the Investigations Subcommittee of the Senate Government Operations Committee. The Senate, in the resolution as adopted, condemned, not censured, McCarthy on the first count. For the second count, it substituted a recital of various McCarthy charges against the Select Committee and condemned the Senator's conduct in making them as "contrary to Senatorial ethics" and as tending "to bring the Senate into dishonor and disrepute, to obstruct the constitutional processes of the Senate, and to impair its dignity."

Eisenhower Pleased. On Dec. 4, President Eisenhower personally congratulated Sen. Arthur V. Watkins (R Utah) for "a very splendid job" as chairman of the Select Committee.

McCarthy Displeased. On Dec. 7, Sen. McCarthy assailed President Eisenhower because he "on one hand congratulates the Senators who hold up the work of our Committee, and on the other hand urges that we be patient with the (Chinese) Communist hoodlums who at this very moment are torturing and brainwashing American uniformed men in Communist dungeons."

UN Resolution. On Dec. 7, the 16 Korean War allies offered a resolution in the General Assembly accusing Red China of violating the Korean armistice by jailing 13 Americans as spies *(see Nov. 22, 1954)* and detaining other captured UN personnel who wanted to be repatriated. On Dec. 10, the General Assembly adopted the resolution and instructed Secretary General Dag Hammarskjold to seek immediate release of the prisoners. On Dec. 13, Peking Radio said the UN had no right to interfere with the conviction and punishment of the Americans.

Warning on Formosa. On Dec. 8, Chou En-lai, Chinese Communist Premier-Foreign Minister, warned the U.S. that it would face "grave consequences" if it did not withdraw "all its armed forces" from Formosa. Chou said Communist China was determined "to liberate Taiwan (Formosa) and liquidate the traitorous Chiang Kai-shek clique." On Dec. 15, the Soviet Union announced "full support" of the Chinese demands.

Peking Visit. On Dec. 30, UN Secretary General Dag Hammarskjold left New York for Peking to try to obtain release of the 13 Americans and other Allied prisoners.

1955

Hammarskjold in Peking -- Red China Threatens Formosa -- Congress Authorizes Use of U.S. Armed Forces to Defend Formosa -- Mutual Defense Treaty with Nationalist China -- Differences Over Offshore Islands of Quemoy and Matsu -- Chou En-lai at Bandung Conference -- Progress Toward Release of Americans in Communist China -- Premier Diem of South Viet Nam Becomes President Diem.

Hammarskjold in Peking. On Jan. 5, UN Secretary General Dag Hammarskjold arrived in Peking to negotiate with Chinese Communist leaders for release of 13 American prisoners. On Jan. 10, Hammarskjold and Chinese Premier-Foreign Minister Chou En-lai issued a joint statement saying that the "talks have been useful and we hope to be able to continue the contact established in these meetings."

Red Raids on Tachen Islands. On Jan. 10, the Nationalist Chinese Defense Ministry announced that the Chinese Communists had launched the largest air attacks of the civil war against the Nationalist-held Tachen Islands, 200 miles north of Formosa.

Hammarskjold Returns. On Jan. 23, UN Secretary General Dag Hammarskjold returned to New York and reported that his visit had been important as "a first stage" in obtaining release of the 13 Americans. Hammarskjold told reporters: "I feel my talks with Mr. Chou En-lai were definitely useful for this purpose. We hope to be able to continue our contact. The door that is opened can be kept open, given restraint on both sides." The Secretary General held a private conference with U.S. Ambassador-to-the-UN Henry Cabot Lodge. Lodge later expressed "disappointment" that the Americans were not immediately released, but he said he was confident that "progress has been made and that our fliers will be free." On Jan. 14, Hammarskjold told a news conference he had made "no deals of any kind" with the Chinese Communists, but that he did feel it would be "useful" if they were allowed to enter the UN.

Nationalist Pledge. On Jan. 14, it was reported that Chinese Nationalist Foreign Minister George K.C. Yeh had pledged, in a private letter to the U.S., that under the U.S.-Nationalist Chinese mutual defense treaty, his country would not invade the Chinese mainland without prior U.S. approval. On Jan. 16, UN Secretary General Dag Hammarskjold said he planned to send a message to Peking informing the Chinese Communist leaders of the Nationalist pledge.

Communists Invade Yikiang. On Jan. 18, Chinese Communist forces invaded Yikiang Island, eight miles north of the Tachen Islands and 210 miles north of Formosa. The small Nationalist force defending the island quickly surrendered. The following day, over 200 Communist aircraft bombed the Tachens and the Nationalist Air Force retaliated by bombing Communist shipping along the China coast. On Jan. 19, President Eisenhower told a news conference he hoped the UN would "exercise its good offices" to obtain a cease-fire in the Formosa Strait.

Chou Threatens Formosa. On Jan. 24, Chinese Communist Premier-Foreign Minister Chou En-lai reiterated his country's intention to invade Formosa and rejected the possibility of a cease-fire. Chou said the U.S. was "using war threats and brandishing atomic weapons to force the Chinese people into tolerating" the "occupation" of Formosa. He demanded that American forces depart from the area.

Eisenhower's Message. On Jan. 24, President Eisenhower sent a special message to Congress requesting emergency authorization to use American armed forces to protect Formosa and the Pescadores Islands. The President said Formosa and the Pescadores "should remain in friendly hands," because, "in unfriendly hands," they "would seriously dislocate the...balance of moral, economic and military forces upon which the peace of the Pacific depends." Eisenhower recounted "a series of provocative political and military actions, establishing a pattern of aggressive purpose" on the part of the Communists. He noted that the Communists had climaxed their military actions with conquest of the island of Yichiang, and said the situation posed "a serious danger." Pending UN action, the President continued, Congress should "improve the prospects for peace" by authorizing the use of American armed forces "if necessary to assure the security of Formosa and the Pescadores." Eisenhower said a resolution to that effect might prevent the Communists from "misjudging our firm purpose and national unity" and "readiness to fight if necessary."

Formosa Resolution. On Jan. 25, the House adopted the Administration resolution (H J Res 159) by a 410-3 roll-call vote and sent it to the Senate without amendment. On Jan. 28, the Senate adopted the resolution by an 85-3 roll-call vote without amendment. The negative votes were cast by Sens. Wayne Morse (D Ore.), William Langer (R N.D.), and Herbert H. Lehman (D N.Y.).

Sen. Morse said Congress, by adopting the resolution, would give the President "a predated authorization" to wage war.

Sen. Hubert H. Humphrey (D Minn.) offered an amendment to restrict the use of armed force specifically to the defense of Formosa and the Pescadores. He said he regretted "that the resolution is not one which we are permitted to design; it is one which we are permitted to accept or reject; and to reject it would be to undermine the President's authority completely and totally." He added that there was not "one iota of evidence" to show that the offshore islands of Quemoy and Matsu, close to the China coast and not in the Pescadores group, were "essential for the defense of Formosa."

Sen. Walter F. George (D Ga.), chairman of the Foreign Relations Committee, replied that turning over Quemoy and Matsu to the Communists would lead to a "disintegration that would...be swift, quick, speedy, and final" and would "cut the heart out" of Nationalist troops.

Morse answered that it "would be a bad historic precedent if we should involve ourselves in a civil war over Quemoy and Matsu" which "the sovereign rights of Red China certainly encompass."

Sen. Russell B. Long (D La.) said "the resolution declares to the world that we are ready to stand with the President in the defense of Formosa and the Pescadores, and if those islands are attacked we are ready to go to war with Red China."

President Signs Resolution. On Jan. 29, President Eisenhower signed H J Res 159 into law (PL 84-4). He said adoption of the resolution was "a step to preserve the peace in the Formosa area," adding that "We are ready to support a United Nations effort to end the present hostilities in the area, but we are also united in our determination to defend an area vital to the security of the United States and the free world."

Cease-fire Rejection. On Jan. 29, the Communist Chinese radio rejected the idea of a cease-fire in the Formosa area. It asked that the UN "take steps to check U.S. aggression against China."

Cease-fire on UN Agenda. On Jan. 31, the UN Security Council voted 9-1 (Russia opposed, Nationalist China abstaining) to place on its agenda a proposal by New Zealand for a Formosa cease-fire. The Council then adopted, 9-1 (Nationalist China opposed, Russia abstaining), a New Zealand resolution to invite Communist China to participate in the discussion.

Red China Refuses Invitation. On Feb. 3, the Chinese Communists rejected the UN invitation to attend discussions on a Formosa cease-fire. They said they would come only if the Nationalist Chinese representatives were "driven out from the Security Council" and replaced by a Communist delegation.

Tachen Withdrawal. On Feb. 5, the U.S. announced that the Nationalist government had decided to withdraw from the Tachen Islands and had requested U.S. protection of the withdrawal operation.

New Soviet Leadership. On Feb. 8, the U.S.S.R. Supreme Soviet announced removal of Georgi M. Malenkov from the premiership and criticized his policy of emphasizing consumer goods production rather than heavy industry. Malenkov admitted his "guilt and responsibility" for "the unsatisfactory state of affairs which has arisen in agriculture." Defense Minister Marshal Nikolai A. Bulganin became the new premier, and the First Secretary of the

Communist Party's Central Committee, Nikita S. Khrushchev, emerged as the strongest figure in the Communist Party.

Senate Ratifies Treaty. On Feb. 9, the U.S. Senate consented, by a 65-6 roll-call vote, to ratification of a mutual defense treaty with Nationalist China. The treaty required the U.S. and Nationalist China to:

(1) Maintain and develop "jointly by self-help and mutual aid" their individual and collective capacity to resist armed attack and Communist subversion directed against them "from without."

(2) Cooperate in economic development.

(3) Consult on implementation of the treaty.

(4) Act to meet an armed attack "in the West Pacific area directed against the territories" of either the U.S. or the Republic of China, including Formosa, the Pescadores Islands, and "such other territories as may be determined by mutual agreement."

In Senate debate, Sen. Wayne Morse (D Ore.) said the treaty "further increases the possibility of war in the Pacific." Sen. Estes Kefauver (D Tenn.) agreed: "I can see no reason for having our nation enter into treaty obligations with the government of Chiang Kai-shek...I do not wish to give the color of sovereignty and permanency to the government of Chiang Kai-shek on Formosa and the Pescadores." Senate Minority Leader William F. Knowland (R Calif.) answered that it was "extremely important" that the U.S. "serve notice that this area will not be used as a blue chip in an international poker game." He said Formosa was "a key part" of the "defense line in the Pacific."

Sen. Alexander Wiley (R Wis.), ranking minority member of the Foreign Relations Committee, asserted that it was "in the national interest that Formosa and the Pescadores be kept in friendly hands.... Either we can defend the United States in the straits of Formosa -- now -- or we can defend it later in San Francisco Bay."

Sen. Herbert H. Lehman (D N.Y.) argued that the Congress had already authorized the President to use U.S. armed forces in defense of Formosa and the Pescadores. "What contribution is made, what strength is taken on, what further pause is given to the Chinese Communists by virtue of this treaty?"

On Feb. 11, President Eisenhower signed the resolution of ratification.

UN Shelves Cease-fire Proposal. On Feb. 14, the UN Security Council tabled New Zealand's Formosa cease-fire proposal.

Nationalist Military Action. On Feb. 22, the Nationalist government on Formosa claimed its largest military victory since leaving the mainland in 1949. The Nationalists said their ships and warplanes had launched successful strikes against Chinese Communist convoys enroute to the Red-held Taishan Islands.

SEATO Meeting. On Feb. 23, the foreign ministers of the eight SEATO nations met in Thailand to formulate defense plans for the member nations. It was the first meeting of the council. The treaty went into effect on Feb. 19.

Chou Offer on Prisoners. On Feb. 28, Chinese Communist Premier Chou En-lai offered to receive an unofficial U.S. delegation to negotiate the release of 13 Americans imprisoned as spies. The U.S. rejected the offer and demanded immediate release of the prisoners.

Dulles Warning to Red China. On March 8, Secretary of State John Foster Dulles, in a nationwide broadcast, warned Communist China not to underestimate U.S. determination to meet aggression in the Far East. Dulles said the SEATO nations "possess plenty of strength" in the area. He added that the U.S. contribution would be primarily in terms of air and sea power and pointed out that American naval and air forces were "equipped with new and powerful weapons of precision, which can utterly destroy military targets without endangering unrelated civilian centers."

Morse Resolution on Offshore Islands. On April 1, Sen. Wayne Morse (D Ore.) introduced a resolution in the Senate to bar the President from employing U.S. forces to defend the islands of Quemoy and Matsu. The resolution was co-sponsored by Democratic Sens. Herbert H. Lehman (N.Y.), Hubert H. Humphrey (Minn.), and Russell B. Long (La.). Morse said the "question is whether we are going deliberately to proceed on a course that involves us in a war on mainland China as an aggressor nation." Minority Leader William F. Knowland (R Calif.) said the resolution tended to "give aid and comfort to communism."

Chinese Free to Leave U.S. On April 2, the State Department announced that 76 Chinese students with technical training who had been refused exit permits after the start of the Korean War, because they might have helped the Communists in Korea, were now "free to depart" from the U.S. The Department denied there was any deal for release of Americans held in China, though "We would like Americans of all categories in China to be released for whatever reason appeals to the Red Chinese authorities."

Dean Urges Recognition. On April 8, Arthur H. Dean, U.S. negotiator in the Korean armistice talks at Panmunjom and a former law partner of Secretary of State Dulles, urged in an article in *Foreign Affairs* that the U.S. recognize Communist China.

Stevenson on Offshore Islands. On April 11, Adlai E. Stevenson told a national radio audience that the U.S. should seek an international declaration "condemning the use of force in the Formosa Strait" and an agreement by free nations "to stand with us in the defense of Formosa against any aggression, pending some final settlement of its status."

The Democratic party's titular leader observed in the same speech that "The possibility of war just now seems to hinge upon Quemoy and Matsu, small islands that lie almost as close to the coast of China as Staten Island does to New York." He asked: "Are the offshore islands essential to the security of the U.S.? Are they, indeed, even essential to the defense of Formosa -- which all Americans have agreed upon since President Truman sent the Seventh Fleet there five years ago?"

Stevenson concluded: "Should we be plunged into another great war, the maintenance of our alliances and the respect and the good will of the uncommitted nations of Asia will be far more important to us than the possession of these offshore islands by Gen. Chiang Kai-shek ever could be."

Dulles' Comment. Secretary of State Dulles remarked at a news conference the following day that Stevenson "suggests, as original ideas, the very approaches which the Government has been and is actively exploring." Dulles cautioned that "The results we want will not be advanced by publicly prodding friendly governments."

Bandung Conference. On April 18, a conference of representatives of 29 Asian and African nations convened in Bandung, Indonesia. The following day, Chinese Communist Premier Chou En-lai, addressing the conference, said:

"Agreements on the restoration of peace in Indo-China reached at the Geneva Conference are endangered. The U.S. continues to create tension in the Formosa area. Countries outside of Asia and Africa are establishing more and more military bases in Asian and African countries. They are creating more and more atomic weapons..." He said the "will of the Chinese people to liberate Formosa and the coastal islands is a just one."

Chou noted that most Asian and African nations, "including China," were "still very backward economically owing to the long period of colonial domination" "That is why," he said, "we demand not only political independence but economic independence as well."

Red China Ready to Negotiate. On April 23, Premier Chou En-lai, in another statement at Bandung, said: "The Chinese people are friendly to the American people. The Chinese people do not want to have war with the U.S.A. The Chinese government is willing to sit down and enter into negotiations with the U.S. Government to discuss the question of relaxing tension in the Far East and especially the question of relaxing tension in the Taiwan (Formosa) area."

U.S. Reaction. The State Department said the same day that the U.S. would agree to negotiations if the Chinese Communists would allow Nationalist China's participation in the discussions as an equal, would release Americans imprisoned in China, and would accept the "outstanding invitation" of the UN Security Council "to participate in discussions to end hostilities in the Formosa region."

On April 26, Secretary of State Dulles said at a news conference: The "first thing is to find out whether there is a possibility of a cease-fire in the area (of Formosa). That is a matter which can be discussed, perhaps bilaterally, or at the UN, or possibly under other circumstances. But I regard a cease-fire as the indispensable prerequisite to anything further. When you get into further matters, then the interests of the Chinese Nationalists would naturally come to play a very large part."

President Eisenhower endorsed Dulles' statement the next day, but Senate Minority Leader William F. Knowland (R Calif.) immediately voiced opposition to negotiations with Red China. Democratic Sens. Walter F. George (Ga.), Majority Leader Lyndon B. Johnson (Texas), Estes Kefauver (Tenn.), and John J. Sparkman (Ala.) all supported the idea.

Conference Adjourns. On April 27, the Bandung Conference adjourned.

Nehru's Announcement. On April 30, Indian Prime Minister Jawaharlal Nehru announced that Indian UN delegate V.K. Krishna Menon had been invited to Peking by Chinese Communist Premier Chou En-lai to discuss the Formosa crisis. Nehru said the Indian government would attempt to avert "the grim alternative that faces us if there are to be no negotiations."

Air Skirmish Near Korea. On May 11, the U.S. lodged a protest with the Korean Armistice Commission against a Chinese Communist attack on U.S. fighter planes "over international waters" near North Korea. The U.S. reported it had shot down two or three Communist planes in the skirmish. The Chinese Communists claimed they had shot down one U.S. plane and damaged two more. The Communists said the U.S. aircraft had violated China's "territorial air" by passing over two Chinese islands off the Manchurian coast.

Four Fliers Released. On May 30, Indian UN delegate V.K. Krishna Menon announced in New Delhi that the Chinese Communists would release four American airmen who had been imprisoned in China for more than two years. Menon said the Chinese still held 11 U.S. fliers who had been convicted of espionage and sabotage. The Indian diplomat had conferred with Chinese Communist Premier Chou En-lai for 11 days in Peking. On June 1, he flew to Washington for discussions on "lowering tensions" between the U.S. and Communist China.

On May 31, UN Secretary General Dag Hammarskjold asked the Chinese Communist government to release all other Americans imprisoned in China. On June 1, the four released fliers said that Hammarskjold's January visit to Peking "had very much to do with our release."

Lattimore Case Dropped. On June 28, Attorney General Herbert Brownell Jr. announced that the Government was dropping its perjury case against Johns Hopkins Prof. Owen Lattimore because "there is no reasonable likelihood of a successful prosecution..."

Johnson Ill. On July 2, Senate Majority Leader Lyndon Baines Johnson (D Texas) suffered a serious heart attack at Middleburg, Va., and was rushed to the Naval Medical Center in Bethesda, Md., where doctors announced that he would be unable to return to Congress during the remainder of the session. Majority Whip Sen. Earle C. Clements (Ky.) took over Johnson's duties.

Aid to North Viet Nam. On July 8, Peking Radio announced a $338 million economic aid program for North Viet Nam. North Vietnamese President Ho Chi Minh had visited Peking to ask for aid and had joined Chinese Communist Premier Chou En-lai in accusing the U.S. of seeking to prevent "peaceful unification" of Viet Nam through elections.

Prisoners Return. On July 10, three of the 23 Americans who had been captured during the Korean War and elected to stay in China left for Hong Kong.

Diem on Elections. On July 16, South Vietnamese Premier Ngo Dinh Diem said he favored free elections for reunification of Viet Nam, but that he was "skeptical concerning the possibility" of elections in North Viet Nam with its "regime of oppression." Diem proposed that the government in Hanoi prove that it placed "the superior interests of the national community above those of communism."

Big Powers Prod Diem. On July 22, the U.S., Britain, and France decided, during the summit conference at Geneva, to recommend that South Viet Nam open pre-election talks with North Viet Nam. Indian Prime Minister Jawaharlal Nehru had complained that South Viet Nam was reluctant to enter into the talks called for by the 1954 Geneva Conference agreements on Indo-China.

U.S. Talks With Red China. On July 25, the U.S. and Communist China announced that discussions between the two countries, carried on in Geneva from time to time since 1954, would be elevated from a consular to an ambassadorial level. The State Department said the action was "in the hope that this would bring about agreement on the return of U.S. civilians detained in China and facilitate further discussions and settlement of other practical matters." The Department added that the change in status of the talks would "not involve diplomatic recognition." On July 27, President Eisenhower told a news conference that the talks might "eventually" reach the foreign minister level.

Chou on Trade and Formosa. On July 30, Chinese Communist Premier Chou En-lai told the National People's Congress in Peking that the "number of American civilians in China is small and their question can be easily settled." He voiced concern over "the extremely unjust policy of blockade and embargo which obstructs trade between countries" and said it should be possible "to remove such barriers so that peaceful trade between all countries will not be hindered."

Chou observed that after "the Korean armistice and the restoration of peace in Indo-China, the situation in the Formosa area has become the most tense in the Far East." He continued: "Provided that the U.S. does not interfere with China's internal problems, the possibility of peaceful liberation of Formosa will continue to increase. If possible, the Chinese government is willing to enter into negotiations with the responsible local authorities of Formosa to map out concrete steps for Formosa's peaceful liberation. It should be made clear that there should be negotiations between the central government and local authorities. The Chinese people are firmly opposed to any ideas or plots of the so-called 'two Chinas.'"

More Fliers Freed. On Aug. 1, Communist China announced that 11 U.S. fliers imprisoned as spies had been released. The Chinese Ambassador to Poland, Wang Ping-nan, who was meeting in Geneva with the U.S. Ambassador to Czechoslovakia, U. Alexis Johnson, confirmed the action and expressed hope it would "have favorable effects on our present talks."

Dulles on Chou's Speech. On Aug. 2, Secretary of State Dulles told a news conference that Chou En-lai's speech "indicated his going further in the renunciation of force than anything he had said before." Dulles went on to say: "What we hope to arrive at by progressive steps is a situation where the Chinese Communists will have renounced the use of force to achieve their ambitions. If they want to use force...that will almost surely start up a war, the limits of which could not be defined in advance."

On Aug. 16, the Secretary expressed disappointment that the Chinese-U.S. talks in Geneva still had not resulted in release of 41 U.S. civilians held in China. He had hoped, in light of Chou's speech, that the matter would be "promptly settled."

Civilians Released. On Sept. 6, Wang Ping-nan, Red China's Ambassador to Poland, announced to U. Alexis Johnson, U.S. Ambassador to Czechoslovakia, that the Chinese Communist government would release 12 of the 41 American citizens held in China. The State Department called the action "encouraging" but reaffirmed demands that all of the civilians be released. On Sept. 10, Wang said the remaining 29 American civilians would be released, but he requested discussions between the two countries at a higher level. Johnson replied that the U.S. would consider the matter after the Americans actually had been released.

UN Turns Down Red China. On Sept. 20, the UN General Assembly adopted a U.S. resolution to defer con-

sideration of representation for Communist China for another year. The vote was 42-12 with 6 abstentions.

Eisenhower Suffers Heart Attack. On Sept. 24, President Eisenhower had a "mild" heart attack while vacationing in Denver, Colo. Doctors called his condition "satisfactory" and said his chances for recovery were "good."

Diem Becomes President. On Oct. 23, a national referendum in South Viet Nam deposed Emperor Bao Dai, who was living in France, and elevated Premier Ngo Dinh Diem to Chief of State. Diem received 98.2 percent of the votes. On Oct. 26, he declared South Viet Nam a republic and proclaimed himself President. He said the country would have a new constitution and an elected National Assembly "before the end of the year."

Eisenhower Leaves Hospital. On Nov. 11, President Eisenhower was discharged from the hospital in Denver and flew back to Washington to continue recuperation from his heart attack.

Stevenson Announces Candidacy. On Nov. 15, Adlai E. Stevenson announced he would be a candidate for the Democratic nomination for President in 1956.

Dulles on Geneva Talks. On Dec. 6, Secretary Dulles said he was disappointed with the progress of the ambassadorial talks in Geneva with the Chinese Communists. He deplored "the lack of actual action under the agreement already reached" on release of U.S. citizens held in Communist China. The Chinese still held 19 Americans and were examining their cases "one by one."

Kefauver Announces Candidacy. On Dec. 16, Sen. Estes Kefauver of Tennessee announced his candidacy for the Democratic Presidential nomination.

Knowland's Demand. On Dec. 17, Senate Minority Leader William F. Knowland (R Calif.) demanded that Presidential candidates of both parties state whether or not they would attempt to block Communist China's admission to the UN, even if it took use of the veto to do it.

1956

Stir Over Dulles Views on Brinkmanship -- Exchanges with Peking on Formosa Question -- Soviet Leaders Assail the Stalin Cult of Personality -- Khrushchev's Denunciation of Stalin -- Washington Turns Down Peking Bid for Dulles-Chou Talks -- Nixon in Saigon -- Chinese Red Troops in Burma -- State Department Bars Acceptance of Chinese Communist Offer of Visas to Newsmen -- Republican and Democratic Party Platforms Oppose Admission of Red China to UN -- General Assembly Defers Question of Chinese Representation.

Peking on U.S. Civilians in China. On Jan. 6, a spokesman for the Chinese Communist Foreign Ministry indicated that the Chinese government was becoming impatient with the Ambassadorial discussions in Geneva, which had recessed for "longer and longer" periods since they began in August 1955. Peking's spokesman said that Chinese-held American civilians "offended against the law in China (and) must be dealt with in accordance with Chinese legal procedures, and no time limit can be set for their release."

Dulles Brinkmanship. On Jan. 11, *Life* Magazine published an article, entitled "How Dulles Averted War," in which Secretary of State John Foster Dulles was quoted as saying it was "a pretty fair inference" that the Eisenhower Administration's "policy of deterrence" had "brought the Korean War to an end...kept the Chinese from sending their Red armies into Indo-China" and "stopped them in Formosa." The article by James Shepley, chief Washington correspondent for *Time-Life*, said that Eisenhower had decided that if truce negotiations failed in Korea, the U.S. would "fight to win," attacking bases in Manchuria and resorting to "tactical use of atomic arms." This decision, the article continued, was relayed to Indian Prime Minister Nehru through Dulles in May 1953, in the belief that Nehru would inform the Chinese Communist leaders. "Within two weeks," Shepley wrote, the Communist negotiators in Korea "began to negotiate seriously."

In the Indo-China war, Secretary Dulles and Admiral Arthur W. Radford, chairman of the Joint Chiefs of Staff, were said to have been given the President's approval to employ U.S. air power to destroy Communist staging areas in China if the Chinese Communists "intervened openly." Shepley added that "Dulles had seen to it that (Communist China and Russia) knew that the U.S. was prepared to act decisively to prevent the fall of all of Southeast Asia."

The article said, in addition, that a war over Formosa was avoided by the Congressional resolution of Jan. 28, l955, authorizing the President to use what force he deemed necessary if the Chinese Communists attacked Formosa or the Pescadores. Shepley reported that Dulles was the author of the resolution and that he had sent a second warning to Communist leaders, via Burmese Prime Minister U Nu, that the U.S. "meant business."

Reaction to Dulles Claims. The *Life* article brought immediate criticism from the Democrats. Sen. Hubert H. Humphrey (D Minn.) told the Senate Jan. 13 that "Mr. Dulles' 'art'...comes precariously close to rejecting the traditional American conviction that we must not strike the first blow (nor) bear the awful responsibility for beginning atomic war." He said the Secretary's policy of "massive retaliation" would cause "untold trouble with our allies."

On Jan. 14, Adlai Stevenson said in Chicago that he was "shocked that the Secretary of State is willing to play Russian roulette with the life of our nation...The art of diplomacy, especially in this atomic age, must lead to peace, not war or the brink of war."

On the same day, Vice President Richard M. Nixon told an audience in Springfield, Ill., that "the test of a foreign policy is its ability to keep the peace without surrendering any territory or principle," and "that great fact about the Eisenhower-Dulles foreign policy will stand out long after the tempest in a teapot over the expression ("brink of war") is forgotten." Both Nixon and Harold E. Stassen, Presidential special assistant on disarmament, criticized Stevenson for describing Dulles' strategy as "Russian roulette."

On Jan. 17, Secretary Dulles told a news conference that "the surest way to avoid war is to let it be known in advance that we are prepared to defend" our interests. He added that the U.S. was "brought to the verge of war" because of Communist threats against Korea, Indo-China, and Formosa.

On Jan. 19, President Eisenhower told a news conference that he had "complete faith" in Dulles as "devoted

to peace" and "to my mind the best Secretary of State I have ever known."

The next day, Sen. Mike Mansfield (D Mont.) said Dulles should have warned the Senate Foreign Relations Committee when the U.S. was on the "brink" of wars. He charged: "For three years we have lived on borrowed time in foreign relations...Nothing has been settled in Korea... (Quemoy and Matsu) may yet lead us into a military involvement with Communist China if not to World War III itself. In Indo-China...the danger of catastrophe is not yet passed."

Dulles answered that "constructive discussion of foreign policy" was "entirely proper and appropriate" up to a certain "danger point" where it might cause "doubt" over U.S. "determination" to fulfill its "commitments."

Peking on Dulles. On Jan. 18, the Chinese Foreign Ministry in Peking released a report on the Geneva ambassadorial discussions because "the U.S. has recently stepped up military activities in the Taiwan (Formosa) area to aggravate the tension, and U.S. Secretary of State Dulles even renewed the clamors for an atomic war against China." The Communist statement said Dulles had "openly cried out recently that in order to hold on to China's territory and infringe China's sovereignty, he would not scruple to start an atomic war."

Washington-Peking Exchanges. On Jan. 21, the State Department released its own report on the Geneva talks because it was "necessary that the record be set straight." Both Washington's and Peking's reports said the U.S. had proposed a joint statement committing the two countries to a mutual renunciation of the use of force. The Communists said they would agree as long as the renunciation did not apply to the "internal affair" of Taiwan. The U.S. said the Chinese were attempting to exempt those areas they planned to seize by force, and that until there was agreement on a declaration renouncing the use of force "generally, and particularly in the Taiwan area," progress toward a Sino-American settlement would be obstructed.

The Communists answered: "Taiwan is China's territory. There can be no question of defense so far as the U.S. is concerned. The U.S. has already used force and the threat of force against China in the Taiwan area....Yet the U.S. has demanded the right of defense in the Taiwan area. Is this not precisely a demand that China accept continued U.S. occupation of Taiwan and that the tension in the Taiwan area be maintained forever?"

The State Department replied that "the Communists so far seem willing to renounce force only if they are first conceded the goals for which they would use force."

Peking further charged that "the great majority" of "tens of thousands of Chinese in the U.S." had "not been able or not dared to apply for returning to China" because of "obstructions and threats...in violations of the agreement." The Chinese called U.S. charges concerning the detention of Americans in China "groundless."

The State Department answered that, four months after Peking had promised their release, "thirteen Americans are still held in Communist prisons." The Department demanded their immediate release "not only for humanitarian reasons but because respect for international undertakings lies at the foundation of a stable international order."

On Jan. 24, Secretary of State Dulles told a news conference: "Negotiations with the Chinese Communists are usually slow and prolonged," but "we are planning to go ahead...and we continue to be patient and persistent in our effort to obtain a greater assurance of peace and renunciation of force in that area."

Controls on China Trade. On Feb. 1, President Eisenhower and British Prime Minister Anthony Eden, who was visiting Washington, announced they had "agreed that trade controls (against Communist China) should continue and should be reviewed...periodically as to their scope, in the light of changing conditions, so that they may best serve the interests of the free world."

Policy Changes in Moscow. On Feb. 14, Soviet Communist Party First Secretary Nikita S. Khrushchev, in a seven-hour speech opening the 20th Soviet Party Congress, said war with "capitalist imperialism" was no longer inevitable, impliedly because of Soviet possession of nuclear weapons. Noting that peaceful coexistence was gaining "increasingly wider international recognition," Khrushchev said: "Indeed, there are only two ways: either peaceful co-existence or the most devastating war in history." Khrushchev also attacked the "cult of personality" or the individual as "alien to the spirit of Marxism-Leninism." This attack foreshadowed Khrushchev's diatribe against Stalin, delivered at a closed session of the Congress on Feb. 24 but not disclosed until several months later. (See June 4)

Trade with Red China. On March 26, Under Secretary of State Herbert Hoover Jr. told the Senate Permanent Investigations Subcommittee that "the Chinese Nationalists are shipping to the Communist Chinese quite a number of millions of dollars' worth of goods every year," but Hoover noted that "if we were arbitrarily to cut off all aid to our allies who were in any way shipping materials to the Communists (as Sen. Joseph R. McCarthy had demanded) it would be a very disadvantageous move on our part."

Events in China. On March 26, Communist news services announced that measures had been taken to combat a "spring famine" in China that had driven many people from their homes.

On March 31, the Chinese Communist Party announced a literacy drive to teach every Chinese citizen how to read and write.

On April 8, Peking announced plans to extend railway lines through areas from northwest China to Tibet, where new oil deposits had been discovered. On April 15, the Peking radio said that key state and joint ownership enterprises in China had expanded production during the first quarter of 1956 by 24.7 percent, 5.3 percent above planned levels.

British to Expand China Trade. On May 16, Britain informed the U.S. that it planned to expand trade with Communist China by "excepting" a number of items currently on the list of strategic goods not to be exported to mainland China. British officials said they would move "cautiously" to avoid selling any important strategic goods to the Communists.

Egypt Recognizes China. On May 16, Egypt extended recognition to the Chinese Communist government. On May 22, Secretary of State Dulles said it was "an action that we regret." On May 24, Egyptian Premier Gamal Abdel Nasser accepted an invitation to visit Communist China and reciprocated by inviting Chinese Premier Chou En-lai to visit Egypt.

Molotov Resigns. On June 1, Soviet Foreign Minister Vyacheslav Mikhailovich Molotov resigned without explanation. He was replaced by Dmitri T. Shepilov, editor of Pravda.

Khrushchev's Attack on Stalin. On June 4, the State Department at Washington made public the text of the secret speech delivered by Soviet Communist Party First Secretary Nikita S. Khrushchev on Feb. 24, 1956, at the 20th Soviet Party Congress. The speech contained a violent and detailed denunciation of the late Premier Joseph V. Stalin and all his works.

President Ill. On June 9, President Eisenhower underwent an emergency operation at Walter Reed Hospital in Washington to relieve an obstruction of the ileum, the lower section of the small intestine. Doctors later in the day said there was no reason why Eisenhower would not be able to run for re-election.

Dulles Rejects Chinese Offer. On June 12, the State Department announced rejection of a Chinese Communist proposal for discussions between Secretary of State Dulles and Chinese Foreign Minister Chou En-lai. The proposal, made May 12, was disclosed in Geneva on June 12 by the Chinese Ambassador to Poland, Wang Ping-nan. The Department said the proposed talks would be held on too short notice. It also pointed out that 13 Americans were still imprisoned in China.

Dulles for Renouncing Force. On June 21, Secretary of State Dulles told an audience in San Francisco: "While the Soviet successors to Stalin at least profess to have renounced the use of force in international affairs, the Chinese Communists still refuse this."

Red China for Greater Leniency. On June 25, the Chinese Communist Party Central Committee adopted a policy of "domestic peaceful coexistence," conceding that "counter-revolutionaries" had been handled too harshly and should be treated with "greater leniency."

Chou's Speech. On June 28, Chinese Communist Premier Chou En-lai told the National People's Congress that "traditional friendships" between the American and Chinese people eventually will lead to U.S. diplomatic recognition of the Communist government. Chou said the Chinese Communist government was "willing to discuss" with Taiwan authorities "specific steps for the peaceful liberation of Taiwan." On June 29, the Nationalist government answered: "What needs liberating now is...the mainland under the bloody Communist reign."

Eisenhower Out of Hospital. On June 30, President Eisenhower was released from Walter Reed Hospital, three weeks after his ileitis operation. On July 10, the President told Republican Congressional leaders that he still intended to run for a second term.

Nixon Trip. On July 6, Vice President Nixon flew to Saigon, South Viet Nam, and praised the administration of President Ngo Dinh Diem in a speech before the Constituent Assembly. On July 8, the Vice President delivered a message from President Eisenhower to Chiang Kai-shek on Formosa reaffirming America's "steadfastness in continuing to support the Republic of China."

Diem's Statement. On July 8, President Diem said the South Vietnamese government would take precautions against a possible Communist invasion of the country on July 20, the day set under the 1954 Geneva agreements for national elections to unite the two Viet Nams. South Viet Nam, which had not signed the Geneva agreements, had refused to participate in the elections on the ground that fair balloting was impossible.

Burma Hostilities. On July 31, the Burmese government charged that several thousand Chinese Communist troops had occupied a large area in northeastern Burma. Burmese officials said there had been sporadic fighting between Communist and Burmese troops, but that the threat was not regarded as very serious and negotiations already had begun with the Chinese Comunists for removal of their forces.

Chou's Interview. On Aug. 5, Chinese Communist Premier Chou En-lai told an Australian newsman that U.S. refusal to recognize the Peking government was ostrichlike. He rejected U.S. participation in any discussions on Formosa, asserting that the island was a Chinese province. Chou said also that China soon could "enlarge the democratic base of our system of government" with more meetings of the National People's Congress, increased self-criticism, and extension of voting privileges.

Travel to China. On Aug. 6, the Chinese Communist government offered visas to 15 U.S. newsmen who had requested them. The following day, the State Department announced it would continue to bar travel to Communist China as long as Americans were held there as "political hostages."

Burma. On Aug. 7, Burmese Premier U Ba Swe said his country would not negotiate with the Chinese Communists until their troops were withdrawn from Burma's border provinces. On Aug. 14, Burmese military authorities said that 4,500 Chinese Communist troops had entrenched themselves in Burma as the first unit of a "planned invasion."

Stevenson and Kefauver Nominated. On Aug. 16, Adlai E. Stevenson was again nominated for President at the Democratic National Convention in Chicago. The next day, the party nominated Sen. Estes E. Kefauver for Vice President. The party's platform stated: "We pledge determined opposition to the admission of the Communist Chinese into the UN,...urge a continuing effort to effect the release of all Americans detained by Communist China." The platform continued, "America's task and interest in Asia is to help the free governments demonstrate that their people can have improved living standards, without yielding to Communist tyranny or domination by anyone." It commented that Secretary of State Dulles "brags of 'brink of war'" rather than making "our peaceful purpose clear beyond dispute in every corner of the world...."

Plane Downed. On Aug. 22, Chinese Communist fighter planes shot down a U.S. patrol aircraft with 16 men aboard 32 miles from the Chinese mainland. The Communists said their pilots had mistaken the plane for a Chinese Nationalist aircraft.

Eisenhower and Nixon Nominated. On Aug. 22, President Dwight D. Eisenhower and Vice President Richard M. Nixon were renominated at the Republican National Convention in San Francisco. Senate Minority Leader William F. Knowland (R Calif.) said in a speech at the convention that he would fight Communist Chinese membership in the UN "as long as I have a voice and a vote" in the Senate.

The Republican platform carried a pledge to "oppose the seating of China in the UN" and denounced "any trade with the Communist world that would threaten the security of the U.S. and our allies."

President's Statement. On Sept. 5, President Eisenhower told a news conference that the position of the U.S. in the world was stronger than when he took office. The President said the French "were involved in a hopelessly losing war in Indo-China" and could have lost the "whole peninsula." The Geneva settlement, Eisenhower said, "at least gave the free world a firm foothold and under stronger leadership...." He continued: "The Korean War was going on (in 1953), and under conditions where it was impossible to win...(We were) suffering losses merely to hold the line we then had. It was settled and we still hold that line."

Mansfield's Answer. On Sept. 6, Sen. Mike Mansfield (D Mont.), a member of the Senate Foreign Relations Committee, said that under Republican leadership one-half of Indo-China had been yielded, and that Laos and Cambodia were beginning to lean toward the Communists. Mansfield added that a Korean peace was "far from settled."

Eisenhower and Nixon Elected. On Nov. 6, President Eisenhower and Vice President Nixon were re-elected in a landslide victory. The Democrats retained control of both chambers of Congress.

UN Bars China. On Nov. 12, the UN General Assembly voted 47-24 (eight abstentions) to postpone consideration of UN membership for Communist China for another year.

New Delhi Talks. On Nov. 28, Chinese Communist Premier Chou En-lai arrived in New Delhi, the second stop of a seven-country tour of Asia. Chou told the Indian Parliament the next day that only through "solidarity" could the newly independent Asian and African countries frustrate attempts to destroy them again, one by one. On Dec. 1, he hinted that Americans imprisoned in Communist China might be released on good behavior. He suggested later that the U.S. would have to make the next move if it wanted release of the prisoners and a general settlement in the Far East.

Nehru Comment. On Dec. 12, Indian Prime Minister Jawaharlal Nehru told American reporters that Chou's "attitude seemed to be one of desiring to have much better relations" with the U.S.

Nehru Visit to U.S. On Dec. 16, Prime Minister Nehru arrived in the U.S. for talks with President Eisenhower. On Dec. 19, Nehru said at a news conference that U.S. foreign policy was "a flexible policy adapting itself to circumstances" and "not as rigid as I thought." The Indian Prime Minister added: "I would say that they (the Chinese Communists) have certain complaints...in the sense of steps taken or not taken." They assert, for example, that they "have gone several steps forward, but there has been no favorable reaction" from the U.S. Nehru pointed out that "legally and constitutionally speaking, there is only one China," and each side "claims to be the real article." He said: "Obviously the Formosan government, at the most, is the Formosan government. It is not China." Nehru observed that India's recognition of Communist China rather than Nationalist China "should indicate our views on the subject."

Chou in Burma. On Dec. 20, Chinese Communist Premier Chou En-lai and Burmese Premier U Ba Swe issued a joint statement saying that they had not resolved the border dispute between their countries, but that it was "nearer to a solution." An interview with Chou, filmed by Edward R. Murrow during his visit to Burma was shown on CBS's "See It Now" Dec. 30. The Chinese Communist Premier reiterated Chinese demands for control of Formosa and the Chinese seat in the UN.

Chinese in U.S. Prisons. On Dec. 22, the U.S. announced that only one of 24 Chinese held in prisons in the U.S. desired to return to Communist China. All 24 had been interviewed by the Red Cross.

1957

Russian-Chinese Joint Policy Statement -- State Department Refusal to Let U.S. Newsmen Go to Red China -- American Policy on Trade with Mainland China -- Eisenhower Pledge of Additional Aid to South Viet Nam -- Mao's "Hundred Flowers" Speech -- New Statement of U.S. Policies Toward China -- Dulles on China and the Bomb -- Anti-Rightist Drive in Communist China -- Young Americans Visit China and Lose Passports -- State Department Lifts China Travel Ban for 24 Newsmen -- Peking Refuses to Admit U.S. Newsmen.

South Korean Demand. On Jan. 7, the South Korean Ambassador to the U.S., You Chan Yung, urged the UN to demand that all Chinese Communist forces abandon North Korea. He said there had been sharp increases in Communist ground and naval forces in North Korea since the armistice.

Unification of Korea. On Jan. 8, the Political Committee of the UN General Assembly adopted a U.S. resolution, 57-8, calling for unification of Korea through UN-sponsored free elections.

Russian-Chinese Policy Statement. On Jan. 18, a joint policy statement signed by Soviet Premier Nikolai A. Bulganin and Chinese Communist Premier Chou En-lai, who was visiting Moscow, said the two nations were "ready to continue rendering support" to the "peoples of the Near and Middle East to prevent aggression and interference in the internal affairs of the countries of this area." The statement charged that the "so-called Eisenhower Doctrine" was a "colonialist" policy designed to "suppress the movement for national independence and enslave the peoples of these countries." (The term "Eisenhower Doctrine" stemmed from the President's request of Congress, Jan. 5, for authority, granted in modified form by a joint resolution approved March 9, 1957, to use military force and economic aid to combat threats of direct or indirect Communist aggression in the Middle East.)

The joint statement noted that Russia and China held "complete unanimity of views" on the international situation; that "American imperialism is trying" to "take the place of the colonialist powers" in the Middle East; that both Russia and China favor the reunification of Germany, Korea and Viet Nam; and that the "great alliance of the Soviet Union and China" was "an important mainstay of peace all over the world."

Chou had arrived in Moscow on Jan. 7. Going on to Warsaw, he declared there, on Jan. 11, that the Soviet Union was the primary leader of the Communist countries and that "strengthening the solidarity of the Socialist camp" was of "utmost importance," because "imperialism has

never stopped its diversionist activities" in the Communist countries. Chou later promised that the "Polish nation may always count on the support of the Chinese nation," adding that while "abnormal relations" could arise between Communist nations, their policies should avoid "fundamental conflicts."

On Jan. 17, before returning to Moscow, Chou visited Hungary and signed a joint declaration with Hungarian leaders in which he supported Soviet suppression of the recent Hungarian revolt and advised the Hungarian people to "stand solidly with the Soviet Union, leader of the Socialist camp."

Ban on China Travel. On Feb. 6, Secretary of State John Foster Dulles told a news conference that the State Department had banned travel to Communist China for reporters because China was "trying to get reporters -- preferably those it picked -- to come," and had "tried to use the illegal detention of Americans" in China to force the State Department's approval of the trips. The Secretary said the U.S. could not allow other governments to "throw into jail American citizens, so they can put a price on their release." He added that "the issuance of passports to a regime which is not recognized is something which is never done."

Green on Recognizing Red China. On Feb. 18, Sen. Theodore F. Green (D R.I.), chairman of the Senate Foreign Relations Committee, said the U.S. "should recognize Red China sooner or later." He explained: "We don't like their form of government, but the country is a great country and organized, and I do not myself see why we should recognize these other Communist countries and withhold recognition of China unless we are going to apply that to other Communist countries."

Green later said his remarks should not be construed as endorsing immediate recognition of Communist China. "This is not the case," he added. "Red China has not purged itself of its aggression of the United Nations in Korea, and it still holds American citizens prisoner against their will. In time -- sooner or later, as I said -- the President -- whose responsibility it is -- must determine if we are to continue forever to live without official contact with 300 million Chinese."

On Feb. 19, Secretary of State Dulles told a news conference it would be "premature, to say the least," to discuss recognizing Communist China, but he added that "none of us are talking here in terms of eternity."

Newsmen's Travel. On March 5, Secretary Dulles told a news conference that newsmen's travel to Communist China "would be bearable by us" but could have "dangerous consequences in other areas." The Secretary said the U.S. would attempt "to satisfy better the demand for news coverage without seeming to drop the barriers down generally."

On March 7, President Eisenhower said he could not "offer at the moment any change in policy" on newsmen's travel. He said the State Department had "studied this very earnestly to see how we could secure from China more news without appearing to be accepting Red China on the same cultural basis as we do...other nations."

Chou's Charges. On March 5, Chinese Communist Premier Chou En-lai said in a statement to the Political Consultative Conference in Peking that the U.S. did not want "to negotiate seriously on the question of tension in the Taiwan area." He charged that the U.S. was "planning to install guided missiles" on Formosa to convert the island into an American "dependency, like Hawaii," and was plotting to "overthrow the (present) Taiwan authorities." Chou again pledged to "liberate" Formosa peacefully.

Dulles' View of Asian Communism. On March 11, Secretary of State Dulles told a meeting of the SEATO Council of Ministers in Canberra, Australia, that communism was "a passing and not permanent phase" in Asia and that U.S. recognition or UN membership for Communist China "would serve no national purpose" and would "encourage influences hostile to us and to our allies."

SEATO Statement. On March 13, the SEATO Council said in a statement issued at Canberra that "while the immediate military threat to peace in Southeast Asia has diminished, forces are still working for the ultimate objective of world domination."

Celler Resolution. On March 18, Rep. Emanuel Celler (D N.Y.), chairman of the House Judiciary Committee, introduced a resolution (H Con Res 153) aimed to permit U.S. newsmen to travel anywhere in the world, including Communist China.

Newsman Testifies. On March 29, William Worthy, reporter for the Baltimore *Afro-American*, who defied the State Department ban on travel to Communist China, protested before the Senate Judiciary Constitutional Rights Subcommittee the Department's delay in processing his application for passport renewal. Also opposing the travel ban were representatives of the American Society of Newspaper Editors, the *Saturday Review*, the American Newspaper Guild, and the American Civil Liberties Union.

Communist China Trade. On April 4, Secretary of Commerce Sinclair Weeks said the U.S. ban on all trade with Communist China would remain intact, but he found "some merit" in the desires of other free world countries for relaxation of the ban, observed by them, on exports of strategic goods to Communist countries. Weeks said he favored a policy of easing some restrictions against China for tighter restrictions against trade with the Soviet bloc.

Travel Ban Criticism. On April 11, J.R. Wiggins, executive editor of the *Washington Post*, told the Senate Foreign Relations Committee that the State Department ban on travel to Communist China should be lifted in the interest of "swift, accurate, and complete information." Julius Frandsen, United Press bureau chief in Washington, agreed with Wiggins.

Trade Controls. On April 20, the State Department notified 14 allied nations participating in the system of controls on trade with Communist China and the European Soviet bloc that the United States would consider "certain modifications" of the general controls but would "continue its unilateral embargo on all trade with Communist China." A Department spokesman said the U.S. had been "repeatedly pressed by its allies" to relax controls and would consider the following modifications:
• Certain items for peaceful use embargoed for shipment to Communist China would be "removed from controls" and given the same status as similar items traded with the European Soviet bloc.
• Other items embargoed for Communist China would remain embargoed and added to the European Soviet bloc list, but with a "lesser degree of control."
• Tightening the "exceptions" procedure used for trade when an embargo was deemed "unfair."

Travel Ban Problem. On April 23, Secretary of State Dulles told a news conference that the State Department was willing to allow a "pool" of American newsmen to visit Communist China provided existing bans on travel by other Americans to the Chinese mainland could be maintained. But he said the Department and leading news executives with whom the problem had been discussed were bankrupt of ideas on how this could be done successfully.

McCarthy Dead. On May 2, Sen. Joseph R. McCarthy (R Wis.), 48, died in Bethesda Naval Hospital of acute hepatitic failure.

Missiles in Formosa. On May 7, the U.S. and the Nationalist Chinese government announced that missiles capable of carrying conventional or nuclear warheads were being based on Formosa "wholly for the defensive purpose of deterring and if necessary repelling attack." On May 11, the Chinese Communist government called the action "another serious, provocative action of the (U.S.) Government in its policy of carrying out aggression against China."

Promise to Diem. On May 9, President Ngo Dinh Diem of South Viet Nam, in the U.S. on a state visit, told Congress that U.S. aid had helped to keep his country free and able to "continue to fight communism." In a joint Eisenhower-Diem communique the next day, Eisenhower pledged additional aid to South Viet Nam within U.S. "constitutional processes."

Dulles on Reporting China. On May 14, Secretary of State Dulles pointed out that American newspapers could send anyone to Communist China so long as he did not travel on a U.S. passport not validated for travel to that country. Dulles added that there were "ample ways" to obtain news from China "without sending American correspondents...into areas where that would involve a conflict with (U.S.) foreign policy." The Secretary concluded that if China released U.S. prisoners "we would certainly take a new look at the situation."

Formosan Riot. On May 24, an anti-American riot erupted in Taipei, Formosa, after a U.S. military court had acquitted an American soldier charged with the murder of a Chinese he said he had caught peeping through a window at his wife while she was taking a bath. The soldier said he shot the victim in self-defense after the Chinese approached him with a club. About 3,000 rioters raided the American Embassy and the U.S. Information Service in Taipei, injuring 13 Americans. On May 25, the city was placed under martial law and occupied by 33,000 Nationalist troops. At least two Chinese were killed during the rioting.

British Trade With China. On May 30, the British government announced it would apply the same restrictions on trade with Communist China as those applied on trade with the Soviet bloc. The same day, the State Department, "most disappointed" by the British move, said the U.S. contemplated no change in its total embargo on trade with Red China. On May 31, Senate Republican Leader William F. Knowland (Calif.) said the British were taking a "calculated risk" of losing Hong Kong by strengthening Communist China with "strategic" materials. Knowland added that while the U.S. might "question the wisdom" of the

British decision, as "good and stout allies, we understand some of the economic reasons behind their action." Senate Democratic Leader Lyndon B. Johnson (Texas) said June 1 that the U.S. would have to re-evaluate the China trade situation.

On June 5, President Eisenhower observed at his news conference: "I don't see as much advantage in maintaining the differential (between restrictions on Soviet and Chinese trade) as some people do, although I have never advocated its complete elimination."

On June 2, Sen. Allen J. Ellender (D La.) said the U.S. should consider lifting its total embargo.

On June 11, Secretary Dulles told a news conference that the President supported continuation of a "differential" on trade with China and East Europe.

On June 16, Sen. Warren Magnuson (D Wash.), chairman of the Senate Interstate and Foreign Commerce Committee, said the possibility of starting American passenger and mail flights to Communist China would be explored at upcoming hearings on U.S. trade policies. "We have got to be realistic," Magnuson said. "We can't keep 400 million people behind an economic bamboo curtain just because we don't like their government." Senate Republican Leader William F. Knowland (Calif.) said he doubted if the hearings would alter Administration opposition to trade exchanges and that "I don't believe that sentiment has changed in the Senate."

Mao's "Hundred Flowers" Speech. On June 18, the Chinese Communist government news agency, *Hsinhua* (New China), published the edited text of a four-hour speech delivered on Feb. 27 by Chairman (President) Mao Tse-tung to a closed session of the Supreme State Conference in Peking. Portions of the address that hinted of differences with Soviet leaders or admitted Chinese errors -- not included in the official text -- were contained in a version of the speech published by the *New York Times* on June 12. According to that version, Mao conceded that the Communists had "liquidated" 800,000 Chinese between October 1949 and early 1954, but he acknowledged that continued use of terrorist tactics might lead to situations much like the "tragedy of Hungary."

In the speech, titled "The Correct Handling of Contradictions Among the People," Mao said it "would be naive to imagine that there are no more contradictions" in China between "the government and the masses." But, he said, "if properly handled, (they) can be transformed into a non-antagonistic" trend and "resolved in a peaceful way." He added: "Ours is a people's democratic dictatorship, led by the working class and based on the working class and based on the worker-peasant alliance." The government's "first function is to suppress the reactionary classes...and those exploiters in the country who arrange themselves against the Socialist revolution."

Mao admitted that "Certain people in our country were delighted when the Hungarian events took place." They hoped that "something similar would happen in China," but "such hopes ran counter to the interests of the masses and therefore could not possibly get their support." Others, he said, desired "the adoption of the two-party system of the West, where one party is in office and the other party out of office." But that system, Mao said, was "nothing but a means of maintaining the dictatorship of the bourgeoisie..."

"While we stand for freedom with leadership and democracy under centralized guidance, in no sense do we mean that coercive measures should be taken to settle ideological matters and questions involving the distinction between right and wrong among the people." Mao urged Chinese Marxists to consider non-Marxist criticism. "As a scientific truth," he said, "Marxism fears no criticism." Counter-revolutionary ideas should be silenced, but other non-Marxist ideas could be met "only by employing methods of discussion, criticism and reasoning." Therefore, the slogan should be "Let a Hundred Flowers Blossom and Let a Hundred Schools of Thought Contend."

Turning to agriculture, the Chinese President conceded that contradictions existed "between the state and the co-operatives" and "within and among the cooperatives themselves." But he insisted that the cooperatives enjoyed the support of 70 percent of the 500 million peasants, and food production had increased rapidly since 1949. In industry, "most" former business owners were being "transformed from exploiters into working people living by their own labor."

Mao admitted that "small numbers of workers and students" and "members of a small number of agricultural cooperatives" had engaged in strikes and caused "disturbances" in 1956 because of "the failure to satisfy certain of their demands for material benefits." He urged leaders to "stamp out bureaucracy," "deal with contradictions in a proper way," and "make use of these disturbances as a special means of improving our work and educating the cadres and the masses" to find "solutions to those questions which have been neglected in the past."

Russia Denounced at Peking. On June 20, the *Hsinhua* (New China) News Agency reported that the vice chairman of the Chinese Communist National Defense Committee, Gen. Lung Yun (a former aide to Chiang Kai-shek), had denounced the Soviet Union for removing "huge quantities of industrial equipment" from China after World War II, and for allowing China "to pay all expenses of the Korean War." Lung pointed out that the United States had "given up her claims for loans she granted to her allies during the first and second world wars, yet the Soviet Union insists that China must pay interest on Soviet loans." He added that "China could not possibly reimburse the Soviet loans within 10 years or more." On June 23, it was reported that the Kuomintang Revolutionary Committee, an organization of former Chinese Nationalists who had defected to the Communists, had denounced Lung and two other generals for "rightist deviation."

Trade Controls Relaxed. On June 21, the Italian government announced relaxation of its restrictions on trade with Communist China. The Danish and French governments had announced revision of their embargo lists earlier in the week.

Korean Military Buildup. On June 21, the UN Korean Command announced in Panmunjom that it would no longer abide by the armistice terms covering amounts of military equipment to be allowed in South and North Korea. The UN Command explained that continued Communist violation of the terms had resulted in a "vastly superior" Communist force in North Korea.

Peking Letter. On June 22, it was reported that a unique letter had been published in the Peking *People's Daily* on May 31. A professor at Peking People's University had written: "To kill Communists and to overthrow you cannot be called unpatriotic, because you Communists are no longer of service to the people. Even if the Communist party is destroyed, China will not perish. This is because we will not become traitors even if there is no guidance of the Communist party."

Refusal for Mrs. Roosevelt. On June 25, Mrs. Franklin D. Roosevelt said the State Department had denied her permission to travel to Communist China and interview Chinese leaders.

Chou's Warning. On June 26, Chinese Communist Premier Chou En-lai warned all Chinese non-Communists they would be classified as "enemies of the people" if they continued to criticize the government. Chou said he hoped they would "repent and accept opportunities of re-molding themselves." Speaking to the National People's Congress in Peking, the Premier denounced elections and multiparty systems as "bourgeois tricks" and warned that the Communist party would "allow no wavering on the basic state system of our country."

Dulles' Policy Pronouncement. On June 28, Secretary of State John Foster Dulles, addressing a convention in San Francisco, made what the State Department called a major policy pronouncement on Communist China. Affirming that the U.S. would continue to oppose Communist Chinese membership in the UN and to withhold diplomatic recognition of the Peking regime, Dulles declared that Red China failed "to pass even those tests which...the Soviet regime seemed to pass."

The consequences of recognizing the Chinese Communists would be: (1) "The many mainland Chinese, who by Mao Tse-tung's own recent admission seek to change the nature of their government, would be immensely discouraged." (2) "The millions of overseas Chinese would feel that they had no Free China to which to look." (3) "The Republic of China would feel crushed by its friend,...and we are honor-bound to give our ally, to whom we are pledged by a mutual defense treaty, a full measure of loyalty." (4) "The free Asian governments of the Pacific and Southeast Asia would be gravely perplexed." (5) "United States recognition of Communist China would make it probable that the Communist regime would obtain the seat of China in the United Nations," which is "not a reformatory for bad governments" but supposedly "an association of those who are already 'peace-loving' and who are 'able and willing to carry out the charter obligations.'"

Dulles pointed out that "diplomatic recognition gives the recognized regime valuable rights and privileges, and, in the world of today, recognition by the United States gives the recipient much added prestige and influence at home and abroad."

"Normal peacetime trade with China, from which the American and Chinese peoples would benefit, could be in the common interest," he conceded. "But it seems that that kind of trade is not to be had in any appreciable volume. Trade with Communist China is not a free trade. It does not provide one country with what its people want but cannot well produce for themselves, in exchange for what other people want but cannot well produce for themselves. Trade with Communist China is wholly controlled by an official apparatus and its limited amounts of foreign exchange are used to develop as rapidly as possible a formidable military establishment and a heavy industry to support it. The primary desire of that regime is machine tools, electronic equipment, and, in general, what will help it produce tanks, trucks, planes, ammunition, and other military items."

The Secretary said there were "basic power rivalries between Russia and China in Asia" but that the Russian and Chinese Communist parties were bound together by close ideological ties. At the same time, "if the ambitions of the Chinese Communists are inflated by successes, they might eventually clash with Soviet Russia."

"Internationally," Dulles concluded, "the Chinese Communist regime does not conform to the practices of civilized nations; does not live up to its international obligations; has not been peaceful in the past; and gives no evidence of being peaceful in the future. Its foreign students are hostile to us and our Asian allies. Under these circumstances it would be folly for us to establish relations with the Chinese Communists which would enhance their ability to hurt us and our friends."

Chinese Problems. On July 1, the Chinese Communist government's Chief Prosecutor told the National People's Congress in Peking that 190,000 counter-revolutionaries had been captured in 1956 and given "lenient treatment."

On July 2, the President of the Chinese Communist Supreme Court told the Congress that "corruption, theft, assault...(and) public disturbances...are comparatively common in rural areas" and in some cities.

Dulles on China and the Bomb. On July 2, Secretary of State Dulles told a news conference he would expect Communist China to abide by any East-West agreement banning nuclear weapons even though it did not sign such a pledge. He doubted if Communist China would manufacture its own weapons unaided because of the expense and possibility of detection.

Humphrey Statement. On July 6, Sen. Hubert H. Humphrey (D Minn.) said it was "essential" for Communist China to be brought into any international disarmament system "at an early stage." Humphrey, in a preface to the Senate Foreign Relations Disarmament Subcommittee's study of Far East military commitments, said Communist China's exclusion from a disarmament system would leave Russia a "loophole" to use in violating treaty obligations. He also said "the time has come" to review U.S. policy on Communist China and to "encourage American newsmen to visit" there.

Trade With Red China. On July 3, Sen. Charles E. Potter (R Mich.) said that "the stakes are too high, the dangers too great" for the U.S. to assume the "calculated risk of trade with Red China." Potter asserted that "Anyone who believes we can trade with Communist China to any appreciable degree in any types of goods without augmenting her war machine is simply deluding himself." On July 9, Secretary of Commerce Sinclair Weeks said the Administration would "not gamble with national security" by a premature removal of this country's total embargo on trade with Communist China. Weeks said Red China "continues to constitute a serious threat to the security of the Far East."

Rightists in China. On July 12, the head of the propaganda section of the Chinese Communist Party's Central Committee warned the National People's Congress in Peking that "rightists" had attempted to "seize leadership" in China by spreading "fantastic anti-Socialist views." On the same day, the Peking *People's Daily*, in an article believed to have been written by Mao Tse-tung, warned that right-wing "demons can be wiped out only when they...come out of their cage."

Rightist Confessions. On July 15, two major critics of the Chinese Communist regime, the Ministers of the Timber Industry and of Communications, gave "confessions" to the National People's Congress in Peking that they had conspired "to attack the Communist party and leadership... (and) replace the proletarian dictatorship and the National People's Congress with bourgeois democracy," which "would have inevitably led to a capitalist comeback" in China. Another "rightist" who admitted to anti-party activity was the Minister of Food.

Moscow Reaction. On July 16, the Soviet Communist Party newspaper, *Pravda*, said that Mao Tse-tung's speech on "contradictions" was "an outstanding event in China's political life" and "furnishes the Chinese people with a new clear-cut orientation in the new situation." The newspaper added that the speech "has multiplied the strength of the millions of supporters of socialism in China who have turned to a decisive offensive against...right-wing bourgeois elements."

Warning to Students. On July 18, the Chinese government's State Council warned that any students whose views "seriously run against socialism face penalties ranging from corrective labor to long periods of work without pay." Reports from Hong Kong had indicated a substantial amount of unrest in the Chinese universities.

Trip to China. On Aug. 14, 41 young Americans left Moscow on a trip to Peking despite warnings from the State Department that the U.S. and Communist China were in a "quasi state of war" and that the trip "would be subversive of (U.S.) foreign policy." The youths attempted to avoid violating American passport laws by obtaining visas from the Chinese Communist government. The 41 were members of a U.S. delegation to Russia's Sixth World Festival of Youth and Students in Moscow. Before leaving on their three-week tour of China, 35 of the youths issued a statement saying they were making the trip to confirm "the right of (U.S.) citizens to travel." On Aug. 21, President Eisenhower said the youths were "doing the country a disservice."

Travel Authorization. On Aug. 22, Secretary of State Dulles authorized 24 news organizations (newspapers, news services, periodicals, and radio-TV networks) to send correspondents to mainland China for a seven-month trial period. The State Department said it was modifying its eight-year travel ban because "new factors have come into the picture, making it desirable that additional information be made available to the American people respecting current conditions within China."

The newsmen's entry hinged on issuance of visas by the Chinese Communist government; the State Department said the U.S. would not accord reciprocal visas to newsmen from Communist China. It warned that those entering China faced "abnormal personal risks." A Department spokesman said renewal of the passport validation, after the seven-month trial period, would depend on whether the newsmen were allowed to report freely.

Sen. J. William Fulbright (D Ark.) had introduced a resolution (S Res 190), Aug. 20, calling on the State Department either to "encourage and facilitate" entry of newsmen into China or refrain from taking reprisals against those entering on their own responsibility.

Chinese Reaction. On Aug. 25, the Peking *People's Daily* called the State Department's plan "completely un-acceptable to the Chinese people." It denounced the U.S. for "insufferable arrogance" in agreeing to "send its correspondents to China just on the basis of its own unilateral decision" and "refusing reciprocal visas to Chinese correspondents." The paper asserted that the U.S. State Department "wants to collect intelligence in China through its correspondents (and) carry out subversive activities." The principle of equality and reciprocity," it added, "requires that newsmen of both sides be allowed to stay in each other's country."

Journalists Purged. On Aug. 26, the *Hsinhua* (New China) News Agency said that 90 journalists had been "ferreted out from press and radio operations all over China" in "a struggle against rightists in the journalistic field." In the following weeks, the Chinese government announced the arrest and execution of a number of counter-revolutionaries and admitted there had been student and peasant uprisings against the government.

Dulles on Newsmen. On Aug. 27, Secretary of State Dulles told a news conference that if any Chinese newsman applied for entry into the U.S., his application would be studied "on its merits." Dulles commented: "So far as I know, we have never laid down any absolute rule that no Chinese Communist could come to this country," but there had been "no application for anyone" from Communist China. The Secretary explained that when travel of American newsmen to China was authorized, no reciprocal offer to admit Chinese Communist newsmen was made because "We wanted to obviate any claim by the Chinese Communists that they would be entitled as a right to send a corresponding number" of reporters to the U.S. "That we could not do under the law," he said, which "hedges about very strictly the possibility of Communists coming to this country." Dulles said there must "be a finding made by the Attorney General to permit any Communist to come. Whether or not he could make these findings I do not know."

On Sept. 1, Sen. William F. Knowland (R Calif.) said in a television interview that the State Department could issue "temporary news certificates" to Chinese Communist reporters and still maintain the ban on Chinese Communist visitors. On Sept. 6, Sens. Bourke Hickenlooper (R Iowa) and Mike Mansfield (D Mont.) of the Senate Foreign Relations Committee endorsed Knowland's suggestion.

On Sept. 10, Under Secretary of State Christian A. Herter said the U.S. had opened the way for an exchange of newsmen with Communist China and the matter "is now up to the Chinese government." Herter added that if Communist China were interested in reciprocal exchange of newsmen, its reporters should apply for admission to the U.S.

On Sept. 24, Secretary Dulles said he was expressing his own opinion in relation to the specific problem of newsmen's entry into Communist China when he said Constitution-guaranteed freedom of the press "relates to publication and not to the gathering of news." Dulles, in a letter to Executive Editor J.R. Wiggins of the *Washington Post* made public Oct. 3, said it was his "firm belief that insofar as the gathering of news can be carried out without prejudice to the national interest, that activity should be facilitated and it is our policy to do that."

Visitors to China Return. On Oct. 5, 14 of the 41 American youths who had visited Communist China returned to Moscow and were informed by a U.S. consular official that their passports were valid only for return to the

U.S.   The State Department had said on Sept. 18 that it would revoke the passports of all 41 youths. The students reported that Chinese Communist Premier Chou En-lai had told them, on Sept. 6, that China's "door is always open" but "it should be on an equal and mutual basis." On the following day, Chou told 10 of the American visitors that the State Department "put an end to the matter by refusing reciprocal rights of coverage to Chinese reporters."

Anti-Rightist Campaign. On Oct. 19, Peking Radio broadcast a report by the Secretary General of the Chinese Communist Party Central Committee at a plenary session of the Committee in Peking. The report said that Communist China's "rectification" campaign had "basically achieved victory." The anti-rightist movement, the report said, was "in complete conformity with the directives of the Central Committee and the instructions" of Mao Tse-tung.

Economy.   Peking announced that 1957 production levels in Communist China would reach 223 percent of 1952 levels.

Saigon Bombings. On Oct. 22, two bombs exploded in Saigon, one in front of a U.S. officers' billet and another under a bus loaded with American enlisted men. Fifteen Vietnamese civilians and 13 U.S. servicemen were injured. South Vietnamese President Ngo Dinh Diem blamed the bombings on Communists, who were attempting to ruin "the friendly relations between the U.S. and Viet Nam."

Mao in Moscow. On Nov. 6, Mao Tse-tung told a special session of the Supreme Soviet in Moscow that Communist China would maintain strong ties with the Soviet Union, although it had the right to travel "separate roads to socialism."

U.S. Trade. On Dec. 16, Assistant Secretary of Commerce for International Affairs Harry Kearns said the World Trade Advisory Committee of the Commerce Department was critical of U.S. policy on trade with Communist China; committee members called the rigid trade ban "unrealistic."

Grain Production in China. On Dec. 25, the Chinese Communist government announced a record grain production of 185 million tons for 1957.

Drive Terminated. On Dec. 29, the Chinese Communist Party announced that the movement against right wingers in China had been terminated because the rightists were now in "complete isolation."

1958

Reds Purge Rightists in China -- Sino-Soviet Trade Pact -- ADA Asks Negotiations for Recognition of Communist China -- China's First Atomic Reactor -- State Department Rejects Concept of Two Chinas -- Red China Threatens Formosa and Offshore Islands -- Pentagon Strengthens U.S. Forces in Formosa Strait -- U.S. Reaffirms Determination to Defend Formosa -- Resumption of U.S.-Chinese Communist Ambassadorial Talks Proposed -- Progress of Red China's Rural Communes -- Foreign Policy in U.S. Mid-Term Campaign -- Chiang Renounces Use of Force to Return to Mainland -- Partial Truce on Offshore Island Bombing -- Mao Tse-Tung Resigns as Chairman of People's Republic.

China Visit. On Jan. 7, the mothers of three Americans held prisoner in China were allowed to visit their sons.

Chou's Warning. On Jan. 10, Chinese Communist Premier Chou En-lai charged in an interview that the U.S., Britain, and Japan were attempting to create a permanent Nationalist government on Formosa in order to "manufacture two Chinas." Chou said that as the U.S. "exerts pressure on us, the more we will resist." "If the (U.S.) insists on waging war, we will fight."

The interview followed repeated reports from the China mainland that the Chinese Communist government continued to arrest governmental and religious leaders as "counter-revolutionaries." On Jan. 17, the vice chairman of the Nationality Affairs Committee said in Peking that "mounting regional nationalism" among minorities had "become a danger that must be taken seriously."

Dulles on China. On Jan. 16, Secretary of State Dulles told the National Press Club that he did not think there was "any occasion at the present time to meet Communist China at the summit," but the U.S. would negotiate with that government or even recognize its regime "any time it will serve the interests of the United States."

Dismissals. On Jan. 31, Chinese Communist President Mao Tse-tung announced the dismissal of three members of the Cabinet: Communications Minister Chang Po-chun, Timber Industry Minister Lo Lung-chi, and Food Minister Chang Nai-chi. All three had criticized the Peking government after Mao Tse-tung's plea, Feb. 27, 1957, to let "a hundred schools of thought contend." On Feb. 1, the National People's Congress was informed that 16 deputies and 38 members of the Congress had been barred from its meeting and dismissed.

Humphrey Statement. On Feb. 4, Sen. Hubert H. Humphrey (D Minn.), chairman of the Senate Special Disarmament Subcommittee, suggested that the U.S. reexamine its policies toward Communist China because "some settlement of the China issue must take place" before any general disarmament agreement can be contemplated seriously.

Rightists Purged. On Feb. 6, a Chinese Communist Party publication containing an article by Lo Jui-ching was received in Hong Kong. The article asserted that 100,000 rightists and counter-revolutionaries had been discovered and purged during an investigation of 1,770,000 persons from June 1955 through October 1957.

Korea. On Feb. 7, Chinese Communist Premier Chou En-lai renewed a proposal that both the UN and Chinese Communist forces withdraw from Korea "within a set period of time."

New Chinese Foreign Minister. On Feb. 11, Chou resigned as China's Foreign Minister and was replaced by Marshal Chen Yi. Chou remained in the government as Premier.

Chinese Withdrawal. On Feb. 19, the Chinese Communist and North Korean governments announced that all Chinese Communist forces would be withdrawn from Korea by the end of 1958. The joint statement said the "Chinese government is taking the initiative in withdrawing its volunteer forces in support of North Korea's demand for withdrawal of all foreign troops in Korea."

The State Department announced the same day that the U.S. would not remove its troops from South Korea but hoped that Communist China "would go further" and "agree to genuinely free elections" to unite the country. On Feb. 22, the South Korean National Assembly voted unanimously for a resolution demanding that the UN Command discard the 1953 truce agreement with North Korea and Communist China.

Soviet Warns SEATO. On March 8, the Soviet Union warned SEATO member nations not to accept U.S. missiles and atomic weapons because they would then bear "serious responsibility" for increased tension in Southeast Asia. On March 11, Secretary of State Dulles told the SEATO Ministerial Council in Manila that Communist pressure "should alert us to the possibility that there may be new aggressive Communist plans for this area, plans which Communist rulers fear SEATO might block."

Saigon Declines. On March 16, the South Vietnamese government rejected an offer from the North Vietnamese government to discuss reduction of armed forces and conclusion of trade agreements.

Wheat to China. On March 31, it was disclosed that Communist China and four companies, three Canadian and one American, had signed an agreement for shipment of Canadian wheat to China.

UN on Korean Elections. On April 9, the UN Command asked Communist China and North Korea to clarify their proposals for unification of Korea through free elections. The Command queried the Communists as to whether they would approve of UN supervision of the elections, and whether they would accept a unified Korean National Assembly based on proportional representation. South Korea's population is almost three times that of North Korea.

Production in China. On April 10, the Peking radio reported that light industrial production had almost doubled during Communist China's first five-year plan (1952-1957). During the same period, the broadcast said, there had been a 39 percent increase in the wages of light industrial workers.

Sino-Soviet Trade Pact. On April 22, Communist China and the Soviet Union signed a trade agreement providing for the increased exchange of Chinese food products and Soviet industrial machinery.

Reds on Korean Settlement. On May 6, the Chinese Communist and North Korean governments said the UN Command would have to withdraw all its forces from South Korea before there could be "a peaceful settlement of the Korean question, including the question of holding free elections."

ADA Resolution. On May 18, Americans for Democratic Action, meeting in annual convention, called for an immediate start on negotiations looking toward recognition of Communist China. An earlier resolution, which would have recommended immediate recognition, was defeated after a floor fight. The final resolution said: "ADA urges immediate initiation of negotiations toward diplomatic recognition of the Peking regime, not as a gesture of moral approval -- which the Chinese Communists obviously do not merit -- but as a means of establishing the normal channels of international communication between the two nations."

Chinese and COMECON. On May 24, the governments of Communist China, North Korea, North Viet Nam, and Mongolia, during a meeting of the Council for Mutual Economic Assistance (COMECON) in Moscow, "expressed their readiness to take an active part in the economic planning of the (European) Socialist countries."

De Gaulle Becomes Premier. On June 1, Gen. Charles de Gaulle became the 26th postwar premier of the French Fourth Republic.

Tito on Red China. On June 15, President Tito of Yugoslavia charged that Chinese Communist leaders were attempting to subvert world peace and dominate Asia through war. He said the Chinese leaders believed that "if 300 million Chinese were killed (in war) there would still remain 300 million Chinese." Tito's comment: "By God! Nobody would survive a new war."

Chinese Minorities. On June 27, the Peking *People's Daily* said "final victory" had been achieved over minority groups attempting to restore capitalism and "regional nationalism" in Sinkiang Province.

Ambassadorial Talks. On June 30, Peking warned that it would abandon the ambassadorial talks with the U.S. in Geneva -- suspended since December 1957, shortly before Ambassador U. Alexis Johnson, the American representative, was transferred to Thailand -- unless the U.S. agreed within 15 days to resume the discussions. The Chinese had refused to accept the U.S. Second Secretary of the London Embassy as a temporary replacement for Ambassador Johnson. The State Department rejected the Chinese warning as an ultimatum but said it was not trying to terminate the meetings or reduce their importance. (*See Sept. 6*)

Peking Restricts Diplomats. On June 30, the Chinese Communist government announced that foreign diplomats in China would not be allowed to travel more than 12 miles from Peking without special permission. This restriction, and arrests of Chinese employed in foreign embassies, were considered indications that the anti-rightist campaign was continuing and had been extended to the Peking area. On July 5, the Peking radio denounced nationalism in Sinkiang Province as a "major dangerous tendency."

China's Atomic Reactor. On July 1, the Peking radio reported that Communist China's first experimental atomic reactor began operating June 13.

UN Command Rejects Korean Withdrawal. On July 2, the member states of the UN Command in Korea told the Chinese Communists that UN forces would not be withdrawn from South Korea until plans for unification of the country through free elections were definitely agreed upon.

Douglas Statement. On July 15, Sen. Paul H. Douglas (D. Ill.) called for strong resistance to the "rise of new efforts to convince the American people of the desirability of closer diplomatic, economic and cultural relations with Communist China."

Nationalist Alert. On Aug. 6, the Chinese Nationalist government ordered a state of emergency on Matsu and the Pescadores Islands because of increasing Communist activity in the Formosa Strait area. A Chinese Communist deputy premier had announced Aug. 1 that Red China intended to build a "powerful army, a powerful air force, and a powerful navy, modernized for the revolutionary task" of "wiping out for good the imperialist system" and terminating the U.S. isolation of China through its "occupation" of Formosa. On Aug. 8, the State Department announced that Communist China was attempting to "increase tension and raise the specter of war" in the Formosa Strait area by increasing the size of its air force on the mainland nearest Formosa.

U.S. Policy Statement. On Aug. 9, the State Department issued a memorandum, which had been circulated to all its embassies, reaffirming the policy of not recognizing Communist China. The memorandum said that "one day (Communist rule in China) will pass" and by "withholding diplomatic recognition from Peiping, (the U.S.) seeks to hasten that passing." The "two Chinas"theory was rejected on the ground that the Nationalist government on Formosa "would not accept any diminution of its sovereignty over China." The memorandum noted also that the Chinese Communists had rejected any solution that included diplomatic recognition of both the Nationalist and the Communist governments. It added that the U.S. would "readjust its present policies" if "the situation in the Far East were so to change in its basic elements as to call for a radically different evaluation of the threat Chinese Communist policies pose to (the U.S.)."

Offshore Islands Shelled. On Aug. 23, the Chinese Communists began intensive shelling of Quemoy, Little Quemoy, and the Tan Islands, just to the south of Quemoy. On the same day, Secretary of State Dulles asserted in a letter to Acting Chairman Thomas E. Morgan (D Pa.) of the House Foreign Affairs Committee that an invasion of the offshore islands would be a "threat to peace in the area." He said that if the Communists did attack the islands, "President Eisenhower will decide as to the...value of certain coastal positions to...Formosa."

On Aug. 27, President Eisenhower declared that the U.S. would not "desert our responsibilities or the statements we have already made" concerning Formosa and the offshore islands. Adding that "the Nationalist Chinese have now deployed about a third of their forces to...these islands,"...the President noted that "that makes a closer interlocking between the defense systems of the islands with Formosa than...before." On Aug. 28, the Nationalists reported that the Chinese Communists were concentrating military sea power in the mainland's coastal bases near Quemoy and Matsu.

Communist Threat to Formosa. On Aug. 29, the Peking radio said that a "landing on Quemoy is imminent," and that the Communists were "determined to liberate Taiwan (Formosa)...as well as the offshore islands." The broadcast told Nationalist forces defending Quemoy to "stop resistance immediately and return to the fatherland" or "be totally destroyed." The same day, the State Department warned that a Communist attempt "to change the situation" in the Formosa Strait by force "could (not) be a limited operation." The Defense Department announced that U.S. forces in the area were being reinforced.

Soviet Support. On Aug. 31, the Soviet Union announced it would send "moral and material aid" to the Chinese Communists in their efforts to overthrow the "aggressors" in the Formosa area.

Mme. Chiang's Speech. On Sept. 3, Mme. Chiang Kai-shek told an American Legion convention in Chicago that when the Chinese Communists "are ready for war, no amount of appeasement will do any good," but that "a clear-cut, strong stand by the U.S. ...will stop the Communists short in their tracks." She pledged that mainland China would be liberated "in my lifetime" and that "the only way to avoid a third world war is for us to get back to the mainland."

U.S. Ready to Use Force. On Sept. 4, Secretary of State John Foster Dulles, in a statement cleared by President Eisenhower, warned Communist China that the President "would not hesitate" to use armed force "in insuring the defense of Formosa" if he deemed such action necessary. The statement, issued following a conference at the Newport, R.I., summer White House, said the President "has not yet made any finding" on the need for armed action, but if he should, "action both timely and effective" would follow.

The statement stressed U.S. obligations, under a 1955 mutual defense treaty with Nationalist China, to help defend Formosa. By joint resolution, also in 1955, Congress authorized the President to employ U.S. armed forces to defend not only Formosa but also "related positions...now in friendly hands." The Dulles statement pointed out that securing of the offshore islands of Quemoy and Matsu "has increasingly become related to the defense of Taiwan." Dulles said any "naked use of force" by the Chinese Communists "would pose an issue far transcending the offshore islands and even the security of Taiwan." It would "forecast a widespread use of force in the Far East which would endanger vital free world positions and the security of the United States."

Red China Proclaims 12-Mile Limit. On Sept. 4, Communist China laid formal claim to all waters within 12 miles of its coasts, and to Quemoy, Matsu, and other islands within the proclaimed limit of its territorial waters. Peking forbade foreign vessels and aircraft to enter the area without permission. The U.S. immediately said it would recognize only the traditional three-mile limit.

Ambassadors to Discuss Formosa. On Sept. 6, Chinese Communist Premier Chou En-lai proposed resumption of the Sino-U.S. ambassadorial talks for discussion of the Formosa question. The U.S. replied the same day that Jacob Beam, U.S. Ambassador to Poland, "stands ready to meet promptly" with the Chinese Communist Ambassador to Poland, Wang Ping-nan, who had conducted the talks for China from their inception at Geneva. The statement said the U.S. would "adhere to the negotiating position... that we will not...be a party to any arrangement which would prejudice the rights of our ally, the Republic of China."

Khrushchev Letter. On Sept. 8, President Eisenhower received a letter from Soviet Premier Nikita Khrushchev warning that an attack on Communist China would be "an attack on the Soviet Union." The White House answered that world order depended on Communist China's avoidance of the use of force; the U.S. "would welcome the Soviet government's concerning itself with this aspect of the matter."

Dulles on Warsaw Talks. On Sept. 9, Secretary of State Dulles told a news conference that a meaningful renunciation of force by Communist China would ease the Formosa Strait crisis, and he said there might be "further consequences." Dulles hinted that the U.S. was ready to offer concessions under such circumstances at the proposed ambassadorial talks in Warsaw. The Secretary said the U.S. would seek agreement along detailed, specific lines but could not itself negotiate the future of Quemoy and Matsu, because those islands belonged to Nationalist China.

Eisenhower Bars Appeasement. On Sept. 11, President Eisenhower said in a radio-television address that it would be appeasement, probably leading to a major war, to allow the Chinese Communists to overthrow the Chinese Nationalists. Although he believed "negotiations and conciliation should never be abandoned in favor of force and strife," the U.S. could not be "either lured or frightened into appeasement." Secretary of Defense Neil H. McElroy, following the President, said the U.S. had "made it clear we would resist an assault on the Quemoys by the Chinese Communists."

Letter to Khrushchev. On Sept. 13, President Eisenhower, replying to a letter received from Soviet Premier Khrushchev on Sept. 8, suggested that he carry out his asserted desire for peace by urging Communist China to discontinue military operations in the Formosa Strait area.

British Policy on Formosa. On Sept. 15, British Labor Party Leader Hugh Gaitskell demanded in a letter to Prime Minister Harold Macmillan that he "make it plain that, even if the U.S.A. becomes involved in a war to defend Quemoy, Britain would not join in." Macmillan replied that Britain "strongly supported" the U.S. "in opposing any attempt to settle the dispute by...force." Macmillan noted that "Our American allies have neither sought nor received promises of military support from us in the Formosan area."

Anti-Communist China Lobby. On Sept. 15, Marvin Liebman, secretary of the Committee of One Million Against the Admission of Communist China to the United Nations, said the organization was "redoubling and tripling our efforts to stem this tide of pro-appeasement sentiment" concerning Communist China. Liebman said the Red shelling of Matsu and Quemoy helped the committee's campaign because "it shows up the Chinese Reds for what we always said they were; proves they are prepared and willing to shoot their way into the United Nations"; and brings the whole issue out into the open for debate.

The Committee of One Million listed 23 Senators as members, including Paul H. Douglas (D Ill.), William F. Knowland (R Calif.), Mike Mansfield (D Mont.), Everett M. Dirksen (R Ill.), Jacob K. Javits (R N.Y.), and A. S. Mike Monroney (D Okla.). It also listed 83 Representatives; four Governors; Robert S. Allen, columnist; H. V. Kaltenborn, radio commentator; Gen. George C. Marshall; Henry R. Luce of *Time* and *Life*; Warren R. Austin, first U.S. Ambassador to the UN; and Adm. Arthur W. Radford, former chairman of the Joint Chiefs of Staff.

Reaction to Formosa Crisis. The impending crisis in the Formosa area brought various reactions from Congressional and other official sources:

On Sept. 6, former Secretary of State Dean Acheson commented that the U.S. seemed to be "drifting, either dazed or indifferent, toward war with China...over issues which the Administration has not presented to the people and which are not worth a single American life." The same day, Vice President Richard M. Nixon said the U.S. "could make no greater mistake than by appearing to be a paper tiger" in the Far East, because "in dealing with dictatorships you do not maintain peace by appearing to be weak but only by maintaining strength militarily and diplomatically."

On Sept. 9, Adlai Stevenson said that recent U.S. foreign policy was "clumsy, erratic, and self-righteous," but the U.S. had a "solemn obligation" to defend Formosa. The same day, Sen. John Sherman Cooper (R Ky.) said the U.S. "should make it clear we will defend Formosa with everything we have, but I do not believe it is in the national interest to go to war over Quemoy and Matsu."

On Sept. 12, Sen. Theodore F. Green (D R.I.), chairman of the Senate Foreign Relations Committee, expressed "profound concern" over the President's policy of employing armed forces "in a way which might risk deeper military involvement." The President, Green said, "has a duty to request policy guidance from Congress."

On Sept. 13, Sen. John F. Kennedy (D Mass.) said that "the weight of military, diplomatic, political, and historical judgment would dictate a contrary policy concerning Formosa." Kennedy was joined by Sen. Ralph W. Yarborough (D Texas), who commented that President Eisenhower was "getting bayonet-happy."

On Sept. 14, former President Harry S. Truman said it would be "folly and dangerous" to abandon Formosa to the Communists as long as they were "aggression-minded." The situation in Quemoy and Matsu, he said, "should be treated as a major element in a global struggle for survival."

On Sept. 15, Sen. Kenneth B. Keating (R N.Y.) said he was "unalterably" opposed to recognition of Communist China and its admission to the UN.

Warsaw Talks. On Sept. 15, the American and Chinese Communist ambassadors to Poland (Jacob D. Beam and Wang Ping-nan) opened talks on the Formosan crisis.

Dulles at UN. On Sept. 18, Secretary of State Dulles told the UN General Assembly that debate on the Formosa and Quemoy-Matsu dispute should be postponed until the outcome of negotiations in Warsaw between the U.S. and Communist China. He expressed hope that the negotiations there would bring a cease-fire but reserved the right to bring the problem to the UN if the Warsaw talks appeared headed for failure.

Aid to Formosa. On Sept. 18, Defense Department spokesmen said the U.S. had sent $90 million in military supplies to Formosa in the three weeks since the Quemoy crisis began. The Pentagon announced also that American pilots were authorized to follow a "hot pursuit" policy against any Chinese Communist plane which might attack them, including following the plane over Communist-held territory.

Nationalist View. On Sept. 19, Nationalist Chinese Premier Chen Cheng told the Nationalist Parliament that the Formosan government would "not accept any resolution reached in Warsaw that might prejudice the rights of (Nationalist) China." He added: "Nobody has the right to make us demilitarize these islands. Communist occupation of Quemoy and Matsu would pose a serious threat to the security of all the Far East area."

Khrushchev Letter Rejected. On Sept. 20, the White House rejected a letter from Soviet Premier Khrushchev because it was "replete with false accusations." The letter said that neither Russia nor Communist China was frightened by what they considered "atomic blackmail," and that there should be no doubt of Russia's intention to support its Chinese allies. On Sept. 21, the official Russian news agency, *Tass*, said the rejection indicated that President Eisenhower was unwilling to "listen to the voice of reason."

Quemoy Casualties. On Sept. 21, the Nationalist government announced that the Chinese Communist bombardment of Quemoy from Aug. 23 to Sept. 21, 1958, had resulted in 3,000 civilian and 1,000 military casualties.

UN Action. On Sept. 23, the UN General Assembly approved, by a 44-28 vote with nine abstentions, a U.S. proposal to postpone for another year any consideration of Communist China's admission to the UN. U.S. Representative to the UN Henry Cabot Lodge on Sept. 22 told the Assembly that the Chinese Communists were "rapidly shooting themselves and shooting the world" out of a peaceful Formosa settlement. He said their bombardment of the offshore islands was "a further disqualification" for UN membership. On Sept. 25, British Foreign Secretary Selwyn Lloyd told the General Assembly "the whole world community should join in insisting that this matter should not be settled by force." His government, Lloyd said, hoped the Warsaw talks would lead to an immediate cease-fire, followed by later negotiations on various claims.

Chiang's Statement. On Sept. 29, Chiang Kai-shek told a news conference that the offshore islands had become a "shield" for the protection of Formosa, rather than a springboard for invasion of the mainland, and for that reason the Nationalist government was determined to defend them. He added that "talks with the Communists under any circumstances are futile, and the Warsaw talks are no exception."

Hint of a Policy Change. On Sept. 30, Secretary of State Dulles hinted at a possible change in Formosa policy. The Secretary said at a news conference that the U.S. would favor reducing Chinese Nationalist forces on the offshore island of Quemoy if the Chinese Communists would agree to a cease-fire. Dulles said that a renunciation of force should apply to both Nationalists and Communists. The U.S., he added, had "no commitment of any kind" to help the Nationalists return to the mainland.

On Oct. 2, Chiang Kai-shek said he opposed any reduction in the island garrisons as the price of a cease-fire. On the same day, Secretary Dulles told newsmen he had sent a message to the U.S. Ambassador in Formosa, Everett F. Drumright, to "straighten out" misconceptions by "the press out there" and the Nationalists that "gave an exaggerated idea of a shift of position on our part."

Eisenhower on Formosa and UN. On Oct. 1, President Eisenhower told his news conference that Secretary Dulles' modification of Formosan policy was not appeasement. "We want a peaceful solution," he said, "and fundamentally anyone can see that the two islands (Quemoy and Matsu) as of themselves, as two pieces of territory, are not greatly vital to Formosa. But of course the Chinese Nationalists hold that if you give way to that, you have given a way to exposing us to great attack and that is a different thing than just concluding that two pieces of territory are the vital issue."

When asked about the possibility of Communist Chinese membership in the UN, the President answered: " ... I have announced myself publicly before you people and others that there are certain historical facts in the history of Communist China that make it impossible for us to consider this question as an arguable one at the moment. For example, they are still branded as aggressors in Korea, and they have taken no effective steps to remove that stigma from the record. They have gone into Viet Nam. They have violated some of the terms of the armistice by continuing to train North Vietnamese and so on for armed purposes, and we don't know whether it's for eventual aggression or not. They have refused in spite of an agreement given as long back...(as) two years ago...that they would release our remaining prisoners from China. They have refused to do so.... And finally, their deportment in the diplomatic field and all the way through has been such that makes this indeed a very difficult thing even to study dispassionately and disinterestedly."

Morse's Statement. On Oct. 1, Sen. Wayne Morse (D Ore.) said that before the Senate ratified a defense treaty with Chiang Kai-shek in 1955, Secretary Dulles was "forced into an understanding" with the late Sen. Walter F. George (D Ga.), then chairman of the Foreign Relations Committee, that the Senate would be asked to ratify any U.S. move to defend Quemoy and Matsu.

Passports. On Oct. 2, a Federal judge upheld the State Department's refusal in 1957 to renew the passport of William Worthy Jr., a newspaperman who violated the ban on travel to Communist China.

Warsaw Meeting. On Oct. 4, the discussions between the U.S. and Communist China in Warsaw were reported to have made no progress toward a solution of the Formosan crisis.

Congressional Telegram. On Oct. 4, a demand for a special session of Congress on the Far East situation was made by 10 Democratic Congressmen in a telegram to the President. They said they had found "the great majority" of their constituents "deeply disturbed with the Administration's Quemoy policy," and they believed "we should disentangle ourselves from Chiang Kai-shek's aspirations on Quemoy, and should endeavor to bring the mantle of the UN over Formosa."

Cease-Fire. On Oct. 6, Communist China's Defense Minister Peng Teh-huai announced over the radio a one-week cease-fire in the Formosa Strait area. He said the Nationalists would be "fully free to ship in supplies (to

Quemoy) on condition that there would be no American escort." Peng reiterated the Chinese Communist position that the warfare was "an internal Chinese matter" and "not a matter between China and the U.S.," so "the question of a cease-fire does not arise" between the two countries. He added that "of all choices, peace is best.... We propose that talks be held to effect a peaceful settlement." On the same day, the Nationalist government rejected the proposal for talks, because the Communists "never will keep their word."

Dulles on Cease-Fire. On Oct. 7, Secretary Dulles said "it was not easy to evaluate" the cease-fire, but that "the development assures world-wide condemnation of the Chinese Communists if they again resume fighting."

U.S. Halts Convoys. On Oct. 8, the State Department announced a halt in convoying of Nationalist Chinese supply vessels to Quemoy as a result of Communist China's Oct. 6 announcement of a one-week cease-fire in the Formosa Strait area. The Department said the halt in convoys followed "full consultation" with the Chinese Nationalists, but that the escort system would be resumed if the Communists resumed their attacks.

Humphrey's Statement. On Oct. 8, Sen. Hubert H. Humphrey (D Minn.), addressing the International Chemical Workers Union (AFL-CIO), said the question of jurisdiction over the offshore islands "should be given to the World Court to decide," and that the possibility of turning Formosa into an independent nation "under the umbrella of United Nations guarantees and protection" should be "thoroughly explored."

Warsaw Talks. On Oct. 9, a State Department spokesman said "our whole purpose" in the Warsaw talks with the Chinese Communist ambassador was to broaden the cease-fire agreement in the Formosa area. He said the Department had ordered Ambassador to Poland Jacob Beam to seek a continuation of the one-week Quemoy cease-fire.

Chiang on Quemoy. On Oct. 10, Nationalist President Chiang Kai-shek said the Nationalists had "won the first round in the battle for Quemoy" and would some day "deliver our compatriots on the mainland from Communist tyranny." He asserted that the Communists had placed themselves in "a hopeless position from which they can never extricate themselves." Another attack would "invite common action by the free world's anti-aggression force."

Growth of Communes. On Oct. 12, a *Hsinhua* (New China) news agency report carried by the *New York Times* stated that by Sept. 30 a reorganization of China's peasantry into communes, replacing private and collective farms, was 90 percent completed. The first experimental commune -- the Sputnik People's Commune -- was set up in Honan Province in April 1958. By Sept. 30 the number of rural communes was reported to have risen to 23,397, containing 112.2 million peasant households or an average of nearly 5,000 families in each commune.

McElroy's Visit to Formosa. On Oct. 12, Secretary of Defense Neil H. McElroy flew to Formosa and was reported to have told Chiang Kai-shek the following day that the U.S. would increase its naval and air power in the area if Chiang would reduce the number of Nationalist troops on the offshore islands. In a speech to Nationalist troops he said they had averted "what might have been a very destructive war."

Cease-Fire Extended. On Oct. 13, Communist China extended its Oct. 6 order for a one-week cease-fire in the Formosa Strait area for two additional weeks "to see what the opposite side is going to do and enable our compatriots on Quemoy, both military and civilian, to get sufficient supplies, including food and military equipment." The statement said the bombardment would "start at once" if the U.S. resumed "escort operations in the Quemoy water area." It added that the dispute was "China's internal affair, and no foreigner has any right to meddle with it."

No Plan to Coerce Chiang. On Oct. 14, Secretary of State John Foster Dulles told a news conference there would be no effort to coerce Nationalist President Chiang Kai-shek into reducing his Quemoy Island garrison. Dulles said the Communists were interested only in "driving a wedge" between the U.S. and the Nationalists, that he had no indications that "a deal could be made with the Communists which was confined to the Quemoy or Matsu situation," and that he did not "want to give the impression that we... plan to press the Republic of China to do something against its own better judgment."

Foreign Policy in Politics. On Oct. 14, at his news conference, Secretary Dulles decried the continuing injection of foreign policy into the current election campaign and said he hoped both parties would "calm down" on foreign policy, though there were "some basic problems which can be discussed in terms of underlying principles." On the same day Vice President Richard M. Nixon replied to an Oct. 11 statement by the Democratic Advisory Council, which criticized "six years of leaderless vacillation" and urged presentation of the Formosa question to the UN. Nixon said the statement was an example of "the same defensive, defeatist, fuzzy-headed thinking which contributed to the loss of China and led to the Korean War."

On Oct. 15, Dulles issued a clarifying statement to halt interpretation of his remarks as direct criticism of Nixon. Dulles said the Democratic statement had evoked Nixon's answer, and "in those circumstances I fully concurred in the need for that answer."

On Oct. 14, former President Harry S. Truman, in a newspaper article, said he intended to "do everything I can to discourage partisan attacks."

On Oct. 15, President Eisenhower said at a news conference that he supported Secretary Dulles on the importance of keeping foreign policy out of "partisan debate." On the same day, Vice President Nixon told reporters in California: "For us who have the responsibility of carrying the weight of this campaign to stand by and to allow our policies to be attacked with impunity by our opponents without reply would lead to inevitable defeat."

On Oct. 16, President Eisenhower sent Nixon a telegram saying that Dulles' Oct. 15 statement "should clear the atmosphere, particularly in pointing out that there is no real difference between the two of you." The President said criticisms of the administrative operation of foreign policy "need to be answered whenever they occur," and that "no one can do this more effectively than you." Six days later, in Wilmington, Del., Nixon voiced his belief that foreign policy was the major issue in the off-year election campaign. Senate Democratic Leader Lyndon B. Johnson asserted a day earlier at Nashville, Tenn., that "Bipartisanship (in foreign policy) should be a two-way street, and it should not run one way during a national crisis and another way during a political crisis."

Bombardment Resumed. On Oct. 20, Communist China, ending its cease-fire a week ahead of schedule, resumed bombardment of the offshore islands. It said the U.S. had broken the truce by escorting Nationalist supply ships to Quemoy the previous day. A U.S. Navy spokesman denied the charge.

Chiang Renounces Force. On Oct. 23, after three days of talks at Taipei, Chinese Nationalist President Chiang Kai-shek and Secretary of State Dulles said in a joint communique that return to the mainland was still Chiang's sacred mission, but that the principal means of accomplishing that mission was through implementation of Sun Yat-sen's three People's Principles (nationalism, democracy and social well-being) "and not the use of force." The U.S. and the Nationalists both "recognized that under present conditions the defense of the Quemoys together with the Matsus is closely related to the defense of Taiwan (Formosa) and Penghu (the Pescadores) islands."

Elaborating on the talks at an Oct. 23 news conference, Assistant Secretary of State Walter S. Robertson said the Nationalists had asked for convoy escorts; he added that "we have reassured them" that "when it is considered by military authorities to be necessary, they will be resumed." Dulles, in an Oct. 17 filmed interview released by the State Department Oct. 23, said the U.S. "was not going to attack or tolerate attacks against the Chinese Communists," but that the Government would "stand firm" to resist any Chinese Communist attacks.

Dulles Statement. On Oct. 24, after reporting to President Eisenhower on his trip to Formosa, Secretary Dulles said that the Nationalist government was "dedicated to the peaceful achievement of its high mission." He added that "Apparently the Communists desire to throw roadblocks in the way of stabilized tranquillity," but that he was "confident that the Chinese Communists will not gain their ends either through their military efforts or their propaganda guile."

Withdrawal From Korea. On Oct. 25, the Chinese Communists announced completion of their troop withdrawal from North Korea.

Every-Other-Day Truce. On Oct. 25, Communist China announced there would be no bombardment of Quemoy airfield, wharf, or beach landing areas on "even dates" of the month (so the offshore islands could get supplies), but that "exception will be taken if there should be escorts." The Communists said they would "not necessarily conduct shelling on odd dates," but they warned the Nationalists to supply the island on even dates "to avoid possible losses."

Dulles on Truce and Talks. On Oct. 28, Secretary Dulles told a news conference that the Chinese Communist announcement of a partial truce showed that "the killing is done for political purposes and promiscuously," and that the Communists "are trying to save themselves from a loss of face and a defeat in the effort which they had initiated but had been unable to conclude successfully." Dulles said the most important achievement of his talks with Chiang Kai-shek was "a fresh formulation of the mission of the government of Free China" with "the emphasis on winning through peaceful processes." He agreed with a statement the day before by Chinese Nationalist Ambassador to the U.S., George K.C. Yeh, that "We will not give up military might for legitimate and self-defense purposes." Dulles commented: "Certainly we do not nor have we ever asked anybody else to do that."

Clarification. On Oct. 31, State Department Press Officer Lincoln White told a news conference that Nationalist China could use force "for self-defense or in the case of a large-scale uprising" on the Communist mainland, despite President Chiang Kai-shek's Oct. 23 renunciation of force. White said his statement was aimed at clarifying "misunderstandings."

Smathers Statement. On Nov. 1, Sen. George A. Smathers (D Fla.) said White's statement was "an illustration of what we Democrats mean when we complain that the State Department marches up the hill one week and down the hill the next." He told newsmen Secretary Dulles should make it clear that the U.S. will not aid any Nationalist attempt to recapture the mainland.

Chen Yi's Statement. On Nov. 1, in an interview with a Canadian newsman in Peking, Chinese Communist Foreign Minister Chen Yi said: "Quemoy, Matsu, Formosa, and the Pescadores must be liberated as a whole. We will not allow the handing over of Quemoy in exchange for placing Formosa under (UN) trusteeship," which "would be nothing but American occupation." "Nor can we accept demilitarization or referring the matter to the (UN) or the International Court of Justice."

Bombardment. On Nov. 3, the Chinese Communists gave Quemoy the worst shelling it had received in two months.

Election. On Nov. 4, the Democrats made important gains in Congressional and gubernatorial elections as a record number of Americans went to the polls for the midterm voting. The Democrats gained 13 Senate seats, 47 House seats, and five Governorships. In California, Sen. William F. Knowland (R) and Gov. Goodwin J. Knight (R) were both defeated. In New York, Republican Nelson A. Rockefeller defeated Gov. Averell Harriman (D) in his bid for re-election.

Eisenhower on China. On Nov. 5, President Eisenhower, said at a news conference, regarding China policy: "As far as I am concerned, our position has not changed as long as Red China continues to do some of the things which we cannot possibly stomach, one of them being that after two years ago promising to give back all our prisoners, and people that we think are illegally held, they still will do nothing about it. And there are a good many other accusations of the same kind."

Beam Returns. On Nov. 10, U.S. Ambassador to Poland Jacob D. Beam returned to the U.S. to report on seven weeks of negotiations with Communist China's Ambassador in Warsaw, Wang Ping-nan. The two envoys were scheduled to resume their talks Nov. 25. Meanwhile, Communist China continued its every-other-day bombardments in the Formosa Strait.

Dulles Speech. On Nov. 13, Secretary of State Dulles told a meeting of the Seattle, Wash., Chamber of Commerce that Communist China's leaders were creating a vast slave state to increase the power of international communism; because they recognized that their activities were "bound to induce hatred on the part of the Chinese people," they were trying to divert hatred away from themselves by directing it against foreigners.

Mao Resigns. On Dec. 17, the Chinese Communist Party Central Committee announced that Mao Tse-tung, 65, would retire as chairman of the Chinese People's Republic when his current term expired in January 1959. The announcement said Mao was resigning to devote full time to his job as Communist party chairman. Chinese Foreign Minister Chen Yi said Mao was retiring "to conserve himself (for) still more important tasks." He denied that difficulties with the commune system -- which was intended to enable Red China to make a "great leap forward" in agricultural and industrial production -- or the failure to gain control of the offshore islands had anything to do with Mao's decision.

Commune Slowdown. On Dec. 18, the Chinese Communist Party Central Committee announced a decision, made Dec. 10, to put off introduction of large-scale communes in big cities pending solution of special problems encountered in urban centers. Meanwhile, the rural communes, where friction between peasants and party workers had arisen, were to be "tidied up, checked over and consolidated."

1959

Sino-Soviet Aid Pact -- Anti-Chinese Revolt in Tibet -- Mao Swims Yellow River -- Dalai Lama Escapes to India -- Liu Shao-chi New Chairman of Chinese People's Republic -- Unrest in China's Communes -- Dulles Dies -- China's Economic Progress -- Laos Asks for UN Emergency Force to Stop North Vietnamese Aid to Laotian Rebels -- Development of Chinese Border Dispute With India -- Khrushchev in Washington -- Lin Piao Named Red China's Defense Minister -- Khrushchev in Peking -- Marshall Dies -- Indian-Chinese Border Clash -- Failure of Nehru and Chou to Find Basis of Negotiation.

Economic Progress. On Jan. 1, Communist China announced that its industrial and agricultural production in 1958 was 70 percent greater than in 1957.

Chou in Moscow. On Jan. 28, Chinese Communist Premier Chou En-lai told the 21st Soviet Communist Party Congress in Moscow that the Soviet Union and Communist China shared "a common destiny" and a friendship that was "eternal and inviolable."

Sino-Soviet Aid Pact. On Feb. 7, Soviet Premier Nikita S. Khrushchev and Chinese Communist Premier Chou En-lai signed a technical aid agreement in Moscow to provide China with $1.25 billion worth of equipment and assistance by 1967 for construction of 78 heavy industrial installations.

Sino-Soviet Unity. On Feb. 14, a joint Soviet-Chinese statement, issued in Moscow by the Chinese-Soviet Friendship Association, asserted that the "unbreakable unity" of China and Russia could not be broken by "American imperialists and...revisionists of Yugoslavia," who were both "spreading infamous insinuations about the 'big leap' in our countries and the development of the people's communes."

Dulles' Health. On Feb. 14, doctors at Walter Reed Army Hospital announced that Secretary of State John Foster Dulles had cancer. Dulles had undergone an operation the day before for a "recently developed hernia." On Feb. 18, President Eisenhower said that if Dulles "believes that he is in shape to carry on, he is exactly the person I want."

China and Disarmament. On Feb. 23, Assistant Secretary of State for Far Eastern Affairs Walter S. Robertson told the Senate Disarmament Subcommittee that Communist China would have to be included in any "sound and workable" disarmament agreement or nuclear test ban treaty.

Robertson said also that, during the Warsaw negotiations, the Chinese Communists had refused to "negotiate on the offshore islands because to them the offshore islands are peanuts." He warned: "What they want is to get rid of a rival Chinese government on Taiwan (Formosa). Their *sine qua non* is that we get out of Taiwan Strait and...out of the western Pacific."

Wang's Statement. On Feb. 24, Gen. Wang Shu-ming, Nationalist Chinese chief of staff, told the *New York Times* that the Nationalists had not reduced the size of their forces on the offshore islands since the Communist bombardment began in August 1958.

Sino-Soviet Trade Pact. On Feb. 26, it was disclosed that the Soviet Union and Communist China had signed a $1.75 billion trade agreement in Moscow. Russia was slated to export industrial equipment to China, while the nature of the Chinese goods sent to Russia was not mentioned.

Tibetan Revolt. On March 20, the Indian External Affairs Ministry in New Delhi confirmed reports that a major armed revolution against the Chinese Communists was taking place in Tibet. The revolt was reported to have erupted when Chinese Communist troops fired on crowds in Lhasa demonstrating in support of Tibet's spiritual and temporal leader, the Dalai Lama, and independence from China. On March 23, Indian Prime Minister Jawaharlal Nehru urged the Chinese Communists not to harm the Dalai Lama because he was "held in high veneration by our people."

Mao Swims. On March 24, a Hong Kong newspaper reported Communist Party Chairman Mao Tse-tung had swum across the Yellow River seven times in September 1958, presumably to disprove reports that he was in ill health.

Tibet. On March 25, the *London Times* reported that the Tibetan cabinet had declared independence from China and demanded that the Chinese withdraw from Tibet. On the same day, Chinese troops were reported to have occupied Lhasa after heavy fighting. They apparently could not re-establish control over the rebels in southern Tibet, where it was believed the Dalai Lama had fled.

On March 28, Chinese Communist Premier Chou En-lai ordered the Tibetan government dissolved and replaced by a regime headed by the Panchen Lama, 21, who said the following day he would serve until the return of the Dalai Lama to Lhasa. Chou charged that Tibetan officials had "colluded with imperialism, assembled rebellious bandits, carried out rebellion," and "put the Dalai Lama under duress." The State Department on March 28 accused China of "barbarous intervention" and of attempting to "destroy the historical autonomy of the Tibetan people."

Nehru's Statement. On March 30, Indian Prime Minister Nehru charged that the Chinese Communists had broken pledges to allow Tibet "full autonomy." He said India sympathized with the Tibetan rebels and would admit refugees from Tibet on an individual basis.

Dalai Lama Escapes. On March 31, the Dalai Lama reached India after a 300-mile journey over the southern mountains of Tibet. He and a party of about 80 had been forced to walk a large part of the way and to travel only at night to avoid Chinese search planes. On the same day, the Peking *People's Daily* said the Chinese Communist army had "swiftly put down the rebellion in the Lhasa area" and was "mopping up the rebels in some other places in Tibet."

Dulles Resigns. On April 15, Secretary of State John Foster Dulles resigned. Doctors had found that cancer had spread to his neck. President Eisenhower, in an emotional press conference, commented: "I personally believe he has filled his office with greater distinction than any man our country has known." On April 18, Eisenhower announced that Christian A. Herter would replace Dulles as Secretary of State. He was sworn in on April 21.

China's Economy. On April 15, Peking announced that all of China's economic goals for 1958, except those for cotton textiles, had been surpassed. On April 17, the Chinese People's Political Consultative Conference, meeting in Peking, appointed several "rightists," previously dismissed, to secondary conference posts.

Dalai Lama's Report. On April 18, the Dalai Lama asserted that failure of the Chinese Communists to respect promised Tibetan autonomy caused the struggle that "assumed serious proportions in 1956." He said that Chinese troops "destroyed a large number of monasteries," that "many Lamas were killed," and that "monks and officials were taken and employed on the construction of roads in China."

Chou on Tibet. On April 18, Chinese Communist Premier Chou En-lai asserted that the Dalai Lama had been "abducted to India." Chou told the Chinese National People's Congress in Peking that "a great victory" had been won for China by suppression of the Tibetan revolt. He

added: "China does not want to threaten or harm anybody, nor ask anybody to change the social-political systems they have chosen."

Liu Elected. On April 27, the National People's Congress in Peking elected Liu Shao-chi as the new chairman (or president) of the Chinese People's Republic. Mao's resignation from the post was announced Dec. 17, 1958. Liu was known as a leading Communist theoretician and organizer.

Nehru on Tibet. On April 27, Indian Prime Minister Nehru said in Parliament that the Indian people had been "greatly distressed" by Communist China's suppression of the Tibetan revolt. Chinese leaders, he observed, had "used the language of the cold war" in attacks on India during and after the revolt.

Commune Unrest. On May 16, sources in Hong Kong reported that the Chinese Communist government had eased control of agricultural production in southern communes due to spreading dissatisfaction among peasants.

Peasant Uprising. On May 25, the Nationalist Chinese reported that 10,000 peasants had revolted near Nanking on May 17 and killed 80 Communist officials. At least 200 rioters were said to have been killed before troops suppressed the uprising.

Dulles Dies. On May 24, former Secretary of State John Foster Dulles died of cancer at age 71.

Nationalist China and Olympics. On May 28, the International Olympic Commission voted "almost unanimously" to withdraw recognition from Nationalist China because "it no longer represents sports in the entire country of China." The president of the IOC, Avery Brundage, an American, said that if Communist China applied for membership, it would be recognized as the "representative of China." On June 2, the State Department charged that the action was "a clear act of political discrimination" against the Nationalist Chinese "to obtain the later admission of the Chinese Communists." On June 3, the House of Representatives voted unanimously to withhold U.S. financial support of the 1960 Winter Olympics at Squaw Valley, Calif., if the IOC refused to allow entry of athletes from any "free nation."

Chinese Athletes. On June 12, the State Department announced it would give visas to any bona fide athletes sent from Communist China to the Winter Olympics in Squaw Valley, Calif.

Food in China. On June 20, the *New York Times* reported that Communist China's 1959 food production had fallen below 1958 levels as a result of floods and drought.

China's Conduct in Tibet. On June 20, the Dalai Lama said Communist China was attempting "complete absorption and extinction of the Tibetan race." He charged that Communist forces had slain 65,000 Tibetans since 1956.

Americans Slain in Viet Nam. On July 8, two Americans were killed and one wounded during a Viet Minh attack on a compound 20 miles northeast of Saigon. The Americans were members of the U.S. Military Assistance Advisory Group in South Viet Nam.

Raids in Laos. On July 30, it was reported that Pathet Lao troops, armed by North Viet Nam, had attacked Laotian army outposts in two northern provinces. Hanoi radio charged the next day that the fighting was caused by "American imperialists," who were responsible for "terrorist raids" on rebel areas in northern Laos. On Aug. 1, the State Department said it viewed "with concern what may be a deliberate effort of insurgent elements,...backed by Communists from outside to provoke a crisis in Laos."

Viet Nam Aid. On July 30, a subcommittee of the Senate Foreign Relations Committee held hearings on allegations of "serious waste" and "outrageous scandal" in the Viet Nam aid program. The allegations were made by Scripps-Howard writer Albert M. Colegrove in a six-article series. Elbridge Durbrow, Ambassador to South Viet Nam, said that Colegrove's articles gave a "distorted picture" of the aid situation and that it was "unfortunate he did not check his facts." Durbrow asserted that Viet Nam's government, with U.S. aid, had brought the country from "chaos to basic stability." Colegrove nevertheless insisted before the subcommittee that the aid program was "scandalous" and a "fiasco." On Aug. 11, Creighton Scott, former adviser to Viet Nam Radio under the aid program, told a House subcommittee that "the whole thing is a stinking mess and might as well be brought out into the open."

Fighting in Laos. On Aug. 4, the Laotian government proclaimed a state of emergency in five of the northern provinces as fighting with the Communist rebels continued. On Aug. 8, Premier Phoui Sananikone said the guerrillas were attempting to establish "a base from which to attack the south and a corridor through which to attack South Viet Nam." He warned the Chinese Communists on Aug. 14 that "they were wrong if they think that Laos can be intimidated." On Aug. 17, the Soviet Union charged that Laos "despite its (neutrality) obligation under the Geneva agreement, has concluded a treaty legalizing the presence of United States military personnel in Laos and handing over control of the Laotian army to (them)." The Chinese Communist Foreign Ministry had charged earlier that the fighting in Laos was "engineered from first to last by the United States."

China's Economic Progress. On Aug. 16, the National Planning Association reported that Communist China distributed $647 million in foreign aid to Asian and Middle Eastern nations from 1952 to 1957 and received $430 million in aid from the Soviet Union during the same period. A report by A. Doak Barnett for the Rockefeller Foundation said that Soviet technical aid had been "indispensable" to China, but that the "Chinese Communists have had to pay their own way in relations with the Russians."

The Barnett report called Communist China's economic progress "very impressive" and its growth since 1958 "revolutionary and ... startling" but said it was "impossible to evaluate (the situation) at this time with any sense of confidence." Barnett said that China's establishment of a commune system and its decentralization of industry constituted the "most radical political, economic and social reorganization ever attempted in so short a time by a large nation." The report predicted that if the communes succeeded, "great opportunities for accelerated development may be opened up for the Peking regime." If they failed, there would be "a very adverse effect upon every aspect of the Chinese Communists' program."

Aid to Laos. On Aug. 25, President Eisenhower told a news conference that the Laotian government had asked the U.S. for aid "to reinforce their police forces, and the units they keep for internal order, and we have got it under study as a matter of urgency." Secretary of State Herter had said on Aug. 24 that the military situation in Laos was "very dangerous." He hoped that UN observers would be sent to the area but added that UN Secretary General Dag Hammarskjold opposed the idea. On Aug. 25, the North Vietnamese Foreign Ministry warned that if U.S. "imperialists" continued "their military interference in Laos," both the U.S. and Laos would suffer "bitter failure" and "bear the full responsibility for all disastrous consequences."

Chinese Statistical Errors. On Aug. 26, the Peking radio broadcast a statement from the Chinese Communist Party Central Committee saying that, owing to "lack of experience in assessing and calculating output of an unprecedented bumper harvest," grain production in 1958 was grossly overestimated. Goals for 1959 had been correspondingly reduced. The broadcast said that 1959 goals for grain production were cut from 525 million to 275 million tons after it was found that the 1958 total was 250 million instead of 375 million tons. Industrial statistics, the report said, also were inaccurate, but 1958 production had still been "a great leap forward."

Indian Border Violations. On Sept. 3, it was reported in New Delhi that Chinese Communist forces had violated India's northern border, and that Indian troops had been dispatched to two Himalayan mountain passes to guard roads from Tibet to Sikkim and India.

Charges Against India. On Sept. 4, Indian Prime Minister Nehru announced that the Chinese had accused India of "aggression" and demanded that India evacuate "one or two areas which they claim to be Chinese territory." Nehru said the general line defining the Tibetan-Indian frontier "has to be accepted," although he would be willing to make some minor revisions. He called the dispute "rather absurd" and said it was "not a question of two or three miles of territory, but (of) national prestige and self-respect."

Laos Appeals to UN. On Sept. 4, Laos appealed to the UN for "dispatch of an emergency force" to counter aggression by North Vietnamese-supported rebels. Laotian Foreign Minister Khampan Panya sent a note to UN Secretary General Dag Hammarskjold asserting that "foreign troops have been crossing the frontier (from North Viet Nam) and engaging in actions against garrison units... stationed along the northeastern frontier of Laos." It charged that "these attacks would not have taken place if the attackers had not come from outside the country and would have not continued" without "reinforcement and supplies...from outside." On Sept. 5, the U.S. warned the Soviet Union and Communist China it would help to counter any "new danger to peace" caused by "further augmentation of the invading force or continued military support thereof by Communists in North Viet Nam."

UN Action. On Sept. 8, the UN Security Council voted 10-1 (Russia opposed), to establish a subcommittee to examine the Laotian complaint.

Chou's Note to India. On Sept. 8, Chinese Communist Premier Chou En-lai sent a note to Indian Prime Minister Nehru offering "friendly negotiations," despite what Chou termed "trespassing and provocations" on the border. Chou said Chinese Communist forces had been forced to disarm Indian troops when they "started pressing forward steadily" during the revolt in Tibet. He added that China was "willing to live in friendship with (the small Himalayan states of) Sikkim and Bhutan...and has always respected the proper relations between them and India."

On Sept. 10, Nehru told the Indian Parliament he would have to study the note "because I do not know how the Chinese mind works."

On Sept. 11, Chou told the Standing Committee of the Chinese National People's Congress that China was willing to negotiate the border dispute, but Chinese Foreign Minister Chen Yi informed the Committee two days later that India had "used two-faced tactics" concerning the border dispute.

On Sept. 12, Nehru reported to Parliament that "this Chinese claim, which was vaguely set down in maps," was "much more serious" than he had previously thought. The Prime Minister said the Chinese position was "quite impossible for India ever to accept, whatever the consequences ...There is no question of mediation, conciliation or arbitration about that." He said India had "undertaken the defense of Sikkim and Bhutan, and anything that happens on their borders is the same as if it happened on the borders of India."

Dalai Lama's Accusations. On Sept. 9, the Dalai Lama, in a statement issued in New Delhi, accused Communist China of "offenses against the universal laws of international conduct" and urged "immediate intervention" by the UN. On Sept. 10, the State Department welcomed the "initiative of the Dalai Lama in bringing the plight of the Tibetan people directly to the attention of the United Nations." The Dalai Lama's statement charged the Chinese with seizing Tibetan property; abducting men, women and children for labor gangs; sterilizing Tibetan men and women with a view to total extermination of the Tibetan race; murdering "thousands of innocent people"; and attempting to "destroy our religion and culture."

Rebel Offer in Laos. On Sept. 10, the Laotian rebels said they were willing to "hold talks and consultations" with the Laotian government and listed a number of conditions. On the same day, Laotian army officials asserted that North Vietnamese troops had swept across the border into Laos.

Soviets Ask Conference. On Sept. 14, the Soviet Union asked that an international conference be "called without delay by the countries that attended the 1954 Geneva Conference" to discuss the hostilities in Laos. The Soviets said the dispute had to be settled "within the framework of the Geneva agreements, which provide the foundations for peace and security in Indo-China."

U.S. Rejects. On Sept. 15, the State Department called the Soviet request "unnecessary and disruptive" and said solution of the Laos problem was "not to be found in international conferences but in cessation of intervention and subversion" by "Laos Communists and their supporters."

Khrushchev Arrives. On Sept. 15, Soviet Premier Nikita Khrushchev arrived in Washington for a two-week visit in the U.S.

Lin Piao Promoted. On Sept. 17, Marshal Lin Piao, 51, close associate of Mao Tse-tung, became Red China's defense minister. Lin's reassignment, along with many others, indicated a major purge in the Chinese government and Communist party.

UN China Action. On Sept. 22, the UN General Assembly adopted, 44-29 with nine abstentions, a U.S. resolution to delay consideration of a UN seat for Communist China for another year. U.S. delegate Walter S. Robertson charged that Communist China "kept itself in power by bloody purges and by the liquidation of some 18 million mainland Chinese in nine years." He said it had promoted "six foreign or civil wars -- Korea, Tibet, Indo-China, the Philippines, Malaya, and Laos" -- and that China's admission to the UN would "make a mockery of our Charter and rob it of all...moral authority." Secretary of State Christian A. Herter had told the General Assembly Sept. 17 that the U.S. was "pledged under the (UN) Charter to resist aggression" and that it would "fulfill this pledge without equivocation." Herter urged the UN to "speak out in clear terms" on the "brutal Chinese Communist repression of the fundamental human rights of the Tibetans."

Khrushchev Leaves. On Sept. 27, Soviet Premier Khrushchev left the U.S. for Moscow. Two days later, he flew to Peking to attend Communist China's 10th anniversary celebrations.

Khrushchev Statements. On Sept. 30, Khrushchev told members of a banquet held in his honor in Peking: "We (Soviet-bloc nations)...must do everything possible to preclude war as a means for settling outstanding questions"; although Communist countries had "created a mighty potential," "this certainly does not mean that...we should test the stability of the capitalist system by force"; "even such a noble and progressive system as socialism cannot be imposed by force of arms against the will of the people," because they "would never understand and would never support (it)."

Laos Asks UN Protection. On Sept. 30, the Laotian Foreign Minister, Kamphan Panya, told the UN General Assembly that North Viet Nam, aided by the Chinese Communists, was attempting "the communization of Laos." He urged that the UN protect his country.

China's Anniversary Celebration. On Oct. 1, Communist China celebrated its 10th anniversary with an enormous parade in Peking, reviewed by Mao, Khrushchev, and other leaders of both countries.

Chinese Defense Minister Marshal Lin Piao told the huge crowd in Peking's Square of Heavenly Peace that China would "never invade anyone nor...allow anyone to invade us." But he reiterated China's determination to "liberate" Formosa "in one way or another" and warned all foreign powers not to intrude.

Chen's Article. On Oct. 4, Chinese Communist Foreign Minister Chen Yi wrote in the Peking *People's Daily* that during the past decade U.S. "imperialists have carried out a series of aggressive acts and war threats against new China, fully revealing that they are the enemy of the Chinese people." He added: "We firmly demand that American troops pull out of the Taiwan area. Taiwan is Chinese territory and the Chinese people are determined to liberate it."

Herter on Sino-Soviet Relations. On Oct. 6, Secretary of State Herter said at a news conference: "There is no question in our minds that the (Soviet Union's) demands for recognition as the leader of the Communist world places upon the Russians a degree of responsibility for the actions of other members of the bloc that is very real." Herter admitted that the Soviet Union followed "a rather different line" from that of Communist China. However, Soviet Premier Khrushchev had "talked quite eloquently" about peaceful coexistence during his trip to China. Chinese Communist Party Chairman Mao Tse-tung "never made any statement" on the subject "either on Mr. Khrushchev's arrival or...departure." The Secretary said it was "very difficult" to determine how "deep the differences" were between the two Communist powers, but from "outward appearances" they "are working very closely together."

Indian-Chinese Notes. On Oct. 3, Indian Prime Minister Nehru sent a note to Chinese Communist Premier Chou En-lai stating that "No discussions can be fruitful unless the posts on the Indian side of the traditional frontier now held by Chinese forces are first evacuated by them and further threats...cease." Chou, replying Oct. 7, said in a note to Nehru that the border dispute between the two countries was "merely an episode in our age-old friendship." On the following day, Nehru told newsmen that he was somewhat optimistic about the Chinese note and that India would not "start military operations...at this stage, when we are dealing with this matter on a political level." He added that another Chinese attack would be "fully resisted."

Panchen Lama in Peking. On Oct. 14, the Panchen Lama, who had been given the title of leader of the Preparatory Committee for an Autonomous Tibetan Region by the Chinese Communists, told the Chinese People's Congress that Tibet had embarked upon a period of "democratic reform" and "peaceful revolution" under Chinese leadership. He called Chinese Communist Party Chairman Mao Tse-tung a "lodestar and living Buddha" for Tibet and said he hoped Indian forces would withdraw "from places that they have invaded." In Tibet the Panchen Lama had traditionally ranked second to the Dalai Lama.

Marshall Dies. On Oct. 16, Gen. George C. Marshall, Chief of Staff of the Army in World War II and later U.S. Ambassador to China, Secretary of State and Secretary of Defense, died in Washington at the age of 78.

Red China as Threat to Peace. On Oct. 16, Assistant Secretary of State for Public Affairs Andrew H. Berding told the National Association of Broadcasters that since the "improvement in the international atmosphere" brought about by the talks between President Eisenhower and Soviet Premier Khrushchev, Red China stood as the world's chief threat to peace. Berding lauded Khrushchev for advising the Chinese Communists not to spread "socialism by force of arms," and he added: "We believe that if the Soviet Union is sincere in wanting to safeguard the peace, it has the leverage...to insure a measure of responsibility on the part of the Chinese Communists."

Russia Supports China. On Oct. 21, it was reported that Soviet Premier Khrushchev had sent a letter to President Eisenhower on Oct. 13 denying that the Soviet Union was responsible for Communist China's actions. Khrushchev's letter added that Russia supported Peking's claims on Formosa and that outside nations should not interfere.

UN Resolution on Tibet. On Oct. 21, the UN General Assembly voted 45-9 with 26 abstentions to approve a resolution expressing "grave concern" over China's repression of Tibet. The resolution neither provided for any UN action nor formally condemned Communist China.

Indian-Chinese Clash. On Oct. 23, India's External Affairs Ministry reported that Chinese Communists had attacked an Indian border patrol and killed at least 17 men in Ladakh, a remote section of Kashmir. A Chinese note to the Indian government said the Indian troops had fired on Chinese soldiers in an area "within China's administrative jurisdiction." On Oct. 24, Indian Prime Minister Nehru said the area was "part of India" and Indians would "defend our territory and our prestige and our honor." He added that he did not think "there will be war with China on this issue." On Oct. 26, the Chinese Communists issued a statement claiming more than 6,000 square miles of territory in Ladakh. The statement said the area had "always been under China's administrative jurisdiction." On Nov. 1, Prime Minister Nehru told an audience in New Delhi that India was making "adequate military preparations."

Khrushchev on Sino-Soviet Relations. On Oct. 31, Soviet Premier Nikita Khrushchev, in a major foreign policy speech to the Supreme Soviet in Moscow, asserted that U.S. leaders had "launched...a psychological attack against the Soviet Union...seeking to distort the nature of the relations between the U.S.S.R. and China and to cast doubt on the sovereignty of (Communist China)," which was a "great sovereign state" following "an independent home and foreign policy" not directed by the Soviet Union. The Soviet Premier added that he "would be happy if there were no more incidents on the Sino-Indian frontier, if the... disputes were settled by...friendly negotiations."

Nehru Warns China. On Nov. 5, Indian Prime Minister Nehru said the Indian-Chinese border dispute did not involve the risk of a "real war" but that India was ready to take "strong action" if necessary. He said he could not "conceive of any power on earth that" would "make me surrender." In a speech on Nov. 10, Nehru said India "cannot allow China to keep a foot on our chest."

UN Report on Laos. On Nov. 6, the UN Security Council subcommittee on Laos, named Sept. 8, reported indications that the Laotian rebels had received "equipment, arms, ammunition, supplies and the help of political cadres" from North Viet Nam.

Chou's Proposals to India. On Nov. 7, Chinese Communist Premier Chou En-lai proposed in a letter to Indian Prime Minister Nehru that "the armed forces of China and India each withdraw 20 kilometers (12.5 miles)...from the so-called McMahon Line in the east (the Tibet-India border), and from the line up to which each side exercises actual control in the west (the Ladakh area of Kashmir)." Both countries would "refrain from again sending their armed personnel to...the zones from which they have (been) evacuated" but would "maintain civil administration...and unarmed police" there. Chou also proposed meeting Nehru to discuss the dispute.

Herter on Border Dispute. On Nov. 12, Secretary of State Herter told a news conference that the U.S. could not "take sides" in the India-China border dispute because it lacked "first-hand knowledge, particularly... (about) the northwestern area, with respect to the definitive border that could rightly be claimed by either side." Herter later apologized to the Indian Chargé d'Affaires for "any possible misconceptions" about his position. He said his comments "were not meant to imply any condonement by the (U.S.) Government of the use of force by the Chinese Communists." He added that the U.S. "strongly sympathizes with India's attempts to resolve the present issues with Communist China peacefully."

Nehru Rejects Chou's Proposals. On Nov. 16, Indian Prime Minister Nehru rejected Chinese Communist Premier Chou En-lai's request for a meeting between the two leaders on the border dispute. Nehru had told the Indian Parliament two days earlier that he had also rejected Chou's proposal for a joint withdrawal of forces from the disputed area because it was "impracticable."

Indian Proposal. On Nov. 20, Indian Prime Minister Nehru read to the Indian Parliament a note he had sent to Communist China proposing that both countries withdraw all their forces from the disputed border areas prior to negotiations. He said his offer was "an interim measure to avoid border clashes" and reiterated his view that the disputed area "has been for long years part of India." Two days later, Nehru suggested to the *Christian Science Monitor* that the conflict had been caused by a Stalinist influence in Chinese foreign policy and by Communist China's inability to understand the world outside its borders.

On Nov. 27, Nehru said in Parliament that while he doubted there was "any country that cares more for peace than the Soviet Union, I doubt that there is any country that cares less for peace than (Communist) China." He warned that if the Indian-Chinese dispute turned to war "we shall become a nation in arms" in a "struggle for life and death" that would "shake Asia and shake the world."

Travel Ban Upheld. On Dec. 7, the U.S. Supreme Court refused to review three lower court decisions sustaining a State Department ban on travel to Communist China. Appeals had been filed by Rep. Charles O. Porter (D Ore.), reporter William Worthy Jr. of the Baltimore *Afro-American*, and Waldo Frank, lecturer and author. The State Department had refused to validate the passports of Porter and Frank for travel in China and had denied Worthy a new passport unless he agreed to respect the ban. In each case the applicants appealed on the ground that the Secretary of State had no authority to restrict the travel of a citizen.

Rockefeller Report on Foreign Policy. On Dec. 7, a broad survey of U.S. foreign policy needs for the future was made public by the Rockefeller Brothers Fund. The report was prepared by a 14-man panel headed by two former assistant secretaries of state, Adolph A. Berle Jr. and Dean Rusk, president of the Rockefeller Foundation.

The members of the panel asserted that no responsible Communist state should be barred from membership in the international community of nations. While not proposing U.S. recognition or UN membership for Communist China, they called for reassessment of China's position in the modern world and cautioned against permitting "emotion or differences of ideology" to stand in the way of improved relations with the Chinese people. However, the report pointed out that "Communist China is in a posture which, in the past historical experience, has almost invariably led to aggression" and it "looks upon the United States as its supreme enemy."

A rift in the alliance between the Soviet Union and Communist China was not to be expected in the near future, the report observed, but the coming decade might see a strain in the relations between the two powers. The panel warned against a policy that might drive China closer to

Russia but said that actions specifically designed to split the two powers probably would fail.

Eisenhower in India. On Dec. 9, President Eisenhower arrived in New Delhi for a four-day state visit.

Nehru Rejects Chinese Offer. On Dec. 21, Indian Prime Minister Nehru told the Indian Parliament he had rejected a new proposal from Chinese Communist Premier Chou En-lai that the two leaders meet to seek a basis for settlement of their border dispute. Nehru said he turned down the offer, made Dec. 17, because of "complete disagreement about the facts" involved. He noted that the Chinese proposal rejected provisions for total military evacuation of the areas concerned and was "merely a reiteration of (Chinese) claims to extensive areas...which, by history, by custom or by agreement have long been integral parts of India." The Indian Prime Minister added that his country would "negotiate to the bitter end" because the "only alternative...is war."

1960

Senate Report Calls Red China a Giant on the March -- Alleged Shortcomings of U.S. Economic Aid Program in Viet Nam -- Bishop Walsh Imprisoned in China -- Chou En-lai Visits India -- South Korean President Rhee Resigns -- Growing Sino-Soviet Split -- Eisenhower in Formosa -- Communists on Coexistence and War -- U.S. Party Platforms on China Questions -- Cuba Recognizes Red China -- Kennedy-Nixon Debates on Quemoy and Matsu -- Kennedy Elected -- Manifesto Unites 81 Communist Parties in Fight Against Capitalism.

Kennedy Announces. On Jan. 2, Sen. John F. Kennedy (D Mass.) announced his candidacy for the 1960 Democratic Presidential nomination.

Report on China. On Jan. 3, Sen. Henry M. Jackson (D Wash.), chairman of a Senate Government Operations subcommittee, issued a report, "National Policy Machinery in Communist China," noting that "the Chinese Communist Party has attained a degree of unity and stability at its higher levels which is unequalled by other major Communist parties." The report said the Chinese Communist leaders had lifted the country "from a prostrate colossus into a giant on the march, in 10 short years."

Brucker on Formosa Defense. On Jan. 10, Secretary of the Army Wilber M. Brucker, visiting U.S. bases on Formosa, said the defense agreement between the U.S. and Nationalist China "included not just Formosa but any part of the Republic of China where aggression would occur by the Communist Chinese."

China's Production. On Jan. 22, the Chinese Communist *Hsinhua* (New China) news agency reported that the Chinese economy in 1959 surpassed the production goals scheduled under the second five-year plan.

Burma-China Agreement. On Jan. 28, Burmese Premier Ne Win and Chinese Communist Premier Chou En-lai signed a border agreement, a 10-year nonaggression pact, and a treaty of friendship.

Newsman Jailed. On Feb. 6, Bill Yim, a *United Press International* newsman accused of "spy activities" in Red China, was reported to have been sentenced to one year in jail. Yim had been arrested while visiting Canton in 1959.

Nehru and Chou. On Feb. 15, a letter from Indian Prime Minister Nehru to Chinese Communist Premier Chou En-lai, inviting the latter to India for talks on the Indian-Chinese border dispute, was made public. Nehru said in the letter that he did not "for the moment...see any common ground between our respective viewpoints." And he told Parliament on Feb. 22 that "certain vested interests (were) opposed to any settlement between China and India" and the dispute could last for "years or generations." On Feb. 26, Chou nevertheless accepted Nehru's invitation. He said that "the friendship between the Chinese and Indian peoples is eternal and...(it was) possible to settle the boundary issue...in a...peaceful manner."

Viet Nam Aid. On Feb. 26, the Senate Foreign Relations Subcommittee on State Department Organization and Public Affairs, headed by Sen. Mike Mansfield (D Mont.), issued a report citing serious shortcomings in the administration of U.S. economic aid to Viet Nam. The report concluded an inquiry begun July 30, 1959, following publication of a series of articles in Scripps-Howard newspapers alleging waste and corruption in the Viet Nam program.

Viet Nam, the report said, had made "great progress under President Ngo Dinh Diem" and the U.S. military aid program had been effective. But nonmilitary aid, which was started in 1955 on a "crash" basis, was "still administered preponderantly as a holding action" without benefit of long-range planning. Aid officials were unable to "project even in the most general terms an ultimate termination date of the program or, at the least, to anticipate when a substantial and progressive scaling down of grant aid may take place." Initiative for specific aid projects, the Subcommittee concluded, should be left to the Vietnamese.

Another target of criticism was the American community of 2,400 U.S. officials and dependents, now "the most conspicuous foreign group" in Saigon. Among its prerequisites, the report said, were a Navy commissary that "does well over $1.5 million business" each year, and housing which in many instances "would appear far above modest and comfortable in the United States." Altogether, the report said, the "total recompense" of U.S. personnel in Viet Nam "far exceeds the levels for Government employees in this country with comparable functions." The report urged the full Foreign Relations Committee to undertake a study of pay and fringe benefits for Americans in overseas service. It also asked the Secretary of State to report by September on steps taken to implement the Subcommittee's recommendations.

China and Disarmament. On March 16, President Eisenhower told a news conference: "If disarmament comes into the realm of practical negotiation and enforcement, you will...unquestionably have to take into account the armaments of Red China." But he added,..."there has to be a very great deal of progress, before we are into the stage of worrying too much about Red China."

Bishop Imprisoned. On March 18, a Communist court in Shanghai sentenced an American Roman Catholic missionary, Bishop James Edward Walsh, 69, to 20 years imprisonment. Walsh, who had been under house arrest since October 1958, was charged with espionage and counter-revolutionary activities. On March 22, the U.S. called the imprisonment of Bishop Walsh "inexcusable" and said it was "one more step in the...persecution of religion in Communist China."

Power in Far East. On March 25, John M. Steeves, Acting Assistant Secretary for Far Eastern Affairs, told the Senate Foreign Relations Committee that a "grave imbalance of power" existed in the Far East and it was "our countervailing presence which redresses this imbalance." He said Communist China could be expected to maintain pressures and tensions in the area, and any signs of weakness on the part of the U.S. would have "grievous effects."

Sino-Soviet Trade. On March 29, the Soviet Union and Communist China signed an agreement to increase their 1960 trade by a 10-percent increase over 1959.

Indian-Chinese Talks. On April 25, Indian Prime Minister Nehru and Chinese Communist Premier Chou En-lai issued a joint statement after a week of talks in New Delhi on the border dispute between their two countries. Nehru and Chou admitted that the talks "did not result in resolving differences that had arisen," but they agreed "to avoid friction and clashes in border areas" while their respective diplomats discussed the differences during the coming summer.

Rhee Resigns. On April 26, South Korean President Syngman Rhee, 85, resigned at the climax of a government crisis marked by extensive student rioting. The crisis was precipitated by charges that the March 15 election won by Rhee and his hand-picked vice presidential candidate, Lee Ki-poong, had been rigged. The State Department said, April 19, that it had notified the South Korean government of "growing and profound" U.S. concern over unrest in that country and had urged restoration of public confidence by actions aimed to protect democratic rights and prevent political discrimination. Shortly before resigning, Rhee ordered new elections. South Korea's foreign minister, Huh Chung, was named Acting President on April 27. He pledged reforms, including elimination of "waste" of aid. The suicides of Lee Ki-poong, his wife and two sons were announced April 28.

Eisenhower's Reaction. On April 27, President Eisenhower told a news conference that the U.S. in no way had interfered in the South Korean crisis. The President said Rhee was a "tremendous patriot" who had "made some mistakes as he grew older."

China-Nepal Agreement. On April 29, Chinese Communist Premier Chou En-lai left Nepal after signing a treaty with Nepalese Premier B.P. Koirala. A joint statement issued after Chou's departure announced ratification of the treaty, which settled Nepalese-Tibetan border disputes. Chou had told a joint session of the Nepalese Parliament on April 28 in Katmandu that the agreement was a step toward "peaceful coexistence between countries of different social systems."

U-2 Incident and Paris Summit. On May 5, the Soviet Union announced that on May 1 a U.S. high-altitude reconnaissance U-2 aircraft had been shot down near Sverdlovsk in the heart of the U.S.S.R. The incident, disclosed by Soviet Premier Nikita S. Khrushchev, produced almost hourly reverberations during the ensuing week. The most sensational was the belated but unequivocal acknowledgment by the U.S. of efforts to penetrate Soviet secrecy by such techniques as overflights.

Khrushchev told the Supreme Soviet May 5 that the flight was an "aggressive provocation aimed at wrecking the summit conference" scheduled to open in Paris on May 16. The Big Four conference did, in fact, collapse almost as it opened, but Khrushchev was the wrecker. He refused to proceed to a discussion of outstanding issues unless President Eisenhower bow to an ultimatum that he apologize for the U-2 flight and agree to punish "those who are directly guilty." The President refused, and two days later both men left Paris and headed for home. Meanwhile, Khrushchev had canceled Eisenhower's scheduled state visit to Russia, which was to begin June 10.

"Liberal Project" Study. On May 23, the "Liberal Project," a group of House Members and scientists, scholars, and political scientists, formed April 15 to expound a liberal point of view, released its first study. "A Re-examination of U.S. Foreign Policy," written by James P. Warburg. On Far Eastern foreign policy, the study said: "We cannot see how our Government can hope to ease tensions, to arrive at fair settlements of disputes or, above all, to achieve disarmament without establishing direct channels of communication with Peking." It recommended that the U.S. withdraw its opposition to Communist China's admission to the UN, "provided that the Peking regime will reaffirm the renunciation of force which it signed at the Bandung Conference of 1955,...undertake the obligations imposed by the Charter of the United Nations, and agree to cooperate in working toward universal total disarmament adequately enforced under world law."

The study also said: The U.S. should recognize Communist China's "unquestionably valid" claim to the offshore islands in return for free evacuation of Chinese Nationalist troops and citizens; the U.S. has "more than fulfilled its obligations to the Nationalist regime" and should ask political amnesty for or offer asylum to Nationalist leaders who wish it; and the U.S. should seek an agreement with Russia and Communist China whereby all three would withdraw from Korea and Viet Nam.

Reaction. On May 24, the Committee of One Million Against the Admission of Communist China to the United Nations said the Liberal Project's objectives, particularly the recognition of Communist China, were "contemptible." The Committee voiced confidence that "the other 427 Members of the House...have learned full well the bitter lessons of appeasement and will continue to maintain and expand the only foreign policy possible to counter Communist aggression -- strength and adherence to the principles of freedom and the preservation of our national security and honor."

Sino-Soviet Split. On May 26 a *New York Times* article by Harrison Salisbury reported a growing split between Communist China and the Soviet Union. Salisbury wrote:

"A violent ideological dispute between the Soviet Union and Communist China was raging on the eve of the (Paris) summit meeting and may now have been resolved in favor of Peking. The conclusion has been reached by some specialists in Soviet affairs after examining texts of an unusual exchange of ideological arguments between Moscow and Peking. The exchange occurred on the 90th anniversary of Lenin's birth, April 22, nine days before the U-2 incident."

"The text of the Chinese arguments," the *Times* article said, "has been published in the April 26 issue of the English-language *Peking Review....* The Soviet presentation was contained in an address at the Lenin Stadium in Moscow by Otto V. Kuusinen, member of the Communist Party's Presidium."

Salisbury thought it "probable that the controversy ...played a major role in the evolution of Premier Khrushchev's policy on the eve of the Paris meeting." He said: "The documents make clear that as late as April 22 the Soviet and Chinese positions were far apart. The Chinese were insisting that little or nothing might be expected from negotiations with the "Imperialist West.""

The Chinese documents were couched in unusually frank terms. "They did not criticize Mr. Khrushchev by name. But in veiled terms he was referred to as a 'revisionist' and 'distorter' of Lenin's teachings. There were slurs against his alleged lack of knowledge of the theory of Marxism-Leninism. The Moscow statement was briefer. It called the Chinese, by implication, 'dogmatists' and restated the known viewpoint of Mr. Khrushchev on the world situation."

Salisbury continued: "The dispute between the Russians and Chinese...arose immediately after Mr. Khrushchev's visit to the United States (in 1959). Mr. Khrushchev contended it was possible to deal with the United States and that President Eisenhower was, essentially, a man of peace. The documents disclosed that the dispute increased rather than diminished in intensity as the summit neared. The Chinese attacked efforts to 'whitewash' or 'prettify' the actions of the United States. They contended that any effort to establish real peace between the 'imperialist and Communist worlds was illusory. The statement bristled with violent revolutionary quotations, taken from Marx, Engels, and Lenin.

"The Soviet presentation supported Mr. Khrushchev's contention that a 'new epoch' had arisen in which it was possible to establish peace between the two systems. It held that the new balance of force in the world had made the old Marxist concept of 'aggressive imperialism' outmoded."

Salisbury concluded that the Chinese had "challenged one of the most basic of Mr. Khrushchev's assumptions -- that there would be no victors in a nuclear war." He reported the Chinese as saying: "The result will certainly not be the annihilation of mankind....On the debris of a dead imperialism the victorious people would create very swiftly a civilization thousands of times higher than the capitalist system and a truly beautiful future for themselves."

Chinese Charge Overflights. On May 27, Communist China charged that American U-2 jets had made at least three flights over the Chinese mainland.

Anti-Peking Campaign in U.S. On June 16, the Committee of One Million Against the Admission of Communist China to the United Nations called on the public to support its campaign to have planks included in the Democratic and Republican platforms expressing opposition to any concessions to the Peking government. The Committee asked citizens to write to their Senators and Representatives, urging support of an anti-Communist China plank drafted by the Committee. The president of the Committee, former Gov. Charles Edison of New Jersey, said the plank had already been endorsed by 212 Members of Congress -- 100 Republicans and 112 Democrats.

Communist Shelling. On June 17, while President Eisenhower was enroute by sea from Manila to Formosa on the second leg of a Far East trip, Chinese Communist batteries fired a record 86,000 artillery shells at Nationalist-held Quemoy Island in what Peking Radio called a "gesture of contempt and scorn" for the President and the United States.

Formosa Visit. On June 18, President Eisenhower arrived in Formosa and told a rally: "You may be assured that our continuing search for peaceful solutions to outstanding international problems does not reflect the slightest lessening of our determination to stand with you, and with all our free neighbors of the Pacific, against any aggression. The United States does not recognize the claim of the warlike and tyrannical Communist regime in Peking to speak for all the Chinese people. In the United Nations we support the Republic of China, a founding member, as the only rightful representative of China in that organization."

Charges of Genocide in Tibet. On June 19, the International Commission of Jurists, a nongovernmental organization, called Communist China guilty of genocide in its suppression of the Tibetan revolt in 1959. A Commission investigation, headed by Purshottam Trikamadas of the Indian Supreme Court, reported that "widespread killings ...unrelated to military action in suppression of the uprising" had occurred. It charged that the Chinese Communists had "killed religious figures" and "forcibly transferred large numbers of Tibetan children to a Chinese materialist environment in order to prevent them from having a religious upbringing."

Communists on Coexistence and War. On June 22, leaders of 12 Communist nations, including Red China, North Viet Nam and North Korea, met in Bucharest, Rumania, and reaffirmed support of Soviet ideas on peaceful coexistence. However, there were indications that the Chinese Communists were reluctant to support a no-war policy. Soviet Premier Khrushchev had told the Rumanian Communist Party Congress a day earlier that "under present conditions, war is not inevitable," and that "he who does not understand this does not believe in the...great attractive force of socialism, which has manifestly demonstrated its superiority over capitalism." Khrushchev explained: "We cannot...always repeat that imperialist wars are inevitable as long as socialism has not triumphed all over the world." Such opinions are "based on what the great Lenin said in completely different historical conditions" and "in our day only madmen and maniacs" advocate a new war. The Soviet Premier had said at an earlier press conference that "Coexistence is the only...path to take; any other way means death and destruction for all of us."

Chinese on Peace. On June 29, the Peking *People's Daily* said: "Only when the imperialist...and capitalist systems...are really abolished can there really be lasting world peace."

Eisenhower on Sino-Soviet Split. On July 6, President Eisenhower discussed the Sino-Soviet split at a news conference: "As these people have gotten more productive, they have a much bigger collection of productive mechanisms. In other words, they have accumulated wealth, and they've also got a great arsenal of powerful weapons; I

think...there comes a time when their views as to the methods they will use to dominate the world...might be changed. And I think there is a change going on there that probably the Red Chinese have not yet decided upon. As of this moment, they seem to be much more belligerent and much more...quarrelsome than are their associates."

Kennedy Nominated. On July 13, the Democratic National Convention in Los Angeles nominated Sen. John Fitzgerald Kennedy, 43, of Massachusetts for President. The following day, Kennedy picked Sen. Lyndon B. Johnson 51, as his running-mate.

The Democratic platform, in its section on China, said: "We deeply regret that the policies and actions of the government of Communist China have interrupted the generations of friendship between the Chinese and American peoples. We reaffirm our pledge of determined opposition to the present admission of Communist China (to the UN) .... Although normal diplomatic relations between our governments are impossible under present conditions, we shall welcome any evidence that the Chinese Communist government is genuinely prepared to create a new relationship based on respect for international obligations, including the release of American prisoners."

Chinese-Cuban Trade. On July 23, Communist China and Cuba entered into a trade agreement under which China agreed to buy 500,000 tons of Cuban sugar each year to be paid for in part by shipments of goods.

Nixon Nominated. On July 27, the Republican National Convention in Chicago nominated Vice President Richard Milhous Nixon, 47, for President. The following day, Nixon picked U.S. Ambassador to the UN Henry Cabot Lodge, 58, as his running-mate.

The Republican platform, in its section on China, said: "Recognition of Communist China and its admission to the United Nations have been firmly opposed by the Republican Administration. We will continue in this opposition."

Chou's "Peace Pact" Offer. On Aug. 1, Chinese Communist Premier Chou En-lai, attending a reception at the Swiss Embassy in Peking, proposed a "peace pact" between China, the U.S., and other Pacific powers to establish a "non-nuclear zone in Asia and the Western Pacific." Chou added that China had not "given up its policy of seeking peaceful relations with countries with different social systems." On the same day, State Department spokesman Lincoln White said Chou's proposal was a "propaganda gesture" and added that the offer had never been discussed at the Chinese-American meetings in Warsaw.

Chou on Capitalism. On Aug. 5, the *Associated Press* reported that a group of Soviet labor leaders had threatened to walk out of a meeting in Peking after Premier Chou told them that "the capitalistic world will not survive another great war" and that "the destruction the Western powers can cause the Communist world is not unrepairable."

Laotian Coup. On Aug. 15, an army rebellion overthrew the government of Premier Tiao Samsonith and a cabinet dedicated to neutralism was formed under Prince Souvanna Phouma. The leader of the military rebellion, Capt. Kong Le, said the new government would "incline neither toward the free world nor the Communist world," but would "lead our country to the path of neutrality."

Cuba-Red China Ties. On Sept. 2, Cuban Premier Fidel Castro announced in Havana that Cuba would become the first Latin American country to recognize Communist China. He said his country would break diplomatic relations with Nationalist China. On Sept. 5, Cuban troops seized a Nationalist Chinese bank in Havana. On Sept. 7, President Eisenhower called Cuba's recognition of Communist China "a very grave error."

Khrushchev at UN. On Oct. 1, Soviet Premier Nikita Khrushchev, attending the 15th UN General Assembly session in New York, said: "There cannot...be any disarmament without (Communist) China; there cannot be any normal (UN) work...without China." At a press conference from the balcony of the Soviet UN mission headquarters, Khrushchev denied there was an ideological split between him and Chinese Communist Party Chairman Mao Tsetung.

Kennedy-Nixon Debate. On Oct. 7, Sen. John F. Kennedy and Vice President Richard M. Nixon held their second radio and television debate of the Presidential campaign. The nominees disagreed about defense of Quemoy and Matsu.

Sen. Kennedy said: "These islands are a few miles, five or six miles off the coast of Red China within a general harbor area, and more than 100 miles from Formosa. We have never said flatly that we will defend Quemoy and Matsu if it is attacked.... I think it is unwise to take the chance of being dragged into a war which may lead to a world war over two islands which are not strategically defensible, which are not...essential to the defense of Formosa."

Vice President Nixon answered: "I think as far as Quemoy and Matsu are concerned that the question is not these two little pieces of real estate. They are unimportant.... It is the principle involved. These two islands are in the area of freedom.... We should not force our Nationalist allies to get off them and give them to the Communists. If we do that, we start a chain reaction, because the Communists aren't after Quemoy and Matsu. They are after Formosa."

UN Vote on Red China. On Oct. 8, the UN General Assembly voted 42-34 (22 abstentions) in favor of a U.S.-backed resolution to take no action at the current session on admission of Communist China. The resolution carried by the smallest margin in the 10 years the Assembly had debated the issue.

Sen. Wayne Morse (D Ore.), a member of the U.S. delegation, told newsmen the next day that the vote showed that Communist China's admission was "inevitable." Morse said that in 1961 the U.S. must "be willing to have the UN negotiate conditions" for such admission. Chairman J. W. Fulbright (D Ark.) of the Senate Foreign Relations Committee told an Oct. 10 news conference he agreed that admission of Communist China was inevitable.

More Debate. On Oct. 13, one of the chief questions at issue in the third Nixon-Kennedy debate was again Quemoy and Matsu. Nixon said that if a Chinese Communist attack on the offshore islands was "a prelude to an attack on Formosa, which would be the indication today,... there isn't any question but that the United States would then again, as in the case of Berlin, honor our treaty obligations and stand by our ally of Formosa." Nixon asserted that surrender of the islands would not lead to peace. On the contrary: "It is something that would lead, in my opin-

ion, to war.... Now what do the Chinese Communists want? They don't want just Quemoy and Matsu. They don't want just Formosa. They want the world. And the question is if you surrender or indicate in advance that you are not going to defend any part of the free world, and you figure that is going to satisfy them, it doesn't satisfy them. It only whets their appetite. And then the question comes -- when do you stop them?"

Sen. Kennedy said in reply: "Mr. Nixon suggests that the United States should go to war if these two islands are attacked. I suggest that if Formosa is attacked, or the Pescadores, or if there is any military action in any area which indicates an attack on Formosa and the Pescadores, then, of course, the United States is at war to defend its (security) treaty (with Nationalist China).... What Mr. Nixon wants to do is commit us, as I understand him,...to the defense of these islands, merely to the defense of these islands as free territory, not as part of the defense of Formosa."

Election. On Nov. 8, Democratic Presidential nominee John F. Kennedy defeated Vice President Richard M. Nixon, the Republican nominee, in the closest Presidential election of the 20th Century. The Democrats maintained their heavy majorities in the Congress and among the nation's Governors.

Attempted Viet Nam Coup. On Nov. 10, a revolt by South Vietnamese paratroopers was quickly suppressed by forces loyal to President Ngo Dinh Diem. The South Vietnamese Defense Ministry had charged on Nov. 8 that North Vietnamese troops were entering the country through Laos "to attack South Viet Nam directly."

Bowles on China. On Nov. 11, Rep. Chester Bowles (D Conn.), a foreign policy adviser to President-elect Kennedy, appeared on a British television program and advocated a "two-China" policy based on "an independent Formosa and an independent (Communist) China." The statement was strongly criticized by Sen. Norris Cotton (R N.H.), and on Nov. 13 Bowles said he thought that "recognition of Red China is impossible."

Communist Manifesto. On Dec. 6, representatives of 81 Communist parties, meeting in Moscow, issued a manifesto proclaiming unity in the fight against capitalism. It was reported that Soviet Premier Khrushchev and Communist Chinese President Liu Shao-chi had debated ideological differences for at least 10 days before a compromise was reached. Because the manifesto's wording was more aggressive than that of previous Soviet statements, it was thought the Russians had made some concessions to Chinese demands. China's views were believed to have had the support of representatives of Communist movements in Latin America, Albania, and some sections of Asia. The Soviet position was said to have been supported by the majority of the participants, most of them from the East European nations.

After declaring that "U.S. imperialism is the main force of aggression and war..." the manifesto said: "The aggressive nature of imperialism has not changed. But real forces have appeared that are capable of foiling its plans of aggression. War is not fatally inevitable. Had the imperialists been able to do what they wanted, they would have already plunged mankind into the abyss of the calamities and horrors of a new world war. But the time is past when the imperialists could decide at will whether there should or should not be war...."

"Peaceful coexistence with countries of different systems or destructive war -- this is the alternative today. There is no other choice. Communists emphatically reject the U.S. doctrine of cold war and brinkmanship, for it is a policy leading to thermonuclear catastrophe....

"Communists have always recognized the progressive, revolutionary significance of national-liberation wars; they are the most active champions of national independence.... The peoples of the colonial countries win their independence both through armed struggle and through non-military methods.... The colonial powers never bestow freedom on the colonial peoples and never leave of their own free will the countries they are exploiting....

"The people's revolution in China dealt a crushing blow at the positions of imperialism in Asia and contributed in great measure to the balance of the world forces changing in favor of socialism. By giving a further powerful impetus to the national-liberation movement, it exerted tremendous influence on the peoples, especially those of Asia, Africa, and Latin America.... The Communist and workers parties unanimously declare that the Communist Party of the Soviet Union has been, and remains, the universally recognized vanguard of the world Communist movement."

Laos. On Dec. 9, the neutralist government of Laos under Prince Souvanna Phouma collapsed under pressure from U.S.-supplied rightist forces attacking Vientiane, the Laotian capital.

Rusk Named. On Dec. 12, President-elect Kennedy announced that Dean Rusk, president of the Rockefeller Foundation, would be his Secretary of State. The next day, Kennedy announced he would nominate Robert S. McNamara as Secretary of Defense.

Chinese Agriculture. On Dec. 29, the Peking radio said that over one-half of Communist China's farmland had been crippled during 1960 by the worst "natural calamities" in a century. The report said millions of acres had been "seriously affected" by droughts, plants diseases, and typhoons. The U.S. Department of Agriculture called the reports exaggerated.

Laotian Appeal. On Dec. 30, the new rightist government in Laos appealed to the UN for assistance against an invasion from North Viet Nam or Communist China. The government asserted that at least seven battalions of North Vietnamese troops had crossed the border and were attacking outposts in northern Laos.

On Dec. 31, the State Department warned that the U.S. "would take the most serious view of any intervention in Laos by the Chinese Communists or Viet Minh armed forces or others in support of the Communist Pathet Lao, who are in rebellion against the royal Laotian government." A State Department press officer said later that the invaders were "non-Laotian forces, presumably coming from North Viet Nam." Sen. Mike Mansfield (D Mont.) had said, Dec. 28, that allocation of "approximately $300 million" in U.S. aid to Laos over an eight-year period was a "gross overcommitment," resulting in nothing "but chaos, discontent, armies on the loose and a large U.S. mission of hundreds of officials in Vientiane."

1961

Threat to Independence of Laos -- Kennedy Inaugurated -- Kennedy Warns on Chinese and Russian Ambitions for World Domination -- Rusk Reaffirms U.S. Commitments to Nationalist China -- Kennedy on Laotian Neutrality -- Johnson's Trip to Asia -- Geneva Conference on Laos Opens -- Restatements of U.S. Opposition to Admitting Red China to UN -- Chinese Praise for Soviet Resumption of Nuclear Testing -- Kennedy on Southeast Asia in UN Address -- United States and South Viet Nam -- Peking-Moscow Squabble Over Stalinism -- UN General Assembly Debate on Chinese Representation.

Laos. On Jan. 1, the Laotian government asserted that Communist-supported forces fighting in northern Laos were supplied by the Soviet Union and Communist China. The *New York Times* reported Jan. 5 that North Viet Nam's participation in the Laotian civil war had been minimal, but that Russian planes were landing supplies and carrying paratroopers for the rebels.

On Jan. 2, the Defense Department announced that President Eisenhower had given orders to "increase the readiness" of American forces in the area of Laos. On Jan. 7, the State Department issued a White Paper urging free nations "to support and maintain the independence of Laos through whatever measures seem most promising." It warned that "if Laos should be seized by the Communists, the effects could be far-reaching and the implication for other small and vulnerable states all too evident."

Burma Treaty with Red China. On Jan. 4, Burmese and Chinese Communist Premiers U Nu and Chou En-Lai, meeting in Rangoon, completed action on a border agreement between the two countries. The two also negotiated an agreement for an $85 million six-year loan for a Chinese technical assistance program.

U.S. Nominees Approved. On Jan. 18, the Senate Foreign Relations Committee approved the nominations of Dean Rusk as Secretary of State and Adlai E. Stevenson as U.S. Ambassador to the UN. On Jan. 19, the Committee approved Chester Bowles as Under Secretary of State.

All three were questioned closely on their attitude toward Communist China. Rusk said Jan. 12 he saw "no promise at the present time that normal relations could be established with the regime in Peiping," primarily because the Chinese Communists set as a prerequisite "the abandonment of the government and people of Formosa." On Jan. 18, Stevenson testified that the U.S. "would have to face the possibility" of Communist China's admission to the UN. He said he had never advocated such a step but it might be "impossible to prevent." Bowles testified Jan. 19 that U.S. recognition of Communist China was "completely unnegotiable" for "the time being" in the light of that government's demands. He said, "We are going to defend Formosa -- whatever the risk, whatever the costs."

Kennedy Inaugurated. On Jan. 20, John Fitzgerald Kennedy, 43, was sworn in as 35th President of the United States.

Farm Failures in China. On Jan. 20, the Chinese Communist Party Central Committee announced that industrial production would be curtailed and new efforts made to expand lagging farm production. The announcement said: "The temporary difficulties in supplying the market caused by the poor harvest and shortage of raw materials for light industry are important problems.... Inasmuch as tremendous (industrial) development has been achieved over the past three years,...the scope of capital construction should be appropriately reduced." Prompt steps would be taken "to help the development of light industry. . . and suburban agriculture."

The Committee blamed the agricultural failures on "bad elements" in the Communist party -- "landlords, bourgeois, and other elements seduced by reactionaries," who had "made use of the difficult conditions created by natural disasters and certain defects." An immediate purge was ordered "throughout the country...area by area" to "clear the party of elements that infiltrated into the party and government departments."

Chinese Declaration. On Jan. 21, the Chinese Communist Party Central Committee published a declaration of policy condemning the U.S. as the "main enemy of the peoples of the whole world." But the declaration added that a "new world war can be prevented by the joint efforts of the powerful forces of our era -- the Socialist camp, the...working class, the national liberation movement." It noted that "revolution is the affair of peoples in various countries" and should not be exported. At the same time, Communists "oppose the imperialist export of counter-revolution" and "imperialist interference in the internal affairs of people. . . who have risen in revolution."

Food for Communist China. On Jan. 25, President Kennedy told a news conference that the U.S. might consider sending food to Communist China if a request should be made. He said: "...the Chinese Communists are exporting food at the present time, some of it to Africa, some. . . to Cuba, and, therefore, that is a factor in their needs for food abroad. Secondly, we have no indication from the Chinese Communists that they would welcome any offer of food. I am not anxious to offer food if it is regarded merely as a propaganda effort by the United States." The President noted that "there has been a rather belligerent attitude expressed towards us in recent days by the Chinese Communists and there is no indication, direct or indirect, public or private, that they would respond favorably to any action by the United States."

State of the Union. On Jan. 30, President Kennedy, in his State of the Union Message to Congress, said: "Our greatest challenge is still the world that lies beyond the 'cold war' -- but the first obstacle is still our relations with the Soviet Union and Communist China. We must never be lulled into believing that either power has yielded its ambitions for world domination."

Interview with Chou. On Jan. 31, *Look* magazine published an interview by Edgar Snow with Chinese Communist Premier Chou En-lai. Chou told the American journalist that although the Soviet Union and Communist China had differences, they agreed on the desirability of disarmament and peaceful coexistence. He said a settlement with the U.S. would be possible only after it had accepted Peking's position that Formosa was a Chinese internal problem. U.S. forces would have to be withdrawn from the island.

Chinese Economy. On Feb. 1, the *New York Times* reported that Communist China was relaxing economic controls over farm workers. The commune system, the *Times*

reported, was slowly disintegrating, and the right of farmers to own small pieces of land and a limited number of livestock had been restored.

Prisoners in China. On Feb. 1, President Kennedy, queried about the five Americans imprisoned in China, replied: "This is a matter of continuing concern, and as long as those men are held, it will be extremely difficult to have any kind of normal relations with the Chinese Communists. There are other matters which affect those relations, too, but this is certainly a point of the greatest possible concern. Now, we have asked for a delay in the meetings which take place in Warsaw between the United States representative and that of the Chinese Communists, from February to March, because they have become merely a matter of form and nothing of substance happens. But I want to make it very clear we are concerned about these men in China.

Rusk on China. On Feb. 6, Secretary of State Dean Rusk told his first Washington press conference that the U.S. had "strong commitments" to Nationalist China, and "that commitment is firm" even though Communist China considers Formosa a "major obstacle" to a settlement with the U.S. Rusk added that the U.S. was studying ways to include Communist China in disarmament discussions and added that "it will not be easy to achieve any realistic or effective disarmament unless all those countries that are capable of producing...large armed forces are brought within the system."

British View. On Feb. 8, Lord Home, British Foreign Secretary, told the House of Lords that "the facts of international life require that Communist China be seated in the United Nations." On Feb. 9, the State Department said the U.S. did not share the British view.

Laotian Neutrality. On Feb. 19, the Laotian government issued a statement declaring: "We. . . proclaim once more the policy of true neutrality that Laos has always sought to follow. Laos will not join in any military alliance ...Laos will not have on its territory either foreign forces or military bases."

Sino-Soviet Rift. On Feb. 19, the New York *Herald Tribune* published an article by Edward Crankshaw, a reporter for the London *Observer*, asserting that the Sino-Soviet split was wider than most Western observers had previously believed. Crankshaw said Western leaders had come into possession of documents, obtained from Soviet-bloc and Western European sources, which indicated that the dialogue between Moscow and Peking had been insulting to the point of obscenity. The controversy, Crankshaw reported, dated back to a January 1960 meeting of the Presidium of the World Peace Council in Rome when the Chinese delegates accused the Soviet Union of attempting to isolate China and make a settlement with the U.S.

Anti-Communists on the Record. On Feb. 19, the Committee of One Million Against the Admission of Communist China to the United Nations announced that a statement upholding its position and also opposing U.S. recognition of Communist China had been signed by 54 Senators and 285 Representatives, including 165 Democrats and 174 Republicans. On Feb. 20, the Committee published the names in an advertisement in the *Washington Post*. Among them were 22 of the 33 members of the House Foreign Affairs Committee, and 9 of the 17 members of the Senate Foreign Relations Committee -- including Majority Leader Mike Mansfield (D Mont.) and Majority Whip Hubert H. Humphrey (D Minn.).

Food for China. On Feb. 23, the White House announced that President Kennedy had rejected a proposal by Rep. Thomas J. Lane (D Mass.) that the U.S. send food to Red China in exchange for release of Americans held prisoner there. It was reported two days later that Chinese Foreign Minister Chen Yi had said that China would not "stoop to beg for food from the United States."

Relations With Russia. On March 1, President Kennedy was asked during a news conference if the reported Sino-Soviet split might result in better relations between the U.S. and U.S.S.R. The President expressed hope that it would and added that "We are attempting, and will be attempting in the coming months to determine whether any effective agreements can be accomplished with the Soviet Union which will permit a relaxation of world tension."

Soviet Loans to China. On March 2, the *New York Times*, commenting on the Sino-Soviet rift, reported that the last known loan granted to Communist China from the Soviet Union was in 1957.

Warsaw Talks Resumed. On March 7, U.S.-Chinese Warsaw talks resumed with U.S. Ambassador to Poland Jacob D. Beam proposing that he and Chinese Ambassador Wang Ping-nan discuss an exchange of newsmen between their two countries, the release of imprisoned Americans in China, and a general settlement of U.S.-Chinese disputes. Wang immediately rejected all three proposals, saying that nothing could be negotiated until the U.S. withdrew its forces from Formosa.

Kennedy on Red China. On March 8, President Kennedy pointed out at a news conference that the Chinese Communists "have been. . . extremely belligerent towards us, and they have been unfailing in their attacks upon the United States." The President said: "Of course, I think part of that has been because they recognize that the United States is committed to maintaining its connections with other countries, committed to its own defense and the defense of freedom.... I would like to see a lessening of... tension.... But we are not prepared to surrender in order to get a relaxation of that."

Laos Fighting. On March 10, it was reported that the Communist Pathet Lao rebels in Laos had launched an offensive in the central section of the country and overwhelmed government forces. The *New York Times* had reported March 3 that the rebels had the aid of Soviet supplies and North Vietnamese advisers. It was reported in Washington March 21 that President Kennedy had ordered an increase in U.S. military aid to the Laotian government.

Kennedy on Laos. On March 23, President Kennedy told a news conference that local Communist forces in Laos had "increasing direction and support from outside" aimed at destroying Laotian neutrality, and if that neutrality was lost the security of all Southeast Asia would be endangered. The President said the U.S. "strongly and unreservedly" supported the goal of a "truly neutral" Laos.

Albanian-Soviet Split. On March 30, it was learned through sources in Belgrade that Albanian Communist Party First Secretary Enver Hoxha, who had supported China in the Sino-Soviet ideological split, had so angered Khrushchev at the November 1960 Moscow congress of Communist leaders that the Soviet Premier shouted: "Comrade Hoxha, you have poured a bucket of dung on me and you will have to wash it off!" Hoxha reportedly refused to attend the Warsaw Pact conference in Moscow on March 27-29 because he feared assassination.

Soviet-Chinese Agreement. On April 7, the Soviet Union and Communist China signed a trade and economic aid agreement the total value of which was reported to be smaller than in either 1959 or 1960. Although China was believed to be in a state of near-famine, the agreement contained no provisions for food shipments, except a loan of 500,000 tons of sugar. The Soviet Union conceded a five-year postponement of payments due from China under previous trade agreements. Chinese Ambassador to Poland Wang Ping-nan admitted in a speech on April 7 that China had suffered great losses in agricultural production because much of the arable land had been "struck by the elements." Wang said that in some areas "the losses were so heavy that no crops were harvested at all." He disclosed that China had reached agreements with Australia and Canada for purchases of grain.

Kennedy-Macmillan Talks. On April 8, President Kennedy concluded three days of talks at the White House with British Prime Minister Harold Macmillan. A joint statement said the two leaders had reached "a very high level of agreement on our estimate of the nature of the problems we face." Differences in U.S.-British policies toward Communist China and its admission to the UN were reported to have been discussed. Kennedy and Macmillan were reported also to have reviewed the situation in Laos and to have taken up the question of Western support for South Viet Nam, plagued by rising Communist infiltration.

Cuban Invasion. On April 17, anti-Castro Cuban rebels launched an attack on Cuba, landing at Cochinos Bay (Bay of Pigs), south of Havana. The force of 1,200 to 1,500 Cuban refugees, reportedly trained and supplied by the U.S. Central Intelligence Agency, encountered unexpectedly strong resistance and was overwhelmed in little more than 48 hours. The U.S. Government became the target of strong criticism at home and abroad. On April 24, a White House statement asserted that the President "bears sole responsibility for the events of the past few days" and "is strongly opposed to anyone within or without the Administration attempting to shift the responsibility."

Call for Laos Cease-Fire. On April 24, after weeks of negotiation, Britain and the Soviet Union called for a cease-fire in Laos, to be followed by a 14-nation conference starting May 12 in Geneva. The Laotian government proposed April 27 that the cease-fire begin the next day, but there was no response from the rebel forces. Shortly thereafter, President Kennedy called Congressional leaders to the White House amid signs that the royal Laotian forces were on the edge of collapse. Sen. J.W. Fulbright (D Ark.), chairman of the Foreign Relations Committee, said April 30 that he would oppose U.S. military intervention in Laos because of the "terrain and conditions."

Canadian-Chinese Agreement. On May 2, Canada announced it had agreed to sell $362 million worth of wheat, barley and flour (six million tons) to Communist China. The Peking radio reported 10 days later that "natural calamities" had caused massive crop losses.

Resolutions on Red China. On May 3, Senate Minority Leader Everett McKinley Dirksen (R Ill.) introduced a concurrent resolution (S Con Res 22) restating opposition to the seating of Communist China in the UN and to diplomatic recognition of Red China. Majority Leader Mike Mansfield (D Mont.) and 15 other Senators co-sponsored the resolution. Identical resolutions were introduced the same day in the House by Rep. Clement J. Zablocki (D Wis.) and 55 other Members (H Con Res 233-288).

Rusk on Laos. On May 4, Secretary of State Dean Rusk said he planned to head the U.S. delegation to a proposed 14-nation conference on Laos beginning in Geneva May 12, assuming the cease-fire was firmly established by then. Rusk also said that the Communists were making a concerted effort, with outside support, to wreck the pro-Western government of South Viet Nam, and he pledged a strong U.S. effort to strengthen that government.

U.S. Space Flight. On May 5, Comdr. Alan B. Shepard became the first U.S. astronaut when his one-ton capsule, "Freedom 7," achieved sub-orbital space flight and returned safely to earth.

Viet Nam. On May 5, President Kennedy told a news conference that dispatch of American troops to Viet Nam was "one of the matters which Vice President Johnson will deal with" in his "consultations with the government of Viet Nam as to what further steps could most usefully be taken."

Johnson's Trip to Asia. On May 9, Vice President Johnson left Washington carrying personal letters from President Kennedy to Asian leaders assuring them of continuing and increased U.S. support. Johnson's first stop was in Saigon, capital of South Viet Nam, where he met May 12 with President Ngo Dinh Diem to discuss the critical problem of infiltration by guerrilla forces from Communist North Viet Nam.

Johnson next visited Manila for talks with President Carlos P. Garcia of the Philippines; a joint communique announced their "complete agreement on the seriousness of the situation in Southeast Asia." From Manila, Johnson flew to Taipei, May 14, where he assured Chinese Nationalist President Chiang Kai-shek of America's continuing support. After a stopover in Hong Kong, Johnson moved on to Bangkok May 16 for talks with Thailand's Premier, Field Marshal Sarit Thanarat, about the precarious situation in adjoining Laos.

Conference on Laos. On May 12, the 14-nation conference on Laos opened in Geneva following a cease-fire between Communist-backed and U.S.-supported forces in Laos. The conference promptly became deadlocked over a procedural question. The Soviets insisted that representatives of the Communist-led Pathet Lao rebels be seated along with spokesmen for the pro-Western Laotian government and for neutralist Prince Souvanna Phouma. Secretary of State Dean Rusk opposed the move as tantamount to recognition of the rebels as a component of the future Laotian government -- a step the U.S. felt would sabotage the objective of creating a truly neutral regime in Laos.

With tension high -- in part because of the presence of Communist China at the conference table -- the principals finally agreed May 15 to seat all three Laotian groups as "spokesmen" for forces operating in Laos. On May 17, both the U.S. and the Soviet Union proposed that all foreign troops be withdrawn from Laos. But the Soviets proposed also that the three-member International Control Commission -- composed of India, Canada, and Poland -- adhere to the rule of unanimity in carrying out its truce-inspection duties, and also that it act only on the instruction of the co-chairmen of the conference, Britain and the Soviet Union. U.S. delegates said such a plan would give the Soviets a "double-barreled veto." By May 20, Secretary of State Rusk and other delegation leaders had returned home, leaving deputies in charge of the negotiations which most observers felt would last several weeks.

Coup in Korea. On May 16, the South Korean government of Premier John M. Chang was overthrown in a surprise coup by an army revolutionary committee headed by Lt. Gen. Chang Do Young. The American Embassy at once announced that U.S. Gen. Carter B. Magruder, commander in chief of the UN Command, had "all military personnel in his command" to support "the only recognized government of the Republic of Korea," and had urged military leaders to "see that control is immediately turned back to the lawful government authorities." The American Chargé d'Affaires added that he wanted to make it "emphatically clear that the United States supports the constitutional government" of Premier Chang.

In Washington, however, the State Department refused to comment on the U.S. position. By May 17, Gen. Chang Do Young claimed full control of the government and country and pledged a return to civilian authority once the junta had eliminated political corruption. On May 18, Premier John M. Chang and his cabinet resigned, giving legal effect to the transfer of power, and the rebels named a 30-man committee to run the country. The committee was headed by Gen. Chang and included chiefs of all of Korea's armed services. Shortly thereafter, U.S. Under Secretary of State Chester Bowles said he "thinks we will" recognize the new regime. The U.S. "can hardly cheer at the upsetting of a constitutional government," said Bowles, but the new regime, "no matter how unconstitutional, is anti-Communist and pro-American."

Kennedy on China. On June 2, President Kennedy, en route to Vienna to meet with Soviet Premier Nikita Khrushchev, was asked during a news conference in Paris how Communist China could normalize its relations with the West and be admitted to the United Nations.

The President replied: "We desire peace and we desire to live in amity with the Chinese people. But I will say that since long before I assumed office, and in the first days of our new Administration before really any actions were taken, the attacks upon our Government and the United States were constant, immediate, and in many cases malevolent.

"The debate which took place last fall between Communist parties indicated that the Chinese planned to take an extremely belligerent attitude and role toward us and those with whom we are associated. We hope that policy changes. We want goodwill. But it takes two to make peace, and I am hopeful that the Chinese will be persuaded that a peaceful existence with its neighbors represents the best hope for us all. We would welcome it. But I do not see evidence of it today."

Kennedy-Khrushchev Meeting. On June 3, President Kennedy and Soviet Premier Khrushchev met in Vienna for two days of discussions. Kennedy later commented that he and the Russian leader had "a very full and frank exchange of views on the issues that now divide our two countries." The President added: "The one area which afforded some...prospect of accord was Laos. Both sides endorsed the concept of a neutral and independent Laos.... And, of critical importance to the current conference on Laos in Geneva, both sides recognized the importance of an effective cease-fire. It is urgent that this be translated into new attitudes at Geneva, enabling the International Control Commission to...make certain that a cease-fire is enforced and maintained."

Laos Conference. On June 12, Chinese Communist Foreign Minister Chen Yi told the 14-nation conference on Laos, meeting in Geneva, that Laos was "a victim of the United States policy of intervention" and warned that Communist China "will never be a party to...enforcing an international condominium over Laos in the name of international control over its neutrality." The delegation from Thailand walked out during Chen Yi's speech.

Khrushchev Letter on China. On July 2, the London *Sunday Times* reported that Soviet Premier Khrushchev had sent a letter to the leaders of all Communist parties denouncing the Chinese for what he felt was an overly aggressive policy. Peking's Formosan policy was said to have come in for special criticism because it risked all-out war. On the same day it was learned that no Soviet officials had attended the celebration in Peking of the 40th anniversary of the founding of the Chinese Communist Party.

Communist Unity. On July 8, the Soviet newspaper *Pravda* published an article by Chinese Foreign Minister Chen Yi in which he said: "No provocations or gossip can shake to the slightest extent the indissoluable cohesion" between the Soviet Union and China, which "resolutely supported the peaceful foreign policy of the Soviet Union" and the 1960 declaration of the Communist parties that "revolution cannot be exported." Chen Yi added that the Chinese Communist leaders "stand resolutely for peaceful coexistence of countries with different social systems." On the following day, Chen Yi said, in a speech at a Peking rally celebrating the 40th anniversary of Mongolian independence, that "China will firmly adhere to a peaceful foreign policy and... fight against the aggressive and war policy of the imperialists."

On July 10, the First Secretary of the Polish Communist Party, Wladyslaw Gomulka, asserted in a speech in the Mongolian People's Republic: "Our enemies counted on the disintegration, or at least the weakening of...(Communist) unity. They tried to take advantage of our ideological discussion to attack the Socialist countries." But, he said, "events have dashed all their expectations."

China Resolution in Senate. On July 28, the U.S. Senate adopted, by a 76-0 roll-call vote, and sent to the House a resolution (S Con Res 34, formerly S Con Res 22) restating Congressional opposition to the admission of Communist China to the United Nations and to U.S. recognition of the Peking government, and Congressional support for continued recognition of the Nationalist Chinese government "as the representative of China in the UN."

The Senate accepted two amendments by Thomas J. Dodd (D Conn.) which, Dodd said, were designed to justify to the world this country's "determination to keep Red China out of the United Nations." The amendments asserted that Communist China should not be seated because it had "flagrantly violated basic human rights," had imposed a brutal regime on the Chinese people, had derived its authority from usurpation and tyranny, and had become the "major source of the international illicit narcotics traffic." Dodd's amendments were in addition to language in the resolution that condemned Communist China's aggression in Korea and Tibet, its failure to release U.S. prisoners, and its hostility to the U.S. and the UN.

During debate Sen. Bourke B. Hickenlooper (R Iowa), in answer to a question from Sen. Norris Cotton (R N.H.), said the Foreign Relations Committee had considered and rejected language which might have been construed as supporting recognition of both Communist China and Nationalist China, the so-called "two-China" policy. Cotton's statement that S Con Res 34 in effect described Nationalist China as the "sole representative" of China at the UN was endorsed by Minority Leader Everett McKinley Dirksen (R Ill.) and Majority Leader Mike Mansfield (D Mont.).

Sen. Wayne Morse (D Ore.) said that had he been present for the debate on S Con Res 34, he would have offered a substitute that would have expressed U.S. willingness to put on the UN's agenda the question of admitting Communist China. "Our case on the merits is so overwhelmingly against the seating of Communist China ...that we ought to be willing to put it on the agenda and present our evidence." The U.S. position, he said, should be that "there is no issue...involving the peace of the world...that we are not willing to have debated...and voted upon in the United Nations."

White House Communique. On Aug. 2, in a joint communique issued following two days of discussions between President Kennedy and Nationalist Chinese Vice President Chen Cheng, Kennedy pledged U.S. support for "continued representation of the Republic of China in the United Nations" and "reaffirmed the U.S. determination to continue to oppose admission of the Chinese Communist regime."

Berlin Wall. On Aug. 13, East German troops, police and factory workers sealed the border between East and West Berlin for reasons of "protection and control." Secretary of State Dean Rusk immediately charged that "Limitation on travel within Berlin is a violation of the four-power status of Berlin and...of the right of free circulation throughout the city. Restrictions on travel between East Germany and Berlin are in direct contravention of the four-power (Paris) agreement" of June 20, 1949. On Aug. 20, American troops began arriving in West Berlin to reinforce the U.S. garrison there.

Atomic Tests Resumed. On Aug. 31, the Soviet Union announced it would break the unofficial moratorium on atomic testing "reluctantly and with regret" because the U.S. "is standing at the threshold of carrying out underground nuclear explosions and only waits for the first suitable pretext to start them." The announcement said the Soviets had designed "super-powerful nuclear bombs" with a yield equal to 100 million tons of TNT. New Soviet testing -- said by the U.S. Atomic Energy Commission to be in the atmosphere -- started Sept. 1.

Chinese Reaction. On Aug. 31, the Chinese Communists praised the Soviet Union for deciding to resume testing "in the interest of the defense of world peace." A statement said the decision was "a cooling dose for hotheaded war

Cost of 'Containment': Aid to Countries Surrounding China

FOREIGN AID BY COUNTRY: JULY 1, 1945 - JUNE 30, 1965

(U.S. Fiscal Years - Figures in Millions of Dollars)

U.S. OVERSEAS LOANS AND GRANTS - NET OBLIGATIONS AND LOAN AUTHORIZATIONS (a)

	Total Military Assistance	Export-Import Bank Long-Term Loans	Total Economic Assistance	Total Economic & Military Assistance
NEAR EAST AND SOUTH ASIA				
Afghanistan	$ 3.1	$ 39.3	$ 304.0	$ 307.1
Ceylon	--	--	90.9	90.9
India	°(b)	406.4	5,882.4 (c)	5,882.4
Nepal	*(d)	--	86.1	86.1
Pakistan	7.8 (e)	35.7	2,937.3	2,945.1
TOTAL: Selected Countries	10.9	$ 481.4	$ 9,300.7	$ 9,311.6
FAR EAST				
Burma	--	--	111.0	111.0
Cambodia (f)	87.1	--	256.0	343.1
China, Republic of	2,530.8	36.0	2.224.7 (g)	4,755.5
Hong Kong	--	--	40.1	40.1
Indochina, Undistributed (f)	709.6	--	825.6	1,535.2
Indonesia	68.9	162.1	799.3 (h)	868.2
Japan	1,075.6 (i)	467.4	2,858.5	3,934.1
Korea	2,290.7	--	4,011.2	6,301.9
Laos (f)	(j)	--	418.5	418.5
Malaysia	0.1	--	37.5	37.6
Philippines	467.7	178.9	1,421.2	1,888.9
Ryukyu Islands	--	--	324.7	324.7
Thailand	4.6 (k)	51.4	433.7	438.3
Viet Nam (f)	1,544.8	--	2,377.5	3,922.3
Far East Regional (l)	1,132.9	--	52.4	1,185.3
TOTAL	$ 9,912.8	$ 895.8	$16,191.4	$26,104.2
OCEANIA				
Australia	$ 117.7	$ 7.4	$ 15.4	$ 133.1
New Zealand	4.7	12.2	16.5	21.2
Trust Territory of the Pacific Islands	--	--	107.4	107.4
TOTAL	$ 122.4	$ 19.6	$ 139.3	$ 261.7
GRAND TOTALS (m) of Selected Countries	$10,046.1	$1,396.8	$25,631.4	$35,677.5

(a) *Export-Import Bank long-term loans are shown in a separate column but are part of the data of total economic assistance since economists both in the U.S. and abroad consider these data part of economic assistance.*

(b) *No military aid to India from 1946-1962. Military aid to India classified since 1963.*

(c) *Excludes $20.0 million loan in FY 1958 financed by Asian Economic Development Fund.*

(d) *No military aid to Nepal from 1946-1964. Military aid to Nepal classified since 1965.*

(e) *Military aid to Pakistan classified except for "Other Military Assistance."*

(f) *Aid to Indochina (Cambodia, Laos and Viet Nam) before partition is shown under "Indochina, Undistributed." Aid after partition is shown under individual countries of Cambodia, Laos and Viet Nam.*

(g) *Includes aid to Mainland China.*

(h) *Includes $101.4 million in aid channeled through the Netherlands.*

(i) *Excludes $540.0 million of materiel provided from Department of Defense stocks.*

(j) *Military data classified since 1963. Cumulative data included in Far East Regional data.*

(k) *Military data classified except for "Other Military Assistance." Cumulative data included in Far East Regional data.*

(l) *Far East Regional figures include loans of Asian Economic Development Funds, and funds for technical assistance programs such as the anti-malaria campaign, irrigation and flood control, training of teachers, etc. Includes cumulative military data for countries which are partially classified.*

(m) *Detail may not add to totals due to rounding.*

(For explanation of tables, see next page.)

plotters but a powerful inspiration to all peoples striving for world peace."

China Resolution in House. On Aug. 31, the House adopted, by a 395-0 roll-call vote, the resolution (S Con Res 34) adopted by the Senate July 28 restating Congressional opposition to admission of Communist China to the United Nations and to U.S. recognition of Communist China. During debate, several Members argued that the language of the resolution was too restrained. Only two Members -- Reps. Thomas L. Ashley (D Ohio) and William Fitts Ryan (D N.Y.) -- spoke against it. Both voted "present" on the roll call. Ashley said the measure constituted "an undesirable and unnecessary" restraint on the President's freedom of action.

Kennedy Orders Atomic Tests. On Sept. 5, President Kennedy ordered resumption of U.S. underground nuclear testing because "We have no other choice."

Khrushchev on Big Bomb. On Sept. 8, the *New York Times* published a lengthy statement by Soviet Premier Khrushchev, given to C. L. Sulzberger to clarify statements

in an earlier interview. Khrushchev said that "We already have" a bomb "equal in capacity to 100 million tons of TNT" and would "test the explosive device for it." He also said that the Soviet Union had given neither nuclear weapons nor long-range missiles to Communist China or any other nation. He denied that any weapons of that type were stationed outside the borders of the Soviet Union unless "possibly in East Germany."

Hammarskjold Killed. On Sept. 18, UN Secretary General Dag Hammarskjold was killed in a plane crash near Ndola, Northern Rhodesia, where he was to meet President Moise Tshombe of Katanga Province to arrange a cease-fire between Katangan and UN Congo forces.

China Debate. On Sept. 21, the UN General Assembly's Steering Committee voted to recommend debate on the question of Chinese representation. In a change of policy, the U.S. supported the proposed debate instead of seeking to have it postponed a year.

Kennedy at the UN. On Sept. 25, President John F. Kennedy took up the question of Southeast Asia in an ad-

---

Explanation of Tables

Foreign aid figures have been compiled by the Agency for International Development (A.I.D.) and are based on the amount of money *planned* over a period of years for a country or a region rather than the amount of money actually spent. For example, A.I.D. figures show the cost of a bridge the first year although the bridge may not be in use until the fifth year. This kind of data is identified by A.I.D. statistical reference as "obligations and loan authorizations." The military data show actual expenditures on a yearly basis but the cumulative total represents the amount of money planned for an individual country for the years of 1950-1965.

Economic Aid

Economic aid to foreign countries is divided by A.I.D. into four sections.

1. A.I.D. commitments for economic and technical assistance as well as earlier agency commitments beginning with the Marshall Plan, April 3, 1948.

2. "Food for Peace" (PL 480) which includes:

Title I -- Planned for Loans and Grants -- provides for the sale of surplus agricultural commodities for foreign currency which in turn can be used for economic development of that foreign country.

Title II -- the use of funds from the sale of U.S. commodities in such emergency situations as famines or floods. Funds from Title II may also be used to "promote economic development."

Title III -- authorization of gifts of surplus commodities to such volunteer American relief organizations as CARE, National Catholic Welfare Conference, Church World Service and other similar groups to distribute food abroad.

Title IV -- deals with dollar credit sales wherein agricultural commodities are sold to the recipient country for American dollars which are paid back on a loan basis within 20 years.

3. Data compiled from reports of the Export-Import Bank for loans of five years or more. The figures exclude credits of less than five years and loans bought by private banks and other institutions. The data also exclude all export guarantees and insurance authorized by the Bank.

4. "Other U.S. Economic Programs" include current programs that do not fall into any of the other categories such as the Peace Corps and also economic assistance which pre-dates the Marshall Plan such as the United Nations Relief and Rehabilitation Administration (UNRRA), "Civilian Relief in Korea" and "Philippines Rehabilitation." Early programs are shown as far as possible on an obligations basis. Programs obligated earlier than June 30, 1945, are not shown in this table although expenditures continued in 1946 and later. Since mainland China was receiving Lend-Lease, this portion of aid to China is not shown. Later programs under the heading of "Other U.S. Economic Programs" also include subscriptions to the Inter-American Bank and Development, IDA, the Peace Corps, Philippine War Damage Claims and the United Nations bond issue.

Military Aid

There are two main categories of military aid data shown in the tables. The first is the Military Assistance Program (MAP) which consists of grants and loans of military equipment, supplies and services. The second category of military aid is termed "Other Military Assistance" and includes the military portion of "China Naval Aid," (PL 454) "Philippines Aid" and "Vessel Loans".

dress before the UN General Assembly: "The first threat on which I wish to report is widely misunderstood: the smoldering coals of war in Southeast Asia. South Viet Nam is already under attack -- sometimes by a single assassin, sometimes by a band of guerrillas, recently by full battalions. The peaceful borders of Burma, Cambodia, and India have been repeatedly violated. And the peaceful people of Laos are in danger of losing the independence they gained not so long ago.

"No one can call these 'wars of liberation.' For these are free countries living under governments. Nor are these aggressions any less real because men are knifed in their homes and not shot in the fields of battle.

"The very simple question confronting the world community is whether measures can be devised to protect the small and weak from such tactics. For if they are successful in Laos and South Viet Nam, the gates will be opened wide.

"The United States seeks for itself no base, no territory, no special position in this area of any kind. We support a truly neutral and independent Laos, its people free from outside interference, living at peace with themselves and with their neighbors, assured that their territory will not be used for attacks on others, and under a government comparable (as Mr. Khrushchev and I agreed in Vienna) to Cambodia and Burma.

"But now the negotiations over Laos are reaching a crucial stage. The cease-fire is at best precarious. The rainy season is coming to an end. Laotian territory is being used to infiltrate South Viet Nam. The world community must recognize -- all those who are involved -- that this potent threat to Laotian peace and freedom is indivisible from all other threats to their own."

U.S. and Viet Nam. On Oct. 2, the State Department said the U.S. was "pressing ahead with urgent measures to increase the ability of the South Vietnamese soldier to defend his country." On the same day, South Vietnamese President Ngo Dinh Diem told the National Assembly at Saigon: "It is no longer a guerrilla war we have to face but a real war waged by an enemy who attacks us with regular units fully and completely equipped and who seeks a strategic position in Southeast Asia in conformity with the orders of the Communist International."

U.S. Involvement. On Oct. 11, State Department spokesman Lincoln White denied reports that the U.S. was considering sending troops to South Viet Nam. White said: "There has been no such decision. Furthermore...Viet Nam assures us...that with U.S. material assistance and training services, it can handle the present Communist aggressive attacks." He admitted he had doubts about South Vietnamese optimism. The U.S. was reported to have 685 men in a U.S. Military Advisory Group in South Viet Nam.

Gen. Taylor to Saigon. On Oct. 11, President Kennedy told a news conference he had asked Gen. Maxwell D. Taylor "to go to Saigon this week to discuss with the President and American officials on the spot ways in which we can perhaps better assist the government of Viet Nam in meeting this threat to its independence."

Kennedy added: "We are going to wait until Gen. Taylor comes back and brings an up-to-date description of the situation, particularly in Viet Nam. As you know, in the last two or three months there has been a large increase in the number of forces that have been involved. There has been evidence that some of these forces have come from

beyond the frontiers. Gen. Taylor will give me and the Joint Chiefs of Staff an educated military guess as to what the situation is that the government there faces. Then we can come to conclusions as to what is the best thing to do."

Chou Warns of U.S. Imperialism. On Oct. 12, Chinese Communist Premier Chou En-lai warned that his country "cannot be indifferent to the increasingly grave situation caused by United States imperialism in South Viet Nam." Chou made the statement at a reception for North Vietnamese Premier Pham Van Dong in Peking.

Moscow on Taylor's Trip. On Oct. 12, the Soviet Union said it was "clear that American plans to send troops to South Viet Nam have another aspect -- the Laotian aspect," and that Gen. Taylor's trip to South Viet Nam was proof of those "openly aggressive" plans.

North Viet Nam's Reaction. On Oct. 14, North Viet Nam protested to the International Control Commission on Viet Nam that Gen. Taylor's mission was planned to "intensify United States intervention in South Viet Nam and prepare the way for introducing United States troops" there.

On the same day, the *Hsinhua* (New China) news agency reported that the President of North Viet Nam, Ho Chi Minh, had met with Chinese Communist Party Chairman Mao Tse-tung and Defense Minister Lin Piao in Peking to discuss the situation in South Viet Nam.

Taylor Departs. On Oct. 15, Gen. Taylor left Washington for South Viet Nam, Thailand, and Laos. Before departing, the General said: "Any American would be reluctant to use troops (in Viet Nam) unless absolutely necessary."

Communist Party Congress. On Oct. 17, the 22nd Congress of the Soviet Communist Party convened in Moscow. Delegations from 83 countries were present. Representatives from Albania and Yugoslavia were notably absent. At the opening session, Soviet Premier Khrushchev denounced Albania for continuing to pursue the "cult of the individual," which in Soviet terms connoted Stalinism.

On Oct. 19, Chinese Communist Premier Chou En-lai took issue with Khrushchev: "If there are quarrels in the Socialist camp we consider that they should be settled through bilateral contacts and that a public denunciation does not contribute to the cohesion of the Socialist camp."

On Oct. 20, foreign Communist delegations began to voice support of Khrushchev's position, but on Oct. 21, the Chinese position was supported by President Ho Chi Minh of North Viet Nam, Premier Kim Il Sung of North Korea, and a representative of the Japanese Communist Party.

On Oct. 26, Khrushchev, again addressing the congress, asserted that Soviet leaders shared "the anxiety of our Chinese friends and...their concern for greater unity," but he insisted that Albania would have to abandon the cult of personality. On Oct. 31, the congress adopted a resolution demanding that Albania's leaders "renounce their erroneous views and...return to the road of unity."

Biggest Bomb Exploded. On Oct. 30, the Soviet Union detonated the largest nuclear weapon in history -- exceeding 50 megatons. The White House announced that "the explosion took place in the atmosphere" and would produce "more radioactive fallout than any previous explosion." On Nov. 2, President Kennedy said the U.S. would consider atmospheric nuclear testing if "it becomes necessary."

New Secretary General. On Nov. 3, U Thant, Burma's Ambassador to the UN, was appointed Secretary General to replace the late Dag Hammarskjold.

Taylor Returns. On Nov. 3, Gen. Maxwell D. Taylor returned to Washington from South Viet Nam and Thailand. He refused to comment on the recommendations he would make to President Kennedy concerning possible use of American forces in Southeast Asia. Taylor did say that he believed South Vietnamese President Ngo Dinh Diem could "prevail against the Communist threat" in South Viet Nam. Before leaving South Viet Nam, Taylor had urged the country to begin "national mobilization" in the "political, economic, military and psychological fields" and voiced "great confidence in the military capability of South Viet Nam to cope with anything within its borders." President Kennedy had sent a message to President Diem, Oct. 26, saying that the United States was "determined to help Viet Nam preserve its independence, protect its people against Communist assassins and build a better life." Reports from Saigon on Nov. 9 indicated that the American aid program had already been increased. On Nov. 13, North Viet Nam demanded that the International Control Commission investigate the American buildup.

Kennedy on Red Split. On Nov. 8, President Kennedy told a news conference: "None of us can talk with precision about the details of relationships between Russia and (Communist) China. It is a matter of surmise and on this experts may differ. Therefore, I don't feel that it is probably useful now for us to attempt to assess it."

China and Albania. On Nov. 8, the Chinese Communist Party Central Committee asserted, in a message to the Albanian Communist Party on its 20th anniversary, that the Chinese-Albanian alliance "can be shaken by no force on earth." Two days later, it was reported in the U.S. press that Enver Hoxha, First Secretary of the Albanian Communist Party, had said on the party's 20th anniversary: "It is not our party but the present Soviet leadership headed by Khrushchev who have slipped from Marxist-Leninist positions by demanding that other Communist parties submit to the Russian views and obey them." He said the Soviet Union was "afraid of imperialism" and had "delayed ...from year to year" a showdown on the Berlin problem.

Purge of Stalinists. On Nov. 11, it was reported from Moscow that ex-Foreign Minister Vyacheslav M. Molotov and ex-Premier Georgi M. Malenkov had been expelled from the Soviet Communist Party because of their associations with Stalin and their 1957 "anti-party" conspiracy against Soviet Premier Khrushchev. On the same day, it was announced that Stalingrad had been renamed Volgograd, and that smaller cities, streets, squares, and highways throughout the Soviet Union and Eastern European countries bearing Stalin's name had been renamed.

Wall Reinforced. On Nov. 19, East German workers began building a permanent wall between East and West Berlin. The following day, the Deputy Mayor of West Berlin, Franz Amrehn, inspected the new wall and commented: "That is a wall for 1,000 years."

China Debate in UN. On Dec. 1, debate on Communist China's membership in the UN began with a warning by U.S. Ambassador Stevenson that "the whole future of the United Nations may be at stake." Stevenson denounced the Chinese Communists for aggression in Tibet, Korea and Viet Nam. Later in the day, the Soviet delegation walked out during a speech by the Nationalist Chinese representative, who called Communist China's leaders "even more bellicose than their Russian comrades, if that is possible." The Soviet Ambassador to the UN, Valerian A. Zorin, had called the Nationalist government on Formosa "a rotten political corpse" kept "alive by sops from the master's table." It was the first time since 1950 that a resolution for Communist China's admission to the UN had been debated in the General Assembly. The question previously had not gone beyond the Assembly's Steering Committee.

Geneva Parley on Laos. On Dec. 2, Soviet Foreign Minister Andrei A. Gromyko and the British Foreign Secretary, the Earl of Home, co-chairmen of the 14-nation conference on Laos meeting in Geneva, said in a joint statement that the conference was "close to reaching an agreement on...the international aspects of the settlement of the Laotian problem."

UN Action on China. On Dec. 15, the UN General Assembly rejected a Soviet resolution for admission of Communist China to the United Nations and expulsion of Nationalist China. The vote was 48 to 37 with 19 abstentions. A second resolution -- to admit Communist China without expelling Nationalist China was rejected the same day by a 45-30 vote with 29 abstentions. A third resolution, sponsored by the U.S. and providing that any new General Assembly resolution dealing with Chinese representation would require a two-thirds majority vote for adoption, was approved 61-34 with seven abstentions.

Tibet and Korea. On Dec. 20, the General Assembly voted 56-11 with 29 abstentions to demand "cessation of practices which deprive the Tibetan peoples of their fundamental human rights and freedoms." The exiled Dalai Lama had charged in a note to UN members Oct. 6 that Chinese jets had machine-gunned 600 Tibetan families seeking to escape into India. The Assembly also adopted on Dec. 20, by a 64-11 vote with 27 abstentions, a resolution urging the UN Commission for the Unification and Rehabilitation of Korea to continue its efforts to "bring about, by peaceful means, the establishment of a unified, independent, and democratic Korea under a representative form of government."

Canadian Wheat. On Dec. 21, the Canadian Minister of Agriculture announced that Canada had signed a new agreement with Communist China for sale of $71 million worth of wheat and barley.

1962

Problem of Laos -- More Aid for Viet Nam -- Red China Warns U.S. -- Chinese-Cuban Trade Agreement -- Communist Offensive in Laos -- U.S. Troops Ordered to Thailand -- Refugees From Red China -- Agreement for Coalition Government in Laos -- Geneva Conference on Laos -- Drop in China's Trade with Soviets -- Indian-Chinese Border War -- Cuban Missile Crisis -- Aid for India -- Sino-Soviet Polemics Over Cuba and India -- Kennedy on U.S. Actions in Viet Nam.

Viet Nam Aid. On Jan. 4, the U.S. and South Vietnamese governments announced that the two countries had agreed to launch "a broad economic and social program aimed at providing every Vietnamese with the means for improving his standard of living." State Department spokesmen said economic aid for South Viet Nam would increase "appreciably" over the $136 million spent in 1961.

Kennedy on Laos. On Jan. 15, President Kennedy was asked during a press conference if the U.S. were taking a chance in supporting a coalition type of government in Laos. The President replied: "We are taking a chance in all of Southeast Asia, we are taking a chance in other areas also. Nobody can make any predictions for sure for the future really on any matter in which there are powerful interests at stake. I think, however, we have to consider what our alternatives are, and what the prospects for war are in that area....There is no easy, sure answer for Laos, but it is my judgment that it is in the best interests for our country to work for a neutral and independent Laos and we are attempting to do that. I can assure you that I recognize the risks that are involved. But I also think that we should consider the risks if we fail, particularly of the possibility of escalation of military struggle in a place of danger."

Laotian Agreement. On Jan. 19, the three princes representing the rightist, neutralist, and leftist factions in Laos announced that they had reached an agreement on formation of a coalition government. The announcement was made by Prince Souvanna Phouma, whose government had collapsed on Dec. 9, 1960, and been replaced by the rightist faction. Souvanna was to become the new premier under the coalition agreement. But on Jan. 25, it was reported that Communist Pathet Lao forces had staged a large attack northwest of Luang Prabang, the royal capital of Laos.

Kennedy's Reaction. On Jan. 31, President Kennedy told a news conference that "if the fighting and hostilities began" in Laos, "the hope of a settlement would substantially diminish." The President cited "the great dangers to both sides in a resumption of hostilities" and added: "We are making every effort to attempt to get an accord before the cease-fire, which appears to be strained somewhat after many months -- to try to get an accord before we have a breakdown of the cease-fire."

On Viet Nam, the President said: "The situation in Viet Nam is one that is of great concern to us. There were, I think last week, nearly 500 incidents, deaths, ambushes, and so on, and it is extremely serious....We are anxious for a peace in that area, and we are assisting the government to maintain its position against this subterranean war."

Laos Discussions Broken Off. On Feb. 2, Prince Boun Oum, rightist premier of the Laotian government, announced that he was breaking off negotiations with the princes representing the neutralist and leftist positions. He said he would boycott the meetings until Communist Pathet Lao troops ceased their attacks.

U.S. in Viet Nam Action. On Feb. 4, South Vietnamese troops attacked a Viet Cong-held village in South Viet Nam's southern tip and captured three guerrillas. The troops were lifted into the area aboard 15 U.S. Air Force helicopters, manned by U.S. crews.

Kennedy on Viet Nam. On Feb. 7, President Kennedy was asked at a news conference how deeply the U.S. was involved in Viet Nam. The President replied: "There is a war going on in South Viet Nam, and I think that last week there were over 500 killings and assassinations and bomb-

ings and the casualties are high. The United States...has been assisting Viet Nam economically to maintain its independence, viability and also sent training groups out there, which have been expanded in recent weeks, as the attacks on the government and the people of South Viet Nam have increased. We are out there on training and transportation, and we are assisting in every way we possibly can the people of South Viet Nam, who with the greatest courage and under danger, are attempting to maintain their freedom."

More Help for Viet Nam. On Feb. 14, President Kennedy told a news conference that the U.S. had enlarged its training mission and its logistics support and was attempting to prevent a Communist take-over in Viet Nam. The U.S. Government, he said, was attempting to make available all the information on its action that was consistent with its security needs and was keeping bipartisan Congressional groups informed.

China and Disarmament. On Feb. 14, at the same news conference, President Kennedy said the Chinese Communists would have to be included in any disarmament agreement among the world powers before the U.S. "would be able to have any confidence in" such an agreement. "I quite recognize the hazards and the difficulties of attempting to bring them in. But if we are making progress,...it is a question which waits for us before the end of the road is reached."

Glenn's Flight. On Feb. 20, U.S. Marine Lt. Col. John H. Glenn, 40, orbited the earth three times in a Mercury space capsule and was safely recovered in the Atlantic Ocean.

Viet Nam Reforms. On Feb. 21, newsmen questioned President Kennedy on reforms in Viet Nam and asked whether the South Vietnamese government had taken the responsibility for carrying them out. The President replied: "(The reforms) are hard to carry out. This country (South Viet Nam) has been in the struggle now for a number of years. It did not have many skilled administrators when it got its independence in 1954. It had been at war, really in a sense, with the Japanese occupation and the war with the French, for almost 15 years before that. So it is a very difficult assignment....But I think it is a matter...which the Vietnamese government must be concerned about. We are prepared to offer every assistance we can in making that government a more effective instrument for the people."

Peking Warns U.S. On Feb. 24, the Chinese Communist Foreign Ministry charged that U.S. action in South Viet Nam was "a direct threat" to North Viet Nam and therefore "seriously affects the security of China and the peace of Asia." It charged that a recently established military command in South Viet Nam was "by no means merely one for military assistance, but an operational command of the United States imperialists for direct participation....The United States is already in an undeclared war in South Viet Nam." Peking urged Britain and the Soviet Union, co-chairmen of the 1954 Geneva Conference, to take "appropriate measures" regarding U.S. intervention in the area. The Soviet Union echoed Chinese sentiments, but the British replied that "The tension in South Viet Nam arises directly from the North Vietnamese (effort)...to overthrow the established government by force."

The U.S. Defense Department had said on Feb. 9 that "this is a war we can't afford to lose" and that "we're drawing a line" against Communist aggression in South Viet Nam. The *New York Times* had reported the day before that the U.S. had 5,000 personnel in South Viet Nam, mostly on an "adviser" basis. The article pointed out that the 1954 Geneva agreements sought to limit South Viet Nam to no more than 685 foreign military advisers and specified amounts of military equipment.

Diem's Palace Bombed. On Feb. 27, two rebellious South Vietnamese Air Force pilots bombed President Ngo Dinh Diem's palace in Saigon, but Diem escaped unharmed. The pilots were flying U.S. fighter-bombers.

Rusk on Vietnamese Peace. On March 1, Secretary of State Dean Rusk told a news conference: "There can be peace overnight in Viet Nam if those responsible for the aggression wish peace. It is as simple as that."

U.S. A-Tests. On March 2, President Kennedy announced that the United States would resume testing nuclear weapons in the atmosphere.

Burmese Coup. On March 2, Burmese Prime Minister U Nu was deposed in a coup led by Defense Minister Gen. Ne Win, who was named prime minister three days later.

Imperialists and Imperialism. On March 7, it was reported from Hong Kong that *Hung Chi*, a Chinese Communist Party journal, had printed an article saying that "unconditional peaceful coexistence" meant "constant concessions toward imperialism," and that it was harmful "not to oppose ...the policies of war and aggression of the United States and other imperialists." An article in the Peking *People's Daily* declared that the anti-Chinese world movement was perpetrated by "imperialists" and "revisionists."

Training of Vietnamese Pilots. On March 9, the State Department said that American pilots had participated in bombing missions against Communist guerrillas in South Viet Nam. The statement said the action was necessary to train the South Vietnamese pilots who accompanied the Americans.

Criticism of Diem. On March 13, the *New York Times* reported that the president of the Committee on National Union in Viet Nam, which led the opposition to President Diem's regime, had sent a letter to the U.S. Ambassador to Viet Nam, Frederick E. Nolting, urging that the U.S. try to get the Diem government to liberalize its policies. The Committee's president, Pham Huy Quat, contended that the Diem government had alienated the majority of the Vietnamese people by suppressing individual rights.

Chinese-Indian Border. On March 16, Indian Prime Minister Nehru told the Parliament in New Delhi that the Chinese Communists had expressed hope that the two countries could reach an "early" settlement of their border dispute. Nehru said he had replied that "Peaceful withdrawal of Chinese forces from territories which have traditionally been a part of India is necessary to lay the foundations for fresh negotiations."

Kennedy on China. On March 29, President Kennedy, asked at a news conference to restate U.S. policy toward Formosa, said: "Quite obviously it is the desire of the people of Formosa that they be returned (to the China mainland), but we have to consider all the responsibilities and problems which all of us bear, and I have not heard that any new proposal is now under consideration."

"Great Leap" Failure. On April 3, Soviet newspapers reprinted a Chinese Communist editorial which disclosed that China had abandoned its attempt to achieve a "great leap forward." The editorial said that "Victory in the struggle against nature cannot be gained by a single leap forward." On Sept. 4, Soviet newspapers printed a statement by Chinese Communist Foreign Minister Chen Yi insisting that "the attempts of the imperialists to split the Soviet camp will never succeed."

Rusk on Split. On April 5, Secretary of State Dean Rusk testified before the Senate Foreign Relations Committee that there was "considerable evidence of deep differences" between the Soviet Union and Communist China. The Secretary said the dispute concerned a "doctrinal debate" between the "hard-line" Chinese and the "peaceful coexistence" theory of the Russians, and that both vied for control of foreign Communist parties and influence in underdeveloped nations. "There is reason to believe," Rusk said, "that mainland China is disappointed in the amount of aid it has received from the Soviet Union."

Trade Agreement. On April 20, Communist China and the Soviet Union signed a trade agreement for an undisclosed amount of goods. The *New York Times* three weeks earlier had carried a report from Polish sources that Communist China currently ranked as the Soviet Union's fourth largest trading partner. It had ranked second in 1960, when Sino-Soviet trade totaled 1.5 billion rubles ($1.38 billion).

Indian Warnings to China. On April 23, India notified Communist China that a 1954 trade agreement, due to expire June 3, would not be renewed until Chinese forces had withdrawn from traditionally Indian territory. The Indian Minister for External Affairs, Mrs. Lakshi Menon, had told the Indian Parliament on April 19 that the Chinese Communists had been warned of "grave consequences" if they "persist in their systematic and deliberate encroachments into Indian territory."

Chinese Cuban Agreement. On April 26, Communist China and Cuba signed a one-year trade agreement providing for Chinese shipments to Cuba of 134,000 tons of food, machinery, and medicine in exchange for 1,120,000 tons of sugar, nickel, copper, tobacco and canned fruits.

Red China Tallies U.S. "Intrusions." On April 27, Peking said: "During the past 15 months of the Kennedy Administration the record of United States intrusions into China's territorial waters and airspace is 52 warships on 40 occasions and 64 sorties by United States aircraft. The criminal violation of China's sovereignty by United States imperialism has further laid bare the piratical nature of the Kennedy Administration." It was "more obsessed and malignant" than the Eisenhower Administration in "pursuing an aggressive policy which is stubbornly hostile to the Chinese people."

Pathet Lao Attacks. On May 3, the Communist Pathet Lao launched an offensive in northwestern Laos, utilizing about four battalions with support from two battalions of North Vietnamese troops. On May 6, the Pathet Lao captured Nam Tha, the northwestern provincial capital; on May 12, the commander in chief of the Royal Laotian Army fled across the Mekong River into Thailand with 2,000 troops and seven U.S. military advisers after the fall of Houei Sai, last government stronghold in the northwest.

Washington Critical. On May 6, the *New York Times* reported that President Kennedy and his advisers felt the

Laotian government had provoked the Pathet Lao attacks by reinforcing the Nam Tha area against the advice of American officials and despite the warnings of Communist leaders. On May 7, State Department press officer Lincoln White said the U.S. and Britain had "been in consultation" and had begun "an immediate effort to have the cease-fire re-established."

Kennedy's Assessment. On May 9, President Kennedy said at a news conference: "The longer this rather frayed cease-fire (in Laos) continues, the more chance we will have of the kind of incidents we have had in the past few days. That is why we were hopeful, after the meetings at Geneva last summer and fall, that the negotiations between the parties involved would take place last fall, and we could organize a government, rather than trying to continue to hold lines which in some cases are exposed, and which are subject to this kind of pressure....

"We are hopeful that we can bring about a restoration of the cease-fire. But we have got to use the time to try to move ahead in our political negotiations. I agree it is a very hazardous course, but introducing American forces, which is the other one...that also is a hazardous course, and we want to attempt to see if we can work out a peaceful solution, which has been our object for many months. I believe that these negotiations should take place quickly. This is not a satisfactory situation today."

Troops to Thailand. On May 15, President Kennedy ordered an immediate buildup of U.S. troops in Thailand to a total of 5,000 and said the move was "considered desirable because of recent attacks in Laos by Communist forces, and the subsequent movement of Communist military units toward the border of Thailand." Mr. Kennedy said "these forces are to help insure the territorial integrity of this peaceful country." He emphasized that "this is a defensive act."

Prior to the President's order, 1,000 troops were in Thailand -- retained there after recent maneuvers by SEATO forces. On May 16, U.S. jet bombers landed in Bangkok to spearhead ground and air forces, and on May 17, a task force of 1,800 Marines arrived. On May 10, a carrier task force of the U.S. Seventh Fleet had been ordered into the Gulf of Siam, off Thailand and Cambodia.

On May 17, the President told a news conference: "We are going into Thailand at the decision of the Thai government, our own decision to provide for the defense of Thailand. The latest information indicated no further breach of the cease-fire. We also have indications that the three princes (representing the rightist, leftist, and neutralist factions) will engage in a conversation shortly. I hope they will produce a government. That is our object. I have always indicated the great hazards of a shooting war in Asia, in the jungles of Asia. It is our object to bring about a diplomatic solution which will make the chances of such a war far less likely."

On the same day, British Prime Minister Harold Macmillan told the House of Commons that Britain was willing to send military aircraft to Thailand if requested.

Khrushchev's Reaction. On May 18, Soviet Premier Khrushchev called the U.S. military action in Thailand "imprudent." He said: "President Kennedy has sent his troops into Thailand, but that will avail him nothing. The Americans will not be able to hold (South) Viet Nam and Laos because they are only uniting themselves with the feudal lords. The French fought nine years in Viet Nam and were kicked out. The Americans may fight 15 years if they want to, but it will not help."

Rusk's Reply. On the same day, Secretary of State Dean Rusk replied: "If Moscow and other Communist capitals would agree to leave those countries alone, the matter could be solved very quickly. And perhaps we could get out before 15 years."

What Peking Said. On May 19, the Peking radio said: "China can absolutely not permit the establishment of a new military bridgehead aimed against her in an area near the Chinese border." The broadcast accused the U.S. of attemptint to turn the Laotian civil war into an all-out conflict to subjugate all of Southeast Asia.

Kennedy on Food for China. On May 23, President Kennedy, questioned on the prospects of a Food for Peace program for mainland China, commented: "There has been no indication of any expression of interest or desire by the Chinese Communists to receive any food from us as I have said from the beginning, and we would certainly have to have some idea as to whether the food was needed and under what conditions it might be distributed. Up to the present, we have no such indications."

Refugees From China. On May 23, President Kennedy announced that the U.S. would admit, under special provisions of the McCarran-Walter Act, "several thousand" Chinese refugees in the Hong Kong area who had been previously cleared by consular officials but could not enter the U.S. because the immigration quota for Chinese nationals was limited to 100 a year. The refugees were to be allowed to enter under the same McCarran-Walter provision as that utilized for admission of Hungarian refugees in 1956 and more recently of Cuban refugees. Preference would be given to those with technical skills in greatest demand or with family ties in the U.S. The President said that admission of some refugees to the U.S. and the continued availability of U.S. food for about half a million Hong Kong refugees would not eliminate "the basic problem which is that of a tremendous country, 650 million people, where food supplies are inadequate."

House Judiciary Immigration and Nationality Subcommittee Chairman Francis E. Walter (D Pa.) on May 24 introduced a bill (HR 11911) to implement the President's plan. It was estimated that 6,000 Chinese might enter the U.S.

The Hong Kong government had been forced to construct a barbed wire barrier to keep additional refugees from entering the overcrowded colony. Around 70,000 were estimated to have entered since May 1, and almost 55,000 had been returned to Communist China. Hong Kong had absorbed one and one-half million refugees since 1952. On May 21, Nationalist China offered to accept all refugees who wished to live in Formosa.

New Laotian Offensive. On May 26, the Communist-led Pathet Lao rebels launched another offensive in southern and northwestern Laos, in what was described by U.S. military advisers as a "concentrated assault" led by North Vietnamese units. It was reported that loyal government forces in the northwest had been forced for the second time to flee into Thailand. In Washington the same day, Kennedy Administration spokesmen confirmed reports that American officials had reproached Laotian government leaders for refusing to negotiate with the Pathet Lao and the neutralist faction on formation of a coalition government, for supplying Nam Tha despite warnings from both the U.S. and the Pathet Lao, and for neglecting the serious military situation.

Harriman on Refugees. On May 29, Assistant Secretary of State for Far Eastern Affairs W. Averell Harriman testified before the House Judiciary Immigration and Nationality Sub-committee that beginning about May 1 the number of Chinese refugees entering Hong Kong had "increased spectacularly." Harriman pointed out that the flow had been going on since 1948 and there were one million Chinese refugees in Hong Kong's population of three million. He said U.S. voluntary agencies in Hong Kong had distributed food, clothing and health supplies to refugees. He noted also that the U.S. was working "as rapidly as possible" to bring in several thousand refugees to help relieve the overcrowded situation in Hong Kong and "would consider sympathetically" requests to help other countries to take in refugees.

Harriman added that the heavy flow of refugees, currently halted by China, resulted from "the cumulative result of 12 years of Communist rule," rather than a sudden worsening in conditions. He said the heavy flow had probably been halted because Communist authorities "could not stand the escape of so many people displeased with conditions in the people's paradise." On the same day, the British Foreign Office reported it had been informed by the Chinese Communist Foreign Affairs Ministry that there would be a quick termination of the flow of refugees into Hong Kong.

Sino-Indian Dispute. On May 31, India protested to China that proposed negotiations between China and Pakistan over the Kashmir border formed a part of China's "aggressive designs" against Indian territory. India asserted that Pakistan had no right to negotiate a Kashmir border agreement because Kashmir belonged to India. The Chinese replied that India was pursuing a policy of "out-and-out power chauvinism." On June 2, India announced it would not renew its trade agreement with Tibet because of China's refusal to discuss Indian-Tibetan border problems.

Call to Admit More Refugees. On June 7, the Emergency Committee for Chinese Refugees, an ad hoc group formed to bring the situation of the Chinese refugees in Hong Kong "to the attention of the American people and the peoples of other free nations, and, by that token, to stimulate specific action," called for "immediate Congressional adoption" of S 3403, a bill providing for an increase in the number of Chinese refugees to be admitted annually to the U.S. from 105 to 5,335. Formation of the Committee was announced by Supreme Court Justice William O. Douglas, news commentator Lowell Thomas, Rep. Walter H. Judd (R Minn.), and Sens. Paul H. Douglas (D Ill.) and John G. Tower (R Texas).

Denunciation of U.S. On June 10, at a banquet in Peking honoring Gen. Kong Le, head of the Laotian neutralist armed forces, Chinese Communist Deputy Premier Ho Lung denounced the U.S. for attempting to turn Laos into a "base for aggression against China."

Mansfield Asks Policy Review. On June 10, Senate Majority Leader Mike Mansfield (D Mont.) called for a review of U.S. policy in Southeast Asia. He said in a speech in Michigan: "We have allies under SEATO, to be sure, but allies either unwilling or unable to assume but the smallest fraction of the burdens of the alliance." Mansfield added that although the U.S. had spent large amounts of money in the area, Laos was "in far more danger today of a collapse into ...communism" and South Viet Nam was "more rather than less dependent" on outside economic and military support.

Laotian Agreement. On June 11, Laos neutralist Prince Souvanna Phouma announced that Prince Boun Oum, the current Premier, and Prince Souphanouvong of the Pathet Lao pro-Communist guerrillas had joined him in signing an agreement establishing a coalition cabinet to rule the nation. Of the 19 cabinet appointees, 11 were neutralists, four rightists, and four Pathet Lao.

Soviet Premier Khrushchev June 12 cabled President Kennedy that the agreement was "good news" for Laos. He said it strengthened the conviction that other international problems could be resolved by "cooperation with mutual account of the interests of all sides." In a June 13 note to Khrushchev, President Kennedy said he shared the view that the agreement was "encouraging." He said "continued progress in the settlement of the Laotian problem" could be helpful in leading toward resolution of other international problems.

Kennedy on Asia Policy. On June 14, President Kennedy was asked at a news conference if a review of policy in Southeast Asia was necessary. He replied: "I know that we have put (in) large sums of money, and the situation there is still hazardous. What is true there, of course, is true all around the world. This is a period of great tension and change. But if the United States had not played a part in Southeast Asia for many years, I think the whole map of Southeast Asia would be different.... Now we have moved to a different plateau, and we are going to see whether that commitment can be maintained. But on the other hand,... withdrawal in the case of Viet Nam and in the case of Thailand might mean a collapse in the entire area."

Indian Complaint. On June 19, India accused Communist China of "daily intruding into Indian territory,...constructing new military bases and extending bases already set up." India said the Chinese had constructed "no less than five new military bases" in the Ladakh section of Kashmir since mid-1960.

Invasion Alerts. On June 20, the Chinese Communists were reported massing troops and military equipment, including aircraft, on the mainland opposite Quemoy and Matsu Islands. On the same day, White House Press Secretary Pierre Salinger admitted the Chinese build-up was causing some concern.

On June 20, the *Christian Science Monitor* reported that President Kennedy and his advisers had considered supporting Chiang Kai-shek's "desire to intervene on the Chinese mainland" but decided in the negative. The article said: "As of now, although the Chinese people are obviously hungry, and although there have been occasional food riots and disturbances, Washington does not believe that the Peking regime has lost its authority over the populace, or that its troops are incapable of putting up stern resistance to an invasion." On June 22, Chen Cheng, Nationalist Vice President and Premier, said in Taipei that the Chinese Communists had lost their control of the people and asserted there were now "brightening prospects of fighting back to the lost mainland."

On June 23, Communist China admitted its military buildup and alerted the country for an invasion from Formosa. On June 24, Under Secretary of State George W. Ball warned Communist China that it would suffer "extremely costly" consequences if it attacked any of the offshore islands. On June 25, Chinese Communist Foreign Minister Chen Yi said China was "watching vigilantly" for a "large-scale military adventure involving the invasion of the coastal areas of the mainland" by U.S. and Nationalist forces. Radio reports from the mainland indicated that the Communists had mobilized the peasants and city workers "to go into action" at any time.

New Laotian Government. On June 22, the new coalition government of Laos was formally installed. The new premier, Prince Souvanna Phouma, declared that the coalition was "resolved to follow the way of peace and neutrality in conformity with the interests...of the Laotian people." He added that it was pledged "not to permit the establishment of any foreign military bases on Laotian territory and not to permit any country to use Laotian territory for military means."

U.S. Warning to Peking. On June 27, President Kennedy told newsmen that the U.S. would "take the action necessary to assure the defense of Formosa and the Pescadores" provided for in the 1955 Congressional "Formosa resolution" if Communist China were to take "aggressive action against" Quemoy and Matsu. Kennedy said that "any threat to the offshore islands must be judged in relation to its wider meaning for the safety of Formosa and the peace of the area."

Troop Withdrawal in Thailand. On July 1, the Defense Department announced that President Kennedy had ordered withdrawal of 1,000 Marines from Thailand. On July 3, Prince Souphanouvong, leader of the pro-Communist Pathet Lao in Laos, demanded that the remainder of U.S. troops leave Thailand.

Soviet Warning to U.S. On July 2, Soviet Premier Nikita Khrushchev warned during a television broadcast from Moscow that "anyone who dares attack" Communist China "will meet a crushing rebuff from the great Chinese people, the peoples of the Soviet Union and the whole Socialist camp." He said this was "not the first time the imperialists are trying to test the power of...Soviet-Chinese friendship." On the same day, Secretary of State Dean Rusk called Khrushchev's statements "nonsense." He said the U.S., instead of being "aggressive," had urged the "abandonment of force in settling matters in the Formosan Strait."

India-China Dispute. On July 21, Communist China accused India of attacking several outposts near the Tibetan border, creating "a new and dangerous situation in the area." India immediately denied the charge and accused China of causing "incidents."

Laos Conference Ends. On July 23, the 14-nation Geneva conference on Laos, which had begun May 16, 1961, ended with the signing of an agreement to guarantee that country's neutrality and independence. The final ceremonies in Geneva were attended by Secretary of State Dean Rusk, Soviet Foreign Minister Gromyko, British Foreign Secretary Lord Home, Chinese Communist Foreign Minister Chen Yi, and representatives from Thailand, Burma, Cambodia, India, South Viet Nam, North Viet Nam, Canada, Poland, France, and Laos. President Kennedy sent a message calling the agreement "a heartening indication that difficult...international problems can in fact be solved by patient diplomacy."

Nehru on China Trouble. On Aug. 13, Indian Prime Minister Nehru said in Parliament that India was "prepared to discuss what measures should be undertaken to remove the tensions that exist" between India and Communist China. He reported that there had been a number of incidents in which Chinese troops had fired on Indian forces. "The situation remains serious...and is likely to remain serious in the future."

U-2 in North Pacific. On Sept. 2, the Soviet Union charged that a U.S. reconnaissance aircraft had flown over the Soviet island of Sakhalin in the northern Pacific. The U.S. admitted that the violation might have occurred but said it was unintentional.

Chinese-Laotian Relations. On Sept. 7, it was announced that Laos and Communist China had established diplomatic relations. Nationalist China severed relations with Laos the same day.

U-2 Over China. On Sept. 9, Communist China said that a "U.S.-made U-2 high-altitude reconnaissance plane of the Chiang Kai-shek gang was shot down this morning by an Air Force unit of the Chinese People's Liberation Army when it intruded over East China." A later statement called the flight part of "an over-all United States U-2 espionage program against Socialist countries, using Japan as the primary base."

On Sept. 10, Nationalist China admitted that one of its two U-2s was missing after a routine flight. A spokesman said that Nationalist China had been flying reconnaissance missions since December 1960 to "find out about conditions on the Communist-held China mainland." On Sept. 11, Secretary of State Rusk told a news conference that "We have not and are not flying any planes over Communist China."

India to Talk With China. On Sept. 19, India accepted an invitation from Communist China to discuss their border dispute, the talks to start Oct. 15 in Peking.

Sino-Soviet Trade Drops. On Sept. 20, the *New York Times* reported that Soviet-Chinese trade in 1961 fell almost 50 percent below the 1960 level to the lowest since 1951. "While Soviet exports to China last year declined from more than $800 million to $360 million, Chinese exports to the Soviet Union declined by only a little more than a third from $840 million to $540 million.... These figures seem to indicate that Moscow has been putting pressure on the Chinese to repay their debts to the Soviet Union."

Soviet Consulates Closed. On Sept. 26, the *New York Times* reported that the Soviet Union had closed its last two consulates in China, at Shanghai and Harbin.

Difficulties in China. On Sept. 28, the Chinese Communist Party Central Committee reported only a "slight gain" in China's agricultural and industrial production in 1962. It said: "Some of our work is not well done. For instance, because of incompetence of leading cadres, some production teams, some factories and some business establishments have produced less or have become unwelcome to (the) masses." The Committee conceded that the "transition from capitalism to communism" would last "scores of years or even longer."

Chou on China's Struggle. On Sept. 30, on the eve of the 13th anniversary of Communist rule in China, Premier Chou En-lai said at a reception in Peking that "the imperialist reactionaries of various countries and modern revisionists" had "launched anti-Chinese campaigns in an attempt to isolate China and compel China to change the just stand it takes in international affairs." But, Chou said, "their attempt is completely futile; it is they themselves...who have become more isolated."

Turning to the economy, the Chinese Premier admitted that the "Socialist construction work of the Chinese people has not been plain sailing." He pointed out that "serious natural disasters for three consecutive years, from 1959 to 1961, and shortcomings and mistakes in work have indeed caused difficulties," but he insisted that "a preliminary foundation has been laid for an independent, comprehensive and modern national economy."

Chinese National Day. On Oct. 1, Communist China celebrated its 13th National Day with an enormous parade in Peking, attended by Communist Party First Secretary Mao Tse-tung and other leaders. Foreign leaders, including Soviet leaders, were noticeably absent. Chinese Communist Foreign Minister Chen Yi told the crowd that "We are still confronted with many difficulties,...yet the most difficult period has already passed."

U.S. Out of Laos. On Oct. 5, the U.S. withdrew its remaining military advisers from Laos, one day before the deadline.

Troops to Leave. On Oct. 9, the State Department announced that the 3,000 U.S. troops remaining in Thailand would be withdrawn.

Optimism in Saigon. On Oct. 9, South Vietnamese President Ngo Dinh Diem told the opening session of the National Assembly in Saigon that the war against the Viet Cong had taken an "incontestable turn" for the better. "Everywhere," he said, "we are taking the initiative...passing to the offensive, sowing insecurity in the Communists' reputedly impregnable strongholds, smashing their units one after another."

Reserve in Washington. On the same day, Secretary of Defense Robert S. McNamara returned to Washington from Honolulu, where he had met with Admiral Harry D. Felt, the U.S. commander in the Pacific, to discuss the rising U.S. military commitment to South Viet Nam. The Secretary said it was "too early" to say whether the war had turned in favor of the South Vietnamese government.

North Vietnamese in Laos. On Oct. 10, the State Department said that North Viet Nam had violated the Geneva agreements by leaving troops in Laos past the Oct. 6 deadline. On Oct. 11, the *New York Times* reported that North Viet Nam had withdrawn some of its troops but had left in Laos a force numbering about 4,000.

Wheat to China. On Oct. 10, Australia announced it had agreed to sell 670,000 tons of wheat to Communist China.

Chinese-Indian Fighting. On Oct. 10, serious fighting broke out between Chinese Communist and Indian troops near the Indian outpost of Dhola on the northeastern frontier. At least six Indians and 22 Chinese were killed in a battle that lasted 12 hours. On Oct. 11, both countries accused the other of starting the fighting, and a Chinese note accused India of "fanning the flames of war." On Oct. 12, Indian Prime Minister Nehru said he had ordered the Indian army to push all Chinese troops out of the Indian territory near the Tibetan border.

A Chinese note Oct. 13 warned India to "pull back from the brink of the precipice." On the same day, the London *Times* reported that Peking was "in a vicious mood." On Oct. 15, Nehru said at a press conference that India would be willing to negotiate when Chinese troops were cleared from its territory. He charged China with attempting to seize territory and then negotiate.

French Sales to China. On Oct. 13, France announced it was selling surplus cereals to Communist China.

Chinese Offensive. On Oct. 20, fighting between Communist China and India intensified as the Chinese launched an offensive that drove Indian forces back in the northeast and also in the Ladakh section of Kashmir. Indian Defense Minister V. K. Krishna Menon charged that the "naked, large-scale aggression" was "premeditated and concerted and obviously undertaken after long preparation and deliberate planning." Communist China charged the same day that India had begun the hostilities.

U.S. Reaction. On Oct. 21, the State Department said the U.S. was "shocked at the violent and aggressive action of the Chinese Communists against India." It added that "our sympathy is with India as it seeks to meet this unprincipled challenge to its national authority." A State Department official said that any Indian request for aid would be "considered sympathetically."

Nehru to the Nation. On Oct. 22, Prime Minister Nehru declared in a broadcast to the Indian nation that China's "aggression" was a "menace that threatens the freedom of our people and the independence of our country." He said India would have to fight "a powerful and unscrupulous opponent" and must direct its energies and resources to the one end of strengthening itself militarily. On Oct. 23, the Peking radio and Chinese forces would continue advancing to prevent Indian troops from "staging a comeback and launching fresh attacks."

Cuban Missile Crisis. On Oct. 22, President Kennedy announced in a nationwide television and radio address that the U.S. had learned that the Soviet Union was establishing medium-range missile bases in Cuba. "To halt this offensive buildup," the President said, "a strict quarantine of all offensive military equipment under shipment to Cuba is being initiated." Kennedy warned that the U.S. would "regard any nuclear missile launched from Cuba against any nation in the Western Hemisphere as an attack by the Soviet Union on the United States requiring a full retaliatory response upon the Soviet Union."

On Oct. 23, the Soviet Union rejected Kennedy's warning and declared that aggressive action by the United States toward Cuba or its sea lanes to the Soviet Union might bring thermonuclear war. On the same day, the Organization of American States adopted a U.S.-sponsored resolution by a vote of 19-0 authorizing the use of force in blockading Soviet weapons en route to Cuba.

On the same day, Cuban Premier Fidel Castro called the blockade "a violation against the sovereign rights of our country and all the peoples" and a prelude to "direct military intervention" in Cuba. On Oct. 24, Communist China called the blockade "flagrant piracy" and urged that all Communist nations unify against "this most serious menace."

On Oct. 24, the blockade, established by a proclamation signed by President Kennedy Oct. 23, went into effect. The proclamation blamed Communist China as well as the Soviet Union for the Cuban crisis. It said that world peace and the security of the Western Hemisphere were "endangered by reason of the establishment by the Sino-Soviet powers of an offensive military capability in Cuba."

Chinese Proposal. On Oct. 24, Communist China proposed that Indian Prime Minister Nehru and Chinese Foreign Minister Chou En-lai meet to settle the border dispute between their countries. The Chinese proposal called for a cease-fire and withdrawal of the forces of both sides a distance of 12 miles from the "line of actual control," India called the offer "a deceptive device that can fool nobody." It demanded withdrawal of Chinese troops from Indian-claimed territory prior to any conference.

On Oct. 26, the Soviet Union termed China's proposal "a display of sincere concern over relations with India and a desire to end the conflict." The statement said the "imperialists dream of inciting these two great powers to quarreling and also to disrupt the friendship of the Soviet Union with fraternal China and with friendly India."

Indian Plea for Aid. On Oct. 26, India declared a state of emergency and appealed to the U.S., Britain, France and Canada for military aid. All four countries immediately responded affirmatively.

Chinese Charge. On Oct. 26, the Peking *People's Daily* said Nehru was attempting to establish an Indian sphere of influence in Asia that "would far surpass that of the colonialist system formerly set up in Asia by the British Empire."

Missile Crisis Ends. On Oct. 28, Soviet Premier Khrushchev announced that he had ordered the dismantling of Cuban missile bases and withdrawal of Soviet missiles from Cuba. President Kennedy called the action, amounting to compliance with his demands, a "statesmanlike decision" and an "important and constructive contribution to peace."

Aid for India. On Oct. 29, Indian Prime Minister Nehru made a direct appeal to the U.S. for arms and military equipment to use in the struggle with Communist China. On the same day, U.S. Ambassador to India John Kenneth Galbraith informed Nehru that the U.S. would airlift infantry weapons to India as quickly as possible and said that heavier weapons would follow if needed. On the same day, British Prime Minister Harold Macmillan told the House of Commons that Britain would be willing to supply India with any military aid needed to combat Communist China's "brutal and ruthless pressure."

China and the UN. On Oct. 30, the UN General Assembly voted 56 to 42 with 12 abstentions to reject a Soviet resolution for Communist China's admission to and Nationalist China's removal from the United Nations. U.S. Ambassador to the UN Adlai E. Stevenson had asserted Oct. 22 that China's "naked aggression" against India was proof of its "scorn" for the UN Charter. India, however, argued that Communist China should be admitted to the UN, where it would be open to the "views and discipline" of the organization.

Chinese on Cuba. On Oct. 31, the Peking *People's Daily* charged indirectly that Soviet Premier Khrushchev had surrendered to the "U.S. imperialist attempt to browbeat the people of the world into retreat at the expense of Cuba."

Indian Communists. On Nov. 1, the Indian Communist Party's National Council adopted a resolution appealing to "all sections of the Indian people to unite in defense of the motherland against Chinese aggression" and supporting Prime Minister Nehru's "stirring appeal for national unity in defense of the country."

U.S. Arms. On Nov. 3, the first planeload of U.S. small arms arrived in India. Within three days, one U.S. plane was landing every three hours.

Peking on Cuba. On Nov. 5, the Peking *People's Daily* gave "full support" to Fidel Castro's rejection of UN supervision over the withdrawal of Soviet missiles from Cuba.

Mid-Term Elections. On Nov. 6, the Democratic party retained heavy majorities in both chambers of the U.S. Congress and among the nation's Governors. Most observers believed that the Democratic victory resulted in part from President Kennedy's handling of the Cuban missile crisis.

Airlift to India Ends. On Nov. 10, the State Department announced that the arms airlift to India had been completed. Chinese troops were reported to have seized 3,000 square miles of the Ladakh territory since fighting broke out on Oct. 20 -- adding it to 12,000 square miles taken since 1957.

Chinese Assail Revisionists. On Nov. 16, the Peking *People's Daily* and other leading Chinese Communist newspapers launched a campaign against "modern revisionists," who, they said, had bowed to U.S. pressure in Cuba and thereby betrayed Marxist principles. The newspaper said it was "nonsense" that "peace had been saved" by the withdrawal of Soviet missiles from Cuba.

On Nov. 17, the *Christian Science Monitor* reported that Peking's charges had included violent personal criticism of Soviet Premier Khrushchev, although he had not been mentioned by name. "But it is no secret that Chinese Communist Party cadres have been identifying Mr. Khrushchev as a 'revisionist' at political discussions for nonparty members throughout the country."

Soviet Reply. On Nov. 18, *Pravda* condemned Khrushchev's critics within the Communist bloc for "pushing mankind toward thermonuclear war." It said the Albanian (and impliedly Chinese) leaders had undertaken "an especially shameful...and provocative campaign in connection with the crisis in the Caribbean." However, "neither bourgeois propagandists nor other falsifiers" with their "unlimited slander" could detract from Khrushchev's contribution to peace.

India Asks More Aid. On Nov. 19, Indian Prime Minister Nehru, in a letter to President Kennedy, detailed the state of India's defenses and appealed for a "massive" U.S. military aid program. On the same day, Chinese Premier Chou En-lai charged that the U.S., "overtly sending military aid to India," planned to "station a big supply mission" there. Chou asserted that such action would only enlarge the area of conflict. He urged all Afro-Asian governments to condemn "foreign intervention" in the Chinese-Indian border dispute.

Cuban Blockade Ended. On Nov. 20, President Kennedy announced that the Soviet Union had agreed to withdraw its IL-28 jet bombers from Cuban bases, and that consequently he had instructed the Secretary of Defense to "lift our naval quarantine" of Cuba.

Chinese Cease-Fire. On Nov. 21, Communist China announced it had ordered all its forces on the Indian-Chinese front to cease their firing at midnight. The announcement said: "Chinese frontier guards will withdraw to positions 20 kilometers (12.5 miles) behind the lines of actual control which existed between China and India on Nov. 7, 1959." The statement said the action was being taken to end the fighting but that China "reserves the right to fight back in self-defense" if Indian forces "continue their attacks" after midnight. The statement concluded that China was willing to negotiate "provided that the Indian government agrees to take corresponding measures." India replied that Communist China's offer was a "treacherous move" and that India would give a "positive response" when China removed its troops from the disputed territory. (See Oct. 24) On Nov. 22, India reported that fighting had ceased.

Indian Position. On Nov. 26, a statement issued by the Indian government said: "While making an apparent show of substantial withdrawals, the Chinese want to retain effective control not only of large areas of Indian territory they had acquired by force prior to Sept. 8, 1962, but also to retain control of further areas both in Ladakh and the North East Frontier Agency that they have occupied since their invasion Sept. 8 and their massive attacks on Oct. 20." The statement added that "withdrawal would leave the Chinese in control of 2,000 square miles of Indian territory they did not control last Sept. 8 in Ladakh." It concluded that if the Chinese were "really keen on a settlement," they should "accept the easier and straightforward Indian position -- restoration of the status quo prior to Sept. 8."

China-Japan Trade Agreement. On Dec. 1, Japan signed a five-year trade agreement with Communist China providing for an exchange of $50 million worth of goods during 1963.

Nehru Rejects China Offer. On Dec. 1, Indian Prime Minister Nehru formally rejected Communist China's proposal for negotiating a settlement of the border dispute between the two countries. On the same day, Communist China announced it was beginning to withdraw its troops "in accordance" with its own cease-fire proposal.

Harriman on Indian Border Trouble. On Dec. 1, Assistant Secretary of State Averell Harriman, returning to Washington from India, said at the airport: "Even if the Chinese Communists go through with the withdrawals,... the Indians look upon the problems with Red China as a long affair."

Soviet-Chinese Differences. On Dec. 3, Frol R. Kozlov, Soviet Communist Party secretary, criticized Communist China at the Rome congress of the Italian Communist Party for "seriously harming the interests" of China and India in the border war between the two countries. Kozlov denounced those who rejected the Soviet policy of peaceful coexistence as adopting "an adventurist position which has nothing to do with Marxism-Leninism." He said that "such a position, even though camouflaged with pseudo-revolutionary phrases, becomes particularly poisonous and dangerous" in the nuclear age. On Dec. 4, the Chinese representative to the congress, Chao Yi-ming, acknowledged "differences" between Chinese and Soviet members of the Communist bloc but insisted that "the nature of imperialism will not change, nor will the policy of aggression." He called the U.S. "the worst enemy of the peoples of the world."

China-Laos Agreement. On Dec. 4, Communist China announced that it had made a long-term loan to Laos for industrial construction and would build a road from China to Laos.

Nehru on Border Dispute. On Dec. 10, Prime Minister Nehru said in the Indian Parliament that India would be willing to refer its border dispute with China to the International Court of Justice if "the (Chinese) aggression is

vacated and the position as it was before Sept. 8, 1962, is restored."

Viet Nam Situation. On Dec. 12, President Kennedy, asked at a press conference for an assessment of the situation in Viet Nam, replied: The U.S. is "putting in a major effort in Viet Nam.... We have about 10 or 11 times as many men there as we had a year ago. We have had a number of casualties. We put in an awful lot of equipment.... In some phases, the military program has been quite successful. There is great difficulty, however, in fighting a guerrilla war. You need 10 to one, or 11 to one, especially in terrain as difficult as South Viet Nam. So we don't see the end of the tunnel, but I must say I don't think it is darker than it was a year ago, and in some ways lighter."

Khrushchev Objects to China's Criticism. On Dec. 12, Soviet Premier Nikita S. Khrushchev denounced the Chinese Communists for criticizing Soviet Cuban policies. It was believed to be the first time a high-ranking Soviet official had publicly assailed the Chinese position on Cuba. Addressing the Supreme Soviet in Moscow, Khrushchev said: "In what way have we retreated, one may ask. Socialist Cuba exists. Cuba remains a beacon of Marxist-Leninist ideas in the Western Hemisphere. The impact of her revolutionary example will grow. The...United States has given a pledge not to invade Cuba. The threat of thermonuclear war has been averted. Is this a retreat?"

The Soviet Premier added: "Will anybody censure the People's Republic of China because fragments of colonialism remain intact (in China)? It would be wrong to push China to any actions which she regards as untimely. If the government of the People's Republic of China tolerates Macao and Hong Kong, there must be weighty reasons for this. It would be ridiculous to use this for an accusation that they are making a concession to the British and Portugese colonialists, that this is appeasement." Khrushchev warned that the world was living above a "mined cellar full of nuclear weapons" and that those who brand imperialism as a "paper tiger" (as had the Chinese Communists) should remember that "the paper tiger has nuclear teeth."

Colombo Peace Effort. On Dec. 12, a conference of six neutral nations -- Ceylon, Burma, Cambodia, Ghana, Indonesia and the United Arab Republic -- which had met in Colombo, Ceylon, to try to settle the Indian-Chinese border dispute, announced agreement on proposals to bring the two nations together for "negotiations to consolidate the cease-fire and settle the boundary dispute between them." The conference statement said that Ceylon's Prime Minister, Mrs. Sirimavo Bandaranaike, would travel to Peking and New Delhi to present the proposals.

Prime Minister Nehru told the Indian Parliament Dec. 12 that India could give "no guarantee" to support the cease-fire indefinitely. "That," he said, "depends on the circumstances. For the present we are accepting the cease-fire, but it all depends on what the Chinese may or may not do in the future." On Dec. 13, Nehru said India was disappointed with the Colombo Conference because it neither condemned nor even mentioned Chinese aggression. "What is obvious to us," Nehru said, "does not seem obvious to the rest of the world."

Tito in Russia. On Dec. 13, Yugoslav President Tito, in the Soviet Union on a "holiday," told the Supreme Soviet in Moscow that during the Cuban crisis Soviet Premier Khrushchev had acted "bravely at the most critical moment, taking into account the interests of all humanity and showing the farsightedness of real statesmen." Referring to Chinese criticism of Soviet Cuban policy, Tito stated: "Unfortunately there are strange views about this policy...which are dangerous, as they might lead certain circles to a false assessment of the motive for this wise and peace-loving action. I think that it is shortsightedness to consider these actions as a sign of weakness."

China Accuses Soviet Leaders. On Dec. 15, an article in the Peking *People's Daily*, reportedly written by Mao Tse-tung, proposed a meeting of the world's Communist parties "to clarify what is right from what is wrong, to strengthen unity and to stand together against the enemy." The article said the Soviet Union had been "scared out of its wits" during the Cuban missile crisis. Soviet leaders were denounced for neutralism in the Chinese-Indian border dispute and for recent friendly relations with the "Tito clique" in Yugoslavia.

The article further accused the Soviet Union of following a policy of "moderation" and making "sensible compromises" with the "saber-rattling enemy" while refusing "to be conciliatory toward fraternal parties and fraternal countries." It declared that "No matter how the imperialists, the reactionaries and the modern revisionists may abuse and oppose us, our stand in upholding Marxism-Leninism and truth is absolutely unshakable."

Opinion of French Reds. On Dec. 19, the General Secretary of the French Communist Party was quoted in *Pravda*: "Chinese comrades, not to speak of Albanians, have...never believed in peaceful coexistence, in the systematic struggle for peace, in the policy leading to disarmament."

"Paper Tigers." On Dec. 19, a member of the Chinese Communist Party Central Committee said in a speech in Peking that the U.S. was the "most vicious enemy of world peace" and that the struggles fought "by the peoples of the whole world prove that imperialism and reactionaries are all paper tigers, which are outwardly strong but inwardly weak."

Chinese Expansionist Ambitions. On Dec. 21, the *India News*, published by the Indian Embassy in Washington, printed a map and text from a Chinese history textbook which claimed as rightfully belonging to China vast stretches of the Soviet Union and all of Nepal, Bhutan, Sikkim, Burma, Thailand, North and South Viet Nam, Laos, Cambodia, Malaya, Singapore, Formosa, North and South Korea, the disputed Indian territories, Sakhalin, the Andaman Islands, the Pescadores Islands, and the Ryukyu Islands.

Chinese-Mongolian Treaty. On Dec. 25, after signing a border agreement with Communist China, the Premier of Outer Mongolia, Yumzhagiin Tsedenbal, said at a banquet in Peking that international disagreements should be solved "exclusively by peaceful means and negotiations." He urged the "continuous consolidation of the unity and solidarity of the Socialist camp, the guarantee for safeguarding world peace and preventing world thermonuclear war." The following day, the *New York Times* noted: "Diplomatic observers described the speech as a forceful affirmation of Outer Mongolia's support for Moscow."

Pakistan-China Agreement. On Dec. 26, Communist China and Pakistan announced "complete agreement in

principle in regard to the alignment of the common border of the China-Sinkiang contiguous area, the defense of which is the responsibility of Pakistan."

Wheat Agreement. On Dec. 28, Australia announced it would sell 50 million bushels more of wheat to Communist China. The following day, the *Washington Post* reported: "The sale would bring total Australian wheat sales to Communist China since December 1960 to about 190 million bushels -- 45 bushels for cash and the balance on terms."

Nationalist Guerrilla Action. On Dec. 31, the Peking radio announced that nine groups of Nationalist Chinese guerrillas had raided the Chinese mainland since October, but that all of them had been exterminated. The broadcast asserted that the guerrillas had operated "under the direct planning and organization of U.S. espionage organizations." On the same day, Nationalist China admitted there had been guerrilla raids, supported by U.S. arms, but insisted that American personnel had not been involved.

Chinese Views. On Dec. 31, the Peking *People's Daily* published a long article in answer to Soviet Premier Khrushchev's Dec. 12 speech to the Supreme Soviet. The article said that peaceful coexistence between socialist and capitalist countries was "inconceivable without struggle," that thermonuclear war "would result in the extinction of imperialism and definitely not in the extinction of mankind," and that disarmament would be possible only when "socialist nations" had "great nuclear superiority."

1963

Sino-Soviet Ideological Feud -- Acceptance of Colombo Proposals for Settling India-China Border Dispute -- Chinese Trade with West -- Fighting in Laos -- Anti-Chinese Riots in Indonesia -- Lodge Appointed Ambassador to South Viet Nam -- Buddhist Demonstrations -- Nuclear Test-Ban Treaty and China's Reaction -- Kennedy on China Threat -- Chinese Denunciation of Khrushchev -- Mme. Nhu on the Buddhist Bonzes -- China and Soviet Nuclear Aid -- Action Against Buddhists -- Mao on Viet Nam -- Kennedy: "It's Their War" -- Peking's Charges of Soviet Subversion in Sinkiang -- Moscow's Charges of Chinese Border Violations -- McNamara-Taylor on Duration of Viet Nam War -- Overthrow and Death of Diem -- Assassination of President Kennedy -- Hilsman Speech on U.S. China Policy.

Chinese on "Revisionism." On Jan. 1, the Chinese Communist Party's theoretical journal, *Red Flag*, published four articles denouncing "modern revisionism" and pledging that Communist China will "incessantly expose the shameful behavior of modern revisionists who have betrayed Marxism-Leninism."

Khrushchev on Communist Differences. On Jan. 1, Soviet Premier Nikita S. Khrushchev said at a New Year's reception in Moscow: "The people in the capitalist world see differences in the socialist camp, but get married and you will see there are differences between husband and wife."

Viet Nam Casualties. On Jan. 2, five U.S. helicopters transporting South Vietnamese troops in the Mekong River delta area were shot down by Viet Cong gunfire. Fourteen of the 15 helicopters involved in the mission were hit by ground fire. Three American military advisers were killed and 10 wounded, bringing the total of U.S. deaths in Viet Nam to 49.

Soviet Reply to China. On Jan. 7, the Soviet Communist Party newspaper, *Pravda*, published a long article replying to attacks by Communist China. It said that China's continued criticisms of Soviet policies might lead to "fragmentation of the international Communist movement," but that "all conditions are present for successfully overcoming these differences." The article contended that the "home made thesis of the 'paper tiger'...is an underestimation of the forces of imperialism," and that what was needed was a "genuine analysis of contemporary imperialism: disclosure of its vices, weaknesses,...and at the same time a sober assessment of its forces, including the huge atomic and other military potential."

Communist Feud: Soviet Round. On Jan. 15, Chinese and Soviet differences surfaced at the sixth congress of the East German Communist Party in East Berlin. The congress was attended by 70 delegations from national Communist parties, most of whom sided with Soviet Premier Khrushchev. Walter Ulbricht, First Secretary of the East German Communist Party, denounced Communist China for "unleashing" the "highly unnecessary" India-China border war without consulting or informing the other Communist countries.

Soviet Premier Khrushchev told the congress, Jan. 16, that a thermonuclear war would destroy the capitalist and socialist worlds alike. He said the "first blow alone" would kill "700 to 800 million people," wipe out "all the big cities," and the consequences would be felt "through many generations, causing disease and death and monstrously deformed human beings." Khrushchev concluded by defending his actions during the Cuban crisis: "It is true that we made a concession, but it was in reply to a concession by the other side" when President Kennedy undertook "an obligation before the whole world" that the U.S. would not invade Cuba.

Communist Feud: Chinese Round. On Jan. 18, the head of the Chinese delegation in East Berlin, Wu Hsiu-chuan, presented Communist China's reply to Khrushchev. According to Jack Altman of *Reuters*, the only Western newsman allowed to cover the congress, Wu was humiliated by other delegates who periodically silenced him by whistling, shouting, and stamping their feet. Despite the commotion, Wu made the following points:

"More and more people in the world have come to realize that U.S. imperialism is...the most ferocious enemy of world peace."

"The Chinese Communist Party and the Chinese government have always stood for peaceful coexistence."

"China has consistently sought a fair and reasonable solution of the Indian border dispute through peaceful negotiation.... Confronted with the massive attacks of the Indian troops, China struck back in self-defense.... Having repulsed the attacks of the Indian forces, China...on her own initiative ceased fire and withdrew her troops."

Wu concluded that there should be an immediate world Communist meeting. There was "danger of a split" if it did not occur.

China Accepts Colombo Proposals. On Jan. 21, Chinese Communist Foreign Minister Chen Yi announced that China would accept the Colombo Conference proposals for settlement of the India-China border dispute "in principle," although it would want to discuss revision of a few points. The proposals, made public Jan. 19, said: (1) India would maintain its present military position in Ladakh, but would not reoccupy territory captured by Chinese Communist forces, which must withdraw 12.5 miles; (2) until there was a final solution, the vacated area would be demilitarized; (3) in the eastern sector, the boundary recognized by both governments would serve as a cease-fire line; and (4) in the middle area, the dispute would have to be solved by peaceful means.

India Accepts. On Jan. 23, Indian Prime Minister Nehru told the Parliament, amidst cries of "appeasement," that India had accepted the Colombo proposals. "The Chinese government," he said, "maintains certain points of their own interpretation of the Colombo proposals. This obviously means that they have not accepted the Colombo proposals as a whole. We on our part are...clear that there can be no talks...to settle the points left for decision by direct discussions between the governments of India and China...unless the government of China accepts in toto the Colombo Conference proposals and their clarifications." Nehru said the proposals "in essence meet our demand that the status quo before Sept. 8 (1962) be restored before talks with China can take place." On Jan. 25, Parliament approved Nehru's action by defeating an opposition resolution 249-59.

Khrushchev's "Happy Family." On Feb. 8, in an interview with Canadian newspaper publisher Roy Thomson, Soviet Premier Khrushchev dismissed Thomson's theory that some day "the Soviet Union, Britain, and America are going to be one happy family opposed to the Chinese Communists." Khrushchev said: "That day will not come. We shall always be friends with the Chinese, and there will come a time when the workers class in Britain and the United States and other countries is victorious. Then we will indeed have one happy family the world over."

Khrushchev's Affection. On Feb. 15, Soviet Premier Nikita Khrushchev, at a Moscow reception given by the King of Laos, embraced Communist China's Ambassador to the U.S.S.R., Pan Tzu-li, and said: "When the last spadeful of earth is thrown on the grave of capitalism, we will throw it with China." Khrushchev added that the two countries were bound in "brotherhood and friendship." The *Washington Post* noted that Khrushchev made the remarks before Western correspondents. "It appeared he wanted the news spread only in the West, for such informal remarks are never reported in the Communist press."

U.S.-Chinese Meetings. On Feb. 20, the Chinese Communist and U.S. Ambassadors to Poland met, in Warsaw, for the 116th time since the talks began at Geneva in 1955.

Laotian Leaders in U.S. On Feb. 21, the King of Laos, Savang Vathana, Premier Souvanna Phouma, and three cabinet ministers arrived in the U.S. They later called on President Kennedy in Washington, who said: "You can count on the friendship...and the determination of the United States to assist you and your countrymen in maintaining your independence."

Soviet Note to Mao. On Feb. 23, the Soviet Communist Party's Central Committee asserted in a letter to Chairman Mao Tse-tung of the Chinese Communist Party that "open, continually exacerbating polemics (were) shaking the unity of the fraternal parties" and that negotiations should establish "a favorable climate" for convening a world Communist conference. The note continued that the "serious differences in the international Communist movement on a series of important questions of principles" were caused by different conditions in the Communist countries.

Viet Nam Report. On Feb. 24, a report on U.S. aid to Southeast Asia, requested by President Kennedy in 1962, was submitted to the Senate Foreign Relations Committee by a four-man panel headed by Senate Majority Leader Mike Mansfield (D Mont.). The report concluded that "there is no interest of the United States in Viet Nam which would justify, in present circumstances, the conversion of the war...primarily into an American war to be fought primarily with American lives." Mansfield noted that the report concentrated on Viet Nam because of the large effort exerted there by the U.S. ($400 million in annual aid and a commitment of 12,000 troops "on dangerous assignment").

The panel recommended that the U.S. conduct a thorough reassessment of its "over-all security requirement on the Southeast Asia mainland" aimed at a reduction in the aid programs, although "extreme caution" should be used. "If the attempt is made to alter the programs via a Congressional meat-ax cut,...it runs the risk of not merely removing the fat but of leaving a gap which will lay open the region to massive chaos and, hence, jeopardize the present Pacific structure of our national security."

"Although not intended for combat," the report pointed out, U.S. troops "have been in combat. More than 50 men have lost their lives -- about one-half in battle -- in Viet Nam" since "the program of intensified assistance" was initiated in 1961. The "intensification (of U.S. assistance) has carried us to the start of the road which leads to the point at which the conflict could become of greater concern and...responsibility to the U.S. than it is to the government and people of South Viet Nam."

Sen. Mansfield, who had visited Viet Nam in 1955, added: "What is most disturbing is that Viet Nam now appears to be as it was then, only at the beginning of coping with its grave inner problems. All of the current difficulties existed in 1955, along with the hope and energy to meet them. But it is seven years later and two billion dollars of U.S. aid later. Yet, substantially the same difficulties remain, if, indeed they have not been compounded."

New Chinese Attack on Soviets. On Feb. 27, Communist China gave a new twist to its attacks on the Soviet bloc. The *People's Daily* accused the Soviet Union of "disregarding international practice" by "perfidiously and unilaterally" tearing up "hundreds of agreements and contracts they had concluded with a fraternal country (China)."

Russia Ready to Aid All Reds. On Feb. 27, Soviet Premier Khrushchev said the Soviet Union desired to live in "peace and friendship with all peoples," but, he added, "if an attack is made on Cuba or on the People's Republic of China, which is being threatened from Taiwan," or on North Korea, North Viet Nam, East Germany, "or indeed any Socialist country, the Soviet Union will come to the assistance of its friends and strike a devastating blow at the aggressors."

Chinese-Pakistani Agreement. On March 2, the foreign ministers of Pakistan and China signed an agreement defining the 300-mile boundary between China's Sinkiang Province and the section of Kashmir controlled by Pakistan

but claimed by India. India immediately protested the agreement.

Chou's Letter to Nehru. On March 3, Chinese Communist Premier Chou En-lai sent a letter to Indian Prime Minister Nehru urging negotiations concerning the border dispute. He said Chinese forces had withdrawn from contested areas and pledged that the border would not become tense again "provided that the Indian side refrains from provocations...and from re-entering the demilitarized zone."

Poison Gas Charge. On March 9, the Peking radio charged that U.S. "interventionists" in South Viet Nam were using "asphyxiation gases" and "noxious chemicals... to poison innocent South Vietnamese people and devastate crops." The broadcast said the Chinese Red Cross had protested use of "chemical poisons by U.S. imperialism to murder civilians and destroy crops in South Viet Nam." On the same day, the State Department replied: "We have never used poison gas in South Viet Nam, and there is no truth in Communist reports that we are using it now." The statement explained that the chemicals used were "nontoxic to humans and animals when used in the prescribed manner, that is, sprayed on trees and underbrush in the open air."

Nehru's Letter to Chou. On March 10, Indian Prime Minister Nehru replied to Chinese Communist Foreign Minister Chou En-lai's request for immediate talks on the border dispute. Nehru said India accepted "without reservations" the proposals of the Colombo Conference and charged that Communist China did not.

Peking Invitation to Khrushchev. On March 10, Communist China disclosed that it had sent a note to the Soviet Union in reply to its request for bilateral talks "on important questions concerning the international Communist movement at present." The Chinese note invited Soviet Premier Khrushchev to visit Peking on his way to Cambodia for a scheduled state visit. (See Feb. 23)

Chinese Trade With West On March 14, the West German Chamber of Commerce announced that a Chinese trade delegation was negotiating with two West German steel and engineering concerns. The statement said Communist China had been seeking contracts with the West since the Soviet Union had withdrawn its technicians from China.

The Peking *People's Daily* had admitted at the beginning of 1963 that industrial output and agricultural production "still remain low and we are confronted with a good many difficulties." The newspaper said that despite a "normal to good" harvest in 1962, the poor harvests of the three previous years meant that agricultural output "still cannot meet the demands of national construction and people's living standards."

In a later article, the *People's Daily* quoted Communications Minister Wang Shao Tao as saying: "The weak spot now is the transport from the townships to the main railroad and road transport stations, harbors, and county administrative centers"; because of "poor communications" and "weak transport services in hilly regions," there was "still a large amount of food grains, edible oil crops and local products that have accumulated for years in a number of important food grain and economic crop-producing regions, while needed materials have not been moved in."

On March 21, a Chinese trade delegation arrived in London for a three-week visit at the invitation of the British government. On the same day, the London *Times* reported: "Chinese trade with the Soviet Union and eastern Europe has fallen sharply in the last three years, partly owing to political differences and partly to bad harvests in China, which have seriously affected Chinese industrial plans. This will mean a switch of Chinese trade to Japan and western Europe."

South Viet Nam vs. Mansfield. On March 24, a group of members of the South Vietnamese National Assembly considered close political allies of President Ngo Dinh Diem's regime denounced the Feb. 24 report of Sen. Mike Mansfield (D Mont.) to the Senate Foreign Relations Committee. They said: "The democracy which is being established in Viet Nam, in spite of all the handicaps of...war, is of the most authentic form.... Any doubt or contention in this regard...(is) unfounded (and) a serious insult" to South Viet Nam's government.

Soviet Invitation. On March 30, the Soviet Communist Party's Central Committee sent a letter to the Central Committee of the Chinese Communist Party turning down China's March 10 invitation to Khrushchev but proposing a high-level meeting between the two countries in Moscow around May 15. The letter reviewed the Soviet position in the current ideological dispute. (*See May 9*)

Laotian Fighting. On March 30, sporadic fighting broke out in Laos between Communist Pathet Lao forces and those of neutralist Gen. Kong Le, a supporter of the coalition government headed by Premier Souvanna Phouma. Kong Le charged that the Pathet Lao forces were "foreign lackeys" attempting "to make...Laos a new kind of colony of international communism." He said: "Foreigners who are the bosses" of the Pathet Lao were "stealthily sending soldiers, weapons, and war equipment" to Laos. He intimated that North Viet Nam's propaganda had caused the hostilities and was "designed to conceal their tricks to bring foreign forces into Laos territory." On April 8, the State Department demanded that "the co-chairmen of the Geneva accords and the International Control Commission...take prompt and effective action to stop the fighting which had been instigated by the pro-Communist Pathet Lao and to insure that the cease-fire is restored."

Foreign Minister of Laos Slain. On April 1, the Foreign Minister of Laos, Quinim Pholsena, was assassinated by one of his own guards, who said later that the Foreign Minister, who had close connections with the Pathet Lao, had wanted "to overthrow the coalition government." On the next day, a Laotian government statement signed by Deputy Premier Souphanouvong and broadcast over a radio station operated by the Pathet Lao asserted that the U.S. had been responsible for the Foreign Minister's death. The statement urged "instilling in the people of Laos a hatred of the United States."

Prisoner Exchange. On April 2, the Chinese Communist Foreign Ministry announced that all 3,213 Indian soldiers captured during the Chinese-Indian border conflict would be released beginning April 11. The Indian government reciprocated on April 14, returning 800 Chinese troops.

Chinese Visit Indonesia. On April 11, Communist China's President (Chairman of the Republic) Liu Shao-chi and Foreign Minister Chen Yi left Peking for a goodwill tour of Southeast Asia. It was Liu's first visit to non-Communist nations. On April 12, they arrived in Indonesia and were greeted by President Sukarno as "comrades in arms." Sukarno pledged Indonesian support of Red China's "just struggle to liberate Taiwan" and to attain its "legitimate rights" in the United Nations.

Rusk on Viet Nam. On April 13, Secretary of State Dean Rusk, interviewed in Washington, warned that the U.S. would have to make "some very serious and possibly harsh decisions" concerning South Viet Nam if the Communist Viet Cong escalated their activities or if the war "drags on unduly." Rusk added that the Administration had "been encouraged by what has been happening in the last several months" and felt that "an important corner had been turned" in the conflict. It was reported April 11 that more U.S. troops were being sent to reinforce the 12,000 Americans already in South Viet Nam.

Diem's Plea to Viet Cong. On April 17, South Vietnamese President Ngo Dinh Diem urged the Viet Cong during a radio address to "return and uphold the just cause of the fatherland and to contribute their efforts along with those of all our people in order to build...a new society... where every citizen will be able to develop totally and in full freedom."

Liu in Burma. On April 20, Chinese Communist President Liu Shao-chi arrived in Burma and in a joint statement with Burmese leaders called for the termination of "outside interference" in Laos.

Sino-Soviet Trade Agreement. On April 20, the Soviet Union and Communist China signed a trade agreement for 1963. The values and quantities involved were not disclosed.

Cease-Fire in Laos. On April 21, Laotian Premier Souvanna Phouma announced that a cease-fire had been arranged between the neutralist and Communist Pathet Lao forces. In the last days of fighting, the Pathet Lao troops had successfully dislodged the neutralists from most of their outposts in the Plaine des Jarres.

Kennedy on Laos. On April 24, President Kennedy said at a news conference that "if Laos fell into Communist hands it would increase the danger along the northern frontiers of Thailand,...would put additional pressure on Cambodia, and would put additional pressure on South Viet Nam, which in itself would put additional pressure on Malaya." The President said he accepted "the view that there is an inter-relationship in these countries and that is one of the reasons why we are concerned with maintaining the Geneva accords as a method of maintaining stability in Southeast Asia."

The President announced that he was sending Under-Secretary of State Averell Harriman to Moscow to discuss the situation in Laos with Soviet leaders. While "the threat to the security of the independent countries of...Southeast Asia" had been "made quite clear by the Chinese," Kennedy said, the Soviet Union had "assumed in the past a special responsibility for the maintenance of a neutral and independent Laos."

Soviet Action. On April 26, the Soviet Union, after a three-hour meeting between Soviet Premier Khrushchev and Under Secretary of State Averell Harriman, announced that it joined the U.S. in support of the 1962 Geneva accords for a neutral and independent Laos.

Liu in Cambodia. On April 27, Chinese Communist President Liu Shao-chi met with Cambodian leaders and in a joint statement pledged China's support for Cambodia's "fight against foreign imperialism." The statement referred to Cambodia's border disputes with Thailand and South Viet Nam.

Liu in North Viet Nam. On May 6, President Liu arrived in North Viet Nam. He told a student audience at the Marxist Institute in Hanoi that "to smash the attacks of modern revisionists, we should first of all seek instruction from Marx, Lenin, and Stalin." Liu added: "An acute struggle between Marxist-Leninists is going on on a worldwide scale over a series of important problems of principle. The polemics are centered on whether the people of the world should carry out revolutions or not, and whether proletarian parties should lead the world's people in revolutions or not." Liu accused "modern revisionists" of "trying their utmost to benumb the revolutionary will of the working class and tamper with the essential contents of socialism and communism as strictly defined by Marxism-Leninism, in an attempt to restore or preserve capitalism."

On May 16, President Liu and North Vietnamese President Ho Chi Minh issued a joint statement denouncing "revisionism, in other words rightist opportunism" as "the principal danger inside the international Communist movement." The statement urged bolstering of the "national defense might of the countries in the socialist camp, including development of a nuclear superiority in the socialist countries," and reaffirmed "the necessity of calling a meeting of representatives of Communist and workers' parties of the whole world to eliminate differences and strengthen unity."

Kennedy on Viet Nam. On May 8, President Kennedy was asked during a press conference why the U.S. had committed itself militarily in Viet Nam, but not in Laos. The President replied: "Because the situations are different; that is why the remedy has been different. We have had a commitment for a good many years to the integrity of South Viet Nam. We are anxious to maintain the neutrality of Laos. It may not be possible to do so, and it may be necessary to seek other remedies, but we have adopted what we consider to be, considering the geography, the history, the nature of the threat, and the ultimate solutions, we have adopted for each country what we regarded as the best strategy, and we will have to wait and see what happens on them."

Buddhist Demonstrations. On May 8, anniversary of the Viet Minh victory over the French in 1954 at Dienbienphu, 9,000 Buddhists demonstrated in the South Vietnamese city of Hue. Troops and police dispersed the demonstrators, and in the process nine people were killed. The demonstrations were to protest an order by South Vietnamese President Ngo Dinh Diem (a Roman Catholic) forbidding Buddhists to display religious signs or parade on the birthday of Buddha (May 8).

On May 15, Buddhist leaders, in a meeting with President Diem, demanded withdrawal of the controversial order, cessation of actions aimed to terrorize Buddhists, and punishment of officials responsible for the death of the nine demonstrators. The last demand was satisfied when the government replaced three officials in Hue, but Buddhist leaders said the demonstrations would continue until all the demands were met.

Chinese Accept Bid to Moscow. On May 9, Chinese Communist Premier Chou En-lai informed the Soviet Ambassador that the Central Committee of the Chinese Communist Party had accepted the March 30 invitation of the Central Committee of the Soviet Communist Party to send a delegation to Moscow to discuss the ideological dispute. The Chinese delegation was to be headed by Teng Hsiao-ping, general secretary of the Central Committee of the party, and Peng Chen, a member of the Presidium of the Central Committee. On May 10, the Peking *People's Daily* attacked the policies of Yugoslavia and the Soviet Union, which it described as "peaceable coexistence and active cooperation" with the West.

Anti-Chinese Riots in Indonesia. On May 10, anti-Chinese riots broke out in Indonesia and continued through the week. Rioters looted, burned and destroyed Chinese shops and homes. On May 17, President Sukarno ordered restrictions on political meetings and imposed a curfew in Bogor, where there had been serious rioting. On May 18, the Indonesian Provisional People's Congress appointed Sukarno as President of Indonesia for life. On May 19, Nationalist China protested the riots and on May 23 Communist China announced it had demanded "effective safeguarding" of Indonesia's Chinese and their property.

Kennedy on Troops in Viet Nam. On May 22, President Kennedy was asked during a news conference to comment on a statement by the brother of South Vietnamese President Ngo Dinh Diem that there were too many American troops in South Viet Nam. The President replied: "Yes, I hope we could...withdraw troops, any number of troops, any time the government of South Viet Nam would suggest it. The day after it was suggested we would have some troops on their way home. That is number one. Number two is we are hopeful that the situation in South Viet Nam would permit some withdrawal in any case by the end of the year, but we can't possibly make that judgment at the present time. There is still a long hard struggle to go."

Appeal to Stop Fighting in Laos. On May 23, the International Control Commission on Laos asked the Soviet Union and Great Britain, co-chairmen of the 1962 Geneva conference, to urge the Pathet Lao and neutralist factions in Laos to cease their fighting, which had broken out again on May 14 in the Plaine des Jarres. On May 29, the U.S.S.R. and Britain responded with an appeal to the two factions to end the hostilities and effect "peace, concord, and strict neutrality."

Aid to India. On May 24, an Indian delegation in Washington announced, after a meeting with President Kennedy, that the U.S. had pledged long-term military aid to India for defense against possible renewed attacks by Communist China.

Chinese Warning to India. On May 27, the Peking *People's Daily* warned India that if its forces "create new border clashes, the Indian government will again be exposed rather than gain any advantage." The newspaper said that if India attempted to regain any of the ground lost to Chinese forces, India "would again pick up a stone to drop on its own feet."

Australian Wheat. On May 31, Australia announced it had sold 46 million bushels of wheat to Communist China, bringing the total of Australian wheat purchased by China since 1960 to 263 million bushels valued at $330 million.

North Korean Visit. On June 6, the North Korean head of state, Choe Yong Kun, arrived in Communist China for a state visit. A joint statement issued later with Chinese Communist President Liu Shao-chi asserted that "both sides were completely identical in their stands and views." The statement denounced "modern revisionism" and "United States imperialism."

South Vietnamese Buddhists. On June 7, after a series of Buddhist demonstrations throughout South Viet Nam, President Ngo Dinh Diem appealed for an end to the strife and admitted that some government officials had been mistaken in their handling of the Buddhist problem.

Nuclear Tests. On June 10, President Kennedy told a commencement audience at American University in Washington, D.C., that the U.S. would not conduct nuclear tests in the atmosphere so long as other states did not do so.

Agreement With Buddhists. On June 15, the South Vietnamese government and dissident Buddhist leaders came to an agreement under which the government was to relax its restrictions on Buddhist activities. On June 17, the English-language newspaper *Times of Viet Nam* charged that "Certain agitators in the group now managing demonstrations and widely distributing...propaganda had contact with Red Chinese bonzes (monks) in 1958, supposedly centering on the tactics for using Buddhists in the Communist strategy in Viet Nam."

Earlier in the week, a Buddhist monk had protested the government's policies by burning himself to death on a Saigon street. On June 16, thousands of Buddhists attempting to attend the monk's funeral rioted, resulting in one death and scores of injuries and arrests. On June 22, the Buddhists warned that the demonstrations would continue unless the government took immediate action to implement the terms of the June 15 agreement.

Chinese Letter to Moscow. On June 16, the Chinese Communist Party's Central Committee publicized a letter sent two days earlier to the Central Committee of the Soviet Communist Party proposing 25 points for discussion at a July 5 meeting in Moscow to discuss Sino-Soviet differences. The letter criticized the Soviet Union for seeking "peaceful coexistence" while ignoring "the revolutionary struggles of the people." It said: "To make no distinction between enemies, friends and ourselves and to entrust the fate of the people and of mankind to collaboration with United States imperialism is to lead the people astray. The events of the last few years have exploded this illusion."

The Chinese asserted that "Certain persons now go so far as to deny the great international significance of anti-imperialist, revolutionary struggles of Asian, African and Latin American peoples...and to hold down those struggles." It concluded that "if the imperialists are forced to accept an agreement to ban nuclear weapons, it decidedly will not be because of their love of humanity but because of the pressure of the people of all countries and for the sake of their own vital interests."

Reaction in Moscow. On June 18, the Central Committee of the Soviet Communist Party condemned the Chinese letter and ordered the Soviet press not to print it. Leonid F. Ilyichev, a secretary of the Central Committee, reiterated Soviet Premier Khrushchev's policy of peaceful coexistence, but added: "There has never been and can never be any peaceful coexistence of ideologies. As long as

antagonistic classes exist, an irreconcilable class struggle has been, is, and will be going on."

On June 21, Khrushchev told the Central Committee that "the leaders of the Communist Party of China had exacerbated in the extreme their differences with the Communist Party of the Soviet Union and the entire Communist movement." He said that "Those who reject the principle of peaceful coexistence of states with different social systems, the principle of peaceful competition, show they do not have faith in the revolutionary strength of the working class, in the mighty power of the ideas of Marxism-Leninism."

Diplomats Ousted. On June 27, the Soviet Union demanded that Communist China recall from Moscow three of its embassy employees and two Chinese students because they had distributed copies of the Chinese Communist Party Central Committee's letter of June 14 despite a ban on its publication in the Soviet Union.

On June 29, the Chinese Foreign Ministry noted that Moscow's action was "unprecedented in the history of the relations between the two socialist countries of China and the Soviet Union." It called the expulsions "unreasonable and unfriendly" and accused the Soviet Union of "deliberately trying to undermine Sino-Soviet unity...and create obstacles to the talks between the Chinese and Soviet parties."

Lodge Appointed. On June 27, President Kennedy announced appointment of Henry Cabot Lodge Jr. as Ambassador to South Viet Nam. Lodge was to replace Frederick E. Nolting Jr.

Chinese Reprove the Russians. On July 1, the Central Committee of the Chinese Communist Party said it would send delegates to the scheduled Moscow meeting with Soviet Communist Party representatives, but it felt "compelled to point out solemnly that the series of measures taken by the Central Committee and leaders of the CPSU (Communist Party of the Soviet Union) constitute a serious step in further worsening Sino-Soviet relations and in manufacturing a split in the international Communist movement."

Soviets Explain. On July 4, the Central Committee of the Soviet Communist Party explained that the five Chinese who had been ousted from the Soviet Union had been interfering in "the internal affairs of our party." A second statement asserted that the Chinese embassy in Moscow had been warned about the unauthorized distribution of leaflets before expulsion was demanded.

Sino-Soviet Talks Begin. On July 5, the Moscow talks between representatives of Communist China and the Soviet Union began. The Soviet delegation was headed by Mikhail A. Suslov, secretary of the Central Committee, and the Chinese delegation by Teng Hsiao-ping, who held the same post in the Chinese party.

"Hot Line" Established. On July 10, it was announced in the U.S. and the Soviet Union that a "hot line" communications system had been established between the Kremlin and the White House and would go into operation on Sept.1.

Chinese Report on Moscow Meeting. On July 13, the Peking *People's Daily* reported in an editorial article that the negotiations in Moscow "have gone contrary to our hopes." Noting that the Soviet press had continually attacked the Chinese position, the editorial said: "It must be frankly pointed out that the present situation is very grave as a result of the steps taken by...the Soviet Communist Party to worsen Sino-Soviet relations. We sincerely hope that the comrades of the Soviet party will...refrain from rash actions and will not push things to the extreme.''

Soviets Blame China. On July 14, the Soviet Communist Party answered China's June 14 letter in an open letter to all members of the Soviet Communist Party. The letter, published in *Pravda*, said: "We are sure that all of our party and the entire Soviet people support us in that we cannot share the views of the Chinese leadership on the creation of a '1,000 times higher civilization' on the corpses of hundreds of millions of people.''

The Russian letter reviewed the history of the Sino-Soviet split, blaming Communist China for every phase, and then refuted one by one the 25 points the Chinese had sought to have debated at the Moscow meeting. It accused the Chinese government of reducing by "almost 67 percent in the past three years" the volume of China's trade with the Soviet Union and asserted that "the Chinese leaders did not tell their people truthfully through whose fault (trade) relations were curtailed.''

Test-Ban Talks. On July 15, talks between the U.S., Great Britain and the Soviet Union on a treaty to limit nuclear tests opened in Moscow.

Buddhists Demonstrations. On July 15, Vietnamese Buddhists announced they would resume protests against government policies toward their religion. In the next few days, they staged large demonstrations in Saigon resulting in a number of injuries and arrests.

Kennedy on Buddhist Protests. On July 17, President Kennedy told a news conference that the South Vietnamese religious dispute was unfortunate because it had "arisen at the very time when the military struggle has been going better than it has been going in many months." The President also said: "I would hope this would be settled, because we want to see a stable government there, carrying on a struggle to maintain its national independence." We strongly believe in that. We are not going to withdraw from that effort. In my opinion, for us to withdraw from that effort would mean a collapse not only of South Viet Nam, but of Southeast Asia. So we are going to stay there.''

Diem Appeals to Buddhists. On July 18, South Vietnamese President Ngo Dinh Diem appealed to Buddhist leaders to negotiate with the government. His offer was rejected the following day. The government then released Buddhist demonstrators who had been jailed in previous demonstrations and removed barbed wire fences that had been placed around Saigon's pagodas. The Buddhist leaders only made additional demands.

Khrushchev on Disarmament. On July 19, Soviet Premier Khrushchev, speaking at a Kremlin reception, voiced optimism about conclusion of a nuclear test-ban treaty and suggested "the freezing of military budgets of states, and even better, the cutting down of these budgets." These and other measures would be the beginning of "an understanding on the vital issue -- general and complete disarmament.''

Chinese on Test Ban. On July 19, an editorial in the Peking *People's Daily* called the nuclear test-ban talks in Moscow a "capitulation in the face of imperialist nuclear blackmail." The editorial noted that Mao Tse-tung had

said in 1957 "that mankind will definitely not be destroyed even if the imperialists insist on a nuclear war" and that World War III would "hasten the complete destruction of the world capitalist system.''

The same article disclosed that on July 16, 1960, the Soviet Union had suddenly told Peking that it had decided to "withdraw all the 1,300 and more Soviet experts in China within a month, to scrap the hundreds of agreements and contracts it had signed, and to discontinue supplies of many important items of equipment and materials." This action "inflicted incalcuable difficulties and losses on China's economy, national defense and scientific research." *(See also Dec. 4, 1963.)*

Sino-Soviet Talks End. On July 21, Moscow and Peking announced in a joint statement that their talks in Moscow had been recessed the day before and were scheduled to continue "at some later time." The statement said the two delegations had failed to reach any agreement except to recess.

Test-Ban Treaty. On July 25, representatives of the Soviet Union, Great Britain and the U.S. initialed a treaty prohibiting nuclear tests in the atmosphere, in outer space, and under water. On the following day, President Kennedy described the action as a "victory for mankind" and "a shaft of light into the dark threat of thermonuclear war.''

Border Dispute. On July 26, the Indian Foreign Ministry announced that Chinese troops had re-entered areas on the Chinese-Indian border abandoned after the 1962 invasion. The announcement followed a long exchange of charges between the two countries concerning border violations. On July 28, the Peking radio denied the Indian charges. Indian Prime Minister Nehru told a mass meeting two days later that "the Chinese intentions in their present military buildup in Tibet are obviously not good.''

Nuclear Weapons Monopoly. On July 26, Kuo Mo-jo, chairman of the China Peace Committee and one of China's leading intellectuals, told a rally in Peking on the tenth anniversary of the Korean armistice that "the present attempt by a small number of countries to control the destiny of the people of the world by means of monopolizing nuclear weapons will almost certainly be smashed in the not too distant future." Kuo added: "We revolutionary people will surely be able to master the new techniques which the imperialists have been able to master.''

Harriman on Test-Ban Treaty. On July 27, Under Secretary of State W. Averell Harriman, who represented the U.S. at the test-ban treaty negotiations, returned from Moscow, reported to the President, and then told reporters that it was "fairly plain" that Soviet Premier Khrushchev had desired the treaty because he "wanted to show...the Chinese that his policy of coexistence could produce some results." Harriman said he also thought that "the Soviet people want to have relief from tensions.''

On July 29, at another press conference, Harriman said he had found Khrushchev "not overly concerned" about Communist China's future nuclear capability. He reported that the Soviet Premier "told me it would be a long, long, time before they had a nuclear capability of any importance." Khrushchev pointed out that there was "quite a difference between an explosion and a substantial arsenal.''

Chinese Reaction to Test Ban. On July 29, the Peking *People's Daily* called the test ban "a treaty consolidating

the status of the nuclear monopoly of the nuclear powers."
On July 31, a statement by the Chinese Communist government termed the treaty "a big fraud to fool the people of the world." The statement said: "If this big fraud is not exposed it can do even greater harm. It is unthinkable for the Chinese government to be a party to this dirty fraud." Peking proposed a conference of world leaders "to discuss the question of complete prohibition of nuclear weapons," the dismantling of all military bases in foreign lands including the withdrawal of "all nuclear weapons and their means of delivery," and the creation of "nuclear weapons-free zones" in Asia, the Pacific, Central Europe, Africa, and Latin America.

Buddhist Rallies. On July 30, South Vietnamese Buddhists staged rallies in Saigon and four other cities in memory of the Buddhist monk who burned himself to death June 11. About 60,000 people participated in the rallies. On the same day, Buddhist leaders rejected an offer of the government to establish a joint committee to investigate Buddhist charges. The leaders said they would not cooperate with the government until it assumed responsibility for the deaths of nine demonstrators killed in Hue on May 8.

On July 31, Buddhist leaders strongly criticized U.S. Ambassador Frederick E. Nolting Jr., who had earlier told a reporter he saw no sign of religious persecution in South Viet Nam and felt that the demonstrations were impeding the war against the Viet Cong.

Kennedy on the China Threat. On Aug. 1, President Kennedy was asked at a news conference to appraise the power and the threat of Communist China. He said that China, with its 700 million people, with a "Stalinist internal regime," with its determination for war "as a means of bringing about its ultimate success," and with its future potential as a nuclear power, might present in the next decade a "potentially more dangerous situation than any we faced since the end of the second war."

China Proposes World Parley. On Aug. 2, Chinese Communist Premier Chou En-lai addressed a letter to the leaders of all nations proposing a world conference to discuss the "complete, thorough, total and resolute prohibition and destruction of nuclear weapons." The letter, sent to President Kennedy through the American embassy in Warsaw, repeated the series of suggestions included in the Chinese statement of July 31.

Canadian Wheat. On Aug. 2, Canada announced it had agreed on another sale of wheat to Communist China. The new agreement provided for shipment of from three million to five million long tons of wheat over a three-year period.

Soviets Condemn China. On Aug. 3, the Soviet Union countered Communist China's July 31 attack on the nuclear test-ban treaty with a statement denouncing the Chinese for "trying to cover up their refusal to sign a nuclear test-ban treaty." It said: "Trying to discredit...the assured success in the struggle for diminishing the war danger, to vilify the peace-loving foreign policy of the Soviet Union, the leaders of China have shown...that their policy leads to the aggravation of international tensions, to the further stepping up of the nuclear arms race, to the still further expansion of its scope and scale. This position is tantamount to actual connivance with those who advocate world thermonuclear war."

Chinese Attack Khrushchev. On the day that the Soviets denounced China, Aug. 3, the Peking *People's Daily* published an editorial entitled "This is the Betrayal of the Soviet People." The editorial accused Soviet Premier Khrushchev of betraying his own people and predicted he would be overthrown. It concluded: "While fraternizing with United States imperialism on the most intimate terms, the Soviet leader and the Soviet press showed their teeth in their hatred of Socialist China. They use the same language as United States imperialism to abuse China. This is a United States-Soviet alliance against China pure and simple."

Mme. Nhu on Buddhists. On Aug. 3, Mme. Ngo Dinh Nhu, sister-in-law of South Vietnamese President Ngo Dinh Diem, said in a speech at Saigon·that the "so-called holy men" (Buddhist leaders) had employed Communist tactics during their anti-government demonstrations. She called the Buddhist practice of self-immolation "murder." "What else can be said when they (the Buddhists) murder their own kin and their own peers in a most barbaric manner under the pretext of defending a faith that has never been under attack." Mme. Nhu's husband, Ngo Dinh Nhu, was President Diem's brother, chief adviser, and head of the secret police. All of them were Catholics. In the next few weeks, a number of Buddhist monks and nuns continued the protest against the Saigon government by burning themselves to death.

Nuclear Treaty Signed. On Aug. 5, the treaty to ban nuclear tests in the atmosphere, outer space, and under water was signed in Moscow by U.S. Secretary of State Dean Rusk, Soviet Minister of Foreign Affairs Andrei A. Gromyko, and British Foreign Secretary Lord Home. President Kennedy Aug. 8 submitted the treaty to the Senate for approval. In an accompanying message the President said the treaty would "assure the security of the United States better than continued unlimited testing on both sides." France and Communist China had refused to sign the treaty.

Chou's Message to Hiroshima. On Aug. 6, Chinese Communist Premier Chou En-lai said in a message to the World Conference Against Nuclear Weapons, meeting in Hiroshima, Japan, that "the danger of nuclear war, instead of being reduced, has increased." Chou declared: "Only by completely, thoroughly, totally, and resolutely prohibiting and destroying nuclear weapons and by taking effective measures agreed upon by all can the threat of nuclear war be removed."

Mme. Nhu's Statement. On Aug. 7, Mme. Ngo Dinh Nhu asserted that the U.S. Embassy in Saigon has "threatened and blackmailed" the South Vietnamese government in an effort to "shut me up." She said that her brother-in-law's government should warn the Buddhists that "those who break laws will be severely treated, and particularly the bonzes (Buddhist monks)." Mme. Nhu then added that the government should "ignore the bonzes, so if they burn 30 women we shall go ahead and clap our hands."

Mao on Civil Rights. On Aug. 12, the Peking *People's Daily* published a statement by Mao Tse-tung appealing to people everywhere to "unite against the racial discrimination practiced by U.S. imperialism and to support the American Negroes in their struggle against racial discrimination." Mao's statement had been requested by Robert F. Williams, a militant U.S. Negro living in Cuba.

China and Soviet Nuclear Aid. On Aug. 15, the Peking radio broadcast a statement from the Chinese government charging that the Soviet Union had reneged during 1959 on an offer two years earlier to give vital information on the production of nuclear weapons: "On June 20, 1959, when there was no hint of the so-called nuclear test-ban treaty, the Soviet government unilaterally scrapped the Oct. 15, 1957, agreement concerning new defense technology (and) refused to supply China with atomic bomb samples and technical materials for the manufacture of atomic bombs, apparently as a gift for...(Soviet Premier Khrushchev) to take to Eisenhower when visiting the United States in September....

"The Soviet government tried to...curry favor with U.S. imperialism by discontinuing assistance to China....China has long ceased to place any hope in the Soviet leaders in developing its own nuclear strength to resist U.S. nuclear threats....It is no new story that Soviet leaders, in collusion with American imperialism, plot to bind China hand and foot."

Japanese Plant for China. On Aug. 20, the Japanese government approved a contract for the construction in Red China of a $20 million synthetic textile plant by a private Japanese company.

Action Against Buddhists. On Aug. 21, after weeks of demonstrations and riots against the government of President Ngo Dinh Diem by dissident Buddhists, South Vietnamese soldiers and police attacked and overran Buddhist pagodas throughout the country. Hundreds of Buddhist monks, including all the important leaders, were reported to have been beaten and arrested. President Diem proclaimed a state of martial law and ordered a dusk-to-dawn curfew. He asserted that "a number of political speculators who had taken advantage of religion" had abused the "government's extremely conciliatory goodwill in settling problems raised by the General Buddhist Association."

In Hue, the largest pagoda was reported to have been destroyed, touching off a battle between troops and about 6,000 residents. In Saigon, government forces raided a pagoda and arrested Buddhist monks and nuns by the hundreds. Some were reported to have been killed. On the same day, the U.S. State Department deplored the action taken against the Buddhists and said it represented "direct violation by the Vietnamese government of assurances that it was pursuing a policy of reconciliation with the Buddhists."

Soviet Reply to China. On Aug. 21, the Soviet news agency, *Tass*, published the Soviet government's reply to Red China's criticism of the Soviet Union on Aug. 15. Moscow said that China's opposition to the nuclear test-ban treaty demonstrated its lack of regard for "how nuclear arms spread among the capitalist states as long as the Chinese leaders got a chance to lay their hands on a nuclear bomb and see what it is like."

The Soviet statement criticized China for publicizing "classified...information relating to the defense of the Socialist community." It noted that even if China were capable of producing "two or three bombs," it would still have to depend on the Soviet Union's "nuclear shield" for protection. But there were "some people in Peking ready to sacrifice half the population of their country, half of entire mankind" in a war involving nuclear weapons.

The government statement was supplemented by numerous sharp attacks on Communist China in the Soviet press.

Chinese Charge. On Aug. 22, the Peking *People's Daily* added fuel to the flames by denouncing the Soviet Union's decision "to ship more weapons of still newer type to the anti-Communist and anti-popular Nehru government (of India) which has become an advance detachment of U.S. imperialism in its campaign against China." It further charged that Soviet Premier Khrushchev's 1959 expression of "regret" over the Sino-Indian border clash "amounted to tipping off the enemy that the socialist camp was not a monolithic whole and that there were great possibilities for deals" with U.S. "imperialism." Two days later, a Soviet newspaper denounced the Communist Chinese for using "their weapons against neutralist India" and reminded them that their security depended on Soviet military power.

U.S. Report on Viet Nam. On Aug. 26, the State Department said in a report on the measures taken against Buddhist demonstrators in South Viet Nam: "Current information makes it clear that these attacks...were carried out by the police, supported by small groups of Special Forces groups not under the command of the Vietnamese forces (both the police and the Special Forces, or palace guards, were under the command of President Diem's brother, Ngo Dinh Nhu). It was apparent that Viet Nam's military leaders were deeply concerned about continued civil unrest as a result of unresolved differences between the government and the Buddhists. They felt that this conflict was beginning to have an adverse effect on the war to defeat Communist subversion....Present information is that the top leadership of the Vietnamese Army was not aware of the plans to attack the pagodas, much less the brutal manner in which it was carried out."

Saigon Takes Exception. On Aug. 28, the South Vietnamese government asserted that the State Department's Aug. 26 report was "entirely and absolutely erroneous." It said: "All responsible army chiefs unanimously and respectfully proposed and obtained from (President Ngo Dinh Diem)...permission to establish martial law, as well as the referred-to-measures (against the Buddhists), and it is the army which has directly taken all measures to accomplish this mission."

Mao on Viet Nam. On Aug. 29, Chairman Mao Tsetung of the Central Committee of the Chinese Communist Party said in a broadcast over the Peking radio: "Setting itself against all the people of South Viet Nam, the U.S.-Ngo Dinh Diem clique now finds itself besieged by them... The Ngo Dinh Diem regime will inescapably end in total isolation and disintegration, and U.S. imperialism will finally have to get out of South Viet Nam."

On the same day, North Vietnamese President Ho Chi Minh said on the radio that the situation in South Viet Nam was "extremely serious and distressing." He urged the South Vietnamese people to "unite, struggle and win."

Peking Talks Back to Moscow. On Sept. 1, the Chinese Communist Party issued a 10,000-word statement in answer to the Soviet statement of Aug. 21. It accused Soviet leaders of "telling lies for a living," for "You know very well that long before we published our last statement you told the Americans secrets between China and the Soviet Union concerning nuclear weapons." Peking added that "Even if we

Chinese people are unable to produce an atom bomb for 100 years, we will neither crawl to the baton of the Soviet leaders, nor kneel before the nuclear blackmail of the U.S. imperialists."

The statement summarized China's views on war: "(1) China wants peace and not war. (2) It is the imperialists and not we who want to fight a war. (3) World war can be prevented. (4) Even in the eventuality that imperialism should impose a war on the people of the world and inflict tragic losses on them, it is the imperialist system and not mankind that would perish and the future of mankind would still be bright."

Soviet Sarcasm. On Sept. 2, the Soviet government newspaper *Izvestia* remarked that the "Chinese leaders made a terrible fuss about the plight of the people suffering under imperialism, but they surprisingly ignore the sufferings of their own countrymen in Hong Kong," dubbed by *Izvestia* a "dangerous growth on the body of China."

Kennedy on Viet Nam War. On Sept. 2, President Kennedy, discussing the Vietnamese war in a television interview, said: "In the final analysis, it's their war. They are the ones who have to win it or lose it. We can help them, give them equipment, send our men out there as advisers, but they have to win it, the people of Viet Nam against the Communists." Kennedy, emphasizing that victory depended on popular support, said that in his opinion the Diem government had "gotten out of touch with the people." He thought it might regain popular support by "changes in policy and perhaps...personnel." Most sources interpreted the President's remarks as an invitation to Diem to oust his brother Ngo Dinh Nhu, and Mme. Nhu, from positions of power.

Chinese Article on Split with Russia. On Sept. 6, the Peking *People's Daily* and the Chinese Communist Party's theoretical journal, *Red Flag*, printed the first installment of a series of articles entitled "The Origin and Development of Differences Between Ourselves and the Communist Party of the Soviet Union." The differences were said to have begun with the 20th Congress of the Communist Party of the Soviet Union in 1956:

"The criticism of Stalin at the 20th Congress...was wrong both in principle and in method. Stalin's life was that of a great Marxist-Leninist, a great proletarian revolutionary. For 30 years after Lenin's death, Stalin was the foremost leader of the CPSU and the Soviet government, as well as the recognized leader of the international Communist movement and the standard bearer of the world revolution. During his lifetime, Stalin made some serious mistakes, but compared to his great and meritorious deeds his mistakes are only secondary....

"It was necessary to criticize Stalin's mistakes. But in his secret report to the 20th Congress, Comrade Khrushchev completely negated Stalin, and in doing so defamed the dictatorship of the proletariat, defamed the Socialist system, the great CPSU, the great Soviet Union, and the international Communist movement....He treated Stalin as an enemy and shifted the blame for all mistakes onto Stalin alone....

"In his report to the 20th Congress, under the pretext that 'radical changes' had taken place in the world situation, Khrushchev put forward the thesis of 'peaceful transition.' He said that the road of the October (1917) Revolution was 'the only correct road in those historical conditions,' but

that as the situation had changed, it had become possible to effect the transition from capitalism to socialism 'through the parliamentary road.' In essence, this erroneous thesis is a clear revision of the Marxist-Leninist teachings on the state and revolution and a clear denial of the universal significance of the road of the October Revolution."

The Chinese article also charged that the Soviet Union had been involved in subversion within China's borders: "In April and May 1962, the leaders of the CPSU used their organs and personnel in Sinkiang, China, to carry out large scale subversive activities in the Ili region and enticed and coerced several tens of thousands of Chinese citizens into going to the Soviet Union. The Chinese government lodged repeated protests and made repeated representations, but the Soviet government refused to repatriate these Chinese citizens on the pretext of 'the sense of Soviet legality' and 'humanitarianism.' To this day, this incident remains unsettled....(It) "pushed Sino-Soviet relations to the brink of a split."

Trouble in Sinkiang. On Sept. 6, Moscow dispatches said that China's charges of subversion in Sinkiang confirmed reports that around 50,000 Kazakh nomads had fled from that province of China into the Soviet Union because of hunger and religious persecution. Hong Kong dispatches said travelers arriving from Sinkiang had reported that Kazakh tribesmen staged an uprising there and appealed to the Soviet Union for arms to fight their Chinese overlords.

(The *New York Times* on Sept. 7 called the incident in Sinkiang "clearly the most delicate matter yet raised in the (Chinese-Soviet) dispute." It explained: "Sinkiang is one of China's colonial possessions and its predominantly Moslem peoples...are no more Chinese than the people of Tibet. Anti-Chinese feeling and revolutionary activity in Sinkiang have ancient historical roots. Under both the czars and the commissars, Russia has often intervened in this area during the past century....There is substantial evidence indicating that Stalin's long-term goal was to absorb Sinkiang into the Soviet Union.")

Viet Nam Unrest. On Sept. 7, around 800 high school students in Saigon were arrested during an anti-government protest. Two days later, an additional 1,500 were arrested after barricading themselves in their school and throwing rocks and desks at police and soldiers. On Sept. 10, 100 more were arrested and the high schools were closed.

On Sept. 4, Mme. Nhu had told newsmen she had the "impression" that a number of American civilians in South Viet Nam were hired by the Central Intelligence Agency. "American military advisers are very useful here," she said, "but these civilians -- we do not need them, for we do not need anybody to administer our country."

Kennedy's Statement. On Sept. 9, President Kennedy, in a television interview on NBC with Chet Huntley and David Brinkley, was asked if the U.S. tends to "get locked into a policy or an attitude and then finds it difficult to alter or shift that policy."

The President replied: "Yes, that is true. I think in the case of South Viet Nam we have been dealing with a government which is in control, has been in control for 10 years. In addition, we have felt for the last two years that the struggle against the Communists was going better. Since June, however, the difficulties with the Buddhists, we have been concerned about a deterioration, particularly in the Saigon area, which hasn't been felt greatly in the outlying areas but may spread. So we are faced with the problem of wanting to protect the area against the Communists. On the other hand, we have to deal with the government there. That produces a kind of ambivalence in our efforts which exposes us to some criticism. We are using our influence to persuade the government there to take those steps which will win back support. That takes some time and we must be patient, we must persist."

Kennedy added that the U.S. had no plans for reducing aid to South Viet Nam. "If you reduce your aid," he said, "it is possible you could have some effect on the government structure there. On the other hand, you might have a situation which could bring about a collapse. Strongly in our mind is what happened in the case of China at the end of World War II, where China was lost, a weak government became increasingly unable to control events. We don't want that."

The President was then asked if he had "any reason to doubt (the) so-called domino theory, that if South Viet Nam falls, the rest of Southeast Asia will go behind it?"

He answered: "No, I believe it. I believe it. I think that the struggle is close enough. China is so large, looms so high just beyond the frontiers, that if South Viet Nam went, it would not only give them an improved geographic position for a guerrilla assault on Malaya, but would also give the impression that the wave of the future in Southeast Asia was China and the Communists."

Church's Resolution. On Sept. 12, Sen Frank Church (D Idaho) introduced a resolution calling for withdrawal of U.S. aid and personnel from South Viet Nam if "cruel repressions" of Buddhists by the government continued. Church asserted that the situation in South Viet Nam had "worsened" while the U.S. effort had increased. "We have been dismayed by (the Diem regime's) persecution of the Buddhists,...by the desecration of their temples, and by the brutality of attacks upon them. We have been denounced by the very members of the ruling family we have helped to keep in power. To persist in support of such a regime can only serve to identify the U.S. with the cause of religious persecution."

At his news conference the same day, President Kennedy remarked: "I have indicated my feeling that we should stay there, and continue to assist South Viet Nam, but I also indicated our feeling that the assistance we give should be used in the most effective way possible. I think that seems to be Sen. Church's view."

Mme. Ngo Dinh Nhu had said on Sept. 11: "President Kennedy is a politician, and when he hears a loud opinion speaking in a certain way, he always tries to appease it somehow. . . .If that opinion is misinformed, the solution is not to bow to it, but the solution should be to inform."

China's Second Article. On Sept. 13, the Peking *People's Daily* and the journal *Red Flag* published the second article in their series on the Sino-Soviet split. Entitled "On the Question of Stalin," the article denounced Soviet Premier Khruschev for using "filthy, vulgar, and malicious language" in his attacks on former Soviet Premier Stalin. "In what position does Khrushchev, who participated in the leadership of the party and state during Stalin's period, place himself when he beats his breast, pounds the table and shouts abuse of Stalin at the top of his voice? In the position of an accomplice to a 'murderer' or 'bandit' or in the same position as a 'fool' or 'idiot'?"

Liu's Statement. On Sept. 15, Chinese Communist President Liu Shao-chi arrived in North Korea for a state visit. He criticized the belief of Soviet leaders that "the philosophy of survival has replaced the revolutionary theories of Marxism-Leninism" and added that "what really counts is the people ...the decisive factor in war is man, not one or two weapons of a new type."

Russia Charges Border Violations. On Sept. 21, the Soviet government, in an article in *Izvestia*, defended the nuclear test-ban treaty and denounced the Chinese position as "a complete apostasy from the common, collectively formulated line of the Communist movement." In addition, the article charged that the Chinese Communists had "systematically" violated the Sino-Soviet border since 1960. It said that 5,000 violations were reported in 1962 and that "there have even been attempts in the most flagrant manner to appropriate individual sections of Soviet territory." A "decisive rebuff" was threatened if Communist China continued its "hostile activities."

Viet Nam Trip. On Sept. 24, Secretary of Defense Robert S. McNamara and Gen. Maxwell D. Taylor, chairman of the Joint Chiefs of Staff, departed for South Viet Nam to investigate reports that President Ngo Dinh Diem was repressing Buddhists. President Kennedy had ordered the two officials to determine how much the internal chaos in South Viet Nam had affected the war against the Viet Cong.

Third Article. On Sept. 25, the Peking *People's Daily* and the journal *Red Flag* published the third article in their series on the Sino-Soviet split. The article entitled "Is Yugoslavia a Socialist Country?" denounced Yugoslavia's leaders for "the restoration of capitalism in Yugoslavia...(a) process in which the Tito clique has become subservient towards U.S. imperialism and Yugoslavia has degenerated into a U.S. imperialist dependency."

North Korean Statement. On Sept. 27, Chinese Communist President Liu Shao-chi and North Korean President Choi Yong Kon issued a joint statement at the completion of Liu's two-week visit to North Korea. The statement affirmed a "complete identity of views" on all policy matters and noted the common opposition of the two countries to the policies of the Soviet Union.

French-Chinese Relations. On Sept. 28, a French economic mission arrived in Peking. Visits by various French officials followed, and the French press reported that China's leaders were openly encouraging France to recognize the Peking regime.

Viet Nam Prediction. On Oct. 2, Secretary of Defense Robert S. McNamara and Chairman of the Joint Chiefs of Staff Maxwell D. Taylor reported to President Kennedy on their return from an eight-day visit to South Viet Nam. Later that day, a White House statement said that "Secretary McNamara and Gen. Taylor reported their judgment that the major part of the U.S. military task (in Viet Nam) can be completed by the end of 1965, although there may be a continuing requirement for a limited number of...training personnel."

The statement said at the same time that "the political situation in South Viet Nam remains deeply serious." Although repressive actions by the Saigon regime had "not yet significantly affected the military effort, they could do so in the future." Under existing conditions, most of the 14,000 U.S. military personnel could be withdrawn by the end of 1965, and 1,000 men might be withdrawn by the end of 1963.

The McNamara-Taylor mission was designed to ascertain the effect on the war effort of repression of Buddhists and student uprisings and other activities of the government headed by Ngo Dinh Diem. It had been reported that there was wide divergence of opinion among Americans in Saigon representing the military, the State Department, the Agency for International Development, the U.S. Information Agency, and the Central Intelligence Agency. During the next few days, it was disclosed that the U.S. had begun "selective" cuts in aid to Viet Nam in the hope of putting pressure on the Diem government.

Newsmen Beaten. On Oct. 5, three U. S. newsmen were beaten by Vietnamese police after they had witnessed the self-immolation of a Buddhist monk in Saigon. The reporters--two NBC men and David Halberstam of the *New York Times*--had unsuccessfully attempted to keep the police from confiscating an NBC camera used to photograph the suicide.

Mme. Nhu in U.S. On Sept. 7, Mme. Ngo Dinh Nhu arrived in the United States for a speaking tour. She said she hoped "to try to understand why we can't get along better." Federal, New York State, and local officials ignored her arrival.

Kennedy on Diem Regime. On Oct. 9, President Kennedy told his news conference that he saw no improvement in the Diem regime since his Sept. 2 remarks on television suggesting that "changes in policy and personnel" were necessary. "I think we are still dealing with the same problems we were dealing with a month ago," he said

Chou on Pact with Soviets. On Oct. 11, Chinese Communist Premier Chou En-lai told a reporter for *Reuters* that the Soviet-Chinese treaty of friendship and alliance was still in effect despite the ideological differences between the two countries. "If any act of aggression occurs against any socialist country," he said, "this would be an act of aggression against the whole socialist camp. It would be impossible not to give support. If a country refused to give support, it would not be a socialist country." Chou had declared earlier that a diplomatic break between the Soviet Union and Communist China was impossible.

U.S. and Aid to Viet Nam. On Oct. 16, the Senate Foreign Relations Committee approved an amendment to the foreign aid authorization bill, included in the bill as finally enacted, expressing the "sense of Congress" that aid should be extended to or withheld from South Viet Nam, as the President determined, only "to further the objectives of victory in the war against communism and the return to their homeland of Americans involved in that struggle." The amendment was a milder version of a resolution proposed by Sen. Frank Church (D Idaho) calling for termination of aid to South Viet Nam unless reforms were instituted by the Diem government (see Sept. 12).

Diem Suppresses Revolt. On Oct. 19, the Diem government announced that it had put down an "organized rebellion by students and intellectuals" aimed at overthrowing the regime. It was reported two days later that the U.S. had given warning that it would cut off aid to the South Vietnamese Special Forces if they were used for political purposes. Renewal of an agreement for surplus food grants was reportedly being held up to bring pressure on the Diem government.

UN Vote on Red China. On Oct. 21, the UN General Assembly voted 57 to 41 with 12 abstentions to bar Communist China from the UN. The resolution to seat China, always sponsored previously by the Soviet Union, was offered by Albania.

Fourth Article. On Oct. 21, the Peking *People's Daily* and the Chinese Communist party's theoretical journal *Red Flag* published the fourth article on the Sino-Soviet split. The article, entitled "The Apologists of Neo-Colonialism," charged Russia with "racism" and with "raising a hue and cry against the yellow peril."

Soviets Denounce Chinese Leaders. On Oct. 24, the Soviet Communist Party's ideological journal *Kommunist* carried an editorial denouncing the leaders of Communist China, who, it said, "want to destroy the international Communist movement and create under their aegis a new movement." It added that "the Communist movement now finds itself threatened by an attempt to replace Leninism with Maoism."

China's Nuclear Program. On Oct. 28, it was reported that Chinese Communist Foreign Minister Chen Yi had told a group of Japanese newsmen in Peking that it would be several years before China began testing nuclear weapons and many years before China could be considered a nuclear power. It was the first public statement by a Peking official concerning China's nuclear program. The Foreign Minister attributed the lag in China's nuclear program to industrial and technological inadequacies, withdrawal of Soviet technicians from Communist China, and the U.S. economic blockade of the country.

North Viet Nam Aid to Laos. On Oct. 29, the State Department charged that North Viet Nam was sending military equipment to the Communist Pathet Lao forces in northeastern Laos in violation of the 1962 Geneva agreement on Laos. A State Department spokesman said the Laotian government had requested the International Control Commission to investigate the alleged shipments, but that Pathet Lao forces would not allow I.C.C. inspectors in the area.

Viet Nam Coup. On Nov. 1, in mid-afternoon, military forces headed by Gen. Duong Van Minh moved into Saigon to oust the government of President Ngo Dinh Diem. At the end of an 18-hour battle, Gen. Minh proclaimed the downfall of the regime, establishment of a military caretaker government, suspension of the Constitution, and initiation of a more vigorous campaign against the Viet Cong guerrillas.

President Diem and his brother Ngo Dinh Nhu reportedly fled to a Catholic church outside Saigon where they surrendered to the rebel forces. The victorious military commanders asserted that Diem and Nhu committed "accidental suicide," while other reports said the two brothers were murdered by their captors.

The military junta Nov. 5 announced that Nguyen Thoc Tho, 55, vice president during the Diem regime, would act as provisional Premier pending democratic elections "when the situation permits." A statement by the victorious generals Nov. 2 said: "The armed forces are not aiming at setting up a military dictatorship, because they are well aware that the best weapon to fight communism is democracy and liberty."

After the revolt, the State Department quickly denied having had any hand in it and stated that it was unaware of preparations for the coup. Unofficially, it was admitted that recent American criticism of the Diem government might have contributed to development of the "proper climate" for a revolt. The Department said it was "shocked" at the deaths of Diem and Nhu. Secretary of State Rusk told the Senate Foreign Relations Committee Nov. 5 that the generals tried unsuccessfully to persuade Diem to surrender and save his life. Rusk also said the Administration hoped to grant formal recognition to the new government "in the near future."

Rep. Clement J. Zablocki (D Wis.), chairman of the House Foreign Affairs, Far East and Pacific Subcommittee, who recently returned from South Viet Nam, said in a House speech Nov. 4: "My best judgment is there must have been some encouragement" of the insurgents by U.S. authorities. Zablocki stated that moves to curtail aid to the Diem government was one thing which could have helped to "trigger" the coup. He said this was a "sign" to Viet Nam's military leaders that the U.S. would help overthrow the regime. Zablocki, commenting on Diem's promises for reforms, said: "I am satisfied...that Diem meant what he said. He impressed us as a dedicated nationalist, sincere, incorruptible, and determined to defeat the Communist Viet Cong."

The wife of Ngo Dinh Nhu was touring the U.S. at the time of the coup, seeking support for the Diem government. In Los Angeles Nov. 2 she declared that the coup would not have been possible without "American incitement or American backing." She called the deaths of her husband and brother-in-law "murders, either with the official or unofficial blessing of the American Government."

U-2 Shot Down. On Nov. 1, the Peking radio announced that a high-altitude reconnaissance U-2 plane "of the Chiang Kai-shek bandit gang" was "shot down by the air force" near Shanghai while flying "on a harassing mission." On Nov. 2, the Nationalist Chinese government admitted the loss of a U-2.

Russians on Rift with China. On Nov. 6, Nikolai V. Podgorny, a secretary of the Central Committee of the Soviet Communist Party and a member of the Presidium, said during a speech: "We sincerely want to normalize the relationship with the Chinese People's Republic, the great, industrious and talented Chinese people with whom we are bound in great friendship. There are no objective reasons which could prevent a return to the good relations which existed in the not too distant past between the U.S.S.R. and the C.P.R."

On the same day, Soviet Premier Khrushchev told a group of visiting American businessmen that the dispute with China "causes us deep concern...(and) merely causes joy on your part....So let us take the whole matter off the agenda, because it is one that concerns only ourselves and China. We will find a method to discuss this with China, and I do not think that your nose would be quite in place in such a discussion." Khrushchev added: "You are rejoicing that we are arguing with the Chinese, but the more pleased you feel now, the worse you will feel later on."

New Viet Nam Regime. On Nov. 7, the U.S. extended diplomatic recognition to the new provisional government in South Viet Nam. Secretary of State Rusk voiced hope that the new regime would "be able to rally the country" against the Communists.

Kennedy on China Trade. On Nov. 14, President Kennedy, asked at a press conference what would be the conditions for a resumption of trade with Communist China, said: "We are not planning on trade with Red China in view of the policy that Red China pursues. If the Red Chinese indicate a desire to live at peace with the United States, with other countries surrounding it, then quite obviously the United States would reappraise its policies. We are not wedded to a policy of hostility to Red China. It seems to me Red

China's policies are what create the tension between not only the United States and Red China but between Red China and India, between Red China and her immediate neighbors to the south, and even between Red China and other Communist countries."

Kennedy expressed concern over a recent threat by Cambodia to reject American foreign aid. "It is my hope," the President said, "that Prince Sihanouk, who must be concerned about the independence and sovereignty of his country...will not decide at this dangerous point in the world's affairs to surrender it."

Fifth Article. On Nov. 19, the Peking *People's Daily* and the theoretical journal *Red Flag* published the fifth in a series of articles on the Sino-Soviet split. The latest article, entitled "Two Different Lines on the Question of War and Peace," contained the following observation: "Guided by this theory of nuclear fetishism and nuclear blackmail, the leaders of the Soviet Communist Party maintain that the way to defend world peace is not for all existing peace forces to unite and form the broadest united front against U.S. imperialism and its lackeys, but for the two nuclear powers, the United States and the Soviet Union, to cooperate in settling the world's problems." The article went on to say: "The U.S. imperialists are the wildest imperialists of modern times, the wildest plotters of a new world war, and the most ferocious enemy of world peace....However hard Khrushchev tries to serve the U.S. imperialists, they show not the slightest appreciation. They continue to expose their own peace camouflage by fresh and numerous activities of aggression and war, and thus they continue to slap Khrushchev in the face and reveal the bankruptcy of his ridiculous theories prettifying imperialism."

Cambodia Rejects U.S. Aid. On Nov. 19, Cambodian Chief of State Prince Norodom Sihanouk ordered termination of all U.S. military and economic aid to his country. He charged that U.S. military advisers and the CIA had been aiding opponents of his government. The State Department immediately denied that charge. From 1955 through June 30, 1963, the U.S. had given Cambodia about $360 million in economic aid and $86 million in military assistance. Current aid totaled about $30 million a year.

On Nov. 20, Chinese Communist Foreign Minister Chen Yi pledged that his country would give Cambodia "resolute support" in its "just and patriotic struggle against imperialism." On Nov. 21, the Chinese Communist government offered its "all-out support" if Cambodia had to repel an "armed invasion instigated by the U.S. and its vassals." The next day, Sihanouk said that although China was Cambodia's "best friend," his country would not become a satellite of China.

Kennedy Assassinated. On Nov. 22, President John Fitzgerald Kennedy was assassinated in Dallas, Texas, and Vice President Lyndon Baines Johnson was sworn in as his successor. Communist China's press and radio announced the assassination without comment. On Nov. 24, President Johnson said he would follow Kennedy's policies in South Viet Nam.

On Nov. 27, Chinese Communist newspapers described Johnson as "a firm supporter of all Kennedy's reactionary policies."

Chilean Copper to China. On Nov. 27, the Chilean government announced it had signed an agreement to sell Communist China 10,000 tons of copper.

Chinese Rice to Indonesia. On Dec. 1, the Indonesian government announced it had signed an agreement to buy from Communist China 40,000 tons of rice to help alleviate food shortages in Indonesia caused by flood and rodent damage.

China and Pakistan. On Dec. 2, the Chinese Communist Minister of Trade pledged, during a visit to Pakistan, that Communist China would support Pakistan in case of "fresh aggression" by India.

Statement on China's Economy. On Dec. 3, after two weeks of secret debate, the National People's Congress, meeting in Peking, issued a statement asserting that Communist China had finally overcome the serious economic recession caused by three years of natural disasters and by the "perfidious action of those who unilaterally tore up agreements and withdrew experts" from China.

World Reds Support Russia. On Dec. 4, representatives of 80 countries attending a Communist-dominated World Peace Council, held in Warsaw, repeatedly rejected pro-Chinese and anti-Soviet resolutions. On Dec. 5, *Reuters* reported: "The final session was several times postponed while delegates tried to work out a compromise to prevent a split in the movement....In their bid for leadership of the smaller countries of Asia, Africa, and Latin America, the Chinese Communists have called for 'active support' of armed 'revolutionary struggles' particularly in South Viet Nam, Laos, Angola, Portuguese Guinea, Venezuela and Guatemala. Asian sources said committee balloting had yielded 27 votes in favor of the broad lines of Soviet policy and five in support of Peking. Voting with the Chinese throughout the meeting were Albania, North Korea, North Viet Nam, Indonesia, and the delegate of one of the Japanese peace organizations."

Canadian Wheat Trade. On Dec. 4, the Canadian Government announced that Communist China had ordered 18,700,000 bushels of wheat from Canada for $35 million.

Chinese Editorial. On Dec. 4, the Peking *People's Daily* charged that the withdrawal from China of Soviet experts and economic aid had been responsible for disarrangement of their original economic plan because it had come at a time when China was having "enormous difficulties." The article said: "They suddenly and unilaterally decided to withdraw (in July of 1960) all their experts, totaling 1,390, who were assisting China in its work, tore up 343 contracts, and annulled 257 items of scientific and technical cooperation. After that, they heavily slashed the supply of whole sets of equipment and crucial parts of installations. This caused heavy losses to China's construction work and dislocated its original plan for the development of the national economy, greatly aggravating our difficulties."

Soviet Editorial. On Dec. 6, the Soviet Communist Party newspaper *Pravda* commented that "the open polemics have gone too far and in many instances overstepped the standards of relations between Communist parties." *Pravda* urged that the dispute be limited to "the normal course of interparty relations."

Sixth Article. On Dec. 11, the Peking *People's Daily* and the Chinese Communist Party's theoretical journal *Red Flag* published their sixth article on the Sino-Soviet split. The article, "Peaceful Coexistence--Two Diametrically Opposed Policies," included a lengthy analysis of "Lenin's and Stalin's policy of peaceful coexistence, which all Marxist-Leninists, including the Chinese Communists, stand for," compared to "the anti-Leninist policy of peaceful coexistence, the so-called general line of peaceful coexistence advocated by Khrushchev and others." Khrushchev was denounced for not understanding that "the imperialists' cold war against the socialist countries (is one of the) manifestations of the international class struggle (which) inevitably goes on, now in an acute and now in a relaxed form." The article added that "the heart and soul of the general line of peaceful coexistence pursued by the leaders of the Soviet Communist Party is Soviet-United States collaboration for domination of the world...(but) all that the leaders of the Soviet Communist Party have received from the U.S. imperialists is humiliation!"

Cambodian Incident. On Dec. 12, Cambodian head of state Prince Norodom Sihanouk ordered the Cambodian Ambassador to the U.S. to close the embassy in Washington and return home. The next day, the U.S. Ambassador to Cambodia was recalled for consultation. Continuing deterioration of U.S.-Cambodian relations resulted from a statement broadcast over the Cambodian government's radio expressing satisfaction at the deaths of South Vietnamese President Ngo Dinh Diem, Thai Premier Sarit Thanarat, and "the great boss of these aggressors."

The U.S. immediately protested, and on Dec. 12 the Cambodian government denied that any reference had been made to the late President Kennedy. On Dec. 14, Prince Sihanouk ordered closing of the Cambodian embassy in London. The British also had protested the broadcast.

Hilsman's Speech on China. On Dec. 13, Assistant Secretary of State for Far Eastern Affairs Roger Hilsman Jr., addressing the Commonwealth Club of San Francisco, said that the U.S. was "determined to keep the door open to the possibility of change (in Communist China), and not to slam it shut against any developments which might advance our national good, serve the free world, and benefit the people of China."

Hilsman declared that the Chinese were "dangerously over-confident" and "wedded to outdated theories, but pragmatic when their existence is threatened." He conceded that "We have no reason to believe that there is a present likelihood that the Communist regime will be overthrown," but he said there was "some evidence of evolutionary forces at work in mainland China" among the intellectuals and the "more sophisticated second echelon of leadership" which would one day come into power. Hilsman added that U.S. defense of Formosa was a matter of basic principle" and there could be no "basic improvement" in U.S.-Chinese relations until Communist China accepted that fact.

Chou in Cairo. On Dec. 14, Chinese Communist Premier Chou En-lai, starting a two-month tour of Africa with Foreign Minister Chen Yi, arrived in the United Arab Republic for a six-day visit. He met with U.A.R President Gamal Abdel Nasser and told a news conference Dec. 20 that he knew nothing of Chinese development of atomic weapons. Chou was reported the same day to have called President Kennedy's assassination a "despicable, shameful act."

On Dec. 21, Chou and Nasser issued a joint statement denouncing "the imperialist policy adopted in the Middle East" and warned against "the threat of such a policy to world peace and security." Nasser supported the Chinese Communist claims to Formosa, and Chou supported the U.A.R. on the Arab refugee problem.

During his visit, Chou admitted that Communist China had "serious differences with the leaders of the Communist Party of the Soviet Union." But, he added, those countries that "want to profit by these differences are doomed to failure," because China and the U.S.S.R. "have between them a Treaty of Friendship, Alliance and Mutual Assistance" and, in case of attack, "the Chinese and Soviet peoples will without fail stand by each other."

Rusk and De Gaulle. On Dec. 16, Secretary of State Dean Rusk and French President Charles de Gaulle met in Paris. It was reported later by U.S. spokesmen that de Gaulle had denied reports that France was going to recognize Communist China.

Soviet Action in UN. On Dec. 17, the Soviet Union voted against a proposal before the UN General Assembly to revise the UN Charter to enlarge the Security Council and the Economic and Social Council to give greater representation to Asian and African nations. The Soviet delegates said they voted against the resolution because they felt there should be no expansion until Communist China became China's representative in the UN.

On Dec. 18, the Peking *People's Daily* said the Soviet Union had misrepresented Communist China by voting against the resolution. The newspaper stated that "the Chinese government has consistently and actively supported the Asian and African nations' efforts to obtain an increase in the number of their seats in the principal UN bodies." On Dec. 21, the Soviet Foreign Ministry criticized Communist China for failing to disclose its position on the resolution until after the vote had been taken.

Acheson Mission. On Dec. 17, Cambodia's Prince Norodom Sihanouk said "it would be useless" for former Secretary of State Dean Acheson to "come to our country" unless the U.S. met certain conditions. The conditions included an apology for a remark said to have been made by a member of the U.S. delegation at the UN about a Cambodian radio broadcast following President Kennedy's assassination. Sihanouk demanded also the closing of an allegedly anti-Cambodian radio station said to be operated by the CIA in Laos or Thailand. The Acheson mission, planned for the purpose of seeking improvement in U.S.-Cambodian relations, never materialized.

McNamara Mission. On Dec. 21, Secretary of Defense Robert S. McNamara reported to President Johnson on his return from a two-day fact-finding mission to South Viet Nam. Following their meeting, it was announced that the previous plan (see Oct. 2, 1966) to withdraw most U.S. military personnel from Viet Nam by the end of 1965 had been abandoned. McNamara reportedly told the President that the Viet Cong had made progress in the wake of the chaos created by overthrow of the Diem regime.

Chou in Algeria. On Dec. 21, Chinese Communist Premier Chou En-lai and Foreign Minister Chen Yi conferred with Algerian President Ahmed Ben Bella. In a speech to National Liberation Front Groups, Dec. 24, Chou asserted that the current international situation was "excellent for revolutionary struggle and the pursuit of national liberation." Declaring that Algeria could be called "the Cuba of Africa," he predicted that there would be more such revolutions in Africa and Latin America. Chou called for "a second Asian African conference," similar to the 1955 conference at Bandung, Indonesia.

Wheat to Russia. On Dec. 26, the U.S. Department of Commerce announced it had approved two export licenses for shipment to Russia a total of 500,000 tons of wheat, valued at $40,640,000.

Chou in Morocco. On Dec. 27, Chinese Communist Premier Chou En-lai and Foreign Minister Chen Yi arrived in Rabat, Morocco, where they met with King Hassan and other officials. The Moroccans had been disturbed by China's support of Algeria in that country's border dispute with Morocco.

On Dec. 29, Chou was interviewed in Rabat by a French television network. He said: "We believe it possible that countries with different social systems should coexist peacefully." He added that war was "not inevitable between the socialist and imperialist camps," but he accused the U.S. of impeding peaceful coexistence by "its policy of hostility towards China" and by holding the "Chinese territory of Taiwan (Formosa)...and maintaining military bases around China and violating Chinese airspace and territorial waters." Chou said he hoped a "normalization of relations" between Communist China and France might result in establishment of cultural and economic ties between the two nations.

Chou in Albania. On Dec. 31, Chou arrived in Tirana, Albania. He and Albanian Premier Mehmet Shehu asserted in a joint statement that it was "now the sacred duty of Communists of all countries to combat modern revisionism and modern dogmatism, and to safeguard the purity of Marxism-Leninism." Shehu praised China for aiding Albania to overcome the effects of the Soviet bloc's economic blockade of his country.

1964

African Tour of Chou and Chen -- France Recognizes Red China -- McNamara on Withdrawing Troops From Viet Nam -- De Gaulle Urges Neutralization of Southeast Asia -- Washington and Hanoi Reject Neutralization -- Rusk on Far East Policy -- White House Pledge to Viet Nam -- Fulbright on Far East Policy -- Khrushchev's Opinion of China's Leaders -- U.S. Troops to Stay in Viet Nam -- Red China's Foreign Minister on Relations With U.S. -- Lodge Resigns as Ambassador to South Viet Nam -- Gulf of Tonkin Crisis -- Congressional Resolution Supporting Johnson's Southeast Asian Policies -- Charges Against Chinese in Africa -- China's First Nuclear Explosion -- Chou in Moscow -- Hints of Wider Viet Nam War -- Ambassador Taylor Confers with President -- Tito on Sino-Soviet Split -- Chou Denounces U.S. Action in Southeast Asia.

China's Chief Task for New Year. On Jan. 1, the Peking *People's Daily* said that an increase in agricultural output would be China's "most important task" in 1964. The editorial said that "all efforts will be devoted" to the increase, even if workers from other occupations have to be transferred to agricultural production.

Message to Viet Nam. On Jan. 1, President Johnson, in a message to Maj. Gen. Duong Van Minh, chairman of the ruling South Vietnamese military junta, said the U.S. would "continue to furnish you and your people with the fullest measure of support in this bitter fight" and "maintain in Viet Nam American personnel and material as needed to assist you in achieving victory." The message added that "As long as the Communist regime in North Viet Nam persists in its aggressive policy, neutralization of South Viet Nam would be another name for a Communist takeover."

Goldwater Announces. On Jan. 3, Sen. Barry Goldwater (R Ariz.) announced he would seek the 1964 Republican Presidential nomination. He previously had summarized his prime foreign policy objective as "total victory" in the face of "the all-embracing determination of communism to capture the world and destroy the United States." Believing that negotiations with the Communists were dangerous, Goldwater favored severance of diplomatic relations with the Soviet Union and liberation of Cuba and Eastern European satellites. He opposed sale of wheat to the U.S.S.R. and was one of eight Republican Senators who voted against ratification of the 1963 limited nuclear test ban treaty. He thought the U.S. should withdraw from the United Nations if Communist China were admitted.

Wheat Sale to Russia. On Jan. 3, the "single biggest sale of wheat in American history," according to the Agriculture Department, was concluded between the Soviet Union and Continental Grain Co., one of several U.S. grain trading companies that had been negotiating with Soviet representatives. The Soviets agreed to pay $78.5 million in cash for 37 million bushels of wheat delivered at Russian ports.

Chou and Chen in Africa. On Jan. 9, Chinese Communist Premier Chou En-lai and Foreign Minister Chen Yi arrived in Tunisia. On the following day, Chou and Tunisian President Habib Bourguiba announced that their countries would establish diplomatic relations and "build up economic and human exchanges."

On Jan. 12, Chou and Chen Yi arrived in Ghana. On Jan. 16, the Chinese Premier joined President Kwame Nkrumah in proposing an Asian, African, Latin American "anti-imperialist" conference and a conference of the world's leaders "if it could be convened for the purpose of prohibiting the development and use of all nuclear weapons and the complete destruction of existing nuclear weapons."

On Jan. 16, the Chinese leaders arrived in Mali, where, on Jan. 21, Chou and President Modibo Keita announced Mali's "determination to move forward on the road to socialism," with increased aid from Communist China. On Jan. 20, a *New York Herald Tribune* dispatch pointed out that the Soviet Union had "spent more than $50,000,000 on economic aid to Mali," while the Chinese Communists to date had "sent 300 to 400 technicians to teach improved methods on rice paddies, and sugar and tea plantations."

On Jan. 21, Chou and Chen arrived in Guinea. Five days later, Chou and President Sekou Toure said they wished "to further develop the relations of friendship and cooperation, in particular in the economic field." Asian and African countries, they added, "must first of all depend on their own efforts and rely on their own people," but "self-reliance does not exclude foreign aid, which is only an auxiliary means" to which "no political conditions or privileges whatsoever should be attached."

Castro on Russia's Side. On Jan. 23, Cuban Premier Fidel Castro, winding up a nine-day visit to the Soviet Union, declared his support for the U.S.S.R. in its ideological dispute with Communist China.

Laos. On Jan. 23, Communist Pathet Lao forces in central Laos launched a new military offensive against rightist and neutralist government forces.

France Recognizes Red China. On Jan. 27, France established diplomatic relations with Communist China. The State Department called the French action "an unfortunate step, particularly at a time when the Chinese Communists

Defense Department Expenditures Since 1948

The Defense Department was established Sept. 17, 1947.

(billions of dollars)

Fiscal Year	
1948	$11,198.0
1949	11,988.0
1950	12,021.0
1951	20,755.0
1952	41,339.0
1953	47,558.0
1954	43,955.0
1955	37,823.0
1956	38,403.0
1957	40,788.0
1958	41,258.0
1959	43,563.0
1960	42,824.0
1961	44,676.0
1962	48,205.0
1963	49,973.0
1964	51,245.0
1965	47,401.0
1966	54,200.0 (Estimated)
1967	58,300.0 (Estimated)

are actively promoting aggression and subversion in Southeast Asia and elsewhere." The statement said the U.S. would "stand firmly by its commitments" to Nationalist China, South Viet Nam, and other countries endangered by Communist China.

McNamara on Far East. On Jan. 27, Secretary of Defense Robert S. McNamara told the House Armed Services Committee that the Administration was hopeful of withdrawing a majority of the 15,000 American troops in South Viet Nam before the end of 1965. McNamara noted that the U.S. effort in South Viet Nam had begun in 1961 and it was "reasonable to expect that after four years of such training, we should be able gradually to withdraw certain of our... personnel." The Secretary said he did not feel the U.S. "should assume the primary responsibility for the war in South Viet Nam," although some U.S. military personnel would "have to stay there until the counter-insurgency operation has been successfully completed."

On the dispute between China and Russia, McNamara said it was "now quite evident that we are witnessing more than a disagreement on ideological matters and on strategy in opposing the free world," and that "what is involved is a direct clash of national interests." Because this clash led to a major cutback of Soviet military aid, the Chinese probably would not undertake any major military campaigns in 1964 but "will certainly continue to support subversion and insurrection in Southeast Asia and will attempt to gain control of revolutionary movements elsewhere in the world."

South Vietnamese Coup. On Jan. 30, Maj. Gen. Nguyen Khanh, commander of the Vietnamese Army's First Corps, led a bloodless rebellion against the military junta which had been in control of the government since the Diem regime was ousted in November 1963. Maj. Gen. Duong Van Minh, leader of the junta, was placed under house arrest in Saigon.

Gen. Khanh told American observers that the coup had been necessary to foil a plot by members of the military junta to neutralize South Viet Nam. Khanh said the junta members had been collaborating with French agents and that formalization of the plot was to have coincided with France's recognition of Communist China. On Jan. 28, however, the South Vietnamese government had issued a statement criticizing the French action as likely to encourage Chinese Communist aggression in Asia.

Chou in Ethiopia. On Jan. 30, Chinese Communist Premier Chou En-lai and Foreign Minister Chen Yi arrived in Ethiopia. On Feb. 1, Chou and Emperor Haile Selassie announced their intention to expand economic and cultural relations of the two countries.

De Gaulle on S.E. Asia Neutralization. On Jan. 31, French President Charles de Gaulle said at a news conference in Paris that French recognition of Communist China was justified because France could no longer ignore "the fact that for 15 years almost the whole of China is gathered under a government which imposes its laws, and that externally China has shown herself to be a sovereign and independent power." Going on to propose neutralization for Southeast Asia, de Gaulle said: "There is in Asia no political reality... that does not concern or affect China. There is...neither a war nor a peace imaginable on this continent without China's being implicated in it. Thus it would be...impossible to envisage, without China, a possible neutrality agreement relating to the Southeast Asian states -- a neutrality, which by definition, must be accepted by all, guaranteed on the international level, and which would exclude both armed agitations...and the various forms of external intervention; a neutrality that...seems...to be the only situation compatible with the peaceful coexistence and progress of the peoples concerned."

Johnson Rejects Neutralization. On Feb. 1, President Johnson, commenting on the possibility of neutralizing Southeast Asia, said at a news conference: "I do not agree with Gen. de Gaulle's proposals. I do not think that it would be in the interest of freedom to share his view....I think that the present course we are conducting is the only answer,... and I think that the operations should be stepped up there." Secretary of State Dean Rusk added at a Feb. 7 news conference that the U.S. would not consider neutralization of South Viet Nam unless North Viet Nam also were neutralized. Rusk noted that De Gaulle's statement had contained "no detailed proposals."

Chou in Somalia. On Feb. 1, Chinese Communist Premier Chou En-lai and Foreign Minister Chen Yi arrived in Somalia. Chou told French newsmen that U.S. "aggression and intervention" had prevented reunification of Viet Nam under the 1954 Geneva agreements. He added that all peaceful countries "should join efforts" to force the U.S. to withdraw from South Viet Nam.

Seventh Article on Splittism. On Feb. 3, the Peking *People's Daily* and the Chinese Communist Party's theoretical journal *Red Flag* published the seventh article in a series on the Sino-Soviet split. Entitled "The Leaders of the Communist Party of the Soviet Union Are the Greatest Splitters of Our Time," the article asserted that the international Communist movement was "confronted with an unprecedentedly serious danger of a split." It said: "Opportunism and

revisionism are the political and ideological roots of splittism. And splittism is the organizational manifestation of opportunism and revisionism. It can also be said that opportunism and revisionism are splittism as well as sectarianism. The revisionists are the greatest and vilest splitters and sectarians in the Communist movement."

"The Soviet Communist Party leaders have completely reversed enemies and comrades...(and) are bent on seeking Soviet-United States cooperation for the domination of the world....By embarking on the path of revisionism and splittism, the Soviet Communist Party leaders automatically forfeited the position of 'head' of the international Communist movement."

Chou and Chen Return to China. On Feb. 5, Chinese Communist Premier Chou En-lai and Foreign Minister Chen Yi returned to Peking. Their trip through 10 African countries and Albania had lasted 55 days.

Formosa Breaks with France. On Feb. 10, the Nationalist Chinese government announced it had broken diplomatic relations with France. The action resulted from French recognition of the Peking regime.

Hanoi Rejects Neutralization. On Feb. 11, two Communist party newspapers in North Viet Nam published a government statement that North Viet Nam would never accept neutralization of its territory. The statement also warned that if the U.S. attacked North Viet Nam, as "certain military circles" in the U.S. had proposed, Communist China would come to its aid.

Cambodian Complaint. On Feb. 11, Prince Norodom Sihanouk of Cambodia charged that two South Vietnamese planes had attacked a Cambodian village and killed five people. Sihanouk said the U.S. was partly responsible because it had "overarmed" South Viet Nam. He again demanded an international conference on Cambodia's neutrality and warned that if the U.S. remained "passive" about the conference, Cambodia "would be compelled to modify our neutrality status and would have to consider assistance pacts with certain great friendly countries."

Khrushchev on Red Unity. On Feb. 14, Soviet Premier Khrushchev told a plenary meeting of the Soviet Communist Party's Central Committee that the U.S.S.R. was attempting to restore "the monolithic unity of the world socialist system." He said: "We have fought and will continue to fight against revisionists, dogmatists, the newly-baked Trotskyites who, while making high-sounding revolutionary phrases about the struggle against imperialism, undermine in fact the unity of the world Communist movement by splitting their activities."

Chou's New Trip. On Feb. 14, Chinese Communist Premier Chou En-lai and Foreign Minister Chen Yi arrived in Burma. On Feb. 18, Chou and General Ne Win, head of Burma's military junta, said in a joint statement that the emerging nations of Africa and Asia should concentrate on building "their independent national economy...(depending) on the efforts of their peoples and their own material resources." The statement warned the emerging nations to "beware of attempts by colonialists and neo-colonialists to dominate newly independent countries by taking advantage of the financial and economic difficulties with which they are faced."

On Feb. 18, Chou and Chen Yi proceeded to Pakistan, where, after talks with President Mohammed Ayub Khan, Chou announced that Communist China would support Pakistan's position on Kashmir.

Argentine Wheat for China. On Feb. 19, Argentina signed an agreement to sell Communist China 400,000 tons of wheat.

Johnson Gives Warning on Viet Nam. On Feb. 21, in a speech at the University of California at Los Angeles, President Johnson hinted at reappraisal of U.S. efforts in Viet Nam. In what was viewed as a major foreign policy statement, the President warned "those engaged in external direction and supply" of Communist fighting there that "this type of aggression is a deeply dangerous game."

Johnson's speech was followed Feb. 24 by announcement that Defense Secretary Robert S McNamara would visit Viet Nam the following week. While Defense Department officials said McNamara's major mission would be to assess the military effectiveness of the new government headed by Maj. Gen. Nguyen Khanh, they added that he would also hear suggestions for expanding the war effort. On the same day, *Tass,* the Soviet news agency, warned that "new and senseless plans" to extend fighting to North Viet Nam would have "the most serious consequences."

China and the Congo. On Feb. 22, the Republic of the Congo (Brazzaville) recognized Communist China.

Rusk on Far East Policy. On Feb. 25, Secretary of State Dean Rusk, addressing a world affairs conference in Washington sponsored by the AFL-CIO International Union of Electrical, Radio and Machine Workers, said: "We have special and very grave concerns about Communist China. And here let me clear away a myth. We do not ignore the Chinese Communist regime....We talk with it regularly through our respective ambassadors to Warsaw. There have been 119 of these talks. And what the Peiping regime itself says to us is among the reasons why we continue to have very grave concerns about it.

"Peiping continues to insist upon the surrender of Formosa as the *sine qua non* of any improvement whatever in the relations with the United States. We are loyal to our commitments to the Government of the Republic of China; and we will not abandon the 12 million people of Free China on Taiwan to Communist tyranny.

"Peiping incites and aggressively supports the aggression in Southeast Asia in violation of the Geneva Agreements of 1954 and the Geneva Accords of 1962.

"Peiping attacked India and occupies a position from which it continues to threaten the subcontinent of South Asia.

"Peiping is attempting to extend its tactics of terror and subversion into Africa and Latin America.

"In other words, Peiping flouts the first condition for peace: leave your neighbors alone.

"And we in the United States have not forgotten Peiping's aggressive intervention in Korea -- an act for which it stands condemned by the United Nations.

"The American people cherished their close and cordial ties with the people of the Chinese mainland. They look forward to the time when it will be possible to renew this historic friendship."

Chou's Demands on U.S. On Feb. 25, while touring in East Pakistan, Chinese Communist Premier Chou En-lai demanded at a press conference that the U.S. withdraw its military personnel from Viet Nam and end its "armed intervention" in Laos. He reiterated the conditions for an improvement in relations between the U.S. and China: a change in America's "hostile policy toward China" and a withdrawal from Formosa and the Taiwan Straits.

Chou in Ceylon. On Feb. 26, Chinese Communist Premier Chou En-lai and Foreign Minister Chen Yi were greeted coolly in Ceylon. On Feb. 29, Chou and Mrs. Sirimavo Bandaranaike, Ceylon's Prime Minister, jointly urged an Asian-African conference, establishment of nuclear free zones in "various parts of the world," and reaffirmation of the Ceylonese view "that Taiwan is an integral part of China."

Johnson's Statement. On Feb. 29, President Johnson was asked at a press conference if an "extension of the fighting in South Viet Nam might bring Communist China or even the Soviet Union into the fight." The President said in reply: "I would answer your question merely by saying that I do not care to speculate on what might happen." He added later: "The speculation on Viet Nam has been going on for some time. I was out there in 1961. There was a good deal of speculation then. In my California speech, I intended to say just what I did, that aggressors who intend to envelop peaceful, liberty-loving, free people, and attempt to do so through aggressive means, are playing a very dangerous game. That is what I said, that is what I meant, and that is a very dangerous situation there and has been for some time."

Khanh Charges Plot. On March 1, South Vietnamese Premier Nguyen Khanh related at a press conference that there had been a plot by French agents to kill him and end the war in Viet Nam through "a neutralist settlement." Khanh said he had "the names of the agents" and would "take them all" when "we know the whole organization." The French embassy in Saigon denied the charge.

Rumania and China. On March 2, a delegation from Rumania began talks with Chinese President Liu Shao-chi in Peking on "the question of unity of the Socialist camp." On March 11, a joint statement said only that the talks had been held "in a friendly atmosphere."

Canadian Barley to China. On March 3, the Canadian government announced the sale of 16.3 million bushels of barley to Communist China.

Viet Cong and Paper Tiger. On March 4, the Peking *People's Daily* ran an article asserting that the "U.S. paper tiger had been punctured and exposed" by the Viet Cong in South Viet Nam. The article added that the Viet Nam experience had proved that "the people of any country...subjected to U.S. aggression can win victory if only they are not overawed by its apparent strength and...know how to struggle."

McNamara Mission. On March 8, Secretary of Defense Robert S. McNamara arrived in Saigon for the fourth time during the Viet Nam war. Before leaving Washington, he had told newsmen there was "evidence that in the last six months the North Vietnamese support of the Viet Cong had increased," and that weapons recently captured from the enemy "were obviously of Chinese Communist manufacture."

The Secretary said also that his mission was a "further affirmation of the U.S. commitment to furnish whatever military training and logistical support is needed by the South Vietnamese to suppress this insurgency and to continue to furnish that support for whatever period is required."

Accompanied by a number of high U.S. officials and Premier Khanh, McNamara visited several hamlets in the Mekong River delta, including Hoa Hao, where he said: "The thing which we want to emphasize is that Khanh has the full and complete support of President Johnson and our whole government and I want to let his people know this."

Premier Khanh had issued a 15-page policy statement March 7 proposing reforms to give South Viet Nam "a solid foundation for the task of national salvation and development." The Premier said: "The previous...program followed the principle of building too many hamlets too quickly.. We shall...insist on quality rather than quantity, giving equal stress to the security factor and to (increasing) the standard of living of the population."

Cambodia Accuses U.S. On March 9, Prince Norodom Sihanouk, Cambodian chief of state, accused the U.S. of torpedoing his plans for an international conference on Cambodia's neutrality. Sihanouk charged that the U.S., Laos, Thailand, and South Viet Nam had conspired to partition his country. He warned he would negotiate border agreements with the "future masters of Viet Nam and Laos," the North Vietnamese and the Laotian pro-Communist Pathet Lao.

Gruening and Morse on Viet Nam. On March 10, Sen. Ernest Gruening (D Alaska) in a Senate speech called the war in Viet Nam "a bloody and wanton stalemate." He said: "The time has come to cease the useless and senseless losses of American lives in an area not essential to the security of the U.S. This is a fight which is not our fight, which we should not have gotten into in the first place." Sen. Wayne Morse (D Ore.) added: "Southeast Asia may very well be essential to the defense of some of our allies, but who are they? They ran out on us. We should never have gone in. We should never have stayed in. We should get out."

On March 11, Sen. Thomas J. Dodd (D Conn.) replied to Morse and Gruening by urging increased efforts "to help turn the war against North Viet Nam, the home base of the aggressor."

Peking Review Article. On March 13, Communist China's English-language weekly magazine, *Peking Review*, published an article blaming the Soviet Union for "serious economic difficulties" suffered by China since 1959. The article said that because of the withdrawal of Soviet technicians and cancellation of contracts, "certain projects were brought to a standstill and a number of installations could not be put into operation.... In these circumstances...a fairly big readjustment in our economy had to be carried out."

Chinese Arms for Cambodia. On March 15, a planeload of arms arrived in Cambodia from Communist China. At the airport, Prince Sihanouk told the Chinese Communist ambassador: "Since our liberation from conditional American aid, our two armies have been able fraternally to extend hands. This is not conceived, as Thailand maintains, to menace the peace and encourage Cambodia to become aggressive. Our only worry is to have sufficient military force to dissuade instigators of imperialistic war who menace the Cambodian peace."

White House Statement on Viet Nam. On March 17, the White House, in a rare public statement following a meeting of the National Security Council, pledged the U.S. "to furnish assistance and support to South Viet Nam for as long as it is required to bring Communist aggression and terrorism under control." The NSC meeting followed a five-day inspection trip to Viet Nam by Defense Secretary McNamara, Chairman of the Joint Chiefs of Staff Gen. Maxwell D. Taylor, and other high ranking officials.

While admitting there "have unquestionably been setbacks" in Viet Nam since McNamara's and Taylor's last visit in October 1963, the White House expressed confidence in the new regime of Maj. Gen. Nguyen Khanh. The statement said the South Viet Nam government had "produced a sound central plan for the prosecution of the war" and recognized

"the crucial role of economic and social as well as military action to ensure that areas cleared of the Viet Cong survive and prosper in freedom."

The statement outlined parts of a new South Vietnamese mobilization plan to increase the numbers, pay and equipment of military and paramilitary forces and create "a highly trained guerrilla force that can beat the Viet Cong on its *own* ground." The White House said that while South Viet Nam now had "the power to clear any part of its territory," Gen. Khanh's new program was designed to "clear and hold, step by step, and province by province."

China Supports Palestine Arabs. On March 17, a Peking *People's Daily* declared that Communist China supported "the restoration of the lawful rights of the Arab people of Palestine," and that "Israel, created and nurtured by the United States, has all along been used as an instrument of aggression against the Arab countries."

Cambodian Village Raided. On March 19, Cambodia charged that U.S. and South Vietnamese soldiers had mistakenly raided a Cambodian village, killing 17 people. The Cambodian government demanded that the U.S. send Cambodia "one bulldozer or a powerful tractor for each of our (17) dead." Secretary of State Rusk denied that American troops had been involved in the attack.

U.S.-Indonesian Relations. On March 24, Secretary of State Dean Rusk warned Indonesian President Sukarno that the U.S. would cut off aid shipments to Indonesia if that country did not settle its "confrontation" with Malaysia. On the following day, Sukarno said in Jakarta: "To hell with your aid! We can do without aid. We'll never collapse. Indonesia is rich in natural resources. Indonesia is rich in manpower with its 103 million inhabitants -- not like Malaysia with its 10 million."

On March 26, a spokesman for the Agency for International Development said the U.S. had made "a clear decision not to give this government (Indonesia) any aid that would directly support its current policies." The U.S. had been sending rice and cotton to Indonesia.

Fulbright on Far East Policy. On March 25, Sen. J.W. Fulbright (D Ark.), chairman of the Senate Foreign Relations Committee, spoke in the Senate on "Old Myths and New Realities," strongly criticizing American foreign policy. He asserted that "We are committed, with respect to China and other areas of Asia, to inflexible policies of long standing from which we hesitate to depart because of the attribution to these policies of an aura of mystical sanctity... "Whatever the outcome of a re-thinking of policy might be, we have been unwilling to take it because of the fear of many government officials, undoubtedly well-founded, that even the suggestion of new policies toward China or Viet Nam would provoke a vehement outcry." Nevertheless, the Senator asked for a re-evaluation of U.S. Far Eastern policy. For himself, he said:

"I do not think that the United States can or should recognize Communist China or acquiesce in its admission to the United Nations under present circumstances. It would be unwise to do so because there is nothing to be gained by it so long as the Peking regime maintains its attitude of implacable hostility towards the United States. I do not believe, however, that this state of affairs is necessarily permanent.... It is not impossible that in time our relations with China will change again, if not to friendship, then perhaps to 'competitive coexistence.' It would therefore be an extremely useful thing if we could introduce an element of flexibility, or, more precisely, of the capacity to be flexible, into our relations with Communist China."

Fulbright said the foremost of the new realities about China "is that there are not really 'two Chinas' but only one, mainland China, and that is ruled by Communists and likely to remain so for the indefinite future." He expressed hope that "a new generation of leaders" both in Communist China and Nationalist China "may put a quiet end to the Chinese civil war."

The Senator said there were "only two realistic options open to us in Viet Nam in the immediate future: the expansion of the conflict in one way or another or a renewed effort to bolster the capacity of the South Vietnamese to prosecute the war successfully on its present scale." He added that whatever course was taken, "it should be clear to all concerned that the United States will continue to meet its obligations and fulfill its commitments with respect to Viet Nam."

McNamara on Worsening Situation. On March 26, Secretary of Defense Robert S. McNamara told the annual dinner of the National Security Industrial Association in Washington that the "situation in South Viet Nam has unquestionably worsened, at least since last fall." In South Viet Nam, he added, the U.S. was "not dealing with factional disputes or the remnants of a colonial struggle against the French, but rather with a major test of communism's new strategy...of sabotage, terrorism and assassination on an unprecedented scale."

China vs. Malaysia. On March 27, an article in the Peking *People's Daily* condemned Malaysia as a "product of neocolonialism" and charged that "with the blessing of U.S. imperialism, the British imperialists have stepped up armed suppression in North Kalimantan (North Borneo) and resorted to military blackmail to threaten Indonesia."

Eighth Article. On March 31, the Peking *People's Daily* and the party's theoretical journal, *Red Flag*, published the eighth of its series of articles on the Sino-Soviet split. Entitled "The Proletarian Revolution and Khrushchev's Revisionism," the article described Soviet Premier Khrushchev as the "greatest capitulationist in history" and said the time had come "to repudiate and liquidate Khrushchev's revisionism," for it was "opening the floodgates for the restoration of capitalism."

Brazil and China. On March 31, the Brazilian army ousted the government of President Joao Goulart and seized power. The *Peking Review* on April 4 called "Washington's dirty work in the Brazilian camp...another ugly chapter in the history of U.S. domination of and interference in Latin America." The new Brazilian government on April 3 had arrested nine Chinese Communists on charges of conspiring with the Brazilian Communist party, which had been banned in 1947. On April 15, the Chinese Communist government demanded release of the nine prisoners and charged that the military government in Brazil was "under the scheming manipulation of U.S. imperialism, is colluding with the Chiang Kai-shek gang, and is planning to take the arrested Chinese to Taiwan."

The nine Chinese Communists were convicted on Dec. 22, 1964, by a Brazilian military tribunal and sentenced to ten-year prison terms. On Dec. 24, the *New York Herald Tribune* noted: "Brazil not only won the distinction of imprisoning the first Red Chinese agents caught in the Western Hemisphere. It also served notice on other American Republics how far afield the Chinese Communists already have

gone, and what they do when they get there." On Feb. 26, 1965, the nine Chinese were deported from Brazil.

Khrushchev on the Chinese. On April 1, 1964, Soviet Premier Khrushchev, said in a speech delivered on a visit to Budapest: "There are people...who call themselves Marxists-Leninists, and at the same time say there is no need to strive for a better life. According to them, only one thing is important -- revolution. What kind of Marxism is this?" The Soviet Premier asserted that the key to communism's victory was increased "productivity of labor in the socialist countries."

Khrushchev on April 3 called Communist China's leaders a "great danger." Two days later, while touring Hungary, he said they were "crazy" to try to develop China economically without outside aid; "only an idiot could pretend that it is easier to build socialism alone than by using the possibilities and support of the fraternal community of peoples who had previously taken the road." Back in Budapest, Khrushchev on April 9 made another speech, televised throughout Europe, in which he charged that the Chinese Communists were "renegades and traitors" whose "spasmodic efforts to subordinate world communism will end in shameful failure."

Chinese Called Racists. On April 1, Bobodzhan G. Gafurov, head of the Soviet delegation at an African-Asian Solidarity Council meeting in Algiers, told a French news agency that the Chinese Communists were attempting to pit the yellow and black races "against the whites," which was "no different from Nazism." Gafurov asserted that in Sinkiang Province "non-Chinese people are persecuted and take refuge in the Soviet Union, where they arrive half naked, starved and destitute."

China as Threat to Red Unity. On April 3, the Soviet government published a report by Mikhail Suslov, the Communist party's chief ideologist, charging that "the policy and activities of the Chinese leaders represent today the main danger to the unity of the world Communist movement." The report denounced Mao Tse-tung as the source of Communist China's "subversive policies."

Laos and China. On April 4, Prince Souvanna Phouma, Premier of Laos, visited Peking and appealed for assistance in bringing peace to his country. Chinese Communist Premier Chou En-lai replied by blaming Laotian difficulties on the U.S. and demanding that U.S. forces be withdrawn from South Viet Nam.

Australian Wheat to China. On April 5, Australia announced the sale to Communist China of 21 million bushels of wheat for about $35.8 million. This transaction brought the three-year total of Australian wheat sold to China to 300 million bushels valued at $448 million.

USIA Report on China. On April 8, the U.S. Information Agency in a report entitled "Asian Communist Bloc Propaganda Offensive" asserted: "Peking sustained a massive propaganda effort in 1963 to increase Chinese influence abroad and to gain friends both inside and outside the Communist bloc in its ideological confrontation with Moscow.... Freed from Moscow's restraining hand and flushed by what it held to be the promise of an economic 'take-off' on the mainland, Peking moved confidently to break out of isolation and to establish its own image internationally. These goals, together with the worsening of Sino-Soviet relations, the persistence of United States pressure of containment in the Far East, and opportunities for exploiting political, social, and economic turmoil in the underdeveloped world, provided the major stimuli for the continuous growth of Peking's propaganda mechanisms."

The report said that Peking, "determined to reduce its dependence on the Soviet bloc...made a prodigious effort in 1963 to seek out technical assistance, capital goods and raw materials from the West and new markets for Chinese exports." China concluded trade agreements with Japan, Britain, the Netherlands, Finland, Italy, Afganistan, Cambodia, Ceylon, Guinea, Iraq, Argentina, Canada, Australia, and Mexico. "In a probable re-export deal designed to increase its influence in Jakarta, Peking announced the sale of 40,000 tons of 'Chinese' rice to Indonesia, soon after purchasing some 100,000 tons of Burmese rice."

Khrushchev Knocks China. On April 12, Soviet Premier Nikita S. Khrushchev said in a radio and television address that it was "imperative" to give the leaders of Communist China a "resolute rebuff" for their "anti-Leninist concepts and subversive actions." Stressing that there should be equality within the Communist bloc, Khrushchev asserted that Communist China -- like Stalin -- had attempted to assume "a special role" in the international Communist movement.

Poles Assail China. On April 13, Polish officials arrived in Moscow for talks with Soviet leaders. A joint statement issued later accused the Communist Party of China of organizing "a brazen and slanderous campaign against the CPSU (Communist Party of the Soviet Union) and its Leninist leadership." The statement nevertheless advocated admission of Communist China to the UN, "ending of the occupation of Taiwan by American troops, and the reunification of this age-old Chinese territory with China."

Congo and China. On April 15, terrorism and violence broke out in the eastern Congo between government and rebel forces. The *New York Times* reported May 3 that the "Communist Chinese embassy in Burundi is believed to be backing the rebel action." On May 6, the Peking *People's Daily* said "the modern revisionists (were) accomplices in the U.S. imperialist crime of repressing the national independence movement in the Congo." On the same day, the *Associated Press* said: "Red China virtually acknowledged today it is deeply involved in the terrorism that has swept the eastern Congo.... The official Peking *People's Daily*...praised the Congo terrorists for resorting to violence rather than Soviet-style peaceful coexistence."

Nixon on Viet Nam. On April 15, former Vice President Richard M. Nixon, returning from a 24-day trip through Asia (described as a business trip for the Pepsi Cola Co.), told reporters that "We should strengthen our policy toward Communist activities in Asia rather than move along the lines suggested by Sen. Fulbright." Nixon later urged that the U.S. take action against Red outposts in North Viet Nam and Laos so that the "enemy can no longer have privileged sanctuary." On April 18, he told the American Society of Newspaper Editors in Washington that South Vietnamese forces should be allowed to follow Communist troops "in hot pursuit" into Laos and North Viet Nam.

At a news conference April 23, President Johnson was asked if Nixon's advice had been based on erroneous information. The President replied: "No, I wouldn't make that comment. I don't know what it was based on. I haven't talked to Mr. Nixon. I assume that he spent a good deal of his time out there looking after Pepsi Cola's interest. I don't know how much real information he got. But at least that is what he said he was doing." Mr. Johnson added that he

wanted "all of the men of the opposition party to know all the facts that dictate the decisions that involve our national interests."

Rusk in Viet Nam. On April 15, Secretary of State Dean Rusk, arriving in South Viet Nam, said: "I am here to make it clear once again that we shall help you to defeat Communist efforts "to impose their own misery on you." Accompanied by Premier Khanh and Ambassador Henry Cabot Lodge, Rusk toured hamlets in the northern part of the country. He told villagers: "Some day that regime in Hanoi will disappear and you and your brothers in the north will be able to join in a free and democratic Viet Nam."

Laotian Coup. On April 19, the Laotian coalition government under Prince Souvanna Phouma was ousted by a rightist military junta. The coup followed the failure of another attempt to unite the three Laotian factions: Pathet Lao, neutralists and rightists. On the same day, the U.S., Great Britain and France denounced the coup as a violation of the 1962 Geneva agreements. On April 22, Communist China charged that the U.S. had engineered the coup. The military junta announced April 23 that Prince Souvanna Phouma had been reinstated as Premier and would form a new coalition government. On May 2, Souvanna Phouma announced formation of a coalition of neutralists and rightists under his leadership.

Nuclear Materials Production. On April 20, President Johnson and Soviet Premier Khrushchev simultaneously announced that both countries would cut down production of nuclear materials. On the following day, Britain joined in the agreement. France refused to join.

Johnson on China. On April 20, in a speech at the *Associated Press* luncheon in New York, President Johnson said: "So long as the Communist Chinese pursue conflict and preach violence, there can be and will be no easing of relationships. There are some who prophesy that these policies will change. But America must base our acts on present realities and not on future hopes. It is not we who must re-examine our view of China. It is the Chinese Communists who must re-examine their view of the world." The President added that no one should "doubt our unalterable commitment to the defense and liberty of free China. Meanwhile, we will say to our historic friends, the talented and courageous people on the Chinese mainland, that just as we opposed aggression against them, we must oppose aggression by their rulers and for the same reasons." The President told his news conference April 23: "I anticipate that we will have stepped-up activity" in Viet Nam. He warned that it "would cost more money."

Troops to Stay in Viet Nam. On April 24, Defense Secretary Robert S. McNamara said at a news conference that the Administration had been forced to give up plans for withdrawing American military personnel from Viet Nam by the end of 1965.

Laotian Fighting. On April 27, the Communist Pathet Lao forces in Laos launched heavy attacks on rightist and neutralist forces. Britain and the Soviet Union, co-chairmen of the 1962 Geneva conference, attempted to arrange another cease-fire.

Mao Assailed by Pravda. On April 28, the Soviet Communist Party newspaper *Pravda* published an editorial asserting that Mao Tse-tung was not the lawful leader of the Chinese Communist Party because, in violation of the party statutes, he had not convened a party congress since 1956. The editorial said Mao was following the example of Stalin, who did not convene a party congress from 1939 till 1952. Pointing out that "The Chinese leadership has not reported to the party the fulfillment of the Five-Year Plan, although the five years since the last congress have elapsed long ago," *Pravda* commented: "They did not have the courage to tell the truth about the disgraceful failure of the fantastic 'great leap forward.'"

Terrorism in Saigon. On May 2, a U.S. naval ship, the WWII escort carrier *Card*, was sunk in Saigon harbor by a hidden bomb attached to the hull by Viet Cong divers. On May 3, a second bomb explosion in Saigon wounded eight U.S. soldiers and one Vietnamese civilian.

Chen Yi on Relations With U.S. On May 3, Chinese Communist Foreign Minister Chen Yi, in answer to questions asked by Western newsmen, said the initiative for better relations between the U.S. and China would have to come from the State Department and that China could only wait patiently. He said the State Department's policy toward Communist China had remained much the same despite eight years of negotiations (in Warsaw), and that the policy was exemplified by American refusal to recognize Communist China and to withdraw its forces from Taiwan. The Foreign Minister asserted that the American people were not at fault, only the U.S. Government since the time of President Truman.

Chen Yi on Nuclear Weapons. On May 3, Chen Yi said also that he did not know when China would have nuclear weapons but that it was only a matter of time. "We are against an atomic monopoly," he added. "Whatever the leading powers of the world can do, whatever level of technology they have reached, we want to catch up and arrive at the same level. We may be unable to catch up with a few very advanced powers in 10, 20, or 30 years, but we will never give up trying to catch up. If this is a strong attitude, it is because China is threatened. When the threat has been removed, we can take another attitude."

Soviet Charges Against China. On May 4, the Soviet government newspaper, *Izvestia*, published a statement accusing Communist China of attempting to use racism as a weapon against the Soviet Union in Asia and Africa, and of constructing "a Chinese wall between white, yellow and black nations." There followed an angry exchange of statements, one of which revealed that the Chinese Communist Party had rejected a Soviet proposal for a world conference of Communist parties to solve the Sino-Soviet dispute. On May 10, the Soviet Union, through *Pravda*, charged that Chinese leaders, especially Mao Tse-tung, wished to usurp the leadership of the international Communist movement. On May 11, another *Pravda* article charged that Communist China's government terrorized the people and perpetuated "poverty and privations of the working masses."

Ho Chi Minh's Warning. On May 10, an interview given by North Viet Nam's President Ho Chi Minh to Wilfred S. Burchett in April was made public. Ho told the Australian newsman that if the U.S. and South Viet Nam attempted to carry the war into the north, North Viet Nam had "powerful friends ready to help." Ho called French proposals for neutralization of the area worth negotiating, but he set withdrawal of American forces as a precondition to any discussion of the matter.

McNamara's Fifth Mission. On May 12, Secretary of Defense Robert S. McNamara arrived in Saigon, via Europe, on his fifth fact-finding mission to South Viet Nam. He was joined there by Chairman of the Joint Chiefs of Staff Gen. Maxwell D. Taylor. After conferring with South Vietnamese Premier Nguyen Khanh and U.S. officials, McNamara announced that the U.S. would send more fighter planes to Viet Nam. He warned that "It's going to be a long war."

On May 14, McNamara and Taylor returned to Washington, conferred with President Johnson and recommended that the U.S. increase its economic and military support of South Viet Nam. In a news conference after seeing the President, McNamara said the Viet Cong had increased its rate of attacks in past weeks, that South Vietnamese military forces would be increased, and that "certain additional U.S. personnel" would have to be sent to Viet Nam, but only in an effort to "expand the training" of Vietnamese troops. The Secretary added that victory was "not going to come soon." He said: "This is a war for the confidence...and security of those people, and that kind of a war is a long, hard war."

Crisis Over Laos. On May 13, Chinese Communist Foreign Minister Chen Yi sent letters to Foreign Ministers R. A. Butler of Britain and Andrei Gromyko of the Soviet Union (the two countries that were co-chairmen of the 1962 Geneva conference on Laos) charging that the U.S. had promoted the rightist military coup of April 19 in Laos to "endeavor to completely undermine the Laotian government of National Union, rekindle the flames of civil war in Laos and to create the division of Laos." Chen Yi said that "Laos is now faced with the dangers of all-out civil war as a result of provocations of United States imperialists and the Laotian right wing." (*See April 19 and April 27.*) The Chinese Foreign Minister proposed a new Geneva conference on the entire Indo-China question.

Meanwhile, Pathet Lao attacks on loyalist forces in Laos were continuing successfully. On May 19, Britain asked Communist China to use its influence to end the hostilities. Peking refused the request a week later and again charged that the U.S. was guilty of aggression in Indo-China. The Chinese proposed that foreign ministers of the countries represented at Geneva in 1962 meet at Pnom Penh, Cambodia, to confer on Southeast Asia, and that they take up the question of Laos first.

On May 21, a day after French President de Gaulle had called for a reconvening of the Geneva conference, Ambassador Adlai E. Stevenson said in the UN Security Council: "There is no need for another such conference. Another Geneva conference, if it reached any agreement at all, would prove no more effective than the agreements we already have." The U.S. later said it was agreeable to "consultations" in the Laotian capital of Vientiane or representatives of the 14 nations that signed the Geneva accords. The consultation approach (initiated by Prince Souvanna Phouma) would permit a quick meeting under terms of the Geneva accords, which provided for consultations in the event of aggression or other threats to Laos.

Senate Majority Leader Mike Mansfield (D Mont.) urged on May 21 that a conference be convoked before the whole of Indo-China collapsed in the "gathering chaos." Secretary of State Rusk suggested in a Washington speech the next day that the wars in Laos and in South Viet Nam were connected and would be expanded to North Viet Nam if the aggression continued.

Chinese-Soviet Trade. On May 16, Communist China announced it had signed a trade agreement with the Soviet Union three days earlier. Russia was to send China aircraft, tractors, trucks, tools, oil and chemicals; China was to send Russia metals, ores, frozen and canned pork, egg products, fruit, wool and silk. The value of the trade agreement was not disclosed.

China and Sudan. On May 16, the President of Sudan, Ibrahim Abboud, arrived in Peking for a state visit and was met by Mao Tse-tung in one of his rare public appearances. During his visit, the Sudanese President signed an agreement with China for export of Sudanese cotton in return for machinery and electrical equipment.

Aid to South Viet Nam. On May 18, in the midst of a deepening Southeast Asia crisis, President Johnson asked Congress for $125 million in additional economic and military aid for South Viet Nam. The President's request for $70 million more in economic aid and $55 million more in military aid was approved May 20 by the House Foreign Affairs Committee. A total of about $500 million for Viet Nam had already been requested in the budget for the fiscal year beginning July 1.

President Johnson told Congress the new funds were needed because the Viet Cong's campaign of terrorism had been stepped up, and because the new government of Prime Minister Nguyen Khanh had come to power since the first aid requests were submitted. It needed more help "to mount a successful campaign against the Communists."

Chinese Aid to Kenya. On May 20, Kenya announced that Communist China had agreed to grant that country $3 million immediately and to give it later a five-year, interest-free loan of $16 million.

Nehru Dies. On May 27, Jawaharlal Nehru, Prime Minister of India during the 17 years since the country became independent, died in New Delhi. Home Minister G. L. Nanda was sworn in as Acting Prime Minister.

Chinese Defection. On May 29, the State Department announced that a diplomat at Communist China's Embassy in Burundi had defected and was being given asylum in the U.S. Embassy there. The Chinese Embassy in Burundi charged that the diplomat, Tung Chih-ping, had been "kidnapped."

The Burundi government attempted to block Tung's departure from the country, but on July 31 the U.S. Embassy announced that Tung had "disappeared." On Aug. 4, he reappeared in New York and told a news conference that China was using Burundi as a "steppingstone to the Congo," because, according to the strategy of Mao Tse-tung, "When we grab the Congo, then we can grab the whole of Africa."

Southeast Asian Crisis. On June 1, high-ranking U.S. officials met in Honolulu to discuss the growing crisis in Southeast Asia. Among those attending were Secretary of State Dean Rusk, Secretary of Defense Robert S. McNamara, Chairman of the Joint Chiefs of Staff Maxwell D. Taylor, CIA director John A. McCone, Ambassador to South Viet Nam Henry Cabot Lodge, Under Secretary of State George W. Ball, and McGeorge Bundy, special assistant to the President.

On June 2, President Johnson told his news conference:

"It may be helpful to outline four basic themes that govern our policy in Southeast Asia.

"First, America keeps her word.

"Second, the issue is the future of Southeast Asia as a whole.

"Third, our purpose is peace.

"Fourth, this is not just a jungle war, but a struggle for freedom on every front of human activity.

"On the point that America keeps her word, we are steadfast in a policy which has been followed for 10 years in three administrations." The President then read a letter dated Oct. 25, 1954, in which President Eisenhower pledged U.S. support to Ngo Dinh Diem, then Premier of South Viet Nam.

On June 3, the Administration officials who had been conferring in Honolulu returned to Washington and reported to President Johnson. They recommended no basic changes in the American military role in Viet Nam but proposed ways to improve operations by the South Vietnamese.

On June 3, in Vientiane, Laos, talks began among six of the fourteen countries that signed the 1962 Geneva accords providing for Laotian neutrality. India, Great Britain, the U.S., Canada, South Viet Nam and Thailand discussed recent violations of the accords by the Communist Pathet Lao forces. The U.S. continued to oppose a French proposal to reconvene the Geneva conference on Laos -- a proposal which Russia and China supported. The U.S. was reportedly interested, however, in a Polish plan, which also had Soviet support, for a six-nation meeting without the U.S. or Communist China. The Polish proposal would include Britain and the Soviet Union, as co-chairmen of the 1962 Geneva conference; India, Canada, and Poland, as the members of the International Control Commission for Laos; and Laos itself, represented by the three factions in its coalition government.

On June 3, President Johnson, in a speech at the Coast Guard Academy in New London, Conn., said that the military strength of the U.S. was greater than "the combined might of all the nations in the history of the world, and... will continue to grow more rapidly than the might of all others." On June 7, the *Christian Science Monitor* noted: "Peking is warned. That, presumably, was the President's purpose."

On June 6, the Pathet Lao rebels in Laos shot down an American reconnaissance plane. On June 7, another was downed. On June 8, U.S. jet fighters attacked Pathet Lao positions in northern Laos. On June 10, the Peking *People's Daily* warned that the U.S. air attacks were "direct military attacks on the Laotian people" and charged that U.S. "armed intervention in Laos is gradually being extended with a view to intimidating the Laotian people into giving up their resistance....By 'escalating' armed intervention in Laos," the paper said, "the U.S. will only sink deeper... into a quagmire and meet with an ever more powerful rebuff." Chinese Communist Premier Chou En-lai had charged June 9 that the U.S. was wrecking the Geneva agreements on Laos and was bringing Laos "to the brink of a total split and general civil war."

On June 13, Communist China sent notes to the Soviet Union and Great Britain requesting that they reconvene a conference including the 14 nations that participated in the 1962 Geneva conference. The notes said that if the U.S. "should continue to be tolerated in going it alone and acting unscrupulously in defiance of the Geneva agreements, not only will it be impossible to restore peace in Laos, but there is a danger that...the war in Indo-China may spread."

On June 15, the Peking *People's Daily* warned that "the peace in Indo-China and Southeast Asia is hanging by a thread" due to continuing U.S. air attacks in Laos. The paper then asked: "We want to question the Johnson Administration. What are you planning to do? Do you intend to force the Chinese people to react to your provocations?"

China and Yemen. On June 1, the President of Yemen, Abdullah al-Sallal arrived in Communist China for a state visit. The next day, Liu Shao-chi, Red China's head of state, pledged his country's support for the people of "Aden, South Yemen and Oman in their just struggles against colonialism." All three countries were under British protection. President al-Sallal answered that Communist China's support had "strengthened the Arab people's struggle to uphold their independence and to oppose the imperialists' scheme of undermining the solidarity of the Arab people." On June 9, Communist China and Yemen signed a treaty of friendship and also agreements for economic and cultural cooperation.

New Indian Leader. On June 2, Lal Bahadur Shastri was appointed Prime Minister of India.

South Korean Riots. On June 3, full-scale riots broke out in Seoul against the government of South Korean President Chung Hee Park. The rioters, mostly students, charged that there was corruption in the government and that Park misused his power. On the same day, Seoul was placed under martial law. Park said the government could "no longer tolerate the excessively destructive activities of student demonstrators, who aim to overthrow constitutional government without presenting any constructive alternatives."

UN and Cambodia. On June 4, the UN Security Council voted 9-0, with the U.S.S.R. and Czechoslovakia abstaining, to send a three-man inspection team to Cambodia to investigate charges of border violations by South Viet Nam and to "consider such measures as may prevent any recurrence of such incidents."

China and Tanganyika. On June 11, a delegation from Tanganyika arrived in Communist China. On June 16, Vice President Rashidi Kawawa, head of the delegation, signed a treaty for cooperation with Communist China. On the following day, he called China the friend of all Africa and said he agreed with Mao Tse-tung that "imperialists are like dirt which will not move until it is swept out." It was learned later that China had given Tanganyika a small grant and an interest-free loan of $28 million.

De Gaulle's Statement. On June 12, French President Charles de Gaulle urged all foreign powers to withdraw from Southeast Asia, adding that "to desire peace for those countries implies for both sides to leave those countries -- Viet Nam, South and North, Cambodia and Laos -- alone to find their own destinies." On the same day, President Johnson and West German Chancellor Ludwig Erhard, who was visiting in Washington, said in a joint statement that South Viet Nam "must be fully supported in its resistance against the Viet Cong."

Warnings on Southeast Asia. On June 18, testimony of Assistant Secretary of State William P. Bundy, given before a House Appropriations subcommittee on May 4, was made public. Bundy told the subcommittee that if the Communist Pathet Lao in Laos seemed destined to win, "the only response we would have would be to put our own forces in there." Bundy said also that the U.S. was

determined to "drive the Communists out of South Viet Nam" even if it had to attack "the countries to the north."

On June 19, Secretary of State Dean Rusk told newsmen in a background briefing that if aggression did not cease in Southeast Asia, Communist China and North Viet Nam risked war with the U.S.

On June 20, the retiring commander of U.S. forces in the Pacific, Admiral Harry D. Felt, said at a news conference in Taipei, Formosa, that the U.S. was willing "to risk war with Communist China because we believe too strongly it cannot and must not win." Questioned further, Felt added that China, in his opinion, "will not risk going to war with the United States...because they know how strong we are."

On June 21, an editorial in *Pravda* declared that if Communist China continued its "dirty anti-Soviet campaign," it should not rely on Soviet assistance during a crisis.

On June 22, a State Department statement said: "There can be little doubt in the minds of the Communist leaders...that we are prepared to help the Vietnamese repel Communist aggression. Our support to Thailand is equally clear....Our position with respect to Laos is equally clear."

On June 24, Chinese Communist Foreign Minister Chen Yi warned that his country would not "sit idly by while the Geneva agreements (on Indo-China) are completely torn up."

China and Japan. On June 20, Chinese Communist Foreign Minister Chen Yi told a Japanese journalist during a radio and television interview: "The present state of Sino-Japanese relations still falls far short of the two people's strong desire for restoring diplomatic relations....The Chinese government has always held that in relations between China and Japan, politics and economics are inseparable." On June 27, Japan and Communist China agreed to exchange trade representatives. The U.S. and Nationalist China both strongly objected.

Lodge Resigns. On June 23, President Johnson accepted the resignation of Henry Cabot Lodge as Ambassador to South Viet Nam and named Gen. Maxwell D. Taylor, chairman of the Joint Chiefs of Staff, to replace him. Gen. Earle G. Wheeler was named to replace Taylor as chairman of the Joint Chiefs of Staff and Lt. Gen. Harold Johnson to replace Wheeler as Army Chief of Staff.

In announcing Lodge's resignation, the President said the U.S. was not seeking "a wider war" but was "determined to use its strength to help those who are defending themselves against terror and aggression." Johnson said he believed that China and North Viet Nam had "no doubt" about American policy in Southeast Asia.

Chinese Aid to Congo Rebels. On June 23, it was reported that two Chinese Communists were serving as advisers to Congolese leftist rebels in Kivu Province. On June 24, the Peking *People's Daily* said the rebellion in Kivu Province was "an excellent revolutionary situation" and added that the rebels would "win still greater victories like the people's armed forces of South Viet Nam."

Chinese Warning on Viet Nam. On July 6, Chinese Communist Foreign Minister Chen Yi said that any attack against North Viet Nam would threaten Chinese security and that "the Chinese people naturally cannot be expected to look on with folded arms" if such an attack occurred.

Thant on Viet Nam. On July 8, UN Secretary General U Thant urged that the 1954 Geneva conference reconvene to negotiate an end to the war in Viet Nam. Thant said that "military methods will not bring about peace in South Viet Nam" and that the "only sensible alternative is the political and diplomatic method of negotiation."

Rumania and China. On July 8, it was announced that Rumania and Communist China had agreed to expand their trade and to step up cooperation in scientific and technical fields.

China to Defend Viet Nam. On July 9, the Peking *People's Daily* announced that Communist China would "defend" North Viet Nam. The editorial added: "The Chinese people have always maintained that it is an unshrinkable proletarian internationalist duty of all Socialist countries to safeguard the peace and the security of the entire Socialist camp, to protect all its members from any imperialist invasion and to defend the Socialist camp."

Ninth Article. On July 13, the Peking *People's Daily* and the Chinese Communist Party's theoretical journal, *Red Flag*, published the ninth article in a series on the Sino-Soviet split. Entitled "On Khrushchev's Phony Communism and its Historical Lessons for the World," the article asserted that the Soviet Premier headed a "privileged stratum" in his country that was attempting to restore capitalism while "the broad masses" were "seething with discontent in the face of oppression and exploitation practiced by the privileged stratum." The article charged that Soviet leaders "appropriated the fruits of the Soviet people's labor" and made annual incomes "a dozen or even a hundred times those of the average Soviet worker and peasant." The Soviet leadership "carried out one purge after another, planting their proteges in all leading posts," until, under Khrushchev, the growth of a "new bourgeoisie" confronted the Soviet Union with "the unprecedented danger of capitalist restoration."

More Americans to Viet Nam. On July 14, the Defense Department announced that 600 more "military advisers" were being sent to South Viet Nam. On July 27, the U.S. announced that 5,000 more men would be sent to Viet Nam, bringing the total of U.S. military personnel there to 21,000.

Soviet Letter. On July 15, the Soviet Communist party made public a letter, sent a month earlier to the Chinese Communist Party, advocating immediate agreement to convoke a world meeting of Communist parties. The letter charged that the Chinese had opposed the meeting because they "could not count on support" from other parties for their views.

Goldwater Nominated. On July 15, the Republican Party nominated Sen. Barry Morris Goldwater of Arizona for President and Rep. William E. Miller of New York for Vice President. On China, the party's platform said: "We are opposed to the recognition of Red China. We oppose its admission into the United Nations. We steadfastly support free China."

Khanh Urges Invasion of North Viet Nam. On July 19, South Vietnamese Premier Nguyen Khanh, during a speech to 100,000 people in Saigon, demanded an invasion of North Viet Nam. Asserting that the Vietnamese people had "called for the war to be carried to the north," Khanh said that "the government cannot remain indifferent before the firm determination of all the people who are considering the push northward as an appropriate means to fulfill our national history." A statement issued the following day in the name of the South Vietnamese government declared: "If Communist China and Communist Viet Nam obstinately continue their war of aggression, the government and entire people of Viet Nam will step up the war with determination until total victory liberates the whole of our national territory."

On July 23, the new U.S. Ambassador to South Viet Nam, Maxwell D. Taylor, conferred with Premier Khanh and reportedly voiced displeasure over Khanh's pronouncements on carrying the war to the north.

De Gaulle's Proposal. On July 23, French President de Gaulle said at a Paris press conference: "It does not appear there can be a military solution in South Viet Nam ....Then, since war cannot bring a solution, one must make peace. This implies a return to the (Geneva) agreement made 10 years ago and that, this time, it should be respected; in other words, that in North Viet Nam, South Viet Nam, Laos and Cambodia, no foreign power intervenes in any way." De Gaulle urged reconvening of the Geneva conference to "organize the necessary control."

The French President proposed that the U.S., the Soviet Union, France and Communist China all withdraw from Indo-China and pledge to guarantee the area's neutrality and independence. He proposed also a "massive economic and technical aid program to the Indo-Chinese ensemble by the nations that can afford this, so that development should replace strife."

On July 24, President Johnson told a news conference in Washington that the U.S. had rejected De Gaulle's proposal. "If those who practice terror and murder and ambush will simply honor their existing agreements," the President said, "there can easily be peace in Southeast Asia immediately. But we do not believe in conferences called to ratify terror, so our policy is unchanged."

Militarization of China. On July 28, the Soviet government newspaper *Izvestia* published a dispatch from its Peking correspondent reporting that China was undergoing "total militarization" and that "military camps" were being established, where, "in addition to military training, (those participating) will digest the spirit of the people's army of liberation" and will be tutored in "correct political foundations." On the following day, the Chinese Communist news agency confirmed the report.

China Rejects World Conference. On July 30, the Chinese Communist Party announced that it had rejected the Soviet party's proposal for a world meeting of Communist parties. The July 28 letter of rejection said: "We will never take part in an international meeting, or any preparatory meeting, which you call for the purpose of splitting the international Communist movement."

Chinese Loan to Pakistan. On July 31, Pakistan announced it was to receive an interest-free $60 million loan from Communist China for purchase of heavy machinery, sugar mills and cement plants, and would repay the loan over a 30 to 40-year period with agricultural and manufactured goods. It was the first such agreement between the two countries, and was concluded at a time when Pakistan's relations with the U.S. had been rapidly deteriorating because the U.S. had supplied India with arms.

Gulf of Tonkin Crisis. On Aug. 2, the U.S. destroyer *Maddox* was attacked by three North Vietnamese PT boats in international waters about 30 miles off the coast of North Viet Nam. The Defense Department said the Seventh Fleet vessel was on a routine patrol in the Gulf of Tonkin when the PT boats attacked with torpedoes and gunfire. Joined by four U.S. aircraft from a carrier, the *Maddox* returned the gunfire and drove off the attacking boats. Informed of the attack, President Johnson held White House briefings with top U.S. military and diplomatic officials.

On Aug. 3, the President announced the following instructions to the Pacific naval command: (1) Continue the patrols in the Gulf of Tonkin; (2) double the destroyer force off North Viet Nam; (3) provide a "combat air patrol" over the destroyers; (4) attack any force which attacks U.S. naval patrols and attack "with the objective of not only driving off the force but of destroying it."

The State Department said it was sending a strong protest to North Viet Nam over "the unprovoked attack on an American ship in international waters." The protest warned the Hanoi government that it should be "under no misapprehension as to the grave consequences which would inevitably result from any further unprovoked offensive military action against United States forces."

On Aug. 4, the Defense Department announced that a second "deliberate attack" had been made by an undetermined number of North Vietnamese PT boats on two U.S. destroyers. The *Maddox* and the *C. Turner Joy* were fired on "while on routine patrol in the Tonkin Gulf international waters about 65 miles from the nearest land." The destroyers and their covering aircraft followed the President's orders of the previous day, returning the attack and apparently sinking at least two of the PT boats.

President Johnson summoned members of the National Security Council and top Congressional leaders for an evening conference at the White House. In a televised address to the nation shortly before midnight, the President announced that "air action is now in execution against gun boats and certain supporting facilities of North Viet Nam which have been used in these hostile operations." He termed the American response "limited and fitting" and emphasized that "we still seek no wider war."

President Johnson announced also that he had given the following instructions to Administration leaders in Washington: Secretary of State Dean Rusk was to make the American position "totally clear to friends, to adversaries, and indeed to all"; UN Ambassador Adlai E. Stevenson was to raise the matter "immediately and urgently" before the Security Council; Congressional leaders of both parties were requested to facilitate prompt passage of a resolution "making it clear that our Government is united in its determination to take all necessary measures in support of freedom and in defense of peace in Southeast Asia."

On Aug. 5, Secretary of Defense Robert S. McNamara told a news conference that 64 air sorties, launched from two Seventh Fleet carriers, were made against North Vietnamese PT boat bases and the supporting oil storage depots in four areas. The Secretary said the strikes resulted in destruction of approximately 25 North Vietnamese vessels, while two American planes were lost and two others damaged.

On Aug. 6, Communist China charged that the U.S. had "gone over the brink of war" in its retaliatory air strikes against North Viet Nam. The Peking radio said

it was up to North Viet Nam to "hit back in self-defense against the armed attack of the U.S. imperialists." Hanoi warned the same day that U.S. "acts of provocation...would be subject to due punishment."

Tonkin Gulf Resolution. On Aug. 7, Congress voted overwhelming approval of the resolution supporting President Johnson's actions in Southeast Asia (H J Res 1145). The House approved the resolution by a 416-0 roll-call vote. The Senate adopted it the same day by a vote of 88-2 with Sens. Wayne Morse (D Ore.) and Ernest Gruening (D Alaska) dissenting.

The resolution recorded that "Congress approves and supports the determination of the President, as Commander-in-Chief, to take all necessary measures to repel any armed attack against the forces of the United States and to prevent further aggression." It stated also that the United States was "prepared, as the President determines, to take all necessary steps, including the use of armed force, to assist any...(state protected by SEATO, including South Viet Nam) requesting assistance in defense of its freedom."

In debate, Rep. Eugene Siler (R Ky.), who paired against the resolution, called it an unnecessary "buck-passing" device designed to seal Congress' lips against future criticism. Rep. H.R. Gross (R Iowa) said: "For whatever value it may have as an expression of unity in this emergency, I will support the resolution. However, I am sick and tired of approving resolutions which try to imply that the United Nations has provided more than token opposition to the halting of the Communist world conspiracy."

Rep. William S. Broomfield (R Mich.) commented: "We have been called a paper tiger by the leaders of Red China, a tiger without real substance. By our actions in answer to provocation earlier this week, we have shown unmistakably in the only language the Communists seem to comprehend, that we decidedly have teeth and we know how to use them."

Rep. John M. Ashbrook (R Ohio) added: "Many of us are glad to see the President take the action in Viet Nam which he did. There are some pertinent questions to ask, however. Does this really represent a policy switch from the no-win, vacillating course of events which our State Department has followed? While I hope it has, I must say I am indeed apprehensive."

Rep. Henry S. Reuss (D Wis.) suggested: "Drawing on peace force patterns established in the Middle East, the Congo, Cyprus, and elsewhere, we should go before the UN and request the establishment of such a peace force for South Viet Nam, to patrol its borders, to restore tranquillity, and to depart when peace comes and free elections can be held."

Emergency Declared at Saigon. On Aug. 7, South Vietnamese Premier Nguyen Khanh declared a state of emergency with tightened government controls over travel, food distribution and curfews. Khanh asserted that Chinese troops were massing along China's southern frontier and that "the coming weeks will decide the destiny of our entire people."

Lodge to Visit Allies. On the same day, former Ambassador Henry Cabot Lodge announced that he would tour allied capitals for President Johnson to explain the situation in South Viet Nam. Following a White House conference with the President, Lodge said that his reports to allied officials would be "in support of our national policy."

Concern Rose Over Deepening U.S. Commitment in Viet Nam

After World War II, French forces reoccupied Viet Nam to begin a drama which ended nine years, 80,000 French casualties and 1.5 billion American dollars later. The leading nationalist underground organization fighting the French in Viet Nam was the Vietminh, headed by Ho Chi Minh, a Moscow-trained intellectual and a member of the French Communist Party since 1921. When the Japanese occupation ended, the Vietminh controlled most of the country and immediately proclaimed the founding of the Democratic Republic of Viet Nam, with Ho as the head of the new government in Hanoi.

By 1954, it was clear that the French were being beaten. In the early part of that year, the Vietminh offensive laid siege to the fortress of Dien Bien Phu, which controlled the highlands between the Mekong River Valley and the Red River delta. For a time, it appeared as if the the United States might intervene, but President Eisenhower and Secretary of State Dulles decided against it. On March 7, 1954, Dien Bien Phu fell to the Communists.

Geneva Conference. On the following day, a conference opened in Geneva to negotiate an armistice in Indo-China. Both Communist China and the Vietnamese government established by the French in Saigon were present, along with representatives of the Vietminh, the Big Four powers, Laos and Cambodia. The conference agreed to divide the country into two sections along the 17th parallel, with the Communist government in the north and the French-supported regime in the south. Vietminh forces were to withdraw from the south within 300 days and the French forces were to leave when the Saigon government ordered. It also was stipulated that nation-wide elections would be held in July 1956 to determine who should govern a reunited Viet Nam. The United States and the South Vietnamese governments refused to sign the agreements.

The 1956 elections never were held. The new South Vietnamese President, Ngo Dinh Diem, claimed the Geneva accords were made without the consent of the Vietnamese people.

U.S. Involvement. After 1954, as Communist China and the Soviet Union supplied North Viet Nam with military and economic aid, the United States filled the vacuum created by the French withdrawal in the south. From 1954 until fiscal 1962, U.S. aid to South Viet Nam amounted to $2.4 billion. By 1960, over 600 American troops were serving as advisers to the South Vietnamese armed forces. By mid-1963, after repeated pleas from President Diem, the number had grown to 12,000. But the numbers of the Viet Cong (the new name for the Vietminh) and the level of guerrilla activity had also increased.

The fortunes of the Viet Cong were further enhanced by the ineffectiveness of the South Vietnamese government and army and the strained relations between Washington and Saigon. President Diem's harsh suppression of all political opposition and his unwillingness to promote reform led to discontent among both the Vietnamese and the Americans.

Upset by the government's actions against Buddhists, suicidal burnings by Buddhist monks, corruption within the government, and inadequate military success against the Viet Cong, the State Department in 1963 gradually curtailed aid to President Diem. But on Nov. 1, an 18-hour, largely bloodless, military coup ended the Diem regime. The State Department denied participation in the coup, but unofficially admitted that it might have encouraged the "proper climate" for such a revolt.

The conflict in Viet Nam went badly for the United States in 1964. A series of South Vietnamese governments seemed unable to rally the people while the U.S. commitment in both men and money was significantly increased.

Gulf of Tonkin. On Aug. 2 and 4 U.S. destroyers patrolling the Gulf of Tonkin off the coast of North Viet Nam reported attacks by Communist PT boats and President Johnson ordered retaliatory air strikes at their bases, resulting in the destruction of 25 boats. On Aug. 5, the President asked Congress to enact a resolution to "give convincing evidence to the aggressive Communist nations, and to the world as a whole, that our policy in Southeast Asia will be carried forward, and that the peace and security of the area will be preserved." Two days later, Congress overwhelmingly passed the resolution.

Escalation. From that time on, the story of U.S. involvement in Viet Nam was one of rapidly increasing cost and commitment. On Feb. 7, 1965, the United States began its bombing of North Viet Nam. When this tactic did not succeed in turning the course of the war, President Johnson ordered a vast increase -- from about 20,000 to over 140,000 -- in American troop strength in the south, and an aggressive prosecution of the land war. Despite highly vocal criticism of his Viet Nam policy by a small number of Senators, Congress approved Mr. Johnson's special requests for funds with little dissension.

But the opposition was persistent. An unfavorable report on Viet Nam by Senate Majority Leader Mike Mansfield (D Mont.) Jan. 6, 1966, and President Johnson's Jan. 31 decision to end a 38-day pause in the bombing of North Viet Nam touched off an even more heated debate, both in Congress and on college campuses. In February, the Senate Foreign Relations Committee conducted nationally televised hearings on the Administration's Viet Nam policy, with testimony from supporters and opponents.

During 1966, as U.S. troop strength jumped to 400,000, the course of the war took a decided turn. The Communists, despite increased assistance from North Viet Nam, could not keep pace with the U.S. buildup and were forced to avoid large-scale confrontations. South Viet Nam found some political stability under Marshal Nguyen Cao Ky, who was able to weather Buddhist-led uprisings in the Spring of 1966. On Sept. 11, 80.8 percent of the registered voters in South Viet Nam elected delegates to a constituent assembly which was then to draft a constitution.

By early 1967, with U.S. forces pushing into the Viet Cong's traditional sanctuary, the Mekong River Delta area, and Communist China preoccupied with Mao Tse-tung's Cultural Revolution, North Viet Nam was giving vague indications of a willingness to negotiate. But the price of U.S. involvement had been high. By Jan. 28, the United States had already lost 7,109 men, and suffered 40,799 casualties.

UN Action. On Aug. 7, the UN Security Council extended an invitation to North Viet Nam to testify on the armed clashes in the Gulf of Tonkin. On Aug. 8, the crisis atmosphere began to ease as the Security Council adjourned the Southeast Asia debate pending a response to its invitation to North Viet Nam.

Response of Hanoi and Peking. On Aug. 9, North Viet Nam rejected the Security Council's invitation, declaring that the Council "has no right to examine U.S. war acts" in Viet Nam. On the same day, the Chinese Communist government asserted that "aggression by United States imperialism against the Vietnamese people means aggression against the Chinese people." A Central Committee official declared that China was "determined by practical needs to volunteer aid to the Vietnamese people."

On Aug. 10, Assistant Defense Secretary Arthur Sylvester confirmed reports that Communist China had been moving Russian-built MIG 15s and MIG 17s into North Viet Nam. Sylvester said that "This has been expected for some time because of known preparations such as lengthening of runways of airfields in the Hanoi area."

Soviet Invitations to Communist Parley. On Aug. 10, *Pravda* announced that the Soviet Union, at the end of July, had invited 25 Communist parties to attend a Dec. 15 preparatory meeting for a world Communist conference on the Sino-Soviet split. The article said that even if "some parties" were absent, the conference would still be held. The article accused the Chinese of being "afraid" to attend and added that their refusal to participate would be an attempt "to give the split a formal status."

Communist China replied Aug. 30: "We will never be taken in by your fine words, never submit to your threats, never be accomplices in your divisive activities and never share with you the responsibility for splitting the international Communist movement."

Tshombe's Statement. On Aug. 20, the new Premier of the Congo, Moise Tshombe, sent a note to UN Secretary General U Thant asserting that Communist China was attempting to exploit the strife in the Congo "to maintain a permanent center of subversion on Congolese soil." Tshombe appealed to the UN for aid in checking the Communist infiltration.

Government Crisis in Viet Nam. On Aug. 28, South Viet Nam's Finance Minister Nguyen Xuan Oanh was named Acting Premier after a week of anti-government demonstrations which forced Premier Nguyen Khanh to step down temporarily as head of the wartime military government.

Khanh on Aug. 7 had banned public demonstrations and established a strict curfew in Saigon. On Aug. 16 he promulgated a new constitution, which was to make him President with virtually dictatorial powers. These steps toward one-man rule touched off strong protests by Buddhist leaders and student groups. Government control collapsed Aug. 23 as rioting spread to all the major cities of South Viet Nam. The Military Revolutionary Council voted Aug. 25 to withdraw Khanh's "Presidential" powers and promised to name a new head of government who would convene a constitutional congress within two months.

Unable to agree on the choice of a new government leader, the 62-man military council appointed a triumvirate made up of Khanh, Gen. Duong Van Minh, and Defense Minister Tran Thien Khiem. The triumvirate named Har-vard-educated Oanh the Acting Premier. Oanh told a news conference that Khanh was still the Premier but was temporarily "incapacitated." Selection of Oanh and the promise of a new constitution brought restoration of order, although peaceful demonstrations continued in Saigon.

U.S. Ambassador Maxwell D. Taylor, after conferring with Khanh, said Aug. 31 that Khanh was "rested and recovered from his heavy workload" and "expects...in the next few days to resume his normal duties as head of the government."

In Washington, Secretary of State Dean Rusk said the upheaval represented "an adjustment in the responsibilities of individuals" and not a change of government "in the usual sense." Khanh returned to Saigon Sept. 3 after conferences with Buddhist leaders and military commanders. A government official announced that he would shortly resume his official duties as Premier, with the reported support of the top military personnel.

Johnson-Humphrey Ticket. On Aug. 26, President Lyndon B. Johnson was chosen Democratic nominee for President. On the same day, he recommended Sen. Hubert H. Humphrey (Minn.) as his running-mate and Humphrey was duly nominated for Vice President. The Democratic platform did not make the usual mention of Communist China but said only: "We will support our friends in and around the rim of the Pacific, and encourage a growing understanding among peoples, expansion of cultural exchanges, and strengthening of ties."

Maps of Red China. On Sept. 2, the Soviet Communist Party newspaper, *Pravda*, ran an editorial accusing Communist China of publishing maps that showed vast sections of the Soviet Union, Outer Mongolia, Burma, Viet Nam, Korea, Thailand, Malaya, Nepal, Bhutan, and Sikkim as parts of China. The editorial asked: "What would happen if all states should follow the Peking recipe and start presenting mutual claims to each other for a revision of historically formed borders....This would mean an inevitable aggravation of international tensions and would be fraught with military conflicts."

On Sept. 3, the *New York Times* reported that Mao Tse-tung had told a group of visiting Japanese Socialists July 10 that "the places occupied by the Soviet Union are too numerous." Communist China on Sept. 3 accused the Soviet Union of "creating constant border incidents" in the Ili area of Sinkiang Province. On Sept. 4, Soviet Premier Khrushchev said in Prague, Czechoslovakia, that Communist China's "territorial claims" on the U.S.S.R. indicated that they might "suggest the dismemberment of the Soviet Union."

Togliatti on Red Split. On Sept. 4, Italy's Communist party, considered the strongest in Western Europe, released a memorandum written by its First Secretary, Palmiro Togliatti, only a few hours before he died while visiting the Soviet Union. The memorandum said that, although he sided with the Soviet Union in its dispute with Communist China, he thought the December meeting of world Communist parties in Moscow was "ill prepared and premature," for it would only result in creation of a "Chinese center" of communism that would split the international Communist movement.

China and Africa. On Sept. 8, Prime Minister of Malawi, Hastings Kamuzu Banda, charged that Chinese Communist Embassy officials in Tanganyika had offered his political opponents either a $50 million economic aid program or the assassination of Banda in exchange for diplomatic recognition of Communist China.

On Sept. 10, Prime Minister Jomo Kenyatta of Kenya was urged by his political opponents to expel Chinese Communist diplomats from the embassy in Nairobi because they had issued a statement criticizing Premier Tshombe of the Congo.

China and Indonesia. On Sept. 9, the Peking *People's Daily* asserted: "Should United States imperialism dare launch aggression against Indonesia, the Chinese people will back Indonesia with all their might." The paper said it was the "common task" of China and Indonesia to "crush Malaysia." On Sept. 3, Malaysia had charged Indonesia with "blatant and inexcusable aggression" and had called for an emergency meeting of the UN Security Council. About 100 Indonesian paratroopers, dropped into two areas of Malaysia on Sept. 1, were promptly killed or captured by Malayan, British or New Zealand troops.

Attempted Coup in Saigon. On Sept. 13, a group of South Vietnamese army officers failed in an attempt to oust Premier Nguyen Khanh. Khanh owed the survival of his regime mainly to the loyalty of Air Commodore Nguyen Cao Ky, who had his planes circle over military units of the rebels until they withdrew.

Opium Traffic. On Sept. 13, *Pravda* charged that Communist China was engaged in illegal opium traffic grossing nearly $500 million a year. The article asserted that the profits were used to pay for anti-Soviet propaganda.

Revisionism in China. On Sept 13, the Chinese Communist Party's theoretical journal, *Red Flag*, published an article denouncing all those who had deviated from Mao Tse-tung's teachings. On Sept. 14, the *New York Times* suggested that a purge of intellectuals similar to the anti-rightist purge of 1958 might be developing. "Analysts believe," the *Times* said, "that such old-guard leaders as Mao Tse-tung, the party chairman, are afraid that Chinese Communist society is harboring trends similar to those that led the Soviet party to emphasize living standards and to compromise its international revolutionary goals."

New Gulf of Tonkin Incident. On Sept. 18, U.S. destroyers engaged in an encounter with apparently "hostile" vessels in international waters 42 miles off the coast of North Viet Nam in the Gulf of Tonkin. According to "preliminary and fragmentary reports," the Pentagon stated at the time, "no damage was reported by American vessels, and no loss of American personnel." Secretary of Defense Robert S. McNamara said in a clarifying statement Sept. 19 that four unidentified vessels "disappeared" after having menaced the two destroyers and drawn fire from them. The Secretary added that "darkness and poor weather" had made identification impossible.

On Sept. 19, North Viet Nam requested an immediate meeting of the International Control Commission to discuss the "American reports of new naval action in the Gulf of Tonkin." It charged that the reports were "pure fabrications prearranged by the United States." On Sept. 20, the Peking *People's Daily* said the U.S. had "engineered" the incident and promised "a helping hand" to North Viet Nam against U.S. "acts of war."

On Sept. 21, the Soviet news agency *Tass* reported that the U.S. destroyers had sunk three of five North Vietnamese ships in the Gulf of Tonkin on Sept. 18. On Sept. 22, the *New York Times* reported that the Defense Department "believes" that radar operations during the battle indicated that "at least one and possibly three unidentified craft were sunk." However, the Administration refrained in official statements from affirming that any of the ships were sunk, because of inconclusive evidence in the form of identifiable debris or visual sightings from reconnaissance planes.

Cambodia's No. 1 Friend. On Sept. 26, Cambodian chief of state Prince Norodom Sihanouk arrived in Peking on a state visit. In a joint statement Oct. 5, China pledged "all out support" of Cambodia in case of "foreign armed aggression." In a Peking speech, Sihanouk thanked China for "new and most important unconditional economic and military aid" and said that China was Cambodia's "number one friend."

China and Africa. On Sept. 28, Alphonse Massemba-Debat, President of the former French Congo Republic, visited Peking. A joint statement Oct. 3 with Chinese Head of State Liu Shao-chi said that China supported the Republic against "imperialist threats, interference and subversion" emanating from the former Belgian Congo. A day earlier, Massemba-Debat had signed a treaty of friendship and an economic agreement with Communist China.

On Sept. 29, the President of Mali, Modibo Keita, arrived in Peking on a state visit. Communist China and Mali already had close economic and cultural ties.

On Sept. 29, Communist China and the Central African Republic established diplomatic relations.

On Oct. 31, Communist China and Zambia established diplomatic relations.

Resistance to Expanding War. On Sept. 28, President Johnson said in a speech at Manchester, N.H., that he was opposed to involving the U.S. in "a war with 700 million Chinese." The President said also that the U.S. was "not going north (in Viet Nam) and drop bombs at this stage." The following day, Assistant Secretary of State William P. Bundy warned in Tokyo that "Expansion of the war outside South Viet Nam, while not of course what we want or seek, could be forced upon us by the increased external pressures of the Communists, including a rising scale of infiltration." Bundy added that the U.S. does not advocate "overthrowing the Communist regime of North Viet Nam, but rather inducing it to call off the war it directs and supports in South Viet Nam."

Rusk on China's Bomb. On Sept. 29, Secretary of State Rusk announced that Communist China might set off its first nuclear explosion "in the near future." He pointed out that "detonation of a first device does not mean a stockpile of nuclear weapons and the presence of modern delivery systems." Rusk said the U.S. "has fully anticipated the possibility of Peiping's entry into the nuclear weapons field and has taken it into full account in determining our military posture and our own nuclear weapons program." Noting that Communist China "not only failed to sign, but strongly opposed the Nuclear Test-Ban Treaty, which has been signed by over 100 countries," the Secretary added that the U.S. "would deplore atmospheric testing in the face of serious efforts made by almost all other nations to protect the atmosphere from further contamination and to begin to put limitations upon a spiraling arms race."

China and Czechoslovakia. On Sept. 29, Communist China announced it had signed an agreement with Czechoslovakia for scientific and technical cooperation.

Peiping & Peking

"The best explanation I have seen of the difference between Peiping and Peking appeared in an article entitled "China Notes" by Hans Koningsberger, which was published in the *New Yorker* of April 23, 1966:

"'By then (1949) Peking (the name means 'Northern Capital') had been rechristened Peiping (which means 'Northern Peace') by Chiang Kai-shek, and the capital had been moved to Nanking. In 1949, when the Communists took the town, they made it the capital once more and gave it back the name Peking. The United States State Department (off and on) and most American mapmakers have gone on talking about the nonexistent town of Peiping and putting it in atlases -- an interesting example of a nominalistic, well-nigh old-Chinese view of reality. It is reminiscent of that Ming emperor who, instead of bothering to build dikes, changed the name of a turbulent river from the Wild One to the Peaceful One. It didn't help.'"

(The above is taken from an article by Roy Copperud in *Editor & Publisher*, Aug. 27, 1966.)

Cairo Conference. On Oct. 5, leaders of 47 non-aligned nations met in Cairo for their second conference (the first was in Belgrade in 1961). On Oct. 7, Indian Prime Minister Lal Bahadur Shastri proposed that the conferees "consider sending a special mission to persuade China to desist from developing nuclear weapons." Shastri also urged the conference to oppose "any changes brought about by use of force as well as by quiet penetration of borders or subversion." On Oct. 10, Communist China called the proposal "provocative" and said: "The Indian government has vainly attempted to use the aid provided by the Khrushchev clique as a fig leaf on its signboard of nonalignment. But whether coming from the United States or the Soviet Union, arms obtained by expansionist India constitute the same threat to her neighbors."

China on Khrushchev. On Oct. 11, Communist China issued a statement again personally attacking Soviet Premier Khrushchev. It said: "A comparison between Khrushchev's statements yesterday and today exposes this big conspirator, careerist and double-faced hypocrite in all his ugliness. Yesterday, using the most obsequious language, he fervently extolled Stalin....Today, in the language of Trotskyites, he maliciously vilifies Stalin....Khrushchev is the biggest revisionist of the present time and the biggest teacher by negative example in the history of the...international Communist movement."

Three Russians in Orbit. On Oct. 12, the Soviet Union orbited a three-man space capsule, the first to contain more than one man. The flight lasted 16 orbits and 24 hours.

Khrushchev Ousted. On Oct. 14, the Soviet Union announced that Nikita S. Khrushchev had resigned as Premier and First Secretary of the Communist party. He was replaced as party secretary by Leonid Brezhnev, 57, and as Premier by Aleksei Kosygin, 60. Observers doubted that Khrushchev's resignation was voluntary. The government announcement said he had requested retirement in view of his "advanced age and deterioration of health."

On Oct. 16, Communist China's leaders extended "warm greetings" to the new Soviet leaders and voiced "our sincere wish" that they "will achieve new successes... in all fields and in the struggle for the defense of world peace." The message also expressed hope that the "fraternal, unbreakable friendship" between Communist China and the Soviet Union will "continuously develop."

Chinese Nuclear Test. On Oct. 16, Communist China successfully tested its first nuclear device. The official statement announcing the test said China "will never...under any circumstances be the first to use nuclear weapons." The statement proposed a "summit conference" of all nations to discuss "complete prohibition and thorough destruction of nuclear weapons."

President Johnson said the test came as "no suprise" and had been "fully taken into account" in the American defense program. He reaffirmed U.S. defense commitments in Asia. In a nationally televised speech Oct. 18, Johnson discussed the change in leadership of the Soviet Union and the Chinese nuclear explosion. He said the U.S. would continue to support the 1963 limited nuclear test-ban treaty and would work to end all nuclear tests and prevent the spread of nuclear weapons.

The President also assured "the nations that do not seek national nuclear weapons" that "if they need our strong support against some threat of nuclear blackmail, then they will have it." He cautioned against overestimating the military significance of the Chinese test: "Many years and great efforts separate the testing of a first nuclear device from having a stockpile of reliable weapons with effective delivery systems. Still more basic is the fact that if and when the Chinese Communists develop nuclear weapons systems, the free world nuclear strength will continue, of course, to be enormously greater."

Aftermath of Test. On Oct. 20, Chinese Communist Premier Chou En-lai, in letters to the leaders of all governments, proposed an international summit meeting on nuclear disarmament. On Oct. 22, UN Secretary General U Thant termed the Chinese test "regrettable" and "deplorable" but said it would be "very worthwhile" for the U.S., the U.S.S.R., Great Britain, France and Communist China to hold disarmament talks.

The following day the State Department replied that existing "channels for a dialogue are open" if China had "anything worthwhile to say." A State Department spokesman, noting that China would have to participate in negotiations "at some stage...if such agreements are to have any real meaning," said "we never have precluded the participation of any country in disarmament negotiations."

On Oct. 30, French President Charles de Gaulle in a message to Premier Chou En-lai, supported the proposed international disarmament conference and stressed that it should be set up "between the responsible and competent powers to discuss the problems of disarmament on a constructive and practical basis." The French President suggested that the conference should discuss means of "effective control," which the Chinese Communists had not mentioned in their original proposal.

New South Viet Nam Government. On Oct. 24, the High National Council of South Viet Nam, charged with preparations for a return to civilian government, chose a civilian, Phan Khac Suu, as Chief of State. Suu, who under the new constitution was limited (for the most part) to performing ceremonial functions, appointed as Premier and administrative head of the government former Saigon Mayor Tran Van Huong.

Premier Nguyen Khanh, responding to demands for a civilian government made by Buddhists and student groups during the August riots, had appointed the 17-man National

Council nearly two months earlier to draw up a new constitution. Khanh had promised at that time to step down as head of the military regime by Oct. 27.

Interview With Chou. On Oct. 24, Chinese Communist Premier Chou En-lai told a group of foreign newsmen that the ousting of former Soviet Premier Khrushchev was "a good thing," and that he hoped relations between the Soviet Union and Communist China would improve as a result. Chou said that Communist China would not "bargain with the nuclear powers" and that the purpose of China's nuclear program was "to break the nuclear monopoly and eliminate nuclear weapons." He added: "It is true that, compared with the nuclear weapons now in the hands of the United States, our bomb is insignificant. But...it is the fruit of our own efforts, of the efforts of Asians." When asked about China's admission to the UN and possible diplomatic recognition by the U.S., Chou replied: "That is a question that will come up even later because the United Nations is still controlled and manipulated by the United States and it is always thinking up all sorts of ways to obstruct restoration to the People's Republic of China of her position in the United Nations as the only legal representative of the Chinese people." He noted: "We have rich experience in dealing with the United States Government. The United States has held talks with the Ambassador of the People's Republic of China for more than nine years, and yet it does not recognize the new China."

New Soviet Goals. On Oct. 26, the Soviet government newspaper *Izvestia* published an article entitled "A Commonwealth of Equals," in which the new administration outlined its goals for unity of the Communist movement with equality and autonomy for each party. On Oct. 30, it was reported in the American and Western European press that a document listing 29 reasons why Khrushchev had been removed as Soviet Premier had been circulated among party officials. One of the main reasons cited was Khrushchev's handling of the Sino-Soviet rift. He was accused of allowing the situation to deteriorate to the point where the leaders of both sides were waging a conflict of personal polemics.

China's Support of Cambodia. On Oct. 27, after repeated charges by the Cambodian government that South Vietnamese and American planes had strafed and bombed Cambodian villages, the government sought Communist China's support against "the criminal aggression of the American-South Vietnamese forces of oppression."

On Oct. 31, Peking replied that it "cannot ignore... grave crimes...against the Cambodian people." On Nov. 9, Chinese Head of State Liu Shao-chi and Premier Chou En-lai wired the Cambodian government leaders that "650 million Chinese" supported Cambodia's "just struggle in defense of independence, neutrality and territorial integrity." China was "indignant at the grave crimes recently committed by the armed forces of the United States and its puppets."

De Gaulle on Nuclear Negotiations. On Oct. 30, French President Charles de Gaulle said in a message to Chinese Communist Premier Chou En-lai that his country would be willing "at any moment" to enter into "any serious negotiations" with the five nuclear powers. France was the only other nuclear power aside from Communist China that had refused to sign the 1963 nuclear test-ban treaty.

Soviet Pledge to India. On Nov. 1, the Indian Minister of Information, Mrs. Indira Gandhi, told a news conference in New Delhi following her return from Moscow that the new leadership in the Soviet Union had pledged to continue the policy of giving India both economic and military aid. Mrs. Gandhi said that, in her opinion, the Soviet policy toward Communist China would remain the same because "great differences make it very difficult for them to come to terms," although the new Soviet leaders might attempt to "smooth the edges" in their dispute.

Viet Cong Raid. On Nov. 1, as South Viet Nam was celebrating the first anniversary of the overthrow of the Diem regime, Communist Viet Cong forces staged a surprise night mortar attack on the U.S. air base at Bien Hoa near Saigon, killing five Americans, wounding 76 others, and destroying or damaging numerous aircraft. On Nov. 3, Communist China called the attack a great victory and said "no modern means or weapons" could save the U.S. from certain defeat.

Chinese-British Trade. On Nov. 2, the British Trade Fair, largest Western trade fair to be held in Communist China, opened in Peking. The president of China's Council for the Promotion of International Trade, Nan Han Chen, urged at the opening ceremony that all obstacles to expansion of Chinese-British trade be eliminated. He said that "United States imperialism is always creating artificial barriers in an attempt to hinder the development of trade" between Britain and China.

U.S. Election. On Nov. 3, President Johnson led the Democratic party to its biggest national victory since 1936. Johnson amassed the largest vote of any Presidential candidate in history and helped the Democrats score major gains in the House of Representatives and increase their already large majority in the Senate.

On Nov. 13, the Peking *People's Daily* commented on "Johnson's make-believe role of a 'searcher for peace' ": "Johnson's utterances show no trace of a 'moderate' looking for relaxation of international tension, but provide every indication that he is the chieftain of a ferocious and sabre-rattling U.S. imperialism....In the face of such a truculent and dangerous enemy, no one should entertain any illusions over the election of Lyndon Baines Johnson. The peoples of the Socialist camp, of Asia, Africa, and Latin America and all other peaceloving countries and peoples should further close their ranks and form the broadest possible united front against U.S. imperialism and its stooges."

Chou in Moscow. On Nov. 5, Chinese Communist Premier Chou En-lai arrived in Moscow, along with delegates from every Communist state except Albania, to celebrate the 47th anniversary of the Bolshevik revolution. On Nov. 6, eve of the anniversary, the Soviet party's First Secretary, Leonid Brezhnev, told the delegates that the new Soviet government would press for improved relations between the Communist and capitalist worlds "to prevent a world thermonuclear war." He also urged greater unity within the Communist world, more East-West trade, and "ever more democracy for the Soviet people."

Constantly mentioning the equality of all the Communist nations and parties, Brezhnev declared that "a world war is not inevitable in contemporary conditions." He advocated "reuniting" Formosa "with its homeland," the Chinese Communist mainland, and withdrawing U.S. troops from South Korea and South Viet Nam in order that "a peaceful reunification...on democratic principles" might be effected in those countries.

On Nov. 7, the Peking *People's Daily* published an editorial advocating unity between Communist China and the Soviet Union so that they may fight "the common enemy

...the nefarious United States imperialists and their lackeys." It also expressed optimism that "the difficulties which have temporarily appeared between China and the Soviet Union and between the two parties...can be gradually resolved."

On Nov. 13, after a series of long talks with the new Soviet leaders, Chinese Communist Premier Chou En-lai returned to Peking. A Soviet statement that day said only that the talks had been held in a "frank, comradely atmosphere."

Southeast Asia Politics. On Nov. 5, the new government of South Viet Nam began to disintegrate as Dr. Nguyen Xuan Chu, chairman of the High National Council, resigned in protest against the cabinet appointments of Premier Tran Van Huong. Chu said the political factions were not adequately represented and that "such a government cannot win the confidence of the population."

On Nov. 9, Prince Norodom Sihanouk, Cambodian chief of state, requested North and South Viet Nam and Laos to join Cambodia in a conference that would denounce U.S. interference in Southeast Asia. Sihanouk said President Johnson "would probably never have the courage to admit to his people that the population of South Viet Nam...has overcome its 'fear of communism' and will accept even communism provided the war stops."

China and Africa. On Nov. 12, the African state of Dahomey announced it would establish diplomatic relations with Communist China. On Dec. 6, the Prime Minister of Malawi, H. Kamazu Banda, announced that his country also would recognize Communist China.

U-2 Flight. On Nov. 16, Communist China announced it had shot down a pilotless U-2 high-altitude reconnaissance plane over south-central China. On Nov. 18, American military sources in Saigon said that the U.S. was launching pilotless reconnaissance aircraft (drones) from mother planes in South Viet Nam on missions over North Viet Nam. They could not report with certainty that any of the drones had been guided over Chinese territory.

Hints of Wider Viet Nam War. On Nov. 21, there were indications in Saigon, based on an interview with U.S. Ambassador to South Viet Nam Maxwell D. Taylor printed in *Life* magazine, that Taylor, upon his return to the U.S. Nov. 26 for conferences, would recommend limited bombing of military targets in North Viet Nam and Laos. In Washington, a State Department spokesman said Nov. 23 that Taylor's statements were "not policy," but merely "possibilities" that "exist as options."

On Nov. 25, Sen. Richard B. Russell (D Ga.), chairman of the Armed Services Committee, said: "I want to explore every avenue before extending the war. We either have to get out or take some action to help the Vietnamese.... We made a mistake in going there, but I can't figure out any way to get out without scaring the rest of the world."

On Nov. 26, Ambassador Taylor, arriving in Washington, refused to discuss whether or not he advocated expanding the war.

On Nov. 27, South Viet Nam's newly arrived Ambassador-designate to the U.S., Lt. Gen. Tran Thiem Khiem, urged in Washington that the U.S. strike North Viet Nam supply bases.

On the same day, Sen. Wayne Morse (D Ore.) called Ambassador Taylor one of the "key warmongers," who was "seeking to extend the war in Asia in the absence of a declaration of war." Morse urged that Taylor and Deputy

Ambassador U. Alexis Johnson be permanently recalled from South Viet Nam because they had been "complete failures" in bringing about internal stability in the country and "are in league with the war expansionists."

Chinese Rejection. On Nov. 22, the Peking *People's Daily* announced that Communist China had rejected UN Secretary General U Thant's proposal that the five nuclear powers hold disarmament talks and that Communist China participate in the 17-nation Geneva disarmament conference. The *People's Daily* said the Geneva conference was "in fact still under the manipulation and control of the United States," and "served as a smokescreen for U.S. imperialist armament expansion and war preparations."

China's Support of Congo Rebels. On Nov. 24, Belgian paratroopers were dropped from U.S. planes in Stanleyville in the Congo to rescue white hostages held prisoner by Congolese rebels. Later in the day, the Congolese government's army, led by white mercenaries, arrived in the city and drove the rebels out. On Nov. 28, Chinese Communist Party chairman Mao Tse-tung personally announced China's full support of the Congolese rebels and called on all the peoples of the world to "unite and defeat the U.S. aggressors." On the next day, 700,000 people demonstrated in Peking against U.S. policy in the Congo.

State of Siege in Saigon. On Nov. 26, South Vietnamese Premier Huong, after five days of anti-government demonstrations and mob violence inspired by political factions excluded from the civilian cabinet, imposed a state of siege in Saigon. Buddhist leaders demanded that the rioters be released and Huong ousted. Huong attributed the disorders to "dissatisfied politicians" and the Viet Cong.

On Nov. 28, South Viet Nam's High National Council demanded cabinet changes in the 22-day-old civilian government. Meanwhile, Thich Tam Chau, chairman of the National Buddhist Council's secular affairs department, warned that his organization would "wait to see whether the High National Council and the chief of state would take positive action" to remove the cabinet. "If not," he added, "the Buddhists will."

On the same day the Buddhist Secular Institute in Viet Nam accused the government of employing the same tactics against Buddhists as those employed by the Diem regime. It announced that it would oppose Hunong's regime through a campaign of noncooperation.

Johnson and Taylor. On Dec. 1, President Johnson met with South Viet Nam Ambassador Maxwell D. Taylor and other high Administration officials to review the situation in South Viet Nam. The President "instructed" Taylor to "consult urgently" with the government of South Viet Nam on measures "to improve the situation in all its aspects." A White House statement issued after the conference said that Taylor found the political situation in Saigon under the new government of Premier Tran Van Huong "still difficult" and reported "accumulating evidence of continuing and increased North Vietnamese support of the Viet Cong."

On Dec. 3, after another talk with the President, Taylor said that a series of new steps would be taken by the U.S. and South Viet Nam to improve Vietnamese military operations. He foresaw no need to increase American military personnel in Viet Nam. Taylor reportedly had discussed various proposals for expanding the war, including American bombing of Communist supply routes and depots in

North Viet Nam and Laos. Reports indicated that the President gave high priority to strengthening the civilian government and making it acceptable to the political factions in Laos before committing the U.S. to expand the war.

On Dec. 12, the Peking *People's Daily* warned that "should U.S. imperialism dare to invade the liberated areas of Laos, Cambodia, or the Democratic Republic of (North) Viet Nam, it will be severely punished." On Dec. 24, that warning was repeated with the added admonition that if the U.S. bombed the Ho Chi Minh trail, "the flames of war will spread to the whole of Indo-China."

Tito on Sino-Soviet Split. On Dec. 7, President Tito of Yugoslavia, addressing the League of Communists of Yugoslavia, acknowledged that there was no real unity in the international Communist movement. Taking up reasons for the disunity, he said the Sino-Soviet dispute was rooted in the "conflicting foreign policies of two great powers." The ideological differences between the two countries, he added, were only a "smoke-screen" to hide the real reasons for the split.

China on the UN. On Dec. 4, the Peking *People's Daily* announced that Communist China would not accept membership in any UN organizations until Nationalist China was ousted from every UN organization.

On the same day, the Foreign Minister of Japan, Etsusaburo Shiina, said in a speech to the UN General Assembly that Communist China's first nuclear explosion was an "open betrayal" of the world's "millions upon millions of people." He added: "We feel grave doubts about the intentions of the Communist Chinese leaders who launch a nuclear test explosion with a view to developing their nuclear arsenal and who in the same breath advocate the holding of a world summit conference on the prohibition of the use of nuclear weapons."

Increased Aid to Viet Nam. On Dec. 11, the South Vietnamese government announced that the U.S. would send increased economic and military aid to South Viet Nam. The State Department immediately added that the action did not mean the war would be extended to North Viet Nam. The South Vietnamese statement said its government had accepted "additional...assistance to improve the execution of the government's program and to restrain the mounting infiltration of men and equipment by the Hanoi regime in support of the Viet Cong."

Plan for World Communist Meeting. On Dec. 12, the Soviet Communist Party newspaper *Pravda* announced that a commission to plan a parley of the world's Communist parties would meet in Moscow on March 1, 1965.

China and Japan. On Dec. 12, the Peking *People's Daily* denounced the government of Japan for its policy toward China. The article specifically criticized the Japanese Foreign Minister's speech to the UN Dec. 4 and accused him of "peddling his 'one China and one Taiwan' stuff." It added: "This is an ugly variant of the 'two Chinas' plot created by U.S. imperialism. This not only helps the U.S. to continue its forcible occupation of Taiwan Province, China's territory, but also exposes the covetous designs of Japanese militarism to lay its hands once again on Taiwan."

Chinese Agriculture. On Dec. 12, it was reported that Communist China had reaped its greatest harvest since 1957, due mainly to good weather and more scientific farming methods. It was reported also that Communist China

had imported more grain during 1964 than in any previous year.

China and Indonesia. On Dec. 14, the *Times* of India reported that Communist China had offered to send military specialists, including those versed in nuclear weapons, to Indonesia.

On Dec. 15, the Indonesian Communist Party announced that it would not participate in the international Communist meeting proposed by the Soviet Union because such a conference could only lead to a total split.

Dissidence in Saigon. On Dec. 19, a group of South Vietnamese military officers overthrew the High National Council, arrested seven of its nine active members, and jailed the leading political opponents of Premier Tran Van Huong. The officers announced that the action had been taken "because we trust the prime minister and the chief of state and we do not (trust) the High National Council."

On Dec. 23, Secretary of State Dean Rusk and U.S. Ambassador Maxwell D. Taylor warned that U.S. aid would be reduced unless South Vietnamese leaders set "aside... personal rivalries or lesser issues in the interest of maintaining the strength and unity of the country." Rusk said that "if there are problems of unity, certain kinds of assistance...are simply not feasible."

Chou Denounces U.S. On Dec. 21, Chinese Communist Premier Chou En-lai denounced the U.S. for "aggression and intervention in Viet Nam, Laos and Cambodia" and for "occupation of South Korea" and said that "if the United States enlarges the war in Indo-China, China will absolutely not sit idly by." Chou also said that the U.S. had been informed through the Warsaw meetings that any "settlement of concrete problems in Sino-American relations is out of the question" until the U.S. withdraws its forces from the Formosa area.

Nuclear Submarine on China Station. On Dec. 26, the Defense Department announced that the first of seven U.S. submarines carrying nuclear-armed rockets was on station off the coast of Communist China. On Dec. 29, Communist China called the action a "naked provocation by United States imperialism against the Chinese people" and an "utterly shameless act of nuclear blackmail."

Chinese Aid to Cambodia. On Dec. 27, Cambodia announced that Communist China had agreed to give it more military aid, including heavy artillery.

1965

Red Front in Thailand -- Bombing of North Viet Nam Starts -- McNamara on the Stakes in Viet Nam -- Proposals for Viet Nam Negotiations -- Marines Land in Viet Nam -- Explosion Outside U.S. Embassy in Saigon -- Johnson's Johns Hopkins Speech -- Five-Day Bombing Pause -- Washington Teach-in -- Chou on Risk of World War -- Commitment of U.S. Troops to Combat -- First B-52 Raids -- Ky Government Installed -- Lodge Replaces Taylor at Saigon Embassy -- Ho Chi Minh's Four Points for Peace -- Lin Piao's Call for People's War Against Imperialists -- Communist China's Conditions for Entering UN -- Trouble in Indonesia -- Anti-War Demonstrations in U.S. -- Chinese-Soviet Exchange -- Christmas Cease-Fire in Viet Nam -- Year-End Peace Offensive -- Viet Nam Buildup in 1965.

Indonesia Leaves UN. On Jan. 1, the Indonesian delegation to the UN announced it had received orders to withdraw from the organization. Indonesian President Sukarno had warned Dec. 31, 1964, that Indonesia would leave the UN if Malaysia took the Security Council seat to which it had been elected Dec. 29. It was the first time any member had quit the organization.

On Jan. 6, the Peking *People's Daily* announced Communist China's support of the Indonesian action and added that Malaysia's election to the Security Council proved that the UN was "an American imperialist instrument of aggression, an infamous organ in the service of old and new colonialism, and a vile place for a few powers to share the spoils." U.S. officials asserted that Indonesia's move gave indication of an emerging "Peking-Jakarta axis" in Southeast Asia. Indonesia's departure took formal effect Jan. 21, when Ambassador L. N. Palar handed UN Secretary General U Thant a letter of resignation.

Soviet for Outlawing Nuclear Weapons. On Jan. 3, the Soviet news agency *Tass* reported that the Soviet Union had informed Communist China of its support for the latter's proposal of a world conference on the outlawing and destruction of all nuclear weapons. The Soviet note, *Tass* reported, said that Russia favored a "radical" disarmament agreement, but would also favor any agreement to "limit" or "slow down" production of nuclear weapons.

Instability in Saigon. On Jan. 4, South Vietnamese Premier Huong asserted in an interview published by the *Indian Express* that the political turmoil in Saigon was "not a clash between Americans and Vietnamese" but a personal feud between U.S. Ambassador Maxwell D. Taylor and Commander in Chief Lt. Gen. Nguyen Khanh.

On Jan. 5, the U.S., in a statement approved in Washington and issued by the American mission in Saigon, said: "The primary concern of the U.S. Government and its representatives is that there be in Saigon a stable government in place, able to speak for all its components, to carry out plans and execute decisions."

On Jan. 9, Gen. Khanh, Premier Huong, and Chief of State Phan Khac Suu signed a compromise declaration in which the armed forces reiterated their Aug. 27, 1964, pledge to leave affairs of state in the hands of the civilian government. A communique issued later said that legislative powers had been turned over to Suu until a legislative assembly could be organized. Ambassador Taylor called the declaration "a promising step in the direction of establishing a stable and effective government."

On Jan. 11, Senate Armed Services Committee Chairman Richard B. Russell (D Ga.) called for a re-evaluation of the American position in Viet Nam. Russell said that "Up to now we have been losing ground instead of gaining it." He feared total failure in Viet Nam unless "a more stable government" was established.

On Jan. 12, Communist China said it might intervene in Viet Nam "if U.S. imperialism continues to prosecute its scheme for expanding its aggressive war in South Viet Nam."

On Jan. 13, Premier Huong, after meeting with military leaders in Saigon, said he intended to bring the military into the government and to convene a national congress in March to cope with the political crisis.

China and Cuba Trade. On Jan. 5, Communist China and Cuba announced a five-year trade agreement designed to make "new contributions to the struggle against imperialism headed by the United States." Under the pact, Cuban sugar, nickel and copper were to be traded for Chinese rice, cotton fabrics, laminated steel, industrial machinery and other products.

Sato in Washington. On Jan. 12, Japanese Premier Eisaku Sato conferred with President Johnson. In a joint statement issued the next day, the President reiterated U.S. support of Taiwan (Formosa) and warned that "Communist China's militant policies and expansionist pressures against its neighbors endanger the peace of Asia." Sato said it was his country's policy to maintain friendly relations with the Nationalist government on Formosa, but "at the same time to continue to promote private contact" with Communist China, especially on matters concerning trade.

U.S. Planes in Laos. On Jan. 13, the U.S. acknowledged that two U.S. Air Force bombers had been shot down over Laos. The disclosure was the first public admission that U.S. forces were engaged in attacks on Communist supply lines beyond the borders of South Viet Nam. The jets were reportedly participating in an air strike by more than 20 U.S. planes which destroyed a key Laotian bridge on the Communist supply route from North Viet Nam. The State Department said Jan. 18 the U.S. was "assisting" Laos to defend its neutrality and independence as guaranteed by the 1962 Geneva accord but violated by the Communists.

Cabinet Reshuffle in Saigon. On Jan. 18, South Vietnamese Premier Huong reshuffled his 75-day-old civilian government, giving Cabinet posts to four generals and removing two ministers who had been the target of Buddhist criticism. An American Embassy spokesman in Saigon called the changes "a positive and helpful step toward stable government."

China and India. On Jan. 18, Communist China in a note to India charged that Indian troops and reconnaissance planes had violated Chinese territory. It was the second such charge made by the Chinese. The Indian government had rejected the first as a "fantastic fabrication." During the first weeks of 1965, the Indian government had arrested more than 800 Communists on charges that they were Chinese agents preparing "subversive and revolutionary action."

Red Front in Thailand. On Jan. 22, the Peking radio announced that a "Patriotic Front," similar to the National Liberation Front in South Viet Nam, had been established in Thailand. Thai Premier Thanom Kittikachorn had warned the previous week that Chinese Communist agents were infiltrating Thailand from Laos.

New UN Proposed. On Jan. 24, Chinese Communist Premier Chou En-lai, during a visit by Indonesian Foreign Minister Subandrio, said: "A revolutionary United Nations may well be set up so that rival dramas may be staged in competition with that body which calls itself the United Nations but which, being under the manipulation of United States imperialism, is capable only of making mischief and can do nothing good."

Canadian Wheat to China. On Jan. 25, Canada announced sale of 27 million bushels of wheat to Communist China.

Viet Nam Coup. On Jan. 27, following a series of Buddhist demonstrations, South Vietnamese military commanders staged a coup d'etat and ousted Premier Tran Van Huong. Deputy Premier Nguyen Xuan Oanh was named Acting Premier.

China and Indonesia. On Jan. 28, Chinese Communist Premier Chou En-lai and Indonesian Foreign Minister Subandrio issued a joint statement declaring that Communist China will "absolutely not sit idly by" if the U.S. or Britain "impose war on the Indonesian people." Indonesia denounced the U.S. "war of aggression in Indo-China" and the futility of "peaceful coexistence" with the Western countries.

Burundi Breaks With China. On Jan. 30, Premier Joseph Bamina of Burundi broke off diplomatic relations with Communist China and ordered the Chinese Ambassador and his staff to leave the country within 48 hours. It had been reported that Chinese were training Congolese rebels in Burundi.

Attempted Laotian Coup. On Jan. 31, army officers from the Laotian rightist faction attempted a coup against the coalition government. They announced that they only "wanted to make some changes" in the leadership of the army, and that their goals were not political. By Feb. 1, troops loyal to the government had defeated the rebel forces.

China and Niger. On Feb. 2, the President of Niger, Hamani Diori, charged that Communist China had plotted and financed an unsuccessful revolt against his government in the fall of 1964. He denounced Chinese Communist influence in Africa.

De Gaulle's Proposal for Revising UN. On Feb. 4, President Charles de Gaulle of France proposed at a news conference that a five-power conference, including Communist China, be convoked to revise the UN Charter.

Kosygin in Peking. On Feb. 5, Soviet Premier Aleksei Kosygin received a cool reception in Peking, where he stopped on his way to Hanoi.

Kosygin in Hanoi. On Feb. 6, Soviet Premier Kosygin arrived in Hanoi. At a dinner that night, North Vietnamese Premier Pham Van Dong urged that Soviet and Chinese Communist leaders forget their differences and join together in the fight against U.S. imperialism.

On the following day, Kosygin told a mass rally in Hanoi that his country would supply North Viet Nam with "all necessary assistance if aggressors dare to encroach upon (its) independence and sovereignty," and he "severely warns the United States against its schemes to provoke acts of war against North Viet Nam."

North Viet Nam Bombed. On Feb. 7, responding to major attacks by Viet Cong guerrillas against U.S. installations in South Viet Nam, American and South Vietnamese aircraft engaged in "joint retaliatory attacks" on North Vietnamese training and staging areas. The attacks continued Feb. 8 and 11. Announcement of the first U.S. attack was made Feb. 7 by President Johnson, who said it had been launched "in response to provocation ordered and directed by the Hanoi regime."

Viet Cong troops had carried out a major raid Feb. 6 against a U.S. airfield and billeting area at Pleiku, South Viet Nam, killing eight Americans and wounding more than 100. They also had made two smaller attacks in two other areas. The raids followed by only a few hours the arrival of Soviet Premier Kosygin in Hanoi.

The Feb. 7 White House statement, issued after a meeting of the National Security Council, said the U.S. attacks had been "carefully limited to military areas," which "intelligence has shown to be actively used by Hanoi for training and infiltration of Viet Cong personnel into South Viet Nam." The statement emphasized that "we seek no wider war" but added that "whether or not this course can be maintained lies with the North Vietnamese aggressors." Government sources said the Soviet Union had been informed of the limited nature and intent of the U.S. attacks.

President Johnson also announced Feb. 7 that he had ordered evacuation of approximately 1,800 American dependents in Viet Nam as a precautionary measure, because "it has become clear that Hanoi has undertaken a more aggressive course of action against both South Vietnamese and American installations." The President said, in addition, that he had ordered U.S. troop reinforcements and deployment of Hawk ground-to-air missile defense battalions in South Viet Nam.

Following the White House announcement, Secretary of Defense Robert S. McNamara told a news conference that the Viet Cong attack had been "a clear challenge of the political purpose of both the U.S. and South Vietnamese governments...which we could not fail to respond to... without misleading the North Vietnamese as to our intent and the strength of our purpose to carry out that intent."

More Action in Viet Nam. On Feb. 9, Viet Cong forces blew up a U.S. Army barracks at Qui Nhon, approximately 275 miles northeast of Saigon. Two Americans were killed, 23 were listed as missing, and 18 were wounded. On Feb. 11, the Defense Department announced that U.S. and South Vietnamese aircraft had bombed two more staging areas in North Viet Nam in retaliation for the latest attack.

Reaction to Bombing of North Viet Nam. The action in Viet Nam received general support from Members of Congress. Senate Majority Leader Mike Mansfield (D Mont.) said: "In view of the circumstances, I think the President did the only thing he could do. He had little choice in the matter." Senate Minority Leader Everett M. Dirksen (R Ill.) said the U.S. retaliatory attacks "could hardly be called an expansion" of the war. Dirksen added: "We're going to carry out our initial purpose and objective. We were asked in there to help preserve their independence and protect their government against Communist subversion and infiltration."

Sen Wayne Morse (D Ore.), strong critic of U.S. policy in Viet Nam, said: "The United States is carrying out the war escalation plans that both the Pentagon Building and the State Department have been manipulating for the past several months. The violations of international treaties by Communist nations and groups in Asia are inexcusable, but they do not justify the United States committing the same wrongs the Communists have been committing."

On Feb. 8, Communist China called the first air strike an "extremely serious provocation by United States imperialism to extend the war to" North Viet Nam "once again in defiance of world condemnation and in an effort to avert total defeat in South Viet Nam."

On Feb. 12, the National Liberation Front, the Viet Cong's political arm, in a radio broadcast urged its guerrilla forces to "fight the enemy with all means and weapons: Weaken their forces as much as possible,...destroy the strategic hamlets, and force the United States imperialists to pay more blood debts."

On Feb. 12, Soviet Premier Kosygin said in a speech at Pyongyang, North Korea, that the "imperialist provocations" in Viet Nam had made the Soviet Union, Communist China and North Korea "unanimous in their desire to support the heroic people of Viet Nam."

In a second statement Feb. 13, Peking recalled that it had "declared long since that aggression against the Democratic Republic of Viet Nam means aggression against China, and the Chinese people have long been prepared and know how to aid the people of Viet Nam and Indo-China in driving out U.S. aggressors."

On Feb. 14, U.S. Ambassador to South Viet Nam Maxwell D. Taylor said during an interview in Saigon that the amount of air activity against North Viet Nam would be "set by the behavior of the Hanoi government." As far as the U.S. was concerned, Taylor added, "the objective is limited -- namely to oblige Hanoi, to persuade Hanoi, to desist in its efforts to maintain the insurgency" in South Viet Nam.

Sino-Soviet Exchange. On Feb. 14, Communist China and the Soviet Union exchanged messages on the 15th anniversary of the signing of their treaty of mutual assistance and friendship. The Chinese note was far more militant, especially against the U.S., than the Soviet message, which did not mention the U.S. as an enemy or Viet Nam as a problem.

On the following day, Chinese Communist Foreign Minister Chen Yi said, during a reception at the Soviet Embassy in Peking, that "peaceful coexistence with United States imperialism, which is pushing ahead its policies of war and aggression, is out of the question." He added that "only in concrete action against United States imperialism and its followers can the Chinese-Soviet alliance be tested and tempered and Chinese-Soviet unity be consolidated and developed."

Chinese Threat to Enter War. On Feb. 15, the Peking *People's Daily* published an editorial warning that if the U.S. sent troops beyond the 17th parallel (the boundary separating North and South Viet Nam), Communist China would enter the Vietnamese conflict and also reopen the Korean War. "If the United States expands the war in Viet Nam," the editorial warned, "the front will extend from Viet Nam to Korea."

Another Coup in Saigon. On Feb. 16, a new civilian government was formed in Saigon, headed by Dr. Pan Huy Quat. Lt. Gen. Nguyen Khanh was ousted as Commander-in-Chief of the Armed Forces and Chairman of the Armed Forces Council. Quat, a former foreign minister, replaced Acting Premier Nguyen Xuan Oanh, who had been appointed by Khanh's Armed Forces Council after it had overthrown Premier Tran Van Huong on Jan. 27.

McNamara on Stakes in Viet Nam. On Feb. 18, Secretary of Defense Robert S. McNamara told the House Armed Services Committee that "the stakes in South Viet Nam are far greater than the loss of one small country to communism.... The choice is not simply whether to continue our efforts to keep South Viet Nam free and independent, but, rather, whether to continue our struggle to halt Communist expansion in Asia." The Secretary asserted that Communist China, while threatening India, Nepal, and other Asian nations, had decided to make South Viet Nam the decisive test. Pointing out that the Soviet Union

at least understood that nuclear war must be avoided, McNamara said: "Accordingly, we intend to pursue every step, no matter how small, which might lead to a peaceful understanding with the Soviet Union that would lessen the danger to us all, and we intend to stand fast against the present implacable animosity of Communist China until that nation, too, realizes that its security and progress can be better served by a more peaceful policy."

Chen Yi Blames U.S. On Feb. 18, Chinese Communist Foreign Minister Chen Yi said during a reception at the Nepalese Embassy in Peking that the "absurd (American) argument that to eliminate the present dangerous situation 'the Viet Cong should cease attacks' and be the first to cease fire" was "sheer drivel." Chen Yi contended that the U.S. was responsible for the situation and insisted that there would be "no peace in Indo-China as long as the aggressive forces of United States imperialism hang on there."

Red China and Tangania. On Feb. 20, Communist China and Tanzania signed a treaty of friendship and, in a joint statement, condemned the "imperialists."

Afro-Asian Seminar. On Feb. 23, the Chinese Communist representative to an Afro-Asian Economic Seminar in Algiers, Nan Han-chen, asserted that "Exploitation and plunder by imperialism and old and new colonialism is the root cause of the poverty and backwardness of the Afro-Asian and Latin American countries." He said that "the fundamental way for the Afro-Asian peoples to achieve complete national liberation is to develop independent national economics on the basis of self-reliance and through assistance to each other based on equality and mutual benefit."

U.S. Bombing in South Viet Nam. On Feb. 24, a U.S. Embassy spokesman in Saigon announced that American jet aircraft manned solely by American crews had taken part in bombing raids against the Viet Cong in South Viet Nam since Feb. 17. The statement said the American attacks, staged "at the request of the government of Viet Nam," were considered "appropriate, fitting and measured" in response to increased infiltration and provocations by the Viet Cong. All previous airstrikes in South Viet Nam had been made by South Vietnamese pilots, sometimes "assisted" by U.S. co-pilots. Defense Secretary Robert S. McNamara said Feb. 25: "Our policy has not changed in the slightest. Our tactics and equipment have changed."

Proposals for Viet Nam Negotiations. On Feb. 24, UN Secretary General U Thant, at a news conference, said he had presented "concrete ideas and proposals" to "some of the principal parties directly involved in the question of Viet Nam," including the U.S. Thant declined to disclose the replies. His proposals included negotiations which "alone," he stressed, "can create conditions which will enable the United States to withdraw gracefully from that part of the world." On Feb. 25, Presidential Press Secretary George Reedy said that any proposal by U Thant was "not before the President."

British Prime Minister Harold Wilson had announced Feb. 23 that his government was "actively engaged in diplomatic consultations of a confidential nature" with the Soviet Union to discover whether the Russians were interested in reviving the British-Soviet co-chairmanship of the 1954 Geneva conference, which established the division of North and South Viet Nam along the 17th parallel.

Soviet Ambassador to France, Sergei A. Vinogradov, after a Paris meeting with French President Charles de Gaulle, on Feb. 23 voiced Russian support of De Gaulle's proposals for a negotiated settlement in Viet Nam. De Gaulle had been advocating such a settlement since Aug. 29, 1963, when he called for an agreement that would leave Viet Nam in unity, peace and independence.

In Saigon, a leading Buddhist monk, Thich (Venerable) Tri Quang, had called on Washington and Hanoi, Feb. 19, to start immediate negotiations for a neutralizing settlement. Four days later, Thich Tam Chau, another top Buddhist leader, publicly requested a cease-fire with the Communists.

White Paper on North Viet Nam Aggression. On Feb. 27, the State Department issued a 14,000-word White Paper documenting North Vietnamese aggression against South Viet Nam. The report, entitled "Aggression from the North," concluded that stepped-up Communist involvement in South Viet Nam could no longer be met by military efforts in the South alone.

The White Paper did not predict new air strikes against North Viet Nam, but it invited the North Vietnamese to choose between peace and an "increasingly destructive" conflict. U.S. officials said the purpose of the paper was to counter pressures at home and abroad for a negotiated settlement. Opponents of U.S. policy in Viet Nam had contended that the conflict was a civil war and the U.S. had no justification for involvement. The White Paper represented a departure from the former insistence that, despite North Vietnamese participation, the war would have to be won in the South.

To document North Vietnamese aggression, the White Paper included case histories of North Vietnamese infiltrators who defected or were captured in the South, photographs of North Vietnamese and Chinese Communist arms caches captured in or on the way to South Viet Nam, captured documents describing infiltration activities, and lengthy appendices detailing arms shipments and troop movements.

Communist Parties Meet in Moscow. On March 1, delegations from 19 Communist parties met in a suburb of Moscow to lay plans for a unity conference of the world's 81 Communist parties. The parties of Albania, Communist China, Indonesia, Japan, North Korea, North Viet Nam and Rumania had turned down invitations to attend. The meeting, held in secret, ended March 5. A public statement, issued March 10, supported the plan for a global conference to re-establish unity in the world Communist movement but only after several years of preparation, which would include bilateral party talks and a preliminary meeting of the 81 parties. The statement called meanwhile for "an end to the public polemics, which have a character which is unfriendly and offensive for fraternal parties."

Air Strikes on North Viet Nam. On March 2, the U.S. joined South Viet Nam in the heaviest air strikes so far against North Viet Nam. At least 100 U.S. and 60 South Vietnamese planes took part. For the first time since selective air attacks on North Vietnamese targets began in August 1964, the strikes were not described as in direct retaliation for specific North Vietnamese or Viet Cong attacks. On March 3, more than 30 U.S. Air Force jets reportedly bombed the Ho Chi Minh trail in eastern Laos.

China and Pakistan. On March 2, President Ayub Khan of Pakistan arrived in Peking on a state visit. On March 5, he told a Peking audience that the war in Viet Nam "should not be allowed to expand" and urged negotiations for "peace in honor to all interested parties." On March 7, Pakistan's President issued a joint statement with Chinese leaders expressing Pakistan's support for Peking's "legitimate rights" in the UN and "for national independence movements and struggles against imperialism and all forms of colonialism in Asia and Africa."

Moscow Students Mob U.S. Embassy. On March 4, 2,000 Russian, Asian (many Chinese), African, and Latin American students broke through police barricades in Moscow to storm the U.S. Embassy in protest against American air strikes on North Viet Nam. The students broke 310 windows, ripped the U.S. seal from the wall, and spattered the building with ink. The 600 policemen were forced to call in 500 troops to quell the rioters. Several soldiers, policemen and demonstrators were seriously injured.

On March 6, the Chinese Communist government, in a note to Moscow, took the Soviets to task for suppressing the demonstration. Peking said it was "entirely legitimate and just for the foreign students in Moscow to stage an anti-American demonstration." It demanded that the Soviet government apologize to the students. On the same day, a crowd of about 400 demonstrated in front of the Soviet Embassy in Peking.

On March 12, the Soviet government, replying to the Chinese note, accused Peking of conducting an "extensive slander campaign" against the Soviet Union. It said that Chinese students in the demonstration were using "iron rods, stones and sharp objects" against "unarmed Soviet policemen."

On March 14, four of the Chinese students allegedly injured in the demonstrations flew to Peking aboard a Soviet airliner. They were greeted by a crowd of 2,000 students, many of whom carried signs saying: "Welcome home to fellow students persecuted by the Soviet government." The Peking *People's Daily* charged the next day that the four students had been mistreated in Soviet hospitals. It said also: "It is unprecedented in history that the government of a Socialist country should have gone so far as to use force in broad daylight to suppress the masses' just struggle against U.S. imperialism and to conduct with ulterior motives, political persecution of seriously wounded students in the hospitals."

Marines Land in Viet Nam. On March 8, 3,500 Marines landed in South Viet Nam to defend the U.S. base at Danang. On March 13, North Viet Nam called the landing "an open declaration of war on the entire Vietnamese people" and said that "We will take all necessary measures to defend ourselves and annihilate the United States aggressors." On the same day, the Peking radio said the action "further blocked the way to a political settlement of the Viet Nam question." The broadcast warned that Communist China would take "all possible measures to support the people of Viet Nam and the whole of Indo-China in carrying out the struggle against the United States aggressors to the very end."

U.S. Wary of Viet Nam Negotiations. On March 9, the State Department announced it had rejected UN Secretary General U Thant's proposals for negotiations on the Viet Nam question. It said the U.S. did not "see any indication that whatever the procedure, the Hanoi regime is prepared to stop trying to take over South Viet Nam by violence."

Johnson on Negotiations. On March 13, President Johnson told his news conference in Washington: "We have not had any indication...from anyone that Hanoi is prepared or willing or ready to stop what it is doing against its neighbors. I think that the absence of this crucial element affects the current discussion of negotiations. On March 17, the Peking *People's Daily* said that discussion of a peaceful settlement in Viet Nam was "nothing but the most flagrant, most shameless war blackmail" by the U.S.

Indonesia and the U.S. On March 19, the Indonesian government seized properties of three American oil companies. It had already taken over two American tire and rubber plants. The U.S. Information Agency had announced March 4 that it was "most reluctantly" closing its five libraries and reading rooms in Indonesia because of government harassment.

Chinese Restraint on Viet Nam. On March 20, Chinese Communist Premier Chou En-lai said in an interview in the Manila *Times* that his country was "against world war and would never provoke it," and that China had "shown restraint" in Viet Nam, although "our restraint has limits." He added that China was not afraid of the U.S. since the latter's forces were scattered all around the globe.

Red China Ready to Intervene. On March 21, Chinese Communist Foreign Minister Chen Yi said, in an interview with an Italian journalist, that Communist China would actively fight in Viet Nam if U.S. troops invaded North Viet Nam or if the North Vietnamese government requested them to enter the war.

"We have made all preparations," Chen Yi said. "The United States began its aggression in 1954. Since then we have prepared to participate some day in this war, when the course of events would oblige us....We have no right to take the initiative. We cannot decide to send our troops today. It would be possible for us, but we do not want to send troops into Southeast Asia beyond our frontiers, to give the imperialists the pretext to shout that the Communist threat is knocking at the door. It is only in case of a legitimate defense that we use our forces and fight. But if the countries which are our friends ask for our help, we will not fail to do it."

Nausea Gas. On March 21, a U.S. military spokesman in Viet Nam said that U.S.-supplied nausea gas was being used against Communist guerrillas. The announcement aroused strong criticism in the press of allied countries as well as in neutralist and Communist countries. The non-poisonous gases reportedly had been used several times against Communist-controlled villages where there were women and children who might be killed by deadly weapons, and against guerrilla positions where South Vietnamese or American prisoners were being held.

On March 22, Hanoi radio charged that "the U.S. aggressors and their henchmen on March 3, 4, and 5 sprayed poisonous chemicals on many hamlets in Ventre Province, affecting more than 30 persons and defoliating vast areas."

A Soviet representative to the UN accused the U.S. April 5 of violating international law by using "poisonous" gases in Viet Nam. A U.S. spokesman replied that poisonous gases had not been used and that there was no intention of

using them. He said the gases in use were non-toxic and were those commonly employed by police forces for riot control.

Chen Yi's Trip. On March 22, Chinese Communist Foreign Minister Chen Yi arrived in Afghanistan to sign an agreement for a long-term $27.5 million no-interest loan to that country. On March 24, he went on to Pakistan to sign a border agreement formalizing the boundary between China and that part of Kashmir controlled by Pakistan. On March 29, the Foreign Minister, now in Nepal, pledged Communist China's aid for Nepal's new five-year plan.

Viet Cong Asks Aid. On March 24, the National Liberation Front, political arm of the Communist Viet Cong, broadcast a statement on Hanoi radio that the people of South Viet Nam "were ready to receive all assistance, including weapons and other war materials, from their friends in the five continents." The statement also said: "If the United States imperialists continue to commit United States combat troops and those of their satellites to South Viet Nam and continue to extend the war to North Viet Nam and Laos, the South Viet Nam National Liberation Front will call on the people of various countries to send youth and army men to South Viet Nam to side with the South Vietnamese people in annihilating the common enemy."

Chinese Ready to Give Aid. On March 25, the Peking *People's Daily* said that Communist China, in response to the March 24 declaration of the National Liberation Front, would "join the people of the whole world in sending all necessary material aid, including arms and other war materials, to the heroic South Vietnamese people who are battling fearlessly." The paper added that China was "ready to send" its "own men whenever the South Vietnamese people want them, to fight together with the South Vietnamese people to annihilate the United States aggressors." It concluded: "The South Vietnamese people will not lay down their arms until the last American soldier leaves their land.... All negotiations with the United States imperialists at this moment are utterly useless if they still refuse to withdraw from South Viet Nam..."

Johnson on the Search for Peace. On March 25, President Johnson said the U.S. looked forward to "the day when the people and governments of all Southeast Asia may be free from terror, subversion, and assassination" and would need no military aid "but only economic and social cooperation for progress in peace." Of a Vietnamese settlement, the President said: "The United States will never be second in seeking a settlement in Viet Nam that is based on an end of Communist aggression. As I have said in every part of the nation, I am ready to go anywhere at any time, and meet with anyone whenever there is promise of progress toward an honorable peace.... We seek no more than a return to the essentials of the agreements of 1954 -- a reliable agreement to guarantee the independence and security of all in Southeast Asia. At present the Communists have given no sign of any willingness to move in this direction, but as they recognize the costs of their present course, and their own true interest in peace, there may come a change."

Moscow-Hanoi Agreement. On March 26, the Soviet Communist Party's Central Committee ratified a defense pact between the Soviet Union and North Viet Nam aimed at "repelling aggression on the part of United States imperialism."

Saigon Embassy Explosion. On March 30, terrorists set off an estimated 250 pounds of explosives in a car parked outside the U.S. Embassy in Saigon, killing 20 persons including two Americans, and injuring 175 others. Windows and brickwork of the five-story building were shattered. President Johnson termed the attack a "terrorist outrage" and said it would only reinforce the Administration's determination to assist South Viet Nam.

The House on April 5 passed, by a 378-0 roll-call vote, a bill (HR 7064) authorizing $1 million for construction of a new embassy building in Saigon. The authorization had been requested April 1 by President Johnson, who said the new building would be a symbol of U.S. resistance in South Viet Nam, a visible sign that "we intend to live up to our commitments."

Neutrals Ask Viet Nam Settlement. On April 1, leaders of 17 neutral nations appealed for a "peaceful solution through negotiations" of the war in Viet Nam "without any preconditions." Copies of the appeal were sent to North and South Viet Nam, the U.S., Communist China, Britain, the Soviet Union, France, the National Liberation Front, Poland and Canada (the last two because they were members of the International Control Commission on Viet Nam).

The statement said a peaceful solution of the Viet Nam conflict was impeded by "foreign intervention in various forms, including military intervention, which impedes the implementation of the Geneva agreements on Viet Nam." It added that "a political solution to the problem of Viet Nam" should be found "in accordance with the legitimate aspirations of the Vietnamese people and in the spirit of the Geneva agreements."

Viet Nam Buildup. On April 2, the Johnson Administration announced it would send more economic aid and more troops to South Viet Nam. A decision was also made at a meeting of the National Security Council to increase the number and intensity of air strikes over North Viet Nam and to extend them farther to the north. The number of American troops currently in South Viet Nam was 27,500.

U.S. Planes Downed. On April 4, two U.S. fighter-bombers were shot down by four North Vietnamese MIGs while bombing a bridge in North Viet Nam.

Bundy Warns Red China. On April 4, McGeorge Bundy, special assistant to the President on national security affairs, said on television that Communist China would be making a bad mistake if it became involved in the Viet Nam war, because the U.S. would not, as in the Korean War, allow planes or forces based in China to enjoy a "privileged sanctuary" there.

Chou's Reply to Thant. On April 6, Chinese Communist Premier Chou En-lai replied through an intermediary to Secretary General U Thant's appeal for negotiations to end the Viet Nam conflict. Chou said that any negotiations would have to be undertaken directly with the Viet Cong rather than with Communist China or North Viet Nam.

Mao's Advice to Arabs. On April 6, in one of his infrequent public appearances, the Chairman of the Central Committee of the Chinese Communist Party, Mao Tse-tung, told an Arab delegation visiting Peking: "Asia is the biggest continent in the world. The West wants to continue to exploit it because the West likes neither us nor you. We must all understand this fact. The Arab battle against the West is actually a battle against Israel, so you Arabs must boycott Europe and America." Mao added that Communist China was winning "in all the battles we are fighting, especially in Viet Nam."

Johnson's Speech at Johns Hopkins. On April 7, President Johnson, in a speech at Johns Hopkins University in Baltimore, Md., said the U.S. was willing to begin "unconditional discussions" to end the war in Viet Nam. The President also proposed a joint development plan for Southeast Asia under United Nations auspices and said the U.S. would contribute $1 billion. The speech was considered in part a response to the April 1 plea by 17 neutral countries for immediate negotiations "without any preconditions" to achieve a solution of the Viet Nam problem.

While saying the U.S. was willing to begin negotiations without prior conditions, Johnson made it clear that any settlement must guarantee "an independent South Viet Nam." He said: "We will not be defeated. We will not grow tired. We will not withdraw, either openly or under the cloak of a meaningless agreement."

The President expressed hope that "all other industrialized nations, including the Soviet Union," would join in a regional program for development of Southeast Asia, and that UN Secretary General U Thant would initiate such a plan "as soon as possible." He announced that he would appoint Eugene R. Black, former president of the International Bank for Reconstruction and Development, to head a special team of Americans "to inaugurate our participation in these programs."

Concerning China, the President said: "Over this war and all Asia is another reality: the deepening shadow of Communist China. The rulers in Hanoi are urged on by Peking. This is a regime which has destroyed freedom in Tibet, which has attacked India and has been condemned by the United Nations for aggression in Korea. It is a nation which is helping the forces of violence in almost every continent. The contest in Viet Nam is part of a wider pattern of aggressive purposes."

Reaction to Johnson's Speech. The Peking radio charged April 9 that the President's speech was "full of lies and deceptions." It said that "while the United States trumpets peace by word of mouth, it is actually pushing on with preparations for expansion of the war." Peking viewed the proposals as "an old device presented in new form for the sole purpose of luring the South Vietnamese people to lay down their arms." But it was confident that "Washington's dream to strike a political bargain with a billion dollars...could not possibly soften the Vietnamese people's resistance."

On the following day, the Soviet Communist Party newspaper *Pravda* called the speech "noisy propaganda" that "cannot change the fact that the United States aggression in Viet Nam is going on and that the situation there is getting worse, endangering peace in Southeast Asia and elsewhere in the world." On April 12, North Viet Nam, in its party newspaper, *Nhan Dan*, said the President's offer "smells of poison gas" and that his economic aid proposal was "bait" held out by "stupid pirates."

Soviet Supplies for Viet Nam. On April 7, it was reported that Communist China and the Soviet Union had reached agreement on shipment of military equipment from Russia through China to North Viet Nam. The report followed repeated stories that Communist China had refused to allow the U.S.S.R. to send supplies to North Viet Nam by rail, forcing the Russians to make shipments by sea (a distance of nearly 12,000 miles) and risk interception by the U.S. Seventh Fleet. On April 1, the Chinese Embassy in Kabul, Afghanistan, had called Soviet reports of a Chinese blockade false and said China had "always given access to all Soviet material for help to Viet Nam to pass through China."

U.S. Reply to Neutrals. On April 8, the Johnson Administration, replying to the 17 neutral nations which had appealed for negotiations on Viet Nam, said the U.S. was "ready and eager to withdraw its forces from South Viet Nam...when conditions have been created in which the people...can determine their own future free from external interference." Belief was expressed that "peace can be achieved in Southeast Asia the moment that aggression from North Viet Nam is eliminated."

Chinese-U.S. Air Clash. On April 9, Communist China asserted that MIG jet fighters of its air force had been involved in a dogfight with 16 U.S. jets over the Chinese island of Hainan in the South China Sea. Peking said that one U.S. jet had been shot down by a missile fired from another U.S. plane. According to the U.S. version, the encounter had taken place 35 miles from Hainan Island, and four U.S. fighter-bombers had shot down one Chinese plane and lost one of their own. The U.S. insisted that the American aircraft had not violated Chinese air space and had not been able to determine whether the other aircraft were Chinese or North Vietnamese.

Peace Corps Leaves Indonesia. On April 14, it was announced that U.S. Peace Corps volunteers would be withdrawn from Indonesia. The Indonesian Communist Party had been pressuring the government to order the 30 volunteers out of the country.

Air Strikes and Missile Bases. On April 15, in the biggest air action of the Viet Nam war, 230 American and South Vietnamese planes struck a suspected Viet Cong outpost 72 miles west of Saigon. U.S. and South Vietnamese planes continued daily air strikes in North Viet Nam. It was reported in Washington that U.S. reconnaissance planes had spotted preparations in North Viet Nam to construct defensive missile sites, presumably for Soviet SAM missiles which could hit aircraft flying as high as 100,000 feet. On April 16, the State Department confirmed the reports.

Johnson Refuses to Halt Bombing. On April 17, President Johnson rejected appeals that he order discontinuance of air strikes over North Viet Nam in the hope that such action would help bring about peace negotiations. The President reiterated his offer of "unconditional negotiations" and criticized the Communists for rejecting the April 7 proposal. "It has been a week of disappointment," he said, "because we tried to open a window to peace, only to be met with tired names and slogans -- and a refusal to talk."

Secretary of State Dean Rusk said that suspension of air raids over North Viet Nam "would only encourage the aggressor and dishearten our friends who bear the brunt of battle."

On April 18, Secretary of Defense Robert S. McNamara said that "we have no indications that a cessation of the bombing would move the North Vietnamese to discussion leading to termination of their aggression in the south."

On the same day, Chairman J. W. Fulbright (D Ark.) of the Senate Foreign Relations Committee commented: "There might be some value in stopping the bombings temporarily. I don't know if it would work, but it seems worth trying."

On April 17, 15,000 demonstrators at a rally and march in Washington protested the bombing of North Viet Nam.

Volunteers for Viet Nam. On April 18, following a meeting of Soviet and North Vietnamese officials in Moscow, the Soviet Union said that if the war in Viet Nam intensified, it would allow Russian volunteers to join the fighting forces of North Viet Nam whenever Hanoi asked for them. Two days later, a similar offer was made by Communist China.

Exchanges on Viet Nam Policy. On April 22, Senate Majority Leader Mike Mansfield (D Mont.) said that delay in getting to the peace table increased "the likelihood that the present limited conflict will spread into general war in Asia."

On April 24, Secretary of State Dean Rusk accused critics of U.S. policy in Viet Nam of showing a "stubborn disregard of plain facts." Referring to recent protests by college professors and students, Rusk said he wondered at the "gullibility of educated men...who are supposed to be helping our young...to learn how to think."

On April 26, Sen. Wayne Morse (D Ore.) called U.S. policy in Viet Nam "immoral and godless." On the same day Senate Majority Whip Russell B. Long (D La.) attacked "modern-day appeasers and isolationists." Long said, "We will do whatever is necessary, including fighting a nuclear war, before we will surrender to anybody there."

On April 26, Secretary of Defense Robert S. McNamara told a news conference that there was "no military requirement for the use of nuclear weapons in the current situation." McNamara, noting that North Vietnamese infiltration of arms and men into South Viet Nam had become "progressively more flagrant and more unconstrained," said it indicated growing Viet Cong dependence on North Viet Nam. The "great bulk" of Viet Cong weapons, the Secretary said, came from external sources, the larger pieces being "mainly Chinese."

Johnson Repeats Peace Talk Offer. On April 27, President Johnson, at a news conference, reaffirmed his offer to engage in unconditional peace talks with "any government, anywhere, any time." He said the U.S. had not changed its "essential position" on Viet Nam -- to obtain a "peaceful settlement," to "resist aggression," and to "avoid a wider war." Responding to a question on possible use of nuclear weapons in Viet Nam, the President said he had "never had a suggestion from a single official of this government...concerning the use of such weapons in this area."

Sino-Soviet Trade. On April 29, the Soviet Union and Communist China signed a trade agreement providing for shipment to China of machine tools, automobiles, airplanes, tractors, and other equipment in exchange for shipment to the U.S.S.R. of fruit, eggs, livestock, chemicals, and shoes.

French-Soviet Statement. On April 29, Soviet Foreign Minister Andrei Gromyko and French Foreign Minister Maurice Couve de Murville wound up three days of talks in Paris. A joint statement urged that the 1954 and 1962 Geneva agreements be implemented to reaffirm the independence of Viet Nam, Cambodia and Laos. The statement said the "situation in the Indo-Chinese Peninsula, and in particular Viet Nam...creates dangers for peace." On April 28, the Soviet government newspaper *Izvestia* had denounced President Johnson and Secretary of Defense McNamara for having "refused to rule out the use of nuclear weapons" in Southeast Asia. *(See April 26 and 27 above.)*

China on Dominican Intervention. On April 30, the Chinese Communist *New China* news agency, commenting on American intervention April 28 in the Dominican Republic, said: "The new intervention on the part of the United States, which came at a moment when United States imperialism was wildly extending its aggression in Viet Nam, threw further light on its hideous feature as the international gendarme."

On May 12, Chinese Communist Party Central Committee Chairman Mao Tse-tung declared: "U.S. military intervention in the Dominican Republic has aroused a new wave against U.S. imperialism among the people of Latin America and the world....In the eyes of the U.S. imperialist aggressor, the United Nations, the Organization of American States and what not are just tools in their hands."

On the following day, an enormous demonstration was held in Peking protesting the American intervention in the Dominican crisis.

Cambodia Breaks With U.S. On May 3, Cambodia severed diplomatic relations with the United States. Prince Norodom Sihanouk, head of state, said the action was taken because of an attack on two Cambodian villages April 28 by South Vietnamese airplanes, and because of a *Newsweek* article criticizing Sihanouk's mother. Sihanouk added that "Diplomatic relations may be restored...if the United States conducts itself correctly towards Cambodia."

Appropriation for Viet Nam. The House May 5 and the Senate May 6, by roll-call votes of 408-7 and 88-3, respectively, passed and sent to the President a bill (H J Res 447) making fiscal 1965 supplemental appropriations of $700 million to meet mounting military requirements in Viet Nam. House and Senate action was completed only two days after President Johnson appealed to Congress in a special message to "provide our forces with the best and most modern supplies and equipment" and to show "prompt support of our basic course: resistance to aggression, moderation in the use of power, and a constant search for peace." The President signed the bill May 7 (PL 89-18).

The President, before sending his message to Capitol Hill May 4, briefed more than 100 members of the House Foreign Affairs Committee, Senate Foreign Relations Committee, and House and Senate Armed Services and Appropriations committees at a morning meeting in the East Room of the White House that was open to newsmen and newsreel cameras.

"This is not a routine appropriation," the President said in his formal message to Congress. "For each member of Congress who supports this request is also voting to persist in our effort to halt Communist aggression in South Viet Nam. Each is saying that the Congress and the President stand united before the world in joint determination that the independence of South Viet Nam shall be preserved and the Communist attack will not succeed."

The President said that U.S. armed forces personnel in Viet Nam had increased from 3,164 men in December 1961 to over 35,000 at the end of April 1965; that U.S. helicopter activity had risen from 30,000 flying hours in the first quarter of 1963 to 90,000 flying hours in the first quarter of 1965; and that U.S. air strikes "against military targets in North Viet Nam" had increased from 160 sorties in February 1965 to over 1,500 sorties in April. He noted also that more than 400 Americans had died in Viet Nam. Although Johnson did not ask for "complete approval" of his Viet Nam policy from Members of Congress, he observed that "an overwhelming vote" on the appropriation would clearly show national unity.

Opposition and apprehension were voiced by a number of Senators: Joseph S. Clark (D Pa.), Frank Church (D Idaho), and Jacob K. Javits (R N.Y.) expressed approval of H J Res 447 but emphasized that their votes should not be construed as endorsing a "command decision" or a "blank check" that would permit the President to use U.S. troops in ground combat in Viet Nam.

Sen. Wayne Morse (D Ore.) said: "I say sadly and solemnly, but out of deep conviction, that today my Government stands before the world drunk with military power" and is about to lay the foundation for "intense Asiatic hatred." H J Res 447 gives "the President power to make undeclared war."

Sen. Albert Gore (D Tenn.) proposed "that after this escalated firepower, the President propose a cease-fire...provided it is met by the Viet Cong with a cease-fire."

Sen. Gaylord Nelson (D Wis.) commented: "Obviously, you need my vote less than I need my conscience....In the cloakrooms and on the floor, numerous distinguished Senators from both sides of the aisle have expressed their concern over the precipitous manner in which we are disposing of this matter."

Viet Nam Buildup. On May 5, the first contingent of 8,000 Marines landed in South Viet Nam, bringing the total number of U.S. personnel to 42,000 men.

SEATO Statement. On May 5, a conference of the member nations of the Southeast Asia Treaty Organization, meeting in London, issued a statement expressing "grave concern" over the aggression "organized, directed, supplied and supported by the Communist regime in North Viet Nam." The statement emphasized that "Defeat of this Communist campaign is essential not only to the security of the Republic of Viet Nam but to that of Southeast Asia." The signatories were the U.S., Britain, the Philippines, Thailand, New Zealand, and Australia. Pakistan refused to sign. France boycotted the meeting in protest against U.S. policy in Viet Nam.

Soviet-Chinese Thrusts. On May 7, at a Moscow rally celebrating the anniversary of VE Day, Soviet Premier Aleksei N. Kosygin, referring to the Chinese Communists, said that "Some people contend that only a new world war can bring about the unity and solidarity of the...international Communist movement." He added: "We decisively reject such a position....We have no more important task than to prevent a new world conflagration." On May 9, the Peking *People's Daily* accused the Soviet leaders of "colluding with the United States aggressors and plotting to sell out the basic interests of the people of Viet Nam and of all other countries, including the Soviet Union."

Johnson on China's Aims. On May 13, President Johnson, speaking to the Association of American Editorial Cartoonists, said that Communist China wanted the Viet Nam war to continue, not for "the fulfillment of Vietnamese nationalism" but "to erode and to discredit America's ability to help prevent Chinese domination over all of Asia." The President repeated his offer of economic assistance to Southeast Asia and again called for "unconditional discussions." He said it would "clearly be in the interest of North Viet Nam to now come to the conference table."

Bombing Pause. U.S. bombing raids on North Viet Nam were suspended from May 13 until May 18. According to news reports, the raids were stopped to give North Viet Nam a face-saving opportunity to accept the President's offer of talks. The Administration made no official statement, but Robert J. McCloskey, State Department press officer, voiced disappointment that North Viet Nam made no move toward negotiations during the bombing suspension. On May 18, North Viet Nam charged that the suspension was "an effort to camouflage American intensification of the war and deceive world opinion."

Second Bomb Test. On May 14, Communist China announced it had exploded its second atomic bomb. The announcement indicated that the bomb had been dropped from the air. China's first successful nuclear test took place Oct. 16, 1964.

The Chinese announcement of the test said: "It is a great victory for Mao Tse-tung's thinking....China is conducting necessary nuclear tests within defined limits and is developing the nuclear weapons for the purpose of coping with the nuclear blackmail and threats of the United States and for the purpose of abolishing all nuclear weapons." Peking pledged that "China will never be the first to use nuclear weapons." It declared that "The Chinese government and people will, as always, continue to strive for the noble aim of the complete prohibition and thorough destruction of nuclear weapons."

The Atomic Energy Commission on May 14 issued a compilation of announced nuclear explosions by the five nuclear countries: United States 337; Soviet Union 127; Britain 24; France 5; Communist China 2.

Rejection of Cease-Fire. On May 14, Communist China labeled "preposterous" a proposal by India on April 24 for a Viet Nam cease-fire to be enforced by Asian and African police detachments. The next day, North Viet Nam called the proposal "an offense" against the North Vietnamese people and charged that India had expressed "erroneous viewpoints that only benefit the United States imperialists."

Teach-Ins. On May 15, a "teach-in" protesting the war in Viet Nam was held in Washington and broadcast by radio and television to college and university campuses throughout the nation. The U.S. policy was condemned and defended by government officials, professors, historians and writers. The teach-in was one of many of a similar kind held in past months.

Eaton's Interviews. On May 20, Soviet Premier Aleksei Kosygin, at a meeting with U.S. industrialist Cyrus S. Eaton, said the Soviet Union had "some internal differences with China, all of which will be ironed out." Kosygin assured Eaton that "We will pool our forces and resources with China in order to meet force with force." The Soviet Premier warned that if the U.S. continued its air strikes against North Viet Nam, the Soviet Union would have "no alternative but to fight...with everything we have."

On May 26, Secretary of State Dean Rusk said at a news conference that he did not "attach undue importance to what Cyrus Eaton" had reported. He noted that "If the Soviet government has views that it wishes to send to the United States Government, there are well-established channels for doing so."

Missile Sites in North Viet Nam. On May 26, Secretary of State Rusk told his news conference that two or more Soviet anti-aircraft missile sites might be under construction in North Viet Nam. Construction of one of the missile sites had been disclosed early in the year by Administration officials. The sites believed under construction were apparently similar to those built in Cuba by Russia in 1962.

Funds for Asian Development. On June 1, President Johnson told a news conference that he was asking Congress for a special appropriation of $89 million to start the economic development program for Southeast Asia that he proposed April 7. "This is the only way that I know in which we can really win not only the military battle against aggression but the wider war for the freedom and for progress of all men," the President said.

China and the Viet Cong. On June 1, the Peking *People's Daily* warned that U.S. air strikes in Viet Nam "threatened China's security in an increasingly serious manner" and that China and North Viet Nam were "all the more entitled" to assist the Viet Cong. The article also charged that the U.S. had "made a farce of the boundaries between Laos, Viet Nam and Thailand" by "turning this entire nation into one battleground where it moves as it wishes."

Australians in Viet Nam. On June 2, the first contingent of Australian troops arrived in South Viet Nam.

Hearing on Viet Nam Asked. On June 3, a group of 28 House Democrats, including seven members of the House Foreign Affairs Committee, in a letter to Committee Chairman Thomas E. Morgan (D Pa.) urged a public hearing on the Administration's Viet Nam policy.

Chou on Risk of World War. On June 3, *Al Mussawar*, Egyptian news magazine, quoted Chinese Communist Premier Chou En-lai as asserting during an interview in Peking that a "world war could not erupt because of war in Viet Nam, or even if Red China itself were attacked by the United States." He said that "even if the United States were to extend military operations into China itself, we will fight it alone without the Soviet Union."

Chou's Trip to Africa. On June 4, Chinese Communist Premier Chou En-lai arrived in Tanzania after a brief stopover in Pakistan. At a reception the same day, Tanzanian President Julius K. Nyerere expressed gratitude for Communist China's aid but cautioned that "From no quarter shall we accept direction or neo-colonialism, and at no time shall we lower our guard against the subversion of our government and people."

At a rally in Dar Es Salaam, Tanzania's capital, Chou said that "in the face of the revolutionary storm sweeping Africa, Asia, and Latin America,... (the U.S.) becomes desperate like a cornered dog and is increasingly revealing its true nature, which is even more ruthless than old colonialism and Hitlerite fascism."

On June 8, Chou and Nyerere urged in a joint statement that an international conference be convoked to discuss elimination of all nuclear weapons. Prior to Chou's visit, Red China had increased its economic and military aid to Tanzania. It was reported that 300 Chinese technicians were in the country and that Chinese were operating a military training camp for the Tanzanian armed forces on Zanzibar.

Before returning to Peking, Chou briefly visited the United Arab Republic and Ethiopia. The African trip was only partly successful because Chou did not receive hoped-for invitations to visit Kenya, Uganda and Zambia.

Combat Role of U.S. Troops. On June 8, Robert J. McCloskey, State Department press officer, said that U.S. military commanders in Viet Nam had recently been given authority to commit U.S. ground troops to combat if their assistance was requested by the South Vietnamese army. But the White House said the next day that there had been "no change in the mission of U.S. ground combat units in Viet Nam." Their primary mission was to "safeguard important military installations." However, the U.S. Commander, Gen. William C. Westmoreland, already had discretionary authority to give troops combat assignments "in support of Vietnamese forces faced with aggressive attack when other effective reserves are not available." Any difference between the State Department and the White House seemed to involve only the question of whether the authority to commit American troops to battle in Viet Nam was old or new.

Viet Nam Protest Rally. On June 8, 17,000 people gathered in New York's Madison Square Garden to protest the war in Viet Nam. Sen. Wayne Morse (D Ore.) told the crowd that President Johnson's "consensus" was "not the consensus of our people, nor even the community of nations; it is a consensus among the State Department, Defense Department, Central Intelligence Agency, and the White House staff."

Threat to Send Volunteers to Viet Cong. On June 9, the Communist *New China* news agency reported that South Viet Nam's National Liberation Front had asserted that President Johnson's "declaration to put Viet Nam and its adjacent waters in the combat zone of the United States armed forces and to order the expeditionary forces to take a direct part in the fight...blatantly violates the 1954 Geneva agreement on Viet Nam." The news agency said the NLF, because of Johnson's action, was "entitled to call for volunteers from the armies of North Viet Nam and other friendly countries to join in the fight against the United States aggression."

On the following day, the North Vietnamese government was reported to have urged its people to "expand the movement of volunteering by joining the army and taking a direct part in destroying the enemy and saving the country." On June 11, the Peking *People's Daily* warned that Communist China "and all other friendly countries reserve their rights to send volunteers of their armies...if necessary to participate in the war against the United States imperialists."

South Viet Nam's Premier Resigns. On June 12, South Vietnamese Premier Phanh Huy Quat resigned and announced that the "responsibility and power" of the government were being turned over to the military. He also said that his civilian regime would remain in office until another government had been formed.

Fulbright Speech on Viet Nam. On June 15, Sen. J.W. Fulbright (D Ark.), chairman of the Senate Foreign Relations Committee, said in a speech on the Senate floor that it was "clear" that "a complete military victory in Viet Nam ...can in fact be attained only at a cost far exceeding the requirements of our interest and our honor" and that "the unconditional withdrawal of American support...would have disastrous consequences." Fulbright concluded, therefore, that American policy should remain "one of determination to end the war at the earliest possible time by a negotiated settlement involving major concessions on both sides." He said that "There may be much to be said for a return to the Geneva accords in 1954, not just in their essentials, but in all their specifications." The accords contemplated union of North and South Viet Nam following elections which were to be held, but were not, in July 1956.

The Fulbright speech was interpreted by some observers as indicating that the Administration was willing to make "major concessions." Fulbright had met with President Johnson June 14, reportedly to discuss Viet Nam.

Rep. Melvin R. Laird (R Wis.), chairman of the House Republican Conference, had said June 14 that "we may be dangerously close to ending any GOP support of our present Viet Nam policy" because the Administration refused to say how far it would go with large-scale use of U.S. ground forces in the war. "We can only conclude that the present policy is aimed not at victory over the Communist insurgency...but rather at some negotiated settlement which would include Communist elements in a coalition government," Laird said.

The Republican leadership in both House and Senate called for increased U.S. military action and warned against concessions. Other Members of Congress, such as Sens. Frank Church (D Idaho), Joseph S. Clark (D Pa.), Gaylord Nelson (D Wis.) and George McGovern (D S.D.) urged negotiations and warned against escalation of the war.

More Troops to South Viet Nam. On June 16, Secretary of Defense Robert S. McNamara announced that U.S. military strength in Viet Nam would be increased to between 70,000 and 75,000 men, including 21,000 ground combat troops. The total current strength in Viet Nam was 54,000 men.

Commonwealth Mission. On June 17, at a conference of the 21-nation British Commonwealth, a Commonwealth mission was established to attempt to find a peaceful solution to the Viet Nam question. It was stipulated that the mission would travel to the capitals of those countries involved directly or indirectly, in the Viet Nam conflict: North and South Viet Nam, the U.S., Communist China, and the Soviet Union. After some bickering, it was decided that the members of the mission would include: Prime Minister Harold Wilson of Great Britain, President Kwame Nkrumah of Ghana, Prime Minister Sir Abubakar Tafawa Balewa of Nigeria, and Prime Minister Eric E. Williams of Trinidad and Tobago.

On June 20, the Peking *People's Daily* commented: "If the Wilson government wants to have another try with this 'mission' of his, all that awaits it is another slamming of the door" because the mission "entirely serves the needs of United States imperialism." (See July 1 below.)

First B-52 Raids. On June 17, 27 long-range heavy jet B-52 bombers of the U.S. Strategic Air Command were employed for the first time to bomb a Viet Cong-infested area, 30 miles from Saigon. The bombers made a round trip flight of over 4,000 miles from Guam to South Viet Nam and back again.

New Saigon Government. On June 21, South Vietnamese Air Vice Marshal Nguyen Cao Ky, 34, became premier following Dr. Phan Huy Quat's resignation June 12. The new government was the 10th in 19 months. Premier Ky on June 24 announced severance of diplomatic relations with France. The move had been opposed by U.S. officials in Saigon, but South Vietnamese Foreign Minister Tran Van Do asserted that Paris "has always directly or indirectly helped our enemies."

Military "Firsts" in Viet Nam. On June 22, U.S. Air Force planes bombed North Viet Nam sites north of Hanoi for the first time. On June 28, U.S. paratroopers and Australian and South Vietnamese troops launched a joint probing operation in Zone D, a Viet Cong stronghold northeast of Saigon, but failed to make substantial contact with the enemy. It was the first time American soldiers had taken the offensive. The U.S., since bombing of North Viet Nam began Feb. 7, had limited air raids to targets in the southern part of North Viet Nam and had limited ground operations to support of the South Vietnamese against Viet Cong assault.

President's UN Address. On June 25, President Johnson in a speech in San Francisco at the 20th anniversary celebration of the signing of the United Nations charter in that city, appealed to the UN to help get North Viet Nam to the conference table for peace negotiations. He said: "I now call upon this gathering of the nations of the world to use all their influence, individually and collectively, to bring to the tables those who seemed determined to make war. We will support your efforts, as we will support effective action by any agent or agency of these United Nations."

Soviet UN Ambassador Nikolai T. Fedorenko denounced the speech as "an odd sermon" intended to place the "responsibility for the crimes committed (in Viet Nam)...not on the aggressor but on the victim of aggression." On June 26, the Peking *People's Daily* asserted that the new Soviet leaders sought to make the United Nations "a center for political transactions between the Soviet Union and the U.S. and a tool for paving the way for Soviet-U.S. cooperation to dominate the world."

France Urges Red China's Entry to UN. On June 26, French Ambassador to the UN Roger Seydoux urged admission of Communist China to the world organization, saying that "So long as the United Nations does not accurately reflect the world as it exists, its effectiveness will be impaired and even its role may be called into question."

North Viet Nam Bars Peace Mission. On July 1, North Viet Nam joined the Soviet Union, Communist China, and the National Liberation Front in refusing to receive a mission established by the British Commonwealth June 17. The mission was set up to seek a peaceful solution of the Vietnamese war. The North Vietnamese statement said: "We do not receive (British Prime Minister) Wilson's mission because we have every reason for doubting Mr. Wilson's 'goodwill' for peace." Hanoi called the mission "only a repetition of Lyndon Johnson's 'peace negotiations' swindle."

To Bomb or Not to Bomb Missile Sites. On July 7, House Minority Leader Gerald R. Ford (R Mich.) called for "immediate, effective" air strikes against missile bases in North Viet Nam. Referring to a July 6 announcement by the State Department that two Soviet anti-aircraft missile sites in North Viet Nam were almost ready for emplacement of weapons, and that two more were nearing completion, Ford said: "Sites designed for firing surface-to-air missiles should be knocked out by United States air superiority before the enemy uses the weapons against the side of freedom." But Senate Majority Leader Mike Mansfield (D Mont.) said July 8 to bomb the missile sites "does not make sense" and would raise "the level of the conflict another notch."

Lodge Again. On July 8, Henry Cabot Lodge, former U.S. Ambassador to South Viet Nam, was named to the post a second time, replacing Gen. Maxwell D. Taylor, whose resignation was announced the same day.

Chinese Submarines. On July 13, a *Wall Street Journal* dispatch from Washington reported that Communist China was developing a fleet of submarines capable of firing nuclear missiles. The report said the subs, of the diesel-electric type, would be operational within two to three years.

Stevenson Death. On July 14, Adlai Ewing Stevenson, U.S. Ambassador to the United Nations since 1961 and the Democratic Presidential candidate in 1952 and 1956, died suddenly in London. On July 20, Supreme Court Justice Arthur J. Goldberg was appointed by President Johnson to take Stevenson's place at the UN.

McNamara's Sixth Trip. On July 16, Secretary of Defense Robert S. McNamara and the new U.S. Ambassador-designate to South Viet Nam, Henry Cabot Lodge, arrived in Saigon and conferred with American and Vietnamese officials there. It was McNamara's sixth trip to Viet Nam.

Aid to North Viet Nam. On July 17, the Chinese Communist *New China* news agency reported that China and North Viet Nam had concluded an agreement under which China would send "equipment, whole sets of installations, and supplies in the national defense and economic fields" to North Viet Nam. During the previous week, similar agreements had been made by North Viet Nam with the Soviet Union and North Korea.

Nationalist Chinese Defector. On July 20, the former President of Nationalist China (from January 1949 until February 1950), who had been in exile in the U.S. for 16 years, arrived in mainland China. Li Tsung-jen, 74, said in Peking, that he sympathized with the Communist regime. He accused President Johnson of deliberately expanding the war in South Viet Nam and "thereby trying to provoke war against the Chinese people." Li added that the U.S. "has been bent on seizing Taiwan (Formosa) for itself and has stopped at no tricks and plots to attain this end." He called for "reunion of Taiwan with the mainland" and declared that the problem was "purely China's internal affair, in which the U.S. must not be allowed to meddle."

McNamara's Views on Viet Nam. On July 21, Secretary of Defense Robert S. McNamara, completing his five-day visit in South Viet Nam, said at a news conference in Saigon: "The over-all situation continues to be serious. As a matter of fact, in many aspects there has been a deterioration since I was last here 15 months ago. The size of the Viet Cong forces has increased; their rate of operations and the intensity of their attacks has been expanded; their destruction of the lines of communications, both rail and sea and road, is much more extensive; and they have intensified their campaign of terror against the civilian population." But he added: "the picture is not all black by any means. The Vietnamese people continue to be willing to fight and

...die in their own defense. The Viet Cong...are suffering increasingly heavy losses, and the U.S. combat forces are adding substantially to the military power of the government." McNamara pledged that the U.S. would do whatever was necessary "to support the people of Viet Nam in their fight to win their independence."

The day before, North Vietnamese President Ho Chi Minh had declared that his country would fight another 20 years if necessary. He urged the U.S. to abandon South Viet Nam.

U.S. Bombing of Missile Sites. On July 24, the war in Viet Nam took on a new dimension with the downing of a U.S. military plane and damaging of three others by Soviet surface-to-air (SAM) missiles. U.S. Air Force fighter-bombers retaliated July 26 by attacking two of the missile sites 40 miles west of Hanoi. One site was destroyed and another badly damaged. Five U.S. planes were lost in the raids.

Troop Increase. On July 28, President Johnson announced at a news conference that U.S. troop strength in Viet Nam would be increased from the current 75,000 to 125,000, and that monthly draft calls would be raised from 17,000 to 35,000. The President said it was not "essential" at present to call up reserve units. He added, however, that if use of the reserves became advisable later, the country would be given "due and adequate notice" before action was taken. The decision to increase the strength of U.S. fighting forces in Viet Nam followed a week-long series of conferences with top military and foreign policy advisers.

Mr. Johnson at the news conference renewed his call for peace negotiations and said he had directed the newly appointed U.S. Ambassador to the United Nations, Arthur J. Goldberg, to present to UN Secretary General U Thant a letter "requesting that all the resources and the energy and the immense prestige of the United Nations be employed to find ways to halt aggression and to bring peace in Viet Nam."

On July 30, Ambassador Goldberg in a letter to the UN Security Council expressed hope that the Council would "somehow find the means to respond effectively to the challenge...in Southeast Asia." He pledged that the U.S. would "collaborate unconditionally with members of the Security Council in the search for an acceptable formula to restore peace and security to that area of the world (Southeast Asia)."

Chinese Criticism. On July 31, the Peking *People's Daily* reiterated charges that the "Khrushchev revisionists" in the Soviet Union were attempting to "work hand-in-glove with the United States imperialism in order to push the scheme for 'peace talks' in Viet Nam."

France and Red China. On Aug. 3, after two weeks of talks with Chinese Communist leaders in Peking, the French Minister of Cultural Affairs, Andre Malraux, told a Hong Kong press conference that the Chinese "leaders are still keeping one window open to (joining) the United Nations that now exists" while "keeping a second window open to a new United Nations." The French government issued a statement Aug. 18 describing Malraux's mission to China as "of very great significance."

NLF Asks Northern Aid. On Aug. 3, the Viet Cong's National Liberation Front, via Hanoi radio, called on "the North Vietnamese people to actively assist the South Vietnamese people in all fields in order to increase our forces and step up the resistance of the war 10 times more vigorously with a view to winning back and preserving the independence of the fatherland." The statement urged "our South Vietnamese compatriots and army men who regrouped in the North (after 1954) to quickly organize their ranks and get ready to return to the South when they are ordered... to fight the U.S. aggressors and save the country and their families."

The NLF also called on South Vietnamese troops to abandon their government and urged Americans "to continue their struggle to prevent the U.S. ruling circles from drafting their sons and brothers to South Viet Nam."

More U.S. Money for Viet Nam. On Aug. 4, President Johnson asked Congress to appropriate an additional $1.7 billion to finance the expanding war in Viet Nam. Defense Secretary Robert S. McNamara, appearing before the Senate Armed Services Subcommittee on Military Appropriations Aug. 4, said the additional funds would help finance the war "through January," after which time requests for more funds would be made.

McNamara proposed that total strength of the armed services be increased by 340,000 over the previously planned strength of 2,640,000 men for fiscal 1966. The Secretary said the increase in U.S. troops in Viet Nam from 75,000 to 125,000, announced by President Johnson on July 28, would take place "almost immediately."

War in Kashmir. On Aug. 5, fighting broke out between India and Pakistan in the disputed state of Kashmir.

Chinese Volunteers. On Aug. 7, Communist China, noting that it had "repeatedly pledged to the Vietnamese people our all-out support and assistance, up to and including the sending...of our men to fight shoulder to shoulder with them," warned "once more that we Chinese people mean what we say." The statement commented that while President Johnson was "announcing the sending of large reinforcements to South Viet Nam, he hypocritically talked about America's willingness to begin unconditional discussions with any government, at any place, at any time."

Anti-U.S. Mobs in Indonesia. On Aug. 7, 7,000 Indonesian youths and students mobbed the U.S. Consulate in Surabaya while Indonesian police looked on. The U.S. Consulate in Medan, Indonesia, had received the same treatment on July 30. Four days before that, President Sukarno asserted that U.S. Viet Nam policy was "discouraging the Indonesian people in their wish to develop friendship with the United States" and that relations between the two countries were "at their lowest level."

Acceptance of Viet Nam Policies. On Aug. 9, President Johnson told reporters there was "no substantial division" in the U.S. or in Congress over the Administration's Viet Nam policies. He warned "any would-be hopeful enemy" not to assume that the U. S. was divided. Asked whether some Members of Congress were "disagreeing privately" with the stepped-up U.S. commitment in Viet Nam, the President replied, "I find that members of my party, and the other party, and people throughout the country frequently disagree with me on a good many things." He added that "unanimity" would never be reached "in situations as difficult as Viet Nam."

Rivers on China's Bomb. On Aug. 11, Rep. L. Mendel Rivers (D S.C.), chairman of the House Armed Services Committee, speaking in Hartford, Conn., said the U.S. must be prepared to use atomic weapons on Communist China before Communist China used them on the United States. "Even if we win the war in South Viet Nam," he said, "I cannot help but think that we are merely postponing the final victory of Red China--unless the nation is prepared to risk the possible consequences of destroying her nuclear capability. And unless we make that decision, it is possible that all our fighting in South Viet Nam will have been in vain."

Sen. Stephen M. Young (D Ohio) called Rivers an "armchair militarist" and termed his speech "bombastic." Rep. Don Edwards (D Calif.) said such a speech was "dangerous and inflammatory" and would "undercut the very basis of American foreign policy." Rep. F. Edward Hebert (D La.), however, thought Rivers had made "a great contribution" to the national defense.

Ho's Terms. On Aug. 12, North Viet Nam's President Ho Chi Minh, in an interview appearing in the Paris newspaper *Le Monde*, said his country would agree to negotiations on the Viet Nam war when the U.S. accepted North Viet Nam's four-point proposal.

The four points were: (1) Total U.S. withdrawal from all of Viet Nam; (2) following "peaceful reunification" of the country, its "two zones must refrain from joining any military alliance with any foreign countries" and "there must be no foreign military bases, troops, or military personnel in their respective territories."; (3) South Viet Nam's "internal affairs...must be settled by the South Vietnamese people themselves in accordance with the program" of the National Liberation Front, the Viet Cong's political arm; (4) the Vietnamese people must be responsible for peaceful reunification of the country "without any foreign interference."

Independent U.S. Fighting. On Aug. 18, U.S. forces staged their first ground action not in support of South Vietnamese troops.

Quarrel Over Commitments. On Aug. 19, controversy arose between President Johnson and House Minority Leader Gerald R. Ford (R Mich.) over a statement by former President Eisenhower denying that his Administration had given South Viet Nam any military "commitments" other than those connected with the Southeast Asia Treaty Organization. President Johnson had frequently cited an Oct. 23, 1954, letter by Eisenhower to President Ngo Dinh Diem of South Viet Nam as an example of the long-term U.S. involvement in South Viet Nam. Eisenhower told a news conference in Washington Aug. 17 that the letter contained no offer of military aid, only economic aid.

Asked to comment on Eisenhower's remarks, White House Press Secretary Bill Moyers said Aug. 18 that President Johnson did not feel there was any division between himself and the former President over South Viet Nam. Moyers said Johnson did not "consider any effort by anyone else to use Gen. Eisenhower to promote such divisions as serving the national interest."

Ford fired back the following statement Aug. 19: "I have just read with indignation and resentment a published statement by the White House Press Secretary alleging that former President Eisenhower is being 'used' by someone as a puppet for political purposes. Gen. Eisenhower and the nation are entitled to an immediate apology from the White House for this irresponsible insinuation. National unity is not strengthened by disparaging a beloved and dis-

tinguished statesman, Gen. Eisenhower."

Eisenhower himself said Aug. 19 and 20 that he fully supported President Johnson's South Viet Nam policies, that "When it comes to the current job, we must follow the President."

North Vietnamese Appeal. On Aug. 23, the International Red Cross announced that North Viet Nam had appealed for medical supplies, blood plasma, and surgical equipment for the Viet Cong.

Republican "White Paper." On Aug. 24, the House Republican Committee on Planning and Research issued a 33-page "White Paper" alleging that U.S. involvement in South Viet Nam dated from a May 1950 decision by the Truman Administration to aid French forces then fighting in Indo-China. The report asserted that there "was no crisis in South Viet Nam when President Eisenhower" left office in January 1961, although late "in 1959, the tempo of guerrilla attacks began to assume significant proportions" and "the year 1961 saw the development of conflict...from covert guerrilla action to open, if still small-scale, war."

The paper contended that President Johnson's 1964 Presidential campaign had encouraged "miscalculation" by the Viet Cong: "In order to make his opponent appear reckless and trigger-happy, the President in several statements set limits to American participation in the Vietnamese conflict." The Republicans were critical also of Mr. Johnson's lack of candor "about Viet Nam" and said that it "confuses the American public."

While seeking to lay the blame for the situation on the Democrats, the report concluded: "The nation by the President's admission is now engaged in war. All Americans must support whatever action is needed to put a stop to Communist aggression and to make safe the freedom and independence of South Viet Nam."

Viet Nam Funds. On Aug. 25, the Senate, by an 89-0 roll-call vote, passed and sent to conference a bill (HR 9221) appropriating $46,877,063,000 for the Defense Department in fiscal 1966. The bill, which had passed the House June 23 by a 407-0 roll-call vote, included a stopgap $1.7 billion appropriation for military operations in Viet Nam.

Coupled with a $700-million fiscal 1965 supplemental appropriation, cleared by Congress May 6 (H J Res 447 -- PL 89-18), HR 9221 brought additional calendar 1965 outlays earmarked for Viet Nam to a total $2.4 billion. HR 9221 was signed into law (PL 89-213) on Sept. 29.

China and Nepal. On Aug. 29, Communist China signed an agreement to grant Nepal $28 million to build a 140-mile east-west highway.

Negotiations and Bombing. On Aug. 29, President Johnson denied news reports that North Viet Nam had signified willingness to start peace negotiations if the U.S. stopped bombing North Viet Nam: "We hear a lot of reports. There is nothing official about them. I expect some newspaperman was speculating."

News reports suggested also that the Administration had made offers to North Viet Nam, through undisclosed third parties, to exchange demonstrations of willingness to slow down the war. Secretary of State Dean Rusk, at an Aug. 27 news conference, said such an assertion was too precisely worded, but he acknowledged that there had been "many" third party contacts with Hanoi. Rusk emphasized that the U.S. was "prepared to consider" ending its bombing attacks on North Viet Nam if such an action would be a "step toward peace."

Senate Majority Leader Mike Mansfield (D Mont.), in a Senate speech endorsed by the White House Sept. 1, said it was important "that we do not assume that we are engaged in Viet Nam against a group or government which has no objective except warfare for the sake of warfare." Comparing the U.S. and North Viet Nam conditions for peace negotiations, Mansfield suggested that the divergences preventing a settlement might not be irreconcilable.

China and the UN. On Sept. 1, the Chinese Communist *New China* news agency reported that China was "firmly opposed to United Nations intervention in the Viet Nam question." It asserted that the U.S. was "seeking to make use of the United Nations" to further its "peace-talk scheme," which had "met with rebuffs everywhere."

Lin Piao's Article. On Sept. 2, 20th anniversary of Japan's surrender to the Allies, Chinese Communist Defense Minister Lin Piao issued a major policy statement which was published in newspapers all over China. The article called for a "people's war" utilizing the same techniques as those carried into effect by Mao Tse-tung in the Chinese civil war of the late 1940s.

"It must be emphasized," Lin said, "that Comrade Mao Tse-tung's theory of the establishment of rural revolutionary base areas and the encirclement of cities from the countryside is of outstanding and universal practical importance for the present revolutionary struggles of all the oppressed nations and peoples, and particularly (those)...in Asia, Africa and Latin America, against imperialism and its lackeys....The countryside, and the countryside alone, can provide the revolutionary bases from which the revolutionaries can go forward to final victory. Precisely for this reason, Comrade Mao Tse-tung's theory...is attracting more and more attention among the people in these regions."

"Taking the entire globe," Lin continued, "if North America and Western Europe can be called 'the cities of the world,' then Asia, Africa and Latin America constitute 'the rural areas of the world.' "

Lin asserted that "imperialists are extremely afraid of Comrade Mao Tse-tung's thesis that 'imperialism and the reactionaries are paper tigers,' and the revisionists are extremely hostile to it. They all oppose and attack this thesis ....But all this cannot in the least diminish its importance." Mao "points out that we must despise the enemy strategically and take full account of him tactically. To despise the enemy strategically is an elementary requirement for a revolutionary. Without the courage to despise the enemy..., it will be simply impossible to make a revolution and wage a people's war."

Lin contended that nuclear weapons could not save U.S. imperialism. "U.S. imperialism has been condemned by the people of the whole world for its towering crime of dropping two atomic bombs on Japan. If it uses nuclear weapons again, it will become isolated in the extreme. Moreover, the U.S. monopoly of nuclear weapons has long been broken; U.S. imperialism has these weapons, but others have them too. If it threatens other countries with nuclear weapons, U.S. imperialism will expose its own country to the same threat."

The deciding factor, in Lin's view, was still the ground forces, and U.S. troops "cannot possibly be endowed with the courage and the spirit of sacrifice possessed by the rev-

olutionary people." He believed that "The spiritual atom bomb which the revolutionary people possess is a far more powerful and useful weapon than the physical atom bomb."

Lin then gave his view of the United States: "Since World War II," he said, "United States imperialism has stepped into the shoes of German, Japanese and Italian Fascism and has been trying to build a great American empire by dominating and enslaving the whole world. It is the most rabid aggressor in human history and the most ferocious common enemy of the people of the world. Every people or country in the world that wants revolution, independence and peace cannot but direct the spearhead of its struggle against U.S. imperialism...

"The struggles waged by the different peoples against U.S. imperialism reinforce each other and merge into a worldwide tide of opposition to U.S. imperialism. The more successful the development of the people's war in a given region, the larger the number of U.S. imperialist forces which can be pinned down and depleted there. When the U.S. aggressors are hard pressed in one place, they have no alternative but to loosen their grip on others. Therefore, the conditions become more favorable for the people elsewhere to wage struggles against U.S. imperialism and its lackeys....U.S. imperialism, like a mad bull dashing from place to place, will finally be burned to ashes in the blazing fire of the people's wars it has provoked by its own actions."

Referring to the Sino-Soviet split, Lin accused the Soviet leaders of "actively preaching that socialism can be built without the proletariat and without the Communist party." Their purpose, he added, was "solely to divert the oppressed nations from their struggle against imperialism" because they, the Soviet leaders, had lost faith in the masses and feared the U.S. "The Khrushchev revisionists regard imperialists like Kennedy and Johnson as 'sensible' and describe us, together with all those who dare to carry out armed defense against imperialist aggression, as 'bellicose'.....War can temper the people and push history forward. In this sense, war is a great school. In diametrical opposition to the Khrushchev revisionists, the Marxist-Leninists and revolutionary people never take a gloomy view of war."

It was Lin's opinion that the U.S. had made Viet Nam a "testing ground for the suppression of the people's war." The Viet Nam conflict was "now the focus of the struggle of the people of the world against U.S. aggression." Lin insisted that China's determination to support the Communists in Viet Nam was "unshakable."

Pakistan-India-China. On Sept. 7, Communist China denounced Indian "aggression" in Pakistan and pledged full support of Pakistan in the struggle on the subcontinent. The Soviet Union on Sept. 7 offered its good offices in the search for a settlement of the dispute. Open warfare between India and Pakistan, which started in Kashmir in August, was intensified in September when the fighting reached into India and Pakistan proper. Violent air and ground action ensued.

U.S. Jet Downed. On Sept. 20, Communist China said its planes had shot down an American jet fighter over Hainan Island and that the pilot had been captured.

Thant Urges Red China's Admission to UN. On Sept. 21, UN Secretary General U Thant urged that Communist China be admitted to the UN. "Both the Viet Nam situation and the disarmament impasse," Thant said, "point once again to the imperative need for the United Nations to achieve universality of membership as soon as possible."

Cease-Fire in Kashmir. On Sept. 22, Pakistan joined India in accepting a UN Security Council demand for a cease-fire in the war over Kashmir and withdrawal of all Indian and Pakistani troops to the positions they occupied on Aug. 5. A UN Observer Mission was established Sept. 23 to supervise the cease-fire. Both countries also announced acceptance of Soviet Premier Aleksei N. Kosygin's offer to mediate the dispute.

Goldberg Opposes Red China in UN. On Sept 23, U S Ambassador to the UN Arthur J. Goldberg appealed to the United Nations to keep Communist China out of the organization. In his first major policy speech to the General Assembly, Goldberg described the "incredible manifesto" of Communist China's Defense Minister Lin Piao, Sept. 2, as "the antithesis of everything this organization stands for." He said the UN had a "common responsibility to demonstrate to those who use violence that violence does not pay." He asked for UN aid in beginning "serious discussions" for a resolution of the Viet Nam conflict.

Soviet Foreign Minister Andrei A. Gromyko in a policy speech to the General Assembly the next day, condemned U.S. "aggression" in Viet Nam and presented a draft declaration on non-interference in the affairs of other states. In the same speech, Gromyko stressed Soviet support of "national liberation wars" in any part of the world. He also submitted a draft treaty on the non-dissemination of nuclear weapons which provided that any nation possessing such weapons must not transfer them "in any form" to any nation not having nuclear weapons. Finally, Gromyko asked that Communist China be given a seat in the UN.

The General Assembly agreed without dissent Sept. 25 to debate the question of seating Communist China.

North Viet Nam Refuses to Negotiate. On Sept. 23, North Viet Nam reaffirmed earlier rejections of U.S offers of peace negotiations. It admitted that U.S. air strikes in North Viet Nam had "disrupted the peaceful labor" of the people, but said they would keep struggling "even if this takes five, ten, or more years."

Chen Yi's Challenge of U.S. and UN. On Sept. 29, Chinese Communist Foreign Minister Chen Yi told a news conference in Peking that his country was "fully prepared against U.S. aggression." He added: "If the U.S. imperialists are determined to launch a war of aggression against us, they are welcome to come sooner, to come as early as tomorrow."

Chen Yi also laid down conditions for entry of Communist China into the United Nations: The UN must oust "the Chiang Kai-shek clique," must cancel its 1951 resolution condemning China and North Korea as aggressors, and adopt a resolution condemning the...(U.S.) as the aggressor (in Korea)." Furthermore, the "UN Charter must be reviewed and revised...by all countries, big and small, all independent states should be included in the United Nations; and all imperialist puppets should be expelled."

As for the Chinese economy, Chen conceded that the second five-year plan had "met with great difficulties," which he blamed on natural disasters, the American trade embargo, and termination of Soviet aid. But, he said, "After three years of readjustment, there has been an all-round turn for the better in the situation....We shall have a good harvest this year, but there are still natural disasters" and "It will take decades -- 30 to 50 years more of efforts to build up China's industry, agriculture and national defense."

Liu's Views of U.S.S.R. and U.S. On Sept. 29, at a Peking dinner for Cambodia's Prince Norodom Sihanouk, Chinese Communist Head of State Liu Shao-chi asserted that the Soviet Union was in collusion with the U.S. and at the same time was attempting to "squeeze" into "Asian-African anti-imperialist ranks." In a joint statement Oct. 3, the two leaders said the UN would disintegrate unless it could shake off the domination of "certain big powers, notably the United States."

Attempted Coup in Indonesia. On Sept. 30, the Indonesian armed forces crushed what appeared to be a coup d'etat against the regime of President Sukarno. Reports from Jakarta indicated that Sukarno was still in control of the government. On Oct. 2, he announced appointment of Gen. Suharto as temporary head of the army in place of Gen. Abdul Haris Nasution, who had been injured when the insurgents attempted to kidnap him.

After a few days, it became apparent that the coup had been led by Lt. Col. Untung, a battalion commander in Sukarno's body-guard, who allegedly was backed by the Indonesian Communist Party. Untung said he had acted to avert overthrow of Sukarno by right-wing elements of the army high command. Coup forces had broadcast Oct. 1 that subversive generals and the CIA had been "very active lately." The U.S. denied CIA involvement.

Through the first weeks of October, the army arrested thousands of members of the PKI (Indonesian Communist Party), charging that they had supported the attempted coup. The PKI denied the charge. On Oct. 8, the army announced it had arrested three Communist youths who had confessed their guilt in the assassination of six army generals during the attempted coup. On Oct. 11, the army said it had captured Lt. Col. Untung. It was reported Oct. 12 that the leader of the PKI in Indonesia, D.N. Adit, had escaped from the country in a Chinese Communist submarine. On Oct. 12, the army announced it had obtained evidence that Communist China had been arming the rebels.

Peking Parade. On Oct. 1, Chairman Mao Tse-tung of the Central Committee of the Chinese Communist Party, other Chinese leaders, and Cambodian Head of State, Prince Norodom Sihanouk, watched an estimated 700,000 people march in a Peking parade celebrating the 16th anniversary of the independence of Communist China.

Draft Quota Raised. On Oct. 14, the Pentagon announced that the draft quota for December had been set at 45,224 men, an increase of 8,774 over the November quota of 36,450. The new quota was the highest since May 1953.

Viet Nam Demonstrations. On Oct. 15-17, student-organized demonstrations against American military involvement in Viet Nam flared across the U.S. An estimated 70,000 people participated in marches and rallies in 40 cities. The biggest demonstrations were in New York City and Berkeley, Calif. Similar protests took place in London, Dublin, Brussels, Copenhagen, Stockholm, Rome and Tokyo.

Protests against the military draft formed a major part of the weekend demonstrations. The antidraft campaign reportedly was led by the Students for a Democratic Society (SDS). It involved numerous new, radical student organizations (called the "New Left"), which opposed the war in Viet Nam and sought to build a mass antidraft movement.

According to news reports, the SDS had organized "draft counseling workshops" in six cities to encourage men of draft age to become conscientious objectors. Beginning Oct. 15, draft opponents picketed draft induction centers. Pamphlets were circulated at Rutgers University and the University of California on how to "beat" the draft by feigning insanity, stupidity, homosexuality, drunkenness, or drug addiction.

A 22-year-old pacifist, David J. Miller, was arrested Oct. 18 for burning his draft card. Miller was the first person charged under a new law (PL 89-152) making it a federal crime to knowingly destroy or mutilate a draft card.

On Oct. 18, Attorney General Nicholas deB. Katzenbach told a news conference in Chicago that there were "some Communists involved" in the antidraft movement and that the Justice Department had begun an investigation of groups behind the movement. Presidential Press Secretary Bill Moyers said the same day that President Johnson "concurred in and approved strongly" of the Justice Department's investigation of antidraft groups. The Internal Security Subcommittee of the Senate Judiciary Committee had issued, Oct. 14, a report on its investigation of the "Anti-Viet Nam Agitation and the Teach-In Movement." In the introduction to the report, Subcommittee Chairman Thomas J. Dodd (D Conn.) charged that control of the anti-Viet Nam movement had "clearly passed from the hands of the moderate elements who may have controlled it at one time, into the hands of Communists and extremist elements who are openly sympathetic to the Viet Cong and openly hostile to the United States."

On Oct. 18, Senate Majority Leader Mike Mansfield (D Mont.) criticized the "sense of utter irresponsibility" shown by the weekend demonstrators. Senate Majority Leader Everett M. Dirksen (R Ill.) said the demonstrations were "enough to make any person loyal to his country weep."

Indonesian Ban on Reds. On Oct. 18, the Indonesian army announced that it had banned activities of the Indonesian Communist Party, the PKI, in the Jakarta area. Since the attempted coup of Sept. 30, many Chinese and their shops had been attacked by mobs. Red China protested that Indonesian troops had invaded the Chinese Commerical Center in Jakarta on Oct. 16. Large-scale arrests of Communists continued.

Viet Nam Dialogue. On Oct. 21, Gen. Curtis E. Le-May, retired former Air Force Chief of Staff, in an address to the National Aeronautics Association in Washington, asserted that the U.S. was doing "too little too late" in Viet Nam and that "we're getting people killed who shouldn't be killed." LeMay said the "wrong targets" were being hit and Hanoi "was not getting the message." He stated that it was time to stop "pecking around the edges" in raids on North Viet Nam and to start hitting "industries, ports, power plants, and transportation," whose destruction would "really hurt" the Hanoi regime.

Senate Foreign Relations Committee Chairman J. W. Fulbright (D Ark.) in an NBC "Meet the Press" interview, Oct. 24, called for a temporary suspension of bombing raids in North Viet Nam as a move toward peace negotiations. Fulbright asserted that the May 13-18 moratorium "was not a very long time to allow any kind of negotiations to get under way" and that present air strikes should be suspended "for a more reasonable time."

Red China and Indonesia. On Oct. 23, the Chinese Communist *New China* news agency reported that In-

donesian soldiers and police had "forced their way into" the Chinese Communist embassy in Jakarta "and pried about the whole place." Indonesian army officers and newspapers had complained that Communist China was sneaking weapons into the country through its embassy.

On Oct. 26, the Chinese ambassador to Indonesia, Yang Chung-ming, met with Indonesian President Sukarno for the first time since the abortive Sept. 30 coup. After the meeting, the Chinese embassy said that "the relations between China and Indonesia remain firm although there are elements trying to alienate China and Indonesia."

Optimism on Viet Nam. On Oct. 25, Presidential Assistant McGeorge Bundy said in a Washington speech that the military situation in South Viet Nam had taken a sharp turn for the better because of the use of U.S. troops and the "decision to use air power, jet air power and strategic bombers." Bundy added that the "prospects of military collapse, which clearly darkened all aspects of the problem nine months ago, has disappeared."

Pro-Administration Demonstration. On Oct. 30, about 25,000 persons paraded down New York's Fifth Avenue to demonstrate support for the Administration's policy on Viet Nam.

Self-Immolation in U.S. On Nov. 2, a critic of the U.S. war effort in Viet Nam, Norman R. Morrison, 31, burned himself to death outside the Pentagon within view of Defense Secretary Robert S. McNamara's third floor office.

On Nov. 9, Robert Allen LaPorte, 22, of the pacifist Catholic Worker movement, set himself afire in front of UN headquarters in New York to protest the Viet Nam war. He died later in a hospital.

Chinese-Soviet Exchange. On Nov. 10, the Peking *People's Daily* and the Chinese Communist theoretical journal, *Red Flag*, asserted that the Soviet Union "regarded U.S. imperialism...as its closest friend and the Marxist-Leninists of the world...as its principal enemy." The article said that efforts by the U.S. and the Soviet Union to curb proliferation of nuclear weapons were only in the interest of maintaining "the monopoly of the two nuclear overlords ...against China and all other independent countries."

On Nov. 16, *Pravda* and *Izvestia* replied that the Chinese article "from beginning to end, is full of impermissible, utterly groundless, slanderous provocative fabrications, permeated with a spirit of hostility toward the Soviet people and toward the Communist Party of the Soviet Union." The Soviets accused the Chinese Communist Party of rejecting "unity of action with the Soviet Communist Party and other Marxist-Leninist parties...against United States aggression."

It had been Soviet policy since the ouster of Premier Khrushchev to ignore the Chinese attacks, but both the Nov. 10 Chinese article and the Soviet reply were given publicity by Soviet news media.

Chinese Fliers Defect. On Nov. 11, three Red Chinese pilots defected to Nationalist China in a Russian-made bomber. The plane crashed while landing and one of the three defectors died.

Reported Hanoi Offer. On Nov. 15, the State Department confirmed a report that the U.S. in late 1964 rejected an offer by North Viet Nam to meet U.S. emissaries in Rangoon, Burma, to discuss ending the Vietnamese war. Robert J. McCloskey, State Department spokesman, said the offer was turned down because, "on the basis of the total evidence available to us, we did not believe at any time that North Viet Nam was prepared for serious talks."

The North Vietnamese offer had been relayed by UN Secretary General U Thant to Ambassador Adlai E. Stevenson in the fall of 1964. The offer was disclosed by television commentator Eric Sevareid in an article published (Nov. 15) in the Nov. 30, 1965, issue of *Look*. In the article, Sevareid wrote in detail of a discussion he had with Stevenson two days before the latter's death on July 14. Sevareid said that Stevenson told him that "Someone in Washington suggested that this attempt be postponed until after the Presidential election." Sevareid added: "When the election was over,... Hanoi was still willing to send its man. But Defense Secretary Robert S. MacNamara...flatly opposed the attempt. He said the South Vietnamese government would have to be informed and that this would have a demoralizing effect on them; that government was shaky enough as it was."

Although the State Department confirmed the initial offer of discussions, it flatly denied that the Presidential election was a factor, that there was a second overture from Hanoi, or that McNamara was in any way involved. The Defense Secretary himself issued a statement declaring that "There is not one word of truth in the remarks made about me or the position attributed to me in the article." U Thant and President Johnson both declined comment.

China's UN Seat. On Nov. 17, the UN General Assembly defeated a resolution to award China's seat in the United Nations to Communist China and expel the representatives of Nationalist China. The vote was a 47-47 tie, with 20 abstentions. Prior to rejecting the change in representation, the General Assembly decided by a vote of 56-49, with 11 abstentions, that the matter was an "important question" requiring a two-thirds majority for adoption. With 94 members present and voting, 63 affirmative votes were needed.

Although the resolution fell far short of adoption, Peking's supporters claimed a political victory in having denied Nationalist China a plurality for the first time since the question was initially voted on in 1950. In each of the previous votes, the U.S.-backed Nationalists had attained wide margins. In 1963, when the question last came to a vote, the Nationalists won by 57-41, with 12 abstentions.

While Peking won six more votes than in 1963, the biggest change was in the number of abstentions. Withholding their votes on the latest resolution were eight 1963 supporters of the Nationalists: Cameroon, Chad, Chile, Cyprus, Iran, Jamaica, Libya, and Rwanda. By contrast, the ranks of Communist China's 1963 proponents held firm, with the exception of Laos, which refused to participate, and Tunisia, which abstained.

On Nov. 19, the Peking *People's Daily* commented: "China may as well stay out of a United Nations like this." It added that the vote had been a "humiliating setback" for the U.S., which had "strained every nerve and worked overtime to get the resolution voted down by a simple majority." The article asserted that the UN "must free itself from the control of the United States, rectify its mistakes, and undergo a thorough...reform." To satisfy Peking, the UN would have to expel the Nationalist Chinese delegation, "resolutely condemn U.S. imperialism," withdraw its resolutions charging Communist China and North Korea with aggression in the Korean War, and revise the Charter to to "include as UN members all independent countries to

the exclusion of all imperialist puppets."

Ho's Letter to Pauling. On Nov. 20, Linus Pauling, winner of both the Nobel Peace Prize and the Nobel award for chemistry, received a letter from North Vietnamese President Ho Chi Minh which called U.S. offers of peace negotiations "deceitful talk." Ho said that, in reality, U.S. policy was "to negotiate from a position of strength, to perpetrate even more horrible massacres and cause even greater devastation to compel the Vietnamese people" to give up their struggle. He added that the "most correct way to a peaceful settlement of the Viet Nam problem" was to accept the conditions set down by the National Liberation Front. Ho's letter was in reply to a letter from Pauling, signed by seven other recipients of the Nobel Peace Prize, appealing for an end to the conflict.

Hanoi's Version. On Nov. 26, North Viet Nam said it had never made any peace feelers regarding the Vietnamese conflict. The statement said: "An American newspaper even fabricated the legend that since last fall Hanoi has two or three times proposed negotiations. This trickery has a double aim: On the one hand to attack the Johnson clique to prepare for forthcoming elections, and on the other to create confusion in world opinion."

Washington March. On Nov. 27, an estimated 20,000 demonstrators joined in a "March on Washington for Peace in Viet Nam." The protesters gathered at the White House bearing placards demanding a U.S. cease-fire. The peace march was accompanied by a four-day Washington convention of delegates from approximately 140 anti-war groups. Their objective was to unify efforts toward ending U.S. participation in the war.

McNamara to Viet Nam. On Nov. 28, Secretary of Defense Robert S. McNamara left for a 30-hour inspection tour of Viet Nam. He announced that American air attacks on North Viet Nam and Viet Cong supply routes would be stepped up to offset Communist military infiltration in the South. The Pentagon had disclosed four days earlier that 240 American servicemen were killed in action during the week of Nov. 14-20, the largest weekly total so far.

China and Disarmament. On Nov. 29, the UN General Assembly approved a resolution urging convocation of a world disarmament conference, "not later than 1967," that would include Communist China. The vote was 112-0 with France abstaining and Nationalist China absent.

On Dec. 1, Communist China declared that "China will never enter into relations with the United Nations and any conference connected with it before the restoration of her legitimate rights in the United Nations and expulsion of the Chiang Kai-shek clique from the organization."

India-China Border Trouble. On Nov. 30, Indian Defense Minister Y. B. Chavan told the Indian Parliament that Communist intrusions across the disputed Chinese-Indian border had been getting steadily bigger. "Where we used to see 10 or 12 Chinese coming across, we now see 50 or 60." On Nov. 28, the two countries had exchanged protest notes, each charging the other with border violations amounting to "aggression."

Chinese Aid to North Viet Nam. On Dec. 5, Communist China and North Viet Nam signed an agreement providing for more loans to North Viet Nam. The amount was not disclosed.

Indonesian Puzzle. On Dec. 1, Indonesian President Sukarno, addressing the People's Provisional Consultative Conference in Jakarta, declared that members of the Indonesian Communist Party, the PKI, were like "rats that have eaten a part of a big cake and tried to eat the pillar of our house." He added, "now let us catch these rats...and I will punish them."

This statement, and others attacking the U.S., added confusion to an already puzzling situation. It was obvious that the Indonesian army had gained power at Sukarno's expense, and that Indonesian Communists had suffered a serious blow. It also seemed clear, in the words of Indonesian Foreign Minister Subandrio Dec. 3, that relations between his country and Communist China "have become strained lately." Subandrio said: "This is because the public feels that China is, if not responsible, at least sympathetic toward the 30th of September Movement (date of the abortive coup)." But on Nov. 20, Sukarno had said that "In our struggle against imperialism, we continue to exist in the Jakarta, Pnompenh, Hanoi, Peiping, Pyonyang axis." It was the opinion of most observers that the military, with considerable popular support, was slowly taking over control but did not yet dare to remove Sukarno because of his popularity.

Poland's Views on China. On Dec. 3, the Polish Communist Party criticized Communist China for its Nov. 10 attack on the Soviet Union, which it termed "incredibly aggressive and lacking any foundation." The statement pointed out that the Soviet Union had "not infrequently approached" Communist China and North Viet Nam "with proposals on the concerting of joint actions to defend" the latter, but "unfortunately, all these suggestions...were turned down by the Chinese." The statement exprssed optimism that the "disruptive activities of the Chinese Communist Party will be overcome."

Church Council on Viet Nam. On Dec. 3, the National Council of Churches called on the U.S. Government to halt the bombing of North Viet Nam long enough to establish a more favorable atmosphere for peace negotiations. The Council's appeal was the first policy statement on the Viet Nam war by a major U.S. religious body.

Hotel Explosion. On Dec. 4, Viet Cong terrorists exploded a bomb in front of a hotel used to house U.S. military personnel in Saigon. Six Vietnamese, one American, and one New Zealander were killed; 137 persons were injured, including 72 Americans.

Christmas Truce Offer. On Dec. 7, South Viet Nam's National Liberation Front, political arm of the Viet Cong, offered a 12-hour Christmas truce. It proposed that all attacks in South Viet Nam cease from six p.m. Dec. 24 to six a.m. Dec. 25, so that Catholic soldiers might "attend mass and celebrate Christmas Eve." The sole condition was that the troops carry no weapons. The U.S. initially discounted the proposal as a propaganda move but did not entirely rule out some sort of Christmas pause. Pope Paul VI made a specific plea Dec. 19 for American acceptance of the NLF offer and expressed hope that a brief cease-fire might lead to peace negotiations.

Johnson and Ho Statements. On Dec. 9, President Johnson in an address to the AFL-CIO convention reiterated American willingness to negotiate peace but appeared to signal a further step-up in the Viet Nam war. The President said he was determined that every prospect for peace in Viet Nam be exhausted "before other hard steps are taken." "Only this week," he added, "we reviewed our efforts for peace in detail. Our efforts...to talk about peace were met with silence from some, shrill propaganda from others."

The Johnson statement followed a newsman's interview with Ho Chi Minh, president of North Viet Nam, broadcast in English Dec. 8 by Radio Hanoi. In the interview, Ho had brusquely turned down U.S. offers of "unconditional discussions," which Ho said were a cover for unacceptable U.S. conditions. He proceeded to restate Hanoi's previous demands: "U.S. imperialism is the aggressor. It must stop its air attacks on the North, put an end to its aggression in the South, withdraw its troops from South Viet Nam, and let the Vietnamese people settle by themselves their own affairs, as provided for in the Geneva agreements."

Anti-Chinese Attacks in Indonesia. On Dec. 10, 2,000 Indonesian demonstrators attacked Communist China's consulate in Medan, North Sumatra. Three persons were killed when police fought to keep the demonstrators from entering the building. Homes and business establishments of Chinese residents also were attacked. On Dec. 18, President Sukarno appealed to Indonesians to stop attacking Chinese in Indonesia, and the Peking regime, because, he said, "we are struggling against imperialism and we cannot do it alone."

Thailand Buildup. On Dec. 12, a dispatch to the *New York Times* from Bangkok reported that the U.S. had begun construction of a huge military base on the Gulf of Siam in Thailand. The dispatch reported also that pro-Communist activity in northern Thailand had increased in the past six months. Communists were said to be using the same tactics in Thailand that the Viet Cong had used in South Viet Nam before the large-scale American buildup there.

Air Strike near Haiphong. On Dec. 15, U.S. planes made their first strike on a major industrial center in North Viet Nam, destroying a thermal power plant 14 miles north of Haiphong, North Viet Nam's major port.

Peace Feeler Report. On Dec. 17, the State Department confirmed reports of another possible North Viet Nam peace feeler. Confirmation came after the *St. Louis Post-Dispatch* reported Dec. 17 that two Italian professors had met secretly with North Viet Nam President Ho Chi Minh on Nov. 11. The professors subsequently communicated with Italian Foreign Minister and UN President Amintore Fanfani. State Department officials denied that the offer had been rejected out of hand, asserting that a written reply to Fanfani by Secretary of State Dean Rusk had been forwarded to Hanoi Dec. 13 requesting clarification of certain "ambiguous" points. The official North Viet Nam news agency on Dec. 18 denounced the Italians' story as "sheer groundless fabrication."

UN Resolution on Tibet. On Dec. 18, the UN General Assembly adopted a resolution urging "cessation of all practices which deprive the Tibetan people of the human rights and fundamental freedom that they have enjoyed." The vote was 43-26 with 22 abstentions. All Communist nations voted against the resolution.

Red China Ready to Fight U.S. On Dec. 20, Chinese Communist Premier Chou En-lai, at a reception in celebration of the fifth anniversary of the founding of the National

Liberation Front in South Viet Nam, accused the U.S. of "making preparations" to extend the war in Viet Nam to all of Southeast Asia and into China. Chou warned that if the U.S. decided on "going along the road of war expansion and having another trial of strength with the Chinese people," China would "take up the challenge and fight to the end."

Draft Reclassifications. On Dec. 21, Lt. Gen. Lewis B. Hershey, director of the Selective Service System, in a letter to House Judiciary Chairman Emanuel Celler (D N.Y.), confirmed plans to induct registrants who had burned their draft cards or joined unlawful sit-ins. Celler had asked Hershey for information on the cases of 10 University of Michigan students who were reclassified 1-A following their arrest for trespassing during an Oct. 15 sit-in at an Ann Arbor draft board.

Hershey said that destroying a draft card or refusing to leave a Selective Service office constituted "interference with the Selective Service System." He said: "We must always distinguish between those who engage in a legal demonstration of political views and those who express those views by willfully violating the Selective Service law...Any deliberate, illegal obstruction of the administration of the law by registrants cannot be tolerated."

Celler asserted that Hershey's statement showed that he was using the draft law to punish and discourage political dissent, thereby "demeaning the draft act" and jeopardizing the honor of the armed forces. Infringements of the draft law, Celler said, should be punished by arrest, indictment and trial.

Sen. Philip A. Hart (D Mich.), a Judiciary Committee member, had said Dec. 15 that Hershey "apparently assumes that sit-ins violate the Selective Service Law, and it is with this assumption of guilt that I have my basic doubt." Hart said draft officials should not be in the position of both judge and jury and asked that Congress deny them power to reclassify student demonstrators.

Soviet-North Vietnamese Agreement. On Dec. 21, the Soviet Union and North Viet Nam signed an agreement providing for shipment of "supplementary technical assistance" and "additional free economic assistance" to North Viet Nam.

Cambodian Sanctuary. On Dec. 21, the State Department confirmed reports that U.S. forces in South Viet Nam had been authorized to pursue Viet Cong or North Vietnamese forces into Cambodia "in the exercise of the inherent right of self-defense to protect their forces." It was disclosed also that U.S. military commanders had been authorized to call in air strikes on North Vietnamese and Viet Cong forces hiding in Cambodia.

Prince Norodom Sihanouk, Cambodian head of state, denied Dec. 27 that his country was being used as a sanctuary for Viet Cong and North Vietnamese troops and accused the U.S. of planning to invade Cambodia. The next day, Red China pledged Cambodia its support in case of a U.S. attack.

Christmas Cease-Fire. On Dec. 22, the U.S. military command ordered a 30-hour Christmas cease-fire, to apply generally unless firing became necessary in self-defense. Similar orders were issued by South Viet Nam's military leaders, who referred to Pope Paul's appeal for a Christmas truce. Pressure immediately mounted to stretch the cease-fire into a lasting truce.

Calls for Continued Truce. On Dec. 23, Senate Majority Leader Mike Mansfield (D Mont.) proposed extension of the truce from 30 hours to one month -- through the three-day Vietnamese lunar New Year celebrations. Vice President Humphrey, Chairman J.W. Fulbright (D Ark.) of the Senate Foreign Relations Committee, and Sen. Jack Miller (R Iowa) also expressed hope that the truce would lead to a longer cessation of hostilities. Sen. Henry M. Jackson (D Wash.), though favoring extension of the Christmas truce, was "not over-optimistic" that peace could be negotiated with the North Vietnamese.

On Dec. 23, Pope Paul in a Christmas appeal for world peace deplored the attitudes of both sides as "obstacles to peace." He said: "No one ought to force his neighbors to resort to armed defense. And no one ought to shirk just and sincere negotiation to restore order and friendship."

On Dec. 24, Sen. Robert F. Kennedy (D N.Y.) proposed that if the Viet Cong substantially honored the cease-fire, the U.S. and South Viet Nam unilaterally extend it into an open-end truce by holding off from being the first to resume hostilities.

On Dec. 26, almost immediately after termination of the 30-hour Christmas truce period, allied ground forces resumed military action in face of heavy Viet Cong attacks, but bombing raids on North Viet Nam remained suspended.

On Dec. 28, a National Liberation Front broadcast proposed a four-day cease-fire between Communist forces and South Vietnamese troops during the lunar New Year, Jan. 20-23. The offer was not extended to U.S. troops, but American officials said the U.S. would observe such a truce if it were agreed to by South Viet Nam.

Peace Offensive. On Dec. 29, despite Administration silence on continuation of the bombing pause begun Christmas Eve, it was apparent that a significant diplomatic operation was under way. U.S. Ambassador to the United Nations Arthur J. Goldberg called on Pope Paul VI on a special mission from the President; Ambassador at Large W. Averell Harriman went to Warsaw with a large entourage of China specialists to discuss Viet Nam with Polish officials in Poland's capacity as a member of the International Control Commission for Viet Nam; and Ambassador Foy D. Kohler met with Soviet President Nikolai Podgorny in Moscow.

Administration officials, breaking the silence, confirmed Dec. 30 that the President had been sending top aides to various world capitals in an all-out effort to bring peace in Viet Nam. The wide range of diplomatic activity soon became evident. Goldberg proceeded to Paris for talks with French President Charles de Gaulle and the North Atlantic Treaty Organization Council, and then flew to London to confer with British Prime Minister Harold Wilson; Harriman continued on to Yugoslavia and India, the latter being another member of the Control Commission; Secretary of State Dean Rusk met with Hungarian officials in Washington. Presidential Assistant McGeorge Bundy flew to Ottawa for consultations with Prime Minister Lester Pearson; Canada was the third member of the International Control Commission.

No positive response to all the activity was discerned in Hanoi's public statements, nor was there any indication that North Viet Nam was reducing its war effort as a prelude to peace talks. On the contrary, Hanoi was getting ready to reject the President's peace offensive (on Jan. 4, 1966) as a "deceptive peace campaign and a trick."

Viet Nam Buildup in 1965. The U.S. military buildup in Viet Nam in 1965 had proceeded at a fast pace. At the end of 1964, the number of U.S. military personnel in Viet

U.S. Troop Involvement in Viet Nam

October 23, 1954 -- President Dwight D. Eisenhower sends message to Premier Ngo Dinh Diem stating that the American Ambassador to Vietnam has been instructed to examine with Diem "...how an intelligent program of American aid given directly to your government can serve to assist Viet Nam in its present hour of trial, provided that your government is prepared to give assurances as to the standards of performance it would be able to maintain in the event such aid were supplied." [1]

November 3, 1954 -- President Eisenhower designates General J. Lawton Collins as Special United States Representative in Viet Nam to coordinate the operations of all U.S. agencies there. [2]

FIRST U.S. MILITARY ASSISTANCE

Shortly after President Eisenhower's message to Diem, a small military mission was established[3] General Maxwell D. Taylor has stated that "almost at once after this agreement in 1954, we established a small mission which gradually grew. For a while the French remained in a training capacity in South Viet Nam. Eventually they withdrew that formal participation and we took over the entire training task of the armed forces." [4]

February 12, 1955 -- The U.S. Military Assistance Advisory Group (MAAG) takes over the training of the South Vietnamese Army after the French had relinquished their command authority. [5]

FIRST U.S. MILITARY CASUALTY

December 1961 -- (Secretary of State, Dean Rusk testifying before Senate Committee on Foreign Relations, February 18, 1966) "I am informed that our first military casualty in South Viet Nam occurred in December 1961."[6]

U.S. TROOPS IN SOUTH VIET NAM

The history of U.S. troop involvement is shown in Defense Department figures:

1954-60	650 (annual average)
December 31, 1960	800
December 31, 1961	3,200
December 31, 1962	11,300
December 31, 1963	16,300
December 31, 1964	23,300
December 31, 1965	184,300
December 31, 1966	389,400
March 11, 1967	423,000

1 *United States Senate Committee on Foreign Relations,* **Background Information Relating to Southeast Asia and Viet Nam** *(2d Revised Edition), 89th Congress, 2d Sess., March, 1966, pp. 75.*
2 *Ibid., p. 76.*
3 *Testimony of General Maxwell D. Taylor, in Hearings on S. 2793, To Amend Further the Foreign Assistance Act of 1961, As Amended, Committee on Foreign Relations, U.S. Senate, 89th Cong., 2d Sess., p. 446.*
4 *Ibid.*
5 *United States Senate Committee on Foreign Relations,* **Background Information Relating to Southeast Asia and Viet Nam,** *p. 2.*
6 *Testimony of Secretary of State Dean Rusk in Hearings on S. 2793, To Amend Further the Foreign Assistance Act of 1961, as Amended, p. 606.*

Nam had been 23,000 and the number of U.S. deaths from hostile action since Jan. 1, 1961, had been 239. By the end of 1965, the number of U.S. military personnel in Viet Nam was nearing 200,000 and the number of deaths from hostile action since January 1, 1961, exceeded 1,500.

In late 1965, the Viet Nam war was compared frequently with the Korean War. In the earlier conflict, the number of U.S. battle deaths from 1950 through 1953 totaled 33,629. In 1952, during the peak of Korean War mobilization, 3,636,-000 U.S. military personnel, representing 5.5 percent of the U.S. labor force, were on active duty. On Oct. 31, 1965, the 2,757,440 military personnel on active duty represented 3.5 percent of the labor force.

1966

Mansfield Report on Viet Nam -- Bombing of North Viet Nam Resumed After Five-Week Pause -- Senate Opens Hearings on Viet Nam -- Johnson Flies to Hawaii to Meet Ky -- Declaration of Honolulu -- Kennan Testifies Before Foreign Relations Committee -- Ridgway Supports Gavin's Proposed Enclave Strategy in Viet Nam -- Maxwell Taylor's Testimony on Viet Nam -- Rusk vs. Fulbright -- Kennedy's Proposals for Viet Nam Negotiations -- McNamara's Posture Statement -- McNamara on China's Nuclear Capability.

Foreign Relations Committee Hearings on China Policy -- Soviet Blast Against Communist China -- Peking Turns Down Bid to Soviet Party Congress -- Buddhist Protests in South Viet Nam -- Rusk Outlines U.S. Policy Toward Red China -- Fulbright on Viet Nam Consequences -- Beginning of China's Cultural Revolution -- Communist China's Third Nuclear Test -- Rise of Lin Piao -- Peking Mayor Peng and Others Purged -- Bombing Near Hanoi and Haiphong -- Johnson on Coming Pacific Era -- Ky Urges Invasion of North Viet Nam.

Mao Tse-Tung Goes for a Swim -- Peking Rally and New Order of Precedence in Communist Hierarchy -- Fulbright on U.S. Purpose in Asia -- Red Guard Rampages -- De Gaulle in Cambodia -- Resistance to Red Guards -- Election in South Viet Nam -- Eisenhower on Threat to Use Nuclear Weapons in Korea -- Alexis Johnson's Analysis of Situation in Red China -- Advocacy of Two-China Policy in UN -- Manila Conference Offer to Hanoi on Troop Withdrawal -- China Tests Atomic Missile -- Support of Asia Policy in Congress -- Sabotage in China -- Red Guard Activity in Peking -- Red China Shuns a Nuclear Non-Proliferation Pact -- Sino-Soviet Border Tension -- UN Vote on Red China -- Space Treaty -- Interview With Chen Yi -- New Phase in Mao's Drive Against Foes -- Lin Piao's Secret Speech -- New Denunciation of Liu and Teng -- U.S. Asks Thant's Aid on Cease-Fire -- Steel Sales by China -- Civilian Casualties in North Viet Nam -- Purge of Workers Urged -- China's Fifth Nuclear Test -- Peking's Prediction of Victory for Mao in 1967.

Red Reaction to Peace Offensive. On Jan. 1, the Peking *People's Daily* assailed U.S. diplomats seeking to find the basis for a negotiated settlement in Viet Nam as "freaks and monsters" who were "raising a lot of dust with their sinister activities." Four days later, it said "the well-intentioned people" who had been contacted by U.S. diplomats should not be fooled by the "peace-talks hoax," which was only a cover for coming expansion of the war by the U.S.

On Jan. 4, the North Vietnamese Foreign Ministry accused the U.S. of engaging in a "large-scale deceptive peace campaign coupled with the trick of 'temporary suspension of air attacks' on North Viet Nam." It said the U.S. had "no right to impose any conditions whatsoever in exchange for stopping its air raids on North Viet Nam." The real purpose of the U.S. in advocating unconditional discussions, the Foreign Ministry's statement asserted, was "to carry out the plot of conducting negotiations from a position of strength and attempting to force on the Vietnamese people acceptance of United States terms." However, North Viet Nam would not abandon its four-point peace proposal.

The statement also complained that the U.S. had "intensified its air attacks on the liberated areas in Laos and imprudently authorized United States troops to intrude into central Laos and into Cambodian territory, thus extending the war from South Viet Nam to these two countries."

China-Cuba Trade. On Jan. 2, Cuban Premier Fidel Castro announced that Communist China was reducing its trade with Cuba from an exchange of $250 million in 1965 to $170 million in 1966.

Viet Nam Casualties. On Jan. 5, the Defense Department released casualty figures showing that 1,365 American servicemen were killed in action in Viet Nam during 1965. Incomplete statistics listed 5,969 men wounded; 149 missing; 25 prisoners of the Communists; and 354 dead from causes other than hostile action. The new figures brought the total killed in action since Jan. 1, 1961, to 1,620; wounded to more than 7,500; and dead from other causes to 458.

Mansfield Report on Viet Nam. On Jan. 7, a report on "The Viet Nam Conflict: The Substance and the Shadow" was made public by the Senate Foreign Relations Committee. The report, submitted by a Senate group headed by Majority Leader Mike Mansfield (D Mont.) following a 35-day fact-finding tour of Europe and Asia, concluded that the situation in Viet Nam offered "only the very slim prospect of a just settlement by negotiations or the alternative prospect of a continuance of the conflict in the direction of a general war on the Asian mainland." Discussing the military outlook, the report made the following points:

"The large-scale introduction of U.S. forces and their entry into combat has blunted but not turned back the drive of the Viet Cong."

"The lines remain drawn in South Viet Nam in essentially the same pattern as they were at the outset of the increased U.S. commitment." Despite the increase, "it is doubtful...that the constricted position now held in Viet Nam by the Saigon government can continue to be held" indefinitely, let alone be extended without more American ground forces.

The Viet Cong "have responded to the increased American role with a further strengthening of their forces...and a general stepping up of military activity." As long as the North Vietnamese and their supporters "are willing and able to meet increased force by increased force," American pressure is only being applied against a military situation that is "open-ended."

"All of mainland Southeast Asia, at least, cannot be ruled out as a potential battlefield .... The war has already expanded into Laos and is beginning to lap over the Cambodian border while pressures increase in the northeast of Thailand."

"The visible alternative at this time...is the indefinite expansion and intensification of the war which will require the continuous introduction of additional U.S. forces."

"With a few exceptions, assistance has not been and is not likely to be forthcoming for the war effort in South Viet Nam from nations other than the United States. On the contrary...the longer the war continues in its present pattern and the more it expands in scope, the greater will become the strain placed upon the relations of the United States with allies both in the Far East and Europe."

Of negotiations, the report said: "Negotiations,...if they do come about, and if they are accompanied by a cease-fire and standfast, would serve to stabilize a situation in which the majority of the population remains under nominal government control but in which dominance of the countryside rests largely in the hands of the Viet Cong."

"Total Viet Cong strength, apparently, is steadily increasing....The Viet Cong, through local recruitment in the South and infiltration from the North, have the capability of a substantial increase in their numbers within a short period of time."

Regarding Communist China, the Mansfield group reported: "Until now the Chinese Communists have not introduced their manpower directly into the conflict although they clearly recognize that the war may reach that point. They recognize, too, that the war may impinge upon China herself at some point and have begun to make preliminary preparations for that eventuality.

"For the present, however, the Chinese appear to take the view that their direct intervention in Viet Nam is not required since: (1) the war in South Viet Nam is a people's war which the Viet Cong are winning; (2) North Viet Nam is successfully defending itself; (3) the more the United States escalates the war, the higher our casualties will be and the more discouraged we will become; and (4) the United States cannot win, in any event, according to Chinese theories.

"It is from Communist China," the report concluded, "that North Viet Nam and the Viet Cong derive the bulk of their outside material support. It is from Communist China that there has also flowed encouragement of resistance to negotiation or compromise. As the war escalates and Hanoi becomes ever more dependent upon Chinese support, a dependence which Soviet aid at best only tempers, the likelihood also increases that North Viet Nam will not be able to negotiate a settlement without at least the tacit consent of China. In fact, that point may have already been reached."

U.S. Bombing in Laos. On Jan. 8, it was reported in Saigon that large numbers of U.S. planes were bombing the Ho Chi Minh trail in Laos daily, trying to stem an increased flow of supplies and men from North Viet Nam to South Viet Nam.

Visitors to Hanoi. On Jan. 9, Staughton Lynd, an assistant professor at Yale; Herbert Aptheker, director of the American Institute of Marxist Studies and an avowed Communist; and Thomas Hayden, one of the founders of the left-wing Students for a Democratic Society, arrived in New

York after spending 10 days in North Viet Nam. Lynd, spokesman for the trio, said at a news conference that Pham Van Dong, the North Vietnamese premier, had told them during an interview that a "political settlement of the Viet Nam problem" could be reached "only when the United States has accepted the four-point stand of the government of...(North Viet Nam), has proved this by actual deeds and ...has stopped unconditionally and for good its air raids and all other acts of war." Then, he said, "it will be possible to consider the reconvening of an international conference of the type of the 1954 Geneva Conference on Viet Nam."

Lynd reported that both North Viet Nam and the National Liberation Front insisted that the U.S. would have to make an "unambiguous decision" to withdraw its forces from Viet Nam before there could be any negotiations. However, Lynd noted, "there is no explicit requirement of the physical withdrawal of all United States troops prior to negotiations." He said that the North Vietnamese were extremely suspicious of U.S. peace moves because they saw "a deep inconsistency between a peace posture looking toward a negotiated settlement and an interventionist posture which has in view the permanent partition of Viet Nam and an expanded war."

Note to Hanoi. On Jan. 10, Presidential Press Secretary Bill D. Moyers confirmed reports that an American official had delivered a note to a representative of North Viet Nam at an undisclosed time and place. The reported purpose of the note was to clarify the U.S. position on negotiations to end the war.

Tashkent Agreement. On Jan. 10, Indian Prime Minister Shastri and Pakistani President Mohammad Ayub Khan signed an agreement in Tashkent, Russia, under which both countries agreed to withdraw from the positions they had occupied during the border conflict. The Soviet Union had acted as mediator in the discussions.

State of the Union. On Jan. 12, the cost of the conflict in Viet Nam dominated the State of the Union Message delivered by President Johnson to a joint session of Congress. The President said that the war, plus domestic and other foreign programs, would require a fiscal 1967 budget of $112.8 billion, the first $100 billion-plus budget in the nation's history. The defense budget was estimated at $53.8 billion, with fiscal 1967 costs for Viet Nam rising $5.8 billion above the estimated fiscal 1966 costs.

The address was almost uniformly somber in tone, returning again and again to the theme of confronting Communist aggression in Viet Nam. It was in sharp contrast to the President's 1965 State of the Union Message, which was directed more toward domestic problems.

In 1966, Johnson said the nation was engaged in a "brutal and bitter" conflict in Viet Nam which "just must be the center of our concerns."

Soviet Aid to Hanoi. On Jan. 14, following a visit to North Viet Nam by a Soviet delegation headed by Aleksandr N. Shelepin, member of the presidium of the Soviet Communist Party's Central Committee, it was announced in Moscow that Russia had agreed to send more military aid to North Viet Nam.

NLF Representation. On Jan. 14, Government officials made it clear that the U.S. would not object to participation of the National Liberation Front in genuinely free elections in South Viet Nam. However, it would not consider the NLF a separate entity from the North Vietnamese in negotiations.

Gavin's Article. On Jan. 16, Lt. Gen. James M. Gavin (ret.), former U.S. Ambassador to France, said in an article in *Harpers* magazine for February that U.S. military objectives in South Viet Nam were stretching the capacity of American forces "beyond reason." To secure the country against Viet Cong insurgency would require "many times as much force as is being employed," Gavin wrote. And if the United States applied the force needed, it would have to expect Communist China to enter the war and reopen the Korean front as well. Gavin proposed that bombing of the North be permanently discontinued and that U.S. military operations be limited to defense of the coastal enclaves already held. Meanwhile, he said, an ultimate solution should be sought at the United Nations or in a Geneva conference. "I do not think...that if we should withdraw from Viet Nam the next stop would be Waikiki. The Kra Peninsula, Thailand, and the Philippines can all be secured. Withdrawal from Viet Nam would pose serious problems, but the problems we would then have to deal with would be far less serious than those associated with an expansion of the conflict."

Chinese Deny Blocking Soviet Shipments. On Jan. 16, the Chinese Communist *New China* news agency denied reports, which it said were of Soviet origin, that the Chinese were blocking transit of Soviet arms shipments through China to North Viet Nam. The news agency asserted that Chinese trains had been provided to transport Russian "military aid supplies and technical personnel" to North Viet Nam. It also said that a Chinese note accusing Russia of attempting to weaken Chinese-North Vietnamese relations "to serve United States imperialism" had been sent to the Soviet embassy in Peking but had been rejected.

Mrs. Gandhi. On Jan. 19, Mrs. Indira Gandhi, 48, was named India's new Prime Minister. The daughter of the late Prime Minister Jawaharlal Nehru, she succeeded Lal Bahadur Shastri, who died Jan. 11 in Tashkent.

More Viet Nam Funds. On Jan. 20, President Johnson transmitted to Congress requests for supplemental appropriations for fiscal 1966 amounting to $12,760,719,000, chiefly to support U.S. and allied operations in Southeast Asia.

Most of the amount requested, $12,345,719,000, was to enable the Defense Department to meet additional costs of the Viet Nam war. The balance, $415 million, was for the Agency for International Development (AID), chiefly for its programs in Southeast Asia.

Army-Party Dispute in Red China. On Jan. 25, all Chinese Communist newspapers and the Peking radio carried a report written by Hsiao Hua, chief of the general political department of the Chinese Liberation Army. The report indicated that a dispute over control of the army had been raging between the military and leaders of the Chinese Communist Party.

Hsiao's report said the basic question was "whether the gun will direct the party or the party will direct the gun." Since the end of the Korean War, he asserted, the army had grown "vain" and "self-satisfied." It was essential to "keep politics in the fore, strengthen our political and ideological work, arm all our commanders and fighters with Mao Tse-tung's thinking, ensure absolute leadership over the army by the party, make our army the party's most responsive instrument, which most faithfully carries out its line, its principles and its policies, thus ensuring that the guns are always in the hands of the most reliable people."

Hsiao suggested that the U.S. and the "modern revisionists," who were "shamelessly" lending their support, could be expected to attack China. China must "make full preparations against the war of aggression which U.S. imperialism may launch at an early date, on a large scale, with nuclear or other weapons, and on several fronts." But, he said, China's "absolute supremacy," derived from its enormous population and its ideological superiority, made it certain that "we can definitely drown the U.S. aggressors in an ocean of people's war."

Congress and Viet Nam. On Jan. 25, President Johnson called a bipartisan group of about 20 Congressional leaders to the White House for an intelligence briefing on Viet Nam. Reports from the secret session said the briefing concerned a North Vietnamese military buildup said to have taken place in the South during the month-long U.S. suspension of bombing raids. The lull in bombing of North Viet Nam had begun Christmas Eve, 1965. Earlier on Jan. 25, it was disclosed that the U.S. had informed allied and neutral governments that it would not be able to postpone resumption of bombing raids indefinitely.

Secretary of State Dean Rusk, at a Jan. 21 press conference, had reported that U.S. efforts to open the way to negotiations on Viet Nam had received "an overwhelmingly favorable response" except from "those who could in fact sit down and make peace." Observers concluded that the Administration was laying the groundwork for a decision to end the bombing pause and increase the U.S. troop commitment in South Viet Nam. Sen. Richard B. Russell (D Ga.), chairman of the Senate Armed Services Committee, ventured to say Jan. 21 that a force of 400,000 to 500,000 men might be needed. Rep. Robert L. F. Sikes (D Fla.), chairman of the House Military Construction Appropriations Subcommittee, asserted the same day that American forces in Viet Nam should be doubled. Sen. Stuart Symington (D Mo.) said Jan. 25 that bombing of North Viet Nam had proved ineffective and should not be resumed unless prime targets such as power plants, oil stores and docks were hit.

Rusk Defends Viet Nam Policy. On Jan. 28, the Senate Foreign Relations Committee started hearings on the Administration's $415-million economic aid supplemental request. The hearings opened the door to discussion of the essentials of U.S. policy in Viet Nam. Secretary of State Rusk told the Committee that every action the Administration had taken was justified in acts of Congress, treaties, resolutions or other actions of record. He cited as special evidence of Congressional support the resolution (PL 88-408) adopted in August 1964, after North Vietnamese torpedo boats attacked American destroyers in the Gulf of Tonkin. The broad language of the resolution authorized "all necessary steps, including the use of armed force" to protect American forces in Southeast Asia. Rusk said the Administration had tried to "expose fully to the public the elements of this problem" but it was hard to get people to listen. "I am a little concerned that formal acts of the Government over a period of years would appear to catch people by surprise at the moment that things get difficult."

Committee Chairman J. W. Fulbright (D Ark.) questioned the Secretary about what Rusk called the United States' "clear and direct commitment to the security of South Viet Nam against external attack" and asked whether in fact the United States was not trying to enforce a "Pax

Americana." The United States, Rusk replied, is not trying to serve as the "policeman of the world"; it makes "selective" decisions to halt inroads of aggressive communism.

Tests for Draft Deferment. On Jan. 28, Lt. Gen. Lewis B. Hershey, director of the Selective Service System, announced that tests and class standing would be restored as criteria for draft deferment of college students. Hershey said that local boards would start using the academic ratings, similar to the procedures adopted during the Korean War and continued until 1961, before the start of the next academic year

Bombing Resumption. On Jan. 31, President Johnson announced in a nationally televised address that U.S. aircraft had resumed bombing of North Viet Nam, ending the pause that began Dec. 24. The strikes, Johnson said, were directed against military targets, such as lines of supply which support the movement of men and arms from North Viet Nam to South Viet Nam.

The President said the end of the bombing pause did not "mean the end of our own pursuit of peace." He said he had instructed U.S. Ambassador to the UN Arthur J. Goldberg to ask for an immediate meeting of the UN Security Council and to present a U.S. resolution "which can open the way to the conference table."

Following Johnson's announcement, Secretary of State Dean Rusk held a news conference at which he reviewed recent U.S. diplomatic efforts to promote peace. Rusk reported that the only responses from Hanoi had been "negative, harsh and unyielding...by deeds as well as words." Perhaps, he said, Hanoi had failed "to understand that the United States will meet its commitment."

Congressional Reaction. President Johnson received generally reluctant support from the Senate for his decision to resume bombing of North Viet Nam, but the House gave him almost solid backing. The Senate, on the other hand, took more kindly than the House to Johnson's decision to ask the UN Security Council to consider the Viet Nam question. Senate Democratic Majority Leader Mike Mansfield (D Mont.) said, "I will do my best to support him to the best of my ability. I fully appreciate the difficulty and agony of the decision which was his, and his alone, to make." Sen. J. W. Fulbright (D Ark.) said the President had made his decision and while the "wisdom of the policy may be questioned, we must back our men in the fight."

U.S. Resolution at UN. On Jan. 31, U.S. Ambassador Arthur J. Goldberg submitted to the UN Security Council a draft resolution asking the Council: (1) to call for immediate discussions among the "appropriate interested governments," without preconditions, on arranging a conference "looking toward" application of the 1954 and 1962 Geneva agreements and the establishment of a durable peace in Southeast Asia; (2) to recommend that the first order of business of such a conference be the arrangement of an effectively supervised cease-fire; and (3) to offer UN mediation to help achieve the purposes of the resolution. The Council on Feb. 2 voted 9-2 (U.S.S.R. and Bulgaria), with four abstentions (France, Mali, Nigeria, Uganda) to take up the resolution.

Goldberg asserted in an interview on Feb. 5 that there was a broad consensus in the Security Council that a reconvened Geneva conference was the proper place to deal with the Viet Nam war.

Foreign Reaction to Bombing. On Feb. 1, North Viet Nam protested to the International Control Commission on Viet Nam that the resumption of U.S. air attacks "had brought about a very serious crisis to peace and security to all countries in Indo-China and Southeast Asia." Hanoi charged that U.S. peace soundings had actually been a cover for "moves to intensify and expand the war of aggression in Viet Nam." On the same day, the Peking radio asserted that the U.S. had "recklessly resumed its bombings ...after the utter failure of its peace hoax."

On Feb. 2, the French government issued a statement saying it could "only regret and disapprove of the resumption of bombing," which was "jeopardizing the cause of peace." The statement also said that, because North and South Viet Nam and Communist China were not members of the United Nations, the UN was "not qualified to intervene."

Chinese Charges Against Soviets. On Feb. 1, the Peking *People's Daily* charged that the purpose of the high-level Soviet mission to North Viet Nam in January was to "say clearly that the Vietnamese people must sit down around a conference table with the American aggressors." Soviet leaders were attacked also for sponsoring the negotiations that led to a settlement between Pakistan and the "Indian aggressors."

News reports from Moscow Feb. 1 stated that a "memorandum" about the 23rd Congress of the Soviet Communist Party (due to begin March 29) accused the Chinese Communists of instigating more than 150 border incidents in 1965. The memorandum asserted that China was engaged in subversive activities along the Soviet-Sinkiang Province border, was sending propaganda to individual Soviet citizens through the mails, and was attempting to force Russia into stirring up trouble for the U.S. elsewhere in the world in order to aid the Viet Cong. A speech by Soviet President Nikolai V. Podgorny, reprinted in the memorandum, included the comment that the only obstacle to better U.S.-Soviet relations was the war in Viet Nam.

On Feb. 2, the Peking *People's Daily* charged that the Soviet Union was supporting U.S. efforts to achieve the "military encirclement of China." The article claimed that Soviet policy "on Viet Nam, India-Pakistan and Japan questions completely conforms with the requirements of United States imperialism, especially with the latter's policy of encircling China." The *People's Daily* had earlier published a map showing the positions of U.S. air bases, troop concentrations, ships and naval bases throughout Asia. The map was entitled: "The Military Encirclement of China by American Imperialism."

Giap Predicts U.S. Defeat. On Feb. 1, North Viet Nam's defense minister and chief military strategist, Gen. Vo Nguyen Giap, said in an article in *Hoc Tap*, North Viet Nam's Communist party journal, that the U.S. "cannot escape the inevitable defeat which is likely to befall any aggressive army facing a whole nation resolute to resist them." Giap asserted that the purpose of U.S. involvement in South Viet Nam was to "control important strategic areas and set up firm bases as springboards" for attacks on "liberated areas" and to "decimate our forces." He said the U.S. also was attempting to "prevent the collapse of the puppet army and administration" of South Viet Nam.

The Vietnamese Communist forces, Giap insisted, had "grown up, and the liberated areas have included the major part of the southern population and territory." Despite the deployment of "hundreds of thousands of troops, (the U.S.) cannot avoid being driven into passivity in strategy, compelled to scatter their forces..., and cannot easily wrest back the initiative they wish, but instead face increasing failure."

Passport Cancellation. On Feb. 3, the State Department announced it had "tentatively withdrawn" the passports of seven citizens for violating the Government's restrictions on travel to North Viet Nam. Among the seven was Staughton Lynd, an assistant history professor at Yale, who visited Hanoi and talked with Premier Pham Van Dong in early January (*See Jan. 9*).

Public Hearings on Viet Nam. On Feb. 3, Sen. J. W. Fulbright (D Ark.), chairman of the Senate Foreign Relations Committee, announced that his committee would hold public hearings on the Administration's Viet Nam policy.

Johnson to Hawaii. On Feb. 4, President Johnson announced that he would fly to Hawaii to meet with leaders of the Saigon government Feb. 6. The surprise announcement was made as the Senate Foreign Relations Committee was opening its hearings on Viet Nam policy.

Senate Hearings Begin. On Feb. 4, the Senate Foreign Relations Committee opened hearings on an Administration bill (S 2793) authorizing $415 million in supplemental fiscal 1966 foreign economic aid, of which $275 million was earmarked for South Viet Nam. The hearings, televised nationally, were used by the Committee as a springboard for a public inquiry into the Administration's "general policy" in Viet Nam. Sen. J. W. Fulbright (D Ark.) opened the session by asserting that a major factor in the deep U.S. involvement in South Viet Nam was the $3 billion in economic aid poured into that country in the past 10 years.

David E. Bell, Administrator of the Agency for International Development (AID), said in response to questions that U.S. economic aid to Viet Nam would increase, rather than decrease, during the coming year. Bell also said there was considerable public support for the Saigon government in South Viet Nam; that murder and terrorism carried out by the Viet Cong had spread into northeast Thailand, and that some of the supplemental aid in S 2793 would provide helicopters, radio communications and weapons for Thailand to strengthen its border patrols and provincial police; and that the "vast majority" of refugees in South Viet Nam were fleeing from Viet Cong terror and not from the "incidental damage" of U.S. action.

Peking Snubs Moscow. On Feb. 6, the Chinese Communist *New China* news agency indicated that Red China would not be represented at the 23rd Congress of the Soviet Communist Party, due to open March 29. The news agency said the purpose of the Congress was "to impose the revisionist line defended by the fifth column of American imperialism into the heart of the international Communist movement."

NLF Representation. On Feb. 6, Ambassador at Large W. Averell Harriman suggested in a broadcast interview that the U.S. might be willing to have the South Viet Nam National Liberation Front participate in peace negotiations as an "independent group," though not as a government delegation. The United States had previously insisted that the NLF could be represented only in a North Vietnamese delegation as an "interested party."

China and Cuba. On Feb. 6, it became clear that the split between Communist China and Cuba had widened. The Cuban Communist Party's newspaper, *Granma*, published an article by Cuban Premier Fidel Castro in which he accused Communist China of "blackmail" and the "betrayal" of the Cuban revolution. He asserted that China had attempted to intervene in Cuba's internal affairs, and that Cuban action to stop a Chinese propaganda campaign on the island was the "true motive for the Chinese conduct."

Castro reported that the Chinese had sent propaganda material to Cuban officials through the mail despite warnings from the Cuban government to desist. "We have clearly told the representatives of the Chinese government that these ways of behaving compare to those employed in our country by the United States embassy when it attempted to intervene in the internal affairs of Cuba....We have liberated ourselves from imperialism which is 90 miles from our coasts and we are not disposed to accept that other powerful state, 6,000 miles away, which comes to impose upon us similar methods."

Johnson in Honolulu. On Feb. 6, President Johnson arrived in Honolulu for talks with Vietnamese leaders. Among the many officials accompanying Mr. Johnson were Secretaries Dean Rusk, Robert S. McNamara, Orville L. Freeman and John W. Gardner. Secretary of Agriculture Freeman later accompanied Vice President Humphrey to Saigon, as did Ambassador at Large W. Averell Harriman and other government officials. Secretary of Health, Education and Welfare Gardner was scheduled to make a trip later to Saigon.

Honolulu Declaration. On Feb. 8, the United States and South Viet Nam issued a Declaration of Honolulu and a joint communique following a three-day meeting between President Johnson and leaders of the Saigon government. The declaration confirmed U.S. commitments to South Viet Nam and stressed not only expansion of military efforts but also political and social reforms in South Viet Nam. The President announced that he had asked Vice President Hubert H. Humphrey to fly to Saigon with the Vietnamese leaders and from there commence a tour of other Southeast Asia nations.

Mr. Johnson, in Los Angeles on his return from Hawaii, reported on the talks from a prepared statement: "We went to Honolulu to meet the leaders of the government of South Viet Nam....The war we are helping them fight must be fought on two fronts. One is military. The other front is the struggle against injustice; against hunger, disease and ignorance; against political apathy and indifference....We talked of very specific things."

Gavin's Testimony. On Feb. 8, Gen. James M. Gavin (ret.), testifying before the Senate Foreign Relations Committee on the Administration's Viet Nam policy, supported views he had expressed in the February 1966 issue of *Harper's* Magazine. In response to questions, Gavin warned that escalation of the Southeast Asian fighting "could hurt our strategic position there and elsewhere" and involve the risk of war with China. He said that "urban bombing" on such North Vietnamese centers as Hanoi and Haiphong would be of little military value. However, he insisted that his proposal that U.S. military operations be limited to holding enclaves along the Viet Nam coast should not be thought of as retreat or a static strategy but rather as a policy of using existing forces to maintain the positions currently controlled while the question of expanding the war was weighed.

Chinese Charge. On Feb. 10, the Chinese Communist theoretical journal *Red Flag* charged that the only reason the Soviet Union was giving aid to North Viet Nam was "to get more of a say on the Viet Nam questions, to sow dissension in Chinese-Vietnamese relations and to help the United States to realize its peace talks plot." The article further charged that the Soviet leadership had allied its country with the U.S. "to enable the U.S. to occupy South Viet Nam permanently and to strike a political deal with it."

Kennan's Testimony. On Feb. 10, former Ambassador George F. Kennan, testifying before the Senate Foreign Relations Committee on the Administration's Viet Nam policy, said the U.S. aim should be to liquidate its military involvement in South Viet Nam "as soon as this can be done without inordinate damage to our own prestige or to the stability in that area." Kennan opposed "deliberate expansion of hostilities on our part directed to the achievement of something called 'victory' " and expressed fear that an attempt to "crush" Hanoi would "have the effect of bringing in the Chinese at some point,...involving us in a military conflict with Communist China in one of the most unfavorable theaters of hostility that we could possibly choose."

It was Kennan's hope that the U.S. would restrict its military operations to the minimum necessary to assure the security of U.S. military forces and maintain "our military presence there" until a peaceful resolution of the conflict was achieved. He said a proper "liquidation of unsound positions" would be more likely to win world respect than to undermine confidence in the U.S. Kennan questioned the extent of the U.S. commitment and when and how it was made. "If we did not incur such an obligation in any formal way, then I think we should not be inventing it for ourselves," he said.

Proposals on Viet Nam. On Feb. 10, Retired Gen. Matthew B. Ridgway added his support to the enclave strategy for Viet Nam proposed by retired Gen. James M. Gavin. "I agree basically," Ridgway said, "with everything that Gen. Gavin said." Commenting at a news conference Feb. 11 on the testimony by Gen. Gavin and former Ambassador George F. Kennan before the Senate Foreign Relations Committee, President Johnson said he did not see "a great deal of difference" between what they had said and what the Government was doing.

Sen. Abraham A. Ribicoff (D Conn.) on Feb. 12 urged President Johnson to arrange a preliminary conference on Viet Nam in Geneva at a specific date. "Let all who are involved in Viet Nam -- including the Viet Cong," Ribicoff proposed, "attend, with no subject barred from the agenda." At such a conference, he said, the U.S. should offer to make a token withdrawal of 10,000 troops to be matched by a similar withdrawal of North Vietnamese forces.

Sen. Jacob K. Javits (R N.Y.) proposed Feb. 13 that the U.S. adopt a military policy of defending important enclaves in Viet Nam. He called also for U.S. recognition of the Communist National Liberation Front as a party to any peace negotiations.

Humphrey's Tour. On Feb. 10, Vice President Hubert H. Humphrey arrived in Saigon at the start of a tour of Asian nations to stimulate new concern for social and economic development in the region. In South Viet Nam, Laos and Thailand, Humphrey emphasized that the U.S. had embarked upon a major development program along with its military support in Southeast Asia. On Feb. 15, he pledged increased military aid to Thailand to bolster and modernize that country's military forces.

U.S. Ready to Admit Chinese Journalists. On Feb. 14, the State Department announced that the U.S. was prepared to allow Chinese Communist journalists to visit the United States. A spokesman said the offer, advanced during one of the regular meetings of U.S. and Chinese diplomats in Warsaw, was not dependent on reciprocal admission of American newsmen by Red China. The spokesman added that Communist China "has neither taken up the offer or rejected it."

De Gaulle's Letter. On Feb. 15, French President Charles de Gaulle informed North Vietnamese President Ho Chi Minh that his government was prepared to "actively take part...in exerting her influence" to end the Viet Nam conflict "as soon as this appears possible." De Gaulle's note was in answer to a letter from Ho on Jan. 24 asking the French President to do what he could to "prevent perfidious new maneuvers" by the U.S. in Southeast Asia. De Gaulle made it clear that he opposed the U.S. policy in South Viet Nam.

Taylor's Testimony on Viet Nam. On Feb. 17, Gen. Maxwell D. Taylor (ret.), special consultant to the President, testified before the Senate Foreign Relations Committee on the Administration's policy in Viet Nam: "We intend to show that the (Communist) 'war of liberation'...(is) doomed to failure." Referring to President Eisenhower's 1959 statement stressing the military importance of defending South Viet Nam, Taylor remarked that he did not believe in that view, often referred to as the "domino" theory. "However, I am deeply impressed with the probable effects world wide, not necessarily in areas contiguous to South Viet Nam, if the 'war of liberation' scores a significant victory there," he said. He also defended the use of air power against military targets. Taylor said he did not believe the war was open-ended, although he could not say exactly what limit there might be on U.S. troop commitments. He rejected the "so-called holding strategy" advocated by Gen. James Gavin as "inglorious" and "disastrous."

The sharpest clash of the day came between Taylor and Sen. Wayne Morse (D Ore.). When Morse said that in his opinion the American people would soon "repudiate our war in Southeast Asia," Taylor observed, "That, of course, is good news to Hanoi." Morse retorted, "I know that is the smear artist that you militarists give to those of us who have honest differences of opinion with you, but I don't intend to get down in the gutter with you and engage in that kind of debate, General." Morse added that Taylor "and the President, in my judgment have been misguiding" the American people "for a long time in this war."

Rusk vs. Fulbright. On Feb. 18, Secretary of State Dean Rusk, testifying before the Senate Foreign Relations Committee, said that "we do not regard ourselves as the policemen of the universe." Rusk said the reason the U.S. was in Viet Nam was part of a long "process of preventing the expansion...of Communist domination by the use of force against the weaker nations on the perimeter of Communist power. He identified the SEATO treaty as the fundamental obligation guiding U.S. actions in South Viet Nam and said the "far-reaching implications of this commitment were well understood by" the Committee and the Senate when the treaty was consented to. Rusk pointed out that under the treaty "the finding that an armed attack has occurred" does not have to be made collectively "before the obligation of each member becomes operative, nor does the treaty require a collective decision on actions." He added that "if the United States determines that the armed attack has occurred,...it is obligated 'to act...' without regard to the views or actions of any other treaty member."

Rusk contended that "our forces are being employed for a limited and well defined objective...," and that the U.S. troop commitment depended primarily on what the enemy committed. For the Communists, Rusk said, "the major question of substance" was U.S. "recognition of the (National Liberation) Front as the sole spokesman for the people of South Viet Nam." Acceptance of the Front, he said, would "in effect mean our acceptance of the Communist position as to the indigenous nature of the conflict and thus our acceptance of a settlement on Hanoi's terms -- which would mean delivering South Viet Nam into the control of the Communist North."

In a later exchange Fulbright said, "It would be one of the greatest victories for us in our prestige if we could... bring about some kind of settlement of this particular struggle." Rusk agreed, but he pointed out that "We can't get anybody into the discussions for the purpose of talking about it." Fulbright said that if that were the case, "there must be something wrong with our diplomacy." Rusk then asked, "Senator, is it just possible that there is something wrong with them?"

Maritime Boycott. On Feb. 18, the executive board of the Maritime Trades Department of the AFL-CIO approved a resolution to boycott ships of foreign nations permitting trade with North Viet Nam. The boycott was scheduled to begin within 30 days unless there was a change in the policies of the countries involved (including, among others, Great Britain, Norway, Sweden, Denmark, France, Italy and Egypt).

Kennedy Proposal for Viet Nam Negotiations. On Feb. 19, Sen. Robert F. Kennedy (D N.Y.) suggested that the U.S. offer the National Liberation Front, and other discontented elements in South Viet Nam, a share of the power and responsibility in that country as the best hope for a negotiated settlement. Kennedy said there were "three things you can do" with those groups, both "Communist and non-Communist, who disire to change the existing political and economic system of the country...-- kill or repress them, turn the country over to them, or admit them to a share of power and responsibility." He chose the last alternative but said that "the manner or degree of participation" cannot "now be described with any precision," and that there must be "international guarantees to back up" any agreement.

Kennedy asserted that "We must reveal enough of our intentions to Hanoi to eliminate any reasonable fear that we ask them to talk now only to demand their surrender." He was "aware that the United States cannot proclaim in advance the precise terms of an acceptable settlement," but the U.S. must show enough of its intentions to persuade "our adversaries" that a "settlement is in their interests as well as our own."

Opinions on Kennedy's Proposal. On Feb. 21 Presidential adviser McGeorge Bundy described Kennedy's plan as neither useful nor helpful. Bundy said he did not think experience showed that Communists and non-Communists could cooperate in the government of a country. Under Secretary of State George W. Ball said there was nothing in Kennedy's plan that the Administration had not already considered and found unacceptable. A coalition government with the Communists, he said, would quickly turn into a Communist government. Vice President Humphrey compared Kennedy's suggestion to putting "a fox in a chicken coop; there aren't any chickens left." On the other hand, Gen. Maxwell D. Taylor (ret.) had "no difficulty" with the Kennedy statement. "I don't read into it many of the things that various commentators have. It's very, very close to what I consider my position."

On Feb. 22, Sen. Kennedy said he was not suggesting that the Communists "automatically be put into power, but if the negotiators feel it is the best way to proceed in forming an interim government, we shouldn't shut the door automatically against them." Later that day, Presidential Press Secretary Bill D. Moyers said there was no disagreement between the Administration and Kennedy "if Sen. Kennedy did not propose a coalition government with Communist participation before elections are held." The major area of agreement seemed to be that the United States should abide by the results of free, supervised elections even if the elections resulted in a Communist government in South Viet Nam.

Chinese Reaction to Rusk's Testimony. On Feb. 20, the Chinese Communist *New China* news agency said that Secretary of State Rusk's testimony before the Senate Foreign Relations Committee Feb. 18 amounted to a "declaration that United States imperialism will not lay down its butcher's knife and that it is determined to seize South Viet Nam by force." The statement added that Rusk had "tried to threaten the Vietnamese and Chinese people with a 'big war,'" but, the statement asserted, they would not yield to U.S. "brinkmanship." It warned that China was "fully prepared to take up the challenge and fight to the end if United States imperialism insists on carrying the war into their country."

Indonesian Turmoil. On Feb. 21, Indonesian President Sukarno announced he had removed 15 anti-Communist military officials from their posts, including Gen. Abdul Nasution, defense minister and head of the armed forces. The action, considered an attempt to counter the violent anti-Communist campaign that had followed the abortive left-wing coup, led to violent demonstrations against the government.

De Gaulle on Viet Nam. On Feb. 21, French President Charles de Gaulle, at a news conference in Paris, said, "Unless one is able...and willing...to banish resistance to the ends of the earth, there is no other way to put an end to this war than by concluding peace among all those interested....The conditions of this peace are known....Locally, the conditions...(are) the end of all foreign intervention and after that the neutrality of the country. France not long ago withdrew her troops and is the better for it today."

Saigon Government Changes. On Feb. 21, South Viet-
namese Premier Nguyen Cao Ky announced creation of 11 new cabinet-level posts and promised that elections would be held in 1967. Ky said he would not be a candidate at that time. He explained that enlargement of the cabinet would enable the government to better carry out the social and economic reforms promised at Honolulu.

Johnson Reply to Critics. On Feb. 23, President Johnson, in a speech at Freedom House in New York, said that the "strength of America can never be sapped by discussion," but he also warned that "no foe...should mistake ...our debate for weakness." Reciting his replies to the "questions that are still being asked," Johnson said, "there is not and there will not be a mindless escalation...(of the Viet Nam war)." There was no risk of war with Communist China, he insisted, as long as "there is any reason left behind the wild words from Peiping." In an apparent answer to Sen. Kennedy's remarks, the President said, "Men ask who has a right to rule in Viet Nam. Our answer: the people must have this right -- the South Vietnamese people ....Washington will not impose upon the people of South Viet Nam a government not of their choice."

Viet Nam Deserters. On Feb. 23, a dispatch to the *New York Times* stated that around 96,000 South Vietnamese soldiers had deserted the army during 1965. Despite the high desertion rate and the deaths and casualties suffered in combat, the size of the South Vietnamese army had grown appreciably during the year. The dispatch noted that the desertion figures, which had been released by the South Vietnamese government, did not include those who had deserted to rejoin their families and then returned to duty.

Posture Statement. On Feb. 23, a censored version of Secretary of Defense Robert S. McNamara's "posture statement," an annual review of U.S. global defense policy, was made public. McNamara's testimony had been given in late January and early February before the Senate Armed Services Committee and the Senate Appropriations Subcommittee on Defense, meeting in joint session.

On Communist China the Secretary said: "The long-range objective of the Chinese Communists is to become dominant in the Asian, African and Latin American countries, and to frustrate the process of peaceful development and free choice in the developing nations. They hope to create a new alignment, especially in the Southern and Eastern Hemispheres, in which Communist China is the ideological leader and the most powerful country....

"Notwithstanding their bellicosity and their cynical protestations that it is permissible for them to move men and guns across borders to attack free governments but not for the forces of freedom to defend themselves, the Chinese Communists have thus far displayed great caution in an effort to avoid direct confrontation with the United States military forces in Asia. As in the case of Moscow, there is no reason to suppose that Peiping does not understand the hazards of a major war. However, there is every reason to conclude that Peiping is determined to press the conflict in Viet Nam at the expense of the Vietnamese people, and that it will follow a similar course at the expense of other peoples whenever it believes an opportunity exists....

"I believe that the leaders of the Soviet Union fully appreciate, as we do, the perils of a general war and the danger of local wars escalating into general nuclear war.

I believe that the leaders of Communist China are also reluctant to challenge the full weight of our military power. But it is clear that we have yet to convince the Chinese Communists that their new drive for world revolution, using what they euphemistically call 'people's wars,' will not succeed....But convince them we must....If we and our free world allies fail to meet the Chinese Communists' challenge in Southeast Asia, we will inevitably have to confront it later under even more disadvantageous conditions. Chinese Communist ambitions, the most important source of tension in the Far East, have remained unchanged and, to a large extent, unrealized in the last year. In Viet Nam, the Indian subcontinent, Indonesia, and the Afro-Asian movement, Peiping's attempts to increase its influence and exclude that of the United States (and the Soviet Union) were largely unsuccessful....Communist China has reacted to these setbacks by assuming a still more militant posture."

Discussing the problem of "nth country" nuclear threats, McNamara said China posed the greatest threat of that kind to the United States. He said, "The Chinese Communists have detonated two nuclear devices and could possibly develop and deploy a small force of ICBMs by the mid to latter part of the 1970s....The development and deployment of even a small force of ICBMs might seem attractive to them as a token, but still highly visible, threat to the U.S., designed to undermine our military prestige and the credibility of any guarantee which we might offer to friendly countries. The prospect of an effective U.S. defense against such a force might not only be able to negate that threat but might possibly weaken the incentives to produce and deploy such weapons altogether."

Concerning Laos, the Secretary said: "The future of Laos continues to be intimately tied to the outcome of the struggle in Viet Nam....The Lao government, led by Prince Souvanna Phouma, has made some progress in the past year over coping with the military threat, and has been successful in maintaining relative political and economic stability....We must recognize, however, that the government's continued ability to defend against the Pathet Lao and the North Vietnamese and to maintain political and economic stability...depends largely on continued military and economic assistance from the United States."

On Cambodia, McNamara was not as optimistic. "Apparently believing that Communist China will achieve predominant influence in Southeast Asia and that North Viet Nam will conquer South Viet Nam, (Prince Norodom) Sihanouk has sought close relations with both Peiping and Hanoi in the hope of retaining at least some semblance of independent existence for Cambodia....We wish to continue to avoid, if possible, any action that would preclude an improvement in relations between Cambodia and the United States or that would threaten to expand the war in South Viet Nam into Cambodia."

Concerning Thailand, McNamara said: "During the past year, Thailand has strengthened her relations with the free world, maintained internal stability and continued its economic progress, becoming an ever more valuable and cooperative partner of the United States....The Thais are keenly aware that in the last year Communist China has blatantly advertised its preparations for subversive insurgency designed to overthrow the Thai government. The Thais are equally cognizant of the implications for all of Southeast Asia of a Communist victory in Viet Nam."

Ghana Coup. On Feb. 24, a military coup d'etat

ousted President Kwame Nkrumah of Ghana while he was en route to Peking. "The military, with the cooperation of the people," a rebel broadcast reported, "has taken over the government. The myth surrounding Kwame Nkrumah has been broken." Arriving in Peking on the same day, Nkrumah declared: "As you can see, the struggle against colonialism, neo-colonialism and imperialism has been intensified as a result of what is happening today."

No Progress at UN. On Feb. 26, after three weeks of deliberation, it was reported that the UN Security Council had been unable to make progress toward agreement on the U.S. resolution to promote a negotiated settlement of the Vietnamese conflict. *(See Jan. 31, 1966)*

Kennedy-Humphrey on Viet Cong. On Feb. 27, Sen. Robert F. Kennedy (D N.Y.) and Vice President Hubert H. Humphrey, appearing on separate television programs, again differed on whether the U.S. should be prepared to concede to the Viet Cong a share of power in a South Vietnamese government.

Kennedy's stand continued to seem obscure to some observers. His argument Feb. 27 was that the U.S. should make clear that the Viet Cong could expect a place in an interim government -- between fighting and elections -- and in an elected government, depending on the voting results, if they made certain concessions. This apparently was the same point he made in a Feb. 19 statement.

Humphrey said the U.S. would not offer the Viet Cong any part in a coalition government, but that they could stand for election after a negotiated settlement. Both contended that they were in agreement with the White House.

Presidential Press Secretary Bill D. Moyers said Feb. 28 there was "no confusion within the Administration" as to the Viet Cong, and that "If Sen. Kennedy did not propose a coalition government with participation prior to election, there is no disagreement."

Chinese Protest to Indonesia. On Feb. 28, Communist China protested to Indonesia regarding an attack on the Chinese consulate in Macassar. The note asserted that the Indonesian government had allowed "hooligans organized by Indonesian right-wing forces" to attack Chinese diplomats and destroy Chinese property. On March 9, a mob of Indonesian students broke into the offices of the Chinese Communist *New China* news agency in Jakarta, destroying the building and the news agency's cars. In another part of the city, student mobs attacked the Chinese consulate, injuring 25 persons. The Chinese embassy again protested.

Defense Authorization. On March 1, Congress moved nearer to action on supplemental defense appropriations by passing several authorization bills. Passage of the measures in the Senate was marked by lengthy and at times acrimonious debate on President Johnson's Viet Nam policies, while the House acted with dispatch and made only limited criticism of the increased U.S. commitment to the war.

The Senate passed, by a 93-2 roll-call vote, a bill (S 2791) authorizing $4,807,750,000 in fiscal 1966 supplemental appropriations for the Defense Department. Wayne Morse (D Ore.) and Ernest Gruening (D Alaska), two of the most vocal critics of the Administration's policy in Viet Nam, cast the negative votes. Next, the Senate by voice vote accepted an almost identical House bill (HR 12889), passed the same day, after substituting the language of S 2791 as approved by the Senate.

Prior to approval of S 2791, the Senate by a 92-5 roll call had adopted a motion by Majority Leader Mike Mansfield (D Mont.) to table (kill) a Morse amendment to repeal the 1964 "Gulf of Tonkin" resolution (PL 88-408). Voting against the tabling motion were J. W. Fulbright (D Ark.), chairman of the Senate Foreign Relations Committee, Eugene J. McCarthy (D Minn.), Stephen M. Young (D Ohio), Morse and Gruening.

Ghana Ousts Communists. On March 1, the new regime in Ghana ordered all Soviet, Chinese Communist and East German personnel and their families to leave the country. About 130 Russian and 150 Chinese departed during the first week of March.

Nkrumah in Guinea. On March 2, Kwame Nkrumah, ousted President of Ghana, arrived in Guinea and was immediately proclaimed by Guinean President Sekou Toure the "head of state in Guinea and secretary general of the Guinean Democratic Party." Toure added: "If there were a conference of African heads of state tomorrow, Comrade Nkrumah would speak in the name of Guinea, because Nkrumah is not a simple African but a universal man."

Nkrumah later declared: "I have come here purposely to use Guinea as a platform to tell the world that very soon I shall be in Accra, in Ghana." On March 4, Ghana broke diplomatic relations with Guinea.

Chinese on U.S. Debate. On March 3, the Peking *People's Daily* called the debate in the U.S. on the Administration's Viet Nam policy only "camouflage" to hoodwink the people." The article said both the "hawks" and the "doves" were a "bunch of fools" who would not "abandon the United States policy of aggression in Viet Nam and Asia" or advocate withdrawal of U.S. forces from Asia.

Taylor's Proposal to Mine Haiphong Harbor. On March 4, a statement by Gen. Maxwell D. Taylor "that the time has been reached" when U.S. forces should mine the harbor of Haiphong was made public. The proposal was included in a supplementary statement submitted to the Senate Foreign Relations Committee after Taylor's testimony Feb. 17.

McNamara on China's Bomb. On March 7, Secretary of Defense Robert S. McNamara told the Joint Congressional Committee on Atomic Energy that he was disturbed about the future nuclear capability of Communist China, especially because of the "aggressive statements of her leaders." McNamara said that within two or three years Communist China would have a nuclear "warhead delivery capability" within a 700-mile radius. Communist China then would be able to support the aggressive statements of its leaders "with instruments of war of the most terrible kind."

China Hearings. On March 8, the Senate Foreign Relations Committee began a series of hearings on U.S. policy towards Communist China. The hearings were an outgrowth of the nationally televised investigation of U.S. policy in Viet Nam.

Committee Chairman J.W. Fulbright (D Ark.), opening the hearings, said: "The immediate purpose of these hearings is educational. At this stage perhaps the most effective contribution the Committee can make is to provide a forum for recognized experts and scholars in the field of China. I hope that these hearings in this way will increase the knowl-

edge of China, our knowledge in Congress and the public's knowledge."

Barnett on China Policy. On March 8, the Senate Foreign Relations Committee heard from its first witness, A. Doak Barnett, professor of government at Columbia University. Barnett said there was "a need for basic changes in the over-all U.S. posture toward Communist China." While supporting the policy of containment of China, Barnett argued that the attempt to isolate China had been unwise and unsuccessful and should be abandoned. He suggested instead a policy aiming at "maximum contacts with and minimum involvement of the Chinese Communists in the international community," complimented by a policy of checking the Chinese military or subversive threats--"containment but not isolation." Barnett urged recognition of the Chinese Communist regime as the de facto government of the Chinese mainland, increased trade in nonstrategic goods with China, and U.S. acceptance of some formula to provide seats in the UN for both Chinas.

Barnett said it was important to recognize Peking's ambitious goals, but it was "equally important to note that...the Chinese Communists do not appear to think primarily in terms of spreading their influence through direct military and territorial expansion." At the same time, it would be a "dangerous error to conclude that Communist China would not risk major war if it genuinely felt that its vital interests were threatened."

French to Leave NATO. On March 9, France formally announced that it planned to withdraw from the North Atlantic Treaty Organization. No date was specified.

Travel to Communist Countries. On March 9, it was disclosed that President Johnson had decided to ease travel restrictions for scholars wanting to visit Albania, China, North Viet Nam, North Korea or Cuba.

Peking Explains. On March 9, the Peking *People's Daily*, apparently referring to Chinese setbacks in Cuba, Ghana and Indonesia, told party members that in some countries the U.S. "might get the upper hand for the time being." It said: "The anti-United States struggle does not advance in a straight line. There will be many ebbs and flows until final victory." The paper added later: "Sometimes the balance of forces in the struggle is, for the time being, unfavorable to the revolution, sometimes the leadership of the revolution may make mistakes of one kind or another.... Twists and turns...should cause no surprise."

Kenya Expels Communists. On March 10, the government of Kenya announced that it had ordered Chinese Communist, Russian and Czech diplomats and journalists to leave the country. No reason for the action was given.

Thi Fired. On March 10, South Viet Nam's National Leadership Committee unanimously voted to oust Lt. Gen. Nguyen Chanh Thi, head of the Army's 1st Corps and a political rival of Premier Nguyen Cao Ky. The Committee said that Thi had acted like a "war lord" and was guilty of insubordination. The U.S. Embassy labeled the action a "step toward political stability" and "a defeat for warlordism."

The Buddhists immediately organized large demonstrations for Thi in Danang, Hue and other cities and demanded that Ky's regime be replaced by a civilian government.

Fairbank on China Policy. On March 10, Dr. John K. Fairbank, director of the East Asian Research Center at

Harvard University, testified before the Senate Foreign Relations Committee.

Fairbank emphasized the influence of history on Communist Chinese behavior. "The problems they face and the methods they use are in large part inherited," he said. "I think we need more perspective on the Chinese style of political behavior." Fairbank stressed in particular the roots of "China's remarkable feeling of superiority," its cultural isolation, and its classical doctrines of social order, which were reflected in the current Communist regime as well as in its foreign policy. He said that "applying all this background to the present moment,...we should not get too excited over Peiping's vast blueprints for the onward course of Maoist revolution." Observers had overreacted to the "blueprint of world revolution put out by Lin Piao last September (1965)." Fairbank said Lin's statement was meant "mainly as compensation for China's recent defeats in many parts of the globe" and was not to be compared with Hitler's *Mein Kampf.*

Shifting to the U.S. role in Asia, Fairbank said that use of American military power in the region should be tempered by constructive "nation-building." He thought that the alternatives to war with Peking were (1) to be more constructive socially and politically in Viet Nam, so that "the non-Communist model of nation-building there can compete more effectively with the Chinese Communist model," and (2) to "dampen Peiping's militancy by getting China into greater contact with the outside world." In addition to proposing admission of China to international organizations, Fairbank pointed out that "the Chinese people positively need certain kinds of aid through exchanges of technology or of goods, like all developing countries."

He concluded: "Containment alone is a blind alley unless we add policies of constructive competition and international contact....Peiping's rulers shout aggressively out of manifold frustrations....Isolation intensifies their ailment and makes it self-perpetuating, and we need to encourage international contact with China on many fronts."

Governors Support Viet Nam Policy. On March 12, Governors of 28 states and three territories adopted a resolution declaring that the Governors "wholeheartedly support and endorse the policies and programs in Viet Nam." The Administration's policies were "sound and the only rational policies to be followed under the circumstances."

Sukarno Yields. On March 12, following weeks of demonstrations in Jakarta, President Sukarno relinquished all governmental power. Lt. Gen. Suharto, army commander, assumed leadership of the country. Sukarno, Foreign Minister Subandrio and other cabinet ministers were placed under house arrest. Suharto immediately banned the PKI, the Indonesian Communist Party. Suharto said the new regime had no "intention of turning our revolution to the right as charged by some people, nor will we return it to the extreme left, because it is already leftist."

Humphrey on China Policy. On March 13, Vice President Hubert H. Humphrey, during a broadcast interview, said that U.S. policy toward China should be one of "containment without necessarily isolation." Humphrey added that the "program of responsible containment, the building of collective security in the West, but at the same time a probing and trying to find ways of communication, has been relatively successful, and I think it is in our interest and in the interest of humanity that the same kind of approach be exercised in Asia." He asserted that departure of the "Mao

generation" from "positions of leadership" was necessary before there could be improved relations between China and the West. "In the meantime, we ought to maintain...a spirit of friendship toward the Chinese people, but recognizing what the regime is, and making that regime understand they cannot achieve their purpose by military power."

Buddhist Protest in Danang. On March 15, the South Vietnamese city of Danang was paralyzed by a strike called by the Buddhists to protest the March 10 dismissal of Lt. Gen. Nguyen Chanh Thi and to express dissatisfaction with the government of Nguyen Cao Ky. Thi arrived in the area the following day and appealed to his supporters to end their protests and unite against the Viet Cong.

Foreign Aid Authorization. On March 15, the Senate and on March 16 the House by voice vote adopted the conference report on an Administration-backed bill (HR 12169) authorizing $415 million in fiscal 1966 supplemental foreign assistance appropriations. Of the total, $315 million was for supporting assistance to help finance the war in Southeast Asia and operations in the Dominican Republic.

Sen. Wayne Morse (D Ore.) spoke in opposition to adoption of the report. He said that at least half of the $275 million programed for Viet Nam "will get into the hands of the Viet Cong" and that "a great deal of this money will be used by one of the most corrupt regimes in Viet Nam we can imagine."

China Trade. On March 16, Dr. John Lindbeck, associate director of the East Asian Research Center at Harvard University, testified before the Senate Foreign Relations Committee on U.S. China policy. Lindbeck pointed out that China's trade had shifted from Communist countries to industrialized non-Communist countries, with Japan replacing Russia as the leading trade partner, but that "not one of China's trading partners can be classed as a strong ally." Lindbeck noted the importance of the removal of Russian influence from China.

Long War Prediction. On March 16, Truong Chinh, a member of the North Vietnamese Communist Party's politburo, said the North Vietnamese people "must enhance solidarity to defeat the U.S. war of destruction, defend North Viet Nam, continue Socialist construction, and actively support the liberation war of the South Vietnamese people." He added that the people would have to "firmly grasp the general strategic line of fighting a protracted war and mainly relying on our own forces." The "South Vietnamese people," he said, "are fully capable of defeating United States aggressors whatever form of aggressive wars...they may use."

More Views on China. On March 18, Brig. Gen. Samuel B. Griffith II (U.S. Marine Corps ret.) testified before the Senate Foreign Relations Committee on U.S. policy toward China. Griffith said that "except by the use of ground forces--predominantly infantry--in immediately peripheral areas, China lacks the conventional means to influence events." He did "not believe China will commit conventional formations in South Viet Nam." Its strategy of national liberation wars "seems to promise large gains for a small investment, and at little risk." Griffith pointed out: "It avoids direct confrontation with the United States. At the same time, it is designed to keep us busy running about from place to place, to engage our energies, impair our national morale and will, weaken our alliances and damage our economy."

On the same day, Morton H. Halperin, assistant professor of government at Harvard, testified on China's nuclear capability and strategy. He said the Communist Chinese expected a "long, drawn-out war" in Viet Nam and would be very disappointed if Hanoi accepted a negotiated settlement which might lead to increased Soviet influence in Southeast Asia. Halperin thought Peking was determined not to provoke "a nuclear attack on China" because it knew how much damage could be inflicted on the country. The Chinese drive for an operational nuclear capability "is related to their long-standing fear of an American nuclear attack." In his view, the U.S. should avoid "overreacting to very limited Chinese capabilities."

European Steel Plant for China. On March 20, Secretary of State Dean Rusk, during a television interview, protested a plan by West German and other European companies to construct a $150 million steel plant in Communist China. Rusk voiced hope that "our friends in Europe would keep this matter under review, and before they get into a situation where they are producing two million tons more of steel for Peiping, that they would give some thought to the problems of peace."

Changes in China. On March 21, Donald S. Zagoria, professor of government at Columbia University, testified before the Senate Foreign Relations Committee on U.S. China policy. He said: The "Chinese Communist regime today faces the most serious and far-reaching foreign policy crisis it has ever confronted....The crisis is of such magnitude as to have seriously weakened Peiping's influence in the underdeveloped countries" and foreshadows basic changes in Chinese Communist policy "in the foreseeable future." Zagoria concluded: "Our only hope to achieve a stable and tolerable relationship with Communist China is to do all we can to promote not a change of the system--which can be done only by war--but a change within the system. The kind of evolution which is already transforming Russia and the East European Communist countries will have to come....We can help to hasten its growth."

On the same day, Harold C. Hinton, associate professor of international affairs at George Washington University, told the Committee there was no reason why the U.S. policy of containing China should put the "United States on some sort of collision course with China," or why China's possession of "more than token nuclear power" would pose a "moral threat to peace in the absence of formal disarmament." Hinton thought it was unlikely that China ever would be able to outstrip either the U.S. or the Soviet Union in strategic military power.

Supplemental Funds for Viet Nam. On March 22, the Senate, by an 87-2 roll-call vote, passed an amended bill (HR 13546) making supplemental defense and foreign aid appropriations for fiscal 1966 totaling $13,135,719,000, primarily for U.S. operations in Southeast Asia. The House the following day concurred in Senate amendments, thereby clearing the bill for the President's signature.

Soviet Letter Attacking Chinese Communists. On March 22, a letter reportedly written by the Soviet Communist Party's Central Committee to the East European parties was published by a West German newspaper (*Die Welt* of Hamburg). An English translation appeared two days later in the *New York Times*. The letter said there was "every reason to assert that it is one of the goals of the policy of the Chinese leadership in the Viet Nam question to originate a military conflict between the U.S.S.R. and the United States...so that they may, as they say themselves, 'sit on the mountain and watch the fight of the tigers.'" Other statements in the letter pertinent to the Viet Nam conflict included the following: "The attitude of the CPR (Chinese People's Republic) leadership toward the struggle of the DRV (Democratic Republic of Viet Nam) and all Vietnamese people against United States aggression is currently causing great damage to the joint cause of the countries of socialism and the worldwide liberation movement."

"The Soviet Union delivers large amounts of weapons to the DRV, including rocket installations, anti-aircraft artillery, airplanes, tanks, coastal guns, warships and other items. In 1965 alone, weapons and other material worth about 500 million rubles ($550 million) were placed at the disposal of the DRV. The DRV is receiving support in the training of pilots, rocket personnel, tank drivers, artillerymen and so on. Our military aid is being rendered to the extent the Vietnamese leadership thinks necessary."

The Soviet leaders had proposed "more than once" to the Chinese leaders "that joint actions to support Viet Nam be organized." But the Chinese leadership opposed such action. "By stating openly that they do not desire joint action with the U.S.S.R. and other Socialist countries, by emphasizing their differences of views with the Soviet Union, and by hindering its aid to the DRV, the Chinese leaders basically encourage the United States aggressors in their war acts against Viet Nam."

The letter asserted that ever since the ouster of Khrushchev in October 1964, the new Soviet leaders had attempted to improve relations with the Chinese Communists: "We submitted an extensive program for normalizing Chinese-Soviet relations at both the party and state level. This program included proposals on implementing bilateral meetings of delegations of the CPSU (Soviet party) and the CCP (Chinese party) on the highest level, on the mutual discontinuation of polemics, concrete proposals on extending Chinese-Soviet trade and scientific, technical and cultural cooperation and on coordinating the foreign policy activities of the CPR and the U.S.S.R."

All of the proposals were ignored. "The Chinese leadership states more and more frequently that the CCP is waging a political struggle against the Soviet Union....They present it as a struggle 'of the state of the proletariat against the state of the bourgeoisie.' The anti-Soviet course has now become an inseparable part of the entire ideological work of the CCP."

Going on to accuse the Chinese leadership of propagating "ever more obstinately the thesis of potential military clashes between China and the Soviet Union," the Russians referred to a recent increase in border conflicts and said they were provoked by the Chinese. "The Chinese government refuses to resume the negotiations suspended in May 1964 on a precise delimitation of the border. It obviously prefers to leave this problem unsettled. At the same time, allegations are being spread to the effect that the Soviet Union unlawfully holds Chinese territory in the Far East." On the contrary, the Russians emphasized, the area in question had always belonged to the U.S.S.R.

Finally, the Soviet Communists accused the Chinese of attempting to split the international Communist movement and lead the world toward war. The letter said that Lin Piao's article on the "struggle of the world village against the world city" was "tantamount to the rejection of the leading role of the working class and constitutes a complete revision of the Marxist-Leninist doctrine of the world-historical mission of the working class."

The letter concluded that the Chinese Communists were seeking to dominate the entire Communist movement and added that while the Chinese criticized others because they were not sufficiently militant, they themselves "show extraordinary caution in their own political deeds, as well as extreme patience toward imperialist powers and their policy, including the policy that is aimed against China itself."

Chinese Refuse Bid to Moscow. On March 23, Communist China refused the Soviet Union's invitation to attend the 23rd Congress of the Soviet Communist Party. The Chinese statement, referring to the Soviet Party's anti-Chinese letter, said that "Since you have gone so far, the Chinese Communist Party...cannot send its delegation to attend this congress of yours."

The Chinese added: "Your clamor for 'united action,' especially on the Viet Nam question, is nothing but a trap for the purpose of deceiving the Soviet people and the revolutionary people of the world. You have all along been acting with the United States in its plot for peace talks, vainly attempting to sell out the struggle of the Vietnamese people against United States aggression and for national salvation and to drag the Viet Nam question into the orbit of Soviet-United States collaboration." Peking asserted also that the Soviet Union had "worked hand in glove with the United States in a whole series of dirty deals inside and outside the United Nations," and was "actively trying to build a ring or encirclement around Socialist China" in a "holy alliance" with the U.S.

North Viet Nam Attends. On March 26, a delegate from North Viet Nam arrived in Moscow to attend the Soviet Communist Party's 23rd Congress. He immediately praised the U.S.S.R. for its aid in the war.

Viet Nam Protests in U.S. On March 26, anti-war demonstrations took place in numerous American cities. The largest was in New York; other demonstrations were staged in San Francisco, Chicago, Washington, Detroit and Cambridge, Mass. The rallies and parades were organized by the National Coordinating Committee to End the War in Viet Nam, with headquarters in Madison, Wis.

China Hearings: Judd, Taylor, Rowe. On March 28, former Rep. Walter H. Judd (R Minn. 1943-63) testified before the Senate Foreign Relations Committee on U.S. policy toward Communist China. Judd said that "Our choice --with Red China just as it was with Japan and Hitler--is not between checking and not checking, it is whether to check early, while we can, and with allies--or try to check the aggression later, when it is stronger, closer, and we have fewer and weaker friends and allies." Specifically, Judd opposed diplomatic recognition of Red China by the United States, opening of trade relations with mainland China, and representation of Communist China in the United Nations.

Judd thought there was little risk of Chinese intervention in the Viet Nam war because, among other things, (1) China would thereby invite destruction of its nuclear facilities--"her greatest trump"; (2) it would not be able to supply "masses" of troops fighting in South Viet Nam; and (3) it could not ignore the presence on its flank of the powerful Chinese Nationalist air and military forces on Taiwan. In

conclusion, Judd said: "This is the time to stand fast for the basic containment policies that have proved sound and more successful during the last 15 years than most people believed possible."

Dr. George E. Taylor, professor of Far Eastern History at the University of Washington, also testified on March 28. Although Red China wanted to avoid a direct collision with the U.S., Taylor said, it would continue to foster so-called wars of national liberation. Stopping China in Viet Nam, he warned, would not prevent other similar wars, nor would a U.S. failure necessarily result in the loss of all of Southeast Asia. The answer to the problem was to "assist in building up viable states" in parts of the world vulnerable to Communist pressure.

Dr. David Nelson Rowe, a Yale professor specializing in Far Eastern Affairs, joined the two previous witnesses on March 28 in advocating a continuing "hard-line" policy toward Red China along with stepped-up bombing attacks on North Viet Nam. Rowe also discounted the prospect that China would intervene in force in Viet Nam, noting that Peking would be loath to give the U.S. a pretext for destroying its nuclear weapons development centers. He called for a "rigid attitude of inflexibility" toward Communist China-- one of "extreme hostility."

Sen. George D. Aiken (R Vt.) directly challenged an assertion by Rowe, included in his prepared statement but not read during the hearings, that the Senate hearings were "paralleling" efforts of "pro-Communists" and "anti-anti-Communists" to soften American policy toward China. Aiken asked Rowe if he really believed "these hearings are being held in the interests of Communist China." Rowe said that he did not, but he pointed to the "one-sided" nature of previous testimony and the use to which the hearings were being put by enemies of the United States.

Goldberg on China Policy. On March 28, Ambassador to the UN Arthur J. Goldberg said that UN members were currently less favorably disposed to seating Communist China than in 1965. He said the reason was due mainly to China itself and its self-imposed isolation. Goldberg said the U.S. was willing to terminate this isolation in limited ways, such as preliminary talks to determine whether a world disarmament conference should be held, a nonproliferation of nuclear weapons agreement, and exchanges of technical personnel.

Soviet Congress. On March 29, the 23rd Soviet Communist Party Congress convened in Moscow. In the opening speech, Communist Party First Secretary Leonid I. Brezhnev stressed unity and called relations with Communist China and Albania "unsatisfactory." He said the Soviet Communist Party condemned "with deep indignation the anti-Communist terror in Indonesia."

China Hearings: Scalapino, Morgenthau. On March 30, Robert A. Scalapino, chairman of the political science department at the University of California, testified before the Senate Foreign Relations Committee on U.S. policy toward China. Scalapino said that "an over-throw of the Communist Party" in China seemed remote, but that changes would occur within the party, in the course of time, from "ideological rigidity" to "pragmatic experimentalism." Such changes, he warned, presented dangers for the U.S. because the resulting pressure on the more rigid members of the ruling group would cause "irrational and distractive behavior" on their part. The U.S. must find policies to abet the changes, shaping them to "discourage extremism and encourage moderation."

Scalapino disagreed with both the thesis that China was essentially a weak nation and not a basic threat to the United States, and the argument that the United States should treat China as a major power. He favored a combination of these two views, concluding that while "China is scarcely a military match for the United States," the "Chinese Communists...have consummated alliances large and small, undertaken aid and technical assistance programs far beyond their economic capacities, and engaged in a range of political activities throughout the world" with the result that other countries have labeled China a "major power designate." He considered that "a significant accomplishment because such a status grants certain rights without conveying the requisite responsibilities." Scalapino said he did not believe the Chinese Communists were prepared to enter into an open war with the United States or intervene fully in the Viet Nam war unless the obliteration of North Viet Nam was threatened.

Scalapino went on to say that the United States should move away from the current policy of "attempted containment by isolation," which he described as a negative and inflexible approach to a complex, difficult problem. He supported such steps as increased citizen exchanges, involvement of China in negotiations on a variety of problems, and establishment of terms for the entrance of China into the United Nations.

Scalapino asserted that the United States bore some burden of the responsibility for both the wars in Korea and Viet Nam by not defining clearly enough U.S. commitments. "Let us not make this type of mistake again.... At this point, for example, we should make it absolutely clear that any attempt to change the status of Taiwan or South Korea by... force will be resolutely countered by the application of American forces." U.S. intentions in South Viet Nam, he said, should continue to be made clear.

Regarding Viet Nam, Scalapino said that if the "tactics" of force succeeded in South Viet Nam, it would be of inestimable value to the extremist movement in China and the Communist world. "Nothing would lead us more quickly into the awful choice," he said, "between precipitous retreat everywhere and World War III" than a Maoist victory in Viet Nam.

For U.S. success in its approach to China and Asia as a whole, Scalapino advocated, among other things, development of a balance of power within Asia to counter the thrust of China. This would replace the balance currently enforced by the United States and the Soviet Union.

Another witness at the China Hearings on March 30, was Hans J. Morgenthau, director of the Center for the Study of American Foreign Policy at the University of Chicago. He identified the question of Taiwan as a "*casus belli*" between the U.S. and China once China has realized its military potential. Morgenthau said that the U.S. policy of isolating China had "obviously failed" and that it was the "United States rather than Communist China which has been isolated." In many respects China was enjoying those things, such as commercial relations with other countries, that the United States was trying to deny her. The issue of isolation, therefore, was irrelevant; the real issue was containment. This was the "crucial point at which the traditional national interests of China and the policy of the United States clash."

Morgenthau suggested that the policy of "peripheral military containment ought to be gradually liquidated." Such containment, he said, which succeeded in Europe, "was bound to fail elsewhere." He said there were two reasons for this: first, because the threat in Europe after World War II was military, whereas elsewhere the threat has been political in nature, working on weak governments and societies; and, secondly, because "China is, even in her present underdeveloped state, the dominant power in Asia"--culturally and geopolitically. The United States could not stop such political and cultural predominance by "nibbling at the periphery of her empire." "To be defeated," Morgenthau said, "China has to be conquered," and he did not think that would be a desirable policy for the United States.

Morgenthau asserted that "peripheral military containment would be ineffective in the long run in view of China's local military superiority....They will not be contained by the armed forces...put into the field on the mainland of Asia. They will only be deterred by the near certainty that China as an organized society will be destroyed in the process of nuclear retaliation." He said that currently China was protected from U.S. nuclear retaliation by her own technological backwardness, "for she does not possess the number of industrial and population centers whose nuclear destruction would spell her defeat." However, the "ultimate instrument for containing China was the same that had contained the Soviet Union: the retaliatory nuclear capability of the United States." It must be "brought home to China...that in the unlikely event that she should embark upon a policy of Asian or world conquest, she is bound to be at war with the United States."

In the opinion of Morgenthau, expansion of Chinese power and influence must be contained by political means, by "strengthening politically, socially and economically the nations of Asia which are within China's reach." He feared that if the United States continued its present policy of "peripheral military containment" it would find itself at war with China.

Ho Praises Soviets. On March 30, Ho Chi Minh sent a letter to the 23rd Soviet Communist Party Congress in Moscow calling it a "brilliant success in laying the material and technical foundation for communism." He praised the "high proletarian internationalism of the Soviet Communist Party" and appealed for unity in the international Communist movement.

Hotel in Saigon Bombed. On April 1, Viet Cong terrorists bombed a Saigon hotel used to house American personnel. The blast killed three Americans and four South Vietnamese and injured 110 Americans and 14 South Vietnamese.

Viet Nam Unrest. On April 4, South Vietnamese Premier Nguyen Cao Ky ordered 4,000 marines to Danang, scene of violent anti-government demonstrations since early March. The troops did not enter the city, but remained at the airbase nearby. On April 9, the Buddhist Institute of Secular Affairs announced an all-out campaign to oust Ky's regime. Unrest in the northern cities of Danang and Hue quickly spread to Saigon and other cities and was exploited by a militant group of Buddhists led by Thich Tri Quang. Tri Quang called not only for ouster of the military junta but also for immediate election of a constituent assembly with interim legislative powers.

Sen. Richard B. Russell (D Ga.), chairman of the Senate Armed Services Committee, had said April 1 that a collapse of the Ky regime should bring an "agonizing reappraisal" of U. S. involvement in the Viet Nam war. "If it becomes clearly evident," he said, "that majority of the Vietnamese do not want our help, I would favor withdrawing immediately, both military forces and economic aid." John Sherman Cooper (R Ky.) and others in the Senate echoed Russell's views.

U.S. officials publicly took a neutral position toward the rival groups maneuvering for power in South Viet Nam. An apparent exception was William P. Bundy, Assistant Secretary of State for Far Eastern Affairs, who on April 8 said that the Buddhist group headed by Thich Tri Quang sought a constitutional system only to dominate it. He recalled that the Buddhist monk had played a part in toppling former Vietnamese governments but had never wanted to take formal power.

Bundy contrasted Thich Tri Quang with Thich Tam Chau, leader of another Buddhist group, whom Bundy called a "more moderate" leader.

Under Secretary of State George W. Ball suggested April 10 that the power struggle was a "groping for a sense of national expression" on the part of the South Vietnamese people, and that it might have been touched off by developments at the Honolulu conference between President Johnson and Premier Ky. At Honolulu, Ball said, a plan for a constitutional convention was discussed. "This was a signal to all the political forces in Viet Nam that there was going to be a test of strength among them."

Peking Says U.S. Planning War. On April 6, the Peking *People's Daily* charged that the U.S. was "planning a war in Asia." The editorial noted that the U.S. had recently indicated its willingness to improve relations with Communist China, but it said these "hints of 'goodwill'...are very obviously...an attempt to undermine the Chinese people's fighting determination and their combat readiness." The paper asserted that the U.S. had "built a 'new crescent cordon' in the Asian and Pacific regions extending from South Korea, through Japan, Taiwan, the Philippines, South Viet Nam, Thailand, Malaysia, and all the way to India." The evidence was "increasingly clear that the United States imperialists are preparing to impose war on the Chinese people."

"Therefore, we must be prepared for a war they may start at some later date, and be even more prepared for a small-scale war. An early war means one that will have to be fought this year or next. A large-scale war means one in which the United States imperialists will use all their strength, sending a few million or even 10 million troops to China." The editorial said that China was ready for a "possible sudden attack by United States imperialism," and that China "had grown stronger in the last 10 years" while the U.S. "had grown weaker."

Withdrawal of Specialists From Europe. On April 7, the Defense Department disclosed plans to withdraw about 15,000 specialists from the Army in Europe and use them to train recruits in the U.S. for service in Viet Nam.

B-52 Raids in North. On April 12, B-52 heavy jet bombers staged bombing raids over North Viet Nam for the first time.

Viet Nam Elections. On April 14, Nguyen Van Thieu, chief of state of the South Vietnamese government, signed a decree providing for election of a South Vietnamese constituent assembly in "three to five months." Press reports said that a tentative agreement had been reached to hold the national elections on Aug. 15.

Ford on Conduct of the War. On April 14, House Republican Leader Gerald R. Ford (Mich.) accused the Johnson Administration of "shocking mismanagement" of the Viet Nam war. Ford said that bomb shortages and shipping bottlenecks were "almost a national scandal." He also criticized as unsuccessful and "hurriedly arranged" President Johnson's Honolulu conference with Premier Nguyen Cao Ky. Defense Secretary Robert S. McNamara denied the existence of any bomb shortage. McNamara disclosed normally secret data on bomb stockpiles, production plans, flight operations and bomb tonnages dropped to prove his assertion that "there isn't any such shortage of bombs."

Senate Republican Leader Everett McKinley Dirksen (Ill.) on April 19 disassociated himself from Ford's charges. Dirksen asked "in what respect" was the management of the war shocking. He said that Ford "went pretty far" with his charges and added, "You don't demean the Chief Magistrate of your country at a time like this when a war is on."

Ford nevertheless renewed his charges April 20 and noted that it had been disclosed April 16 that the Government had repurchased bombs in West Germany for more than it sold them for in the first place.

Offer to Chinese Scholars. On April 14, the State Department disclosed that several American universities had been notified that scientists and scholars from Communist China would be permitted to visit the United States. The offer was rejected by Communist China two days later.

China and Indonesia. On April 15, a mob of 2,000 Chinese citizens of Indonesia raided the Chinese embassy in Jakarta following an anti-Peking rally attended by over 40,000 Chinese Indonesians. The mob ransacked the building, but its employees were protected by Indonesian soldiers.

The Indonesian and Chinese press had been exchanging attacks for several weeks. An Indonesian broadcast a few days before the embassy incident said: "Various attacks by Peking against Indonesia have unmasked China's real intentions. China planned to regard Indonesia as a satellite."

On April 16, Communist China protested the embassy riot and charged that "rightwing reactionary soldiers" and "American imperialists" were responsible. On the same day, the Indonesian Ambassador to Peking defected to Red China.

U.S. Asian Policy. On April 17, the House Foreign Affairs Subcommittee on the Far East and the Pacific made public a part of testimony given before the Subcommittee March 16 by Secretary of State Dean Rusk.

After outlining basic questions at issue between the U.S. and Communist China, Rusk summed up the elements of future U.S. policy toward China. It was a policy of containment designed to avoid encouraging "Peiping -- or anyone else -- to believe that it can reap gains from its aggressive actions and designs." The policy was also one of non-isolation, Rusk said, "if Peiping abandons its belief that force is the best way to resolve disputes and gives up its violent strategy of world revolution." If that should happen, the Secretary said, "we would welcome an era of good relations."

More specifically, Rusk cited ten elements "in our policy." These were: (1) firmness in assisting allied nations which sought U.S. help against Chinese aggression; (2) continued assistance to the nation-building process in Asia; (3) honoring of commitments for the defense of the Republic of China on Taiwan; (4) continued efforts to prevent the expulsion of the Republic of China from the United Nations, and opposition to Communist China's UN membership;

(5) reassurance to Peiping that the U.S. did not intend to attack the mainland; (6) avoidance of the assumption that hostility between the U.S. and Communist China was "unending and inevitable"; (7) enlargement of possibilities for unofficial contacts between Communist China and the United States, including permission for American universities to invite Chinese scientists to visit them; (8) continued direct diplomatic contacts with the Chinese Ambassador in Warsaw; (9) willingness to discuss with Peiping and other countries the critical problems of disarmament and nonproliferation; and (10) exploration and analysis of all available information on Communist China in order to keep U.S. policies up to date.

On April 18, the *New China* news agency called Secretary Rusk's ten elements "a mixture of hostility to China and deception" and said that "the real aim (of the U.S.) is to be hostile to and launch aggression against China and to contain and encircle it." The Nationalist Chinese government characterized the Secretary's policy statement as appeasement.

Mansfield Proposal for Peace Parley. On April 18, Senate Majority Leader Mike Mansfield (D Mont.) proposed that negotiations for peace in Viet Nam should be sought with "greater vigor" in the Asian area, given the failure of the UN and of the co-chairmen of the Geneva conferences to bring about such negotiations. Mansfield said that "there would be no better place to locate a peace table" than in Japan or Burma or another "Asian setting." He said the "peace table" should consist of "ourselves, Hanoi, Peiping, and such elements in South Viet Nam as may be essential to the making and keeping of a peaceful settlement." Arthur J. Goldberg, U.S. Ambassador to the United Nations, and Robert J. McCloskey, State Department press officer, welcomed Mansfield's remarks and endorsed the idea of a conference called by Asian nations.

On April 21, the Chinese Communist *New China* news agency dismissed Mansfield's proposal, saying that the "Johnson Administration and Congress notables resort to the 'peace talks' hoax again in an attempt to force the Vietnamese people into submission by the dual tactics of increasing 'military pressure' and making peace gestures."

China and the UN. On April 19, Arthur J. Goldberg, U.S. Ambassador to the UN, speaking at the National Press Club in Washington, outlined the minimum conditions under which the U.S. would agree to Communist China's admission to the United Nations. Peking would have to abandon its demand for expulsion of Taiwan; withdraw its demand that the UN rescind its condemnation of Red China for aggression in Korea and brand the U.S. as the aggressor; withdraw its demand that the UN be reorganized and that unnamed "lackeys" of the United States be expelled; and promise to observe the provisions of the UN Charter. While indicating that the Administration was reconsidering its past position on Communist China's admission, Goldberg said: "This is a highly intricate question, and no change in our policy has been made. Our tactics, of course, are under review." He said also that "along many avenues, even in the face of numerous rebuffs," the U.S. was trying to get Communist China to "come into the mainstream of the international community."

Viet Nam Debate: Three Senators. On April 21, Sen. J. W. Fulbright (D Ark.), chairman of the Senate Foreign Relations Committee, said in a lecture April 21 at Johns Hopkins University School of Advanced International Studies, that the U.S. was "gradually but unmistakably...

succumbing to the arrogance of power" and that those protesting the Viet Nam war "deserve our sympathy and respect." Fulbright also said the Senate "should undertake to revive and strengthen the deliberation function" in foreign policy-making which it had left atrophy during the past 25 years.

Sen. Albert Gore (D Tenn.) in a Senate speech the same day proposed that the U.S. initiate negotiations for a cease-fire during the political campaign and elections in South Viet Nam. Gore said, "Surely we should take every step -- commensurate with the security of our men -- to effect a proper election." Sens. Joseph S. Clark (D Pa.) and Jacob K. Javits (R N.Y.) endorsed the proposal.

Sen. Richard B. Russell (D Ga.), chairman of the Senate Armed Services Committee, said April 21 that he hoped "our bombing operations will be intensified to take in all of the military targets in Viet Nam." He thought "we should use our full strength to push this war to a conclusion."

Viet Nam Debate: Galbraith. On April 22, Harvard economist and former U.S. Ambassador to India John Kenneth Galbraith, in a keynote address to the Americans for Democratic Action convention, criticized current U.S. policies in Viet Nam as too militant. Galbraith ascribed the policies to "the permanent diplomatic and military establishment" and "the New York foreign policy syndicate...the Dulles, McCloy, Lovett communion." He included Secretary of State Dean Rusk in the latter group but excluded President Johnson, who, according to Galbraith, was acting as "a force of restraint" in formulation of U.S. Viet Nam policy. The former ambassador favored a reduction of the U.S. military role. He said Viet Nam was "not important to us"; that the U.S., rather than trying to "roll the Viet Cong back from vast areas that they have controlled now for up to 10 years," must "remain on the defensive in whatever area we can hold with the present force"; that the U.S. "should permanently suspend air attacks on the North"; and that the purpose of this "holding action is to allow the best possible bargain between the non-Communist groups ...and the Viet Cong."

Air Fight. On April 23, in the first major air battle of the Viet Nam war, U.S. jet fighters shot down two North Vietnamese MIG-17s about 70 miles north of Hanoi. No U.S. losses were reported.

Ho Calls on U.S. to Withdraw. On April 26, North Vietnamese President Ho Chi Minh told the National Assembly in Hanoi: "Our people are resolved to fight until final victory. Again we say to President Johnson: If the United States really wants peace it must withdraw all U.S. and satellite troops from South Viet Nam and stop the aggressive war there." Ho called also for immediate and unconditional suspension of U.S. bombing in North Viet Nam.

No Privileged Sanctuary. On April 26, the State Department reiterated Secretary of State Dean Rusk's 1965 warning that the "idea of sanctuary is dead." The statement indicated that enemy planes participating in the air war over Viet Nam would be pursued to their home bases, even if they were in another country. The statement was directed specifically to Communist China. On April 28, the statement was amended by an announcement that the decision as to whether U.S. aircraft would pursue Chinese Communist warplanes into China would be made by the President.

The second statement came a day after Sen. Robert F.

Kennedy had warned in the Senate that it would be "neither prudent nor wise to undertake risks of a still wider war until some progress has been made toward achieving that stability that is essential for the successful prosecution of our efforts in Viet Nam."

Fulbright on Viet Nam Consequences. On April 28, Sen. J. W. Fulbright (D Ark.) said in a speech before the Bureau of Advertising of the American Newspaper Publishers Association that "East-West relations now hinge on the war in Viet Nam." Fulbright added that the long-term consequences of the Viet Nam war were as important for the U.S. position in Europe as they were for future U.S. relations in Southeast Asia. If the fighting continues, he said, it might lead to a direct conflict with the Communist powers. The war already had affected the American policy of "building bridges to the East." Fulbright also questioned whether the U.S. could support a war in Asia and also accomplish domestic social reforms.

In Praise of Mao. On May 1, the *New York Times* reported that Chinese Communist Party Chairman Mao Tse-tung had not appeared in public for five months and that there had been no indication as to his whereabouts. The article noted, however, that Peking had been making a large-scale propaganda effort to impress on all peasants the importance of Mao's teachings and writings "as a guide in their jobs and in their personal lives." It added that "The character of the campaign suggests that the party hierarchy is attempting to deify Mr. Mao and to elevate his works to the rank of dogma in much the same way that the Soviet Communist Party immortalized Lenin."

Although Mao was absent from the May Day celebrations in Peking, the *New China* news agency reported that the people shouted: "Long live Chairman Mao!" and "sang and danced to express their love and respect for the great revolutionary leader."

China's Cultural Revolution. On May 1, *Reuters* reported from Peking that the Chinese Communists had launched a new campaign to remold the thinking of Chinese intellectuals "and make them toe the party line." It said that Chinese Communist Premier Chou En-lai had declared at a rally the previous day that there should be a long struggle to abolish "bourgeois ideology in the academic, educational and journalistic fields, in art, literature and all other fields of culture."

Cambodian Border Fighting. On May 3, the U.S. Military Command in Saigon acknowledged for the first time that American ground forces had fired on targets in Cambodia, delivering "a heavy volume of artillery" fire into a Viet Cong position on the Cambodian side of the Cai Bac River which forms the border. A U.S. note to Cambodia May 17 asserted that two American soldiers had been killed by Viet Cong fire from Cambodia and that U.S. troops had returned the fire as "a measure of self-defense." On May 23, the Chinese Communist *New China* news agency reported that the Cambodian government had rejected the note and accused the U.S. of attempting "to turn the victims into aggressors."

Transit of Soviet Aid to Viet Nam. On May 4, the Peking radio broadcast a Chinese Foreign Ministry statement that "China has never hampered the transit of Soviet aid materials to North Viet Nam." Peking insisted that "All military aid materials Viet Nam asked for and the Soviet Union delivered to China have been transported to Viet Nam by China with

priority, at high speed and free of charge."

Purge in China. On May 4, the Hong Kong correspondent of the *New York Times* reported: "A widespread cultural purge with clearly stated political overtones is underway within the Chinese Communist Party." An article in the People's Liberation Army's newspaper that day asserted that the activities of certain "anti-party, anti-Socialist" intellectuals were "not an accidental phenomenon."

The intellectuals were "responding to the great international anti-Chinese chorus of imperialists, modern revisionists and various reactionaries to revive the Chinese reactionary class, which has been struck down." The article said the cultural debate was not simply academic; it was a "struggle to the death" to abolish bourgeois ideology.

The correspondent of the *Times* reported that "Political commissars have been accusing leading members of the intelligentsia of pretending to follow the party line while resisting the regime's efforts to 'remold their thinking'" in strict accordance with the dogmas of Mao Tse-tung. The Chinese Communist ideological journal, *Red Flag*, had admonished Chinese intellectuals to get rid of their "lordly attitude" and yield to the criticism of the people.

The *Times* story noted that "leading intellectuals had been jolted by the public humiliation in April of Kuo Mo-jo, the country's most prominent scholar and the regime's spokesman on cultural affairs for many years." It added: "Intellectuals have interpreted" Kuo's April 14 speech "as a warning that no one in the cultural fields is safe from the party purge. Mr. Kuo has been a literary and political collaborator of Chairman Mao. It is not known what part, if any, Mr. Mao took in impelling his old associate to make his unexpected speech of self-criticism."

On May 6, the *Times* correspondent reported evidence of dissension in Communist China "on questions of policy in the economic and military fields as well as on cultural questions" and "speculation that the current convulsions may be surface manifestations of a struggle for succession." The dispatch noted that all those in contention for leadership were friends of Mao Tse-tung and shared his views, and that resistance was more likely to come from moderates on lower levels of the hierarchy.

"Prominent figures in literature, art and education are feeling the brunt of the campaign against deviationism," the story said, "but other party members holding important posts in the economy and the armed forces have also been subjected to severe criticism. In castigating these individuals, usually unidentified, the press dwells consistently on the theme that the Maoist revolution will be subverted unless the ideologically lax can be made to bend to party discipline."

On May 5, the Peking *People's Daily* had urged China's youth to oppose "the anti-party, anti-Socialist ideology of bourgeois and revisionists" and warned: "Imperialism pins its hope of 'peaceful evolution' on the third and fourth generations. China's young people must...remember class hatred and carry the proletarian revolutionary cause through to the end."

Fulbright vs. Javits. On May 5, Sen. J. W. Fulbright (D Ark.), in his final lecture at Johns Hopkins University's School for Advanced International Studies, restressed the theme of two prior lectures and of a speech in New York April 28 -- the United States was in danger of succumbing to an "arrogance of power" as a mighty nation. Relating this "arrogance of power" to U.S. policy in Viet Nam, Fulbright said he did not doubt the sincerity of Administration leaders when they proclaimed that the U.S. aimed to create conditions under which South Viet Nam could freely determine its future; but he doubted the ability of the United States to "go into a small, alien, undeveloped Asian nation and create stability where there is chaos,...democracy where there is no tradition of it, and honest government where corruption is almost a way of life."

Sen. Jacob K. Javits (R N.Y.) said May 5 that the bipartisan foreign policy of the United States since World War II had been "basically sound" and that "its motives have been an 'acceptance of power,' not an 'arrogance of power'." He asserted that Fulbright's thesis was "largely negative and offers no guidelines for action."

Rusk and Ky. On May 8, Secretary of State Dean Rusk said that news reports quoting South Viet Nam's Premier Nguyen Cao Ky as saying May 7 that he intended to stay in power "at least for another year" had misconstrued Ky's remarks.

In a televised interview, Rusk said he did not expect that Ky was "going to try to stand in the way of the constitutional and electoral processes which he himself...initiated last Jan. 15, well before the Honolulu conference." According to Rusk, Ky simply predicted that it would be 1967 before the cycle of elections for a constituent assembly, the drafting of a constitution, a campaign and election for a national assembly and, finally, the installation of the assembly would be completed.

Denunciations in Peking. On May 9, the Peking radio disclosed that Teng Jo, director and former editor of the Peking *People's Daily*, had been denounced by the Chinese Communist leadership for bourgeois tendencies and Soviet revisionism. Three Peking newspapers were attacked for letting themselves be used by Teng "to send poison arrows against the socialist system."

Also denounced was Prof. Wu Han, Peking's vice mayor and a leading playwright, who was accused of being a "right-wing opportunist." It was indicated, in addition, that the Mayor of Peking, Peng Chen, may have been purged. Peng had been considered a possible contender to succeed Mao Tse-tung.

The three papers that were attacked immediately published joint statements: "We beg to accept these criticisms and would earnestly welcome it if the broad masses of newspapers and periodicals throughout the country make all-out criticisms of our wrongdoings." The papers said they would correct their mistakes and "participate in the great socialist cultural revolution."

China's Third Nuclear Test. On May 10, Communist China announced that it had set off its third nuclear test explosion the day before. The statement said the test was that country's first to "contain thermonuclear material."

On the same day, the *New China* news agency reported that Chinese Communist Premier Chou En-lai had said that China would "not take the initiative to provoke war with China.

"Should the United States impose a war on China, it can be said with certainty that, once in China, the United States will not be able to pull out, however many men it may send over and whatever weapons it may use, nuclear weapons included. Since the 14 million people of South Viet Nam can cope with over 200,000 United States troops, the 650 million people of China can undoubtedly cope with 10 million of them. No matter

how many United States aggressor troops may come, they will certainly be annihilated."

The Chinese Premier promised that "If any country in Asia, Africa or elsewhere meets with aggression headed by the United States, the Chinese government and the people definitely will give it support and help."

Mao and the Albanians. On May 10, the *New China* news agency reported that Chinese Communist Party Chairman Mao Tse-tung had met with Albanian leaders in Peking a few days earlier. A picture of Mao and the Albanians was published. During their visit, the Albanians were reported to have joined the Chinese in warning the North Vietnamese "against remaining friendly with the Russians." They were said to have insisted that there could be "no neutrality in the dispute and that the struggle against Soviet revisionism must be carried through to the end."

Johnson on Use of U.S. Power. On May 11, President Johnson, in remarks at the dedication of the new building of Woodrow Wilson School of Public and International Affairs, Princeton University, asserted that "the issue for this generation...has to do with the obligations of power." Apparently replying to statements by Sen. J. W. Fulbright (D Ark.), the President said that "America's involvement" abroad could best be measured "by a single proposition: not one single country where we have mounted a major effort to resist aggression...today has a government servile to outside interests." Johnson observed also: "The exercise of power in this century has meant for the United States not arrogance but agony. We have used our power not willingly and recklessly but reluctantly and with restraint."

U.S. Rejection of Chinese Proposal. On May 11, the State Department disclosed that the U.S. had rejected in 1965 a Chinese Communist proposal that the U.S. and China formally agree that neither nation would be the first to use nuclear weapons against the other. A Department spokesman said the offer was rejected because the Chinese "profess to believe that such a public declaration without controls would constitute a sufficient guarantee" whereas "we do not, and we have given our views to the Chinese."

On May 17, Secretary of State Dean Rusk said the U.S. had rejected the Chinese proposal because "mere declarations on such matters would not be adequate." The United States, he pointed out, had "put forward...far-reaching proposals about limiting nuclear weapons and freezing and possibly reducing nuclear weapons delivery vehicles." Rusk added that it had been suggested to the Chinese that they "ought to be associated with the preparatory committee... (that) might try to work out arrangements for a world disarmament conference, but we've had no indication...that they're willing to do that."

Rise of Lin Piao. On May 15, the *New York Times* correspondent in Hong Kong reported that Communist China's Defense Minister, Lin Piao, appeared to be emerging as the most likely successor to Chairman Mao Tse-tung. The correspondent reported also that Communist China's most recent purge, which many analysts believed was begun by Lin, had spread throughout the country.

"There have been indications," the *Times* dispatch said, "that Mr. Mao has been grooming Mr. Lin as his successor for some time. Since 1960 their names have frequently been coupled in important statements. This was most apparent in January at a conference of the political department of the army, when Hsiao Hua, its director, said that Mr. Lin 'creatively applies Chairman Mao's pattern of military thought.' No other member of the hierarchy has been elevated to the degree that he is acknowledged as an interpreter of the Mao doctrine."

Demonstration in Washington. On May 15, some 10,000 people demonstrated in Washington against the war in Viet Nam and pledged themselves to fight politically for candidates in the coming elections who would support a slowdown of the Viet Nam conflict, looking toward a cease-fire.

Danang Seized by Ky's Troops. On May 15, to the surprise of the United States, South Vietnamese Premier Nguyen Cao Ky ordered 1,000 government troops into the northern city of Danang to seize power from the rebellious, Buddhist-inspired 1st Army Corps. In fighting that ensued between South Vietnamese and South Vietnamese, 10 were killed and 12 wounded. By the end of the day, government forces occupied all strategic points in the city. In Saigon, leading Buddhist monks called the move an "act of treachery" that would "surely lead to civil war."

On the same day, a State Department spokesman said: "We have been aware that the government of Viet Nam was concerned over its lack of full authority in the Danang-Hue area. However, we had no information they were contemplating the movement of troops to Danang."

After a week of fighting in which 75 persons were killed and around 500 wounded, the last of the rebels surrendered. Meanwhile, thousands of Buddhists demonstrated in Saigon.

Intrusion Into China. On May 17, the Chinese Communist *New China* news agency asserted it could prove that five U.S. planes shot down a Chinese training plane over Chinese territory. "We can tell them," the news agency said, "that the fragments of the missiles used by the U.S. pirate planes to attack the Chinese trainer plane after they had intruded into China's air space, and the seven auxiliary fuel tanks jettisoned by them, have fallen in the area northeast of Makwan, in the Chinese province of Yunnan. The tanks bear the marks: 'Mfd. by Sargent-Fletcher Co., El Monte, Calif.'"

Asian Policy. On May 19, the House Foreign Affairs Subcommittee on the Far East and the Pacific issued a report on open hearings, held between Jan. 25 and March 10, 1966, on U.S. policy toward Asia. The Subcommittee concluded that China was rapidly becoming a great world power and as such was bound to influence both events in Asia and the future of peace and order in the world; the Communist regime in China appeared to be firmly entrenched; and Communist China was not interested at present in attaining peaceful accommodation with the remainder of the world except on terms which clashed with principles of the Western world.

The report asserted that the West should "stake its security" on the probability that, in the course of time, common devotion to the Communist ideology and the cause of Communist world domination would heal the Sino-Soviet split. The report pointed out that despite American industrial-military superiority, "our country's ability to influence the course of events on the Asia mainland is essentially limited."

The Subcommittee recommended that the United States, despite rebuffs, continue to seek peaceful contacts with Red China while at the same time taking steps to block any aggressive expansion on its part. To do this, it said, would require increased assistance and cooperation from this country's European allies and increased U.S. efforts to help strengthen "the independent countries of the (Asian) continent -- from India and Pakistan to Japan and Korea."

UAW on China. On May 21, the annual convention of the United Auto Workers (AFL-CIO), in a break with AFL-CIO policy, called for diplomatic recognition of Communist China.

Johnson on War Weariness. On May 21, President Johnson, commenting at a news conference on civil unrest in South Viet Nam, said: "We believe everything possible should be done to bring the various factions to an understanding of the need for unity while the constitutional process is moving forward.... We regret any diversion from that task and from efforts to defeat the Communist attempt to take over South Viet Nam."

The President dealt also with domestic criticism of the war, saying: "The longer we are there, the more sacrifices we make. The more we spend, the more discontent there will be. The more wish and desire there will be to get out. Leading the parade is the President." Johnson felt that those who approved of "what we are doing, are almost twice as many as all these various factions" in opposition. He identified the opposing factions as those who were dissatisfied and who "would run out," those "who would run further in," and those who would sit and do nothing -- which only gets you into "further trouble."

U Thant's Appeal. On May 24, UN Secretary General U Thant appealed to the U.S., North and South Viet Nam, the Viet Cong and Communist China to scale down the fighting in Viet Nam and negotiate a settlement. Speaking at a convention of the Amalgamated Clothing Workers of America (AFL-CIO) in Atlantic City, he said: "The world has been watching the inexorable escalation of the war in Viet Nam with increasing anxiety.... Little by little, larger forces and more powerful armaments have been introduced, until an anguished and perplexed world has suddenly found that a limited and local conflict is threatening to turn into a major confrontation."

Thant observed that "the fear of a much larger conflict may still have a restraining influence upon the demands of military strategy," but he was apprehensive lest "the temptation to win a military success may still prove stronger than the more prudent call to reason." He said also: "As the war worsens, its justification in terms of a confrontation of ideologies is becoming more and more misleading. For democratic principles, which both sides consider to be at stake in Viet Nam, are already falling a victim to the war itself."

Another Purged. On May 25, the *New York Times* correspondent in Hong Kong reported that another high party functionary had been purged in Red China's campaign against "anti-party and anti-Socialist elements." The victim was Li Chi, director of the propaganda department of the Communist party's Peking branch. Li was attacked as a Soviet revisionist and for protecting other anti-party elements.

The *Times* dispatch said that observers in Hong Kong felt that evidence was accumulating that the broadening purge was the outgrowth of a power struggle among the top leaders. The disarray in Peking was thought to have adversely affected national policy planning and general administration of the country. The correspondent noted that the third five-year plan, instituted at the beginning of the year, had not been mentioned again and "may not have in fact been implemented."

Anti-U.S. Riots. On May 26, a mob of Buddhist students sacked and burned the U.S. library and cultural center in Hue; on June 1, the U.S. consulate in Hue met the same fate. Student leaders said the attacks were in protest against U.S. support of the Ky government. On May 29-31, in Saigon, five Buddhists burned themselves to death. The bodies of two were placed in a chapel where an overhead banner read: "Sacrifice and sacrifice much more in order to warn the irresponsible and heartless people about the crimes of the Americans and the Thieu-Ky lackeys."

Purge Extended. On May 28, *Reuters* news service reported from Peking that the "anti-party, anti-Socialist" purge in Red China had reached the Communist party's Central Committee. Articles appearing in the Peking *People's Daily* and in Shanghai papers accused one of the 11 deputy directors of the Central Committee's Propaganda Department of being a "protector" of anti-party intellectuals.

The articles asserted that a drama written by Chou Hsin-fang, head of the Shanghai Opera Company, was "a big rightist, opportunist attack on the party." But, the articles said, he and other dissident writers had "a protector, who is the deputy director of the Propaganda Department of the Central Committee," and "not only did he provide inspiration and material for this play, but he also praised it after seeing it." *Reuters* reported that the play suggested that the Communist party "take a rest."

Japanese Communists. On May 30, Japanese police experts on communism reported that Japanese Communists, disturbed by the experience of the Indonesian party and by Peking's advocacy of violent tactics, were moving toward a neutral position in the ideological split between Soviet and Chinese Communists.

Saigon Government Reforms. On May 30, President Johnson, in a Memorial Day address at Arlington National Cemetery, deplored self-immolations in South Viet Nam and said this "unnecessary loss of life obscures the progress being made toward a constitutional government" in that country. The President told a news conference June 1 he was confident that formation of a constitutional government in South Viet Nam was attainable.

Earlier on June 1, the South Vietnamese government and the Buddhist hierarchy had announced an agreement to end the prevailing political crisis. The agreement left Gen. Nguyen Cao Ky in office but diluted the power of the nine other generals in the 10-man ruling junta. The agreement provided for doubling the size of the junta, or National Liberation Council, by adding 10 civilians by June 6, and for setting up by June 19 a Peoples and Armed Forces Council of 60 civilians and 20 military men to advise the junta. (Both actions were carried out on schedule.)

More Purged. On June 2, the Peking *People's Daily* denounced the president of Peking University, Lu Ping, and two other university officials for attempting to suppress the "strong revolutionary demands" of faculty members and students for participation in what was now called the "cultural revolution." On the same day, the Yugoslav news agency reported that Peng Chen, mayor of Peking, and Lo Jui-ching, chief of the army's general staff, had been removed from their offices (*see June 3, 1966*).

Proposals to Peking and Hanoi. On June 2, it was reported in Washington that the U.S., through its ambassadorial contacts with Communist China in Warsaw, had raised the possibility of agreeing to China's previous offer (see May 11, 1966) that the two countries pledge not to use nuclear arms against each other, if Communist China in return would sign the 1963 limited test-ban treaty. It was reported also that the U.S. had made an offer to North Viet Nam, through Warsaw, to stop bombing that country if Hanoi would halt all military movements into South Viet Nam and agree to some system of international verification.

Action Against Buddhists. On June 2, South Vietnamese Premier Nguyen Cao Ky ordered troops into the northern city of Hue, which had been in a state of rebellion against the Saigon government since mid-May. Buddhist resistance in the city was passive for the most part, but large and violent anti-government demonstrations were staged in Saigon. By June 19, resistance had been brought under control in both Hue and Saigon. On June 20, the most militant Buddhist leader, Thich Tri Quang, was placed under arrest and flown to Saigon. He had been on a hunger strike since June 8.

Peng and Others Purged. On June 3, the Chinese Communist press confirmed that Peng Chen, a member of the Politburo of the Chinese Communist Party's Central Committee, mayor of Peking and at one time considered a possible successor to Mao Tse-tung, had been removed from office. It was announced that Li Hsueh-feng, first secretary of the Chinese Communist Party's North China bureau, had been chosen to take Peng's place on the party's Peking Municipal Committee. Ousting of Lu Ping, president of Peking University, and of Peng Pei-yung, a member of the higher education department of the municipal committee, also was confirmed.

On June 5, the Peking *People's Daily* charged that the two educators had attempted "to lead students astray onto the road of revisionism and train them as successors for the bourgeoisie." It noted that "the struggle by the bourgeoisie to win the younger generation away from the proletariat is an important part of a class struggle in a Socialist society." On the same day, it was reported that students of Peking University had staged a demonstration, denouncing Lu Ping and shouting "Long live Mao Tse-tung!"

Humphrey on China. On June 8, Vice President Hubert H. Humphrey, speaking at graduation exercises at West Point, said that the U.S. sought "and will continue to seek to build bridges, to keep open the doors of communication to the Communist states of Asia and, in particular, Communist China." He added that "the peace and development of Asia will be high on our national agenda for the rest of the century."

Humphrey said the "so-called hawks" would have to learn that "military power is not enough," that it "can be wholly unavailing if not accompanied by political effort and by the credible promise to ordinary people of a better life." The "so-called doves," he added, must learn that "there is no substitute for force in the face of a determined enemy who resorts to terror, subversion, aggression, whether concealed or open."

Concerning Viet Nam, the Vice President said, "If we can succeed there -- if we can help sustain an independent South Viet Nam, free to determine its own future even in its rather disruptive and confusing way -- then our prospects and the prospects for free men throughout Asia will be bright indeed."

China Group Formed. On June 9, it was announced in New York that more than 60 leading experts on Asia had formed an organization dedicated to informing the public about Communist China. The organization was to be called the National Committee on United States-China Relations. Its chairman was Prof. Robert A. Scalapino, a political science professor at the University of California and one of those who testified before the Senate Foreign Relations Committee on U.S. China policy.

Anti-Communist Forces in Red China. On June 10, the Chinese Communist Party's theoretical journal, *Red Flag*, said that "anti-Communist forces" in China "still have powerful strength, large amounts of funds, extensive social and international connections and counter-revolutionary experience to carry out their anti-party activities." The article asserted: "Anti-Communist intellectuals have established many positions from which they launch attacks on the party; they have newspapers, magazines, lecturing platforms, and publication houses. And their arms are extremely long, stretched to almost every field in the cultural world." *Red Flag* warned that "Unless we take this problem into serious consideration and take necessary measures, our party and our nation may change color and hundreds of thousands of heads may fall on the ground."

Red Flag emphasized that to be a good Marxist one must "place Mao Tse-tung's thought right in the forefront and absorb comrade Lin Piao's 'very important instructions on the study and application of Chairman Mao's works.'"

Struggle for Power in China. On June 10, it was disclosed that the purge in Communist China had reached into provincial areas, affecting officials and journalists either suspected of or known to be proteges of the ousted mayor of Peking, Peng Chen.

On June 11, an *Associated Press* dispatch from Hong Kong said: "Marshal Lin (Piao) has knocked out Peng Chen,...but it is obvious that Lin's real target is President Liu Shao-chi. Liu has long been tabbed as Mao's likely successor to the party chairmanship.... Elimination of Peng Chen was a necessary step to undermining Liu. Peng has been a close and apparently trusted associate of Liu since the early 1930s.... Professional observers in Hong Kong now believe that the major power struggle will be between 57-year-old Lin and 67-year-old Liu, with one probably being eliminated as a political force within the next 12 months."

On June 12, the Toronto *Globe and Mail* reported from Peking that the words of China's army chief, Defense Minister Lin Piao, had become "the official interpretation of the thoughts of Chairman Mao Tse-tung." The report said it might "also be significant that while the Defense Minister and the army have been given increasing prominence in the press, Liu Shao-chi, the head of state, has been silent in recent weeks."

More Troops to Viet Nam. On June 11, Secretary of Defense Robert S. McNamara in a joint news conference with Secretary of State Dean Rusk said that 18,000 more American troops had been authorized for movement to Viet Nam in the next 45 days, bringing the total there to 285,000.

Youth Purge. On June 15, the Chinese Communist *New China* news agency reported that the current purge had been extended to the Communist Youth League with dismissal of at least two top officials. The Toronto *Globe*

A.I.D. and Military Estimates for Fiscal 1966

NEAR EAST AND SOUTH ASIA

	Economic Aid (Millions of dollars)	Military (Millions of dollars)
Afghanistan	$ 11.0	$ 4
Ceylon	7.5	--
India	309.9	classified
Nepal	3.3	classified
Pakistan	127.2	classified
Total	$ 458.9	$ .4

FAR EAST

Burma	$ 0.3	$ --
Cambodia	--	--
China, Republic of	--	81.0
Hong Kong	--	--
Indonesia	--	.9
Japan	--	28.1
Korea	146.8	151.7
Laos	55.2	classified
Malaysia	--	.1
Philippines	3.7	25.4
Ryukyu Islands	--	--
Singapore	--	--
Thailand	43.4	classified
Viet Nam	589.8	409.0
Far East Regional (a)	15.0	94.1
Total	$ 854.0 (b)	$790.3

OCEANIA

Australia	$ --	$ 19.5
New Zealand	--	.2
Trust Territory	--	--
Total	$ --	$ 19.7

Grand Total: Of Selected Countries	$1,312.9	**Grand Total:** Of Selected Countries $810.4

(a) Far East Regional includes 12.1 million for Nam Ngum Dam.
(b) Detail many not add to totals due to rounding.
(c) Data included in Far East Regional.
(d) Obligations figure is a later figure than an estimate.

and Mail reported the same day: "The announcement of the dismissal of the leaders of the Youth League caused the biggest demonstration yet. It brought tens of thousands of youths into the streets and created a frenzied display of color, music, slogans, chanting and noise. Traffic was disrupted and slowed to a crawl as marchers converged on the Communist party's headquarters in Peking. They blew bugles, banged a variety of drums, crashed their cymbals and struck gongs."

Asian Council. On June 16, nine non-Communist nations established the Asian and Pacific Council (ASPAC) at a meeting in Seoul, South Korea. The members included South Korea, Nationalist China, Japan, South Viet Nam, Malaysia, Thailand, the Philippines, Australia and New Zealand. Laos was represented by an observer. In a joint statement the nine nations voiced their determination "to preserve their integrity and sovereignty in the face of external threats." They also supported "the inherent right of the Vietnamese people to self-defense and to choose their own way of life and their own form of government free from external aggression and subversion."

Progress of the Purge. On June 16, the Peking radio announced that Kuang Ya-ming, rector of Nanking University, had been ousted from his post because of his "ignoble and villainous conspiracy to suppress the revolutionary movement" in the university.

On the same day, the Peking *People's Daily* reported that the people who had been purged, and their supporters, were "not reconciled to voluntary withdrawal from the political arena." It added: "A big, blooming and contending campaign must be used as a weapon against the bourgeois representatives who oppose Mao Tse-tung."

On June 17, Chinese Communist Premier Chou En-lai told a luncheon audience in Bucharest, Rumania, that China was undergoing a "cultural revolution." He said: "We want to liquidate entirely by this great cultural revolution all the old ideas, the entire old culture, all the old habits and customs created by the exploiting classes in the course of thousands of years to poison the people," and "We want to create and form in the ranks of the broad masses of the people, the new ideas, the new culture, the new habits and customs of the proletariat."

Chou asserted that the "main cutting edge of this cultural revolution is turned against a handful of bad elements that are waging dirty anti-Communist activity under the cover of a false communism."

Mansfield Urges Meeting With China. On June 16, Senate Majority Leader Mike Mansfield (D Mont.), in a speech at Yeshiva University in New York City, said that what was needed in the face of the current danger in South Viet Nam was an "initiative for a direct contact between the Peking government and our own Government on the problem of peace in Viet Nam and Southeast Asia." He favored a meeting on the foreign minister level. Mansfield called it "unrealistic to describe the situation in South Viet Nam in a clear-cut ideological context" or to view the conflict "as wholly one of an aggression of the North against the South."

Senate Minority Leader Everett McKinley Dirksen (R Ill.), commenting June 18 on Mansfield's proposal, said that for the U.S. to initiate a conference "with the sinner" would appear to be a fruitless undertaking and a "humiliating experience."

Johnson on War Policy. On June 18, President Johnson, at a news conference, read one of his strongest statements to date on Viet Nam. Pointing out that the conflict had become more intense, he declared that the national interest required the Administration to persist in its present policy. That policy was "to bring to bear the ground, naval and air strength required to achieve our objective."

China Rejects Nuclear Agreement. On June 20, the Peking *People's Daily* announced that Communist China had rejected a proposal that the two countries pledge not to use nuclear weapons against each other and that China adhere to the nuclear test-ban treaty *(see June 2, 1966).* The Chinese statement called the proposal another one of America's "big frauds" and added that China would "determinedly continue to develop nuclear weapons" and would not attend any disarmament conference.

De Gaulle to Moscow. On June 20, French President Charles de Gaulle arrived in Moscow for a state visit.

Failure of Peace Overtures. On June 22, the State Department announced that recent peace overtures to Hanoi -- including one by Canada -- had made no progress.

Chinese Education Overhaul. On June 24, the *New York Times* correspondent in Hong Kong reported that Communist China was overhauling its entire system of higher education to eliminate "breeding grounds for counter-revolution," and to guarantee that the ideology of Mao Tse-tung would be passed on to younger generations. "There are hints," the *Times* correspondent said, "that Ho Wei, Minister of Education, and Chiang Nan-hsiang, Minister of Higher Education, have been dismissed from their posts. Their names are no longer mentioned in the press."

Bombing Near Hanoi and Haiphong. On June 29, U.S. Air Force and Navy planes conducted daylight raids against petroleum facilities near Hanoi, Haiphong, and Do Son, North Viet Nam. The raids involved bombing closer to Hanoi, the North Vietnamese capital, and Haiphong, a major port, than any before and amounted to an escalation of the war. Defense Secretary Robert S. McNamara said at a news conference a few hours after the attacks that the raids were carried out "to counter a mounting reliance by North Viet Nam on the use of trucks and powered junks to facilitate...infiltration of men and arms into South Viet Nam." McNamara insisted that "every effort was made" to prevent injury to the civilian population of the city. The bombed facilities, he said, were respectively two miles from Haiphong, three miles from Hanoi, and one-half mile outside Do Son. They represented 60 percent of North Viet Nam's "remaining oil storage capacity." McNamara reported that one American plane was lost and one MIG aircraft was "probably destroyed." Early estimates indicated that damage to the bombed facilities was heavy.

British Prime Minister Harold Wilson said his government "disassociated Britain" from bombings touching upon populated areas even if directed against oil installations. The London government continued to give general support to the United States position in Viet Nam. *Tass,* official news agency of the Soviet Union, described the bombing as "proof of the further criminal escalation of the war." President Ho Chi Minh of North Viet Nam declared his country would fight to the end despite the U.S. raids.

On June 30, U.S. planes hit more oil depots in the Hanoi area. On the same day, President Johnson, speaking in Omaha, said the strikes "will continue to impose a growing burden and a high price on those who wage war against the freedom of their neighbors."

Red China's Three Purges. On July 1, the Peking *People's Daily* disclosed that there had been three major internal struggles in Communist China since 1950. It said the current "Great Proletarian Cultural Revolution" was the most significant because the new party opponents were "more insidious and cunning" than their predecessors.

The article reported that in 1953 one group attempted to stage a "counter-revolutionary comeback" through a "revisionist coup d'etat," but it was "thoroughly exposed and smashed" by Mao. The second struggle occurred in 1958, during the ill-fated "Great Leap Forward," when a "handful of ambitious careerists and schemers, who had the support of the Khrushchev revisionist clique, put forward at a party meeting in 1959 a thoroughly revisionist program in the vain hope of dragging our country back to the capitalist road."

Reassurance to Taiwan. On July 3, Secretary of State Dean Rusk, upon arrival at the airport in Taipei, Taiwan, pledged that "we are constant in our relations and in our alliance to the Republic of China, that we oppose the seating of the Peiping regime in the United Nations, and I have no doubt that that will be the basis of our relationship in weeks, and months, and years to come." Rusk's statement quelled fears in the Chiang Kai-shek government that the United States was considering a more flexible or "soft-line" policy toward Communist China.

Evacuation from Hanoi. On July 4, the *New China* news agency reported that the North Vietnamese government had ordered evacuation of all residents of Hanoi "except those who had tasks of production or fighting to assure the defeat of U.S. war escalation."

Infiltration of Laos. On July 4, the Peking radio reported that the Chinese Communist Foreign Ministry had charged the United States with "making active preparations for sending its ground forces into Laos." The statement said also: "At the instigation of the United States, military personnel of Thailand and South Viet Nam have successfully infiltrated into the areas of central and lower Laos." The State Department called the Chinese charges "pretty far out."

New Faces. On July 4, the Toronto *Globe and Mail* reported from Peking that Tao Chu, first secretary of the Chinese Communist Party's Central-South Bureau, and Yeh Chien-ying, deputy chairman of the National Defense Council, had been chosen to replace victims of the "cultural revolution" in top posts. Tao, the report said, was to be the new head of the Central Committee's Propaganda Department, replacing Lu Ting-yi, the previous propaganda chief. Yeh was reported to have been picked as the new Chief of the General Staff, succeeding Lo Jui-ching.

Changes in Indonesia. On July 5, the 520-member People's Consultative Congress, meeting in Jakarta, unanimously voted to strip President Sukarno of his title "President for Life." The Congress also authorized Lt. Gen. Suharto to organize a new cabinet.

Chinese Charge Against Soviets. On July 10, Chinese Communist Foreign Minister Chen Yi charged at a Peking rally that the Soviet Union was "making military deployments along the Chinese border in coordination with United States imperialist encirclement of China." He said:

"Fabrications are made and lies and slander spread everywhere, accusing China of obstructing transit of aid material to Viet Nam in an attempt to undermine the unity between the peoples of China and Viet Nam and to sabotage the Vietnamese people's war of resistance against

United States aggression and for national salvation.... The facts are very clear. The Soviet revisionist ruling clique is redoubling its efforts to take united action with United States imperialism in a big way to sabotage the revolutionary struggle of all peoples of the world."

Doors Closed. On July 11, the Chinese Communist government suspended most visas and closed China's doors to foreign travelers, with the exception of visitors whose business was considered essential to the Chinese state. The action was generally interpreted as a move to keep the "cultural revolution" under as close wraps as possible.

President on China and a Pacific Era. On July 12, President Johnson asserted in a nationally televised speech to the American Alumni Council at White Sulphur Springs, W.Va., that eventual reconciliation with Communist China was necessary and possible, and that the U.S. would persist in efforts to reduce tensions between the two countries. "A peaceful mainland China is central to a peaceful Asia," the President said. "A hostile China must be discouraged from aggression. A misguided China must be encouraged toward understanding of the outside world and toward policies of peaceful cooperation."

Throughout the address, President Johnson stressed the responsibilities of the United States as a Pacific power. He declared that "We will not retreat from the obligations of freedom and security in Asia," and he voiced faith that "if we stand firm in Viet Nam against military conquest,... the emerging order of hope and progress in Asia will continue to grow and grow." Looking forward to a "Pacific era" based on cooperation and peaceful competition among nations, Johnson emphasized that "As a Pacific power, we must help achieve that outcome."

Defense Authorization. On July 13, President Johnson signed a bill (S 2950) authorizing appropriation of $17.5 billion for military procurement and defense research in fiscal 1967. The bill had been passed the day before by the House, 359-2, and by the Senate, 81-1. Dissenting votes were cast by Reps. George E. Brown Jr (D Calif.) and Jeffery Cohelan (D Calif.) and by Sen. Wayne Morse (D Ore.). The dissenters were protesting escalation of the war in Viet Nam.

P.O.W. Pilots. On July 14, Secretary of State Rusk told a Senate Judiciary subcommittee (on refugees) that if the North Vietnamese tried and convicted American pilots held prisoner in North Viet Nam, it would be a "very, very grave development." On July 15, 18 Senators considered critical of U.S. policy in South Viet Nam signed a letter urging North Viet Nam "to refrain from any act of vengeance against the American airmen." The letter said that punishment of the pilots "would incite a public demand for retaliation swift and sure, inflicting new levels of suffering...and fixing more firmly still the seal of an implacable war."

On July 16, UN Secretary General U Thant warned North Viet Nam that "the possible trial of American prisoners is certain to generate still more intense escalation of the war" -- to the point where it might bring on World War III. On July 20, Pope Paul declared that mistreatment of the prisoners would result in "very grave consequences."

On July 23, North Vietnamese President Ho Chi Minh, responding to a telegram from CBS News, said there was "no trial in view" for the captured Americans.

Travel to Red China. On July 16, the State Department relaxed restrictions on tourist travel to Communist China. The only condition imposed by the new regulations was that the traveler's business or professional stature be such that his trip would benefit the United States. Communist China, meanwhile, refused to grant visas to Americans.

Ho on Long War. On July 17, North Vietnamese President Ho Chi Minh, speaking over the Hanoi radio, ordered a "partial mobilization" of the country and declared that negotiations to end the war were "out of the question." The 76-year-old Communist leader said that "although some cities may be destroyed (by U.S. planes), we will eventually score a victory and will start reconstructing the destroyed cities." He added that the war might last "20 years or longer" but that victory would finally be gained.

On July 19, the Chinese Communist army newspaper, *Chieh-fang Chun Pao* quoted Communist party Chairman Mao Tse-Tung as ordering the army to "thoroughly strengthen war preparedness...so as to be ready at all times for combat action...with the Vietnamese people to wipe out the murderous American bandits completely."

Two-China Policy. On July 20, Sen. Edward M. Kennedy (D Mass.) said in the Senate that both Communist China and Nationalist China should be seated in the United Nations. Later in the day, President Johnson told a news conference that although the Administration would "do everything we can to increase our exchanges" with Communist China, it was not ready to adopt a "two-China" policy.

Liu Warns U.S. On July 22, Chinese Communist Head of State Liu Shao-chi urged the United States to avoid further escalation of the Viet Nam conflict. "If you think you can unscrupulously escalate the war of aggression, without meeting due punishment," Liu's statement said, "then you will find it too late to repent." The theme was repeated the same day at a huge anti-American rally in Peking.

Senate Urged to Advise on Asian Policy. On July 22, Sen. J. William Fulbright (D Ark.), chairman of the Senate Foreign Relations Committee, observed on the Senate floor that "under the emerging Asian doctrine the United States is taking on the role of policeman and provider for all of non-Communist Asia." He asserted that President Johnson's July 12 address to the American Alumni Council represented "a radical departure in American foreign policy in that it is virtually unlimited in what it purports to accomplish and unilateral in its execution."

Fulbright went on to say: "Without reference to the United Nations and with only perfunctory reference to the non-functioning SEATO treaty, the United States on its own has undertaken to win a victory for its proteges in the Vietnamese civil war and thereon to build a 'Great Society' in Asia, whatever that may turn out to mean." He urged "that the Senate, which used to be asked for its advice and consent on major foreign commitments, consider some of the sweeping implications of the 'Asian doctrine' before it becomes an irrevocable national commitment undertaken without the consent or even the knowledge of the Senate."

Ky Calls for Invasion of North. On July 25, South Vietnamese Premier Nguyen Cao Ky, in an interview published in *U.S. News & World Report*, urged an invasion of North Viet Nam and declared that without it "there will be no peace." Asked about Communist China's possible entry into the war, Ky said: "Sooner or later we as free men have to face Communist China. And I think it is better to face them now than in five or 10 years."

On the following day, State Department spokesman Robert J. McCloskey, commenting on Ky's statement, said: "I would say our position of not seeking any wider war has been repeatedly made clear and remains our position. We do not threaten any regime."

Big Splash. On July 25, the *New China* news agency reported that Communist party Chairman Mao Tse-tung, 72, had demonstrated his "wonderful health," after recovering from a long illness, by swimming for nine miles in the Yangtze River in view of thousands of spectators, many of them foreigners. The news agency reported that when residents of a town near where Mao took his plunge heard the "happy news," they all reacted by saying: "Our respected and beloved leader Chairman Mao is in such wonderful health. This is the greatest happiness for the entire Chinese people and for revolutionary people throughout the world." The agency added that cheers of "Long live Chairman Mao!" were heard from both banks of the river for well over four hours.

DMZ Bombed. On July 30, U.S. aircraft bombed the demilitarized zone between North and South Viet Nam for the first time. U.S. officials claimed that the zone had been used by North Vietnamese and Viet Cong as a sanctuary and infiltration route.

Another Purged. On Aug. 1, it was learned in Hong Kong that the chief of the Chinese Communist Army's General Staff, Lo Jui-ching, had become a victim of the purge sweeping China. Lo, who was also a deputy premier, had reportedly opposed the rise to power of Defense Minister Lin Piao. *(See June 2, 1966, p. 189.)*

Mao's Orders to Army. On Aug. 2, the Chinese Communist army newspaper *Chieh-fang Chun Pao*, published an editorial that included "extremely important directions" from Chairman Mao Tse-tung. Mao ordered that the Chinese army and the Chinese people be brought into closer contact, with soldiers carrying out some civilian tasks and the general populace learning from the army.

The editorial said that Mao had ordered soldiers to gain knowledge of politics, military affairs and culture. "They can also engage in agricultural production and side occupations, run some medium and small factories and manufacture a number of products to meet their own needs or exchange with the state at equal values," Mao was quoted as saying. "They can also do mass work and take part in the Socialist education movement in factories and villages."

On Aug. 3, the *New China* news agency said Mao's orders were "a call to turn all fields of work into great revolutionary schools where people take part in both industry and agriculture and military as well as civilian affairs."

This new campaign led to speculation that China was on the verge of a great social and economic upheaval comparable to the "Great Leap Forward" of the late 1950s.

Draft Record. On Aug. 4, the Defense Department announced that its draft call for October would be 46,200 -- highest for any month since the Korean War.

Lost Planes and Long War. On Aug. 7, the United

States lost seven aircraft over Viet Nam in one day -- a record. On the same day, a U.S. Marine Corps study asserted that the North Vietnamese could continue the war in Viet Nam indefinitely at their present rate of casualties in South Viet Nam.

Purge Directives. On Aug. 9, the Peking radio announced that the Chinese Communist Party's Central Committee had adopted a series of resolutions calling for formation of committees to expand the "proletarian cultural revolution" -- China's current purge -- throughout the nation's cities and farm communes. The resolutions denounced "anti-party and anti-Socialist" elements in educational, social and cultural fields and urged that they be removed.

"We must reform our educational system," the broadcast said. "We must reform our culture and art and destroy those in the upper strata who represent opposition to the economic basis of Socialist societies. In this way the Socialist system can be strengthened."

The resolutions also said it was forbidden to "force in any way a minority who holds different views to submit,... because sometimes the truth is with the minority."

Chinese in Viet Nam. On Aug. 11, U.S. officials announced that 50,000 uniformed Chinese Communist troops were in North Viet Nam, engaged mainly in repairing supply routes between Hanoi and military bases in China. Previous reports had placed the number of Chinese at 30,000 to 40,000.

Policy Debate in Peking. On Aug. 12, a correspondent for the Toronto *Globe and Mail* reported from Peking that the Chinese Communist Party's hierarchy was engaged in a heated policy debate in the wake of efforts by the Central Committee Aug. 9 to extend, yet moderate, the current purge. The debate was thought to concern who should be involved in policy-making and how much the thought of Chairman Mao Tse-tung should be emphasized.

"If the press is any indication," the story said, "the men around the Defense Minister, Lin Piao, one of the country's brilliant military leaders, may have suffered a setback in their efforts to propagate the fundamentalist view that the army should control and set the pattern for a campaign to turn men into combination workers, peasants, soldiers and intellectuals."

The *Globe and Mail* correspondent reported that the largest street demonstrations to be seen in Peking in 17 years had been continuing all week. On Aug. 11, he said, "columns of marchers as long as half a mile filed past government headquarters forming a sea of red flags dotted with hundreds of portraits of Mr. Mao. Significantly, the demonstrators chanted declarations of support for the Central Committee's declaration, which appears to be aimed at taming a revolution that has become unruly."

Independence of North Korean Reds. On Aug. 12, the North Korean Communist Party's official newspaper, *Rodong Shinmoon,* declared in an editorial that the North Korean party was independent of the Chinese and Soviet parties alike. "Revolution," the editorial said, "can neither be exported nor imported, and outside influence plays only a secondary role." Criticism was directed against both the Soviet Union and Communist China, but the accent seemed to be on the latter.

Peking Communique. On Aug. 13, the Peking radio broadcast a communique on the work of the first plenary session of the Chinese Communist Party's Central Committee since 1962. The session lasted from Aug. 1-12. The communique stated that "The plenary session fully approves the series of brilliant policies of decisive and fundamental importance put forward by Comrade Mao Tse-tung over the past four years." It also implied that China might be on the verge of launching another "Great Leap Forward," although the new policies were described as being of a more "gradual" nature than those instituted in 1958.

The communique placed heavy emphasis on China's split with the Soviet Union: "A clear line of demarcation must be drawn in dealing with modern revisionist groups with the leadership of the Communist Party of the Soviet Union as the center, and it is imperative to resolutely expose their true feathers as scabs. It is impossible to have united action with them." The plenary session agreed that "our party's comprehensive public criticisms of Khrushchev revisionism over the last few years have been entirely correct and necessary."

During the next few days, huge demonstrations were staged outside Communist party headquarters in Peking in support of the communique, Mao, and the Central Committee.

Revealing Rally in Peking. On Aug. 18, the *New China* news agency, reporting the names of Chinese Communist leaders who had attended a Peking rally, indicated that Liu Shao-chi, head of state, had been replaced as China's number two leader (after Mao Tse-tung) by Defense Minister Lin Piao. Listing the names of Chinese leaders in their order of importance, the news agency put Lin Piao next to Mao, and Liu in eighth place.

Analysts in Hong Kong speculated that the 22 persons named by the news agency were the members of a new politburo, ratified during the recent session of the party's Central Committee. Aside from Mao and Lin, the list included, in the following order, Premier Chou En-lai, Deputy Premier Tao Chu, theoretician Chen Po-ta, the party's Secretary General, Teng Hsiao-ping, Kang Sheng, secret police chief, Liu Shao-chi, and 14 others. Six members of the old politburo were not named on the new list.

In a speech at the rally, held to celebrate the Cultural Revolution, Lin Piao called Mao Tse-tung "the most outstanding leader of the proletariat and the greatest genius of the present era." He declared that "We will strike down those in power who take the road of capitalism, strike down the reactionary bourgeois authorities,...oppose all actions to suppress the revolution, and strike down all monsters and demons." Lin promised also to "destroy all the old ideas, old cultures, old customs and old habits of the exploiting classes" and to "sweep away all vermin."

Although foreign correspondents in Peking were not allowed to attend the rally, it was televised live, enabling newsmen to see close-ups of Mao and Lin, both of whom were described as looking healthy. Stanley Karnow of the *Washington Post* reported: "It was Lin's first public appearance in the Chinese capital in three years and his first exposure ever to such a crowd. But from the style of his presentation, there was little doubt that he had been chosen to succeed Mao, now approaching 73."

Rusk on Viet Nam Commitment. On Aug. 22, Secretary of State Dean Rusk told an annual meeting of the Veterans of Foreign Wars in New York that U.S. withdrawal from South Viet Nam would "surely" lead to a third world war.

The Secretary said also that the United States would have been committed in Viet Nam to the same extent if President Kennedy had lived. Kennedy, Rusk asserted, had "never faltered" to commit U.S. strength in Viet Nam.

Fulbright on Purpose of U.S. in Asia. On Aug. 23, Sen. J. William Fulbright (D Ark.), chairman of the Senate Foreign Relations Committee, asserted during a committee session that the "real purpose" of the U.S. was to stay in Asia indefinitely to counter-balance the influence of Communist China. The Senator added that the massive construction of military bases in Thailand afforded proof of his point. "It is almost incredible to think that we are doing this as a temporary operation," he said.

Nixon for Asian Conference. On Aug. 23, former Vice President Richard M. Nixon told newsmen in Washington that he strongly favored an all-Asian peace conference on Viet Nam. Nixon joined a growing list of Republicans in support of the proposal. He said he thought both Communist China and North Viet Nam should be included in such a conference.

Red Guards. On Aug. 23, *Reuters* reported that thousands of young Chinese had stormed Christian churches in Peking, defacing Biblical paintings, plastering the walls with slogans and shattering windows. In a Protestant church, a large bust of Mao Tse-tung was erected.

The Red Guards attacked stores and private homes containing items considered too bourgeois or extravagant. Even flowers were banned because they were not "revolutionary." People who wanted to ride in pedicabs were ordered to pull the driver instead of vice versa. Place names were being changed; the famous Square of Heavenly Peace had become "East Is Red Square."

On Aug. 25, Red Guards raided a Roman Catholic convent used as a school for the children of foreign diplomats, who were on vacation at the time.

On Aug. 26, Red Guards joined art students in removing famous art objects from the Peking Central Art Academy and destroying them. The city's better restaurants were ordered to serve only cheap meals, the barbers to refrain from giving "bizarre" haircuts, and the tailors from making Western-style clothing.

On the same day, the *New China* news agency said "the revolutionary rebel spirit" of the Red Guards had "sparked off a prairie fire that is sweeping the whole of China,...burning down all the decadent influences of the bourgeois and feudal classes as well as all old ideas, old culture, old customs and old habits."

Anti-Russian Rally. On Aug. 29, thousands of Red Guards marched past the Soviet Union's embassy in Peking in an all-day demonstration against "revisionism." Although the parade was well-disciplined, Chinese soldiers and police guarded the building against possible attack. In a ceremony at the start of the demonstration, the Red Guards changed the name of the street on which the embassy is situated from Growing Prestige Street to Anti-Revisionism Street.

Doom of U.S. Imperialism. On Aug. 30, the Peking *People's Daily* published an editorial charging that the Soviet Union, India, Japan, and the United States were attempting to encircle China. The editorial doomed the effort to failure:

"The tying down of large numbers of United States troops by the Asian people creates a favorable condition for the further growth of the anti-United States struggle of the people in other parts of the world. With all the people rising to attack it, one hitting at its head and the other at its feet, United States imperialism can be nibbled up bit by bit.

"By transferring the main weight of its force to Asia, United States imperialism is courting disaster. Instead of extinguishing the flames of the Asian people's revolution, it gives the Asian peoples an excellent opportunity to put up a good fight.

"To be quite frank, if United States imperialism kept its forces in Europe and America, the Asian people would have no way of wiping them out. Now, as it is so obliging as to deliver its goods to the customer's door, the Asian people cannot but express welcome."

DeGaulle's Apprehension. On Aug. 30, French President Charles de Gaulle declared in Pnompenh, Cambodia, that the war in Viet Nam might lead to the world's worst disaster. Hundreds of thousands of Cambodians greeted the French President, who was in Pnompenh for three days of talks with Cambodian Chief of State Prince Norodom Sihanouk.

Defector's Statement. On Aug. 30, a defecting member of the Chinese Communist commercial mission in Syria, Miao Chen-pai, said upon his arrival in New York that the Chinese leadership was "still very cautious" about confronting the United States in Viet Nam. On China's current purge, Miao thought that "all those who question the effectiveness of Mao Tse-tung's extreme policies will be deprived of their power and voice." The fall of Peng Chen, former Mayor of Peking, could be traced to a statement he had made to a meeting of propaganda officials in September 1965. "Mr. Peng suggested that everyone in the face of truth was equal," Mr. Miao said, "that everyone should be given freedom to speak and that even if Chairman Mao is wrong, then, he too, must be criticized." The defector reported also that "many setbacks" for China, internationally and domestically, had created "widespread opposition" to Chairman Mao and his policies.

Soviet Condemnation of Red China. On Aug. 31, the Soviet Communist Party's Central Committee condemned the Chinese Communist leadership for breaking up the international Communist movement and appealed directly to the Chinese people for renewed unity. The resolution adopted by the Central Committee was the first official Soviet statement condemning the Chinese Communist leadership since former Soviet Premier Nikita S. Khrushchev was removed from office in October 1964.

"It is becoming increasingly more obvious," the resolution said, "that the leadership of the People's Republic of China, using the concoctions about the U.S.S.R.'s collusion with United States imperialism and the restoration of capitalism in the Soviet Union as a cover, is provoking a sharp deterioration of relations between the U.S.S.R. and the Chinese People's Republic.... Things have gone so far that mass outrages have been organized near the Soviet Embassy in Peking."

Red Guards Cautioned. On Aug. 31, the militant Red Guards held another rally in Peking and were reviewed by Mao, Lin Piao, and other leaders. A directive issued the same day stated that the Red Guards had been overly zealous in their anti-bourgeois campaign. They were reminded that ultimate authority rested with the Communist

Party's Central Committee. The directive said the youths had made some "mistakes" and had attacked "revolutionary families." It also warned that the homes of party functionaries and military officers were not to be raided. At the rally, Lin hailed the Red Guards as "the shock fighting force...in the great cultural revolution," but he cautioned them to carry on their campaign against counter-revolutionaries "by reasoning and not by coercion or force."

Thailand Hearings. On Aug. 31, Sen. J. William Fulbright (D Ark.), chairman of the Senate Foreign Relations Committee, announced that his Committee would hold hearings on the U.S. involvement in Thailand. "We ought to know what we are getting into," the Senator said. "Are we to have another Viet Nam?"

Interview with NLF Spokesman. On Aug. 31, a taped interview in Algiers with a representative of South Viet Nam's National Liberation Front, political arm of the Viet Cong, was shown on NBC's Huntley-Brinkley Report. The NLF representative said negotiations on the Viet Nam conflict would be "inappropriate" while American troops remained in Viet Nam. He said the Americans sought negotiations only to "obtain at the conference table what they could not obtain on the battlefield." The NLF spokesman added: "For our people, peace means that there is no longer any aggressor on Vietnamese soil. As long as the American troops still hang onto our country, the South Vietnamese people will fight them until the achievement of independence, democracy and peace."

De Gaulle's Speech. On Sept. 1, French President Charles de Gaulle told a crowd of more than 100,000 in Pnompenh, Cambodia, that the United States would gain if it withdrew its forces from South Viet Nam. If it took such action, he said, "what an audience would the United States recapture from one end of the world to the other, and what an opportunity would peace find on the scene and everywhere else."

The French President asserted that "continuous reinforcement in Viet Nam meant that the war was coming increasingly closer to China" and becoming "increasingly provoking in the eyes of the Soviet Union." With emotion, he said France would not side with the United States in a general war in Asia. He said also that France would not attempt to initiate peace talks unless the United States pledged to withdraw its forces from South Viet Nam.

On the following day, De Gaulle and Cambodian Chief of State Prince Norodom Sihanouk signed a joint communique calling on all interested powers to pledge non-interference in the internal affairs of Viet Nam and for a cessation of all acts of war in that country.

Chinese Bellicosity. On Sept. 2, the *New China* news agency reported that Communist China had assured North Viet Nam that "every preparation" had been made to deal "joint blows at the U.S. aggressors until final victory is achieved." On the same day, the Peking *People's Daily* published an article attributed to the Red Guards declaring: "We Red Guards not only are staging an all-out rebellion on the domestic scene, but are ready to step into the international arena to fight to the end and make thoroughgoing rebellions together with the oppressed peoples and nations of the whole world.

"At the moment, the U.S. gangsters are slaughtering our Vietnamese brothers and the Vietnamese people are valiantly fighting a war of resistance. We pledge ourselves to provide powerful backing for the heroic Vietnamese people." The article added: "Listen, you United States gangsters! Since we are fighters, we Red Guards are ready to fight a war at any time. We are a powerful reserve force of the heroic, invincible Chinese People's Liberation Army. If the United States imperialists dare to invade our beloved country, we will break their backs."

On Sept. 3, first anniversary of the publication of Lin Piao's famous article urging underdeveloped countries to wage a people's war against the capitalist countries, the Peking *People's Daily* carried another article declaring a "people's war of annihilation" on capitalist nations and "Soviet revisionists." The article stated that the Chinese army had completed one year's intensive training, preparing it for the time when it would carry the Communist revolution into other countries and "liberate" the world. The article, which many analysts in Hong Kong called "a most significant statement," declared: "All China is the base for the world revolution. Just as the liberated areas within our country were the base for the successful Chinese revolution."

Lin Piao to Lead Red Guards. On Sept. 4, the Peking radio announced that Defense Minister Lin Piao, heir apparent to Mao Tse-tung, had been designated by the Red Guards as their leader. It was reported also that Premier Chou En-lai had been named an adviser to the militant youth group.

On the same day, *Reuters* reported that the Red Guards had closed a Peking cemetery for foreigners and renamed it "anti-imperialist, anti-revisionist orchard."

Johnson on Troop Withdrawal. On Sept. 5, President Johnson, in an indirect reply to French President Charles de Gaulle, said the United States would offer a timetable for withdrawal of its troops from South Viet Nam when one was offered by the North Vietnamese. The President added: "We cannot walk away from the simple fact that the peace and security of many nations are threatened if aggressors are permitted to succeed in a strategic area of the world, if vital treaties are broken and if men and arms are moved illegally across international boundaries to conquer small nations."

Chinese Report and Warning. On Sept. 5, the *New China* news agency reported that U.S. airplanes on Aug. 29 had sunk one Chinese ship in the Gulf of Tonkin and damaged another, killing nine Chinese seamen and injuring seven others. U.S. officials said the report would be investigated. According to the news agency, the Chinese Ministry of National Defense had said the attack was one of many. It added: "Once again we seriously warn the U.S. aggressors: These blood debts will have to be repaid in blood. Armed with Mao Tse-tung's thought, the Chinese people will not let U.S. imperialists perpetrate their evil unpunished."

Flurry Over China Talks on Viet Nam. On Sept. 6, Chinese Communist Foreign Minister Chen Yi was reported by Japanese sources to have told a group of Japanese legislators that China was "not necessarily dismissing" the idea of talks with the United States over Viet Nam. Two days later, however, a spokesman for the Japanese legislators said that "Peking has 'no intention whatever' to talk with the United States for peace in Viet Nam." The Japanese legislators were quoted as saying that the Chinese had pledged to "fight 10 or 15 years and (that) China will back up and aid North Viet Nam." The Japanese added that "it should be understood that this means there must be no hint of negotiations with the United States."

Resistance to Red Guards. On Sept. 6, the Peking correspondent of the Toronto *Globe and Mail*, reported that the activities of China's Red Guards were meeting some opposition:

"Among thousands of posters plastered on walls and windows throughout the city (Peking) are frank accounts of resistance in which local or regional Communist party committees were implicated in resisting the authority of Chairman Mao Tse-tung and his Central Committee. One poster told of a sharp clash between peasants and students of the Lanchow Railway School, in which local party officials were implicated. A manhunt for a Lanchow man subsequently was launched in Peking. He was described as counter-revolutionary. In the city of Tsingtao on the Yellow Sea, resistance by no fewer than 40,000 persons was reported. Similar reports came in from such widely separated points as Tientsin and Changsha. The posters did not make clear whether there was any bloodshed."

Hanoi and Moscow. On Sept. 9, a Moscow dispatch to the *New York Times* reported that North Viet Nam had "moved reluctantly into the Soviet political sphere of influence...after Communist China allowed its once-predominant influence in Hanoi to be dissipated." The Chinese purge, the report said, "is believed to have disillusioned the North Vietnamese with their Chinese alliance and, consequently, raised their dependence on Moscow."

Warning on Red Guards. On Sept. 11, the Peking *People's Daily* published an editorial warning Communist party officials and government employees not to interfere with the activities of the Red Guards. This was the first official admission that the militant youth group was encountering organized opposition. The editorial acknowledged that the Red Guards had made mistakes, but it was firm in stating that "No matter what the pretext, fighting between the students and farmers and laborers must not be permitted."

Election in Viet Nam. On Sept. 11, 80.8 percent of South Viet Nam's registered voters went to the polls to elect a constituent assembly to draft a new constitution. South Vietnamese Premier Nguyen Cao Ky said the election "certainly announces the beginning of the end" for the Communists. On the following day, President Johnson called the large turnout of voters a "good sign."

Trouble Over Red Guards. On Sept. 12, a Japanese newspaper's correspondent in Peking reported that units of the Chinese army had been called out to control a crowd of 100,000 people protesting activities of the Red Guards in Kweilin, in southeastern China. The report said that similar clashes had occurred all over the country. "The main cause of resistance put up by local party committees and citizens against the Red Guard," the report said, "is that Red Guards from Peking visit districts suddenly and start propaganda against local party committee members," who defend themselves by attempts to "suppress the activities of Red Guards from Peking through the use of the pressure of local people."

On Sept. 14, the Peking correspondent for the Japanese newspaper *Asahi* reported that "The confusion of the Red Guards is coming from the attempt to make the local people grasp the meaning of the 'great cultural revolution.'"

Red Guards Want to Hear Mao. On Sept. 14, the Soviet news agency *Tass* reported that Red Guards in Peking were demanding that Chairman Mao Tse-tung speak at the Oct. 1 national holiday celebrations. "We want to hear the voice of Chairman Mao to receive his instructions," the youths were reported to have said. There had been reports in Hong Kong newspapers that Mao was suffering from throat cancer and could not speak at length.

Peking Rally. On Sept. 15, more than one million Red Guards and soldiers crowded into the Square of Heavenly Peace (renamed the East is Red Square) in Peking to hear Premier Chou En-lai urge them to halt temporarily their anti-bourgeois campaign and join the peasants in the countryside in harvesting the crops. Lin Piao, defense minister and Mao's heir apparent, also urged the crowd to "uphold Chairman Mao's teachings, strengthen the power of the revolution by uniting with the workers, peasants and soldiers, and firmly concentrate on production."

On the same day, the Peking *People's Daily* said in an editorial that the Cultural Revolution may be "suspended temporarily during the busiest period of the autumn harvest." It added: "It is not necessary for Red Guards and revolutionary teachers and students from colleges and middle schools to go to factories and rural areas to exchange revolutionary experiences and interfere with arrangements there."

Number of U.S. Troops in Viet Nam. On Sept. 15, a U.S. military spokesman in Saigon announced current U.S. military strength in South Viet Nam slightly exceeded 308,000.

Philippines and Viet Nam. On Sept. 15, substantial increases in U.S. economic aid to the Philippines were announced. On the following day, the first contingent of Philippine troops arrived in South Viet Nam. On Sept. 16, Philippine President Ferdinand E. Marcos, addressing the National Press Club in Washington, said he supported the U.S. effort in Viet Nam but was "concerned about the apparent failure of economic development measures in Viet Nam to date."

Chinese Charge Plane Attack. On Sept. 16, Communist China charged that two U.S. warplanes had attacked across the Chinese border, wounding three peasants. The Chinese asserted that the U.S. planes had been scared away by Chinese Air Force fighters. On the same day, Secretary of State Dean Rusk said the United States would investigate the charges. *(See Sept. 5, 1966.)*

U.S. to Oppose Red China at UN. On Sept. 16, Secretary of State Dean Rusk told a news conference that the United States would again oppose admission of Communist China to the United Nations. "We do not see the basis on which the United Nations is in a position to vote Peking into membership at this point," Rusk said. He added, however, that the Administration's current policy goals centered around the possibility of visitor exchanges with Communist China to help "break through the walls of isolation that Peking has built around itself."

Ike on Nuclear Weapons in Korea. On Sept. 18, former President Dwight D. Eisenhower disclosed in a television interview that the United States had secretly threatened during the Korean War to use nuclear weapons against Communist China, and that it had "a great effect" in speeding up the armistice negotiations.

"I let it be known that if there were not going to be an armistice,...I would no longer regard this war as being limited (and) deny ourselves the right to attack wherever we saw enemy coming at us -- meaning that we were not going to be bound by the kind of weapons that we would use. I don't mean to say that we'd have used those great big things and destroyed cities, but we would use them enough to win and we, of course, would have tried to keep them on military targets, not civil targets." *(See also Oct. 3, 1966.)*

North Korea and Red China. On Sept. 18, the Soviet newspaper *Pravda* published an article from the North Korean Communist Party newspaper *Rodong Shinmoon* criticizing recent political events in Communist China and implying that the North Korean party had defected from the Chinese camp.

Struggle Against Mao. On Sept. 18, the Chinese theoretical journal *Hung Chi* said that powerful elements within the Communist party were waging a struggle against Mao Tse-tung and his heir apparent, Defense Minister Lin Piao.

Sacking of Mme. Sun's House. On Sept. 20, militant Red Guards in Shanghai ransacked the home of Soong Ching-ling, the widow of Dr. Sun Yat-sen, founder of the Chinese Republic. The 75-year-old Miss Soong, vice president of the People's Republic and an older sister of Mme. Chiang Kai-shek, was accused by the youth group of favoring capitalism. It was not known whether Miss Soong was in her house when her possessions were confiscated by the invading youths.

Reason for Purge. On Sept. 20, a Peking radio broadcast described the purge sweeping China as "a life-or-death fight between capitalists who attempted to revive their ideology and those who put down the revival." The broadcast said that party officials and intellectuals had been planning an anti-party coup d'etat. "Our victory is essential," the broadcast said, "because it is closely inter-related with the future and fate of the world revolution."

Soviet Students Sent Home. On Sept. 20, Communist China ordered all Soviet students studying in the country to leave because their teachers were preoccupied with the "cultural revolution." An unstated reason was that virtually the whole of Red China's educational system was shutting down temporarily. Closing of the upper schools freed millions of students to join the Red Guards and promote the "cultural revolution."

Denunciation of Soviets. On Sept. 22, a Russian newspaper correspondent reported that Red Guards had hung a poster near the Soviet embassy in Peking attacking the Soviet Union. "All the old and new hatred is graven on our hearts," the poster said. "We won't forget it in a hundred, a thousand or ten thousand years. When the moment comes, we will tear the skin from you, rip out your guts, burn your bodies, and throw the ashes to the winds."

U.S. Offer to De-escalate. On Sept. 22, U.S. Ambassador Arthur J. Goldberg told the UN General Assembly that the United States would be willing to begin de-escalating the war in Viet Nam if the Communists would give assurances that they would do the same. Goldberg said the United States would first halt the bombing of North Viet Nam, and then start withdrawing troops from South Viet Nam as a second step.

On the following day, Soviet Foreign Minister Andrei A. Gromyko told the General Assembly that the U.S. peace offer gave "no signs testifying to the seriousness of the intention of Washington to seek for a settlement of this problem and to stop the aggression against the Vietnamese people." He said, "The aggressor has come to Viet Nam, the aggressor should leave."

Pravda Report on Red Guards. On Sept. 23, the Soviet Communist Party newspaper *Pravda* published a report from Peking that Red Guards were beating and murdering officials of the Chinese Communist Party. The dispatch said that many Red Guard leaders were attempting to dissociate themselves from such extreme acts. A Sept. 25 *Pravda* dispatch said the Red Guards had ordered "the destruction of all books which did not conform to the spirit of Chairman Mao's ideas." The Soviet correspondent added: "There are no school children in the streets of Peking this September. The children have been given a different task -- 'to study, popularize and defend Chairman Mao's ideas.'"

Soviet Exports to the East. On Sept. 25, the Soviet government announced that its exports both to Communist China and to North Viet Nam had sharply increased in 1965, with the bulk of the increase consisting of industrial machinery, power generating equipment, and road excavating machines. There was also an increase in shipments of military equipment to North Viet Nam. Soviet imports from China were notably reduced, Moscow said.

Chinese Arms to Arabs. On Sept. 25, Communist China was reported to be shipping small amounts of weapons to the Palestine Liberation Organization of the Arab countries. "Reports of shipments," a Washington dispatch to the *New York Times* said, "have not been completely confirmed, but it is generally accepted among analysts of the Middle East that China has assisted the Pan-Arab army, either through direct shipment of arms or by supplying money to the Palestine Liberation Organization to buy them."

Proposals of Vietnamese Communists. On Sept. 28, the Hanoi radio broadcast an interview with the President of the National Liberation Front, Nguyen Huu Tho, in which he said the organization's goal was to "found a broad democratic coalition government consisting of representatives of all social strata, nationalities, religious communities and patriotic personalities." Tho said that all people, excluding some of those currently connected with the South Vietnamese government, would be able to participate in a new government. "There will be no grudge for their former activities, political tendencies and viewpoints, nor any discrimination as to nationalities or religious communities." He did say, however, that participants in the government would have to agree to oppose the United States, "win back national sovereignty, realize the rights of freedom and democracy, put an end to the U.S. policy of intervention and aggression, and achieve peace and neutrality in South Viet Nam."

On the following day, North Viet Nam broadcast a sweeping rejection of all U.S. peace efforts to date and said the only way to end the war was for the United States to cease its "aggressions." The broadcast added: "While advertising their good will for peace at the United Nations (see Sept. 22), the United States aggressors are planning a greater buildup of United States forces and new war acts on the South Viet Nam battlefield. It is obvious that this tortuous peace campaign is only aimed at deceiving the world's people."

Peking on People's Wars. On Sept. 29, the *New China* news agency declared that the world was ripe for "people's wars," and that "revolutionary people," owing allegiance to China and "the invincible thought of Mao Tse-tung," would "gain the entire world." The news agency said that "armed struggles of the Asian people against U.S. imperialism and its lackeys are on the upsurge in various regions and are further developing in scope and strength."

Poles Denounce China. On Sept. 29, the Polish Communist Party, which had resisted Soviet attempts to exclude Red China from the international Communist movement, for the first time strongly denounced China for disrupting the unity of the Communist nations.

Goldberg. On Sept. 30, U.S. Ambassador to the UN Arthur J. Goldberg, after an hour with President Johnson, told newsmen that the United States was still somewhat optimistic about North Viet Nam's reaction to recent peace proposals (see Sept. 28). "It would have been unrealistic to expect immediately a considered reply to the serious proposals we made at the General Assembly," Goldberg said. "It is highly natural that the earlier replies be largely propagandistic in nature." The Ambassador pointed out that although Hanoi's reaction had generally been harsh, the proposals had not been rejected. The U.S. offer was made by Goldberg in the UN General Assembly on Sept. 22.

China Regime's Survival Questioned. On Sept. 30, eve of the 17th anniversary of the People's Republic of China, Stanley Karnow of the *Washington Post* reported that many China analysts doubted whether the present regime could survive.

"For the first time since the Communists took over China in 1949," Karnow said, "even the most sober specialists are speculating on the possibility that Chinese leader Mao Tse-tung and his heir apparent, Lin Piao, could be overthrown by an opposition that has, from all accounts, grown significantly within recent months. Should this come to pass, it might plunge China into a chaos reminiscent of the 1920s, when the country was torn by rival warlords and political factions."

Through "intensive spiritual indoctrination," the dispatch reported, Mao hopes to mobilize the Chinese people for an economic leap forward. Supported by only a minority of the Communist party hierarchy, he turned to Lin Piao, who had been spectacularly successful in indoctrinating the army "in much the same fashion Mao wished to see all of China indoctrinated." Mao and Lin then launched the "cultural revolution" to cleanse the party apparatus of all those who disagreed with them.

However, Karnow said, there was growing opposition to the purge and its storm troopers, the Red Guards. In a number of provinces, Red Guards had been beaten and jailed by local party leaders and their followers. "How far this tumult will go is difficult to foresee. Until now, however, it has dramatized the fact that China is not the Communist monolith it once was, and Mao himself may prove a victim of its new disunity."

Chinese Holiday. On Oct. 1, 17th anniversary of the founding of the Chinese People's Republic, more than 50 Soviet-bloc diplomats, their wives and families, left the reviewing stand during the mammoth ceremonies in Peking. They were protesting a charge by Defense Minister Lin Piao that the Soviet Union was plotting with the United States in Viet Nam.

"We must turn the whole country into a great school of Mao Tse-tung's thought," Lin declared, adding that China was ready to wage "the struggle against U.S. imperialism and its lackeys and the struggle against modern revisionism, with the leadership of the Communist Party of the Soviet Union as its center, to the end."

In the parade, about 5,000 goose-stepping soldiers were followed by an estimated two million Red Guards, taking more than four hours to pass the reviewing stand where Mao, Lin and other officials were standing. Although the Red Guards made constant requests, Mao refused to speak.

At a banquet the night before, it was noted that Head of State Liu Shao-chi was absent, but he attended the National Day ceremonies.

Intra-Party Conflict in China. On Oct. 3, the Chinese Communist Party's ideological journal, *Hung Chi*, said there were still officials who were attempting to "usurp the leadership of the party, the army, and the government." It added: "They are the most dangerous enemy and the main one." The article described the opposition group as a handful of people who had been "hit by sugar-coated bullets of the bourgeoisie" and were "no longer representatives of the proletariat." Because the "overthrown exploiting classes" were "placing their hopes of a comeback chiefly on them," it was "only by striking down those people within the party who are in authority and who are taking the capitalist road" that it would be possible to "smash plots by the exploiting classes for a restoration, consolidate the dictatorship of the proletariat more completely, and promote development of the socialist cause."

Eisenhower on Nuclear Weapons. On Oct. 3, former President Dwight D. Eisenhower, asked at a Washington news conference if he would preclude the use of atomic weapons in Viet Nam, said: "I would not automatically preclude anything. When you appeal to force to carry out the policies of America abroad, there is no court above you." Discussing his part in ending the Korean War, Eisenhower added: "When I came to the White House, we had almost a monopoly in atomic power -- in certain phases we did have a monopoly -- and there was great respect of what we might do. But I never openly threatened to use atomic weapons. I said we would no longer be restrained by gentlemen's agreements outside the Yalu River, or across the Yalu, and whatever was needed to win that war or make them sign that armistice right now, I would do whatever was necessary and avoid making promises on restrictions of weapons I would use." (See also Sept. 18, 1966.)

The former President conceded that he did not know how he would "fight the war today," but he said: "I would do it just as soon as I could. I would bring this to a conclusion because, as Senator Dirksen pointed out, there's the blood of a lot of young men involved and whenever we have had casualties in order to carry out the policy of America abroad, America as a whole has made it the first order of business to get that war done first."

Soviet Aid to North Viet Nam. On Oct. 3, the Soviet news agency, *Tass*, reported that the Soviet Union and North Viet Nam had concluded agreements for economic assistance and military aid. No figures were released. Soviet Deputy Premier Vladimir N. Novikov, after signing the agreements, was reported to have said: "The Soviet Union and other socialist countries will not leave the Vietnamese people in trouble. This has been seen and felt by the aggressors. Let them have no illusions on this score."

On the same day, it was reported that U.S. officials had evidence that Soviet advisers in North Viet Nam were helping to operate the country's air defenses, described by many military experts as the most sophisticated in the world.

French Information on Viet Nam. On Oct. 4, it was reported from Washington that French Foreign Minister Maurice Couve de Murville had told President Johnson during a 90-minute White House meeting that North Viet Nam had given up all hope of winning the war in South Viet Nam. But the Foreign Minister was reported also to have warned that the North Vietnamese would not negotiate at present because they thought they could maintain a force of 50,000 troops in South Viet Nam, thereby wearing down American forces, and because U.S. terms for peace remained "fuzzy." Couve de Murville had met with representatives of the National Liberation Front and of North Viet Nam while visiting Cambodia with French President Charles de Gaulle late in August.

Kohler on Blockading North Viet Nam. On Oct. 4, U.S. Ambassador to the Soviet Union Foy D. Kohler told the Senate Foreign Relations Committee, which was considering his nomination as Deputy Under Secretary of State for Political Affairs, that to establish an American blockade of North Viet Nam would be a "dangerous step" because it would carry the risk of a direct confrontation with the Soviet Union.

Senators' Plea. On Oct. 4, Sens. John O. Pastore (D R.I.), vice chairman of the Senate-House Atomic Energy Committee, Jacob K. Javits (R N.Y.), and Gale McGee (D Wyo.) appealed to the Administration to avoid a situation in Viet Nam where the United States might have to use nuclear weapons. The Senate reaction was sparked by former President Eisenhower's remarks the previous day that he would not "automatically preclude anything," even the use of nuclear weapons in Viet Nam.

Sen. Pastore said: "I implore Lyndon B. Johnson, the President; I implore Robert S. McNamara, the Secretary of Defense; I implore Dean Rusk, the Secretary of State; and I implore the Joint Chiefs of Staff not to maneuver the United States in Viet Nam into a position where we have to use nuclear or thermonuclear weapons. If we do, all I can say is God help us, God help us!"

Analysis of China's Position. On Oct. 4, U. Alexis Johnson, the new Ambassador to Japan and former Deputy Under Secretary of State, told the 18th annual Far East Conference in Washington that Communist China's loss of prestige in the economic and political fields might force it to move toward a "live-and-let-live" policy toward the rest

of the world. Noting that the non-Communist nations of Asia were making rapid economic progress, Johnson said that Communist China had made no progress in gross national product per capita since 1956. He added that the spread of Chinese-style communism had suffered a disastrous defeat in Indonesia and would again in Viet Nam. The latter event, he said, might be a turning point for China, forcing the people to give up violence and attempt to live peaceably with their neighbors.

Communist China's economic failure, Johnson said, "has, I believe, long since dispelled in the area the notion that Peking holds any special key to rapid economic development. Politically, Peking is faced with uncertainty as to how to proceed in the face of a major series of setbacks internationally over the last few years. It stands in growing isolation even within the international Communist movement. Its own population, including major elements of the Chinese Communist Party, are exhibiting increasing skepticism as to the validity and effectiveness of the ideological prescriptions for China's ills."

Ky to Thant. On Oct. 5, South Vietnamese Premier Nguyen Cao Ky sent a letter to UN Secretary General U Thant saying that the South Vietnamese government would accept any solution for peace so long as the liberty and independence of South Viet Nam was assured. Ky promised that once North Viet Nam's "aggression" ceased, his government would ask U.S. forces to leave South Viet Nam.

Hanoi's Terms. On Oct. 6, an unidentified unaligned nation, represented in Hanoi, informed the United States that the North Vietnamese government would not consider a pause in U.S. bombing of North Viet Nam a sufficient inducement to start negotiating a settlement of the conflict. The source reportedly said that complete cessation of the bombing would be necessary.

Chinese Students to Leave Russia. On Oct. 7, the Soviet Union announced it had ordered all 65 Communist Chinese students in the U.S.S.R. to leave the country by the end of October. Peking on Sept. 20 had told Russian students in China to return home because their teachers were preoccupied with the "cultural revolution."

Soviet Rejects Call for Geneva Conference. On Oct. 8, the Soviet Union announced at the United Nations that it had rejected a British proposal that the two countries reconvene the Geneva Conference on Viet Nam. Britain and the U.S.S.R. were co-chairmen of the 1954 Geneva Conference.

Hanoi's Response to Thant's Proposals. On Oct. 10, the North Vietnamese government rejected UN Secretary General U Thant's proposal that ground fighting in Viet Nam be de-escalated. However, it endorsed Thant's proposal that U.S. bombing of North Viet Nam be halted. *Nhan Dan*, official newspaper of the North Vietnamese Communist Party, said: "Thant has not made the necessary distinction, namely that American imperialism is the aggressor and the Vietnamese people is the victim of aggression. He demands that this people should curb its struggle for independence and freedom."

Glorification of Lin. On Oct. 11, a Hong Kong dispatch to the *New York Times* reported that "a campaign has been launched in China to glorify Lin Piao, the defense minister, and underline his new role as heir apparent to

Mao Tse-tung, the Communist party's chairman." Interpreting this move as "a significant shift in emphasis on the part of Peking," the dispatch observed: "Until recently Mr. Lin was content to stand in Mr. Mao's shadow and be acknowledged simply as the party leader's chief aide and spokesman. Today he is being praised in his own right and his name is appearing more frequently in the press as the authoritative voice of the hierarchy. Mr. Lin increasingly appears to be taking on the mantle of China's strong man while the deification of Mr. Mao appears to be removing him from the mundane affairs of the state and party. Analysts say it has become difficult to tell just where Chairman Mao's authority ends and Mr. Lin's begins."

Kosygin Accuses China. On Oct. 13, Soviet Premier Aleksei N. Kosygin, in a speech in Sverdlovsk, accused Communist China of preventing a North Vietnamese victory in the Viet Nam war by blocking efforts of socialist countries to assist North Viet Nam. He said: "If American imperialism had met such general resistance from all the countries of socialism, with a unity of policy, there would be no doubt but that its outrages in Viet Nam would have been brought to a halt in a short time." Kosygin went on to say: "The policies of China have become a serious obstacle in the struggle for this sacred cause.... They are causing great concern to all Communist and progressive people, to whom the defense of the Vietnamese people's freedom and independence is dear, because these policies are resulting in ever greater damage to the interests of the Vietnamese and the interests of world socialism."

On the same day, the Italian Communist Party condemned Communist China for the first time, objecting mainly to the "cultural revolution."

New Record in Air Strikes. On Oct. 15, U.S. warplanes flew a record 175 missions (including 450 to 500 individual plane strikes) against North Viet Nam. On the same day, it was announced that the number of U.S. planes shot down over the north had passed the 400 mark.

Peking Attacks U.S. and U.S.S.R. On Oct. 16, the Peking *People's Daily* denounced President Johnson's policies toward Eastern Europe and charged that the Soviet Union had "long ceased to support world revolution." It accused the President of attempting to accelerate capitulation of the Soviet bloc to capitalism and of seeking Soviet cooperation in reducing tensions in Europe so that more American troops could be transferred to Viet Nam. The *People's Daily* article charged that the Soviet Union and the U.S. were trying to create an "anti-Communist, anti-people, counter-revolutionary, and anti-China new holy alliance."

Reports of Anti-Mao Activity. On Oct. 16, Czechoslovakia's news agency, *Ceteka*, reported that posters had appeared in Peking accusing some groups of Red Guards of attacking party Chairman Mao Tse-tung. According to the news agency, one poster quoted a Red Guard as saying: "If we look at the social origin of Chairman Mao, we see he comes from the family of a rich farmer." Another accused a Red Guard of saying that Defense Minister Lin Piao was "no revolutionary." Reports from travelers arriving in Hong Kong indicated that there was anti-Mao activity among some Red Guards during a rally in Canton in September. It was also reported that the 2571st birthday of Confucius had only brought scorn from the Red Guards, who marched through Canton denouncing the Chinese philosopher as a "demon," "snake," and "devil."

LBJ Trip. On Oct. 17, President Johnson flew from Washington to Honolulu on the first leg of a trip to be climaxed by a conference at Manila with the leaders of six other nations. Upon arrival in the Hawaiian capital, the President said he was "convinced that we have reached a turning point in Asia's history, in Asia's relations with the United States, and in Asia's relations with the rest of the world." He added: "All hatred among nations must end in reconciliation, and we look to the day when the policies of mainland China will permit such a reconciliation."

Another Red Guard Rally. On Oct. 18, Red China's leader Mao Tse-tung and his heir apparent Defense Minister Lin Piao reviewed a rally of 1,300,000 Red Guards in Peking. Many observers viewed the rally, and those which preceded it, as a much-needed demonstration of support for Mao and Lin, who seemed to be encountering continuing resistance to their policies within the Peking hierarchy.

Chen Yi Denounced. On Oct. 19, Japanese correspondents in Peking reported that Red Guards had plastered the Chinese Foreign Ministry with posters reading: "Bombard the party committee of the Foreign Ministry and burn to death Vice Premier and concurrently Foreign Minister Chen Yi!"

On the same day, travelers from China reported in Hong Kong that around 100 Communist officials had been killed and 300 injured when an explosion ripped through the Sin Hua Theatre in Swatow, in southern China. The officials had been among a crowd of 1,000 celebrating the Oct. 1 National Day.

The official Soviet news agency, *Tass*, had reported the day before that Red Guards had beaten and tortured at least 140 people in a hospital in Tsingtao, a large port on the Yellow Sea, 260 miles southeast of Peking.

Two-China Policy Urged. On Oct. 20, the United Nations Association, an independent, non-partisan organization devoted to support of the United Nations, published a study of the problem of China, the United Nations and United States policy. The study, prepared by a panel of 27 prominent persons, urged that the United States adopt a "two-China policy," permitting representation of both Communist China and Nationalist China in the United Nations.

The panel warned that if the United States continued to oppose the entry of Communist China, the General Assembly might vote Nationalist China out of the organization and assign China's seat to the Communist regime. To save Nationalist China's membership, the study said, the United States should promptly adopt a "two-China policy." Communist China might initially reject an offer of UN membership if Nationalist China were to remain in the organization, but the panel felt that the offer "could strengthen the position of moderate voices in Peking and thereby have some influence in the changes" of leadership expected to occur in the Chinese hierarchy.

Chinese Appeal to Defend Mao. On Oct. 20, the Peking *People's Daily* appealed to the Chinese people "to defend the proletarian revolutionary line represented by Chairman Mao Tse-tung and resolutely oppose the reactionary bourgeois line; even at the cost of our lives defend Chairman Mao and the Central Committee of the party and the thought of Mao Tse-tung."

The editorial declared: "We will strike down whoever

opposes Chairman Mao and Mao Tse-tung's thought.... We must resolutely strike down the small handful of those within the party who are in positions of power and have taken the capitalist road, counter-revolutionary revisionists and all monsters and demons; we must hit them hard, completely discredit them and never let them rise again."

Publication of such an appeal inevitably led to speculation that Mao Tse-tung and Lin Piao, his heir apparent, were meeting determined resistance to the current "cultural revolution."

LBJ in Australia. On Oct. 21, President Johnson arrived in Melbourne, Australia, where he was given a tumultuous welcome. Among the thousands of welcomers, however, were numerous anti-Viet Nam war demonstrators, two of whom threw sacks of paint on the President's car. On the following day, the President traveled to Sydney, where he was again met by large and friendly crowds. From there, he flew to Brisbane, where he told crowds: "We are ready to stop the bombing of North Viet Nam. We are ready to produce a schedule for the withdrawal of our troops -- whenever the other side tells us what it is prepared to do to move toward peace in Viet Nam."

Nationalist Reaction to Two-China Plan. On Oct. 21, the Nationalist Chinese representative to the United Nations, Liu Chieh, said the proposal that the United States move toward a "two-China policy," offered by a panel of prominent citizens Oct. 20, was "ill-timed" and "unrealistic." Liu added that the proposal would "encourage the extremists in the Chinese Communist Party to believe that their policy has proved effective and that Peking is to be accepted into the United Nations because of that policy."

Manila Conference. On Oct. 25, Gen. William C. Westmoreland, commander of U.S. troops in South Viet Nam, told the Manila Conference that additional troops would be needed in Viet Nam to meet the "increase in the flow of invaders from the North." Seven nations were represented at the conference: Australia, New Zealand, the Philippines, South Korea, South Viet Nam, Thailand and the United States. President Johnson, representing the United States, told the conference: "The determination of all is that aggression must fail. Let the bullies of the world know that when they do attack their neighbors, the friends of their neighbors will be there to resist."

Manila Offer to North Viet Nam. On Oct. 25, the seven nations meeting at Manila offered North Viet Nam a timetable for mutual withdrawal of all foreign forces from Viet Nam. A joint communique, signed at the end of the conference, said that all infiltration into South Viet Nam would have to cease. Allied troops would be "withdrawn after close consultation, as the other side withdraws its forces to the North, ceases infiltration and the level of violence thus subsides." The allied forces would be pulled out "as soon as possible and not later than six months after the above conditions have been fulfilled."

On the following day, the North Vietnamese, Chinese Communist and Soviet governments all denounced the Manila meeting as a "war conference" and declared that the United States was preparing to escalate the conflict.

Subandrio Sentenced. On Oct. 25, Indonesia's former Foreign Minister Subandrio was sentenced to death on charges of subversion and complicity in the abortive Oct. 1,

1965 pro-Communist coup, which subsequently led to slaughter of an estimated 500,000 pro-Chinese Communists.

New Information on Red Guards. On Oct. 25, Anna Louise Strong, an 80-year-old American who was an honorary member of Communist China's Red Guards, acknowledged in her newsletter from Red China that a minority of the Red Guards had attacked Mao Tse-tung, but she said they had not endangered his position. Miss Strong, who lived in Peking and had been a longtime supporter of Chairman Mao, reported: "Mao himself has been criticized. In one middle school, somebody put up a poster flatly disagreeing with Mao's policies. The school's Cultural Revolution Committee felt they had to give the writer a large group of bodyguards against other outraged students. The top leaders came to explain that the right of a minority, however small and unpopular, to dissent must be protected."

Miss Strong reported also that Chinese Premier Chou En-lai was the Red Guard's official adviser and was credited with toning down some of the earlier extreme views. "Flowershops, goldfish, gay children's clothes, and walks in the park are no longer thought 'bourgeois'." A "conservative guess" as to the number of Red Guards in China would be 10 million.

LBJ in Viet Nam. On Oct. 26, President Johnson paid a surprise visit to Camranh Bay, a large and well-secured U.S. base in South Viet Nam. The visit, which was shrouded in secrecy, lasted two and one-half hours. The President told soldiers, many of whom had just returned from patrols, that they had "the respect, the support and the prayers of a grateful President and a grateful nation."

Ky Will Fight, Not Negotiate. On Oct. 26, South Vietnamese Premier Nguyen Cao Ky, arriving in Saigon from Camranh Bay, which he had visited along with President Johnson, told reporters that his government would neither negotiate with nor form a coalition government with the Communists. "We will fight to the end," Ky declared.

Chinese Act of Defiance in Moscow. On Oct. 26, 37 of the Chinese students ordered to leave the Soviet Union performed a last act of defiance. After arguing for hours with Soviet guards, the students, all of whom wore Red Guard arm bands, placed two wreaths outside the mausoleum housing the body of Lenin. The second wreath was intended for Stalin's grave, behind the mausoleum, but Soviet guards refused to let the students approach the area.

China Tests Atomic Missile. On Oct. 27, the *New China* news agency announced that Communist China on Oct. 26 had "successfully conducted over its own territory a guided missile-nuclear weapons test." The agency said the test demonstrated that "China's defense capabilities are advancing at even greater speed." The test was "another new important achievement scored by the Chinese people in further strengthening" the country's national defense.

"China's purpose in developing nuclear weapons," the news agency asserted, "is precisely to oppose the nuclear monopoly and nuclear blackmail by the United States and the Soviet Union acting in collusion." It added that China's tests of nuclear weapons and of the guided missile afforded "great encouragement to the heroic Vietnamese people,...who are waging a war of resistance against U.S. aggression, and to all the revolutionary peoples of the world who are now engaged in heroic struggles."

As early as the summer of 1965, U.S. scientists had predicted that it would be only a short time before the Chinese tested a missile. The range of the weapon was judged to be about 500 to 700 miles, which would make Japan, Formosa, the Philippines, Southeast Asia, India and Pakistan potential targets.

Targets of Red Guard. On Oct. 27, David Oancia of the Toronto *Globe and Mail* reported from Peking that Chinese Head of State Liu Shao-chi and the General Secretary of the Communist party, Teng Hsiao-ping, had been criticized in the latest posters circulated by the Red Guards. "Others again criticized," Oancia reported, "included Li Hsueh-feng, chief of the Communist party's Peking municipal committee, and his deputy, Wu Teh. They took over the Peking branch following the purge last June of Peng Chen and his colleagues and an associated drive to reform Peking University."

Support of Asia Policy in Congress. On Oct. 28, a *Congressional Quarterly* survey of Members of Congress showed that 313 Senators and Representatives, 58.5 percent of the membership, favored the basic course the United States was taking in Viet Nam. But 141 members, or 26.4 percent of the Senate and House, favored more decisive military action; 81 members, or 15.1 percent of the total, favored increased stress on peace talks.

De Gaulle Denounces U.S. Policy. On Oct. 28, French President Charles de Gaulle, in his semi-annual press conference, denounced U.S. Viet Nam policy. "We find it totally detestable that a small country should be bombed by a very big one," he said, "and we find it not less detestable that the soldiers of both sides should suffer losses."

LBJ in Thailand and Malaysia. On Oct. 28, President Johnson arrived in Bangkok, Thailand, from Manila, received a friendly, but subdued welcome, and conferred with Thai officials. The President confirmed U.S. plans for increased aid to combat Communist insurgency in northeastern Thailand. On the following day, Johnson flew to Kuala Lumpur, capital of Malaysia. His visit there was marred by the death of a Chinese youth, shot by police during a demonstration against U.S. policy in Viet Nam.

Ho on Conditions in North Viet Nam. On Oct. 30, the North Vietnamese press agency reported that Ho Chi Minh had told a French editor during an interview that American bombing of his country had caused "some losses," but that "we have adapted our economy to the present situation." The North Vietnamese president said rice production was up and that communications and transportation were still functioning. He asserted that President Johnson had deceived the American people with false optimism about the war. The North Vietnamese people, he said, were prepared to fight another 10 years.

Warning to Mao's Opponents. On Oct. 31, the *Manchester Guardian* reported that for the first time the Chinese Communist leadership had warned against any compromise with its internal opposition. The warning, printed in all Peking daily newspapers, was viewed by Western observers as an indication that the faction in China opposing Mao Tse-tung and Lin Piao had urged a compromise in the struggle for leadership. An article in a Peking magazine reportedly said: "The dog that has fallen should be beaten

and not allowed to rise again lest it should inflict mortal injuries on the real revolutionaries."

LBJ in Seoul. On Oct. 31, President Johnson arrived in Seoul, capital of South Korea, and received the largest and most exuberant welcome of his Asian trip. After conferring with South Korean officials, the President at a state banquet pledged continued U.S. aid and support for South Korea. On the following day, he flew to Alaska.

Brezhnev on China and Viet Nam. On Nov. 1, Soviet Communist Party Chairman Leonid Brezhnev said in a speech in Tbilisi, the Georgian capital, that Red China was blocking efforts to create a united Communist front against American "aggression" in Viet Nam. The Soviet leader failed to mention conditions for ending the war, causing speculation in some Western capitals that the Kremlin might be ready to modify its policy on Viet Nam.

Sabotage in China. On Nov. 1, *Reuters* reported that the Peking press for the first time had conceded the existence of a "hostile class enemy" capable of committing acts of sabotage throughout the country. The latest such act reported by the *New China* news agency occurred on Oct. 10. A soldier guarding a railroad bridge in East China's Chekiang Province shoved a log off the tracks just before a train carrying Red Guards passed over. The soldier was killed. The news agency blamed the incident on "an inveterately hostile class enemy opposed to the current great proletarian revolution." On the same day, David Oancia of the Toronto *Globe and Mail* reported from Peking: "The attention given the new hero in the press and broadcasts can only partly be explained as a desire to illustrate the necessity to strengthen security arrangements. This has resulted in armed patrols and troops being in evidence at points where they were never seen before the cultural revolution moved into the phase where Red Guard activities seized the attention of practically everyone." Oancia reported also that the Red Guard newspaper had admitted that "rival groups of Red Guards exist and that the differences between them no longer are trivial."

Peking Rally. On Nov. 2, Communist party Chairman Mao Tse-tung attended a mass rally in Peking's Square of Heavenly Peace following the return of 65 Chinese students from the Soviet Union. As usual, Defense Minister Lin Piao spoke on Mao's behalf.

LBJ's Return. On Nov. 2, President Johnson returned to Washington from his 17-day, 31,500-mile tour of Asian nations. Upon arrival at Dulles International Airport, the President told waiting crowds that he was "much more confident and hopeful" that peace would come to Asia.

Troop Strength in South Viet Nam. On Nov. 3, the U.S. Military Command in Saigon announced that U.S. troop strength in South Viet Nam had reached 345,000, not counting about 50,000 Navy men offshore in vessels of the Seventh Fleet.

Peking on Nuclear Test. On Nov. 3, the Peking *People's Daily* asserted that China's successful test of a nuclear-tipped missile dealt "a direct blow to the two nuclear overlords, the United States and the Soviet Union." The paper's editorial said the test sabotaged efforts by the United States and the Soviet Union to conclude a nuclear nonproliferation treaty. "The latest Chinese test was exactly a fatal blow to this scheme of these two mischievous partners...who are thinking of promulgating a law by which you, and only you and no others, may have (nuclear weapons). Now we want to answer you with the earth-shaking noise of a nuclear explosion. You have it, and we too, must have it."

Another Rally. On Nov. 3, two million Red Guards and soldiers packed Peking's Square of Heavenly Peace for the second rally in as many days. Party Chairman Mao Tse-tung was followed onto the reviewing balcony by China's new leaders, including Defense Minister Lin Piao, Premier Chou En-lai, Chen Po-ta, Tao Chu, and Chiang Ching (Mrs. Mao Tse-tung). Two more men who were reportedly leaders of the faction opposing Mao and Lin, Head of State Liu Shao-chi and Communist Party General Secretary Teng Hsiao-ping, appeared together a little later. In the only speech, Lin Piao said there could be no coexistence between "bourgeois reactionaries" and those who supported Mao's thought.

Pravda on Communist Split. On Nov. 4, the Soviet Communist Party newspaper, *Pravda*, said that Communist China "expected to engineer a split in the world Communist movement and to win some parties over to its side." The statement added: "These expectations have not and could not come true. The Communists of the world denounce and reject the dissentious line of the Chinese Communist leaders."

McNamara on Troops for Viet Nam. On Nov. 5, Secretary of Defense Robert S. McNamara told a news conference at the LBJ Ranch that the United States would continue to build up its military forces in South Viet Nam during 1967, but that the number of new troops committed would be "substantially less" than in 1966. Therefore, the Secretary said, draft calls were expected to be lower in 1967.

Red Guard Activity in Peking. On Nov. 6, David Oancia of the Toronto *Globe and Mail* reported from Peking that Red Guards had demonstrated outside the offices of the Peking branch of the Communist Party, demanding an audience with Li Hsueh-feng, head of the party's municipal committee, or his deputy, Wu Teh. Both men had been assigned by the party's Central Committee to purge the party's Peking branch of members opposing Mao Tse-tung. By the end of the day, the Red Guards had swarmed into the building.

At the same time, posters were circulated criticizing Tao Chu, new head of the Communist party's Propaganda Department and one of the directors of the Cultural Revolution. Trucks full of soldiers were placed outside the Propaganda Department's main offices in Peking. "The atmosphere was charged with a feeling of drama," Oancia reported, "but its precise nature could not be delineated last night. It may not be beyond the realm of possibility that the two developments are related and that a massive policy struggle involving Tao Chu's Propaganda Department and Li Hsueh-feng's Peking committee is under way. Li has been under persistent fire for more than a month on charges that he has betrayed the trust placed in him as Peng Chen's successor to follow the Maoist revolutionary line."

Walkouts in Moscow. On Nov. 6, Chang Teh-tsuen, acting head of Peking's embassy in Moscow, stormed out of a Kremlin rally during a speech in which Communist China was accused of aiding the American effort in Viet

Nam by splitting the Communist movement. The speech, by a member of the Soviet Politburo, also denounced U.S. policy in Viet Nam. "It is a pity," the Soviet official said, "that Chinese leaders are rejecting all proposals...for joint actions against imperialism, against aggression of the United States in Viet Nam. Behind a screen of ridiculous fabrications about a 'collusion' between the U.S.S.R. and the American imperialists, about the 'restoration' of capitalism in the Soviet Union, the Chinese leadership is developing a political struggle against our country and activity."

On the following day, Chang Teh-tsuen and his aides walked away from the diplomatic stand in Moscow's Red Square during festivities celebrating the 49th anniversary of the Bolshevik Revolution. Chang's exit came when Marshal Rodion Y. Malinovsky, Soviet Defense Minister, told the crowds: "We regret that the leaders of China oppose the unity of action by the socialist countries in support of the Vietnamese people. This hampers the cohesion of all progressive forces of the world in fighting off American aggression in Viet Nam and it encourages United States imperialism to commit new crimes."

U.S. Elections and the War. On Nov. 8, Republican candidates in the mid-term elections won three additional U.S. Senate seats and 47 additional House seats. The election results indicated continuance of broad support in Congress for President Johnson's Viet Nam policies. The voters, rather than electing opponents of the war, chose new Representatives who seemed more in favor of stepped-up military efforts in Viet Nam than were their predecessors.

Red Guard Demands. On Nov. 8, the Peking correspondent of the Toronto *Globe and Mail* reported that a thousand Red Guards had demonstrated outside the offices of Chinese Communist leaders in Peking demanding to see Premier Chou En-lai. Chou did not appear. On the walls surrounding the Central Committee's offices were numerous posters referring to Tao Chu, new head of the Propaganda Department, who had recently moved up from 95th to fourth place in the Communist party's hierarchy.

"The poster battle over Tao Chu could be of critical importance for the future of the Great Proletarian Cultural Revolution. Tao is one of the chief executors of the policy line enunciated by Mao and Lin (Piao), described now as Mao's closest comrade-in-arms. In quantity, there was about an even division in the posters attacking and defending him." The report continued: "Why the Red Guards demanded to see Chou was not precisely clear, but it seemed to be part of the increasingly evident pattern of growing defiance shown by members of the paramilitary youth organization. Recent State Council edicts have made plain the desire of the leaders to bring the Red Guard activities under greater control." The dispatch said the State Council had ordered the Red Guards to leave Peking as soon as possible and had asked for "greater coordination of the movements of youths around the country under army supervision."

Red Guard Logistics. On Nov. 8, Stanley Karnow of the *Washington Post* reported that the Red Guards were "causing havoc in China's inadequate transportation system." The Chinese leadership had therefore instructed the youth group to emulate the Long March of 1934-35 and travel by foot rather than rail. A Nov. 8 dispatch by the *New China* news agency reported that "thousands upon thousands" of the youths were marching throughout the country, spreading the thoughts of Chairman Mao. "In a recent statement," Karnow reported, "Chinese Premier Chou En-lai calculated that 30 percent of China's road and rail facilities have lately been devoted to moving the youths in and out of Peking for assorted rallies and other demonstrations. A clue to the magnitude of the movement is suggested by the official claim that a total of six million youngsters attended the five main rallies held in the Chinese capital between Aug. 18 and Nov. 3." After that, there were two more such rallies.

Defense Against Missiles. On Nov. 10, Secretary of Defense Robert S. McNamara told a news conference at the LBJ Ranch in Texas that the Soviet Union had developed an anti-ballistic-missile system and that he and President Johnson were conferring on whether the United States should do likewise. He said it was "much too early to make a decision" on deployment of an anti-missile system against Chinese missiles.

Soviet Troop Movements. On Nov. 10, the *Washington Post* reported that Communist sources in the United Nations had indicated that several divisions of Soviet troops had been switched from Eastern Europe to the Sino-Soviet border. As a result, the number of Soviet troops deployed in Asia was believed to exceed the number stationed in Eastern Europe.

Defector. On Nov. 10, the Chinese Nationalist government announced that the head of the editorial department of Hong Kong's Chinese Communist newspaper had defected to Taiwan after visiting many areas in Communist China and "seeing with my own eyes the disasters brought about by the Red Guards."

Talking to Hanoi. On Nov. 11, Ambassador W. Averell Harriman, after conferring with President Johnson in Texas, told newsmen that all the East European nations were "talking to Hanoi" in an attempt to bring an end to the Viet Nam war. Harriman said that the leaders he had seen on a recent trip all indicated that the "confusion in Peking reducing China's influence" had created a better atmosphere for approaching the North Vietnamese government.

China's Prestige. On Nov. 13, Max Frankel pointed out in an article in the *New York Times* on Communist China's prestige: "In just a year the upheavals inside China have changed its reputation from that of a formidable challenger of the United States throughout Asia and of the Soviet Union inside the Communist world to that of a hobbled giant riddled by dissent and thus incapable of sustained growth and self-assertion."

In a separate article, Frankel maintained that the split in the Chinese hierarchy was not yet resolved and that "the Chinese drama is far from over." He said: "The conflict runs so deep that it appears it cannot be resolved without further major changes of personalities and policies, a convulsion that is bound once again, as in the period of the Great Leap Forward eight years ago, to sacrifice economic progress to political controversy." The war in Viet Nam, Peking's relations with Moscow and general problems of national defense, Frankel noted, were among the issues being vehemently debated in China. "But the overriding pressures and preoccupations are domestic, related above all to the problem of governing China and, if anything, divert attention and energy from foreign affairs."

Proposal for World Communist Meeting. On Nov. 14, in the presence of Soviet Communist Party Chairman Leonid I. Brezhnev, Bulgaria's Premier and party leader, Todor Zhivkov, proposed a world conference of Communist parties to deal with the Chinese Communist "heresy." Zhivkov told a Bulgarian party congress in Sofia that "conditions are ripe" for holding the conference to "unmask and fight present-day dogmatism which in essence is a sign of nationalism and adventurism." In the next few days, it appeared as if the Soviet-Bulgarian plan to hold a conference would fail. The only Communist parties supporting the move were the Czechoslovakian and the French, along with a handful of other smaller parties.

Nuclear Non-Proliferation Treaty. On Nov. 15, an article in the Peking *People's Daily* declared that Communist China would never agree to a treaty banning the spread of nuclear weapons. The article said the proposed treaty had been "cooked up" by the United States and the Soviet Union in the United Nations and was "all part and parcel of the big collusion between the United States and the Soviet Union on a global scale." The treaty plan, the article said, meant that "nuclear weapons should be regarded as a thing to be monopolized by the two nuclear overlords, the United States and the Soviet Union, and that they and they alone should be allowed to possess such weapons, and not anyone else."

Red Guards Curbed. On Nov. 20, Victor Zorza of the *Manchester Guardian* reported that the Chinese government had told Red Guards to stop holding unofficial courts and using torture to obtain "confessions." The move was one of a number the Chinese government had made in the past few weeks in an effort to curb Red Guard excesses. A week earlier, the government had urged the militant youths to leave Peking and not to interfere with agricultural or industrial production.

Purge Hints. On Nov. 20, a correspondent of the Yugoslav news agency reported that posters in Peking were calling for a meeting to "finally unmask the bourgeois-reactionary line of Liu Shao-chi (head of state), Teng Hsiao-ping (general secretary of the Communist party), and Li Hseuh-feng (head of the Peking branch of the party)."

China and the UN. On Nov. 21, U.S. Ambassador to the UN Arthur J. Goldberg announced American support of an Italian draft resolution for a study of Chinese representation in the world organization. Goldberg emphasized that the U.S. had not changed its position that Nationalist China should remain in the UN. Many observers, however, professed to see some modification of the hitherto inflexible U.S. policy on the China question. Italy's resolution proposed creation of a special committee to explore Communist China's attitude on entry into the UN. Nationalist China's strong opposition to the resolution pointed up Taiwan's fear that a two-China policy might eventually emerge from the new move.

Sino-Soviet Border Tension. On Nov. 21, the *New York Times* reported from Washington that Soviet diplomats had openly discussed with American officials the growing concern of Moscow over a nuclear-armed Communist China. According to the *Times*, a U.S. official described recent talks between Secretary of State Dean Rusk and Soviet Foreign Minister Andrei A. Gromyko as the "most direct, honest, objective and non-ideological in several years." The official added, "Mr. Gromyko made clear that the break with China is quite fundamental and that Russia is now more interested than ever in settling other outstanding issues."

The Soviet Foreign Minister "was said to feel that none of the border disputes (with China) were worth a war, but that in a period of continuing ill-will between the two countries, there was always the danger that neither would be willing to back off from a small border clash and that such clashes could escalate and lead to a nuclear explosion." Reports of a large Soviet military buildup on the Sino-Soviet border continued.

Troop Needs in Viet Nam. On Nov. 21, the U.S. commander in Viet Nam, Gen. William C. Westmoreland, said in an interview with U.S. *News & World Report* that North Vietnamese were infiltrating South Viet Nam at the increased rate of 7,000 per month despite heavy U.S. bombing attacks. As for the future of the war, the General said "the initiative has swung to our side," but he added that "we will need more troops." Without mentioning how many, he said: "We must gear ourselves for the long pull. We must be prepared to field appropriate forces and sustain these forces as long as required. The enemy thinks in terms of protracted conflict. We must also think in terms of a protracted commitment."

Denial. On Nov. 22, the Texas White House and the State Department both vigorously denied reports that Soviet Foreign Minister Andrei Gromyko had confided in U.S. officials that Moscow was concerned about tension along the Sino-Soviet border.

French on China and the UN. On Nov. 22, the French representative to the United Nations told the General Assembly that France opposed the Italian resolution for study of Chinese representation in the UN and the two-China theory. Delegate Roger Seydoux said the Peking regime was clearly entitled to China's UN seat; all negotiations dealing with disarmament and other matters would have "a certain unreality" without Chinese Communist participation.

Red Guard Discord. On Nov. 22, *Reuters* reported that the Red Guard newspaper, *The East is Red*, had urged members of the youth group to "smash the headquarters of the Red Guards of the capital's colleges and universities who are 'royalists.' " In this case, the term "royalist" meant reactionary. The newspaper said that one of the units of the Peking faction of the Red Guards "took the side diametrically opposed to the proletarian revolutionary line represented by Chairman Mao Tse-tung, consciously or unconsciously implemented and maintained a reactionary line, and became stubborn obstacles to the Cultural Revolution."

Canada on China and the UN. On Nov. 23, Canadian External Affairs Minister Paul Martin told the UN General Assembly that Communist China should be seated in the Security Council and General Assembly, but that Nationalist China should remain seated in the General Assembly.

Liu Assailed. On Nov. 23, David Oancia of the Toronto *Globe and Mail* reported from Peking that a new series of Red Guard posters contained extremely strong attacks on Head of State Liu Shao-chi, 68, a man who had been Mao Tse-tung's heir apparent until early 1966. The posters disclosed that both Liu and his wife had been deprived of some of their party positions at the meeting of the Central Committee in August. The posters also attacked the party's General Secretary, Teng Hsiao-ping, as the number two conspirator behind Liu.

Extended Vacation for Red Guards. On Nov. 24, the Soviet news agency *Tass* reported that Chinese Premier Chou En-lai had informed students that "studies at educational establishments will not begin until at least the summer vacations next year." The schools had originally been scheduled to reopen in December 1966. The dispatch said the Red Guards had welcomed Chou's announcement by plastering the city with posters reading: "There are another ten months ahead of us for carrying on the Cultural Revolution."

Another Red Guard Rally. On Nov. 25, nearly two million Red Guards and soldiers jammed into Peking's Square of Heavenly Peace for another rally witnessed by Party Chairman Mao Tse-tung and his heir apparent Lin Piao. This one lasted two days. Also on the reviewing stand near Mao were Head of State Liu Shao-chi and the party's General Secretary, Teng Hsiao-ping, both of whom had recently been strongly attacked by the Red Guards. The *New China* news agency later announced that the rally would be the last until spring due to cold weather.

Soviet Attack on Mao. On Nov. 27, the Soviet Communist Party newspaper *Pravda* published its sharpest attack on Mao Tse-tung. An editorial urged that opponents in China of Mao Tse-tung's "erroneous course" take action against the aging leader. "The interests of unity of all revolutionary forces in the struggle against imperialism," it said, "demand that the nationalistic, anti-Soviet policy and the attempts to distort Marxism-Leninism and replace it by the ideology and practice of Mao Tse-tungism should be overcome." The editorial also denounced the "systematic brainwashing of China's population in an anti-Soviet spirit." Pointing to what *Pravda* considered hypocrisy, the editorial said: "Alleging that all contacts of the Soviet Union with the United States are a 'collusion' with imperialism, the Chinese leaders at the same time do not miss a chance to develop relations with capitalist countries, including the United States."

On the same day, the Hungarian Communist Party called on other parties to join the Soviet Union in the "common cause" against Communist China.

Soviet Denial of Border Tension. On Nov. 28, a statement by the Soviet Embassy in Washington said an article in the *New York Times* of Nov. 22 concerning tension on the Sino-Soviet border was "absolutely groundless." The statement asserted that the article "was evidently designed for the use by certain circles who are looking for any pretext to smear the Soviet Union and who are interested in worsening Soviet-Chinese relations."

Chinese Attack on Soviets. On Nov. 28, the Peking *People's Daily* assailed *Pravda's* attack on Mao the preceding day and called the Soviet leadership "a group of renegades" who would eventually be ousted. Repeating charges that the United States and the Soviet Union were acting in "collusion," the article described U.S. power as "nothing formidable." It said: "The more you are afraid of it, the fiercer it becomes. But if you are not afraid of it, dare to worry it, dare to provoke it, dare to stand up to it, dare to cross swords and battle with it, this clawing and snarling beast, United States imperialism, will be subdued and defeated."

UN Vote on China. On Nov. 29, the UN General Assembly defeated 46-57 an Albanian-sponsored resolution to assign China's seat in the UN to the Communists and expel the Nationalists; 17 members abstained. The vote was interpreted as an appreciable gain for U.S. policy, because the 1965 contest over Chinese representation had ended in a 47-47 tie vote with 20 abstentions. Many African and Asian delegations, reacting to what they called Red China's "aggressive" or "subversive" policies, abandoned their previous pro-Peking stand.

The Assembly also rejected, 34-62 with 25 abstentions, the Italian resolution for a study of the question of Chinese representation. Many observers thought such a study might lead to a recommendation that both Chinese governments be seated in the UN.

Viet Nam Truces. On Nov. 29, the South Vietnamese government announced that its forces and those of its allies would observe three separate truces: two of 48 hours each during Christmas and the solar New Year, and one of 96 hours in February.

Victory for Mao Claimed. On Nov. 29, the *New China* news agency reported that Chinese Communist Premier Chou En-lai declared at a reception in the Albanian Embassy that Mao Tse-tung's faction had won out in the "great proletarian revolution." The agency quoted Chou as saying: "The proletarian revolutionary line represented by Comrade Mao Tse-tung has triumphed and the bourgeois line of opposing revolution has been defeated. We must put politics in command, go among the masses and, together with them, do a better job of the Great Proletarian Cultural Revolution."

Brezhnev on Communist Meeting. On Nov. 29, Soviet party leader Leonid I. Brezhnev, addressing the ninth Congress of the Hungarian Communist Party, said Western press reports that the Soviet Union would attempt to banish Red China from the Communist movement during a proposed meeting of pro-Soviet parties were "utter nonsense."

"When Communists call for a new meeting," he said, "they have in mind a comradely discussion of urgent problems of international development to analyze jointly the great changes that have taken place in the world in the last six years and to elaborate a common line for the future. The question can be posed in no other way."

Lin Piao's Exclusive Position. On Nov. 30, the Peking *People's Daily* made clear in a front-page article that Lin Piao was now the only vice chairman of the Chinese Communist Party. Previously, four other men, in addition to Lin, had held the title: Liu Shao-chi, Chou En-lai, Chu Teh, and Chen Yun. All four had lost the title of vice chairman, and Chou alone remained in listings of the party hierarchy, where he continued to hold third place.

Sino-Soviet Border. On Dec. 1, Henry S. Bradsher of the *Associated Press* reported from Moscow that the Soviet people were being told in semi-public meetings that "China has been trying to occupy some Soviet frontier territory and has staged border provocations." The dispatch added that "While opinion against China is being stoked by revelations of border trouble and allegations of secret Chinese agree-

ments with the West, Viet Nam is being played down, especially in the press."

The *AP* report said that speakers at the semi-public meetings "say Chinese forces — it is not clear whether they were troops or organized civilians — have crossed the Soviet border and tried to build installations." The audiences are told that "Soviet troops have surrounded and forced the Chinese back across the border but no mention of bloodshed was heard and no date or location was specified." The report said the speakers "accuse China of having a secret agreement with the United States: If the Soviet Union and China get into war, the United States agrees not to help Moscow."

Kosygin in Paris. On Dec. 1, Soviet Premier Aleksei Kosygin arrived in Paris for talks with French President Charles de Gaulle. At the airport the Russian leader said: "The period characterized by a certain emptiness in Franco-Soviet relations, whatever its origins may have been, belongs to the past."

U Thant to Stay. On Dec. 1, U Thant announced he would stay on for another five-year term as Secretary General of the United Nations.

Chinese Primary Schools to Reopen. On Dec. 2, reports from Peking indicated that the Chinese Communist Party's Central Committee had ordered the country's primary schools to reopen. They had been closed for seven months. Primary schools include children from the ages of six to 12. It was reported that secondary schools, colleges and universities would remain closed.

Red Guards Ordered Home. On Dec. 3, the Chinese Communist Party's Central Committee ordered Red Guards remaining in Peking and other cities to return home. The order said the army would be responsible for seeing that the Guards left the cities by the appointed times.

Red Guard Violence. On Dec. 3, the Soviet news agency *Tass* reported that hundreds of people had been injured and several killed in China during recent fights between Red Guards and workers. The news agency said the most recent such disorders had taken place in Shanghai, where workers had rioted against the militant youth group after the Guards had tortured a local party official.

Macao Riot. On Dec. 3, a mob of pro-Communist Chinese stormed through the Portuguese enclave of Macao on the south China coast, beating officials and police and sacking the city hall.

V.C. Attacks in Saigon. On Dec. 4, a Viet Cong unit mounted a mortar attack on Tansonnhut Air Base near Saigon, and another blew up an American billet in the downtown area. On the same day, the U.S. Military Command announced that eight planes and 13 airmen had been lost over North Viet Nam two days earlier. On Dec. 5, the Viet Cong attempted another attack at Tansonnhut but were repelled by U.S. sentries.

Thant's Peace Efforts. On Dec. 4, UN Secretary General U Thant said in an interview in *Newsweek* that the United States thwarted his efforts to bring about peace talks between Washington and Hanoi three times between late 1964 and early 1965. Thant told columnist Emmet John Hughes that U.S. officials remained silent about the first peace probe, rejected the second because they thought Hanoi was insincere, and rejected the third on the ground that such talks would weaken the South Vietnamese government.

Travel Restrictions. On Dec. 4, the *New York Times* reported that the State Department was considering lowering existing travel barriers to five Communist countries: Communist China, Albania, North Korea, North Viet Nam and Cuba. "While no final decision has been made," the dispatch said, "it appears likely that the prohibition will be lifted on travel to Communist China and Albania. Less certain is whether the ban on travel to North Viet Nam, North Korea and Cuba will be removed." The article continued: "In the last year, the restrictions have been progressively modified for certain categories of people to the point where a denial of a request to travel to the five Communist countries is now more an exception than the rule."

More Fulbright Hearings. On Dec. 4, Sen. J. William Fulbright (D Ark.), chairman of the Senate Foreign Relations Committee, announced that his committee would hold hearings early in the first session of the 90th Congress on worldwide U.S. policies, including conduct of the Viet Nam war. Fulbright said officials would be asked for information on developments in Communist China.

Mrs. Mao's Ascent. On Dec. 4, the Peking radio reported that Mao Tse-tung's wife, Chiang Ching, had demanded that all those opposing her husband be "wiped out once and for all." The broadcast said Miss Chiang had been appointed as a consultant to the General Political Department of the Chinese army. She was reported to have strongly criticized the Peking branch of the Communist party for being "as rotten as ever." The Peking branch had been one of the first targets of the Cultural Revolution in June when its secretary, Mayor Peng Chen, was relieved of his post.

Chiang Ching was quoted as saying: "The old Peking municipal party committee was collaborating with reactionary powerholders . . . . The new Peking municipal committee is also resisting revolution. It is the same old stuff as the old committee. They are reactionary, two-faced; they insult Chairman Mao. They must be wiped out once and for all. For if we do not wipe them out, how can we carry on the revolution?"

Macao Riots. On Dec. 5, reports from Macao said Chinese Communist gunboats had appeared off shore following rioting by pro-Communist Chinese that resulted in seven deaths, hundreds of injuries and mass looting. On Dec. 6, the *New China* news agency commented: "The intensification of the brutality, as shown in the latest incidents, indicated that the Portuguese authorities have the effrontery of placing themselves in a position of hostility to all Chinese compatriots in Macao."

Air Attack on Rail Yard. On Dec. 6, U.S. fighter-bombers attacked a railroad yard on a line connecting North Viet Nam with Communist China. The attack was interpreted by some observers as an escalation of the air war against North Viet Nam.

Soviet Training on China Border. On Dec. 6, the *New York Times* reported from Moscow that the Soviet Union had launched a campaign to "rally patriotic sentiment and to sharpen military preparedness among the peoples of the Soviet Union's three central Asian republics that border

on China." The report said "military-patriotic schools" had been organized in those areas to prepare high school students "to become artillerymen, tank crewmen, radio operators and border guards."

More War Funds. On Dec. 6, President Johnson disclosed in Austin, Texas, he would ask Congress to appropriate $9 billion to $10 billion more to pay for the war in Viet Nam during fiscal 1967. The supplemental appropriation, Johnson noted at a news conference, would bring the defense total for fiscal 1967 to $67 billion or $68 billion, the biggest defense budget since the $79.8 billion of 1945.

Call for Trial of Anti-Mao Men. On Dec. 6, it was reported from Peking that posters demanded the arrest and trial of persons opposing Communist party Chairman Mao Tse-tung. The Toronto *Globe and Mail* correspondent wrote that men like Peng Chen, former head of Peking's party committee, "Lu Ting-yi, the former propaganda chief; Lo Jui-ching, once the army's chief of staff, and top officials in the Ministry of Culture apparently are to be brought to trial."

French Communists on China. On Dec. 6, the French Communist Party's newspaper, *L'Humanite*, published a front-page editorial supporting Soviet attacks on the Chinese Communist Party. The editorial described the Cultural Revolution as an "antiparty operation" directed against "many organizations" within the party.

Kosygin on U.S. and Viet Nam. On Dec. 6, Soviet Premier Aleksei N. Kosygin, visiting France, told reporters in Lyons that he saw a "community of interests" between the United States and the Soviet Union," but he added: "The United States is bombing defenseless people in Viet Nam. We don't see any indication of the way the United States is going to end the war. If it were ended, relations would improve. . . .We want a better understanding with the United States."

Peng Chen Arrested. On Dec. 7, the Yugoslav news agency, *Tanjug*, reported that Peng Chen former mayor of Peking, had been taken into custody. According to the dispatch, the Red Guards announced over loud speakers: "Peng Chen was arrested three days ago, and upon first meeting Red Guards he proved to be a paper tiger."

Timetable for China's Missiles. On Dec. 7, a study published by the Western European Union Assembly's Committee on Defense Questions and Armaments predicted that Communist China would explode an H-bomb by 1968 and have missiles capable of carrying such weapons 1,500 miles by 1970. According to the study, China would "very probably" have intercontinental ballistic missiles, capable of hitting targets anywhere in Europe, the Soviet Union, or the United States, by 1975 to 1980. On the same day, Secretary of State Dean Rusk, upon arriving in Taipei, Taiwan, said it would be a matter of years before Communist China would pose a real nuclear threat.

Panel on China Policy. On Dec. 7, the State Department announced appointment of a 10-member civilian panel to help "stimulate ideas" on U.S. policy toward Communist China. The panel included several Sinologists who had criticized U.S. policy during the Senate Foreign Relations Committee hearings on China in March 1966.

Space Treaty. On Dec. 8, President Johnson announced at a news conference in Texas that the United States and the

Soviet Union had agreed on terms of a UN-sponsored treaty to bar the orbiting of weapons of mass destruction or their installation on celestial bodies. The president said the treaty was "the most important arms control development since the limited test-ban treaty of 1963." The treaty will come to force upon ratification by the United States, the Soviet Union, Great Britain, and at least two other countries.

Resistance to Red Guards. On Dec. 8, the Soviet news agency *Tass* reported that at least 31 people had been killed and 380 injured in clashes between Red Guards and residents of Wusih (eastern China), Shanghai and Chungking.

Opinions of Chen Yi. On Dec. 10, the *Associated Press* carried an interview with Chinese Foreign Minister Chen Yi by a Brazilian lawyer who had defended nine Chinese Communists accused of spying in Brazil. In the interview, Chen Yi was quoted as saying: "The Soviets have 13 divisions on the Chinese frontier, moved there from Eastern Europe. We do not fear a Soviet-American attack. The Chinese people are prepared for the war and confident of final victory.... The Soviet Union plots world domination with the United States. Politically, the Soviets and North Americans are already united. The Red Guard is attacked in the same terms in the *New York Times* and *Pravda*, often with the same lying adjectives. It is impossible to deny the abundant evidence which proves the anti-Chinese union between the United States and the U.S.S.R."

Chen said of the Red Guards: "The Western press cut the official name of the organization which brings together the young revolutionaries. It is called the Guard of Red Defense and has as its mission the study and propagation of the thinking of Mao Tse-tung, through the elimination of some leadership groups which are not identified with the reality of the Chinese Communist movement and who follow the path of capitalism."

The Chinese Foreign Minister said that Viet Nam was a good example of the U.S. military failure "since 300,000 super-equipped men with the support of powerful land, sea and air forces have failed to defeat the guerrillas of a poor country." He accused the Soviets of wanting "to sell peace negotiations because they know that the Vietnamese and Chinese are united side by side against the imperialists, who will join forces to halt the march of nations toward communism."

Chen was pessimistic about U.S.-Chinese relations. "In the last ten years," he said, "we have had ambassadorial-level meetings with the United States which could have brought forth a Chinese-North American agreement. But invariably the representatives of Washington reject the precepts of peaceful coexistence and refuse to withdraw their forces from Formosa and the Strait of Taiwan . . . . We must first resolve the most important problem, Taiwan. And then, at the opportune moment, we will claim Macao and Hong Kong, today referred to by the Red Guards as the vacationland of the imperialists."

China on Kosygin's Aims in France. On Dec. 12, the *New China* news agency commented on Soviet Premier Aleksei N. Kosygin's trip to France: "While working strenuously for Soviet-U.S. collusion, the Soviet revisionist leading clique has been continuing to develop its relations with France so as to bring about relaxation in Europe, coordinate with the United States in the transfer of the emphasis of its

strategy to the East, and join hands with the United States to oppose China. At the same time, the Soviet Union has further tried to gain French assistance in pushing its 'peace talks' fraud in Viet Nam."

Mao's Campaign Against Opponents. On Dec. 12, a Washington dispatch to the *New York Times* reported that analysts believed that Communist Party Chairman Mao Tse-tung was beginning a new stage of his campaign to rid the party of his opponents. The new stage seemed to include arrest and trial of his opponents, such as Peng Chen, former mayor of Peking, who was reported to have been arrested Dec. 7. "The first stage came last August at the plenary meeting of the party's Central Committee, which laid down a 16-point declaration on the conduct of the Cultural Revolution. A week later, the new hierarchy was announced, disclosing Mr. Lin (Piao) as China's second-ranking leader and downgrading such traditional figures as the chief of state, Liu Shao-chi and Teng Hsiao-ping, the party's secretary general. When this did not prove sufficient to quell the opposition, Mr. Mao turned to the Red Guard movement as an instrument of control. But analysts . . . . believe it got out of hand without achieving decisive results."

Lin Piao's Secret Speech. On Dec. 13, Robert S. Elegant of the *Los Angeles Times* reported from Hong Kong that a speech by Defense Minister Lin Piao at the August 1966 meeting of the Chinese Communist Party Central Committee contained the original order for a purge of the party apparatus. Recent publication of the speech in Red Guard leaflets disclosed that Lin had ordered "a general examination, a general alignment and a general reorganization" of the party's structure. The Defense Minister said he spoke with the consent of Chairman Mao Tse-tung, who was present but did not speak. Lin added that those who opposed the conditions of the purge would be dismissed from their posts. "On the present occasion, we are going to dismiss a number of people, promote a number of people, and . . . . there will be a general reorganization."

Another correspondent, R. H. Shackford of *Scripps-Howard,* had reported a week earlier that there were signs that Lin Piao was falling out of favor with Mao. "After weeks of dominating the public scene along with Mao," Shackford reported, "Lin Piao is seen and heard from less and less. Latest reports from Peking say wall posters now are cautiously critical of the man whom Mao was believed to have selected as his heir." The dispatch noted: "This coincides with intensification of a campaign to 'get' Mao's former heir presumptive, President Liu Shao-chi, and with the sudden public prominence of Madame Mao, the former Shanghai actress who now is known as Comrade Chiang Ching." Shackford wrote that Chinese propaganda had given special prominence to Madame Mao's Nov. 28 speech to a Peking rally, in which she mentioned Lin Piao only once. "Madame Mao admitted great mistakes in the Cultural Revolution, told how the Red Guards (Lin Piao's creation) got out of hand, and even conceded Mao was in a 'minority.' "

Shackford concluded: "Some analysts think Lin Piao is in trouble not because he violated old Maoist precepts but because, after six months of running the Cultural Revolution and the Red Guard movement, Lin Piao has failed to 'get' the men who presumably led the opposition to Mao -- Liu Shao-chi and Teng Tsiao-ping. What's baffling is that these two formerly powerful men still remain unpurged, although they no longer are listed as members of the all-powerful seven-man standing committee of the Politburo. But both men now are being criticized by name whereas formerly much of the criticism was by innuendo. Now it is clear that when Madame Mao and Lin Piao talk about 'those in authority who are taking the capitalist road' they mean Liu and Teng."

Soviet Statement on China. On Dec. 13, the Soviet Communist Party's Central Committee, after a two-day meeting, issued a statement asserting that the "anti-Soviet policy of Mao Tse-tung and his group has entered a new, dangerous stage." The statement also said that "favorable conditions are now being created for a new international conference" on the China problem. On the same day, the *New York Times* reported that the Soviet Union "appears to be overcoming the reluctance" of some Communist parties and outright opposition of others to take part in a world meeting "by emphasizing that the meeting would be aimed at strengthening Communist unity, not at isolating the Chinese from the world movement."

Workers in the Red Guards. On Dec. 13, David Oancia of the Toronto *Globe and Mail* reported from Peking an editorial in the official newspaper of the Chinese Communist Party's Central Committee had said that "broad masses" of workers were joining the Red Guards. The editorial, written by Chen Po-ta, leader of the Cultural Revolution, denounced those who claimed to be revolutionary, yet who actually "enjoy being officials and lords, forgetting about the revolutionary past," and who "made use of the prestige of Chairman Mao and the party to mobilize groups of masses to protect themselves." On the same day, the Soviet news agency *Tass* and the Yugoslav news agency *Tanjug* reported from Peking that separate groups of Red Guards had been fighting each other in the capital's streets, each accusing the other of being "fascist."

Attacks on Hanoi. On Dec. 13, the Communist press charged that American fighter-bombers had attacked residential sections of Hanoi for the first time in the air war. U.S. officials in Saigon immediately denied the charge, insisting that U.S. planes bombed only military targets. The Soviet news agency *Tass* said: "Scores of buildings were destroyed in the fire that ensued. Smoke from the fires is hanging over the city. Scores of ambulances are taking the wounded to hospitals and first aid centers. It is the first time in the two years of the undeclared air war that American planes bombed residential areas within the Hanoi city limits."

On Dec. 14, the Hanoi radio charged that American planes had bombed the city for the second day, causing more than 100 casualties and severe damage to buildings in the residential and foreign diplomatic areas of the city. The report said also that eight American planes had been shot down. A U.S. military spokesman in Saigon said he could not "deny or confirm" the charge. "We have nothing to indicate that this indeed did occur," he said, adding that a bombing error was unlikely because the planned targets were long distances from where the North Vietnamese asserted the bombs had fallen. On the same day, the Peking *People's Daily* called the incident another "crazy escalation" of the war.

Truce in Viet Nam. On Dec. 14, the Viet Cong radio reported that the National Liberation Front had rejected a suggestion that the Christmas and New Year's truces in Viet Nam be extended through the Vietnamese new year in February.

Liu and Teng Assailed. On Dec. 14, the Japanese newspaper *Asahi* reported from Peking that Tao Chu, head of the Propaganda Department and fourth-ranking member of the Communist hierarchy, had denounced Head of State Liu Shao-chi and the party's General Secretary, Teng Hsiao-ping, in a Peking speech. It was the first time the two men had publicly mentioned a Communist party official. Previous attacks on Liu and Teng had been confined to the press and Red Guard posters. According to the Japanese report, Tao charged that Liu and Teng had associated themselves with Soviet "reactionary bourgeois thought" and were in conflict with the thought of Chairman Mao Tse-tung.

Soviet Defense Spending Raised. On Dec. 15, the Soviet Union announced it would increase its defense spending in 1967 by 8.2 percent due to "aggressive" U.S. policies, especially in Viet Nam. On the same day, *United Press International* reported that U.S. officials had indicated "that Russia's increased military budget undoubtedly reflected concern over the situation" along the Sino-Soviet border. Both China and the Soviet Union, the report said, had heavily reinforced the border area "where China still claims 600,000 square miles of Soviet territory."

U.S. Denial of Hanoi Bombing. On Dec. 15, American officials in Washington and Saigon emphatically denied North Vietnamese charges that U.S. planes had bombed residential areas within Hanoi's city limits, but they admitted there could have been some destruction in areas outside the city. The officials said it was possible that explosions in Hanoi had been caused by falling Soviet SAM anti-aircraft missiles intended for American planes.

Thant's Warning on Bombing. On Dec. 15, UN Secretary General U Thant issued a statement deploring "the loss of lives and the worsening of the situation resulting from the intensification of the bombing of North Viet Nam." The statement warned "that if this trend were allowed to continue, it might lead to a wider war with dangerous consequences."

Anti-Peng Rally. On Dec. 15, *Reuters* reported from Peking that Red Guard newspapers confirmed that the former mayor of Peking, Peng Chen, had been presented at a Red Guard rally in a Peking stadium Dec. 15 as a leader of the "revisionist clique" in China. Others named as revisionists, but evidently not presented to the crowd, were Lu Ting-yi, former Minister of Culture and head of the Propaganda Department, and Lo Jui-ching, former army chief of staff.

Charges of Damage in Hanoi. On Dec. 16, Communist China charged that American planes had seriously damaged Peking's embassy in Hanoi on Dec. 14. The Rumanian Embassy and offices of the *New China* news agency in Hanoi also were said to have been damaged by U.S. fighter-bombers. A Chinese statement warned the United States that it would "certainly receive redoubled punishment for your crime." A State Department spokesman replied: "The Department of Defense has informed us that there is no basis for allegations that U.S. ordnance fell on the city of Hanoi."

Soviet Newsmen Expelled. On Dec. 16, the *New China* news agency reported that Peking had ordered three of the six Soviet journalists in China to leave the country by Christmas. The dispatch said the action was "in accordance with the principle of reciprocity," for the Chinese had only three correspondents in Moscow. But the news agency added that the Soviet reporters had "done all they could to spread rumors and slanders about China's Great Proletarian Cultural

Revolution," providing "U.S.-led imperialism with a good deal of material for its anti-China propaganda."

China Assails Thant and Pope. On Dec. 16, the Peking radio assailed Secretary General U Thant of the United Nations and Pope Paul VI as "reactionaries" who were attempting to "cajole the Vietnamese people into capitulation." The broadcast said the "bombing of Hanoi shows forcefully that 'peace' for U.S. imperialism means the surrender of the Vietnamese people."

Embassy Evidence in Hanoi. On Dec. 17, the North Vietnamese news agency reported that Peking's ambassador to Hanoi, Chu Chi-wen, had escorted journalists around the Chinese embassy in Hanoi to show them evidence of American air raids. The news agency described the damage: "Part of the tile roof was demolished, window panes shattered, water pipes and walls riddled by missile splinters." The report said also that newsmen were shown parts of the American air-to-ground missiles which hit the embassy.

U.S.-Chinese Trade. On Dec. 17, Dennis Bloodworth of the *London Observer* reported from Singapore that Communist China had sold "several thousand tons of steel" for use in construction of U.S. military bases in South Viet Nam. Bloodworth reported that about $1 million worth of round and flat steel bars were purchased in Singapore and transshipped to Saigon in early 1966, "when only Peking could plug a crucial gap in American supplies by meeting the specifications, the quantities and the six-week delivery date that would satisfy hard-pressed U.S. military purchasing officers." The Chinese Communists, the report said, were paid for the steel through banks in Hong Kong.

Bloodworth added that disclosure of the steel purchases had "provoked suspicions that cement manufactured in Haiphong, the main port of North Viet Nam, may also have been reaching Air Force construction sites in South Viet Nam." The report said large deliveries of cement had been arriving in Singapore from Haiphong during the past year, "coinciding with bulk sales of cement from Singapore to Saigon." Bloodworth concluded that "Hong Kong constitutes the vital junction at which East and West touch, and the leakage of the Chinese steel story follows accusations published in *Izvestia* last month that the Chinese Communists were trading with their arch-enemies on a grand scale through the British Crown Colony while denouncing Moscow for alleged collusion with Washington."

Javits Quits Committee. On Dec. 17, Sen. Jacob K. Javits (R N.Y.) announced he had withdrawn from the Committee of One Million Against the Admission of Communist China into the United Nations. In a letter to the Committee's secretary, Marvin Liebman, Sen. Javits said: "I deeply believe that I must now, in any case, withdraw from membership in the interest of my duty as United States Senator to retain freedom of action regarding Communist China." On the same day, Liebman sent memorandums to all Congressional members of the Committee stating that the Committee would no longer use their names on letterheads and other publications.

Chinese Editorial. On Dec. 17, a *New York Times* dispatch from Hong Kong reported that *Hung Chi*, the Chinese Communist Party's ideological journal, had published an editorial indicating that Mao Tse-tung and Defense Minister Lin Piao felt it might be "impossible to control the regular party organization without continuing

help from such mass organizations as the youthful Red Guards." The editorial compared the "handful of people within the party who are in authority and are taking the capitalist road" to "time bombs planted within our party." It said that "once the conditions were ripe, they would explode and start a coup d'etat of the Khrushchev type."

Mao Drive Against Foes. On Dec. 18, Stanley Karnow of the *Washington Post* asserted in a dispatch from Hong Kong that China's political crisis seemed to be "entering a fresh phase" in which Chairman Mao Tse-tung and Marshal Lin Piao were launching a "last-ditch drive . . . to rout their foes inside the entrenched Chinese Communist Party organization." Karnow observed that as Mao and Lin launched their new effort, the Red Guards had "returned to violent tactics, reportedly clashing with party loyalists in the provinces and forcing dismissed party figures in Peking to face public humiliation." But he added that Mao's faction had lost strength among provincial party leaders who had successfully defended themselves against the Red Guard movement, which seemed to have lost some of its enthusiasm. "More important," the dispatch added, "party operatives opposed to Mao made inroads among them (the Red Guards). Using Mao's own writings, which are ambiguous, they were able to confuse the teen-agers' loyalties and split their ranks, with the result that China has lately presented a spectacle of charges and counter-charges flying in all directions."

U.S. Asks Thant's Aid on Cease-Fire. On Dec. 19, the United States asked UN Secretary General U Thant to take "whatever steps" he considered necessary to bring about talks for a cease-fire in Viet Nam. U.S. Ambassador to the United Nations Arthur J. Goldberg in a letter to Thant assured him that "the United States will cooperate fully with you in getting such discussions started promptly and in bringing them to a successful conclusion."

China's Army Warned. On Dec. 19, the *New China* news agency reported that the Chinese army had been warned by its newspaper, *Liberation Daily*, to prepare for surprise attacks by the United States and the Soviet Union.

Steel Sales by China. On Dec. 20, a *New York Times* dispatch from Singapore stated that some of the iron and steel brought into that port from Red China was being "sold quietly to South Viet Nam for American use." The dispatch added: "There is no official confirmation of such sales, but they are reported to be considerable. Major importers and distributors here would neither confirm nor deny such sales. However, they confirmed reports that Chinese iron and steel were being re-exported from Singapore through agents with overseas connections. Privately, some of them confirm the sales to Viet Nam. No one is willing to confirm such sales openly because they are illegal and there is an embargo on strategic goods that would help the American war effort in Viet Nam."

On the same day, it was reported from London that Chinese Communist diplomats there had denied the stories, referring to them as "absolute slander."

Mao's Minority On Dec. 20, a Washington dispatch to the *New York Times* reported increasing evidence that the "hard-line faction of Chairman Mao Tse-tung is in the minority at the upper levels of the Chinese Communist Party." The dispatch noted that a number of Sinologists regarded that possibility as "the most likely explanation for the duration and intensity of the power struggle in Peking."

New Posters. On Dec. 21, *Reuters* reported from Peking that new posters there called for dismissal of Chief of State Liu Shao-chi and Party General Secretary Teng Hsiao-ping. *Reuters* reported from Moscow that the Soviet press was stepping up its charges that Communist China was colluding with Washington on the Viet Nam war.

Chinese Advice. On Dec. 20, the Peking *People's Daily* published an editorial urging North Viet Nam and the National Liberation Front (Viet Cong) to fight the war in Viet Nam to the end and avoid all negotiations with the United States. The editorial said: "To realize the complete liberation and unification of their fatherland and defend the fruits of their victory, it is necessary for the Vietnamese people to carry through to the end the struggle against U.S. aggression and for national salvation and, without a single exception, to drive all of the U.S. aggressors out of their national soil."

Chinese Steel. On Dec. 21, the U.S. Embassy in Singapore said it was "skeptical" of reports that the United States had been buying steel from Communist China for use in Viet Nam. According to *United Press International:* "Trade figures showed that during the first six months of 1966, Singapore imported some $700,000 worth of steel bars from Communist China. During the same period, Singapore exported about $600,000 worth of steel bars to South Viet Nam." The *UPI* report added that "A leading manufacturer estimated that his mill alone had shipped some 5,000 tons of steel worth $500,000 to Saigon since January."

Chou on the Purge. On Dec. 21, the *New China* news agency reported that Chinese Premier Chou En-lai had told a Peking military rally that the "people in authority" who opposed the leadership of Chairman Mao Tse-tung "will never accept defeat and will always struggle desperately." Chou urged the Red Guards and other Maoists to "catch hold of and overthrow the counter-revolutionaries." Although the Premier claimed that the purge of anti-Maoists was "forging ahead vigorously," he admitted that "it has not been smooth sailing."

North Korean Pilots in Hanoi. On Dec. 21, the *Washington Post* reported that U.S. officials had confirmed reports that "25 to 40 North Korean airmen" had been assigned to fly aircraft for North Viet Nam. This report concurred with another that the Soviet Union was sending North Viet Nam an additional 100 MIG Jet Fighters.

Chinese Nuclear Rockets. On Dec. 21, a Japanese newspaper reported that Japanese businessmen well acquainted with developments in Communist China had predicted that the Chinese would test a series of nuclear-tipped rockets during 1967, one of them fired from a nuclear-powered submarine. French businessmen in China substantiated the report that Communist China was developing the submarine.

Wheat to India. On Dec. 22, the United States announced a long-delayed decision to make emergency food shipments to India. The Soviet Union, Canada, and Australia were committed to ship 600,000 tons of grain. The U.S. shipments would total 900,000 tons.

North Viet Nam to Fight On. On Dec. 22, the North Vietnamese news agency reported that Vo Nguyen Giap, North Vietnamese defense chief, had said North Viet Nam would keep fighting "no matter how many more troops the U.S. aggressors may bring" to Viet Nam.

Rumored Suicides. On Dec. 22, a Japanese correspondent in Peking reported rumors that three victims of the Cultural Revolution had committed suicide. The three were: Lo Jui-ching, former army chief of staff; Yang Shang-kun, alternate member of the Secretariat of the party's Central Committee; and Lu Ting-yi, former Minister of Culture and head of the Central Committee's Propaganda Bureau. On the following day, a spokesman for the Chinese Foreign Ministry said: "The press and news agencies of capitalist countries have usually spread all sorts of foul rumors. It is entirely unnecessary for us to confirm them." On the same day, *Tanjug*, the Yugoslav news agency, reported that Lo Jui-ching had been arrested.

Holiday Truce. On Dec. 24, a 48-hour holiday truce went into effect in Viet Nam but was marred in the early hours by sporadic fighting.

Reports from Hanoi. On Dec. 24, Harrison E. Salisbury, an assistant managing editor of the *New York Times*, reported on damage caused in Hanoi by American air strikes. Salisbury had entered North Viet Nam aboard an aircraft operated by the International Control Commission on Viet Nam.

The veteran newsman wrote: "Christmas Eve found residents in several parts of Hanoi still picking over the wreckage of homes said to have been damaged in the United States raids of Dec. 13 and 14. United States officials have contended that no attacks in built-up or residential Hanoi have been authorized or carried out. They have also suggested that Hanoi residential damage in the two raids could have been caused by defensive surface-to-air missiles that misfired or fell short." Salisbury added: "This correspondent is no ballistics specialist, but inspection of several damaged sites and talks with witnesses make it clear that Hanoi residents certainly believe they were bombed by United States planes, that they certainly observed United States planes overhead, and that damage certainly occurred right in the center of town."

The *Times* correspondent described damage in certain residential areas of Hanoi and concluded: "Contrary to the impression given by United States communiques, on-the-spot inspection indicates that American bombing has been inflicting considerable civilian casualties in Hanoi and its environs for some time past....It is the reality of such casualties and such apparent by-products of the United States bombing policy that lend an atmosphere of grimness and foreboding to Hanoi's Christmas cease-fire. It is fair to say that based on evidence of their own eyes, Hanoi residents do not find much credibility in United States bombing communiques."

Wheat to Pakistan. On Dec. 24, the Pakistani government announced that Communist China was sending 100,000 tons of wheat and 50,000 tons of rice to Pakistan. The United States had previously announced it would send 500,000 tons of wheat to Pakistan.

Chinese Christmas. On Dec. 25, according to *Reuters*, for the first time in many years, no services were held in any of China's churches, all of which had been closed by the Red Guards in August.

Truce Ends. On Dec. 26, the holiday truce ended. An hour later, American heavy bombers struck 28 miles from Saigon.

Mao's Birthday. On Dec. 26, despite pleas from Red Guards for mass demonstrations, Chairman Mao Tse-tung's 73rd birthday was officially ignored. According to *Reuters*, the Chinese leader "apparently decided to keep to the tradition of never officially marking the birthday of Communist Chinese leaders." Peking newspapers published their usual commentaries on the party Chairman's thoughts but made no mention of his age. A full-page article in the Peking *People's Daily* was headed "Chairman Mao is the red sun in the hearts of revolutionary people throughout the world."

Liu's "Confession." On Dec. 26, reports from Peking indicated that Chinese Head of State Liu Shao-chi had "confessed" to taking an erroneous course. Red Guard newspapers and posters published the text of the confession, which was described as insincere and superficial. Liu, considered one of the leaders of the faction opposing Chairman Mao Tse-tung, had been the target of repeated Red Guard demands that he be dismissed. Official party publications were silent about Liu's statement. However, the Yugoslav news agency *Tanjug*, reported that Liu and General Secretary Teng Hsiao-ping were facing arrest soon. The report said that both men "do not have much time left in liberty."

Raid Damage at Namdinh. On Dec. 26, Harrison Salisbury of the *New York Times* reported from Namdinh, third largest city of North Viet Nam, that American reconnaissance planes had flown over the city while he was there. Describing damage done by earlier bombing, he said: "The cathedral tower looks out on block after block of utter desolation; the city's population of 90,000 has been reduced to less than 20,000 because of evacuation; 13 percent of the city's housing, including the homes of 12,464 people have been destroyed; 89 people have been killed and 405 wounded." Salisbury commented: "No American communique has asserted that Namdinh contains some facility that the United States regards as a military objective. It is apparent, on personal inspection, that block after block of ordinary housing, particularly surrounding a textile plant, has been smashed to rubble by repeated attacks by Seventh Fleet planes." The reporter added that the only possible products of military value made in the city were uniforms, and that the textile plant had been bombed 19 times by American planes. He concluded: "President Johnson's announced policy that American targets in North Viet Nam are steel and concrete rather than human lives seems to have little connection with the reality of attacks carried out by United States planes."

Mme. Liu's "Confession." On Dec. 27, it was reported from Peking that Mme. Liu Shao-chi, wife of the Chinese head of state (President), had written a 3000-word confession in which she said: "I betrayed the Communist party and Chairman Mao's trust, solicitude, and teachings. This has greatly troubled me." Her husband had reportedly confessed his "crimes" the day before. On the same day, a Red Guard rally of 100,000 in Peking denounced Liu as the "Khrushchev of China" and the "Boss of Capitalism."

Purge of Workers Urged. On Dec. 27, an editorial in the Peking *People's Daily* urged mine and factory workers to purge themselves of anti-Maoists. The editorial conceded there was considerable opposition to Mao and his heir apparent, Lin Piao, in China's industrial establishment.

Fifth Nuclear Test. On Dec. 28, Peking announced that the Chinese had exploded their fifth nuclear device, apparently larger than the first four. U.S. experts said the initial

evidence indicated that the test constituted a new step toward development of a hydrogen bomb.

Chen Denounced. On Dec. 28, reports from Peking said that Chinese Foreign Minister Chen Yi had been denounced in Red Guard posters. A Japanese dispatch said that Chen's wife and son also had been criticized.

Defense Minister Arrested. On Dec. 28, *Reuters* reported that Peng Teh-huai, commander of Red China's forces in the Korean War and a former defense minister, had been arrested by Red Guards. Peng had been accused in Red Guard posters of following the bourgeois line.

Tao Chu Attacked. On Dec. 29, Red Guard posters in Peking attacked Tao Chu, who had recently risen from obscurity to fourth place in the Chinese hierarchy. The posters asserted that "Tao Chu is a new bourgeois element." In July 1966, Tao took over as head of the party's Propaganda Department; he had been a Vice Premier since January 1965.

Chinese Warning on Hong Kong. On Dec. 29, the *New China* news agency reported that Communist China had warned Great Britain it was "courting disaster" by allowing U.S. Navy ships to visit Hong Kong. The dispatch said Britain was "toeing the U.S. line and turning Hong Kong into a U.S. military base."

Student Letter to Johnson. On Dec. 29, presidents of student organizations and campus editors from 100 colleges and universities sent a letter to President Johnson voicing concern and doubt over U.S. involvement in the Viet Nam war. "Unless this conflict can be eased, the United States will find some of her most loyal and courageous young people choosing to go to jail rather than to bear their country's arms," the letter said. "There are many who are deeply troubled for every one who has been outspoken in dissent.... There is increasing confusion about both our basic purpose and our tactics, and there is increasing fear that the course now being pursued may lead us irrevocably into a major land war in Asia -- a war which many feel could not be won without recourse to nuclear weapons, if then."

China's Harvest. On Dec. 29, the *New York Times* reported that experts on Chinese agriculture disagreed with Peking's contention that the 1966 harvest in China was the largest in history. Most of the specialists were said to feel that the 1966 crop was smaller than that of 1965, due mainly to natural disasters in south China.

Labor Takeover. On Dec. 30, reports from Tokyo indicated that supporters of Mao Tse-tung and Lin Piao had taken over the powerful All China Federation of Trade Unions. The move was considered a blow to the fortunes of Head of State Liu Shao-chi, leader of the group opposing Mao and Lin. Liu was thought to have gained most of his support from the trade unions.

Death Demanded for Peng. On Dec. 30, it was reported from Tokyo that the Red Guards were demanding that the former Mayor of Peking, Peng Chen, and three other officials purged during the Cultural Revolution be put to death. The three others were Lo Jui-ching, former army commander; Lu Ting-yi, former culture minister; and Yang Shang-kun, a former member of the Standing Committee of the Chinese Communist Party.

Chinese Bomb. On Dec. 30, the U.S. Atomic Energy Commission announced that the recent Chinese nuclear test "involved thermonuclear material" and the "dirtiest" and most powerful type of nuclear weapon.

Truce Begins. On Dec. 30, a two-day New Year's cease-fire began in Viet Nam.

U Thant's New Year's Message. On Dec. 30, UN Secretary General U Thant stated in a New Year's message: "I am convinced that if peace were soon restored there would be a rebirth of faith in our ability to promote the well-being of all. World cooperation would be considerably advanced, for conditions are favorable for a breakthrough in international cooperation which is being held back by the dark barriers of war."

Johnson on Civilian Casualties. On Dec. 31, in a news conference at the LBJ Ranch, President Johnson said: "I would like to repeat again that it is the policy of this government to bomb only military targets. We realize that when you do that, inevitably and almost invariably there are casualties, there are losses of lives.... We do everything we can to minimize them, but they do occur in North Viet Nam as they do in South Viet Nam.... But only military targets have been authorized."

1967

Prediction of Victory for Mao in 1967 -- Bombing Question in the Search for Peace in Viet Nam -- Red Guard Denunciation of Chou -- Violence in Nanking -- Communist China's Ambassadors Called Home -- Thant Dismisses Importance of Viet Nam to West's Security -- Opposition to Mao in China -- Control of Army Tightened -- Waning of China's Influence in Asia -- Turning Point in Cultural Revolution -- Report of U.S.-China Deal -- Anti-Mao Tactics -- Anti-Maoist Gains -- Violence in Kiangsi -- Reported Order to Use Army Against Mao's Opponents -- Fighting in the Provinces -- Violence in Sinkiang -- Anti-Soviet Demonstrations in Peking -- Kennan on U.S.-Soviet Relations -- Maoists and Army Dissidents.

Victory Prediction. On Jan. 1, the Peking *People's Daily* predicted that Chairman Mao Tse-tung and his supporters would win a "decisive victory" over their opponents in 1967.

NLF Truce Offer. On Jan. 1, the National Liberation Front in South Viet Nam announced it would observe a seven-day truce during the Lunar New Year in February. Secretary of State Rusk said the same day that the United States would have to consult with its allies in Viet Nam before agreeing to the truce.

Dogfight. On Jan. 2, seven Russian-built MIGs were shot down over North Viet Nam by American fighter planes using heat-seeking missiles. No U.S. planes were lost.

British Peace Proposal. On Jan. 2, South Viet Nam accepted in principle a British proposal to hold a Viet Nam parley on British territory. The United States had already accepted the proposal, but the Hanoi radio called it an attempt to "deceive world opinion."

U Thant's View. On Jan. 3, after two weeks of secret maneuvering, UN Secretary General U Thant was reported to have become convinced that a halt in the bombing of North Viet Nam would lead to negotiations to end the war in South Viet Nam. The *New York Times* reported that Thant

had hopes, "based on what were described as hard facts, of a positive response from North Viet Nam once the United States unconditionally ended the bombing." The response was expected at the United Nations to take the form of a de-escalation of North Vietnamese military operations.

Salisbury Interview at Hanoi. On Jan. 3, in an interview with *New York Times* assistant managing editor Harrison Salisbury, North Vietnamese Premier Pham Van Dong said that "The moment the United States puts an end to the war, we will respect each other and settle every question." It was reported the same day that many officials in Washington thought the Premier's statement indicated a shift in North Vietnamese policy toward peace.

Peking Posters. On Jan. 3, David Oancia of the Toronto *Globe and Mail* reported from Peking that top-level military, scientific, labor and Communist party personnel were being denounced in Red Guard wall posters throughout the capital. Some of the military men and scientists criticized were men directly involved in China's nuclear development program.

Prisoners Freed. On Jan. 4, the Viet Cong released two American civilian construction workers and a Filipino woman who had been in captivity for six months. The three were said to be in bad physical condition.

New Peace Hint. On Jan. 5, a high-ranking North Vietnamese diplomat in Paris told a group of French journalists that if the United States would "definitively and unconditionally stop the bombing of North Viet Nam, his government would be willing to "examine and study" American proposals for peace. On the same day, the Johnson Administration indicated that it was seeking clarification of North Vietnamese terms for peace negotiations.

Mao's 1958 Resignation. On Jan. 6, Japanese correspondents in Peking reported that Red Guard posters asserted that Mao Tse-tung's resignation in 1958 as President of the People's Republic had been forced by pressure from a faction in the Chinese Communist Party headed by the present President, Liu Shao-chi. The posters indicated that Mao had been fighting to regain the position ever since 1958. He was quoted as saying that President Liu and the party General Secretary Teng Hsiao-ping, "treated me as if I were their dead parent at a funeral." Mao said Teng had attempted to create his own "independent kingdom."

Tao Purged. On Jan. 6, Japanese correspondents reported that Tao Chu, the propaganda chief who had risen to prominence during the first stage of the purge, had been denounced by Mao's wife and led through the streets of Peking in disgrace by the Red Guards. Tao, considered one of the architects of the Cultural Revolution, had only been in his post for four months.

Chou Denounced. On Jan. 6, Premier Chou En-lai was denounced in Peking's Red Guard posters. David Oancia of the Toronto *Globe and Mail* wrote: "Residents of the capital reported that gunfire shattered the usual nighttime calm for more than five minutes in the vicinity of the railway station. There was no confirmation or explanation of this today, but there were posters reporting clashes among factory workers in the city's western district." Some of the posters declared that Premier Chou should be "burned to death."

Meanwhile, Japanese correspondents reported bloody clashes all over China between supporters and opponents of Chairman Mao and his heir apparent, Lin Piao. Other reports said anti-Mao elements were putting up posters calling Mao a "fanatic."

Pope Paul and Chinese Communists. On Jan. 6, Pope Paul VI said he would like to renew old contacts on the Chinese mainland and "discuss peace" with Chinese Communist leaders.

Hanoi Stands Fast. On Jan. 6, in the midst of speculation that North Viet Nam had changed its position on peace negotiations, a statement was issued making it clear that Hanoi still insisted on acceptance of its four-point program.

Violence in Nanking. On Jan. 7, reports from Peking said that bloody battles between Red Guards and masses of workers had placed Nanking "in the grip of terror." The Czechoslovak news agency, *Ceteka*, reported that 60,000 prisoners had been taken by both sides, and that many of them had been tortured. "Their fingers, noses and ears were chopped off. Their tongues were cut out," the dispatch said. Japanese news sources reported that 54 people had been killed, 900 wounded and 6,000 arrested. The reports said the trouble had begun when an estimated 100,000 workers in Nanking, led by the local party secretary, attacked the city's Red Guard headquarters. A huge battle ensued, lasting at least three days.

Ky Willing to Meet Ho. On Jan. 7, South Vietnamese Premier Nguyen Cao Ky, visiting the northern city of Hue, said he would be willing to meet with North Vietnamese Premier Ho Chi Minh "anywhere, anytime" if it would bring peace. On Jan. 8, R. W. Apple of the *New York Times* reported from Saigon: "For the first time in the war against the Viet Cong, the primary attention of this capital is beginning to swing from the fighting itself to the prospect for negotiations."

Rioting in Red China. On Jan. 8, Japanese sources reported that uprisings on the Chinese mainland had spread to the Chusan Islands, southeast of Shanghai, where thousands of farmers had attacked Red Guards. On the same day, the Peking radio announced that anti-Maoist "bourgeois elements" had attempted to cut off Shanghai's water and electricity. Other reports indicated that many workers had walked off their jobs. Much of the urban unrest was attributed to an attempt by Mao Tse-tung and his supporters to organize a mass movement of workers, known as the "Red Rebel Workers," to supplement the Red Guards in their struggle against Mao's enemies. Reports from Peking, published in the *New York Times*, asserted that "people have been buried alive near Peking, that the Peking security police has been taken over by Red Guards, and that the wife of President Liu Shao-chi had been kidnapped and held briefly by students."

Peking's Ambassadors Called Home. On Jan. 9, reports from foreign capitals throughout the world indicated that most of Communist China's ambassadors to other countries were being ordered home.

Taiwan's Reaction. On Jan. 9, it was reported from Taiwan that Nationalist Chinese officials considered the bloody clashes on the mainland a prelude to civil war. Reports from Washington indicated that this view was not shared by State Department officials, many of whom felt that Red China's army would be the key factor in determining the outcome of the power struggle.

Johnson on Far East. On Jan. 11, in his annual State of the Union address, President Johnson predicted "more cost, more loss and more agony" for the United States in the Viet Nam war. He added: "We shall continue to hope for a reconciliation between the people of mainland China and the world community -- including working together in all the tasks of arms control, and security, and progress on which the fate of the Chinese people, like their fellow men elsewhere, depends."

U Thant Differs on Viet Nam. On Jan. 10, UN Secretary General U Thant told a news conference that he did not agree with the U.S. argument that Viet Nam was vital to the interests and security of the West, nor did he believe in the so-called domino theory that if Viet Nam fell to the Communists, other countries would follow.

Hanoi Invites Inspection. On Jan. 10, an assistant managing editor of the *New York Times*, Harrison Salisbury, reported from Hong Kong that the "North Vietnamese government has reached a momentous decision -- to open its doors and invite the world in to inspect the results of American bombings."

Labor Strikes. On Jan. 10, the Peking radio and press indicated that strikes were continuing in Shanghai and Foochow. Japanese correspondents in Peking reported that Chinese Premier Chou En-lai, who had opposed extending the Cultural Revolution to industry and the labor unions for fear of upsetting the economy, was attempting to moderate the campaign while remaining in the pro-Mao faction. Wall posters in Peking quoted Chou as saying: "We must thoroughly smash the bourgeois reactionary line represented by Liu (President Liu Shao-chi) and Teng (General Secretary Teng Hsiao-ping), but it should be distinguished from excessive individual attacks against them."

No Nationalist Invasion. On Jan. 10, the State Department made it clear that Chiang Kai-shek's Nationalist forces could not make any military moves against Communist China without U.S. approval. This put the damper on reports that Chiang hoped to take advantage of the political crisis on the mainland and invade with his 600,000-man army.

Mao's and Lin's Support. On Jan. 10, diplomatic reports reaching London asserted that Communist Party Chairman Mao Tse-tung still had the support of the Chinese masses but retained the loyalty of less than one-third of the members of the Politburo. The reports indicated that Mao himself remained in the background while his heir apparent, Lin Piao, was "running the show" in the name of Mao. It was said that Lin, however, could no longer depend on army support.

Soviet Preparation. On Jan. 10, the Soviet Defense Ministry's newspaper, *Krasnaya Zvezda*, reported that Soviet armed forces were being prepared for a possible confrontation with Communist China.

Opposition to Mao. On Jan. 11, the Chinese Communist official press asserted that political and economic sabotage had been carried out in an effort to discredit the regime of Mao Tse-tung. The press called on the Chinese people "to take concerted action and beat back the new counterattack" by Mao's opponents. Press reports indicated that local party officials in Shanghai and other cities had used party funds and personnel to spread opposition to Mao and Lin Piao among workers and students.

Another Purged. On Jan. 11, David Oancia of the Toronto *Globe and Mail* reported that Po I-po, one of Communist China's leading economists, had been jailed by the Red Guards. The report said Po had been arrested in Canton, brought to Peking, and was being "held under what are reported to be extremely rugged conditions along with the former mayor of Peking, Peng Chen; the former army chief, Lo Jui-ching; the propaganda director, Lu Ting-yi; a Central Committee member, Yang Shang-kun; and former Defense Minister Peng Teh-huai, who was replaced by Lin Piao in 1959." It was also reported from sources at the United Nations that Red Guard groups were being trained to undergo a series of "long marches" into the countryside to spread the doctrine of Mao Tse-tung.

Nuclear Priority in China. On Jan. 11, Richard Helms, director of the Central Intelligence Agency, told the Joint Congressional Committee on Atomic Energy that Communist China was giving "highest priority" to the development of nuclear weapons and medium-range missiles that could deliver warheads to targets 1,000 miles from China's borders.

Control of Army Tightened. On Jan. 12, the Peking press reported that Chairman Mao Tse-tung and Lin Piao had rearranged the power structure controlling the army to give Defense Minister Lin and Chen Po-ta, head of the Cultural Revolution, tighter control. Opposition to Mao within the army's ranks was conceded. It was also announced that Mao's wife, Chiang Ching, was appointed as an adviser to the new committee in charge of running the army.

Waning of China's Influence. On Jan. 12, a *New York Times* dispatch from the United Nations suggested that the new political crisis in Communist China was significantly "changing the balance of power in Asia." The dispatch said that "From Moscow and Kabul, eastward to Seoul and Tokyo, governments are contemplating the possibility that internal conflict will inhibit China's ability to initiate military or political action and will reduce the influence of Chinese communism on Communist parties in neighboring countries."

Action to Isolate Mao's Enemies. On Jan. 13, the Peking radio reported that groups loyal to Mao Tse-tung and Lin Piao had taken over the Shanghai railroad system and the city's major power plant after a "very keen" struggle. On the same day, the *New China* news agency indicated that action would be taken throughout the country to isolate those local officials who did not support Mao and who had been, according to reports, bribing workers and farmers with party funds to discredit the Cultural Revolution.

Peking Newspaper Reorganized. On Jan. 13, after an absence of two weeks, the Peking's *People's Daily* resumed publication. The first issue of the reorganized paper devoted its front page to a huge picture of Chairman Mao Tse-tung.

Thant vs. Seven Ambassadors. On Jan. 13, seven Asian ambassadors to the United Nations told Secretary General U Thant that they did not agree with his view that South Viet Nam was not important to the security of other nations, especially the nations of Southeast Asia. Thant in turn informed the representatives of Japan, Laos, Malaysia, Nationalist China, the Philippines, South Korea and Thailand that he did not believe in the domino theory -- that if South Viet Nam fell to the Communists, other threatened nations would do the same. The ambassadors disagreed, and one of them was reported to have said that if South Viet Nam fell to the Communists, the others might even fall together instead of one after another.

No Bombing of MIG Bases. On Jan. 13, the Chairman of the Joint Chiefs of Staff, Gen. Earle G. Wheeler, stated that U.S. pilots would refrain from bombing four airfields in North Viet Nam used by Russian-supplied MIG fighter planes.

Air Battle. On Jan. 13, the Nationalist government on Taiwan announced that four of its jet fighters had shot down two Chinese Communist MIG jet fighters over the Taiwan Strait. The Nationalists said their planes all returned safely.

Liu Retracts Confession. On Jan. 14, Japanese correspondents in Peking reported that Chinese President Liu Shao-chi had asked permission of the Communist party to retract the "self-criticism" he had made at an October 1966 party meeting. In that statement, Liu had apologized for building his own support rather than mobilizing the masses in favor of Mao Tse-tung.

New Plane Record. On Jan. 14, U.S. planes set a record for the number of single-plane attacks in South Viet Nam; the day's total was 549.

Turning Point in Cultural Revolution. On Jan. 15, the Peking radio, announcing that the Cultural Revolution had reached "a new turning point," urged all supporters of Chairman Mao Tse-tung to "take political and economic authority into your own hands." The night before, Chinese Premier Chou En-lai had told a banquet audience in Peking that Mao had ordered "an all-out general offensive" against his opponents.

The radio said that opponents of Mao and Lin Piao had formed "an army of defenders of Red state power" and warned: "The struggle between the proletarian revolutionaries and the handful of those persons within the party in authority taking the capitalist road is acute, complicated and tortuous." The broadcast said also that supporters of Mao Tse-tung had finally wrested control from his enemies in Shanghai, and it exhorted other pro-Mao elements to do the same. It was reported that a purge of the army had begun, and that resistance to the Cultural Revolution had been "sharp and complicated."

U.S.-China Deal. On Jan. 15, Rene Dabernat, foreign editor of *Paris-Match*, said in an interview in *U.S. News and World Report* that Communist China had informed the United States through Paris, in the spring of 1966, that it would not become involved in the Viet Nam war if the United States refrained from invading China or North Viet Nam and from bombing the latter's Red River dikes. Dabernat said that subsequent public statements by President Johnson and other U.S. officials demonstrated that they had "agreed to these conditions." The State Department replied with a "no comment," but other officials acknowledged that the United States had received a number of messages from Communist China through a number of different third parties.

Details of Nanking Fighting. On Jan. 15, the Soviet Communist Party newspaper *Pravda* reported that "bricks, tables, chairs, practice grenades, fire extinguishers and even boiling water" were used during the fighting in Nanking, which involved more than 100,000 workers, on Jan. 3 and 4. "Ambulances and trucks which came to the area of the clash could not take away all the wounded and dead," the paper said. Reports of the violence in Nanking did not appear in the Soviet press until almost a week after they were published in Western newspapers.

New Bombing Near Hanoi. On Jan. 16, U.S. fighter-bombers resumed bombing of targets in the Hanoi area, the first since Dec. 19.

Hanoi's Appetite. On Jan. 16, Secretary of State Rusk was questioned for four hours by the Senate Foreign Relations Committee behind closed doors. Reporters asked him afterward for his reaction to North Vietnamese President Ho Chi Minh's statement that the North Vietnamese would "never surrender our independence for the sake of peace." Rusk replied: "No one is trying to take anything from North Viet Nam except their appetite for South Viet Nam."

Anti-Mao Tactics. On Jan. 16, Japanese reports said that wall posters in Peking accused officials opposed to Mao Tse-tung of urging peasants and farmers to go to the cities to make "irrational economic requests." It was also reported that a number of Mao's supporters in the provinces had been imprisoned by his opponents.

Army Dissension. On Jan. 17, the Peking radio accused Chinese army officers of confining their troops to quarters to keep them from studying the thoughts of Mao Tse-tung. This and other charges increased speculation that Mao did not have effective control of the army. An earlier broadcast by the Peking radio said that army units throughout the country were being asked to swear loyalty to Mao.

Sukarno Asked to Resign. On Jan. 17, Indonesian Foreign Minister Adam Malik called on President Sukarno to resign because of his suspected participation in the unsuccessful October 1965 coup. Malik added that if Sukarno did not resign, he would have to face "extremely grave issues."

Ho Lung Accused. On Jan. 17, David Oancia of the Toronto *Globe and Mail* reported that leaflets distributed in Peking accused Vice Premier Ho Lung of being "the biggest time bomb at the side of Chairman Mao Tse-tung and Vice Chairman Lin Piao, the boss behind the scenes of the counter-revolutionary Lo Jui-ching, the representative of the Liu-Teng line inside the army." Lo Jui-ching, former chief of staff of the army, was currently being held captive by the Red Guards.

Peking Stores Closed. On Jan. 18, it was reported from Peking that Red Guards and adult Revolutionary Rebels had shut down all stores in Peking in an attempt to force workers who had come to the city to go back to their jobs and get production rolling again. Pro-Maoists asserted that "bourgeois reactionary elements," seeking to make things difficult for Mao, had been bribing workers to leave their jobs and journey to the capital. A day earlier, the *New China* news agency had warned of the "existence of reactionary revisionists in the communes (who are) attempting to deceive the peasants with their economic principles." Other reports said the acting general manager of the *New China* news agency had been dragged through the capital's streets by the Red Guards for "reactionary bourgeois activity," and that officials of the Peking *People's Daily* had been criticized.

Red Guard Threats. On Jan. 19, *Reuters* and the Yugoslav news agency, *Tanjug*, reported from Peking that a Red Guard newspaper asserted that anti-Maoist officials had made secret contact with the Soviet Embassy in Peking. The paper warned the leaders of the anti-Mao faction, President Liu Shao-chi and party General Secretary Teng Hsiao-ping, "If you continue your stubborn opposition and if you do not capitulate, you will have the same fate" as the other members of the conspiracy. The other members included the

former Peking mayor, Peng Chen; the ousted propaganda chief, Lu Ting-yi; and the former army chief of staff, Lo Jui-ching. Along with Liu and Teng, the Red Guard newspaper said, they had attempted to oust Mao Tse-tung, but had failed.

Reuters reported that in many areas, the Red Guards had seized control of factories, only to find they could not operate them. The dispatch said that anti-Maoist elements had welcomed such seizures because it gave the Red Guards plenty of rope to hang themselves.

Lo's Suicide. On Jan. 20, a Chinese army wall newspaper reported that the former army chief of staff, Lo Jui-ching, had committed suicide. It was his second attempt. A Red Guard newspaper the day before had shown a picture of Lo in the hands of his Red Guard captors, who were twisting his arm behind his back. The former mayor of Peking, Peng Chen, also in the photo, was shown in a similar position.

Another Denounced. On Jan. 20, Hsiao Hua, director of the army's political department and former right-hand man to Defense Minister Lin Piao, was assailed by Chairman Mao's wife and in posters as an opponent of the Cultural Revolution.

Shanghai Struggle. On Jan. 20, the Peking radio reported that the struggle between opponents and supporters of Mao Tse-tung had intensified in Shanghai. Anti-Maoists had sent "great numbers" of peasants into the city to demand higher wages. The broadcast added that there had been a "great loss" in farm production.

Soviet Appeal. On Jan. 20, the Soviet Communist Party newspaper *Pravda* urged Communists throughout the world to oppose the hard-line policies of Mao Tse-tung and his companions, which, the paper said, were "directly aimed at splitting world communism." Meanwhile, Red Guard newspapers continued to charge that the Soviet Union was acting in collusion with Mao Tse-tung's opponents to oust him from office.

Peasants Told to Stay Home. On Jan. 21, the Peking radio and the Peking *People's Daily* carried orders to Chinese peasants to remain in their villages and stay away from the cities. The order was believed to be aimed specifically at Shanghai, where reports continued to emphasize clashes between workers and peasants. The Peking broadcast charged that opponents of Mao were sending the peasants into the cities to demand higher wages -- a tactic denounced by Maoists as "economism." More than three million peasants were reported to have entered Shanghai alone.

Anti-Maoist Gains. On Jan 21, reports from a number of coastal provinces indicated that anti-Maoist forces were gaining momentum; new units of Red Guards who opposed Mao were reportedly being formed and army units were said to be defecting. Wall posters in Peking continued to denounce Vice Premier Ho Lung and Hsiao Hua, director of the army's general political department. But other posters said that Premier Chou En-lai had called the denunciation of Hsiao a mistake and had warned against spreading false rumors through wall posters. In another broadcast, the Peking radio disclosed that both aircraft production and foreign trade had declined as a result of the internal upheaval.

Fulbright's Proposals. On Jan. 21, Sen. J. William Fulbright (D Ark.), chairman of the Senate Foreign Relations Committee, offered an "alternative to Viet Nam" in a newly published book. Entitled "The Arrogance of

Power," it outlined an eight-point program for ending the conflict and neutralizing Southeast Asia. Fulbright suggested that the United States talk South Viet Nam into seeking negotiations with North Viet Nam, and itself propose ceasefire talks with North Viet Nam and the Viet Cong. The Arkansas Democrat called also for promotion of Viet Cong independence from the North Vietnamese, self-determination in South Viet Nam, eventual reunification of Viet Nam, and neutralization of Southeast Asia.

Chinese Space Program. On Jan. 21, *Red Banner,* the newspaper of the Red Guards connected with the Peking Aviation Institute, said that Communist China would orbit its first spacecraft in 1967. The article said also that China would conduct more nuclear missile tests during the year.

Violence in Kiangsi. On Jan. 22, a local radio station in China's Kiangsi Province reported that soldiers, peasants and workers were fighting Red Guards in that south central province. The broadcast accused the Guards' opponents of "great violence...vicious white terror," and of having "gravely disrupted order." It added that a "great number of persons" had been injured and that "instant arrest" of persons attacking the Guards had been ordered, although later reports indicated that police and army units were ignoring the order. The broadcast said that Red Guards had been streaming into the province for the past few days and had made the standard charges against the local party officials. But opponents of Mao Tse-tung among the peasants and workers, led by "a large number of party officials of high and low rank," formed ranks and overwhelmed the Guards.

Mao's Order on Use of Army. On Jan. 23, wall posters in Peking reported that Chairman Mao Tse-tung had ordered his Defense Minister, Lin Piao, to use the 2.5 million-man army when necessary to defeat Mao's opponents. "After Chairman Mao had read about incidents in Anhwei Province," the posters read, "he issued a directive to Lin Piao that in the future the army should support left revolutionary masses if this would become necessary. The so-called idea of non-intervention by the army is a false idea. It does not correspond to the real situation." On the same day, the Peking radio said: "The current power struggle is merciless. There is no place...for moderation. Therefore, reactionary powerholders may not be executives any longer. Revolutionary rebels must completely, radically seize all executive powers."

Anti-Maoist Violence. On Jan. 23, the radio station in Kiangsi Province, controlled by pro-Maoists, reported that "brutal suppression of revolutionaries" was continuing and that banks, newspapers, and radio stations had been seized by the anti-Maoists. Electricity and water supplies had been cut off and factories and mines closed down. More fighting was reported also in Inner Mongolia, Manchuria, Tientsin, Paoting, and Kwangtung Province.

U.S. War Costs. On Jan. 24, President Johnson sent Congress the federal Budget for fiscal 1968. The Budget Bureau estimated that defense spending in the fiscal year would rise to $73.1 billion, including $21.9 billion attributed solely to the cost of continuing the war in Viet Nam. From July 1, 1964, to June 30, 1968, incremental costs of the war were estimated to total $47.2 billion.

Provincial Battles. On Jan. 24, the Peking radio reported that an armed rebellion in Shansi Province had been crushed and the party organization completely purged. The broadcast gave the most detailed account to date of violence in the provinces. It was also the first time the overthrow of an anti-Maoist party organization had been reported. The radio said that "tens of thousands" of people who had "used weapons and ammunition" against Mao's "revolutionary rebels" had been stirred up by local officials who bribed them with offers of more pay and material benefits. The Peking *People's Daily* reported that suppression of the revolt had been accomplished with the help of the army. "The Liberation Army stationed in Shansi Military District stood for the proletarian revolution line represented by Mao Tsetung and supported the Revolutionary Rebel Faction's fight to seize control," the paper said. However, the Peking radio's broadcast said that "a handful of people in the Shansi Communist Army Committee" had been responsible for the uprising.

In other reports, travelers returning from Canton claimed they saw youths burning books of Mao's thoughts, posters attacking Mao's wife, and fighting in the city's streets. A Peking radio broadcast confirmed that army units had been used to quell a revolt in Fangshan (near Peking), where anti-Maoists had "arrested several hundred revolutionaries and subjected them to Fascist torture."

Thai Charge Against China. On Jan. 24, Thailand accused Communist China of directing guerrilla operations in Northeastern Thailand. The charge followed a roundup of suspected Communists in the area by Thai police, who said that most of the suspects were Thai-born Chinese.

Call For Army Loyalty to Mao. On Jan. 25, an editorial calling on the army to give complete loyalty to Chairman Mao Tse-tung appeared on the front pages of every major newspaper in Peking. The editorial described the army as the "pillar of the dictatorship of the proletariat." According to *Reuters,* there was "no evidence in the capital of any preparations for large-scale armed intervention or of any significant increase in troop activity."

Anarchy and Revolution. On Jan. 25, the *New China* news agency reported: "Everywhere on both banks of the Yellow River, north and south of the Yangtze, all of China is (in) a frenzy...Only one word can describe the circumstances. That word is 'anarchy.' Without anarchy there can be no revolution!"

U.S.-Chinese Meeting. On Jan. 25, the U.S. and Chinese ambassadors to Poland met in Warsaw for a secret three and one-half hour talk. Neither the U.S. Ambassador, John A. Gronouski, nor the Chinese Ambassador, Wang Kuochuan, would discuss the content of the talk. The next meeting was scheduled for June 7, 1967.

McNamara on Viet Cong Losses. On Jan. 26, the Senate Armed Services Committee and Senate Appropriations Defense subcommittee released Secretary of Defense Robert S. McNamara's annual defense posture statement. The Secretary said in the statement that the Viet Cong was losing so many men in the Viet Nam conflict that it was having to rely on North Viet Nam for increases in troop strength.

Fighting in China's Provinces. On Jan. 26, reports from a number of Chinese provinces indicated that pro-Maoist forces had been successful in ousting some local officials opposed to the Cultural Revolution. In Shansi Province, however, there were reports of continued fighting although revolutionary elements there supposedly had been subdued two weeks earlier. A Mao-controlled radio station in Kiangsi Province reported that a 200,000-man "private" army had been defeated by pro-Maoists and that the guilty officials had been removed. Clashes in Hopei and Sinkiang Provinces also were reported.

Chinese-Russian Clash in Moscow. On Jan. 26, the Chinese Communist Embassy in Moscow protested to the Kremlin that 61 Chinese students had been attacked "without provocation" by Russian soldiers when they sought to place a wreath at the Lenin Mausoleum in Red Square. The Soviet government answered that the protest was made up of "unpardonable lies." It accused the Chinese students of provoking the "wild scene." On the same day, huge crowds gathered outside the Soviet Embassy in Peking, shouting such slogans as "Down with the Soviet pigs!"

Sinkiang Violence. On Jan. 27, Japanese correspondents in Peking reported that 100 people had been killed and only one of eight army units had remained loyal to Chairman Mao Tse-tung in distant Sinkiang Province. Posters on the capital city's walls said that "machine guns, rifles, infantry mortars and hand grenades are being used," but they did not say by whom. The posters accused Wang En-mao, the party and military chief of the area, of being behind the rebellion. In another area of the huge province, anti-Mao forces were reported to have been in control of 12 tanks. Factories were said to have been shut down.

Sino-Soviet Charges and Counter-Charges. On Jan. 28, the Chinese Embassy in Moscow held a press conference at which some of the Chinese students injured in a fracas with Soviet police in Moscow's Red Square on Jan. 25 testified as to what happened. One of the students called the Soviet leaders "bastards." Another declared: "We will crush the dog's heads." At a press conference the same day at the Soviet Foreign Ministry, the Russians gave their version of the incident, asserting that the students had provoked the incident to impair Sino-Soviet relations.

Anti-Soviet Demonstrations in Peking. On Jan. 28, Chinese soldiers took part in an enormous demonstration outside the Soviet Embassy in Peking. The troops wielded rifles and fixed bayonets in the third demonstration in as many days. The Embassy's walls were plastered with posters reading "Shoot Brezhnev" and "Fry Kosygin." On Jan. 29, hundreds of thousands again marched in front of the Soviet Embassy in Peking. Meanwhile, the Soviet government said in a note of protest to the Chinese Embassy in Moscow: "The Soviet side reserves the right to take the necessary measures if the Chinese authorities fail to provide normal conditions for the activity of the Soviet representation."

Chinese Demonstration in Paris. On Jan. 29, for the second time, French police clashed with Chinese students demonstrating outside the Soviet Embassy in Paris. In the first demonstration, police arrested Chinese students and detained them in a police station overnight for splashing red paint on the Embassy.

Holidays Canceled. On Jan. 29, the Peking radio announced that workers' holidays for the Chinese New Year

had been canceled, and that all elementary students had been ordered back to school on Feb. 9. A Peking wall poster announced that Premier Chou En-lai had ordered all Chinese students studying abroad to return home.

Kennan on U.S.-Soviet Relations. On Jan 30, former U.S. Ambassador to the Soviet Union George F. Kennan told the Senate Foreign Relations Committee that the irreparable disunity of the Communist world presented the United States with a perfect opportunity to take "greatly exciting" steps to improve U.S.-Soviet relations.

Taylor on Viet Nam. On Jan. 30, the former U.S. Ambassador to South Viet Nam, Gen. Maxwell D. Taylor, told newsmen that there would be "some new developments in the course of this year...some changes for the better." The former chairman of the Joint Chiefs of Staff, who had just returned from a trip through Southeast Asia, said there was "a new feeling" in South Viet Nam, "a feeling that the logjam is breaking a little bit."

Control of Peasants by Viet Cong. On Jan. 30, it was reported from Saigon that U.S. troops in the Iron Triangle area had captured a Viet Cong document admitting to loss of control over more than one million South Vietnamese peasants since early 1965. The document asserted, however, that the Viet Cong still controlled three-fourths of the country's population.

"Great Alliance." On Jan. 30, the Peking *People's Daily* called on supporters of party Chairman Mao Tse-tung to form a "great alliance" after first settling "petty bourgeois" differences among themselves. "Only when such an alliance is forged is it possible to engage successfully in a struggle to seize power," the newspaper said. "Any hasty attempt to seize power without this alliance is either empty talk or an ill-considered action that is bound to be unsuccessful."

Reischauer Against Bombing. On Jan. 31, former U.S. Ambassador to Japan Edwin O. Reischauer told the Senate Foreign Relations Committee that U.S. bombing of North Viet Nam was a "psychological blunder." Reischauer said he was "a supporter of the Administration's objectives in Viet Nam," but he urged a "prudent de-escalation" of the war. "I believe that we have tended to overestimate (Communist China's) strength and its immediate menace to our interests and to its neighbors."

Demonstrations. On Jan. 31, Chinese demonstrated outside the French Embassy in Peking, protesting the treatment of Chinese students who had been demonstrating against the Soviet Embassy in Paris. There were reports that Chinese in Hanoi demonstrated in front of the Soviet Embassy there. Large and noisy demonstrations continued in front of the Soviet and Yugoslav embassies in Peking.

Maoists and Army Dissidents. On Jan. 31, 1967 the Peking radio announced that pro-Maoist forces had triumphed over their opponents in the port of Tsingtao. Anti-Maoists, the broadcast said, had been supported by "some army troops."

Biographies

BIBLIOGRAPHY ON CHINESE LEADERS AND EVENTS

Barnett, A. Doak. *Communist China and Asia: Challenge to American Policy.* New York: Harper Brothers, 1960.

Barnett, A. Doak. *Communist China: The Early Years, 1949-55.* New York: Frederick A. Praeger, 1964.

Boorman, Howard L. Editor, *Men and Politics in Modern China.* New York: Columbia University, 1960.

Boorman, Howard L. "Mao Tse-tung: The Lacquered Image," *The China Quarterly,* November-December 1963.

Ch'en, Jerome. *Mao and the Chinese Revolution.* London, Oxford University Press, 1965.

China Year Book, 1965-66. Taiwan, China Publishing Co.

Chinese Information Service, 1270 Avenue of the Americas, New York, N.Y.: *Chiang Kai-shek, President of the Republic of China.*

Clubb, O. Edmund. *20th Century China.* New York and London, 1964.

Communist China, 1955-59: Policy Documents With Analysis. Cambridge, Harvard University Press, 1962.

Congressional Quarterly. *Congress and the Nation.* Congressional Quarterly Inc., Washington, D.C., 1965.

Fairbank, John K., Edwin O. Reischauer, Albert M. Craig. *East Asia: The Modern Transformation.* Boston: Houghton Mifflin Company, 1965.

Fairbank, John K. *The United States and China.* Cambridge: Harvard University Press, 1958.

Fitzgerald, C.P. *The Chinese View of their Place in the World.* London: Oxford University Press, 1964.

Hahn, Emily. *China Only Yesterday, 1850-1950.* New York: Doubleday, 1963.

Hinton, Harold C. *Leaders of Communist China.* Santa Monica: Rand Corporation, 1956.

Isaacs, Harold R. *The Tragedy of the Chinese Revolution.* Stanford University Press, 1951.

Lifton, Robert J. "Thought Reform of Chinese Intellectuals," *The Journal of Asian Studies,* Vol. XVI, November, 1965, pp. 75-88.

MacNair, H.F. and D.F. Lach. *Modern Far Eastern International Relations.* New York: D. Van Nostrand Co., Inc., 1960 and 1965.

Mehrert, Klaus. *Peking and Moscow.* New York: G. P. Putnam's Sons, 1963.

North, Robert C. *Moscow and Chinese Communists.* Stanford: Stanford University Press, 1953.

Payne, Robert. *Portrait of a Revolutionary: Mao Tse-tung.* New York: Abelard, 1962.

Perleberg, Max. *Who's Who in Modern China.* Hong Kong: Ye Old Printerie, Ltd., 1954.

Raskin, Marcus G. and Bernard B. Fall. *The Viet Nam Reader.* New York: Random House, 1965.

Schram, Stuart R. *The Political Thought of Mao Tse-tung.* New York: Frederick A. Praeger, 1963.

Schwartz, Benjamin I. *Chinese Communism and the Rise of Mao.* Cambridge: Harvard University Press, 1951.

Siao-yu. *Mao Tse-tung and I were Beggars.* Syracuse University Press, 1959.

Smedley, Agnes. *The Great Road: The Life and Times of Chu Teh.* New York: Monthly Review Press, 1956.

Snow, Edgar. "Interview With Mao," *The New Republic,* Feb. 27, 1965, pp. 17-23.

Snow, Edgar. *The Other Side of the River.* New York: Random House, 1962.

Snow, Edgar. *Red Star Over China.* New York: Random House, 1938.

Strong, Anna Louise. *The Chinese Conquer China.* New York Country Life Press, 1949.

Tong, Hollington K. *President Chiang Kai-shek, An Abridged Biography.* China Publishing Co., Taiwan, No Date.

U.S. State Department. The China White Paper Report: *United States Relations With China, 1944-1949.*

U.S. State Department. *Transcript of Round Table Discussions on American Policy Toward China,* 1949.

Vinacke, Harold M. *A History of the Far East in Modern Times.* New York: Appelton-Century-Crofts, Inc., 1946.

Wales, Nym. *Inside Red China.* New York: Doubleday Doran and Co., Inc., 1939.

Wales, Nym. *Red Dust: Autobiographies of Chinese Communists as Told to Nym Wales.* Stanford: Stanford University Press, 1952.

White, Theodore H. and Annalee Jacoby. *Thunder Out of China.* New York: William Sloane Associates, Inc., 1946.

Who's Who in Communist China. Hong Kong: Union Research Institute, 1966.

REFERENCES

Who's Who
Deadline Data
Editorial Research Reports
Foreign Broadcast
   Information Service

Facts on File
Congressional Quarterly
Current Biography

MAGAZINES

Look
Diplomat
Time
Newsweek
Foreign Affairs

Fortune
Saturday Evening Post
Life
U.S. News and World Report
Harpers

U.S. NEWSPAPERS

Washington Post
Christian Science Monitor
Wall Street Journal
United Press International
Los Angeles Times

New York Times
New York Herald Tribune
St. Louis Post-Dispatch
Associated Press
World Journal Tribune (N.Y.)

CHINESE SOURCES

The Peking People's Daily (Jenmin Jih Pao)
Red Flag (Hung Chi)

The Peking Review
New China News Agency (Hsinhua)
Liberation Army Daily (Chieh-fang Chun Pao)

OTHER FOREIGN PUBLICATIONS

Voice of the People (Albania)
The London Times
The Toronto Globe and Mail
The Manchester Guardian
Indian Express
The Manila Times
Le Monde (French)
Granma (Cuban)
Nhan Dan (North Vietnamese)
The Times of Viet Nam (South Vietnamese Government)
Asahi (Japanese)
Reuters (British)
Pravda
Izvestia
Tass
Rodong Shinmoon (North Korean)
Ceteka (Czechoslovakian)
Tanjug (Yugoslav)

Mao Tse-tung:
The Revolutionary

Biographies of China's Leaders

Mao Tse-tung, born Dec. 26, 1893, came out of an unjust world with a single solution--Marxism. He has been called the first successful heretic of the Communist world. He is an anti-Confucian who writes poetry in classical style. He is an intellectual who distrusts intellectuals. He who hated his father has become a father "image."

Mao Tse-tung's first successful act of rebellion occurred in his own family circle. He has described a typical argument with typical "Marxist" humor.

> When I was about thirteen my father invited many guests to his home...a dispute arose between the two of us. My father denounced me before the whole group, calling me lazy and useless. This infuriated me. I cursed him and left the house...I reached the edge of a pond and threatened to jump in if he came any nearer. In this situation demands and counter-demands were presented for cessation of the civil war... I agreed to give a one-knee (kow tow), if he would promise not to beat me. Thus the war ended, and from it I learned that when I defended my rights by open rebellion my father relented, but when I remained meek and submissive he only cursed and beat me the more.

The Early Years--1893-1920

Born into a prosperous peasant family in the village of Shao-Shan in Hunan province, Mao Tse-tung was one of four children--three sons and a daughter. All of the children became Communists. All met violent deaths--except for Mao. The young Mao entered a society whose articulate members were deeply disturbed by the role of China in the twentieth century. He himself has remembered vividly a pamphlet that he read in his school years which began, "Alas, China will be subjugated!" telling of Japan's occupation of Korea and Formosa and the loss of China's hegemony in Indochina. During the years of his youth, China went from a monarchy to republic to restoration of a monarchy to an anarchic state of warlordism.

Cruelty seemed to be a way of life in Mao's China. He witnessed many barbarisms, both at home and in the outside world. Almost every reference to his father mentions the cursing of his son. Mao tells in a matter-of-fact way of seeing the corpses of two revolutionists lying in the street "...when I went to call on a friend."

Mao halted his education at the age of 13 to work on his father's farm. He later continued his education and successfully passed examinations to enter the Hunan Provincial First Normal School in 1913. He early displayed a highly disciplined mind, having spent several months in self-education, reading in the Hunan provincial library such authors as Adam Smith, Charles Darwin, John Stuart Mill, Rousseau,

Spencer and Montesquieu. He also read poetry and the romances of old China which had been a great love of his since he was a small boy forced to hide such reading from his primary school teacher and his father.

Young Mao Tse-tung graduated from Normal School in June 1918, having been active in the Changsha Student Assn. and the New People's Study Society, which were primarily nationalistic groups, although the New People's group was to form the seed-bed for many future Communists.

During his five year stay at Normal School, Mao had become a favored student of Yang Chen-chi, whose daughter he married in 1920 or 1921. Professor Yang thought so well of Mao that he once gave the young student a grade of 100 "plus 5."

In 1918, Professor Yang was invited to teach at Peking University and Mao Tse-tung followed him there in autumn of that year. Through Yang's good offices, Mao found a job as assistant librarian to Li Ta-chao, who later became with Mao a co-founder of the Chinese Communist Party. Mao Tse-tung has spoken many years later of the snubs he received from famous scholars because of his lowly position and "southern dialect."

Communist Functionary--1921-1927

On a second trip to Peking in 1920, Mao Tse-tung seems to have made the transition from pure nationalist to Marxist. He read three books that especially influenced him--*The Communist Manifesto, Class Struggle* by Kautsky and a *History of Socialism* by Kirkupp. He previously had met and fallen in love with Yang Kai-hui, the daughter of his former professor. They were married in 1920 or 1921 and Mao brought his bride to Hunan where he taught school and propagandized for Marxism.

Mao Tse-tung states that he was one of twelve delegates present in Shanghai July 1921 when the First National Congress of the Communist party met for the first time.

During the early years of the party, Mao was a functionary carrying out the policy of the Second Comintern and the Chinese Communist Party in cooperation with the Kuomintang. He was elected to membership of the party's Central Committee in June 1923 and was also alternate member of the Kuomintang Central Executive Committee during the honeymoon period between the Communist party and the Kuomintang. He worked in various posts, moving between Changsha, the capital of Hunan Province, Canton and Shanghai, organizing workers and peasants. He temporarily gave up his Kuomintang offices in 1925 and concentrated on peasant organization in Hunan.

In March 1927, Mao Tse-tung made his historic *Report of an Investigation into the Peasant Movement in Hunan* in which he stressed the potential of the peasantry for revolution. Since both the Comintern and Chinese Communist leadership were still cooperating with the Kuomintang, they appear to have rejected Mao's report because of his emphasis upon the peasants as the vanguard of the revolution. Mao Tse-tung has since put the blame for Communist losses during this period upon certain Chinese leaders and the Russian adviser, Borodin.

After Chiang Kai-shek's coup against the Communists at Shanghai in April 1927, Mao was sent back to Hunan to organize. He took part in the Autumn Harvest Uprising, September 1927, which was suppressed by military forces. He then became an outlaw and retreated in October to Chingkanshan, located in the mountains on the Hunan-Kiangsi border. He organized the First Regiment of the First Workers and Peasants Revolutionary Army. He had already been dismissed from the Politbureau in November 1927.

Mao has said that his group did not agree with certain Chinese Communists' policy of "...burning and killing of landlords. The First Army Front Committee refused to adopt such tactics." He was joined in April 1928 by the troops of Chu Teh. They combined forces to constitute the Fourth Red Army. By January 1929, nationalist encirclement tactics forced the Communists to retreat. They settled in January 1929 at Juichen in southeastern Kiangsi and gradually built a soviet base. At this time it is believed that Mao began the formulation of theories regarding organization and leadership. He wrote *On the Rectification of Incorrect Ideas in the Party*, December 1929, his first exposition on party ideological matters. He also wrote *A Single Spark Can Start a Prairie Fire* (January 1930) in which he expected that the present unrest in China would lead to a "prairie fire" of revolution.

Military tactics also were evolving into the basic guerrilla rules which were successful for the Red Army--that of harassing often and attacking only when strong enough.

1. When the enemy advances, we retreat!
2. When the enemy halts and encamps, we trouble them!
3. When the enemy seeks to avoid battle, we attack!
4. When the enemy retreats, we pursue!

After an abortive assault on Changsha in July 1930, which had been ordered by the Chinese leadership, Mao's wife and sister were both executed by order of Ho Chien, governor of Hunan. Mao later wrote a poem to his wife for a friend who also was in mourning. The opening lines are:

I lost my proud poplar, and you your willow.
Poplar and willow soar lightly to the heaven of heavens....

Guerrilla Leader (1930-1935)

During the years 1930-1934, Chiang Kai-shek directed five successive campaigns against the Red Army, which Mao Tse-tung survived by means of his guerrilla methods. An anti-Mao revolt, the Futien Incident (December 1930) seems to have been a struggle for power among the Chinese leadership of the guerrilla forces. The anti-Mao group was arrested and liquidated. Historian Benjamin I. Schwartz has commented: "It is clear even from official sources that Mao Tse-tung did not achieve his position of pre-eminence in the Soviet areas without harsh and bloody conflict." By the end of 1931, Mao Tse-tung had won the position of Chairman of the Chinese Soviet Republic.

The building up of strong bases brought power to the Soviet areas which were based on the peasantry rather than the familiar Marxist doctrine of concentrating on the proletariat in urban centers as other Chinese Communists urged. Schwartz comments, "It was the beginning of a heresy in act never made explicit in theory." Since then, Mao noted that nowhere in Lenin's writings can there be found a hint that the Communist party can exist without its urban base. Historians differ as to the extent of Mao's heresy and whether he was in fact a "heretic."

The Long March -- October 1934-October 1935

Communist statistics on the Long March of 1934-35 are impressive. The Red Army marched some 6,000 miles. There was an average of a battle almost every day. The Communists began with more than 90,000 men in southern Kiangsi and arrived in northern Shensi with less than 20,000 men. They crossed 18 mountain ranges and 24 rivers. They then fought two years before making Yenan the capital of the new Soviet.

The Long March was important, not only as an example of mass determination and heroism, but also as marking the advent of Mao to dominant power and decisive control of the central apparatus of the Chinese Communist Party.

Mao in Power -- The Yenan Years -- 1935-1949

Mao Tse-tung had achieved power without the aid of the Soviet Union and had quietly disregarded, whenever possible, the capture-the-cities strategy of the Communist leadership at this time. But historians point out that the Communist party's advent to final power was achieved primarily by the fact that there were Japanese troop movements in Northern China in 1935 which brought forth a general response from the Chinese people. The Communists quickly exploited these feelings. They projected the idea that they were spokesmen for Chinese nationalism while Chiang Kai-shek sought allies outside of China. Mao proceeded to form a competitive administrative system behind the Japanese lines. By December 1935, the Politburo in Shensi called for a united front with the Kuomintang against the Japanese armies. At this time, Mao gave a series of lectures on *Strategic Problems of China's Revolutionary War* at the Red Army Academy, which was an analysis of the strategy and tactics to be used to defeat the Nationalist military operations.

The beginning of full-scale Japanese aggression in China occurred on July 7, 1937. By July 15, an agreement was reached between the Chinese Communists and Chiang Kai-shek to collaborate against Japan.

The years in Yenan brought forth a number of writings by Mao which are still in use in China. These include: *On the Protracted War* (May 1938), in which Mao envisaged three stages of China's war against Japan: 1. Strategic Defense, 2. Strategic Stalemate, 3. Strategic Counter-Offensive; and *On New Democracy* (1940), which justified the united front, but only as a temporary phase. The ultimate goal was a socialist revolution. The Yenan Forum on Art and Literature in May 1942 put forth the idea that literature is meant for the masses and should be used for the political education of the Chinese people.

The so-called "rectification" program or what is called "brain-washing" in the West was developed during these years. Robert J. Lifton made a study of this program, which became especially active in the years 1948-1952. The program consisted of a course of approximately six months in which the last stage was a final confession of some 5 to 25,000 words usually requiring ten days preparation. The student had to read the confession to the group and could be under cross-examination for five days. Lifton observed,

> . . .in almost every case, its central feature is the denunciation of the father, both as a symbol of the exploiting classes and as an individual.

Lifton also noted that "thought reform" was in the Confucian tradition to the extent that man can and should be re-educated and that he must follow the correct ideological path as the guide to human conduct. The Communists also used the traditional Chinese educational style of constant repetition and the use of exact models. One Chinese remarked on the similarity of the final confession with the old-style Chinese state examination. The untraditional elements in "thought reform" were the open denunciation of the father and the encouragement of "informing" on one's comrades. An early example of the process of "thought reform" may be glimpsed in a speech by Mao Tse-tung in 1942, in which he suggested treatment for those who were "in error" by ". . .administering a shock and shouting at the patient, 'You are ill!' so that he is frightened into a sweat, and then we tell him gently that he needs treatment."

The closed society of the guerrilla environment of Mao and his fellow Communists during these years may have contributed to his seeming lack of knowledge about the United States. He told a reporter in 1947 that there would be a depression in the United States: "I study the market reports very closely. One day soon I'll find in them the first signs of the coming depression. That'll be the beginning of the end of the capitalist system." He was convinced that the "toiling masses" would "march on Washington and overthrow the Wall Street government."

It should be noted that the rectification program during the Yenan period was not a blood purge, although aimed in part at people who had antagonized Mao. The major purpose seemed to be the clarification of doctrine so that it might be clearly implemented in understandable terms to the peasants in the soviet area.

In 1943, Mao had been elected Chairman of the Politburo and the Central Committee. He was also head of a five-man Secretariat of the Central Committee.

In 1945, when World War II ended, the Communists controlled 19 bases with a population of over 90 million people. Both Mao and Chiang Kai-shek sent their troops in, after the departing Japanese army, to gain control of as much territory as possible. All attempts at conciliation were unsuccessful, including the American mediation through Patrick Hurley and George C. Marshall.

By the summer of 1946, there was civil war in China. This was the year that Mao also formulated the famous phrase that all "reactionaries" were "paper tigers."

By the successful use of their tested guerrilla methods, of mobilizing the populace and avoiding unfavorable battles, the Communists entered Peiping as victors on Jan. 25, 1949. They changed the name to Peking.

Leader of Communist China -- 1949-1966

On October 1, 1949, the People's Republic of China was proclaimed by Mao Tse-tung in Peking. Mao's achievement since 1949 has been described as primarily the ability to put all parts of the new order together under an unprecedented degree of central control dominated by Communist theory and practice.

Domestic Policies

Domestic policies after the Communists took power were marked by mounting extremism seemingly encouraged by Mao Tse-tung. The peasants were brought into cooperatives soon after a speech by Mao in July 1955. By 1956, nine-tenths of the peasantry were reported in these associations.

"The Great Leap Forward" in 1958 was an attempt to mobilize workers and peasants for the development of agriculture and industry as speedily as possible. The first commune was established in April 1958 and named "Sputnik." Intellectuals and "dissidents" were mobilized by a series of

"Let A Hundred Flowers Blossom... A Hundred Schools of Thought Contend!"

The text of the speech by Mao Tse-tung to the Supreme State Conference on May 2, 1956, in which he was believed to have set forth this slogan, was not published. Lu Ting-yi, director of the Propaganda Department of the Central Committee of the Chinese Communist Party referred to Mao Tse-tung's speech when Lu spoke on May 26, 1956, to a group of scientists, social scientists, doctors, writers and others in Peking. His speech appeared in the *People's Daily* on June 13, 1956. The following is an excerpt of his remarks:

To artists and writers, we say "Let a hundred flowers blossom." To scientists, we say "Let a hundred schools of thought contend." This is the policy of the Chinese Communist Party. It was announced by Chairman Mao Tse-tung at the Supreme State Conference.

In applying this policy we have gained some experience, but it is still far too scanty. Furthermore, what I am saying is merely my own personal understanding of this policy. . . .

campaigns beginning in 1951. Confessions, apologies, and the reform or elimination of opponents were achieved by labor camp, suicide or execution. Hundreds of thousands accused of being counter-revolutionaries were publicly executed in this period.

Some analysts believe that Mao and his associates may have "brain-washed" themselves into believing that "thought reform" had succeeded with the intellectuals. This is one explanation of the brief, "Let a hundred flowers blossom. . ." unpublished speech of Mao Tse-tung in May 1956 (see box). The open criticism of party policies lasted for one month in the spring of 1957 and was harshly suppressed. A similar campaign of "rectification" of the party cadres was launched about the same time to curb the over-enthusiasm of local Communists in following orders from the top leadership.

In the 1960's, some experts felt that China's economic development was moving ahead. The average Chinese was better fed and better clothed. Some specialists suggested that the relative affluence of the Chinese people might have brought about the most recent campaign of "thought reform" and party purges. In any case, Mao admitted in February 1965 that there was a possibility that Chinese young people could "negate the revolution" by making peace with "imperialism."

Foreign Affairs

Militant revolutionary aims also were evident in Chinese foreign policy during the years 1949-1952. Mao visited Moscow in 1949, having announced a policy of "leaning to one side" against "capitalist imperialism." China intervened in the Korean War and invaded Tibet in October 1950.

The militancy of these years was followed by a phase of diplomatic persuasion exemplified by China's taking part in the Geneva Conference of 1954 and Chou En-lai's theme of "peaceful co-existence" expressed at the Bandung Conference of April 1955.

Mao and his associates intervened apparently in the Polish and Hungarian crises of 1956. Allegedly, Mao advised the Poles to develop their own brand of socialism. But late in 1957, after the Hungarian revolt, Mao no longer emphasized individual roads to communism, but rather a hard line. He supported the Soviet Union and spoke of opposing "revisionist tendencies." Speaking to Chinese students in Moscow November 1957, after the successful launching of the Russian "Sputnik," he said that the "east wind prevails over the west wind" and called for a new militancy in East-West relations. These words were followed by the Quemoy crisis in 1958 and the suppression of rebellion in Tibet. In 1959, Peking had precipitated a border crises with India and was backing guerrillas in Laos. Mao's personal role during the years 1958-63 was considered obscure although it was believed that he was at the center of decision-making in Peking. The growth of Chinese disenchantment with Russia was openly acknowledged in 1963, and Khrushchev was damned as a "revisionist."

Mao Tse-tung retired as Chairman of the People's Republic in 1959 but held on to the all-important post of chairman of the Communist Party Central Committee. In the mid-1960s, he was reported as ill and convalescing and was not seen in public from November 1965 until May 1966, when he met the Premier of Albania and subsequently other foreigners.

A film of Mao greeting African and Asian writers in July 1966 showed him apparently improved in appearance. This film was followed by pictures and stories of his swimming nine miles for 65 minutes in the Yangtze July 16, 1966. Anna Louise Strong has said that Mao was directing the latest purge, the Great Proletarian Cultural Revolution, and that it was his "crowning gift" to the revolution. Mao Tse-tung, the rebellious son, had become the center of a cult of mass admiration, reminiscent of the adulation of Stalin. His "swim" in the Yangtze displayed almost legendary fortitude, according to the *New China* news agency. He reportedly even stopped at one point to teach a young woman the backstroke. Foreign witnesses were quoted as saying that "Chairman Mao's good health and long life is the happiness of all the oppressed peoples of the world."

Mao's Personal Life

Mao Tse-tung has been married four times: the first was an "arranged" marriage and he has stated that he never lived with the bride. His second wife, Yang Kai-hui, was executed in 1930. His third wife was Ho Tzu-chen who accompanied him on the Long March. They were divorced in 1937. Mao then married Lan Ping in 1939. She was described as a "comely moving-picture actress, later known as Chiang Ching, from Shanghai."

Mao had several children. One son was killed fighting in Korea. Another son was an engineer living in the provinces and a daughter was a student at Peking University.

In personal appearance, Mao was described as above average height for a Chinese. Although he was thin as a young man, he gained weight over the years. He was a heavy smoker but cut down in later years. He always lived simply. In the Yenan days, he lived in a two-room "cave" dwelling with a few pieces of furniture. He has been described as having the habits of a peasant. Edgar Snow told of interviewing Lin Piao with Mao present: "It was extremely hot inside the little room. Mao lay down on the bed, pulled off his pants, and for twenty minutes carefully studied a military map on the wall. . . ."

In the 1960s, Mao Tse-tung lived in one of a group of palace buildings formerly occupied by court mandarins. His comforts were described as roughly equivalent to those of a successful American businessman living in a New York suburb.

Estimates of Mao

One analyst said that Mao and his associates evolved a very sophisticated view of power as the product of many complex factors including military, political, economic and psychological elements with special emphasis upon the psychological ingredients.

Another specialist saw Mao as a combination of Lenin and Garibaldi. A left-wing historian gave the highest credit to Mao for his originality in synthesizing ideas and for making slogans that were understood by great masses of people, but questioned these "simplifications" in the building of socialism in a more complex society. Furthermore, the writer, Stuart R. Schram, expressed the fear that Mao's "thoughts" might become the source of mechanical and dogmatic repetition rather than a creative answer to the specific problems of Communist China. Mao Tse-tung himself once said, "Any ideology -- even the very best, even Marxism-Leninism itself -- is ineffective unless it is linked with objective realities, meets objectively existing needs and has been grasped by the masses of the people."

Lin Piao: Communist General

Mao Tse-tung once said, "Our principle is that the party commands the gun, and the gun will never be allowed to command the party." Lin Piao, Marshal of the Red Army, Defense Minister, Vice Premier of the government, member of the standing committee of the Politburo, and deputy chairman of the Military Affairs Committee, was a "gun" for Mao Tse-tung ever since they came together in 1928 at Chingkangshan.

According to Lin Piao's own account, he was born in Hupeh Province in 1908 of a "lower middle-class family," which fit party bias toward peasant and proletarian backgrounds. His father was in fact the owner of a small handcraft factory. Lin attended Whampoa Military Academy in 1924, where he studied under the famed Soviet general of the Siberian Civil War, Vassily K. Blucher, who was acting as Chiang Kai-shek's Chief of Staff. Lin was recognized as a brilliant student at Whampoa. When he graduated in 1925, he participated as a lieutenant in the Northern Expedition and then became a captain.

Lin stated that, during 1925, he became a Communist. Lin said that Chiang Kai-shek, commandant of the Academy, demanded that the students at Whampoa choose either the Kuomintang or the Communist party. Lin made his choice for the Communists and resigned. However, he served in the Nationalist Army as an officer. Under Chu Teh's command in the Kuomintang army, Lin took part in the Nanchang Uprising in August 1927 which was an abortive Communist attempt to take the city. This date also marked the beginning of the Red Army in China. He then retreated under Chu Teh's command to Swatow where they were again defeated. After further defeats including the Canton Uprising, Chu Teh and Lin Piao, with a remnant of some 1,000 troops, led their soldiers to Chenchow where they made contact with Mao Tse-tung's brother, Mao Tse-tan, and arrived in the vicinity of Chingkangshan to join Mao's group and merge the Red

Army probably in April 1928. In 1930, Lin took command of the Fourth Red Army. By 1932, he received the command of the First Red Army Group at the age of 25. He said proudly that he had never been defeated since he held this command although he had fought in more than 100 battles.

Long March Leader

Lin led the First Red Army Corps on the Long March which lasted 370 days, covering a distance of some 6,000 miles from October 1934 to October 1935. Lin's corps acted as the vanguard in the crossing of the Wu River. His troops captured Tsunyi literally without firing a shot in January 1935. According to one source, Red Army soldiers dressed in Kuomintang uniforms came to the town claiming to be survivors from a battle and begged to be let in. The gates were opened and the Red Army took the town. It was at Tsunyi that Mao Tse-tung emerged as the leader of the Chinese Communist Party. The Long March was so rigorous that Lin Piao almost died on the edge of Tibet during a severe snowstorm.

In Yenan, Lin was considered one of the half-dozen military geniuses of recent Chinese history. He was President of the Chinese People's Anti-Japanese Political and Military Academy in 1937, when he married Liu Hsi-hing, who was a student at the Academy. In the same year, he was the commander in a brilliant victory over Japanese troops at Pinghsinkwan. At this time, Lin went to see a Japanese captain who had been taken prisoner. When Lin entered, the captain remained seated and is said to have ordered Lin to get him chicken, eggs and rice to eat. Lin replied: "Do not misunderstand the kindness with which we treat you. It does not mean that we are your inferiors. We serve you rice while we ourselves eat millet. I hear that you struck a peasant who came to look at you. We won't kill you for this, but if you ever strike a Chinese again, we will whip you in public."

He was severely wounded in 1937 or 1938 and is supposed to have spent four years in the Soviet Union recuperating from his wounds.

After the defeat of Japan, Lin commanded the Northeast Liberation Army which took Manchuria. He rose steadily in party and government ranks since 1949. He was the Commander of the Chinese troops when China entered the Korean War in 1950. Lin was appointed a Vice Premier in 1954 and then became a member of the Politburo and a marshal of the armed forces until that title was abolished in 1965. When the Defense Minister was purged in 1959, Lin received that post. He then set to work to "reform" those army officers who chafed at political interference in military affairs. Lin was alleged to have forced high ranking officers to serve for a while as orderlies and privates so as not to lose their allegiance to the proletariat. Lin Piao was described by a sympathetic observer as a "more compliant and less colorful figure" than Marshal Peng Teh-huai whom he replaced.

World Attention

Lin Piao came under world scrutiny after the publication of his essay, "Long Live the Victory of People's War!" on Sept. 2, 1965. His article was concerned with the theory that the "countryside" of the world (the underdeveloped countries) can provide the basis for revolutionary movements which would encircle the "cities of the world" (North America and Western Europe).

Some experts considered Lin a leading contender in the 1966 struggle for power in Peking in the high party ranks.

Others saw him as Mao's own choice in the succession pointing out that he was photographed repeatedly in 1966 with Mao, that a letter written by Lin and published in all major Chinese papers June 19, 1966, was signed with his untitled signature -- an honor which Lin alone shares with Mao Tsetung. In August 1966, the reported roster of leaders at a mass rally listed Lin in second place after Mao which reinforced the speculation as to Lin Piao's growing importance.

He was described as short and frail, nervous and a driving personality. He also was considered very anti-foreign and possibly anti-Russian. Little is known about his private life.

Chou En-lai: The Red Mandarin

Chou En-lai was like Kipling's *The Cat That Walked By Himself*. He kept his own counsel and always managed to land on his feet in the swirling world of Communist party politics. Except for one public admission of "cowardly rotten opportunism" before the Fourth Plenum of the Chinese Communist Party in January 1931, he managed to be at the center of power in the party since the early 1920s.

Early Years

He was born in Kiangsu Province in 1898. His family was part of the Chinese "Establishment," since his grandfather was a wealthy official in the Manchu Dynasty and his father a teacher while his mother was a well-educated woman. En-lai means "advent of grace," which he was named, according to some sources, because his father had just passed an examination for the higher bureaucracy of the Mandarinate.

Chou En-lai attended the American missionary college, Nankai University, where he was considered a brilliant student. He met his future wife, Teng Ying-chao, at the University. Chou entered into China's politics and took part in the student rebellion of 1919, known as the May 4th Movement. He and his future wife were arrested and he spent a year in Tientsin Prison, according to one account. Upon his release from prison, Chou went abroad to work and study in France and then visited the French branch of the Chinese Communist Party in February 1921. Chou spent a year in Weimar, Germany, where Chu Teh, the future Communist general, met him. At this time, a visitor found Chou En-lai as "a slender man of more than average height with gleaming eyes and a face so striking that it bordered on the beautiful....Chou was a quiet and thoughtful man, even a little shy as he welcomed his visitors."

Leadership and Defeats

The Communist line in the early twenties involved close cooperation with the Kuomintang. Chou became Chiang Kai-shek's deputy political commissar of the newly-formed Whampoa Military Academy in 1924. He was on friendly terms with Mao Tse-tung in nearby Canton where they both were connected with a training college of organizers for the peasant movement sponsored by the Kuomintang.

Chou stated that he was sent to Shanghai to prepare a workers' insurrection for Chiang Kai-shek. On March 21, 1927, Chou called a general strike which closed down all of the industries of the city. Chiang took Shanghai March 22.

However, a few days later, on April 6, Shanghai police raided the office of the Soviet military attache and found many documents showing a direct connection between the U.S.S.R. and various Chinese Communist activities. One observer has pointed out that this could hardly have been a surprise to Chiang but apparently the Generalissimo had decided he could do without further Soviet support at this juncture. On April 12, Chiang Kai-shek's troops led an attack on the Shanghai labor unions. Some 5,000 Communists, labor leaders and others were killed. Chou En-lai became a fugitive. He was captured by Chiang's Second Division and orders were issued for his execution. But, according to one account, he escaped through the help of a former student from Whampoa.

Chou then went to Nanchtang to help organize the August 1st Uprising of 1928, which lasted for four days, followed by the evacuation of the Communist troops on August 5. There followed a series of the temporary occupations of towns, only to be followed by defeats and retreats. Late in 1928, Chou was forced to flee to Hong Kong suffering from malaria. He then went underground and later made a trip to Russia on a party matter. He returned to China for the Third Plenum September 1930 in Lushan. Here he seems to have supported the leadership which was soon to be condemned and discredited by the Comintern and the Chinese Communist Party. By January 1931, Chou En-lai spoke of his "cowardly opportunism" but also got a place for himself on the new Central Committee. At about the same time, he also was reported in charge of the successful liquidation in Shanghai of the family of Ku Shun-chang, in retribution for Ku's betrayal of a close friend of Mao Tse-tung.

Chou En-lai then seems to have joined Mao by November 1932, when he led the operations against the Fourth Encirclement of the Soviets around Hupei and Kiangsi. Although his leadership was successful, the Fifth Campaign of the Nationalists forced the Chinese leaders to make the decision to begin the Long March in October 1934. Chou was sick only once on the Long March, but his wife Teng Ying-chao, whom he had married in 1925 after his return from Europe, contracted tuberculosis. Chou again emerged on the winning side with Mao in the struggle for power of the Chinese Communist leadership at this time.

The Yenan Years

With the capture of Yenan in December 1936, Chou worked as the able lieutenant of Mao Tse-tung. Edgar Snow saw him in 1936 in a small village in control of a radio station through which Chou kept in direct touch with all important points in the Soviet area. His headquarters was a "bombproof hut." Another visitor considered him the best dancer at Yenan. "He was perfection in the waltz -- sometimes a too restrained perfection," according to Anna Louise Strong.

By far his most successful role has been his flair for diplomacy. He was part of the delegation in December 1936 sent by Mao to Sian, where the "Young Marshal" Chang Hsüeh-liang held Chiang Kai-shek prisoner. Here, Chou exhibited the charm which he has shown very often to diplomats when he is supposed to have said to Chiang Kai-shek: "Mr. Chairman, I have come to sign betrothal articles for the remarriage of the Kuomintang and the Communist party so that together we can defeat the common enemy, Japan." Chou then spent time in Nanking, Hankow and Chungking, in liaison with the Kuomintang. With the outbreak of the civil war between the Nationalists and the Communists, Chou took part in the truce talks instigated by the United States. Although Mao considered that Patrick Hurley, the United States envoy, had acted in bad faith, Chou sent a letter dated December 6, 1944, in which he said that Chairman Mao Tse-tung had asked him to express deep thanks and appreciation for Hurley's "sympathy and energetic efforts" on behalf of unity in China.

Premier of Red China

Since October 1949, when Chou En-lai stood next to Mao Tse-tung at the victory parade of the Chinese Communists in Peking, he has been in the top group of decision-makers listed either third or fourth in precedence. He has been described as a planner rather than an ideologist and is considered by some authorities to be part of the group among the leadership which is inclined toward gradualism in the achievement of Communist goals. For example, there is a difference between Chou's proposals in late 1956 for orderly and more gradual economic development and what has been described as the "frantic...tempo of the 'great leap forward,'" proclaimed by Liu Shao-chi in early 1958.

That these differences are concerned with means and not with ends is illustrated by Chou's public utterances and behavior since 1949. He warned the United States in October 1950 that if it thought the Chinese weak, it was making the same error as the Kuomintang: "...whoever would wipe out and destroy the interest of this quarter of the human race, and foolishly think to settle arbitrarily any Eastern question directly related to China, then he will certainly break his head and spill his blood."

Chou En-lai opened the campaign for "ideological reform" of the intellectuals on September 29, 1951, which was followed by the publication of "confessions" of well-known Peking professors, such as the Dean of the College of Law at Peking University, who said he had made the "serious mistake of holding on to my views."

In July 1957, Chou on the dais, as the vice-chairman of the Peasants and Workers Party, broke down and cried as he addressed the Chinese Parliament. He had been attacked as belonging to the "rightist opposition." One observer has reported the scene: "...I saw the speaker wipe away his tears with a handkerchief. This went on for a while -- a few sentences, then sobs and tears. Every time he dried his eyes he had to take off his glasses." Chou was reported by several sources as carrying on an animated conversation during the entire time.

In June 1966, Chou En-lai described the current purge as a "cultural revolution" to create a "new culture" of the proletariat and peasantry. At a luncheon toast in Bucharest, he said: "We want to liquidate entirely by this great cultural revolution all the old ideas, the entire old culture...created by the exploiting classes in the course of thousands of years...."

He has been an able spokesman for Communist China abroad, where he represented his country at the Geneva Conference in 1954. Chou played a leading role at this meeting, since it was clear that Peking had the power to decide whether there would be war or peace in Viet Nam. His proposals and private meetings with French Prime Minister Pierre Mendes-France broke a deadlock at one point. Chou En-lai told a writer that in Geneva he met John Foster Dulles in a lounge where the two men were alone. Chou extended his hand but stated that Dulles put his hands behind his back, shook his head and left the room. "That was really carrying even reaction to extremes," said Chou.

Chou En-lai was a striking success at the Bandung Conference of 1955, according to many observers. Even when there were arguments whether Communist colonialism should be condemned along with Western colonialism, he was seemingly unperturbed: "We do not hide the fact that we believe in communism...there is no need at this conference to publicize one's ideology."

Chou broke off a tour he was making through South Asia to fly to Moscow and then to Poland and Hungary in January 1957. According to some sources, Chou told the Poles that China would support them provided that they did not break publicly with Russia as did Yugoslavia in 1948. Chou supported the Russian position in Hungary. One analyst has explained the difference in China's position toward Poland and Hungary as, in part, due to the Chinese desire to share with Russia the hegemony of all of the Communist parties but with no one else.

On October 1961, Chou was in Moscow at the twenty-second Congress of the Communist Party of the Soviet Union. The break between Moscow and Peking was evidenced by Chou's laying of a wreath at Stalin's coffin which read, "To the great Marxist-Leninist." This action was matched by Khrushchev's attacks on the leaders of Albania. Before Chou's sudden departure, he appealed to the Russians to stop their open criticism of another Communist party. It is not surprising that, in 1964, Chou stated in an interview that he approved of the downfall of Khrushchev.

Home Life

Chou En-lai and his wife have been variously described as living in a small apartment and also a one-story house in Peking. Their furnishings included a piano, a hi-fi and a television set, as well as a bust of Mao Tse-tung. He neither drank nor smoked. His wife, who was an alternate member of the Central Committee, once spoke of their courtship: "We fell in love only after he went to Europe...he proposed to me after three years of correspondence." One of the few times Chou En-lai has expressed public regret was at the death of John Foster Dulles. Chou said Dulles was such a "downright reactionary" that it was easy to anticipate his reactions.

Liu Shao-chi: Organizer

Liu Shao-chi, Communist China's Chief of State, has been referred to as the "organization man," the individual responsible for much of the difficult, behind-the-scenes work of the party over the last 40 years. Once at the pinnacle of power as second-in-command to Mao Tse-tung, and viewed as the heir apparent, Liu, in 1966, became a chief target of the militant Red Guard movement and was openly denounced in posters and pamphlets for obstructing the Cultural Revolution.

In the struggle for power in Communist China, Liu was dropped from 2nd to 8th place in the roster of leaders at Peking rallies after a meeting of the Central Committee in August 1966. He was replaced in the second position at that time by Lin Piao.

Liu is associated with the more moderate elements of the Chinese Communist Party (CCP), proposing a pragmatic and less doctrinaire approach to China's domestic and economic problems. In his fall from favor, he was accused of clinging to the "reactionary bourgeois thought" of former

Soviet Premier Nikita Khrushchev -- or peaceful co-existence -- as opposed to the Mao line of revolutionary violence.

Liu, whose seniority in the Chinese Communist movement parallels that of Mao, was charged in late 1966 with issuing orders in the name of the party in June of that year, when Mao was absent from Peking, which violated Mao's policy line and almost "perverted" the Cultural Revolution. Liu at that time organized work teams to conduct the early phases of the Cultural Revolution and to oversee the activities of the Red Guards. The work teams have since been disbanded, but critics of Liu, including Mao's wife, Chiang Ching, stated that the teams tried to restrain the Guards to prevent damage to the national party organization.

This attempt on the part of Liu to assume control of the Cultural Revolution, according to Stanley Karnow of the *Washington Post*, "has become a key to the current resistance to Mao, and it may ultimately contribute to the collapse of Maoism." On Dec. 26, 1966, reports from Peking indicated that Liu had "confessed" his crimes to the Red Guards and that he and Teng Hsiao-ping, the party's Secretary General, did "not have much time left in liberty." On Jan. 14, 1967, however, Japanese correspondents reported that Liu had retracted this "self-criticism," an indication that he and Teng were faring well in the power struggle.

Early Life

Liu was born in Hunan (Mao's native province) in 1898, to well-to-do peasant parents. He studied first at Peking's National University and in 1919, under Comintern auspices, went to Moscow where he attended Sun Yat-sen University as part of a radical group known as Toilers of the East. He joined the CCP in Moscow in 1921, the year it was founded.

Soon after Liu's return to China, he organized his first strike -- among the coal miners -- before he was 25 years old. By 1925, Liu was vice president of the newly founded China Labour Federation at Canton. He spent the next ten years in the labor movement, recruiting and organizing workers and leading trade unions in underground activities. Liu was closely associated with Chou En-lai during this period.

Revolutionary Activities

In 1932, Liu moved to the Kiangsi Soviet area, where Mao was establishing himself. When Communist headquarters was transferred to Yenan in the north, Liu took part in the "Long March" (1934-35). Having joined the party Politburo in 1931, he became Central Committee representative to the 8th and 5th Corps and eventually political commissar of the 3rd Corps. In 1941 he was appointed political commissar of the New Fourth Army.

Liu spent the years 1935-45 engaged in organizational work in Yenan. When the Kuomintang and the Communists formed their united front to fight the Sino-Japanese War, Liu helped the Communists to consolidate their following and expand the areas under their control. By 1943 he was Vice-Chairman of the People's Revolutionary Military Council and Secretary of the Party Secretariat.

The basis for study during the first Party Rectification Campaign in 1942 was provided in two lectures delivered by Liu to the Party School in Yenan. The lectures, *On the Training of a Communist Party Member*, delivered in 1939, and *On Struggle Within the Party*, delivered in 1941, were followed by an article published in 1943 entitled *Liquidate the Menshevik Ideology Within the Party*. They became

Communist classics, concerning themselves theoretically with events during Mao's successful rise to power. Placed in charge of the massive rectification campaign by Mao, Liu wrote in the 1943 essay: "The...campaign of self-education and self-criticism in the party is unprecedented in the history of the past 22 years. It has given our party a unique impetus towards the Bolshevik road."

Rise in the Party Structure

Liu's success in handling this phase of the party's development led to his appointment the following year as General Secretary of the party, a post he held until 1954. At the 7th Party Congress in 1945, he was re-elected to the Party Central Committee and to the Politburo. He delivered the report on the new Party Constitution which adopted "democratic centralism" as the form of administration.

When the Sino-Japanese war ended in 1945, Liu acted as party Chairman when Mao went to Chungking to negotiate an agreement for peaceful coexistence with Chiang Kai-shek. In 1949, when Mao visited the Soviet Union, Liu was again leader of the party, but on this occasion he was also acting head of State.

After the Nationalist government was driven from the mainland and the Communists were establishing their position, Liu held numerous official posts and made important pronouncements to the party on most major issues. He was named to the Constitution and Electoral Law Drafting Committees in 1953, which produced the Constitution of the Chinese People's Republic and endorsed "democratic centralism" as the form of State administration. Under the new laws, Liu was elected deputy for Peking and member of the Standing Committee of the National People's Congress.

In 1956, at the 8th Party Congress, Liu was elected a Vice-Chairman, of the Politburo's Standing Committee, an elite five-man group introduced for the first time that year. He again delivered the political report to the Congress which placed the emphasis on the "democratic" side of centralism.

Internal Activities

When the policies of the Great Leap Forward in agriculture and industry were launched during 1957 and 1958, Liu was extremely active inside China. He toured much of the country and, at the second session of the Eighth Party Congress in May 1958, he revealed by implication troubles within the party over economic, and possibly other, policies. He defended the 1956 leap forward and stressed that only by speeding up advance could the state be consolidated.

International Activities

Liu was active on the international level as well. In 1952, he attended the 19th Soviet Party Congress in Moscow where he remained for three months. In 1960, he headed the Chinese party and government delegation to Moscow for the 43rd October Revolution anniversary, and spent a month touring other cities such as Leningrad, Minsk and Irkutsk. He attended the meeting of 81 Communist and Workers' Parties, which issued the 1960 Statement and Appeal to the Peoples of the World. In 1963, he held talks with Ho Chi Minh in Hanoi, and he visited Indonesia, his first trip to a non-Communist nation. In 1964, he headed the CCP delegation meeting with representatives from Rumania and Japan. In March 1966, Liu, accompanied by Foreign Minister Chen Yi, paid a state visit to West Pakistan. At that time, Liu declared Peking's support for Pakistan in its dispute with India over Kashmir. The following month, Liu and Chen visited Afghanistan on the personal invitation of King Mohammad Zahir Shah, who visited Peking in 1964.

Private Life and Appraisals

Little is known of Liu's private life. He is believed to have been married twice, and in recent years appeared in public with an attractive young wife. Mrs. Liu also came under attack in the 1966 purge. One observer described Liu as "precise, stubborn and imperturbable." (Article in *Diplomat* Magazine, September 1966, by Howard Boorman.) Another said that Liu maintains a "sour puritanism." (Article in the *New York Times*, July 23, 1966.) In general, Liu is considered thorough and intellectually able, but lacking Mao's warmth and flair.

Liu's chief ally in the 1966 resistance to Mao was Teng Hsiao-ping, Secretary General of the CCP. Teng's biography follows.

Teng Hsiao-ping

Teng Hsiao-ping was a veteran Communist, but a relative newcomer to the top echelons of political power in Communist China. Holding minor, regional posts before 1950, he rose rapidly since then in government and party ranks. In 1954, he became secretary-general of the Central Committee of the Chinese Communist Party (CCP), a position with responsibility for top-level administration and coordination of party affairs. In addition, Teng became a member, in 1956, of the important seven-man Standing Committee of the Politburo, the policy-determining core of the party structure.

Teng became one of the principal targets in the 1966 Red Guard movement and was denounced as against Mao thought and the "cultural revolution."

Born in 1904 in Szechuan, Teng Hsiao-ping, known also as Teng Wen-pin, went to France in 1920 to study under the Work-Study plan. There he made his first contact with communism when he joined the French-educated group of young Chinese Communists, which included Chou En-lai and Chen Yi. Unlike these men, however, Teng did not play a prominent role in the Chinese Communist Party's early development.

After spending several years in France, where he learned to speak fluent French, Teng, in 1924, went to the Soviet Union for a few month's stay. After his return to China, he became dean, in 1926, of a military school in Shensi, which was established by Feng Yu-hsiang, a friend he met in the Soviet Union while both were visiting there. The military academy became a center for radical activities in Shensi province.

Regional Activities

In the period between 1928 and 1930, Teng played a leading roll in organizing and leading the Seventh Red Army in Kwangsi and in transmitting instructions from senior party officials to these guerrilla forces.

Teng held minor posts in the propaganda section of the CCP General Political Department between 1932 and 1934. These assignments were in the Communist-controlled districts in Kiangsi, where Mao Tse-tung had established himself. In this period, Teng edited the CCP army newspaper, *Hung-chi (Red Star)*. He also served as instructor at the Red Army Academy in Juichin in 1933, where he lectured on "The Construction of the Communist Party."

Teng took part in the Long March from Kiangsi to Shensi (1934-35). During the march, Teng headed the propaganda section of the First Red Army Group. At Shensi, he became successively, director, vice-chairman, and chairman of propaganda, political department, First Army Corps.

With the outbreak of the Sino-Japanese war in 1937, the Communist forces were reorganized into the Eighth Route Army, composed of three divisions. Teng became political commissar of the 129th division, which was responsible for Communist military-political operations in the Shansi-Hopei-Shantung-Honan border area. At this time, Teng was also a member of the Central Committee's North China Bureau.

Between 1943 and 1945, Teng was the director of the general political department of the People's Revolutionary Military Council at Yenan. This group represented the top planning organization of the Chinese Communist military establishment.

Teng gained membership for the first time to the Central Committee of the party in 1945. This was the occasion of the Seventh National Congress of the CCP meeting at Yenan. The Central Committee was expanded at this time to include members from the group of Communist military commanders and political commissars who attained prominence during the war against Japan.

In the civil war period between 1946 and 1948, Teng continued in these positions. In addition, he served as deputy commander and political commissar of the re-named Second Field Army of the People's Liberation Army. When the Communists came to power in 1949-50, the Second Field Army moved through the central Yangtze region and occupied the entire southwest. Teng then became political commissar, Southwest Military Region, a post he held until 1954.

National Activities

Since 1950, Teng moved swiftly from the level of regional political activity in the Communist military establishment to the "highest echelon of national leadership in Communist China."

In 1952, Teng was called to Peking. His first central post was that of vice premier and member of the State Planning Committee (until its reorganization in 1954). He served briefly from 1953-54 as Minister of Finance, and also joined as vice-chairman, the Committee of Finance and Economic Affairs.

During the 1954 reorganization of the national government at Peking, Teng served on the committees responsible for the drafting of the 1954 Constitution of the People's Republic of China and the national election law. He was secretary general of the Central Election Committee.

At this time, Teng was a member of the first National Committee of the Chinese People's Political Consultative Conference (CPPCC), and from February 1953, a member of its standing committee. From 1954-59, Teng served on the standing committee of the Second CPPCC. He was not re-elected to the Third CPPCC in 1959, but in April of that year, Teng was re-elected vice premier of the State Council and vice chairman of the National Defense Council. In 1959, Teng joined the National People's Congress (NPC) as deputy for Szechan. (He was not elected to the new parliament (NPC) in 1954.)

Party Accomplishments

Teng became the secretary general of the Central Committee in May 1954. In April 1955, he became a member of the Politburo, ten years after his initial appearance as a member of the Central Committee in Yenan. During the Eighth Party Congress in 1956, a Politburo Standing Committee was established for the first time and Teng was nominated to membership. He thus became the only member of the Chinese Communist Party who was concurrently a member of the Politburo, of its Standing Committee and of the Party Secretariat.

Teng delivered the report at the Eighth Party Congress on the new party constitution, which emphasized the "democratic" side of "centralism." He also reported to the Central Committee in September 1957 on the Rectification Campaign, a result of earlier criticism during the liberalization period. The campaign was designed to eliminate bureaucracy from the party. In May 1958, Teng reported on revisionism to the second half of the Eighth Party Congress.

In 1958, Teng attended the Provincial Communist Party Committee meeting in Liaoning, when an anti-party clique was smashed. As secretary general of the party, Teng was the leader of all provincial party organizations.

International Activities

Teng Hsiao-Ping was among the top party leadership at various international meetings since 1950. In July 1955, he was a member of the CCP delegation which held talks with the North Vietnamese government. In February 1956, he was the ranking deputy to Chu Teh (then vice chairman of the Central People's government at Peking), who led the Chinese delegation to the 20th Congress of the Communist Party of the Soviet Union (CPSU) in Moscow.

Teng ranked second to Mao Tse-tung in November 1957, when a Chinese delegation attended the 40th anniversary celebration of the Russian revolution in Moscow. In 1960, he was deputy chief of the CCP delegation to celebrate the revolution. Teng remained in Moscow at this time to attend the Conference of Communist Parties in November, when a compromise was reached between the differences in interpretation of Chinese and Soviet Marxism. In July 1963, Teng led a CCP delegation to the Soviet Union, again to conduct high-level party talks. He maintained at this meeting a hard line on Sino-Soviet relations.

Teng met with Asian Communist party leaders on many occasions since 1958. He signed a joint communique with the secretary general of the Japanese Communist party in March 1959, and with the Italian Communist delegation in April of that year. He gave a reception in March 1959 for an Indonesian party delegation, and was present in June 1960 at a meeting with Mao and the Indonesian Communist leader, Aidit. In 1961, he received Singhalese party leaders, and with Mao, the Panchen Lama of Tibet, and Ho Chi Minh of North Viet Nam.

Teng was acting premier during Premier Chou En-lai's tour of Africa and Southeast Asia in the winter of 1963-64. He served in this capacity again in March 1965. In Sep-

tember 1964, he was elected deputy for Peking to the Third National People's Congress.

Appraisals

Teng Hsiao-Ping has been identified as a "close comrade-in-arms" of Mao Tse-tung from May 1958 until 1966. He was described as a hard-liner. "He simply wants to take over the country, and apparently thinks the way to do it is to concentrate on the development of China rather than getting diverted into a war with the United States over Viet Nam, or conquering Asia, or winning an argument with the Russians about who is the true disciple of Lenin." Teng was also described as "adroit, argumentative, articulate and ambitious."

Chiang Kai-shek: The Undaunted

I look for no reward, not even Heaven, but I look for the happiness of men; to lead those who have strayed, to enlighten those who live in the darkness of error, to banish from the earth all pain and suffering.
(Fo-Cho-Hing-Tsan-King)

This quotation is said to have been admired by Chiang Kai-shek as a young man. It is believed by many to express the central credo of this paradoxical figure: one who converted to Christianity and still embraces Confucian philosophy, who is quick to admit failure, yet is said to be ruthless with his critics, who has daily Bible readings yet is considered by some to have turned his back on corruption.

Chiang grew up in a time of treachery and violence in his country. He began his career with the determination of restoring China to its ancient greatness, but all his politics revolved about the concept of force.

The military conquest of his rivals in the early days was accomplished while Chiang set himself as a moral example as head of the state. It is said that no one can understand Chiang Kai-shek without understanding Confucius. Sanctions of government power in this philosophy are based on a single, consistent pattern of authoritarian ideas. There is emphasis on right conduct on the part of the ruler. This tenet prompted many admissions of personal failure from Chiang, followed by apologies and offers to resign throughout his career.

Despite this Confucian humility, Chiang doesn't think in terms of public opinion or popular approbation. In the mid-1960s, looking at his country across a 110-mile strait from the island of Formosa, Chiang considered that his right to rule the Chinese people was assured by his "infallible judgment and his view of himself as the indispensable man."

The Early Years -- 1887-1925

Chiang was born on October 31, 1887, at Chikow in Chekiang Province into the family of wine merchant Chiang So-an and his third wife. Chiang's father died when he was nine and his boyhood was impoverished and difficult.

China, during this time, was in a period of "unprecedented chaos and disaster." It was prey to corruption, internal fighting among warlords preserving their own dynasties and "every humiliation foreign arms could heap on her." Chiang, moved by the national disaster, chose to become a soldier.

At the age of 19, Chiang entered China's first military academy at Paoting, near Peking. He was an outstanding student, and by the end of the first year he was selected by the imperial Chinese government as one of the cadets to be sent to Japan for advanced military training. Chiang spent the next four years, 1907-1911, at the Imperial Military College in Tokyo, where he was first a student, then a Japanese artillery officer.

In Japan, Chiang first met Chen Chi-mei, a noted revolutionary leader, who was said to have initiated him into revolutionary activities. Under Chen's sponsorship, Chiang joined the secret society, Tungmenghui, in 1907. It was at one of the meetings of this organization that Chiang first met Dr. Sun Yat-sen, known as the "father" of the Chinese revolution.

Chiang was still in Japan at the time of the "Wu-chang Uprising" on Oct. 10, 1911, which deposed the Manchu Dynasty. The subsequent proclamation of a Chinese Republic on Feb. 12, 1912, with Dr. Sun as provisional President, brought Chiang back to China. He was already a staunch supporter of Dr. Sun.

For the next ten years, the political structure of China was a "patch-work of confusion." Regimes were overthrown and re-established, only to be overthrown again. Both Sun and Chiang during this period spent some time in exile in Japan.

The years of failure and exile in the decade following the Manchu collapse convinced Sun that what was needed to unify China was not only a political instrument, organized by him as the Kuomintang, but a military one as well.

In the early twenties, Dr. Sun established contact with Lenin. In 1932, a Soviet political mission arrived in Canton, which was the capital of the newly established Republic of South China, and by now "the seat of an incandescent revolutionary movement." A Russian agent, Michael Borodin, became Sun's political adviser.

Chiang, meanwhile, had been sent to Canton in 1917, after several years of leading "an obscure existence as a small stockbroker in Shanghai." In Canton, Chiang was already the young hero of the revolution, and was attached to general headquarters, according to biographical accounts.

In August 1923, Sun sent Chiang, who was now Chief of Staff, to the Soviet Union to study its political and social system. He remained in Moscow for six months and returned in early 1924. Unlike Dr. Sun, however, Chiang was never attracted by the Communist ideology.

On his return, Chiang organized and became the first commandant of the Whampoa Military Academy. The Academy was to produce men who would wield force, not for its own sake, but for a new China. Chiang told his cadets -- who included Chou En-lai and Lin Piao -- that the great common bond between the revolutionary Kuomintang and Soviet Russia was their mutual determination "to vanquish imperialism and liberate the peoples enslaved by it."

A Soviet marshal, Vassily Blucher, was assigned as Chiang's chief adviser. (Blucher was also known as Galen. He later became the commander of the Russian armies in Manchuria.) Training in military tactics as well as in tactics of political propaganda gave the young army officers an unusual fighting spirit coupled with a revolutionary zeal.

Dissension had begun to overtake the Kuomintang leaders, but Sun was able to keep the party together during his lifetime. When he died on March 12, 1925, the Kuomintang was under a Central Executive Committee composed of right-wing leader Hu Man-min, the Borodin-supported

> *No adequate biography of Chiang Kai-shek will appear in our times. Many of those who could best tell of his career are dead; the others are either his bonded servants, who see him as a saint, or his desperate enemies, who seek only his destruction. It has been too dangerous too long in China to record the facts of Chiang's career, so that now all that is known, apart from a few idolatrous official biographies, consists of morsels of gossip.*
>
> **Theodore White and Annalee Jacoby in** Thunder Out of China. *(p. 38)*

Wang Ching-wei, and Chiang, who was also chairman of the Military Affairs Commission.

Hu Man-min died soon afterwards, leaving the other two men poised to fight for control of the party. Chiang, from the early 1920s, began to suppress peasant unions and to indicate in various ways his hostility towards the Communists and Kuomintang members who supported them.

In 1925, Chiang staged a military coup, which was followed by the flight of Wang, and the naming of Chiang as Commander-in-Chief, Northern Expeditionary Force.

The Northern Expedition -- 1926-1927

The "Northern expedition" was a campaign of the revolutionary armies of the Kuomintang to march from Canton to the Yangtze Valley with the goal of reclaiming China from the warlords. It was the dream of Sun Yat-sen since 1917 and was adopted as the objective of the Kuomintang. The expedition was finally launched in the summer of 1926, with the plan of attack devised by the chief Russian military adviser, Gen. Blucher.

Chiang was given dictatorial powers by the Kuomintang for the duration of the Northern expedition. He declared that the party "would follow the program that Sun had laid down: a phase of military supervision first, then a period of political tutelage, and finally a constitutional government."

From his march to the Yangtze Valley, Chiang became aware that certain groups, principally wealthy Chinese in Shanghai, were looking to him to give the Kuomintang a more conservative leadership. In return they could offer him a base of support for his armies and his party. Chiang discovered he no longer needed to be dependent on Russian aid.

As Chiang prepared to enter Shanghai in March 1927, he was aided by a Communist-led union, which first disarmed and then expelled the warlord garrison. Chiang, a month later turned on the union and suppressed it in a ruthless massacre. Similar massacres of workers belonging to radical labor movements followed, deflecting the Kuomintang from its leftward orientation.

Within a year of the Shanghai coup, communism was illegal in China. After the capture of Nanking in March 1927, Chiang named that city the new capital. He invited the support of all those who were opposed to communism and Russian domination.

This was the year that split Sun Yat-sen's followers. Yet both the Kuomintang and the Communists claim to be his true heirs. His 100th birthday in 1965 was celebrated by both Communist China and Taiwan.

The Nanking Government -- 1927-1937

For ten years in the period between 1927 and 1937, the new Nationalist government saw a period of "modern and effective growth." In Chiang Kai-shek, the government "had a leader who met the demands both of ancient tradition and of modern polities."

The Nanking government was recognized by both the United States and Great Britain during 1928. In that year also, Chiang was named Chairman of the State Council and Generalissimo of the Chinese Fighting Forces.

The domestic achievements of the Nationalist government were many. The labor movement, agriculture and education all made considerable headway. Payments on the general public debt were resumed and eventually "China was enabled to announce the final balancing of its budget."

Credited with this achievement was T. V. Soong, Chiang's brother-in-law, who, as a world-renowned financier, established Chinese finance on the Western system. He founded the Bank of China and as Minister of Finance for the Nanking government, was responsible for negotiating large United States loans to China.

It was the decade from 1927 to 1937 which saw the advance of the Japanese into Manchuria and North China and, on the domestic side, the launching of Nationalist campaigns against the Chinese Red Army.

This was also the period of the New Life Movement, which was the title of a book written in 1937 by Chiang and his wife, Madame Chiang, the former Mei-ling Soong, who was the American-educated daughter of Charles Jones Soong, Chinese Christian and businessman. The Chiangs were married in Shanghai in December 1927, and soon afterwards, Chiang himself was converted to the Methodist faith.

The Movement, begun in 1934, stressed the reform of China through personal virtue. "It attacked uncleanliness, sloppy dress, unpunctuality and bad manners generally." Nine years later, in 1943, Chiang published his "China's Destiny," which again encouraged Confucian virtues and urged "moral regeneration and the patriotic subordination of the individual to the state."

The integrity and efficiency of the Nanking government were nonetheless subject to criticism, according to Robert C. North in "Moscow and Chinese Communists." "In facing the Japanese invasion, Kuomintang leaders had resorted to a series of special measures -- the expansion of the New Life

Chiang's Anti-Americanism

In 1926, an American reporter, Lewis Gannett, interviewed Chiang Kai-shek, then commander-in-chief of the Chinese Nationalist armies. During the interview, Gannett quoted Chiang as saying:

"Thinking men in China hate America more than they hate Japan. Japan talks to us in ultimatums; she says frankly she wants special privileges. . . .We understand that and we know how to meet it. The Americans come to us with smiling faces and friendly talk, but in the end your government acts just like the Japanese. And we, disarmed by your fair words, do not know how to meet such insincerity. This is what is behind the anti-Christian movement in China. Your missionaries write 'charity' over their doors, and I do not deny that many of them are good men who do good work. But in the end they make it easier for American policy to follow that of the other imperialist powers. So because we have been deceived by your sympathetic talk, we end by hating you most."

Movement devoted to a regeneration of Confucian teachings, the formation of the rigidly disciplined San Min Chu I Youth Corps, the granting of extraordinary powers to Chiang, the arbitrary designation (rather than election) of a portion of National Congress membership, the re-introduction of party cells, and the further development of party purging facilities through the party supervisor's net. . . all of them features which impressed many Westerners as essentially nondemocratic and potentially authoritarian in spirit."

In effect, the new Kuomintang government was considered a dictatorship, with Chiang himself as the driving spirit.

The struggle against the Communists in this period was "savage and relentless." In areas Chiang controlled, "his police butchered Communist leaders, families of known Communist leaders were wiped out; students were watched and spied on, and possession of Communist literature was made a crime punishable by death."

By 1934, the Communists broke out of Chiang's blockade line and embarked on the spectacular Long March, streaming across China from the south to re-establish themselves in the northwest. This feat was accomplished by the end of 1935 in the areas north of Yenan in Shensi province. Shensi later became the Communists' chief base.

United Front Against Japan -- 1936-1938

Principal factions within the Chinese Communist Party hoped to form an anti-Japanese united front from the time the Japanese army seized Manchuria in 1931. In August of 1935, the Seventh World Congress of the Comintern proclaimed a world-wide united front policy against fascism, and the Chinese Communist Party decided to include the Kuomintang within the united front. Stalin, it appeared, went further and insisted that although Chiang had not renounced his anti-Communist policies, only Chiang could lead a united front. The matter remained in abeyance until the following year.

The call for Chinese unity against the threatening advances of Japan began by 1936 to penetrate the Nationalist army. The government's troops, blockading the Shensi soviet troops under Mao Tse-tung, had come to agree with the Communists' view that all Chinese should stop fighting each other and unite against their common enemy.

In December 1936, Chiang flew to Sian, headquarters of the blockading troops, to "prod" his commanders into activity against Mao's troops. (It was said that Chiang's policy of virtual non-resistance to the Japanese was largely determined by the desire to concentrate on the struggle against Communism.) Chiang flew into a trap at Sian, and was kidnapped by one of his commanders, the "Young Marshal," Chang Hsueh-liang.

The Chinese Communist party, under a delegation headed by Chang and Chou En-lai, then a representative of the party, succeeded in bringing about an agreement whereby Chiang was released on Christmas day -- two weeks after his "kidnapping." This was the first time Chiang had met with the Communists personally since 1927.

Chiang's position at the outset was that there was nothing about which to negotiate. His unwillingness to discuss matters with his captors was softened somewhat by the arrival in Sian of Madame Chiang and her brother, T.V. Soong. (One writer has said she was accompanied by an "Australian friend.") At that time, another writer said: "The great problem was that of finding a basis of agreement between himself and his captors which would enable them, on their side, to release him without fear of the consequences to themselves, and on his side, to maintain his prestige as commander-in-chief and head of the government."

What actually happened at this meeting was never recorded in full. The release was ostensibly unconditional. It appeared, however, that Chiang gave verbal pledges to stop civil war, to form a united front with the Communists against Japan and to effect certain reforms in his regime.

Chiang returned to Nanking amid unprecedented national rejoicing. His detention made him more than ever a symbol of national unity. Yet four days later, Chiang submitted his resignation, albeit a nominal one, which was "elaborately declined." He said: "Since I am leading the military forces of the country, I should set a good example for my fellow servicemen. It is apparent that my work failed to command the obedience of my followers; for otherwise the mutiny, which nearly resulted in the collapse of the foundation of the state, would not have occurred . . . I sincerely hope that the central executive committee will censure me for my negligence of duties. After the Sian incident, it is no longer fit for me to remain in office."

The following year saw much negotiating between the two groups. The Kuomintang began to implement the commitments made at Sian and the Communists for their part suspended anti-Kuomintang activity. Chiang's release paved the way for Chinese unity against Japan -- an essential weapon in combating the full-scale hostilities opened six months later by the Japanese army on July 7, 1937, in North China.

Chiang remained commander-in-chief with the advent of Japanese hostilities. Peking, Shanghai and Nanking were lost within the year. The Chinese capital was moved to Hankow. In 1938, Hankow and Canton fell. Chiang moved the capital to Chungking in 1939, 1,000 miles inland.

The War Widens -- 1939-1945

The united front began to disintegrate by 1939. Once the central government was forced to retreat to Chungking, it began to drift steadily to the right, a position which led to a "war within a war" and a long period of civil war strife. "Chiang continued to fear the Communists more than he feared the Japanese. He feared social reforms more than he feared military defeats."

Japan's attack on America at Pearl Harbor on Dec. 7, 1941 presented new considerations. On Dec. 8, Chiang declared war on both Germany and Italy. In a brief message to President Roosevelt, Chiang said: "To our new common battle we offer all we are and all we have, to stand with you until the Pacific and the world are freed from the curse of brute force and endless peril."

In January 1942, President Roosevelt sent Major General Joseph W. (Vinegar Joe) Stilwell to China to command a large body of Chinese and American troops. Chiang by this time was appointed Supreme Commander for Allied Powers in the China Theater and Stilwell was named by the Generalissimo as his chief-of-staff.

Stilwell favored the united front of Chiang and the Communists and continued to press for a coalition government in which the Communists would be represented. Stilwell disagreed with Chiang on other matters relating to the war and the two men clashed openly. When Stilwell was relieved of his command, to be replaced by General Wedemeyer in 1944, Chiang had the dispatches of foreign correspondents translated into Chinese and censored them himself.

The Civil War -- 1945-1949

The Japanese surrender in August 1945 occurred at the time a race was developing between Chiang and the Communists for control of territory occupied by the Japanese armies. Chiang's hold on North China was insecure, and it was said that, were it not for the presence of American marines and American transport, the Kuomintang would have been unable to move into the major ports and cities. Four years of civil war ensued, during which time negotiations between the Kuomintang and the Chinese Communist Party were conducted under American auspices.

Criticism of Chiang had begun to infect Chungking by 1944. His critics "believed that Chinese energies were being held back by the nature of Chiang's political balances and commitments, that he could not balance corruption, duplicity and extortion to get a net effect of strength. Energy could come only from the people, and Chiang's alliances bound him to the oppressors of the people."

Discontent with Chiang Kai-shek's government had spread among the peasants as well by 1944. Reports -- half gossip, half fact -- of peasant uprisings began to reach the capital. Chiang had the press silenced, and signs hung in country tea houses: "It is forbidden to discuss national affairs." Critics were singled out and terrorized by Chiang's secret police.

Chiang's assessment of his role during this period was that he was leading China to democracy. Any references to himself as a dictator made him furious. When Chou En-lai, the chief Communist representative in Chungking, told him that the Communists would turn over control of their army only to a democratic government, Chiang replied, "Would you call *me* undemocratic?"

Chiang became the first constitutional president of China when the first National Assembly under a new Constitution convened in the spring of 1948. His reign as a democrat ended after six months. The continuation of the civil war, the Communist victory in Manchuria in late 1948, and the threat of losing Nanking to the Communists sent Chiang into retirement on Jan. 21, 1949.

The "retirement" was short-lived, lasting less than two months. Chiang returned to head the Supreme Policy Council at Canton and to resume command of the Kuomintang army. The mainland positions began to collapse before the Communist advance in the early months of 1949. During the last four months of 1948, the Nationalists lost a million men -- mostly by desertion -- and half a million rifles. By December of 1949, Chiang was forced to retreat from the mainland and move to Taipei on the island of Formosa, where he arrived on Dec. 10, 1949.

When Chiang relinquished the presidency in January 1949, he was still "Tsungtsai" of the Kuomintang and head of the Kuomintang Emergency Committee. Acting President, Li Tsung-jen, refused to go to Taiwan and the Legislative Yuan asked that Chiang return to the presidency. On March 1, 1950, Chiang Kai-shek resumed the office of president of Nationalist China.

Taiwan -- The Island Refuge -- 1949-1966

Taiwan consists of 14,000 square miles of productive farm land and flourishing industry. Its economic progress over the years has been striking, despite the fact that about four-fifths of the national revenues are spent on national defense. The domain's total area is smaller than the smallest province of mainland China, and its population of over 12 million (ten million native-born Taiwanese and two million Nationalist exiles) is about one-sixtieth of that controlled by Peking.

In addition, the Nationalists hold a number of lesser islands, namely those of the Matsu group and Quemoy. Quemoy is only 2,300 yards from Red China, and it is here that the Nationalists and the Communists shout at each other through electronic loud-speakers, an exchange described by a news correspondent as "my old mandarin can lick your old mandarin."

Martial law has been in effect ever since the Nationalists retreated to Taiwan, but in practice, wide areas of government were left to civil rule. Chiang, however, retained control over the main instruments of power, delegating some of the functions only to a small group of trusted collaborators. He oversaw the armed forces, where every important officer candidate must be approved by him (the officer corps is 96 percent mainlanders); the Kuomintang, whose members were placed throughout the government structure; and the police system, the secret operations of which were under a close Chiang subordinate.

Chiang's Personal Life

Chiang Kai-shek lives in a large house surrounded by trees and a high wall in suburban Taipei. The house is an unostentatious one, decorated by a few of Madame Chiang's own Chinese ink paintings. Chiang dresses in the high-necked tunic devised by Sun Yat-sen, with plain buttons and no insignia of rank. At home, he likes to relax in the traditional gown of the Chinese gentleman of long ago.

Chiang makes few public appearances, mostly for ceremonial functions. He does most of his work at home where officials come at his bidding, although several times a week, in a convoy of limousines carrying aides and body-guards, he drives to his office in the Ministry of National Defense.

Lean and erect, Chiang has a remarkably unlined face for his 80 years. His head is almost bald and he has a closely cropped white mustache. He celebrates his birthdays quietly and follows the Chinese custom of eating the traditional "longevity noodles." His birthday invites island-wide celebrations, with toasts proposed for Chiang's health at "thousands of dinners."

Chiang was married twice. The first marriage, when Chiang was 15, was arranged by relatives, and terminated in divorce nine years later in 1911. This marriage produced Chiang's only child, Chiang Ching-kuo, said by observers to be his political heir as leader of the Nationalist government. Chiang and his second wife, Mei-ling Soong, whom he married in December 1927, have no children.

Return to the Mainland

Return to the mainland has become the entire rationale for Chiang's leadership and the existence of his regime. "Either we exist to return to the mainland or we have no existence worth mentioning," Chiang said. He lives with the single-minded dedication to this objective and no opposition to this policy is permitted on the island. Return is very much a cardinal tenet of faith and Chiang sees himself as providing leadership for the perennially imminent attack on the mainland. The Nationalist army, however, has been described as "too big for defense and too small for attack." It is considered top-heavy with brass, having "about 400 more generals and 700 more colonels than the United States Army, which is more than twice its size."

In 1960, Chiang apologized for failure to recover the mainland. In an address to the opening session of the National Assembly, he said, "So great is my fault that I wish sincerely to surrender myself to you for punishment." The Assembly responded with cries for a third six-year term for the President. He has since been re-elected to a fourth term on March 21, 1966.

On that occasion he said: "As I am approaching 80, I would prefer retirement and return to private life. But I have been encouraged by the constant thought that I should redeem myself for what I have thus far failed to do for our nation. I feel my obligation unfulfilled so long as the Chinese mainland is not recovered."

Estimates of Chiang

One observer said that Chiang's regime failed to meet the needs for social change in Chinese society. The revolutionary ideals which brought the Kuomintang into existence were the very ones with which Chiang could not cope.

Another analyst said that Chiang played a transitional role between old and new, acting both in the traditional pattern of a dynastic founder and in the modern fashion of a party leader. "His strength has lain in these traditional qualifications: courage and determination to retain power, moral fervor and austerity that give him personal prestige, loyalty to those who are loyal to him, ruthlessness and subtlety in balancing his rivals against one another."

The view of experts in the mid 1960s was that Chiang's return to the mainland from his "temporary" island was not a realistic goal. Furthermore, there was a growing feeling that Nationalist China must agree to some political compromise in order to preserve its own self-interest.

Madame Chiang Kai-shek: The Missimo

Madame Chiang Kai-shek, wife of the Generalissimo, was described by some as charming, witty, eloquent and the personification of "Free China." She was seen by her critics as imperious, ambitious, calculating and a hard-boiled politician.

Madame Chiang was born Mei-ling Soong in Shanghai, the fourth of six children of Charles Jones Soong, a prominent Chinese Christian and businessman. There were conflicting reports of her age. On a visit to the United States in 1965, Madame Chiang said this on the subject: "What does it matter whether I am 64 or 67 or something else? You can tell the age of a person not by the calendar but by his, or her, purpose in life, character and willingness to be of service to the world." Records from Wellesley College, from which she graduated with honors in 1917, give the date of her birth as June 5, 1897.

Madame Chiang was a member of a distinguished family. When the Soong sisters were growing up in Shanghai, there was a saying: "One (now Mrs. H.H. Kung) loves money, one (Madame Chiang) loves power, and one (now widow of Sun Yat-sen) loves China." (Mme. Chiang and Mme. Sun, who lives in Shanghai, have not seen each other since 1940.)

Soon after her marriage to Chiang Kai-shek in 1927, Madame Chiang began with the Generalissimo a campaign to unite China against the warlords and the Communists.

In 1936, when Chiang was kidnapped by a commander of his own troops in the famous Sian Incident, Mme. Chiang flew to Sian to help win his release. It was said that, at that time, she instructed an aide to shoot her "without hesitation if the rebels got out of hand."

Mme. Chiang founded the Chinese Air Force when the Japanese attacked China, and until her retirement in 1938, she was Secretary General of the Air Ministry.

During World War II, she made several visits to the United States seeking help for her country. In 1943, after 26 years in China, she returned to this country and addressed a joint session of Congress in what was considered a memorable and moving speech.

Madame Chiang was present with her husband at the Cairo conference in November 1943 to discuss plans for the defeat of Japan, with President Roosevelt and Prime Minister Winston Churchill. She frequently broke into the discussions, whether or not invited, saying, "If you allow me, I shall put before you the Generalissimo's real thoughts." It is said this period represented the peak of Madame Chiang's career.

In his private papers, Lt. General Joseph W. (Vinegar Joe) Stilwell described Madame Chiang as "direct, forceful, energetic, loves power, eats up publicity and flattery, pretty weak on history. Great influence on Chiang Kai-shek, mostly along the right lines, too."

Considered one of the first ladies of the world, Madame Chiang in 1966 devoted most of her time to charities, particularly orphanages which she helped establish. She shared the confidence of her husband that the Nationalists on Formosa would retake the China mainland. "Some troops get tired of waiting, but our troops are different, they have a cause," she said in a visit to the United States in September 1965. Her last previous visit to the United States was in 1958.

Leading Figures in United States-Far East Developments

Following are capsule biographies of the leading figures in the events which took place in the Far East during the 1940s, 1950s and 1960s. Names are alphabetized according to the practice of the nationalities involved. Generally, the first names control the positions of the Chinese, Laotians and Tibetans; last names those of Westerners, Cambodians, Burmese and Vietnamese.

D. N. Aidit. Leader of the Indonesian Communist Party (PKI) before its abortive coup in October 1965; believed to have been assassinated in Central Java after the attempted coup, but his death was not confirmed; became active in political youth movements at the age of 16; studied politics in a Jakarta school during the Japanese occupation; became a member of the PKI, 1943, became its secretary general, 1954; close adviser to President Sukarno and held the formal rank of minister without portfolio since 1962, although he had no cabinet functions. Aidit headed the oldest Communist party in Asia and the largest outside the Soviet Union and Communist China. There were unconfirmed rumors in December 1966 that his wife, also a party member, and daughter had been captured.

Dr. Herbert Aptheker. Leading theoretician of U.S. Communist Party; has filled various party posts; one of 16 authors whose books were removed from State Department libraries abroad, 1953; author of several historical books, including "A Documentary History of the Negro People in the United States"; currently professor American Institute for Marxist Studies; candidate for Congress in Brooklyn, 1966; accompanied Thomas Hayden and Professor Staughton Lynd on trip to Hanoi, December 1965.

Mohammed Ayub Khan. President of Pakistan since 1958; studied military tactics in England and commissioned to the Royal Fusiliers, 1928; commanded a battalion in Burma during World War II; appointed commander-in-chief of Pakistan Army, 1951; defense minister, 1954; helped President Iskander Mirza oust Pakistani government, and days later seized power himself, driving Mirza into exile, 1958; instituted sweeping land reform program and government reorganization as president. Communist China's support of Pakistan in its dispute with India over Kashmir resulted in an increasing Pakistani drift toward Peking in 1965. This was arrested somewhat by the 1966 Tashkent agreement between India and Pakistan and the subsequent upheaval in China.

Bao Dai. French-oriented chief of state of Viet Nam 1949-55, when Premier Ngo Dinh Diem's nationalistic government was formally voted into power; emperor of Annam (later made into part of Republic of Viet Nam) 1926; placed under custody of Japanese in 1945; abdicated same year and went to live abroad three years; returned as head of Viet Nam state in 1949, but gradually lost control of Congress and Nationalist forces which considered him too pro-French, appointed Ngo Dinh Diem as premier, 1954; living in exile on the French Riviera, 1966.

A. Doak Barnett. Political scientist; born in Shanghai, China; fellow at Institute of Current World Affairs in China and Southeast Asia after attending Yale University; correspondent for the *Chicago Daily News,* 1947-50, 1952-53; headed foreign area studies branch of Foreign Service Institute, State Department, 1956-57; research fellow at the Council on Foreign Relations, 1958-59; program associate at the Ford Foundation, 1959-61, authoring a report on Chinese economic development; professor of Political Science at Columbia University, 1961- ; director, Association of Asian Studies, 1962-65; author of a number of books on China; appeared before 1966 Senate Foreign Relations Committee hearings on U.S. China policy.

Jacob D. Beam. Career Foreign Service officer and specialist in Eastern European Affairs; chief counselor, U.S. Embassy in Indonesia, 1949-51, and Yugoslavia, 1951-52; acting head U.S. Embassy in Moscow, 1952-53; Deputy Assistant Secretary of State

for European Affairs, 1955-57; U.S. Ambassador to Poland representing the United States in negotiations with Communist China, 1957-61; assistant director, International Relations Bureau of the Arms Control and Disarmament Agency, 1962-66; U.S. Ambassador to Czechoslovakia, 1966-

Eugene R. Black. Graduated from University of Georgia in 1917; joined Atlanta banking firm in 1931, and later served with Chase Manhattan Bank in New York City, 1933-47; executive director for the U.S. International Bank for Reconstruction and Development, 1947-49; continuing as president, 1949-62; special assistant to UN secretary general and adviser on foreign aid to the State Department, 1962-66; led U.S. mission to South Viet Nam to apply civil aid programs, 1966. President's adviser on Southeast Asian development since 1965, advising U.S. support of Asian Development Bank and encouraging Asian effort in developing resources of the Mekong valley.

Prince Boun Oum. Rightist Premier of Laos, 1960-61; educated in French schools; member of Royal Council and later minister of defense when French granted Laos a measure of autonomy; agreed to coalition government after pressure by U.S., which had formerly backed him, 1961; received U.S. support as successor to Deputy Premier Phoumi Nosavan in coalition government, 1965.

Gen. Omar Bradley. Educated at U.S. Military Academy, graduating in 1915; commissioned as Second Lieutenant in U.S. Army infantry, 1915; during World War II was commanding general in Northern Tunisia campaign, Sicilian operations, and served in European campaigns including the Normandy invasion, 1944; Administrator for Veterans' Affairs, 1945-47; U.S. Army chief of staff, 1948; chairman of Joint Chiefs of Staff, 1949-53, leading opposition to Gen. Douglas MacArthur's plan to involve Communist China in the Korean conflict; chairman of the board of the Bulova Watch Company, 1958.

Leonid I. Brezhnev. First Secretary of the Soviet Communist Party 1964- ; educational background in agriculture and engineering; rose rapidly during Stalin purge (1936-38); elected to the Central Committee in 1952; elected deputy to U.S.S.R. Supreme Soviet, 1954; became chairman of the Presidium of the U.S.S.R. in 1960; replaced Nikita Khrushchev as party secretary, October 1964.

Nikolai A. Bulganin. Achieved prominence as a leading political officer in the Soviet Army during World War II; named Politburo member in 1946 and defense (Armed Forces) minister, 1947-49, 1953-55; "elected" premier in 1955 when Communist party head Nikita S. Khrushchev gained control of the Soviet government; reportedly joined anti-Khrushchev faction and several months later, in March 1958, replaced by Khrushchev as premier; later expelled from Presidium (formerly Politburo) and Communist Party Central Committee.

William C. Bullitt. U.S. Ambassador to the Soviet Union, 1933-36, and to France, 1936-41; Ambassador-at-large, 1941-42; decorated for wartime service in French army; advocated extensive U.S. military and technical aid to the Nationalist Chinese government in 1948 to ensure the defeat of Communist forces; died February 1967 in Paris.

McGeorge Bundy. Special assistant to the President for national security affairs, 1961-66; Army intelligence officer; administrator of the Marshall Plan and a research analyst on foreign policy; dean of faculty at Harvard in 1953; leading figure in Viet Nam policy formation in Johnson Administration; joined Ford Foundation as president, 1966.

William P. Bundy. Assistant Secretary of State for Asian and Pacific Affairs, 1964- ; joined Central Intelligence Agency, 1951; investigated by Sen. Joseph R. McCarthy (R Wis.) after making a contribution to the defense of Alger Hiss; staff director of President Eisenhower's Commission on National Goals, 1960; as defense deputy, coordinated arms shipments to India in 1962 conflict with Communist China; Assistant Secretary of Defense for International Security Affairs, 1963; entered State Department in 1964 and became a principal spokesman for Johnson Administration policy in Southeast Asia.

James F. Byrnes. U.S. House of Representatives, 1911-25; practiced law in Spartanburg, S.C., 1925-31; U.S. Senate, 1931-41; Supreme Court associate justice, 1941-42; director of Economic Stabilization, 1942; director of War Mobilization, 1943; U.S. Secretary of State, 1945-47, playing an important role in post-war U.S.-Soviet-Chinese relations; Governor of South Carolina, 1951-55.

Gen. Chang Chun. Influential conservative member of Kuomintang in 1930s; opposed cooperation with Communist movement; served as Minister of Foreign Affairs before World War II; in mid-1940s became more liberal; represented Nationalists in 1946 peace discussions with Gen. George C. Marshall and Communist Gen. Chou En-lai; Premier of first coalition government, 1947-48, cabinet member, 1948-49.

John M. Chang. Premier of South Korea, 1960-61; studied at Manhattan College in U.S.; school principal in Seoul; elected to Representative Democratic Council after World War II; Ambassador to U.S. and premier under government of Dr. Syngman Rhee; led opposition to Rhee in 1956, elected vice president; survived assassination attempt in 1958.

Chang Nai-chi. A leader of anti-Japanese resistance in 1930s; held various commercial posts in Chinese Communist government; minister of food, 1956; criticized "sectarian and doctrinaire way of thinking and working style of Chinese Communist Party," charging that "the national bourgeoisie in essence is now no different from working class" and "as an enemy, bureaucracy is more dangerous than capitalism"; after admitting theoretical errors, officially branded a "rightist" and ousted from many positions, 1958.

Chang Po-chun. Long-time Chinese Communist politician, administrator, diplomat and frequent critic of ideological rigidity; called for the establishment of a "political designing institute," referred to as the "Chang Po-chun and Lo Lung-chi alliance"; branded a "rightist" and excluded from 1958 session of National People's Congress; removed from minister of communications post in 1958.

Thich Tam Chau. Leader of the Unified Buddhist Secular Affairs Institute in South Viet Nam; head of the moderate faction of Buddhists who opposed Thich Tri Quang during the 1966 Buddhist uprising against the Ky regime.

Chen Cheng. Premier and vice president of Nationalist China until his death in March 1965; long military career; chief lieutenant and one-time heir apparent of Chiang Kai-shek.

Chen Po-ta. Since 1958, editor-in-chief of the Chinese Communist Party theoretical journal *Hung Chi (Red Flag);* ranked fifth after Mao in 1966 listings; full member of the CCP Central Committee since 1946, and since 1956, an alternate member of the Politburo; became political secretary to Mao at the outbreak of the Sino-Japanese war in 1937; attended with Mao negotiations in Moscow on Sino-Soviet Treaty of Friendship, 1949-50; vice-president of Chinese Academy of Sciences since 1949; elected delegate representing social science organizations to 2nd, 3rd and 4th Chinese People's Political Consultative Conferences (CPPCC), and to its Standing Committee, 1954 to present; elected deputy for Shanghai municipality to 2nd National People's Congress, 1958, and re-elected to 3rd NPC, 1964; deputy director, Propaganda Department, CCP Central Committee, 1957 to present; author of many books, including *The Thought of Mao Tse-tung, On the Cultural Front, Chiang Kai-shek, Don't Disrupt the Industrial Organization;* considered the one most capable of interpreting the thought of Mao and identified in July 1966 as the "leader of the group in charge of the Cultural Revolution under the party's Central Committee."

Chen Yi. Foreign Minister of Communist China since 1958; studied law and commerce at Peking University and later in France; joined Communist party in 1923; led troops seizing nationalist capital of Nanking, 1949; mayor of Shanghai, 1949-58. Although criticized by some Red Guard posters in late 1966, Chen's position in Mao's faction nevertheless appeared stable.

Chen Yun. Vice Premier of China's State Council since 1954; vice chairman of Central Committee of the Chinese Communist Party and member of Standing Committee of Politburo since 1956; started career as labor organizer in Shanghai where he met Liu Shao-chi; joined CCP, 1925; elected to Central Committee, 1931, and to Politburo, 1934; participated in Long March, 1934-35; left for U.S.S.R., returning after outbreak of Sino-Japanese War, 1937; held various government and party posts with assignments in the economic areas of government; currently considered China's principal economic planner; minister of heavy industry, 1949-50; chairman of Economic-Financial Committee, 1949-54, member of State Planning Committee, 1952-54; accompanied Chou En-lai to Moscow to negotiate for return of China Railway, 1952; led Chinese "observer" group to Moscow to important intra-Communist bloc economic and military meetings, 1958; acting premier during Chou's visits abroad, 1955, 1957; elected deputy for Shanghai municipality to 2nd National People's Congress, and to 3rd NPC, 1964; was disgraced by resisting the economic policies of Mao's Great Leap Forward, but restored to favor by subsequent reappointment as vice premier in 1965; dropped in the listings of the hierarchy, 1966.

Claire L. Chennault. Army pilot; retired in 1937; served as an adviser to Chiang Kai-shek, 1937-41; head of the Flying Tigers; recalled to active duty and promoted to brig. general, 1942; organized and commanded the China Air Task Force, 1942; activated 14th Air Force and commanded 1943-45; major general, 1943; retired, 1945; president and director of the Civil Air Transport, Inc., 1948-55; chairman and director of the Asiatic Aviation Co., Ltd., 1955-58; died in 1958.

Chiang Ching. Former Shanghai movie actress known as Lan Ping, became Mao's fourth wife in 1939; lived in relative obscurity until 1966, when she appeared in Peking as deputy chairman of the Proletarian Cultural Revolution, in whose name the 1966 purges were conducted; also holds position as cultural advisor of the Chinese Army; considered an important figure in the Communist hierarchy in her own right; reportedly a member of the Central Committee, ranking 25th behind Mao in the Peking listings.

Chiang Kai-shek. President of Nationalist China. *See page 232.*

Mme. Chiang Kai-shek. *See page 236.*

Chiang Nan-hsiang. Chinese minister of higher education, 1965-66, ousted in 1966 purge; joined Communist party on the recommendation of Chou En-lai and led student movement against the Japanese in North China; began career in youth affairs as department chief in Youth Work Committee, 1949; vice minister of education, 1960-64.

Chou En-lai. Premier of Communist China. *See page 228.*

Chow Shu-kai. Nationalist China's ambassador to the United States since April 1965, succeeding Dr. Tingfu F. Tsiang; educated at London and Cambridge Universities; began diplomatic career as an attache at the Chinese embassy in London; ambassador to Spain, 1962-65.

Chu Teh. Chairman of the Standing Committee of the National People's Congress since 1959; vice-chairman of the People's Republic of China, 1954-59; currently vice-chairman of the Politburo, ranking 9th in the 1966 roster of Peking officials; joined the Chinese Communist Party at age of 36 with encouragement from Chou En-lai, after almost 20 years of independent guerrilla fighting; became member of CCP Central Committee and chairman of its Revolutionary Military Committee in 1930; became member of the Politburo in 1945, and of its standing committee in 1956; served as commander-in-chief, Chinese People's Liberation Army, 1946-54; elected deputy for Szechwan Province to National People's Congress, 1954, 1958 and

1964; headed CCP delegation to Warsaw and Budapest, 1959; participated in talks with D. N. Aidit, chairman of the Indonesian Communist Party, 1963. Criticized in some Red Guard posters in late 1966 and early 1967, but defended by Chou En-lai.

Gen. Mark W. Clark. Commander-in-chief, U.S. occupation forces at the end of World War II and a State Department representative at 1947 Austrian treaty negotiations; head of U.S. Sixth Army on Pacific Coast, 1947-49; succeeded Gen. Matthew B. Ridgeway as commander-in-chief, UN Forces in Korea in 1952 until conclusion of fighting and truce talks in Panmunjom.

Dalai Lama. Religious ruler of Tibet; rose to power from peasant origins; enthroned in 1940; assumed full power in 1950 and fled to India, after abortive resistance to Chinese, 1959; leader of all Buddhist sects in Tibet.

Arthur H. Dean. Succeeded John Foster Dulles in 1949 as senior partner of New York firm specializing in international law; chairman of the Institute of Pacific Relations, 1950-52; appointed special deputy to Secretary of State Dulles, with rank of ambassador, to negotiate for a Korean political peace conference, 1953-54; subsequently recommended U.S. recognition of Communist China and support of British plan to seat "two Chinas" in the UN; U.S. delegate to UN General Assembly, 1961-62, and chairman, U.S. delegation to 1961-62 Geneva nuclear test ban negotiations and 1962 Disarmament Conference.

Brig. Gen. Christian de Castries. Commander of French fortress at Dienbienphu when it fell to Viet Minh rebels on May 7, 1954; taken prisoner, freed after four months in Communist prisoner-of-war camps; said he was convinced Viet Minh were independent of Communist China but were "animated" by nationalism; assigned to West Germany in 1955, reportedly causing some protest from Germans because of his alleged order to destroy Freudenstadt during World War II.

Ngo Dinh Diem. President of South Viet Nam, 1955-63; studied for Roman Catholic priesthood at age 15 but gave it up and attended a school for civil servants; rose to the post of minister of the interior in the cabinet of Emperor Bao Dai, 1933; resigned when he discovered the real power was held by a French adviser; returned to Saigon in 1954 after four years of exile in Japan, the United States, Belgium, and France; accepted Bao Dai's (now chief of state) request that he assume premiership, 1954; ousted Bao Dai as chief of state in 1955 elections; remained in power, with heavy U.S. support due to his staunch anti-Communist stands and social reform programs, until intense Buddhist opposition and a military coup resulted in his "accidental suicide" in November 1963.

Pham Van Dong. Designated vice president of Ho Chi Minh's rebel Vietnamese government in 1949 and head of the Viet Minh delegation to the 1954 Geneva conference on Indo-China; named premier and foreign minister of North Viet Nam in 1955; relinquished the foreign ministry position in 1961 but retained the premiership through early 1967.

Justice William O. Douglas. Appointed associate justice of U.S. Supreme Court, 1939, by President Roosevelt; one of the founders of the Emergency Committee for Chinese Refugees, 1962. Advocated demilitarization of Taiwan and admission of Communist China to the United Nations in 1965; State Department granted request for permission to travel to Peking in 1966, a trip he never took.

Everett Francis Drumright. U.S. Ambassador to Republic of China (Taiwan), 1958-62; served as foreign service officer in the Far East 1931-43, 1948-52; appointed deputy assistant secretary for Far Eastern Affairs, 1953; consul general with personal rank of minister, Hong Kong, 1954-58.

Eldridge Durbrow. U.S. Ambassador to Viet Nam, 1957-61; foreign service officer; counsel in various European countries, 1930-37; joined State Department in 1942 in Eastern European Affairs division.

Anthony Eden (First Earl of Avon). Conservative member of British House of Commons, 1923-57; foreign secretary, 1935-38,

1942-45, and while serving as Winston Churchill's deputy prime minister, 1951-55; succeeded Churchill as prime minister, 1955-57; maintained Conservative support of U.S. Formosa policy while advocating "abandonment" of Quemoy and Matsu and inclusion of both Nationalist and Communist China in the UN.

Prof. John K. Fairbank. Member of Harvard University history department since 1936, director of Harvard's East Asian Research Center; on leave with State Department, 1941-46, serving as special assistant to U.S. Ambassador in Chungking, China, 1942-43, in Far East section of Office of War Information, 1944-45, and as director of U.S Information Service in China, 1945-46; trustee of the American Institute of Pacific Relations, 1947-51. Charged with having Communist ties by two former Communists, Louis Budenz and Elizabeth Bentley, during 1951-52 Congressional hearings; charges were dropped after Fairbank's denial. Leading witness at 1966 Senate Foreign Relations Committee hearings on U.S. China policy.

Nikolai Fedorenko. Soviet Union's permanent representative to the UN since 1963; head of the Far Eastern Department of the Foreign Ministry, 1952-55; deputy foreign minister, 1955-58; Ambassador to Japan, 1958-62; professor of history of Chinese literature.

Bobodzhan G. Gafurov. Leading Soviet intellectual; former journalist and considered an expert on Asian history; party official and full member of U.S.S.R. Academy of Sciences; director of Institute of Asian Peoples; led the U.S.S.R. delegation to the 24th anniversary celebration of the International Congress of Orientalists in Munich, 1957; president of International Congress of Orientalists in Moscow, 1960.

Indira Gandhi (Priyandarshini Nehru). Prime Minister of India 1966- ; daughter of Prime Minister Jawaharlal Nehru; president of the Congress party, 1959; co-ordinated civil defense efforts in India-China conflict, 1962; became prime minister in January, 1966, on death of Lal Bahadur Shastri; advocated Indian neutrality and called for negotiations on Viet Nam conflict.

Gen. James M. Gavin. Graduated from West Point, 1929, became an expert on parachuting tactics; chief of staff of allied forces in southern Europe, 1951; retired disputing "New Look" policies in 1957; appointed by President Kennedy as ambassador to France, 1961-62; criticized Johnson Viet Nam policy, calling for an "enclave" strategy of holding only key bases in South Viet Nam, testified before Senate Foreign Relations Committee during 1966 Viet Nam hearings and again in February 1967, when he called for cessation of U.S bombing of North Viet Nam.

Gen. Vo Nguyen Giap. Commander-in-chief of the army and vice president of North Viet Nam; self-taught military theoretician; educated at a French college in Hue and arrested at age 18, when disturbances broke out; joined Communist party when released; received a doctorate of law, 1938; fled to China when Japan attacked and the French outlawed the party; organized first underground Viet Minh troops, 1941; served in Ho Chi Minh's first cabinet, 1945; engineered victory over French at Dienbienphu, 1954.

John A. Gronouski. U.S. ambassador to Poland, 1965- ; commissioner of taxation in Wisconsin, 1960-63; Postmaster General of the United States, 1963-65; considered main U.S. diplomatic link with the Chinese Communists because of his regular talks with Chinese diplomats in Warsaw, 1966-

Dag Hammarskjold. Entered Swedish diplomatic service in 1946 as a financial specialist; became deputy foreign minister, cabinet member and head of Sweden's UN delegation 1951-53; elected UN secretary general in 1953, serving until his death in an air crash in 1961; although Soviet UN delegates supported his re-election to a second term in 1957, they became increasingly critical of his "independent" action; during the 1960 Congo crisis, they denounced him as a "tool of the imperialists."

Han Hsien-chu. Named deputy chief of the General Staff of the Chinese army in late 1966; chief of the army on the Fukien front line, across from Taiwan, 1960-66; alternate member of the Communist Party Central Committee since 1958.

Thomas Hayden. Leading figure in "New Left" movement; one of the founders of Students for Democratic Society; associated with the Student Non-Violent Coordinating Committee; organizer for New Community Union Project, Newark, N.J.; accompanied Dr. Herbert Aptheker and Prof. Staughton Lynd on trip to Hanoi in December 1965.

Roger Hilsman. Key policy-making official in the Kennedy and Johnson Administrations as director of the Bureau of Intelligence and Research for the State Department, 1961-63, and Assistant Secretary of State for Far Eastern Affairs, 1963-64, advocated an open-door policy to negotiations with Communist China and played an important role in the formulation of U.S. policies in South Viet Nam; resigned to return to academic life, reportedly prompted by loss of influence rather than by policy differences; in 1966, professor of government, Columbia University.

Ho Chi Minh. *See Minh, Ho Chi.*

Ho Lung. Purged in early 1967 from his posts as vice premier and one of three deputy chairmen, positions he held since 1954; started career as a bandit and organizer of peasants; joined the Chinese Communist Party in 1926, after his application for membership had been denied more than ten times; headed Second Red Army Corps which acted as rear-guards of the Long March, 1934-35; commander of the 120th division of the Eighth Route Army, 1938; became member of the CCP Central Committee in 1945, and of the Politburo in 1956; served as a member of the Presidium of the Third Session, Second People's Congress, 1962; participated in talks between Chou En-lai and Indonesian President Sukarno, 1961; acted as vice-head of the party and government delegation to Moscow to attend celebrations of the 47th anniversary of the October Revolution, 1964.

Ho Wei. Chinese Minister of Education, 1964-66, victim of 1966 purge; long career of underground activities before completion of Communist occupation; mayor of Canton, 1952-54; assistant minister of foreign affairs, 1954-57; ambassador to North Viet Nam, 1957-62.

Gen. Ho Ying-chin. Conservative Nationalist Chinese leader and fairly constant supporter of Chiang Kai-shek since 1931; minister of war, defense minister and commander-in-chief of Nationalist troops under Chiang during 1930s and 1940s. Premier for a short time in 1949.

Gen. Enver Hoxha. First Secretary of Albanian Party of Labor since 1954; rose through ranks of Albanian Communist Party after experience as a school teacher; head of Albanian Liberation Movement since 1939; participated in Albanian liberation of 1944; minister of foreign affairs, 1946-53.

Hsiao Hua. Director of the General Political Department of the Chinese Communist Party since 1964; received early training with Mao Tse-tung; connected with Young People's Section of the Communist party's Political Department, 1929-35; commanded troops during the Long March and continued military activities until occupation was completed; gained rank of full general, 1955; former right-hand man to Defense Minister Lin Piao; criticized by Mao's wife and in Red Guard wall posters in early 1967, but defended by Premier Chou En-lai.

Hsieh Fu-chin. Minister of Public Security in China since 1959, and political commissar of Public Security Forces since 1964; vice-premier of State Council and member, National Defense Council, since 1965; became member of the Chinese Communist Party Central Committee September 1956; graduate of Red Army College and served as political commissar of the Eighth Route Army, 129th Division, 1937, and of the Shansi-Hopei-Shantung-Honan Field Army, 1947; elected deputy to First National Peoples' Congress (1954) for Yunnan, and to Third NPC (1964); accompanied Chou En-lai to Algeria for talks with Ben Bella, and on visit to Albania, 1965; attended talks between Chou and Nasser in Cairo, and between Chou and General Ne Win, chairman of the Burmese Revolutionary Council, in Rangoon, 1965.

Hsu Hsiang-chien. Vice-chairman of China's National Defense Council since 1954; participated in the Northern Expedition, 1926; joined the Chinese Communist Party, 1927; met Mao Tse-tung and joined the Central Red Army, 1935; became vice-commander of the 129th division, when the Red Forces were reorganized into the Eighth Route Army, 1937; became member of the CCP Central Committee, 1945; elected deputy for the People's Liberation Army to First, Second and Third National People's Congresses (1954, 1958, 1964); served as vice-chairman of Standing Committee of Third NPC since January 1965; participated with Mao receiving representatives of the Conference of Political Workers in the People's Liberation Army, 1963; member, Central People's Government Council, 1949-54.

Tran Van Huong. Premier of South Viet Nam, 1964-65; instructor of French and Vietnamese, 1926-37; with anti-French forces, 1945, but resigned, rejecting Viet Minh as Communists; appointed mayor of Saigon, 1954, and resigned shortly thereafter because of political differences with President Diem; joined anti-Diem group in 1959; named mayor of Saigon by Premier Khanh, 1964; ousted as premier by Armed Forces Council, 1965.

Maj. Gen. Patrick J. Hurley. Secretary of War in Hoover Administration, 1929-33; minister to New Zealand, 1942; President Roosevelt's personal representative to the Soviet Union, Afghanistan, India and China, 1942-43; returned to China in 1944 with personal rank of Ambassador to ease deadlocked Kuomintang-Communist negotiations; appointed U.S. ambassador to China, 1944-45; failed to sustain agreements between Chiang Kai-shek and Mao Tse-tung; strongly urged additional U.S. aid to Chiang in 1949 and blamed Secretary of State Dean Acheson for Truman Administration's "appeasement" of communism in Asia.

Philip C. Jessup. U.S. Representative to the UN General Assembly, 1948-52, and ambassador-at-large, 1949-53; Columbia University faculty, international law, 1927-61; served as an advisor to U.S. diplomatic officials; judge on the International Court of Justice since 1961 and member of the governing counsel of the International Institute for the Unification of Private Law since 1964; edited U.S. State Department White Paper explaining relations with China during the 1940s; accused by Sen. Joseph R. McCarthy (R Wis.) of disloyalty.

Louis A. Johnson. Assistant Secretary of War, 1931-40; U.S. Secretary of Defense, 1949-50; aroused widespread Congressional criticism by "paring the fat" from the defense budget while the United States incurred setbacks in Korea and refused military aid to Formosa.

U. Alexis Johnson. U.S. foreign service officer stationed in Japan, Korea, China, Manchuria and the Philippines, 1935-42, 1945-50; Deputy Assistant Secretary of State for Far Eastern Affairs, 1951-53; U.S. ambassador to Czechoslovakia and representative for ambassadorial-level discussions with Communist Chinese, 1953-58. Ambassador to Thailand and SEATO council member, 1958-61; Deputy Under Secretary of State (for political affairs) 1961-64; deputy ambassador to Viet Nam serving under Ambassador Maxwell D. Taylor, 1964-65; appointed ambassador to Japan, confirmed by Senate, Aug. 31, 1966.

Vice Admiral Charles Turner Joy. Commander of Naval amphibious group in Chinese waters, 1945-46; became vice admiral and commander of U.S. Naval Forces in the Far East in 1949; appointed chief UN negotiator for the first year of Korean armistice talks, 1951-52; retired in 1954 after two years as superintendent, U.S. Naval Academy.

Rep. Walter H. Judd (R Minn. 1943-63). Staunch opponent of dealings with China and other Communist nations; graduated from University of Nebraska School of Medicine in 1923 and studied surgery as a Mayo fellow at the University of Minnesota, 1932-34; medical missionary in China, 1925-31 and 1934-38; co-founder of Committee of One Million Against the Admission of Communist China to the UN; testified before the Senate Foreign Relations Committee's 1966 hearings on U.S. China policy.

Kang Sheng. Alternate member of the Chinese Politburo since 1956 and an "adviser" to the group leading the Cultural Revolution; vice-chairman of Standing Committee of National People's Congress since 1965; joined the Chinese Communist Party while a university student in Shanghai and led three student uprisings in 1926; studied in the Soviet Union, 1930-35; held minor party posts until 1945, when he became a member of the Central Committee; elected deputy for Shantung to National People's Congress in 1958; re-elected to six-year term, 1964; represented China at international meetings in Moscow, 1959, Warsaw and Rumania, 1960, Korea, 1961; participated in talks between Mao and Indonesian Communist leader D. N. Aidit, 1963; member of delegation holding talks with Rumanian, Japanese and Belgian Communist parties, 1964, and with Moroccan Communist Party, 1965; ranked 7th in roster of Peking leaders in August 1966.

Brig. Gen. Nguyen Khanh. Prime Minister of South Viet Nam, 1964-65; served in French Colonial Army after military education in Viet Nam, France, and the United States; took part in coup against President Diem, 1963.

Tran Thien Khiem. Member of South Viet Nam ruling triumvirate, 1964; educated as Roman Catholic; firm supporter of President Diem and helped put down 1960 revolt against the regime; became chief of staff of general staff in Saigon, 1962; supported Buddhists in ouster of Diem, 1963; removed from triumvirate and served as ambassador to U.S., 1964; ambassador to Taiwan since 1965.

Nikita S. Khrushchev. Became known as Ukranian Communist Party organizer and first secretary, 1938-49, named Politburo member in 1939; brought to Moscow as head of CP regional committee in 1949 to effect a far-reaching agricultural reorganization; became CP first secretary soon after Premier Joseph V. Stalin's death in 1953 and, by 1955, was considered the most powerful Soviet government official; assumed Premiership in 1958; October 1964, removed from government and party offices and retired on maximum government pension; repeatedly attacked by Chinese Communists as head of the "revisionist" faction within the international Communist movement.

Kim Il Sung. Head of North Korean Communist Party and People's Government, 1946-; educated at China's Whampoa Military Academy; entered North Korea with Soviet Army in 1945 as handpicked Korean Communist leader; named supreme commander of North Korean forces in the war against United Nations forces, 1950-53; consistently supported the Chinese Communist position during the first phase of the Sino-Soviet split, but indicated in 1966 that the North Korean Communist Party had shifted its allegiance to Moscow.

Sen. William F. Knowland (R Calif. 1945-59). Newspaper publisher (*Oakland Tribune*); served on the Armed Services (1949-52) and Foreign Relations Committees, 1953-58; Senate Republican leader, 1955-59; strongly opposed the Truman Administration's "weak China policy" and Eisenhower Administration's negotiating with Communist China; staunch supporter of Chiang Kai-shek; during his Senate career sometimes referred to as the "Senator from Formosa" and the most vocal spokesman for the "China Lobby"; supported the Committee of One Million Against the Admission of Communist China to the UN.

Foy Kohler. Began career as foreign service officer in 1931; assistant chief in the division of Near Eastern affairs in 1944; served in U.S. Embassy in Soviet Union, 1947-48; chief of the International Broadcasting Division of the State Department, and director of the Voice of America broadcasts in 1949; assistant administrator for International Information Administration and on policy planning staff of the State Department, 1952; counselor at Turkish Embassy, 1953-56; served on International Cooperation Administration, 1956-58; Deputy Secretary of State for European affairs, 1958-59, and Assistant, 1959-62; U.S. Ambassador to Soviet Union, 1962-66; appointed Deputy Undersecretary of State for political affairs, confirmed by Senate Oct. 12, 1966.

Capt. Kong Le. Engineered 1960 coup toppling pro-Western Laotian regime; later supported neutralist government of Prince Souvanna Phouma and Pathet Lao forces supporting the neutralists; military training with French and Americans; joined the Laotian army under the French in the 1950s.

Wellington Koo. Nationalist Chinese diplomat whose career started in 1915 at age 27, representing the new Republic of China as minister to Mexico, the United States, and Cuba; served as Chinese representative to the League of Nations, 1920-22, 1932-39; served in a variety of high government posts in Peking, including prime minister, finance minister and minister of foreign affairs, 1922-27; ambassador to France, 1936-40; to Great Britain, 1941-46; to the United States, 1946-56; chairman of the Chinese delegation to the UN Assembly, 1946; the Republic of China's representative on the International Court of Justice at the Hague, ending a nine-year term in February 1967.

Aleksei N. Kosygin. Premier of Soviet Union since October 1964, succeeding Khrushchev; joined Red Army at age 15; worked way up through industry and economic planning councils rather than the party's-political structure; considered an expert on economic planning; only member of Leningrad group to survive Stalin purge of 1949; in disfavor from 1953-57 and dropped from presidium although retaining several planning posts; later renamed to presidium and became first deputy premier in 1960; viewed as a moderate and was the first presidium member to defend withdrawal of Soviet missiles during Cuban crisis of 1962 saying "compromise with the West" was sometimes necessary; holds Soviet Union's two highest decorations, Order of Lenin and Hero of Socialist Labor.

Frol Kozlov. Soviet party and government official; secretary of the Communist party, 1960; closely associated and believed chosen heir of Chairman Khrushchev; lost decision-making powers in 1963, after reported differences with Khrushchev; died in 1965.

Kuang Ya-ming. Rector of Nanking University, 1963-66, reportedly ousted in 1966 Cultural Revolution; deputy director of East China Propaganda Department, 1952-54; began first of three university presidencies in 1955.

Kuo Mo-jo. Leading Chinese Communist writer and intellectual; began studies in Japan, graduating from Tokyo's Imperial University in 1920; started prolific writing career in 1927; numerous honorary degrees from Asiatic and European universities; one of the first victims of the Cultural Revolution in 1966.

Otto V. Kuusinen. Secretary and member of Soviet Presidium from 1957 until his death May 17, 1964; became member of the Communist Party Central Committee, 1941, and chairman of the U.S.S.R. Parliamentary Group in 1958; started revolutionary activity in Social-Democratic Party of Finland as leader of its left-wing faction; helped direct Communist revolution in Finland, 1917-18, and founded Finnish Communist Party in 1918; headed "Democratic Government of Finland," 1939-40; chairman, Presidium, Karelo-Finnish Supreme Soviet, 1940-56; simultaneously deputy chairman, Presidium, U.S.S.R. Supreme Soviet until 1958; author of many works on the history of international communism.

Nguyen Cao Ky. Premier of South Viet Nam since June 12, 1965; gained air force training from French colonial administration; rose quickly through military and government ranks after overthrow of President Diem, 1963; top aide to Premier Khanh, 1964. Although controversial because of some of his statements, Ky weathered an uprising by militant Buddhists in 1966 and was able to bring some stability to the government in Saigon. By early 1967, his regime seemed as firmly entrenched as ever, and there were reports that he would run for president in the forthcoming elections.

Joseph Laniel. Founder of France's postwar Rightist Independent Party; premier of the 19th French cabinet since World War II and the first since 1946 to include Gaullist party members, 1953; worked for European unity and Indo-Chinese independence within the French Union; resigned in June 1954 when refused vote of confidence in his handling of the Indo-Chinese war.

Owen Lattimore. Engaged in business and research in China, 1920-35; appointed director, Johns Hopkins School of International

Relations, 1939-53; served as political adviser to Chiang Kai-shek, 1941-42; was cleared of Sen. Joseph R. McCarthy's charges of being a top Soviet agent and of influencing State Department policy to favor the Chinese Communists, but indicted for perjury in 1952; perjury charges dropped by the Government and case dismissed in June 1955; appointed professor of Chinese Studies, Leeds University (England), 1963- .

Gen. Curtis LeMay. Retired Air Force officer; commander-general of the USAF in Europe, 1947; commander-in-chief of the Strategic Air Command, 1957-61; attained rank of general in 1951, chief of Air Force staff, 1961-65; retired in 1965; advocate of more intensive bombing of North Viet Nam.

Li Fu-chun. Vice Premier of China's State Council since 1954 and considered one of the principal economic planners of the country, holding positions under Vice Premier Chen Yun; became a member of the Central Committee of the Chinese Communist Party in 1934, and of the Politburo in 1956; elected to Standing Committee of the Politburo in November 1966, ranking 10th in the Peking listings as of that date; studied in France under the work-study program, and one of the founders, with Chou En-lai, of the French CCP, 1921; studied in Moscow at University for Toilers of the East, 1923-24; became political commissar on Long March, 1934-35; held regional political and economic positions, and on national level, began planning Chinese Communist economic development programs; minister of heavy industry, 1950-52; vice-chairman of financial-economic committee of government Administration Council, 1950-54; head of Office of Industry and Communications within State Council since 1959; attended Moscow economic and military meetings as First Deputy to Chen Yun with Chinese "observer" group among intra-Communist bloc; elected deputy for Hunan to Second National People's Congress, 1958.

Li Hsueh-feng. Succeeded deposed Peng Chen as mayor of Peking and party secretary of the Peking municipal branch, 1966; denounced by the Red Guards and Mao's wife in late 1966; closely associated with party General Secretary Teng Tsiao-ping, one of Mao's principal adversaries; member of the Chinese Communist Party Central Committee since 1956; vice chairman of the Standing Committee of the Third National People's Congress since 1965; early career started as an alternate member to the Executive Council, Central-Soviet Provisional Government, 1934; directed work of the local party organizations in southeastern Shansi, 1937; political commissar, 1940-49.

Gen. Li Tsung-jen. Nationalist Chinese liberal and frequent critic of Chiang Kai-shek; became vice president under Chiang in 1948 and acting president during Chiang's retirement, 1949-50; fled to the United States in late 1949; officially exiled by the Kuomintang in 1950; left U.S. for mainland China in 1965 and announced his allegiance to the Peking regime, denouncing U.S. actions in Viet Nam.

Trygve Lie. Norwegian Social Democratic leader; foreign minister, 1940-46; chairman of Norwegian UN delegation and first secretary general of the United Nations, 1946-53; Norwegian ambassador "en mission speciale," 1959; minister of industry, 1963-64, of commerce, 1964-65.

Lin Piao. Defense Minister and deputy chairman of the Chinese Communist Party. See page 227.

Liu Po-chang. Leading military tactician of Communist China and member of the Politburo since 1956; deputy chairman of the Defense Council. Although Liu was omitted from a roster of 201 leading members of the Chinese Communist Party and the government at an August 1966 Peking rally, indicating he may have been a victim of the Cultural Revolution, he appeared in March 1967 as one of a select group working with Premier Chou En-lai, who at that time seemed to have assumed control of China's governmental and party affairs.

Liu Shao-chi. Chief of State of Communist China. See page 229.

Lo Jui-ching. Chief of Staff of General Army, victim of the Cultural Revolution; reported arrested in December 1966, and to have committed suicide January 1967; early revolutionary career with

graduation from Whampoa Military Academy; studied at Sun Yat-sen University in Moscow; joined the Chinese Communist Party in 1926; accompanied Mao on the Long March, 1935; trained in secret police work, established the CCP intelligence organization in Peking, 1946; member, Board of Directors, Sino-Soviet Friendship Assn., 1949-54; minister of public security, 1949-59; vice premier of State Council, 1959; secretary of CCP Central Secretariat, 1962; vice chairman under Mao, 1965; disappeared from public view in November 1965 after writing a series of articles pointing to the dangers of China's isolation from the rest of the world.

Lo Lung-chi. Western-educated intellectual and Communist political activist; legal and propaganda expert; proposed Rectification Committee in 1957 to hear appeals of political prisoners who believed they were wrongly accused; was branded "rightist" and reportedly "confessed" his crimes, July 15, 1957; was removed from post as timber minister in 1958.

Robert Lovett. Special assistant to the Secretary of War, 1940-41; Assistant Secretary of War for Air, 1941-45; Undersecretary of State, 1947-49; Deputy Defense Secretary, 1950-51; succeeded Gen. George C. Marshall as Secretary of Defense, 1951-53.

Lu Ping. President of Peking University, 1960-66, ousted in 1966 purge as a result of criticism appearing in *Liberation Army Daily*, a newspaper under Defense Minister Lin Piao's control; studied at Peking University and engaged in propaganda activities before completion of Communist occupation; vice minister of railways, 1954-57; vice president of Peking University, 1957-60.

Lu Ting-yi. Director of Propaganda Department of the Chinese Communist Party Central Committee, 1949, and minister of culture of the State Council, 1965; victim of the Cultural Revolution; reports in late 1966 of being brought to trial; graduated from Sun Yat-sen University in Moscow; participated in Long March and directed operations with Mao and Chou En-lai in North Shensi Province; member of CCP Central Committee since 1945 and alternate member of CCP Politburo since 1956; vice premier of State Council since 1959.

Henry R. Luce. Editor and publisher; founder of *Time*, 1923, *Fortune*, 1930, *Life*, 1936, *Sports Illustrated*, 1954; born in China in 1898 and regarded as a staunch supporter of Chiang Kai-shek; organized United China Relief, 1940; received numerous decorations, including the Order of Auspicious Star from China, 1947; member of Committee of One Million Against the Admission of Communist China to the UN. Died Feb. 28, 1967.

Gen. Lung Yun. World War II aide to Chiang Kai-shek; removed and imprisoned by Chiang as a provincial warlord governor in 1945; emerged in mid-1950s as vice chairman of the Kuomintang Revolutionary Committee, an organization of former Nationalists associated with the Communist regime, and vice chairman of the Chinese Communist National Defense Committee; denounced as a "rightist" in 1957 after criticizing the Soviet Union for removing "huge quantities of industrial equipment" from Manchuria following World War II and recommending that Communist China decrease the amount of foreign aid it gave away to other nations; permanently dropped from the National Defense Council in 1959 by newly-elected President Liu Shao-chi.

Prof. Staughton Lynd. Leading figure in "New Left" movement; son of noted U.S. sociologists Robert S. and Helen M. Lynd; educated at Harvard University, University of Chicago, and Columbia University; dishonorably discharged from Army in 1954, after entering as a non-combatant conscientious objector; U.S. Supreme Court decision later forced Army to grant him an honorable discharge; assistant professor of history at Yale University; accompanied Thomas Hayden and Dr. Herbert Aptheker on trip to Hanoi, December 1965.

Georgi M. Malenkov. Reportedly Stalin's secretary during late 1920s and influential in his purges of the 1930s and 1940s; became full Politburo (changed to Presidium in 1952) member in 1946 and succeeded to Stalin's offices, including the Premiership, in 1953; "resigned" in 1954 to become deputy premier and minister of power stations, when Khrushchev emerged as the strongest Soviet official;

dismissed by Khrushchev from all offices and Presidium in 1957 and from the Communist party in 1961.

Jacob A. Malik. Soviet ambassador to Japan, 1942-45; deputy foreign minister, 1946-55; chief Soviet delegate to the UN Security Council, 1948-52; led 1950 Russian boycott of the United Nations following rejection of the Soviet resolution to replace Nationalist China on the Security Council.

Mao Tse-tung. Chairman of the Chinese Communist Party. *See page 223.*

Neil H. McElroy. President of Procter & Gamble, 1948-57; succeeded Charles E. Wilson as Secretary of Defense, 1957-59; cancelled Wilson's economy restrictions on fiscal 1958 defense spending and accelerated U.S. missile and satellite programs; retired to become board chairman of Procter & Gamble, 1959- .

Pierre Mendes-France. Cabinet member in Gen. Charles de Gaulle's 1944-45 provisional French government; UN Economic and Social Council representative, 1947-50; Radical Socialist leader of the opposition succeeding Joseph Laniel in June 1954 as premier of France's 20th post-war government; in power until February 1955, when his North African policy was refused a vote of confidence; chief opponent of De Gaulle's 1958 return to power, organizing the moderate-leftist Union of Democratic Forces in opposition to the Fifth Republic's constitution.

V. K. Krishna Menon. India's first high commissioner in Great Britain, 1947-52; became chief Indian delegate to the UN General Assembly, 1952-62; instrumental in breaking deadlocked Korean armistice negotiations; India's defense minister, 1957-62, when severely criticized for failing to equip the Indian army for Chinese military action; ousted as defense minister and cabinet member in 1962; also lost UN position; opposed election of Lal Bahadur Shastri following Nehru's death in 1964; defeated as a non-party candidate for India's lower House (Loc Sabha) in February 1967.

Duong Van Minh. Member of South Viet Nam ruling triumvirate, 1964-65; entered French colonial army in 1940 and fought the Japanese in World War II; fought with French during Indo-China war; served with Diem regime; had considerable support from Buddhists and students; ousted in 1965.

Ho Chi Minh. President of North Viet Nam; seaman for the French during World War I; traveled to the United States and worked as a chef in London and a photographer in France; tried in vain to appeal the Vietnamese case to President Woodrow Wilson; joined French Communist Party in 1921, and as an expert on colonial affairs traveled extensively in Europe; studied in Moscow; returned to Viet Nam and founded Indo-China Communist Party, 1930; organized Viet Minh united front against the Japanese; reportedly asked U.S. aid in creating a nationalist government but was rebuffed, 1945; fought the French colonial army after World War II and claimed victory after siege at Dienbienphu, 1954; established North Vietnamese government in Hanoi; considered to have Soviet rather than Chinese sentiments in Communist ideological dispute.

Vyacheslav M. Molotov. Soviet foreign minister, 1939-49; deputy prime minister, 1949-53. A strong supporter of Stalin's anti-Western foreign policy, Molotov became foreign minister again at Stalin's death in 1953, and member of a small "committee dictatorship" ruling the Soviet Union. He "resigned" in 1956, soon after Khrushchev gained control of the government; expelled from Presidium, 1957.

Hans J. Morgenthau. Writer and teacher of international politics; appointed to faculty of law at University of Frankfurt, 1931; fled native Germany for Switzerland, 1933; moved to United States and became instructor at Brooklyn College, 1937; University of Chicago political science faculty, 1943 to date; leading exponent of "unemotional" and "pragmatic" foreign policy; leading academic critic of Johnson Viet Nam policy; called for the establishment of peace by political rather than military means.

Lt. Gen. Nam II. North Korean Army chief of staff and senior member of five-man Communist delegation to 1951-53 Korean Armistice Conference; became North Korean foreign minister in 1953.

Nan Han-chen. Joined Chinese Nationalist Revolutionary Army, 1926, and Communist party, 1927; worked in anti-Japanese underground; served Communist government as an economic expert and has handled many of China's international financial agreements; governor, People's Bank of China (about 1950).

G. L. Nanda. Interim Indian prime minister on death of Jawaharlal Nehru, 1964; identified with labor as a moderate Socialist and economist; jailed by British authorities for political activity, 1932 and 1942-44.

Gen. Abdul Haris Nasution. Indonesian military figure; led nationalist troops against Dutch colonialists, 1945; rose quickly through ranks of nationalist army; strongly anti-Communist but rejected pro-Western label; key figure in overpowering of President Sukarno and purge of Indonesian leftists, 1966.

Jawaharlal Nehru. Long-time member of Mohandas Gandhi's nonviolent, noncooperation movement; president of the All India Congress Committee in 1929, 1936, 1937 and 1946, when he formed an interim cabinet in preparation for 1947 independence from Great Britain; India's first prime minister and foreign minister from 1947 until his death in 1964; maintained a policy of neutrality between Western nations and the Communist bloc.

Frederick E. Nolting Jr. Ambassador to Viet Nam, 1961-63; assistant chief of Northern European Affairs, 1948-49; coordinator of aid programs for the Far East, 1950, and member of the U.S. delegation to the UN, 1951; special assistant to the Secretary of State for mutual security affairs, 1953-55; State Department in NATO affairs, 1955-62; special intelligence survey for U.S. Government, 1963-64; joined New York financial firm in 1964.

U Nu. Elected Burma's provisional premier in 1947; negotiated 1948 independence of Union of Burma from Great Britain; retained leadership of parliamentary government and moderately socialist ruling parties, 1948-56, 1957-58, when Ne Win seized power in a military coup.

Dr. Nguyen Xuan Oanh. Acting premier of South Viet Nam caretaker governments, 1964 and 1965; Harvard-educated economist.

Lambertus N. Palar. Indonesian diplomat; leading figure in Netherlands Labor Movement, 1929-47; Netherlands Parliament, 1945-47; came to Indonesia in 1947 and served as a permanent representative to the UN, 1950-53 and 1962-65, when Indonesia pulled out of the UN; explained Indonesia's withdrawal as a result of the election of the Federation of Malaysia to the Security Council; ambassador to the United States, 1965-66; former ambassador to U.S.S.R., India, West Germany and Canada; teaching at the East-West Center, the University of Hawaii, 1966- .

Panchen Lama. Assumed power in Tibet during Chinese intervention, 1959, supplanting the Dalai Lama, spiritual and temporal ruler who was exiled and sought refuge in India; deposed in 1965 for resisting Chinese violations of Tibetan traditions.

Khamphan Panya. Laotian diplomat and ambassador to U.S.S.R. since 1963; former professor of law and medicine; deputy secretary-general of High Council of French Union, 1954-55; ambassador to India, 1956-58; minister of foreign affairs, 1958-60, public works, 1961-62.

Chung Hee Park. President of South Korea; taught school and then attended a Japanese military academy and fought with the Japanese in World War II; after the war entered the American sponsored Korean military academy; accused of being a Communist, court-martialed and condemned to death, but escaped with a dishonorable discharge from the service; called to active duty in Korean conflict but did not see combat action; believed to be real power behind the 1961 military coup ousting Dr. Syngman Rhee; elected to four-year presidential term in 1963.

Linus Pauling. Leading American scientist; awarded the Nobel Prize for Chemistry in 1954; accused by Senator Joseph R. McCarthy (R Wis.) of being a Communist because of long-time pacifist interests, 1954; received the Nobel Peace Prize in 1962, because of his efforts for the 1963 Test Ban Treaty.

Peng Chen. Mayor of Peking and head of the Peking municipal committee of the Chinese Communist Party, 1951-65; ousted in May 1966 as one of the first victims of the Cultural Revolution; active as mayor in the 1951 purges of counter-revolutionaries; central committee and Politburo member since 1956; started revolutionary career in north China where he joined the CCP in 1926; led guerrilla activities against the Japanese; became vice-principal with Lin Piao (Mao was principal) of Yenan Party School, and took charge of rectification movement, 1942; senior political commissar in Manchurian military command headed by Lin, 1945-48; led CCP delegation to Rumania, 1960, to North Korea and North Viet Nam, 1962, and to Indonesia, 1965; December 1966 posters in Peking demanded that Peng face trial for his "crimes"; Red Guards announced his arrest in the same month; reports indicated he had attempted suicide a number of times.

Peng Teh-huai. Early activity as military revolutionary; joined forces with Mao, 1928, and went on to become a leader of the Communist military forces; minister of defense, 1954-59; purged in 1959; disappeared from public view in May 1960; believed to have supported continued reliance on the Soviet Union for equipment and guidance, and to have resisted heavy political controls over the army; dropped in early 1965 from his posts as vice premier and member of the National Defense Council.

Christian Pineau. Socialist party leader in France's Fourth Republic; was asked to assume premiership in 1952 and 1955, but failed to command a majority in Parliament; appointed foreign minister by Premier Guy Mollet in 1956; remained in the post in three succeeding governments until the 1958 accession of President Charles de Gaulle; influential in European unity and Anglo-French-U.S. agreement on Far and Middle Eastern policy questions.

Po I-po. Leading economic expert in Communist China since 1949; seized and imprisoned by the Red Guards in January 1967 for "capitalist" tendencies; one of the first few officials to become a victim of the Cultural Revolution; until his arrest was an alternate chairman of the State Economic Commission; supervised the operations of many ministries, including mining, metallurgy and petroleum and defense construction.

Nikolai V. Podgorny. President of the Soviet Union, December 1964- ; rose to present positions from background in food administration; accompanied Premier Khrushchev to the United States in 1960; became a member of the Presidium, 1960; named to the Communist Party's Secretariat, 1963; considered a moderate.

Pu Yi. Manchu boy emperor Hsuan Tung, known also as Henry Pu Yi; born in 1906 as nephew of the late Emperor Kuang Hsu, whom he succeeded to the throne on Kuang's death in 1909; abdicated in 1912, but restored to the throne for 10 days in July 1917; resided in the Japanese concession in Tientsin from 1924-31, then left for Manchuria where he was proclaimed Regent of Manchukuo; enthroned in 1934 as Emperor Kang-te of Manchukuo; captured in 1945 by the Russian army and sent to Siberia; returned to China in 1950 and placed in a special camp for war criminals; released in 1959 to work as a gardener; appointed in 1960 to do historical research at the Chinese Academy of Sciences; currently living in Peking.

Thich Tri Quang. South Vietnamese Buddhist monk; militant nationalist; key figure in Buddhist inspired collapse of several Saigon governments, including Diem regime, 1963; leader of the unsuccessful campaign against the Ky regime by militant Buddhists in 1966.

Dr. Elpidio Quirino. Leader of Philippine Liberal party; Japanese prisoner during World War II; became vice president and foreign secretary of the Philippine Republic in 1946; succeeded to the presidency, 1948-53; consistently supported U.S. international policies; sought U.S. support for Chiang Kai-shek's proposed anti-Communist alliance of Pacific Nations.

Admiral Arthur W. Radford. Commander of the Pacific Fleet in 1949; given specific control of the Philippine-Formosan area and advocated blockade of Communist China; chairman of the Joint Chiefs of Staff, 1953-57; retired to a position with the Bankers Trust Co., 1957; supporter of the Committee of One Million Against the Admission of Communist China to the UN.

Sir Benegal N. Rau. Member United Nations International Law Commission and chairman of atomic energy subcommittee in 1948; named India's permanent delegate to UN in 1949; strongly advocated atomic energy control; took leading part in attempting to settle Korean War; favored UN recognition of Communist China, arguing it would become subject to obligations shared by other members; refused to serve on UN Good Offices Committee after it had passed a 1951 resolution condemning Chinese as "aggressors."

Dr. Syngman Rhee. Leader of Korea's nationalist anti-Communist Liberal party and president of the Korean "Provisional Government in exile," under Japanese occupation, 1919-41; founder and first president of the Republic of Korea, 1948-60; forced into exile by pressure for political and social reforms, 1960; died in Honolulu, Hawaii, July 1965.

John Hammond Richardson. Executive officer in the Defense Department, 1953-55; special assistant to several U.S. ambassadors, 1955-62; served as first secretary and special assistant to U.S. ambassador to South Viet Nam, since 1962.

Gen. Matthew B. Ridgway. Served in China and the Philippines in the 1930s and at the end of World War II; requested by Gen. Douglas MacArthur as second in command in Korea, 1950-51; succeeded MacArthur as commander-in-chief of the Far East, 1951-52; appointed supreme commander of the Allied Powers in Europe, 1952-53, and Army chief of staff, 1953-55; board chairman of the Mellon Institute of Industrial Research, 1955-60; director, Apollo Industries, Inc., and Fairbanks Whitney Corp.; advocated "enclave theory," withdrawing U.S. forces from all but strategic bases in South Viet Nam, 1966.

Walter S. Robertson. Chief of U.S. Lend-Lease Mission to Australia, 1943-44; economic advisor to the State Department, 1945; served in U.S. Embassy in Chungking, 1945-46, as a minister and counselor of economic affairs, decorated for work on Gen. George C. Marshall's 1946 commission to end hostilities between Nationalist and Communist Chinese; member of the public advisory commission to the China Aid Program, 1948; played a major role in the early years of SEATO, in the 1955 Manila Pact and the 1956 Colombo Plan Conferences as Assistant Secretary of State for Far Eastern Affairs, 1953-59; governor of the N.Y. Stock Exchange, 1961-64.

Dean Rusk. U.S. Secretary of State 1961- ; joined State Dept. in 1945, later specializing in United Nations affairs; appointed Assistant Secretary of State for Far Eastern Affairs in March, 1950; in 1951 speech, called for unyielding support of Chiang Kai-shek regime on Formosa; president of Rockefeller Foundation, 1952-60.

Eisaku Sato. Premier of Japan 1964- ; brother of former Premier Nebusuke Kishi; upper class background and educated as a lawyer; elected to Diet, 1954; became leader of ruling Liberal-Democratic Party; considered anti-Communist and pro-West.

John Stewart Service. Spent early life in China, 1909-24; returned as a Foreign Service officer in the Far East, 1935-46; assigned to State Department in 1948; despite being cleared of Sen. Joseph R. McCarthy's (R Wis.) charges, was dismissed with "reasonable doubt" of his loyalty in 1951; reinstated as senior foreign officer, 1957-62; curator, University of California Center for Chinese Studies, 1962-

Lal Bahadur Shastri. Prime Minister of the Republic of India, July 1964 to January 1966, when he died of a heart attack; organized first general election of independent India in 1951; entered national Parliament and later appointed minister for transport and railways, 1952; Indian envoy to Nepal, 1963; assumed prime ministership on Nehru's death.

Alexander N. Shelepin. Soviet party and government official; head of Department of Propaganda and Agitation during World War II; skilled administrative organizer; member of the Secretariat and Presidium who developed a reputation as "trouble-shooter" in the international Communist movement; removed from government positions, which dealt primarily with the policing of internal society, in late 1965 to concentrate on undefined party duties; appointed to head Soviet delegation to Hanoi at the end of 1965, believed to be an attempt to strengthen Moscow's position in the ideological dispute with Peking.

Dmitri T. Shepilov. Career Communist party theoretician specializing in foreign affairs and propaganda; editor of Soviet newspaper, *Pravda*, 1952-56; replaced Vyacheslav M. Molotov as Foreign Minister, June 1956-February 1957, reportedly easing Soviet relations with less orthodox Communist countries; identified with Molotov's mid-1957 "anti-party plot" to depose Khrushchev and sent to a teaching post in the Soviet Far East.

Prince Norodom Sihanouk. Premier of Cambodia; elected to Cambodian throne to replace an uncle, 1941; held prisoner by Japanese during World War II; ruled as a constitutional monarch after the war; sent into exile in Thailand for five months in 1953 in a move to force the French into granting concessions to Cambodia; abdicated in 1955 and placed his father on the throne with himself as premier; became head of state (but not king) when his father died, 1960; staunch nationalist who frequently denounced the United States as well as Communist China and the Soviet Union.

Gen. Walter Bedell Smith. Chief of Staff under Gen. Dwight D. Eisenhower in the European Theatre, 1945; appointed by President Truman as ambassador to the Soviet Union, 1946-49; member of the U.S. delegation to the Paris Peace Conference, 1946; CIA director, 1950-53; in 1951 named acting chairman of cold-war Psychological Strategy Board; retired from the Army to become Undersecretary of State to John Foster Dulles, 1953-54; died in August 1961.

Edgar Snow. Leading authority on Chinese Communist internal affairs and leaders; after beginning writing career with the *Kansas City Star*, was assistant editor of *China Weekly Review*, 1929-30, and correspondent for the *Chicago Tribune*, 1929; correspondent for Consolidated Press Association, 1930-34, *London Daily Herald*, 1932-41, and *New York Sun*, 1934-37; first correspondent to interview Communist leaders during the Chinese civil war; covered World War II for the *Saturday Evening Post*, associate editor, 1943-51; special research consultant at Harvard University, 1956; *Look* Magazine's China correspondent, 1960-61; reporter for *Le Nouveau Candide* of Paris, 1964-65; author of numerous books and monographs on China, including "Red Star Over China" and "The Other Side of the River."

Soong Ching-ling. Widow of Dr. Sun Yat-sen and his close political collaborator during his lifetime; elder sister of T.V. Soong and of Mme. Chiang Kai-shek; vice-president of Communist China since 1959; educated in the United States (Wesleyan College for Women); opposed anti-Communist policy of the Nationalist government and led leftist group in the Kuomintang in 1927; went to the Soviet Union with Michael Borodin, who was chief Soviet adviser to China, 1927-29; resumed use of maiden name during World War II and remained in Peking when Nationalists fled the mainland in 1949; moved steadily upward in Chinese Communist government, named deputy chairman of the government, 1949; awarded Stalin Peace Prize, 1951; home in Shanghai reportedly was vandalized in September 1966 by Red Guards who accused her of pretending to be a revolutionary but actually favoring capitalism.

T.V. Soong. Brother of Madame Chiang Kai-shek and Madame Sun Yat-sen; educated at Harvard (A.B. 1915) and Columbia (Ph.D.); held important financial, political and diplomatic posts in Nationalist China, 1928-1950, when the Kuomintang removed him as president of the Bank of China on Formosa; frequently associated with the U.S. "China Lobby" in the 1950s, taking an active role in negotiating aid for Nationalist China.

Prince Souvanna Phouma. Premier of Laos; Western-educated in engineering, entered Public Works Service of Indo-China, 1931; at the end of World War II, initiated "free Laos" movement with his half-brothers, Prince Pethsarath and Prince Souvanouvong; between Japanese defeat and return of the French was provisional prime minister; when French returned, went into exile in Thailand, returned in 1951 when Laos was granted independent statehood within the French Union; as government official, denounced Pathet Lao actions led by Souvanouvong, declaring his support for neutral-

ist policy; elected premier of independent Laos, 1956; named as ambassador to Italy when Communist strength forced him to give way to coalition government; returned in 1960 as president of the National Assembly and again became premier after military coup in August; went into exile after rightist military coup in December; returned as premier in 1962 when Western powers agreed to support the formation of a neutralist coalition.

John M. Steeves. Served with the Far Eastern Affairs bureau of the State Department until 1948; in U.S. embassies in India, Japan, and Indonesia, 1948-54; political adviser to U.S. officials in the Pacific, 1955-59; deputy to the Assistant Secretary of State for Far Eastern Affairs, 1959-62; U.S. Ambassador to Afghanistan, 1962-

Gen. Joseph W. Stilwell. Appointed chief of staff for Chiang Kai-shek's forces and U.S. Army representative in China, February 1942; his plans for military reform were opposed by Chiang, who requested his removal from office; replaced by Maj. Gen. Albert C. Wedemeyer, October 1944.

Dr. John Leighton Stuart. U.S. missionary-educator in China, 1905-46; president of Yenching University, Peking, 1919-46; U.S. ambassador to China, 1946-53; acted in collaboration with President Truman's personal representative, Gen. George C. Marshall; fled from Communist-occupied U.S. embassy on mainland, 1949; author of "Essentials of New Testament Greek," a Greek-Chinese-English dictionary of the New Testament; died in September 1962.

Subandrio. Foreign Minister of Indonesia from 1957 until his arrest in March 1966 for complicity in the 1965 abortive Communist coup. During the October trial, evidence revealed that Subandrio had accepted an offer from Communist China to send arms to Indonesian "peasants and workers" who supported the Communists. Despite Subandrio's pleas that he was only following government policy, he was sentenced to death Oct. 25. His case was under appeal in early 1967. He was born in 1913 into an aristocratic family; received a medical education in Jakarta; first entered the international scene in 1947 when he was sent to London to rally world support for Indonesia during the struggle with the Dutch; after independence, was appointed first ambassador to Great Britain, 1949, and first ambassador to the Soviet Union in 1954. He also served as head of Indonesia's Central Intelligence Bureau and first deputy premier, as well as foreign minister.

Lt. Gen. Suharto. Leader of military coup ousting President Sukarno in Indonesia, 1966; led guerrilla commandos in the war for independence against the Dutch; protege of anti-Communist Gen. Abdul Haris Nasution; helped suppress Communist coup, 1965.

Sukarno. President of Indonesia; began revolutionary activities in 1927; jailed for subversion by Dutch colonial officials, 1928-32; exiled from 1933 until released by Japanese in 1942; proclaimed Republic of Indonesia, 1945, and took control; lost power in anti-Communist military coup in 1966, but remained as figurehead; threatened with trial in early 1967, but refused to go into exile.

Sun Fo. Son of Sun Yat-sen; influential liberal Kuomintang member and part of a faction rivaling Chiang Kai-shek's assumption of Kuomintang leadership after Sun Yat-sen's death in 1925; held many high posts in the Nationalist government including the premiership, November 1948-March 1949.

Sun Yat-sen. Known as the "father" of the Chinese revolution; became provisional president of the first Chinese Republic in February 1912 after the October 1911 "Wu-chang Uprising," which overthrew the Manchu Dynasty; power was short-lived and Sun spent most of the next ten years in exile, with the exception of a short period in September 1917 when he established and headed a provisional government in South China; died in 1925.

Mikhail Suslov. Soviet party and government official; served as public information officer beginning in 1946; chief editor of

Pravda, 1949-50; elected chairman of Commission for Foreign Affairs and played key role in suppressing the Hungarian revolt, 1956; a party secretary in 1966.

Phan Khac Suu. South Viet Nam Chief of State, 1964 and 1965; Minister of Agriculture under Emperor Bao Dai, 1949; minister in first government of President Diem, 1954; later opposed Diem and was jailed after an abortive coup against Diem in 1960; ousted as chief of state, later reappointed; resigned after brief service, 1965; announced Presidential candidacy, March 1967.

U Ba Swe. Burmese defense minister in Premier U Nu's cabinet, 1952-56; succeeded Nu as premier, 1956-57, pledging to continue Burma's independent foreign policy; served as deputy premier when U Nu returned to power, 1957-58; lost power along with U Nu in Ne Win's military coup in 1958; later became party leader, but never regained governmental power.

Tao Chu. Rose from obscurity to the fourth position in the Chinese Communist hierarchy during 1966, only to be consumed by the purge he had directed; appointed head of the Propaganda Department, 1966; considered one of the architects of the Cultural Revolution; vice premier of the State Council since 1965; member of the Central Committee of the Chinese Communist Party since 1956; served in the National Revolutionary Army during the Northern Expedition in 1926; responsible for a dramatic rescue of 18 CCP imprisoned cadres during the civil war, receiving praise of the Central Committee; served as political commissar in 1950 of the South China Military Region and the Kwangsi Military Region, and since 1958, of the Canton Military Region; governor of Kwangtung, February 1955 - August 1957; member of the CCP delegation to the 22nd Congress of the CPSU in Moscow in October 1961; elected deputy for Kwangtung to the National People's Congress in September 1964; participated in talks between Premier Chou En-lai and Indonesian Foreign Minister Subandrio in May 1965; considered protege of Defense Minister Lin Piao; purged in early 1967.

Gen. Maxwell Taylor. Special consultant to the President 1966- ; assigned to 82nd Airborne Division in World War II, becoming a brigadier general, 1942; major general with 101st Airborne in 1944, leading troops in the Normandy invasion; after war became superintendent of West Point, 1945; appointed chief of staff of the American Forces in Europe, 1949; commanded Eighth Army in Korea, 1953; chief of staff of U.S. Army, 1955; retired from active duty in 1959; military representative to President Kennedy, 1961; chairman of the Joint Chiefs of Staff, 1962-64; United States Ambassador to South Viet Nam, 1964-65.

Teng Hsiao-ping. Secretary General of the Chinese Communist Party. *See page 231.*

U Thant. Secretary General of the United Nations; educated in native Burma; was a schoolmaster, then returned to study law at University of Rangoon; during World War II criticized colonialism as a free-lance journalist; appointed director of broadcasting in the newly established Burmese government, 1948; Burmese delegate to the seventh session of the United Nations General Assembly, 1952; head of Burmese UN delegation, 1957; in UN debate over Quemoy Matsu conflict, held that U.S. was partly responsible by not recognizing Peking government and that China was guilty of aggressive tactics; replaced the late Dag Hammarskjold as UN secretary general, Nov. 3, 1961, for a five-year term; in Viet Nam conflict has been a strong supporter of negotiations.

Lt. Gen. Nguyen Chanh Thi. Powerful member of South Viet Nam governing junta ousted in 1966 amidst his open opposition to Ky regime; rose through military ranks from humble origins in central Viet Nam; served with French colonial forces in Indo-China war; staged abortive coup against President Diem and fled to Cambodia, 1960; returned to Viet Nam on overthrow of Diem regime, 1963, and assumed leadership of northern forces in South Viet Nam; currently in exile in the United States.

Maj. Gen. Nguyen Van Thieu. Powerful military figure of Ky regime in South Viet Nam; commanded Bienhoa province troops, north of Saigon, 1962-64; key figure in coup ousting President

Diem, 1963; headed National Leadership Committee in South Viet Nam, 1965.

Nguyen Huu Tho. Chairman since 1962 of the Presidium of the Central Committee of the National Liberation Front (NLF), the political arm of the Viet Cong; received law degree in France in the early 1930s and returned to practice in the Saigon area; active from 1947-49 in trying to bring about negotiations between the French and the North Vietnamese Communists; stated in an Hanoi broadcast in September 1966 conditions for a political settlement in Viet Nam, which some officials viewed as a possible softening because he was not insistent on the NLF as the "sole interlocutor," but as having a "decisive voice" in any political solution concerning South Viet Nam.

Nguyen Thoc Thu. Provisional premier of South Viet Nam after coup ousting President Diem, 1963; raised as a Buddhist in southern portion of Viet Nam; joined civil service in 1930; served Diem as minister of the national economy, vice president, and minister of the interior; governed his native province, 1948-54, under Emperor Bao Dai; reportedly selected by military leaders of the 1963 coup because of his considerable mediating abilities; ousted in 1964 coup.

Tsiang Tingfu F. Nationalist Chinese chief of delegation to the United Nations, 1947-62; ambassador to the U.S., 1962-65; ambassador to the Soviet Union, 1936-38; director of political affairs of the Chinese Executive Yuan (cabinet) in Chungking, 1938-44; educated in America, professor of history and author of several books on Chinese history; died in 1965.

Tsien Hsue-shen. Nuclear scientist who directed Communist China's nuclear research program and regarded the individual most responsible for the development of China's nuclear capacity. Born in Shanghai in 1909, Tsien was a brillant undergraduate student in mechanical engineering at Chiaotung University. He won a scholarship to study in the United States on his graduation in 1934, and entered the Massachusetts Institute of Technology. In 1936, he received a master of science degree in aeronautical engineering from that institution. In 1939, he was awarded a Ph.D. from the California Institute of Technology. Tsien was a full professor of aeronautical engineering at MIT from 1947-49 and became the Robert H. Goddard Professor of Jet Propulsion at Caltech in 1949. During World War II, Tsien was given the rank of colonel in the Air Force and in 1945 accompanied Theodore von Karman to Germany to study German progress in missiles. Tsien became director of the rocket section, U.S. National Defense Scientific Advisory Board, and a member of a group of scientists assigned to study how the next war would be fought in the air. Their report, called "Toward New Horizons -- Science as the Key to Air Supremacy," became the basis of the American missile program in succeeding years. Tsien had top U.S. security clearance at this time. In 1950, Tsien was arrested and charged with Communist party membership pre-dating his arrival in this country. His arrest followed the seizure by federal agents of 1,800 pounds of papers and books on rocketry and space physics that Tsien had consigned for shipment to himself in Shanghai. Tsien denied the charges. He was ordered deported, but proceedings were delayed for five years on the grounds that Tsien possessed so much knowledge of potential value to an enemy that it would be "inimical to the best interests of the United States" to let him leave. Tsien resumed teaching at Caltech until 1955, when American officials judged his secret knowledge to have become dated. He returned to China in that year and was immediately named to the Chinese Academy of Sciences, assigned to work on developing weaponry. Soon after his return, an announcement was made that Tsien had joined the Communist party.

Gen. James A. Van Fleet. Headed Truman Doctrine U.S. military mission to Greece and directed Greek army's buildup against the Communist rebels 1948-1950; took over 8th Army forces in Korea April 1951, when Gen. Matthew B. Ridgway succeeded Gen. Douglas MacArthur as Far Eastern commander; retired 1953; in 1952, called Korean War a "blessing" because it spurred free world to crush communism; frequently criticized "hold-the-line" policy in Korea, recommending 1953 use of atomic weapons if truce were violated and full-scale war resumed; complaint before Senate Armed Services Committee 1953 of ammunition shortages during war resulted in investigation; urged in 1954 breaking off diplomatic relations with Russia; author of "Black Book Against China"; supported Committee of One Million Against the Admission of Communist China to the UN.

John Carter Vincent. Foreign Service officer stationed primarily in China, 1925-35, 1941-43; held positions in State Department's division of Far Eastern Affairs, 1935-39, 1943-44, becoming division director in 1945. Cleared by Senate of 1950 disloyalty charge by Sen. Joseph R. McCarthy (R Wis.); appointed consul general in Tangier, Morocco, 1951; retired in 1953, shortly after Secretary of State Dulles investigated and dismissed a second McCarthy charge.

Andrei Y. Vishinsky. First deputy Soviet foreign minister, 1940-46, 1953; foreign minister, 1949-53; chief Soviet spokesman at major UN meetings and many Big Four conferences from 1946 until his death in 1954; vigorously denounced U.S. "aggression" in China, Formosa and Korea.

Bishop James Edward Walsh. Ordained as a priest in the Roman Catholic Church, 1915; directed parochial school in Pennsylvania, 1916-18; assigned to mission in China, 1918; consecrated titular bishop of Sata and vicar apostolic of Kongmoon, China, 1927; returned to U.S. and served as superior general of the Catholic Foreign Mission Society, Maryknoll, N.Y., 1936-46; general secretary of the Catholic Central Bureau since 1948 in Shanghai; interned by Chinese Communists in 1950 for "counter-revolutionary activities"; released in 1966.

Wang Kuo-chuan. Red China's ambassador to Poland since April 1964; participated in talks between China and the United States in Warsaw since July 1964. Served as ambassador to East Germany from June 1957 to January 1964; signed China-East Germany Commodity Exchange and Payments Protocol in 1960 and 1962. Attended First Chinese People's Political Consultative Conference (CPPCC) in September 1949 as the representative of "peasant bodies from various liberated areas."

Wang Ping-nan. Red China's vice minister of foreign affairs since 1964; served as ambassador to Poland from 1955-1964; studied in Germany where he joined the Chinese Communist Party and Berlin Branch, Communist Third International, becoming active leader of Chinese students in Germany in 1925; visited Soviet Union in 1936, and on return to China was one of the planners of the 1936 kidnapping of Chiang Kai-shek by the warlords; served as Chou En-lai's personal secretary and representative, 1938-45; member and secretary of Communist delegation during CCP and Kuomintang peace talks in Nanking in 1946; assistant minister of foreign affairs, 1954-55, and member of Chinese delegation to 1954 Geneva Conference.

Gen. Wang Shu-ming. Chief of the Nationalist Chinese delegation to the United Nations Military Staff Committee; graduated from Chiang Kai-shek's Whampoa Military Academy in 1924 and attended aviation and military flying schools until 1932; served as commander of 2nd Bomber Squadron, Chinese Air Force in 1934, commandant of Air Force Academy in 1941 and of Air Staff College in 1942; deputy commanding general and chief of staff, Chinese Air Force, 1946; commander-in-chief, Chinese Air Force, 1952; Nationalist China's chief of staff, 1957-59.

Lt. Gen. Albert C. Wedemeyer. Replaced Gen. Joseph W. Stilwell as commander of U.S. Forces in China Theater and as chief of staff, November 1944-46; led Presidential fact-finding mission, with rank of ambassador, to China and Korea, 1947; supported Gen. Douglas MacArthur's views on the Far East; retired from active duty, July 1951; vice president and dir. of Avco Manufacturing Co., 1951-54; mem. of the board of directors of National Airlines, Inc., Financial Industrial Fund, Inc., and Axe Science and Electronics Corp.

Gen. William C. Westmoreland. Commander of U.S. forces in Viet Nam since 1963; attended U.S. Military Academy; stationed in Hawaii, 1936-41, but saw action mostly in Europe during World War II; worked with airborne divisions, 1946-53; secretary to Army general staff, 1955-58, after serving as deputy; superintendent of West Point, 1960-63, after service with airborne training divisions.

Gen. Ne Win. Chairman of the Burmese Revolutionary Council that took control of the government on March 2, 1962; chief of General Staff of the Army, 1960- ; joined Allied forces in 1945; deputy prime minister, 1949-50; prime minister and minister of defense, 1958-60.

Wu Han. Prominent Chinese historian, literary figure and vice mayor of Peking until 1966; engaged in underground work for the Communists while teaching at National Tsinghua University, 1946-48; secretary general of first all-China Federation of Democratic Youth (ACFDY), 1949-53; vice-chairman, ACFDY, 1953-58; member of Board of Directors, Sino-Soviet Friendship Assn., 1949-54; member of Chinese Academy of Sciences since 1955; led cultural delegations to India, 1956, Nepal and Iraq, 1962; charged with bourgeois tendencies and Soviet revisionism in 1966 purge and removed from his post as vice-mayor of Peking.

Wu Hsiu-chuan. Studied in Moscow and France, 1927-30, returned to China to become a professor in Shanghai; joined Red Army in 1932; director of U.S.S.R. and East European Affairs Dept., Ministry of Foreign Affairs, Government Administration Council, 1949-52; denounced United States before UN Security Council as aggressor against Taiwan, 1950; ambassador to Yugoslavia, 1955-58; participated in talks with Laotian Premier Souvanna Phouma, 1961.

Wu Teh. Deputy and acting mayor of Peking, succeeding Peng Chen, who was deposed in the 1966 purge; denounced by the Red Guards and Mao's wife in late 1966; early career started as labor union organizer in eastern Hopei mines; reported to Mao in Yenan, 1940; continued as leader in labor movement, member of 6th Executive Committee of all-China Federation of Trade Unions (ACFTU), 1948-53; mayor of Tientsin, 1953-55; president, University of Tientsin, 1952-57; alternate member of the Chinese Communist Party's Central Committee since 1956, political commissar of Kirin Military Region since 1958; secretary of Secretariat, CCP Northeast Bureau since 1963; associated with Lin Piao in party leadership.

Yang Hsien-chen. Communist philosopher and member of the Chinese Communist Party Central Committee since 1958; studied at Russian Language Institute, Peking, and in the U.S.S.R. and Germany; did translating in the U.S.S.R. Far East Bureau until the Chinese Communists came to power, 1949; returned to China and became vice president of the CCP Marxist-Leninist Institute; taught theoretical cadres for the Party Center, 1953; deputy chief, Division of Theoretical Education, CCP Propaganda Dept. 1954; in 1964, the CCP used the political line of "one divides into two" to show the split from the Soviet Communist Party; a debate ensued. Yang was believed to have encouraged the writing of an article "Two Combine into One," published May 29, 1964, against this theory and in opposition to the party's political line. He was subjected to severe criticism, continuing into the summer of 1965.

George K.C. Yeh. Appointed Nationalist Chinese foreign minister in 1950, when Premier Chen Cheng formed his first cabinet of comparatively young and liberal Kuomintang leaders in Formosa; replaced as foreign minister in 1958; named ambassador to the United States, 1958-62.

Valerian Zorin. Soviet diplomat; ambassador to Czechoslovakia during Communist coup, 1945-48; deputy foreign minister, 1948-55 and 1956-60; permanent representative to UN, 1952-53 and 1960-63; left UN reportedly as a result of 1962 Cuban missile confrontation; ambassador to France in 1966.

Texts and Documents

Documents and Texts Bearing on United States–China Relations

TRUMAN POLICY STATEMENT

Following is the text of a statement made by President Truman on United States policy toward China on Dec. 15, 1945, on the eve of the mission to China by Gen. George C. Marshall (see p. 39):

The Government of the United States holds that peace and prosperity of the world in this new and unexplored era ahead depend upon the ability of the sovereign nations to combine for collective security in the United Nations organization.

It is the firm belief of this Government that a strong, united and democratic China is of the utmost importance to the success of this United Nations organization and for world peace. A China disorganized and divided either by foreign aggression, such as that undertaken by the Japanese, or by violent internal strife, is an undermining influence to world stability and peace, now and in the future. The United States Government has long subscribed to the principle that the management of internal affairs is the responsibility of the peoples of the sovereign nations. Events of this century, however, would indicate that a breach of peace anywhere in the world threatens the peace of the entire world. It is thus in the most vital interest of the United States and all the United Nations that the people of China overlook no opportunity to adjust their internal differences promptly by means of peaceful negotiation.

The Government of the United States believes it essential:

(1) That a cessation of hostilities be arranged between the armies of the National Government and the Chinese Communists and other dissident Chinese armed forces for the purpose of completing the return of all China to effective Chinese control, including the immediate evacuation of the Japanese forces.

(2) That a national conference of representatives of major political elements be arranged to develop an early solution to the present internal strife — a solution which will bring about the unification of China.

The United States and the other United Nations have recognized the present National Government of the Republic of China as the only legal government in China. It is the proper instrument to achieve the objective of a unified China.

The United States and the United Kingdom by the Cairo Declaration in 1943 and the Union of Soviet Socialist Republics by adhering to the Potsdam Declaration of last July and by the Sino-Soviet Treaty and Agreements of August 1945, are all committed to the liberation of China, including the return of Manchuria to Chinese control. These agreements are made with the National Government of the Republic of China.

In continuation of the constant and close collaboration with the National Government of the Republic of China in the prosecution of this war, in consonance with the Potsdam Declaration, and to remove possibility of Japanese influence remaining in China, the United States has assumed a definite obligation in the disarmament and evacuation of the Japanese troops. Accordingly the United States has been assisting and will continue to assist the National Government of the Republic of China in effecting the disarmament and evacuation of Japanese troops in the liberated areas. The United States Marines are in North China for that purpose.

The United States recognizes and will continue to recognize the National Government of China and cooperate with it in international affairs and specifically in eliminating Japanese influence from China. The United States is convinced that a prompt arrangement for a cessation of hostilities is essential to the effective achievement of this end. United States support will not extend to United States military intervention to influence the course of any Chinese internal strife.

The United States has already been compelled to pay a great price to restore the peace which was first broken by Japanese aggression in Manchuria. The maintenance of peace in the Pacific may be jeopardized, if not frustrated, unless Japanese influence in China is wholly removed and unless China takes her place as a unified, democratic and peaceful nation. This is the purpose of the maintenance for the time being of United States military and naval forces in China.

The United States is cognizant that the present National Government of China is a "one-party government" and believes that peace, unity and democratic reform in China will be furthered if the basis of this Government is broadened to include other political elements in the country. Hence, the United States strongly advocates that the national conference of representatives of major political elements in the country agree upon arrangements which would give those elements a fair and effective representation in the Chinese National Government. It is recognized that this would require modification of the one-party "political tutelage" established as an interim arrangement in the progress of the nation toward democracy by the father of the Chinese Republic, Doctor Sun Yat-sen.

The existence of autonomous armies such as that of the Communist army is inconsistent with, and actually makes impossible, political unity in China. With the institution of a broadly representative government, autonomous armies should be eliminated as such and all armed forces in China integrated effectively into the Chinese National Army.

In line with its often expressed views regarding self-determination, the United States Government considers that the detailed steps necessary to the achievement of political unity in China must be worked out by the Chinese themselves and that intervention by any foreign government in these matters would be inappropriate. The United States Government feels, however, that China has a clear responsibility to the other United Nations to eliminate armed conflict within its territory as constituting a threat to world stability and peace — a responsibility which is shared by the National Government and all Chinese political and military groups.

As China moves toward peace and unity along the lines described above, the United States would be prepared to assist the National Government in every reasonable way to rehabilitate the country, improve the agrarian and industrial economy, and establish a military organization capable of discharging China's national and international responsibilities for the maintenance of peace and order. In furtherance of such assistance, it would be prepared to give favorable consideration to Chinese requests for credits and loans under reasonable conditions for projects which would contribute toward the development of a healthy economy throughout China and healthy trade relations between. China and the United States.

Wedemeyer Report

Following is the text of the report made to President Truman by Lt. Gen. Albert C. Wedemeyer on Sept. 19, 1947, following a mission to China from July 16 to Sept. 18, 1947 (see p. 43):

Members of the Mission

Capt. James J. Boyle, Aide-de-Camp -- Secretary, War Department; Capt. Horace Eng, Aide-de-Camp -- Interpreter, War Department; Lt. Colonel Claire E. Hutchin, Jr, Military Advisor, War Department; David R. Jenkins, Fiscal Advisor, Treasury Department; Philip D. Sprouse, Political Advisor, State Department; Rear Admiral Carl A. Trexel, Engineering Advisor, Navy Department; Melville H. Walker, Economic Advisor, State Department; Mark S. Watson, Press and Public Affairs Advisor, Baltimore "Sun"; Lt. Gen. A. C. Wedemeyer, Special Representative of the President of the United States.

REPORT TO THE PRESIDENT

CHINA

Part I – General Statement

China's history is replete with examples of encroachment, arbitrary action, special privilege, exploitation, and usurpation of territory on the part of foreign powers. Continued foreign infiltration, penetration or efforts to obtain spheres of influence in China including Manchuria and Taiwan (Formosa), could be interpreted only as a direct infringement and violation of China's sovereignty and a contravention of the principles of the Charter of the United Nations. It is mandatory that the United States and those other nations subscribing to the principles of the Charter of the United Nations should combine their efforts to insure the unimpeded march of all peoples toward goals that recognize the dignity of man and his civil rights and, further, definitely provide the opportunity to express freely how and by whom they will be governed.

Those goals and the lofty aims of freedom-loving peoples are jeopardized today by forces as sinister as those that operated in Europe and Asia during the ten years leading to World War II. The pattern is familiar -- employment of subversive agents; infiltration tactics; incitement of disorder and chaos to disrupt normal economy and thereby to undermine popular confidence in government and leaders; seizure of authority without reference to the will of the people -- all the techniques skillfully designed and ruthlessly implemented in order to create favorable conditions for the imposition of totalitarian ideologies. This pattern is present in the Far East, particularly in the areas contiguous to Siberia.

If the United Nations is to have real effect in establishing economic stability and in maintaining world peace, these developments merit high priority on the United Nations' agenda for study and action. Events of the past two years demonstrate the futility of appeasement based on the hope that the strongly consolidated forces of the Soviet Union will adopt either a conciliatory or a cooperative attitude, except as tactical expedients. Soviet practice in the countries already occupied or dominated completes the mosaic of aggressive expansion through ruthless secret police methods and through an increasing political and economic enslavement of peoples. Soviet literature, confirmed repeatedly by Communist leaders, reveals a definite plan for expansion far exceeding that of Nazism in its ambitious scope and dangerous implications. Therefore in attempting a solution to the problem presented in the Far East, as well as in other troubled areas of the world, every possible opportunity must be used to seize the initiative in order to create and maintain bulwarks of freedom.

Notwithstanding all the corruption and incompetence that one notes in China, it is a certainty that the bulk of the people are not disposed to a Communist political and economic structure. Some have become affiliated with Communism in indignant protest against oppressive police measures, corrupt practices and mal-administration of National Government officials. Some have lost all hope for China under existing leadership and turn to the Communists in despair. Some accept a new leadership by mere inertia.

Indirectly, the United States facilitated the Soviet program in the Far East by agreeing at the Yalta Conference to Russian re-entry into Manchuria, and later by withholding aid from the National Government. There were justifiable reasons for these policies. In the one case we were concentrating maximum Allied strength against Japanese in order to accelerate crushing defeat and thus save Allied lives. In the other, we were withholding unqualified support from a government within which corruption and incompetence were so prevalent that it was losing the support of its own people. Further, the United States had not yet realized that the Soviet Union would fail to cooperate in the accomplishment of world-wide plans for post-war rehabilitation. Our own participation in those plans has already afforded assistance to other nations and peoples, friends and former foes alike, to a degree unparalleled in humanitarian history.

Gradually it has become apparent that the World War II ob-

jectives for which we and others made tremendous sacrifices are not being fully attained, and that there remains in the world a force presenting even greater dangers to world peace than did the Nazi militarists and the Japanese jingoists. Consequently the United States made the decision in the Spring of 1947 to assist Greece and Turkey with a view to protecting their sovereignties, which were threatened by the direct or inspired activities of the Soviet Union. Charges of unilateral action and circumvention of the United Nations were made by members of that organization. In the light of its purposes and principles such criticisms seemed plausible. The United States promptly declared its intention of referring the matter to the United Nations when that organization would be ready to assume responsibility.

It follows that the United Nations should be informed of contemplated action with regard to China. If the recommendations of this report are approved, the United States should suggest to China that she inform the United Nations officially of her request to the United States for material assistance and advisory aid in order to facilitate China's post-war rehabilitation and economic recovery. This will demonstrate that the United Nations is not being circumvented, and that the United States is not infringing upon China's sovereignty, but contrary-wise is cooperating constructively in the interest of peace and stability in the Far East, concomitantly in the world.

The situation in Manchuria has deteriorated to such a degree that prompt action is necessary to prevent that area from becoming a Soviet satellite. The Chinese Communists may soon gain military control of Manchuria and announce the establishment of a government. Outer Mongolia, already a Soviet satellite, may then recognize Manchuria and conclude a "mutual support agreement" with a *de facto* Manchurian government of the Chinese Communists. In that event, the Soviet Union might accomplish a mutual support agreement with Communist-dominated Manchuria, because of her current similar agreement with Outer Mongolia. This would create a difficult situation for China, the United States and the United Nations. Ultimately it could lead to a Communist-dominated China.

The United Nations might take immediate action to bring about cessation of hostilities in Manchuria as a prelude to the establishment of a Guardianship or Trusteeship. The Guardianship might consist of China, Soviet Russia, the United States, Great Britain and France. This should be attempted promptly and could be initiated only by China. Should one of the nations refuse to participate in Manchurian Guardianship, China might then request the General Assembly of the United Nations to establish a Trusteeship, under the provisions of the Charter.

Initially China might interpret Guardianship or Trusteeship as an infringement upon her sovereignty. But the urgency of the matter should encourage a realistic view of the situation. If these steps are not taken by China, Manchuria may be drawn into the Soviet orbit, despite United States aid, and lost, perhaps permanently, to China.

The economic deterioration and the incompetence and corruption in the political and military organizations in China should be considered against an all-inclusive background lest there be disproportionate emphasis upon defects. Comity requires that cognizance be taken of the following:

Unlike other Powers since V-J Day, China has never been free to devote full attention to internal problems that were greatly confounded by eight years of war. The current civil war has imposed an overwhelming financial and economic burden at a time when resources and energies have been dissipated and when, in any event, they would have been strained to the utmost to meet the problems of recovery.

The National Government has consistently, since 1927, opposed Communism. Today the same political leader and same civil and military officials are determined to prevent their country from becoming a Communist-dominated State or Soviet satellite.

Although the Japanese offered increasingly favorable surrender terms during the course of the war, China elected to remain steadfast with her Allies. If China had accepted surrender terms, approximately a million Japanese would have been released for employment against American forces in the Pacific.

I was assured by the Generalissimo that China would support to the limit of her ability an American program for the stabilization of the Far East. He stated categorically that, regardless of moral encouragement or material aid received from the United States, he is determined to oppose Communism and to create a democratic form of government in consonance with Doctor Sun Yat-sen's principles. He stated further that he plans to make sweeping reforms in the government including the removal of incompetent and corrupt officials. He stated that some progress has been made along these lines but, with spiraling inflation, economic distress and civil war, it has been difficult to accomplish fully these objectives. He emphasized that, when the Communist problem is solved, he could drastically reduce the Army and concentrate upon political and economic reforms. I retain the conviction that the Generalissimo is sincere in his desire to attain these objectives. I am not certain that he has today sufficient determination to do so if this requires absolute overruling of the political and military cliques surrounding him. Yet, if realistic United States aid is to prove effective in stabilizing the situation in China and in coping with the dangerous expansion of Communism, that determination must be established.

Adoption by the United States of a policy motivated solely toward stopping the expansion of Communism without regard to the continued existence of an unpopular repressive government would render any aid ineffective. Further, United States prestige in the Far East would suffer heavily, and wavering elements might turn away from the existing government to Communism.

In China (and Korea), the political, economic and psychological problems are inextricably mingled. All of them are complex and are becoming increasingly difficult of solution. Each has been studied assiduously in compliance with your directive. Each will be discussed in the course of this report. However, it is recognized that a continued global appraisal is mandatory in order to preclude disproportionate or untimely assistance to any specific area.

The following three postulates of United States foreign policy are pertinent to indicate the background of my investigations, analyses and report:

The United States will continue support of the United Nations in the attainment of its lofty aims, accepting the possible development that the Soviet Union or other nations may not actively participate.

Moral support will be given to nations and peoples that have established political and economic structures compatible with our own, or that give convincing evidence of their desire to do so.

Material aid may be given to those same nations and peoples in order to accelerate post-war rehabilitation and to develop economic stability, provided:

That such aid shall be used for the purposes intended.

That there is continuing evidence that they are taking effective steps to help themselves, or are firmly committed to to so.

That such aid shall not jeopardize the American economy and shall conform to an integrated program that involves other international commitments and contributes to the attainment of political, economic and psychological objectives of the United States.

Part II - China

Political

Although the Chinese people are unanimous in their desire for peace at almost any cost, there seems to be no possibility of its realization under existing circumstances. On one side is the Kuomintang, whose reactionary leadership, repression and corruption have caused a loss of popular faith in the Government. On the other side, bound ideologically to the Soviet Union, are the Chinese Communists, whose eventual aim is admittedly a Communist state in China. Some reports indicate that Communist measures of land reform have gained for them the support of the majority of peasants in areas under their control, while others indicate that their ruthless tactics of land distribution and terrorism have alienated the major-

ity of such peasants. They have, however, successfully organized many rural areas against the National Government. Moderate groups are caught between Kuomintang misrule and repression and ruthless Communist totalitarianism. Minority parties lack dynamic leadership and sizable following. Neither the moderates, many of whom are in the Kuomintang, nor the minority parties are able to make their influence felt because of National Government repression. Existing provincial opposition leading to possible separatist movements would probably crystallize only if collapse of the Government were imminent.

Soviet actions, contrary to the letter and spirit of the Sino-Soviet Treaty of 1945 and its related documents, have strengthened the Chinese Communist position in Manchuria, with political, economic and military repercussions on the National Government's position both in Manchuria and in China proper, and have made more difficult peace and stability in China. The present trend points toward a gradual disintegration of the National Government's control, with the ultimate possibility of a Communist-dominated China.

Steps taken by the Chinese Government toward governmental reorganization in mid-April 1947 aroused hopes of improvement in the political situation. However, the reorganization resulted in little change. Reactionary influences continue to mold important policies even though the Generalissimo remains the principal determinative force in the government. Since the April reorganization, the most significant change has been the appointment of General Chen Cheng to head the civil and military administration in Manchuria. Projected steps include elections in the Fall for the formation of a constitutional government, but, under present conditions, they are not expected to result in a government more representative than the present regime.

Economic

Under the impact of civil strife and inflation, the Chinese economy is disintegrating. The most probable outcome of present trends would be, not sudden collapse, but a continued and creeping paralysis and consequent decline in the authority and power of the National Government. The past ten years of war have caused serious deterioration of transportation and communication facilities, mines, utilities and industries. Notwithstanding some commendable efforts and large amounts of economic aid, their overall capabilities are scarcely half those of the pre-war period. With disruption of transportation facilities and the loss of much of North China and Manchuria, important resources of those rich areas are no longer available for the rehabilitation and support of China's economy.

Inflation in China has been diffused slowly through an enormous population without causing the immediate dislocation which would have occurred in a highly industrialized economy. The rural people, 80 percent of the total Chinese population of 450 million, barter food-stuffs for local handicraft products without suffering a drastic cut in living standards. Thus, local economies exist in many parts of China, largely insulated from the disruption of urban industry. Some local economies are under the control of Communists, and some are loosely under the control of provincial authorities.

The principal cause of the hyper-inflation is the long-continued deficit in the national budget. Present revenue collections, plus the profits of nationalized enterprises, cover only one-third of governmental expenditures, which are approximately 70 percent military, and an increasing proportion of the budget is financed by the issuance of new currency. In the first six months of 1947 note-issue was tripled but rice prices increased seven-fold. Thus prices and governmental expenditures spiral upwards, with price increases occurring faster than new currency can be printed. With further price increases, budget revisions will undoubtedly be necessary. The most urgent economic need of Nationalist China is a reduction of the military budget.

China's external official assets amounted to $327 million (US) on July 30, 1947. Privately-held foreign exchange assets are at least $600 million and may total $1500 million, but no serious attempt has been made to mobilize these private resources for rehabilitation purposes. Private Chinese assets located in China include probably $200 million in gold, and about $75 million in US currency notes. Although China has not exhausted her foreign official assets, and probably will not do so at the present rates of imports and exports until early 1949, the continuing deficit in her external balance of payments is a serious problem.

Disparity between the prices of export goods in China and in world markets at unrealistic official exchange rates has greatly penalized exports, as have disproportionate increases in wages and other costs. Despite rigorous trade and exchange controls, imports have greatly exceeded exports, and there consistently has been a heavy adverse trade balance.

China's food harvests this year are expected to be significantly larger than last year's fairly good returns. This moderately encouraging situation with regard to crops is among the few favorable factors which can be found in China's current economic situation.

Under inflationary conditions, long-term investment is unattractive for both Chinese and foreign capital. Private Chinese funds tend to go into short-term advances, hoarding of commodities, and capital flight. The entire psychology is speculative and inflationary, preventing ordinary business planning and handicapping industrial recovery.

Foreign business enterprises in China are adversely affected by the inefficient and corrupt administration of exchange and import controls, discriminatory application of tax laws, the increasing role of government trading agencies and the trend towards state ownership of industries. The Chinese Government has taken some steps toward improvement but generally has been apathetic in its efforts. Between 1944 and 1947, the anti-inflationary measure on which the Chinese Government placed most reliance was the public sale of gold borrowed from the United States. The intention was to absorb paper currency, and thus reduce the effective demand for goods. Under the circumstance of continued large deficits, however, the only effect of the gold sales program was to retard slightly the price inflation and dissipate dollar assets.

A program to stabilize the economic situation was undertaken in February 1947. The measures included a wage freeze, a system of limited rationing to essential workers in a few cities, and the sale of government bonds. The effect of this program has been slight, and the wage freeze has been abandoned. In August 1947, the unrealistic official rate of exchange was replaced, for proceeds of exports and remittances, by a free market in foreign exchange. This step is expected to stimulate exports, but it is too early to determine whether it will be effective.

The issuance of a new silver currency has been proposed as a future measure to combat inflation. If the government continued to finance budgetary deficits by unbacked note issue, the silver would probably go into hoards and the price inflation would continue. The effect would be no more than that of the gold sales in 1944 -- 1947, namely, a slight and temporary retardation of the inflationary spiral. The proposal could be carried out, moreover, only through a loan from the United States of at least $200 million in silver.

In the construction field, China has prepared expansive plans for reconstruction of communications, mines and industries. Some progress has been made in implementing them, notably in the partial rehabilitation of certain railroads and in the textile industry. Constructive results have been handicapped by a lack of funds, equipment and experienced management, supervisory and technical personnel.

On August 1, 1947, the State Council approved a "Plan for Economic Reform." This appears to be an onmibus of plans covering all phases of Chinese economic reconstruction but its effectiveness cannot yet be determined.

Social - Cultural

Public education has been one of the chief victims of war and social and economic disruption. Schoolhouses, textbooks and other equipment have been destroyed and the cost of replacing any considerable portion cannot now be met. Teachers, like other public servants, have seen the purchasing power of a month's salary shrink to the market value of a few days' rice ration. This applies to the entire educational system, from primary schools, which provide a medium to combat the nation's grievous illiteracy, to universities, from which must come the nation's professional men, technicians and administrators. The universities have suffered in an additional and no less serious respect -- traditional academic freedom. Students participating in protest demonstrations have been severely and at times brutally punished by National Government agents without pretense of trial or public evidence of the sedition charged. Faculty members have often been dismissed or refused employment with no evidence of professional unfitness, patently because they were politically objectionable to government officials. Somewhat similarly, periodicals have been closed down "for reasons of military security" without stated charges, and permitted to reopen only after new managements have been imposed. Resumption of educational and other public welfare activities on anything like the desired scale can be accomplished only by restraint of officialdom's abuses, and when the nation's economy is stabilized sufficiently to defray the cost of such vital activities.

Military

The overall military position of the National Government has deteriorated in the past several months and the current military situation favors Communist forces. The Generalissimo has never wavered in his contention that he is fighting for national independence against forces of an armed rebellion nor has he been completely convinced that the Communist problem can be resolved except by force of arms. Although the Nationalist Army has a preponderance of force, the tactical initiative rests with the Communists. Their hit-and-run tactics, adapted to their mission of destruction at points or in areas of their own selection, give them a decided advantage over Nationalists, who must defend many critical areas including connecting lines of communication. Obviously large numbers of Nationalist troops involved in such defensive roles are immobilized whereas Communist tactics permit almost complete freedom of action. The Nationalists' position is precarious in Manchuria, where they occupy only a slender finger of territory. Their control is strongly disputed in Shantung and Hopei Provinces where the Communists make frequent dislocating attacks against isolated garrisons.

In order to improve materially the current military situation, the Nationalist forces must first stabilize the fronts and then regain the initiative. Further, since the Government is supporting the civil war with approximately seventy percent of its national budget, it is evident that steps taken to alleviate the situation must point toward an improvement in the effectiveness of the armed forces with a concomitant program of social, political and economic reforms, including a decrease in the size of the military establishment. Whereas some rather ineffective steps have been taken to reorganize and revitalize the command structure, and more sweeping reforms are projected, the effectiveness of the Nationalist Army requires a sound program of equipment and improved logistical support. The present industrial potential of China is inadequate to support military forces effectively. Chinese forces under present conditions cannot cope successfully with internal strife or fulfill China's obligations as a member of the family of nations. Hence outside aid, in the form of munitions (most urgently ammunition) and technical assistance, is essential before any plan of operations can be undertaken with a reasonable prospect of success. Military advice is now available to the Nationalist on a General Staff level through American military advisory groups. The Generalissimo expressed to me repeatedly a strong desire to have this advice and supervision extended in scope to include field forces, training centers and particularly logistical agencies.

Extension of military aid by the United States to the National Government might possibly be followed by similar aid from the Soviet Union to the Chinese Communists, either openly or covertly -- the latter course seems more likely. An arena of conflicting ideologies might be created as in 1935 in Spain. There is always the possibility that such developments in this area, as in Europe and in the Middle East, might precipitate a third world war.

Part IV - Conclusions

The peaceful aims of freedom-loving peoples in the world are jeopardized today by developments as portentous as those leading to World War II.

The Soviet Union and her satellites give no evidence of a conciliatory or cooperative attitude in these developments. The United States is compelled, therefore, to initiate realistic lines of action in order to create and maintain bulwarks of freedom, and to protect United States strategic interests.

The bulk of the Chinese are not disposed to Communism and they are not concerned with ideologies. They desire food, shelter and the opportunity to live in peace.

China

The spreading internecine struggle within China threatens world peace. Repeated American efforts to mediate have proved unavailing. It is apparent that positive steps are required to end hostilities immediately. The most logical approach to this very complex and ominous situation would be to refer the matter to the United Nations.

A China dominated by Chinese Communists would be inimical to the interests of the United States, in view of their openly expressed hostility and active opposition to those principles which the United States regards as vital to the peace of the world.

The Communists have the tactical initiative in the overall military situation. The Nationalist position in Manchuria is precarious, and in Shantung and Hopei Provinces strongly disputed. Continued deterioration of the situation may result in the early establishment of a Soviet satellite government in Manchuria and ultimately in the evolution of a Communist-dominated China.

China is suffering increasingly from disintegration. Her requirements for rehabilitation are large. Her most urgent needs include governmental reorganization and reforms, reduction of the military budget and external assistance.

A program of aid, if effectively employed, would bolster opposition to Communist expansion, and would contribute to gradual development of stability in China.

Due to excesses and oppressions by government police agencies basic freedoms of the people are being jeopardized. Maladministration and corruption cause a loss of confidence in the Government. Until drastic political and economic reforms are undertaken United States aid can not accomplish its purpose.

Even so, criticism of results achieved by the National Government in efforts for improvement should be tempered by a recognition of the handicaps imposed on China by eight years of war, the burden of her opposition to Communism, and her sacrifices for the Allied cause.

A United States program of assistance could best be implemented under the supervision of American advisors in specified economic and military fields. Such a program can be undertaken only if China requests advisory aid as well as material assistance.

Part V -- Recommendations

It is recommended:

That the United States Government provide as early as practicable moral, advisory, and material support to China in order to contribute to the early establishment of peace in the world in consonance with the enunciated principles of the United Nations, and concomitantly to protect United States strategic interests against militant forces which now threaten them.

That United States policies and actions suggested in this report be thoroughly integrated by appropriate government agencies with other internation commitments. It is recognized that any foreign assistance extended must avoid jeopardizing the American economy.

China

That China be advised that the United States is favorably disposed to continue aid designed to protect China's territorial integrity and to facilitate her recovery, under agreements to be negotiated by representatives of the two governments, with the following stipulations:

That China inform the United Nations promptly of her request to the United States for increased material and advisory assistance.

That China request the United Nations to take immediate action to bring about a cessation of hostilities in Manchuria and request that Manchuria be placed under a Five-Power Guardianship or, failing that, under a Trusteeship in accordance with the United Nations Charter.

That China make effective use of her own resources in a program for economic reconstruction and initiate sound fiscal policies leading to reduction of budgetary deficits.

That China give continuing evidence that the urgently required political and military reforms are being implemented.

That China accept American advisors as responsible representatives of the United States Government in specified military and economic fields to assist China in utilizing United States aid in the manner for which it is intended.

CHINA AID ACT OF 1948

Following is the text of Title IV of PL 80-472, the Foreign Assistance Act of 1948, authorizing $463 million for aid to China -- $338 million for economic aid and $125 million for military aid. President Truman had requested $570 million in economic aid only. The bill was signed by Mr. Truman on April 3, 1948. (See p. 45)

Sec. 401. This title may be cited as the "China Aid Act of 1948."

Sec. 402. Recognizing the intimate economic and other relationships between the United States and China, and recognizing that disruption following in the wake of war is not contained by national frontiers, the Congress finds that the existing situation in China endangers the establishment of a lasting peace, the general welfare and national interest of the United States, and the attainment of the objectives of the United Nations. It is the sense of the Congress that the further evolution in China of Principles of individual liberty, free institutions, and genuine independence rests largely upon the continuing development of a strong and democratic national government as the basis for the establishment of sound economic conditions and for stable international economic relationships. Mindful of the advantages which the United States has enjoyed through the existence of a large domestic market with no internal trade barriers, and believing that similar advantages can accrue to China, it is declared to be the policy of the people of the United States to encourage the Republic of China and its people to exert sustained common efforts which will speedily achieve the internal peace and economic stability in China which are essential for lasting peace and prosperity in the world. It is further declared to be the policy of the people of the United States to encourage the Republic of China in its efforts to maintain the genuine independence and the administrative integrity of China, and to sustain and strengthen principles of individual liberty and free institutions in China through a program of assistance based on self-help and cooperation: *Provided*, That no assistance to China herein contemplated shall seriously impair the economic stability of the United States. It is further declared to be the policy of the United States that assistance provided by the United States under this title should at all times be dependent upon cooperation by the Republic of China and its people in furthering the program: *Provided further*, That assistance furnished under this title shall not be construed as an express or implied assumption by the United States of any responsibility for policies, acts, or undertakings of the Republic of China or for conditions which may prevail in China at any time.

Sec. 403. Aid provided under this title shall be provided under the applicable provisions of the Economic Cooperation Act of 1948 which are consistent with the purposes of this title. It is not the purpose of this title that China, in order to receive aid hereunder, shall adhere to a joint program for European recovery.

Sec. 404. (a) In order to carry out the purposes of this title, there is hereby authorized to be appropriated to the President for aid to China a sum not to exceed $338,000,000 to remain available for obligation for the period of one year following the date of enactment of this Act.

(b) There is also hereby authorized to be appropriated to the President a sum not to exceed $125,000,000 for additional aid to China through grants, on such terms as the President may determine and without regard to the provisions of the Economic Cooperation Act of 1948, to remain available for obligation for the period of one year following the date of enactment of this Act.

Sec. 405. An agreement shall be entered into between China and the United States containing those undertakings by China which the Secretary of State, after consultation with the Administrator for Economic Cooperation, may deem necessary to carry out the purpose of this title and to improve commercial relations with China.

Sec. 406. Notwithstanding the provisions of any other law, the Reconstruction Finance Corporation is authorized and directed, until such time as an appropriation is made pursuant to section 404, to make advances, not to exceed in the aggregate $50,000,000, to carry out the provisions of this title in such manner and in such amounts as the President shall determine. From appropriations authorized under section 404, there shall be repaid without interest to the Reconstruction Finance Corporation the advances made by it under the authority contained herein. No interest shall be charged on advances made by the Treasury to the Reconstruction Finance Corporation in implementation of this section.

Sec. 407. (a) The Secretary of State, after consultation with the Administrator, is hereby authorized to conclude an agreement with China establishing a Joint Commission on Rural Reconstruction in China, to be composed of two citizens of the United States appointed by the President of the United States and three citizens of China appointed by the President of China. Such Commission shall, subject to the direction and control of the Administrator, formulate and carry out a program for reconstruction in rural areas of China, which shall include such research and training activities as may be necessary to appropriate for such reconstruction: *Provided,* That assistance furnished under this section shall not be construed as an express or implied assumption by the United States of any responsibility for making any further contributions to carry out the purposes of this section.

(b) Insofar as practicable, an amount equal to not more than 10 per centum of the funds made available under subsection (a) of section 404 shall be used to carry out the purposes of subsection (a) of this section. Such amount may be in United States dollars, proceeds in Chinese currency from the sale of commodities made available to China with funds authorized under subsection (a) of section 404, or both.

Approved April 3, 1948.

STATEMENT ON AID

Following is the text of a statement issued by the State Department March 21, 1949 -- a "Summary of United States Government Economic, Financial, and Military Aid Authorized for China Since 1937":

Since the commencement of hostilities between China and Japan in 1937 the United States Government has authorized aid to China in the form of grants and credits totalling approximately $3,523 million, of which $2,422 million has been in the form of grants and $1,101 million as credits. About 40 percent of the total, or $1515.7 million, was authorized prior to V-J Day to contribute toward the stabilization of China's wartime economy and to enable the Chinese Government to obtain military, agricultural and industrial goods essential to the conduct of the war with Japan.

United States Government grants and credits to China authorized since V-J Day have amounted to approximately $2,007.7 million, representing sixty percent of the total, of which $1,596.7 million has been as grants and $411 million on credit terms. This aid was designed to assist the Chinese Government in the reoccupation of liberated areas and the repatriation of Japanese, to meet some of China's urgent relief and rehabilitation needs, and, in the case of the present ECA program, to help retard the rate of economic deterioration in China and to encourage the adoption of effective self-held measures on the part of the Chinese Government. The Chinese Government has elected to use $125 million authorized by the China Aid Act of 1948 (included in the total of grants above) to purchase items of a military nature.

The totals of United States aid given above do not include sales to the Chinese Government of United States Government military and civilian-type surplus property which have been made since V-J Day, except where these sales were made on credit terms.

United States aid to China reviewed herein does not reflect assistance through provision of advisory personnel in cultural, economic and military fields; nor does it include United States contributions through certain United Nations' programs in China -- the International Children's Emergency Fund, the International Refugee Organization, the World Health Organization, and advisory social welfare services.

U.S. Economic, Financial, Military Aid to China Since 1937

(In millions of U.S. dollars)	Credits (1)	Grants (2)	Sales of U.S. Government Excess and Surplus Property Procurement value (3)	Realization by U.S. Initial (4)	Ultimate (5)
Pre- V-J Day:					
ECONOMIC					
1. Export-Import Bank Credits Authorized		$120.0			
2. Stabilization fund agreement, 1941		50.0			
3. 1942 Treasury Credit (PL 442)		500.0			
TOTAL ECONOMIC AID		$670			
MILITARY					
4. Lend-lease ($845.7 million)	$825.7	20.0			
TOTAL MILITARY AID	$825.7	20.0			
TOTAL PRE-V-J DAY AID	$825.7	$690.0			
Post-V-J Day:					
ECONOMIC					
5. Lend-lease "pipeline" credit		51.7			
6. UNRRA -- U.S. Contribution	474.0				
7. BOTRA -- U.S. Contribution	3.6				
8. Export-Import Bank Credits Authorized		82.8			
9. Civilian Surplus Property Transfers (Under August 30, 1946, bulk sale agreement)		55.0	$900.0	$120.0	$175.0
10. OFLC dockyard facilities sales		4.1	n.a.		4.1
11. Maritime Commission ship sales		16.4	77.3	9.8	26.2

(In millions of U.S. dollars)	Grants (1)	Credits (2)	Sales of U.S. Government Excess and Surplus Property Procurement value (3)	Realization by U.S. Initial (4)	Ultimate (5)
Post V-J Day --Continued					
12. U.S. Foreign Relief Program	46.4				
13. ECA Program	275.0				
TOTAL ECONOMIC AID	$799.0	$210.0	$977.3	$129.8	$205.3
MILITARY					
14. Lend-lease ($694.7 million)	513.7	181.0			
15. Military Aid Under SACO	17.7				
16. Sale of excess stocks of U.S. Army in West China		20.0	n.a.	(a)	(a)20.0
17. Ammunition Abandoned and Transferred by U.S. Marines in North China (over 6,500 tons)	(b)				
18. Transfer of U.S. Navy Vessels (PL 512)	c 141.3				
19. Sales of surplus military equipment (total accepted by Chinese Govt.)			100.8	6.7	6.7
20. $125 Million Grant Under China Aid Act of 1948	125.0				
TOTAL MILITARY AID	$797.7	$201.0	$100.8	$6.7	$26.7
TOTAL POST-V-J DAY AID	1,596.7	411.0	1,078.1	136.5	232.0
GRAND TOTAL	$2,422.4	$1,101.0	$1,078.1	$136.5	$232.0

a Down payment covered under item 9.   *b No estimate of total value available.*
c Vessels valued at procurement cost.

Acheson States 'Basic' U.S. Far East Policy in 1950

Following is the text of a speech made by Secretary of State Dean Acheson before the National Press Club on Jan. 12, 1950. In its publication of basic foreign policy documents, the State Department characterized the speech as "The basic position of the United States -- review of the position as of 1950." (See p. 48)

Foundations of Policy

This afternoon I should like to discuss with you the relations between the peoples of the United States and the peoples of Asia, and I used the words "relations of the peoples of the United States and the peoples of Asia" advisedly. I am not talking about governments or nations because it seems to me what I want to discuss with you is this feeling of mine that the relations depend upon the attitudes of the people; that there are fundamental attitudes, fundamental interests, fundamental purposes of the people of the United States, 150 million of them, and of the peoples of Asia, unnumbered millions, which determine and out of which grow the relations of our countries and the policies of our governments. Out of these attitudes and interests and purposes grow what we do from day to day.

Now, let's dispose of one idea right at the start and not bother with it any more. That is that the policies of the United States are determined out of abstract principles in the Department of State or in the White House or in the Congress. That is not the case. If these policies are going to be good, they must grow out of the fundamental attitudes of our people on both sides. If they are to be effective, they must become articulate through all the institutions of our national life, of which this is one of the greatest -- through the press, through the radio, through the churches, through the labor unions, through the business organizations, through all the groupings of our national life, there must become articulate the attitudes of our people and the policies which we propose to follow. It seems to me that understanding is the beginning of wisdom and therefore, we shall begin by trying to understand before we announce what we are going to do, and that is a proposition so heretical in this town that I advance it with some hesitation.

Now, let's consider some of the basic factors which go into the making of the attitudes of the peoples on both sides. I am frequently asked: Has the State Department got an Asian policy? And it seems to me that that discloses such a depth of ignorance that it is very hard to begin to deal with it. The peoples of Asia are so incredibly diverse and their problems are so incredibly diverse that how could anyone, even the most utter charlatan believe that he had a uniform policy which would deal with all of them. On the other hand, there are very important similarities in ideas and in problems among the peoples of Asia and so what we come to, after we understand these diversities and these common attitudes of mind, is the fact that there must be certain similarities of approach, and there must be very great dissimilarities in action.

To illustrate this only a moment: If you will consider as an example of the differences in Asia the subcontinent of India and Pakistan, you will find there an area which is roughly comparable in size and population to Europe. You will find that the different states and provinces of that subcontinent are roughly comparable in size to the nations of Europe and yet you will find such differences in race, in ideas, in languages, and religion, and culture, that compared to that subcontinent, Europe is almost one homogeneous people.

Or take the difference, for instance, between the people and problems of Japan and Indonesia, both in the same Asian area. In Japan, you have a people far advanced in the complexities of industrial civilization, a people whose problems grow out of overpopulation on small islands and the necessity of finding raw materials to bring in and finding markets for the finished goods which they produce. In Indonesia, you find something wholly different -- a people on the very threshold of their experience with these complexities and a people who live in an area which possesses vast resources which are awaiting development. Now, those are illustrations of complexities.

Emerging Independence

Let's come now to the matters which Asia has in common. There is in this vast area what we might call a developing Asian consciousness, and a developing pattern, and this, I think, is based upon two factors which are pretty nearly common to the entire experience of all these Asian people.

One of these factors is a revulsion against the acceptance of misery and poverty as the normal condition of life. Throughout all of this vast area, you have that fundamental revolutionary aspect in mind and belief. The other common aspect that they have is the revulsion against foreign domination. Whether that foreign domination takes the form of colonialism or whether it takes the form of imperialism, they are through with it. They have had enough of it, and they want no more.

These two basic ideas which are held so broadly and commonly in Asia tend to fuse in the minds of many Asian peoples and many of them tend to believe that if you could get rid of foreign domination, if you could gain independence, then the relief from poverty and misery would follow almost in course. It is easy to point out that that is not true, and of course, they are discovering that it is not true. But underneath that belief, there was a very profound understanding of a basic truth and it is the basic truth which underlies all our democratic belief and all our democratic concept. That truth is that just as no man and no government is wise enough or disinterested enough to direct the thinking and the action of another individual, so no nation and no people are wise enough and disinterested enough very long to assume the responsibility for another people or to control another people's opportunities.

That great truth they have sensed, and on that great truth they are acting. They say and they believe that from now on they are on their own. They will make their own decisions. They will attempt to better their own lot, and on occasion they will make their own mistakes. But it will be their mistakes, and they are not going to have their mistakes dictated to them by anybody else.

The symbol of these concepts has become nationalism. National independence has become the symbol both of freedom from foreign domination and freedom from the tyranny of poverty and misery.

Since the end of the war in Asia, we have seen over 500 million people gain their independence and over seven new nations come into existence in this area.

We have the Philippines with 20 million citizens. We have Pakistan, India, Ceylon, and Burma with 400 million citizens, southern Korea with 20 million, and within the last few weeks, the United States of Indonesia with 75 million.°

This is the outward and visible sign of the internal ferment of Asia. But this ferment and change is not restricted to these countries which are just gaining their independence. It is the common idea and the common pattern of Asia, and as I tried to suggest a moment ago, it is not based on purely political conceptions. It is not based purely on ideological conceptions. It is based on a fundamental and an earthy and a deeply individual realization of the problems of their own daily lives. This new sense of nationalism means that they are going to deal with those daily problems -- the problems of the relation of man to the soil, the problem of how

---

°The Philippine Republic achieved full independence, July 4, 1946; Pakistan and India became separate dominions in the British Commonwealth, Aug. 15, 1947, India becoming a sovereign republic, Jan. 26, 1950; Ceylon was accorded dominion status in the British Commonwealth, Feb. 4, 1948; Burma became independent, Jan. 4, 1948; the Republic of Korea was proclaimed, Aug. 15, 1948; and Indonesia achieved its independence, Dec. 28, 1949.

much can be exacted from them by the tax collectors of the state. It is rooted in those ideas. With those ideas they are going forward. Resignation is no longer the typical emotion of Asia. It has given way to hope, to a sense of effort, and in many cases, to a real sense of anger.

Recent Developments in China

Now, may I suggest to you that much of the bewilderment which has seized the minds of many of us about recent developments in China comes from a failure to understand this basic revolutionary force which is loose in Asia. The reasons for the fall of the Nationalist Government in China are preoccupying many people. All sorts of reasons have been attributed to it. Most commonly, it is said in various speeches and publications that it is the result of American bungling, that we are incompetent, that we did not understand, that American aid was too little, that we did the wrong things at the wrong time. Other people go on and say: "No, it is not quite that, but that an American general did not like Chiang Kai-shek and out of all that relationship grows the real trouble." And they say: "Well you have to add to that there are a lot of women fooling around in politics in China."

Nobody, I think, says that the Nationalist Government fell because it was confronted by overwhelming military force which it could not resist. Certainly no one in his right mind suggests that. Now, what I ask you to do is to stop looking for a moment under the bed and under the chair and under the rug to find out these reasons, but rather to look at the broad picture and see whether something doesn't suggest itself.

The broad picture is that after the war, Chiang Kai-shek emerged as the undisputed leader of the Chinese people. Only one faction, the Communists, up in the hills, ill-equipped, ragged, a very small military force, was determinedly opposed to his position. He had overwhelming military power, greater military power than any ruler had ever had in the entire history of China. He had tremendous economic and military support and backing from the United States. He had the acceptance of all other foreign countries, whether sincerely or insincerely in the case of the Soviet Union is not really material to this matter. Here he was in this position, and 4 years later what do we find? We find that his armies have melted away. His support in the country has melted away. His support largely outside the country has melted away, and he is a refugee on a small island off the coast of China with the remnants of his forces.

As I said, no one says that vast armies moved out of the hills and defeated him. To attribute this to the inadequacy of American aid is only to point out the depth and power of the forces which were miscalculated or ignored. What has happened in my judgment is that the almost inexhaustible patience of the Chinese people in their misery ended. They did not bother to overthrow this government. There was really nothing to overthrow. They simply ignored it throughout the country. They took the solution of their immediate village problems into their own hands. If there was any trouble or interference with the representatives of the government, they simply brushed them aside. They completely withdrew their support from this government, and when that support was withdrawn, the whole military establishment disintegrated. Added to the grossest incompetence ever experienced by any military command was this total lack of support both in the armies and in the country, and so the whole matter just simply disintegrated.

The Communists did not create this. The Communists did not create this condition. They did not create this revolutionary spirit. They did not create a great force which moved out from under Chiang Kai-shek. But they were shrewd and cunning to mount it, to ride this thing into victory and into power.

That, I suggest to you, is an explanation which has certain roots in realism and which does not require all this examination of intricate and perhaps irrelevant details. So much for the attitudes of the peoples of Asia.

U.S. Attitude Toward Asia

Let's consider for a moment another important factor in this relationship. That is the attitude of our own people to Asia. What

is that fundamental attitude out of which our policy has grown? What is the history of it? Because history is very important, and history furnishes the belief on the one side in the reality and truth of the attitude.

What has our attitude been toward the peoples of Asia? It has been, I submit to you, that we are interested -- that Americans as individuals are interested in the peoples of Asia. We are not interested in them as pawns or as subjects for exploitation but just as people.

For 100 years some Americans have gone to Asia to bring in what they thought was the most valuable thing they had -- their faith. They wanted to tell them what they thought about the nature and relationship of man to God. Others went to them to bring to them what they knew of learning. Others went to them to bring them healing for their bodies. Others and perhaps fewer went to them to learn the depth and beauty of their own cultures, and some went to them to trade with them. But this trade was a very small part of American interest in the Far East, and it was a very small part of American interest in trade. It was a valid interest; it was a good interest. There was nothing wrong about it, but out of the total sum of the interests of the American people in Asia, it was a comparatively small part.

Through all this period of time also, we had, and still have, great interests in Asia. But let me point out to you one very important factor about our interests in Asia. That is that our interests have been parallel to the interests of the people of Asia. For 50 years, it has been the fundamental belief of the American people -- and I am not talking about announcements of government but I mean a belief of people in little towns and villages and churches and missionary forces and labor unions throughout the United States -- it has been their profound belief that the control of China by a foreign power was contrary to American interests. The interesting part about that is it was not contrary to the interests of the people of China. There was not conflict but parallelism in that interest. And so from the time of the announcement of the open door policy[1] through the 9-power treaty[2] to the very latest resolution of the General Assembly of the United Nations[3] we have stated that principle and we believe it. And similarly in all the rest of Asia -- in the Philippines, in India, in Pakistan and Indonesia, and in Korea -- for years and years and years, the interests of Americans throughout this country have been in favor of their independence. This is where their independence societies, and their patriotic groups have come for funds and sympathy. The whole policy of our government insofar as we have responsibility in the Philippines was to bring about the accomplishment of this independence and our sympathy and help. The very real help which we have given other nations in Asia has been in that direction, and it is still in that direction.

The Factor of Communism

Now, I stress this, which you may think is a platitude, because of a very important fact: I hear almost every day someone say that the real interest of the United States is to stop the spread of communism. Nothing seems to me to put the cart before the horse more completely than that. Of course we are interested in stopping the spread of communism. But we are interested for a far deeper reason than any conflict between the Soviet Union and the United States. We are interested in stopping the spread of communism because communism is a doctrine that we don't happen to like. Communism is the most subtle instrument of Soviet foreign policy that has ever been devised, and it is really the spearhead of Russian imperialism which would, if it could, take from these people what they have won, what we want them to keep and develop, which is their own national independence, their own individual independence, their own

---

[1] See Secretary Hay's instructions of Sept. 6, 1899, and Mar. 20, 1900; United States Relations with China, with Special Reference to the Period 1944-1949 (Department of State publication 3573; 1949), pp. 414-416.

[2] Treaty of Feb. 6, 1922; ibid., pp. 438-442.

[3] Res. 291 (IV), Dec. 8, 1949; A Decade of American Foreign Policy, pp. 726-727.

development of their own resources for their own good and not as mere tributary states to this great Soviet Union.

Now, it is fortunate that this point that I made does not represent any real conflict. It is an important point because people will do more damage and create more misrepresentation in the Far East by saying our interest is merely to stop the spread of communism than any other way. Our real interest is in those people as people. It is because communism is hostile to that interest that we want to stop it. But it happens that the best way of doing both things is to do just exactly what the peoples of Asia want to do and what we want to help them to do, which is to develop a soundness of administration of these new governments and to develop their resources and their technical skills so that they are not subject to penetration either through ignorance, or because they believe these false promises, or because there is real distress in their areas. If we can help that development, if we can go forward with it, then we have brought about the best way that anyone knows of stopping this spread of communism.

It is important to take this attitude not as a mere negative reaction to communism but as the most positive affirmation of the most affirmative truth that we hold, which is in the dignity and right of every nation, of every people, and of every individual to develop in their own way, making their own mistakes, reaching their own triumphs but acting under their own responsibility. That is what we are pressing for in the Far East, and that is what we must affirm and not get mixed up with purely negative and inconsequential statements.

Soviet Attitude

Now, let me come to another underlying and important factor which determines our relations and, in turn, our policy with the peoples of Asia. That is the attitude of the Soviet Union toward Asia, and particularly towards those parts of Asia which are contiguous to the Soviet Union, and with great particularity this afternoon, to north China.

The attitude and interest of the Russians in north China, and in these other areas as well, long antedates communism. This is not something that has come out of communism at all. It long antedates it. But the Communist regime has added new methods, new skills, and new concepts to the thrust of Russian imperialism. This (These) Communistic concept(s) and techniques have armed Russian imperialism with a new and most insidious weapon of penetration. Armed with these new powers, what is happening in China is that the Soviet Union is detaching the northern provinces (areas) of China from China and is attaching them to the Soviet Union. This process is complete in Outer Mongolia. It is nearly complete in Manchuria, and I am sure that in inner Mongolia and in Sinkiang there are very happy reports coming from Soviet agents to Moscow. This is what is going on. It is the detachment of these whole areas, vast areas -- populated by Chinese -- the detachment of these areas from China and their attachment to the Soviet Union.

I wish to state this and perhaps sin against my doctrine of non-dogmatism, but I should like to suggest at any rate that this fact that the Soviet Union is taking the four northern provinces of China is the single most significant, most important fact, in the relation of any foreign power with Asia.°

Two Rules of U.S. Policy

What does that mean for us? It means something very, very significant. It means that nothing that we do and nothing that we say must be allowed to obscure the reality of this fact. All the efforts of propaganda will not be able to obscure it. The only thing that can obscure it is the folly of ill-conceived adventures on our part

°*For background material regarding Soviet penetration of northern areas of China, see Department of State Bulletin, Feb. 6, 1950, pp. 218-219. See also Secretary Acheson's statement of Mar. 31, 1950, regarding Sinkiang; ibid., Apr. 10, 1950, p. 568.*

which easily could do so, and I urge all who are thinking about these foolish adventures to remember that we must not seize the unenviable position which the Russians have carved out for themselves. We must not undertake to deflect from the Russians to ourselves the righteous anger, and the wrath, and the hatred of the Chinese people which must develop. It would be folly to deflect it to ourselves. We must take the position we have always taken -- that anyone who violates the integrity of China is the enemy of China and is acting contrary to our own interest. That, I suggest to you this afternoon, is the first and the greatest rule in regard to the formulation of American policy towards Asia.

I suggest that the second rule is very like the first. That is to keep our own purposes perfectly straight, perfectly pure, and perfectly aboveboard and do not get them mixed-up with legal quibbles or the attempt to do one thing and really achieve another.

The consequences of this Russian attitude and this Russian action in China are perfectly enormous. They are saddling all those in China who are proclaiming their loyalty to Moscow, and who are allowing themselves to be used as puppets of Moscow, with the most awful responsibility which they must pay for. Furthermore, these actions of the Russians are making plainer than any speech, or any utterance, or any legislation can make throughout all of Asia, what the true purposes of the Soviet Union are and what the true function of communism as an agent of Russian imperialism is. These I suggest to you are the fundamental factors, fundamental realities of the attitude out of which our relations and policies must grow.

Military Security in The Pacific

Now, let's in the light of that consider some of these policies. First of all, let's deal with the question of military security. I deal with it first because it is important and because, having stated our policy in that regard, we must clearly understand that the military menace is not the most immediate.

What is the situation in regard to the military security of the Pacific area, and what is our policy in regard to it?

In the first place, the defeat and the disarmament of Japan has placed upon the United States the necessity of assuming the military defense of Japan so long as that is required, both in the interest of our security and in the interests of the security of the entire Pacific area and, in all honor, in the interest of Japanese security. We have American -- and there are Australian -- troops in Japan. I am not in a position to speak for the Australians, but I can assure you that there is no intention of any sort of abandoning or weakening the defenses of Japan and that whatever arrangements are to be made either through permanent settlement or otherwise, that defense must and shall be maintained.

This defensive perimeter runs along the Aleutians to Japan and then goes on to the Ryukyus. We hold important defense positions in the Ryukyu Islands, and those we will continue to hold. In the interest of the population of the Ryukyu Islands, we will at an appropriate time offer to hold these islands under trusteeship of the United Nations. But they are essential parts of the defensive perimeter of the Pacific, and they must and will be held.

The defensive perimeter runs from the Ryukyus to the Philippine Islands. Our relations, our defensive relations with the Philippines are contained in agreements between us. Those agreements are being loyally carried out and will be loyally carried out. Both peoples have learned by bitter experience the vital connections between our mutual defense requirements. We are in no doubt about that, and it is hardly necessary for me to say an attack on the Philippines could not and would not be tolerated by the United States. But I hasten to add that no one perceives the imminence of any such attack.

So far as the military security of other areas in the Pacific is concerned, it must be clear that no person can guarantee these areas against military attack. But it must also be clear that such a guarantee is hardly sensible or necessary within the realm of practical relationship.

Should such an attack occur -- one hesitates to say where such an armed attack could come from -- the initial reliance must be on the people attacked to resist it and then upon the commitments of the entire civilized world under the Charter of the United Nations which so far has not proved a weak reed to lean on by any people who are determined to protect their independence against outside aggression. But it is a mistake, I think, in considering Pacific and Far Eastern problems to become obsessed with military considerations. Important as they are, there are other problems that press, and these other problems are not capable of solution through military means. These other problems arise out of the susceptibility of many areas, and many countries in the Pacific area, to subversion and penetration. That cannot be stopped by military means.

Susceptibility To Penetration

The susceptibility to penetration arises because in many areas there are new governments which have little experience in governmental administration and have not become firmly established or perhaps firmly accepted in their countries. They grow, in part, from very serious economic problems, some of them growing out directly from the last war, others growing indirectly out of the last war because of the disruptions of trade with other parts of the world, with the disruption of arrangements which furnished credit and management to these areas for many years. That has resulted in dislocation of economic effort and in a good deal of suffering among the peoples concerned. In part this susceptibility to penetration comes from the great social upheaval about which I have been speaking, an upheaval which was carried on and confused a great deal by the Japanese occupation and by the propaganda which has gone on from Soviet sources since the war.

Here, then, are the problems in these other areas which require some policy on our part, and I should like to point out two facts to you and then discuss in more detail some of these areas.

The first fact is the great difference between our responsibility and our opportunities in the northern part of the Pacific area and in the southern part of the Pacific area. In the north, we have direct responsibility in Japan and we have direct opportunity to act. The same thing to a lesser degree is true in Korea. There we had direct responsibility, and there we did act, and there we have a greater opportunity to be effective than we have in the more southerly part.

In the southerly part of the area, we are one of many nations who can do no more than help. The direct responsibility lies with the peoples concerned. They are proud of their new national responsibility. You can not sit around in Washington, or London, or Paris, or The Hague, and determine what the policies are going to be in those areas. You can be willing to help, and you can help only when the conditions are right for help to be effective.

Limitations of U.S. Assistance

That leads me to the other thing that I wanted to point out, and that is the limitation of effective American assistance. American assistance can be effective when it is the missing component in a situation which might otherwise be solved. The United States cannot furnish all these components to solve the question. It can not furnish determination, it can not furnish the will, and it can not furnish the loyalty of a people to its government. But if the will and if the determination exists and if the people are behind their government, then, and not always then, is there a very good chance. In that situation, American help can be effective and it can lead to an accomplishment which could not otherwise be achieved.

Japan. -- Now, with that statement, let's deal very briefly -- because the time is going on and I am almost equaling my performance in the Senate and House -- let's deal very briefly with some of the problems. Let's take the situation in Japan for a moment. There are three great factors to be faced. The security matter I have dealt with. Aside from that, there are the economic questions and the political questions. In the political field, General MacArthur has been very successful and the Japanese are hammering out with some backsliding, and regaining and backsliding again of progress, a political system which is based on nonmilitaristic institutions.

In the economic field, we have not been so successful. That is in very large part due to the inherent difficulty of the problem.

The problem arises with the necessity of Japan being able to buy raw materials and sell goods. The former connections of Japan with the mainland and with some of the islands have been disrupted. That has produced difficulties. The willingness of other countries to receive Japanese goods has very much contracted since the war.

Difficulties of currency have added to those problems. But those matters have got to be faced and have got to be solved. Whether they are solved under a treaty or if the procedural difficulties of that are too great under some other mechanism, they must be solved along lines which permit the Japanese greater freedom -- complete freedom if possible -- to buy what they need in the world and to sell what they have to offer on the mainland of Asia, in southeast Asia, and in other parts of the world. That is the nature of the problem and it is a very tough one. It is one on which the occupation authorities, the Japanese government, ourselves, and others are working. There can be no magic solution to it.

Korea. -- In Korea, we have taken great steps which have ended our military occupation, and in cooperation with the United Nations, have established an independent and sovereign country recognized by nearly all the rest of the world.[1] We have given that nation great help in getting itself established. We are asking the Congress to continue that help until it is firmly established, and that legislation is now pending before the Congress.[2] The idea that we should scrap all of that, that we should stop half way through the achievement of the establishment of this country, seems to me to be the most utter defeatism and utter madness in our interests in Asia. But there our responsibilities are more direct and our opportunities more clear. When you move to the south, you find that our opportunity is much slighter and that our responsibilities, except in the Philippines and there indirectly, are very small. Those problems are very confusing.

Philippines. -- In the Philippines, we acted with vigor and speed to set up an independent sovereign nation which we have done.[3] We have given the Philippines a billion dollars of direct economic aid since the war. We have spent another billion dollars in such matters as veterans' benefits and other payments in the Philippines. Much of that money has not been used as wisely as we wish it had been used, but here again, we come up against the matter of responsibility. It is the Philippine Government which is responsible. It is the Philippine Government which must make its own mistakes. What we can do is advise and urge, and if help continues to be misused, to stop giving the help. We cannot direct, we should not direct, we have not the slightest desire to direct. I believe that there are indications that the Philippines may be facing serious economic difficulties. With energetic, determined action, they can perhaps be avoided or certainly minimized. Whether that will be true or not, I can not say, but it does not rest within the power of the American Government to determine that. We are always ready to help and to advise. That is all we can and all we should do.

Asia -- Elsewhere in southeast Asia, the limits of what we can do are to help where we are wanted. We are organizing the machinery through which we can make effective help possible. The western powers are all interested. We all know the techniques. We have all had experiences which can be useful to those governments which are newly starting out if they want it. It cannot be useful if they don't want it. We know techniques of administration. We know techniques of organizing school districts, and road districts, and taxation districts. We know agricultural and industrial techniques, all of which can be helpful, and those we are preparing to make available if they are wanted, where they are wanted, and under circumstances where they have a fighting chance to be successful.

---

1 The independence of Korea was proclaimed Aug. 15, 1948. For the resolution of the U.N. General Assembly relating to Korean independence, see Res. 122 (ll), Nov. 14, 1947; A Decade of American Foreign Policy, pp. 677-678.

2 See infra, pp. 2527-2528.

3 The independence of the Philippine Republic was proclaimed July 4, 1946, by the President of the United States; see A Decade of American Foreign Policy, pp. 860-861.

We will not do these things for the mere purpose of being active. They will not be done for the mere purpose of running around and doing good, but for the purpose of moving in where we are wanted to a situation where we have the missing component which, if put into the rest of the picture, will spell success.

The situation in the different countries of southeast Asia is difficult. It is highly confused in Burma where five different factions have utterly disrupted the immediate government of the country. Progress is being made in Indochina where the French, although moving slowly, are moving. There are noticeable signs of progress in transferring responsibility to a local administration and getting the adherence of the population to this local administration. We hope that the situation will be such that the French can make further progress and make it quickly, but I know full well the difficulties which are faced by the Foreign Minister of France and my admiration and respect for him are so great that I would not want one word I say to add a feather to the burden that he carries.

In Malaya, the British have and are discharging their responsibility harmoniously with the people of Malaya and are making progress.

Indonesia. -- In Indonesia, a great success has been achieved within the last few weeks and over a period of months. The round table conferences at The Hague in which great statesmanship and restraint were displayed, both on the Dutch and the Indonesian side, have resulted in this new government being formed.1 Relations of this government with the Dutch will be very good, and the Dutch can furnish them great help and advice, and we will be willing to stand by to give whatever help we can rightly and profitably give. That situation is one which is full of encouragement although it is full of difficulty also.

India and Pakistan. -- As one goes to the end of this semicircle and comes to India and Pakistan, we find really grave troubles

1 *The independence of Indonesia was effected Dec. 28, 1949; see ibid., pp. 802-804.*

facing the world and facing these two countries there, both with respect to Kashmir, and to the utter difficulties -- economic difficulties growing out of the differences in devaluation, settlement of monetary plans back and forth, et cetera. We know that they have assured one another, and they have assured the world, that as stubborn as these difficulties may be and difficult as they may be of solution, they are not going to resort to war to solve them. We are glad to hear those assurances and the whole world is glad to hear it, but we know also that the problems are in such a situation and in such an area that they are most inflammable, and we believe that in addition to these most desirable assurances there should be some accommodation of wills to bring about a result as soon as possible.

In India and in Pakistan we are willing to be of such help as we can be. Again, the responsibility is not ours. Again we can only be helpful friends. Again the responsibility lies with people who have won their freedom and who are very proud of it.

The New Day For Asia

So after this survey, what we conclude, I believe, is that there is a new day which has dawned in Asia. It is a day in which the Asian peoples are on their own, and know it, and intend to continue on their own. It is a day in which the old relationships between east and west are gone, relationships which at their worst were exploitation, and which at their best were paternalism. That relationship is over, and the relationship of east and west must now be in the Far East one of mutual respect and mutual helpfulness. We are their friends. Others are their friends. We and those others are willing to help, but we can help only where we are wanted and only where the conditions of help are really sensible and possible. So what we can see is that this new day in Asia, this new day which is dawning, may go on to a glorious noon or it may darken and it may drizzle out. But that decision lies within the countries of Asia and within the power of the Asian people. It is not a decision which a friend or even an enemy from the outside can decide for them.

Dulles States 'Basic' U.S. Position on Far East in 1955

Following are excerpts, as published by the State Department, of a speech made by Secretary of State John Foster Dulles on Feb. 16, 1955, before the Foreign Policy Assn. in New York. The Department cited this speech as a "review of (the basic U.S. Far East and Southeast Asia) positions as of 1955."

Far East Security Treaties

In the Far East the United States has responded to the desire of others that we join with them to assure their security. During the last 4 years, the United States has become party to security treaties with Korea, Japan, the Republic of China on Formosa, the Philippines, Australia and New Zealand. Also we have joined the eight-power Manila Pact for the security of Southeast Asia.

The total of these treaties is a mutual security system which, starting from the Aleutian Islands in the North, runs in a great arc to the South Pacific. This constitutes a defensive bulwark for freedom in that part of the world.

What has thus been done by many nations is important. Also important is the manner in which the United States has played its part, particularly during recent days.

When the Congress convened last January, it was organized by the Democratic Party. So when the Manila Pact and the China treaty were submitted, they were submitted by a Republican President to a Democrat-controlled body. The same was true of President Eisenhower's request for Congressional authority to use the armed forces of the United States in the Formosa area.

Nevertheless, the two treaties were ratified and the Congressional authority was granted. This was done promptly and with virtual unanimity.

These events demonstrate a national unity and capacity of action which is needed in the world today. Too often representative processes lead to such partisanship and such consequent delays that hostile forces are encouraged to believe that democracies are inherently ineffective. The Government of the United States has shown the contrary. Partisanship was wholly subordinated to the national good, so that action of great importance could be taken with deliberation, but with decisiveness.

For this the nation can be grateful to the leadership and to the general membership of both parties in the Congress. I know that they would expect me to pay special tribute to Walter F. George, who, as Chairman of the Senate Foreign Relations Committee, carried the heaviest aggregate burden of responsibility in relation to the three acts to which I refer.

We can all take pride, as Americans, in this demonstration of national unity and capacity. Because of it, free men throughout the world can face the future with better hope and new confidence.

Mutual Defense Treaty With China

Let me turn now to deal with some of the substantive problems which arise out of the two Far Eastern treaties to which I have referred -- the China treaty and the Manila Pact.

The United States is firmly committed to the defense of Formosa and the Pescadores. These islands became part of the Japanese Empire in 1895.1 They continued as such for half a cen-

1 *Treaty of April. 17, 1895; British and Foreign State Papers, vol. 87, pp. 795-805.*

tury, until they were relinquished by Japan as a result of her defeat in war[1] -- a defeat principally wrought by the efforts and sacrifices of the United States.

These islands form an important part of the Western Pacific defense system which I have described. The people of the islands eagerly seek our help.

Thus Formosa and the Pescadores have been properly a matter of concern to the United States.

In 1945 our long-time ally, the Republic of China, was entrusted with authority over these islands.[2] In 1950, when the aggression against Korea occurred, President Truman ordered our Pacific fleet to defend Formosa against possible Chinese Communist attack. Now, that determination has been converted into our Mutual Defense Treaty with the Republic of China.

It is important to note that the treaty, except as it relates to United States territories, covers only the islands of Formosa and the Pescadores, and an armed attack directed against those islands. The Congressional authority is to secure and protect Formosa and the Pescadores against armed attack, and to make secure and to protect "related positions and territories" as the President judges "this would be required or appropriate in assuring the defense of Formosa and the Pescadores."

The President did not use our armed forces to help the Chinese Nationalists to hold the Tachen Islands and Yushan and Pishan, lying some 200 miles north of Formosa. These islands were virtually unrelated to the defense of Formosa and the Pescadores. We helped the Chinese Nationalists to evacuate these islands and regroup their forces, so as to avoid a bloody and wasteful battle which would have inflamed public emotions. Thus, Nationalist China and the United States have made an important contribution to the cause of freedom.

The Chinese Communists have been the initiators of violence in this area. They have already formally declared their intention to take Formosa by force. If the Chinese Nationalists now oblige by making it easier for the Chinese Communists to conquer Formosa, will they be less apt to do so? I doubt it.

The United States has no commitment and no purpose to defend the coastal positions *as such*. The basic purpose is to assure that Formosa and the Pescadores will not be forcibly taken over by the Chinese Communists. However, Foreign Minister Chou says they will use all their force to take Formosa and they treat the coastal islands as means to that end. When the Nationalists voluntarily evacuated the Tachen islands, the Chinese Communists' comment was: "The liberation of these islands has created favorable conditions for our People's Liberation Army in the liberation of Formosa."

Thus the Chinese Communists have linked the coastal positions to the defense of Formosa. That is the fact which, as President Eisenhower said in his message to Congress about Formosa, "compels us to take into account closely related localities." Accordingly, we shall be alert to subsequent Chinese Communist actions, rejecting for ourselves any initiative of warlike deeds.

It is hardly to be expected that the Chinese Communists will renounce their ambitions. However, might they not renounce their efforts to realize their goals by force?

Such renunciation of force is one of the basic principles of the United Nations, and the United States had hoped, and still hopes, that the United Nations may be able to effect a cessation of the pre-

sent hostilities. President Eisenhower, in his message to Congress dealing with this matter, made clear that the United States would welcome action by the United Nations which might bring an end to the active hostilities in the area. The Government of New Zealand has brought this situation before the Security Council,[3] and the United States, in the interest of peace, went to the length of voting to invite the Chinese Communists to come to the Security Council to discuss the matter.

In 1950, the Chinese Communists had accepted a Security Council invitation in relation to Korea.[4] However, this time the Chinese Communists contemptuously rejected the invitation.

We sincerely hope that this decision of the Chinese Communists is not irrevocable and that they will abide by the principles of the United Nations rather than challenge by force the defensive obligations of this country. In any event, we believe that their attitude toward the United Nations Security Council has not ended the responsibility of that body which, by the Charter, has the "primary responsibility for the maintenance of international peace and security."

It should not, moreover, be carelessly assumed that peace and security will be promoted merely by the non-Communist nations indefinitely granting one-sided concessions to the Communist nations.

A great danger in Asia is the fear of many non-Communist peoples that the United States has no real intention of standing firmly behind them. Already that fear has mounted to the danger point. We accepted in Korea an armistice which the Chinese Communists boisterously misrepresent as a "victory" for them. We acquiesced in an Indochina armistice which reflected the defeat of the French Union forces at Dien Bien Phu. We aided the Tachen evacuation. The reasons were compelling; nevertheless the result added a few square miles to the Communist domain.

If the non-Communist Asians ever come to feel that their Western Allies are disposed to retreat whenever communism threatens the peace, then the entire area could quickly become indefensible.

As the situation now exists, neither the cause of freedom, nor United States security, nor world peace and security would be promoted by undermining the faith of the free Asian peoples in our strength and in our willingness to use that strength to restrain those who violently menace liberty. The American people have, through the Congress, made their own resolution clear. That is a verdict which the Government accepts as sound and which it will soberly execute.

Security of Southeast Asia

Let me turn now to Southeast Asia. In a few hours I shall be going to Bangkok to attend the first meeting of the Council created under the Manila Pact for the Security of Southeast Asia.

We shall at Bangkok deal with the problem of organizing the Treaty Council. Also we shall begin to deal with the three substantive problems assigned to the Council, namely, military security, security against subversion directed from without, and economic welfare. I cannot anticipate what the decisions will be, but I am confident that our gathering will show the advantages of cooperation between the East and the West.

Some Asians retain a fear, derived from past colonial relationships, that close ties with the Western powers will lead to their being dominated by the Western powers. It is essential that that fear should be dispelled.

An important step in that direction was taken at Manila when, at the inspiration of President Magsaysay, the eight powers there signed the Pacific Charter. Thereby we dedicated ourselves to promoting self-government and to securing independence for all countries whose peoples desire it and are able to undertake its responsibilities. Also, we agreed to cooperate in the economic, social, and cultural fields in order to promote higher living standards, economic progress, and social well-being.

---

1 See instrument of surrender, Sept. 2, 1945; A Decade of American Foreign Policy, pp. 625-626.

2 See General Order No. 1, Sept. 2, 1945; The Political Reorientation of Japan, September 1945 to September 1948; Report of Government Section, Supreme Commander for the Allied Powers, vol. II, p. 442.

3 See letter of Jan. 28, 1955, from the Representative of New Zealand to the President of the Security Council; Department of State Bulletin, Feb. 14, 1955, p. 253.

4 United States Participation in the United Nations: Report by the President to the Congress for the Year 1950 (Department of State publication 4178; 1951), pp. 40-41.

However, words alone are not enough. It is necessary to infuse these words with the breath of life. That, I hope, will be done at Bangkok. Those who gather there will meet as equals. We shall, I think, find ways to diminish the risk of armed attack against the treaty area and the danger of subversion from without. Also we shall begin to study economic problems. These are not capable of any dramatic and spectacular solution, but they do respond to steady, painstaking, and sympathetic efforts.

The first task is to deal with fundamentals. That we are already doing, particularly in the basic realm of education. United States universities and colleges are cooperating with Asian institutions in Thailand, the Philippines, and Pakistan. Many United States technicians are serving in Asia in economic, educational, and health tasks, and the number is being increased. Our cooperation is already beginning to show results in better food and better health, and we are together taking the first steps to expand trade, to increase private investment, and to raise standards of living.

In such ways, we can justify man's faith in freedom.

There should indeed be no cleavage between the Western and Asian nations. Our concept of the nature of man had its beginning in Asia, where East and West met. We believe that all men are the creation and concern of a universal God and that He has endowed every person with a right to develop in accordance with the dictates of his individual reason and conscience.

That religious faith, politically translated into the Magna Charta, the French Declaration of the Rights of Man, and our own Declaration of Independence, was, as Lincoln said of our Declaration, nothing exclusive but designed to provide "liberty, not alone to the people of this country, but hope for the world for all future time." [1]

---

1 President Lincoln's speech of Feb. 22, 1861, delivered in Independence Hall, Philadelphia; Roy P. Basler, ed., The Collected Works of Abraham Lincoln, vol. IV, (New Brunswick, N.J., 1953), p. 240.

We also realize that, if human liberty is to be a reality, there must be an economic as well as a political foundation. The impoverished and the destitute cannot be truly free. So we recognize that economic values are essential to give reality to the normal and political values that we cherish.

Such a philosophy is indeed very different from that of Soviet communism.

Soviet communism denies the principal of human equality and instead substitutes the principal of class rule.

It denies that men are capable of self-government and substitutes the principle of dictatorship, the so-called dictatorship of the proletariat.

It denies nationalism, except as it can be used as a slogan to drive a wedge between East and West and prepare the way for an absorption of the peoples by international communism.

It preaches a new doctrine of segregation. The peoples of Asia, it is said, must be segregated from the peoples of the West. The new nations of Asia must be segregated from association with others.

The guile behind this is obvious. The Soviet and Chinese Communists know that their combined power can dominate the Eurasian continent. If the other nations of Europe and Asia stand alone, they will be unable to resist the iron embrace of international communism.

At the Berlin Conference last year, Mr. Molotov denounced NATO and proposed a European security system which would exclude the United States.[1] Now, the Soviet and Chinese Communists denounce the Manila Pact, because it may bring to Southeast Asia the strength needed to resist Communist aggression.

The Bangkok Conference will enable the free nations of the West and of the East to begin a vital demonstration. They can show that, through association as sovereign equals, they can each help the other to independence, security, and well-being.

That result accords with the high ideals with which our nation was founded. It is in keeping with what our people have sought throughout their history. So our delegation goes to Bangkok with confidence, because we know that our mission is sustained by national faith and a national purpose.

Rusk 1966 Statement of U.S. Policy Toward Communist China

Following is the statement made by Secretary of State Dean Rusk on U.S. Communist China policy, March 16, 1966, before the Far East and the Pacific Subcommittee of the House Foreign Affairs Committee:

Mr. Chairman, during the last month and a half this distinguished committee and its corresponding members in the other house have heard testimony on Communist China from a number of prominent scholars and distinguished experts on Asia.

I welcome these hearings. For Communist China's policies and intentions, in all their aspects, need to be examined -- and reexamined continually.

China Specialists in Government

The Department of State and other agencies of the Government do collect, study, and analyze continually with the greatest care all the information obtainable on Communist China in order to make -- and, when the facts warrant, revise -- judgments of Peiping's intentions and objectives. Highly trained Chinese-language officers here in Washington and overseas -- men who specialize in Chinese history and communism -- are working full time analyzing and appraising Peiping's moves. Numerous private scholars, some of whom have appeared before this committee in recent weeks, are consulted by the Department of State. And there are, of course, many specialists on Communist China in other agencies of the Government. These capable individuals -- in and out of Government -- systematically interchange and cross-check their analyses and

estimates to provide what I believe is the most complete and most accurate picture of Communist China, its leaders, and its policies, available to any non-Communist government in the world.

Three Caveats

Before going further, I would like to enter three caveats:

First, the experts do not always agree, especially in their estimates of Chinese Communist intentions.

Second, the leaders we are discussing are both Chinese and Communist. Some of their words and acts can perhaps be best understood in terms of Chinese background -- Chinese traits or historic Chinese ambitions. Others can perhaps be better understood in terms of their beliefs and ambitions as Communists. They are deeply committed to a body of Communist doctrine developed by Mao Tse-tung. Still other words and acts may be consistent with both the Chinese and doctrinaire Communist factors.

We have faced a similar problem over the years with respect to the Soviet leadership. Some of their words and acts could be explained chiefly in terms of historic Russian imperial ambitions or Russian traits or practices. Others have been clearly attributable to Marxist-Leninist doctrine, or to interpretations of that doctrine by Stalin and more recent leaders. Some sovietologists put more emphasis on the traditional nationalist or imperial factors, others put more on the Marxist-Leninist factors. There is no way to determine the exact weight which ought to be given to each of these two influences.

Likewise, with regard to the Chinese Communists, there has been considerable disagreement over the respective dimensions of the two streams of influence: Chinese and Marxist-Leninist-Maoist. Over the years some of the experts on China may not have appreciated adequately Marxist-Leninist-Maoist doctrine. Likewise, some of the experts on Chinese Communist doctrine may tend to underestimate the Chinese factors in the behavior and intentions of the Peiping regime.

The third caveat is this: Predicting what the Chinese Communists will do next may be even more hazardous than usual at this juncture. They themselves appear to be taking stock. We know that some high-level talks have been going on and that they have called some of their ambassadors back for consultation.

Chinese Communist Setbacks

We know -- the whole world knows -- that the Chinese Communists have suffered some severe setbacks internationally during the past 14 months. They were unable to persuade the Afro-Asians to accept their substantive views on the Second Bandung Conference. They have found themselves in difficulty in several African countries. Their diplomatic missions have been expelled from Burundi, Dahomey, and the Central African Republic. Their technicians have been expelled from Ghana. The Governments of Kenya and Tunisia have warned them against promoting revolution in Africa.

During the fighting between India and Pakistan, the Chinese Communists marched up hill and down again. They have been disappointed by the Tashkent agreement and the steps taken in accord with it. They were strongly opposed to the agreement between Japan and the Republic of Korea, which was ratified by both countries. They have suffered a major setback in Indonesia -- the Indonesian Communist Party has been decimated.

Generally, in their struggle with Moscow for leadership of the world Communist movement, the Chinese Communists appear to have lost ground. Even their relations with Castro's Cuba have sunk to the level of mudslinging.

And, probably most important of all, Peiping sees the power of the United States committed in Southeast Asia to repel an aggression supported -- and actively promoted -- by Peiping.

Will the Chinese Communist reaction to all these setbacks be a wild lashing out? Or will it be a sober decision to draw back and even to move toward peaceful coexistence?

We, of course, hope it will be the latter. But we cannot be sure what Peiping intends to do. We do not expect the worst but we must be prepared for it.

Our Relations With Peiping

I will not try here today to review in detail the record of our relations with the Peiping regime. In the months after the Chinese Communist takeover in 1949 we watched to see whether the initial demonstration of intense hostility toward the United States and toward Americans who were still resident in China was momentary, or reflected a basic Peiping policy. Then came the aggression against the Republic of Korea, to which, at a second stage, the Chinese Communists committed large forces, thus coming into direct conflict with the United Nations and the United States.

We have searched year after year for some sign that Communist China was ready to renounce the use of force to resolve disputes. We have also searched for some indication that it was ready to abandon its premise that the United States is its prime enemy.

The Chinese Communist attitudes and actions have been hostile and rigid. But a democracy, such as ours, does not accept rigidity. It seeks solutions to problems, however intractable they may seem.

Sino–United States Ambassadorial Talks

We have discussed various problems with the Chinese Communists at international conferences such as the Geneva conferences of 1954 and 1962.

In 1955 we began with them a series of bilateral conversations at the level of ambassadors, first in Geneva and later in Warsaw. It was our hope that by direct, systematic communication we might be able to reduce the sharpness of the conflict between us. There now have been 129 of these meetings, the latest of which took place in Warsaw today.

These exchanges have ranged widely, covering many subjects affecting our two countries. At first there was a little progress in dealing with small specific issues, such as the release of Americans being held in Communist China. Although an understanding was reached in this limited area, Peiping refused to fulfill its commitment to release all the Americans.

I think it is accurate to say that no other non-Communist nation has had such extensive conversations with the Peiping regime as we have had. The problem is not lack of contact between Peiping and Washington. It is what, with contact, the Peiping regime itself says and does.

Although they have produced almost no tangible results, these conversations have served and still serve useful purposes. They permit us to clarify the numerous points of difference between us. They enable us to communicate in private during periods of crisis. They provide an opening through which, hopefully, light might one day penetrate. But the talks have, so far, given no evidence of a shift or easing in Peiping's hostility toward the United States and its bellicose doctrines of world revolution. Indeed, the Chinese Communists have consistently demanded, privately as well as publicly, that we let them have Taiwan. And when we say that we will not abandon the 12 or 13 million people on Taiwan, against their will, they say that, until we change our minds about that, no improvement in relations is possible.

Today we and Peiping are as far apart on matters of fundamental policy as we were 17 years ago.

The Basic Issues

In assessing Peiping's policies and actions, and the problems they present to American foreign policy and to the free peoples of the world, we must ask ourselves certain key questions:

What does Peiping want, and how does it pursue its objectives?

How successful has it been, and how successful is it likely to be in the future?

Is it on a collision course with the United States?

What are the prospects for change in its policies?

What policies should the United States adopt, or work toward, in dealing with Communist China?

What Does Peiping Want?

First, the Chinese Communist leaders seek to bring China on the world stage as a great power. They hold that China's history, size, and geographic position entitle it to great-power status. They seek to overcome the humiliation of 150 years of economic, cultural, and political domination by outside powers.

Our concern is with the way they are pursuing their quest for power and influence in the world. And it is not only our concern but that of many other countries, including in recent years the Soviet Union.

Peiping is aware that it still lacks many of the attributes of great-power status, and it chafes bitterly under this realization.

Arming To Become a "Great Power"

The Chinese Communists are determined to rectify this situation. They already have one of the largest armies in the world. They are now developing nuclear weapons and missile delivery systems. They are pouring a disproportionately large proportion of their industrial and scientific effort into military and military-related fields.

What is all this military power for? Some believe it to be for defensive purposes alone:

To erect a token "deterrent" nuclear capability against the United States or the U.S.S.R.;

To demonstrate symbolically that "China must be reckoned with";

To react to an imaginary, almost pathological, notion that the United States and other countries around its borders are seeking an opportunity to invade mainland China and destroy the Peiping regime.

But such weapons need not serve a defensive role. They can be used directly by Peiping to try to intimidate its neighbors, or in efforts to blackmail Asian countries into breaking defense alliances with the United States, or in an attempt to create a nuclear "balance" in Asia in which Peiping's potentially almost unlimited conventional forces might be used with increased effect.

These weapons can ultimately be employed to attack Peiping's Asian neighbors and, in time, even the United States or the Soviet Union. This would be mad and suicidal, as Peiping must know, despite cavalier statements that mainland China can survive nuclear war. Nevertheless, a potential nuclear capability, on top of enormous conventional forces, represents a new factor in the equilibrium of power in Asia that this country and its friends and allies cannot ignore.

Peiping's use of power is closely related to what I believe are its second and third objectives: dominance within Asia and leadership of the Communist world revolution, employing Maoist tactics. Peiping is striving to restore traditional Chinese influence or dominance in South, Southeast, and East Asia. Its concept of influence is exclusive. Foreign Minister Ch'en Yi reportedly told Prince Sihanouk recently that his country's "friendship" with Cambodia would be incompatible with Cambodian ties with the United States. Peiping has tried to alienate North Viet Nam and North Korea from the Soviet Union. It has had uneven success in such maneuvers. But it has not abandoned this objective. Where Peiping is present, it seeks to exclude all others. And this is not only true in its relations with its neighbors but in the Communist world as well.

Direct Aggression

Peiping has not refrained from the use of force to pursue its objectives. Following Korea, there were Tibet and the attacks on the offshore islands in the Taiwan Straits. There have been the attacks on India. It is true that, since Korea, Peiping has moved only against weaker foes and has carefully avoided situations which might bring it face to face with the United States. It has probed for weaknesses around its frontier but drawn back when the possibility of a wider conflict loomed.

While the massive and direct use of Chinese Communist troops in overt aggression cannot be ruled out, Peiping's behavior up to now suggests it would approach any such decision with caution.

If the costs and risks of a greater use of force were reduced by, for example, our unilateral withdrawal from the region, Peiping might well feel freer to use its power to intimidate or overwhelm a recalcitrant opponent or to aid directly insurgent forces.

Mao's Doctrine of World Revolution

As I have said, the Chinese Communist leaders are dedicated to a fanatical and bellicose Marxist-Leninist-Maoist doctrine of world revolution. Last fall, Lin Piao, the Chinese Communist Minister of Defense, recapitulated in a long article Peiping's strategy of violence for achieving Communist domination of the world. This strategy involves the mobilization of the underdeveloped areas of the world -- which the Chinese Communists compare to the "rural areas" -- against the industrialized or "urban" areas. It involves the relentless prosecution of what they call "people's wars." The final stage of all this violence is to be what they frankly describe as "wars of annihilation."

It is true that this doctrine calls for revolution by the natives of each country. In that sense it may be considered a "do-it-yourself kit." But Peiping is prepared to train and indoctrinate the leaders of these revolutions and to support them with funds, arms, and propaganda, as well as politically. It is even prepared to manufacture these revolutionary movements out of whole cloth.

Peiping has encouraged and assisted -- with arms and other means -- the aggressions of the North Vietnamese Communists in Laos and against South Viet Nam. It has publicly declared its support for so-called national liberation forces in Thailand, and there are already terrorist attacks in the remote rural areas of northeast Thailand. There is talk in Peiping that Malaysia is next on the list. The basic tactics of these "wars of liberation" have been set forth by Mao and his disciples, including General Giap, the North Vietnamese Communist Minister of Defense. They progress from the undermining of independent governments and the economic and social fabrics of society by terror and assassination, through guerrilla warfare, to large-scale military action.

Peiping has sought to promote Communist coups and "wars of liberation" against independent governments in Africa and Latin America as well as in Asia.

Words Versus Actions

Some say we should ignore what the Chinese Communist leaders say and judge them only by what they do. It is true that they have been more cautious in action than in words -- more cautious in what they do themselves than in what they have urged the Soviet Union to do. Undoubtedly, they recognize that their power is limited. They have shown, in many ways, that they have a healthy respect for the power of the United States.

But it does not follow that we should disregard the intentions and plans for the future which they have proclaimed. To do so would be to repeat the catastrophic miscalculation that so many people made about the ambitions of Hitler -- and that many have made at various times in appraising the intentions of the Soviet leaders.

I have noted criticism of the so-called analogy between Hitler and Mao Tse-tung. I am perfectly aware of the important differences between these two and the countries in which they have exercised power. The seizure of Manchuria by Japanese militarists, of Ethiopia by Mussolini, and of the Rhineland, Austria, and Czechoslovakia by Hitler, were laboratory experiments in the anatomy and physiology of aggression. How to deal with the phenomenon of aggression was the principal problem faced in drafting the United Nations Charter, and the answer was: collective action. We do ourselves no service by insisting that each source of aggression or each instance of aggression is unique. My own view is that we have learned a good deal about this phenomenon and its potentiality for leading into catastrophe if the problem is not met in a timely fashion.

The bellicosity of the Chinese Communists has created problems within the Communist world as well as between Peiping and the non-Communist world.

Recently a leading official of a Communist state said to me that the most serious problem in the world today is how to get Peiping to move to a policy of "peaceful coexistence."

Chinese Communist Fear of Attack

At times the Communist Chinese leaders seem to be obsessed with the notion that they are being threatened and encircled. We have told them both publicly and privately, and I believe have demonstrated in our actions in times of crisis and even under grave provocation, that we want no war with Communist China. The President restated this only last month in New York. We do not seek the overthrow by force of the Peiping regime; we do object to its attempt to overthrow other regimes by force.

How much Peiping's "fear" of the United States is genuine and how much it is artificially induced for domestic political purposes only the Chinese Communist leaders themselves know. I am convinced, however, that their desire to expel our influence and activity from the western Pacific and Southeast Asia is not motivated by fears that we are threatening them.

I wish I could believe that Communist China seeks merely a guarantee of friendly states around its borders, as some commentators have suggested. If it was as simple as this, they would have only to abandon their policies which cause their neighbors to seek help from the United States.

The trouble is that Peiping's leaders want neighboring countries to accept subordination to Chinese power. They want them to become political and economic dependencies of Peiping. If the United States can be driven from Asia, this goal will be in their grasp. The "influence," therefore, that Peiping's present leaders seek in Asia is indeed far reaching.

Dominance in the Communist Movement

I had the privilege almost exactly a year ago of commenting at some length before this committee on the Sino-Soviet dispute. The essential nature of this conflict has not changed in this year. It has, if anything, intensified and widened. Its Russo-Chinese national aspects have become more conspicuous. Both sides have clearly given increased thought to the implications of a wider war in Southeast Asia for their mutual treaty obligations. I don't know what the Soviets would actually do with respect to their treaty with Communist China, but Peiping does not seem to be counting on Soviet support.

Peiping's Desire

One of Peiping's most fundamental differences with Moscow centers on its desire to maintain the sharpest possible polarization between the Communist world and the United States. Peiping argues that we are the "enemy of all the people in the world." Its national interests in Asia are served by maximizing Communist (and world) pressure on us and by attempting to "isolate" us. For this reason alone the Chinese would probably have opposed any Soviet attempts to reach understandings with us. In addition there are ideological and psychological reasons for Sino-Soviet rivalry:

The intense and deadly antagonisms that have always characterized schisms in the Marxist world;

Mao's belief that after Stalin's death the mantle of world Communist leadership should rightfully have passed to him and the Chinese Communist party;

Peiping's obsession, also held or professed by the leaders of the Soviet Union during the 30 years after the Bolshevik revolution, with a fear of being threatened and encircled;

The mixture of the psychology of the veterans of the long march and Chinese traditional attitudes which has led Peiping's leaders to believe that through a combination of patience, struggle, and "right thinking" all obstacles can be conquered; and

Peiping's professed belief that the Soviets are joining with the United States in keeping China in a position of inferiority and subordination.

All these have merged to give the Sino-Soviet dispute a flavor and an intensity which rival even the current Chinese Communist antagonism for the United States itself.

How Successful Has Peiping Been?

We can see that the Communist Chinese have set vast goals for themselves, both internally and externally. The disastrous results of the so-called great leap forward have forced them to acknowledge that it will take them generations to achieve their goals.

They have wrought considerable changes on the mainland of China. Perhaps their greatest feat has been to establish their complete political authority throughout the country. They have made some progress in industrialization, education, and public health -- although at the expense of human freedom, originality, and creativity. But their efforts to improve agriculture and to mold the Chinese people into a uniform Marxist pattern have been far less successful.

The economic, political, and social problems still confronting the Chinese Communist leaders today are staggering.

Economic Problems

Peiping's economic power will almost certainly increase over the coming years. But even with relatively effective birth control programs the population of mainland China may reach 1 billion by 1985.

Where is the food to come from? Where are the resources for investment to come from? Can the rapidly increasing military and economic costs of great-power status be carried by Chinese society at the same time that other economic tasks vital to China's economic survival are carried out? I do not denigrate in the slightest native Chinese ingenuity and capacity for incredibly hard work when I suggest that the solutions to these problems are in the gravest doubt.

Internal Political Problems

Even more important to Peiping's leaders than these economic problems, however, are the will and morale of their own people. The current leaders -- Mao, Liu Shao-ch'i, Chou En-lai, and others -- are an intensely committed group of men whose entire lives symbolize their willingness to postpone the satisfactions of the present for the promised glory of the future.

Every generation is suspicious that the youth of today is not what it was in the good old days. But this has become another obsession of Peiping's old men. Their comments to visitors, as well as the reports of refugees, have all emphasized their distrust of the youth of the country. They fear that their grand designs and goals -- both domestic and foreign -- will not be pursued with zeal by the next generation.

I believe their concern may be both genuine and warranted. How pleased can young college graduates be to be sent off to rural China for years for ideological hardening? How attractive is it to the Chinese peasant and worker to be called on for years of sacrifice to bring revolution to Africa or Latin America? Will Chinese scientists accept the dogma that scientific truth can be found only in the pages of Mao Tse-tung's writings? How can professional Chinese Communist army officers and soldiers be persuaded that the words of Mao represent a "spiritual atomic bomb" more powerful than any material weapon?

I am unaware of any new revolution brewing on the Chinese mainland. I have no evidence that the current regime does not, in practical terms, control effectively all of mainland China. But there is evidence of a growing psychological weariness that in years to come could produce a significant shift in the policies of a new generation of leaders.

The dramatic succession of foreign policy failures during the last year, both in the Communist and non-Communist world, must be having some effect on the confidence of the people in the wisdom of their leaders and even on the leaders themselves.

I do not predict any quick changes in China. Nor are there simple solutions. Peiping's present state of mind is a combination of aggressive arrogance and obsessions of its own making. There are doubtless many reasons, cultural, historical, political, for this state of mind. Psychologists have struggled for years in an effort to characterize what is a normal personality. The definition of what a normal state personality might be is beyond my abilities. I would be inclined, however, to advance the view that a country whose behavior is as violent, irascible, unyielding, and hostile as that of Communist China is led by leaders whose view of the world and of life itself is unreal. It is said that we have isolated them. But to me they have isolated themselves -- both in the non-Communist and Communist world.

We have little hope of changing the outlook of these leaders. They are products of their entire lives. They seem to be immune to agreement or persuasion by anyone, including their own allies.

It is of no help in formulating policy to describe Peiping's behavior as neurotic. Its present policies pose grave and immediate problems for the United States and other countries. These must be dealt with now. The weapons and advisers that Peiping exports to promote and assist insurrections in other countries cannot be met by psychoanalysis. At the present time there is a need for a counterweight of real power to Chinese Communist pressures. This has had to be supplied primarily by the United States and our allies.

We should be under no illusion that by yielding to Peiping's bellicose demands today we would in some way ease the path toward peace in Asia. If Peiping reaps success from its current policies, not only its present leaders but those who follow will be emboldened to continue them. This is the path to increased tension and even greater dangers to world peace in the years ahead.

China as a Great Power

We expect China to become some day a great world power. Communist China is a major Asian power today. In the ordinary course of events, a peaceful China would be expected to have close relations -- political, cultural, and economic -- with the countries around its borders and with the United States.

It is no part of the policy of the United States to block the peaceful attainment of these objectives.

More than any other Western people, we have had close and warm ties with the Chinese people. We opposed the staking out of spheres of influence in China. We used our share of the Boxer indemnity to establish scholarships for Chinese students in the United States. We welcomed the revolution of Sun Yat-sen. We took the lead in relinquishing Western extraterritorial privileges in China. We refused to recognize the puppet regime established by Japan in Manchuria. And it was our refusal to accept or endorse, even by implication, Japan's imperial conquests and further designs in China that made it impossible for us to achieve a *modus vivendi* with Japan in 1940-41.

We look forward hopefully -- and confidently -- to a time in the future when the government of mainland China will permit the restoration of the historic ties of friendship between the people of mainland China and ourselves.

Elements of Future Policy

What should be the main elements in our policy toward Communist China?

We must take care to do nothing which encourages Peiping -- or anyone else -- to believe that it can reap gains from its aggressive actions and designs. It is just as essential to "contain" Communist aggression in Asia as it was, and is, to "contain" Communist aggression in Europe.

At the same time, we must continue to make it plain that, if Peiping abandons its belief that force is the best way to resolve disputes and gives up its violent strategy of world revolution, we would welcome an era of good relations.

More specifically, I believe, there should be 10 elements in our policy.

First, we must remain firm in our determination to help those Allied nations which seek our help to resist the direct or indirect use or threat of force against their territory by Peiping.

Second, we must continue to assist the countries of Asia in building broadly based effective governments, devoted to progressive economic and social policies, which can better withstand Asian Communist pressures and maintain the security of their people.

Third, we must honor our commitments to the Republic of China and to the people on Taiwan, who do not want to live under communism. We will continue to assist in their defense and to try to persuade the Chinese Communists to join with us in renouncing the use of force in the area of Taiwan.

Fourth, we will continue our efforts to prevent the expulsion of the Republic of China from the United Nations or its agencies. So long as Peiping follows its present course it is extremely difficult for us to see how it can be held to fulfill the requirements set forth in the charter for membership, and the United States opposes its membership. It is worth recalling that the Chinese Communists have set forth some interesting conditions which must be fulfilled before they are even willing to consider membership:

- The United Nations resolution of 1950 condemning Chinese Communist aggression in Korea must be rescinded;
- There must be a new United Nations resolution condemning U.S. "aggression";
- The United Nations must be reorganized;
- The Republic of China must be expelled;
- All other "imperialist puppets" must be expelled. One can only ask whether the Chinese Communists seriously want membership, or whether they mean to destroy the United Nations. We be-

lieve the United Nations must approach this issue with the utmost caution and deliberation.

Fifth, we should continue our efforts to reassure Peiping that the United States does not intend to attack mainland China. There are, of course, risks of war with China. This was true in 1950. It was true in the Taiwan Straits crises of 1955 and 1958. It was true in the Chinese Communist drive into Indian territory in 1962. It is true today in Viet Nam. But we do not want war. We do not intend to provoke war. There is no fatal inevitability of war with Communist China. The Chinese Communists have, as I have already said, acted with caution when they foresaw a collision with the United States. We have acted with restraint and care in the past and we are doing so today. I hope that they will realize this and guide their actions accordingly.

Sixth, we must keep firmly in our minds that there is nothing eternal about the policies and attitudes of Communist China. We must avoid assuming the existence of an unending and inevitable state of hostility between ourselves and the rulers of mainland China.

Seventh, when it can be done without jeopardizing other U.S. interests, we should continue to enlarge the possibilities for unofficial contacts between Communist China and ourselves -- contacts which may gradually assist in altering Peiping's picture of the United States.

In this connection, we have gradually expanded the categories of American citizens who may travel to Communist China. American libraries may freely purchase Chinese Communist publications. American citizens may send and receive mail from the mainland. We have in the past indicated that if the Chinese themselves were interested in purchasing grain we would consider such sales. We have indicated our willingness to allow Chinese Communist newspapermen to come to the United States. We are prepared to permit American universities to invite Chinese Communist scientists to visit their institutions.

We do not expect that for the time being the Chinese Communists will seize upon these avenues of contact or exchange. All the evidence suggests Peiping wishes to remain isolated from the United States. But we believe it is in our interests that such channels be opened and kept open. We believe contact and communication are not incompatible with a firm policy of containment.

Eighth, we should keep open our direct diplomatic contacts with Peiping in Warsaw. While these meetings frequently provide merely an opportunity for a reiteration of known positions, they play a role in enabling each side to communicate information and attitudes in times of crisis. It is our hope that they might at some time become the channel for a more fruitful dialogue.

Ninth, we are prepared to sit down with Peiping and other countries to discuss the critical problems of disarmament and nonproliferation of nuclear weapons. Peiping has rejected all suggestions and invitations to join in such talks. It has attacked the test ban treaty. It has advocated the further spread of nuclear weapons to non-nuclear countries. It is an urgent task of all countries to persuade Peiping to change its stand.

Tenth, we must continue to explore and analyze all available information on Communist China and keep our own policies up to date. We hope that Peiping's policies may one day take account of the people of Asia and her own people for peace and security. We have said, in successive administrations, that when Peiping abandons the aggressive use of force and shows that it is not irrevocably hostile to the United States, then expanded contacts and improved relations may become possible. This continues to be our position.

These, I believe, are the essential ingredients of a sound policy in regard to Communist China.

I believe that they serve the interests not only of the United States and of the free world as a whole -- but of the Chinese people. We have always known of the pragmatic genius of the Chinese people, and we can see evidence of it even today. The practices and doctrines of the present Peiping regime are yielding poor returns to the Chinese people. I believe that the Chinese people, no less their neighbors and the American people, crave the opportunity to move toward the enduring goals of mankind: a better life, safety, freedom, human dignity, and peace.

TEXT OF MANSFIELD REPORT ON VIET NAM SITUATION

Following is the complete text of a report on Viet Nam to the Senate Foreign Relations Committee by Sens. Mansfield (D Mont.), Muskie (D Maine), Inouye (D Hawaii), Aiken (R Vt.) and Boggs (R Del.). The report, titled "The Viet Nam Conflict: The Substance and the Shadow," was issued Jan. 6, 1966, as a committee print. (See p. 171)

A. Vietnam: The Substance of War

1. Introductory

The most important new factor in the war in Vietnam has been the introduction of large numbers of U. S. troops into South Vietnam and their direct entry into combat. This augmentation of the U. S. military role in Vietnam was a response to a near-desperate situation early in 1965. There is no question that the Government of Vietnam in Saigon was faced with a rapidly deteriorating position at that time.

After the assassination of Ngo Dinh Diem, repeated coups had weakened the cohesiveness of the central authority and acted to stimulate public disaffection and indifference to the war. At the same time, there was a greatly accelerated military drive by strengthened Vietcong forces. Their control expanded over large areas of the country, particularly in provinces adjacent to the western borders. Communications and transportation between population centers became increasingly hazardous, except by Vietcong sufferance. In short, a total collapse of the Saigon government's authority appeared imminent in the early months of 1965.

U. S. combat troops in strength arrived at that point in response to the appeal of the Saigon authorities. The Vietcong counter response was to increase their military activity with forces strengthened by intensified local recruitment and infiltration of regular North Vietnamese troops. With the change in the composition of opposing forces the character of the war also changed sharply.

2. Military forces of the Government of Vietnam

The Government of Vietnam now has approximately 635,000 men under arms. Of this number, however, only about 300,000 are regular troops of the Army, Navy, Air Force and Marines, with about 88 percent being Army troops. A general reserve of six airborne battalions and five marine battalions is equipped to fight anywhere in the country.

The Vietnamese Government has six fighter-bomber squadrons. It also has a small navy, composed of sea, river, and coastal forces.

In the total of 635,000 men there are also regional forces of about 120,000 men which act as a constabulary in the 43 Provinces. Each Province chief, who has a military as well as a civil capacity, has a number of regional force companies under his command. Popular forces number about 140,000. Lightly armed, this group is recruited as a rule from local youth to act as defenders of villages and hamlets. A civilian irregular defense group is recruited by the Vietnamese Special Forces. It numbers about 25,000 and is posted in border areas for patrol purposes. Finally, there is a national police of about 50,000 men.

The total of 635,000 men in all categories is expected to be expanded in the current year, although a substantial increase is not anticipated. The sources of expanded recruitment are not great and, in any event, are shared with the Vietcong. Moreover, a high desertion rate continues, despite determined efforts to reduce it.

3. U.S. and international forces in Vietnam

In 1962, U.S. military advisers and service forces in South Vietnam totaled approximately 10,000 men. This number had increased by May of 1965 to about 34,000. At that time the American force was still basically an advisory organization. Americans, in regular combat units, were not yet engaged on the ground. U.S. helicopter companies were in use but only to supply tactical transportation to regular Vietnamese units and the U.S. jet fighter-bombers in the country with the exception of two or three squadrons of aircraft were not engaged in support of the Vietnamese Armed Forces.

By December 1965, however, there were approximately 170,000 U.S. troops in South Vietnam. Additionally, there were about 21,000 soldiers and marines from the Republic of Korea, an infantry battalion and battery of artillery, comprising some 1,200 men, from Australia, and a New Zealand artillery battery of about 150 men.

The augmented U.S. ground forces were composed of two Army divisions, the 1st Infantry Division and the 1st Air Cavalry Division, and two separate brigades, the 1st Brigade, 101st Airborne Division, and the 173rd Airborne Brigade. The Australian and New Zealand troops were attached to the latter group. A full U.S. Marine division reinforced by a separate regiment was in Vietnam with the support of six Marine fighter-bomber squadrons.

The small Vietnamese coastal force was augmented by a number of U.S. naval ships and Coast Guard vessels. The U.S. 7th Fleet was off the Vietnamese coast. Planes from its carriers were active in the air campaign against North Vietnam. They were also reinforcing the U.S. Air Force and Vietnamese fighter-bomber squadrons in operations in South Vietnam.

Ten U.S. Air Force and Marine fighter-bomber squadrons were operating from five jet airfields in Vietnam; a sixth field was under construction. B-52 bombers from Guam were providing additional air strength, concentrating on more remote Vietcong bases which had previously been immune to harassment or attack.

The magnitude of the expanded U.S. military effort has required a vastly enlarged support complex. Starting almost from scratch in May of 1965, a logistic system has been built. There are four major logistic support areas. One is in the Saigon region, including Bien Hoa and Vung Tau. The other three are located along the coast, at Cam Ranh Bay, at Qui Nhon in Binh Dinh Province, and at Da Nang. The rapid infusion of American forces has strained the facilities of the new logistic system to the utmost, with long delays in unloading and moving equipment not unusual. There have also been and still are shortages of important items of supply despite efforts to eliminate these shortages.

4. Relationship of United States and Vietnamese forces

From the point of view of American policy and practice, the war itself remains a Vietnamese war. The American command emphasizes that U.S. forces in Vietnam are there to support the Vietnamese and their Armed Forces in the effort to resist aggression by infiltration from the north and terrorism and subversion from within. Vietnamese sovereignty and the paramount role of the Vietnamese are meticulously respected and the supporting nature of the U.S. role is stressed.

There is no combined or unified command of the international forces in Vietnam. United States and Vietnamese forces work together through coordination and cooperation. The commander of the U.S. forces maintains close liaison with the Vietnamese Minister of Defense and the Chief of the Joint General Staff. Strategy and plans are devised together. Parallel instructions are then issued to the respective commanders through corps and division to regimental level. In the execution of an operation a joint command post is set up or liaison officers are exchanged and terrain is apportioned for tactical areas of operation. According to American military commanders these arrangements have proved to be practical and workable.

5. Vietcong-North Vietnamese forces

In December 1965, the best available estimates placed Vietcong strength in South Vietnam at 230,000 men. This figure is double that of 3 years ago. Total Vietcong strength, apparently, is steadily increasing despite the serious casualties which these forces have suffered during the past few months.

Of the present total, approximately 73,000 are main force soldiers, including 14,000 regular PAVN (People's Army of North Vietnam) troops from North Vietnam. The Vietcong forces also include about 100,000 militia, some 17,000 support troops who operate along lines of communication, and approximately 40,000 political cadres. It is estimated that the Vietcong, through local recruitment in the south and infiltration from the north, have the capability of a substantial increase in their numbers within a short period of time.

Infiltration of men from North Vietnam through Laos has been going on for many years. It was confined primarily to political cadres and military leadership until about the end of 1964 when North Vietnam Regular Army troops began to enter South Vietnam by this route. It is anticipated that with the multiplication of routes through Laos the rate of infiltration is likely to increase threefold from the present estimated 1,500 per month. The monsoon, which earlier was considered to be of great significance in its effect on the reinforcement capabilities of the Vietcong as well as on the ability of both sides to prosecute the war, has proved in experience to be of minor consequence if, indeed, of any consequence at all.

6. Current state of the war

By November 1965, American troops were directly involved in battle to a much greater degree than at any other time in the history of the Vietnamese conflict. At the same time, the intensity of the war itself reached a new high. The Vietcong initiated 1,038 incidents during the last week of November and the total number of incidents which had increased steadily throughout 1965, reached 3,588 in that month. These incidents involved armed attacks up to regimental strength as well as terrorism and sabotage of various kinds and antiaircraft fire against U.S. aircraft. In the later months of 1965 the trend was toward larger attacks, except in the Mekong Delta where there were numerous small-scale actions.

With the increase in the intensity of the conflict, there were increased numbers of casualties among all participants. In the month of November 1965, alone, 469 Americans were killed in action, a figure representing about 35 percent of all Americans killed in action in the war until that date. In addition 1,470 Americans were listed as wounded and 33 as missing. During the same month the South Vietnamese Army reported 956 soldiers killed in action, 2,030 wounded, and 355 missing. The Vietcong, for their part, are estimated to have lost 5,300 men killed in the month and, in addition, 595 were taken prisoner. Many of these casualties were regulars of the North Vietnamese Army.

7. The security situation in South Vietnam

The presence of U.S. combat forces has acted to arrest the deterioration in general security in Government-controlled parts of South Vietnam. It has also improved the ability of the Vietnamese Government to hold Saigon, the strategic heart of the country, the coastal bases, and certain other key areas in the country. In the latter connection, it should be noted that a strategic route (19) from the coast to the western highlands has been reopened for convoyed ground traffic to Pleiku, a major military strong point in the western highlands. On certain other roads, an improvement in security is also reported.

8. Vietcong reactions

Faced by a blunting of their military efforts, the Vietcong have reacted strongly to the new situation. Beginning in June an estimated 1,500 North Vietnamese troops per month have entered South Vietnam through Laos and this number is rapidly increasing. The estimates are that at least seven regiments of regular troops from North Vietnam are now in the country with more on the way. At the same time the Vietcong have in recent months greatly stepped up the recruiting, induction, and training of South Vietnamese in the densely populated delta region. They have increased their small-scale attacks in that area, aiming apparently at isolated outposts and at demoralizing the regional and popular forces as well as harassing lines of supply and communication.

The stepped-up activity of the Vietcong in the countryside has been paralleled by an effort on the part of the Government forces to strengthen their control over the population in the base areas and their immediate environs. These base areas themselves are held in some force. At the U.S. Marine base at Da Nang, for example, the perimeter of security has been pushed out about 10 miles. The bulk of the U.S. Marine forces, however, is now preoccupied in defense within that perimeter. Nevertheless, it is still possible for the Vietcong to bypass the defenders and penetrate the area in sporadic

hit-and-run raids. Communications between the base areas along the coast are still subject to Vietcong ambush and attack.

In Saigon, heavily defended as it is, the rattle of automatic weapons fire or the explosion of mortar shells in the outskirts of the city are not uncommon sounds by day or by night. Vietcong ability to carry out terroristic attacks within the city itself is from time to time made evident. Indeed, it is considered by some that Saigon with its many vulnerabilities to sabotage and terrorism and Hanoi with its exposure to air attack are mutual hostages, one for the other.

9. Impact of increased American forces on the Vietnamese

The arrival in Vietnam of American combat troops in large numbers has had an immediate positive psychological effect on Government-held areas. Not only has there been an improvement of morale in the Government and the Armed Forces, there has also been a return of confidence among Vietnamese civilians. This is especially true in Saigon where the increased American presence is taken as insurance against an imminent collapse of the existing structure.[1] Politically and commercially minded Vietnamese, seeing that the United States had so far committed itself, have found renewed courage and confidence.

Of great significance is the fact that there has been a period of Government stability in Vietnam following the arrival of additional U.S. troops. This stability is more essential than ever for the maintenance of public confidence after the debilitating consequences of the repeated coups which followed the assassination of President Diem. It is also vital for the effective prosecution of the war and the formulation and carrying out of social, economic, and political reform programs.

10. The government of Gen. Nguyen Cao Ky

The new leadership in Government which is drawn largely from military circles, is young and hopeful, but with little knowledge of politics. Gen. Nguyen Cao Ky, the Prime Minister, recognizes that a purely military solution to the problems of Vietnam is not possible. Security and social and economic reform, in his view, must proceed hand in hand in order to gain the support of the people.

The new leaders express the intention of moving toward some form of representative civilian government, taking into account the history and needs of the Vietnamese people. They speak of a consultative assembly to prepare the way for a constitution and hearings throughout the country on the constitution with a new to a referendum at the end of 1966. The referendum, according to their concepts, would be followed by elections to a legislative body by the end of 1967, if by that time elections can be held without intimidation in as much as two-thirds of the country. Some observers believe that, perhaps, not more than 25 percent of the villages under Government control in South Vietnam would be free from intimidation at an election at the present time.

In addition to prosecuting the war, the Government of Vietnam is seeking to initiate measures to protect and improve the welfare of the population. With the indispensable assistance of U.S. aid, food and other commodities are being imported into the country to meet current needs and to insure that the price of staples such as rice, fish, and canned milk remain within the reach of the people.

11. The pacification or civic action program

A new effort is also being made to bring the people of the villages into closer and firmer rapport with the Government. In the period following the fall of the government of Ngo Dinh Diem, the so-called pacification or civic action program which brought govern-

---

[1]*The illustrative story is told of the Vietnamese professional man who sold his house in Saigon in January of 1965 in despair over the deteriorating situation, only to buy back the same house later in the year, following the arrival of American troops, for twice the price at which he had sold it.*

ment, police, economic, and social organization into the hamlets, was allowed in large measure to lapse. Due to subsequent changes of government, there were eventually only a very few people left to carry on this work. Military necessity required the Government to concentrate on attempting to stop Vietcong military advances.

The present Government is once again seeking to create an organization to carry out a program of pacification or civic action. Screening the cadres left from the programs of previous governments, a basic group has been selected. Together with additional groups to be trained it is expected that a total number adequate to meet the needs for pacification teams in the priority areas chosen by the Government of Vietnam will be available by the end of 1966.

The present plan for pacification work is regarded by observers as more thorough and more realistic than previous efforts. It contemplates teams remaining in each village for an initial period of several months with subsequent followups over a period of at least 1 year. The belief is that the inhabitants can generally be sufficiently won over to the side of the Government in that period and conditions established where elections for local officials can be held. It is realized, however, that even then the work cannot be considered as completed.

12. Other programs

In addition to giving strong support to the pacification program, the new Government has numerous other plans to better the lot of the people. There are, for example, projects to improve the pay of the troops, construct low-cost housing, and redistribute land. In this connection a program has been inaugurated to give 700,000 acres of land to 180,000 farmers. It is generally recognized that Government programs of this kind, many of which have been attempted in various forms before, will require years before any substantial political effect upon the population can be anticipated.

13. Economic aspects of the conflict

The Government of Vietnam has also instituted a resources control program in an effort to restrict the Vietcong's ability to get the things they need to carry on the war. In most parts of Vietnam, which is a naturally rich and productive country, it is not difficult to obtain enough food to support life. This is particularly true in the fertile and densely populated delta of the south with its great rice fields and network of interconnecting canals. The Vietcong obtain money by many means, including taxation and extortion, and they can and do use these funds to purchase food in the countryside and medicines in district and provincial towns. The Vietcong can and do attack trucks and convoys on the roads and seize the weapons, ammunition, and the other goods which they may carry.

By a system of rationing, identity cards, and resource control, including checkpoints and mobile control teams, however, the Government hopes to stop the Vietcong from obtaining key commodities such as food and medicines in key areas such as the highlands, which is a deficit region. In other areas it is hoped that the system will make goods less available for the Vietcong and more difficult for them to obtain.

It must be said that there is also a reverse side to this picture. The Vietcong, operating in the countryside, have the ability to restrict the flow of food to cities and population centers such as Saigon. Vegetables, for example, come to Saigon from Dalat in the central highlands. Sugar also comes to Saigon along the same road which is controlled in part by the Vietcong. It is common knowledge that commodities reaching Saigon's markets by road from the Dalat area have paid a tax to the Vietcong before reaching the city and that unless the tax is paid they will not reach the city. The fact is plain: Much of Saigon's indigenous food and commodity supply depends on the sufferance of the Vietcong and on payments to them.

The ravages of war and terrorism, however, are taking a toll of the country's productive capacity. Rice fields and rubber plantations in areas that are being bombed and fought over no longer produce

their contribution to feed the people and to nourish the economy. Fledgling enterprises in outlying areas, cut off from supplies and from markets by interrupted communications, wither and fail.

Along with increased Vietcong activity in the delta in recent months, there has been growing Vietcong restriction on the flow of rice from that region to the Saigon market. The result is that Vietnam, a rice surplus region, in 1966, will have to import at least 300,000 tons of rice from abroad under U.S. aid programs to feed the population of the cities and towns under the Government's control.

Although, as has been said, the arrival of large numbers of American troops has gone far to restore business confidence in the cities of Vietnam, there have been adverse effects as well. One of these is the creation of a labor shortage, particularly among skilled workers, as men have been drained away from normal areas of employment to the base complexes and other regions where construction projects are being pushed to create the logistic structure and other facilities required by the American forces.

Inflationary pressures resulting from the war and the changed U.S. role have thus far been kept within bounds. Saigon itself, however, has an overstimulated atmosphere of almost hectic prosperity, in some respects, as the impact of spending by American servicemen and the effect of U.S. defense expenditure make themselves felt. There are also the beginnings of the rumblings of personal discontent and antagonism which generally characterize the reaction in any nation to the sudden infusion of a large body of foreign forces.

14. Summation

In sum, the overall control of the country remains about the same as it was at the beginning of 1965. It is estimated that about 22 percent of the population is under Vietcong control and that about 18 percent inhabits contested areas. About 60 percent of the population in the country is, at present, under some form of government control, largely because of its hold on Saigon and other cities and large towns.

The population of the cities has been augmented by a great number of refugees. Hundreds of thousands in number, they are for the greater part composed of people who have fled to the cities in an effort to escape the spreading intensity of the war. In this sense, they are unlike the refugees who came from North Vietnam in 1954. These earlier refugees consciously chose to leave their ancestral homes and come south permanently, rather than accept a Communist regime. The new refugees, for the most part, are believed merely to be waiting for an end to the fighting in order to return to their homes and land.

The Vietcong have stepped up sabotage, terrorism, and hit and run attacks in the Government-held areas which are, principally, cities and major towns and indeterminate, but limited, extensions outward from them. Harassment by United States and Vietnamese air attack and airborne forces has increased in the firmly held Vietcong areas of South Vietnam which are almost entirely rural. And, of course, North Vietnam has been brought under air attack.

In general, however, what the Saigon government held in the way of terrain in the early months of 1965 (and it was already considerably less than was held at the time of the assassination of Ngo Dinh Diem), is still held. What was controlled then by the Vietcong is still controlled by the Vietcong. What lay between was contested at the outset of 1965 and is still contested.

B. Vietnam and the Nations of Asia

Other nations of Asia generally view the conflict in Vietnam with great concern. Those countries nearest to Vietnam see in the spread and increasing intensity of the warfare a heightened danger of a spillover into their territory. They sense that the longer the conflict continues and the more it escalates the greater becomes this danger to themselves. Furthermore, they fear the effect upon their own future should all of Vietnam become a Communist state.

Laos already finds itself deeply although unwillingly involved on the fringes of the war in Vietnam. The fighting within Laos, which continues despite the 1962 Geneva Agreement, is now a closely interwoven part of the Vietnamese struggle. The connection is most pronounced in the eastern part of Laos which lies within the control of the Communist Pathet Lao forces. This region, the so-called Laotian panhandle, is a natural infiltration route for men and supplies from North Vietnam into South Vietnam. A long border abutting on South Vietnam makes it possible for troops and equipment from Hanoi to reach far south through Communist-controlled territory in Laos with a minimum of risk before being diverted across the border into South Vietnam by any number of lateral communications routes. New roads have been constructed through this mountainous terrain along which men and supplies can pass, for the most part undetected, protected as they are in some regions by double canopies of jungle foliage. These roads are not easily susceptible to aerial interdiction.

Cambodia, in a different manner and to a much lesser extent than Laos, is already directly touched by the fighting in Vietnam. There are repeated charges that Cambodian territory is being used as a base for Vietcong operations. That is possible in view of the remoteness and obscurity of the border but there is no firm evidence of any such organized usage and no evidence whatsoever that any alleged usage of Cambodian soil is with the sanction much less the assistance of the Cambodian Government. Prince Sihanouk responded immediately to a recent allegation that the Cambodian port of Sihanoukville is being used to transship supplies to the Vietcong by calling for an investigation by the International Control Commission which was set up under the Geneva Accords of 1954.

Cambodia's overwhelming concern is the preservation of its national integrity which, in times past, has been repeatedly violated by more powerful neighbors and is still subject to occasional forays from a minor dissident movement (the Khmer Serai) which has been allowed to base itself in the neighboring nations. Cambodia seeks recognition and respect of its borders by all parties to the conflict. It asks to be left to live in peace so that it may concentrate on its own problems and internal development. The Cambodians have made great internal progress, largely through their own efforts supplemented by a judicious use of aid from the United States in the past and from other nations both in the past and at the present time. They have a peaceful and productive nation with an intense sense of national unity and loyalty to Prince Sihanouk.

The fact that fighting in South Vietnam has raged close to the border and there have, as a result, been occasional border incursions and bombing of Cambodian territory has caused the deepest concern to the Cambodian Government. Cambodia can be expected to make the most vigorous efforts to resist becoming directly involved in the struggle surging through South Vietnam and to repel to the best of its capability direct and organized invasions of its territory which may stem from the mounting tempo of the war.

Thailand, the only country on the southeast Asian mainland directly allied with the United States, seeks to cooperate with the United States as an ally while avoiding a spillover of the war into Thai territory. That course is becoming increasingly difficult to maintain. Thailand has a large number of North Vietnamese living in its northeast region bordering on Laos. This element retains an affinity for Hanoi and is susceptible to its influence. Moreover, in the recent past Peiping has brought to the forefront a Thai leader in exile and has increased the intensity of its propaganda attacks against Thailand. Reports of terrorism and sabotage in the northeast of Thailand are increasing.

The Vietnamese war was brought very close to Thai territory in November 1965. A Pathet Lao military thrust toward the Laotian town of Thakkek on the Mekong, which was supported by North Vietnamese troops, was fortuitously driven back by Government forces. Had it not been repelled, the war, in effect, would have reached the point where it made direct contact with Thailand's frontier.

Nations in Asia more geographically remote from the war in South Vietnam are nonetheless conscious of the dangers to the entire area as the struggle in South Vietnam becomes more prolonged and

ever more intense. These countries range from neutral and non-aligned Burma through such allies of the United States as the Philippines and Japan.

Each of the countries of Asia has its own internal problems. Each has varying degrees of internal stability. Each has as a principal concern, the avoidance of direct involvement in the Vietnamese conflict. With the exception of Korea, there is little likelihood of substantial material help from these sources in providing military assistance in South Vietnam. Others are either unwilling or reluctant to become involved in a military sense or are unable to do so because of inner difficulties or the broader strategic requirements of the Asian situation. Even with respect to Korea, it is obvious that any withdrawal of forces for use in Vietnam creates new problems of military balance as between North and South Korea. It should not be overlooked that peace in the Korean peninsula is still held together only by a tenuous truce.

The Asian nations generally are aware of their own relative powerlessness to influence the main course of events, or, in the final analysis, to control their own destinies should the conflict in Vietnam ultimately develop into a confrontation between the United States and Communist China with all that such an eventuality might imply for the peace of Asia and the world. In Japan, for example, there is a deep anxiety over the possible consequences to that nation of such a confrontation if it should materialize. The memory of the escalation of the limited Manchurian incident of 30 years ago into a seemingly interminable war on the mainland of China is not yet dead in Japan.

To sum up, then, the nations of Asia recognize the immense importance to themselves of what is transpiring in Vietnam. But they also recognize their own limitations in the face of it. Their immediate preoccupation, in any event, is with their own internal problems and development. Throughout the area there is a continuing interest in activities involving peaceful cooperation for economic development. The Peace Corps is generally welcomed wherever it operates and, notably, in the Philippines. The new Asian Development Bank is being launched with considerable enthusiasm. The Mekong project has warm support throughout the region and considerable interest in Cambodia, which is central to the concept.

It is clear that none of the nations of the area desires the domination of either China or the United States. Given a choice, it is doubtful that any nation would like to see the influence of the United States withdrawn completely from southeast Asia. Generally speaking, the nations of the area welcome peaceful ties with the United States and our participation in the development of the region if that participation does not become overwhelming.

C. The Soviet Union and Eastern Europe

Without exception the Soviet Union, Poland, and Rumania give full and firm support to the postion of Hanoi and the Vietcong They are quick in their denunciation of the U.S. role in South Vietnam and vehement against U.S. bombing in North Vietnam.

Part of this solidarity is undoubtedly derived from ideological affinities. Whatever attitudes they may manifest toward Communist China and they vary, it is clear that responsibility for the continuation of the conflict in Vietnam is assigned to the United States and this is regarded as an impediment to improvement in political relations with this country.

There is no reason to believe that the Soviet Union, in present circumstances, sees its way clear or, in fact, is anxious to play a significant role to assist in bringing an end to hostilities in Vietnam. The Soviet Union has steadfastly refused to join with the United Kingdom, the other Cochairman of the 1954 Geneva Conference, in calling for a reconvening of that Conference. They have emphasized repeatedly in public statements as well as in other ways that they have no intention of taking an initiative for peace in Vietnam at this time.

The countries of Eastern Europe have reason for concern over the continuation of the conflict in Vietnam and its escalation. Some of these reasons have to do with their own national preoccupations and the situation in Europe. Both Poland and Rumania, for example, have a very substantial trade with the Western World and remain interested in increased trade with the United States should conditions permit. Both might well be disposed to make a contribution to a settlement of the Vietnam problem to the extent their capabilities permit but only should they see some possibility of success.

D. Communist China

Behind the war in Vietnam, behind the fears and preoccupations of other Asian nations and through the attitudes of the Eastern European countries and the Soviet Union runs the shadow of Communist China.

Until now the Chinese Communists have not introduced their manpower directly into the conflict although they clearly recognize that the war may reach that point. They recognize, too, that the war may impinge upon China herself at some point and have begun to make preliminary preparations for that eventually.

For the present, however, the Chinese appear to take the view that their direct intervention in Vietnam is not required since: (1) the war in South Vietnam is a people's war which the Vietcong are winning; (2) North Vietnam is successfully defending itself; (3) the more the United States escalates the war the higher our casualties will be and the more discouraged we will become; and (4) the United States cannot win, in any event, according to Chinese theories.

It is from Communist China that Hanoi and the Vietcong derive the bulk of their outside material support. It is from Communist China that there has also flowed encouragement of resistance to negotiation or compromise. As the war escalates and Hanoi becomes ever more dependent upon Chinese support, a dependence which Soviet aid at best only tempers, the likelihood also increases that North Vietnam will not be able to negotiate a settlement without at least the tacit consent of China. In fact, that point may already have been reached.

E. Concluding Comments

A rapid solution to the conflict in Vietnam is not in immediate prospect. This would appear to be the case whether military victory is pursued or negotiations do, in fact, materialize.

Insofar as the military situation is concerned, the large-scale introduction of U.S. forces and their entry into combat has blunted but not turned back the drive of the Vietcong. The latter have responded to the increased American role with a further strengthening of their forces by local recruitment in the south and reinforcements from the north and a general stepping up of military activity. As a result the lines remain drawn in South Vietnam in substantially the same pattern as they were at the outset of the increased U.S. commitment. What has changed basically is the scope and intensity of the struggle and the part which is being played by the forces of the United States and those of North Vietnam.

Despite the great increase in American military commitment, it is doubtful in view of the acceleration of Vietcong efforts that the constricted position now held in Vietnam by the Saigon government can continue to be held for the indefinite future, let alone extended, without a further augmentation of American forces on the ground. Indeed, if present trends continue, there is no assurance as to what ultimate increase in American military commitment will be required before the conflict is terminated. For the fact is that under present terms or reference and as the war has evolved, the question is not one of applying increased U. S. pressure to a defined military situation but rather of pressing against a military situation which is, in effect, open ended. How open is dependent on the extent to which North Vietnam and its supporters are willing and able to meet increased force by increased force. All of mainland southeast Asia, at least, cannot be ruled out as a potential battle-

field. As noted, the war has already expanded significantly into Laos and is beginning to lap over the Cambodian border while pressures increase in the northeast of Thailand.

Even if the war remains substantially within its present limits, there is little foundation for the expectation that the government of Vietnam in Saigon will be able, in the near future, to carry a much greater burden than it is now carrying. This is in no sense a reflection on the caliber of the current leaders of Vietnam. But the fact is that they are, as other Vietnamese Governments have been over the past decade, at the beginning of a beginning in dealing with the problems of popular mobilization in support of the Government. They are starting, moreover, from a point considerably behind that which prevailed at the time of President Diem's assassination. Under present concepts and plans, then, what lies ahead is, literally, a vast and continuing undertaking in social engineering in the wake of such military progress as may be registered. And for many years to come this task will be very heavily dependent on U.S. foreign aid.

The basic concept of present American policy with respect to Vietnam casts the United States in the role of support of the Vietnamese Government and people. This concept becomes more difficult to maintain as the military participation of the United States undergoes rapid increase. Yet a change in the basic concept could have a most unfortunate impact upon the Vietnamese people and the world at large. What is involved here is the necessity for the greatest restraint in word and action, lest the concept be eroded and the war drained of a purpose with meaning to the people of Vietnam.

This danger is great, not only because of the military realities of the situation but also because, with a few exceptions, assistance has not been and is not likely to be forthcoming for the war effort in South Vietnam from nations other than the United States. On the contrary, as it now appears, the longer the war continues in its present pattern and the more it expands in scope, the greater will become the strain placed upon the relations of the United States with allies both in the Far East and in Europe.

Many nations are deeply desirous of an end to this conflict as quickly as possible. Few are specific as to the manner in which this end can be brought about or the shape it is likely to take. In any event, even though other nations, in certain circumstances, may be willing to play a third-party role in bringing about negotiations, any prospects for effective negotiations at this time (and they are slim) are likely to be largely dependent on the initiatives and efforts of the combatants.

Negotiations at this time, moreover, if they do come about, and if they are accompanied by a cease-fire and standfast, would serve to stabilize a situation in which the majority of the population remains under nominal government control but in which dominance of the countryside rests largely in the hands of the Vietcong. What might eventually materialize through negotiations from this situation cannot be foreseen at this time with any degree of certainty.

That is not, to say the least, a very satisfactory prospect. What needs also to be borne in mind, however, is that the visible alternative at this time and under present terms of reference is the indefinite expansion and intensification of the war which will require the continuous introduction of additional U.S. forces. The end of that course cannot be foreseen, either, and there are no grounds for optimism that the end is likely to be reached within the confines of South Vietnam or within the very near future.

In short, such choices as may be open are not simple choices. They are difficult and painful choices and they are beset with many imponderables. The situation, as it now appears, offers only the very slim prospect of a just settlement by negotiations or the alternative prospect of a continuance of the conflict in the direction of a general war on the Asian mainland.

FULBRIGHT SPEECH ON 'OLD MYTHS AND NEW REALITIES'

Following is the text of a speech delivered March 25, 1964, in the Senate by Sen. J. W. Fulbright (D Ark.), chairman of the Senate Foreign Relations Committee, on foreign policy:

There is an inevitable divergence, attributable to the imperfections of the human mind, between the world as it is and the world as men perceive it. As long as our perceptions are reasonably close to objective reality, it is possible for us to act upon our problems in a rational and appropriate manner. But when our perceptions fail to keep pace with events, when we refuse to believe something because it displeases or frightens us, or is simply startlingly unfamiliar, then the gap between fact and perception becomes a chasm and action becomes irrelevant and irrational.

There has always -- and inevitably -- been some divergence between the realities of foreign policy and our ideas about it. This divergence has in certain respects been growing rather than narrowing and we are handicapped, accordingly, by policies based on old myths rather than current realities. This divergence is, in my opinion, dangerous and unnecessary -- dangerous because it can reduce foreign policy to a fraudulent game of imagery and appearances, unnecessary because it can be overcome by the determination of men in high office to dispel prevailing misconceptions by the candid dissemination of unpleasant but inescapable facts.

Reasons For Growing Divergence

Before commenting on some of the specific areas where I believe our policies are at least partially based on cherished myths rather than objective facts, I should like to suggest two possible reasons for the growing divergence between the realities and our perceptions of current world politics. The first is the radical change in relations between and within the Communist and the free worlds and the second is the tendency of too many of us to confuse means with ends and, accordingly, to adhere to prevailing practices with a fervor befitting immutable principles.

Although it is too soon to render a definitive judgment, there is mounting evidence that events of recent years have wrought profound changes in the character of East-West relations. In the Cuban missile crisis of October 1962, the United States proved to the Soviet Union that a policy of aggression and adventure involved unacceptable risks. In the signing of the test ban treaty each side in effect assured the other that it was prepared to forego, at least for the present, any bid for a decisive military or political breakthrough. These occurrences, it should be added, took place against the background of the clearly understood strategic superiority -- but not supremacy -- of the United States.

'Peaceful Coexistence'

It seems reasonable, therefore, to suggest that the character of the cold war has, for the present at least, been profoundly altered: by the drawing back of the Soviet Union from extremely aggressive policies; by the implicit repudiation by both sides of a policy of "total victory;" and by the establishment of an American strategic superiority which the Soviet Union appears to have tacitly accepted because it has been accompanied by assurances that it will be exercised by the United States with responsibility and restraint. These enormously important changes may come to be regarded by historians as the foremost achievements of the Kennedy Administration in the field of foreign policy. Their effect has been to commit us to a foreign policy which can accurately -- though perhaps not prudently -- be defined as one of "peaceful coexistence."

Another of the results of the lowering of tensions between East and West is that each is now free to enjoy the luxury of accelerated strife and squabbling within its own domain. The ideological thunderbolts between Washington and Moscow which until a few years ago seemed a permanent part of our daily lives have become a pale shadow of their former selves. Now instead the United States waits in fascinated apprehension for the Olympian pronouncements that issue from Paris at six-month intervals while the Russians respond to the crude epithets of Peking with almost plaintiff rejoinders about "those who want to start a war against everybody."

These astonishing changes in the configuration of the postwar world have had an unsettling effect on both public and official opinion in the United States. One reason for this, I believe, lies in the fact that we are a people used to looking at the world, and indeed at ourselves, in moralistic rather than empirical terms. We are predisposed to regard any conflict as a clash between good and evil rather than as simply a clash between conflicting interests. We are inclined to confuse freedom and democracy, which we regard as moral principles, with the way in which they are practiced in America -- with capitalism, federalism, and the two-party system, which are not moral principles but simply the preferred and accepted practices of the American people. There is much cant in American moralism and not a little inconsistency. It resembles in some ways the religious faith of the many respectable people who, in Samuel Butler's words, "would be equally horrified to hear the Christian religion doubted or to see it practiced."

'Devil in the Kremlin'

Our national vocabulary is full of "self-evident truths," not only about "life, liberty, and happiness," but about a vast number of personal and public issues, including the cold war. It has become one of the "self-evident truths" of the postwar era that just as the President resides in Washington and the Pope in Rome, the Devil resides immutably in Moscow. We have come to regard the Kremlin as the permanent seat of his power and we have grown almost comfortable with a menace which, though unspeakably evil, has had the redeeming virtues of constancy, predictability, and familiarity. Now the Devil has betrayed us by traveling abroad and worse still, by dispersing himself, turning up now here, now there, and in many places at once, with a devilish disregard for the laboriously constructed frontiers of ideology.

We are confronted with a complex and fluid world situation and we are not adapting ourselves to it. We are clinging to old myths in the face of new realities and we are seeking to escape the contradictions by narrowing the permissible bounds of public discussion, by relegating an increasing number of ideas and viewpoints to a growing category of "unthinkable thoughts." I believe that this tendency can and should be reversed, that it is within our ability, and unquestionably in our interests, to cut loose from established myths and to start thinking some "unthinkable thoughts" -- about the cold war and East-West relations, about the under-developed countries and particularly those in Latin America, about the changing nature of the Chinese Communist threat in Asia and about the festering war in Vietnam.

The master myth of the cold war is that the Communist bloc is a monolith composed of governments which are not really governments at all but organized conspiracies, divided among themselves perhaps in certain matters of tactics, but all equally resolute and implacable in their determination to destroy the free world.

I believe that the Communist world is indeed hostile to the free world in its general and long-term intentions but that the existence of this animosity in principle is far less important for our foreign policy than the great variations in its intensity and character both in time and among the individual members of the Communist bloc. Only if we recognize these variations, ranging from China which poses immediate threats to the free world to Poland and Yugoslavia which pose none, can we hope to act effectively upon the bloc and to turn its internal differences to our own advantage and to the advantage of those bloc countries which wish to maximize their independence. It is the responsibility of our national leaders both in the executive branch and in Congress, to acknowledge and act upon these realities, even at the cost of saying things which will not win immediate widespread enthusiasm.

'Normal' Dealings with Soviet Union

For a start, we can acknowledge the fact that the Soviet Union, though still a most formidable adversary, has ceased to be totally and implacably hostile to the West. It has shown a new willingness to enter mutually advantageous arrangements with the West and, thus far at least, to honor them. It has therefore become possible to divert some of our energies from the prosecution of the cold war to the relaxation of the cold war and to deal with the Soviet Union, for certain purposes, as a normal state with normal and traditional interests.

If we are to do these things effectively, we must distinguish between communism as an ideology and the power and policy of the Soviet state. It is not communism as a doctrine, or communism as it is practiced within the Soviet Union or within any other country, that threatens us. How the Soviet Union organizes its internal life, the gods and doctrines that it worships, are matters for the Soviet Union to determine. It is not Communist dogma as espoused within Russia but Communist imperialism that threatens us and other peoples of the non-Communist world. Insofar as a great nation mobilizes its power and resources for aggressive purposes, that nation, regardless of ideology, makes itself our enemy. Insofar as a nation is content to practice its doctrines within its own frontiers, that nation, however repugnant its ideology, is one with which we have no proper quarrel. We must deal with the Soviet Union as a great power, quite apart from differences of ideology. To the extent that the Soviet leaders abandon the global ambitions of Marxist ideology, in fact if not in words, it becomes possible for us to engage in normal relations with them, relations which probably cannot be close or trusting for many years to come but which can be gradually freed of the terror and the tensions of the cold war.

In our relations with the Russians, and indeed in our relations with all nations, we would do well to remember, and to act upon, the words of Pope John in the great Encyclical, *Pacem in Terris:* "It must be borne in mind," said Pope John, "that to proceed gradually is the law of life in all its expressions, therefore, in human institutions, too, it is not possible to renovate for the better except by working from within them, gradually.... Violence has always achieved *only* destruction, not construction, the kindling of passions, not their pacification, the accumulation of hate and ruin, not the reconciliation of the contending parties. And it has reduced men and parties to the difficult task of rebuilding, after sad experience, on the ruins of discord."

Communist Bloc Polycentrism

Important opportunities have been created for Western policy by the development of "polycentrism" in the Communist bloc. The Communist nations, as George Kennan has pointed out, are, like the Western nations, currently caught up in a crisis of indecision about their relations with countries outside their own ideological bloc. The choices open to the satellite states are limited but by no means insignificant. They can adhere slavishly to Soviet preferences or they can strike out on their own, within limits, to enter into mutually advantageous relations with the West.

Whether they do so, and to what extent, is to some extent at least within the power of the West to determine. If we persist in the view that all Communist regimes are equally hostile and equally threatening to the West, and that we can have no policy toward the "captive nations" except the eventual overthrow of their Communist regimes, then the West may enforce upon the Communist bloc a degree of unity which the Soviet Union has shown itself to be quite incapable of imposing -- just as Stalin in the early postwar years frightened the West into a degree of unity that it almost certainly could not have attained by its own unaided efforts. If, on the other hand, we are willing to reexamine the view that all Communist regimes are alike in the threat which they pose for the West -- a view which had a certain validity in Stalin's time --, then we may be able to exert an important influence on the course of events within a divided Communist world.

Victims of Our Own Convictions

We are to a great extent the victims, and the Soviets the bene-

ficiaries, of our own ideological convictions, and of the curious contradictions which they involve. We consider it a form of subversion of the free world, for example, when the Russians enter trade relations or conclude a consular convention or establish airline connections with a free country in Asia, Africa, or Latin America -- and to a certain extent we are right. On the other hand, when it is proposed that we adopt the same strategy in reverse -- by extending commercial credits to Poland or Yugoslavia, or by exchanging ambassadors with a Hungarian regime which has changed considerably in character since the revolution of 1956 -- then the same patriots who are so alarmed by Soviet activities in the free world charge our policy makers with "giving aid and comfort to the enemy" and with innumerable other categories of idiocy and immorality.

It is time that we resolved this contradiction and separated myth from reality. The myth is that every Communist state is an unmitigated evil and a relentless enemy of the free world; the reality is that some Communist regimes pose a threat to the free world while others pose little or none, and that if we will recognize these distinctions, we ourselves will be able to influence events in the Communist bloc in a way favorable to the security of the free world. "It could well be argued," writes George Kennan, "...that if the major Western powers had full freedom of movement in devising their own policies, it would be within their power to determine whether the Chinese view, or the Soviet view, or perhaps a view more liberal than either would ultimately prevail within the Communist camp."

There are numerous areas in which we can seek to reduce the tensions of the cold war and to bring a degree of normalcy into our relations with the Soviet Union and other Communist countries -- once we have resolved that it is safe and wise to do so. We have already taken important steps in this direction: the Antarctic and Austrian treaties and the nuclear test ban treaty, the broadening of East-West cultural and educational relations, and the expansion of trade.

Increased East-West Trade

On the basis of recent experience and present economic needs, there seems little likelihood of a spectacular increase in trade between Communist and Western countries, even if existing restrictions were to be relaxed. Free world trade with Communist countries has been increasing at a steady but unspectacular rate and it seems unlikely to be greatly accelerated because of the limited ability of the Communist countries to pay for increased imports. A modest increase in East-West trade may nonetheless serve as a modest instrument of East-West detente -- provided that we are able to overcome the myth that trade with Communist countries is a compact with the Devil and to recognize that, on the contrary, trade can serve as an effective and honorable means of advancing both peace and human welfare.

Whether we are able to make these philosophic adjustments or not, we cannot escape the fact that our efforts to devise a common Western trade policy are a palpable failure and that our allies are going to trade with the Communist bloc whether we like it or not. The world's major exporting nations are slowly but steadily increasing their trade with the Communist bloc and the bloc countries are showing themselves to be reliable customers. Since 1958 Western Europe has been increasing its exports to the East at the rate of about 7 percent a year, which is nearly the same rate at which its over-all world sales have been increasing.

West Germany is by far the leading Western nation in trade with the Sino-Soviet bloc. West German exports to bloc countries in 1962 were valued at $749.9 million. Britain was in second place -- although not a close second -- with exports to Communist countries amounting to $393 million in 1962. France followed with exports worth $313.4 million and the figure for the United States -- consisting largely of surplus food sales to Poland under Public Law 480 -- stood far below at $125.1 million.

Our allies have made it plain that they propose to expand this trade, in nonstrategic goods, wherever possible. West Germany in the last sixteen months has exchanged or agreed to exchange trade missions with every country in Eastern Europe except Albania. Britain has indicated that she will soon extend long-term credits to

Communist countries, breaching the five-year limit which the Western Allies have hitherto observed. In the light of these facts, it is difficult to see what effect the tight American trade restrictions have other than to deny the United States a substantial share of a profitable market.

Value of Trade in Reducing Tensions

The inability of the United States to prevent its partners from trading extensively with the Communist bloc is one good reason for relaxing our own restrictions, but there is a better reason: the potential value of trade -- a moderate volume of trade in nonstrategic items -- as an instrument for reducing world tensions and strengthening the foundations of peace. I do not think that trade or the nuclear test ban, or any other prospective East-West accommodation, will lead to a grand reconciliation that will end the cold war and usher in the brotherhood of man. At the most, the cumulative effect of all the agreements that are likely to be attainable in the foreseeable future will be the alleviation of the extreme tensions and animosities that threaten the world with nuclear devastation and the gradual conversion of the struggle between communism and the free world into a safer and more tolerable international rivalry, one which may be with us for years and decades to come but which need not be so terrifying and so costly as to distract the nations of the world from the creative pursuits of civilized societies.

There is little in history to justify the expectation that we can either win the cold war or end it immediately and completely. These are favored myths, respectively, of the American right and of the American left. They are, I believe, equal in their unreality and in their disregard for the feasibilities of history. We must disabuse ourselves of them and come to terms, at last, with the realities of a world in which neither good nor evil is absolute and in which those who move events and make history are those who have understood not how much but how little it is within our power to change.

Mr. President, in an address on February 18 at Bad Godesburg, the United States Ambassador to Germany, Mr. George McGhee, spoke eloquently and wisely about the character and prospects of relations between the Communist and the free worlds. I ask unanimous consent that Ambassador McGhee's address, "East-West Relations Today," be inserted in the Record at the end of my remarks.

Latin American Myths

Latin America is one of the areas of the world in which American policy is weakened by a growing divergency between old myths and new realities.

The crisis over the Panama Canal has been unnecessarily protracted for reasons of domestic politics and national pride and sensitivity on both sides -- for reasons, that is, of only marginal relevance to the merits of the dispute. I think the Panamanians have unquestionably been more emotional about the dispute than has the United States. I also think that there is less reason for emotionalism on the part of the United States than on the part of Panama. It is important for us to remember that the issue over the Canal is only one of a great many in which the United States is involved, and by no means the most important. For Panama, on the other hand, a small nation with a weak economy and an unstable government, the Canal is the preeminent factor in the nation's economy and in its foreign relations. Surely in a confrontation so unequal, it is not unreasonable to expect the United States to go a little farther than half way in the search for a fair settlement.

We Americans would do well, for a start, to divest ourselves of the silly notion that the issue with Panama is a test of our courage and resolve. I believe that the Cuban missile crisis of 1962, involving a confrontation with nuclear weapons and intercontinental missiles, was indeed a test of our courage, and we acquitted ourselves extremely well. I am unable to understand how a controversy with a small and poor country, with virtually no military capacity, can possibly be regarded as a test of our bravery and will to defend our interests. It takes stubbornness but not courage to reject the entreaties of the weak. The real test in Panama is not of our valor but of our wisdom and judgment and common sense.

We would also do well to disabuse ourselves of the myth that there is something morally sacred about the treaty of 1903. The fact of the matter is that the treaty was concluded under circumstances that reflect little credit on the United States. It was made possible by Panama's separation from Colombia, which probably could not have occurred at that time without the dispatch of United States warships to prevent the landing of Colombian troops on the isthmus to put down the Panamanian rebellion. The United States not only intervened in Columbia's internal affairs but did so in violation of a treaty concluded in 1846 under which the United States had *guaranteed* Colombian sovereignty over the isthmus. President Theodore Roosevelt, as he boasted, "took Panama," and proceeded to negotiate the Canal treaty with a compliant Panamanian regime. Panamanians contend that they were "shotgunned" into the treaty of 1903 as the price of United States protection against a possible effort by Colombia to recover the isthmus. The contention is not without substance.

It is not my purpose here to relate the events of sixty years ago but only to suggest that there is little basis for a posture of injured innocence and self-righteousness by either side and that we would do much better to resolve the issue on the basis of present realities rather than old myths.

The central reality is that the treaty of 1903 is in certain respects obsolete. The treaty has been revised only twice, in 1936 when the annual rental was raised from $250,000 to $430,000 and other modifications were made, and in 1955 when further changes were made, including an increase in the annual rental to $1.9 million, where it now stands. The Canal of course contributes far more to the Panamanian economy in the form of wages paid to Panamanian workers and purchases made in Panama. The fact remains, nonetheless, that the annual rental of $1.9 million is a modest sum and should probably be increased. There are other issues, relating to hiring policies for Panamanian workers in the Zone, the flying of flags, and other symbols of national pride and sovereignty. The basic problem about the treaty, however, is the exercise of American control over a part of the territory of Panama in this age of intense nationalist and anticolonialist feeling. Justly or not, the Panamanians feel that they are being treated as a colony, or a quasi-colony, of the United States, and this feeling is accentuated by the contrast between the standard of living of the Panamanians, with a per capita income of about $429 a year, and that of the Americans living in the Canal Zone, with a per capita income of $4,228 a year. It is the profound social and economic alienation between Panama and the Canal Zone, and its impact on the national feeling of the Panamanians, that underlies the current crisis.

No 'Dishonor' in Redress for Panama

Under these circumstances, it seems to me entirely proper and necessary for the United States to take the initiative in proposing new arrangements that would redress some of Panama's grievances against the treaty as it now stands. I see no reason -- certainly no reason of "weakness" or "dishonor" -- why the United States cannot put an end to the semantic debate over whether treaty revisions are to be "negotiated" or "discussed" by stating positively and clearly that it is prepared to negotiate revisions in the Canal treaty and to submit such changes as are made to the Senate for its advice and consent.

I think it is necessary for the United States to do this even though a commitment to revise the treaty may be widely criticized at home. It is the responsibility of the President and his advisers, in situations of this sort, to exercise their own best judgment as to where the national interest lies even though this may necessitate unpopular decisions.

An agreement to "negotiate" revisions is not an agreement to negotiate any particular revision. It would leave us completely free to determine what revisions, and how many revisions, we would be willing to accept. If there is any doubt about this, one can find ample reassurance in the proceedings at Geneva, where several years of "negotiations" for "general and complete disarmament" still leave us with the greatest arsenal of weapons in the history of the world.

Cuban Myths

The problem of Cuba is more difficult than that of Panama, and far more heavily burdened with the dead weight of old myths and prohibitions against "unthinkable thoughts." I think the time is overdue for a candid reevaluation of our Cuban policy even though it may lead to distasteful conclusions.

There are and have been three options open to the United States with respect to Cuba: first, the removal of the Castro regime by invading and occupying the island; second, an effort to weaken and ultimately bring down the regime by a policy of political and economic boycott; and finally, acceptance of the Communist regime as a disagreeable reality and annoyance but one which is not likely to be removed in the near future because of the unavailability of acceptable means of removing it.

The first option, invasion, has been tried in a half-hearted way and found wanting. It is generally acknowledged that the invasion and occupation of Cuba, besides violating our obligations as a member of the United Nations and of the Organization of American States, would have explosive consequences in Latin America and elsewhere and might precipitate a global nuclear war. I know of no responsible statesman who advocates this approach. It has been rejected by our Government and by public opinion and I think that, barring some grave provocation, it can be ruled out as a feasible policy for the United States.

Our Cuban Policy a 'Failure'

The approach which we have adopted has been the second of those mentioned, an effort to weaken and eventually bring down the Castro regime by a policy of political and economic boycott. This policy has taken the form of extensive restrictions against trade with Cuba by United States citizens, of the exclusion of Cuba from the inter-American system and efforts to secure Latin American support in isolating Cuba politically and economically, and of diplomatic efforts, backed by certain trade and aid sanctions, to persuade other free world countries to maintain economic boycotts against Cuba.

This policy, it now seems clear, has been a failure, and there is no reason to believe that it will succeed in the future. Our efforts to persuade our allies to terminate their trade with Cuba have been generally rebuffed. The prevailing attitude was perhaps best expressed by a British manufacturer who, in response to American criticisms of the sale of British buses to Cuba, said: "If America has a surplus of wheat, we have a surplus of buses."

In cutting off military assistance to Great Britain, France and Yugoslavia under the provisions of Section 620 of the Foreign Assistance Act of 1963, the United States has wielded a stuffed club. The amounts of aid involved are infinitesimal; the chances of gaining compliance with our boycott policy are nil; and the annoyance of the countries concerned may be considerable. What we terminated with respect to Britain and France, in fact, can hardly be called aid; it was more of a sales promotion program under which British and French military leaders were brought to the United States to see -- and to buy -- advanced American weapons. Terminating this program was in itself of little importance; Britain and France do not need our assistance. But terminating the program as a sanction against their trade with Cuba can have no real effect other than to create an illusory image of "toughness" for the benefit of our own people.

Trade with Cuba

Free world exports to Cuba have, on the whole, been declining over recent years, but over-all imports have been rising since 1961.

Mr. President, I ask unanimous consent that there be inserted in the *Record* at the conclusion of my remarks two tables provided by the Department of State showing the trade of selected free world countries with Cuba from 1958 to 1963. The figures shown in these tables provide little basis for expecting the early termination of free world trade with Cuba. The export table shows United States exports to Cuba in both 1962 and 1963 exceeding those of any other free world country. These American exports consisted almost entirely of ransom payments for the Bay of Pigs prisoners and should not be confused with normal trade.

I should like to make it very clear that I am not arguing against its feasibility. The effort has been made and all the fulminations we can utter about sanctions and retaliation against free world countries that trade with Cuba cannot long conceal the fact that the boycott policy is a failure.

Why Boycott Policy Failed

The boycott policy has not failed because of any "weakness" or "timidity" on the part of our Government. This charge, so frequently heard, is one of the most pernicious myths that have been inflicted on the American people. The boycott policy has failed because the United States is not omnipotent and cannot be. The basic reality to be faced is that it is simply not within our power to compel our allies to cut off their trade with Cuba, unless we are prepared to take drastic sanctions against them, such as closing our own markets to any foreign company that does business in Cuba, as proposed by Mr. Nixon. We can do this of course, but if we do, we ought first to be very sure as apparently Mr. Nixon is, that the Cuban boycott is more important than good relations with our closest allies. In fact, even the most drastic sanctions are as likely to be rewarded with defiance as with compliance. For practical purposes, all we can do is to ask other countries to take the measures with respect to Cuba which we recommend. We have done so and in some areas have been successful. In other areas, notably that of the economic boycott, we have asked for the full cooperation of other free world countries and it has been largely denied. It remains for us to decide whether we will respond with a sustained outburst of hollow and ill-tempered threats, all the while comforting ourselves with the myth that we can get anything we want if we only try hard enough -- or, in this case, shout loud enough --, or we can acknowledge the failure of our efforts and proceed, coolly and rationally, to reexamine the policies which we now pursue in relation to the interests they are intended to serve.

The prospects of bringing down the Castro regime by political and economic boycott have never been very good. Even if a general free world boycott were successfully applied against Cuba, it is unlikely that the Russians would refuse to carry the extra financial burden and thereby permit the only Communist regime in the Western hemisphere to collapse. We are thus compelled to recognize that there is probably no way of bringing down the Castro regime by means of economic pressures unless we are prepared to impose a blockade against *nonmilitary* shipments from the Soviet Union. Exactly such a policy has been recommended by some of our more reckless politicians, but the preponderance of informed opinion is that a blockade against Soviet shipments of *nonmilitary* supplies to Cuba would be extravagantly dangerous, carrying the strong possibility of a confrontation that could explode into nuclear war.

Castro Regime Not Intolerably Dangerous

Having ruled out military invasion and blockade, and recognizing the failure of the boycott policy, we are compelled to consider the third of the three options open to us with respect to Cuba: the acceptance of the continued existence of the Castro regime as a distasteful nuisance but not an intolerable danger so long as the nations of the hemisphere are prepared to meet their obligations of collective defense under the Rio Treaty.

In recent years we have become transfixed with Cuba, making it far more important in both our foreign relations and in our domestic life than its size and influence warrant. We have flattered a noisy but minor demagogue by treating him as if he were a Napoleonic menace. Communist Cuba has been a disruptive and subversive influence in Venezuela and other countries of the hemisphere, and there is no doubt that both we and our Latin American partners would be better off if the Castro regime did not exist. But it is important to bear in mind that, despite their best efforts, the Cuban Communists have not succeeded in subverting the hemisphere and that in Venezuela, for example, where communism has made a major effort to gain power through terrorism, it has been repudiated by a people who in a free election have committed themselves to the course of liberal democracy. It is necessary to weigh the desirability of an objective against the feasibility of its attainment, and when we do this with respect to Cuba, I think we are bound to conclude that Castro is a nuisance but not a grave threat to the United States and that he cannot be gotten rid of except by means that are wholly disproportionate to the objective. Cuban Communism does pose a grave threat to other Latin American countries, but this threat can be dealt with by prompt and vigorous use of the established procedures of the inter-American system against any act of aggression.

I think that we must abandon the myth that Cuban communism is a transitory menace that is going to collapse or disappear in the immediate future and face up to two basic realities about Cuba: first, that the Castro regime is not on the verge of collapse and is not likely to be overthrown by any policies which we are now pursuing or can reasonably undertake; and second, that the continued existence of the Castro regime, though inimical to our interests and policies, is not an insuperable obstacle to the attainment of our objectives, unless we make it so by permitting it to poison our politics at home and to divert us from more important tasks in the hemisphere.

- - - - - - - - - - - -

Violence in Latin America

The policy of the United States with respect to Latin America as a whole is predicated on the assumption that social revolution can be accomplished without violent upheaval. This is the guiding principle of the Alliance for Progress and it may in time be vindicated. We are entitled to hope so and it is wise and necessary for us to do all that we can to advance the prospects of peaceful and orderly reform.

At the same time, we must be under no illusions as to the extreme difficulty of uprooting long-established ruling oligarchies without disruptions involving lesser or greater degrees of violence. The historical odds are probably against the prospects of peaceful social revolution. There are places, of course, where it has occurred, and others where it seems likely to occur. In Latin America, the chances for such basic change by peaceful means seem bright in Colombia and Venezuela and certain other countries; in Mexico many basic changes have been made by peaceful means, but these came in the wake of a violent revolution. In other Latin American countries the power of ruling oligarchies is so solidly established and their ignorance so great that there seems little prospect of accomplishing economic growth or social reform by means short of the forceful overthrow of established authorities.

I am not predicting violent revolutions in Latin America or elsewhere. Still less am I advocating them. I wish only to suggest that violent social revolutions are a possibility in countries where feudal oligarchies resist all meaningful change by peaceful means. We must not, in our preference for the democratic procedures envisioned by the Charter of Punta del Este, close our minds to the possibility that democratic procedures may fail in certain countries and that where democracy does fail violent social convulsions may occur.

Possibility of Violent Revolution

We would do well, while continuing our efforts to promote peaceful change through the Alliance for Progress, to consider what our reactions might be in the event of the outbreak of genuine social revolution in one or more Latin American countries. Such a revolution did occur in Bolivia, and we accepted it calmly and sensibly. But what if a violent social revolution were to break out in one of the larger Latin American countries? Would we feel certain that it was Cuban or Soviet inspired? Would we wish to intervene on the side of established authority? Or would we be willing to tolerate or even support a revolution if it was seen to be not Communist but similar in nature to the Mexican revolution or the Nasser revolution in Egypt?

These are hypothetical questions and there is no readily available set of answers to them. But they are questions which we should be thinking about because they have to do with problems that could become real and urgent with great suddenness. We should be considering, for example, what groups in particular countries might conceivably lead revolutionary movements, and if we can identify them, we should be considering how we might com-

municate with them and influence them in such a way that their movements, if successful, will not pursue courses detrimental to our security and our interests.

- - - - - - - - - - - -

Myths on the Far East

The Far East is another area of the world in which American policy is handicapped by the divergence of old myths and new realities. Particularly with respect to China, an elaborate vocabulary of make-believe has become compulsory in both official and public discussion. We are committed, with respect to China and other areas in Asia, to inflexible policies of long standing from which we hesitate to depart because of the attribution to these policies of an aura of mystical sanctity. It may be that a thorough reevaluation of Far Eastern policies would lead us to the conclusion that they are sound and wise, or at least that they represent the best available options. It may be, on the other hand, that a reevaluation would point up the need for greater or lesser changes in our policies. The point is that, whatever the outcome of a re-thinking of policy might be, we have been unwilling to undertake it because of the fear of many government officials, undoubtedly well founded, that even the suggestion of new policies toward China or Viet Nam would provoke a vehement public outcry.

Relations with China Can Change

I do not think that the United States can or should recognize Communist China or acquiesce in its admission to the United Nations under present circumstances. It would be unwise to do so because there is nothing to be gained by it so long as the Peking regime maintains its attitude of implacable hostility toward the United States. I do not believe, however, that this state of affairs is necessarily permanent. As we have seen in our relations with Germany and Japan, hostility can give way in an astonishingly short time to close friendship; and as we have seen in our relations with China, the reverse can occur with equal speed. It is not impossible that in time our relations with China will change again, if not to friendship then perhaps to "competitive coexistence." It would therefore be an extremely useful thing if we could introduce an element of flexibility, or, more precisely, of the capacity to be flexible, into our relations with Communist China.

Only One China—Communist

We would do well, as former Assistant Secretary Hilsman has recommended, to maintain an "open door" to the possibility of improved relations with Communist China in the future. For a start we must jar open our minds to certain realities about China, of which the foremost is that there are not really "two Chinas" but only one, mainland China, and that it is ruled by Communists and likely to remain so for the indefinite future. Once we accept this fact, it becomes possible to reflect on the conditions under which it might be possible for us to enter into relatively normal relations with mainland China. One condition, of course, must be the abandonment by the Chinese Communists, tacitly if not explicitly, of their intention to conquer and incorporate Taiwan. This seems unlikely now, but far more surprising changes have occurred in politics, and it is quite possible that a new generation of leaders in Peking and Taipei may put a quiet end to the Chinese civil war, opening the possibility of entirely new patterns of international relations in the Far East.

Should such changes occur, they will open up important opportunities for American policy, and it is to be hoped that we will be able and willing to take advantage of them. It seems possible for example, that an atmosphere of reduced tensions in the Far East might make it possible to strengthen world peace by drawing mainland China into existing East-West agreements in such fields as disarmament, trade and educational exchange.

These are long-range prospects, which may or may not materialize. In the immediate future, we are confronted with possible changes in the Far East resulting from recent French diplomacy.

French recognition of Communist China, though untimely and carried out in a way that can hardly be considered friendly to the

United States, may nonetheless serve a constructive long-term purpose by unfreezing a situation in which many countries, none more than the United States, are committed to inflexible policies by long-established commitments and the pressures of domestic public opinion. One way or another, the French initiative may help generate a new situation in which the United States, as well as other countries, will find it possible to reevaluate its basic policies in the Far East.

Conflict in Viet Nam

The situation in Viet Nam poses a far more pressing need for a reevaluation of American policy. Other than withdrawal, which I do not think can be realistically considered under present circumstances, there are three options open to us in Viet Nam: first, the continuation of the anti-guerrilla war within South Viet Nam along with renewed American efforts to increase the military effectiveness of the South Vietnamese Army and the political effectiveness of the South Vietnamese Government; second, an attempt to end the war through negotiations for the neutralization of South Viet Nam or of both North and South Viet Nam; and finally, the expansion of the scale of the war, either by the direct commitment of large numbers of American troops or by equipping the South Vietnamese Army to attack North Vietnamese territory, possibly by means of commando-type operations from the sea or air.

It is difficult to see how a negotiation, under present military circumstances, could lead to the termination of the war under conditions that would preserve the freedom of South Viet Nam. It is extremely difficult for a party to a negotiation to achieve by diplomacy objectives which it has conspicuously failed to win by warfare. The hard fact of the matter is that our bargaining position is at present a weak one, and until the equation of advantages between the two sides has been substantially altered in our favor, there can be little prospect of a negotiated settlement which would secure the independence of a non-communist South Viet Nam.

Recent initiatives by France calling for the "neutralization" of Viet Nam have tended to confuse the situation without altering it in any fundamental way. France could perhaps play a constructive mediating role if she were willing to consult and cooperate with the United States. For somewhat obscure reasons, however, France has chosen to take an independent initiative. This is puzzling to Americans, who recall that the United States contributed $1.2 billion to France's war in Indochina of a decade ago, which was 70 percent of the total cost of the conflict. Whatever its motivation, the problem posed by French intervention in Southeast Asia is that while France may set off an unforeseeable chain of events, she is neither a major military nor economic force in the Far East and is therefore unlikely to be able to control or greatly influence the events which her initiative may precipitate.

It seems clear that there are only two realistic options open to us in Viet Nam in the immediate future: the expansion of the conflict in one way or another or a renewed effort to bolster the capacity of the South Vietnamese to prosecute the war successfully on

its present scale. The matter calls for thorough examination by responsible officials in the executive branch, and until they have had an opportunity to evaluate the contingencies and feasibilities of the options open to us, it seems to me that we have no choice but to support the South Vietnamese Government and Army by the most effective means available. Whatever specific policy decisions are made, it should be clear to all concerned that the United States will continue to meet its obligations and fulfill its commitments with respect to Viet Nam.

These, I believe, are some, although by no means all, of the issues of foreign policy in which it is essential to reevaluate longstanding ideas and commitments in the light of new and changing realities. In all the issues which I have discussed, American policy has to one degree or another been less effective than it might have been because of our national tendency to equate means with ends and therefore to attach a mythological sanctity to policies and practices which in themselves have no moral content or value except insofar as they contribute to the achievement of some valid national objective. I believe that we must try to overcome this excessive moralism, which binds us to regard new and unfamiliar ideas with fear and mistrust.

Too Much Caution and 'Shock'

We must dare to think about "unthinkable" things. We must learn to explore all of the options and possibilities that confront us in a complex and rapidly changing world. We must learn to welcome rather than fear the voices of dissent and not to recoil in horror whenever some heretic suggests that Castro may survive or that Khrushchev isn't as bad a fellow as Stalin was. We must overcome our susceptibility to "shock" -- a word which I wish could be banned from our newspapers and magazines and especially from the *Congressional Record*.

If Congress and public opinion are unduly susceptible to "shock", the Executive Branch, and particularly the Department of State, is subject to the malady of chronic and excessive caution. An effective foreign policy is one which concerns itself more with innovation abroad than with conciliation at home. A creative foreign policy -- as President Truman, for one, knew -- is not necessarily one which wins immediate general approval. It is sometimes necessary for leaders to do unpleasant and unpopular things, because, as Burke pointed out, the duty of the democratic politician to his constituents is not to comply with their every wish and preference but to give them the benefit of, and to be held responsible for, the exercise of his own best judgment.

We must dare to think about "unthinkable things," because when things become "unthinkable," thinking stops and action becomes mindless. If we are to disabuse ourselves of old myths and to act wisely and creatively upon the new realities of our time, we must think and talk about our problems with prefect freedom, remembering, as Woodrow Wilson said, that "The greatest freedom of speech is the greatest safety because, if a man is a fool, the best thing to do is to encourage him to advertise the fact by speaking."

Testimony by Experts at Fulbright Hearings on China

Following are statements by various experts who appeared March 8-30, 1966, before the Senate Foreign Relations Committee, chaired by Sen. J.W. Fulbright (D Ark.). The subject of the hearings was "U.S. Policy with Respect to Mainland China."

BARNETT STATEMENT

The following is the statement of A. Doak Barnett, professor of government and acting director of the East Asian Institute at Columbia University. Dr. Barnett was born in 1921 in Shanghai, China, and lived in China until 1936. He appeared before the Senate Foreign Relations Committee on March 8, 1966. (See p. 179)

Mr. Chairman and members of the committee, I would like first of all to express my very great appreciation for this opportunity to

meet with you and discuss some of the problems of the U.S. relations with China and to examine policy alternatives that, in my opinion, our Government should consider.

How to Deal with China

The question of how to deal with China is now -- and certainly will continue to be during the decade ahead -- one of the most crucial foreign policy issues facing us. It will demand not only firmness, determination, and commitment, but also flexibility, understanding, and patience. Rigid dogmatism cannot point the way toward sound policies. We need creative and imaginative thinking about a wide range of questions -- not only about how to contain and check China's pressures on its neighbors and how to achieve a more stable military balance in Asia, basic as these questions are, but also about how to avoid war, minimize conflict, and reduce tension; how to meet the multiple nonmilitary challenges which China poses; how to evolve policies which can exert a moderating influence on Peking's leaders; how to accommodate to Communist China's legitimate interests as a major power; how to reestablish a reasonable basis for contact and discourse between the United States and mainland China; how to create a broader consensus among non-Communist nations on reasonable approaches to dealing with the Chinese; and how over time to involve Communist China increasingly in more responsible roles in the general international community.

Areas of Inquiry

Mr. Chairman, you suggested to me that when initiating these hearings I attempt to outline briefly some of the broad areas of inquiry that the committee, the American Government, and the American people might well consider in any systematic effort to re-examine the problems of U.S. relations with China, and I will try to do this.

I hope that I will be given perhaps a little bit more time for my opening statement than may be normal in view of the fact that I am trying to deal with a very wide range of subjects here briefly.

It is my understanding that while the committee does intend, during the course of these hearings, to probe the interconnections between our policy toward China and the pressing problems that we now face in Vietnam, the intention is to examine China policy, also, in a broader and longer term perspective, and that is the kind of perspective that I have adopted primarily this morning.

You also invited me to present some of my own views on key issues and problems, and I consider it a privilege to have this opportunity to do so.

U.S. Posture Toward Communist China

I would like, right at the start, to state my own belief that there is a need for basic changes in the overall U.S. posture toward Communist China. For almost 17 years we have pursued a policy that might best be characterized as one aimed at containment and isolation of Communist China.

In my view, the element of containment -- using this term in a very broad sense to include both military and nonmilitary measures to block threats posed by China to its neighbors -- has been an essential part of our policy and has been, in some respects at least, fairly successful. Our power has played an important and necessary role in creating a counterbalance to Communist China's power in Asia, and we have contributed significantly to the task of gradually building stable non-Communist societies in areas that lie in China's shadow. But the U.S. attempt to isolate Communist China has been, in my opinion, unwise and, in a fundamental sense, unsuccessful, and it cannot, I believe, provide a basis for a sound, long-term policy that aims not only at containing and restraining Chinese power but also at reducing tensions, exerting a moderating influence on Peking, broadening the areas of non-Communist agreement on issues relating to China, and slowly involving Communist China in more normal patterns of international intercourse.

I strongly believe, therefore, that the time has come -- even though the United States is now engaged in a bitter struggle in Vietnam -- for our country to alter its posture toward Communist China and adopt a policy of containment but not isolation, a policy that would aim on the one hand at checking military or subversive threats and pressure emanating from Peking, but at the same time would aim at maximum contacts with and maximum involvement of the Chinese Communists in the international community.

Such a policy would involve continued commitments to help non-Communist regimes combat Communist subversion and insurrection, as in Vietnam, and continued pledges to defend areas on China's periphery, including Taiwan. But it would involve changes in many other aspects of our policies.

Proposals For Future U.S. Policies

While continuing to fulfill our pledge to defend Taiwan against attack, we should clearly and explicitly acknowledge the Chinese Communist regime as the de facto Government of the China mainland and state our desire to extend de jure recognition and exchange diplomatic representatives with Peking if and when it indicates that it would be prepared to reciprocate.

We should press in every way we can to encourage nonofficial contacts. We should, instead of embargoing all trade with the China mainland, restrict only trade in strategic items and encourage American businessmen to explore other opportunities for trade contacts. And within the United Nations we should work for the acceptance of some formula which would provide seats for both Communist China and Nationalist China. In taking these steps, we will have to do so in full recognition of the fact that Peking's initial reaction is almost certain to be negative and even hostile and that any changes in our posture will create some new problems. But we should take them, nevertheless, because initiatives on our part are clearly required if we are to work, however slowly, toward the long-term goal of a more stable, less-explosive situation in Asia and to explore the possibilities of trying to moderate Peking's policies.

Some people believe that a policy combining the differing elements I have suggested, that is, containment but also increased attempts to deal directly with Peking -- would involve contradictory and inconsistent elements. I would argue that, on the contrary, in terms of our long-term aims the seemingly contradictory elements would in fact be complementary and mutually reinforcing.

Others argue that a change of posture such as the one I have suggested might be interpreted as a sign of weakness and irresolution on our part, and therefore be dangerous, particularly if taken while we are engaged in a major struggle against Communist insurrection in Vietnam. I would argue that our commitments and actions in Vietnam make it wholly clear, to both friend and foe, that we are not acting out of weakness and that while we search for areas of possible agreement and accommodation we will also continue in our determination to protect the interests of ourselves and our friends, to oppose violence as a means of political change, and to assist in the growth of viable, progressive, non-Communist regimes, in Asia, as elsewhere.

Desirable Areas of Inquiry

I hope that later in our discussion we will have an opportunity to examine in more concrete terms some of the detailed aspects of our China policy, but before proceeding further perhaps I should try to outline briefly, in response to your suggestion, Mr. Chairman, some of the broad areas of inquiry that it would be desirable to cover in any examination of U.S. relations with China that attempts to probe background factors as well as immediate issues.

Briefly stated, I think it is necessary to examine: the historical background to the Chinese revolution, including both the general characteristics of the historic confrontation between China and the West and the causes of the rise of communism in China; the internal situation in Communist China since 1949, including the domestic political situation, recent trends, and possible changes in the future, and the state of the Chinese economy; and Communist China's general international position and foreign policy, with special attention to the Sino-Soviet split and China's military strength and potential.

I can do no more than make a few comments on each of these complicated subjects and I know you will be pursuing them all later, but if time permits I would like to do that much.

Historical Background

It is important, I think, to view recent developments in China and the present state of American-Chinese relations in some kind of historical perspective. The perspective of the policymaker must, of necessity, be very different from that of the historian, and analysis of the past does not necessarily provide answers to the urgent policy issues of the present. But unless one has some understanding of the broad forces that have been at work overtime, it is difficult to evolve a rational or coherent framework even for policies designed to meet immediate problems.

For roughly 2,000 years prior to the mid-19th century, China was the center of one of the great world civilizations. It was relatively isolated from comparable centers in Europe and elsewhere; it considered itself superior to all of its neighbors, and it played a role of unchallenged primacy in the world as Chinese leaders knew it.

Then, in the mid-19th century, its isolation was shattered by the restless, expanding, technologically superior nations of the West, and it became an arena for, and pawn of, competing imperial and colonial powers. The "Chinese revolution," if one uses this term in a broad sense, started at that time, in response to the traumatic impact of the West as well as to mounting domestic problems. It has been underway, therefore, for over a hundred years. In this revolution the Chinese people have been groping, painfully and slowly, to find effective means to modernize and develop their country, to build a strong, modern nation-state, and to reassert China's role in the world.

It is worth noting that to date there has been no extended period of peaceful relations between China and the Western World on the basis of reasonable equality. Before the mid-19th Century, the Chinese held a superior position and attempted, unsuccessfully, to fit the Western powers into its traditional imperial system of relations with subordinate states. During the next hundred years, the Western Powers held a superior position and attempted, also without great success, to fit China into the modern international system of relations. The still unresolved problem for the future is whether both China and the West can, in time, reach an acceptable peaceful accommodation within the modern nation-state system, on the basis of relationships in which the rights and obligations of both will be recognized.

Part of the legacy of the past hundred years is the intense nationalism and self-assertiveness that all Chinese -- whatever their ideology -- now feel. All Chinese, non-Communist as well as Communist, are now determined to end China's recent position of inferiority and see their country achieve recognized major power status.

There seems little doubt in my mind that in due time it will. The question is whether both China and the West can discover and reasonably accept roles for the Chinese in the international community as a whole -- or whether China and the West must face an indefinite period of dangerous confrontation and high risk of major military conflict.

One obviously cannot look at the Chinese historical background simply in the terms I have suggested, however.

China has been, and still is, undergoing not just a revolution, but more specifically a Communist revolution, led by men dedicated to promoting their own pattern of revolutionary struggle and change abroad as well as at home. It is important for us to understand the reasons for Communist success in China and the impact of their success elsewhere.

Reasons for Chinese Communist Successes

The explanations for Chinese Communist successes in the 1930's and 1940's are numerous, but I would say that the most important ones were the following.

One was the Sino-Japanese War, which had a shattering effect on China and helped to create a revolutionary situation.

Another was the failure of the non-Communist leaders in China to achieve unity in their own ranks, to define and pursue effective programs designed to cope with such basic problems as landlordism, inflation, and corruption, or to build a firm grassroots base of support -- a failure which in effect created a vacuum into which the Communists moved.

Still another was the Communists' own success in building an unprecedently disciplined and strong revolutionary organization, in appealing to nationalism and reformism especially during the war, in developing a shrewd revolutionary strategy, and in implementing their programs with determination and, whenever necessary, ruthlessness.

Peking's leaders now maintain that their experience provides a primary model for revolutions throughout the underdeveloped world.

It is a model calling for the creation of Communist-led peasant armies, the establishment of so-called liberated areas as bases for revolutionary struggle, the creation of broad anti-imperialist united fronts, and the overthrow of existing non-Communist regimes by violence. There is little doubt that the Chinese model has had, and will continue to have, an impact far beyond China's borders; revolutionary leaders in many parts of the world look to it for inspiration. We need, therefore, to understand it, and to grasp not only how it helps to explain Communist successes in China, but also how it may influence events elsewhere.

We should not, however, magnify its significance. Careful analysis indicates, I think, that the particular constellation of factors and forces which made it possible for Mao Tse-tung's strategy to succeed in China are not widely duplicated, and there are many reasons to believe that the Chinese model cannot be exported as easily as Mao and some of his colleagues have hoped. The available evidence also suggests that while the Chinese leaders would like to see their model widely emulated, their capacity to promote, and willingness and ability to support, Chinese-style revolutions elsewhere is definitely limited.

Developments In China Since 1949

The historical background is important, but obviously the primary focus of any inquiry into current problems must be on developments in China in the 17 years since Communist takeover. Communist China in 1966 is a very different country in many respects from China in 1949.

Perhaps the first thing that should be noted about the political situation in China is that the Communists have created a very strong totalitarian apparatus that has unified and exercises effective control over the entire China mainland, and they have used their power to promote uninterrupted revolution aimed at restructuring the nation's economy, social structure, and system of values.

While the impact of the regime has been harsh and painful for millions of Chinese, the Communists have built a strong base of organized support, partly on the basis of appeals to nationalism as well as promises of future accomplishments. They have also demonstrated a remarkable capacity to make and implement decisions and an impressive ability to mobilize people and resources. Not surprisingly, however, there are many tensions in the society and, in my opinion, fairly widespread -- even though largely unarticulated -- dissatisfaction with numerous Communist policies and methods of rule. But there is no significant organized opposition and no foreseeable prospect of its developing. In short, the regime is not a passing phenomenon. In time it may change its character, but it will continue to exist, as we will continue to have to deal with it, for the predictable future.

Possible Future Policies of China

There are some important questions one can raise, however, about the future. I believe that among the leaders in China there are significant differences on policies, under the surface -- especially differences regarding domestic policies but some of them are relevant to foreign policy issues as well -- and that one can differentiate between groups that might be labeled the technical bureaucrats or managers and the specialists in power, politics, and ideology.

I further believe that these differences are reflected, even today, in the complex mixture of policies in China, and that in the future they are likely to become increasingly important, especially after the death of Mao.

The biggest question about the future arises from the fact that Communist China is on the verge of an historic transition period in which virtually the entire top leadership will pass from the scene in a relatively brief period of time. To date the unity as well as longevity of the Chinese Communist leaders has been remarkable, but what has been an asset to the regime in the past is now becoming a liability, as the leaders steadily age and resist bringing younger men into the top inner circle.

When Mao and other top leaders die, therefore, I would expect China to enter a period in which there could be a great deal more fluidity and uncertainty about both leaders and policies than in recent years. It would be reasonable to expect, I think, that the outcome of the competition between leaders and policies that is likely to occur, and the resulting balance between what one might call radicals and moderates will be definitely influenced by the perceptions that the new leaders have of the international environment as it affects China. While it may not be possible for outsiders to exert very much influence on the outcome, our hope, certainly, should be that the balance will in time shift in favor of technical bureaucrats promoting relatively moderate policies.

Review of China's Economic Performance

The economic performance of the Chinese Communist regime to date has been a very mixed one, characterized by some notable successes, some serious failures, and some basic unanswered questions. When the Chinese Communists first came to power they were impressively successful in bringing order out of economic chaos, and in initiating an ambitious development program. During their first 5-year plan, under a Stalinist-type program, China's annual increase in GNP -- about 6 or 7 percent -- was as rapid or more rapid than that of any other important underdeveloped nation at the time. But the momentum of growth started to decline by 1957, the last year of the first plan -- as a result of the lag in agricultural output, the steady increase in population, and the ending of Soviet credits.

And in 1958 Peking's leaders embarked on their radical and reckless Great Leap Forward and commune program, hoping to achieve the impossible by unprecedented political and ideological mobilization.

The failures of the Leap produced an economic crisis of major proportions in China, which lasted from 1959 through 1961. The result, in effect, was a Communist version of a great depression. It compelled the regime to abandon many of its most extreme policies and ambitious goals, and Peking redefined its economic policies to include some sensible elements, showing realism and pragmatism.

Emphasis was placed on the need to promote agriculture, various sorts of incentives were restored, needed food was imported from the West, major industrial projects were postponed, and in general more modest goals were adopted.

Since 1962 there has been a slow but steady recovery of both agricultural and industrial production in China, and today overall Chinese output is comparable to what it was just before the Leap -- although it is still not that high in per capita terms. The primary stress on development agriculture continues, and its results, plus continuing grain imports, have greatly eased the food situation.

This year a new 5-year plan, the third, has begun and even though no details on the plan have yet been published, undoubtedly there is renewed growth in industry -- although at a more gradual pace than in earlier years.

In any overall assessment of the Chinese economy since 1949, several things would have to be noted. The Communists have not yet converted China into a major industrial power, but they have begun to build a significant industrial base.

At one point, in 1960, steel output was claimed to be 18 million tons; production now is below peak capacity but is probably between 8 and 10 million tons. Moreover, since the regime decides how output will be used, current production fully supports the Nation's military power and further industrialization. There has been no appreciable overall increase in living standards in China since 1949, but, except during the worst post-Leap years, the regime has met the population's minimum requirements, distributed available goods fairly equitably, and kept the economy running -- a not insignificant accomplishment in China.

However, the Communists have not found panaceas capable of rapidly solving the Nation's most basic economic problems. Agriculture continues to lag, and it will take time for present improvement

programs to change the situation. And the population steadily rises; a birth control program has been initiated, but quick results cannot be expected.

As a consequence of the Sino-Soviet split, and the ending of Soviet technical assistance as well as credits, the Chinese Communists have decided to glorify the virtues of economic "self-reliance."

On a more practical level, however, they have pragmatically adapted to the changed situation and have done all they could to expand trade with Japan and a variety of Western nations. As a result, Communist China's international economic orientation has fundamentally changed, and now a majority of its trade is with the non-Communist world. Even though to date this fact has not greatly affected Peking's overall foreign policy, the shift has slowly created new and diversified patterns of relations which could be of some significance over time.

Foreign Policy

In examining Peking's general foreign policy, the first thing to note is that China's leaders obviously have very ambitious long-term goals. Moved by intense nationalism, they aim to build a strong base of power at home and to strengthen China's security; they also hope to recover what they consider to be "lost territories" (including Taiwan); and they are determined to play the role of a major power on the world stage.

At the present time, they view the United States as the major obstacle and threat to many of their aims and interests -- and call, therefore, for the removal of American power from Asia -- but they also regard the Soviet Union at present as a serious obstacle to Chinese aspirations and therefore compete with it, too, whenever, and wherever feasible.

As first generation revolutionary leaders, and true believers in the Maoist version of Marxism-Leninism, Peking's leaders are also dedicated to the promotion of revolutionary struggles, especially in the underdeveloped world. Their public pronouncements now tend to concentrate on this aim and in at least some areas, such as Vietnam, they are prepared to give significant support to revolutionary forces, even though they have avoided direct Chinese military intervention.

While it is important to recognize Peking's ambitious goals, it is equally important to note that, on the basis of available evidence and Communist China's performance to date, the Chinese Communists do not appear to think primarily in terms of spreading their influence through direct military and territorial expansion; they appear to recognize the limits to their capabilities for military action outside of China's borders; they have usually been quite realistic in assessing the power balance in concrete situations; they have generally been calculating and even cautious in avoiding military "adventurism" and limiting their risks; they have tended to think in long-range terms about their most ambitious goals; and they have repeatedly been flexible and pragmatic (at least until recently) in adapting their strategy and tactics to fit changing situations in pursuit of their short-run goals.

If one analyzes the Chinese Communists' overall foreign policy strategy since 1949, one can identify at least three major periods in which their approach to the outside world has been distinctive. In the period immediately after 1949, Peking -- like Moscow at the time -- adopted a militant posture of struggle against the entire non-Communist world and called for revolutions wherever possible in the underdeveloped countries.

By contrast, in the mid-1950's, during the so-called Bandung period, it adopted a much more moderate and flexible strategy and promoted friendly relations with a wide variety of non-Communist countries, especially in the underdeveloped world.

Then, in the late 1950's it shifted back to a militant posture and renewed its calls for worldwide revolutionary struggle. Further shifts of this sort are certainly possible, in the future as in the past.

Even in the recent period of militancy, moreover, Peking's doctrinaire and rigid ideological statements have not fully represented Chinese Communist policies, which in practice have included a variety of elements. In fact, even its major ideological statements on strategy have not been wholly consistent. For example, while Peking's leaders have sounded the trumpet for "people's wars" wherever feasible and for the mobilization of the "rural areas of the world" (the underdeveloped nations) against the "cities of the world" (North America and Western Europe), at the same time they have called for closer links with many countries in the so-called intermediate zone -- including Japan and many Western countries -- since their practical requirements, dictated by economic considerations, make it seem desirable to promote trade and other contacts with these nations.

Possibility of Change

On balance, nevertheless, Peking's primary stress in the most recent period has been a revolutionary militancy. But developments of recent months must have raised questions in the minds of at least some of the policy planners in Peking as to whether they should continue present policies or consider a new shift in overall foreign policy strategy.

Where the Chinese Communists have been dogmatically and rigidly militant in the recent period, they have suffered a series of major setbacks and policy defeats -- in relations with the Soviet Union, at the Algiers Conference last fall, and in such widely scattered countries as Indonesia, Cuba, and Ghana. It seems probable also, that Peking's leaders misestimated the likely extent of American involvement and commitment in Vietnam.

Recent events demonstrate, in short, that Peking's ability to manipulate or control even those situations where receptivity to Chinese influence has been greatest is severely limited. It remains to be seen whether Peking's leaders will grasp this fact and modify their policies as a result. Mao and some other top leaders may well resist doing so. But changes in Chinese policies are certainly within the realm of possibility -- after Mao's death if not before.

What is required, it seems to me, to maximize the possibility of a desirable sort of shift in Peking's posture and policies, is a combination of two elements: developments in Vietnam as well as elsewhere that will help to convince Chinese Communist leaders that excessive militancy is counterproductive, but at the same time indications in the general international environment, as they see it, that there are other reasonable and promising policy options -- that they can see some possibility of expanding China's role in international affairs and achieving at least some of China's legitimate aspirations by moderate rather than militant means.

In any careful examination of Communist China's international role, two subjects certainly deserve special attention: the Sino-Soviet dispute and its implications for the rest of the world, and China's military position and potential.

Sino-Soviet Dispute

The Sino-Soviet dispute as it has evolved in recent years is clearly one of the most important developments in the international politics of the 1960's -- just as the formation of the Sino-Soviet alliance was in the 1950's. There can be no doubt that the conflicts between Peking and Moscow now are very real, very bitter, and very deep. The dispute has involved basic clashes of national interests as well as major ideological differences, and it has resulted in worldwide competition between the two countries.

In a fundamental sense the Sino-Soviet dispute has weakened Peking's international position, which has been to our advantage in many respects, since it imposes increased restraints on the Chinese Communist regime. But not all of the results of the dispute have been good from our point of view. It appears, for example, to have been a significant factor reinforcing Peking's tendency in recent years to maintain a highly militant posture.

We cannot, moreover, rely on the dispute to solve our own basic problems in relations with the Chinese. In certain situations, Soviet interests and policies may run parallel to ours, as appears to be the case even in Vietnam today, to a very limited degree. But we cannot expect such parallelism to be dependable or believe that it will

result -- as some suggest -- in a kind of Soviet-American anti-Chinese axis. Even when a degree of parellelism does exist, it cannot be expected to resolve all the difficult problems of dealing with the Chinese. Furthermore, although it is difficult to see in the predictable future any full restoration of the type of Sino-Soviet relationship that existed in the early 1950's, it is certainly possible that Communist China, particularly under new leaders, might decide to try to repair at least some of the damage that has been done to the alliance in recent years. In any case, the United States will itself have to work toward a solution of at least some of our problems with Communist China; the Sino-Soviet dispute will not solve them for us.

China's Military Position and Potential

Turning to the question of Communist China's military position, several things should be noted. First of all, the Peking regime has developed China into a significant military power, with large, modernized, conventional land forces and a sizable air force. However, these forces appear to be designed mainly for defense, and Peking lacks many of the prerequisites for successful operation outside of China against the forces of a major power such as the United States. The strength of Communist China's military establishment far exceeds that of its Asian neighbors, though, and its mere existence argues for the maintenance of adequate counterbalancing forces in Asia, which at the present time must be provided largely by the United States.

Despite Peking's formal entrance into the "nuclear club" and despite the fact that Communist China will probably acquire some sort of missile delivery system in the not distant future, the Chinese Communists are not close to achieving superpower status.

For the predictable future, therefore, Peking's leaders are likely to use China's limited nuclear arsenal primarily for political purposes -- although they doubtless also hope that they will be able to deter and cancel out the significance of American nuclear power in Asia.

Peking's leaders will probably continue to be sensitive to the actual balance of military strength, and reluctant to take excessive risks; for a while, in fact, the vulnerability of their embryonic nuclear establishment may actually impose additional restraints on them.

However, it would be a dangerous error to conclude that Communist China would not risk major war if it genuinely felt that its vital interests were threatened. In regard to Vietnam particularly, there is considerable evidence, I believe, that while Peking hopes to avoid any major conflict with the United States it fears that American escalation will create situations demanding escalation on the Chinese side, which could lead to major conflict.

In recent months, in fact, Peking has repeatedly warned its own people of the dangers of American attacks and major war, and there appears to be a genuine apprehension that this may take place. No one can say with certainty what actions might provoke an increased Chinese response. Since Peking appears to view North Vietnam, like North Korea, as a vital buffer area, it is likely that if the Chinese concluded there was a major threat to the existence of the North Vietnamese regime, the result could be large-scale, direct Chinese intervention. There is no guarantee, however, that even less drastic forms of American escalation -- such as bombing of North Vietnam's major cities -- might not impel the Chinese to escalate their involvement in smaller ways which might lead to much higher risks of direct American-Chinese clashes that are not desired by either side.

In view of this uncertainty, it is essential that the United States exercise great restraint in the use of its power, especially in North Vietnam, and demonstrate by deeds as well as words that we are determined to avoid provoking any direct American-Chinese conflict.

Change in U.S. China Policy

Let me, at this point, return again to questions relating to U.S. policy.

On February 23, President Johnson clearly stated that our desire is to avoid major conflict with China. "Some ask," he said, "about the risks of wider war, perhaps against the vast land armies of Red China. And again, the answer is 'No.' Never by any act of ours -- and not if there's any reason left behind the wild words from Peking. We have threatened no one, and we will not. We seek the end of no regime, and we will not." He declared that we will employ a "measured use of force," with "prudent firmness," and that "there will not be a mindless escalation."

This is a wise posture for us to adopt -- although to insure against major war resulting from miscalculation we must firmly hold the line against further escalation in practice as well as theory. This stand is excellent, as far as it goes. But in my opinion we should go still further, especially in regard to policy toward China, and, as I suggested earlier, we should alter our basic posture toward the Chinese Communist regime from one of containment plus isolation to one of containment without isolation.

I indicated earlier that such a change of posture would call for re-examination of many specific aspects of our current policy toward China, and I would like now to make just a few comments on some of these.

The China Issue In The UN

The China issue in the United Nations is in many respects an urgent question, since unless we can soon evolve a new and sounder position on this issue, we are likely to be defeated in the General Assembly, and then our entire policy of isolation of Peking will begin to unravel as a result of a major political defeat, even before we can, on our own initiative, attempt to redefine our posture.

Last fall, we were barely able to get enough votes to sustain our position. Conceivably we might do so once or twice again; but it is equally conceivable that next fall the General Assembly might, despite our opposition, vote to seat Peking in the present China seat occupied by the Chinese Nationalist regime. If this takes place there is little likelihood that the Nationalists could later be brought back into the United Nations, since this would then be a question of admitting a new member, which is subject to the veto.

It would be to our interest, therefore, to take the initiative in the General Assembly in promoting a solution in which the Assembly would declare that there are now two successor states ruling the territory of the original China which joined the United Nations when it was formed in 1945, and that both should have seats in the Assembly. Neither the Chinese Communists nor the Chinese Nationalists are presently willing to accept such a solution, and conceivably both might boycott the United Nations for a period of time, if such a solution were adopted. Nevertheless, it is a realistic and reasonable position for the international community as a whole to adopt, and I believe that, if it were adopted, there would be numerous pressures operating over time to induce Peking and Taipei eventually to re-examine their positions and consider accepting seats even under these conditions.

If and when Communist China does assume a seat in the United Nations, its initial impact is likely to be disruptive, but I firmly believe that over the long run it is nonetheless desirable to involve Peking in this complicated political arena where it will have to deal on a day-to-day basis with such a wide variety of countries and issues. It will soon learn, I think, that dogmatic arrogance will result only in self-isolation and that even a major nation must make compromises to operate with any success in the present world community.

Foreseeable Modification of U.S. Taiwan Policy

A shift of American policy on the United Nations issue -- and, in fact, any significant change in our posture toward Peking -- will inevitably require some modification of our policy toward the Nationalist regime on Taiwan. For many reasons -- political, strategic, and moral -- we should continue defending Taiwan against attack and should firmly support the principle of self-determination in regard to the 13 million inhabitants of the island. But we will not be able to continue sustaining the fiction that the Nationalist regime is the government of mainland China.

Our view of the Nationalist regime should be one in which we recognize it as the legal government of the territories it now oc-

cupies, essentially Taiwan and the Pescadores, rather than as the government of all China; this, one might note, is essentially the position which the Japanese Government already maintains in regard to the Nationalists. We should do all we can to obtain representation for the Taipei regime in the United Nations and to urge the international community to accept and support it as the government of its present population and territory. But we cannot indefinitely sustain the fiction that it is the government of all China.

Desirability of Contacts

The desirability of increased unofficial contacts with Communist China has already been accepted, at least to a limited degree, by the U.S. Government, and there is now a sizable number of American newsmen, and some doctors and medical scientists, who would be permitted to visit mainland China if the Chinese Communists would grant them visas. The present obstacles to limited contacts, in short, are created by Peking, not by us. But despite Peking's current intransigence, we should continue searching for every possible opportunity for contact, in the hope that Peking will eventually modify its present stand, and should encourage scholars, businessmen, and others, as well as newsmen and doctors, to try to visit mainland China.

As a part of our effort to increase unofficial contacts with Communist China we should, in my opinion, end our embargo on all trade and permit trade in nonstrategic items. The present significance of our embargo, it should be stressed, is wholly symbolic, since no other major trading nation maintains such an embargo, and Peking is able, therefore, to purchase in Japan, Germany, England, or elsewhere any goods that are denied to it by us. The ending of our embargo might well be largely symbolic, too, since the Chinese Communists are likely to prefer trading with countries other than the United States. Nevertheless, it is conceivable that over time some limited trade contacts might develop, and be desirable from our point of view.

De Facto Recognition

The question of de jure recognition of Communist China -- which in some discussions of China policy is given more attention than it deserves -- is really a question for the future rather than the present. Until Peking indicates a willingness to exchange diplomatic representatives with us, there are no strong arguments for our unilaterally extending official recognition that would not be reciprocated.

Our aim, certainly should be to work toward eventual establishment of normal diplomatic relations, but it is likely to be some time -- even if we alter our own overall position -- before that is possible. We can and should, however, clearly indicate now -- in much more explicit fashion than we have to date -- that we do recognize the Peking regime in a de facto sense. One might argue that our frequent ambassadorial meetings with the Chinese Communists in Warsaw already constitute a form of de facto recognition, but officially we have refused to acknowledge any sort of recognition -- de jure or de facto -- and we should now do so.

American Public Opinion

No discussion of China policy would be complete without at least a word on American public opinion. Although there are many persons in the United States -- in the Government, in universities, and elsewhere -- who are relatively well informed about Communist China, there is no doubt that the American people as a whole know far too little about China, or about the problems of evolving effective policies to deal with it. At the same time, issues relating to China policy have been among the most emotional in American public life ever since the late 1940's. It is probably fair to say that there has been less responsible public discussion of China policy than of any other foreign policy issue of comparable importance. I believe, therefore, that the holding of these hearings is of very great importance, and I hope that they will stimulate nationwide interest and will encourage widespread discussion of U.S. policy toward China.

It is sometimes assumed that, because issues relating to China policy have tended to be viewed emotionally, it has not been politically wise to discuss them. I do not really know to what extent this has been true in the past, or to what extent it has inhibited responsible public debate. I do believe, however, that public opinion has been slowly changing and is increasingly receptive to a reexamination of China policy. In support of this view, I would like to call your attention to a book just published, called "The American People and China." It is written by T. A. Steele, formerly of the New York Herald-Tribune, and published by the Council on Foreign Relations as part of its broad study, which will result in almost a dozen books, on the United States and China in World Affairs. Steele concludes that "American public opinion would, on the whole, welcome a public reappraisal in Congress and among the people, of our China policy" and he also concludes that public opinion would be responsive to both congressional and Presidential leadership on this issue. I believe he is right, and I hope, therefore, that these hearings will mark the start of the most important public reexamination of China policy since the Communist takeover of China in 1949.

FAIRBANK STATEMENT

The following is the statement of John K. Fairbank, professor of history and director of the East Asian Research Center at Harvard University. He appeared before the Committee on March 10, 1966. (See p. 179)

I greatly appreciate this opportunity. I have read the testimony of Mr. Barnett in the earlier meeting and I generally agree with it. I propose this morning to pursue certain historical aspects which I think might make a contribution to our general perspective on the origins of the Chinese attitude toward the West and so I would like to present this condensed statement as the basis for further discussion.

China Unrealistic About U.S.

Dealing with the Peking rulers is so frustrating because they are so implacably doctrinaire. They call us all lackeys of "Wall Street capitalist imperialism," lumping together indiscriminately Democrats and Republicans, professors and public servants, even the executive and legislative branches, all of us due for extinction by the laws of Marxist history.

Peking is not only unrealistic about us, Chairman Mao even thinks of himself as the successor to Marx, Lenin, and Stalin. Whereas in actual fact, as the ruler of China, he is much more the successor of the emperors who ruled at Peking until 1912 when Mao was already 18 years of age.

To hear the Peking leaders talk you would think they were an offshoot of European socialism. Actually the problems they face and the methods they use are in large part inherited from Chinese history.

We Americans talk every day about our Founding Fathers of the 18th century. Our Founding Fathers lived in the period of the Emperor Ch'ien-lung, who ruled for 60 years at the height of the 2,000-year development of imperial monarchy. Chairman Mao doesn't seem to know it, but he owes something of his style and world view to his predecessors in Peking in ages past. Since we have now given up calling communism a great international monolith, everywhere and always the same, it is high time for us to examine the Chineseness which is now showing through the communism in Peking.

I am a professional historian but we all know that everybody is his own historian, and history can be cited selectively on all sides of every question. I think we need more perspective on the Chinese style of political behavior. What did the world look like from Peking? How was power held there down to 1912, within the lifetime of many of us? How did Peking handle her foreign relations, and what kind of heritage is operating today in Peking's motives and methods toward the outside world?

China's Feeling of Superiority

I imagine we would all agree on a first point -- China's remarkable feeling of superiority. Here was a very big, ancient, isolated, unified, and self-sufficient empire, stretching from the latitude of Hudson's Bay to Cuba or from the Baltic Sea to the Sahara Desert, with a great deal of domestic commerce to meet its needs, cut off from west Asia by the high mountains and deserts of central Asia and thus isolated throughout most of its history, preserving a continuity of development in the same area over some 3,000 or 4,000 years, during most of which time the Chinese state has been a unified entity.

As we might expect, this biggest, most isolated and distinctive, most long-continued culture and society developed a strong tendency to look inward, an attitude of ethnocentrism or Sinocentrism, China being the center of the known world and of civilization, the non-Chinese being peripheral and inferior, China being superior to all foreign regions.

It is fascinating to note how this cultural isolation is still reinforced by the Chinese writing system. Because it uses ideographic characters, it cannot easily take in foreign words by sound but only by representing the foreign ideas in Chinese characters, yet the Chinese characters have their own meaning already.

Our current research finds that foreign ideas have come into Chinese most easily when the Chinese have already had the same general idea. The writing system makes for continuity and inertia in Chinese ways. Unlike Japan, Korea, or Vietnam, who all had a phonetic writing system combined with Chinese characters, the Chinese cannot take in foreign words purely by transcribing their sound even today.

A second point is that the old Peking rulers were the custodians and propagators of a true teaching, the Confucian classical doctrines of social order, an orthodoxy which told every man how to behave in his proper place and kept the social pyramid intact with the Emperor on top. The Emperor was himself the high priest of a cult of social order. The three main bonds of the Confucian social order were the filial piety of children to their superior parents, the admirable devotion of wives to their superior husbands, the loyalty of scholar-officials to their superior, the Emperor.

This system did not believe in the equality of all men, which was obviously untrue. It believed in selecting the talented, training them in the orthodoxy, and promoting them as officials to keep the populace under control and maintain the system. We need not labor the point that China today still has a ruling class selected for their abilities who propagate a true teaching under a sage ruler and strive to keep the various social classes in order.

The Myth of Rule-By-Virtue

If we try to generalize about the ideological sanction for holding power in China, I think we must conclude that China was ruled by a great Confucian political fiction, the myth of rule-by-virtue. According to this, the right conduct of a superior man, acting according to the correct principles, set an example which moved others and commanded their respect and allegiance. In particular, the Emperor's right conduct, the most perfect example among mankind, was thought to exert and influence over all beholders. His virtuous conduct commanded their loyalty, providing they also understand the correct principles of conduct as laid down in the classics. Persons too uneducated to be so moved could, of course, be dealt with by rewards and punishments.

This national myth of rule-by-virtue fills the Chinese historical record. It corresponded in political life, I suppose, to the Western concept of the supremacy of law and the natural rights of the individual and his civil liberties under law, which I take to be still one of our chief articles of faith, including the idea of self-determination for nations. Ancient China never developed these concepts of supremacy of law and natural rights or civil liberties. Instead it spread the Confucian faith as to proper conduct in all relationships and so reinforced the ruler's claim that he ruled by his virtuous example.

In their foreign relations the Chinese rulers down to 1912 extended their domestic doctrines across their frontiers and applied the national myth of rule-by-virtue to their foreign relations. Foreign rulers could have contact with the Peking monarch only by sending tribute to him and having their envoys perform the three kneelings and nine prostrations of the kowtow ritual. This elaborate and prolonged ceremony, kneeling and prostrating oneself at command in front of the emperor -- quite a lot of exercise -- was absolutely insisted upon by the court to preserve the image of China's superiority and show the foreigner his proper place in the world hierarchy. It became well established that all foreign relations must be tributary relations, reinforcing the myth of Chinese supremacy and particularly the myth that foreign rulers were attracted by emperor's virtue and "turned toward him" to offer their submission to the center of civilization. This grandiose concept reminds one of other ancient kings. The interesting thing is that the Chinese state was able to preserve it intact down to this century. The last tribute mission came from Nepal in 1908.

When China was weak, she could still maintain the fiction of supremacy by maintaining the rituals and the written records.

For example, 3,000 Mongol horsemen might come to Peking on a so-called annual tribute mission, being royally entertained and given expensive gifts at great cost to the Government, having as much fun as a Shriner's convention and letting the Chinese court call it tribute just to keep its fictions intact. In short, the tribute system was sometimes maintained by giving gifts.

The long record of Chinese foreign relations shows the importance attached to the political myths of China's superiority and rule by virtue. Maintaining this ideological orthodoxy in written form helped the emperor keep power in fact, because the recorded "facts" sustained the theory. It was like the advertisement for paint -- "Save the surface (or the record) and you save all."

We can conclude, I think, that the ideological component of power in China has been proportionately greater than in the West. Calling everything by its orthodox name helped keep things in order. The emperors were constantly spelling out the true doctrines, having them read in the Confucian temples and studied by all scholars. Heterodoxy and deviation could not be permitted, or if they did exist, could not be acknowledged to exist.

Even when the foreigners were more powerful, the myth of China's superiority had to be solemnly recorded and preserved in ritual. This stress on orthodoxy strikes one today when Peking is continuing its nationwide indoctrination in Chairman Mao's true teachings.

Applying all this background to the present moment, I suggest we should not get too excited over Peking's vast blueprints for the onward course of the Maoist revolution. Some American commentators who really ought to know better have overreacted to the visionary blueprint of world revolution put out by Lin Piao last September in Peking (about the strangling of the world's advanced countries or "cities" from the underdeveloped countries or "countryside.") This was, I think, a reassertion of faith, that the Chinese Communists own parochial example of rural-based revolution is the model for the rest of the underdeveloped world to emulate. It was put out mainly as compensation for China's recent defeats in many parts of the globe.

To compare it to Hitler's "Mein Kampf" would be quite misleading. Rule-by-virtue required that the rulers proclaim their true teaching, claiming that it will still win the world even if they themselves are too weak to support it in practice.

China's Modern Disaster

The disaster that hit China in the 19th century is one of the most comprehensive any people ever experienced. The ancient tradition of China's superiority, plus this modern disaster, has undoubtedly produced one first-class case of frustration. It cannot seem right that a civilization once at the top should have been brought so low.

The 19th century disaster began with a great population increase during the peaceful 18th century, a consequent weakening of administrative efficiency and maybe some popular demoralization, evident in the beginning of opium smoking.

In the Opium War of 1840 the Chinese were fighting against the opium trade, conducted by both foreigners and Chinese, while the British were fighting in the broad sense against the tribute system, demanding that China drop her claim to superiority and join the modern international trading world, the same thing we are waiting for today more than a century later.

The Opium War and the unequal treaties in the 1840's gave our merchants and missionaries a privileged status as agents of "westernization" in the Chinese treaty ports. Throughout the next century, Western influence gradually disintegrated the old Chinese civilization. As the disaster gained momentum, Western gunboats proved that China had to have scientific technology, and then had to have Western industries, for which it was necessary to have Western learning, and eventually Western institutions and even a Western type of government.

The prestige of the Confucian classics evaporated. The Confucian type of a family structure began to crack. China's superiority vanished, even culturally.

The generation of Chinese that lived through this long-continued disaster, which happened in our grandfathers' time, experienced a deepening crisis. The sacred values of proper conduct and social order proved useless. The ancient faith in China's superiority as a civilization was slowly strangled. The privileged foreigners came in everywhere and gradually stirred up a Chinese nationalism.

So complete was the disaster that a new order had to be built from the ground up. Western doctrines of all kinds were tried out. The thing that proved effective was the Leninist type of party dictatorship, an elite recruited under discipline according to a new orthodoxy, organized something like an old Chinese secret society, united in the effort to seize power and recreate a strong state. This nationalistic aim overrode every other consideration. The kind of Western individualism propagated by our missionaries had no chance.

The retrospective humiliation and sense of grievance over the enormous disaster of the 19th century has made modern Chinese feel that their country was victimized, so it was, by fate.

Circumstances made China the worst accident case in history. But Marxism-Leninism offers a devil-theory to explain it: how "capitalist imperialism" combined with "feudal reaction" to attack, betray, and exploit the Chinese people and distort their otherwise normal development toward "capitalism" and "socialism." Thus a great Communist myth of "imperialist" victimization becomes the new national myth.

Maoism As A Minor Tradition

It would not be naive to agree that China's early sense of superiority had some justification, and that her modern sense of victimization also has some justification. To have been so advanced and superior and then to find herself so backward and weak was a shattering experience. Now that Maoism is in power, we see the continued desire to set a model for mankind, to be the center from which civilization is derived. We can also see the tactic of having relations with other powers only insofar as they fit into the Chinese world view.

But what has happened to the old Confucian tradition of balance, harmony, and tolerance for private variations in faith and custom? The training of bureaucrats who were also humanists, artists, and scholars to carry on the established order was the major tradition, dominant over most of the centuries, whereas the present regime seems to be in a minority rebel tradition of dynastic founders, more like a band of sworn brothers rising from the countryside as leaders of peasant rebellion, animated by an extreme fanaticism.

The Peking leaders of today remind one of the leaders of the Taiping rebellion of the 1850's who picked up Christianity as a foreign ideology, rebuilt it to suit their needs, and took over half the country. The Taipings came from the back country, not from the foreign trade centers. They began as a secret society with a cult, invoked the radical tradition in the Chinese classics, and sought a utopian collective or communal society, at one time even segregating in the sexes. But the Taiping leaders were so dogmatic and doctrinaire that they alienated both the Chinese scholar class who might have helped them and the foreign merchants and missionaries who also might have helped them. Their simple fanaticism and xenophobia led them to pluck disaster from the jaws of victory.

In the course of time Peking should see a resurgence of the more humanistic and bureaucratic tradition of government by well-educated administrators who keep society in balance. While the past is gone forever, the present is not permanent either. Eventually we may expect the Chinese revolution to mellow down a bit.

American Sentiment About Our China Policy

As Americans we can only begin to imagine how the Chinese have suffered, from being on the receiving end of modernization rather than the giving end. It has been hard for them to take, because under their traditional code there should be reciprocity between people, one should not accept gifts without paying them back. For China to be always receiving from the West not only hurts national pride, being on the receiving end with no chance of repaying the favors of missionaries, for example, also hurts personal self-respect.

We Americans, being on the giving end of modernization, got a great deal more fun out of Sino-American relations. In the privileged status thrust upon them by the treaty system, most Americans enjoyed their contact with China, the chance to be an upper class foreigner riding in a rickshaw while still remaining an egalitarian grass-roots democrat in one's own conscience. For an average American to go abroad and find himself a rich man by comparison with the local people is also quite enjoyable. The Chinese were very polite, and countless Americans made warm friends among them. The American people built up a genuine, though sometimes patronizing, fondness for China.

Unfortunately, this now turns out to have been an unrealistic and rather naive attitude for two reasons. In the first place, the Americans were conscious of their own good intentions and less conscious of the humiliation that their superior circumstances often inflicted upon their Chinese friends.

In the second place, the Americans were able in the 19th century to share all the special privileges of foreigners in China under the unequal treaties without fighting for them. The British and others fought the colonial wars and the Americans enjoyed the fruits of such aggression without the moral responsibility. By 1900 the British, the French, and the Japanese had all fought wars with China; the Russians had seized territory; and all of them, together with the Germans, had seized special privileges in spheres of influence.

The Americans had done none of these things and came up instead with the "open-door" doctrine, which soon expanded to include not only the open door for trade but also the idea of China's integrity as a nation. Thus we Americans prided ourselves on championing China's modernization and self-determination. We considered ourselves above the nasty imperialism and power politics of the Europeans. We developed a self-image of moral superiority. The "open door" and benevolence toward Chinese nationalism became the bases of our Far Eastern policy until war with Japan brought us up against the realities of power politics. Then we began to realize, for almost the first time, that the power structure of east Asian politics had been held together by the British Navy in the 19th century, and by the British and Japanese Navies under the Anglo-Japanese alliance from 1902 to 1922.

Today we find ourselves in an enormous situation trying to maintain the power balance in east Asia. It is reminiscent in some ways of the colonial wars of the 19th century, a type of situation that

we generally succeeded in avoiding in that era. I do not contend that we today are simply 19th-century imperialists come back to life, any more than Chairman Mao is actually a resurrected Son of Heaven in a blue boiler suit. But I don't believe we can escape our historical heritage entirely, any more than he can. We have been part and parcel of the long-term Western approach to east Asia and ought to see ourselves in that perspective, just as any view of our China policy has to include a perspective on our program in Vietnam.

Echoes of Colonial War in Vietnam

Our Vietnam war differs from colonial wars of the past in certain basic ways, but still the similarities are rather striking. Colonial wars in east and southeast Asia had half a dozen common features:

First, an expansive ideological interest on the part of the modernizing colonial power -- whether it was British faith in "commerce as the handmaiden of civilization," the French "civilizing mission" in support of Catholic Christianity, Russia's sacred mission to "liberate" the oppressed peoples of the Orient, Japan's "coprosperity sphere," or merely the "white man's burden" and "manifest destiny."

Second, a rival to keep ahead of in power politics -- witness the long-continued Anglo-French rivalry in southeast Asia, Russo-Japanese rivalry in Korea and Manchuria, Anglo-Russian rivalry all across Asia, and so on.

Third, marked uncertainties of policy, much debated at the time -- but which usually wound up in a refusal to back down or scuttle out. As the czar said of Vladivostok in 1860, "Where the flag has once been raised, it must not be lowered."

Fourth, a superior logistic capacity and firepower -- evident all the way from the British iron-hulled steam gunboats of the Opium War that could sail against wind and tide to the Japanese tank-and-divebomber teams of the 1930's. This superior killing capacity gave colonial wars their particular brand of inhumanity.

Fifth, a local regime to work with -- either inherited like Vietnam's Nguyen dynasty from 1885 to 1945, or Korea's Yi dynasty from 1905 to 1910, or else built up anew; but in either case staffed by native and foreign administrators working together.

Sixth, a period of military "pacification" after the foreign power moved in. Britain in Upper Burma after 1886 needed 5 years and 40,000 troops to suppress the resistance. After the French had defeated China and seized North Vietnam (Tonkin) in 1885, their network of posts and punitive flying columns needed 10 years to "pacify" the guerrillas. After the United States seized the Philippines in 1898, military suppression of Aguinaldo's Philippine Republic took 3 years. When Japan moved into Formosa in 1895 she needed 7 years to suppress the resistance. In Korea, Japan faced 3 years of nationwide rebellion even before 1910.

Finally, disruption and modernization of the old colonial society -- accelerated change on all levels, neither wholly bad nor wholly good, and still much disputed in retrospect.

Most of these criteria seem to apply to Vietnam today. "Self-determination" and "defense against aggression" are ideals we all, I am sure, deeply believe in, yet they have expansive implications. In Vietnam we are bent on forestalling the Chinese Communist model of nation building by subversion and regimentation, which we regard as a dangerous rival to our own trade-and-aid model. Our firepower is superb and our killing capacity is superior. We have a local regime to work with. The American buildup in South Vietnam is so massive it comes very close to a colonial takeover, even though it is firmly intended to be only temporary.

"Pacification" is naturally scheduled to ensue for several years, probably in the towns more than the back country, together with the further disruption of Vietnamese society and its further modernization. The Americans bring with them their culture, its goods and its ills. Refugee shantytowns and traffic jams in the Saigon metropolis are only the most superficial evidence of shattering changes in the urban part of South Vietnam that we can hope to dominate.

Of course, this war is not for colonial territory nor our own aggrandizement. Asian nationalism and nuclear capacity are great new factors. Times have changed. The age of imperialism has given way to the age of nationalism, which we now champion, although we supported the French in Vietnam not so long ago. National interest is now tied in with international stability.

But Vietnam today gives us a more severe crisis of moral conscience partly because during most of our history we felt morally superior to the imperialist powers of the 19th century.

May I read that again -- Vietnam today gives us a more severe crisis of moral conscience partly because during most of our history we felt morally superior to the imperialist powers of the 19th century. Why must our land of the free now send its boys to kill and be killed in a civil war so far away? I would not claim that the history of power politics in east Asia automatically gives us the justification, but I do believe it helps explain how we got in. The problem of power relations has to be faced. Perhaps power has to be used in smaller wars if we are to avoid bigger wars. In any case, in Vietnam we seem unlikely either to lose or to win completely. Therefore I think the most important issue is our nonmilitary, or more-than-military program there.

Containment and Competition in Southeast Asia

The main fact about our containment of the Chinese revolutionary influence in South Vietnam is that it is only in part military. In larger part, it is a competition in how to help in nation building. Warfare is only the visible top of the iceberg. Most of the problem is not only political but also social, how to mobilize the people and organize their participation in politics.

The real test for us is not whether we can fight but whether we can be more constructive than destructive while we are fighting, right now and not later on. At present we seem more destructive. Whatever our level of effort, the balance of it should be weighted much, much more than it is on the side of helping civil action, recruitment and training for "pacification," and the other good things envisioned at Honolulu.

This kind of military containment plus social competition in helping to build up a new nation in South Vietnam, is obviously a much harder task than our original containment plus Marshall plan effort in industrialized Europe. We should not expect a comparable success. Yet to burn up Vietnam and go away and leave it will not smell as good as to make the much greater effort to help build up the society wherever we can.

Some argue, feeling culturally closer to Europe, that Vietnam is beyond our proper realm of concern. I don't agree. The Western powers have played major roles in southeast Asia for 400 years even if we have not. The West has made its contribution while also precipitating the nationalist revolutions. American merchants and missionaries joined in making this Western contribution. We cannot now condemn and disown the old British Empire, for instance, just because we let the British fight dirty colonial wars while we got the profits. We were and are involved in east Asian power politics at least as much as in those of Europe, cultural differences notwithstanding.

Stuck in a dirty war today, we would do well to lower our self-esteem, be not so proud, acknowledge our Western inheritance of both good and evil, and see ourselves as hardly more noble and not much smarter than the British and French in their day. We must be steadfast and restrained. We cannot take east Asia or ourselves out of power politics. The real test, I repeat, is whether we can be more constructive than destructive in areas of Vietnam we can influence.

Conclusion

My conclusion is that the alternative to war with Peking, over Vietnam or elsewhere, lies along two lines of effort -- one is to achieve a better balance between destruction and construction in our own efforts in Vietnam, so that the non-Communist model of nation building there can compete more effectively with the Chinese Communist model of nation building. The other line of effort is to defuse or dampen Peking's militancy by getting China into greater contact with the outside world, more connected with the international scene and more interested in participating in it like other countries.

How to get the Peking leadership into the international order, instead of their trying to destroy it according to their revolutionary

vision, is primarily a psychological problem. Therapy for Peking's present, almost paranoid, state of mind must follow the usual lines of therapy: it must lead the rulers of China gradually into different channels of experience until by degrees they reshape their picture of the world and their place in it.

The remolding of Chairman Mao, the greatest remolder of others in history, is not something I would advocate as feasible. But I think it is high time we got ourselves ready to deal with his successors and with their successors in years ahead.

In practice this means getting Peking into a multitude of activities abroad. China should be included in all international conferences, as on disarmament, and in international associations, both professional and functional, in international sports, not just ping-pong, and in trade with everyone, including ourselves, except for strategic goods. One thinks naturally of the U. N. agencies and participation in the Security Council as well as the Assembly. Yet all this can come only step by step, with altercation all along the way -- not an easy process but a lot more constructive than warfare.

American policy should work toward a gradual shift from trying to isolate Peking, which only worsens our problem, to a less exposed position where we can acquiesce in the growth of contact between Peking and other countries and let them suffer the impact of Peking's abrasiveness.

In gradually manipulating Peking into an acceptance of the international world, as an alternative to trying to subvert it, we must motivate Chinese behavior according to China's needs:

(1) One of these is the craving for greater prestige in the world to redress the balance of the last century's humiliations. For China to be in the center of the world's councils would seem to a Chinese patriot only right and proper.

(2) We can also use the Peking government's need for prestige to maintain itself domestically. It is still true that the virtue of the rulers, as advertised in their acknowledged achievements, is a vital element sustaining any regime in China.

(3) In addition, the Chinese people positively need certain kinds of aid through exchanges of technology or of goods, like all developing countries.

(4) Peking may also be motivated by the opportunity to manipulate foreigners against one another. This traditional way of dealing with outsiders can be attempted in any conclave like the United Nations. But any number can play this game, and, in fact, it is the essence of diplomacy.

As these types of motives come into play, we may expect the Peking regime to be involved in bilateral relationships and be influenced by others whose desire is for peace rather than violence. In the end all this may make coexistence more attractive and feasible.

Opening the door for China's participation in the world scene is only one part of an American policy. The other part is to hold the line. The Chinese are no more amenable to pure sweetness and light than other revolutionaries. Encouraging them to participate in the U.N. and other parts of the international scene has to be combined with a cognate attitude of firmness backed by force. Military containment on the Korean border, in the Taiwan Straits, and somehow in Vietnam cannot soon be abandoned and may have to be maintained for some time. But containment alone is a blind alley unless we add policies of constructive competition and of international contact.

In short, my reading of history is that Peking's rulers shout aggressively out of manifold frustrations, that isolation intensifies their ailment and makes it self-perpetuating, and that we need to encourage international contact with China on many fronts.

SCHWARTZ STATEMENT

The following is the statement of Benjamin I. Schwartz, professor of history and government at Harvard University. He appeared before the Committee on March 16, 1966.

Mr. Chairman, and members of the committee, I have been asked to comment briefly on the history of the rise of the Chinese Communists to power in 1949 and on the fall of the Nationalist government.

My talk will mainly concern the past although my interests are also very much involved in the present. I think that it is most appropriate that the two be linked since the success of the one side was to a considerable extent the result of the failure of the other. Were it not for certain fundamental and very specific failures on the Nationalist side, the Maoist revolutionary strategy might not have succeeded.

Since much attention has been focused recently on Mao Tse-tung's formula for revolutionary success I would like to dwell for a moment on the failures of the Nationalists.

Failures of Nationalist Chinese

In 1911, China witnessed the collapse of one of the most imposing political systems the world has ever known. What collapsed was not merely a government but the whole cosmology on which that government was based. In the ensuing vacuum, political power gravitated into the hands of local militarists. We then have the immense anarchy and chaos of the so-called warlord period. It is, I believe, a warranted assumption that during this period of chaos and political decay, the social and economic situation of the vast masses of China -- in the aggregate -- continued to deteriorate.

In 1927, the Kuomintang government ostensibly carried out the political and military unification of China. This speedy unification was, however, based on a network of flimsy agreements with many of the local militarists themselves -- agreements which proved highly evanescent. In fact, the Government in Nanking controlled directly only certain provinces of central China. This situation had, of course, not been created by the Nationalist government and the tendency of this government to direct much of its energy during the next few years to the task of achieving the genuine military unification of China may seem entirely justifiable.

Unfortunately, the resources available to this government were limited and the concentration of major energies in this task meant that other vital tasks were neglected.

Furthermore, the Kuomintang itself, which was the supreme political body of the society, was not a highly integrated movement. It was riven by cliques among which there was little lateral cohesion. The reasons for this failure of the Kuomintang to achieve inner unity still remain to be studied but the fact that the party rested on what has been called a "balance of weakness" can hardly be denied. One aggravating factor was undoubtedly the fact that these political cliques were often able to establish links with the independent military groupings mentioned above.

On the whole, the ideology of the Kuomintang did not prove to be an overwhelming galvanizing force, either within or outside of the party. One of its ingredients was, of course, nationalism, and nationalism is, as we know, one of the most potent engines in the world. The Nationalist government was, however, unable -- particularly after the Japanese onslaught -- to feed its engine with the fuel of success.

Kuomintang Programs Limited

During its early years, the Kuomintang did carry out positive programs in the realm of communications, education, foreign affairs, et cetera, but these programs were also limited in conception. They were largely urban in orientation and paid little attention to the vast rural hinterland which was hardly affected by the Nationalist rise to power. Local power in these areas, by default remained in the hands of the incumbent holders of power.

No doubt, the rural situation in the vast territory of China was not uniform. It was obviously better in some areas than others. It was not, however, substantially improved anywhere by Government action. The Government's conception of the priority of tasks involved the assumption that the task of military and political unification, the tasks of industrialization and various forms of urban modernization, must come first. Since the Government was unable, during the whole

period of its tenure on the mainland, to solve the problem of military unification or to launch a substantial industrialization program, it never did turn its attention seriously to the problem of the rural areas. There are those who contend that it could probably not have carried out substantial programs of reform in the countryside even if it had desired to do so because it had become indissolubly linked to the local holders of power and privilege. Whether this is so or not, the fact remains that even in terms of policy, rural reform was not high on the list of priorities.

It should also be pointed out that in spite of its orientation to military tasks, the Nationalist government did not carry out substantial reforms in the military area itself. Taking the period of Nationalist control as a whole, one must say that too little was done to improve the condition of the average soldier, to improve the practices of recruitment or the relations between the military and the civilian population.

Many of the deplorable practices of the warlord period had carried on into the post-1927 period. The failure in this area may have been due in part to the military crises in which the Government was constantly involved. There was the seemingly commonsense argument that one does not proceed to carry out sweeping reforms within a military force currently involved in combat. Even more important was the notion that one does not scrutinize the behavior of military officers who have manifested their unquestioned loyalty.

The Kuomintang government was not a totalitarian government in the Communist sense. The intellectually articulate classes were not completely repressed. There was, however, sporadic and arbitrary repression. There was not sufficient repression to prevent intellectuals and students from communicating with each other and exchanging views but there was sufficient suppression (including occasional executions) to embitter and alienate many of them.

It should also be noted that during the period from 1931 to 1937 the Nationalist government was unable to take full advantage of the patriotic anti-Japanese sentiment of the intellectuals and students. It was the considered view of the leadership that it was futile for China to attempt to confront Japanese power before carrying out military unification at home. While this policy may again on the surface appear eminently sensible, the campaigns against the Communist areas and against local militarists provided the unfortunate spectacle of Chinese fighting Chinese rather than fighting the common Japanese enemy.

Strengths of Maoist Strategy

It is within the context of this situation that the Maoist strategy of revolution gradually emerged. The development of this strategy on the part of Mao and others was a gradual and groping process, there was no preexistent blueprint. Neither Communist theory nor Russian practice provided any clear "operational code." The Chinese Communist Party in 1927 was by no means committed to an exclusive concentration on rural areas. The emergence of rural bases, the emergence of a concentration on peasant support, on the creation of peasant military forces and on guerrilla warfare was precisely a response to some of the Nationalist weaknesses mentioned above

The Kuomintang was weakest in the countryside and in an environment of military disunity, the Communists in a sense took on the coloration of their environment.

The Nationalists, indeed, often referred to them as a peculiar breed of warlords. Yet they were neither warlords nor "agrarian reformers." From their communism they derived a profound faith that history was on their side and they on its side. They also derived the concept of the Communist Party as the instrument of history, as a monolithic group united by an iron discipline and a fixed purpose. Their image of the future was also profoundly influenced by Soviet communism.

By the forties, Mao Tse-tung and others had succeeded in creating a Communist Party which corresponded in the main to this ideal type. Land reform played a considerable role in their program but this does not mean that their policies were uniformly popular with the peasantry or that their dreams for the future were in any way determined by the perspectives of the peasants.

Whether popular or unpopular, they succeeded during the

course of the thirties and forties in involving the peasantry in their organizational network and in tapping their energies.

Above all, I would stress some of the policies which they developed in the military area. They paid enormous attention to the political indoctrination and morale of the average soldier and, within the limits of the situation, to his physical well-being. They also laid constant stress on proper relations between the military and civilian population. In accounting for their victory after 1945, I would be inclined to place more weight on this factor than on the efficacy of land reform as such.

Effect of Japanese Assault

Having pointed out some of the weaknesses of the Kuomintang and some of the strengths of the Maoist strategy of revolution, as I see them, I should immediately add that had there been no Japanese assault on China, it is not inconceivable that the Kuomintang might have survived and that the Maoist strategy might have failed.

In the course of time, the Nanking government might have achieved a decisive preponderance of military power in China. Whether this would then have led it to cope successfully with all its other manifold problems we shall never know, but we do know that governments often survive without solving all their problems.

The Communist strategy of revolution -- at least as it had developed before 1935 -- did not prove invulnerable. For all its weaknesses, the Nationalist government was able to muster sufficient military power to squeeze the Communists out of the areas occupied by them in southeastern China.

Mao Tse-tung has claimed that this happened because he was not at the time in control of the party and because his own policy views were not being followed. Be that as it may, the Red army was forced to save itself by retreating to the northwest where it arrived with its number greatly reduced. Most impartial observers might well have maintained during the 1935-36 period that the Communist strategy had arrived at a dead end.

The Japanese war against China after 1937 proved, however, to be like a disease which attacks a frail body at its weakest points. The net effect of the war was to aggravate the weaknesses of the Nationalist government. All thought of achieving the military control of north China had to be abandoned. The dependence on holders of military power increased and the government became more dependent than in the past on the rural power structure. As the war progressed the government became convinced that the major battles against Japan would be won elsewhere. This led to a passive posture in the war and to policies more concerned with postwar problems of unification than with wartime tasks. Farsighted as such policies may have been, they did nothing to improve morale or to encourage reform within the military establishment.

Communist Experience

The Communists, on the other hand, were able to apply their considerable experience in organizing rural areas to the situation in north China. Once again they were able to spread their power through the countryside while the enemy -- now the Japanese -- controlled cities and lines of communication. The fact that the enemy was now the foreign aggressor made it possible for the Communists to add an important string to their bow. They were now able to make a strong appeal to nationalistic sentiment (which they undoubtedly shared) and to call for support among many elements -- particularly intellectuals and students who were deeply impressed by their anti-Japanese activities.

One may, of course, raise the question whether Chinese Communist military activities against the Japanese would have made much difference if Japanese power had not been destroyed elsewhere.

From the point of view of many nationalistic Chinese, however, there was the fact, that they were actively engaged with the enemy while the Nationalist government continued in its passive posture. It is not easy to know how much this Communist patriotic approach affected the attitude of the masses but there can be no doubt that it actually attracted many intellectuals and students to the Com-

munist areas and created an attitude of at least favorable neutrality in wide circles outside of these areas.

By the end of the war the Communists had managed to establish their political authority in some depth over wide areas of the North China plain.

This, of course, gave them ready access to Manchuria which had in actuality never been under firm Nationalist control.

Nationalist Government in Postwar Period

The Nationalist government carried into the postwar period its overwhelming concern with the immediate achievement of military, political, and even economic unification. Yet the factors which had made for low morale in both its political and military establishment had not been overcome during the course of the war.

They had, in fact, been aggravated.

One is tempted to speculate in retrospect on what might have happened if the Nationalist government had concentrated during the years between 1927 and the later forties on reform in depth within the areas under its firm control rather than on the will-o'-wisp pursuit of the military unification of the whole of China.

If it had been able to establish its power in depth in given areas, these areas might have been proven a solid base for a much more effective unification effort. This would have involved at a bare minimum a sweeping reform of the military establishment and some sort of beneficent impact on the life of the peasant village.

The notion that national unification was the task of first priority is one which has a certain commonsensical plausibility. Unfortunately, ordinary "commonsense" and true statesmanship do not always coincide. Whether the Nationalist government could have carried out such a policy is a question which cannot be answered here.

In considering some of the general implications of this story, I think it must be emphasized that the success of the Maoist strategy in China must be explained in terms of the specific history of modern China and not in terms of vague generalities about underdeveloped countries in general.

Success of Communist Strategy

The political and military fragmentation of modern China, the whole phenomenon of "warlordism," the failure to carry out military reform even in those armies under firm government control played an enormous role in the ultimate success of Chinese Communist strategy.

Furthermore as a result of the Japanese aggression, the Chinese Communists were able to wed their rural strategy to a genuine national appeal. In the eyes of many Chinese, they were able to make themselves the spokesmen of a genuine Chinese nationalism even while remaining Communists. It is by no means true that all the circumstances here described can be found in all underdeveloped countries.

Warlordism and military fragmentation is by no means a universal phenomenon in the third world. Many of these states, in spite of their many debilities, do succeed in creating a fairly unified, cohesive, and disciplined army.

Furthermore, few of these new nations now confront a foreign enemy on their own soil.

Peking has been attempting to create in the third world an attitude toward the United States which would be the equivalent of Chinese attitudes toward Japan during the forties. This effort is not likely to succeed unless we actually choose to perform the role which Peking has assigned to us.

The notion that the Chinese model of revolution is a kind of magic formula which will work everywhere in the "underdeveloped world" once certain buttons are pressed in Peking is a notion based on the same fear of the diabolical cleverness of Communists which we used to direct to Moscow. Not only does the strategy require the existence of a local political situation favorable to its success. It requires the existence of a self-reliant, capable, indigenous leadership willing to adopt and adapt it to local conditions.

Peking may now believe that it can create such revolutionary elites through embassy staffs and manuals. Its own experience should have taught it otherwise. In Vietnam, which provides the only case until now of the successful adaptation of the Chinese strategy, one has had not only specific favorable circumstances but a leadership in Hanoi which has essentially made itself.

The fact that neither the United States nor the U.S.S.R. have been quite successful in persuading the third world to accept their models on the third world, is in itself no proof that the Chinese will succeed in doing so.

ZAGORIA STATEMENT

The following is the statement of Donald S. Zagoria, associate professor of government and senior fellow, Research Institute on Communist Affairs, Columbia University. He appeared before the Committee on March 21, 1966. (See p. 181)

Mr. Chairman and members of the committee, let me say at the outset that I greatly value this opportunity to meet with you to submit my views on China's foreign policy and the problems it poses for the United States, and I would like to add that personally, I would like to congratulate you, Senator Fulbright, and your committee for your attempts to focus the attention of the American people on the problem of China. I personally believe that these hearings have so far performed a very useful service and I hope that our testimony today may contribute to shedding a little more light on the problems that Communist China poses for the United States.

China Faces Foreign Policy Crisis

U.S. foreign policy, and all considerations of it, must bear in mind a crucial fact of international life: that the Chinese Communist regime today faces the most serious and far-reaching foreign policy crisis it has ever confronted. This crisis is largely the outgrowth of rigidly dogmatic postures assumed in recent years by Mao and his closest collaborators. The crisis is of such magnitude as to have seriously weakened Peking's influence in the underdeveloped countries, cast doubt on the legitimacy and viability of even the regime's reasonable international aspirations, and greatly sharpened existing divergencies among Communist movements all over the world. It is a crisis which will not be resolved without basic changes in Chinese Communist policy -- changes which may not come until after Mao's death, but which could occur sooner and, in any case, in my opinion, are bound to happen in the forseeable future.

The dimensions of this crisis are global -- Indonesia, Cuba, Kenya -- wherever we look in Asia, Latin America, and Africa, the Peking regime stands accused of unwarranted intervention and arrogance, its representatives are asked to go home, and its intentions are viewed with growing suspicion.

Within the international Communist movement, where Peking a year or two ago could count on some 20 allies and sympathizers, and seemed ready to set up a new Communist international alliance of Afro-Asian-Latin American parties, Chinese influence is now at an all-time low. Even the intransigent Albanians are beginning to have second thoughts about the wisdom of Mao's strategy and doctrine. Meanwhile the split with Moscow deepens.

The current crisis in Communist China's foreign policy has its roots in 1957 when Mao, incorrectly assuming that the development of Soviet ICBM capabilities had wrought a decisive change in the world balance of power, abandoned Peking's previous caution and embarked on a more militant course to achieve his primary foreign policy goals; elimination of U.S. military power from Asia, repossession of Taiwan, and international recognition of Communist China as a great power.

It soon became clear that the Soviet Union, on whose support Mao had unquestionably counted, was unwilling to back Mao's ambitious aims at the risk of war with the United States. Quite to the contrary, it soon made overtures for a detente with the United States. The "spirit of Camp David" and Khrushchev's subsequent efforts to persuade Peking to accept a modus vivendi envisaging Chinese

Nationalist control of Formosa pressed home to Mao the fact that the Russians could not be depended on to help push the United States out of Asia. This difference of approach to the U.S. presence is among the fundamental causes of the Sino-Soviet split and explains the bitterness of Chinese feelings toward the Soviet leadership.

Peking then turned to the underdeveloped countries, encouraging nationalist and local Communist leaders in these countries to join in an anti-American alliance. Mao's plans could not be carried out without replacing Soviet by Chinese authority in the Communist and leftist groups of Afro-Asia and Latin America. However, Mao's gambit has fallen flat all along the line: radical nationalists receptive to Peking's game are disappearing from power, and Communist parties in Africa, Asia, and Latin America are deeply divided and increasingly disenchanted with Mao.

What amounts, then, to effective containment of Communist China has been accomplished primarily by the Peking leadership itself. In a few short years, the Chinese leadership has split with the only other major Communist power in the world, it has alienated itself from the international Communist movement and from the emergent nationalist forces of the developing countries, and it has not only failed to attain most of its pressing national goals but it has even prejudiced them. The rumblings of discontent with Mao's policies are plainly audible in China today.

Cause of China's Failures

China's failures are essentially the result of its erroneous assessment of the forces at work in the Afro-Asian world. National self-realization rather than instant social revolution or an anti-American crusade is the immediate goal sought by the new countries, and Peking's product mix of subversion, helpful revolutionary hints, and polemics on the evils of imperialism has inevitably found only a limited market where economic development and nation-building are the primary concerns. By the same token, Peking cannot compete with Russia or the United States when it comes to economic and military aid.

Similarly, Peking's loss of influence in the international Communist movement is the direct consequence of Chinese intransigence, which even the most radical Communist parties have come to regard as unrealistic. Mao's failure last year to cooperate in a reported Soviet plan to send a limited number of Russian troops into North Vietnam and to station Soviet fighter planes in southern Chinese airfields provides a striking example of Peking's unwillingness to accept realistic alternatives in a situation of deep concern to the international Communist movement.

With such a move Moscow had apparently hoped to reassure China as to its physical security, discourage U.S. bombing of North Vietnam and, at the same time, exert pressures for negotiations on all participants in the Vietnamese fighting. Peking promptly charged that the Soviet leaders were out to make a "deal" with the Americans, and suggested that, instead, Soviet supplies to Vietnam be sent by sea and that the Russians open a "second front" in Europe, preferably in Berlin. Moscow countered by accusing the Chinese of unwillingness to help take united action against imperialist aggression -- an accusation which found a wide echo in many Communist parties. The suspicion is growing among them that Peking is willing to fight the Americans to the last Vietnamese.

Interpretation of Lin Piao's Statement

The extent of the crisis facing the Chinese Communist leadership in the field of foreign policy is dramatically pointed up in the now-notorious statement made by Marshal Lin Piao last September. Ironically, there are two -- and, in my opinion, only two -- countries in the world where Lin Piao's revolutionary smorgasbord is regarded as some kind of magic weapon: one is China, and the other is the United States.

Two, in my opinion, equally erroneous interpretations of Lin Piao's statement are current, and both, it seems to me, to miss the point. On the one hand there are those who dismiss it as 4th of July rhetoric. On the other are those part-time Pekinologists who call this Lin Piao's "Mein Kampf," blithely ignoring the fact that it is basically a rehash of what Chinese Communist leaders have been saying on and off since at least 1949.

The analogy with "Mein Kampf" comes, therefore, a little late, to say the least. But, more importantly, it is harmful and misleading because it equates Maoist and Nazi ideology in such a way as to evoke the specter of overt Chinese Communist military and territorial expansion in Asia. Neither in the Lin Piao statement nor in the multitude of similiar statements made in the past is there any suggestion of Chinese Communist intentions to engage in direct, Hitler-style expansionism.

In fact, a cardinal point of Lin Piao's message is the Vietcong and other Communist revolutionaries throughout the world must make their revolutions on their own, that they should not count on Chinese or any other outside assistance. Far from giving notice of any intention to intervene aggressively, Lin Piao is rationalizing Peking's unwillingness to go to the aid of the Vietcong, in a struggle which -- let there be no doubt -- the Chinese Communist regard as just and which is taking place on their very borders.

The difference between Hitler and Mao, then, is that "Mein Kampf" was a blueprint for what Germany herself, under Hitler, would do; Lin Piao's statement, on the contrary, is designed to tell other Communist parties what they should do, to recommend strategy. It is, thus, simply not Fourth of July oratory.

Reaction

However, most of the Communist parties now recognize that Lin Piao's advice is largely inappropriate to their local situations, and they are not about to act on it. The ingredients of the Chinese Communist revolutionary model which has long been put forward as a "do it yourself" model for foreign Communists -- are well known: a disciplined Communist Party, a broad united front, a protracted guerrilla struggle originating in the rural hinterland and based on armed peasantry -- the whole led by Communists right from the outset.

How many foreign Communist Parties are in a position to implement the model? With the exception of Vietnam, the answer is none, as of this moment, and for very good reasons: Not one Communist party in Africa, Asia or in Latin America has a strong base, either in the society in general or among the peasants in particular -- an indispensable prerequisite for launching a Maoist-style guerrilla war. The one party which came closest to having such a mass base, the PKI in Indonesia, has recently been decimated by the Indonesian Army and is unlikely to recover in the forseeable future.

In India, Communism is strong in certain areas but it has not been able to generate a mass basis of support among peasants in the countryside. In Africa, Communist parties are for the most part non-existent, and Peking had to build on a variety of the most unlikely patchwork of local oppositionists, at least one of whom took $70,000 from them and then opened up a bar at which, we may assume, instruction in Marxism-Leninism is not regularly supplied.

This is, of course, not to argue that the appeal of revolutionary communism has been entirely unsuccessful in the underdeveloped countries. Apart from the startling conquest of mainland China, it has been able to generate mass movements in Vietnam, Cuba, and until recently in Indonesia. But the factors that account for its gains in these areas are not exactly paralleled in other underdeveloped countries of the world. The single most important element in the advance of communism in Vietnam, as in China itself, was that the local Communist party captured a nationalist movement during and after World War II in the course of a national struggle against a foreign invader.

Second, the nationalist opposition to the Communists both in China and Vietnam was divided, unimaginative and without effective organization at the rice-root level. Current Vietcong success in South Vietnam is inextricably related to the fact that Ho Chi Minh, like Mao, was able to capture a weak nationalist movement during the last war.

Communist success in China and Vietnam should not, however, obscure the more fundamental fact that the Communists have been unable to seize control of a nationalist movement anywhere in Asia, Africa, or Latin America since the start of World War II. (Castro was not a Communist when he took power; he converted to Communism afterward in order to obtain Soviet protection against American at-

tack.) This is not a mere historical accident. It suggests that the Chinese and Vietnamese successes are not easy to duplicate even in the favorable circumstances of an anticolonial armed struggle. Witness the fact that in none of the recent or current instances of such a struggle -- Algeria and Angola, for example -- have local Communists played a leading role.

In those Afro-Asian countries which have already achieved independence -- and these, of course, constitute the vast majority -- it is even more difficult for local Communists to exploit nationalism to their advantage or to outmaneuver the nationalists and the army in the post-independence struggle for power. In the one instance where they were able temporarily to exploit nationalism, namely Indonesia, they could not convert this into lasting power. Even in the many new countries which have been torn by strife at the top or have failed to solve the problems of modernization, the Communists are nowhere close to power.

Assessment of Nationalism

It is ironic that both Peking and Washington have in the past seemed to share the view that somehow nationalists in the developing countries would prove to be a pushover for the disciplined Communists. This has turned out to be a completely wrong assessment. On the contrary, the containment of Communism in the underdeveloped areas has been accomplished in the main not by Western military action, though this has made some real economic aid or the attractions of Western democracy but rather by the growth of a variety of nationalist regimes who have no particular desire to imitate either Western or Communist economic and political institutions.

Since the Chinese Communist leadership has in the past shown itself flexible enough to adjust policies when they go wrong, I see no reason not to expect that they will be able to recognize their plight and adapt accordingly. True, what we have thus far seen from Peking is not the sign of change in direction but rather the rationalization of past mistakes. But this cannot suffice. The Chinese will not stay indefinitely in the corner they have painted themselves into.

Foreign Policy Options

What options do they have? They could try to reach a rapprochement with the Soviet Union. But so long as Mao lives, this is unlikely. They could improve relations with the United States. It is interesting in this respect to note that a recent French emissary in Peking was told that the Americans were, after all, only an enemy, and a respected one, whereas the Russians were traitors and traitors could never be forgiven. The clear impression was that it might eventually, and I stress the word "eventually" because I do not expect or anticipate an early improvement in Chinese-American relations, that the clear impression was that it might eventually be easier to adjust relations with the United States than with Russia.

Thirdly, Peking could try to revive the "Bandung spirit" of the mid-1950's when it sought to portray itself not as a revolutionary power but as a friend of the entire Afro-Asian world. But it is not likely to do any of these things until the issue of Vietnam is decided because the old guard still cherishes the hope that a success in Vietnam could turn back the tide.

Peking and Hanoi

It nourishes this hope despite deteriorating relations with Hanoi. Let me at this point clarify certain things about the relationship among Peking, Hanoi, and the South Vietnamese Liberation Front:

There is, I believe, general agreement among informed observers that Hanoi is fully independent of Peking. The precise relationship between Hanoi and the Liberation Front is a more controversial matter. It is clear, in my opinion, that the Liberation Front is controlled by a South Vietnamese Communist Party called the People's Revolutionary Party. It is also clear that the People's Revolutionary Party is a branch of the parent Lao Dong Communist Party in North Vietnam. What is not clear is how much the South Vietnamese Communists and the Liberation Front have emancipated themselves from North Vietnamese control.

Important tactical differences between Hanoi and the Front have been apparent for some time. In general, Hanoi shows greater flexibility than the Front whose position is closed to the intransigence of

Peking. It is quite likely that the South Vietnamese Communists, having been abandoned by their northern comrades at the Geneva conference in 1954, are extremely fearful that Hanoi may do it again.

In other words, the Communists, and especially the South Vietnamese Communists in the firing line, have their own Yalta complex.

Peking and Hanoi, I want to stress, have both overlapping and conflicting interests in South Vietnam. They share an interest in eliminating American power and influence from South Vietnam but Peking has a much greater interest in a protracted war. For Peking, the war in South Vietnam which, to be sure, it did not itself start, nevertheless provides a test case for its "liberation war" strategy. More important, it provides an opportunity to humiliate, divert, and to weaken the United States without any cost to itself.

This is why Peking, although concerned about the possibility of an American attack on China, is nevertheless not eager for a negotiated settlement in Vietnam. Hanoi, on the other hand, has a clearly more limited interest: namely, the unification of Vietnam under Communist hegemony, a goal that might -- under certain conditions -- be achieved through negotiations rather than through protracted war against a determined and superior enemy.

These different perspectives have resulted in differences in emphasis on the possibility of negotiations and the preconditions for them -- differences that have gone largely unnoted in most of the American press. Peking has repeatedly been at pains to warn against U.S. deceit and far more vehemently than Hanoi has denounced all proposals to end the war in Vietnam short of U.S. disengagement. Moreover, Hanoi's conditions for negotiations have in general been more ambiguous and flexible than Peking's.

The crucial and, as far as U.S. policy is concerned, complicating factor is that Hanoi's leadership is itself divided. Hanoi has its own version of hawks and doves. Hanoi's hawks -- who remain predominant -- seem to believe that the massive introduction of American power into South Vietnam has not greatly diminished Communist prospects for success, while the doves believe that it has. Peking has consistently sought to strengthen Hanoi's hawks and the Chinese Communists have recently expressed considerable apprehension that the Hanoi dove faction is, with Soviet backing, on the rise.

Courses of U.S. Action in Vietnam

In this situation there are some things the United States can, and in my opinion, should do. First, it seems to me imperative that we recognize -- even if the Chinese Communists do not -- that Communist successes in South Vietnam are not easily duplicable. They are the product of conditions that are extremely unusual in the former colonial world. This is not an argument for precipitate withdrawal from South Vietnam, a course of action that would under no circumstances be consistent with the best interests of the United States.

But the price we are willing to pay, and the risks we are willing to accept for an eventual settlement will depend in part on whether we regard South Vietnam as the first of a series of dominoes or as an exception to the general rule that the heyday of communism in the underdevelopment areas has passed.

Second, it appears that our best hope in Vietnam is to strengthen those groups in Moscow and Hanoi who have a more flexible approach to negotiations against the bitter-enders supported by Peking. These moderates can be strengthened by two complementary lines of American policy. First, our words and our actions could substantiate their realistic assessment that the United States cannot be forced out of South Vietnam and that a military victory for the Vietcong is in fact impossible. Second, our words and our actions could assure them that the United States is not insisting on unconditional surrender. On the first count, we have already made significant progress. A year or two ago Peking, Hanoi, and even Moscow seemed to believe that the United States would tire of the war and withdraw. It is now apparent that the moderate groups of the Communist world have revised their estimates. In my view, more effort must now be expended on the second line of approach.

Neutralization of Southeast Asia

While on the subject of Vietnam, I want to make a specific proposal for neutralizing mainland southeast Asia after the Vietnam war is concluded. We can insure genuine neutralization of the area, it seems to me, only if the smaller countries concerned believe that their security is provided for. If we merely talk about neutralization while withdrawing our military power, they will obviously be forced to accommodate to China on Chinese terms. We must convince all of these countries that the United States, preferably in conjunction with international authority and with the Soviet Union, will help them to resist any threat to their security by an outside power. To do this, I think we need two things: first, the continued physical presence of effective American power even if it takes the form of the 7th Fleet; second, bilateral contingency plans which will set down the conditions for American action and the manner in which such action will be undertaken. I do not believe that it is practical to talk about such neutralization, however, until after the Vietnam war is concluded. Too much emphasis on neutralization at this point, before adequate preparation is made with the countries involved, would be bound to have a disquieting effect on them.

Change of U.S. China Policy

Finally, I would like to endorse enthusiastically the changes in our policy toward China recommended to this committee by Professors Barnett and Fairbank. As I indicated, it seems to me likely that Peking's failures in foreign policy must inevitably lead the Chinese Communists to undertake a painful readjustment of their strategy and tactics that have brought them to the brink of international bankruptcy. If Mao were a British Prime Minister, he would by this time have been elevated to the House of Lords. There are credible reports that the Chinese leaders are increasingly divided on foreign policy, and when Mao dies, it is quite likely that we will witness as furious a succession struggle in China as we saw in the Soviet Union after the death of Stalin. I think it is now generally recognized that we missed the opportunity to strengthen the hand of the moderates in the Stalin succession struggle and we should not repeat the same mistake in our policy toward China. A change in our policy toward China now could provide an alternative to those Chinese leaders who believe that Mao's policy has been too rigid.

It might be countered by some that if China is in such serious difficulty, why is there any need for a change in our policy? I believe such a change is necessary at some point if we are ever to achieve stability in Asia and to solve a host of international questions that cannot be resolved without Chinese participation, including arms control and disarmament. In the past, objections have been raised to a change in U.S. policy on the grounds that it would be interpreted as weakness by the other side. But if this is the case, what better time is there for such a change when it is quite clear that we are not leading from weakness?

Moreover, there are many countries and people, particularly in Asia, who believe that Chinese intransigence and militance is largely the result of isolation by the United States. We can prove that they are wrong only by ending our policy of isolation. If the Chinese continue, as they have done in the past to isolate themselves by their own inept policies, at least the onus will be on them.

Finally, and not least important, our only hope to achieve a stable and tolerable relationship with China is to do all we can to promote not a change of the system -- which can be done only by war -- but a change within the system. The kind of evolution that is already transforming Russia and the East European Communist countries will have to come one day in China too. We can help to hasten its growth.

HINTON STATEMENT

The following is the statement of Harold C. Hinton, associate professor of international affairs at George Washington University. He appeared before the Committee on March 21, 1966. (See p. 181)

Mr. Chairman and members of the committee, I am honored by this invitation to appear before you. I should like to emphasize that

I am speaking solely for myself and not for the Institute for Defense Analysis, with which I am affiliated, or for the Department of Defense, for which the Institute performs contract research.

Background

The Chinese Communist Party came to power in 1949 determined not only to wipe out China's past humiliations at the hands of what it called foreign imperialism but to make China the leading state in Asia and a model and source of support for other Communist revolutions in Asia. The scope of its ambitions was soon broadened to include the whole of the underdeveloped areas and even the attainment of the status of a world power. The United States, which was tentatively moving toward diplomatic recognition of Communist China in the last months of 1949, found its intentions frustrated by the Chinese Communist determination to cast the United States in the light of the major enemy for reasons both foreign and domestic, including a desire to isolate Western-oriented Chinese and facilitate their reindoctrination.

A first step in Communist China's quest for influence was the acquisition of all territory claimed as Chinese. In 1936 Mao Tse-tung had said that Taiwan, or Formosa, should be independent after its liberation from Japan, but he changed his mind as the United States and Britain promised Taiwan to China in 1943, the Chinese Nationalists made it their main base and refuge after 1949, and the United States began to protect it in 1950. Shortly afterward Communist China intervened in the Korean conflict in order to keep American ground forces away from its Manchurian frontier. It succeeded in this, but its intervention together with the developing Sino-American confrontation in the Taiwan Strait, led the United States to shift the emphasis of its military policy in the Far East from containment of the Soviet Union to containment, or as the Chinese would say encirclement, of Communist China.

China Versus the U.S. in Asia

Thus Communist China's overeager promotion of its own security and influence, although it enhanced its influence somewhat by creating in many quarters an exaggerated impression of its readiness to resort to force, also created a greater and continuing threat to Chinese security. Much the same is happening now as the United States constructs major air bases in Thailand in response to a Vietnamese crisis in which Communist China has chosen to involve itself to a limited degree.

Since 1950 a major deterrent to hostile action against Communist China by the United States or anyone else is the widespread belief that China's large conventional forces, which it refuses to reduce under any international disarmament agreement, hold the non-Communist countries of mainland Asia hostage for the good behavior of its enemies. To a degree, therefore, Communist China can count on Asian countries as well as others to exert restraining pressures on the United States. In reality, Communist China's ability to invade other Asian countries is severely limited by logistics and is almost canceled by the threat of American retaliation and the political liabilities that would follow an actual invasion, as distinct from a mere threat or assumed capability to invade. At various times in the past year and a half, Communist China has said that it would fight the United States on the ground in Indochina if the United States attacked China, whether on land or merely in the air is not clear, if the United States invaded North Vietnam or northern Laos, or if the National Liberation Front with Hanoi's consent requested such Chinese intervention. Since none of these preconditions is likely to materialize, direct Communist Chinese intervention in Vietnam is also unlikely, except in the highly improbable event of some major miscalculation or irrational decision on the Chinese side.

Chinese Alliance with U.S.S.R.

For a number of reasons that included its determination to confront the United States in Asia, the Chinese leadership chose to ally itself with the Soviet Union in 1950. The alliance was seriously strained by the Korean crisis and still more by the massive retaliation doctrine and the entry of West Germany into NATO, which riveted Soviet attention on Europe more than ever and reduced almost to the vanishing point Soviet willingness to take serious risks on behalf of China, even in defense of its security and still less in support of its offensive ambitions such as the taking of Taiwan. In 1956, therefore, Communist China decided that it must have nuclear weapons and delivery systems of its own. It succeeded in getting substantial Soviet technical aid and equipment toward this end in exchange for acquiescence in Soviet efforts to achieve a test ban agreement. A Chinese demand for the turning over of finished Soviet nuclear weapons as an interim measure seems to have foundered, however, on a Soviet counterdemand for joint defense arrangements that would have amounted to Soviet controls. The Soviet Union canceled its nuclear aid, and China in return withdrew its support for a test ban agreement, its objections rising to a crescendo when the Soviet Union actually signed such an agreement in 1963. Over and above the specific issue of the test ban, China objects to any sort of American-Soviet detente, because it diminishes still further the Soviet incentive to give China active support against the United States without reducing Sino-American tensions in any way.

Undaunted, Communist China has continued its drive to become a nuclear power. Indeed, there is strong evidence that it is the only country in the world that is seriously trying to join the United States and the Soviet Union as a thermonuclear superpower. The current Chinese leadership apparently intends to use whatever pressures and exact whatever sacrifices are necessary to put China at least over the hump on the way to thermonuclear weapons and suitable delivery systems, just as Stalin did for the Soviet Union, and is greatly worried that younger Chinese may not share its taste for hardship and nuclear status symbols. The Chinese quest for nuclear weapons, as well as Chinese pressures on the Soviet Union within the framework of the international Communist movement that are at least partly in retaliation for what the Chinese regard as Soviet betrayal of the Sino-Soviet alliance, have contributed heavily to a deterioration of Sino-Soviet relations that since 1963 has occasionally taken on dramatic proportions. One manifestation of this deterioration has been a border dispute that has sometimes approached the level of at least local war.

China's Relations

China has done fairly well in its recent relations with the developed non-Communist countries, including Japan and excluding the United States, primarily because its revolutionary activities there are minor and ineffectual and it gives priority to its national interests, which stress trade and the acquisition of technological information. China's trade with these countries, and with Japan and West Germany in particular, is trending upward. On the other hand, the Chinese interest in the developed countries is by no means entirely economic. China hopes to lure them away from the United States, and keep them away from the Soviet Union, in order to use them if possible against both. French recognition in January 1964 was a major diplomatic feather in China's cap, and shortly afterward the Chinese gave signs of an interest not only in signing a trade agreement with West Germany but in establishing diplomatic relations with it, not for the sake of harming East Germany but for the sake of putting pressure on Khrushchev, with whom their relations were almost unbelievably bad at that time. Nothing came of this Chinese interest in relations with West Germany, as it turned out.

Communist China's policy toward the underdeveloped areas consists essentially, although not entirely, of overtly inciting and covertly aiding Chinese-style armed revolutions, not necessarily Communist led but aimed at "imperialist" influence in the country in question, within the limits of supposed feasibility. The purpose seems to be twofold: not only to promote eventually the spread of Communism, but to weaken the United States and distract it from the Far East by involving it in crises and brushfire wars elsewhere in the underdeveloped areas. The best known formulation of this strategy is Marshal Lin Piao's article of September 3 last on "people's war," in which he says that the Japanese army in China produced its own defeat by driving the Chinese people into the arms of the Communists, that the United States is now doing in the underdeveloped areas as a whole exactly what the Japanese did in China, and that the peoples of the underdeveloped areas, therefore, can and should imitate the Chinese people's example without relying for decisive aid on Communist China or any other external source. So central to Lin's argument, and yet so fantastic, is the analogy between imperial Japan and the United States that one is tempted, even before examining the evidence, to conclude that the Chinese hope for widespread anti-imperialist risings in the underdeveloped countries is poorly founded.

Chinese Foreign Policy Reversals

If the year 1964 had witnessed such Chinese gains as French recognition, the fall of Khrushchev, and the first Chinese nuclear test, 1965 saw the beginning of a series of major Chinese setbacks in the underdeveloped areas. Of these the first in point of both time and importance was the massive American escalation in Vietnam beginning in February 1965, which tended to cast China in the role of a paper dragon unable and unwilling to intervene effectively in a struggle that is of great political importance to it and is being conducted almost on its doorstep. In the Kashmir crisis of late 1965, China intervened loudly but ineffectively on behalf of Pakistan in a way that tended to distract international attention from Kashmir, where Pakistan wanted it to rest, without giving the Chinese enough leverage to accomplish their objective of obstructing Pakistani acceptance of the United Nations cease-fire resolution and of Soviet mediation. It appears that the Chinese gave some aid and advice to the Communist coup that was attempted in Indonesia last September 30, and regardless of whether such was the case they have suffered enormously from the bloody losses inflicted on what had been the largest Communist Party in the non-Communist world and one that seemed to stand a good chance of coming to power in a mood to be cooperative with China. In sub-Saharan Africa, the Chinese have been expelled to one degree or another during the past year from Burundi, Dahomey, Upper Volta, the Central African Republic, and Ghana because of their energetic efforts to promote subversion on the theory that Africa is "ripe for revolution." Farther north, the Chinese have also been caught in subversive activities in Egypt, and more serious still they helped to torpedo the Afro-Asian Conference at Algiers rather than attend it together with the Soviet Union and Malaysia and in the probable absence of resolutions that would condemn both American policy in Vietnam and the receipt of aid by Afro-Asian countries from non-Afro-Asian countries -- meaning mainly the United States and the Soviet Union.

In Latin America, the standing of Communist China in leftwing circles has suffered greatly because Castro has been moving away from the Chinese and toward the Russians since late 1964. This trend, which the Chinese only aggravated by putting pressures on Castro, has resulted in a loud and open quarrel in the early months of this year.

Outlook for China's Foreign Policy

Communist China's setbacks in the underdeveloped areas in the past year have been so serious that it may well be that a major rethinking of Chinese foreign policy is in process, such as occurred in the Soviet Union after the Cuban missile crisis. If so, the outcome is likely to be less rather than more Chinese pressure on other countries, since it does not appear that China has any rabbits in its hat in this field. In fact, a long-term mellowing is the most likely outlook for future Chinese policy, unless the United States gives China reason to act differently by relaxing its containment policy, which has already contributed substantially to moderating Chinese foreign policy much as it did Soviet foreign policy during the last years of Stalin's life, and for that matter as it has since. There is no compelling reason to assume that American persistence in containment of Communist China -- notably, by giving it reason to stay out of Vietnam even if the military situation there continues on balance to develop adversely to the Communist side -- will put the United States on some sort of collision course with China. Nor is there any reason to think that the possession of more than token nuclear power, which will accrue not to the present Chinese leadership but to its successors, will pose a mortal threat to peace in the absence of formal disarmament. In the nuclear age, power confers vulnerability as well, and, therefore, tends to lead to responsibility and the acceptance of at least tacit arms control agreements.

It is still less likely that Communist China will ever be able to equal or surpass the United States or the Soviet Union in strategic military power. Communist China will remain a problem and at times perhaps a threat, but not an unmanageable one so long as the United States is willing to do what may be necessary to keep it manageable.

Containment of China

Mr. Chairman, if I may add a few words to my prepared statement, I should conclude that just as the maintenance of a military balance with respect to the Soviet Union requires an American military presence on the European continent, so the maintenance of a military balance with respect to China requires an American military presence in continental east Asia. This presence should, of course, be used to contain Chinese power, political as well as military, not to attack it on its home ground. It will be recalled that Abraham Lincoln's policy, whose rejection by extremists on both sides brought on the Civil War, was to contain slavery within its existing borders rather than abolish it outright, on the theory that in time it would mellow or break up. It seems to me that this is one dogma of the past that is adequate to the stormy present.

JUDD STATEMENT

The following is the statement of Dr. Walter H. Judd, (R Minn.), former Member of the U.S. House in the 78th to 87th Congresses. Dr. Judd was also the American delegate to the 12th General Assembly of the United Nations. He appeared before the Committee on March 28, 1966. (See p. 182)

Mr. Chairman, and members of the committee, thank you very much for your kindness in inviting me to testify here this morning.

As you said, 27 years ago, I was given the opportunity to testify before this committee on essentially the same subject as today. It was then called "Neutrality, Peace Legislation, and Our Foreign Policy." The question was how to get and keep freedom and peace in Asia and thus security and peace for the United States. The threat then was Japan's aggressive military expansionism. After months under the Japanese in China, I had become convinced that the best hope for our peace and security lay in stopping the vital aid, assistance, and comfort being supplied by us to the aggressor, while doing all we properly could to strengthen and help the free peoples resisting that aggressor. Many considered such a policy too dangerous and costly -- a confrontation with Japan might lead to war. Our Government was persuaded, until it was too late, to try to placate the aggressor. Perhaps we could change his attitudes toward us and others by carrying on normal trade and showing him our good will. Perhaps that might start an evolutionary process in Japan's military leadership leading to better relationships.

The policy did not lead to peace; it led to Pearl Harbor.

The same general approach to aggression in Asia is being advocated today as on that earlier occasion. Communist governments and their fronts are waging war against free peoples worldwide. At the moment the hot-test spot, and the test case for us, is Vietnam -- as at other times the test case has been Japan, Greece, Berlin, Korea, Quemoy, Lebanon, Cuba.

But the issue is not Vietnam; it is how are disputes to be settled -- by resolution through civilized means, or by armed force?

The state is not Vietnam; it is Asia -- and ourselves and the world.

The problem is not Vietnam; it is aggressive Communist expansionism -- this time from North Vietnam, backed up by the Soviet Union and Communist China.

Mr. Chairman, no great expansionist movement has ever stopped until it was checked. Our choice -- with Red China just as it was with Japan and Hitler -- is not between checking and not checking. The choice is whether to check early, while we can, and with allies -- or try to check the aggression later when it is stronger, closer, and we have fewer and weaker friends and allies.

The urgent question, I think, is how to check it with least risk and cost.

U.S. China Policy Since 1950

Since the beginning of the Korean war in 1950, America's policy toward Communist China under the Truman, Eisenhower, Kennedy, and Johnson administrations has been a hard headed realistic attempt to protect the security interests of the United States by resisting any steps that would further increase Chinese Communist influence and power. An indispensable part of the policy has been to support and strengthen all non-Communist governments around China that are trying to preserve their independence and thereby to keep their manpower, territory, bases, and resources out of Communist control.

Some say that policy has failed because Red China is still there and is as hostile and as dedicated to world domination by armed force as ever. Yes, it is there; but where would the countries around Red China have been without this policy of containment of the aggressor and support of the free? There are great problems ahead for Korea, Taiwan, the Philippines, Burma, as well as South Vietnam, Malaysia, and Indonesia. But all of them are still free. And who can believe they would have been free, and with at least the possibility of solving their problems, if it had not been for our firm containment of China?

U.S. Policy Changes

From what I have seen in the press, most of the changes in American policy toward Communist China proposed by various witnesses before this committee appear to be based on certain assumptions which do not seem to me to be justified:

1. That the Communist regime now in control of the China mainland is here to stay.

But the same was said of Hitler, of Khrushchev, of Sukarno, of Nkrumah. People are not so sure now that Castro will last forever. Despots generally appear invincible -- "until the last 5 minutes."

2. That the United States is stubbornly keeping Red China isolated and therefore we are responsible for its hostility and belligerence. The reverse is the truth; it is Red China's hostility and belligerence in its international attitudes and actions, that are responsible for its isolation.

General George Marshall wrote on January 7, 1947, after he had spent a year trying the very policies now being recommended of friendliness, conciliation, bringing the Chinese Communists into the Chinese Government and into the world community:

I wish to state to the American people that in the deliberate misrepresentation and abuse of the action, policies, and purposes of our Government this propaganda (against the United States) has been without regard for the truth, without any regard whatsoever for the facts, and has given plain evidence of a determined purpose to mislead the Chinese people and the world and to arouse a bitter hatred of Americans.

Mr. Chairman, if I may interject, it can perhaps be thought of in baseball terms. To the Communists, China is first base. The countries around China, where live a third of the people of the world, are second base. Africa and Latin America are third base. But ordinarily you don't go to third base to stop; you go to third base to try to get home. Homeplate, of course, is the United States and Western Europe. They proclaimed precisely this strategy as you know in the recent Lin Piao reaffirmation of the original statement made repeatedly by Mao Tse-tung.

Mr. Chairman, I come from Minnesota and Maury Wills is not one of our chief heroes up there. When he is on first base, do we say, "Well, he is tough. Let's give him second base, and maybe that will please him so, and make him so grateful that he won't try to get to third base"?

No, we try to keep him on first base. In essence that is what our policy under four administrations has been -- to keep Red China on first base. How do you accomplish that? We must not do anything to strengthen Red China. Secondly, we must do all we properly can to strengthen the countries around China that are resisting its expansion.

Mr. Chairman, I don't believe the American people will ever accept the assumption that any tyranny is here to stay, or that we will accept as permanent the subjugation of any people, no matter how powerful the despots may look at the moment.

The cause of Red China's hostility is not its isolation, but the Communist doctrine of the necessity for use of armed force to achieve world revolution. To remove China's isolation now would prove that the doctrine is correct and should be adhered to by them even more tenaciously.

3. That there is a better hope of getting Red China to change its attitudes and activities by giving in to it on matters like diplomatic recognition, trade, and admission to the United Nations than by resolute continuance of the policy of containment as long as Red China refuses to act like a responsible member of civilized society.

4. That changing our policy vis-a-vis Red China just might start an evolutionary process there.

But, of course, it might just as easily reduce the chances of such an evolutionary process. Everybody desires and hopes for "evolution" in Red China. The debate should be over what measures are most likely to produce it.

For example (a) giving Red China greater prestige, influence, entree; that is, making it stronger? Or keeping it as weak and isolated as possible?

(b) Concessions from its intended victims -- like the United States? Or pressures from its present victims -- the Chinese within Red China, those on Taiwan and in southeast Asia, Muslims in Indonesia and Malaysia, et cetera?

(c) Proving that Red China's truculence and stubborn defiance of the world succeeds? Or showing that it will fail?

(d) Taking the mountain -- United Nations -- to Mao? Or patiently and nonbelligerently insisting that Mao come to the mountain of better international conduct if he wants the benefits to Red China of membership in the international community?

What has caused the reported mellowing and evolution inside Yugoslavia, Rumania, the Soviet Union? Influences from without? Or their failures within?

If economic and other pressures from within and without are compelling some Communist governments to moderate their policies, at least toward their own people, shouldn't we keep the pressures up rather than reduce them by helping those Governments to solve their problems?

Changes in China Policy

Let us look now at the changes in policy toward Red China suggested by some. They are mostly three: official diplomatic recognition by the United States, expansion of trade relations, and admission of Communist China to the United Nations. What would be the probable results of such changes, the gains, and the loses?

Almost no one, so far as I have seen, goes further than to express the vague hope that some time after these steps, perhaps after Mao dies or in another generation or two, Red China may "mellow, moderate, mature, evolve." But there is no evidence on which to base the hoped-for changes.

What benefits, economic or political, has Great Britain received from her granting of diplomatic recognition in 1950? Or France 2 years ago?

Prime Minister Nehru of India recognized Communist China in 1949 and worked out with Chou En-lai the "Five Principles of Peaceful Coexistence." He remarked to me that we Americans didn't get along very well with the Chinese Communists because we are not Asians, implying that he being a fellow Asian could. I replied that I feared he would find that the Chinese Communists will not act as Asians but as world revolutionists. He was Red China's chief apologist and advocate -- at the U.N. and elsewhere. How did his fellow Asians in Peking respond to his being their best friend? They invaded India, and left Mr. Nehru a broken man.

It is suggested that with diplomatic recognition we might get more information about conditions in Red China. But we have been getting plenty of information by a variety of means, especially from the thousands of escapees each year. Red China has not allowed newspaper correspondents of any nationality to travel freely in that land unless it had reason to believe in advance that they were generally favorable. Our trouble is not lack of information but erosion of our steadfastness, our patience, our will -- as Mao boasted would be the case.

Resulting Losses

In contrast, there is no uncertainty as to the losses that would result from the suggested weakening of American policy.

Here are some:

1. It would pull the rug out from under our loyal allies on Taiwan. The Chinese are a realistic, even fatalistic, people. With no hope for reunion in freedom with their brethren on the China mainland, they would have little or no choice but to prepare for the inevitable.

Americans who advocate admitting Red China and then add glibly, "Of course we would support the defense of Taiwan," may be salving their own consciences but I think no Asians will be deceived. Twelve million Chinese could hardly maintain indefinitely the will or the capacity to resist 700 million, with the world organization for peace itself rejecting the 12 million and accepting the 700 million.

In 1944 an American Foreign Service officer stationed with the Communists in North China recommended in a secret memorandum that our Ambassador to China be sent on an official visit to the Communist headquarters. He added:

Public announcement that the President's representative had made a visit to the Communist capital at Yenan would have significance that no Chinese would miss -- least of all the Generalissimo.

He was right. When Ambassador Hurley was ordered to make the trip to Yenan, millions of Chinese understood that their cause was lost. Without full American support they could not hope to recover after the war with Japan and put down the Communist rebellion. Obviously America was going to give official status to that rebellion and was announcing we would be impartial toward our ally and its enemy.

The result was deterioration of our ally's morale. It would be the same on Taiwan. At least some of those now advising such a course understand this psychological factor as well as did the Foreign Service officer. It enables them to appear resolutely in favor of containing Red China while recommending a course almost certain to lead to that policy's failure.

2. With weakening or loss of Taiwan our Pacific island chain of defenses would be breached. It is doubtful that the Philippines could long resist Communist pressures and blandishments. Filipinos remember that it was from Taiwan that their country was invaded by the Japanese. It would take vast intervention with American forces to save that new nation for which we certainly have a special responsibility in the Pacific. I have not found any responsible Filipino leaders who favor recognition of Communist China, or its admission to the U.N.

3. The 15 million or so Chinese living in southeast Asia would be shaken. They occupy key positions of power and influence in Vietnam, Malaya, Thailand, Burma, Indonesia, the Philippines. The governments of those countries could not refuse to recognize Communist China once we did. That would mean every Chinese embassy and consulate in southeast Asia, and the world for that matter, would become a protected center of Communist espionage, propaganda, sabotage and subversion of the host government -- as recently exposed in Indonesia and Ghana. Through these embassies and consulates the Chinese minorities would be under direct and almost irresistible pressure to support the aggressive policies of the Mao regime. The stability of the strategic countries of southeast Asia would inevitably be weakened.

4. If the United States were to show that it is not a dependable ally in Asia, our allies elsewhere, including those in Europe, would know they cannot count on us either. What would happen to the whole system of collective security we have been building at such cost and effort, and which this committee has taken such effective leadership in developing, and which is absolutely indispensable to our own survival as a free nation? Why should any country any-

where stand by us if it is not sure we will stand by it?

5. It would tell the neutrals and "uncommitted" nations that they were right all along and that they might as well give in to the winning side at once.

6. Perhaps worst of all, it would tell the 700 million people on the China mainland that we are accepting their subjugation, that we think there is more hope for peace for ourselves in deals with their oppressors than in standing steadfastly with them, the oppressed.

During the war and postwar years the United States relaxed under the skillfully built-up illusions that the Soviet Union was a "peace-loving democracy," eager and willing to cooperate to build a world of order and peace, and that the Chinese Communists were just agrarian reformers. Now they are strong and able boldly to threaten us. Perhaps our best hope of getting out of our present predicament and peril without a nuclear holocaust lies in the urge to be free that lives in the hearts of a billion human beings behind the Communist curtains. Unless these peoples are able from within to force their Communist regimes to change and eventually to abandon Communist world objectives, there is little hope of our avoiding an ultimate all-out clash. Is it intelligent or realistic to adopt a foreign policy that can cause those millions behind the curtains to abandon hope? If the strong accept the Communist overlords, how long can the weak continue to resist them?

Resumption of Trade Relations

What would be the gains from resumption of trade relations? Based on the experience of others and on the announced purposes of the Communists, the gains would be minimal.

The Communists themselves have made clear on numerous occasions that their unwavering purposes are:

First, to get military and industrial equipment and supplies which they cannot yet obtain within the Communist bloc -- not in order that they can trade more with us in the future, but so that they can become self-sufficient and not need to trade with us at all.

Second, to take advantage of a favorable trade or price situation wherever there is one that they cannot match even by exploitation of their own people and of their satellites.

Third, to induce countries to become more and more dependent on trade with the Soviet bloc, and therefore more at its mercy. This applies particularly to Germany and Japan.

Fourth, to divide the free world powers.

Our own objectives in trade are to improve the lives of people, to improve relations between the countries involved, to promote peace and prosperity in the world, and in the process earn a profit much of which becomes capital for further expansion of production and trade with further improvements of living standards.

But none of these is or can be the objective of a Communist regime. All trade is conducted by Communist state organizations and monopolies that have as their single objective the strenghtening of the state. They cannot trade under the accepted rules of the free world without ceasing to be Communist. They cannot cease to be Communist without their movement collapsing. Trade is as much a weapon of their expansionism as are missiles. It is to be expanded or contracted, to be directed here or shifted there, as those at the top determine to be advantageous in promoting the Communist world revolution.

This was dramatically illustrated some years ago when Japan established trade relations with Communist China. It soon found that Red China would not actually carry on trade unless Japan bowed to Red China's political wishes.

In 1953 when Pakistan appeared to be veering toward the United States, Red China cut its purchases of Pakistan cotton from $84 million to $7 million in 1 year.

Where trade between Communist China and other countries does exist, it is only on sufferance of the Communist government and will be extinguished when it has served its purpose. This has never been denied by the Chinese Communist leaders. On the contrary, they have avowed on numerous occasions that complete nationalization of industries and trade and collectivization of agriculture has to come, but in stages -- which means just as fast as they feel themselves strong enough to impose it. Would it be in our interest, economic or otherwise, to help them do it faster?

Admission to the UN

What would be the result of admitting Communist China to the United Nations? I cannot see any important benefits for us or for the United Nations, but the benefits for the Communists would be enormous.

I understand Prof. David Rowe is to discuss with you this afternoon the various ways in which Red China might conceivably be brought into the U.N., including the so-called two-China policy. But the one way I am sure will not be accepted is the two-China device. It is the kind of neat formula that certain types of minds like to play around with in disposing of other people and their problems.

It is a neat formula; all it ignores is the people involved and what they want or will take. I should also add that none of the proposed methods of admitting Red China will be adopted if the United States is determined in opposing them.

One or another might be adopted if the United States lets the impression go out that the United States itself will vote against admission but it will be all right with us if others vote for it. If, however, we believe that Red China is a danger to us, then we cannot permit its admission because admission would represent for Red China the greatest possible diplomatic victory. It would give the Mao regime the stamp of legitimacy and add immeasurably to its prestige and power all over the world. Why has every Communist government, party and front in the world worked tirelessly for 15 years for Red China's admission if that would be bad for Communism and good for us?

Some say, "But Communist China is a fact. We must be realistic. We cannot hide our heads in the sand and ignore it or pretend it is not there." But that is not a description of our policy. On the contrary, it is just because we recognize that Red China is indeed a fact, and such a powerful and dangerous fact, that intelligent concern for our own and the world's future requires its exclusion from the United Nations until it is willing to meet the qualifications for membership. To admit it prior to that time would only make it more powerful and more dangerous.

The Communist regime in China avowedly is dedicated to the isolation and destruction of the United States. Should Americans help it get into a better position to work for that objective? It is a complete non sequitur to say that because "Red China is there" therefore it ought to be admitted to the U.N. There are gangsters in some of our cities. We do not argue that therefore the city councils, courts, and police force should take the gangsters in. Rather we demand that lawless elements be kept out of the forces responsible for maintaining law and order, or "peace and security" -- which the U.N. Charter states is the purpose for which that organization was established.

It is said that the 700 million Chinese are entitled to be represented in the U.N. Certainly. But the Peking regime does not represent the Chinese people any more than the Quisling regime in Norway represented the Norwegian people. Mao has got to destroy the Chinese culture and its values -- moderation, gentlemanliness, primary loyalty to the family, reasonableness, the middle of the road, good manners, which are the essentials of that culture; or he knows it will transform and absorb communism. Mao and the Communists are wholly un-Chinese. How can they represent the Chinese people? Whenever the Chinese people have opportunity to choose their own representatives in free elections, those representatives will undoubtedly be admitted promptly to the United Nations. Incidentally, is it not strange that free elections are demanded in Vietnam "to determine the people's wishes," even during a cruel internal war, but such elections are not demanded in mainland China?

To keep Red China isolated and weaker than it would otherwise be is not denying or ignoring its existence: It is the realistic way to deal with its existence.

It is said that the United Nations ought to be a universal organization with all existing governments in it. But the charter makes perfectly clear that the U.N. was never intended to be a universal orga-

nization. That concept was discussed at San Francisco -- and rejected. Why would the Charter have article 6 which provides for expelling a member which has consistently violated the principles contained in the present Charter, if the organization was supposed to be universal?

Article 4 reads:

Membership in the United Nations is open to all other peace-loving nations which accept the obligations contained in the present Charter, and, in the judgment of the organization, are able and willing to carry out these obligations.

What obligations? Article 2 reads, in part:

All members shall settle their international disputes by peaceful means, and

All members shall refrain in their international relations from the threat or use of force against the territorial integrity or political independence of any state, or in any other matter inconsistent with the purpose of the United Nations.

For more than 10 years we have been negotiating with the Chinese Communists, trying to get them, among other things, to accept the membership obligations prescribed in the U.N. Charter and to agree to refrain from the threat or use of force in their relations with their neighbors. They would then be eligible for U.N. membership. But they have refused.

So, it is grossly untrue to say that the United States is stubbornly, blindly, arbitrarily keeping Communist China out of the United Nations, as is sometimes claimed. Red China is stubbornly keeping itself out. It simply refuses to qualify. I don't know any university that will admit a student without his meeting its entrance requirements -- even if he has a gun.

The Soviet Position

Some ask, "But what's the difference between Communist China and the Soviet Union? The Soviet Union doesn't refrain from the threat or the use of force either. Look at the missiles it put into Cuba."

The answer is that the Soviet Union got into the United Nations at the time of its founding when it was pretending to be peace-loving and willing to cooperate for peace in international affairs. Red China does not even pretend. In fact, the essence of its quarrel with Moscow is over its unwavering insistence on the use of armed force.

It is said that if the United Nations is not to admit Communist China, then it ought to expel the Soviet Union. This is a good logical argument, but it is a useless one. The Soviet Union can veto its own expulsion.

If Communist China were to be admitted, it could not be expelled either, no matter what its conduct.

The fact that there are already some bad actors in the U.N. is all the more reason why it should not, knowingly, bring any more in.

Perhaps it might be useful to establish a new universal organization -- a league of all existing governments, lawless as well as law abiding. But the United Nations is not such an organization. Let us not destroy its character as a union of peace-loving states pooling their strength against lawlessness and aggression from whatever source.

It is hard to understand how some can advocate world peace through world law and at the same time advocate brazen violation of the nearest to world law that we have, the Charter of the United Nations. One would expect that those genuinely wanting to build respect for international law and order would advocate amending the Charter according to its own provision, rather than cynical nullification of it.

If some members of an organization break its rules and standards, that is not fatal to the organization. But if the organization itself votes to scrap its own rules and standards in a vain effort to appease some lawless members, that is starting down the road to its own destruction. I do not want to see the United Nations destroyed, as was the League of Nations, by its own action in violating its own principles.

It is suggested that if we recognize Communist China and admit it to the United Nations, it might improve the functioning of that and related international organizations. There is far more evidence that it would hamper their functioning. The only time the United Nations has ever been able to operate as it was intended to on a matter as serious as aggression was in 1950 when the Soviet Union was absenting itself from the Security Council in an effort to pressure the United Nations into admission of Red China -- and thus was unable to veto U.N. action against the Communist aggression in Korea.

It is clear that Communist governments do not join the United Nations with the same purpose in mind as we and other governments have; namely, to help make it an effective instrument for resolving international disputes. Obviously the Soviet Union joined in order to make sure that the U.N. does not work effectively. The reason is clear: It has a world organization of its own, the Communist Party, with organized, disciplined, efficient units in every country. The Communists intend to win for their world organization. What could be more advantageous than to have seats in the other world organization also, particularly in the Security Council, where perfectly legally under the Charter, they can keep the rival organizations, the United Nations, crippled and ineffective whenever they wish to. Almost all of the more than 100 Soviet vetoes have been against measures that were favored by the overwhelming majority of U.N. members and were in the direction of peace.

Reasons for Chinese Admission

It is contended that it is necessary to have Communist China in the United Nations because no agreement on disarmament can be effective without its participation. But until there is some prospect of an agreement with the Soviet Union which already has deliverable nuclear weapons, what point is there in including Red China which most experts believe cannot have the capacity to deliver powerful nuclear weapons in a decade or more? If and when the day comes, and I hope and pray it may, that the Soviet Union will agree to effective disarmament proposals -- which means with inspection -- there will be some point in negotiation with Red China on this subject. But it is not necessary to have Red China in the U.N. in order to negotiate with her, on this or any other matter. We have had over 130 negotiations in the last 11 years -- almost one a month -- far more than any other non-Communist government has had.

It has been said that the Chinese Communist regime should be accepted because the Chinese people under it are "better off" economically. Such is not the case, as compared with Chinese in Free China. But even if it were true, it would not prove the point. People were better off economically under Hitler than in any other nation in Europe. Did the groups who now urge acceptance of Red China advocate acceptance of Hitler on that ground?

Then there is the old diversionary argument, "What about Chiang Kai-shek? Well, what about him? History will decide his proper place and I predict it will be a high one. But our policy is not and has not been based on Chiang; if he were gone tomorrow, America's interests would be precisely the same. We are trying to help free peoples remain free; therefore, it is to our interest to support all peoples who will make determined efforts in that direction. The free Chinese on Taiwan certainly are making such efforts -- and succeeding. They are now ahead economically of every other country in Asia except Japan. We were able to stop our economic assistance to Free China last July.

So, if one examines the results of the proposed changes in American policy toward China, it is apparent that the benefits would be minimal, if any. The dangers to the countries still free in China, to the United Nations itself, and to our own security and peace, would be certain and serious indeed.

On the other hand, the policy of keeping Red China contained and isolated has proved successful in promoting the vital security interests of the United States.

Senator Hickenlooper. Mr. Chairman, Dr. Judd, the second sentence in the last paragraph as you read it "the dangers to the countries still free in China." In my copy it says Asia.

Dr. Judd. I mean the countries around China.

Senator Hickenhooper. You read it "China."

Dr. Judd. You are correct. The "dangers to the country still free in Asia," --

Senator Hickenlooper. Thank you.

Dr. Judd. Men have always found ways to bring down tyrants -- and the Chinese will bring down theirs -- if only we are not beguiled into throwing the ball game away in the last quarter by failing to stand fast -- "5 minutes longer." We are called upon by history to prove that free citizens have greater fortitude, stronger nerves, and steadier patience and faith than do tyrants -- faith in man and faith in God.

How to Contain China

So the key question for us is how best to keep Communist China contained until it fades or changes. What should we do to implement that basic policy in the period just ahead, and in the most crucial area of immediate contest -- Vietnam?

1. We must recognize and state frankly that we are at war, however much it was unsought and unprovoked by us.

Furthermore, this is the only war the United States was in danger of losing. Why are we in danger of losing this war? Because we are not fighting it in earnest. Why are we not fighting it in earnest? Because it is not called war, it is called peace.

2. We must develop a national will to wage this war with greater vigor and skill by all the measures -- economic and social as well as military -- that are required of us by the enemy's new and different tactics. I will pass over a discussion of the measures most suitable for use in Vietnam. Prof. George Taylor, I am sure, will deal with them most competently.

3. We must develop a greater unity in support of the total war effort and the heroic sacrifices being made in Vietnam by our own brave men and by valiant Vietnamese and other allies. It is unrealistic to ask or expect Vietnamese leaders to be more united in support of American policy than American leaders are. It is unreasonable to expect greater stability on this matter in Saigon than there is on Capitol Hill in Washington.

Furthermore, we cannot expect our allies in Vietnam to sacrifice their lives just to improve the position of the United States for bargaining with their enemy, the Vietcong. For us to negotiate with the Vietcong, as has been suggested, would undermine and demoralize the Government of South Vietnam as surely as negotiation with the Chinese Communists at Yenan in the 1944-46 period undermined the Chinese Government in Chungking.

4. We must remember that the objective of a war is political; namely, to change the will of the adversary, killing as few people as possible. How are we likely to change the will of this adversary in Hanoi? By constantly repeated assurances that we will not make him suffer, no matter what he does? The administration has stated repeatedly that we have "no desire for the overthrow of Hanoi or Peking." Is it any wonder that Ho Chi Minh has felt no need to negotiate? By going all out in South Vietnam, perhaps he can win the struggle for Asia by humiliation of the United States. If he does not succeed, then he can go back to the 17th parallel with no penalty to himself and his regime.

Surely the most effective way to change the will of the enemy is to make him know that his aggression, if continued, will become so costly and dangerous to his own position and power that it is to his advantage to call it off. It is troubles in North Vietnam, not killings in South Vietnam, that are likely to influence Hanoi.

Proposed Action

To achieve this objective of changing the will of the enemy I would stress several main steps:

First, we must continue what we are doing militarily in South Vietnam -- that is, we must hold, and then advance, cleaning out Vietcong and pacifying liberated areas.

Second, we must achieve economic, educational, health, and thereby political improvements, even while fighting a cruel war with every village a potential battlefield. The people of Vietnam are no less important in this "people's war" than the military. Whenever it is shown to the rank and file that there is more for them to gain by supporting their Government in Saigon assisted by the United States, more and more of them will support it.

To stay in their villages and near their land, as they would like most of all to do, is becoming intolerable. They often are under Government forces during the day and under the Vietcong at night, with both men and women now being drafted to fight or to carry loads for the Communists.

If they go over to the Vietcong, the latter simply do not have the resources to give the people better living conditions or any kind of security.

We can bring them over to our side. We can run rings around the Communists more easily in this field than in any other. Even in refugee camps, the people can have better food and better medical care and more hopes of some education for their children than they can under the Communists or in no man's land.

Relieved from fear of Communist reprisals, the people can give the Government the vitally important information they have about Communist bases, hideouts, and planned operations. This could start a tide that in shorter time than most now believe possible could force the Vietcong to pull back from their present positions and induce thousands of them to give up.

Gen. Edwin F. Black, whom I have known for several years as one of the most astute workers in this field and who has served two tours in Vietnam, has written:

The end to the people's war will come when the people make their choice.

A third essential step is to do our utmost to interdict supplies coming from or through North Vietnam. The one thing that seems to me unjustifiable is to ask an American or a Vietnamese soldier to risk his life for freedom, unless his Government is doing everything it possibly can to cut down the supply of men and weapons which enable the enemy to take his life. Whatever the risks here, they must be taken.

Fourth, we should openly let the South Vietnamese do what they can to make trouble in North Vietnam, as they wanted all along to do. It would give an enormous boost to morale to let South Vietnam conduct even a small "liberation front" in North Vietnam, making it more difficult for North Vietnam to operate its fraudulent "liberation front" in South Vietnam.

Fifth, should we bomb cities in the north? Not as we did in Germany and Japan. But we should bomb war plants, powerplants, oil tanks, whatever is important to North Vietnam's war. Why not openly announce to North Vietnam and the world a list of military targets that are going to be destroyed sometime in the next few weeks or months. Won't Ho Chi Minh please get his people out of those plants or away from those areas because we don't want to kill North Vietnamese people; we want only to reduce his capacity to kill South Vietnamese people and to kill Americans. There would be criticism. But the cheers in our country and around the world for such action would make the jeers sound pretty feeble by comparison.

Red China's Entrance into War

Why haven't we done these things? Because an almost hysterical fear has been built up that, among other things, it might lead to war with Red China and "we must not get into a land war with Red China's masses."

Well, all things are possible; and there is no course without risk. But let us weigh realistically the small likelihood of such intervention against the absolutely certain dangers involved in going on as we are.

1. Red China would be inviting and justifying our destruction of her nuclear facilities -- her greatest trump in this world power struggle. There is nothing in South Vietnam that is a fraction as valuable to Red China as those nuclear facilities.

2. How would Red China supply masses of troops in South Vietnam? A Communist army, just like Napoleon's, moves on its stomach. The Communists are having all they can do to supply the Vietminh and Vietcong forces already in South Vietnam.

3. Red China cannot forget for a moment the presence on her flank of powerful air and military forces on Taiwan. Most of mainland China's lines of communications run north and south and are within easy reach of the airbases we have helped the Chinese build on that island for the very purpose they are now serving -- a powerful deterrent to Red China's entering the war and getting itself too far extended to the south.

Some 700,000 to a million Red Chinese are tied down opposite Taiwan, on guard against possible action from that base. Red China also has to keep large numbers of troops on the long border with India, on the longer border with the Soviet Union, on the borders of Korea, and hundreds of thousands of soldiers are required to maintain order in Tibet, Mongolia, and at home.

4. If Red China were to get involved in southeast Asia, she would have to concentrate on it to a degree that would almost certainly make her lose her bitter struggle with the Soviet Union for control of the world Communist movement. That struggle is enormously more important to Red China than anything in Vietnam. Red China talks war -- but hasn't done one reckless thing. The Soviet Union talks peace -- but puts missiles into Cuba aimed at the United States, and it is supplying the sinews of war to North Vietnam.

Policy of Confrontation

Despite powerful considerations like the above, many in our country seem almost paralyzed by two words, "confrontation" and "escalation." They assert, without evidence to support it, that a firm confrontation with Communist aggression will lead to escalation into nuclear war -- "and we must not have nuclear war."

Just to say that, of course, makes more likely the nuclear war we want to avoid. It encourages the Communists to believe we will surrender rather than have nuclear war, and that therefore at the right moment they can cow us into submission by the threat of it. It may well be that the outcome of this world struggle will be determined by which side appears to be less afraid of nuclear war.

There is no such thing as power if there is not the will to use it.

Let us, however, look not only at reasons like the above but at the record:

Eleven times in the last 20 years under three administrations we have accepted a confrontation with Communist expansionism -- this is the 12th. Eleven times the United States has simply said, "No, this we cannot take."

Did any one of those 11 confrontations lead to escalation, as was threatened by the Communists and feared by us? No, each led to de-escalation. Each led to improvement of the situation. Each time the Communists said, in effect, "So sorry. We just wanted to know." And shifted to some other field. There followed a lessening, not increase, of tensions.

What has led to escalation? Not confrontations, but hesitation, indecision, division, vacillation, appearance of fear. From the standpoint of inviting or prolonging war with Communists, it is as dangerous to look like a paper tiger as to be one.

So, I have no difficulty in deciding which is the wiser and safer course for the United States to follow with respect to Communist China.

The true way to influence our enemies is to stand steadfastly by our friends.

How foolish and shortsighted it would be to abandon the policy of patience, firmness, and strength in support of human freedom and of our commitments to friends and allies, the course which when consistently followed has brought peace, in order to make changes in policy which would inevitably weaken our friends and allies -- the very advocacy of the changes has already shaken some of them -- and would inevitably strengthen our enemies.

Can we really believe that for us to prove to the Chinese Communists that their tough, unyielding belligerence gets results is the way to get them to abandon that belligerence?

Admission of China to the UN

Particularly would it be shortsighted and foolish to give such a smashing and wholly unnecessary victory to Red China, right now when it is in such trouble worldwide. Does it make sense to accept its representatives into our country and into the United Nations just when its representatives are being exposed and expelled from countries in Africa, Latin America, and Asia -- countries that followed the very policies toward Red China we are now being urged to adopt?

Each year since 1954 it has been so confidently predicted that Red China's admission was "inevitable," probably at the next session of the General Assembly, that many came to believe it. Well, a dozen years have gone by and it has not yet happened. Last year saw the high water mark of support. In these last months the tide has been turned against Red China by its own actions. Countries that voted for admission are having their eyes opened. This is no time for us to close ours.

Mr. Chairman, administrations change, but facts do not. And the facts with respect to Red China's lack of qualifications for membership in the U.N. remain the same under President Johnson as under Presidents Truman, Eisenhower, and Kennedy.

May I quote three points stressed before the U.N. General Assembly by the late Ambassador Adlai Stevenson, who could hardly be called a blind reactionary or isolationist. Saying that "the whole future of the United Nations may be at stake," he urged the members to consider with great care the fact that --

"The step advocated (admission of Red China) once taken, is irreversible. We cannot try it and then give it up if it fails to work. We must assume that, once in our midst, the Peking representatives would stay -- for better or for worse.

"Secondly, there are ample grounds to suspect that a power given to such bitter words and ruthless actions as those of the Peking regime, far from being reformed by its experience in the United Nations, would be encouraged by its success in gaining admission to exert, all the more forcefully, by threats and maneuvers, a most disruptive and demoralizing influence on the organization at this critical moment in its history.

"Thirdly, its admission, in circumstances in which it continues to violate and defy the principles of the Charter, could seriously shake public confidence in the United Nations -- I can assure you it would do so among the peoples of the United States -- and this alone would significantly weaken the organization."

In summary, seating of Red China in the United Nations would be illegal. It would require violation of the organization's charter.

It would be immoral. It would almost certainly mean removal of a member that abides by the charter to seat a nonmember that brazenly refuses to abide by the Charter. It would abandon 700 million people to Communist subjugation. It would properly be regarded as an attempt to buy peace for ourselves by sacrificing our principles and other peoples' freedom.

And it would bring no practical benefits. On the contrary, there would be definite and disastrous losses -- with our allies; with the neutrals; with the peoples of Asia and everywhere else who desire to retain their freedom; and with the long-suffering millions now under Communist rule who long to regain their freedom. Do not break the hearts of the oppressed and their continued will to resist from within by accepting their oppressors.

Free Asia will crumble once it believes the Communists are winning. Admission of Red China to the United Nations would mean to much of Asia, as it should mean to us, that the Communists have all but won.

Having spent more than $100 billion to strengthen the will and capacity of free nations and peoples to resist communism, would it make sense now to strengthen communism?

The whole Communist movement worldwide is in serious trouble today. Why change the policies that have contributed to its difficulties both abroad and at home, and thereby provided the free world its first ray of hope in years? We must always keep the door open to any genuine change on their part -- as proved by deeds. We must keep the door resolutely closed to Communist threats, tricks, or promises not supported by performance.

Mr. Chairman, this is the time to stand fast for the basic containment policies that have proved sound and more successful during

the last 15 years than most people believed possible. There is no course that does not involve serious risk; we are dealing with a ruthless and resourceful enemy. But such a course as outlined involves, I believe, far less risk.

Unless someone can suggest policies that offer better prospects of success, based on something more substantial than speculation, wishful thinking, or just hope, I can see no sound, sensible, or logical reason to change present policies and every reason to continue them, always being flexible in our tactics as required by developments as they come along.

Keep Red China on first base.

TAYLOR STATEMENT

The following is the statement of George E. Taylor, director of the Far Eastern and Russian Institute at the University of Washington. He appeared before the Committee on March 28, 1966. (See p. 182)

Mr. Chairman, and members of the committee, I am honored by this opportunity to appear before your committee to discuss some aspects of U.S. relations with Communist China. Since I speak as a member of the academic profession, it might not be out of place for me to refer briefly to the basis of all academic work, the availability of information and materials.

U.S. Information

The high quality of the testimony which has been heard by this committee stems, in my view, from the fact that the United States is better informed about Communist China today than is any other country in the free world. Our Government provides daily translations of the mainland press and periodicals for general use, it translates for its own purposes a great variety of specialized Chinese printed material, some of which it puts at the disposal of scholars. There are about a dozen major universities with libraries and staff sufficient to provide the student with advanced graduate training on China. Courses in the Chinese language can be taken at hundreds of universities and colleges. The financial support provided by private foundations and by the National Defense Education Act has been instrumental in providing us with hundreds of scholars well trained in the Chinese language and one or more of the disciplines. Our library holdings on Communist China are very extensive, and we probably publish more studies of Communist China than all other non-Communist countries put together. The combined resources of England, France, and Germany, both human and material, are small indeed when compared with those of the United States.

The American scholar, it has been pointed out, cannot go to Communist China and therefore loses a valuable asset. This is true; the Communists will not allow him. There is no substitute for being on the ground, but in some cases there is no great advantage in being there either. Most of the correspondents of other countries who have resided in Peking are quite frank about the difficulties and frustrations facing the journalistic profession in that country. Hong Kong is a far more valuable source of information about Communist China than is Peking. Ironically enough, an American journalist, Edgar Snow, has written a comprehensive book on Communist China containing very unusual information because he had access to men in high positions and had written about the Communists before the war. So if going to Peking is of any advantage, the Americans have already taken as much advantage of it as any of those who have recognized Communist China. Japan does not recognize Communist China but as many Japanese have visited there, probably, as have citizens of the Soviet Union. Recognition, therefore, is not necessary for scholars, journalists, and politicians to visit a Communist country if the country so wishes. The main difficulty of getting information about China stems not from the fact that Americans are not allowed to visit there, but from the extraordinary efforts made by the Communist regime to prevent both its own people and other peoples from knowing those things it wishes to conceal. I would not be surprised if Peking found our economic studies to be more accurate than their own. I wish to mention this point about information because there are those who feel that we would be much better informed if we recognized Communist China and could send our scholars and journalists to that country. Unless there were a radical change in the attitude of the Communist regime the evidence does not suggest, considering the price we would have to pay, either that access to the mainland would make that much difference or that access depends upon recognition.

I wish to make it clear, Mr. Chairman, that I would be happy to go to China tomorrow and I know the State Department would let me go, if I could get a visa.

I am not suggesting that we have sufficient information about Communist China, merely that we have as much if not more than anyone else. In the academic profession, while we all read the same materials, we do not arrive at the same conclusions. I find myself in general agreement with the descriptive material presented in this testimony -- that Communist China's domestic problems are serious and exacting, her military as well as economic resources are not those of a great power, her adventurous excursions in foreign policy have been costly and discouraging, and that she is not getting along very well with the Soviet Union in either party or state relations. But I cannot follow some of the policy recommendations of my colleagues because I think that they are based on debatable premises, and it is the premises that are crucial.

Limited Stability

Much is made of the assumption that we have stabilized our relations with the Soviet Union and that the same can be done with Communist China. The Soviet model is so much taken for granted that it is never clearly defined. It is asserted that we now have a stable and tolerable relationship with the Soviet Union and that this has come about through an evolutionary process marked by changes within the Communist system. There certainly have been considerable changes and there is a sort of stability.

But in my view the present stability is brittle in the extreme and is based mainly on the superior military power of the United States and its allies and on a common interest in avoiding one kind of war, and one only, nuclear conflict between the United States and the U.S.S.R. Moscow still favors subversion and "just" wars of national liberation. The balance can change because it does not rest merely on a counting of nuclear bombs. There are other factors in the balance such as the state of economy, the state of our alliances, the quality of our leadership. As we showed at the time of the Cuban crisis, a shift in the nuclear balance of power can be prevented by the use of conventional weapons. Nor can we fail to note that the present stability includes a war with the Soviet Union by proxy, in Vietnam, and Soviet cooperation with Cuba in an effort to subvert Latin America, whose governments are so alarmed by Cuban activities that many have broken off diplomatic relations.

Two sets of reasons are usually given for the new Soviet behavior. There are those who think that the stability of our relations with the Soviet Union is due to changes in the mode of production which have been reflected in changes in the ideological superstructure. They would phrase it differently but it is still vulgar Marxism. As the Communists put on fat, according to this theory, they acquire a democratic dislike for muscle. Such scholarly investigation as we have of this subject, to say nothing of the record, suggests that the question of whether or not there have been basic changes in the political objectives of the Soviet Union is still open to serious question.

Then there are those who think that present Soviet behavior arises from the fact that we have followed a policy of containment combined with recognition and membership in the U.N. The same formula applied to China should produce the same results. It is proposed to continue the containment, offer recognition, and cease to block the way into the U.N. This is doubtful analogy on which to base action. Nor is there any real parallel between Communist China and the U.S.S.R., or surety that the same techniques will bring the same results. But the U.S.S.R. could be used as an interesting case study of what happens when a Communist party is treated with generosity and goodwill, as during World War II, and allowed to operate within an organization for the maintenance of peace.

In my view it is safer to proceed on the premise that there is no world community, as the phrase goes, into which we can induce the Chinese to enter. Unfortunately we live in a world in which there are at least two violently opposed concepts of international relations, of political and social organization, and of world order. The dialog between them is still minimal. Everything we do with Communist China has to be seen in this context. Whatever the relations between Peiping and Moscow, as far as the world community is concerned, they share the same outlook. The problem then is one of how to define our relations with the Chinese section of the Communist world. It is clearly necessary, in this dangerous world, to do this.

Influence on Policy

Further to clarify my premises, I do not think, for example, that the evidence supports the fashionable view that the Communist world is falling apart and that Communist states have the same sort of foreign policy objectives as any other nation state or can be expected to pursue them in the same manner. The social and political content of nationalism is determined by the institutional power configuration and this is what is new and lasting about communism. It is because it is the nature of power that determines foreign policy -- to put the matter very briefly -- that I feel so little hope of any changes in Chinese Communist policies that are not forced on her. It is necessary to mention this because there is a great reluctance on the part of China specialists, perhaps because they love the Chinese so much, to admit that the Chinese Communists are really Communists.

The agrarian reformers of the forties are now the aging paranoids of the sixties, to be handled, it would seem, by group therapy. If they were really nationalists masquerading as Communists, then Chinese tradition as well as the humiliations of 19th-century imperialism would be relevant to their mood, but in my view the Communists represent a complete break with the past. Their world view is not conditioned by the imperial past although they are willing to exploit it. A comparison with some real nationalists will point up the differences. It was the National Government that won the ending of imperial privileges in 1942 and lost the chance of building up a modern China largely as a result of the Japanese invasion. We might have difficulties with them if they were in power on the mainland, but I doubt they would be sponsoring the Vietcong or fomenting trouble over the rest of the world.

There is nothing about Chinese nationalism that calls for the hate campaign of the Chinese Communists against the United States, for the militarization of a quarter of the people of the earth, for the racial invective that pervades so much of their propaganda, even in Hong Kong, or for the support of revolutionary movements in southeast Asia, Africa, and Latin America spelled out in the Central Committee decisions of 1963 and reaffirmed in the Lin Piao statement. A true nationalism would call for attention to domestic problems and would certainly avoid a quarrel with a powerful neighbor.

Nature of U.S. Policy

In conducting this very valuable review of our relations with China we have to reckon with a commonly held view that U.S. policy has been doctrinaire, rigid, uncompromising, emotional, and unrealistic, even that it was manufactured not in the State Department but in the China lobby. An examination of the record shows that this is not very good history. American policy toward Communists states in general and China in particular has been pragmatic and flexible. In this regard we may note the rapid adaptation to Tito in 1948, the opening of cultural exchange with the U.S.S.R. and our carefully graduated responses to the East European satellites. With Communist China we were about ready for recognition when the Korean war broke out. More recently we have offered to discuss disarmament, negotiate a settlement of southeast Asia, and permit Americans to travel to the mainland. In this connection I admire the temperate tone and placid reasoning of the position paper signed recently by some of my colleagues. It is good to have debate and to differ as honest men.

The policy problem is how to regulate our relations with Communist China in such a way as to provide for the peaceful and independent development of southeast Asia and to secure her cooperation in the maintenance of world peace.

Lin Piao Statement

Like most of the witnesses, I am strongly in favor of containing Chinese Communist aggression. We do not all agree, however, on what we are containing, in fact one gets the impression that some witnesses think that there is almost nothing to contain. Most have referred to the most recent statement of Chinese Communist political goals, the Lin Piao position paper of September 1965, but it is variously interpreted. The Aesopian dialogue of the Communist world is not always easy to follow and this effort was clearly designed to achieve several purposes at the same time. In my view it should be taken seriously as a general indication of the objectives and strategy of the Peking wing of the movement. It is not impossible that this strategy could be made to work. It is based on the assumption that the revolution is not going to occur in the great industrial states, that the Achilles heel of the West is the third world, that the promotion of wars of national liberation in Africa, Latin America, and southeast Asia will distract and waste the energies of the Western Powers, confuse their peoples, and demoralize their leaders.

Some believe that Communist China is too weak to carry out such a grandiose strategy, that in fact she is now reeling from shattering defeat. When the Soviets came to the assistance of the Chinese Nationalists in 1923 they were not a strong power, but they almost succeeded in taking over the Nationalist movement at a cost of 1,000 advisers and about $3 million. The Chinese Communists were not very stong when they provided the Vietminh with the heavy weapons that made possible the conquest of Dienbienphu, nor when they intervened in North Korea, nor when they promoted a Communist attempt to take over Malaya in 1948. May I also suggest that the Chinese Communists were involved in the attempted coup d'etat in Indonesia last October and that it came very close to succeeding? If it had succeeded it would have been followed by an intensification of the war against Malaya, Thailand would have been caught in the pincers, and our position in Vietnam would have been very precarious.

The main question that the leaders and peoples of southeast Asia are asking is, Who is going to win? Under the above conditions it would have seemed that the Chinese brand of communism was in the ascendent; Lin Piao's statement would have looked like a curtain raiser rather than noisy bragging or defensive defiance. China is obviously in no position to seek a head-on collision with the United States and is most unlikely to give us the opportunity to declare war on her, but she is quite capable of fostering wars of national liberation wherever opportunities are provided. We have chosen to assist in blocking one of these wars in South Vietnam, under the most unfavorable conditions for us that could possibly have been selected. If we succeed there it will not stop the Chinese from aiding others to promote similar wars of national liberation; if we fail we do not necessarily lose the whole of southeast Asia but it would be that much harder to defend.

Building of Viable States

How do we contain this sort of threat, when the rich countries are getting richer and the poor, poorer; when population growth outstrips economic growth in most of the underdeveloped countries? Certainly not by denying its existence. In the Philippines, made to order for Mao's strategy, American help and advice was of decisive importance. That was in 1951. In Malaya British forces and political programs preserved the country from a Chinese Communist takeover, but it took 10 years to do it. India, Burma, and Indonesia took care of the problem themselves and arrived at their own compromises. In Vietnam the Communists were not stopped until 1954 when they had half the country and the nationalist movement split into two opposed camps. In Japan the Communists are far from weak, but they were robbed of an agrarian base by land reform measures undertaken during the occupation.

The answer is clearly to assist in building up viable states in the many parts of the world that might come under Communist pressure, Chinese or Soviet. To do this is going to require not force backed by a political program, but a political program backed by force, the sort of program that was given some substance recently at Honolulu. It is best to start before massive force is required but if we come in late, as we have in Vietnam, then force is necessary to hold the line so that the real war -- on the intellectual, economic, and social fronts -- can be won.

To bring stability and prosperity to the third world requires a combination of tremendous human dedication, enormous technical and economic help, and far-reaching social and political changes. To disrupt the process takes comparatively small material resources when they are combined with a forceful and appealing program -- and with organization. Peking has such a program, expects reverses, and has persuaded several Communist parties in other nations that it has the right answer for the future shape of Communist expansion.

Purposes of U.S. Containment

How far should containment go? Clearly, far enough to prevent the exploitation of wars of national liberation. What is the ultimate purpose? I have argued that it is naive to expect containment to reform a Communist country. We must obviously make it clear to Peking that we welcome and are always ready to accept any overtures directed toward improvement of relations. But the real problem is the future of the National Government of the Republic of China. We are the only great power involved in the Chinese civil war. But there are other civil wars in the world today which have been created or intensified by Communist action -- two Germanies, Koreas, Mongolias, Vietnams -- that are of equal if not greater urgency and magnitude. They also raise problems of representation. The difference is that one of the Chinas has a permanent seat on the Security Council and the other China has, in effect, been at war with the U.N. since 1950. If the civil conflict cannot be resolved, the problem of policy comes down to the question of what sort of international status we are willing to accord to the National Government and to the People's Democratic Republic. The United States will not allow the Communists to take Taiwan by force or assist the Nationalists in returning to the mainland unless we are at war with Peking, so the status quo is what we have to live with, as do the Koreans, Germans, Mongols, and Vietnamese, to say nothing of the Irish. Someday, sometime, the international status of the two parts of China must correspond to the facts of power, but there is no hurry. At the present time there is no advantage to the United States in talking about recognition or admission to the U.N. and there are a great many disadvantages. Why help the Peking regime when it is in trouble? What conceivable interest do we have in assisting this regime to become a great power?

Peking is Isolating United States

It is said that we should not isolate Peking. It is Peking that is trying to isolate us. Communist China is far from being isolated; she has diplomatic relations of a sort with about 40 countries and is trading with many she does not recognize, such as Japan and Canada. She is very much in the international community where it counts, in fact much too much. The terms she has announced for taking a seat in the U.N. are so outrageous that they must have been designed to show her contempt for that organization. Her terms for recognition are humiliating in the extreme, although she would be delighted to have us help her finish off the civil war by reducing or eliminating the international status of the National Government. If the Chinese Communists really want to live in peace with the world they are quite capable of making a move in that direction.

In the meantime, it should not be beyond the wit of man to devise ways and means of putting the burden of proof, as far as peaceful intentions are concerned, on the Peking regime, so long as nothing is done to damage American credit in Asia and our willingness to stand by our friends and our principles.

ROWE STATEMENT

The following is the statement of David N. Rowe, professor of political science at Yale University. Dr. Rowe was born in Nanking, China, in 1905 and lived in central China until mid-1922. He appeared before the Committee on March 28, 1966. (See p. 182)

I want to discuss here briefly the China problem today in U.S. policy-making.

Why does this problem exist (in the United States)?

It exists, of course, because the Korean war proved that Communist China was willing to fight the free world in order to achieve Communist expansionist aims in Asia vis-a-vis Korea. (Japan was the real objective and the most important one.)

The formula has been repeated in --

(a) Tibet -- anti-India and Nehru.

(b) Laos -- 250,000 Chinese Communist troops massed on the Laos frontier in 1961-62 to bring a settlement favorable to Communist China.

Again on the Indian frontier which, of course, involved an actual Sino-Indian war, with Communist Chinese troops fighting Indian troops.

Finally, Communist Chinese support for North Vietnam aggression against South Vietnam. The Sino-Russian ploy; North Vietnam (the North Korean of this episode) is immune from destruction at the hands of the United States and its allies, because of its joint Sino-Soviet backing. Communist China stands directly behind North Vietnam's aggression militarily, to prevent such military action against North Vietnam as is necessary to the attainment of our military objectives in and for South Vietnam. Thus, Communist China achieves for North Vietnam immunity from the consequences of its aggression in South Vietnam which the previous Sino-Soviet techniques and strategies of support for North Korea failed to achieve, and this without any cost thus far in Communist Chinese manpower.

Thus, Sino-Soviet "indirect" aggression in South Vietnam depends upon their joint success in preventing the United States from taking military action against North Vietnam adequate to achieve the defense of South Vietnamese independence.

The chief Sino-Soviet weapon in this psychological warfare struggle is the threat of massive Chinese manpower intervening as "Peoples Volunteers" in the Vietnamese war.

How did we deal with this threat and fact in the Korean war?

(a) By making no direct attacks on the Chinese Communist home base.

(b) By application of massive firepower to Communist Chinese mass attacks in Korea, resulting in such heavy Communist Chinese casualties as to make them insupportable indefinitely. This led to truce talks of great length -- so that most U.S. casualties were incurred during the truce talk period.

The difference this time is that we have publicly announced that never again would there be a privileged sanctuary in Communist China in case we got into another war directly with Communist Chinese military forces under whatever guise and in whatever conditions.

Thus, the risk to the Communist Chinese regime is incalculably greater this time than in the case of Korea, albeit the current actual costs to them are negligible.

Therefore, the prevention of a military showdown now between the United States and Communist China is the main aim of Communists everywhere. Why?

(a) If such a showdown came soon it would destroy Communist China as such and constitute the single most catastrophic setback in history to the course of the Communist world revolution.

(b) If such a showdown can be prevented for 5 to 10 years, the pro-Communist-China and anti-anti-Communist elements in this country count on the development of Communist Chinese thermonuclear power to produce a standoff and make Communist China then invulnerable to U.S. destruction, by means of the retaliatory threat. They count on this stage lasting 10 or 20 years during which either one and probably both of two things would happen.

1. The United States would prove unable to develop any effective deterrent to so-called "indirect aggression" and to "peoples war" with the result that all of Asia would come under Chinese Communist domination and control, and the impact on Africa and Latin America would be disastrous.

2. Under the deterrent of terror the political and psychological pressures toward a "detente" with Communist China similar to present illusions along that line with the U.S.S.R. would engender a thorough and complete "coexistence" policy vis-a-vis the Communist Chinese.

The Communist Chinese need "coexistence" much worse than do the Russians. Why? The lack of massive external support and their huge and insoluble internal problems, doom them forever to weakness and mediocrity and complete totalitarianism and military adventurism. They are trying their hardest now to soften our approach to them under the blackmail of aggression and war to gain at no cost to them politically, what they need in outside economic and technical support from the West and particularly from the United States of America. This is why their friends in the United States are trying hard to soften the U.S. approach to Communist China.

Themes of Soft Approach

What are the main themes now being pushed by the pro-Communist China and anti-anti-Communist elements along this line?

A. (Theme: The historical causation line.) The Communist Chinese foreign policies are merely a logical result of China's frustrations and suffering at the hands of the outside world for the last century or more.

Question. Why are these frustrations and hostile reactions focused on the United States, the one nation with the longest and best record of pro-Chinese aims and actions for 125 years?

Answer. Because our past pro-Chinese policy and our present anti-Communist policies are identical. Both involve (as with our war against Japan 1941-45) the defense of the territorial integrity and sovereignty of small and/or weak countries in Asia. The Chinese Communists today are the chief declared opponents of this policy of ours, as Japan was previously.

Question. In this framework, why should anyone react emotionally to the word "Munich" when it is used similarly to evoke a hostile reaction to any sellout of our friends in southeast Asia? (That is, was a surrender to fascism appeasement and surrender, a surrender to communism neither?)

Answer. Is this reaction hypocritical, merely naive, or knowingly wrong headed?

Softening of Communist Chinese

B. (Theme: The "inevitable softening of the Communist Chinese.") This line is pushed hard by all the pro-Communist China and anti-anti-Communist elements. Even Fidel Castro gives them aid and comfort by blasting the current Chinese Communist leaders as "senile" and anticipating a less dangerous Communist Chinese leadership to come with the demise of Mao.

Question. Was Khrushchev better than Stalin, and is the present leadership of the U.S.S.R. better than Khrushchev?

Answer. No.

Two-Chinas Policy

C. (Theme: The "two Chinas" line.) This is tantamount to saying we can play with enemies without alienating friends. Whatever the distant future holds we cannot know. But for the responsible policy-making future there can be no two-Chinas policy for the United States or anyone else. For example, the United Kingdom has tried to adopt a two-Chinas policy: recognition of Peiping and trying to do business with Taipei. Result: it has neither China. The Communist Chinese have never entered full diplomatic relations with the United Kingdom, and the United Kingdom cannot really cooperate with the Republic of China or Taiwan, the single most rapidly advancing and developing area in Asia. By contrast, the United States without recognition of Peiping, has much higher level diplomatic contacts with the Chinese Communists than Britain, and is the main ally and collaborator with the Republic of China on Taiwan.

Question. Should anyone believe there can be any formal United States-Communist China diplomatic relationship without U.S. abandonment of the Republic of China?

Answer. No.

Question. Can any U.S. administration advocate abandonment of the Republic of China without committing political suicide?

Answer. This is what two-Chinas policy advocates really are urging the administration toward, some knowingly and others unwittingly. That is, the two-China policy means, to start, full diplomatic and other relations with Communist China, and with a trend toward this once set in motion we can easily abandon the Republic of China on Taiwan, particularly since it would break relations with us if we recognized Communist China.

Truth of Chinese Statements

D. (Theme: The "they don't mean what they say" line.) Anyone who believes in drawing the lessons of history, should not object if we say the world would have been better off if more people had taken seriously such historical documents as the Marxist manifesto, Hitler's "Mein Kampf" or the pre-World War II utterances of the Japanese imperialists. The current utterances of the Communist Chinese leadership seems just as dangerously unrealistic today as the previously cited ones did then. They are therefore hard to give credence to.

For example, in the same March 19, 1966, issue of the New York Times in which witnesses before this committee were quoted as describing Communist China as being "fundamentally weak" and "inward looking" and "desirous of avoiding a military confrontation with the United States," the Times carried (on the last page in the upper right-hand corner) a statement by Kuo Mo-jo, Vice Chairman of the Standing Committee of the National Peoples Congress, as follows:

Listen, U.S. imperialists: The 650 million people of China are prepared. If you insist on another trial of strength, suit yourselves. Come when you like, alone or with others. We will not shut you out; we will wipe you out as many as you come.

Questions. When men talk madness -- as the Communist Chinese do -- would it not be wise to assume they mean it until and unless they prove otherwise by their acts? Yes. Are the Communist Chinese proving otherwise by their acts? No -- they do just the opposite. Witness: Korea, the Taiwan Straits, the Indian frontier, Laos, and Thailand, as well as Vietnam.

Simultaneous Hard and Soft Line

E. (Theme: The "simultaneous hard and soft" line.) "Containment, but not isolation." The friends of Communist China and the anti-anti-Communists are constantly describing our post-World War II policy toward the U.S.S.R. as combining these two features and advocating that we adopt such a policy toward Communist China. What is the truth?

1. Our immediate postwar policy toward the U.S.S.R. was not one of containment but of surrender. Eastern Europe and Outer Mongolia were surrendered to the U.S.S.R. with the connivance of the United States and even with highest pressures being brought to bear by the United States on our allies to surrender to the U.S.S.R. landgrabs, as in the case of Nationalist China and of Mongolia. This was an effort to appease Stalin and get him to accept this as his price for cooperating with us. He took the price, but did not cooperate.

2. The containment policy was then resorted to and it has prevented further territorial takeover. However, this whole policy is now threatened by French action in re NATO, and the chief deterrent to armed action by the U.S.S.R. in Europe is now the mutual thermonuclear threat.

3. Accordingly, we have generally not applied the policy of surrender of territory to Communist China, and in every case but

one, have resisted Communist Chinese efforts to push outward. This case was Laos in 1961-62, and much of our trouble in Vietnam stems from the application to Laos of the formula of appeasement and surrender through the device we tried to use in China 1946-47 to prevent a Communist Chinese takeover pure and simple; that is, the coalition government with Communists in it. Sino-Soviet cooperation helped bring about the surrender in Laos and thus to mark out South Vietnam and Thailand as the next Communist targets.

4. As far as Communist China is concerned containment means isolation: the two are one and inseparable and the crux of this problem is Taiwan. The Communist Chinese price for nonisolation -- which is a two-sided matter, not solely under our control -- is the handing over of Taiwan to them; that is, destruction of containment. Any U.S. administration which would even suggest any such thing would commit political suicide by producing a major catastrophe in Asian affairs.

Question. Do those who suggest the ending of Communist China's isolation in re the United States, the United Nations, and so forth, know what they are saying? Are they merely stupid? Or hypocritical? Or are they trying to be "smart"?

Allied Support

F. (Theme) The line "we have no support among our allies" for our southeast Asian policy. This line was, for example, advanced in re the Japanese by that great authority (?) on Japanese affairs, Mr. George Kennan. Mr. Kennan today seems to know even less about Far Eastern affairs than he did 17 years ago, when I asked him what Asia would mean in our future struggle with communism. He replied then that the struggle with communism would be settled somewhere along a line drawn between Stettin in the north and Trieste in the south. Of course, since then we have had Greece and Turkey in Europe; Korea, the Taiwan Straits, and the 17th parallel in Vietnam; not to mention Laos, and the Indian frontier, in Asia.

But today Mr. Kennan is our latest "Johnny-come-lately" on Japan. Mr. Kennan says we are seriously alienating our Japanese friends by our military actions in Vietnam. He thus shows his profound ignorance of the Japanese people who suffer as we do ourselves in this country, from the presence of a lunatic fringe of cowards, pacifists, appeasers, and just plain, simple Communists and pro-Communists. In spite of this they basically understand and respect what we are doing in Vietnam. They know their own security depends upon us, and our resolution and will to suffer and die for what we believe in. Despite their "lunatic fringe" problem the Japanese people are sound and sensible. They understand the need of armed defense. Their own small "self-defense" forces are slowly but steadily growing in strength and improving.

Even business firms today are sending their new employees for short periods of living and working with the armed forces before starting work, in order to bolster their morale and acquaint them again with the spirit of disciplined organization so lacking in upper level educational institutions today both there and elsewhere. They increasingly support their defense arrangements with us, and this is because of, not in spite of, the war in Vietnam. In the past 2 years the number of Japanese who support their alinement with the West has increased materially, and the number advocating so-called neutralism has decreased. This "new mood" is the result, I believe, of our firmness in southeast Asia, an area vital to Japan from an economic point of view.

The Japanese people will respect and honor success on our part in Vietnam. Like others, they view with apprehension any irresolution, lack of determination, or willingness to pull out and surrender, on our part. This is generally true of all Asians, from Japan clear around through Korea, Taiwan, the Philippines, southeast Asia, and south Asia. This is one of the many reasons why we cannot and must not fail in Vietnam.

Other friends and allies, including Korea, the Republic of China, the Philippines, Australia, and New Zealand are helping in various ways in Vietnam, and will doubtless help still more in the future. If and when the need arises, the arrangements have no doubt been already worked out for the Republic of China, on Taiwan, to become directly involved. But, whether this will be required only time can tell.

As to allies and friends in Europe and elsewhere the vast preponderance of them approve what we are doing whether they say or not. Secretary Rusk is right on this.

Better Relationship

G. (Theme) The line "if we can get to know enough about China and the Chinese people we can promote better relationships with the Chinese Communists."

This, in my opinion, is the exact opposite of the truth. Actually, the more we study Chinese history and culture the more we can see that the Chinese Communists are revisionists who have chosen to reemphasize the worst that can be found in the Chinese tradition instead of the best. What are some of these things? Totalitarianism, authoritarianism and autocracy, conspiratorial politics, dogmatic subjectivity, the perversion of education into sheer indoctrination, the exaltation of political dogma, and the corresponding debasement of technology, true science, and scientific expertise. They have chosen these emphases, and allied them with the religious subjectivism of Marxism, which appeals to them because it demands so little in the way of abandonment of those reprehensible features of the Chinese tradition that they have seized upon in their fanatical desperation and urgency to change China and the Chinese overnight. This latter characteristic they assert over and over again in such terms as "the great leap forward," "socialism within 5 years," "do 20 years work in 2," and so forth.

Such hopeless and futile experiments at doing something with nothing, as the backyard steel furnace debacle, are also illustrative of this trend, as well as of the subjectivist dogmatism of the upper level Chinese Communist leadership. No wonder the Chinese intellectuals reacted in such a hostile way to this leadership in the brief interval of the so-called "Hundred Flowers" episode when they were encouraged to express their opinions, only to be ruthlessly suppressed by Mao Tse-tung when he realized the truth; namely, that they were not for him but against him. With true subjective self-deception he had convinced himself that the intellectuals were on his side. But they were not, and are not today. In the last 2 years 160,000 intellectuals have been seized by the regime and forced into so-called "reform through labor" camps. (See the Sydney Herald; March 17, 1966, for reference to this.) This means for most of them merely slow death by overwork and starvation. This has gone virtually unnoticed in the West, at a time when even some European Communists are openly rebelling at the recent arrest, "trial," and condemnation to forced labor of only two Soviet intellectuals.

Indeed, the notion that to know the Chinese Communists better will make it easier for us to tolerate them is no more true than if we were to say that to know Italy better would make it easier for us to tolerate the Mafia. The fact is we already know enough about both the Mafia and the Chinese Communists to know one thing, and that is that we do not need to know any more in order to justify our policies of opposition and hostility. Of course, we can always use more knowledge on what can be described as a tactical level, such, for example, as is being supplied by U-2 overflights from Taiwan. But we are not likely to learn much from proposals to allow our scholars and students of China to visit Communist China, and for two reasons:

1. The Chinese Communists are not going to allow anyone to come there unless they are convinced that he is a dependable friend of communism and of Chinese communism in particular. They have been following this policy for years.

2. Under these circumstances what knowledge is brought back is likely to be either superficial or biased along pro-Chinese Communist lines.

ARFEP

The campaign along the lines analyzed above, is being carried out in this country at a pitch of intensity unmatched in recent propaganda history. The so-called teach-in; more extensively used in the earlier phases of the anti-Vietnamese war campaign, has not been emphasized in this one. Instead, full-blown new organizations have been established on a nationwide basis, including ARFEP, or Americans for a Review of Far Eastern Policy. This organization was started on the Yale campus by a group of students and faculty members. It has been spread across the country from there by a well-manned organization of promoters and organizers. Recently a large advertisement advancing its views appeared, for example, in a San Francisco newspaper, as emanating from the northern California chapter of ARFEP.

Certain features of this organization appear very clearly. For example, what they mean by a "review" of our Far Eastern policy usually turns out to be nothing but propaganda in favor of Communist China in the shape of support for its admission to the United Nations, U.S. recognition of the Red regime, full U.S. relations in trade, cultural relations, et cetera, well calculated to advance the aims, purposes, and interests of Communist China. This propaganda also, at times, is heavily in derogation of our ally, the Republic of China, President and Madame Chiang Kai-shek, and so forth.

Secondly, the main centers of organization and the main personnel involved are the colleges and universities. I do not know how many ARFEP centers and branches there are, or how many persons have signed up or are otherwise formally or informally affiliated with them. Nor can we fully know at present just what activities they engage in. The following is a no doubt incomplete list of activities: signing petitions and placing advertisements in newspapers; holding small and unadvertised seminars conducted by faculty members on China and China policy questions, with both sides represented (a minor feature); conducting what amounts to a speaker's bureau to supply speakers from one campus to another.

Conferences on China

What we do not know is the extent to which ARFEP is behind the second main feature of the current campaign, that is the current rash of conferences on various aspects of China and U.S. policy toward Communist China being held on college and university campuses from coast to coast.

For example, in Portland, Ore., two such conferences, involving a number of educational institutions on a cooperating basis, are being held within a month of each other this spring. At these and other such meetings, speakers are brought in from long distances for substantial honoraria plus travel costs, necessitating very substantial budgets in the amount of thousands of dollars. Where does this money come from?

At a "National Conference on the United Nations and China" to be held next month at the University of Pennsylvania, the fee and travel cost paid to one speaker alone, will approximate one thousand dollars. At this conference, where they hope for a maximum of 800 registrants, a $10 registration fee is being assessed toward expenses. But it is doubtful that the cost of the conference can be met in this way. Where will the balance come from?

It should be noted that at the University of Pennsylvania conference, not one single academic specialist on China will be present to speak on the program in favor of the official U.S. policy toward Communist China. This defense is relegated to official representatives of the U.S. Government and of the Republic of China. This repeats the pattern so clearly seen elsewhere, of putting up as academic experts on China only those in opposition to the official policy, and "balancing" them with "official spokesmen" who can be discounted in advance as such. Thus, the false impression is created that the "public" represented by the academic experts, is uniformly opposed to the policy of our Government at this time. This is false, and utterly false.

At a conference at Harvard under the auspices of the Collegiate Council for the United Nations on March 25 to 27, Prof. Owen Lattimore of the Institute of Pacific Relations fame was scheduled to speak on the "Chinese Revolution. Causes and Consequences."

Position Paper

Also, from an organizational point of view, new and political uses are now being made of an organization that predictably would be used for pro-Chinese Communist purposes if and when the time came to do so. This is the Association of Asian Studies. When I say its current political uses were predictable, I mean just that. I refer you to my statement on this organization made in testimony under oath before the Internal Subcommittee of the Senate Committee on the Judiciary, on March 27, 1952 (pp. 4010-4013). I referred then to the Far Eastern Association, which is now the Association of Asian Studies, and I characterized it as designed, at least in part, to take over the political propaganda functions of the Institute of Pacific Relations in case the latter institution came to grief, as I believe it subsequently did, over questions of the pro-Communist bias of its activities.

Well, my prophecy on this matter in 1952 has taken almost exactly 14 years to prove out, but prove out it has. We now see, on March 21, 1966, that "all the signers" of a pro-Chinese Communist position paper published on that date in the New York Times, are from among the about 2,700 members of the Association of Asian Studies. Of these 2,700 persons, 198 labeled, in many cases incorrectly, by the Times as "China experts" signed the statement which now places the Association of Asian Studies squarely in the policy-making arena. Of the total membership of 2,700, some 300, that is, about one-ninth, "responded to the paper" signed eventually by 198 of them, that is, about 7.3 percent of the total membership. To the views of this small minority of the total membership the New York Times of March 21, 1966, devoted a full column on its front pages and nearly an entire inner page (p.12): In an editorial on March 23, 1966, the Times stated that "this shows where the weight of informed American opinion lies." Such are the distortions of propagandistic journalism.

Committee of One Million

The least the Times could do would be to give equal weight and coverage to the some 330 signers, as of January 1966, of the "Declaration in Opposition to Any Concessions to Communist China" sponsored by the Committee of One Million (not 2,700) against the admission of Communist China to the United Nations. I say this in view of the fact that all of these some 330 signers are Senators or Representatives in Congress, representing I do not know how many millions of American voters. But the Times would not even print a letter submitted to it in February 1966, by two Senators in opposition to a Times editorial on the subject of China and the United Nations. The two Senators wrote as members of the steering committee of the Committee of One Million, which no doubt accounts for the failure of the Times to print it.

What the Times will print is well exemplified by the letter in its columns for March 18, 1966, by Prof. Vera M. Dean of New York University. In this letter the lady professor, while expressing her views on various policy matters, also expresses her hopes. Among these, as she puts it, is that the ghosts, as she describes them, of Senator McCarthy and the Committee of One Million on China should be exorcised, and that former China experts who she says were driven from the State Department by McCarthyism should be sought out to advise the President and Secretary Rusk. Leaving this latter point aside, the lady professor should be informed that before she can exorcise the ghost of the Committee of One Million it will have to die and produce such a ghost. Far from dying, the committee is very much alive today, and shows no signs of dying. All reports to the contrary are highly premature, to say the least. As time goes on I am sure the committee itself will do everything in its power to continue its efforts by all means at its disposal. It should see to it that Professor Dean is aware of these efforts. Or is she merely whistling to keep up her courage?

U.S. Policy Alternatives

In this situation and from this background in what policy area should our best and strongest efforts be made, to counter the current attempts to support Communist China and its program for Asia and the world? We are talking here, of course, of U.S. policy alternatives.

I do not believe the matter of possible U.S. recognition, trade and cultural relations, et cetera, is central. It is quite doubtful that, under current circumstances, any administration in Washington would move toward such policies. More real is the danger that we will succumb to the folly of supinely accepting the supposed inevitability theory, and submit to the admission of Communist China to the United Nations. In fact, so central do I believe this whole question to be to the problem of standing up to Communist China's grandiose demands in world affairs, as Prof. John Fairbank puts it, that I believe here is where major emphasis should lie in respect to China policy today.

Therefore, I propose to devote a considerable part of my written presentation to analyzing the problem of Chinese representation in the United Nations. I submit this paper of which there are two features:

1. An expanded version of what I have just read.
2. Continuation: an analysis of the problem of Chinese representation in the United Nations.

That concludes my introductory formal statement.

SCALAPINO STATEMENT

The following is the statement of Robert A. Scalapino, professor of political science and the chairman of the political science department at the University of California at Berkeley. Dr. Scalapino is also editor of the monthly journal, Asian Survey. *He appeared before the committee on March 30, 1966. (See p. 182)*

Mr. Chairman, I am honored to participate in this inquiry into the nature of contemporary China and American-Chinese relations. In holding these hearings, you and your distinguished committee have performed a significant function, in my opinion. I would like to believe that we are entering a new era in the United States, one which will be marked by much more intimate, frank, and continuous exchange between Government officials and public officeholders on the one hand, and private scholars and specialists on the other. There are some individuals on both sides who fear that such contact will be corrupting. They would impose a policy of isolation, or limit communication to confrontation. Personally, I regard these approaches as more likely to be corrupting since they restrict both perspectives and knowledge. Hence, I welcome expanded contacts of many types.

You have requested that I devote my attention primarily to the issue of American policy toward China. In approaching this issue, I should like to set forth very briefly certain premises which I hold concerning China that are germane to any consideration of policy.

Major Changes

The question is often asked, "Can we anticipate major changes in China in the near future?" If by major changes, one means an overthrow of the Communist Party, the chances seem to me remote, barring global war or some other major and unforeseeable crisis. This is not because dissidence is absent in China. We have no accurate method of measuring such dissidence, but I am inclined to believe that if one could measure the total spectrum of opposition -- from the most passive "grumblers" to the active or potential "subversives" -- it would be relatively high, despite the fact that certain groups have clearly benefited from the revolution and are grateful.

The point, however, is that Communists more than most modern rulers have mastered the science of power. Consequently, dissidence can be relatively high and still pose no serious threat to a regime such as that of Peking because the dissidents cannot find or develop an organizational outlet. Without depreciating the significance of ideology or policy, I regard organization as still the most important weapon of the Communists, especially when it can operate in an unorganized or disorganized environment.

Thus if change is to occur in China it is most likely to come through communism, and via top party circles. Any American policy should be based upon this assumption. It is possible, of course, that at some point, the Red army can pose a threat since it represents the one organizational alternative to the party of any significance, and the trend toward modernization is more likely to separate the military and the party than to bring them closer together. In the era of guerrilla warfare and its immediate aftermath, the party has dominated the military via the type of political-military leadership represented by Mao Tse-tung himself. That era is coming to a close.

There is a growing struggle which in its essence poses the primitivism implicit in Maoist political-military doctrines against the professionalism that is implicit in the whole modernization program. Already, some military men have been placed in major opposition to party leaders. As it unfolds, however, this struggle will involve the bureaucracy in all of its aspects, civilian as well as military, and it is likely to be settled within the party, especially since most of the key disputants will either be in the top echelons of the party or have access to these. I cannot easily envisage a situation where the military and the party would enter into struggle as separate, self-contained units.

Thus, in all probability, the most meaningful question is that so frequently posed recently, "Will a younger generation of party leaders diverge considerably from the group of old Bolsheviks currently holding absolute power, so that the resulting changes, while taking place within the party, will nonetheless be profound and, in general, in the direction of realism and moderation?"

This is a crucial question, and one that cannot be answered with any complete certainty. My own belief is that such changes will occur, but that the critical element of timing will depend heavily upon both the international and the external environment. Even under the best of circumstances, I am inclined to feel that the struggle for a more pragmatic, realistic, and moderate political elite in China will be long and arduous, extending considerably beyond one generation. But the rate and nature of change will certainly be affected by the degree to which a wide range of subtle external pressures and alternatives can be developed.

In certain terms, we are conducting a holding operation in Asia, and one of the variables with which we must contend is the race in China itself between the acquisition of power and the acquisition of responsibility. Our policies and those of other foreign states, while not representing the sole determinants of this race, are vitally important elements.

One final point regarding change in China might be added. No political regime can be totally rigid and survive. Clearly, current Chinese leaders have been forced to make substantial adjustments to various programs that have failed, at home and abroad. That will continue. Indeed, just as the Maoists had to retrench in the aftermath of the failure of the Great Leap Forward at home, so now they are engaged in a reassessment of the Great Leap Forward abroad which has also failed on a major scale. No democratic regime, incidentally, could possibly have survived the colossal failures in foreign policy suffered by Peking in the last few years.

Importance of Ideology

Thus, tactical adjustments and modifications will be made because there is literally no alternative. One must distinguish, however, between belated responses to inescapable realities and the frame of mind which is bound to a minimum of dogma, the mind fundamentally responsive to a wide range of alternatives. China is still ruled by hardcore ideologues who hold to the thesis that being "red" is more important than being "expert," and who have now been driven to the deification of Maoism as the repository of all significant truth. Even a casual reading of Chinese journals today reveals the staggering degree to which ideological rigidity has produced a cult of irrationality centering upon Mao. Is crop failure threatened? The answer lies in Mao's writings, asserts Hung Ch'i. Is the student having trouble in solving a mathematical equation? Read Mao's collected works, suggests Jen-min Jih-pao.

Perhaps a basic fragility is revealed in a regime that is forced increasingly to rely upon the omnipotence of one man and descend into such irrational depths in the process. But the current scene in China has universal implications. In most emerging societies, a broad and supremely important conflict ensues at some point between elements we may roughly call ideologues and pragmatists. First-generation revolutionaries are generally strongly ideological, highly politicized, possessed of certain "charismatic" qualities, and lacking in most advanced technical skills. Their primary task is nation building, often via mass mobilization. At some point, however, they must give way to an elite who are more pragmatic than ideological, more bureaucratic than charismatic, and more concerned with the technical and administrative skills essential to progress in economic and social terms. The implications of this process for American foreign policy, I would suggest are far reaching.

The era of the ideologues is likely to be at once dynamic and disappointing -- disappointing in the sense that many of the broad goals projected will not be realized. Expectations will be high. Performance will generally be low, with the means employed often not in accordance with the ends sought. Consequently, mounting pressures upon the elite in power will ensue. The temptation on their part to engage in irrational, distractive behavior will increase. But there will also be ultimate pressures for realistic policies that can achieve results.

It is certainly incumbent upon the United States in these circumstances to take a positive position in affirmation of the broad goals constantly voiced in this era: nationalism; the acceptance of, and involvement in, the world community; democracy; social justice and economic development. It is equally important that we devise policies that in concrete terms will discourage extremism and encourage moderation, primarily by making clear the risks of the former, and setting forth the opportunities of the latter. And these opportunities must involve precisely the types of interaction and assistance that would abet the movement from ideological rigidity toward pragmatic experimentalism. This general approach, I would submit, is appropriate to our China policy, as to our policy elsewhere, because it relates to the general nature of change.

Nature of Chinese Power

There are two other general questions relating to China upon which I should like to comment prior to discussing the specifics of our China policy. There has been some debate over the nature of Chinese Communist power and intentions. Some emphasize the thesis that China is essentially a weak nation, one thoroughly frightened by the massive power and encirclement policies of the United States, and most likely to respond to us only in a defensive sense -- hence constituting no basic threat to us, our allies, or the neutrals. Others argue that we should treat China as a major power and one that clearly has aggressive, expansionist aspirations threatening the whole of the non-Communist world.

In my opinion, the truth is approached as one combines these two views treating them as more complementary than in conflict. China is weak in a variety of ways. Her economic recovery from the disasters of a few years ago is scarcely complete, and despite remarkable feats in certain areas of production and distribution, overall increases -- particularly in agrarian production -- appear to be modest, especially when measured against population growth. Moreover, the changing of the political guard is at hand and even if the resulting changes may not be dramatic, some internal tension must be present in the Chinese Communist Party at this point, heightened by the significant setbacks in foreign policy. Finally, China is scarcely a military match for the United States, and she undoubtedly fears American power.

American power confronts China on the east and south. Soviet power lies on the west and north. Without question the existence of this power contributes to a psychology that is at once fearful and blatantly defiant. It would be extremely unwise, however, to deduce from this that such power being removed, Chinese foreign policy would subsequently be characterized by passivity or moderation. Were it not for American and Soviet power in Asia, the Chinese Communists would almost certainly have advanced much further toward their basic goals there, although I do not for a moment regard American and Soviet interests and objectives in the area as identical.

Chinese Foreign Policy Goals

What are the Chinese goals? Three have been oft proclaimed: To remove all Western influence from Asia; to encourage by a variety of means an ideologically politically uniform Asia cast in the image of "the new China"; and to enlist this "progressive" Asia in the global struggle against both the "revisionists" and the "imperialists." The words are those of the Chinese.

These are scarcely the goals of an elite that is primarily oriented toward defense, and posing its objectives in very limited terms. It is quite true, however, that these goals -- and some of the actions that have accompanied them -- have triggered a reaction, not alone from us but from many others as well. Thus today, China must calculate defensively because the United States, and in some degree the Soviet Union, will not permit her to calculate offensively on any significant scale.

Her defensive calculations undoubtedly include a determination in each specific instance as to what she can and cannot tolerate from the standpoint of her own national interests, and what risks, correspondingly, she is prepared to run. Personally, I do not believe that the Chinese Communists are prepared to take the risks of an open war with the United States at this time except under the most extraordinary of circumstances or under conditions where they misinterpret American signals. Specifically, I regard it as highly unlikely that China will intervene fully in the Vietnam war unless the obliteration of North Vietnam is threatened. Even then, it will be an extremely difficult decision for Peking because she knows she would be subjected to massive destruction, and such a war would run completely counter to her basic policy which has been aimed at provoking an American-Soviet confrontation in the course of involving the United States simultaneously in a series of "national liberation wars."

The fact, however, that China is forced to react defensively and partly from fear at this point should not obscure the very strong commitment which the current generation of Chinese leaders have had to global influence. From the moment they emerged into full control, these leaders committed themselves and their society to the cultivation of power in all of its forms: military, political, psychological, and economic. Contrast their attitude toward power and their actions, for example, with those of Nehru and Nehru's India. Nehru eschewed armaments, avoided alliances, and on occasion, seemed to shun even active political diplomacy. Mao and his comrades, on the other hand, were prepared to make major sacrifices for the sake of political and military power, including the development of a nuclear arsenal.

Since the Communist era began in China, no Asian state has been capable of matching Chinese power unaided, and it is wise to remember that there is not a pacifist bone in a Maoist body. The Chinese Communists, moreover, have consummated alliances large and small, undertaken aid and technical assistance programs far beyond their economic capacities, and engaged in a range of political activities throughout the world that caused most nations, friend and foe, to label China "major power designate." That is a significant accomplishment, incidentally, because such a status grants certain rights without conveying the requisite responsibilities.

When all of these activities are surveyed, I do not understand how anyone can regard Chinese actions or goals of the past decade as defensive, either in character or intent. The recent major failures of that policy, indeed, are due to precisely the opposite problem: the Chinese Communists sought to force the pace, undertaking actions in Asia, Africa, and Latin America that were interpreted by others as aggressive, ultranationalist and dangerous. As noted earlier, it is quite likely that Peking will now be forced to retrench in foreign policy as they have previously been forced to retrench in domestic policy. The basic ingredients -- the fundamental source-springs -- of Chinese foreign policy, however, are likely to remain. It will be important, therefore, to distinguish between short-run tactics and long-range goals.

Major Source-Springs

What have been the major source-springs of Chinese foreign policy under the Communists? Three forces seem to me of central importance: Tradition, nationalism, and MLM -- Marx-Lenin-Maoism. In certain respects, the current Chinese leaders still think of their problem as how to handle the barbarians. They still divide the world into those who accept Chinese culture (now to be read "ideology") and those who live outside the pale. The former are the "civilized" or the "progressive" people, to use their terms; the latter are barbarians, be they "revisionists," "imperialists," or "neutrals." The barbarian must be handled by a combination of persuasion and coercion. One uses visits to the imperial capital, exchanges of gifts, and many other devices to awe and impress; and one uses strong words and, when necessary and possible, strong actions to cajole and coerce. Some of China's difficulties today are unquestionably due to a continuance among her present generation of mandarin rulers of an "imperial complex," an engrained sense of cultural superiority and the attitude of condescension toward other peoples that invariably accompanies this.

The nationalist quotient in Chinese foreign policy is, of course, extremely high. In many respects, China is behaving in much the same fashion as have other major societies en route to power. First, she has sought to define and defend her boundaries as she interprets these; secondly, she has sought to create a buffer state system around her; and finally, she has sought hegemony in the world in which she lives: the Asian world, the non-Western world, and the Communist world.

In pursuit of these objectives, the Chinese Communists have been no more able to follow a totally consistent foreign policy than the leaders of other major states. The main thrust of Chinese Communist foreign policy, as suggested earlier, has been characterized by revolutionary fervor, global commitment, and relatively inflexible division of the world into comrades and enemies. The line has been hard, advanced by practicing ideologues fiercely impatient with the existing order and anxious to challenge it in radical fashion. And yet, for tactical reasons and out of necessity, these leaders have adopted a great variety of approaches. On occasion, they have not hesitated to consort with "feudalists" and support "reactionary" regimes; sometimes, they have used the soft line, as at the time of Bandung; not infrequently, they have been caught in such un-Marxian stances as making an appeal to race. Indeed, one is forced to conclude that the one element of major consistency is that which runs through the policies of all nations: the consistent expression of what appears to the political elite as in their national interests. And it is precisely this fact that offers hope of some flexibility, even among hard-core ideologues.

At its roots, the Sino-Soviet dispute itself is closely connected with the phenomena of nationalism. We now know that nationalism has not only survived Communism, but in many respects triumphed over it. The Sino-Soviet cleavage illustrates the fact that two nations supposedly sharing a common ideology but differing substantially in cultural traditions, timing of revolution, stage of development, generation of leadership and degree of power are almost certain to have different views of the world and of their own needs. Hence, they will have different concepts of national interest which, in the case of Marxists, will be translated into different interpretations of what is truth; namely, what is orthodox Marxism-Leninism. (In fact, of course, all modern Marxists are revisionists of the highest order.)

Sino-Soviet Dispute

The Sino-Soviet dispute centers upon the issue of how to treat the United States, although there are other significant issues as well. The Soviet Union basically believes in nation-to-nation competition with the United States, counting upon the ultimate superiority of Soviet productivity and power. Thus it argues that the appropriate method of confrontation is peaceful coexistence, meaning all-out economic, political and social competition but the avoidance of nuclear war. There is, to be sure, an element of ambiguity in the Soviet position surrounding its defense of national wars of liberation, which may be variously defined and supported. Nevertheless, its standard criticisms of the Peking line is that the Chinese leaders have rejected peaceful coexistence, and pursue a left-adventurist policy that risks global war.

China, on the other hand, not being able to conceive of the possibility of nation-to-nation competition with the United States in the near future, and having no basic responsibility for the maintenance of peace or the prosecution of a nuclear war, argues the classical Bolshevik thesis that America must be challenged by the technique of unfolding the world revolution. The Chinese theme is that primary emphasis must be placed upon mobilizing the non-Western World for a rapid, continuous assault upon the "capitalist West, led by the United States." Thus, the Russians are rebuked for their refusal to take massive risks on behalf of global revolution, and they are now charged by Peking with active collaboration with Washington for purposes of world domination. At the moment, China asserts that Vietnam is the supreme test of the validity of her position and her principles. The United States is a paper tiger which, if challenged resolutely and in accordance with Maoist principles, will collapse as a result of internal and external pressures. Maoism will be vindicated on the battlefields of Vietnam -- and in the streets of the United States -- against the combination of American imperialism and Soviet sabotage. That is the Chinese position.

Course of U.S. Policy

As the nationalist component in Chinese foreign policy is surveyed, I would suggest that the following conclusions pertinent to policy might be advanced. One critical problem is that of striking a balance between providing Chinese nationalism with legitimate outlets and guarding against those aggressive potentials that lie embedded in any nationalist movement, and particularly one possessed of active messianic goals like that of China. There are some who argue that Chinese domination of Asia is appropriate or in any case, inevitable. Their thesis is that Asia is the legitimate sphere of influence for China, just as the Western Hemisphere is for us. I am not prepared to accept this argument in any of its major contentions, as it is usually advanced. The simple spheres of influence concept is misleading in terms of fact, unrealistic in terms of current political trends, and untenable in terms of basic morality.

There can be no question that the United States, of all modern nations, has had the greatest unchallenged preponderance of power historically in its own region. Yet even the United States has lived for various periods of time with hostile states in this hemisphere, and with states having intimate ties with foreign powers -- from the time of British Canada to the time of Moscow-oriented Cuba. Certainly, the Russians have never had any total dominance of their near neighbors -- witness the existence of Finland, Turkey, Greece, and Iran, among others. My own belief, indeed, is that the existence of some elements of competition and neutrality in the vicinity of a major power is healthy. A major state totally secure in its own region may not only be oblivious to the problems of its neighbors, but may also be unduly free to undertake expansionist activities afield. Thus, I do not believe that Chinese dominance of Asia is either inevitable or desirable -- and neither, I suspect, do the peoples of India, Japan, Indonesia, and the Soviet Union, among others.

This is not to say, however, that China should be denied -- or can be denied -- all elements of security. Already, China has a certain buffer state system: North Korea shields the Manchurian complex, at least from the East; North Vietnam stands in front of the Kwantung area; China now controls Tibet; and many of the border states of south and southeast Asia -- notably Afghanistan, Pakistan, Nepal, Burma, and Cambodia can either be accounted neutral or friendly. Over time and under conditions where a general balance of power in Asia had been achieved, it might be possible to extend that belt of neutrality to other states. Indeed, nothing should be ruled outside the range of future possibility, including large-scale disarmament and a reliance upon collective security agreements by the major Asian states. Progress on any of these fronts, however, now depends primarily upon China: her willingness to renounce force as a means of effecting international change; her preparedness to enter into negotiations on a wide range of issues; her capacity to accept compromise as an essential ingredient in international agreement; and her ability to abandon the thesis that the destruction of the United States as it is presently constituted takes priority over all other foreign policy objectives.

Marx-Lenin-Maoism

The final source-spring of Chinese Communist foreign policy, I have labeled MLM. The Maoists think of themselves as orthodox Marxist-Leninists, indeed, as the only legitimate leaders of the world Marxist movement. At the same time, however, they pride themselves upon having "applied Marxism-Leninism creativity" to the conditions of China. Perhaps it is accurate to define the Maoist element in Chinese Marxism as the practical development of a five-stage revolutionary progression which places heavy reliance initially upon intellectual leadership and a peasant-based radical movement that has its roots in the countryside.

The Maoist revolutionary formula begins with the creation of a Communist Party which must never lose control of the revolutionary movement. That party proceeds to guide the creation of a united front, using nationalist and socioeconomic appeals, but relying heavily upon organization, and using freely the instruments of coercion as well as those of persuasion. When the front has been prepared, the movement into guerrilla warfare is the next stage, and then the advance to positional warfare. When military victory has been attained, the so-called People's Democratic Republic is established under the complete control of the Communist Party.

Long before Lin Piao's speech of last summer, it was clear that the Chinese Communists regarded this revolutionary formula broadly applicable to the world scene -- from the Congo to Vietnam. In very high degree, indeed, the old Bolsheviks of China, so strongly isolated from world reality, have seen the world mirrored in their own ideological-revolutionary image and history. The need for a true Communist party means that one must fight such false Marxists-Leninists as the Russians. The united front with its emphasis upon a union of peasants, workers, intellectuals, and national bourgeois under the leadership of the vanguard party spells out the Chinese determination to unite the world peasantry (the Afro-Asian societies) and certain susceptible bourgeois elements (clearly France was once in mind) under Peking's banners.

Thus, MLM makes Chinese Communist foreign policy something more than merely another expression of nationalism in action. It defines both the scope and the techniques of policy in a unique way. China is interested in Albania as well as Korea; in Mali as well as in Vietnam. The definition of national interest, the conceptualization of problem, the vocabulary of dispute are all colored by MLM. It would be as dangerous to underestimate the Marxist quotient in Chinese foreign policy at this point as to accord it total influence.

Failure of Isolation Policy

The above considerations seem to me germane as we examine American policy toward China. Nearly 6 years ago, Mr. Chairman, I had the privilege of writing the northeast Asia section of a report on U. S. foreign policy in Asia which was submitted to this committee. At that time, I defined our current policy as one of attempted containment by isolation, and I suggested a variety of reasons why, in my opinion, we should move away from such a negative, inflexible approach to an admittedly complex, difficult problem.

Naturally, I am gratified to note that in recent months and weeks, there have been increasing signs that our Government is seeking a more broadly gauged policy. Some of the steps which I advocated in 1959 are now being initiated or at least actively contemplated. These include a willingness to allow American scholars, scientists, journalists, and certain other citizens to travel to China; positive steps to seek the involvement of China in international negotiations on such problems as disarmament, nuclear weapon control, and similar issues of world importance; and the establishment of terms under which mainland China might come in to the United Nations.

Because these steps, and others which should follow will be strongly debated, I should like to reiterate the reasons why I believe such actions, on balance, are highly desirable. A policy of containment by isolation robbed the United States of initiative or leverage, and tended to posit our rigidity against that of Peking. This in turn served to separate us from our allies and the neutrals, making collective thinking and action with respect to China vastly more difficult. It also rendered far less effective the type of multiple external pressures that are essential if the element of extremism in Chinese foreign policy is to be effectively curbed or countered.

Our past policy has been insufficient in certain other respects. To foster isolation is to foster fanaticism. Isolation, indeed, is one of the major weapons of a police state, and there is no reason as to why we should be a party to its support. On the contrary, a truly sophisticated American foreign policy will always aim at complicating the decision-making processes of a totalitarian state. To be able to engage in selective diplomacy and to bear negligible responsibilities in the world community represent significant tactical advantages which we should not bestow lightly. Such a situation also encourages a purist, uncompromising, and irrational attitude, an air of complete unrealism.

A policy of containment by isolation, in short, not only provides an inadequate approach from the standpoint of international political realities, but it is also highly unsatisfactory from the standpoint of its impact upon the Chinese nation itself. In immediate terms, therefore, we must move from such a policy toward one that heightens the element of choice for the Chinese political elite by providing additional incentives for moderation and firm, explicit deterrents to extremism. We must find a way of making peaceful coexistence the only conceivable path for the next generation of Chinese leaders and we must do this without abandoning any of the basic rights or requirements of the non-Communist world.

I do not claim that this will be easy or that it can be done quickly. The thrust of my earlier analysis was that we face a China both militantly nationalist and strongly ideological at present, a China whose leaders have committed a series of excesses from which they must now beat some retreat, but who still appear to be intent upon cultivating power in all of its aspects and quite prepared to use violence to effect revolutionary change throughout the world. At this point, presumably, the Chinese leaders are sufficiently realistic to want to avoid war with the United States, and even with less powerful forces. The time may not be too long, however, before China's military capacities come closer to matching her political visions. We must prepare for that eventuality now.

There are a few individuals who would argue that we should forcefully remove the Chinese military threat before it becomes serious. But preventive war in my opinion, is politically impossible even if one were to waive all questions of morality. We are a democratic society, and neither our people nor our officials would sanction such a policy. Moreover, preventive war by its very nature would fail because it ignores the response of the world community as well as of the people most immediately affected, and provides therefore no basis for erecting a meaningful world order.

Positive Steps in U.S. Policy

The only realistic approach in my opinion, is the complex one of creating an elaborate structure of opportunities and deterrents, and in this task we must have the cooperation of other nations, particularly those of non-Communist Asia. Our first steps seem clear enough. Progressively, we must make it clear by concrete actions that if China is isolated, the initiative lies with her, that we are prepared to enter into cultural relations with her, engage in trade on the same basis as with other Communist nations, and negotiate with her on all matters of international importance. At the same time, we should accept in principle the desirability of universal membership in the United Nations, a principle which among other things would make natural the acceptance of both China and Taiwan as de facto states deserving international representation. Bilateral recognition between the United States and China is not, in my opinion, a first priority item under present circumstances. Once again, however, I believe that we should move toward the establishment of a general principle, namely the complete divorcement of recognition from the question of moral or political approval.

Having supported the above actions, let me make it emphatically clear that I am under no illusions about the initial Chinese response. Peking will not help us develop a new China policy because basically she likes our old one, and does not want us to change. As has already been implied, she believes that our present policy isolates us more than her; makes the United States available as a perfect scapegoat both before her own people and before others; and prevents or at least mitigates the types of pressures developing upon her from the outside that might otherwise be created.

Thus, we can assume that the torrent of abuse against us will continue to flow out of China, and that initial responses to our overtures will be almost completely negative. As in so many other situations today, this will test our patience and our sophistication. We must neither be driven back into rigidity nor panicked into making unwarranted concessions. Suppose, for example, that at this time, China does not permit American scientists or scholars other than those prepared to support the Peking regime into the country. Upon whom does the onus lie, if our doors are kept open. Suppose China refuses to accept a United Nations seat once terms such as those suggested above have been established, and that seat lies vacant for a time. Upon whom will the pressures mount?

Risks of Extremism

Thus far, however, I have advanced and defended only one side of the policy proposed earlier. But it is my firm belief that moderation will be encouraged only if the risks of extremism are made both credible and clear. When the history of this era is written, it may be that the two Asian wars in which we have been engaged since 1950 were both the products of Communist miscalculation for which we must assume some share of responsibility. When the Communists planned their aggression in Korea, did they have any strong reason to believe that the United States would act to protect South Korea, given the manner in which we had recently stated our Asian defense commitments? And when the Communists planned their military campaign in South Vietnam did they have any real reason to believe that the United States would undertake major military efforts to aid South Vietnam, in view of the statements of numerous American leaders about land wars on the Asian continent? Let us not make this type of mistake again. Let us make clear our definition of aggression and neo-aggression, and make clear also our commitments and resolves so that miscalculations can be reduced to an absolute minimum.

At this point, for example, we should make it absolutely clear that any attempt to change the status of Taiwan or South Korea by means of the use of externally directed or assisted force will be resolutely countered by the application of American force. We should also continue to make it unmistakably clear that we do not intend to allow these tactics to succeed in South Vietnam. In my opinion, nothing would be more calculated to pump life into the extremist movement within China and within the Communist world than a Maoist victory in Vietnam -- and nothing would lead us more quickly into the awful choice between precipitous retreat everywhere and World War III. The Chinese have repeatedly emphasized the fact that Vietnam is a supreme test of Maoist principles in statements to their own people, to other Asians, and to fellow Communists. We can be certain that the path toward moderation and peace will be infinitely longer and more painful if extremism pays in this crucial test.

Total U.S. Asian Policy

If we are to be successful in gradually developing a new approach to China, we must also look closely at our total Asian policy, because obviously there must be a close interrelation between our approach to China and our approach to Asia as a whole. Time permits only the suggestion of a few basic long-range considerations which I believe to be of importance in this respect. First, if we look at the present political situation in its broadest dimensions, two powers largely external to Asia -- the United States and the Soviet Union -- are each in somewhat different ways playing a critical role in balancing the thrust of China, primarily because no Asian nation -- or combination of nations -- is currently prepared to play that role. It is recognized on all sides, however, that ultimately a balance of power must be developed within Asia, if diversity and peace are to be rendered possible, and our most basic planning and support must be directed toward this end.

Second, a major world power like the United States is destined by virtue of its strength and resources to be somewhat apart from other nations. In this era, we are required to bear heavier responsibilities, be subjected to heavier criticism, and on occasion to make grave decisions, the execution of which falls primarily upon us, or upon us alone. In many cases, moreover, the decision not to act is at least as fateful as the decision to act. Thus, we cannot escape from a powerful element of unilateralism, and I see no point in naively or romantically railing against this fact. We are going to do certain things alone, or almost alone, if they are done at all. At the same time, it is incumbent upon us -- now more than ever before -- to develop programs and also an attitude of mind soliciting international opinions and support, especially from nations like Japan and India, nations that should be taking more responsibility in world affairs and in the affairs of Asia than is currently the case.

Third, until we find better methods of enabling freedom and socioeconomic development to go together, we will be under substantial handicaps in the struggle to preserve open societies. I am personally convinced that we have the brains and much of the data needed to make significant progress on this problem, and in the course of making that progress, providing answers to a host of crucial questions that relate to certain basic aspects of American foreign policy. At the present time, for instance, we are not posing the critical questions in very precise or meaningful terms. I regard such questions as should we be policeman -- or Santa Claus -- to the world as very crude expressions of problems that should be raised in much more precise manner. Obviously, we should not be and we are not involved equally in every nation of the world -- or even in every region. But under what conditions -- assuming that the initiative is largely ours -- should we be involved, and how? If we can mount at great cost an Apollo project to reach the moon, I would suggest that we should mount a similar project to reach our own planet in this, the most critical century since life first evolved here. We should have in operation now a high-level group of scholars, scientists, and officials probing the basic questions of development and change, peace and war, forms of effective national and international interaction, and this group should be established with some type of permanence so that its hypotheses can be tested periodically revised.

U.S. Status and Responsibilities

I should like to conclude with two final observations that relate to our status in the modern world and our responsibilities. Perhaps we have underestimated the psychological and intellectual problems of moving from a position of regional influence to one of global power. Our intellectual center of gravity, for example, and also the center of our decision-making process continues to evidence strong Europocentric tendencies. I would not for a moment depreciate the ability or the values of those in our scholarly and governmental community whose interests, training, and knowledge relate primarily to the Western world. I would, however, suggest that in an age when

our responsibilities are global and when a region like Asia is so crucial to our own national interest and that of the rest of the world, some redress in the balance of internal authority in this country is desirable. For example, I would suspect that when the testimony of the Asian scholars heard during these hearings is reviewed, it will reveal a somewhat different emphasis -- and on certain issues a different thrust -- than would have been the case had European specialists been the primary witnesses.

Finally, I cannot avoid the observation that perhaps our gravest problem today is the fact that our culture conflicts in certain significant respects with the requirements of our status and power. To some extent, incidentally, this is also true of our main competitors, the Russians and the Chinese. Whereas power in the mid-19th century was held by small states which had come to the industrial revolution early and had accumulated their resources externally, power in the mid-20th century is held by continental-mass societies whose resources lie largely within themselves, and each of whom has had a long history of relative self-sufficiency, a reasonably high quotient of ethnocentrism, and a strong commitment to isolation not easily removed. Whatever our political and ideological differences, we, the Russians, and the Chinese share these traits.

All-or-Nothing Philosophy

Beyond that, ours is a culture that has placed an enormous premium upon speed and efficiency. I suspect that the critical test of American success or failure in world leadership in the years that lie immediately ahead will hinge upon whether we can modify those cherished qualities in accordance with the dictates of the world in which we live. This requires patience and, more than patience, an appreciation of the signal importance of being able to move from 10 to 11, or 8 to 7, in the broad range of policy alternatives, rather than being forced to operate only on the basis of 0 to 100. I regard this as the single most important test of American maturity. If we continue to live by the all or nothing philosophy -- either "all in" or "all out" -- we cannot possibly sustain our values or our interests. This is to use a neolithic approach to the problems of a nuclear age.

This problem merits the most searching scrutiny particularly because our mass media too frequently encourages the 100 or 0 approach by focusing upon the extremities of every issue, thus heightening the sense of crisis and making proper timing and appropriate means to ends so difficult. The time has come, in short, to explore in the greatest possible depth the relation of both the mass media and Government to foreign policy formulation in an age when we must preserve democracy at home and, at the same time, undertake the massive obligations implicit in being the world's greatest power. In the process, we might be able to redefine our responsibilities as well as our rights, both as citizens and as officials.

I am aware that such an inquiry would go far beyond the issue of China, or even Asia, but it seems particularly appropriate to suggest it as I conclude. In no theater of the world is a correct sense of timing and the capacity to utilize effectively the most minute graduations of policy more critical to our future and that of others.

The Conservative Reaction to the China Hearings

Following is one of several articles concerning U.S. China policy appearing in the National Review of May 1966, with an Introduction by Theodore Lit. The article's author, Franz Michael, is a professor of international affairs and Sino-Soviet studies at George Washington University. He taught in Hangchow, China, from 1934 to 1938, was a professor of Far Eastern history and government and assistant director of the Far Eastern and Russian Institute at the University of Washington from 1942 until 1964.

Introduction

Theodore Lit

The war in Vietnam has brought into sharper focus the perennial question of Communist China; the question, that is, of what should be done -- if anything -- about admission to the United Nations, diplomatic recognition, increased trade, cultural exchange.

In this connection, it is astonishing to note how little things have changed since the late 1940s when Mao Tse-tung & Co. were helped to power by the band of China experts in the Institute of Pacific Relations (IPR) and in the State Department.

Then they were saying that the Chinese Communists were merely agrarian reformers and that the element in China to be most concerned about was the "corrupt" Chiang Kai-shek and the warlords. Our China experts of the left-Liberal persuasion helped the Communists seize a continent.

Now they are concerned with legitimizing the Red China regime in the concert of nations. Their help is being extended precisely at the time when Communist China finds its fortunes at low ebb -- at home and abroad, economically and diplomatically.

These friends and members of the Red China lobby point to the Soviet Union as a happy example of the co-existence spirit which the free world might expect from Communist China, if only the mainland regime were accorded the minimal international courtesies -- diplomatic recognition, admission to the United Nations, expanded trade.

The final abandonment of Nationalist China which such a policy would entail creates no crisis of conscience among these self-described realists, for the main enemy in the Far East continues to be Chiang Kai-shek.

One of the ironies of the situation lies in the fact that the very people who in large measure are personally and historically responsible for the political disaster on the Chinese mainland are today hailed as experts by the communications media, the universities and important members of the Congress.

Thus, despite the brilliant and scholarly exposure of the IPR and its collaborators by the Senate Internal Security Subcommittee more than a decade ago, once again we hear the confident voices of such experts as Owen Lattimore, John K. Fairbank, John Stewart Service and Oliver Edmund Clubb. A sorry confirmation of Hegel's observation to the effect that the one thing we learn from history is that we do not learn from history!

The recent hearings by the House Committee on Foreign Affairs and the Senate Foreign Relations Committee furnished a platform for many spokesmen for the Red China lobby, all of whom peddled the new line of "containment without isolation," the now fashionable euphemism for appeasement.

The Opposition

Fortunately, the hearings also featured testimony by some spokesmen for a realistic approach to the China question. Among these, four in particular developed a vigorous and closely reasoned rebuttal to the vagaries of the Red China lobby. The four are: Professor David Nelson Rowe of Yale University, former Representative Walter H. Judd, Professor Franz Michael of Georgetown University and Professor George E. Taylor of the University of Washington.

Although these scholars represent a minority view in the American intellectual community, their testimony articulates American public opinion on Red China (an opinion mobilized in large degree, since 1953, by the Committee of One Million).

Significantly, the national platforms of the Democratic and Republican parties oppose the admission of Red China to the UN; a Gallup poll of January 1966 shows 67 per cent of the American people are opposed to the admission of Red China to the UN; the Congress has repeatedly gone on record opposing concessions to Peking.

All of which opens the nagging question: Why does the Liberal Establishment pursue an appeasement policy toward Communist regimes?

The appeasement policy is not based on a principled pacifism, in view of the fact that the Liberals enthusiastically supported the war against Nazi Germany. Nor does the appeasement policy spring *exclusively* from a fear of a mutually destructive nuclear war. It should be remembered that the Liberals also pushed for an appeasement line during the early postwar period when the United States enjoyed a *monopoly* of nuclear bombs.

The answer is indirectly suggested in a statement by Senator J. W. Fulbright in the first of his Johns Hopkins University lectures. Commenting on the national debate on the Vietnam war, the chairman of the Senate Foreign Relations Committee warned: "It is by no means certain that the relatively healthy atmosphere in which the debate is now taking place will not give way to fears, and tolerance and freedom of discussion will give way to a false and strident patriotism."

Senator Fulbright's qualification of patriotism is not to be taken too literally. This is the Aesopian language of the modern, sophisticated Liberal. For it is patriotism -- normal, healthy patriotism -- which propels the average American to oppose international Communism. And it is this normal healthy patriotism which, in the nature of things, would be heightened in the course of a genuine, all-out struggle against international Communism. The Liberal senses the violent contradiction between patriotism -- of any degree -- and the intellectual power position of the Establishment. It is patriotism -- more than Communism -- which the Liberal Establishment sees as the main enemy.

To be sure, there is always the possibility that normal, healthy patriotism, under a condition of great international stress, may be transformed into the "false and strident" patriotism that Fulbright evokes. It is this added risk from which the Liberal particularly shrinks, preferring instead, through an appeasement policy, the risk of a Communism triumphant.

If this be so, there can be no genuine debate between the Liberal and the anti-Communist communities. Yet it is important that the formal argument against appeasing Communist China be widely disseminated. For the argument finally finds its way to grassroots Americans and fortifies them in their conviction that there is no substitute for victory. And it does correct the thinking of those members of the Liberal Establishment who are sensitive to the persuasive power of right reason.

Unfortunately, but not surprisingly, the press, radio and television gave only meager coverage to the genuinely expert testimony of these witnesses.

China, Viet Nam & U.S. Policy

Franz Michael

The Sino-Soviet conflict has to be seen within the framework of Communism, as a power struggle within the Communist world, and not as an expression of national interests by competing states of an international order of the past.

In discussing today the problems our own policy faces with regard to Communist China, in Vietnam and in Asia in general, I believe it to be of foremost importance that we accept the fact that our opponent, or rather our opponents, are not national states or traditional powers with traditional ambitions, but components of that Communist movement that is out to conquer the world by whatever means and to transform it in its image. I believe that the most fatal mistake that we can make is to assume that Communism is dead, that a Communist ideology is dead, and that we deal with powers which pursue traditional national interests and have to be dealt with on that basis. Lately it has often been argued that the behavior of the Communist Chinese leadership can be explained, at least in part, in terms of the imperial Chinese tradition of past centuries; that if we only could understand this tradition and help to break down the barriers that have kept its present representatives from understanding the world, we would then be able to deal with them on rational terms, that is, terms that are rational within our concept of rationality.

I believe nothing could be further from the truth. There could be no greater contrast, ethically and intellectually, let alone politically, than that between the emperors of Confucian China of old and the Communist Party's Marxist-Leninist China of today. The two are not even historically related. Between the period of the rule of the emperors of old and that of the Communists of today, China was under the National Government which accepted the Western concept of the nation-state. When the Communists took over in 1949 they did not abolish a Confucian imperial order but the law courts, the codes, the educational system, the Western economy and the Western thought that had been the basis of a Nationalist China that was well on the way to taking its place in the world until the Japanese attack in World War II, and the civil war that followed, destroyed it.

Communizing China

The Communists, after their conquest of power, had two major purposes: to communize China internally and to contribute to the world Communist revolution externally. It is the latter purpose which poses the problems we are facing today in Asia. Any attempt to ignore this Communist purpose is done at our risk. It is simply unrealistic to assume that by gestures or offers, by trade or discussions we will sway the Communists to accept our world of live and let live. They are realists, of course, who will not go into ventures they regard as hopeless. They will move when they regard the time and the situation as opportune; and they will bide their time when, in their terms, the revolutionary wave has subsided. But we have to understand that their logic is not our logic. When we negotiate, we have to remember that their purpose is not ours. And until the Communist purpose of world domination has changed, all that can be arranged is at best a truce.

The hope has been expressed that what is sometimes called the "out-moded doctrine of Marxism-Leninism" is losing its grip on Communist leadership, or that at least the next generation of leaders will no longer believe in world revolution. This can only be regarded as wishful thinking. There is no evidence whatsoever that the main tenets of the gospel itself have been affected in Communist thinking by this or the younger generation, whatever shifting strategy may recommend itself to them at the time.

But, of course, the strategies have been shifting. Karl Marx's original predictions of the increasing misery of the industrial proletariat have been completely disproved by developments in the industrial countries, and then the Bolshevik revolution occurred in what was at best a marginal area of industrialization. The hopes which its leader, Lenin, placed on a Communist revolution in Germany in 1919, 1920 and 1922, proved false. It was Lenin who then shifted to strategy number two in the Communist grand plan for world conquest. His theory of Imperialism as the Highest Stage of Capitalism permitted the use for Communist purposes of revolutionary tensions in what we call today the developing countries of the world. The strategy for Communist conquest in China and today in Vietnam and elsewhere, was Lenin's. It is the strategy of what the Communists call "wars of national liberation." It feeds on two elements. One is agrarian discontent or what is called the agrarian revolution in these predominantly agricultural countries. The other is the emerging nationalism of a small, Western-educated elite, regarded by the Communists as bourgeois-capitalist or nationalist-capitalist, but "anti-imperialist." The use of peasant discontent and of nationalist aspirations for Communist purposes must, however, not lead us astray. Mao Tse-tung, who followed this Leninist-Stalinist policy, was not an agrarian reformer nor was he a heretic. And Ho Chi Minh and the Vietcong today are Communists and not nationalists with Communist trimmings.

The two strategies of proletarian revolution and of national liberation movements or wars of liberation are by no means irreconcilable. But the matter of coordinating them may pose problems. And the question of emphasis today, where there are two headquarters in the overall Communist movement has become a part of the expression of the conflict for power. Communist advance in the industrial world today is not possible through proletarian uprisings as once conceived after World War I, nor did the Communists prove able to exploit their participation in the resistance movements during World War II in France and Italy for eventual take-over. And since there is now a universal fear of hydrogen war, blustering threat of same, as once used by a Soviet, has been excluded since it became clear that the United States would stand for

Berlin or any part of Europe. So the strategy has shifted to what is called "peaceful coexistence." In Khrushchev's words:

> Peaceful coexistence does not imply conciliation between socialist and bourgeois ideologies . . . The peaceful coexistence of states with different social systems presupposes an unremitting ideological, political, and economic struggle of the working people inside the countries of the capitalist system, including armed struggle when they find that necessary (sic!) and the steady advance of the national liberation movement among the peoples of the colonial and dependent countries.

'Peaceful Coexistence'

Their "peaceful co-existence" does not mean the end of confrontation with Communism, but it is confrontation in an area where our superiority -- once we understand the threat -- should not make us fear the battle, so much better to be fought in the intellectual rather than in the military field.

But it is different with the wars of liberation. This type of warfare, focused today in Vietnam, is the strategy that the Soviets have as much approved as the Chinese. If they are somewhat reluctant to go all out for it as the Chinese Communists do, it is in order not to compromise the peaceful co-existence strategy for which they want to be known. In my view, Ho Chi Minh has not only received Soviet support from the beginning, but will be backed as long as the Soviets believe that this particular national liberation war looks favorable. The Chinese Communists, however, have gone all out for this strategy. Its priority in today's Communist advance was openly stated by the Indonesian Communist leader D. N. Aidit, who lost his life recently in the Communist coup in Indonesia. It has become most memorably proclaimed in the often-quoted statement of the Chinese Communist military leader Lin Piao, who compared the national liberation wars in the developing countries to the strategy once used in China by the encirclement of the cities through Communist control of the rural areas in preparation for eventual take-over of the whole country. In the same way the rural areas of the world -- the countries of Asia, Africa, and South America -- are to be taken over first by the encirclement of the industrial nations now regarded as the cities of the world. The most important sentence is perhaps the one in which Lin Piao compared the effectiveness of the two strategies:

> Since World War II, the proletarian revolutionary movement has for various reasons been temporarily held back in the North American and West European capitalist countries, while the people's revolutionary movement in Asia, Africa and Latin America has been growing vigorously.

It is this Communist advance that we are facing today. Should it succeed in Vietnam it will continue elsewhere; in Southeast Asia, the Middle East, Africa and South America. That, at least, is the Communist intent. But things have not been going well for the Chinese Communists both in Asia and in Africa, and the Chinese setbacks have, in my view, something to do with the proof of our willingness to resist in Vietnam.

Since we are facing a Communist strategy and not Chinese nationalist imperialism, or for that matter, Soviet nationalist advance, such Communist insurgencies as in Vietnam have to be locally based. But a local insurgency is only possible as a part of the Communist conspiracy, using the organizational and ideological framework that is uniform for all Communism. On this basis the local Communists receive not only political support from the movement but also outside aid in the form of equipment, financing, military expertise and leadership and, where feasible, direct military support. Where they were left alone as in Malaya or in the Philippines, such Communist insurgencies could be defeated. The problem today is to defeat such an insurgency in Vietnam where it is receiving that outside support.

We have today begun to understand that this insurgency is not simply military action which requires a military answer. One of its most important ingredients and one that is not contained in Mao Tse-tung's homilies on guerrilla warfare is the use of terror. This terror is not the use of atrocities for atrocity's sake or as some have held, "the killing of some unpopular landlords or administrators." It is rather the systematic elimination of the leadership of the communities to be taken over by the Communists through assassinations of the most educated and most respected local leaders: the local school teacher, the village head, the monk, and the families of these people. It is also directed against all those who refuse to cooperate, who refuse to provide intelligence and service. Its aim is not only to intimidate the communities, to show on which side one can survive, it is also directed at depriving the communities of their leadership so that the Communist cadres can take the place of those who have been killed.

To fight this strategy requires more than simple military action. What is necessary, of course, is the ability to protect the population from this threat. Before this protection can be guaranteed, all the destruction of the guerrilla forces is at best a temporary reprieve. But there is much more at issue.

The problem of the developing countries of Asia is the problem of a vast transformation. A revolutionary transformation indeed, which will take place and is taking place in these countries under whatever auspices. Under the impact of the modern world, its ideas and its economics, the traditional agrarian societies of this world of old agrarian civilizations are disintegrating. The Western-educated small elites are the first to have been affected by Western ideas, Western education and Western forms of life. But the gap has widened between these Westernizing cities and the rural areas, mostly neglected and often contemptuously disregarded or exploited by the newly emerging elites. It is this gap that the Communists have been exploiting. What is needed, regardless of the Communist threat, is the re-integration of the societies and nations of the world of developing states, a revolution within their old tradition based on their own beliefs and ideas. This revolution does not consist simply of technical change. Modern hygiene, health measures, the fight against malaria, hospitals, schools, new agrarian methods, are only technical forms of changes. What matters is the cultural framework in which this transformation takes place, and "cultural" in this sense is more than the outward manifestations of a material world. It has been said that Communism is strong because of its political organization. And the fight against Communism is truly an organizational battle. But the Communist organization is based on Communist ideology and Communist purposes. If there were no ideology there would be no Communist Party and no Communist threat. The problem of the countries of the developing world is to integrate revolutionary changes into their cultural tradition. In the solution to this problem we can and should assist. To do so we need an understanding of the beliefs and ideas of the great Asian cultural traditions in order to comprehend the setting in which these changes will take place. A true nationalism in these countries -- not the Communist exploitation of it -- must be founded on these cultural traditions.

We have to realize, for instance, that democratic elections which we rightly regard as the free expression of a people's will require a social framework that does not necessarily exist in the countries concerned. Without a viable organization in the communities there is a serious problem of political organization. Political parties in our sense are a new development and need time and the foundation upon which to grow.

I believe our government's policy has today recognized the need of "capturing the revolution." The economic, social and political reforms initiated in South Vietnam, the special teams that are to compete with the National Liberation Front -- our real enemy -- lead us in the right direction.

I would regard it as a deadly mistake to give administrative recognition in negotiations -- let alone beforehand -- to the very foe who is aiming to destroy the society we are trying to build. Truly free elections, once they can be held, need not be feared.

But Vietnam is not an isolated issue. It is only the focal point in what I would regard as the present main front in the battle between Communist totalitarian aspirations and the support of our kind of revolution, in a world that we want to keep free for the pluralism of cultures and traditions, in Asia as well as elsewhere.

CHINESE REACTION TO HEARINGS

The following is the text of an April 10, 1966, dispatch by the New China News Agency from Peking concerning the Communist Chinese reaction to the March Senate Foreign Relations Committee hearings on China and U. S. policy:

The so-called China question has become the focus of attention in the United States in the past two months. U. S. scholars and ideamen in the service of the ruling classes and responsible officials have extended their views in a great debate on China policy.

Beginning from the latter part of January, the House Far East and West Pacific Subcommittee held several public hearings on China policy. From the beginning of March, the Senate Foreign Relations Committee invited a number of "experts on the China question" to testify. Discussions on the "China question" have also been held in American universities, "learned societies" and other "nongovernmental" bodies, and among religious groups. The U. S. President and some high officials have also spoken on China policy on many occasions.

This is a continuation of the debate on the Viet Nam question of some time ago.

Consequences arising from the constant escalation of the war of aggression in Viet Nam by the Johnson Administration are the immediate cause for the discussion on the "China question." This aggressive adventure has not only met with strong opposition from the American people but also aroused anxiety among certain sections of U.S. ruling circles. They fear that this would lead to a "clash with China" and that such a "clash" will be for the United States "the worst possible catastrophe that could occur in the remainder of this century."

There is a more profound reason why the China policy is so widely discussed in the United States. The U. S. imperialist policy of hostility toward China has failed to prevent China from advancing by leaps and bounds along the path of socialist revolution and socialist construction and to check the ever expanding influence of the Chinese revolution. The anti-China betrayal of the revisionist Soviet leadership does not help the United States at all. China, which holds high the banner of anti-imperialism has become the greatest obstacle to the execution of the counterrevolutionary global strategy of U.S. imperialism. U.S. Assistant Secretary of State for Far Eastern Affairs William Bundy said on 12 February that the foreign policy aims of China and the United States are "totally antithetic" and there is "a very fundamental conflict" between them. He admitted that "Communist China is without doubt the most serious and perplexing problem that confronts our foreign policy today."

It can thus be seen that the present debate reflects not the "powerfulness" of the United States but its weakness and defeat and its helplessness and dilemma in face of the great Chinese people. Some influential Americans also criticized the U. S. China policy as fundamentally unsuccessful and "long since out of date." They called for a "fundamental review of our China policy." It is against such a background that the Johnson Administration wants to make use of the debate as a smokescreen to sidetrack the strong dissatisfaction at home and abroad with the U. S. anti-China policy and to conceal the continuance of the policy of hostility and aggression against China.

The debate shows that the difference between these ideamen is about what counterrevolutionary method should be adopted. They are unanimous in persisting in the policy of hostility and aggression toward China. That is why none of them could put forth a feasible formula. After repeated deliberations and consideration, the experts ended in agreeing to the continuation and stepping up of the "containment" policy. They added the phrase "without isolation" after the word "containment," hence the so-called formula "containment without isolation."

Let's see what kind of substance this formula has. The "containment" policy is the core of U.S.-China policy. *Newsweek* of 7 March said, "The necessity for containment of China has become an axiom of U. S. foreign policy." Since taking office, the Johnson Administration has pushed this policy a step forward. It has openly declared that China is the principal enemy of the United States, and has shifted the focus of its global strategy from Europe to Asia. Besides building up more vigorously the "crescent defense line" stretching from South Korea to Thailand, it pins its hopes more and more on collusion with the Khrushchev revisionists, Japanese militarists, and Indian reactionaries to "contain" China. William Bundy said in his 12 February speech that the "containment" of China "is the essence of what we are trying to do."

There is also an aim in the U. S. policy of "containment" which cannot be publicized. By raising the anti-China black banner, the United States wants further to tighten its control over the countries around China, suppress the revolutionary movements in those countries, and turn them into U. S. military bases.

What then is "without isolation" all about? A.D. Barnett, acting director of Columbia University's East Asian Institute, said as the first witness at the Senate Foreign Relations Committee hearing on 8 March that while adhering to its military "containment" of China, the United States should aim at "maximum contacts with and maximum involvement of the Chinese Communists in the international community." This idea was very favorably received in U.S. political quarters. U.S. Vice President Hubert Humphrey said in a speech on 19 March, "We must achieve the containment of Asian communism without isolating the Chinese people." The idea of "dual approach" advanced by Professor Zagoria, another Columbia University "expert on China," amounts to the same thing.

In reality, the "containment without isolation" formula is a manifestation of the U. S. imperialist counterrevolutionary dual tactics on China policy. In short, this means on the one hand continued aggression against and encirclement of China, containment and isolation of China, while on the other, indulging in the vain hope to bring about "peaceful evolution" in China so that revolutionary China will degenerate gradually. "Containment" is the main thing in dual tactics.

Commenting on this formula, the *Christian Science Monitor* said on 6 March that the U.S. policy of "containing" China militarily "has not changed. On the contrary, it has stiffened as a result of the war in Viet Nam." However, the Johnson government wanted this policy "applied together with a long-range political policy" to "lead them (Chinese Communists) down the path that the Russians followed between Stalin and Brezhnev, away from violence and toward an enforced responsibility." This reveals the counterrevolutionary character of the policy of "containment without isolation."

However, U.S. imperialism has found a wrong target. The Chinese people have long seen through the aggressive nature of U.S. imperialism. Whether by its "tough" tactics or by its "soft" tactics or by the simultaneous application of both tactics, U.S. imperialism cannot hope to browbeat or deceive the Chinese people. Even the U.S. ruling circles themselves are not sure whether or not these tactics will bear fruit. William Bundy said on 16 March that in so far as the policy of "containment without isolation" was concerned, the United States had been acting on it for sometime. But he admitted that there was no indication that China would change its policy.

Helplessly and hopelessly, Harvard Professor John Fairbank, the so-called veteran "China specialist," and others again put forward the long discredited "Two Chinas" formula. Some others proposed that "unconditional discussions" be held and "diplomatic relations" established with China before the future of Taiwan is discussed. However, even Dean Rusk himself had to admit that as far as the "Two Chinas" proposal was concerned, "It was useless" because China had rejected it.

U.S. imperialism's persistent hostility towards the Chinese people is determined by its reactionary and aggressive nature. There is nothing strange about it. What is strange is that U.S. imperialism even hopes to find a "way out" of the blind alley of its China policy. The great debate in the United States over Washington's China policy shows once again that it is mere illusion. Look how many politicians, "scholars" and "specialists" took part in these discussions. However, nothing fruitful has come out of them. Nor will there by any result if more discussions are held. Gentlemen in Washington, there is nothing you can do about it!

SCHLESINGER SPEECH

The following is a portion of an address by historian and former Presidential adviser Arthur Schlesinger Jr. on the interpretation of history and the formulation of public policy. The lecture, given at the Institute of Contemporary History in London on May 31, 1966, cautions against drawing "false analogies" between historical events:

For the democratic policy-makers, history generally serves as a negative rather than a positive model: it instructs us not in the things that we must do, like Marxism, but in the things we must not do -- unless we wish to repeat the folly of our ancestors.... In the years since the Second World War, the policy consciousness, at least in Britain and the United States, has been dominated by the Munich analogy -- the generalization, drawn from the attempt to accomodate Hitler in 1938, that appeasement always assures new aggression. I trust that a graduate student some day will write a doctoral essay on the influence of the Munich analogy on the subsequent history of the 20th century. Perhaps in the end he will conclude that the multitude of errors committed in the name of Munich may almost exceed the original error of 1938. Certainly Munich was a tragic mistake, and its lesson was that the appeasement of a highly wound-up and heavily-armed totalitarian state in the context of a relatively firm and articulated continental equilibrium of power was likely to upset the balance and make further aggression inevitable. But to conclude from this that all attempts to avert war by negotiation must always be Munichs is wrong....

Sixteen years after Munich President Eisenhower wrote Churchill, "If...Indochina passes into the hands of the Communists, the ultimate effect on our and your global strategy and position...could be disastrous...We failed to halt Hirohito, Mussolini and Hitler by not acting in unity and in time. That marked the beginning of many years of stark tragedy and desperate peril. May it not be that our nations have learned something from that lesson?" Eisenhower was invoking the Munich analogy to persuade the British to join the Americans in backing the French in Indochina. I need not remind this audience that Churchill was unmoved by Eisenhower's argument. He saw no useful parallel between Hitler, the man on the bicycle who could not stop, a madman commanding vast military force and requiring immediate and visible success, and the ragged bands and limited goals of Ho Chi Minh. Nor could he see any useful parallel between Europe, a developed continent with well-defined national frontiers, interests and identities and a highly-organized equilibrium of power, and Southeast Asia, an underdeveloped subcontinent filled with fictitious states in vague, chaotic and unpredictable revolutionary ferment. So Churchill rejected Eisenhower's analogy -- which did not, of course, prevent Churchill's successor as Prime Minister two years later from seeing Nasser and the Middle East in terms of 1938 and committing his nation to the Suez adventure. This time it was Eisenhower who rejected the Munich analogy.

Today the same analogy haunts us again, echoing in the corridors of Washington, with China cast in the role of Nazi Germany. "In the forties and fifties," President Johnson has said, "we took our stand in Europe to protect the freedom of those threatened by aggression. Now the center of attention has shifted to another part of the world where aggression is on the march. Our stand must be as firm as ever." The instrument of this aggression, we are told, is the war of national liberation. If this technique is permitted to succeed in Vietnam, it will be tried elsewhere. If it is defeated in Vietnam, the Chinese will know that we will not let it succeed in other countries and they will have to reconsider their policies. As Adlai Stevenson put it in a letter published after his death, "I do not think that the idea of Chinese expansionism is so fanciful that the effort to check it is irrational. . . .My hope in Vietnam is that relatively small-scale resistance now may establish the fact that changes in Asia are not to be precipitated by outside force. This was the point in the Korean War. This is the point of the conflict in Vietnam." The Secretary of State has even compared the recent manifesto by the Chinese Defense Minister, Marshall Lin Piao, to *Mein Kampf*.

This is not the place to comment on the Vietnam riddle -- except to suggest that it is not to be solved by bad historical analogies. I see no evidence, for example, that we face in Southeast Asia a premeditated and coordinated plan of Chinese aggression for which the Viet Cong constitute the spearhead, nor do the Chinese appear to have the overwhelming military power or the pent-up mania for immediate expansion which would justify comparison with Hitler. As for the Lin Piao document, a careful reading shows that, far from being a Chinese blueprint for revolution around the earth, it is a message to guerrilla movements in other lands that they are on their own. But the fact that the analogy is invalid does not necessarily invalidate every aspect of the policy. I would, for example, be opposed to any precipitate American withdrawal from Vietnam. I strongly support President Johnson's objective of a negotiated settlement, and it is common sense to recognize that the other side will not negotiate so long as it thinks it can win.

My point rather is to suggest the persistence of the cast of mind which seeks to make policy through stereotype, through -- historical generalization wrenched illegitimately out of the past and imposed mechanically on the future -- and does so in face of Churchill's warning: "No case of this kind can be judged apart from its circumstances." I well remember President Kennedy expressing to me after the Cuban missile crisis in 1962 his fear that people would conclude from his victory that all we would have to do thereafter in dealing with the Communists was to be tough and they would collapse. The missile crisis, he pointed out, had three distinctive features: it took place in an area where we enjoyed local conventional superiority, where Soviet national security was not directly engaged and where the Russians lacked a case which they could convincingly sustain before the world. Things would be different, he said, if the situation were one where the Communists had the local superiority, where their national security was directly engaged and where they could persuade themselves and others they were in the right. Kennedy, who, like Churchill, had the skeptical mind of a first-class historian, was without illusion about the infallibility of historical analogy. Or, as Mark Twain put it in *Pudd'n'head Wilson*, "We should be careful to get out of an experience only the wisdom that is in it -- and stop there; lest we be like the cat that sits down on a hot stove lid. She will never sit down on a hot stove lid again -- and that is well; but also she will never sit down on a cold one any more."

In confronting the choices of our own time, our leaders would be well advised to emulate this skepticism. For history offers us no short cut to clairvoyance. If history teaches us anything, it is rather that the future is full of surprises and outwits all our certitudes. If 25 years ago, in May 1941, a speaker had predicted that before the end of the decade of the forties Germany and Japan would be well on the way to becoming close friends and allies of Britain and the United States, he would have been considered mad. If 15 years ago, in May 1950, as the Russians and Chinese were signing their 30 year pact of amity and alliance, a speaker had predicted that by the end of the fifties they would be at each other's throats, he too would have been considered mad. The chastening fact is that many of the pivotal events of our age were wholly unforeseen: from the Nazi-Soviet pact and the Tito-Stalin quarrel of years ago to such events in today's newspapers as the anticommunist upsurge in Indonesia and the overthrow of Nkrumah in Ghana -- and his resurrection in Guinea.

Occasionally I read in the press that leading political figures in Washington are shaping their actions today by calculations with regard to the Democratic presidential nomination in 1972. I am sure that these men themselves are under no delusion about the hopelessness of such an undertaking. 1972 is tonight as far away from us as 1960 -- and no one reflecting on the unpredictability of the last six years in the United States could sensibly suppose that the next six are going to be any more predictable. I have often thought that a soothsayer trying to forecast the next three American Presidents in early 1940 would hardly have named as the first President after Roosevelt a man who was then an obscure back-

bench senator from Missouri, anticipating defeat by Governor Lloyd Stark in the Democratic primaries; as the second, an unknown lieutenant colonel in the United States Army; and, as the third, a kid still at college. Yet that sequence began to unfold in less time than between now and 1972.

The salient fact about the historical process, so far as the short run is concerned, is its inscrutability. One must bear this in mind, I believe, when asked to accept drastic decisions now on the basis of someone's speculation as to what the behavior of Communist China will be a dozen years from now. In its coarsest form, this is the argument that we must have a showdown with China before it gets the bomb. This is the old preventive-war thesis we used to hear so often in the late forties: yet I do not think anyone can rationally contend that we would be better off today had we dropped the bomb on Russia twenty years ago. Having been wrong so often in the past, how can we be so sure we have achieved such infallibility now that we would risk the future of the world on a guess?

Who can possibly predict the course the Chinese Revolution will take in the years ahead? The study of revolution has shown us that the emotional and doctrinal pitch of revolutions waxes and wanes; that, while revolutions at first may devour their children in the end the children sometimes devour the revolutions; that even totalitarian revolutions fail at total mass indoctrination; that a successful revolution begins to develop a stake in the status quo; that post-revolutionary generations have their own identities and aspirations; that the possession of a major nuclear arsenal has thus far had a sobering effect on the possessor; that nations follow their historic interests much more faithfully than they do their ideologies; and that there is no greater error than to try and deduce the policy of future from the rhetoric of the present. Nor does the example of Hitler and *Mein Kampf* change this. Hitler was indeed the man on the bicycle; he had to keep moving; the Nazi revolution never got beyond the first messianic phase; its natural condemned it to *Gotterdamerung*. We must not forget that the Chinese revolutionary regime has already lasted five years longer than the whole life of the Third Reich -- and we have seen in the case of the Soviet Union the permutation and erosion time and national interest have worked on what were once thought to be final motives and permanent objectives. With an equation so overflowing with variables, how can any one forecast now the behavior of China twenty years from now?

History, in short, offers the statesman a broad and indispensable sense of the massive movements. But it does not give him a detailed forecast of particular relationships or policies. Too often it equips his decisions with good rather than real reasons, holding out a mirror in which he contentedly sees his own face. This is not an argument against the knowledge of history; it is an argument against the shallow knowledge of history. The single analogy is never enough to penetrate a process so cunningly compounded not only of necessity but of contingency, fortuity, ignorance, accident, chance and luck. And the statesman who is sure that he can divine the future invites his own retribution. "The hardest strokes of heaven," Hebert Butterfield has written, "fall in history upon those who imagine that they can control things in a sovereign manner, playing providence not only for themselves but for the far future -- reaching out into the future with the wrong kind of far-sightedness, and gambling on a lot of risky calculations in which there must never be a single mistake."

What, then, should be the impact of history on policy? What has history to offer the statesman? Richard Goodwin, who served Presidents Kennedy and Johnson so well as a White House Special Assistant, has suggested two cautions:

"First, at every step you have to leave as many options open as possible and decide as little as possible; because you may be wrong, you have to leave yourself with opportunities to change your mind, to make different decisions in the future."

"Secondly, since almost all important policy judgments are speculative, you must avoid risking too much on the conviction that you are right."

Of course, agnosticism about the future cannot be permitted to sever the nerve of action in the present, but present action must confront the concrete situation and the specific circumstance. The curse of international affairs is the statesman who sees himself as philosopher and moralist -- we have had some such in Washington -- and proposes to resolve all questions according to a higher law visible only to himself and others of the *illuminati*. Let us pledge ourselves to an economy of means, renounce self-righteousness and not try to settle questions which do not need to be settled. Your countrymen and mine find it especially hard to forsake the pleasures of preaching to lesser breeds, but it still might be worth the effort for both of us. The hard fact is that with all our superiority, we cannot intelligently base decisions on a non-existent chart of the future; so we might as well stick to what we know.

I read the other day a sagacious letter written 70 years ago by the young Winston Churchill to a New York politician of the time, Bourke Cockran. "The duty of government," Churchill said, "is to be first of all practical. I am for makeshifts and expediency. I would like to make the people who live on this world at the same time as I do better fed and happier generally. If incidentally I benefit posterity -- so much the better -- but I would not sacrifice my own generation to a principle however high or a truth however great."

Such an approach may seem too modest -- even, perhaps, too cynical -- for those ideological statesmen whose self-righteousness has adorned our age -- those confident moralists prepared with the deepest conscience and commitment to sacrifice their generation on the altar of their own metaphors. But history, never wholly silent, raises questions about the infallibility of their historical models, whether positive or negative -- questions about both the all-encompassing ideology and the single analogy. Far from enabling us to look piercingly into the future, history, if we read it aright, offers us an even more valuable gift: it makes us -- or should make us -- understand the extreme difficulty, the intellectual peril, the moral arrogance of supposing that the future will yield itself so easily to us.

Properly understood, history must lead statesmen to a profound and humbling sense of human frailty -- to a recognition of the fact, so often and so tragically destructive of our most sacred certitudes, that the possibilities of history are far richer and more various than the human intellect is likely to conceive -- this; and the final understanding that, despite the limitations of our knowledge and the obscurity of our situation, we are never relieved from the necessity of meeting our responsibilities. Freedom and fatality: still the essence of the human condition.

China and the War—A Roundtable Discussion

The following is the edited transcript of a CBS News special report entitled "Viet Nam Perspective: China and the War," as broadcast March 13, 1966. The guests included Sen. J. W. Fulbright (D Ark.), chairman of the Senate Foreign Relations Committee; Dr. John K. Fairbank, professor of history and director of the East Asian Research Center at Harvard University; Dr. Alice L. Hsieh, senior staff member of the Rand Corporation and an expert on Chinese nuclear power; and Charles Taylor, of the Toronto Globe and Mail, a resident correspondent in Peking for a year and a half. Administration experts from the White House and State Department had been invited to join in the discussion by CBS, but refused. The moderator was Marvin Kalb.

MARVIN KALB: When you hear the term "Red China," what are the first impressions that come to your mind? I'd like to start with Dr. Hsieh.

DR. HSIEH: Well, the first thing I think of is that it is the latest stage in a revolutionary process that has been taking place for well over a hundred years in China, and that it is not a static stage and that we need to look and to study at the possible future stages that this revolutionary process may take in the next 10 to 25 years.

KALB: Charles Taylor.

TAYLOR: I think it is a silly phrase. It is one I don't use. My newspaper doesn't use it. I think relatively few Canadians would use it. China is China. Why not just call it that? But I don't think it is something that bothers the Chinese. They are proud of being Red.

KALB: Senator Fulbright.

FULBRIGHT: Well, the first thing that comes to mind was the period of the late Senator McCarthy in the Senate when this matter became of considerable importance to us. A man named Kohlberg, who used to denounce me regularly because of my lack of enthusiasm for the China Lobby. So that my first impression's that way. Then I think of the Opium War, one of the great periods, one of the great accomplishments of Great Britain, about 125 years ago. But I don't know China, never having been there.

KALB: And Professor Fairbank, who shared the Committee's attention last week with Columbia's Professor A. Doak Barnett.

MR. FAIRBANK: I think Red China is a cold war term and in my mind it is sort of the opposite of the People's China, which is the other sort of cold war term. Very pro-Red China is sort of anti.

Personally I confess I haven't been able to use China, I have been using Communist China, but I would favor settling for just China.

KALB: That comment by Senator Kennedy, about 20,000 Chinese being in North Vietnam already, I don't believe has ever come up in the public testimony before your Committee, Senator. Is that the figure that you have heard before?

FULBRIGHT: Well, it was mentioned but they are construction workers primarily. I believe Dr. Fairbank mentioned some number similar to that.

FAIRBANK: I have seen this in the press.

FULBRIGHT: Rebuilding bridges and roads and perhaps manning some of the missile sites, but presumably they are Russians.

KALB: Well, there is a point of view in Washington which has been expressed at this stage basically quietly, privately, that we are not really arguing the question of whether China will intervene in the war in Vietnam, that intervention has taken place but on a minor scale, and we are somewhat seeing this thing develop slowly. Would you accept that on the basis of what you have been hearing?

FULBRIGHT: No, I would not. No one has said there are any combat troops -- I have heard no such allegation; that these are workers who come in and it is so minor I wouldn't call have an intervention at all. I think, on the contrary, the evidence we have had, the witnesses have indicated they didn't believe China had intervened or intended to intervene without much greater provocation than she has so far had.

KALB: Charles Taylor, do you get the impression last year in China, were there visible signs of Chinese preparation for intervention?

TAYLOR: Not for intervention. All the signs that you see are defensive. Of course, they are not going to let any foreigner go anywhere where there might be preparations for offensive actions. I was down in Kunming just above the North Vietnamese border just after the bombings of North Vietnam started, but since then I believe that has been closed to foreign journalists, but what you can see in China leads you to the belief that the preparations are defensive. The main preparation is building up a mass militia, which is clearly a defensive operation.

KALB: Mr. Fairbank, why do you think that we are sort of all talking about a problem like Chinese intervention in the war in Vietnam -- and I get the distinct impression on the basis of the testimony -- as well as Mr. Taylor's comments now -- that this is a defensive operation on their part?

FAIRBANK: I think we have an absolutely amazing lack of perspective on the whole situation. It is fantastic. Here you have this Chinese quarter of the human race -- everybody agrees there's 650 million people or 700 million people -- here they are in their more or less normal boundaries and they have no troops outside, except maybe these railroad troops or whatever it is in the north, and here we are expanding, as we do all over the world. Not just militarily, but economically. In trade, we are much more trading abroad than they are. We are much more touring abroad than they are. We are all over the lot, and here is our large force in South Vietnam. How can they not regard us as, you might say, expansive? And how can we not, therefore, try to see things from their point of view and try to get a different picture of what we are doing?

In other words - I am not saying, you know, that we have to stop what we are doing because I don't have an alternative, but we have to have a different perspective on it. We have to realize that we are really moving out, and that as a country we are, all around the world, in a commercial way, our airplanes everywhere, our airfields - you know, planes - and people, news, CBS, everything. Life Magazine is going to publish in Tokyo, in Japanese. They are going to have everything that we have got. And if you sit in Peking and you feel that this is imperialism -- by the book of Marxism or Maoism, why, you can be scared to death. It is just all over the lot. We don't think it is imperialism, but we ought to have a different perspective on ourselves.

KALB: I think that possibly in this connection, if we were to glance back here at this map, I think if a Chinese leader sitting in Peking, if he were to check out of his reality, he would probably find large American forces in Korea, Japan, Formosa, a quarter of a million men now in South Vietnam and stretching around; they might have some sense of fear, and possibly this is all defensive.

DR. HSIEH: May I take some exception to this, Marvin, because I think for some time it has been my belief that the Chinese do not really fear an unprovoked attack from the United States. If you look back at the Soviet Union, I think beginning in 1956 they had developed a confidence that the United States was not going to attack the Soviet Union on an unprovoked basis. I think by 1957, the Chinese had developed this type of confidence, that the United States was not going to pursue a policy roll-back, or unprovoked attack.

If they had not developed this type of confidence, I do not believe that they would have challenged the Soviet Union in the Sino-Soviet rift to the extent they did in the period following 1956-57, and to have turned down the Soviet Union's demands for the so-called unreasonable military control in China.

I feel what the Chinese are concerned about is that if they take certain actions, they would then be -- if they take actions that would provoke the United States, then they would be subject to retaliatory action by the United States.

KALB: Do you think they know what those actions might be? Aren't we living in a rather gray world here where we are not sure what actions on either side might provoke the other?

DR. HSIEH: Well, I think they have attempted to some degree to communicate these to us, what they would consider, what actions we would take, let's say, in South Vietnam that might provoke a response on their part.

As I recall, it was well over a year and half ago that Ch'en Yi at one time talked about a possible U.S. invasion of North Vietnam as being a point that might bring a Chinese response. Also he mentioned the preservation of the North Vietnamese regime. More recently there has been less said about, "If the United States attacks us, we will counter-attack." I mean this is a gray area, but I think these are the three points where the Chinese might feel they would be compelled to intervene to make some response to U.S. action.

FAIRBANK: This is important to discuss, but it seems to me you need more perspective on the Chinese situation. That is, what are they up to in their national life, and what is the content of day-to-day activity?

I would like to hear from Mr. Taylor for just a moment. Here is the question I would like to ask: This enormous mass of people organized under the biggest government that ever has been put together by man, with a party of 20 million people trying to run the thing, this is an enormous problem in itself for the people in charge. In other words, they are still domestically concerned, primar-

ily domestically concerned. Carrying on a revolution, remaking people, remaking a country, building and everything else. And the question of foreign policy cannot be the main thing in their minds. I don't see how it possibly can be. It seems to me that foreign policy is the question of keeping their borders intact and avoiding attack from abroad.

The thing that you do from day to day is not plan how to take over the world. They are not like the Germans in the midst of competing nations; they are an empire apart, a civilization apart. They have this enormous land with any province as big as a European country, and this is where they have always had their being and their concerns have always been domestically centered. That is why they haven't been so expansive in the past, when they could have been and weren't. I just wonder today if that isn't the same mood in the Peking capital.

MR. TAYLOR: I agree very strongly. I think that is very important, because when you get outside of China, expecially in the West, especially in this country, everybody is concerned about China and Vietnam-China beyond its borders and so on. But when you live in Peking even as a foreign resident, restricted, you do get the impression that what worries the leaders basically are domestic concerns, economic concerns, and perhaps more important, political concerns. They just launched their third Five Year Plan after three years of recovery from their very bad period in '59 to '61, which carried through into '62. They are very much concerned about the morale, as you know, the morale of the young people -- will they be sufficiently revolutionary enough?

KALB: Senator Fulbright, why is it that we are apparently as a nation, are overestimating? Why are we so absorbed with this concept of China, the Korean outlaw, the inevitable expansionist power? This is the area of confrontation.

FULBRIGHT: Well, I wish I knew why. I don't see any good reason for it. I think it is an irrational reaction. Perhaps from the frustration and disappointment that arose at the time of Korea. And their intervention in Korea and the question of communism, and particularly the Democrats being soft on communism, became a part of our domestic political dogma here, and it was, as you know, used quite effectively, and I think this has been stepped up.

The China Lobby is an extraordinarily effective organization. You have one of the strongest publications in the field, the Time Magazine and Life -- the Luce publications have been hammering this away for years and years and they convince people that this is a major threat to our security.

KALB: But you find that this is very much the line that one hears at the State Department, and is this to say . . .

FULBRIGHT: That is right.

KALB: . . . that the State Department is somewhat influenced by the China Lobby?

FULBRIGHT: Oh, very much so. Well, in the days of McCarthy, you will remember -- this is what I said when you mentioned China -- this is the period when I first became aware of this kind of activity. This is a very serious matter. I have never been so concerned or, in a way, dismayed at the Senate as in the days of McCarthy. You weren't here, I don't believe, then, were you?

KALB: I was at the university then.

FULBRIGHT: This was a terrible period in the Senate and in our political life. It was disgraceful. You remember Cohn and Schine, the two of the boys with McCarthy going about Europe and just made us look terrible all over the world as an irresponsible nation, and I was never so ashamed.

We had lots of difficulty in that time, and it did something to the State Department. I think it destroyed their morale. It frightened people that they couldn't speak out and couldn't give honest reports without fear of this retaliation. They put in people in the security part. Mr. McLeod was well thought to be there for that purpose. Dr. Fairbank knows a little about this.

FAIRBANK: I keep thinking about perspective. I don't want to leave this question. This fascinates me, of course. I have a personal interest in it. But as a matter of perspective, here is this Chinese society as a sort of a land animal, a continental land animal.

It doesn't go overseas particularly -- until modern times Chinese didn't go abroad. Even in modern times they were just going to Western colonial places. Here is this American amphibious animal, which goes all over the world as part of the expansion of Europe.

I want to be a little world-historical here. It seems to me you have got to have a perspective that we don't now use in our public conversation. The Americans, in other words, are carrying on a process that has been going on for several hundred years, which has steadily invaded all parts of the globe. We just happen to be the people now that have the higher technology to lead the way in some parts of the world. Russia is doing it in other parts. But the Chinese have seen this going on, they are a different kind of a society, which has been at home all this time, has had a superior civilization, as it felt. It is ancient, continuous in one place, with certain stabilities that it built in. The Chinese did not get into the business of expanding when they might have, when the Europeans started to expand. The Chinese held back. They could have done it, but they didn't. They weren't that kind of country, they were concerned about the bureaucrat collecting the taxes from the peasant. Whereas the Westerners, like ourselves, and the Europeans first, were concerned about the merchant overseas and getting funds, and the armies and the king and all these other elements in society.

The pluralistic society of the West, in short, is a much more dynamic and expansive thing, as we see in ourselves today, and the Chinese have this built-in capacity in their history to be a sort of a land-based, stay-at-home, highly integrated, collectivised sort of society, where people are really under control and everything is organized. They have a great sense of order as we can now see.

Well, now this is the kind of perspective that it seems to me we have got to keep in mind when we try to look at what the Chinese reaction may be to us. I don't mean to say that this is the only thing to consider. History is just one thing to crank in, but I think we are short of it.

FULBRIGHT: I agree we are very short of it.

DR. HSIEH: I would like to suggest that while I can't adhere to the theory that the Chinese have revolutionary objectives and aims at world conquest and taking over Latin America, or Africa, I do feel that the Chinese have certain objectives within the region of Asia, which is the establishment of hegemony in the area, and which means in turn the removal of U.S. power and influence from the area.

FULBRIGHT: I would agree to that.

KALB: Does that mean that the aim of Chinese policy now -- if I interpret you right -- being the removal of America's presence and influence from the areas that they consider close to them and important to them, isn't the next logical step that the United States-- and this is repeated over and over again, and they certainly must know it -- it is said that we are not getting out of that area until we have helped in the creation of a situation that we feel satisfactory to us. Doesn't that again put us on this collision with China?

DR. HSIEH: I agree with you, it continues the confrontation. Because where we are, they want.

TAYLOR: Let me ask a question as a foreigner, that is perhaps presumptuous. The goal of establishing hegemony around its borders and getting rid of the United States would, I am certain, be the goal of any strong Chinese government. It would be the goal of Chiang Kai-shek were he in power in Peking today. Now when you in the United States talk about containing China, are you talking about containing Chinese communism or are you talking about containing China? Are you afraid and unwilling to countenance a strong China? Is there, in other words, unconsciously an element of racism in your approach?

KALB: Dr. Hsieh, what do you think?

DR. HSIEH: I know I would say it is more creating a situation in the Far East where the nations there can pursue their futures on the basis of their own self-determination.

Let us take, for example, the way Peking has, because of its military power -- it is the strongest military power among the Asian nations -- has been able to intimidate Burma, Cambodia, so that it pursues a pro-Peking policy. But I would say what the Chinese would hope to do would be to use their influence to neutralize U.S.

allies in the area, I don't know if I have quite answered your question.

KALB: Does that mean with the use of military force?

DR. HSIEH: I would say the political use of military force.

KALB: I see.

FAIRBANK: Would you set this formula, that the Americans, as the expanding front of this European expansion that I was mentioning a moment ago, are pushing for the free world kind of development, as we call it? I think we can agree on what that means, more or less; international trade, self-determination. We have a whole formula for it. It is our ideology and I am all for it, except I think it doesn't necessarily fit overseas situations always. It has to be adjusted, and there are some shortcomings.

Anyway, we are doing this expanding and at some point we come up against the Chinese who are obviously a great power in the process of developing power, and are going to be in their region and protect their frontiers and to some extent will certainly expand their influence outside of their frontiers.

Now, here you have a zone which may be the Indian border, or it may be Malaya or it may be where we now are, which is a meeting point between power systems and, really, societies, and the problem is how to get some kind of an agreed basis for some kind of zone, some kind of point of demarcation so that the two sides are not concerned about the other person being over there, and this person being over here.

KALB: Professor Fairbank, I wanted to ask; is it really true, is the Chinese language a barrier? Cannot Western ideas get through because of the absence of certain ideographs?

FAIRBANK: We are up against, I am sure, a problem in communication, and the Chinese language is, I think, a real barrier to their contact with outside ideas.

Now, if you look at Chinese characters, if you study them, you will see they have a form conveying the idea and there is no other language like this in modern operation around the world, as far as I know. Every other language can take in -- every other writing system, we are talking about writing systems -- can take in foreign words by sound. The Japanese can do this because they have a syllabary. Koreans can do it. Europeans. Everybody can do it. Sanskrit; everybody can do this by sound. The Chinese cannot take it in by sound because they have to write it in ideographic characters, and if you start using ideographic characters purely for sound purposes you get utter confusion. Is it for sound or for meaning? Any characters should be for meaning unless it is distinctly visible as a name. So the tendency is for foreign words to come into Chinese, being translated into Chinese characters.

Now, this means in effect that if you don't have in those characters meanings that suit the foreign word, it is difficult to get the foreign idea in.

KALB: To give an example, I was once told that when President Truman was President and the Chinese were trying to refer to him, they couldn't get anything close to sounding like Truman and it ended up something "Toolamun."

FAIRBANK: That is right. Marshall is "Marshar." Roosevelt is "Roosafew" and so on. Anybody you want to name has his equivalent characters in Chinese and they don't sound anything like the original name because Chinese characters are not the same sound system as Western languages. So here you have this problem of bringing in Western ideas and the result of the Chinese language having this built-in ideographic nature is, I think, that it can take in most easily those foreign ideas that are already in the language.

KALB: What do you mean?

FAIRBANK: Well, an idea of authority, of rule, of power. If it comes, say, in the Soviet system -- if it comes in, and there is a more or less equivalent Chinese idea, you can use the equivalent Chinese characters and you express the idea and it has all of its ramifications more or less equivalent. But if you take this character for freedom, or you take the word for "nations," which they didn't used to have -- now they have developed one which is "country family" -- or "nationalism" which is "people racism," and so on. All these things have to be brought in and they become Chinese in the process. Now, this is the cultural barrier I am saying that exists.

Everything that comes into China has to be Sinophied. It is a most amazing thing and the Chinologists get Sinophied the same way. You get caught in this different culture and it has its own way of looking at things, and the people who are in it in a way can't get out of it. So we just have to recognize here is a problem of communications. It is a little bit greater than with any other country.

KALB: Charles, did you find in your 18 months that you were Sinophied? Could you get through to the Chinese?

TAYLOR: It is very difficult because you are restricted as a foreigner in China to more or less official contacts. The average Chinese is not meant to come up and speak to you on the street even if you do have a language in common that you can converse in. In conversations with officials, to tend to -- it sounds like the old record playing over and over again. They are not free to digress from the official line, with only a very few exceptions. They would get in trouble for doing so.

That is why -- another reason why communication is very difficult. Even those countries -- and there are many countries that have representation in Peking. Let it not be said that China is isolated just because the United States does not have an embassy there and China is not in the United Nations. There are roughly 45 countries that have diplomatic representatives of one sort or another in Peking. But even those people, even the ones who are friendly, have friendly political relations with the Chinese Communists, or non-Communists, whatever they may be, have difficulty getting through. They are not taken aside and told what China is up to; they are treated with great correctness and politeness, but there is no intimacy in their relationship.

And this is not something that has just come since 1949, as I think Professor Fairbank would agree. This is a highly developed technique for dealing with the foreigner that the Chinese developed over the centuries and that they became particularly good at through necessity after the Opium War period, after the last half of the last century, and in many ways today the foreigner in China is treated as the foreigner was treated by the last dynasty, and this is a very great problem in communication. It is very difficult to get through.

KALB: Dr. Hsieh?

DR. HSIEH: I agree with everything that has been said but I would like to add that the Chinese, in varying ways, do manage to signal certain messages to the United States in varying ways. For example, in their public statements following their first nuclear detonation. If one read these statements very closely, being familiar with the esoteric way that the Chinese tend to communicate, or Chinese Communists tend to communicate, one became very well aware that they were playing their first nuclear detonation, and their second one too, in an extremely low key fashion, thus suggesting to us, or attempting to signal to us that there was going to be no major change in a military policy of very low risk.

KALB: This is a terribly interesting thing. You know there is a study going on at Harvard right now by Dr. Ezra Vogel, based on an interview project with many Chinese, and if I understand some of the results of that study, he has discovered that Chinese Communist cadremen, as well as intellectuals, based on this process of criticism and self-criticism, actually develop excellent thought processes. They are not apart from the mainstream of international communication, can communicate, are able to communicate. In fact, as a result of this study, seemed to be more able to communicate possibly than many other people.

DR. HSIEH: I was going to say, I think there is also a communication between Communist countries too, and in this I would like to second what Professor Barnett said in the (China) hearings with regard to Lin Piao's well-known statement by now -- article of September 3rd of last year, that this was not, as it has been so generally represented, as a blueprint for world conquest, of a transposition of the Chinese strategy of the '30's, of surrounding, of using the countryside to surround the cities, transposing this to using the underdeveloped areas to surround the Western capitalist countries, but a message -- a communication to Hanoi and the Vietcong, suggesting to them a modification, in effect de-escalation of the pace and tempo of the military operations in South Vietnam.

KALB: We had heard here in Washington, I think even Secretary Rusk, possibly before your committee, I am not certain, referred to this Lin Piao statement as the "*Mein Kampf*" of China. Was that before the committee?

FULBRIGHT: That's right.

KALB: And this was a rather startlingly different point of view as to what they were doing. A de-escalation process as opposed to a practical declaration of war.

DR. HSIEH: I think it has long been the feeling -- there has been one school of thought which has taken the point of view that Peking has been masterminding the operations in South Vietnam. Now, for some years now it has been my own feeling that it is not Peking, but Hanoi, that is setting the pace and the tempo and the level of violence in South Vietnam, and that the Chinese Communists were becoming extremely concerned about the increase in the level of operations in South Vietnam, that it would bring about just the type of result that has occurred, an increase in U.S. manpower in South Vietnam, and that when they saw this occurring in the summer of last year, they made this major communication to Hanoi where they used the analogy of the Japanese invasion of China in the '30's, and more or less suggesting that it was no longer in Vietnam a war of national liberation, but a war of national -- of resistance, and that the United States was there to stay and was prepared to consolidate its power there and that the Vietcong should adopt the type of policy the Chinese Communists used, that of relying on revolutionary bases, guerrilla warfare, et cetera, and that also they made very clear, as Professor Barnett has already pointed out, that the Vietnamese were very much on their own and it was a process of self-reliance.

KALB: Senator, on the basis of all of the testimony before your committee, could you give us a kind of consensus, if I might use that word, on the whole concept of Hanoi being the central agent for this all, the role of the Chinese in this? Is there really a legitimate fear in the Administration as expressed before your committee, that the Chinese are the people pulling the strings in all this?

FULBRIGHT: Well, I cannot give a consensus, but I feel myself this is the Administration point of view. Dean Rusk just expressed that a moment ago on that excerpt, and it seems to me that that is what they are primarily concerned with. They have said on various occasions, "This is an opportunity to prove to the Chinese that wars of liberation will not succeed. If we don't prove that here, they will do it in many other places."

I may say I don't subscribe to this, but this is the point of view of the Secretary of State. I don't subscribe to his analysis as to the nature of the war and how it began. That is a very interesting subject, perhaps, though it is not appropriate to go into it here, and we also -- as to what you do about it, I am very interested in this idea that the Chinese think we are preparing to stay there. I have thought all along if they thought we were going to stay there and were able to stay there that this would be the greatest incentive to perhaps a proposal for neutralization of Southeast Asia. Whereas, if we carry the war on at too high a tempo and increase it, that this will result either in an escalation that would involve them or a revulsion in this country against the war that would cause us to pull out.

I think the latter they have hoped would occur, and I think this is a very neat point. I don't know what the answer is yet, but that was the reason I at least held out the proposal that we might look forward to a neutralization that would take us out, our military presence out, along with their own agreement to stay out.

KALB: Mr. Fairbank, I am kind of interested in this point just now raised by the Senator. Do you think the Chinese can be taught a lesson in Vietnam? I mean, are the Chinese the kind of people that will recognize that they are being taught a lesson?

FAIRBANK: Well, if you put it in those terms, it is not very happy is it? They don't want to learn lessons, but they have learned lessons in the past. When the gunboats were superior to what they had, and now the helicopters are superior to what they had, and I think we can probably do that.

Let's try perhaps not to just leave it on this one level: Do you teach them a lesson or don't you, or can you or can't you stop them, because I think we can stop them in the Vietnam situation. The question in my mind is whether, picking up something that was said a moment ago on the excerpt, whether you can reduce their militancy so that they are not so concerned to be subversive.

Now, it is in the nature of things that their militancy ought to die away after a while. A revolution, even if it is made perpetual by the totalitarian methods, is supposed to gradually tire people out and I think this is happening in China.

TAYLOR: But slowly. Slowly. I think you have to distinguish here between the Communist element and the nationalistic element because, although it is conceivable, as the Chinese leaders say themselves, that the revisionism, as they call it -- in other words, what happened in the Soviet Union -- will come to China after they go, there are still these great national problems that remain and that any Chinese government is not going to be happy with until they are settled. Above all, the question of Taiwan, which we hadn't really mentioned, but which is much more crucial to the Chinese than the question of Vietnam, because Taiwan to them, rightly or wrongly, is Chinese soil and any rapproachment, anything you do in this country, as I believe you should and will do toward a rapprochement with China, will founder until this question is solved.

KALB: On this other point, though, getting back to the central issue of simply communicating with them, in your experience in Peking did you find that the Chinese with whom you came in contact were automatons, devoted, unyieldingly devoted to the Communist dogma, unable to talk to you in any other area?

TAYLOR: No, I wouldn't put it that strongly. Certainly not, they are not automatons. They are flesh and blood people. When you deal with your interpreters, with people you meet as you travel around, you can get some human warmth out of them. They will tell you about their families, this sort of thing. Of course, they are people. But they are very restricted and when they are talking to a foreigner they are talking to a foreigner as a representative of the Chinese State and the Chinese people, and they can get into trouble if they diverge from the official line.

FAIRBANK: Marvin, I think we don't have the same idea of this problem of communication. It is essentially a cultural problem. There are different values on the two sides so that things mean something different when the words come through.

You were talking about these cadres that communicate to an investigator. Well, sure they do. They communicate very well about anything human, personal, operational, practical, indentifiable, tangible. But in the background there is something like this, that the cadre that you are talking to will tell you how the thing is set up, and in the process there will be no indication that there is a concept of individual rights such as we have from our schooling and our institutions in the back of his mind, or in the minds of any of his fellows. The concept of individual rights in China is a different thing. It is a very small thing compared to the demands of the collective group, the whole society. How can one individual be as important as the total? Therefore, the individual is out, and the whole concept of individual rights, which goes back to the Western church, Christianity, the sacredness of the individual soul, all of this is very deeply imbedded in our institutional expansion. And so when we are trying to communicate, it is a thing like this, this background value, that is setting out the misunderstanding. We don't resonate on the same wave lengths because of these cultural differences. It is not just practical communication of ideas about practical things; it is the values attached.

KALB: Well, the different values for the individual in society. There is, I think, a fairly widespread idea in the United States -- and maybe it is even true, I don't know -- that if the Chinese soldiers get killed by the tens of thousands, the mothers back there in the villages of China are -- they may shed one tear, but really don't care, because there is a lower value placed on human life. Now, this is generally heard in this country. Is this accurate? Is there any reason to feel that?

FAIRBANK: I think that is baloney. I think there is a different

view of the individual's place in society and in the cosmos. The individual is a smaller thing than with us. You don't glorify individualism as we used to do in our romantic period and Renaissance and all that. They haven't had a Renaissance in the same way. So when you hear about these people that come forward in waves and are shot down, or keep on coming forward, you don't call this just that they don't care. It is rather that they care more for their country or their cause or whatever it is than they do for themselves. They don't have a concept that the individual is so important, and Buddhism, for instance, leads them to merge with the "all." Confucianism leads them to defer to their superiors, to the group; not push individualism, which is selfish. And so a mother will be just as unhappy, I am sure; but there is no sanction for the individual trying to survive in a situation that calls for his sacrifice, so he sacrifices himself. And they will do it, and this is why they are so tough to fight.

KALB: I assume -- I want to check your impressions on this, Charles. Did you get the impression that any of this has changed? Is this all part of China, irrespective of ideology?

TAYLOR: Nobody knows the extent to which Communism is changing the Chinese because they have only been in power for sixteen and a half years. They have only been an effective political force of any sort since the mid-to-late '20's. It is too soon to tell in the history of China how deeply it is affecting them. I wouldn't even like to guess. You do see signs of what one might call the traditional Chinese with all the attitudes that Professor Fairbank has listed remaining, and you see in some aspects that we are capable to judge, such as their treatment of foreigners, they are acting in a very traditional Chinese way; much remains.

KALB: What about the family? You hear reports about efforts to break up the family.

TAYLOR: That is putting it much too strong. What they are trying to do is not so much to break up the family as to maintain that the state is the unit to which the loyalty of the people must be directed rather than the family.

This perhaps to a Westerner sounds very horrific, but it is not all that horrific in a Chinese context, in terms of what they have to do today; the tremendous tasks they have to do. It is not all that horrific in terms of what the Chinese family has been. Perhaps you would not agree, but it has been at times an instrument of repression as well as a very noble exemplar of a certain tradition.

I am not trying to say they don't act against the family in very cruel ways. Sometimes they do. Young people are sent off by the hundreds of thousands each year, young teenagers, to settle permanently in the countryside, hundreds of thousands of miles away from where their family home is, and they are told they will not have a chance to see their family for two or three years, when they may have a short holiday.

Now, this is -- a lot of them go out, I think, with genuine idealism and devotion but it is very hard on the parents and there is some indication that a great minority of the kids go out hating it because they feel, "Why should I leave the city and go and settle in Sinkiang, or somewhere way out in the boondocks?"

KALB: It is an interesting thing that many people who discuss China these days get -- present company excluded -- get their impressions from the experience in the Soviet Union, and very, very often in Russia you will attend propaganda rallies where you will hear all of the expressions come out, two hours' worth: and when it is all over, the Russians kind of shrug their shoulders and walk away from this all and it doesn't seem to get in. I almost have a feeling sometimes that Russian audiences have kind of a protective umbrella which keeps them away from the stuff.

In China does it get through? Certainly that is the impression the Russians leave with us. Russians who come back from China say, "These are not our kind of people at all. They really believe every single thing that they are told."

TAYLOR: I think it got through much more in the early years, inevitably, when the campaigns and the thought reform was something new and rather frightening and in some ways rather exciting to Chinese, especially Chinese intellectuals, but it has gone on and on and the techniques never change from one campaign to another, the techniques of criticism and self-criticism, the techniques of thought reform don't change; but I don't know. You have to get inside a Chinese to really know. Again that's a problem of cultural barriers. But from what I have been told from people who know the Chinese better than I do, and who lived there longer than I did, and from Chinese I have talked to outside of China, freely, I think the Chinese are starting to learn to live with the campaigns and to let more and more of it wash over their heads and to retain their own thoughts.

FAIRBANK: Could I ask Charles a question? There is always the fear that a revolution will turn outward, which I don't think the Chinese revolution has turned yet, and I don't think it is going to, probably; but there is always that fear, that if the problems of holding things together domestically become too great. Now this problem of holding China together is partly a problem of morale, isn't it? Isn't that why everybody has to obey the orthodoxy in words and the words have to always be the same and everybody saying the same thing so that they're united. You don't have the problem of diversity and all the difficulties it would raise. It is the only way that you can control 700 million people in a structure with a bureaucracy and the words coming down from a central point. Now in that situation, morale being so important, and support of the government being essential for its survival -- because a go-slow can wreck any regime in China, isn't that true? Have you seen any signs that the regime in Peking is using foreign affairs in the typical Chauvinist way of stirring things up in the minds of the people in order to maintain support of the regime? Hasn't it been one of their tactics from the beginning? Isn't it built into the Communist system of attacking imperialism as the enemy -- you unite against this enemy, it is everywhere, and so on?

TAYLOR: I think that is true, and it does happen. When you go to a factory in China -- it may be making ball bearings or machine tools or anything -- you will see big banners that say roughly, "Raise our production so that we can help our struggling South Vietnamese brethren fight the United States imperialists." And they will even have big blackboards with charts on them and under the same slogans, and people will be making more ball bearings in order to do this.

So external factors are used to whip up internal morale and to keep a sense of cohesiveness which is very important. But I still think the Chinese do have legitimate external grievances, that it is not entirely artificial.

KALB: I would like to ask Dr. Hsieh a question on that.

DR. HSIEH: I was hoping neither of you were suggesting that the Chinese engage in external adventures in order to whip up internal morale, as many people thought at the time of the 1958 Quemoy crisis, that this was being initiated by the Chinese in order to force the Commune movement. Because this is a theory that I highly question. I don't think you meant that.

TAYLOR: No, I don't think they have been adventuresome. Whatever you would care to mention, Korea, Tibet, the Indian border crisis or the Taiwan Straits crises, they have been basically limited actions and they have only moved when they felt their security and territorial integrity was threatened.

FULBRIGHT: These are the instances cited by the Administration to justify the allegations of aggressiveness, these very instances you have mentioned. You differ then with our Secretary of State?

TAYLOR: Yes, sir, I do.

* * * * * * * *

DR. HSIEH: Persistent in American thinking is this image of Chinese recklessness. I mean, it was exaggerated particularly in the course of the Sino-Soviet dispute when the Soviet Union developed this contrast between a China dedicated to war and the Soviet Union more or less dedicated to peace and peaceful coexistence, and China's military policies have been characterized by considerable, an extreme amount of caution, reflecting a strategy and a doctrine that is based on a very realistic estimate of the military situation, and an extremely careful calculation of risks.

KALB: It seems to me that this is all very much a reflection -- the pros and cons, the disputes over facts -- of the frustration that kind of covers the entire country. There are even some people here who advocate preventive war against the Chinese right now, that

you knock out their nuclear installations before they make too much trouble.

* * * * * * * *

This whole question, of course, about China and the bomb is the one that I suspect terrifies an awful lot of people and probably because we don't know very much about the area.

Dr. Hsieh, you have worked on this at great length. Is the Defense Secretary's estimate that China can make a delivery system capable of inflicting great damage upon the United States within one decade, within a ten year span?

DR. HSIEH: I am not in a position to disagree with an estimate of this nature. I don't think there is any doubt but that the Chinese intend to develop both thermonuclear weapons and missile delivery systems, both of a -- probably of a medium-range ballistic missile delivery system in preference to an ICBM, though I do think that there is a likelihood that they would at least attempt to test an ICBM somewhere along the line, for reasons of political propaganda purposes.

But I think, when we talk about these estimates, we also have to ask ourselves the very next, and I think the more important question: How are the Chinese likely to use a nuclear delivery system of any order? My own studies have indicated that when they possess a nuclear delivery system, they are going to be no more reckless then than they are today; that is, provided that the United States maintains its military presence in the Pacific area and by its determination indicates, makes very clear to the Chinese, that the risks of any aggressive use of their nuclear missile capability would involve extremely high risks.

KALB: Dr. Hsieh, I think you have just hit on a second major theme that has come up this afternoon. One is that China basically is not in an expansionist time right now. It is not interested in expansion, but much more in the development of its internal affairs. And the second that even if they did have all of these weapons, their policy would more than likely be very prudent.

Isn't it possible, isn't it just possible -- and since we are only raising questions here, we might take this up -- that China could, for reasons that we can not determine now, go from an essentially defensive nature to an essentially offensive nature, using these weapons? Don't these things happen in history?

FAIRBANK: Well, you could say this is possible, and I think it behooves us to try to get ahead of any such situation. I wouldn't put it about as possible -- as probable -- all possibilities of disaster stare us in the face -- but probabilities, it seems to me, are still for the Chinese to be concerned with their domestic situation, which is on their necks day by day and if their population problem keeps on exploding as it seems to be, that situation domestically is not easily going to be solved. Their capacity to go overseas in adventures is not going to probably increase any faster than the capacity of other powers like Japan, ourselves, or India or other countries, to counter this kind of thing.

So it seems to me that instead of looking at Armageddon in the face, we should look at how to ameliorate our relations with China, how to mitigate some of the terrible altercations that lie ahead of us. How to get set for a contact with China in diplomatic channels as well as talking about the military side, because this is obviously going to come in some form sometime and we might as well prepare ourselves.

Now it is not going to be any field day, and happy denouement. Some people say, "Well, let's recognize them and get it over with." Recognition they might not accept for a long time. Then others say, "Ask them into the UN and settle it that way." That is no settlement, that is just the beginning of trouble. And yet you've got to have a development on a non-military side, as well as this military holding operation -- I believe it is a holding operation -- to stalemate the situation in South Vietnam.

KALB: Senator Fulbright, do you feel that your colleagues are ready now to think in realistic terms about even an offer to the Chinese that they come to the UN, the possibility of recognition, the possibility of trade, et cetera? Are we capable of that right now?

FULBRIGHT: When you say "right now," after all, these hearings have been going on only a week, you know, and this is a little sudden. It takes longer than that to get accustomed to this idea. I said a moment ago I was very pleased that the reaction to just these two hearings was so mild. No one has objected, to my knowledge yet, and so I don't know how this will develop. I think it is quite possible that by this fall, if these hearings continue and get the kind of exposure that you are giving them here today, and others have given them, that our objections to their admission might be softened or even withdrawn. That may be the first step and a very modest one. I think if we just say, "Well, we stand aside," or we don't try to use any influence to prevent it, that this offer may be made.

Now, as I understand Dr. Fairbank's statement, he is very dubious about their accepting. That is all right. Nevertheless, the offer has been made, and the suggestions you made the other day in the hearings about the small steps that might be taken to open up some means of communication to people going there -- exchanges, perhaps, of literature, anything, trade, perhaps, might be possible. We are the only ones.

I may say it was with great unhappiness in many parts of their country that Canada got all the wheat business both in China and in Russia and that we didn't get any.

We had a big fight about this on Russia. I think it may be too soon to talk about China because these other steps must be made.

In fact, the purpose of these hearings is to open this subject up and I have every confidence, if there is not some terrible tragedy or expansion in Southeast Asia, that they will have their effect, and I think the Senate may come along and the country will.

KALB: Senator, the thing that interests me about this is that the Senate has, had some trouble getting this consular convention with the Russians through, and this is something that has been sitting around for almost two years. And this, theoretically -- the Russians have almost moved around in the American mind to the position of being a virtual ally against China.

FULBRIGHT: That's a very unfortunate thing. My committee dealt with this last year -- about a year ago -- and voted it out with I think only two dissenting votes. It was on the floor ready for action, but Mr. J. Edgar Hoover made a statement in an appropriation hearing that was very damaging, and this is an election year, and after surveying the situation there were a number of Senators who really didn't feel strongly against it, but just would rather not have to defend it in an election year, and so they talked the leadership out of bringing it up: so it hasn't been brought up. It takes two-thirds, you see.

Now, that is difficult always to get in the Senate, so my prediction is they are not going to bring it up.

This war, of course, the Vietnamese war, has poisoned the whole atmosphere of doing anything rational in this area with the Russians or anything else. I think it is one of the greatest prices we are paying for the Vietnamese war is the destruction of the movement -- the stopping of the movement toward relaxation in Eastern Europe and Russia. This is one of the penalties, the temporary, at least, abandonment of that agreement.

FAIRBANK: Has there ever been a case where in the midst of a war a nation has been able to pursue a more rational policy rather than a less rational one?

FULBRIGHT: That is very rare.

KALB: Well, this is what we are asking of the Administration right now, isn't it, Professor?

FAIRBANK: It is. It is what we have to do unless we want more fighting.

FULBRIGHT: I don't wish to mislead you. The Administration itself is today prepared to say they would withdraw their objection to the admission of China. Don't think they would. I am assuming that these discussions, if they continue -- and people seem to be much more interested in them than some had expected -- that this will make a difference.

TAYLOR: I think it should be -- people in this country should be aware that when these gestures are made, as I am sure they will be made, with generosity and reason, they will almost certainly be rejected, and probably in very insulting -- to you -- insulting terminology: very rude terminology. Again it is partly a question of language. The Chinese do express them-

selves in a very heightened form, but this -- because you are as impulsive as you are generous, I am just afraid that when you do make these first tentative gestures and get a scornful rejection from Peking, you will tend to pull back. You mustn't because it will take time and you have got to start from these small things and work up to the bigger ones.

KALB: As I listen to you talk now, I have the feeling we are dealing not with a nation but with an area inhabited by 700 million neurotics. There is that kind of an impression one can get easily.

FAIRBANK: They are just Chinese; they are not neurotic.

FULBRIGHT: They are having a nervous breakdown. We can all enjoy one of these occasionally. We had one a hundred years ago, a very bad one. We all have them from time to time.

FAIRBANK: It seems to me, Marv, we have to caution ourselves in looking at China against one of our great vices, which is to give. We are the most generous nation ever made, and our expansion -- much of this expansion that they call imperialism is actually giving things away, and we go to the defense of South Vietnam in a generous mood. A gesture, and our boys get killed to help those people. Now, this is very difficult for the Chinese to take. I mean they don't want to be on the receiving end of gifts. It is demeaning to them if we say, "Now, we give you this and now we have an AID program for you too." This is something they will absolutely reject, as Charles is saying, because of their pride, and they have a very different attitude toward all of this than we do and we really have to study their background and -- this is a plug for Chinese history; they have got to be understood better if we are going to deal with them without intense altercation -- and the kind of feeling that we had when China went Communist, that they had rejected us. After all, our good deeds, a century of good works, and they threw us out; kicked us in the teeth. Now, they will do this again, kick us many times and that is just what we have to deal with, and it is in ourselves and in them that the altercation arises between the two. We have to understand ourselves better.

TAYLOR: And we have to understand how profoundly humiliated they feel when they think of their history in the last century and how much they resent all the Western powers for what was done to them at that time.

FULBRIGHT: Well, it was pretty bad.

TAYLOR: It was.

FAIRBANK: May I say something? I don't think it was so bad. I think it is much worse in retrospect than it was in fact. It came about in fact because the Chinese cooperated with it, and this is one of the great facts of Chinese history we have got to understand. They cooperated with the invaders. The Japanese turned and they learned from us and drove us out. That is, they got rid of the unequal treaties, and they became a military power later, but the Chinese were not nationalistic at that time. They cooperated with the British. Whenever the British attacked somebody in the Opium War, they had a Chinese coolie corps at $1 a head any time. In other words, this was a different type of society.

FULBRIGHT: How do you mean, in the Opium War -- except for the corrupt local officials who you can always bribe and everybody does -- do you think the government cooperated in the Opium War?

FAIRBANK: No. The government was sufficiently riddled with corruption so that the Chinese Opium trade was on both sides. The local people could be bought by the British any time because the local people were not citizens of the nation in the modern sense. They were just coolies.

FULBRIGHT: But the national government, if I read it right at all, didn't cooperate at all and when they sent Commissioner Lin, he didn't cooperate with them.

FAIRBANK: No. I don't mean at that point that you had cooperation, but after 1860 you had cooperation.

FULBRIGHT: No, I am talking of the Opium War in 1839.

FAIRBANK: I was speaking of the Chinese populace. The populace, the ordinary people. They did not act like modern patriots. It is a pre-modern situation.

DR. HSIEH: I would like to go back to the point made earlier about the varying gestures we could make to the Chinese. I too would like to warn against expecting too much too soon in response from them. We have already had the experience of their turning down of Dr. Rosen, the ear specialist. We have seen what happened last year, last fall, that the closer they come to gaining membership in the United Nations, the higher they raise the ante for their acceptance of membership, now insisting on not only the expulsion of the Republic of China, Taiwan, but also the annulment of the resolution condemning China during the Korean War for aggression, and demanding a complete reorganization of the United Nations.

And there is also some evidence that I would like to refer to that is present in the (word indistinct) documentation. This is the publication of the Political Department of the People's Liberation Army, in which it is suggested that they see a resolution of the confrontation with the United States as an entire package which includes recognition of China, including the restoration of Taiwan to China, and membership in the United Nations, all of this comprising one-package, and this is more or less their terms.

TAYLOR: And I think they will, whether or not it is a package, they will reject all sort of piecemeal approaches until they see some sort of a breakthrough on Taiwan.

KALB: Does that mean in your opinion, Charles, that until such time as the United States and the Government of Nationalist China are prepared to make some fundamental sacrifice in terms of their position on Formosa, that no meaningful kind of negotiation or communication with the Communists can take place?

TAYLOR: They say so more or less and I believe that this is their point of view.

FAIRBANK: Could I suggest on that -- it seems to me we have the real religion of self-determination and we can't ask that Taiwan be given over, because I don't think Taiwan is ever going to vote to go over or want to go over to the mainland in the next foreseeable future.

Now here you have a real conflict of cultural values. Isn't perhaps the best thing to do, just try to bypass this question as much as we can, in this sense: Leave the fleet in the Strait and don't demand that Taiwan declare itself just a government of Taiwan, which is humiliating to it. They probably wouldn't comply. Don't demand that Peking acknowledge the independence of Formosa or Taiwan. Just leave the question to the side and try to get something going elsewhere? This is a Chinese question and between the two of them they have a similar view that Taiwan is part of the mainland. Both governments feel that, and they both accuse us, if we talk about independent Taiwan, of being either a spy or a traitor.

FULBRIGHT: Do you agree they will not take any small step? I mean, for example, to give a visa to anyone at all from this country? Do you agree with Mr. Taylor that they won't do any of these . . .

FAIRBANK: I don't know how long they will hold out on the question of Taiwan. It seems to me we should make all sorts

of considered overtures and use various methods to get them into contact, of the sort you have mentioned.

FULBRIGHT: It seems to me we should make the effort even if they do reject it.

FAIRBANK: Exactly.

FULBRIGHT: I don't understand why -- is it just because of the wheat that they are so friendly to you, or at least they apparently are?

TAYLOR: We have no record of -- we are a small country, Senator. We have no record of what they call imperialist aggression, not because we are any different from you as people, but because we are a small country.

FULBRIGHT: Well, you are a big country with few people, that is all. You have no need of any greater country. I don't think you are any less aggressive, probably. Certainly not in the trade field. Mr. Hamilton came down. You can tell me all about that. Apparently he treated you all very well.

TAYLOR: Well, they are very realistic too. We sell them a lot of wheat each year and they don't demand political recognition because we do not recognize them

FULBRIGHT: You don't recognize them?

TAYLOR: No.

FULBRIGHT: I certainly think we ought to make these gestures, even if they are turned down.

FAIRBANK: Yes. I am all for these gestures. I am just saying that in the case of Taiwan, the one Taiwan issue . . .

FULBRIGHT: Oh, you would leave it out, yes.

FAIRBANK: Our idea, of course, is that Taiwan deserves to be independent. The government of Taiwan refuses that. So does the mainland. Leave it to them.

KALB: I will have to interrupt. Our time is just about out.

I think we would probably all agree that for the most of the past 16 years in this country Communist China has been a taboo topic. People rarely talked about China and when they did it was always in fairly stale cliches. They apparently remember the days of Senator McCarthy.

Now, because suddenly war between China and the United States is possible, growing out of the Vietnam conflict, people have begun to talk about China with some sense of reality. Even within the Administration a new spirit of change is apparent, just below the highest levels of authority, and a possibly historic change in American policy could even evolve out of the present discussion. Not a dramatic change, but a quiet one, perhaps slipping in on the nation on cat's paws. Perhaps one might even be bold enough in this spirit of change to question an old saying of Napoleon that "China is a sleeping giant." He said, "Let her sleep, for if she wakes the world will tremble."

The fact is, China has awakened, but the world, armed with knowledge about China, need not tremble.

The Article by Lin Piao on People's Wars

The following is the partial text of "Long Live the Victory of the People's War," an article by Lin Piao, vice chairman of the Chinese Communist Party's Central Committee, vice premier and minister of national defense. The article, released on Sept. 3, 1965, was written in commemoration of the 20th anniversary of victory "in the Chinese people's war of resistance against Japan."

In the first part of the article, Lin reviewed Mao's strategy for a people's war, asserting that China's victory in the war against Japan was "a victory for people's war, for Marxism-Leninism and the thought of Mao Tse-tung."

The Chinese revolution is a continuation of the Great October Revolution (in Russia). The road of the October Revolution is the

common road for all people's revolutions. The Chinese revolution and the October Revolution have in common the following basic characteristics: 1) both were led by the working class with a Marxist-Leninist party as its nucleus; 2) both were based on the worker-peasant alliance; 3) in both cases state power was seized through violent revolution and the dictatorship of the proletariat was established; 4) in both cases the socialist system was built after victory in the revolution; and 5) both were component parts of the proletarian world revolution.

Naturally, the Chinese revolution had its own peculiar characteristics. The October Revolution took place in imperialist Russia, but the Chinese revolution broke out in a semicolonial and semi-feudal country. The former was a proletarian socialist revolution, while the latter developed into a socialist revolution after the complete victory of the new democratic revolution. The October Revolution began with armed uprisings in the cities and then spread to the countryside, while the Chinese revolution won nationwide victory through the encirclement of the cities from the rural areas and the final capture of the cities.

Mao's Contribution

Comrade Mao Tse-tung's great merit lies in the fact that he has succeeded in integrating the universal truth of Marxism-Leninism with the concrete practice of the Chinese revolution and has enriched and developed Marxism-Leninism by his masterly generalization and summation of the experience gained during the Chinese people's protracted revolutionary struggle.

Comrade Mao Tse-tung's theory of people's war has been proved by the long practice of the Chinese revolution to be in accord with the objective laws of such wars and to be invincible. It has not only been valid for China, it is a great contribution to the revolutionary struggles of the oppressed nations and peoples throughout the world.

The people's war led by the CCP, comprising the war of resistance and the revolutionary civil wars, lasted 22 years. It constitutes the most drawn-out and most complex people's war led by the proletariat in modern history, and it has been the richest in experience.

In the last analysis, the Marxist-Leninist theory of proletarian revolution is the theory of the seizure of state power by revolutionary violence, the theory of countering war against the people by people's war. As Marx so aptly put it, "force is the midwife of every old society pregnant with a new one."

It was on the basis of the lessons derived from the people's wars in China that Comrade Mao Tse-tung, using the simplest and the most vivid language, advanced the famous thesis that "political power grows out of the barrel of a gun."

He clearly pointed out: The seizure of power by armed force, the settlement of the issue by war is the central task and the highest form of revolution. This Marxist-Leninist principle of revolution holds good universally, for China and for all other countries.

Imperialist Wars

War is the product of imperialism and the system of exploitation of man by man. Lenin said that "war is always and everywhere begun by the exploiters themselves, by the ruling and oppressing classes." So long as imperialism and the system of exploitation of man by man exist, the imperialists and reactionaries will invariably rely on armed force to maintain their reactionary rule and impose war on the oppressed nations and peoples. This is an objective law independent of man's will.

In the world today, all the imperialists headed by the United States and their lackeys, without exception; are strengthening their state machinery, and especially their armed forces. U.S. imperialism, in particular, is carrying out armed aggression and suppression everywhere.

What should the oppressed nations and the oppressed people do in the face of wars of aggression and armed suppression by the imperialists and their lackeys? Should they submit and remain slaves in perpetuity? Or should they rise in resistance and fight for their liberation?

Comrade Mao Tse-tung answered this question in vivid terms. He said that after long investigation and study the Chinese people discovered that all the imperialists and their lackeys "have swords in their hands and are out to kill. The people have come to understand this and so act after the same fashion." This is called doing unto them what they do unto us.

In the last analysis, whether one dares to wage a tit-for-tat struggle against armed aggression and suppression by the imperialists and their lackeys, whether one dares to embark on revolution. This is the most effective touchstone for distinguishing genuine from fake revolutionaries and Marxist-Leninists.

Paper Tiger

In view of the fact that some people were afflicted with the fear of the imperialists and reactionaries, Comrade Mao Tse-tung put forward his famous thesis that "the imperialists and all reactionaries are paper tigers."

He said: All reactionaries are paper tigers. In appearance the reactionaries are terrifying, but in reality they are not so powerful. From a long-term point of view, it is not the reactionaries but the people who are really powerful.

The history of people's war in China and other countries provides conclusive evidence that the growth of the people's revolutionary forces from weak and small beginning into strong and large forces is a universal law of development of class struggle, a universal law of development of people's war. A people's war inevitably meets with many difficulties, with ups and downs and setbacks in the course of its development, but no force can alter its general trend towards inevitable triumph.

Comrade Mao Tse-tung points out that we must despise the enemy strategically and take full account of him tactically. To despise the enemy strategically is an elementary requirement for a revolutionary. Without the courage to despise the enemy and without daring to win, it will be simply impossible to make revolution and wage a people's war, let alone to achieve victory.

It is also very important for revolutionaries to take full account of the enemy tactically. It is likewise impossible to win victory in a people's war without taking full account of the enemy tactically, and without examining the concrete conditions, without being prudent and giving great attention to the study of the art of struggle, and without adopting appropriate forms of struggle in the concrete practice of the revolution in each country and with regard to each concrete problem of struggle.

Dialectical and historical materialism teaches us that what is important primarily is not that which at the given moment seems to be durable and yet is already beginning to die away, but that which is arising and developing, even though at the given moment it may not appear to be durable, for only that which is arising and developing is invincible.

Why can the apparently weak newborn forces always triumph over the decadent forces which appear so powerful? The reason is that truth is on their side and that the masses are on their side, while the reactionary classes are always divorced from the masses and set themselves against the masses.

This has been borne out by the victory of the Chinese revolution, by the history of all revolutions, the whole history of class struggle, and the entire history of mankind.

The imperialists are extremely afraid of Comrade Mao Tse-tung's thesis that "imperialism and all reactionaries are paper tigers," and the revisionists are extremely hostile to it. They all oppose and attack this thesis and the Philistines follow suit by ridiculing it. But all this cannot in the least diminish its importance. The light of truth cannot be dimmed by anybody.

Comrade Mao Tse-tung's theory of people's war solves not only the problem of daring to fight a people's war, but also that of how to wage it.

Mao's Virtues

Comrade Mao Tse-tung is a great statesman and military scientist, proficient at directing war in accordance with its laws. By the line and policies, the strategy and tactics he formulated for the people's war, he led the Chinese people in steering the ship of the people's war past all hidden reefs to the shores of victory in most complicated and difficult conditions.

It must be emphasized that Comrade Mao Tse-tung's theory of the establishment of rural revolutionary base areas and the encirclement of the cities from the countryside is of outstanding and universal practical importance for the present revolutionary struggles of all the oppressed nations and peoples, and particularly for the revolutionary struggles of the oppressed nations and peoples in Asia, Africa, and Latin America against imperialism and its lackeys.

Many countries and peoples in Asia, Africa, and Latin America are now being subjected to aggression and enslavement on a serious scale by the imperialists headed by the United States and their lackeys. The basic political and economic conditions in many of these countries have many similarities to those that prevailed in old China. As in China, the peasant question is extremely important in these regions. The peasants constitute the main force of the national-democratic revolution against the imperialists and their lackeys. In committing aggression against these countries, the imperialists usually begin by seizing the big cities and the main lines of communication, but they are unable to bring the vast countryside completely under their control. The countryside, and the countryside alone, can provide the broad areas in which the revolutionaries can maneuver freely. The countryside, and the countryside alone, can provide the revolutionary bases from which the revolutionaries can go forward to final victory. Precisely for this reason, Comrade Mao Tse-tung's theory of establishing revolutionary base areas in the rural districts and encircling the cities from the countryside is attracting more and more attention among the people in these regions.

Cities and Countryside

Taking the entire globe, if North American and Western Europe can be called "the cities of the world," then Asia, Africa, and Latin America constitute "the rural areas of the world." Since World War II, the proletarian revolutionary movement has for various reasons been temporarily held back in the North American and West European capitalist countries, while the people's revolutionary movement in Asia, Africa, and Latin America has been growing vigorously. In a sense, the contemporary world revolution also presents a picture of the encirclement of cities by the rural areas. In the final analysis, the whole cause of world revolution hinges on the revolutionary struggles of the Asian, African, and Latin American peoples who make up the overwhelming majority of the world's population. The socialist countries, should regard it as their internationalist duty to support the people's revolutionary struggles in Asia, Africa, and Latin America.

The October Revolution opened up a new era in the revolution of the oppressed nations. The victory of the October Revolution built a bridge between the socialist revolution of the proletariat of the west and the national-democratic revolution of the colonial and semicolonial countries of the east. The Chinese revolution has successfully solved the problem of how to link up the national-democratic with the socialist revolution in the colonial and semicolonial countries.

Comrade Mao Tse-tung has pointed out that, in the epoch since the October Revolution, anti-imperialist revolution in any colonial or semicolonial country is no longer part of the old bourgeois, or capitalist world revolution, but is part of the new world revolution, the proletarian-socialist world revolution.

Revolution

Comrade Mao Tse-tung has formulated a complete theory of the new democratic revolution. He indicated that this revolution which is different from all others, can only be, nay must be, a revolution against imperialism, fuedalism, and bureaucrat-capitalism waged by the broad masses of the people under the leadership of the proletariat.

This means that the revolution can only be, nay must be, led by the proletariat and the genuinely revolutionary party armed with Marxism-Leninism, and by no other class or party.

This means that the revolution embraces in its ranks not only the workers, peasants and the urban petty bourgeoisie, but also the national bourgeoisie and other patriotic and anti-imperialist democrats.

This means, finally, that the revolution is directed against imperialism, feudalism, and bureaucrat-capitalism.

The new democratic revolution leads to socialism, and not to capitalism.

Comrade Mao Tse-tung's theory of the new democratic revolution is the Marxist-Leninist theory of uninterrupted revolution.

Two Stages

Comrade Mao Tse-tung made a correct distinction between the two revolutionary stages, that is, the national-democratic and the socialist revolutions; at the same time he correctly and closely linked the two. The national-democratic revolution is the necessary pre-

paration for the socialist revolution, and the socialist revolution is the inevitable sequel to the national-democratic revolution. There is no great wall between the two revolutionary stages. But the socialist revolution is only possible after the completion of the national-democratic revolution. The more thorough the national-democratic revolution, the better the conditions for the socialist revolution.

The experience of the Chinese revolution shows that the tasks of the national-democratic revolution can be fulfilled only through long and tortuous struggles. In this stage of revolution, imperialism and its lackeys are the principal enemy. In the struggle against imperialism and its lackeys, it is necessary to rally all anti-imperialist patriotic forces, including the national bourgeoisie and all patriotic persons. All those patriotic persons from among the bourgeoisie and other exploiting classes who join the anti-imperialist struggle play a progressive historical role; they are not tolerated by imperialism but welcomed by the proletariat.

It is very harmful to confuse the two stages, that is, the national-democratic and the socialist revolutions. Comrade Mao Tse-tung criticized the wrong idea of "accomplishing both at one stroke," and pointed out that this utopian idea could only weaken the struggle against imperialism and its lackeys, the most urgent task at the time. The Kuomintang reactionaries and the Trotskyites they hired during the war of resistance deliberately confused these two stages of the Chinese revolution, proclaiming the "theory of a single revolution" and preaching so-called "socialism" without any Communist Party. With this preposterous theory they attempted to swallow up the Communist Party, wipe out any revolution and prevent the advance of the national-democratic revolution, and they used it as a pretext for their nonresistance and capitulation to imperialism. This reactionary theory was buried long ago by the history of the Chinese revolution.

The Revisionist Line

The Khrushchev revisionists are now actively preaching that socialism can be built without the proletariat and without a genuinely revolutionary party armed with the advanced proletarian ideology, and they have cast the fundamental tenets of Marxism-Leninism to the four winds. The revisionists' purpose is solely to divert the oppressed nations from their struggle against imperialism and sabotage their national-democratic solution, all in the service of imperialism.

The Chinese revolution provides a successful lesson for making a thoroughgoing national-democratic revolution under the leadership of the proletariat; it likewise provides a successful lesson for the timely transition from the national-democratic revolution to the socialist revolution under the leadership of the proletariat.

Mao Tse-tung's thought has been the guide to the victory of the Chinese revolution. It has integrated the universal truth of Marxism-Leninism with the concrete practice of the Chinese revolution and creatively developed Marxism-Leninism, thus adding new weapons to the arsenal of Marxism-Leninism.

Ours is the epoch in which world capitalism and imperialism are heading for their doom and socialism and communism are marching to victory. Comrade Mao Tse-tung's theory of people's war is not only a product of the Chinese revolution, but has characteristics of our epoch. The new experience gained in the people's revolutionary struggles in various countries since World War II has provided continuous evidence that Mao Tse-tung's thought is a common asset of the revolutionary people of the whole world. This is the great international significance of the thought of Mao Tse-tung.

U.S. Imperialism

Since World War II, U.S. imperialism has stepped into the shoes of German, Japanese, and Italian fascism and has been trying to build a great American empire by dominating and enslaving the whole world. It is actively fostering Japanese and West German militarism as its chief accomplices in unleashing a world war. Like a vicious wolf, it is bullying and enslaving various peoples, plundering their wealth, encroaching upon their countries' sovereignty, and interfering in their internal affairs. It is the most rabid aggressor in human history and the most ferocious common enemy of the people of the world. Every people or country in the world that wants revolution, independence, and peace cannot but launch the spearhead of its struggle against U.S. imperialism.

Just as the Japanese imperialists' policy of subjugating China made it possible for the Chinese people to form the broadest possible united front against them, so the U.S. imperialists' policy of seeking world domination makes it possible for the people throughout the world to unite all the forces that can be united and form the broadest possible united front for a converging attack on U.S. imperialism.

At present, the main battlefield of the fierce struggle between the people of the world on the one side and U.S. imperialism and its lackeys on the other is the vast area of Asia, Africa, and Latin America. In the world as a whole, this is the area where the people suffer most from imperialist oppression and where imperialist rule is most vulnerable. Since World War II, revolutionary storms have been rising in this area, and today they have become the most important force directly pounding U.S. imperialism. The contradiction between the revolutionary peoples of Asia, Africa and Latin America and the imperialists headed by the United States is the principal contradiction in the contemporary world. The development of this contradiction is promoting the struggle of the people of the whole world against U.S. imperialism and its lackeys.

Since World War II, people's war has increasingly demonstrated its power in Asia, Africa, and Latin America. The peoples of China, Korea, Vietnam, Laos, Cuba, Indonesia, Algeria, and other countries have waged people's wars against the imperialists and their lackeys and won great victories. The classes leading these people's wars may vary, and so may the breadth and depth of mass mobilization and the extent of victory, but the victories in these people's wars have very much weakened and pinned down the forces of imperialism, upset the U.S. imperialist plan to launch a world war, and become mighty factors defending world peace.

Favorable Conditions

Today, the conditions are more favorable than ever before for the waging of people's wars by the revolutionary peoples of Asia, Africa, and Latin America against U.S. imperialism and its lackeys.

Since World War II and the succeeding years of revolutionary upsurge, there has been a great rise in the level of political consciousness and the degree of organization of the people in all countries, and the resources available to them for mutual support and aid have greatly increased. The whole capitalist-imperialist system has become drastically weaker and is in the process of increasing convulsion and disintegration. After World War I, the imperialists lacked the power to destroy the newborn socialist Soviet state, but they were still able to suppress the people's revolutionary movements in some countries in the parts of the world under their own and so maintain a short period of comparative stability. Since World War II, however, not only have they been unable to stop a number or countries from taking the socialist road, but they are no longer capable of holding back the surging tide of the people's revolutionary movements in the areas under their own rule.

U.S. imperialism is stronger, but also more vulnerable, than any imperialism of the past. It sets itself against the people of the world, including the people of the United States. Its human, military, material, and financial resources are far from sufficient for the realization of its ambition of dominating the whole world. U.S. imperialism has further weakened itself by occupying so many places in the world, overreaching itself, stretching its fingers out wide and dispersing its strength, with its rear so far away and its supply lines so long. As Comrade Mao Tse-tung has said, "Wherever it commits aggression, it puts a new noose around its neck. It is besieged ring upon ring by the people of the whole world.

When committing aggression in a foreign country, U.S. imperialism can only employ part of its forces, which are sent to fight an unjust war far from their native land and therefore have a low morale, and so U.S. imperialism is beset with great difficulties. The people subjected to its aggression are having a trial of strength with U.S. imperialism neither in Washington nor New York, neither in Honolulu nor Florida, but are fighting for independence and freedom on their own soil. Once they are mobilized on a broad scale, they will

have inexhaustible strength. Thus their superiority will belong not to the United States but to the people subjected to its aggression. The latter, though apparently weak and small, are really more powerful than U.S. imperialism.

The struggles waged by the different peoples against U.S. imperialism reinforce each other and merge into a torrential world wide tide of opposition to U.S. imperialism. The more successful the development of people's war in a given region, the larger the number of U.S. imperialist forces that can be pinned down and depleted there. When the U.S. aggressors are hard-pressed in one place, they have no alternative but to loosen their grip on others. Therefore, the conditions become more favorable for the people elsewhere to wage struggles against U.S. imperialism and its lackeys.

Everything is divisible, and so is the colossus of U.S. imperialism. It can be split up and defeated. The peoples of Asia, Africa, Latin America, and other regions can destroy it piece by piece, some striking at its head and others at its feet. That is why the greatest fear of U.S. imperialism is that people's wars will be launched in different parts of the world, and particularly in Asia, Africa, and Latin America, and why it regards people's war as a mortal danger.

Nuclear Weapons

U.S. imperialism relies solely on its nuclear weapons to intimidate people. But these weapons cannot save U.S. imperialism from its doom. Nuclear weapons cannot be used lightly.

U.S. imperialism has been condemned by the people of the whole world for its towering crime of dropping two atom bombs on Japan. If it uses nuclear weapons again, it will become isolated in the extreme. Moreover, the U.S. monopoly of nuclear weapons has long been broken; U.S. imperialism has these weapons, but others have them too. If it threatens other countries with nuclear weapons, U.S. imperialism will expose its own country to the same threat. For this reason, it will meet with strong opposition not only from the people elsewhere but also inevitably from the people in its own country. Even if U.S. imperialism brazenly uses nuclear weapons, it cannot conquer the people, who are indomitable.

However fully developed modern weapons and technical equipment may be and however complicated the methods of modern warfare, in the final analysis the outcome of a war will be decided by the sustained fighting of the ground forces, by the fighting at close quarters on battlefields, by the political consciousness of men, by their courage and spirit of sacrifice. Here the weak points of U.S. imperialism will be completely laid bare, while the superiority of the revolutionary people will be brought into full play. The reactionary troops of U.S. imperialism cannot possibly be endowed with the courage and the spirit of sacrifice possessed by the revolutionary people. The spiritual atom bomb which the revolutionary people possess is a far more powerful and useful weapon than the physical atom bomb.

Vietnam

Vietnam is the most convincing current example of a victim of aggression defeating U.S. imperialism by a people's war. The United States has made South Vietnam a testing ground for the suppression of people's war. It has carried on this experiment for many years, and everybody can now see that the U.S. aggressors are unable to find a way of coping with people's war. On the other hand, the Vietnamese people have brought the power of people's war into full play in their struggle against the U.S. aggressors. The U.S. aggressors are in danger of being swamped in the people's war in Vietnam. They are deeply worried that their defeat in Vietnam will lead to a chain reaction. They are expanding the war in an attempt to save themselves from defeat. But the more they expand the war, the greater will be the chain reaction. The more they escalate the war, the heavier will be their fall and the more disastrous their defeat. The people in other parts of the world will see still more clearly that U.S. imperialism can be defeated, and that what the Vietnamese people can do, they can do too.

History has proved and will go on proving that people's war is the most effective weapon against U.S. imperialism and its lackeys. All revolutionary people will learn to wage people's war against U.S. imperialism and its lackeys. They will take up arms, learn to fight battles and become skilled in waging people's war, though they have not done so before. U.S. imperialism, like a mad bull dashing from place to place, will finally be burned to ashes in the blazing fires of the people's wars it has provoked by its own actions.

World Changes

Great changes have taken place in China and the world in the 20 years since the victory of the war of resistance against Japan, changes that have made the situation more favorable than ever for the revolutionary people of the world and more unfavorable than ever for imperialism and its lackeys.

When Japanese imperialism launched its war of aggression against China, the Chinese people had only a very small people's army and a very small revolutionary base area, and they were up against the biggest military despot of the east. Yet even then, Comrade Mao Tse-tung said that the Chinese people's war could be won and that Japanese imperialism could be defeated. Today, the revolutionary base areas of the peoples of the world have grown to unprecedented proportions, their revolutionary movement is surging as never before, imperialism is weaker than ever, and U.S. imperialism, the chieftain of world imperialism, is suffering one defeat after another. We can say with even greater confidence that the people's wars can be won and U.S. imperialism can be defeated in all countries.

The peoples of the world now have the lessons of the October Revolution, the anti-fascist war, the Chinese people's war of resistance and war of liberation, the Korean people's war of resistance to U.S. aggression, the Vietnamese people's war of liberation and their war of resistance to U.S. aggression, and the people's revolutionary armed struggles in many other countries. Provided each people studies these lessons well and creatively integrates them with the concrete practice of revolution in their own country, there is no doubt that the revolutionary peoples of the world will stage still more powerful and splendid dramas in the theater of people's war in their countries and that they will wipe off the earth once and for all the common enemy of all the peoples, U.S. imperialism, and its lackeys.

The struggle of the Vietnamese people against U.S. aggression and for national salvation is now the focus of the struggle of the people of the world against U.S. aggression. The determination of the Chinese people to support and aid the Vietnamese people in their struggle against U.S. aggression and for national salvation is unshakable. No matter what U.S. imperialism may do to expand its war adventure, the Chinese people will do everything in their power to support the Vietnamese people until every single one of the U.S. aggressors is driven out of Vietnam.

The U.S. imperialists are now clamoring for another trial of strength with the Chinese people, for another larger-scale ground war on the Asian mainland. If they insist on following in the footsteps of the Japanese fascists, well then, they may do so, if they please. The Chinese people definitely have ways of their own for coping with a U.S. imperialist war of aggression. Our methods are no secret. The most important one is still mobilization of the people, reliance on the people, making everyone a soldier and waging a people's war.

We want to tell the U.S. imperialists once again that the vast ocean of several hundred million Chinese people in arms will be more than enough to submerge your few million aggressor troops. If you dare to impose war on us, we shall gain freedom of action. It will then not be up to you to decide how the war will be fought. We shall fight in the ways most advantageous to us to destroy the enemy and wherever the enemy can be most easily destroyed. Since the Chinese people were able to destroy the Japanese aggressors 20 years ago, they are certainly still more capable of finishing off the U.S. aggressors today. The naval and air superiority you boast about cannot intimidate the Chinese people, and neither can the atom bomb you brandish at us. If you want to send troops, go ahead, the more the better. We will annihilate as many as you can send, and can even give you receipts. The Chinese people are a great valiant people. We have the courage to shoulder the heavy burden of combating U.S. imperialism and to contribute our share in the struggle for final victory over this most ferocious enemy of the people of the world.

Taiwan

It must be pointed out in all seriousness that after the victory of the war of resistance, Taiwan will be returned to China.

The occupation of Taiwan by U.S. imperialism is absolutely unjustified. Taiwan province is an inalienable part of Chinese territory. The U.S. imperialists must get out of Taiwan. The Chinese people are determined to liberate Taiwan.

In commemorating the 20th anniversary of victory in the war of resistance against Japan, we must also point out in all solemnity that the Japanese militarists fostered by U.S. imperialism will certainly receive still more severe punishment if they ignore the firm opposition of the Japanese people and the people of Asia, again indulge in their pipedreams, and resume their old road of aggression in Asia.

U.S. imperialism is preparing a world war. But can this save it from its doom? World War I was followed by the birth of the socialist Soviet Union. World War II was followed by the emergence of a series of socialist countries and many nationally independent countries. If the U.S. imperialists should insist on launching a third world war, it can be stated categorically that many more hundreds of millions of people will turn to socialism; the imperialists will then have little room left on the globe; and it is possible that the whole structure of imperialism will collapse.

Conclusion

We are optimistic about the future of the world. We are confident that the people will bring to an end the epoch of wars in human history. Comrade Mao Tse-tung pointed out long ago that war, this monster, "will be finally eliminated by the progress of human society, and in the not too distant future, too. But there is only one way to eliminate it and that is to oppose war with war, to oppose counter-revolutionary war with revolutionary war."

All peoples suffering from U.S. imperialist aggression, oppression, and plunder, unite! Hold aloft the just banner of people's war and fight for the cause of world peace, national liberation, people's democracy, and socialism!

Victory will certainly go to the people of the world!

Long live the victory of people's war!

Mao's Essays

The following are the texts of two essays and an excerpt from a third by Mao Tse-tung that Chinese are urged to study. They appeared in the Dec. 10, 1966 issue of the New York Times.

In Memory of Norman Bethune (1939)

A member of the Communist party of Canada, Comrade Norman Bethune was over 50 when, sent by the Communist parties of Canada and the United States to help China in the Anti-Japanese War, he made light of a distance of thousands of miles and arrived in China.

He came to Yenan last spring, went to work in the Wutai Mountains, and unfortunately died a martyr to his duties.

What kind of spirit is this that made a foreigner regard, without any selfish motive, the cause of the Chinese people's liberation as his own?

It is the spirit of internationalism, the spirit of Communism, and every Chinese Communist must learn from this spirit. Leninism teaches that the world revolution can succeed only if the proletariat of the capitalist countries supports the struggle for liberation of the people of the colonies and semi-colonies and the proletariat of the colonies and semi-colonies supports the struggle for liberation of the proletarians of the capitalist countries.

Comrade Bethune has followed this Leninist line in his practice. We Chinese Communists must also carry out this line. We must unite with the proletarians of all the capitalist countries, with the proletarians of Japan, Britain, the United States, Germany, Italy and all other capitalist countries; only then can we overthrow imperialism, liberate our nation and people and liberate the nations and peoples of the world. This is our internationalism, the internationalism with which we oppose both national chauvinism and narrow patriotism.

Comrade Bethune's spirit of doing everything for others' benefit and nothing for his own was shown in his extreme sense of responsibility in his work and his extreme warm-heartedness towards his comrades and the people. Every Communist must learn from him. Quite a number of people are irresponsible in their work, "picking up the light and shirking the heavy," *i.e.*, shoving the heavy loads onto others and choosing the light ones for themselves.

When anything comes up, they think of themselves first and of others only afterwards. When they have exerted themselves a little, they swell with pride and brag about it in case others should not know. Towards their comrades and the people, they are not full of enthusiasm but cold and reserved, indifferent and apathetic.

Such people are not really Communists, or at least cannot be counted as pure Communists. None who returned from the front failed to express their admiration for Bethune whenever his name was mentioned, and none remained unmoved by his spirit. None of the soldiers and civilians in the Shansi-Chahar-Hopeh border area, who had been treated by Dr. Bethune or had seen with their own eyes how he did his work, were unmoved. Every Communist must learn from Comrade Bethune this spirit of a true Communist.

Comrade Bethune was a doctor; he practiced medicine as his profession and he was always improving his skill; and among the Eighth Route Army's whole medical personnel he stood very high for his skill. This is an excellent lesson for that crowd of people who wish to change their work the moment they see something different, and for those who despise technical work as of no consequence, as a blind-alley occupation.

I saw Comrade Bethune only once. Afterwards he wrote me many letters. But as I was busy, I wrote back only one letter and do not know if he ever received it. I feel deeply grieved over his death. Now all of us commemorate him; thus we can see how profoundly people are moved by his spirit. We must all learn from him the spirit that is so completely free from selfishness. Starting from this point one can become a person of great use to the people. A man's ability may be great or small, but if only he has this spirit, he is already a noble-minded man, a pure man, a moral man, a man who has left vulgar taste behind, a man who is useful to the people.

Serve the People (1944)

Our Communist party and the Eighth Route and New Fourth Armies under its leadership belong to the camp of revolution. This camp devotes itself to the liberation of the people and works entirely for their interests. Comrade Chang-Szu-teh (the dead soldier being honored) belonged to our camp.

Death awaits all men but its significance varies with various persons. The ancient Chinese writer Szuma Ch'ien said:

"Although death befalls all men alike, in significance it may be weightier than Mount Tai or lighter than a swan's down."

In significance, to die for the interests of the people is weightier than Mount Tai, but to work hard and die for the Fascists, for those who exploit and oppress the people, is lighter than a swan's down. Comrade Chang Szu-teh died for the interests of the people, and his death is indeed weightier in significance than Mount Tai.

If we have shortcomings, we are not afraid to have them pointed out and subjected to criticism, because we are serving the people. Anyone may do this to us, no matter who he is. So long as he is right, we will correct ourselves immediately. If what he proposes will benefit the people, we will accept it.

The idea of "picked troops and simplified administration," for example, was put forward by Mr. Li Ting-ming, a nonparty man; since he made a good suggestion that would benefit the people, we have adopted it. If, in the interests of the people, we persist in doing what is good as well as rectifying what is wrong, our camp will surely thrive.

We come from all corners of the country, and have met together on the road leading to a common revolutionary goal. Along this road we shall yet march with the vast majority of the Chinese people. Today (in 1944) we are already exercising leadership over a population of 91 million in the base areas, but this is not enough, and to liberate the entire nation the number must be further increased.

In times of difficulty our comrades must be able to see our achievements and the bright side of things and screw up their courage. Since the Chinese people are suffering and we have the duty to save them, we must exert ourselves in struggle. Struggle necessarily entails sacrifice, and death is a common occurrence.

But if we keep in mind the interests of the people and the sufferings of the great majority, then we see that to die for the people's sake is to die a worthy death. Nevertheless, we ought to avoid as much as possible unnecessary sacrifices. Our cadres should be concerned about every soldier, and all people in the revolutionary ranks should care for each other and love and help each other.

From now on, if anyone in our ranks who has done some good work passes away, there should be a funeral procession and a memorial meeting to render him honor, whether he is a cook or a soldier. This should become a regular practice. And it should also be introduced among the common people. When someone dies in a village, hold a memorial meeting for him. This will serve to express our mourning for the deceased and to unite all the people.

The Foolish Old Man Who Removed the Mountains (1945)

There is an ancient Chinese fable called "The Foolish Old Man Who Removed the Mountains."

It tells of an old man who lived in northern China long, long ago and was known as the foolish old man of the north mountain. His house faced south and beyond his doorway stood the two great peaks, Tai-hang and Wang-wu, obstructing the way.

He called his sons, and hoe in hand they began to dig up these mountains with great determination.

Another graybeard, known as the wise old man, saw them and said derisively:

"How silly of you to do this. It is quite impossible for you few to dig up these two huge mountains."

The foolish old man replied:

" When I die, my sons will carry on, when they die, there will be my grandsons, and then their sons and grandsons, and so on to infinity. High as they are, the mountains cannot grow any higher and with every bit we dig, they will be that much lower. Why can't we clear them away?'

Having refuted the wise old man's wrong view he went on digging every day, unshaken in his conviction. God was moved by this, and he sent down two angels, who carried the mountains away on their backs.

Today, two big mountains lie like a dead weight on the Chinese people. One is imperialism, the other is feudalism. The Chinese Communist party has long made up its mind to dig them up. We must persevere and work unceasingly, and we, too, will touch god's heart. Our god is none other than the masses of the Chinese people. If they stand up and dig together with us, why can't these two mountains be cleared away?

Reprint of 'Little Red Book' with Mao's Quotations

Following is a photographic reprint of the first few pages from the English version of "Quotations from Chairman Mao Tse-tung," which, in the Chinese version, is carried and read by millions of Chinese students, peasants, workers, Red Guards, etc. The pages, about 3-1/2 by 5 inches in size, were bound by a bright red plastic cover with the title embossed in it. With a red ribbon attached as a marker, the 311-page booklet closely resembles a common prayer book or missal.

WORKERS OF ALL COUNTRIES, UNITE!

QUOTATIONS FROM
CHAIRMAN
MAO TSE-TUNG

★

FOREIGN LANGUAGES PRESS
PEKING 1966

First Edition   1966

Printed in the People's Republic of China

Study Chairman Mao's writings, follow his teachings and act according to his instructions.

Lin Piao

A facsimile of the above statement by Comrade Lin Piao in his own handwriting appears on the previous page.

CONTENTS

I.	The Communist Party	1
II.	Classes and Class Struggle	8
III.	Socialism and Communism	23
IV.	The Correct Handling of Contradictions Among the People	45
V.	War and Peace	58
VI.	Imperialism and All Reactionaries Are Paper Tigers	72
VII.	Dare to Struggle and Dare to Win	82
VIII.	People's War	88
IX.	The People's Army	99
X.	Leadership of Party Committees	104
XI.	The Mass Line	118
XII.	Political Work	134
XIII.	Relations Between Officers and Men	148
XIV.	Relations Between the Army and the People	153
XV.	Democracy in the Three Main Fields	157
XVI.	Education and the Training of Troops	165
XVII.	Serving the People	170
XVIII.	Patriotism and Internationalism	175
XIX.	Revolutionary Heroism	181
XX.	Building Our Country Through Diligence and Frugality	186
XXI.	Self-Reliance and Arduous Struggle	194
XXII.	Methods of Thinking and Methods of Work	203
XXIII.	Investigation and Study	230
XXIV.	Ideological Self-Cultivation	237
XXV.	Unity	251
XXVI.	Discipline	254
XXVII.	Criticism and Self-Criticism	258
XXVIII.	Communists	268
XXIX.	Cadres	276
XXX.	Youth	288
XXXI.	Women	294
XXXII.	Culture and Art	299
XXXIII.	Study	304

Unless otherwise stated, the page number given for the source of a quotation refers to the first English edition of the book or pamphlet cited as published by the Foreign Languages Press, Peking.

In cases where a word or phrase linked to the preceding text has been omitted in the opening sentence of the quotation, an asterisk is placed after the source. This is also done in a number of places where the English rendering has been reworded to make up for omission of context or to improve the translation.

Translator

I. THE COMMUNIST PARTY

The force at the core leading our cause forward is the Chinese Communist Party.

The theoretical basis guiding our thinking is Marxism-Leninism.

> Opening address at the First Session of the First National People's Congress of the People's Republic of China (September 15, 1954).

If there is to be revolution, there must be a revolutionary party. Without a revolutionary party, without a party built on the Marxist-Leninist revolutionary theory and in the Marxist-Leninist revolutionary style, it is impossible to lead the working class and the broad masses of the people in defeating imperialism and its running dogs.

> "Revolutionary Forces of the World Unite, Fight Against Imperialist Aggression!" (November 1948), *Selected Works*, Vol. IV, p. 284.*

Without the efforts of the Chinese Communist Party, without the Chinese Communists as the mainstay of the Chinese people, China can never achieve independence and liberation, or industrialization and the modernization of her agriculture.

> "On Coalition Government" (April 24, 1945), *Selected Works*, Vol. III, p. 318.*

The Chinese Communist Party is the core of leadership of the whole Chinese people. Without this core, the cause of socialism cannot be victorious.

> Talk at the general reception for the delegates to the Third National Congress of the New-Democratic Youth League of China (May 25, 1957).

A well-disciplined Party armed with the theory of Marxism-Leninism, using the method of self-criticism and linked with the masses of the people; an army under the leadership of such a Party; a united

front of all revolutionary classes and all revolutionary groups under the leadership of such a Party — these are the three main weapons with which we have defeated the enemy.

> "On the People's Democratic Dictatorship" (June 30, 1949), *Selected Works*, Vol. IV, p. 422.

We must have faith in the masses and we must have faith in the Party. These are two cardinal principles. If we doubt these principles, we shall accomplish nothing.

> *On the Question of Agricultural Co-operation* (July 31, 1955), 3rd ed., p. 7.*

Armed with Marxist-Leninist theory and ideology, the Communist Party of China has brought a new style of work to the Chinese people, a style of work which essentially entails integrating theory with practice, forging close links with the masses and practising self-criticism.

> "On Coalition Government" (April 24, 1945), *Selected Works*, Vol. III, p. 314.*

No political party can possibly lead a great revolutionary movement to victory unless it possesses revolutionary theory and a knowledge of history and has a profound grasp of the practical movement.

> "The Role of the Chinese Communist Party in the National War" (October 1938), *Selected Works*, Vol. II, p. 208.

As we used to say, the rectification movement is "a widespread movement of Marxist education". Rectification means the whole Party studying Marxism through criticism and self-criticism. We can certainly learn more about Marxism in the course of the rectification movement.

> *Speech at the Chinese Communist Party's National Conference on Propaganda Work* (March 12, 1957), 1st pocket ed., p. 14.

It is an arduous task to ensure a better life for the several hundred million people of China and to build our economically and culturally backward country into a prosperous and powerful one with a high level of culture. And it is precisely in order to be able to shoulder this task more competently and work better together with all non-Party people who are actuated by high ideals and determined to institute reforms that we must conduct rectification movements both now and in the future, and constantly rid ourselves of whatever is wrong.

> *Ibid.*, pp. 15-16.*

Policy is the starting-point of all the practical actions of a revolutionary party and manifests itself in the process and the

end-result of that party's actions. A revolutionary party is carrying out a policy whenever it takes any action. If it is not carrying out a correct policy, it is carrying out a wrong policy; if it is not carrying out a given policy consciously, it is doing so blindly. What we call experience is the process and the end-result of carrying out a policy. Only through the practice of the people, that is, through experience, can we verify whether a policy is correct or wrong and determine to what extent it is correct or wrong. But people's practice, especially the practice of a revolutionary party and the revolutionary masses, cannot but be bound up with one policy or another. Therefore, before any action is taken, we must explain the policy, which we have formulated in the light of the given circumstances, to Party members and to the masses. Otherwise, Party members and the masses will depart from the guidance of our policy, act blindly and carry out a wrong policy.

> "On the Policy Concerning Industry and Commerce" (February 27, 1948), *Selected Works*, Vol. IV, pp. 204-05.*

Our Party has laid down the general line and general policy of the Chinese revolution as well as various specific lines for work and specific policies. However, while many comrades remember our Party's specific lines for work and specific policies, they often forget its general line and general policy. If we actually forget the Party's general line and general policy, then we shall be blind, half-baked, muddle-headed revolutionaries, and when we carry out a specific line for work and a specific policy, we shall lose our bearings and vacillate now to the left and now to the right, and the work will suffer.

> "Speech at a Conference of Cadres in the Shansi-Suiyuan Liberated Area" (April 1, 1948), *Selected Works*, Vol. IV, p. 238.*

Policy and tactics are the life of the Party; leading comrades at all levels must give them full attention and must never on any account be negligent.

> "A Circular on the Situation" (March 20, 1948), *Selected Works*, Vol. IV, p. 220.

II. CLASSES AND CLASS STRUGGLE

Classes struggle, some classes triumph, others are eliminated. Such is history, such is the history of civilization for thousands of years. To interpret history from this viewpoint is historical materialism; standing in opposition to this viewpoint is historical idealism.

> "Cast Away Illusions, Prepare for Struggle" (August 14, 1949), *Selected Works*, Vol. IV, p. 428.

In class society everyone lives as a member of a particular class, and every kind of thinking, without exception, is stamped with the brand of a class.

"On Practice" (July 1937), *Selected Works*, Vol. I, p. 296.

Changes in society are due chiefly to the development of the internal contradictions in society, that is, the contradiction between the productive forces and the relations of production, the contradiction between classes and the contradiction between the old and the new; it is the development of these contradictions that pushes society forward and gives the impetus for the supersession of the old society by the new.

"On Contradiction" (August 1937), *Selected Works*, Vol. I, p. 314.

The ruthless economic exploitation and political oppression of the peasants by the landlord class forced them into numerous uprisings against its rule. . . . It was the class struggles of the peasants, the peasant uprisings and peasant wars that constituted the real motive force of historical development in Chinese feudal society.

"The Chinese Revolution and the Chinese Communist Party" (December 1939), *Selected Works*, Vol. II, p. 308.*

In the final analysis, national struggle is a matter of class struggle. Among the whites in the United States it is only the reactionary ruling circles who oppress the black people. They can in no way represent the workers, farmers, revolutionary intellectuals and other enlightened persons who comprise the overwhelming majority of the white people.

"Statement Supporting the American Negroes in Their Just Struggle Against Racial Discrimination by U.S. Imperialism" (August 8, 1963), *People of the World, Unite and Defeat the U.S. Aggressors and All Their Lackeys*, 2nd ed., pp. 3-4.*

It is up to us to organize the people. As for the reactionaries in China, it is up to us to organize the people to overthrow them. Everything reactionary is the same; if you don't hit it, it won't fall. This is also like sweeping the floor; as a rule, where the broom does not reach, the dust will not vanish of itself.

"The Situation and Our Policy After the Victory in the War of Resistance Against Japan" (August 13, 1945), *Selected Works*, Vol. IV, p. 19.

The enemy will not perish of himself. Neither the Chinese reactionaries nor the aggressive forces of U.S. imperialism in

China will step down from the stage of history of their own accord.

"Carry the Revolution Through to the End" (December 30, 1948), *Selected Works*, Vol. IV, p. 301.

A revolution is not a dinner party, or writing an essay, or painting a picture, or doing embroidery; it cannot be so refined, so leisurely and gentle, so temperate, kind, courteous, restrained and magnanimous. A revolution is an insurrection, an act of violence by which one class overthrows another.

"Report on an Investigation of the Peasant Movement in Hunan" (March 1927), *Selected Works*, Vol. I, p. 28.*

Chiang Kai-shek always tries to wrest every ounce of power and every ounce of gain from the people. And we? Our policy is to give him tit for tat and to fight for every inch of land. We act after his fashion. He always tries to impose war on the people, one sword in his left hand and another in his right. We take up swords, too, following his example. . . . As Chiang Kai-shek is now sharpening his swords, we must sharpen ours too.

"The Situation and Our Policy After the Victory in the War of Resistance Against Japan" (August 13, 1945), *Selected Works*, Vol. IV, pp. 14-15.

Who are our enemies? Who are our friends? This is a question of the first importance for the revolution. The basic reason why all previous revolutionary struggles in China achieved so little was their failure to unite with real friends in order to attack real enemies. A revolutionary party is the guide of the masses, and no revolution ever succeeds when the revolutionary party leads them astray. To ensure that we will definitely achieve success in our revolution and will not lead the masses astray, we must pay attention to uniting with our real friends in order to attack our real enemies. To distinguish real friends from real enemies, we must make a general analysis of the economic status of the various classes in Chinese society and of their respective attitudes towards the revolution.

"Analysis of the Classes in Chinese Society" (March 1926), *Selected Works*, Vol. I, p. 13.

Our enemies are all those in league with imperialism — the warlords, the bureaucrats, the comprador class, the big landlord class and the reactionary section of the intelligentsia attached to them. The leading force in our revolution is the industrial proletariat. Our closest friends are the entire semi-proletariat and petty bourgeoisie. As for the vacillating middle bourgeoisie, their right-wing may become our enemy and their left-wing may become

our friend — but we must be constantly on our guard and not let them create confusion within our ranks.

Ibid., p. 19.*

Whoever sides with the revolutionary people is a revolutionary. Whoever sides with imperialism, feudalism and bureaucrat-capitalism is a counter-revolutionary. Whoever sides with the revolutionary people in words only but acts otherwise is a revolutionary in speech. Whoever sides with the revolutionary people in deed as well as in word is a revolutionary in the full sense.

Closing speech at the Second Session of the First National Committee of the Chinese People's Political Consultative Conference (June 23, 1950).

I hold that it is bad as far as we are concerned if a person, a political party, an army or a school is not attacked by the enemy, for in that case it would definitely mean that we have sunk to the level of the enemy. It is good if we are attacked by the enemy, since it proves that we have drawn a clear line of demarcation between the enemy and ourselves. It is still better if the enemy attacks us wildly and paints us as utterly black and without a single virtue; it demonstrates that we have not only drawn a clear line of demarcation between the enemy and ourselves but achieved a great deal in our work.

To Be Attacked by the Enemy Is Not a Bad Thing but a Good Thing (May 26, 1939), 1st pocket ed., p. 2.*

We should support whatever the enemy opposes and oppose whatever the enemy supports.

"Interview with Three Correspondents from the Central News Agency, the *Sao Tang Pao* and the *Hsin Min Pao*" (September 16, 1939), *Selected Works*, Vol. II, p. 272.

Our stand is that of the proletariat and of the masses. For members of the Communist Party, this means keeping to the stand of the Party, keeping to Party spirit and Party policy.

"Talks at the Yenan Forum on Literature and Art" (May 1942), *Selected Works*, Vol. III, p. 70.

After the enemies with guns have been wiped out, there will still be enemies without guns; they are bound to struggle desperately against us, and we must never regard these enemies lightly. If we do not now raise and understand the problem in this way, we shall commit the gravest mistakes.

"Report to the Second Plenary Session of the Seventh Central Committee of the Communist Party of China" (March 5, 1949), *Selected Works*, Vol. IV, p. 364.*

President Johnson's 1966 Address on Asian Policy

Following is the partial transcript of President Lyndon B. John son's July 12, 1966, address on Asian policy, broadcast by radio and television to the American Alumni Council. (See p. 192)

...Throughout my entire life I have taken seriously the warning that the world is engaged in a race between education and chaos. For the last two and a half years I have lived here with the daily awareness that the fate of mankind really depends on the outcome of that race.

So I came here tonight because you are committed in the name of education to help us decide that contest. And that is the most important victory we can ever win.

We have set out in this country to improve the quality of all American life. We are concerned with each man's opportunity to develop his talents. We are concerned with his environment -- the cities and the farms where he lives, the air he breathes, the water he drinks. We seek to enrich the schools that educate him and, of course, to improve the governments that serve him.

We are at war against the poverty that deprives him, the unemployment that degrades him, and the prejudice that defies him.

As we look at other parts of the world, we see similar battles being fought in Asia, in Africa, and in Latin America. On every hand we see the thirst for independence, the struggle for progress -- the almost frantic race that is taking place between education, on the one hand, and disaster on the other.

In all these regions we, too, have a very big stake.

Nowhere are the stakes higher than in Asia. So I want to talk to you tonight about Asia and about peace in Asia.

Crucial Arena

Asia is now the crucial arena of man's striving for independence and order and for life itself.

This is true because three out of every five people in all this world live in Asia tonight.

This is true because hundreds of millions of them exist on less than 25 cents a day.

This is true because Communists in Asia tonight still believe in force in order to achieve their Communist goals.

So if enduring peace can ever come to Asia, all mankind will benefit. But if peace fails there, nowhere else will our achievements really be secure.

By peace in Asia I do not mean simply the absence of armed hostilities. For wherever men hunger and hate there can really be no peace.

I do not mean the peace of conquest. For humiliation can be the seedbed of war.

I do not mean simply the peace of the conference table. For peace is not really written merely in the words of treaties, but peace is the day-by-day work of builders.

Peace of Conciliation

The peace we seek in Asia is a peace of conciliation between Communist states and their non-Communist neighbors; between rich nations and poor; between small nations and large; between men whose skins are brown and black and yellow and white; between Hindus and Moslems and Buddhists and Christians.

It is a peace that can only be sustained through the durable bonds of peace: through international trade; through the free flow of peoples and ideas; through full participation by all nations in an international community under law; and through a common dedication to the great tasks of human progress and economic development.

Is such a peace possible?

With all my heart I believe it is. We are not there yet. We have a long way to journey. But the foundations for such a peace in Asia are being laid tonight as never before. They must be built on these essentials:

Pacific Power

First is the determination of the United States to meet our obligations in Asia as a Pacific power.

You have heard arguments the other way. They are built on the old belief that "East is East and West is West and never the twain shall meet;"

--that we have no business but business interests in Asia;

--that Europe, not the Far East, is really our proper sphere of interest;

--that our commitments in Asia are not worth the resources they require;

--that the ocean is vast, the cultures alien, the languages strange, and the races different;

--that these really are not our kind of people.

But all of these arguments have been thoroughly tested. And all of them, I think, have really been found wanting.

They do not stand the test of geography -- because we are bounded not by one, but by two oceans. And whether by aircraft or ship, by satellite or missile, the Pacific is as crossable as the Atlantic.

They do not stand the test of common sense. The economic network of this shrinking globe is too intertwined -- the basic hopes of men are too interrelated -- the possibility of common disaster is too real for us to ever ignore threats to peace in Asia.

They do not stand the test of human concern, either. The people of Asia do matter. We share with them many things in common. We are all persons. We are all human beings.

And they do not stand the test of reality, either. Asia is no longer sitting outside the door of the 20th century. She is here, in the same world with all of us, to be either our partner or our problem.

Americans entered this century believing that our own security had no foundation outside our own continent. Twice we mistook our sheltered position for safety. Twice we were dead wrong.

And if we are wise now, we will not repeat our mistakes of the past. We will not retreat from the obligations of freedom and security in Asia.

Losing Game

The second essential for peace in Asia is this: to prove to aggressive nations that the use of force to conquer others is a losing game.

There is no more difficult task, really, in a world of revolutionary change -- where the rewards of conquest tempt ambitious appetites.

As long as the leaders of North Viet Nam really believe that they can take over the people of South Viet Nam by force, we must not let them succeed.

We must stand across their path and say: "You will not prevail. But turn from the use of force and peace will follow."

Every American must know exactly what it is that we are trying to do in Viet Nam. Our greatest resource, really, in this conflict -- our greatest support for the men who are fighting out there -- is your understanding. It is your willingness to carry perhaps for a long time -- the heavy burden of a confusing and costly war.

We are not trying to wipe out North Viet Nam.

We are not trying to change their government.

We are not trying to establish permanent bases in South Viet Nam.

And we are not trying to gain one inch of new territory for America.

However long it takes, I want the Communists in Hanoi to know where we stand.

First, victory for your armies is impossible. You cannot drive us from South Viet Nam by your force. Do not mistake our firm stand for false optimism. As long as you persist in aggression, we are going to resist.

Second, the minute you realize that a military victory is out of the question and you turn from the use of force, you will find us ready and willing to reciprocate. We want to end the fighting. We want to bring our men back home. We want an honorable peace in Viet Nam. In your hands is the key to that peace. You have only to turn it.

Free Asia

The third essential is the building of political and economic strength among the nations of free Asia.

For years they have been working at that task. And the untold story of 1966 is the story of what free Asians have done for themselves, and with the help of others, while South Viet Nam and her allies have been busy holding aggression at bay.

Many of you can recall our faith in the future of Europe at the end of World War II when we began the Marshall plan. We backed that faith with all the aid and compassion we could muster.

Well, our faith in Asia tonight is just as great. And that faith is backed by judgment and by reason. For if we stand firm in Viet Nam against military conquest, we truly believe that the emerging order of hope and progress in Asia will continue to grow and to grow.

Out very able Secretary of State, Dean Rusk, has just returned from a trip through the Far East. He told me yesterday afternoon of many of the heartening signs he saw as the people of Asia continue to work toward common goals. And these are just some of them.

In the last year:

--Japan and Korea have settled their longstanding disputes and established normal relations with promise for closer cooperation;

--One country after another has achieved rates of economic growth that are far beyond the most optimistic hopes we had a few years ago;

--Indonesia and its more than 100 million people have already pulled back from the brink of communism and economic collapse;

--Our friends in India and Pakistan -- 600 million strong -- have ended a tragic conflict and have returned to the immense work of peace;

--Japan has become a dramatic example of economic progress through political and social freedom and has begun to help others;

--Communist China's policy of aggression by proxy is failing;

--Nine Pacific nations--allies and neutrals, white and colored--came together on their own initiative to form an Asian and Pacific Council;

--New and constructive groupings for economic cooperation are under discussion in southeast Asia;

--The billion dollar Asian Development Bank which I first mentioned in Baltimore in my televised speech a few months ago is already moving forward in Manila with the participation of more than 31 nations;

--And the development of the Lower Mekong River Basin is going forward despite the war.

Throughout free Asia you can hear the echo of progress. As one Malaysian leader said: "Whatever our ethical, cultural, or religious backgrounds, the nations and peoples of southeast Asia must pull together in the same broad sweep of history. We must create with our own hands and minds a new perspective and a new framework. And we must do it ourselves."

For this is the new Asia, and this is the new spirit we see taking shape behind our defense of South Viet Nam. Because we have been firm--because we have committed ourselves to the defense of one small country--other countries have taken new heart.

And I want to assure them tonight that we never intend to let you down. America's word will always be good.

Reconciliation

There is a fourth essential for peace in Asia which may seem the most difficult of all: reconciliation between nations that now call themselves enemies.

A peaceful mainland China is central to a peaceful Asia.

A hostile China must be discouraged from aggression.

A misguided China must be encouraged toward understanding of the outside world and toward policies of peaceful cooperation.

For lasting peace can never come to Asia as long as the 700 million people of mainland China are isolated by their rulers from the outside world.

We have learned in our relations with other such states that the weakness of neighbors is a temptation, and only firmness, backed by power, can really deter power that is backed by ambition. But we have also learned that the greatest force for opening closed minds and closed societies is the free flow of ideas and people and goods.

For many years, now, the United States has attempted in vain to persuade the Chinese Communists to agree to an exchange of newsmen as one of the first steps to increased understanding between our people.

More recently, we have taken steps to permit American scholars, experts in medicine and public health, and other specialists to travel to Communist China. And only today we, here in the Government, cleared a passport for a leading American businessman to exchange knowledge with Chinese mainland leaders in Red China.

All of these initiatives, except the action today, have been rejected by Communist China.

We persist because we know that hunger and disease, ignorance and poverty, recognize no boundaries of either creed or class or country.

We persist because we believe that even the most rigid societies will one day awaken to the rich possibilities of a diverse world.

And we continue because we believe that cooperation, not hostility, is really the way of the future in the 20th century.

That day is not yet here. It may be long in coming, but I tell you it is clearly on its way, because come it must.

Earlier this year the Foreign Minister of Singapore said that if the nations of the world could learn to build a truly world civilization in the Pacific through cooperation and peaceful competition, then --as our great President Theodore Roosevelt once remarked-- this may be the greatest of all human eras--the Pacific era.

As a Pacific power, we must help achieve that outcome.

Because it is a goal worthy of our American dreams and it is a goal that is worthy of the deeds of our brave men who are dying for us tonight.

So I say to you and I pledge to all those who are counting on us: You can depend upon us, because all Americans will do their part.

SOUTH VIET NAM CONSTITUTION

Following is the complete text of the South Viet Nam Constitution, voted on March 18, 1967, by the Constituent Assembly and promulgated April 1 by the Viet Nam Armed Forces Council. (It was signed that day by Chief of State Nguyen Van Thieu.)

PREAMBLE

Confident that the patriotism, indomitable will, and unyielding traditions of the people will assure a radiant future for our country;

Conscious that after many years of foreign domination, followed by the division of our territory, dictatorship and war, the people of Viet-Nam must take responsibility before history, to perpetuate those hardy traditions and at the same time to welcome progressive ideas in order to establish a republican form of Government of the people, by the people, and for the people whose purpose is to unite the nation, unite the territory and assure independence, freedom, and democracy with justice and altruism for the present and future generations;

We, 117 deputies of the National Constituent Assembly, representing the people of Viet-Nam, after debate, approve this Constitution.

CHAPTER I - BASIC PROVISIONS

Article 1.
1. Viet-Nam is a territorially indivisible, unified and independent republic.
2. Sovereignty resides in the People.

Article 2.
1. The State recognizes and guarantees the basic rights of all citizens.
2. The State advocates equality of all citizens without discrimination as to sex, religion, race or political party.
3. It is the duty of every citizen to serve the national interests.

Article 3.
The functions and powers of the Legislative, Executive and Judicial Branches must be clearly delineated. The activities of these three branches must be coordinated and harmonized to realize public order and prosperity on the basis of freedom, democracy and social justice.

Article 4.
1. The Republic of Viet-Nam will comply with those provisions of international law which are not contrary to its national sovereignty and the principle of equality between nations.
2. The Republic of Viet-Nam is determined to oppose all forms of aggression and strives to contribute to the building of international peace and security.

Article 5.
1. The Republic of Viet-Nam opposes communism in every form.
2. Every activity designed to propagandize or carry out communism is prohibited.

CHAPTER II - RIGHTS AND DUTIES OF CITIZENS

Article 6.
1. The State respects human dignity.
2. The State will protect freedom, the lives, property and honor of every citizen.

Article 7.
1. The State respects and protects the security of each individual and the right of every citizen to plead his case before a court of law.
2. No one can be arrested or detained without a legal order issued by an agency which has judicial powers conferred upon it by law except in cases of flagrant violation of the law.
3. The accused and his next of kin must be informed of the accusation against him within the time limit prescribed by law. Detentions must be controlled by an agency of the judiciary.
4. No citizen can be tortured, threatened or forced to confess. A confession obtained by torture, threat or coercion will not be considered as valid evidence.
5. A defendant is entitled to a speedy and public trial.
6. A defendant has the right to a defense lawyer for counsel in every phase of the interrogation, including the preliminary investigation.
7. Any person accused of a minor offense who doesn't have a record of more than three months imprisonment for an intentional crime may be released pending trial provided he (or she) is employed and has a fixed residence. Women pregnant more than three months accused of minor offenses who are employed and have a fixed residence may be released pending trial.
8. Accused persons will be considered innocent until sentence recognizing his guilt is handed down. In event of doubt, the court will rule in favor of the accused.
9. If unjustly detained, a citizen has the right to demand compensation for damages after his release, in accordance with the provisions of the law.
10. No one can be detained for indebtedness.

Article 8.
1. The private life, home, and correspondence of every citizen will be respected.
2. No one can enter, search or confiscate a person's property unless in possession of orders from a court or when necessary to the defense of security and public order according to the spirit of the law.
3. Privacy of correspondence will be protected by law. Any restriction imposed on this right must be determined by law.

Article 9.
1. The State will respect and guarantee freedom of religious belief and freedom to preach and practice religion of every citizen as long as it does not violate the national interest and is not harmful to public safety and order or contrary to good morals.
2. No religion will be recognized as the State religion. The State will be impartial in the development of various religions.

Article 10.
1. The State recognizes freedom of education.
2. Basic education is compulsory and free of charge.
3. University education will be autonomous.
4. Talented persons who do not have means will be given aid and support to continue their studies.
5. The State encourages and supports research and creative work by citizens in the fields of science, letters and the arts.

Article 11.
1. Culture and education must be considered matters of national policy, on a national, scientific, and humanistic basis.
2. An appropriate budget must be reserved for the development of culture and education.

Article 12.
1. The State respects freedom of thought, speech, press and publishing, as long as it does not harm personal honor, national security, or good morals.
2. Censorship will be abolished except for motion pictures and plays.
3. Press regulations will be prescribed by law.

Article 13.
1. Every citizen has the right to meet and form associations in accordance with conditions and procedures prescribed by law.
2. Every citizen has the right to vote, run for office and participate in public affairs on an equal basis and in accordance with conditions and procedures prescribed by law.
3. The State recognizes the political rights of every citizen including the right to petition freely and engage in overt, non-violent and legal opposition.

Article 14.
Every citizen will enjoy freedom to choose his place of residence and freedom of movement including the right to go and return from abroad. These freedoms can be restricted by law only for reasons of public health, security or defense.

Article 15.
1. Every citizen has the right and duty to work and receive fair remuneration enabling him and his family to live in dignity.
2. The State will endeavor to create employment for all citizens.

Article 16.
Freedom to join labor unions and to strike will be respected within the framework and regulations prescribed by law.

Article 17.
1. The State recognizes the family as the foundation of society. The State will encourage and facilitate the formation of families and will assist expectant mothers and infants.
2. Marriage must be based on mutual consent, equality and cooperation.
3. The State will encourage family cohesion.

Article 18.
1. The State will endeavor to establish a system of social security.
2. It is the duty of the State to establish a system of social welfare and public health.
3. It is the duty of the State to support the nation's warriors both spiritually and materially, as well as to support and raise the nation's orphans.

Article 19.
1. The State recognizes and guarantees the freedom of private property.
2. The State will advocate a policy of making the people property owners.
3. Expropriation or requisition by the State for the common good must be accompanied by speedy and just compensation at price levels existing at time of expropriation or requisition.

Article 20.

1. Freedom of trade and competition will be recognized but it cannot be exercised to secure monopoly or control of the market.

2. The State will encourage and assist economic cooperation which has the nature of mutual economic assistance.

3. The State will give special support to those elements of society which have a low standard of living.

Article 21.

The State advocates raising the standard of living of rural citizens, and especially helping farmers to have farmland.

Article 22.

On the basis of equality between duties and rights, workers have the right to choose representatives to participate in the management of business enterprises particularly with respect to matters concerning wages and conditions of work within the framework and procedures prescribed by law.

Article 23.

1. Military personnel elected to public office or serving in positions in central government must be demobilized or take leave of absence without salary, according to their choice.

2. Military personnel on active duty are not permitted to engage in political party activity.

Article 24.

1. The State recognizes the presence of minorities in the Vietnamese community.

2. The State respects the habits and customs of the minority compatriots. Customary courts will be established to pronounce judgments on some disputes involving habits and customs of minority compatriots.

3. A law will prescribe special rights in order to assist minority compatriots.

Article 25.

Every citizen has the duty to defend the country and the republic.

Article 26.

Every citizen has the duty to defend the constitution and respect the law.

Article 27.

Every citizen has the duty to fulfill his military obligations as prescribed by law.

Article 28.

Every citizen has the duty to pay taxes in accordance with the provisions of law.

Article 29.

Any restriction upon the basic rights of the citizens must be prescribed by law and the time and place within which such a restriction is in force must be clearly specified. In any event the essence of all basic freedoms cannot be violated.

CHAPTER III - NATIONAL ASSEMBLY

Article 30.

1. Legislative authority is vested by the people in the National Assembly.

2. The National Assembly includes two houses, the Lower House and the Upper House.

Article 31.

1. The Lower House includes from 100 to 200 representatives.

2. Representatives are elected by universal suffrage, direct and secret ballot. Candidates run as individuals from separate constituencies no larger than province.

3. Representatives serve for four years. They may be re-elected.

4. The election for a new Lower House will be completed at least one month prior to the completion of the term of the old Upper House.

Article 32.

Citizens meeting the following qualifications may run for the Lower House:

1. Vietnamese citizenship at birth, or having held Vietnamese citizenship at least seven years, or recovered Vietnamese citizenship for at least five years, counting from the day of election;

2. At least 25 years old on the day of the election;

3. Enjoying full rights of citizenship;

4. Having draft status in order;

5. Meeting other conditions specified in the electoral law.

Article 33.

1. The Upper House will include from 30 to 60 members.

2. Senators are elected at-large by universal suffrage, direct and secret ballot. The election will be by list voting and on basis of plurality. Each list will include from 1/3 to 1/6 of the total membership of the Upper House.

3. Senators will serve for six years. One half of the Senate will be re-elected every three years. Senators may be re-elected.

4. Members of the first Upper House will be divided into two groups by drawing lots. The first group will serve six years, the second group three years.

5. The election of one half of the Upper House must take place at least two months before the term of that half of the Upper House ends.

Article 34.

Candidates for the Upper House must be citizens 30 years of age by election day, must meet all the conditions prescribed in the senatorial election law and those prescribed in Article 32.

Article 35.

1. If for any reason a vacancy occurs in the Lower House more than two years prior to the end of the term, an election will be held within three months to choose a replacement.

2. If for any reason a vacancy occurs in the Upper House, the election of the replacement will be held concurrent with the next regular election of one-half of the Upper House.

Article 36.

Procedures and conditions for the candidacies and election of representatives and senators, including ethnic minority representatives, will be prescribed by law.

Article 37.

1. Representatives or senators cannot be prosecuted, pursued, arrested or judged for any statement or vote in the National Assembly.

2. During their entire term of office, except in cases of flagrant violation of the law, representatives and senators cannot be prosecuted, pursued, arrested or judged without the approval of three-fourths of the total number of representatives or senators.

3. In cases of flagrant violation of the law, prosecution or detention of representatives or senators must cease if the House concerned so decides.

4. Representatives and senators have the right to keep secret the origin of documents presented to the National Assembly.

5. Responsibilities of representatives or senators are not compatible with any other elected position.

6. Representatives and senators may serve as instructors at universities and advanced technical schools.

7. Under no circumstances may a representative or senator or his spouse bid in or sign a contract with a Government agency.

Article 38.

1. In cases of treason or other serious crime, representatives or senators may be removed from office by the House concerned.

2. Removal from office must be proposed by 2/3 of the total number of representatives or senators.

3. The resolution to remove a member from office must be approved by 3/4 of the total number of representatives or senators.

4. The representative or senator concerned has the right to defend himself in debate during all phases of the removal procedure.

Article 39.

The National Assembly has the authority to:

1. Vote legislation.

2. Ratify treaties and international agreements.

3. Determine declarations of war and holding of peace talks.

4. Determine declaration of a state of war.

5. Control the Government in the carrying out of national policy.

6. Within the framework of each House, pass on the validation of the election of representatives or senators.

Article 40.

1 Each House, with the agreement of 1/3 of its membership, has the right to request the Prime Minister or Government officials to appear before it to answer questions regarding the execution of Government policy.

2. Committee chairmen in each House have the right to request Government officials to appear before sessions of their committees to report on problems relating to various ministries.

Article 41.

The senate has the right to open investigations regarding the execution of national policy and to request public agencies to produce documents necessary in its investigations.

Article 42.

1. The National Assembly has the right to recommend the replacement of part or all of the Government by a two-thirds majority vote of the total number of representatives and senators.

2. The recommendation is binding unless the President has special reasons for rejecting it.

3. In the event of rejection by the President, the National Assembly has the right to vote final approval of the recommendation by a three-quarters majority vote of the total number of representatives and senators. This recommendation by the National Assembly is binding from the day it is voted.

Article 43.

1. Representatives and senators have the right to introduce bills.

2. The President may introduce bills.

3. Bills must be submitted to the office of the Lower House.

4 If the Lower House approves or rejects a bill, it must transmit the bill to the office of the Upper House within three consecutive days.

5. If the Upper House agrees with the viewpoint of the Lower House, the bill will be transmitted to the President for promulgation or will be abolished.

6. If the Upper House does not agree with the viewpoint of the Lower House, it must return the bill to the Lower House within three consecutive days along with an explanation for its action.

7. In the latter case, the Lower House has the right to vote final approval of the bill with a two-thirds majority of its total membership.

8. If the Lower House is unable to reach a two-thirds majority, the viewpoint of the Upper House will be considered as approved.

9. The time limit for debating and voting on a bill in the Upper House may not exceed half the time required to debate and vote on the bill in the Lower House.

Article 44.

1. Bills approved by the National Assembly will be transmitted to the President within three consecutive days.

2. The President must promulgate the law within 15 days from the date of receipt.

3. If the National Assembly appraises the matter as urgent, the bill must be promulgated within 7 consecutive days.

4. If the President does not promulgate the bill within the specified period of time, the bill will automatically become law and will be promulgated by the Chairman of the Upper House.

Article 45.

1. Within the period allowed for promulgation the President has the right to send a message outlining his reasons and requesting the National Assembly to reconsider one or more articles of the bill.

2. In this case, the National Assembly will meet in joint plenary session to vote final approval of the bill with an absolute majority of the total number of representatives and senators. If the National Assembly votes to reject the amendment proposed by the President, the bill will automatically become law and will be transmitted to the President for promulgation.

Article 46.

1. The draft budget must be submitted to the office of the Lower House prior to September 30.

2. Representatives and senators have the right to propose additional expenditures but must at the same time propose equivalent new receipts.

3. The Lower House must vote on the budget prior to November 30 and transmit the approved version to the Upper House by December 1 at the latest.

4. The Upper House must vote on the draft budget before December 31.

5. During the abovementioned period, if the Upper House reconsiders one or more provisions of the draft budget, then the procedures outlined in Article 43 will be applied. In the event that the draft budget has not been finally voted by December 31, the President has the right to sign a decree authorizing expenditure of one-twelfth of the previous budget until the Lower House has voted final approval of the draft budget.

Article 47.

Regulations.

1. Each House will meet in regular and extraordinary sessions.

2. Every year each House will meet in two regular sessions, one session beginning on the first Monday of April; the other beginning on the first Monday of October. A session cannot last for more than ninety days. However, the Lower House can prolong its session in order to vote final approval of the draft budget.

3. Either House may meet in extraordinary sessions when so requested by the President or one-third of the representatives or senators. When extraordinary sessions are convened by the President, the President will set the agenda.

Article 48.

1. Each House will meet in open session except when more than half the members present in the House request a closed session.

2. In open sessions complete reports of the debate and documents presented will be printed in the official journal.

Article 49.

1. Each House will elect its chairman and permanent officers.

2. Each House may establish permanent committees.

3. Each House is responsible for establishing its own internal rules.

4. The officers of the two Houses will meet together to determine procedures for maintaining liaison between Houses.

Article 50.

1. The chairman of the Upper House will convene and preside over joint plenary sessions of both Houses.

2. If the chairman of the Upper House is unable to perform this function, it will be carried out by the chairman of the Lower House.

CHAPTER IV - THE EXECUTIVE

Article 51.

Executive authority is vested by the people in the President.

Article 52.

1. The President and Vice-President run together on one list and are elected by the entire nation by direct and secret ballot.

2. The term of office of the President and Vice-President is four years. The President and Vice-President can be re-elected once.

3. The term of office of the President and Vice-President ends precisely at 12:00 noon on the last day of the forty-eighth month from the day they took office and the term of the new President and Vice-President begins at that time.

4. The election of the new President will be held on a Sunday, four weeks before the incumbent's term ends.

Article 53.

Citizens meeting the following conditions may run for President and Vice-President:

1. Must have Vietnamese citizenship from day of birth and continuous residence in Viet-Nam for ten years as of date of election. Time spent on official assignment abroad or in political exile is considered as residence in Viet-Nam.

2. Must be 35 years of age as of election day.

3. Must have legal draft status.

4. Must enjoy full rights of citizenship.

Article 54.

1. The supreme court will establish a list of candidates, will control the fairness of the election and will announce the result.

2. Candidates will receive equal means in the electoral campaign.

3. Procedures and conditions governing candidacies and election of the President and Vice-President will be prescribed by law.

Article 55.

When assuming office the President, witnessed by the supreme court and National Assembly, shall take the following oath before the nation:

"I solemnly swear before the nation to protect the fatherland, respect the Constitution, serve the interests of the people, and to the best of my ability fulfill my duties as President of the Republic of Viet-Nam."

Article 56.

1. Duties of the President and Vice President may terminate prior to the end of their terms of office in the following circumstances:

   a. Death

   b. Resignation

   c. Impeachment

   d. Serious and prolonged illness such that the incumbent can no longer carry out his duties. This disability must be recognized by three-fourths of the total membership of the two Houses of the National Assembly after complete medical examination.

2. In the event that the duties of the President are terminated more than one year prior to the end of his term of office, the Vice President will temporarily assume the Presidency for a period not to exceed three months in order to organize the election of a new President and Vice President for a new term of office.

3. In the event that the duties of the President are terminated within one year prior to the end of his term of office, the Vice President shall assume the Presidency for the remainder of the term, except in cases of impeachment of the President.

4. If for any reason the Vice-President is unable to assume the Presidency, the chairman of the Upper House will assume the office for a period not to exceed three months in order to organize an election for a new President and Vice President.

Article 57.

The President promulgates laws within the period determined in Article 43.

Article 58.

1. The President appoints the Prime Minister. Upon the proposal of the Prime Minister, the President appoints members of the Government.

2. The President has the right to organize all or part of the Government on his own initiative, or upon the recommendation of the National Assembly.

Article 59.

1. The President appoints, with the approval of the Upper House, chiefs of diplomatic missions and rectors of universities.

2. The President represents the nation in international relations and receives letters of accreditation of diplomatic envoys.

3. The President signs and, after ratification by the National Assembly, promulgates treaties and international agreements.

Article 60.

The President is the supreme commander of the Armed Forces of the Republic of Viet-Nam.

Article 61.

1. The President grants all types of decorations.

2. The President has the right to grant amnesty and pardon for criminals.

Article 62.

1. The President determines national policy.

2. The President presides over the Council of Ministers.

Article 63.

1. The President communicates with the National Assembly by message. In each regular session, and whenever the President considers it necessary, he will advise the National Assembly of the situation in the country and of the Government's domestic and foreign policies.

2. The Prime Minister and other Government officials may participate in sessions of the National Assembly or its committees in order to present and explain matters relating to national policy and its execution.

Article 64.

1. In special situations, the President may sign decrees declaring states of emergency, curfew or tension over part or all of the territory of the country.

2. The National Assembly must meet no later than twelve days after the date of promulgation of the decree in order to ratify, amend or reject it.

3. If the National Assembly rejects or amends the President's decree, the special situations which were decreed will end or be modified accordingly.

Article 65.

In a state of war, and when elections cannot be held, the President, with the approval of two-thirds of the National Assembly, has the right to prolong the terms of office of some of the elected bodies of the country and to appoint some province chiefs.

Article 66.

1. The Vice President is chairman of the Culture and Education Council, the Economic and Social Council and the Ethnic Minority Council.

2. The Vice President cannot hold any other position in the Government.

Article 67.

1. The Prime Minister directs the Government and the administrative agencies of the nation.

2. The Prime Minister is responsible before the President for carrying out national policy.

Article 68.

1. The President, Vice President, Prime Minister and members of the Government cannot hold any position in the private sector whether it is remunerated or not.

2. Spouses of persons holding the above positions may not participate in Government bids or contracts.

Article 69.

1. It is the task of the National Security Council to: examine all matters relating to national defense; propose measures appropriate to the maintenance of national security; propose the declaration of states of emergency, curfew, tension or war; propose declarations of war or holding of peace talks.

2. The President is chairman of the National Security Council.

3. A law shall prescribe the organization and procedures of the National Security Council.

LOCAL ADMINISTRATION

Article 70.

1. The principle of local separation of power is recognized for legal regional entities: villages, provinces, cities, and the capital.

2. The organization and regulation of local administration shall be prescribed by law.

Article 71.

1. Deliberative bodies and the heads of executive agencies of local administrative units will be popularly elected by direct and secret ballot.

2. At the village level, village chiefs may be elected by village councils from among village council members.

Article 72.

The heads of executive agencies of local administrative units are:
Villages -- Village Chief

Provinces -- Province Chiefs
Cities -- Mayor
Capital -- Mayor

Article 73.

The deliberative bodies of local administrative units are:
Villages -- Village Council
Provinces -- Province Council
Cities -- Municipal Council
Capital -- Municipal Council

Article 74.

The Government will appoint two civil servants who have the responsibility to assist mayors, province chiefs and village chiefs in administrative and security matters, as well as other administrative personnel.

Article 75.

Members of deliberative bodies and heads of executive agencies of local administrative units may be dismissed by the President if they violate the constitution, laws of the nation, or national policy.

CHAPTER V - JUDICIARY

Article 76.

1. Independent judicial power is vested in the Supreme Court and is exercised by judges.

2. A law shall establish the organization and administration of the judiciary.

Article 77.

Every court must be established by law with an element which judges and an element which prosecutes, both of which are professionally qualified. Courts must respect rights of defense.

Article 78.

1. The responsibilities of judges and prosecuting judges are clearly delineated, and the two are governed by separate regulations.

2. Judges make decisions according to their consciences and the law, under the control of the Supreme Court.

3. Prosecuting judges monitor the application of the law in order to protect public order, under the control of the Ministry of Justice.

Article 79.

Presiding judges can be relieved of their functions only in cases of mental or physical incapacity, conviction or violation of discipline.

Article 80.

1. The Supreme Court includes from 9 to 15 judges chosen by the National Assembly and appointed by the President from among a list elected by the association of judges, association of prosecutors and association of lawyers.

2. Judges of the Supreme Court must be judges or lawyers who have served at least ten years in the judiciary.

3. The term of office of judges of the Supreme Court is six years.

4. The number of electors of the association of judges, association of prosecutors and association of lawyers must be equal.

5. The organization and regulation of the Supreme Court will be prescribed by law.

Article 81.

1. The Supreme Court is empowered to interpret the constitution, to decide on the constitutionality of all laws and decree-laws, and to decide on the constitutionality and legality of decrees and administrative decisions.

2. The Supreme Court is empowered to decide on the dissolution of a political party whose policy and activities oppose the republican regime.

3. In these cases, the Supreme Court will meet in plenary session. Representatives of the legislative or executive branches may participate in order to present their viewpoints.

4. Decisions declaring the unconstitutionality of a law or the dissolution of a political party require a three-fourths vote of the total number of Supreme Court judges.

Article 82.

The Supreme Court is empowered to decide appeals from lower courts.

Article 83.

The Supreme Court has a separate budget and is empowered to establish regulations governing the judiciary.

Article 84.

1. The Judicial Council has the following responsibilities:
To propose the appointment, promotion, transfer and disciplining of judges;
To advise the Supreme Court in matters relating to the judiciary.

2. The Judicial Council will be composed of judges elected by the association of judges.

3. The organization and regulation of the Judicial Council will be prescribed by law.

CHAPTER VI - SPECIAL INSTITUTIONS

Article 85.
The Special Court is empowered to remove from office the President, Vice President, Prime Minister, Ministers, Secretaries of State, Supreme Court Justices and members of the Inspectorate in cases of treason or other high crimes.

Article 86.
1. The Special Court is chaired by the Chief Justice of the Supreme Court and consists of five representatives and five senators.
2. When the Chief Justice of the Supreme Court is accused the chairman of the Upper House sits as presiding judge.

Article 87.
1. A motion to bring charges and citing reasons therefore must be supported by more than one half of the total number of representatives and senators. The motion must be signed by two-thirds of the total number of representatives and senators. In the particular case of the President and Vice President the motion must be signed by two-thirds of the total number of representatives and senators and it must be approved by a majority vote of three-quarters of the total number of representatives and senators.
2. The functions of the accused must be suspended from the date of approval of the motion by the National Assembly until the decision of the Special Court is rendered.
3. The Special Court decides removal from office by a three-quarters majority vote of its membership. In the particular case of the President and Vice President, the decision must be by a four-fifths majority vote of total membership.
4. The accused will enjoy the rights of defense during the entire proceedings.
5. After having been removed from office the accused may be tried by an ordinary court.
6. A law will establish the organization, administration and procedures of the Special Court.

Article 88.
The Inspectorate is empowered to:
1. Inspect, control and investigate personnel of all public and private agencies directly or indirectly engaged in corruption, speculation, influence peddling or acts harmful to the national interest.
2. Inspect accounts of public agencies and commercial enterprises.
3. Audit the property of personnel of public agencies including the President, Vice President, Prime Minister, representatives, senators, Chief Justice of the Supreme Court and the chairman of the Inspectorate.
4. In the cases of the chairman and members of the Inspectorate, the audit of personal property will be conducted by the Supreme Court.

Article 89.
1. The Inspectorate is empowered to propose disciplinary measures against government personnel or to request prosecution by competent courts.
2. The Inspectorate has the right to publicly announce the results of its investigations.

Article 90.
1. The Inspectorate includes from 9 to 18 inspectors, one-third designated by the National Assembly, one-third by the President, and one-third by the Supreme Court.
2. Inspectors will enjoy those guarantees necessary for them to carry out their responsibilities.

Article 91.
1. The Inspectorate has an autonomous budget, and is empowered to establish regulations governing its internal organization and the inspectorate branch.
2. The organization and regulation of the Inspectorate will be prescribed by law.

Article 92.
1. The Armed Forces Council advises the President in matters relating to the armed forces, especially promotion, transfer and disciplining of soldiers of all ranks.
2. The organization and regulation of the Armed Forces Council will be prescribed by law.

Article 93.
1. The Culture and Education Council has the responsibility to advise the Government in the drafting and execution of cultural and educational policy. A national academy will be established.
2. With the approval of the National Assembly, the Culture and Education Council may select representatives to brief the National Assembly on related matters.
3. The Culture and Education Council may contribute ideas before the National Assembly debates laws relating to culture and education.

Article 94.
1. The membership of the Culture and Education Council includes: one-third designated by the President; two-thirds elected by public and private cultural and educational organizations and by parent-teachers associations.
2. The term of office of the Culture and Education Council is four years.
3. The organization and regulation of the Culture and Education Council will be prescribed by law.

Article 95.
1. The Economic and Social Council has the responsibility to advise the Government in economic and social matters.
2. With the approval of the National Assembly, the Economic and Social Council may select representatives to brief the National Assembly on related matters.
3. The Economic and Social Council may contribute ideas before draft laws and economic and social programs are debated.

Article 96.
1. The membership of the Economic and Social Council includes: one-third designated by the President; two-thirds nominated by industrial and commercial organizations and by labor unions having an economic and social character.
2. The term of office of the Economic and Social Council is four years.
3. The organization and regulation of the Economic and Social Council will be prescribed by law.

Article 97.
1. The Ethnic Council, representing the ethnic minorities living on the territory of Viet-Nam, has the responsibility to advise the Government in matters affecting ethnic minorities.
2. With the approval of the National Assembly, the Ethnic Council may select representatives to brief the National Assembly on related matters.
3. The Ethnic Council may contribute ideas before draft laws, programs, and plans affecting ethnic minorities are debated.

Article 98.
1. The membership of the Ethnic Council includes: one-third designated by the President; two-thirds elected by the ethnic minorities.
2. The term of office of the Ethnic Council is four years.
3. The organization and regulation of the Ethnic Council will be prescribed by law.

CHAPTER VII - POLITICAL PARTIES AND OPPOSITION

Article 99.
1. The Nation recognizes that political parties have an essential role in a democratic system.
2. Political parties may be organized and may operate freely, according to the procedures and conditions prescribed by law.

Article 100.
The Nation encourages progress toward a two-party system.

Article 101.
The Nation recognizes the formalization of political opposition.

Article 102.
Regulations governing political parties and political opposition will be prescribed by law.

CHAPTER VIII - AMENDING THE CONSTITUTION

Article 103.
1. The President or an absolute majority of the total number of representatives or an absolute majority of the total number of senators has the right to propose amendments to the constitution.
2. The proposal must cite reasons and must be submitted to the office of the Upper House.

Article 104.
A joint committee will be established to research the proposed amendment and report to joint plenary sessions of the Assembly.

Article 105.
The resolution to amend the constitution must be supported by two-thirds of the total number of representatives and senators.

Article 106.
The President promulgates a law amending the constitution according to the procedures prescribed in Article 34.

Article 107.
Article 1 of the constitution and this Article may not be amended or deleted.

CHAPTER IX - TRANSITIONAL PROVISIONS

Article 108.
The Provisional Charter of June 19, 1965 is automatically invalidated from the date of promulgation of the constitution.

(Continued on p. 348)

ABBREVIATIONS

ADA -- Americans for Democratic Action; PKI -- Indonesian Communist Party; CCP -- Chinese Communist Party; CPSU -- Communist Party of the Soviet Union; KMT -- Kuomintang; AID -- Agency for International Development; ASPAC -- Asian and Pacific Council; SEATO -- Southeast Asia Treaty Organization.

Index

A

ABBOUD, IBRAHIM - 140
ABBREVIATIONS - 338
ACHESON, DEAN
  Cambodia mission - 132
  China: policy - 11; recognition - 47, 48; UN membership - 49; white paper - 47
  Far East policy conf. - 47
  Far East policy speech, text - 257
  Formosa policy - 48, 87
  Korean conflict - 54
  Secy. of State (appt.) - 11
  Testimony - 57, 58
AFGHANISTAN - 155
AFL-CIO - 176
AGRICULTURE DEPT. - 133
A.I.D. (FY '66 ESTIMATE) - 190
AIDIT, D.N. (BIOG.) - 165
AIKEN, GEORGE D. (R VT.) - 51, 182
ALBANIA - 103, 108, 131, 132, 187
AL-SALLAL - See: Sallal
ALEMAN, MIGUEL - 62
ALGERIA - 132
ALLEN, ROBERT S. - 87
ALTMAN, JACK - 119
AMER. CHINA POLICY ASSN. - 23
AMER. CHINA POLICY COMM. - 12
AMERICANS FOR DEM. ACTION (ADA) - 85
AMERICANS FOR REAPPRAISAL OF OUR FAR EASTERN POLICY - 24
AMREHN, FRANZ - 109
ANTI-VIET NAM MOV. - 165, 166, 167, 182, 188, 213
APPLE, R.W. - 215
APTHEKER, HERBERT - 171
  Biog. - 238
ARGENTINA - 9, 134
ASHBROOK, JOHN M. (R OHIO) - 25, 143
ASHLEY, THOMAS L. (D OHIO) - 17, 18, 106
ASIAN AND PACIFIC COUN. (ASPAC) - 191
ATCHESON, GEORGE A. JR. - 39
ATOMIC ENERGY COMM. - 159, 213
ATTLEE, CLEMENT R. - 55
AUSTIN, WARREN R. - 55
AUSTRALIA
  ASPAC - 191
  China, trade - 9; wheat agrmt. - 115, 118, 122, 137
  Johnson (Pres.) visit - 202
  Manila conf. - 202
  India, wheat - 212
  SEATO - 70; Viet Nam - 158
  Viet Nam, troops - 159

B

BADGER, OSCAR C. - 58
BALEWA, SIR ABUBAKAR TAFAWA - 160
BALL, GEORGE W. - 113, 140, 177, 184
BAMINA, JOSEPH - 152
BANDA, HASTINGS KAMUZU- 145, 149
BANDARANAIKE, MRS. SIRIMAVO - 117, 135
BANDUNG CONF. - 74
BAO DAI - 75
  Biog. - 238
BARDEN, GRAHAM A. (D N.C.) - 16
BARNETT, A. DOAK - 4, 24, 93, 179
  Biog. - 238
  China testimony, text - 278
BARR, DAVID C. - 58
BEAM, JACOB D. - 86, 87, 91, 103
  Biog. - 238
BELL, DAVID E. - 20, 174
BEN BELLA, AHMED - 132
BENTON, WILLIAM (D CONN.) - 60
BERDING, ANDREW H. - 95
BERLE, ADOLPH A. JR. - 96
BEVIN, ERNEST - 39, 48
BIBLIOGRAPHY - 222
BLACK, EUGENE R.
  Biog - 238

BLOODWORTH, DENNIS - 211
BLUM, LEON - 41
BOLTON, FRANCES P. (R OHIO) - 45
BOURGUIBA, HABIB - 133
BOWLES, CHESTER - 100, 101, 104
BOYLE, WILLIAM M. - 25
BOXER REBELLION - 6, 7
BRADLEY, OMAR N. - 51, 57, 60, 64
  Biog. - 238
BRADSHER, HENRY S. - 207
BRAZIL - 137
BREZHNEV, LEONID I. - 147, 182, 203, 207
  Biog. - 238
BRIDGES, H. STYLES (R N.H.) - 11, 12, 44, 58, 60
BRINKLEY, DAVID - 127
BROOMFIELD, WILLIAM S. (R MICH.) - 143
BROWN, GEORGE E. JR. (D CALIF.) - 192
BROWNELL, HERBERT JR. - 74
BRUCKER, WILBER M. - 96
BRUNAUER, ESTHER - 14
BRUNAUER, STEPHEN - 14
BRUNDAGE, AVERY - 92
BUDENZ, LOUIS F. - 50
BULGANIN, NIKOLAI A. - 72, 73, 79
  Biog. - 238
BULLITT, WILLIAM C. - 44, 61
  Biog. - 238
BUNDY, MC GEORGE - 140, 156, 166, 169, 177
  Biog. - 238
BUNDY, WILLIAM P. - 141, 146, 184
  Biog. - 238
BURCHETT, WILFRED S. - 139
BURMA
  China, treaties - 96, 101
  Chou En-Lai visit - 134
  Colombo conf. - 117
  Communist hostilities - 78, 79
  Coup - 111
  Geneva conf., Laos - 114
BURUNDI - 140, 152
BUTLER, JOHN MARSHALL (R MD.) - 54
BUTLER, R.A. - 139
BUTTERWORTH, W. WALTON - 12
BYRNES, JAMES F. - 39
  Biog. - 239

C

CAIRO CONF. - 36
CAIRO CONF. (NON-ALIGNED NATIONS) - 147
CAMBODIA
  China aid - 130, 136, 146, 148, 150, 169
  Colombo conf. - 117
  Embassies closed - 131
  Geneva conf., Laos - 114
  Geneva conf. '54 - 68
  Geneva declaration '54 - 69
  Indo-China armistice - 69
  SEATO Treaty - 70
  U.S. aid rejected - 130
  U.S., relations broken - 158
  Viet Cong sanctuary - 169
CAMEROON - 167
CANADA
  China, trade - 9
  China in UN - 206
  China, wheat agrmt. - 9, 103, 109, 125, 131, 135, 151
  Geneva conf., Laos - 114, 140
  India, mil. aid - 116
  India, wheat - 212
CAPEHART, HOMER E. (R IND.) - 11
CAPITALS OF CHINA - 30
CARTER, EDWARD C. - 24
CASTRO, FIDEL - 100, 115, 133, 171
CELLER, EMANUEL (D N.Y.) - 80, 169
CENTRAL AFRICAN REPUBLIC - 146
CEYLON - 117, 135
CHAD - 167
CHANG CHUN - 39, 43, 45
  Biog. - 239
CHANG HSUEH-LIANG - 36
CHANG, JOHN M. - 104
  Biog. - 239
CHANG NAI-CHI - 84
  Biog. - 239

CHANG PO-CHUN - 84
  Biog. - 239
CHANG TEH-TSUEN - 204
CHAO YI-MING - 117
CHAU, THICH TAM - 149, 154, 184
  Biog. - 239
CHAVAN, Y.B. - 167
CHAVEZ, DENNIS (D N.M.) - 17
CHEN CHENG - 87, 105, 113
  Biog. - 239
CHEN CHIH-MAI - 25
CHEN PO-TA - 194, 204, 210
  Biog. - 239
CHEN YI
  Africa tour - 131, 132, 133, 134
  Biog. - 239
  Burma, Pakistan, Ceylon trip - 134, 135
  China in UN - 165
  Chinese nuclear program - 129
  Colombo proposals - 119
  Denounced - 213
  Foreign minister - 84
  Formosa policy - 90, 94, 113
  Gov. Gen., Formosa - 42
  Interview - 209
  Japan, relations - 141
  Laotian crises - 139
  Nuclear weapons - 139
  Red Guard denunciation - 201
  Sino-Soviet relations - 105, 153
  Soviets charged - 192
  U.S.-Chinese relations - 139
  Viet Nam peace negotiations - 196
  Viet Nam, warning - 141, 155, 165
CHEN YUN - 207
  Biog. - 239
CHENNAULT, CLAIRE L. - 11, 44, 46
  Biog - 239
CHIANG CHING - 204, 208, 209, 216
  Biog. - 239
CHIANG KAI-SHEK
  Admission of failure - 43
  Biog. - 232-236
  Cairo conf. - 36
  Civil war cease-fire - 41; truce - 39
  Communists ousted - 36
  Leashed - 53; unleashed - 64
  Mao, agrmt. - 38
  Nanking govt. organized - 35
  Offshore Islands, defense - 88, 89
  Political consultative conf. - 39
  Presidency reclaimed - 49
  Renunciation of force - 90
  Retirement - 46
  U.S., aid request - 45
  Victory message - 38
CHIANG KAI-SHEK, MME. - 45, 46, 86
  Biog. - 236-237
CHIANG NAN-HSIANG - 191
  Biog. - 239
CHILE - 130, 167
CHINA AID ACT (1948) - 11, 15, 45
  Text and statement - 255
CHINA EMERGENCY COMM. - 12, 23
CHINA FED. OF TRADE UNIONS - 213
CHINA LOBBY
  Communist agents, list - 26 27
  Factsheet - 23-28
  Investigation - 25, 58
  Nationalist agents, list - 26-27
CHINA AND THE WEST (FACT- SHEET) - 4-9
CHINA, PEOPLE'S REPUBLIC OF (COMMUNIST)
  Afghanistan, loan - 155
  Americans imprisoned - 70, 73, 74, 75
  Anti-French demon. - 219
  Anti-Soviet demon. - 195, 219
  Argentina, wheat agrmt. - 134
  Arms to Arabs - 198
  Army-party dispute - 172
  Asian and Pacific peace conf. - 62, 63
  Atomic reactor - 85
  Australia, wheat agrmts. - 115, 118, 122, 137
  Brazil, agents arrested - 137
  British recognition - 8, 48
  British trade - 77, 80, 81, 120, 148
  Burma, treaties - 96, 101
  Cambodia, aid pledge - 130, 136, 146, 148, 150, 169
  Canada, wheat agrmts. - 103, 109, 125, 131, 135, 151
  Capitals (box) - 30
  Chile, copper agrmt. - 130

China lobby, fact sheet - 23-28
Colombo proposals - 119
Congo recognition - 135
Cuba dispute - 175
Cuba, trade agrmts. - 99, 111, 151, 171
Cuban missile crisis - 116
Cuban recognition - 100
Czechoslovakia, agrmt. - 146
Dahomey, dipl. rel. est. - 149
Dominican Rep. crisis - 158
Economy - 84, 85, 89, 91, 92, 93 96, 101, 102, 114, 120, 131, 132, 150, 213
Egyptian recognition - 77
Europ. steel plant constr. - 9, 181
Formosa cease-fire - 88, 89
Formosa threatened - 72, 86
France, relations - 128
French recognition - 8, 133
Geneva accords - 62
Geneva conf. '54 - 67, 68, 69
Geneva conf., Laos - 104, 140
Geneva declaration '54 - 69
Geneva talks, U.S. - 74, 75, 76, 85
Govt. inaugurated - 47
Govt. proclaimed - 8, 47
Great Leap failure - 111
India, border dispute - 93, 94, 95, 96, 97, 111, 114, 115, 116, 124, 151, 167
Indo-China, conf. - 69
Indonesia supported - 146, 150, 151, 152
Indonesia, protest - 178, 184
Invasion alerts - 113
Japan denounced - 150
Japan, trade agrmts. - 117
Kenya, loan - 140
Korean conflict - 52, 53, 54, 55, 56, 57, 58
Korean withdrawal - 84, 90
Laos, dipl. rel. est. - 114
Laos, loan - 117
Malawi recognition - 149
Manila conf. - 202
Mongolia, border agrmt. - 118
Nepal, aid - 163
Nepal, treaty - 97
Netherlands recognition - 8
NLF aid plea answered - 155
North Viet Nam, aid - 74, 161, 168
Norway recognition - 8
Nuclear non-prolif. treaty - 205
Nuclear program - 129, 191, 208, 212, 216
Nuclear tests - 147, 159, 187, 202, 203, 213
Pakistan, pledge to - 131, 164
Pakistan: border agrmt. - 118, 120, 155; loan - 142; wheat - 212
Peasant revolt - 92
Regime's survival questioned - 199
Revolutionary wars - 196, 199
Rusk testimony, reaction - 177
Sabotage - 203
Sino-Soviet policy statement - 79
Soviet newsman expelled - 210
Soviet recognition - 47
Soviet students ousted - 198
Space program - 218
Sweden recognition - 8
Switzerland recognition - 8
Tanganyika, treaty - 141
Tanzania, treaty - 153
Test-ban treaty - 124, 191
Travel ban - 192
UN membership issue - 21, 22, 28, 49, 54, 66, 70, 75, 78, 88, 94, 100, 106, 109, 116, 129, 165, 167, 207; demand - 53
U.S.-Chinese trade - 211, 212
U.S. and East Europe - 201
U.S. peace offensive - 170
U.S. trade policy - 77, 80
U.S. in Viet Nam - 110, 184, 195, 196, 210, 212, 216
USIA report - 137
U.S.S.R., aid agrmt. - 91
U.S.S.R., trade agrmts. - 85, 91, 97, 103, 111, 121, 140, 157, 198
U.S.S.R., treaty - 49
Viet Nam cease-fire - 159
Viet Nam war entry - 153, 155, 160, 162
Warsaw talks, U.S. - 87, 88, 103, 119, 218
Yemen, treaty - 141
Zambia, Central African Rep., dipl. rel. est. - 146
see also - Cultural Revolution, Red Guard, Sino-Soviet Rift
CHINA, REPUBLIC OF (NA- TIONALIST)
  Acheson policy speech - 48

CHINA, REPUBLIC OF (NAT'L) (CONT.)
Anti-U.S. demon. - 42, 80
Arrival in Formosa - 48
ASPAC - 191
China lobby, factsheet - 23-28
Civil war - 37-48
Civil war truce - 39, 40
Communist threats - 41, 46, 53, 71, 72, 86
Const. - 37, 41, 44
Dulles statement - 70
Elections - 44
Established - 35
France, relations broken - 134
Govt. reorg. - 43
Great power status - 36
Indo-China, withdrawal - 39
Joins UN Security Coun. - 37
Laos, relations broken - 114
MacArthur statement - 53
Marshall report - 42
Nat'l. Assembly - 41, 44
Open rebellion proclaimed - 43
Pledge to U.S. - 72
Pol. Consultative Conf. - 39
Sino-Soviet agrmt. - 38
State of emergency - 85, 86
Truman policy - 8, 48
Two-China policy - 202
UN representation issue, 21, 22, 28, 49, 54, 66, 70, 75, 78, 88, 94, 100, 106, 109, 116, 129, 165, 167, 207
U.S.: aid program - 44, 45; arms aid - 43, 87; missiles installed - 80; pact - 15, 71; protection granted - 15-16; treaty - 17, 41, 73; war surpluses - 41; white paper - 47
U.S.S.R., relations broken - 47
U.S.S.R., treaty - 38
CHINA WHITE PAPER - 47, 11
CHINESE COMMUNIST PARTY (CCP)
Anti-rightist campaign - 82, 83, 84, 85, 191, 192
Appeal to UN - 41
Communist manifesto - 100
Intra-Party conflict - 199, 205, 207, 209
Land reform - 43
Origin - 7, 35
Plenary session rept. - 194
Policy declaration - 102
Purges - 186, 187, 188, 189, 190, 193, 194, 198, 209, 214
Red Guard ordered home - 207
Relations with KMT - 7, 35, 36
Revisionism denounced - 146
see also - Cultural Revolution, Red Guard, Sino-Soviet Rift
CHINESE LIBERATION ARMY - 172
CHINH, TRUONG - 180
CHOU EN-LAI
Africa tours - 131, 132, 133, 134, 159
Appeal to Red Guards - 197, 212
Asian tour - 78, 79
Bandung conf. - 74
Biog. - 228-229
Burma, Pakistan, Ceylon trip - 134, 135
Chinese economy - 114
Civil war negotiations - 41
Cultural revolution - 186, 191, 212, 215
Denounced - 214
Dropped in hierarchy - 207
Formosa negotiations - 74, 75, 79 80
Formosa threatened - 71, 72
Geneva conf. '54 - 68, 69
Geneva talks, U.S. - 86
Indian border dispute - 93, 94, 95, 97, 120
Interview - 148
Intl. disarmament meeting - 147
Korean negotiations - 64
Moscow trip - 148
Nuclear war danger - 125
"Peace pact" offer - 99
Premier, foreign minister - 47
Re-named politburo member - 194
Red Guard adviser - 196
Sino-Soviet policy statement - 79
Sino-Soviet talks - 62
Students ordered home - 219
Tibetan govt. dissolved - 92
U.S. denounced - 150
U.S. warned - 71, 168, 187
Viet Nam negotiations - 156
World parley proposed - 125
CHOU HSIN-FANG - 189
CHOW SHU-KAT
Biog. - 239
CHRONOLOG. CHART OF CHINESE HIST. - 29
CHU CHI-WEN - 211

CHU, NGUYEN XUAN - 149
CHU TEH - 207
Biog. - 239
CHUNG, HUH - 97
CHURCH, FRANK (D IDAHO) - 19, 20, 128, 129, 158
CHURCHILL, WINSTON - 36, 37, 60, 68, 69
CLAPP, GORDON R. - 24
CLARK, JOSEPH S. (D PA.) - 20, 158, 185
CLARK, MARK W. 61, 63
Biog. - 240
CLEMENTS, EARLE C. (D KY.) - 74
CLERGYMEN'S EMERGENCY COMM. ON CHINA - 24
CLUBB, O. EDMUND - 24
COFFIN, WILLIAM SLOANE - 24
COHELAN, JEFFERY (D CALIF.) - 192
COLEGROVE, ALBERT M. - 93
COLLINS, LAWTON - 62
COLOMBO CONFERENCE - 117
COMMERCE DEPT. - 132
COMM. TO DEFEND AMER. BY AIDING ANTI-COMMUNIST CHINA - 23
COMM. FOR A DEMO. FAR EASTERN POLICY - 23
COMM. ON NATL. AFFAIRS - 23
COMM. OF ONE MILLION - 24-25, 87, 98, 102
COMMITTEES, HOUSE
Foreign Affairs
Asian policy report - 22, 188
Bullitt testimony - 44
Chennault testimony - 44
China report - 45
Formosa resolution - 16
Marshall testimony - 44
Rusk testimony - 4, 184
Viet Nam aid - 19
Wedemeyer testimony - 44
Military Affairs
China trip, members - 43
COMMITTEES, SENATE
Appropriations
China in UN - 15
McNamara statement - 218
Armed Services
Acheson testimony - 57, 58
Far Eastern policy hearings - 13, 15, 57
Formosa resolution - 16
MacArthur inquiry - 57, 58, 59; testimony - 57
Marshall testimony - 57
McNamara statement - 218
Wake Island conf. report - 57
Wedemeyer report - 57; testimony - 58
Foreign Relations
Acheson testimony - 57, 58
Asia policy study - 17, 18
China policy hearings - 21-22, 179, 180, 181, 182, 183
China, security treaty - 17
Far Eastern policy hearings - 13, 15, 57
Foreign aid auth. - 129
Formosa resolution - 16
Korea, security treaty - 15
MacArthur inquiry - 57, 58, 59
MacArthur testimony - 57
Mansfield report - 20, 171; text - 261
Marshall testimony - 44, 57
McCarthy inquiry - 49, 50, 51, 53
Repub. criticism, Far East policy - 53
SEATO treaty - 70
Tydings subcomm. - 14
Viet Nam aid, reports - 18, 97, 120
Viet Nam hearings - 20, 93, 173, 174, 175, 176
Wake Island conf. report - 57
Wedemeyer testimony - 58
Judiciary
Anti-Viet Nam mov. - 166
Fairbank testimony - 60
Lattimore report - 61; testimony - 60
Rules and Administration
McCarthy report - 63, 64
COMMUNIST PARTY OF THE SOVIET UNION (CPSU) - 100, 108, 147, 182
see also - Sino-Soviet Rift
COMMUNIST YOUTH LEAGUE - 190
CONGO (STANLEYVILLE) - 149
CONGO, REPUBLIC OF (BRAZZA-VILLE) - 135

CONGRESS
General
Arms to China, res. - 12
Asia policy support - 203
China aid - 45, 46
Defense auth. - 192
Far East policy (factsheet) - 11-20
Foreign aid auth. - 180
Formosa resolution - 16, 72
Korean aggressor res. - 12, 55
Legislation on China (box) - 15
Tonkin Gulf resolution - 20, 143
Viet Nam suppl. approprs. - 20, 158, 163, 181
House
Bombing resumption - 173
China in UN, res. - 12, 17, 18, 106
Embassy constr. auth. - 156
Senate
Bombing resumption - 173
China treaty - 73
China in UN, res. - 18, 105
Defense, suppl. approps. - 178
McCarthy censured - 71
CONNOLLY, EUGENE - 24
CONNALLY, TOM T. (D TEXAS) - 11, 47
COOPER, JOHN SHERMAN (R KY.) - 87, 184
COTTON, NORRIS (R N.H.) - 100, 105
COUN. FOR MUTUAL ECO. ASSIST. (COMECON) - 85
COUVE DE MURVILLE, MAURICE - 157, 200
CRANKSHAW, EDWARD - 102
CUBA
China, trade agrmts. - 9, 99, 111, 151, 171
Dispute with China - 175
Invasion - 103
Missile crisis - 115, 116
Recognition of Peking - 100
CULTURAL REVOLUTION
Ambassadors ordered home - 215
Anti-Peng rally - 210
Appeal to defend Mao - 201
Army dissension - 217
Army warned - 211
Chen Yi denounced - 213
Chou denounced - 214
Control of army - 216
Creation - 9-10
Cultural purge - 186
Holidays canceled - 219
Intra-party conflict - 199, 205, 207, 209
Kuang Ya-ming purged - 191
Labor strikes - 215
Labor takeover - 213
Li Chi purged - 188
Liu, Teng denounced - 210, 212
Liu's confession - 213, 216
Lo Jui-ching purged - 193
Lu Ping, Peng Pei-yung purged - 189
Mao in minority - 10, 211, 215
New stage begun - 209
Newspaper reorg. - 216
Opposition to Mao - 10, 215, 216, 217, 218, 219
Peasants warned - 217
Peng Chen purged - 187, 189
Provincial battles - 218, 219
Reason for purge - 198
Red Guard arrests - 213, 215
Riots - 10, 215, 216, 218
Suicides rumored - 212
Tao Chu purged - 212
Teng Jo, Wu Han denounced - 187
Travel ban - 192
Trial of anti-Maoists - 208
Turning point - 216
Victory prediction - 214
Youth League, purge - 190
see also - Red Guard
CYPRUS - 167
CZECHOSLOVAKIA - 44, 146

D

DABERNAT, RENE - 216
DAHOMEY - 149
DALAI LAMA- 91, 92, 94
Biog. - 240
DAVIES, JOHN - 39
DE CASTRIES, CHRISTIAN - 68
Biog. - 240
DE GAULLE, CHARLES
Cambodia visit - 195, 196
Moscow visit - 191

Nuclear negotiations - 147, 148
Offer to Ho Chi Minh - 176
Premier - 85
Recognition of Peking - 134
Rusk meeting - 132
UN charter - 152
U.S. policy demounced - 203
Viet Nam - 142, 177
DE LACY, HUGH (D WASH.) - 24
DEAN, ARTHUR H. - 66, 73
Biog. - 240
DECLARATION OF HONOLULU - 175
DEFENSE DEPT.
Draft quota raised - 165, 193
Expend. (box) - 133
Formosa aid - 87
Thailand troops - 114
Tonkin Gulf crisis - 143
Viet Nam casualties - 110
Viet Nam, U.S. involve. - 110, 142
DEFENSE PRODUCTION ACT (1950) 51
DEMOCRATIC LEAGUE - 44
DENMARK - 8, 81, 176
DEWEY, GOV. THOMAS E. (R N.Y.) - 55
DIEM, NGO DINH
Biog. - 240
Martial law estab. - 126
Ouster - 129
Palace bombed - 111
Premier - 69
President - 75
Reunif., elections - 74, 77
Viet Nam war - 106, 115
DIENBIENPHU - 66, 67, 68
DIORI, HAMANI - 152
DIRKSEN, EVERETT M. (R ILL.)
Anti-Viet Nam movement - 166
China in UN - 18
China res. intro. - 104
Comm. of One Million - 87
Ford criticism of war - 184
McCarthy inquiry - 54
Viet Nam air war - 152
DO, TRAN VAN - 161
DODD, THOMAS J. (D CONN.) - 18, 25, 105, 136, 166
DOMINICK, PETER H. (R COLO.) - 25
DONG, PHAM VAN - 106, 152, 214
Biog. - 240
DOUGLAS, PAUL H. (D ILL.) - 25, 85, 87, 113
DOUGLAS, JUSTICE WILLIAM C. - 59, 113
Biog. - 240
DRUMRIGHT, EVERETT F. - 88
Biog. - 240
DULLES, JOHN FOSTER
Asian communism - 80
Brinkmanship - 76
China: blockade - 64; policy - 82; policy speech, text - 261; recognition - 17, 67, 79, 80, 84; travel ban - 79, 80, 83; UN membership - 66, 67, 69, 80; warned - 65, 73
Formosa cease-fire - 74, 89
Formosa, defense - 86, 88, 90
Formosa pact - 71
Geneva conf. '54 - 67, 68
Illness - 91
Indo-China, U.S. aid - 67
Indo-China war - 66
Korea, security treaty - 15
Massive retaliation doctrine - 66, 67
McCarthy denounced - 66
Resignation, death - 92
Southeast Asia policy - 67, 68
SEATO treaty - 70
DURAN, GUSTAVO - 14
DURBROW, ELBRIDGE - 93
Biog. - 240

E

EATON, CYRUS S. - 159
EDEN, ANTHONY - 69, 77
Biog. - 240
EDISON, GOV. CHARLES (D N.J.) - 25, 98
EDWARDS, DON (D CALIF.) - 163
EGYPT - 77, 176
EISENHOWER, PRES. DWIGHT D.
China: blockade - 64; disarmament - 97; security pact - 15; trade - 77, 81; UN membership - 15, 69, 88
Churchhill, talks - 69
Congressional telegram - 88
Elections - 63, 78
Formosa: defense - 86, 87, 88; protection - 16, 72; resolution - 72; visit - 99
Geneva Conf. '54 - 69
Illness - 75, 77
Inaug. - 64
Khrushchev letter - 86, 87, 88
Korea, security treaty - 15
Korea policy - 62
Korean trip - 63

EISENHOWER, PRES. DWIGHT D. (CONT.)
Laos, aid - 93
McCarthy re-elec. - 62
McCarthy, Senate censure - 71
Nominations - 62, 78
Nuclear weapons, Korea - 198, 199
Seventh fleet order rescinded - 64
Sino-Soviet rift - 99
Southeast Asia defense - 70
South Viet Nam, aid - 70, 80
U-2 incident - 98
U.S. in Indo-China - 65, 67
Viet Nam position - 16

ELEGANT, ROBERT S. 6-7, 209
ELLENDER, ALLEN J. (D LA.) - 81
EMERGENCY COMM. FOR CHINESE REFUGEES - 113
ERHARD, LUDWIG - 141
ETHIOPIA - 134, 160

F

FAIRBANK, JOHN K. - 4, 21, 24, 60, 179
Biog. - 240
China testimony, text - 284
Roundtable discussion on China, text - 317
FANFANI, AMINTORE - 168
FEDORENKO, NIKOLAI T. - 161
Biog. - 240
FELT, HARRY D. - 115, 141
FENG YU-HSIANG - 35
FERGUSON, HOMER (R MICH.) - 54
FIELD, FREDERICK VANDER-BILT - 27-28
FINLAND - 8
FLANDERS, RALPH E. (R VT.) - 16, 71
FORD, GERALD R. (R MICH.) - 161, 163, 184
FOREIGN AGENTS REGIS. ACT OF 1938 - 25
FORMOSA - 42
see also - China Republic of (Nationalist)
FRANCE
China, relations - 128
China trade - 6, 9, 81
China in UN - 161, 206
Chinese demon. - 219
French Communist party - 208
Geneva conf. '54 - 67, 68, 69
Geneva conf., Laos - 114
Geneva declaration '54 - 69
India, mil. aid - 116
Indo-China, conf. - 69
Indo-China, U.S. aid - 65, 67
Indo-China war - 41, 60, 66, 67, 68, 69, 70
NATO, withdrawal - 179
Recog. of Peking - 8, 133
SEATO - 70
Viet Nam indepen. pledged - 68
FRANDSEN, JULIUS - 80
FRANK, WALDO - 96
FRANKEL, MAX - 205
FRAZIER, E. FRANKLIN - 24
FREEMAN, FULTON - 39
FREEMAN, ORVILLE L. - 175
FULBRIGHT, J. WILLIAM (D ARK.)
Appeal to Senate - 193
Bombing moratorium - 166
China: policy - 11; policy hearings - 21, 179; recognition - 17, 18; UN membership - 100
Far East policy speech - 19, 136; text - 273
Roundtable discussion on China, text - 317
Thailand hearings - 196
Travel res. intro. - 83
Viet Nam: consequences - 186; policy hearings - 174, 176; policy speeches - 20, 160, 185, 186; proposals - 217
FULTON, JAMES G. (R PA.) - 12

G

GAFUROV, BOBODZHAN G. - 137
Biog. - 240
GAITSKELL, HUGH - 87
GALBRAITH, JOHN KENNETH - 116, 185

GANDHI, INDIRA - 148, 172
Biog. - 240
GANDHI, MOHANDAS K. - 44
GARCIA, CARLOS P. - 104
GARDNER, JOHN W. - 175
GARSIDE, B.A. - 25
GAVIN, JAMES M. - 20, 172, 175
Biog. - 240
GENEVA CONF. OF 1954 - 67, 68, 69
GENEVA DECLARATION OF 1954 - 18, 69
GEORGE, WALTER F. (D GA.) - 17, 72, 74
GERMANY, WEST - 9, 120, 181
GHANA - 117, 133, 178, 179
GIAP, VO NGUYEN - 174, 212
Biog. - 240
GILMORE, ROBERT - 24
GLENN, JOHN H. - 110
GOLD, BEN - 24
GOLDBERG, ARTHUR J.
Appeal to Thant - 211
China policy - 182
China in UN - 22, 165, 185, 205
De-escalation of war - 198
U.S. ambass. to UN, appt. - 161
Viet Nam peace mission - 169
Viet Nam peace negotiations - 162, 185, 199
Viet Nam res. - 173
GOLDWATER, BARRY (R ARIZ.) - 133, 142
GOMPERTS, JACK - 24
GOMULKA, WLADYSLAW - 105
GOODWIN, WILLIAM J. - 25
GORE, ALBERT (D TENN.) - 17, 158, 185
GOULART, JOAO - 137
GREAT BRITAIN
China trade - 5, 6, 9, 77, 80, 81, 148; delegation - 120
Formosa policy - 87
Geneva conf. '54 - 67, 68, 69
Geneva conf., Laos - 114, 140
Geneva declaration '54 - 69
India, mil. aid - 116
Laos cease-fire, Geneva conf. called - 103
Nuclear materials prod. - 138
Recog. of Peking - 8, 48
SEATO - 70; Viet Nam - 158
Space treaty - 208-209
Test-ban talks, treaty - 124, 125
Viet Nam, Commonwealth mission - 124
Viet Nam proposal - 214
GREAT LEAP FORWARD - 9, 192, 194, 205
GREAT PROLETARIAN CULTURAL REVOLUTION - *see* Cultural Revolution
GREEN, THEODORE F. (D R.I.) - 14, 17, 79, 87
GREW, JOSEPH C. - 25
GRIFFITH, SAMUEL B. II - 180
GROMYKO, ANDREI A. - 109, 114, 125, 139, 157, 165, 205
GRONOUSKI, JOHN A. - 218
Biog. - 240
GROSS, ERNEST A. - 62
GROSS, H.R. (R IOWA) - 143
GRUENING, ERNEST (D ALASKA) - 20, 136, 143, 178
GUINEA - 133

H

HALBERSTAM, DAVID - 129
HALPERIN, MORTON H. - 24, 181
HAMMARSKJOLD, DAG - 71, 72, 74, 106
Biog. - 240
HAN HSIEN-CHU
Biog. 240
HANSON, HALDORE - 14, 50
HARRIMAN, W. AVERELL
Chinese refugees - 112
Election defeat - 90
NLF and peace negotiations - 174
Sino-Indian border dispute - 116
Test-ban treaty - 124
Viet Nam peace negotiations - 205
Warsaw mission - 169
HARRISON, WILLIAM K. JR. - 61
HART, PHILIP A. (D MICH.) - 169
HASSAN, KING - 132
HAYDEN, THOMAS - 171
Biog. - 241
HEAD, DAVID C., REV. - 24
HÉBERT, F. EDWARD (D LA.) - 163
HELMS, RICHARD - 216

HENDRICKSON, ROBERT C. (R N.J.) - 51
HERSEY, JOHN - 24
HERSEY, LEWIS B. - 169, 173
HERTER, CHRISTIAN A. - 83, 92, 93, 94, 95
HICKENLOOPER, BOURKE B. (R IOWA) - 14, 18, 25, 54, 83, 105
HILSMAN, ROGER - 24, 131
Biog. - 241
HINTON, HAROLD C. - 181
China testimony, text - 292
HISS, ALGER - 45
HO CHI MINH - *see* Minh, Ho Chi
HO LUNG - 113, 217
Biog. - 241
HO WEI - 191
Biog. - 241
HO YING-CHIN - 46, 47
Biog. - 241
HOBERECHT, EARNEST - 48
HOLLAND, SPESSARD L. (D FLA.) - 12
HOLLAND, WILLIAM L. - 24
HOME, LORD - 102, 109, 114, 125
HONG KONG - 9
HOOVER, HERBERT JR. - 77
HOXHA, ENVER - 103, 109
Biog. - 241
HSIAO HUA - 172, 217
Biog. - 241
HSIEH, ALICE L.
Roundtable discussion on China, text - 317
HSIEH FU-CHIN
Biog. - 241
HSU KSIANG-CHIEN
Biog. - 241
HUGHES, EMMET JOHN - 207
HUMPHREY, VICE PRES. HUBERT H.
Asian tour - 176
China and disarmament - 82
China policy - 4, 180, 189
Dulles brinkmanship - 76
Formosa policy - 17, 89
Formosa res. - 16, 72
Kennedy (R.F.) proposal - 177, 178
Nomination - 120
Offshore Islands res. - 73
Viet Nam approps. - 20
Viet Nam policy - 189
HUNGARY - 206
HUNTLEY, CHET - 127

HUONG, TRAN VAN - 147, 149, 151, 152
Biog. - 241
HURLEY, PATRICK J. - 36, 38, 47, 58
Biog. - 241

I

ILYICHEV, LEONID F. - 123
INDIA
Aid appeal - 116
China, border dispute - 93, 94, 95, 96, 97, 111, 114, 115, 116, 124, 151, 167
China in UN - 116
Colombo proposals - 119
Geneva conf., Laos - 114, 140
Independence - 43
Kashmir dispute - 162, 164, 165
Sino-Pakistan talks protested - 113
Tashkent agreement - 172
U.S. mil. aid - 116, 122
U.S. wheat shipment - 212
U.S.S.R. pledge - 148
INDO-CHINA WAR
Armistice agreements - 69
Casualties - 70
Dienbienphu - 66, 67, 68
French-Chinese meeting - 69
Geneva conf. '54 - 67, 68
Outbreak - 41
U.S. involvement - 65, 67
Washington conf. - 60
INDONESIA
Abortive coup - 165
American prop. seized - 155
Anti-Chinese riots - 122, 168, 178, 184
Anti-U.S. riots - 162
Ban on Communists - 166
Colombo conf. - 117
Indonesian Communist party (PKI) - 165, 166, 180
Sukarno, loses power - 180, 192
UN, withdrawal - 151
World Peace Council - 131

INSTIT. OF PACIFIC RELATIONS - 24
INTERNL. CONTROL COMM. - 104, 121, 129, 140, 174
IRAN - 167
ITALY - 22, 81, 176, 201
IVES, IRVING M. (R N.Y.) - 51

J

JACKSON, HENRY M. (D WASH.) - 18, 96, 169
JAFFE, PHILIP - 59
JAMAICA - 167
JAPAN
ASPAC - 191
China attack - 36
China, trade - 9, 117
Japanese Communists - 189
Manchuria occupation - 36
Peace treaty - 59
Pearl Harbor attack - 36
U.S.S.R. declaration of war - 37
Surrender - 38
JAVITS, JACOB K. (R N.Y.)
Appeal to Admin. - 200
Comm. of One Million - 87, 211
Fulbright speech - 187
NLF and peace negotiations - 175
Viet Nam approps. - 20, 158
Viet Nam peace negotiations - 185
JENNER, WILLIAM E. (R IND.) - 12, 56
JESSUP, PHILIP C. - 14, 47, 49, 59
Biog. - 241
JOHNSON, BYRON L. (D COLO.) - 17
JOHNSON, HAROLD - 141
JOHNSON, LOUIS A. - 58
Biog. - 241
JOHNSON, PRES. LYNDON BAINES
Asian policy speech, text - 333
Asian trips - 104, 202, 203
Assumed office - 130
China policy - 4, 138, 151, 192
China trade - 81
China in UN - 69
Chinese nuclear test - 147
Declaration of Honolulu - 175
Defense auth. - 192
Dispute with Ford - 163
Election - 148
Formosa negotiations - 74
Honolulu conf. - 175
Illness - 74
Johns Hopkins speech - 156
Manila conf. - 201, 202
Nominations - 99, 145
Nuclear materials prod. - 138
Southeast Asia, aid - 20, 159
Space treaty - 208
State of Union Message '66 - 172
Tonkin Gulf crisis - 143
Travel restrictions eased - 179
Two-China policy - 193
UN address - 161
U.S. as Pacific power - 192
U.S. power - 187
Viet Nam: aid requests - 19, 20, 140, 158, 162, 172, 208; air war - 152, 157, 173, 191, 214; buildup ordered - 156, 162; expansion of war - 146; French report - 200; peace efforts - 155, 157, 162, 168, 169, 214; policy - 16, 140, 142, 155, 191, 215; policy support - 162, 173, 180; reply to critics - 177, 188; troop withdrawal - 196; U.S. involvement - 132, 134, 135, 158
JOHNSON, U. ALEXIS - 75, 85, 200
Biog. - 241
JOY, CHARLES TURNER - 58
Biog. - 241
JUDD, WALTER H. (R MINN.) - 11, 21-22, 23, 25, 113, 182
Biog. - 241
China testimony, text - 294
JUSTICE DEPT. - 25

K

KALTENBORN, H.V. - 87
KANG SHENG - 194
Biog. - 242
KARNOW, STANLEY - 194, 199, 204, 211

KASHMIR - 162, 164, 165
KATZENBACH, NICHOLAS DE B. 166
KAWAWA, RASHIDI - 141
KEARNS, HARRY - 84
KEATING, KENNETH B. (R N.Y.) - 87
KEFAUVER, ESTES (D TENN.) - 16, 17, 73, 74, 78
KEITA, MODIBO - 133, 146
KENNAN, GEORGE F. - 20, 175, 219
KENNEDY, EDWARD M. (D MASS.) - 193
KENNEDY, PRES. JOHN F.
  Asia policy - 113
  Assassination - 130
  Atmospheric tests - 111, 123
  Atomic tests - 106
  Candidacy - 96
  China: disarmament - 110; food for - 102, 103, 112; policy statement - 103; threat - 125; trade - 130
  Chinese refugees - 112
  Cuban missile crisis - 115, 116
  Diem regime, assessment - 129
  Election - 100
  Formosa policy - 17, 87, 105, 111, 114
  Inaug. - 101
  Khrushchev meeting - 104
  Kennedy-Nixon debates - 100
  Laos cease-fire, negotiations - 112
  Laos policy - 103, 110, 121
  Macmillan, talks - 103
  Nomination - 99
  Test-ban treaty - 124, 125
  Thailand, troops - 112
  UN address - 106
  U.S.-Chinese relations - 104
  Viet Nam, McNamara-Taylor rept. - 128
  Viet Nam position - 16, 127
  Viet Nam, U.S. involve. - 110, 117, 122, 124, 127
KENNEDY, ROBERT F. (D N.Y.) - 169, 176, 177, 178, 185
KENYA - 140, 179
KENYATTA, JOMO - 146
KENYON, DOROTHY - 14
KERR, CLARK - 24
KHAMPAN PANYA - 93
KHAN, MOHAMMED AYUB - 134, 154, 172
  Biog. - 238
KHANH, NGUYEN
  Biog. - 242
  Compromise declaration - 151
  Coup - 133
  Govt. crisis - 145
  National coun. appt. - 147
  North Viet Nam, invasion - 142
  Ouster - 153
  Plot charged - 135
  State of emergency - 143
KHIEM, TRAN THIEN - 145, 149
  Biog. - 242
KHRUSHCHEV, NIKITA S.
  Biog. - 242
  Coexistence - 99
  Cuba, Chinese position - 117
  Cuban missile crisis - 116
  Emergence - 73
  Kennedy-Khrushchev meeting - 104
  Letter to Eisenhower - 86, 88
  Nuclear materials prod. - 138
  Ouster - 147
  Sino-Soviet relations - 95, 134, 137, 138
  Test-ban treaty - 124
  Thailand, U.S. troops - 112
  20th party Cong. speech - 77
  U-2 incident - 98
  U.S. visit - 94
KI-POONG, LEE - 97
KIM IL SUNG - 128
  Biog. - 242
KITTIKACHORN, THANOM - 151
KNIGHT, GOV. GOODWIN J. (R CALIF.) - 90
KNOWLAND, WILLIAM F. (R CALIF.)
  Acheson appt. - 11
  Biog. - 242
  China: aid - 12; blockade - 15; policy - 11; trade - 80, 81; travel ban - 83; U.S. treaty - 73; UN membership - 15, 69, 75, 78
  Comm. of One Million - 87
  Formosa - 48
  Formosa negotiations - 74
  MacArthur dismissal - 56
  Offshore Islands res. - 73
KOHLBERG, ALFRED - 23, 24
KOHLER, FOY D. - 169, 200
  Biog. - 242
KOIRALA, B.P. - 97
KON, CHOI YONG - 128

KONG LE - 99, 113, 121
  Biog. - 242
KOO, WELLINGTON
  Biog. - 242
KOREA, NORTH
  Chinese troop withdrawal - 84
  Communist party - 194, 198
  Geneva conf. '54 - 67, 68
  North Viet Nam, aid - 161
  UN res., unification - 79, 109
  World Peace Council - 131
  see also - Korean Conflict
KOREA, SOUTH
  Anti-govt. riots - 141
  ASPAC - 191
  Coup - 104
  Geneva conf. '54 - 67, 68, 69
  Manila conf. - 202
  Troop offer - 67
  UN res., unification - 79, 109
  U.S. Treaty - 15
  see also - Korean Conflict
KOREAN CONFLICT
  Armistice - 65
  Casualties - 19 (box), 65
  Geneva conf. '54 - 67, 68, 69
  Invasion of South - 51
  Negotiations - 58, 59, 60, 61, 62, 63, 64, 65
  Political conf. planned - 65, 66
  POW issue - 61, 62, 63, 64, 65, 67
  Prisoner riots - 61
  Summary of events (box) - 52
  UN atrocity res. - 66
KOSYGIN, ALEKSEI N.
  Biog. - 242
  China accused - 201
  French visit - 207, 208
  Hanoi visit - 152
  Kashmir dispute, mediation - 165
  North Viet Nam, support - 159
  Premier - 147
  U.S.-Soviet relations - 208
KOZLOV, FROL - 117
  Biog. - 242
KUANG YA-MING - 191
  Biog. - 242
KUBLAI KHAN - 4
KUN, CHOE YONG - 123
KUO MO-JO - 124, 186
  Biog. - 242
KUOMINTANG - 7, 35, 36, 44
KUOMINTANG REVOLUTIONARY COMM. - 81
KUUSINEN, OTTO V.
  Biog. - 242
KY, NGUYEN CAO
  Biog. - 242
  Buddhist-govt. agrmt. - 189
  Cabinet enlarged - 177
  Danang, Hue unrest - 183, 188, 189
  Khanh supported - 146
  Letter to Thant - 200
  North Viet Nam, invasion - 193
  Premier - 161
  Viet Nam peace negotiations - 202, 215

L

LANE, THOMAS J. (D MASS.) - 103
LANGER, WILLIAM (R N.D.) - 11, 16, 17, 72
LANIEL, JOSEPH - 68
  Biog. - 242
LAOS
  Appeals to UN - 93, 94, 101
  ASPAC - 191
  Cease-fire - 121
  China, dipl. rel. established - 114
  China loan - 117
  Coalition govt. formed - 110, 113, 114
  Coups - 99, 138
  Geneva conf. '54 - 68
  Geneva conf., Laos - 104, 114, 140
  Geneva declaration '54 - 69
  Govt. collapse - 101
  Indo-China armistice - 69
  Neutrality statement - 102
  Pathet Lao attacks - 92, 111, 112
  SEATO treaty - 70
  State of emergency - 93
  U.S. mil. advisors withdrawn - 115
  Viet Minh invasion - 67; resistance - 64
LAPORTE, ROBERT ALLEN - 166
LATTIMORE, OWEN
  Biog. - 242
  Charge dismissed - 69
  Govt. case dropped - 74
  Indictment - 63
  Institute of Pacific Rel. - 24
  McCarthy charges - 14, 24, 49, 50
  Testimony - 60

LEHMAN, HERBERT H. (D N.Y.) - 16, 17, 72, 73
LEMAY, CURTIS - 166
  Biog. - 243
LI, DUN J. - 4, 6, 8
LI CHI - 188
LI FUCHUN
  Biog. - 243
LI HSUEH-FENG - 189, 203, 204, 205
  Biog. - 243
LI TSUNG-JEN - 44, 45, 46, 48, 49, 161
  Biog. - 243
LIBERAL PROJECT - 96
LIBYA - 167
LIE, TRYGVE - 49, 51, 63
  Biog. - 243
LIEBMAN, MARVIN - 25, 87, 211
LIN PIAO
  Appeal to Red Guards - 197
  Biog. - 227-228
  Formosa - 94
  New position - 194, 200, 207, 215
  People's wars, article, text - 324
  Policy statement - 164
  Purge - 190, 194, 209
  Red Guard leader - 9, 196
  Successor to Mao - 187
LIN TSE-HSU - 6
LINDBECK, JOHN - 180
LIPPMANN, WALTER - 47
LIU CHIEH - 202
LIU PO-CHANG
  Biog. - 243
LIU SHAO-CHI
  Biog. - 229-231
  Burma visit - 121
  Cambodia, North Viet Nam trip - 122
  Confession - 213, 216
  Denounced - 203, 206, 210, 212, 213
  Dropped in heirarchy - 10, 194, 207, 209

  Politburo member - 194
  President - 92
  Purge - 190, 205
  Soviet leaders, criticism - 128

  U.S. warned - 193
LIU SHAO-CHI, MME. - 213, 215
LLOYD, SELWYN - 88
LO JUI-CHING
  Anti-rightist campaign - 84
  Biog. - 243
  Death demanded - 2?3
  Named revionist - 210
  Purge - 189, 192, 193, 208
  Suicide rumored - 212, 217
LU LUNG-CHI - 84
  Biog. - 243
LODGE, HENRY CABOT
  China in UN - 88
  Honolulu meeting - 140
  MacArthur dismissal - 56
  McCarthy investig. - 14
  Pres'l. mission - 143
  Resignation - 141
  U.S. Ambass., South Viet Nam - 123, 161
  U.S.S.R. indictment - 64
LOEB, WILLIAM - 23
LONG MARCH - 36
LONG, RUSSELL B. (D LA.) - 15, 72, 73, 157
LOVESTONE, JAY - 23
LOVETT, ROBERT - 46, 59
  Biog. - 243
LOWENSTEIN, ALLARD K. - 24
LU PING - 189
  Biob. - 243
LU TING-YI - 192, 208, 210, 212, 213
  Bigo. - 243
LUCE, HENRY R. - 27
LUNG YUN - 81
  Bigo. - 243
LYND, STAUGHTON - 171, 172, 174
  Biog. - 243

M

MACAO - 207, 208
MAC ARTHUR, DOUGLAS
  Congressl. address - 12, 13, 57
  Korea, statement - 61
  Report to UN - 54
  Senate inquiry - 59
  Testimony - 57
  Truman dismisses - 12, 56, 57
  UN Commander, Korea - 53
  Wake Island conf. - 54
  Warning to UN - 56
MACMILLAN, HAROLD - 87, 103, 112, 116
MAGNUSON, WARREN G. (D WASH.) - 81
MAGRUDER, CARTER B. - 104
MALAWI - 145, 149
MALAYA - 9
MALAYSIA - 191

MALENKOV, GEORGI M. - 65, 72, 109
  Biog. - 243
MALI - 133
MALIK, ADAM - 217
MALIK, JACOB A. - 48, 53, 58
  Biog. - 244
MALINOVSKY, RODION Y. - 204
MALRAUX, ANDRE - 162
MANCHU DYNASTY - 7
MANCHUKUO - 36
MANCHURIA
  Independence - 36
  Nationalist-Communist hostilities - 38, 39, 40, 42, 44, 45
  Occupied - 36
MANSFIELD, MIKE (D MONT.)
  Anti-Viet Nam mov. - 166
  China: resolution - 104; travel ban - 83; UN membership - 18
  China lobby investg. - 11, 12
  Comm. of One Million - 87
  Dulles brinkmanship - 76
  Indo-China tour - 65
  Laos aid - 101
  Southeast Asia policy - 113
  Viet Nam: air war - 152, 173; extended truce proposed - 169; peace negotiations - 164, 185, 191; reports - 18, 19, 20, 120, 171
  Viet Nam report, text - 261
MAO TSE-TUNG
  Biog. - 223-227
  Cabinet dismissals - 84
  CCP leadership - 36
  CCP organized - 7, 35
  Chairman of Rep. resign. - 91, 214
  Chiang, agrmt. - 38
  China white paper, criticism - 47
  Civil war truce - 39
  Eight point program - 46
  Essays, text - 328
  "Hundred Flowers" speech - 81
  Inter-party conflict - 207, 209
  Long March - 8, 36
  Meeting with Albanians - 187
  Orders to army - 193
  Peking rally - 194
  Policy papers - 47
  Red Guard opposition - 201
  Report to CCP - 44
  Southern China dominated - 7-8, 36
  Swim - 91, 193
  Viet Nam position - 126
MAP - 30-31
MARCOS, FERDINAND E. - 197
MARSHALL, CLIFFORD B. - 24
MARSHALL, GEORGE C.
  China: arms aid - 43; aid program - 44, 45; civil war mediation - 39, 41; policy directives - 45; report - 42
  Comm. of One Million - 87
  Death - 95
  Institute of Pacific Rel. - 24
  Meeting with Chou En-Lai - 41
  Presl. rep., China - 38
  Resignation - 59
  Secy. of State - 42
  Testimony - 57
MARTIN, JOSEPH W. JR. (R MASS.) - 56
MARTIN, PAUL - 22, 206
MASSEMBA-DEBAT, ALPHONSE - 146
MC CARRAN, PAT (D NEV.) - 11, 24, 46, 60
MC CARRAN-WALTER ACT - 112
MC CARTHY, JOSEPH R. (R WIS.)
  Charges - 49, 50, 59, 51, 63
  Death - 14, 80
  Far East policy - 12, 14
  Lattimore case - 14
  MacArthur dismissal - 12, 56
  Renomination - 62
  Senate censure - 14, 71
  Truman denounced - 12
MC CLELLAN, JOHN L. (D ARK.) - 12
MC CLOSKEY, ROBERT J. - 159, 160, 166, 185, 193
MC CONE, JOHN A. - 140
MC CORMACK, JOHN W. (D MASS.) - 12
MC ELROY, NEIL H. - 87, 89
  Biog. - 244
MC FARLAND, ERNEST W. (D ARIZ.) - 12
MC GEE, GALE W. (D WYO.) - 200
MC KEE, FREDERICK C. - 23
MC MAHON, BRIEN (D CONN.) - 12, 14, 50, 58
MC NAMARA, ROBERT S.
  Chinese nuclear capability - 179
  Honolulu conf. - 175
  Honolulu meeting - 140
  Posture statements - 177, 218
  Secy. of Defense - 101
  Sino-Soviet rift - 133
  Soviet ABM system - 205
  Tonkin Gulf crisis - 143
  Viet Nam air war - 152, 157, 191
  Viet Nam defense funds - 20

MC NAMARA, ROBERT S. (CONT.)
  Viet Nam missions, reports - 128, 132, 135, 139, 161, 167
  Viet Nam, U.S. involve. - 133, 138, 153, 160, 190, 204
MENDES-FRANCE, PIERRE - 68, 69
  Biog. 244
MENON, MRS. LAKSHI - 111
MENON, V.K. KRISHNA - 74, 115
  Biog. - 244
MEYER, WILLIAM H. (D VT.) - 17
MIAO CHEN-PAI - 195
MICHAEL, FRANZ
  China article, text - 312
MILLER, DAVID J. - 165
MILLER, JACK (R IOWA) - 169
MILLER, WILLIAM E. (R N.Y.) - 142
MINH, DUONG VAN - 129, 132, 145
  Biog. - 244
MINH, HO CHI
  Biog. - 244
  Four-point proposal - 163
  Indo-China war - 42, 56
  Letter to Pauling - 167
  Liu, joint statement - 122
  Soviets praised - 183
  U.S. withdrawal demanded - 185
  Viet Minh peace bid - 66
  Viet Nam peace negotiations - 168, 193
  War capability - 203
MISSIONARIES - 5, 6
MOLOTOV, V.M. - 39, 42, 68, 77, 109
  Biog. - 244
MONRONEY, A.S. MIKE (D OKLA.) - 87
MORGAN, THOMAS E. (D PA.) - 25, 86
MORGENTHAU, HANS J. - 183
  Biog. - 244
MOROCCO - 132
MORRISON, NORMAN R. - 166
MORSE, WAYNE (D ORE.)
  China lobby investg. - 25, 58
  China, treaty - 17, 73
  China in UN - 100, 105
  Declaration of Conscience - 51
  Defense funds - 178, 192
  Far East policy - 15
  Formosa, defense - 88
  Formosa res. - 16, 72
  MacArthur dismissal - 56
  Offshore Islands res. intro. - 73
  Taylor testimony - 176
  Tonkin Gulf res. - 143
  Viet Nam: air war - 152; approps. - 158, 180; expansion of war - 149; position - 20, 136, 157; protest rally - 160
MOSCOW CONFERENCE - 39
MOW, P.T. - 25
MOYERS, BILL - 163, 166, 172, 177
MURROW, EDWARD R. - 79
MUTUAL DEFENSE ASSIST. ACT OF 1949 - 12

N

NAM IL - 58
  Biog. - 244
NAN HAN-CHEN - 148, 153
  Biog. - 244
NANDA, G.L. - 140
  Biog. - 244
NASSER, GAMAL ABDEL - 77, 131
NASUTION, ABDUL HARIS - 165, 177
  Biog. - 244
NATIONAL COMM. ON U.S.-CHINA - 24, 190
NATIONAL COUN. OF CHURCHES - 168
NATIONAL LIBERATION FRONT (NLF)
  Aid requests - 162
  Chinese aid offer - 155
  Interview - 196, 198
  Truce extension rejected - 210
  Truce offers - 168, 214
  U.S. concession on representation - 174
NATIONAL SECURITY COUNCIL - 65, 136, 152
NEHRU, JAWAHARLAL
  Biog. - 244
  China border dispute - 93, 94, 95, 96, 97, 111, 114, 115, 117, 120
  China trip - 70
  Colombo proposals - 119
  Death - 140
  Formosa Crises - 74
  Korean cease-fire - 56
  Tibet, revolt - 92
NELSON, GAYLORD A. (D WIS.) - 20, 158
NEPAL - 6, 97, 163
NETHERLANDS - 8
NEW ZEALAND - 70, 158, 191, 202
NHU, NGO DINH - 19, 125, 126
NHU, MME. NGO DINH - 19, 125, 127, 128, 129, 130
NIGER - 152
NIGERIA - 160

NIXON, VICE PRES. RICHARD M.
  Asian peace conf. proposed - 195
  Asian trip - 138
  Elections - 63, 78
  Far East policy - 87
  Indo-China, U.S. involve. - 68
  Kennedy-Nixon debates - 100
  Nominations - 62, 78, 99
  Truman, Acheson accused - 69
  Viet Nam trip - 77
NKRUMAH, KWAME - 133, 160, 178, 179
NOLTING, FREDERICK E. JR. - 111, 123, 125
  Biog. - 244
NORTH ATLANTIC TREATY ORGANIZATION (NATO) - 179
NORWAY - 8, 176
NOVIKOV, VLADIMIR N. - 200
NU, U - 101, 111
  Biog. - 244
NYERERE, JULIUS K. - 159

O

OANCIA, DAVID - 203, 204, 206, 210, 214, 215, 217
OANH, NGUYEN XUAN - 145, 152, 153
  Biog. - 244
O'DONNELL, EMMETT - 58
OFFSHORE ISLANDS
  British policy - 87
  Casualties - 88
  Chiang statement - 88, 89
  Communist cease-fire - 88, 89
  Invasion - 72
  Nationalist withdrawal - 72
  Shelled - 71, 86, 90
  State of emergency - 85
  U.S. position - 7, 86, 87
OPEN DOOR POLICY - 7
OPIUM WAR - 5-6
OUM, BOUN (PRINCE) - 110, 113
  Biog. - 238
OUTER MONGOLIA - 38, 118

P, Q

PAKISTAN
  China, border agree. - 118, 120
  China pledge - 131, 164
  Chinese loan - 142
  Chinese wheat shipment - 212
  Independence - 43
  Kashmir dispute - 162, 164, 165
  SEATO - 70; Viet Nam - 158
  Tashkent agreement - 172
  U.S. wheat shipment - 212
PALAR, LAMBERTUS N. - 151
  Biog. - 244
PAN TZU-LI - 119
PANCHEN LAMA - 92, 95
  Biog. - 244
PANYA, KHAMPHAN - 94
  Biog. - 244
PARK, CHUNG HEE - 141
  Biog. - 244
PASTORE, JOHN O. (D R.I.) - 200
PATRIOTIC FRONT - 132
PAULING, LINUS - 167
  Biog. - 244
PEARL HARBOR - 36
PEARSON, LESTER - 169
PEIPING (BOX) - 147
PEKING (BOX) - 147
PENG CHEN
  Biog. - 246
  Death demanded - 213
  Moscow mission - 122
  Named revisionist - 219
  Purge - 187, 189, 190, 195, 208
PENG PEI-YUNG - 189
PENG TEH-HUAI - 88, 213, 216
  Biog. - 245
PENG-YUNG - 189
PEOPLES LIBERATION ARMY - 211, 216, 217, 218, 219
PHILIPPINES - 70, 158, 191, 197, 202
PHOLSENA, QUINIM - 121
PHOUI SANANIKONE - 93
PHOUMA, SOUVANNA - see Souvanna Phouma
PINEAU, CHRISTIAN
  Biog. - 245
PO I-PO - 215
  Biog. - 245
PODGORNY, NIKOLAI V. - 130, 169, 174
  Biog. - 245

POLAND - 114, 138, 140, 168, 199
POLING, REV. DANIEL A. - 24
POLO, MARCO - 4-5
POPE PAUL VI - 168, 169, 215
PORTER, CHARLES O. (D ORE.) - 17, 96
PORTUGAL - 5
POTSDAM CONFERENCE - 37
POTTER, CHARLES E. (R MICH.) - 82
PRESIDENTS' POSITIONS AND ACTIONS ON VIET NAM (BOX) - 16
PROLETARIAN CULTURAL REVOLUTION - see Cultural Revolution
PU YI - 7, 35, 36
  Biog. - 245
QUANG, THICH TRI - 154, 183, 184
  Biog. - 245
QUAT, PHAM HUY - 111, 153, 160
QUEMOY-MATSU - see Offshore Islands
QUIRINO, ELPIDIO - 47
  Biog. - 245

R

RADFORD, ARTHUR W. - 67, 76
  Biog. - 245
RANDOLPH, A. PHILIP - 24
RAU, BENEGAL N. - 55
  Biog. - 245
RAYBURN, SAM (D TEXAS) - 16
RED GUARD
  Anti-Mao activity - 201
  Anti-Maoists warned - 217
  Cautioned - 195, 205
  Chen Yi denounced - 201, 213
  Chou denounced - 214
  Churches closed - 212
  Deaths demanded - 213
  Demonstrations - 204
  Intra-group conflict - 203, 206, 217
  Leadership - 196
  Li Hsueh-feng denounced - 203, 204
  Liu Shao-chi denounced - 203, 206
  Opposition - 197
  Ordered home - 207
  Origin - 9
  Peking rallies - 197, 201, 204, 205, 206
  Peking stores closed - 217
  Peng Teh-huai arrested - 213
  Po I-Po arrested - 215
  Rampages - 10, 195, 198, 201, 207, 209, 215, 218
  Soviets denounced - 198
  Strong report - 202
  Tao Chu denounced - 204, 213, 214
  Teng Hsiao-ping denounced - 203
  Workers join - 210
  Wu Teh denounced - 203
REEDY, GEORGE - 153
REISCHAUER, EDWIN O. - 219
REPUB. PLANNING AND RESEARCH COMM. WHITE PAPER - 163
REUSS, HENRY S. (D WIS.) - 143
RHEE, SYNGMAN - 62, 65, 70, 97
  Biog. - 245
RIBICOFF, ABRAHAM A. (D CONN.) - 175
RICCI, MATTEO - 5
RICHARDSON, JOHN HAMMOND
  Biog. - 245
RIDGWAY, MATTHEW B. - 56, 58, 61, 175
  Biog. - 245
RINGWALT, ARTHUR - 39
RIVERS, L. MENDEL (D S.C.) - 162
ROBERTSON, WALTER S. - 65, 90, 91, 94
  Biog. - 245
ROBESON, PAUL - 24
ROCKEFELLER BROTHERS FUND - 96
ROCKEFELLER, GOV. NELSON A. - 90
ROOSEVELT, ELEANOR (MRS. FRANKLIN D.) - 82
ROOSEVELT, PRES. FRANKLIN D. - 36, 37
ROWE, DAVID NELSON - 182
  China testimony, text - 303
RUMANIA - 135, 142
RUSK, DEAN
  Asian policy - 135, 184
  Biog. - 245
  China policy - 4

China testimony, text - 263
China in UN - 197
Chinese nuclear capability - 146, 208
Chinese proposal rejected - 187
De Gaulle, talks - 132
European aid to China - 181
Formosa policy - 102
Geneva conf., Laos - 104, 114
Honolulu conf. - 175
Honolulu meeting - 140
Indonesia, relations - 136
Pledge to Chiang - 192
Rockefeller rept., foreign policy - 96
Secy. of State - 101
Sino-Soviet rift - 111
Test-ban treaty - 125
Viet Nam: air war - 157; approps. - 20; peace negotiations - 163, 173; peace offensive - 169; policy defended - 173; trip - 138; U.S. involvement - 121, 141, 176, 194
RUSSELL, MAUD - 24
RUSSELL, RICHARD B. (D GA.) - 13, 15, 59, 149, 173, 183, 185
RUSTIN, BAYARD - 24
RWANDA - 167
RYAN, WILLIAM F. (D N.Y.) - 18, 106

S

SALINGER, PIERRE - 113
SALISBURY, HARRISON - 98, 212, 213, 214, 215
SALLAL, ABDULLAH AL - 141
SALTONSTALL, LEVERETT (R MASS.) - 56
SAMSONITH, TIAO - 99
SATO, EISAKU - 151
  Biog. - 245
SCALAPINO, ROBERT A. - 24, 182, 190
  China testimony, text - 306
SCHLESINGER, ARTHUR JR. - 63
  Speech, text - 315
SCHUMAN, FREDERICK L. - 14
SCHUMAN, ROBERT - 60
SCHUTZER, ARTHUR - 24
SCHWARTZ, HARRY - 5, 8
  China testimony, text - 287
SCOTT, CREIGHTON - 93
SCOTT, HUGH D. JR. (R PA.) - 25
SELASSIE, HAILE - 134
SERVICE, JOHN STEWART - 14, 39, 49, 59
  Biog. - 245
SEVAREID, ERIC - 167
SEYDOUX, ROGER - 161, 206
SHACKFORD, R.H. - 209
SHAPLEY, HARLOW - 14
SHARP, MITCHELL - 9
SHASTRI, LAL BAHADUR - 141, 147, 172
  Biog. - 245
SHEEHAN, TIMOTHY P. (R ILL.) - 16
SHEHU, MEHMET - 132
SHELEPIN, ALEXANDER N. - 172
  Biog. - 245
SHEPARD, ALAN B. - 104
SHEPILOV, DMITRI T. - 77
  Biog. - 246
SHEPLEY, JAMES - 76
SHIINA, ETSUSABURO - 150
SHORT, DEWEY (R MO.) - 64
SIHANOUK, NORODOM (PRINCE)
  Acheson mission - 132
  Biog. - 246
  De Gaulle visit - 196
  Embassies closed - 131
  Neutrality - 134
  Peking visit - 146
  U.S. charged - 196
  U.S. aid rejected - 130
  Viet Cong sanctuary, denied - 169
SIKES, ROBERT L.F. (D FLA.) - 173
SILER, EUGENE (R KY.) - 16, 143
SINGAPORE - 9
SINO-SOVIET RIFT
  Chinese diplomats ousted - 123
  Chinese letter - 123
  Chinese statements - 116, 118, 120, 125, 126, 127, 128, 129, 130, 131, 134, 136, 137, 142, 145, 147, 158, 162, 166, 174, 175, 192, 195, 201, 206
  Chinese student demon. - 219
  Communist manifesto - 100
  Crankshaw article - 102
  East German party cong. - 119

Khrushchev letter - 105
Moscow meeting - 123, 124
Peking invitation - 120
Soviet bid refused - 182
Soviet consulates closed - 114
Soviet invitation - 121; accepted -
  122
Soviet letter - 124
Soviet note to Mao - 119
Soviet statements - 119, 125, 126,
  128, 129, 131, 137, 138, 139, 145, 158
  166, 174, 181, 204, 206, 210, 217
Trade decrease - 114
World conf. rejected - 142
World Peace Council - 131
SMATHERS, GEORGE A. (D FLA.)
  - 90
SMITH, H. ALEXANDER (R N.J.) -
  25
SMITH, MARGARET CHASE (R
  MAINE) - 14, 51
SMITH, PAUL C. - 24
SMITH, WALTER BEDELL - 67, 69
  Biog. - 246
SNOW, EDGAR - 102
  Biog. - 246
SOMALIA - 134
SOONG CHING-LING - 198
  Biog. - 246
SOONG, T.V. - 38, 42
  Biog. - 246
SOUPHANOUVONG (PRINCE) -
  113, 114, 121
SOUTHEAST ASIA COLLEC. DEF.
  TREATY OF 1954 - 15, 17, 70, 73
SOUTHEAST ASIA TREATY
  ORGAN. (SEATO) - 85, 158
SOUVANNA (PRINCE), PHOUMA
  Appeal to Peking - 137
  Assumed power - 99
  Biog. - 246
  Coalition govt. - 110, 113
  Govt. collapse - 101
  Govt. installed - 114
  Ouster, reinstatement - 138
  U.S. visit - 119
SPARKMAN, JOHN J. (D ALA.) -
  62, 69, 74
SPROUL, ROBERT B. - 24
STALIN, JOSEPH - 37, 56, 63, 64
STASSEN, HAROLD - 23, 47, 76
STATE DEPT.
  Cambodian sanctuary - 169
  China: arms aid - 43; recognition -
    86; trade - 80; travel ban - 4, 78,
    79, 80, 83, 176, 193, 208; white
    paper - 11, 47
  China lobby investg. - 25
  China policy, panel - 208
  Chinese proposal - 187
  Diem ouster - 129
  East-West trade rept. - 9
  Far East policy conf. - 47
  Geneva talks, China - 74, 75, 76,
    85
  India, mil. aid - 116
  Laos white paper - 101
  North Viet Nam aggression, white
    paper - 154
  North Viet Nam offer - 166
  North Viet Nam peace feeler - 168
  Passport cancellation - 174
  Peace overtures - 191
  Privileged sanctuary - 185
  Thant proposals - 154
  Sino-Indian dispute - 115
  U.S.-China deal - 216
  Viet Nam air war - 210
  Viet Nam aid increase - 110
  Viet Nam and Buddhists, report -
    126
  Warsaw talks, China - 89
STEEVES, JOHN M. - 18, 97
  Biog. - 246
STENNIS, JOHN C. (D MISS.) -
  15, 67
STERLING, J. WALLACE - 24
STEVENSON, ADLAI E.
  Death - 161
  Laotian crises - 139
  McCarthy charges - 63; denounced
    - 62
  Nomination - 62, 78
  Offshore Islands position - 73, 87
  U.S. Ambass., UN - 101
STILWELL, JOSEPH W. - 36
  Biog. - 246
STIMSON, HENRY L. - 36
STRONG, ANNA LOUISE - 202
STUART, JOHN LEIGHTON - 40,
  42
  Biog. - 246
STUDENTS FOR A DEMOCRATIC
  SOCIETY (SDS) - 165
SUBANDRIO - 152, 168, 180, 202
  Biog. - 246
SUDAN - 140

SUHARTO - 165, 180
  Biog. - 246
SUKARNO
  Abortive coup - 165
  Biog. - 246
  Loss of power - 180, 192
  Mil. officials removed - 177
  PKI - 168
  Pledge to China - 121
  President - 122
  Resig. demanded - 217
  UN, withdrawal - 151
  U.S. aid denounced - 136
  U.S.-Indonesian relations - 162
SULZBERGER, C.L. - 106
SUN FO - 43, 45, 46
  Biog. - 246
SUN YAT-SEN - 7, 35
  Biog. - 246
SUN YAT-SEN, MME. - 40
SUSLOV, MIKHAIL - 123, 137
  Biog. - 246
SUU, PHAN KHAC - 147, 151
  Biog. - 247
SWE, U BA - 78, 79
  Biog. - 247
SWEDEN - 8, 176
SWITZERLAND - 8
SWOPE, GERARD - 24
SYLVESTER, ARTHUR - 145
SYMINGTON, STUART (D MO.) -
  173
SYRIA - 195

                    T

TACHEN ISLANDS - 71, 72
TAFT, ROBERT A. (R OHIO) - 48, 55, 58
TAIWAN - see China, Republic of (Nationalist)
TANGANYIKA - 141
TANGKU TRUCE - 36
TANZANIA - 153, 160
TAO CHU - 192, 194, 204, 210, 213, 214
  Biog. - 247
TAYLOR, CHARLES
  Roundtable discussion on China, text - 317
TAYLOR, GEORGE E. - 182
  China testimony, text - 300
TAYLOR, MAXWELL O.
  Biog. - 247
  Escalation proposal - 179
  Honolulu meeting - 140
  Johnson (Pres.), conf. - 149
  Kennedy (R.F.) proposal - 177
  Korean commander - 64
  Resignation - 161
  Testimony - 176
  U.S. Ambass., Viet Nam - 141
  Viet Nam: air war - 153; approps. - 20; missions
    - 106, 108, 128, 136, 139; views - 219
TENG HSIAO-PING
  Biog. - 231-232
  Denounced - 203, 210, 212
  Dropped in heirarchy - 209
  Moscow mission - 122, 123
  Politburo member - 194
  Purge threat - 205
TENG JO - 187
THAILAND
  ASPAC - 191
  China charged - 218
  Geneva conf., Laos - 114, 140
  Manila conf. - 202
  Patriotic Front - 152
  SEATO - 70; Viet Nam - 158
  U.S. troop withdrawal - 114
  Viet Minh resistance - 66
THRANARAT, SARIT - 104, 131
THANT, U
  Biog. - 247
  China in UN - 164
  Ky letter - 200
  New Year's message - 214
  UN Secy. Gen. - 109, 207
  Viet Nam peace negotiations - 142, 153, 188, 214
  Viet Nam, views - 215, 216
THI, NGUYEN CHANH - 179
  Biog. - 247
THIEU, NGUYEN VAN - 184
  Biog. - 247
THO, NGUYEN HUU - 198
  Biog. - 247
THO, NGUYEN THOC - 129
  Biog. - 247
THOMAS, LOWELL - 113
THOMAS, NORMAN - 24
THOMSON, ROY - 119
THORPE, ELLIOTT R. - 50
THYE, EDWARD J. (R MINN.) - 51
TIBET - 57, 91, 92, 95, 109
TITO - 85, 117, 150
TOBEY, CHARLES W. (R N.H.) - 51
TOGLIATTI, PALMIRO - 145

TONKIN GULF RESOLUTION - 143
TOURE, SEKOU - 133, 179
TOWER, JOHN G. (R TEXAS) - 113
TRADERS - 5, 6
TREATY OF NANKING - 6
TREATY OF VERSAILLES - 7
TREATY OF WANG-HSIA - 6
TRIKAMADAS, PURSHOTTAM - 99
TRINIDAD AND TOBAGO - 160
TRUMAN, PRES. HARRY S.
  Attlee conf. - 55
  China aid program 11, 13, 11, 15, 16
  China policy - 39; text of statement - 251
  Formosa, aid - 48
  Formosa, defense - 8, 53, 87
  Hydrogen bomb - 64
  Korean conflict - 51, 52, 53, 55, 63
  Loyalty files - 14, 51
  McCarthy denounced - 50
  MacArthur dismissal - 12, 56, 57
  Potsdam conf. - 37
  Presidential oath - 37
  Re-election - 45
  Wake Island conf. - 54
  Wedemeyer report - 43, 57
TSEDENBAL, YUMZHAGIIN - 118
TSHOMBE, MOISE - 106, 145
TSIANG TINGFU F.
  Biog. - 247
TSIEN HSUE-SHEN
  Biog. - 247
TUNG CHIH-PING - 140
TUNISIA - 133
TWO-CHINA POLICY - 9, 28, 201, 202
TYDINGS, MILLARD E. (D MD.) - 14, 51

                  U, V

ULBRICHT, WALTER - 119
UNITED ARAB REPUBLIC - 117, 131, 160
UNITED AUTO WORKERS (AFL-CIO) - 188
UNITED NATIONS
  Atrocity res. - 66
  Cambodia inspection team - 141
  Charter - 37
  Chinese representation - 22, 28, 49, 54, 66, 70,
    75, 78, 88, 94, 100, 106, 109, 116, 129, 165,
    167, 207
  Formosa cease-fire - 72, 73
  Intl. disarmament conf., res. - 167
  Kashmir cease-fire - 165
  Korea, political conf. planned - 65, 66
  Korean armistice terms broken - 81
  Korean conflict - 8, 51, 52, 54, 55, 56, 61, 85
  Korean unification res. - 79, 109
  Laos report - 95
  Prisoner release res. - 71
  Tibet, res. - 95, 109, 168
  Votes on Chinese rep. (box) - 21
UNITED NATIONS ASSOC. - 201
UNTUNG - 165
U.S. AGENCY FOR INTL. DEVELOPMENT
  (A.I.D.) - 136, 172
U.S. FOREIGN AID (BOX) - 107
U.S. INFORMATION AGENCY (USIA) - 137, 155
U.S. INVOLVE. IN MIL. SITUATIONS (BOX) -
  13
U.S. PEACE CORPS - 157
U.S. SUPREME COURT - 96
U.S. TROOP INVOLVE. IN VIET NAM (BOX) -
  170
USS PANAY - 36
U.S.S.R.
  Albanian-Soviet split - 103, 108
  Atomic tests resumed - 105
  Bolshevik revolution - 7
  China aid agree - 91
  China, trade - 85, 91, 97, 103, 111, 121, 140,
    157, 198
  China, treaty - 49
  China in UN - 70
  Chinese students ousted - 200
  Communist manifesto - 100
  Cuban missile crisis - 115, 116
  Disarmament talks - 151
  Geneva accords on Laos - 121
  Geneva conf. '54 - 67, 68, 69
  Geneva conf. call rejected - 200
  Geneva conf., Laos - 104
  Geneva declaration '54 - 69
  Hydrogen bomb test - 65
  India, wheat - 212
  Japan, war declared - 37
  Laos cease-fire, Geneva conf. called - 103
  Manila conf. denounced - 202
  Military budget - 210
  Moscow party conf. - 154
  Nationalist China, treaty - 38
  New goals announced - 148
  North Viet Nam, aid - 161, 169, 198, 200
  North Viet Nam, def. pact - 155

North Viet Nam, volunteers - 157
Nuclear test - 108
Pledge to India - 148
Sino-Soviet border tension - 205, 206,
  207, 208, 213
Sino-Soviet policy statement - 79
Space treaty - 208-209
Test-ban talks, treaty - 124, 125
U-2 incident - 97
UN charter - 132
UN walkout - 48

U.S. Embassy mobbed - 154
U.S. wheat sales - 132, 133
  see also - Sino-Soviet Rift
UTLEY, FREDA - 23
VAN FLEET, JAMES A. - 64
  Biog. - 247
VANDENBERG, ARTHUR H. (R
  MICH.) - 11, 47
VATHANA, SAVANG - 119
VIET NAM, NORTH
  China war entry - 153, 155, 160, 162
  Chinese troops - 194
  Elections, local - 64
  Geneva conf. '54 - 68
  Geneva conf., Laos - 114
  Geneva declaration '54 - 69
  Indo-China armistice - 69
  Manila offer - 202
  Peace hint - 214
  Peace mission barred - 161
  Peace negotiations rejected - 165,
    200, 215
  Salisbury report - 212, 213
  Soviet volun. offered - 157
  U.S.S.R. aid - 161, 169, 198, 200
  U.S.S.R., def. pact - 155
  Thant proposal - 200
  U.S. peace offensive denounced -
    171, 199
  World Peace Council - 131
VIET NAM, SOUTH
  Abortive coup - 146
  Action against Buddhists - 126,
    183, 188, 189
  Air war - 152, 154, 157, 161, 162,
    168, 171, 184, 185, 191, 193, 197,
    201, 208, 210, 212, 214, 216, 217
  ASPAC - 191
  British proposal - 214
  Buddhist demonstrations - 122, 123,
    124, 179, 180, 183, 188, 189
  Buddhist-govt. agree. - 189
  Buddhist Inst. of Secular Affairs -
    183
  Chinese steel sales - 211, 212
  Civilian govt. chosen - 147
  Coups - 129, 133, 151, 153
  Danang, Hue unrest - 183, 188, 189
  Declaration of Honolulu - 175
  Elections - 64, 184, 197
  Geneva conf. '54 - 68
  Geneva conf., Laos - 114, 140
  Geneva declaration '54 - 69
  Govt. changes - 177
  Govt. crisis - 145
  Indo-China armistice - 69
  Ky govt. installed - 161
  Manila conf. - 202
  Mansfield report denounced - 121
  Natl. Coun. overthrown - 150
  Natl. Leadership Comm. - 179
  Natl. Liberation Coun. - 189
  Peoples and Armed Forces Coun. -
    189
  SEATO treaty - 70
  State of Siege - 149
  Truces observed - 169, 207, 212,
    214
  U.S. casualties - 19 (box), 118
  U.S. commitment (box) - 144
  U.S. Embassy explosion - 156
  U.S. Pres'l. positions, actions - 16
  U.S. troop involvement - 169, 170
  Viet Cong document - 219
VINCENT, JOHN CARTER - 59, 60,
  63, 64
  Biog. - 248
VINOGRADOV, SERGEI A. - 154
VISHINSKY, ANDREI Y. - 49, 63,
  66
  Biog. - 248

                  W

WALLACE, VICE PRES. HENRY A. - 36
WALSH, JAMES EDWARD - 97
  Biog. - 247
WALTER, FRANCIS E. (D PA.) - 112
WANG EN-MAO - 219
WANG KUO-CHUAN - 218
  Biog. - 248

WANG PING-NAN - 42, 75, 77, 87, 103
  Biog. - 248
WANG SHAO TAO - 120
WANG SHU-MING - 91
  Biog. - 248
WARBURG, JAMES P. - 98
WARD, ANGUS - 12
WASHINGTON ARMS CONF. - 7
WATKINS, ARTHUR V. (R UTAH) - 71
WAYMACK, W.W. - 24
WEDEMEYER, ALBERT C.
  Biog. - 248
  China mission - 37, 43
  China report - 41, 43, 57; text - 251
  Testimony - 44, 58
WEDEMEYER REPORT - 43, 57
  Text - 251
WEEKS, SINCLAIR - 80, 82
WEI TAO-MING - 43

WELLES, SUMNER - 24
WESTMORELAND, WILLIAM C. - 160, 202, 206
  Biog. - 248
WHEELER, EARLE G. - 141, 216
WHERRY, KENNETH S. (R NEB.) - 11, 53
WHITE, LINCOLN - 90, 99, 106, 112
WIGGINS, J.R. - 80, 83
WILEY, ALEXANDER (R WIS.) - 73
WILLAIMS, ERIC E. - 160
WILLIAMS, ROBERT F. - 125
WILSON, CHARLES E. - 67
WILSON, HAROLD - 153, 160, 191
WIN, NE - 96, 111, 134
  Biog. - 248
WONG WEN-HAO - 45
WORTHY, WILLIAM JR. - 80, 88, 96
WREN, HEATON L. - 24
WU HAN - 187
  Biog. - 248

WU HSIU-CHUAN - 119
  Biog. - 248
WU TEH - 203, 204
  Biog. - 248
WYATT, WILSON W. - 63

Y, Z

YALTA CONFERENCE - 37
YANG CHUNGMING - 166
YANG HSIEN-CHEN
  Biog. - 248
YANG SHANG-KUN - 212, 213
YARBOROUGH, RALPH W. (D TEXAS) - 17, 87
YEH CHIEN-YING - 192
YEH, GEORGE K.C. - 72, 90
  Biog. - 248

YEMEN - 141
YEN HSI-SHAN - 47
YIKIANG ISLAND - 72
YIM, BILL - 96
YOUNG, CHANG DO - 104
YOUNG, STEPHEN M. (D OHIO) - 163
YUAN SHIHKAI - 35
YUGOSLAVIA - 169
YUNG, YOU CHAN - 79
ZABLOCKI, CLEMENT J. (D WIS.)
  - 9, 18, 104, 130
ZAGORIA, DONALD S. - 181
  China testimony, text - 290
ZAMBIA - 146
ZHIVKOV, TODOR - 205
ZORIN, VALERIAN - 109
  Biog. - 248
ZORZA, VICTOR - 205
ZWICKER, RALPH W. - 71

VIET NAM CONSTITUTION
(Continued from p. 339)

Article 109.
During the transitional period, the national assembly popularly elected on September 11, 1966, representing the people of the nation, will, in the legislative sphere:

1. Draft and approve: laws for the election of the President, Vice President, Upper House, and Lower House, laws organizing the Supreme Court and Inspectorate; political party and press regulations.

2. Ratify treaties.

Article 110.
From the time the first President assumes office, the national assembly popularly elected on September 11, 1966 assumes legislative powers until the first National Legislative Assembly is convened.

Article 111.
During the transitional period, the National Leadership Committee and the Central Executive Committee will continue in power until the first President and Vice President assume office.

Article 112.
During the transitional period, courts presently in operation will continue to exercise judicial authority until the judicial organs prescribed in this constitution are established.

Article 113.
The assembly elected on September 11, 1966 will establish a list of candidates, will control the propriety and will announce the result of the election of the first President and Vice President.

Article 114.
During the first presidential term the President may appoint province chiefs.

Article 115.
The election of the President and Vice President must be organized no later than six months from the date of the promulgation of this constitution.

Article 116.
The election of the National Assembly and the organization of the Supreme Court and Inspectorate must be carried out no later than twelve months from the date the first President assumes office.

Article 117.
The other structures prescribed by the constitution must be established no later than two years from the date the first National Assembly is established.